SAT®:
Total Prep
2018

SAT®:
Total Prep
2018

PUBLISHING

New York

This publication is designed to provide accurate and authoritative information in regard to the subject matter covered. It is sold with the understanding that the publisher is not engaged in rendering legal, accounting, or other professional service. If legal advice or other expert assistance is required, the services of a competent professional should be sought.

© 2017 by Kaplan, Inc.

Published by Kaplan Publishing, a division of Kaplan, Inc.
750 Third Avenue
New York, NY 10017

10 9 8 7 6 5 4 3 2 1

ISBN-13: 978-1-5062-2134-2

Table of Contents

Additional resources available at www.kaptest.com/satbookresources

Introduction to the SAT

The first step to achieving SAT success is to learn about the structure of the test and why it's so important for your future. The SAT, like any standardized test, is predictable. The more comfortable you are with the test structure, the more confidently you will approach each question type, thus maximizing your score.

SAT STRUCTURE

The SAT is 3 hours long, or 3 hours and 50 minutes long if you choose to complete the optional Essay Test. It is made up of mostly multiple-choice questions that test two subject areas: Math and Evidence-Based Reading and Writing. The latter is broken into a Reading Test and a Writing & Language Test.

Test	Allotted Time (min.)	Question Count
Reading	65	52
Writing & Language	35	44
Math	80	58
Essay (optional)	50	1
Total	180 OR 230 (w/ essay)	154 OR 155 (w/ essay)

SAT SCORING

SAT scoring can be pretty complex. You will receive one score ranging from 200 to 800 for Evidence-Based Reading and Writing and another for Math. Your overall SAT score will range from 400 to 1600 and is calculated by adding these two scores together. You will receive a separate score for the Essay Test, if you choose to take it.

In addition to your overall scores, you will receive subscores that provide a deeper analysis of your SAT performance. The SAT also gives you a percentile ranking, which allows you to compare your scores with those of other high school students who took the test. For example, a student with a percentile of 63 has earned a score better than 63 percent of test takers.

WHERE AND WHEN TO TAKE THE SAT

The SAT is offered every year on multiple Saturday test dates. Typically, exams are offered in October, November, December, January, March, May, and June. You can take the SAT multiple times. Some states offer special administrations of the SAT on different dates. Sunday tests are available by request for students requiring religious or other exemptions. The SAT is administered at high schools around the country that serve as testing centers. Your high school may or may not be a testing center. Check www.collegeboard.org for a list of testing centers near you. Note that you must register for the SAT approximately one month in advance to avoid paying a late fee. Some SAT test dates also offer SAT Subject Tests. You may not take both the SAT and the Subject Tests in a single sitting.

THE SAT MATH TEST

The SAT Math Test is broken down into a calculator section and a no-calculator section. Questions across the sections consist of multiple-choice, student-produced response (Grid-in), and more comprehensive multi-part question sets.

	Calculator Section	No-Calculator Section	Total
Duration (minutes)	55	25	80
Multiple-choice	30	15	45
Grid-in	8	5	13
Total Questions	38	20	58

The SAT Math Test is divided into four content areas: Heart of Algebra, Problem Solving and Data Analysis, Passport to Advanced Math, and Additional Topics in Math.

SAT Math Test Content Area Distribution	
Heart of Algebra (19 questions)	Analyzing and fluently solving equations and systems of equations; creating expressions, equations, and inequalities to represent relationships between quantities and to solve problems; rearranging and interpreting formulas
Problem Solving and Data Analysis (17 questions)	Creating and analyzing relationships using ratios, proportions, percentages, and units; describing relationships shown graphically; summarizing qualitative and quantitative data

SAT Math Test Content Area Distribution	
Passport to Advanced Math (16 questions)	Rewriting expressions using their structure; creating, analyzing, and fluently solving quadratic and higher-order equations; purposefully manipulating polynomials to solve problems
Additional Topics in Math (6 questions)	Making area and volume calculations in context; investigating lines, angles, triangles, and circles using theorems; and working with trigonometric functions

A few math questions might look like something you'd expect to see on a science or history test. These "crossover" questions are designed to test your ability to use math in real-world scenarios. There are a total of 18 "crossover" questions that will contribute to subscores that span multiple tests. Nine of the questions will contribute to the Analysis in Science subscore, and nine will contribute to the Analysis in History/Social Studies subscore.

THE SAT READING TEST

The SAT Reading Test will focus on your comprehension and reasoning skills when presented with challenging extended prose passages taken from a variety of content areas.

SAT Reading Test Overview	
Timing	65 minutes
Questions	52 passage-based multiple-choice questions
Passages	4 single passages and 1 set of paired passages
Passage Length	500–750 words per passage or passage set

Passages will draw from U.S. and World Literature, History/Social Studies, and Science. One set of History/Social Studies or Science passages will be paired. History/Social Studies and Science passages can also be accompanied by graphical representations of data such as charts, graphs, tables, and so on.

Reading Test Passage Types	
U.S. and World Literature	1 passage with 10 questions
History/Social Studies	2 passages or 1 passage and 1 paired-passage set with 10–11 questions each
Science	2 passages or 1 passage and 1 paired-passage set with 10–11 questions each

The multiple-choice questions for each passage will be arranged in order from the more general to the more specific so that you can actively engage with the entire passage before answering questions about details.

Skills Tested by Reading Test Questions	
Information and Ideas	Close reading, citing textual evidence, determining central ideas and themes
Summarizing	Understanding relationships, interpreting words and phrases in context
Rhetoric	Analyzing word choice, assessing overall text structure, assessing part-whole relationships, analyzing point of view, determining purpose, analyzing arguments
Synthesis	Analyzing multiple texts, analyzing quantitative information

THE SAT WRITING & LANGUAGE TEST

The SAT Writing & Language Test will focus on your ability to revise and edit text from a range of content areas.

SAT Writing & Language Test Overview	
Timing	35 minutes
Questions	44 passage-based multiple-choice questions
Passages	4 single passages with 11 questions each
Passage Length	400–450 words per passage

The SAT Writing & Language Test will contain four single passages, one from each of the following subject areas: Careers, Humanities, History/Social Studies, and Science.

Writing & Language Passage Types	
Careers	Hot topics in "major fields of work" such as information technology and health care
Humanities	Texts about literature, art, history, music, and philosophy pertaining to human culture

Writing & Language Passage Types	
History/Social Studies	Discussion of historical or social sciences topics such as anthropology, communication studies, economics, education, human geography, law, linguistics, political science, psychology, and sociology
Science	Exploration of concepts, findings, and discoveries in the natural sciences including Earth science, biology, chemistry, and physics

Passages will also vary in the "type" of text. A passage can be an argument, an informative or explanatory text, or a nonfiction narrative.

Writing & Language Passage Text Type Distribution	
Argument	1–2 passages
Informative/Explanatory Text	1–2 passages
Nonfiction Narrative	1 passage

Some passages and/or questions will refer to one or more informational graphics that represent data. Questions associated with these graphical representations will ask you to revise and edit the passage based on the data presented in the graphic.

The most prevalent question format on the SAT Writing & Language Test will ask you to choose the best of three alternatives to an underlined portion of the passage or to decide that the current version is the best option. You will be asked to improve the development, organization, and diction in the passages to ensure they conform to conventional standards of English grammar, usage, and style.

Skills Tested by Writing & Language Test Questions	
Expression of Ideas (24 questions)	Development, organization, and effective language use
Standard English Conventions (20 questions)	Sentence structure, conventions of usage, and conventions of punctuation

THE SAT ESSAY TEST (OPTIONAL)

The SAT Essay Test will assess your college and career readiness by testing your abilities to read and analyze a high-quality source document and write a coherent analysis of the source supported with critical reasoning and evidence from the given text.

The SAT Essay Test features an argumentative source text of 650–750 words aimed toward a large audience. Passages will examine ideas, debates, and shifts in the arts and sciences as well as civic, cultural, and political life. Rather than having a simple for/against structure, these passages will be nuanced and will relate views on complex subjects. These passages will also be logical in their structure and reasoning.

It is important to note that prior knowledge is not required.

The SAT Essay Test prompt will ask you to explain how the presented passage's author builds an argument to convince an audience. In writing your essay, you may analyze elements such as the author's use of evidence, reasoning, style, and persuasion; you will not be limited to those elements listed, however.

Rather than writing about whether you agree or disagree with the presented argument, you will write an essay in which you analyze how the author makes an argument.

The SAT Essay Test will be broken down into three categories for scoring: Reading, Analysis, and Writing. Each of these elements will be scored on a scale of 1 to 4 by two graders, for a total score of 2 to 8 for each category.

TEST-TAKING STRATEGIES

You have already learned about the overall structure of the SAT as well as the structure of the three tests it entails: Reading, Writing & Language, and Math. The strategies outlined in this section can be applied to any of these tests.

The SAT is different from the tests you are used to taking in school. The good news is that you can use the SAT's particular structure to your advantage.

For example, on a test given in school, you probably go through the questions in order. You spend more time on the harder questions than on the easier ones because harder questions are usually worth more points. You probably often show your work because your teacher tells you that how you approach a question is as important as getting the correct answer.

This approach is not optimal for the SAT. On the SAT, you benefit from moving around within a section if you come across tough questions, because the harder questions are worth the same number of points as the easier questions. It doesn't matter how you arrive at the correct answer—only that you bubble in the correct answer choice.

STRATEGY #1: TRIAGING THE TEST

You do not need to complete questions on the SAT in order. Every student has different strengths and should attack the test with those strengths in mind. Your main objective on the SAT should be to score as many points as you can. While approaching questions out of order may seem counter-intuitive, it is a surefire way to achieve your best score.

Just remember, you can skip around within each section, but you cannot work on a section other than the one you've been instructed to work on.

To triage the test effectively, do the following:

- First, work through all the easy questions that you can do quickly. Skip questions that are hard or time-consuming.

- For the Reading and Writing & Language Tests, start with the passage you find most manage-able and work toward the one you find most challenging. You do not need to go in order.

- Second, work through the questions that are doable but time-consuming.

- Third, work through the hard questions.

- If you run out of time, pick a Letter of the Day for remaining questions.

A Letter of the Day is an answer choice letter (A, B, C, or D) that you choose before Test Day to select for questions you guess on.

STRATEGY #2: ELIMINATION

Even though there is no wrong-answer penalty on the SAT, elimination is still a crucial strategy. If you can determine that one or more answer choices are definitely incorrect, you can increase your chances of getting the correct answer by paring the selection down.

To eliminate answer choices, do the following:

- Read each answer choice.

- Cross out the answer choices that are incorrect.

- Remember: There is no wrong-answer penalty, so take your best guess.

STRATEGY #3: GUESSING

Each multiple-choice question on the SAT has four answer choices and no wrong-answer penalty. That means if you have no idea how to approach a question, you have a 25 percent chance of randomly choosing the correct answer. Even though there's a 75 percent chance of selecting the incorrect answer, you won't lose any points for doing so. The worst that can happen on the SAT is that you'll earn zero points on a question, which means you should always at least take a guess, even when you have no idea what to do.

When guessing on a question, do the following:

- Always try to strategically eliminate answer choices before guessing.

- If you run out of time, or have no idea what a question is asking, pick a Letter of the Day.

COMMON TESTING MYTHS

Since its inception, the SAT has gone through various revisions, but it has always been an integral part of the college admissions process. As a result of its significance and the changes it has undergone, a number of rumors and myths have circulated about the exam. In this section, we'll dispel some of the most common ones. As always, you can find the most up-to-date information about the SAT at the College Board website (https://www.collegeboard.org).

Myth: **There is a wrong-answer penalty on the SAT to discourage guessing.**

Fact: While this statement was true a few years ago, it is no longer true. Older versions of the SAT had a wrong-answer penalty so that students who guessed on questions would not have an advantage over students who left questions blank. This penalty has been removed; make sure you never leave an SAT question blank!

Myth: **Answer choice C is most likely to be the correct answer.**

Fact: This rumor has roots in human psychology. Apparently, when people such as high school teachers, for example, design an exam, they have a slight bias toward answer choice C when assigning correct answers. While humans do write SAT questions, a computer randomizes the distribution of correct choices; statistically, therefore, each answer choice is equally likely to be the correct answer.

Myth: **The SAT is just like another test in school.**

Fact: While the SAT covers some of the same content as your high school math, literature, and English classes, it also presents concepts in ways that are fundamentally different. While you might be able to solve a math problem in a number of different ways on an algebra test, the SAT places a heavy emphasis on working through questions as quickly and efficiently as possible.

Myth: **You have to get all the questions correct to get a perfect score.**

Fact: Many students have reported missing several questions on the SAT and being pleasantly surprised to receive perfect scores. Their experience is not atypical: Usually, you can miss a few questions and still get a coveted perfect score. The makers of the SAT use a technique called scaling to ensure that an SAT score conveys the same information from year to year, so you might be able to miss a couple more questions on a slightly harder SAT exam and miss fewer questions on an easier SAT exam and get the same scores. Keep a positive attitude throughout the SAT, and in many cases, your scores will pleasantly surprise you.

Myth: **You can't prepare for the SAT.**

Fact: You've already proven this myth false by buying this book. While the SAT is designed to fairly test students regardless of preparation, you can gain a huge advantage by familiarizing yourself with the structure and content of the exam. By working through the questions and practice tests available to you, you'll ensure that nothing on the SAT catches you by surprise and that you do everything you can to maximize your score. Your Kaplan resources help you structure this practice in the most efficient way possible, and provide you with helpful strategies and tips as well.

HOW TO USE THIS BOOK

WELCOME TO KAPLAN!

Congratulations on taking this important step in your college admissions process! By studying with Kaplan, you'll maximize your score on the SAT, a major factor in your overall college application.

Our experience shows that the greatest SAT score increases result from active engagement in the preparation process. Kaplan will give you direction, focus your preparation, and teach you the specific skills and effective test-taking strategies you need to know for the SAT. We will help you achieve your top performance on Test Day, but your effort is crucial. The more you invest in preparing for the SAT, the greater your chances of achieving your target score and getting into your top-choice college.

Are you registered for the SAT? Kaplan cannot register you for the official SAT. If you have not already registered for the upcoming SAT, talk to your high school guidance counselor or visit the College Board's website at www.collegeboard.org to register online and for information on registration deadlines, test sites, accommodations for students with disabilities, and fees.

PRACTICE TESTS

Kaplan's practice tests are just like the actual SAT. By taking a practice exam you will prepare yourself for the actual Test Day experience. One diagnostic test and a second practice test are included in this book. There are three additional practice tests as part of your online resources. See the Digital Resources section to learn how to access these. You can score your tests by hand using the score conversion tables in this book, or log into your online resources for easy online scoring.

EXTRA PRACTICE

You need to reinforce what you learn in each chapter by consistently practicing the Kaplan Methods and Strategies. Each chapter contains additional practice problems that reinforce the concepts explained in that chapter. These questions are great practice for the real SAT. Answers & Explanations are provided in the back of the book.

SMARTPOINTS

Each chapter contains a breakdown of SmartPoints. By studying the information released by the College Board, Kaplan has been able to determine how often certain topics are likely to show up on the SAT, and therefore how many points these topics are worth on Test Day. If you master a given topic, you can expect to earn the corresponding number of SmartPoints on Test Day. The breakdown of SmartPoints for Math, Reading, and Writing & Language are summarized in the following tables. You can also see how these topics align to chapters in this book.

Math			
SmartPoint Category	**# of Points**	**Sub-Categories**	**SAT Chapter**
Linear Equations	110	Linear Equations, Graphs, Word Problems	Ch. 2
Systems of Linear Equations	50	Systems of Equations, Word Problems, Intersecting Graphs	Ch. 3
Inequalities	40	Inequalities, 1-D Graphs of Inequalities, 2-D Graphs of Inequalities	Ch. 4
Rates, Ratios, Proportions, and Percentages	80	Rates, Ratios, Proportions, Measurement/ Units, and Percents	Ch. 5
Scatterplots	40	Scatterplots, Lines of Best Fit, Modeling Data	Ch. 6
Statistics and Probability	50	Descriptive Statistics, Probability, TwoWay Tables, Graphical Organizers	Ch. 7
Exponents	80	Exponents, Radicals, Rational Expressions/ Equations, and Polynomial Operations	Ch. 8
Functions	50	Functions and Graphs of Functions	Ch. 9

Quadratics	40	Quadratic Equations, Modeling Data, Parabolas, Systems of Mixed Equations	Ch. 10
Geometry	40	Lines, Angles, Triangles, Similarity, Congruence, Proofs, Circles, 3D Shapes	Ch. 11
Imaginary Numbers	10	Imaginary Numbers	Ch. 12
Trigonometry	10	Trigonometry	Ch. 12
TOTAL	**600**		

Reading			
SmartPoint Category	**# of Points**	**Sub-Categories**	**SAT Chapter**
Command of Evidence	60		Ch. 15
Vocab-in-Context	60		Ch. 16
Rhetoric	50	Analyzing Word Choice, Overall Text Structure, Part-Whole Text Structure, Point of View, Purpose, Claims & Counterclaims, Reasoning, and Evidence	Ch. 17
Inference	35	Determining Implicit Meanings, Using Analogical Reasoning	Ch. 18
Synthesis—Analyzing Quantitative Information	35		Ch. 14
Synthesis—Paired Passages	25		Ch. 14
Global	10	Determining Central Ideas & Themes, Summarizing	Ch. 15
Detail	15	Determining Explicit Meanings	Ch. 18
Connections	10	Understanding Relationships	Ch. 16
TOTAL	**300**		

Writing & Language			
SmartPoint Category	**# of Points**	**Sub-Categories**	**SAT Chapter**
Effective Language Use	60	Precision, Concision, Style & Tone, Syntax	Ch. 22
Sentence Formation	60	Sentence Boundaries, Subordination & Coordination, Parallel Structure, Modifier Placement	Ch. 23
Organization	50	Logical Sequence; Introductions, Conclusions, and Transitions	Ch. 20
Usage	40	Pronouns, Possessive Determiners, Pronoun-Antecedent Agreement, Subject-Verb Agreement, Noun Agreement, Frequently Confused Words, Logical Comparison, Conventional Expression (Idioms), Shifts in Construction	Ch. 24
Development	40	Proposition, Support, Focus	Ch. 21
Punctuation	40	End-of-Sentence Punctuation, Within-Sentence Punctuation, Possessive Nouns & Pronouns, Items in a Series, Nonrestrictive & Parenthetical Elements, Unnecessary Punctuation	Ch. 25
Quantitative	10		Ch. 19
TOTAL	**300**		

DIGITAL RESOURCES

To access your online resources:

1. Go to kaptest.com/booksonline.

2. Follow the on-screen instructions. Have this book available.

Join a Live Online Event

Kaplan's SAT Live Online sessions are interactive, instructor-led prep lessons that you can participate in from anywhere you have Internet access.

SAT Live Online sessions are held in our state-of-the-art visual classroom: Actual lessons in real time, just like a physical classroom experience. Interact with your teacher using chat, whiteboards, and polling. Just like courses at Kaplan centers, SAT Live Online sessions are led by top Kaplan instructors.

To register for an SAT Live Online event, visit https://www.kaptest.com/SAT/enroll. From here you can view all of our SAT course offerings—from prep courses, to tutoring, to free events.

SAT Live Online events are scheduled to take place throughout the year. Please check the registration page with dates and times.

SAT PRACTICE TESTS

As part of your online resources, you have access to three additional full-length practice tests. We recommend you complete these practice tests as you make your way through the content of this book. After completing each practice test, you'll receive a detailed online score report. Use this summary to help you focus and review the content areas that comprise your greatest areas of improvement.

SAT Videos and Quizzes

Your online resources also include a variety of videos and quizzes. The following icons indicate what is available for you online.

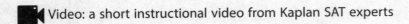 Video: a short instructional video from Kaplan SAT experts

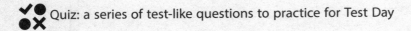 Quiz: a series of test-like questions to practice for Test Day

I'M OVERWHELMED. WHERE DO I START?

No matter what, read Introduction to the SAT. Then, take Practice Test 1 in this book to identify the SmartPoint categories that you need to address in order to get the most points on Test Day. Then, use this table to help you prioritize and find the right practice in your book.

Math SmartPoint Category (# of SmartPoints)	Chapter
Linear Equations (110)	Chapter 2
Rates, Ratios, Proportions, and Percentages (80)	Chapter 5
Exponents (80)	Chapter 8
Systems of Linear Equations (50)	Chapter 3
Statistics & Probability (50)	Chapter 7
Functions (50)	Chapter 9
Inequalities (40)	Chapter 4
Quadratics (40)	Chapter 10
Geometry (40)	Chapter 11
Trigonometry (10)	Chapter 12
Imaginary Numbers (10)	Chapter 12

Reading SmartPoint Category (# of SmartPoints)	Chapter
Synthesis (60)	Chapter 14
Vocab-in-Context (60)	Chapter 16
Citing Textual Evidence (60)	Chapter 15
Rhetoric (50)	Chapter 17
Inferences (35)	Chapter 18
Detail (15)	Chapter 18
Global (10)	Chapter 15
Connections (10)	Chapter 16

Writing & Language SmartPoint Categories (# of SmartPoints)	Chapter
Effective Language Use (60)	Chapter 22
Sentence Formation (60)	Chapter 23
Organization (50)	Chapter 20
Punctuation (40)	Chapter 25
Development (40)	Chapter 21
Usage (40)	Chapter 24
Quantitative (10)	Chapter 19

PART ONE

Math

Math Introduction

BY THE END OF THIS UNIT, YOU WILL BE ABLE TO:

1. Identify the arithmetic and algebra concepts needed to get the most out of this book

2. Determine which calculators are best to use on the SAT

3. Develop best practices for effective use of your calculator

Math

PREREQUISITE SKILLS & CALCULATOR USAGE

Chapter 1

Even More

Math Foundations

Key

 Book Assignment

 Online Video Assignment

 Online Quiz Assignment

CHAPTER 1

Prerequisite Skills & Calculator Usage

CHAPTER OBJECTIVES

By the end of this chapter, you will be able to:

- Identify skills necessary to obtain the full benefits of the math section of this book and to hone skills not fully developed

- Use efficiency tips to boost your Test Day speed

- Distinguish between questions that need a calculator and questions in which manual calculations are more efficient

- Utilize strategies that can help when you don't know how to start a question

- Identify how expert test takers use their calculators in a balanced way

COURSE PREREQUISITES

This course focuses on the skills that are tested on the SAT. It assumes a working knowledge of arithmetic, algebra, and geometry. Before you dive into the subsequent chapters where you'll try test-like questions, there are a number of concepts—ranging from basic arithmetic to geometry— that you should master. The following sections contain a brief review of these concepts.

Algebra and Arithmetic

- Order of operations is one of the most fundamental of all arithmetic rules. A well-known mnemonic device for remembering this order is PEMDAS: Please Excuse My Dear Aunt Sally. This translates to Parentheses, Exponents, Multiplication/Division, Addition/Subtraction. Note: Multiplication and division have the same priority, as do addition and subtraction. Perform

Math

multiplication and division from left to right (even if it means division before multiplication) and treat addition and subtraction the same way.

$$\left(14 - 4 \div 2\right)^2 - 3 + (2 - 1)$$
$$= \left(14 - 2\right)^2 - 3 + 1$$
$$= 12^2 - 3 + 1$$
$$= 144 - 3 + 1$$
$$= 142$$

- Three basic properties of number (and variable) manipulation—commutative, associative, and distributive—will assist you with algebra on Test Day. These properties are outlined next.

1) Commutative: Numbers can swap places and still provide the same mathematical result. This is valid only for addition and multiplication.

$$a + b = b + a \rightarrow 3 + 4 = 4 + 3$$
$$a \times b = b \times a \rightarrow 3 \times 4 = 4 \times 3$$

BUT: $3 - 4 \neq 4 - 3$ and $3 \div 4 \neq 4 \div 3$

2) Associative: Different number groupings will provide the same mathematical result. This is valid only for addition and multiplication.

$$(a + b) + c = a + (b + c) \rightarrow (4 + 5) + 6 = 4 + (5 + 6)$$
$$(a \times b) \times c = a \times (b \times c) \rightarrow (4 \times 5) \times 6 = 4 \times (5 \times 6)$$

BUT: $(4 - 5) - 6 \neq 4 - (5 - 6)$ and $(4 \div 5) \div 6 \neq 4 \div (5 \div 6)$

3) Distributive: A number that is multiplied by the sum or difference of two other numbers can be rewritten as the first number multiplied by the two others individually. This does *not* work with division.

$$a(b + c) = ab + ac \rightarrow 6(x + 3) = 6x + 6(3) = 6x + 18$$
$$a(b - c) = ab - ac \rightarrow 3(y - 2) = 3y + 3(-2) = 3y - 6$$

BUT: $12 \div (6 + 2) \neq 12 \div 6 + 12 \div 2$

Note: When subtracting an expression in parentheses, such as in $4 - (x + 3)$, distribute the negative sign outside the parentheses first: $4 + (-x - 3) \rightarrow 1 - x$. Be particularly careful with these, as negative signs are easily lost in calculations.

- Make sure you can correctly manipulate negative numbers and that you understand the additive inverse property: Subtracting a positive number is the same as adding its negative. Likewise, subtracting a negative number is the same as adding its positive.

$$r - s = r + (-s) \rightarrow 22 - 15 = 22 + (-15) = 7$$
$$r - (-s) = r + s \rightarrow 22 - (-15) = 22 + 15 = 37$$

- You should be comfortable manipulating both proper and improper fractions. To add and subtract fractions, first find a common denominator, then add the numerators together. Multiplication is straightforward: Multiply the numerators together, then repeat for the denominators. Cancel when possible to simplify the answer. Dividing by a fraction is the same as multiplying by its reciprocal. Once you've rewritten a division problem as multiplication, follow the rules for fraction multiplication to simplify.

addition/subtraction: $\dfrac{2}{3} + \dfrac{5}{4} \rightarrow \left(\dfrac{2}{3} \times \dfrac{4}{4}\right) + \left(\dfrac{5}{4} \times \dfrac{3}{3}\right) = \dfrac{8}{12} + \dfrac{15}{12} = \dfrac{23}{12}$

multiplication: $\dfrac{5}{8} \times \dfrac{8}{3} = \dfrac{5}{\cancel{8}} \times \dfrac{\cancel{8}^{1}}{3} = \dfrac{5 \times 1}{1 \times 3} = \dfrac{5}{3}$

division: $\dfrac{3}{4} \div \dfrac{3}{2} = \dfrac{\cancel{3}^{1}}{\cancel{4}_{2}} \times \dfrac{\cancel{2}^{1}}{\cancel{3}_{1}} = \dfrac{1 \times 1}{2 \times 1} = \dfrac{1}{2}$

- Know what absolute value is: the distance a number is from 0 on a number line. Because absolute value is a distance, it is always positive or 0. Absolute value can *never* be negative.

$$|-17| = 17, |21| = 21, |0| = 0$$

- Follow properties of equality: Whatever you do to one side of an equation, you must do to the other. For instance, if you multiply one side by 3, you must multiply the other side by 3 as well.

- The ability to solve straightforward, one-variable equations is critical on the SAT. Here's an example:

$$\frac{4x}{5} - 2 = 10$$

$$\frac{4x}{5} = 12$$

$$\frac{5}{4} \times \frac{4x}{5} = 12 \times \frac{5}{4}$$

$$x = 15$$

Note: $\dfrac{4x}{5}$ is the same as $\dfrac{4}{5}x$. You could see either form on the SAT.

- You should be able to extract numbers (and infer their relevance) from word problems like this one:

Annabel bought six pairs of shoes during a sale at her favorite boutique. If this purchase tripled the number of pairs of shoes she had before she went shopping, how many pairs of shoes did Annabel own before she visited the sale?

Solution: Let p represent the number of pairs of shoes Annabel had before the sale. She adds six pairs ($+6$) to this value, which is equal to triple her original shoe pair count ($= 3p$). Your equation should read $p + 6 = 3p$. Solving for p reveals $p = 3$, so Annabel had three pairs of shoes before she went shopping at the sale.

- You will encounter irrational numbers, such as common radicals and π, on Test Day. You can carry an irrational number through your calculations as you would a variable (e.g., $4 \times \sqrt{2} = 4\sqrt{2}$).

Only convert to a decimal when you have finished any intermediate steps and when the question asks you to provide an *approximate* value.

For Extra Efficiency

You might be a math whiz, but unless you're Isaac Newton (the inventor of calculus), you can likely benefit from knowing a few extra things that will boost your speed on Test Day.

- Don't abuse your calculator by using it to determine something as simple as $15 \div 3$ (we've seen it many times). Besides, what if you're in the middle of the no-calculator section? Save time on Test Day by reviewing multiplication tables. At a bare minimum, work up through the 10s. If you know them through 12 or 15, that's even better!

- You can save a few seconds of number crunching by memorizing perfect squares. Knowing perfect squares through 10 is a good start; go for 15 or even 20 if you can.

- The ability to recognize a few simple fractions masquerading in decimal or percent form will save you time on Test Day, as you won't have to turn to your calculator to convert them. Memorize the content of the following table.

Fraction	Decimal	Percent
$\frac{1}{10}$	0.1	10%
$\frac{1}{5}$	0.2	20%
$\frac{1}{4}$	0.25	25%
$\frac{1}{3}$	$0.33\overline{3}$	$33.3\overline{3}$%
$\frac{1}{2}$	0.5	50%
$\frac{3}{4}$	0.75	75%

Tip: If you need the decimal (or percent) form of a multiple of one of the fractions shown in the table, such as $\frac{2}{5}$, just take the fraction with the corresponding denominator ($\frac{1}{5}$ in this case), convert to a decimal (0.2), and multiply by the numerator of the desired fraction to get its decimal equivalent: $\frac{2}{5} = \frac{1}{5} \times 2 = 0.2 \times 2 = 0.4 = 40\%$.

- Many students assume that every math problem encountered can be solved with a proportion. Proportions are not appropriate for every question. Know when to use them and when not to; review chapter 5 for more information. You must be able to recognize the type of question you have *and* use the right math tools to solve it.

Graphing

- Basic two-dimensional graphing is performed on a coordinate plane. There are two axes, *x* and *y*, that meet at a central point called the origin. Each axis has both positive and negative values that extend outward from the origin at evenly spaced intervals. The axes divide the space into four sections called quadrants, which are labeled I, II, III, and IV. Quadrant I is always the upper-right section, and the rest follow counterclockwise.

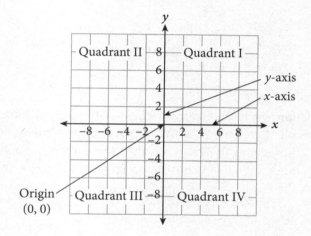

- To plot points on the coordinate plane, you need their coordinates. The *x*-coordinate is where the point falls along the *x*-axis, and the *y*-coordinate is where the point falls along the *y*-axis. The two coordinates together make an ordered pair written as (*x*, *y*). When writing ordered pairs, the *x*-coordinate is always listed first (think alphabetical order). Four points are plotted in the following figure as examples.

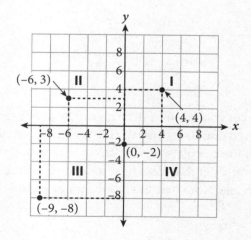

- When two points are vertically or horizontally aligned, calculating the distance between them is easy. For a horizontal distance, only the *x*-value changes; for a vertical distance, only the *y*-value changes. Take the positive difference of the *x*-coordinates (or *y*-coordinates) to determine the distance. Two examples are presented here.

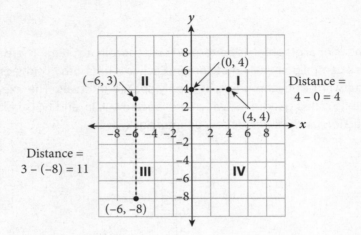

- Two-variable equations have an independent variable (input) and a dependent variable (output). The dependent variable (often *y*), depends on the independent variable (often *x*). For example, in the equation $y = 3x + 4$, *x* is the independent variable; any *y*-value depends on what you plug in for *x*. You can construct a table of values for the equation, which can then be plotted.

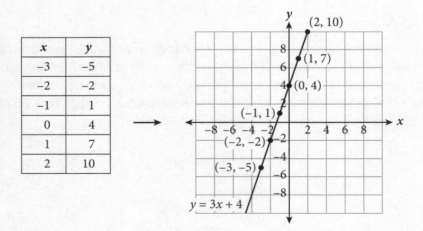

x	y
−3	−5
−2	−2
−1	1
0	4
1	7
2	10

- You may be asked to infer relationships from graphs. In the first of the following graphs, the two variables are time and population. Clearly the year does not depend on how many people live in the town; rather, the population increases over time and thus depends on the year. In the second graph, you can infer that plant height depends on the amount of rain; thus, rainfall is the independent variable. Note that the independent variable for the second graph is the

Math

vertical axis; this can happen with certain nonstandard graphs. On the standard coordinate plane, however, the independent variable is always plotted on the horizontal axis.

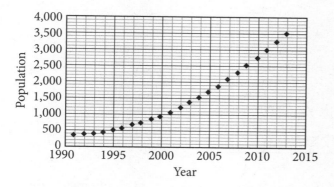

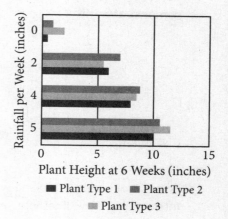

- When two straight lines are graphed simultaneously, one of three possible scenarios will occur:

  1) The lines will not intersect at all (no solution).

  2) The lines will intersect at one point (one solution).

  3) The lines will lie on top of each other (infinitely many solutions).

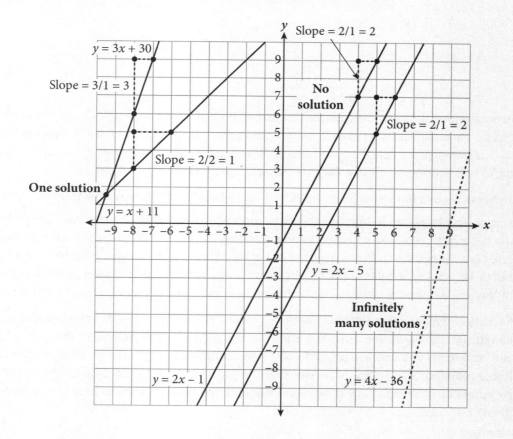

Math

Geometry

- Adjacent angles can be added to find the measure of a larger angle. The following diagram demonstrates this.

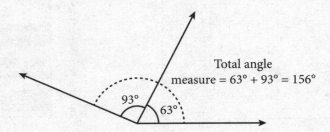

- Two distinct lines in a plane will either intersect at one point or extend indefinitely without intersecting. If two lines intersect at a right angle (90°), they are perpendicular and are denoted with ⊥. If the lines never intersect, they are parallel and are denoted with ∥.

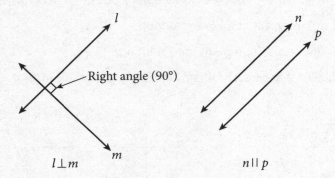

- Perimeter and area are basic properties that all two-dimensional shapes have. The perimeter of a polygon can easily be calculated by adding the lengths of all its sides. Area is the amount of two-dimensional space a shape occupies. The most common shapes for which you'll need these two properties on Test Day are triangles, parallelograms, and circles.

- The area (A) of a triangle is given by $A = \frac{1}{2}bh$, where b is the base of the triangle and h is its height. The base and height are always perpendicular. Any side of a triangle can be used as the base; just make sure you use its corresponding height (the longest perpendicular line you can draw within the triangle). You can use a right triangle's two legs as the base and height, but in non-right triangles, if the height is not given, you'll need to draw it in (from the vertex of the angle opposite the base down to the base itself at a right angle) and compute it.

- Parallelograms are quadrilaterals with two pairs of parallel sides. Rectangles and squares are subsets of parallelograms. You can find the area of a parallelogram using $A = bh$. As with triangles, you can use any side of a parallelogram as the base; in addition, the height is still perpendicular to the base. Use the side perpendicular to the base as the height for a rectangle or square; for any other parallelogram, the height (or enough information to find it) will be given.

- A circle's perimeter is known as its circumference (C) and is found using $C = 2\pi r$, where r is the radius (distance from the center of the circle to its edge). Area is given by $A = \pi r^2$. The strange symbol is the lowercase Greek letter pi (π, pronounced "pie"), which is approximately 3.14. As mentioned in the algebra section, you should carry π throughout your calculations without rounding unless instructed otherwise.

- A shape is said to have symmetry when it can be split by a line (called an *axis of symmetry*) into two identical parts. Consider folding a shape along a line: If all sides and vertices align once the shape is folded in half, the shape is symmetrical about that line. Some shapes have no axis of symmetry, some have one, some have multiple axes, and still others can have infinite axes of symmetry (e.g., a circle).

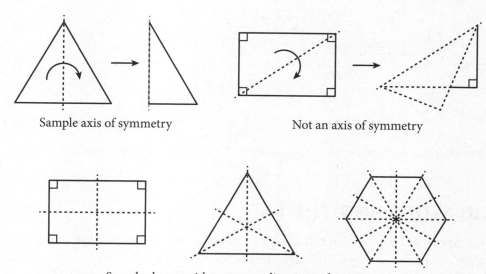

Sample axis of symmetry   Not an axis of symmetry

Sample shapes with corresponding axes of symmetry

- Congruence is simply a geometry term that means identical. Angles, lines, and shapes can be congruent. Congruence is indicated by using hash marks: Everything with the same number of hash marks is congruent.

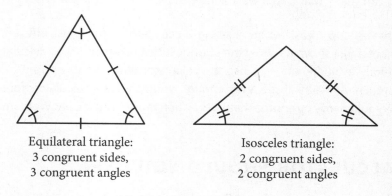

Equilateral triangle:
3 congruent sides,
3 congruent angles

Isosceles triangle:
2 congruent sides,
2 congruent angles

Math

- Similarity between shapes indicates that they have identical angles and proportional sides. Think of taking a shape and stretching or shrinking each side by the same ratio. The resulting shape will have the same angles as the original. While the sides will not be identical, they will be proportional.

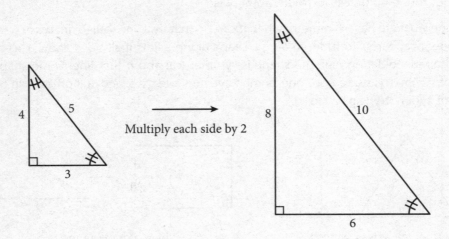

Multiply each side by 2

If you're comfortable with these concepts, read on for tips on calculator use.

CALCULATORS AND THE SAT

Educators and parents believe that calculators serve a role in mathematics, but they are concerned that students rely too heavily on calculators. They believe this dependence weakens students' overall ability to think mathematically. Therefore, the SAT has a policy on calculator use to promote the idea that students need to be able to analyze and solve math problems both with and without a calculator. One math section will allow you to use a calculator, while the other will require you to solve problems without technology. The makers of the SAT walked 12 miles uphill in the snow to school, so why should you have things any easier? Think of this chapter as your personal pair of snow boots that can make that uphill walk a little more comfortable for you.

Many students never stop to ask whether using a calculator is the most efficient way to solve a problem. This chapter will show you how the strongest test takers use their calculators strategically; that is, they carefully evaluate when to use the calculator and when to skip it in favor of a more streamlined approach. As you will see, even though you can use a calculator, sometimes it's more beneficial to save your energy by approaching a question more strategically. Work smarter, not harder.

WHICH CALCULATOR SHOULD YOU USE?

The SAT allows four-function, scientific, and graphing calculators. No matter which calculator you choose, start practicing with it now. You don't want to waste valuable time on Test Day looking for the exponent button or figuring out how to correctly graph equations. Due to the wide range of mathematics topics you'll encounter on Test Day, **we recommend using a graphing calculator**, such as the TI-83/84. If you don't already own one, see if you can borrow one from your school's math department or a local library.

A graphing calculator's capabilities extend well beyond what you'll need for the test, so don't worry about memorizing every function. The next few pages will cover which calculator functions you'll want to know how to use for the SAT. If you're not already familiar with your graphing calculator, you'll want to get the user manual; you can find this on the Internet by searching for your calculator's model number. Identify the calculator functions necessary to answer various SAT math questions, then write down the directions for each to make a handy study sheet.

WHEN SHOULD YOU USE A CALCULATOR?

Some SAT question types are designed based on the idea that students will do some or all of the work using a calculator. As a master test taker, you want to know what to look for so you can identify when calculator use is advantageous. Questions involving statistics, determining roots of complicated quadratic equations, and other topics are generally designed with calculator use in mind.

Other questions aren't intentionally designed to involve calculator use. Solving some with a calculator can save you time and energy, but you'll waste both if you go for the calculator on others. You will have to decide which method is best when you encounter the following topics:

- Long division and other extensive calculations
- Graphing quadratics
- Simplifying radicals and calculating roots
- Plane and coordinate geometry

Practicing long computations by hand and with the calculator will not only boost your focus and mental math prowess, but it will also help you determine whether it's faster to do the work by hand or reach for the calculator. If you tend to make quick work of long division and multiple-digit multiplication by hand, you can still use the calculator afterward to check your work.

Graphing quadratic equations is a big reason most of you got that fancy calculator in the first place; it makes answering these questions a snap! This is definitely an area where you need to have an in-depth knowledge of your calculator's functions. The key to making these questions easy with the calculator is being meticulous when entering the equation.

Another stressful area for students is radicals, especially when the answer choices are written as decimals. Those two elements are big red flags that trigger a reach for the calculator. Beware: Not all graphing calculators have a built-in radical simplification function, so consider familiarizing yourself with this process.

Geometry can be a gray area for students when it comes to calculator use. Consider working by hand when dealing with angles and lines, specifically when filling in information on complementary, supplementary, and congruent angles. You should be able to work fluidly through those questions without using your calculator.

> ✔ **Expert Tip**
>
> If you choose to use trigonometric functions to get to the answer on triangle questions, make sure you have your calculator set to degrees or radians as necessitated by the question.

Your calculator will come in handy when you need to work with formulas (volume, distance, arc length, etc.) and want to check your work. Because the SAT uses π instead of 3.14…, there is no need to enter the decimal form into your calculator.

TO USE OR NOT TO USE?

A calculator is a double-edged sword on the SAT: Using one can be an asset for verifying work if you struggle when doing math by hand, but turning to it for the simplest computations will cost you time that you could devote to more complex questions. Practice solving questions with and without a calculator to get a sense of your personal style as well as strengths and weaknesses. Think critically about when a calculator saves you time and when mental math is faster. Use the exercises in this book to practice your calculations so that by the time Test Day arrives, you'll be in the habit of using your calculator as effectively as possible!

UNIT TWO

Heart of Algebra

BY THE END OF THIS UNIT, YOU WILL BE ABLE TO:

1. Apply the Kaplan Method for Math to math questions on the SAT

2. Solve linear equations and inequalities

3. Graph linear equations and inequalities

4. Solve systems of linear equations and inequalities

5. Translate word problems into math

The Kaplan Method for Math & Linear Equations

CHAPTER OBJECTIVES

By the end of this chapter, you will be able to:

1. Apply the Kaplan Method for Math to Heart of Algebra questions

2. Recognize, simplify, and solve linear equations efficiently

3. Translate complex word problems into equations

4. Interpret the most commonly tested types of linear graphs

SMARTPOINTS

Point Value	SmartPoint Category
Point Builder	Kaplan Method for Math
110 Points	Linear Equations

Math

THE KAPLAN METHOD FOR MATH & LINEAR EQUATIONS

Chapter 2

Homework

Extra Practice: #1-42

Even More

The Kaplan Method for Math

Translating English to Math

Math Quiz 1

Key

 Book Assignment

 Online Video Assignment

 Online Quiz Assignment

THE KAPLAN METHOD FOR MATH

Because the SAT is a standardized test, students who approach each question in a consistent way will be rewarded on Test Day. Applying the same basic steps to every math question—whether it asks you about geometry, algebra, or even trigonometry—will help you avoid minor mistakes as well as tempting wrong answer choices.

Use the Kaplan Method for Math for every math question on the SAT. Its steps are applicable to every situation and reflect the best test-taking practices.

The Kaplan Method for Math has three steps:

> Step 1: Read the question, identifying and organizing important information as you go
>
> Step 2: Choose the best strategy to answer the question
>
> Step 3: Check that you answered the *right* question

Let's examine each of these steps in more detail.

Step 1: Read the question, identifying and organizing important information as you go

This means:

- **What information am I given?** Take a few seconds to jot down the information you are given and try to group similar items together.

- **Separate the question from the context.** Word problems may include information that is unnecessary to solve the question. Feel free to discard any unnecessary information.

- **How are the answer choices different?** Reading answer choices carefully can help you spot the most efficient way to solve a multiple-choice math question. If the answer choices are decimals, then painstakingly rewriting your final answer as a simplified fraction is a waste of time; you can just use your calculator instead.

- **Should I label or draw a diagram?** If the question describes a shape or figure but doesn't provide one, sketch a diagram so you can see the shape or figure and add notes to it. If a figure is provided, take a few seconds to label it with information from the question.

✔ **Expert Tip**

Don't assume you understand a question as soon as you see it. Many students see an equation and immediately begin solving. Solving math questions without carefully reading can take you down the wrong path on Test Day.

Step 2: Choose the best strategy to answer the question

- **Look for patterns.** Every SAT math question can be solved in a variety of ways, but not all strategies are created equally. To finish all of the questions, you'll need to solve questions as *efficiently* as possible. If you find yourself about to do time-consuming math, take a moment to look for time-saving shortcuts.

- **Pick numbers or use straightforward math.** While you can always solve an SAT math question with what you've learned in school, doing so won't always be the fastest way. On questions that describe relationships between numbers (such as percentages) but don't actually use numbers, you can often save time on Test Day by using techniques such as Picking Numbers instead of straightforward math.

> ✔ **Expert Tip**
>
> The SAT won't give you any extra points for solving a question the hard way.

Step 3: Check that you answered the *right* question

- When you get the final answer, **resist the urge to immediately bubble in the answer**. Take a moment to:
  - Review the question stem
  - Check units of measurement
  - Double-check your work

- The SAT will often ask you for quantities such as $x + 1$ or the product of x and y. **Be careful on these questions!** They often include tempting answer choices that correspond to the values of x or y individually. There's no partial credit on the SAT, so take a moment at the end of every question to make sure you're answering the right question.

LINEAR EQUATIONS

Linear equations and linear graphs are some of the most common elements on the SAT Math Test. They can be used to model relationships and changes such as those concerning time, temperature, or population.

The graphs of these equations are as important as the equations themselves. The graphs you will see most are either linear or lines of best fit. A sample graph is shown:

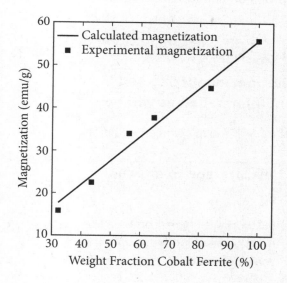

When working with a graph like this, you may not know anything about magnetization or cobalt ferrite, but you do see a graph with a straight line on it. That straight line is your clue that you're dealing with a linear equation.

Being able to work with, understand, and interpret linear equations will make up a substantial part of your Math score. In this chapter, we will explore all of those scenarios so you'll be ready to tackle linear equations in whatever form you encounter them on the test.

Many students inadvertently switch on "math autopilot" when solving linear equations, automatically running through the same set of steps on every equation without looking for the best way to solve the question. On the SAT, however, every second counts. You will want to use the *most* efficient strategy for solving questions. Take a look at the following example:

1. $$\frac{4 + z - (3 + 2z)}{6} = \frac{-z - 3(5 - 2)}{7}$$

What is the value of z in the equation above?

A) -61

B) $-\dfrac{61}{27}$

C) $\dfrac{61}{27}$

D) 61

Math

The following table shows Kaplan's strategic thinking on the left, along with suggested math scratchwork on the right. Keeping your notes organized is critical for success on the SAT, so start practicing now setting up well-organized scratchwork.

Strategic Thinking	Math Scratchwork
Step 1: Read the question, identifying and organizing important information as you go This question is straightforward: You're given an equation and need to solve for z.	
Step 2: Choose the best strategy to answer the question Straightforward algebra will work well here. Combine like terms on both sides of the equation first, being mindful of negative signs. Once you've combined, cross-multiply to eliminate the fractions, and then isolate z.	$$\frac{4 + z - (3 + 2z)}{6} = \frac{-z - 3(5 - 2)}{7}$$ $$\frac{1 - z}{6} = \frac{-z - 9}{7}$$ $$7 - 7z = -6z - 54$$ $$-z = -61$$ $$z = 61$$
Step 3: Check that you answered the *right* question You've determined that z is equal to 61; therefore, (D) is correct.	$$z = 61$$

You could have approached a question like this in many ways, but remember, the goal is to get the correct answer quickly. The faster you solve algebraic equations, the more time you'll be able to devote to challenging questions, setting you up to earn more points on Test Day.

✔ Remember

As you practice, always ask yourself: "Is there a faster way to solve this question?" Use the Answers and Explanations at the back of this book to check!

When solving an equation, always keep in mind the fundamental principles of equality: Because both sides of an equation are equal, you need to do the same thing to both sides so that equality is preserved. Try solving another linear equation for extra practice:

2. $3y + 2(y - 2) = -25$

What value of y satisfies the equation above?

A) $-\dfrac{29}{5}$

B) $-\dfrac{21}{5}$

C) $\dfrac{21}{5}$

D) $\dfrac{29}{5}$

Work through the Kaplan Method for Math step-by-step to solve this question. The following table shows Kaplan's strategic thinking on the left, along with suggested math scratchwork on the right.

Strategic Thinking	Math Scratchwork
Step 1: Read the question, identifying and organizing important information as you go	
This looks similar to the first question: It's asking you to find the value of y.	$3y + 2(y - 2) = -25$
Step 2: Choose the best strategy to answer the question	
Straightforward algebra is the fastest route to the answer. Start by distributing the 2. Continue by collecting like terms until you isolate y.	$3y + 2y - 4 = -25$ $5y - 4 = -25$ $5y = -21$ $y = -\dfrac{21}{5}$
Step 3: Check that you answered the *right* question	
You found y, so you're done! Choice (B) is correct.	

Notice that none of the answer choices are integers. The SAT may challenge you by designing questions so that the answer is in a form you do not expect. If you arrive at an answer in an unusual form, don't be alarmed. Fractions and decimals are often correct on the SAT.

Looking carefully at how the SAT uses fractions and decimals can guide your strategy in solving linear equations. The presence of fractions in the answer choices likely means you'll need to rely on techniques for combining and simplifying fractions to get to the right answer. Seeing decimals in the answer choices, on the other hand, likely indicates that you can rely on your calculator and save time on Test Day.

Try to determine the best strategy for solving the next question.

3. $3(y - 8) + 3(6x + 2) = 24 + 3y$

    Which approximate value of x satisfies the equation above?

    A)   0.80

    B)   1.33

    C)   2.33

    D)   The value cannot be determined from the given information.

Work through the Kaplan Method for Math step-by-step to solve this question. The following table shows Kaplan's strategic thinking on the left, along with suggested math scratchwork on the right.

Strategic Thinking	Math Scratchwork
Step 1: Read the question, identifying and organizing important information as you go The question is asking you to solve for a variable. Note that there are two variables present.	$3(y - 8) + 3(6x + 2)$ $= 24 + 3y$
Step 2: Choose the best strategy to answer the question Before blindly choosing D because there are two variables and only one equation, determine whether the y terms can be eliminated. Divide both sides by 3, and then combine like terms. You'll see that the y terms cancel, leaving one equation with one variable. Isolate x. The presence of decimals in the answer choices means your calculator will be a great asset here. Don't worry about reducing the fraction; just punch it into your calculator to find its decimal equivalent.	$y - 8 + 6x + 2 = 8 + y$ $-8 + 6x + 2 = 8$ $-6 + 6x = 8$ $6x = 14$ $x = \dfrac{14}{6}$
Step 3: Check that you answered the *right* question Double-check the question stem. You've found the value of x, which is 2.33, making (C) correct.	$x = 2.33$

Notice in the previous question that careful use of your calculator can eliminate the need to complete time-consuming tasks by hand. Be conscious of the format of the answer choices—decimal answers are a great clue that you can use your calculator.

> ✔ **Note**
>
> Many graphing calculators have a built-in function that will let you input and solve algebraic equations like the previous one. Consider learning how to use it before Test Day by reading the instruction manual or searching online.

LINEAR WORD PROBLEMS (REAL-WORLD SCENARIOS)

Another way linear equations can be made to look complicated is for them to be disguised in "real-world" word problems, where it's up to you to extract and solve an equation. When you're solving these problems, you may run into trouble translating English into math. The following table shows some of the most common phrases and mathematical equivalents you're likely to see on the SAT.

Word Problems Translation Table	
English	**Math**
equals, is, equivalent to, was, will be, has, costs, adds up to, the same as, as much as	=
times, of, multiplied by, product of, twice, double, by	×
divided by, per, out of, each, ratio	÷
plus, added to, and, sum, combined, total, increased by	+
minus, subtracted from, smaller than, less than, fewer, decreased by, difference between	−
a number, how much, how many, what	x, n, etc.

Linear word problems are made more difficult by complex phrasing and extraneous information. Don't get frustrated—word problems can be broken down in predictable ways. To stay organized on Test Day, use the **Kaplan Strategy for Translating English into Math:**

- Define any variables, choosing letters that make sense.

- Break sentences into short phrases.

- Translate each phrase into a mathematical expression.

- Put the expressions together to form an equation.

Let's apply this to a straightforward example: Colin's age is three less than twice Jim's age.

- **Define any variables, choosing letters that make sense:** We'll choose C for Colin's age and J for Jim's age.

- **Break sentences into short phrases:** The information about Colin and the information about Jim seem like separate phrases.

- **Translate each phrase into a mathematical expression:** Colin's age $= C$; 3 less than twice Jim's age $= 2J - 3$.

- **Put the expressions together to form an equation:** Combine the results to get $C = 2J - 3$.

This strategy fits into the larger framework of the Kaplan Method for Math: When you get to **Step 2: Choose the best strategy to answer the question** and are trying to solve a word problem as efficiently as possible, switch over to this strategy to move forward quickly.

The Kaplan Strategy for Translating English into Math works every time. Apply it here to a test-like example:

4. Malia and Omar want to find the shortest route from their school to a local burger hangout. The length of Route A is 1.5 times the length of Route B and $\frac{3}{4}$ the length of Route C. If Route C is 3 kilometers long, then Route A is how many kilometers longer than Route B?

    A) 0.75

    B) 1.5

    C) 2

    D) 2.25

Work through the Kaplan Method for Math step-by-step to solve this question. The following table shows Kaplan's strategic thinking on the left, along with suggested math scratchwork on the right.

Strategic Thinking	Math Scratchwork
Step 1: Read the question, identifying and organizing important information as you go The question is asking you to solve for the difference between the lengths of Routes A and B.	C is 3 km A is $\frac{3}{4}$ of C and 1.5 times B
Step 2: Choose the best strategy to answer the question This looks like a word problem, so go through each step of the Kaplan Strategy for Translating English into Math. Use the route labels for your variables. Note each comparison of the routes in your scratchwork, and then translate them into math. Work carefully through the algebra to find the lengths of routes A and B.	$A = \frac{3}{4} \times C$ $= \frac{3}{4} \times 3 = \frac{9}{4}$ $= 2.25$ $A = 1.5B$ $2.25 = 1.5B$ $1.5 = B$
Step 3: Check that you answered the *right* question One more step to go. Subtract the length of Route B from the length of Route A to yield (A) as your match.	$A - B = 2.25 - 1.5$ $= 0.75$

Math

LINEAR GRAPHS

Working with equations algebraically is only half the battle. The SAT will also expect you to work with graphs of linear equations, which means using lines in slope-intercept form and point-slope form.

One of the most important quantities you'll be working with when graphing a linear equation is the slope. Slope is given by the following equation: $m = \dfrac{y_2 - y_1}{x_2 - x_1}$, where (x_1, y_1) and (x_2, y_2) are coordinates of points on the line. To remember this, think: slope $= \dfrac{\text{rise}}{\text{run}}$.

One of the most common forms of a linear equation is *slope-intercept form*, which is used to describe the graph of a straight line. The formula is quickly recognizable: $y = mx + b$. The variables y and x represent the coordinates of a point on the graph through which the line passes, while m tells us what the slope of the line is and b represents the point at which the line intersects the y-axis.

Remember: A line with a positive slope runs up and to the right ("uphill"), and a line with a negative slope runs down and to the right ("downhill"). In the following figure, lines n and l have positive and negative slopes, respectively.

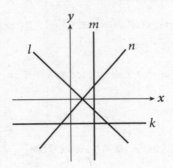

Occasionally, you will encounter a line with a slope of 0—meaning it does not rise or fall from left to right. These lines are easy to spot because they are horizontal and are parallel to the x-axis (line k in the figure shown). Lines that are parallel to the y-axis, such as line m in the figure, have slopes that are "undefined." The lines themselves exist, but their slopes cannot be calculated numerically.

The slope of a graph can also tell you valuable information about the rate of change of numbers and variables associated with the line. A positive slope signifies an increase in a variable, while a negative slope indicates a decrease. *Large* numerical values for slope indicate rapid changes, while *small* numerical values point to more gradual changes. Imagine that the balance in your checking account is B, and that it changes with the number of days that go by, D. Think about how each of the following models would impact your life.

$$B = 100D + 75$$
$$B = 0.25D + 75$$
$$B = -100D + 75$$
$$B = -0.25D + 75$$

The first equation probably looks pretty good. The second equation isn't as great. An extra quarter a day isn't going to do much for you. The third equation would quickly drive you into bankruptcy, while the fourth equation might be cause for concern after a while.

The *y*-intercept, on the other hand, is often less significant, typically representing the initial condition in a model—that is, where the model begins. In the checking account example, the beginning balance was $75 in all four models. Notice, the *y*-intercept didn't change at all.

Look at the following question to see how the SAT might test your ability to match a linear equation with its graph.

5. Line *A* passes through the coordinate points $\left(-\dfrac{2}{5}, 0\right)$ and $(0, 1)$. Which of the following lines will line *A* never intersect?

A)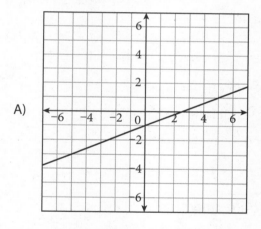

B)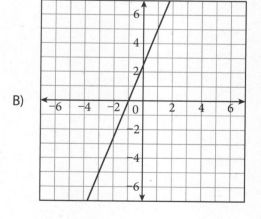

C)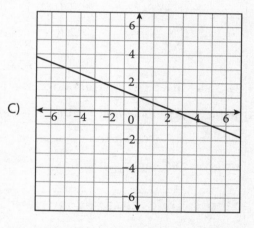

D)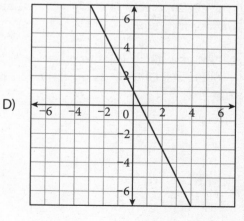

Math

Approach this question by using the Kaplan Method for Math. Try to ask yourself similar questions as you work through questions like this on Test Day.

Strategic Thinking	Math Scratchwork
Step 1: Read the question, identifying and organizing important information as you go This question is asking you to determine which line will never intersect the one that contains the two points provided in the question stem.	
Step 2: Choose the best strategy to answer the question Using your calculator will take too long, so use the slope formula and your critical thinking skills instead. Start by finding the slope of the line in the question stem. Because the slope is positive, you can eliminate C and D, which both contain lines with negative slopes. Two lines that never intersect are parallel and therefore have the same slope, so determine which of the remaining answer choices also has a slope of $\frac{5}{2}$. There is no need to calculate the slopes; simply counting units on the graphs will suffice.	$\left(-\frac{2}{5}, 0\right), (0, 1)$ $m = \dfrac{y_2 - y_1}{x_2 - x_1}$ $\quad = \dfrac{1 - 0}{0 - \left(-\frac{2}{5}\right)} = \dfrac{1}{\frac{2}{5}} = \dfrac{5}{2}$ $m_{\text{Choice A}} = \dfrac{2}{5}$ $m_{\text{Choice B}} = \dfrac{5}{2}$
Step 3: Check that you answered the *right* question Only (B) contains a line that will not intersect the one described in the question stem. Notice you didn't have to do any additional work, such as finding y-intercepts. Only do as much as you need to—this saves time on Test Day.	

Some questions are a little more challenging. They're usually similar in structure to the "checking account" equation described earlier, but they can involve more complicated scenarios. This next question requires you to choose the best model for a given "real-world" situation. See if you can match the graph to an appropriate model. Watch out: It's a science "crossover" question, so you'll need to be particularly careful to separate the question from the context.

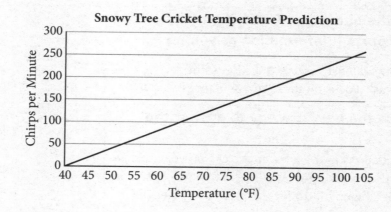

6. Snowy tree crickets have long been used to determine the ambient air temperature. The correlation between ambient air temperature and their chirp frequency is highly consistent. The graph shows the correlation between ambient air temperature, t, in degrees Fahrenheit and the number of chirps, c, per minute that a snowy tree cricket makes at that temperature. Based on the graph, which of the following best represents this scenario?

A) $c = 4t - 160$

B) $c = \dfrac{1}{4}t - 160$

C) $c = \dfrac{1}{2}t - 40$

D) $c = 4t + 160$

Math

Although you may enjoy learning about science with your math, you don't need to waste time digesting extraneous information. The following table shows the strategic thinking that can help you solve this question.

Strategic Thinking	Math Scratchwork
Step 1: Read the question, identifying and organizing important information as you go Only the last two sentences of the question stem describe the graph and your task. Focus on these two sentences.	
Step 2: Choose the best strategy to answer the question Graphing the equations in the answer choices on your calculator would be time-consuming; in addition, the y-intercept of the line is not visible, thereby introducing another hurdle. Opt for examining the answer choices closely instead. Pick a couple points on the line to determine the slope. You'll find it equals 4, so eliminate B and C. Now, read the axis labels carefully. The horizontal axis begins at 40 (not 0), and the line is trending downward, so the y-intercept (when $x = 0$) must be well below 0 on the vertical axis. Eliminate D.	$(40, 0)$ and $(65, 100)$ $m = \dfrac{100 - 0}{65 - 40} = \dfrac{100}{25} = 4$
Step 3: Check that you answered the *right* question Choice (A) is the only option remaining. You're done! Note that you didn't have to calculate b to find the correct answer, so you saved some time.	

While scatterplots will be described in more detail in subsequent chapters, this next question shows that the principles covered here for graphing linear equations can be equally applied to the line of best fit on a scatterplot. See what you can conclude from the slope and y-intercept of the equation of the line of best fit. Note that this question is an example of a very complex word problem—don't be intimidated! If you can tackle this problem, you'll be able to handle the most difficult SAT word problems.

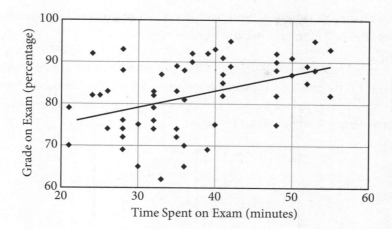

7. A physics professor presented the scatterplot above to his first-year students. What is the significance of the slope of the line of best fit?

    A) The slope represents the rate at which time spent on an exam increases based on a student's exam performance.

    B) The slope represents the average grade on the exam.

    C) The slope represents the rate at which a student's exam grade increases based on time spent on the exam.

    D) The slope has no significance.

Use the Kaplan Method for Math to make short work of this question. The following table shows the strategic thinking that can help you solve complex questions like this one.

Strategic Thinking
Step 1: Read the question, identifying and organizing important information as you go
You must determine the significance of the slope of the line of best fit on the scatterplot.
Step 2: Choose the best strategy to answer the question
Look for answer choices you can easily eliminate based on what you know about lines. A line's slope is a rate, so you can eliminate B and D. Examine A and C next. According to the graph, time spent on the exam is the independent variable (because it is graphed on the horizontal axis), and the exam grade is the dependent variable. Pick the answer choice that reflects this.
Step 3: Check that you answered the *right* question
You've determined the significance of the slope of the line of best fit. The correct answer is (C).

Notice that even complicated-looking questions involving linear graphs often boil down to the same basic concepts of slope and *y*-intercept. Master those ideas and you'll be able to handle any linear graph you'll see on the SAT.

Math

Now you'll have a chance to try a few more test-like questions. Use the scaffolding as needed to guide you through the question and get the right answer.

Some guidance is provided, but you'll need to fill in the missing parts of explanations or the step-by-step rnath to get to the correct answer. Don't worry—after going through the examples at the beginning of this chapter, these questions should be completely doable. If you find yourself struggling, however, review the worked examples again.

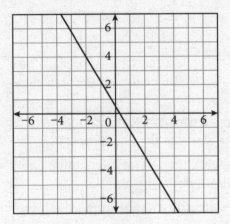

8. The line $y = -\dfrac{7x}{4} + \dfrac{1}{2}$ is shown in the graph. If the line is shifted down 2 units and then reflected over the x-axis, which of the following graphs represents the new line?

A)
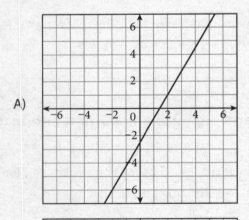

C)
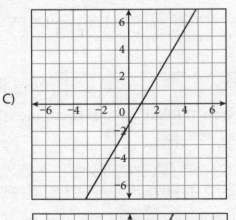

B)
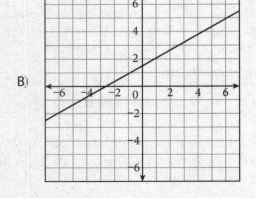

D)
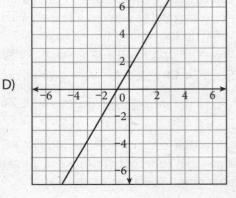

The following table can help you structure your thinking as you go about solving this problem. Kaplan's strategic thinking is provided, as are bits of structured scratchwork. If you're not sure how to approach a question like this, start at the top and work your way down.

Strategic Thinking	Math Scratchwork
Step 1: Read the question, identifying and organizing important information as you go You're asked for the graph that corresponds to the described changes made to $y = -\dfrac{7x}{4} + \dfrac{1}{2}$.	
Step 2: Choose the best strategy to answer the question While you could apply the transformations to the entire line, picking a test point will be faster. For example, draw a dot at $(-2, 4)$ on the original line and apply the changes to that point. Cross off any choices that don't pass through the new point. You might need to pick more than one point if your initial choice doesn't eliminate all of the incorrect answer choices.	
Step 3: Check that you answered the *right* question Did you get (D)? If so, you're correct! Beware of C—it results from a reflection over the wrong axis.	

Here's another test-like example to try.

9. Three years ago, Madison High School started charging an admission fee for basketball games to raise money for new bleachers. The initial price was $2 per person; the school raised the price of admission to $2.50 this year. Assuming this trend continues, which of the following equations can be used to describe the cost of admission, c, y years after the school began charging for admission to games?

A) $c = 6y + 2$

B) $c = \dfrac{y}{6} + 2.5$

C) $c = \dfrac{y}{6} + 2$

D) $c = \dfrac{y}{2} + 2$

The following table can help you structure your thinking as you go about solving this problem. The Kaplan strategic thinking is provided, as are bits of structured scratchwork. If you're not sure how to approach a question like this, start at the top and work your way down.

Strategic Thinking	Math Scratchwork
Step 1: Read the question, identifying and organizing important information as you go You need to identify the equation that correctly relates cost to years after the admission charge implementation.	
Step 2: Choose the best strategy to answer the question Look carefully; you're implicitly given two sets of coordinates. You can use these to find a key piece of a linear equation and eliminate two answer choices. The school started charging admission at a certain point in time; the price at this point is the y-intercept. Use this to pick the correct answer.	$(\underline{\quad}, \underline{\quad})$ $(\underline{\quad}, \underline{\quad})$ $m = \underline{\qquad} = \underline{\qquad}$ eliminate $\underline{\quad}$ and $\underline{\quad}$ $b = \underline{\quad}$
Step 3: Check that you answered the *right* question Did you come up with (C)? If so, great job! You're correct.	$\underline{\quad}$

✔ **Note**

Because the question says "three years ago," it may be tempting to use $(-3, 2)$ and $(0, 2.5)$ as your coordinates. Before you do this, think about what that means: This translates to the first admission charge being $2.50, as it's impossible to have a negative year. Choice B is a trap waiting for students who attempt this route!

Now that you've seen the variety of ways in which the SAT can test you on linear equations, try the following three questions to check your understanding. Give yourself 3.5 minutes to answer the questions. Make sure you use the Kaplan Method for Math on every question. Remember, you'll need to emphasize speed and efficiency in addition to simply getting the correct answer.

10. If the line $y = -5x + 8$ is shifted down 3 units and left 2 units, what is the slope of the new line?

A) -5

B) 0

C) 3

D) 5

11. If $\frac{3}{4}y = 6 - \frac{1}{3}c$, then what is the value of $2c + \frac{9}{2}y$?

12. If m is a constant between 0 and $\frac{1}{2}$ (exclusive), which of the following could be the graph of $x - y = m(2x + y)$?

A)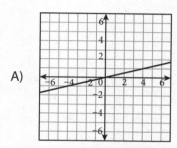

B)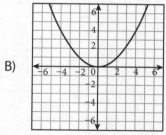

C)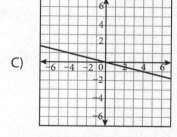

D)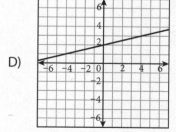

Answers and Explanations for this chapter begin on page 881.

EXTRA PRACTICE

The calculator icon means you are permitted to use a calculator to solve a question. It does not mean that you *should* use it, however.

1. If $2x + 5 = 11$, what is the value of $2x - 5$?

   A) -11

   B) -6

   C) 1

   D) 11

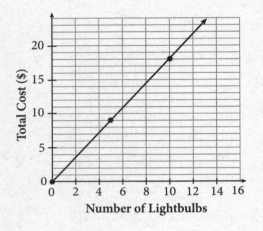

2. A hardware store sells lightbulbs in different quantities. The graph shows the cost of various quantities. According to the graph, what is the cost of a single lightbulb?

   A) $0.56

   B) $1.80

   C) $2.50

   D) $3.60

3. A local restaurant is hosting a dance-a-thon for charity. Each couple must dance a minimum of three hours before earning any money for the charity. After the first three hours, couples earn $50 per half-hour of continuous dancing. Which expression represents the total amount earned by a couple that dances h hours, assuming they dance at least three hours?

   A) $25h$

   B) $100h$

   C) $50(h - 3)$

   D) $100h - 300$

Price of One Pound	Projected Number of Pounds Sold
$1.20	15,000
$1.40	12,500
$1.60	10,000
$1.80	7,500
$2.00	5,000
$2.20	2,500

4. Which of the following equations best describes the linear relationship shown in the table, where g represents the number of pounds of grain sold and d represents the price in dollars of one pound of grain?

A) $g = 1.2d + 12,500$

B) $g = 12,500d + 15,000$

C) $g = -12,500d + 17,500$

D) $g = -12,500d + 30,000$

$$2\left(x - \frac{5}{2}\right) = c\left(\frac{4}{5}x - 2\right)$$

5. If the equation above has infinitely many solutions and c is a constant, what is the value of c?

A) -2

B) $-\dfrac{4}{5}$

C) $\dfrac{5}{4}$

D) $\dfrac{5}{2}$

6. If a is a rational number where $a > 1$, which of the following could be the graph of $y = ay + ax + x + 1$?

A)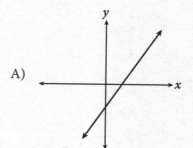

B)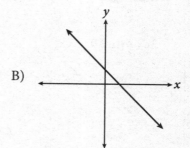

C)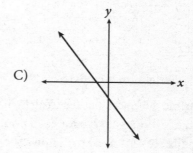

D)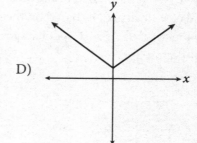

Math

7. What value of n satisfies the equation
$\frac{7}{8}(n - 6) = \frac{21}{2}$?

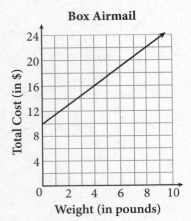

Box Airmail

8. A freight airline charges a flat fee to airmail a box, plus an additional charge for each pound the box weighs. The graph above shows the relationship between the weight of the box and the total cost to airmail it. Based on the graph, how much would it cost in dollars to airmail a 40-pound box?

Expected Property Values
2014-2038

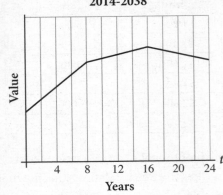

9. A realtor is studying the graph above, which shows the expected value of properties in her area over the next 24 years. If t represents the number of years after 2014, in what year should the increase in property values start to slow down?

A) 2008

B) 2018

C) 2022

D) 2030

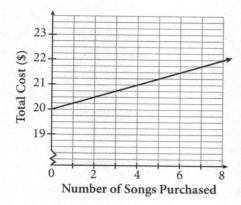

Number of Songs Purchased

10. The graph above shows the cost of joining and buying music from a music subscription service. What does the *y*-intercept of the line most likely represent?

   A) The cost per song

   B) The cost to join the service

   C) The cost of buying 20 songs

   D) The cost of 20 subscriptions to the service

11. Andrew works at a travel agency. He gets paid $120 for a day's work, plus a bonus of $25 for each cruise he books. Which of the following equations represents the relationship between one day of Andrew's pay, *d*, and the number of cruises he books, *c*?

   A) $c = 25d + 120$

   B) $c = 120d + 25$

   C) $d = 25c + 120$

   D) $d = 120c + 25$

12. Which value of *x* makes the equation
   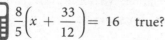 $\frac{8}{5}\left(x + \frac{33}{12}\right) = 16$ true?

   A) 7.25

   B) 8.75

   C) 12.75

   D) 13.25

13. Henry just set up direct deposit from his employer to his checking account. The equation $y = 360x - 126.13$ represents the balance in Henry's account if he deposits his weekly paycheck for *x* weeks. Based on this equation, which of the following statements is true?

   A) Henry earns $126.13 per week.

   B) Henry made an initial deposit of $126.13.

   C) Before setting up the direct deposit, Henry had overdrawn his account.

   D) When Henry set up the direct deposit, he already had $360 in his account.

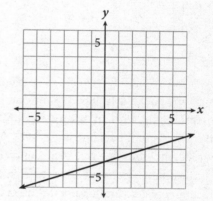

14. The graph shown represents which of the following equations?

   A) $y = -3x + 4$

   B) $y = -\frac{1}{3}x + 4$

   C) $y = \frac{1}{3}x - 4$

   D) $y = 3x - 4$

Math

Minutes Charging	10	15	30
Percent Charged	34	41.5	64

15. Jose is using his laptop and wants to recharge it before the battery completely runs out. He recorded the battery charge for the first 30 minutes after he plugged it in to get an idea of when it would be completely charged. The table above shows the results. Which linear function represents the percent battery charge on Jose's laptop x minutes after he plugged it in?

A) $f(x) = 1.5x + 19$

B) $f(x) = 2x + 14$

C) $f(x) = 2.5x + 9$

D) $f(x) = 10x + 34$

16. A laser tag arena sells two types of memberships. One package costs $325 for one year of membership with an unlimited number of visits. The second package has a $125 enrollment fee, includes five free visits, and costs an additional $8 per visit after the first five. How many visits would a person need to use for each type of membership to cost the same amount over a one-year period?

A) 20

B) 25

C) 30

D) 40

17. Which of the following equations has no solution?

A) $\frac{3}{8}(x - 2) = \frac{8}{3}(x + 2)$

B) $-\frac{3}{2}(2x - 8) = 3x - 12$

C) $4\left(\frac{3}{4}x + 5\right) = 3x + 20$

D) $6\left(\frac{2}{3}x + 5\right) = 4x + 5$

18. Vera is on her school's track and field team. In a practice long-jump competition against her teammates, she gets 5 points for landing over the closer line and 10 points for landing over the farther line. She gets a total of 7 jumps and lands x times over the farther line and the rest of the times over the closer line. Which of the following functions represents Vera's total score?

A) $f(x) = 10x$

B) $f(x) = 5x + 35$

C) $f(x) = 10x + 5$

D) $f(x) = 70 - 5x$

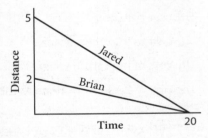

19. Brian and Jared live in the same apartment complex and they both bike to and from work every day. The figure above shows a typical commute home for each of them. Based on the figure, which of the following statements is true?

A) It takes Brian longer to bike home because his work is farther away.

B) It takes Jared longer to bike home because his work is farther away.

C) Jared and Brian arrive home at the same time, so they must bike at about the same rate.

D) Jared bikes a longer distance than Brian in the same amount of time, so Jared must bike at a faster rate.

20. When graphing a linear equation that is written in the form $y = mx + b$, the variable m represents the slope of the line and b represents the y-intercept. Assuming that $b > 0$, which of the following best describes how reversing the sign of b would affect the graph?

    A) The new line will be shifted down b units.

    B) The new line will be shifted down $b \times 2$ units.

    C) The new line will be a perfect reflection across the x-axis.

    D) The new line will be a perfect reflection across the y-axis.

21. Which of the following equations is linear?

    A) $y = \dfrac{3}{x}$

    B) $\sqrt{x} + y = 0$

    C) $\dfrac{1}{2}x - \dfrac{5}{8}y = 11$

    D) $y = x^2 + 2x - 4$

22. Which of the following does not represent a linear relationship?

    A) $y = \dfrac{x}{5}$

    B)

x	y
-4	12
0	2
4	-6
8	2
12	12

    C) $x = \dfrac{9}{7}y + 4$

    D) $y = 4x + 7$

23. The local Farmers' Market usually sells potatoes for $0.90 per pound. On Fridays, they sell potatoes at a 30% discount. The market also sells cantaloupes for $3.50 each. Which of the following represents the total cost, c, if a customer buys 2 cantaloupes and p pounds of potatoes on a Friday?

    A) $c = 0.63p + 7$

    B) $c = 0.9p + 7$

    C) $c = 0.3p + 3.5$

    D) $c = 0.9p + 3.5$

24. If paintbrushes cost $1.50 each and canvases cost 6 times that much, which of the following represents the cost, in dollars, of p paintbrushes and c canvases?

    A) $7.5pc$

    B) $10.5pc$

    C) $9c + 1.5p$

    D) $10.5(p + c)$

25. In states that produce natural gas, the state government typically imposes two types of taxes on producers: a local impact fee, which is a flat tax paid per well drilled, and a severance tax, which is based on the market value of the total volume of gas extracted, v. If a producer's total bill for one well is given by the equation $T = 0.004v + 50{,}000$, then the value 0.004 could represent which of the following?

    A) The local impact fee

    B) The market value of the gas extracted

    C) The total tax bill minus the local impact fee

    D) The amount of the severance tax as a percentage

Math

26. Which value of x makes the equation

$\frac{3}{2}(x + 7) = 6$ true?

A) -5

B) -3

C) 9

D) 11

27. A company is sponsoring a celebrity charity walk. For each celebrity who participates, the company will donate a flat amount to the charity of the celebrity's choice, plus an additional amount for every mile the celebrity walks. If the amount donated to charity on behalf of one celebrity is represented by $y = 100x + 250$, what does the number 250 best represent?

A) The flat amount donated

B) The total amount donated

C) The amount donated per mile

D) The number of miles the celebrity walked

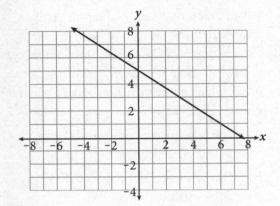

28. What is the slope of the line shown in the graph above?

A) $-\frac{3}{2}$

B) $-\frac{2}{3}$

C) $\frac{2}{3}$

D) $\frac{3}{2}$

$$\frac{3(n - 2) + 5}{4} = \frac{11 - (7 - n)}{6}$$

29. In the equation shown, what is the value of n?

A) $-\frac{1}{11}$

B) $\frac{5}{11}$

C) 1

D) $\frac{11}{7}$

30. A printing press running around the clock can print 54,000 black and white pages per day. Based on this information, what could the function $f(x) = 2,250x$ represent?

   A) The number of pages the press can print in x days

   B) The number of pages the press can print in x hours

   C) The number of days it takes the press to print x pages

   D) The number of hours it takes the press to print x pages

31. A store "breaks even" when its sales equal its expenses. Jon has just opened a new surfboard store at the beach. He buys each surfboard wholesale for $80 and has fixed monthly expenses of $3,600. He sells each surfboard for $120. How many surfboards does Jon need to sell in a month to break even?

   A) 18

   B) 30

   C) 45

   D) 90

32. Nadim is hosting a party and is hiring a catering company to make and serve the food. The caterer charges a flat fee for serving the food plus a per person rate for the meals. If the equation used to calculate the total cost of Nadim's party is $y = 11x + 300$, then which of the following most likely represents the number of people attending the party?

   A) x

   B) y

   C) 11

   D) 300

33. The graph of which of the following linear equations has an undefined slope?

   A) $x = 3$

   B) $y = 0$

   C) $x = -y$

   D) $x - y = 0$

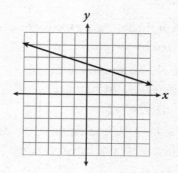

34. If the equation of the line shown in the graph above is written in the form $y = mx + b$, which of the following is true?

   A) $m < 0$ and $b < 0$

   B) $m < 0$ and $b > 0$

   C) $m > 0$ and $b < 0$

   D) $m > 0$ and $b > 0$

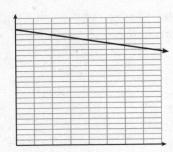

35. Which of the following scenarios could be supported by the graph shown?

   A) As the algae content in a lake increases, the number of fish decreases.

   B) As the algae content in a lake decreases, the number of fish decreases.

   C) As the algae content in a lake increases, the number of fish increases.

   D) As the algae content in a lake increases, the number of fish remains constant.

x	−9	0	3	9
y	11	8	7	?

36. If the values in the table represent a linear relationship, what is the missing value?

   A) 5

   B) 6

   C) 11

   D) 13

37. What was the initial amount of fuel in an airplane's tank, in gallons, if there are now x gallons, y gallons were used for the last flight, and 18,000 gallons were added when the plane was refueled?

   A) $y + x − 18,000$

   B) $y + x + 18,000$

   C) $x − y − 18,000$

   D) $y − x + 18,000$

$$\frac{1}{4}(10h) - \frac{3}{2}(h+1) = -\frac{2}{3}\left(\frac{9}{2}h\right) + 6$$

38. What is the value of h in the equation above?

   A) $\dfrac{9}{8}$

   B) $\dfrac{15}{8}$

   C) There is no value of h for which the equation is true.

   D) There are infinitely many values of h for which the equation is true.

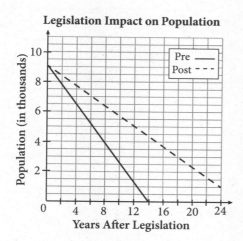

Legislation Impact on Population

39. The federal government in the United States has the authority to protect species whose populations have reached dangerously low levels. The graph above represents the expected population of a certain endangered species before and after a proposed law aimed at protecting the animal is passed. Based on the graph, which of the following statements is true?

A) The proposed law is expected to accelerate the decline in population.

B) The proposed law is expected to stop and reverse the decline in population.

C) The proposed law is expected to have no effect on the decline in population.

D) The proposed law is expected to slow, but not stop or reverse, the decline in population.

40. Some cars are more fuel-efficient than others. Which graph could represent the fuel efficiency of an efficient car, e, and a less efficient car, i?

A)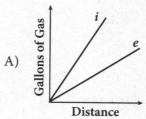

B)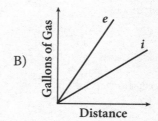

C)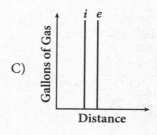

D)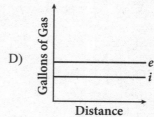

$$0.55x - 1.04 = 0.35x + 0.16$$

41. In the equation above, what is the value of x?

42. For what value of y does the graph of
$\dfrac{3}{2}y - 2x = 18$ cross the y-axis?

CHAPTER 3

Systems of Equations

CHAPTER OBJECTIVES

By the end of this chapter, you will be able to:

1. Distinguish between independent and dependent equations

2. Solve two-variable systems of linear equations

3. Determine the most efficient way to solve systems of equations

4. Translate word problems into multiple equations

SMARTPOINTS

Point Value	SmartPoint Category
50 Points	Systems of Linear Equations

Math

SYSTEMS OF EQUATIONS

Chapter 3

Homework

Extra Practice: #1-12

Key

 Book Assignment

 Online Video Assignment

 Online Quiz Assignment

SYSTEMS OF EQUATIONS

The linear equations detailed in the previous chapter are well suited for modeling a variety of scenarios and for solving for a single variable in terms of another that is clearly defined (e.g., what is the cost of a data plan if you consume 4 GB of data in a month). However, sometimes you will be given a set of multiple equations with multiple variables that are interdependent. For example, suppose a $50/month cell phone plan includes $0.05 text messages and $0.40 voice calls, with a cap of 1,000 combined text messages and voice calls.

This scenario can be represented by the following system of equations:

$$\$0.05t + \$0.40v = \$50$$
$$t + v = 1,000$$

Solving such a system would enable you to determine the maximum number of text messages and voice calls you could make under this plan, while optimizing total usage. To solve systems of equations, you'll need to rely on a different set of tools that builds on the algebra you're already familiar with. The following question shows an example of such a system in the context of a test-like question.

1. If $28x - 5y = 36$ and $15x + 5y + 18 = 68$, what is the value of x?
    A) 1
    B) 2
    C) 3
    D) 4

You might be tempted to switch on math autopilot at this point and employ substitution, solving the first equation for y in terms of x:

$$y = \frac{1}{5}(-36 + 28x)$$

You could plug the resulting expression back into the other equation and eventually solve for x, but remember, the SAT tests your ability to solve math problems in the most efficient way. The following table contains some strategic thinking designed to help you find the most efficient way to solve this problem on Test Day, along with some suggested scratchwork.

Strategic Thinking	Math Scratchwork
Step 1: Read the question, identifying and organizing important information as you go This question is straightforward: You're being asked to solve for *x*.	
Step 2: Choose the best strategy to answer the question None of the coefficients in either equation is 1, so combination will be faster than substitution. Begin by writing the second equation in the same form as the first. The coefficients of the *y* terms are equal in magnitude but opposite in sign, so add the equations. Once the *y* terms are eliminated, solve for *x*.	$28x - 5y = 36$ $15x + 5y + 18 = 68$ $28x - 5y = 36$ $+\quad 15x + 5y = 50$ ─────────── $43x = 86$ $x = 2$
Step 3: Check that you answered the *right* question You've solved for *x*, the requested quantity. You can confidently select (B).	$x = 2$

> ✔ **Note**
>
> Explanations for each simplifying step are not always included in this chapter. If you get stuck, review the information on simplifying and solving equations in chapter 2.

INDEPENDENT VERSUS DEPENDENT EQUATIONS

Generally, when you are given a system involving *n* variables, you need *n independent* equations to arrive at fixed values for these variables. Thus, if you have a system of two variables, you need two independent equations to solve for each of the variables. Three variables would require three independent equations, and so on.

Systems of equations are extremely useful in modeling and simulation. Complex mathematical problems such as weather forecasting or crowd control predictions often require 10 or more equations to be simultaneously solved for multiple variables. Fortunately, you won't encounter anything this daunting on Test Day.

Before we outline the process for solving two-variable systems of equations, let's clarify one of the key requirements. Earlier, it was stated that you need two independent equations to solve for two variables, but what exactly is an independent equation? Consider the equation $4x + 2y = 8$. You could use properties of equality to transform this equation in a number of different ways. For example, you could multiply both sides by 2, resulting in the equation $8x + 4y = 16$.

While it seems as though we've just created an additional equation, this is misleading, as the second equation has the same core variables and relationships as the first equation. This is termed a dependent equation, and two dependent equations cannot be used to solve for two variables. Look what happens when we try to use substitution. Start by isolating y in the original equation; the result is $y = 4 - 2x$.

Substituting that into the second equation, notice what happens:

$$8x + 4(4 - 2x) = 16$$
$$8x + 16 - 8x = 16$$
$$16 = 16$$

Although 16 does in fact equal 16, this doesn't bring us any closer to solving for either of the variables. In fact, if you arrive at a result like this when solving a system of equations, then the two equations are *dependent*. In this case, the system has infinitely many solutions because you could choose any number of possible values for x and y.

> ✔ **Note**
>
> When two equations are dependent, one equation can be obtained by algebraically manipulating the other equation. Graphically, dependent equations both describe the same line in the coordinate plane and therefore have the same slope and the same y-intercept.

At other times, you'll encounter equations that are fundamentally incompatible with each other. For example, if you have the two equations $4x + 2y = 8$ and $4x + 2y = 9$, it should be obvious that there are no values for x and y that will satisfy both equations at the same time. Doing so would violate fundamental laws of math. In this case, you would have a system of equations that has no solution. These two equations define parallel lines, which by definition never intersect.

Knowing how many solutions a system of equations has will tell you how graphing them in the same coordinate plane should look. Remember, the solution of a system of equations consists of the point or points where their graphs intersect.

If your system has...	...then it will graph as:	Reasoning
no solution	two parallel lines	Parallel lines never intersect.
one solution	two lines intersecting at a single point	Two straight lines have only one intersection.
infinitely many solutions	a single line (one line directly on top of the other)	One equation is a manipulation of the other—their graphs are the same line.

Because you could encounter any of these three situations on Test Day, make sure you are familiar with all of them.

Let's examine a sample problem to investigate the requirements for solving a system of equations:

$$\begin{cases} 5x - 3y = 10 \\ 6y = kx - 42 \end{cases}$$

2. In the system of linear equations above, k represents a constant. If the system of equations has no solution, what is the value of $2k$?

A) $\dfrac{5}{2}$

B) 5

C) 10

D) 20

Work through the Kaplan Method for Math step-by-step to solve this question. The following table shows Kaplan's strategic thinking on the left, along with suggested math scratchwork on the right.

Strategic Thinking	Math Scratchwork
Step 1: Read the question, identifying and organizing important information as you go You are looking for the value of $2k$, given the condition that the system of equations has no solution (which means the lines are parallel).	
Step 2: Choose the best strategy to answer the question If the two variables have identical coefficients in both equations, they should be equal to different constants. (This means they have the same slope but different y-intercepts.) Start by manipulating the second equation so that it is in the same format as the first. After manipulating the second equation, divide it by 2 to yield a -3 coefficient for y to match the coefficient of y in the first equation. Now, $\dfrac{k}{2}$ must equal 5, the coefficient of x in the first equation. Solve for k.	$5x - 3y = 10$ $6y = kx - 42$ $-kx + 6y = -42$ $kx - 6y = 42$ $\dfrac{k}{2}x - 3y = 21$ $\dfrac{k}{2} = 5$ $k = 10$
Step 3: Check that you answered the *right* question Be careful: You're asked for $2k$, not k. Multiply both sides by 2 to get $2k = 20$, which is (D).	$2k = 20$

SOLVING SYSTEMS OF EQUATIONS: COMBINATION & SUBSTITUTION

Now that you understand the requirements that must be satisfied to solve a system of equations, let's look at some methods for solving these systems effectively. The two main methods for solving a system of linear equations are substitution and combination (sometimes referred to as *elimination by addition*).

Substitution is the most straightforward method for solving systems, and it can be applied in every situation. Unfortunately, it is often the longest and most time-consuming route for solving systems of equations as well. To use substitution, solve the simpler of the two equations for one variable, and then substitute the result into the other equation. You could use substitution to answer the following question, but you'll see that there's a quicker way: combination.

Combination involves adding the two equations together to eliminate a variable. Often, one or both of the equations must be multiplied by a constant before they are added together. Combination is often the best technique to use to solve a system of equations as it is usually faster than substitution.

Unfortunately, even though most students prefer substitution, problems on the SAT are often designed to be quickly solved with combination. To really boost your score on Test Day, practice combination as much as you can on Practice Tests and in homework problems so that it becomes second nature.

3. If $\frac{1}{4}x + 2y = \frac{11}{4}$ and $-6y - x = 7$, what is half of y?

Prepare

Work through the Kaplan Method for Math step-by-step to solve this question. The following table shows Kaplan's strategic thinking on the left, along with suggested math scratchwork on the right.

Strategic Thinking	Math Scratchwork
Step 1: Read the question, identifying and organizing important information as you go Read carefully: You need to find *half* of y.	
Step 2: Choose the best strategy to answer the question Resist the urge to automatically use substitution. The presence of fractions in the question stem tells you that you should use combination (because substitution will be very messy). Multiply the first equation by 4 to clear the fractions, reorder the second equation so that x comes first, and then add the equations together and solve for y.	$\frac{1}{4}x + 2y = \frac{11}{4}$ $-6y - x = 7$ $4\left(\frac{1}{4}x + 2y = \frac{11}{4}\right) \rightarrow$ $x + 8y = 11$ $+ \quad -x - 6y = 7$ $\overline{\qquad\qquad 2y = 18}$ $y = 9$
Step 3: Check that you answered the *right* question Don't stop yet: You need to find half of y. Grid in 9/2 or 4.5, and you're done.	$\frac{y}{2} = \frac{9}{2} = 4.5$

Combination can also be used when the test makers ask you for a strange quantity, as in the following problem:

4. If $7c - 2b = 15$ and $3b - 6c = 2$, what is the value of $b + c$?

    A)   −27

    B)   −3

    C)   8

    D)   17

Work through the Kaplan Method for Math step-by-step to solve this question. The following table shows Kaplan's strategic thinking on the left, along with suggested math scratchwork on the right.

Strategic Thinking	Math Scratchwork
Step 1: Read the question, identifying and organizing important information as you go You are being asked to find the value of $b + c$. The question stem provides two equations involving b and c.	$7c - 2b = 15$ $3b - 6c = 2$
Step 2: Choose the best strategy to answer the question The fact that you're solving for $b + c$ suggests that there's a short-cut that will save time on Test Day. Add the equations together to yield $b + c$ equal to a constant. Before you add, don't forget to write the variable terms in the same order for each equation.	$\begin{aligned} -2b + 7c &= 15 \\ +\quad 3b - 6c &= 2 \\ \hline b + c &= 17 \end{aligned}$
Step 3: Check that you answered the *right* question Choice (D) correctly reflects the sum of b and c.	$b + c = 17$

That was much easier and faster than substitution. With substitution, you could spend more than two minutes solving a question like this. However, a bit of analysis and combination gets the job done in much less time.

Math

TRANSLATING WORD PROBLEMS INTO MULTIPLE EQUATIONS

While solving systems of equations can be relatively straightforward once you get the hang of it, sometimes you'll encounter a complex word problem and need to translate it into a system of equations and then solve. It sounds a lot scarier than it actually is. Remember to use the Kaplan Strategy for Translating English into Math to set up your equations, and then solve using either substitution or combination.

> ✔ **Note**
>
> The Kaplan Strategy for Translating English into Math can be found in chapter 2.

Let's take a look at an example:

5. At a certain toy store, tiny stuffed pandas cost $3.50 and giant stuffed pandas cost $14. If the store sold 29 panda toys and made $217 in revenue in one week, how many tiny stuffed pandas and giant stuffed pandas were sold?

    A) 18 tiny stuffed pandas, 11 giant stuffed pandas

    B) 11 tiny stuffed pandas, 18 giant stuffed pandas

    C) 12 tiny stuffed pandas, 17 giant stuffed pandas

    D) 18 tiny stuffed pandas, 13 giant stuffed pandas

Work through the Kaplan Method for Math to solve this question step-by-step. The following table shows Kaplan's strategic thinking on the left, along with suggested math scratchwork on the right.

Strategic Thinking	Math Scratchwork
Step 1: Read the question, identifying and organizing important information as you go You need to find the number of tiny stuffed pandas and giant stuffed pandas sold.	tiny: $3.50 each giant: $14 each 29 total sold $217 in revenue
Step 2: Choose the best strategy to answer the question This is a word problem, so use the Kaplan Strategy for Translating English into Math. Because both toys are pandas, p is likely to be a confusing choice for a variable. Instead, use t for tiny and g for giant. Break off each piece of relevant information into a separate phrase. Translating each phrase into a math expression will create the components of a system of equations. After piecing together the system of equations, use combination to quickly eliminate g. Multiply the first equation by -14 before combining with the second. Solve for t. Choices B and C have different values for t, so eliminate them. Plug 18 into the first equation for t, and then solve for g.	$t = $ tiny $g = $ giant tiny: $3.50 $\rightarrow 3.5t$ giant: $14 $\rightarrow 14g$ 29 total sold $\rightarrow \ = 29$ $217 in revenue $\rightarrow \ = 217$ $t + g = 29$ $3.5t + 14g = 217$ $\ -14t - 14g = -406$ $+\ \ \ \ 3.5t + 14g = 217$ $\overline{-10.5t = -189}$ $t = 18$ $t + g = 29$ $18 + g = 29$ $g = 11$
Step 3: Check that you answered the *right* question The only answer choice that contains both quantities you found is (A).	$t = 18, g = 11$

Math

Watch out for B, a trap answer designed to catch students who switched the variables, possibly due to choosing an ambiguous letter such as *p*. Choosing descriptive variable names might sound silly, but in the high-stakes environment of the SAT, you must do everything you can to avoid careless errors and subsequent lost points.

> ✔ **Note**
>
> Always choose variable names that make sense to you. Countless students struggle on multi-part problems due to disorganized notes. Don't let that happen to you. Move beyond *x* and *y* when selecting variable names.

Other questions of this type will simply ask you to choose from a series of answer choices that describes the system of equations—they won't actually ask you to calculate a solution! These questions can be great time-savers. Consider the following example:

6. A state college has separate fee rates for resident students and nonresident students. Resident students are charged $421 per semester, and nonresident students are charged $879 per semester. The college's sophomore class of 1,980 students paid a total of $1,170,210 in fees for the most recent semester. Which of the following systems of equations represents the number of resident (*r*) and nonresident (*n*) sophomores and the amount of fees the two groups paid?

   A) $r + n = 1{,}170{,}210$; $421r + 879n = 1{,}980$

   B) $r + n = 1{,}980$; $879r + 421n = 1{,}170{,}210$

   C) $r + n = 1{,}980$; $421r + 879n = 1{,}170{,}210$

   D) $r + n = 1{,}170{,}210$; $879r + 421n = 1{,}980$

Work through the Kaplan Method for Math to solve this question step-by-step. The following table shows Kaplan's strategic thinking on the left, along with suggested math scratchwork on the right.

Strategic Thinking	Math Scratchwork
Step 1: Read the question, identifying and organizing important information as you go You're asked for the system of equations that represents the given situation.	
Step 2: Choose the best strategy to answer the question This question is wordy, so use the Kaplan Strategy for Translating English into Math. The first step (assigning variables) has been done for you, so you can go right to breaking up the question stem into smaller pieces. Convert these into math, and then assemble your equations.	$r =$ resident $n =$ nonresident r: \$421 in fees n: \$879 in fees 1,980 students \$1,170,210 collected r: \$421 $\rightarrow$ 421r n: \$879 $\rightarrow$ 879n $r + n = 1{,}980$ $421r + 879n = 1{,}170{,}210$
Step 3: Check that you answered the _right_ question Choice (C) is the only answer choice that contains both equations you built.	

Be careful! Choice B is close but switches the fee structure, drastically overcharging the in-state students! Always pay close attention to the differences between answer choices to avoid traps on Test Day.

Math

Now you'll have a chance to try a few more test-like questions. Use the scaffolding as needed to guide you through the question and get the right answer.

Some guidance is provided, but you'll need to fill in the missing parts of explanations or the step-by-step math to get to the correct answer. Don't worry—after going through the examples at the beginning of this chapter, these questions should be completely doable. If you find yourself struggling, however, review the worked examples again.

7. A bead shop sells wooden beads for $0.20 each and crystal beads for $0.50 each. If a jewelry artist buys 127 beads total and pays $41 for them, how much more did she spend on crystal beads than wooden beads?

    A) $11
    B) $15
    C) $23
    D) $26

The following table can help you structure your thinking as you go about solving this problem. Kaplan's strategic thinking is provided, as are bits of structured scratchwork. If you're not sure how to approach a question like this, start at the top and work your way down.

Strategic Thinking	Math Scratchwork
Step 1: Read the question, identifying and organizing important information as you go You're asked how much more the jewelry artist spent on crystal beads than on wooden beads.	
Step 2: Choose the best strategy to answer the question Use the Kaplan Strategy for Translating English into Math. Variables are easy to pick for this question. Think about what letters the words start with. Separate each numerical piece into its own phrase, then convert to math. Assemble a system of equations, then solve. You can use either substitution or combination to solve for the quantity of each bead type. Remember to think critically about which approach would be faster in this situation. Determine how much the jewelry artist spent on each type of bead, then take the difference.	wooden: _____ crystal: _____ _____ per wooden _____ per crystal _____ total bought _____ spent _____ per wooden → _____ _____ per crystal → _____ _____ total bought → _____ _____ spent → _____ _____ + _____ = _____ _____ + _____ = _____ _____ = _____ _____ = _____ $_____ on wooden $_____ on crystal _____ − _____ = _____
Step 3: Check that you answered the *right* question If you came up with (A), you're absolutely correct.	_____

8. If $y = -x - 15$ and $\dfrac{5y}{2} - 37 = -\dfrac{x}{2}$, then what is the value of $2x + 6y$?

Larger numbers don't make this question any different; just be careful with the arithmetic. Again, the following table can help you structure your thinking as you go about solving this problem. Kaplan's strategic thinking is provided, as are bits of structured scratchwork. If you're not sure how to approach a question like this, start at the top and work your way down.

Strategic Thinking	Math Scratchwork
Step 1: Read the question, identifying and organizing important information as you go You're asked to find the value of $2x + 6y$.	
Step 2: Choose the best strategy to answer the question Start by rearranging the equations so that they're in the same general format. Because you're asked for an expression, look for a shortcut. Don't bother trying to solve for either x or y individually. A good strategy: Clear the fractions from the second equation so you can use combination. Once the fractions are gone, confirm that adding the second equation to the first will yield the expression you need.	$y = -x - 15$ $\dfrac{5y}{2} - 37 = -\dfrac{x}{2}$ _____ + _____ = _____ _____ + _____ = _____ _____ (_____ + _____ = _____) _____ + _____ = _____ + _____ + _____ = _____ ―――――――――――― _____ + _____ = _____
Step 3: Check that you answered the *right* question If your answer is 59, you're correct!	_____

Now that you've seen the variety of ways in which the SAT can test you on systems of linear equations, try the following questions to check your understanding. Give yourself 4.5 minutes to tackle the following three questions.

$$\begin{cases} 6x + 3y = 18 \\ qx - \dfrac{y}{3} = -2 \end{cases}$$

9. In the system of linear equations above, q is a constant. If the system has infinitely many solutions, what is the value of q?

   A) -9

   B) $-\dfrac{2}{3}$

   C) $\dfrac{2}{3}$

   D) 9

10. If $12x + 15y = 249$ and $5x + 13y = 124$, then what is the value of $\dfrac{y}{x}$?

11. A pizzeria's top-selling pizzas are The Works and The Hawaiian. The Works sells for $17, and The Hawaiian sells for $13. Ingredient costs for The Works are $450 per week, and ingredient costs for The Hawaiian are $310 per week. Assuming the pizzeria sells an equal number of both pizzas in one week, at what point will profits for one pizza overtake the other?

   A)   After selling 35 pizzas each, The Hawaiian profits will overtake The Works profits.

   B)   After selling 145 pizzas each, The Hawaiian profits will overtake The Works profits.

   C)   After selling 35 pizzas each, The Works profits will overtake The Hawaiian profits.

   D)   After selling 145 pizzas each, The Works profits will overtake The Hawaiian profits.

Answers and Explanations for this chapter begin on page 891.

EXTRA PRACTICE

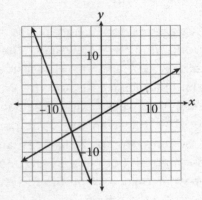

1. If (A, B) is the solution to the system of equations shown above, and A and B are integers, then what is the value of $A + B$?

   A) −12

   B) −6

   C) 0

   D) 6

$$\begin{cases} 4x + 3y = 14 - y \\ x - 5y = 2 \end{cases}$$

2. If (x, y) is a solution to the system of equations above, then what is the value of $x - y$?

   A) $\dfrac{1}{4}$

   B) 1

   C) 3

   D) 18

3. Charlie starts to solve a system of linear equations graphically. He puts both equations into slope-intercept form and notices that the lines have the same slope. Based on this information only, which of the following statements is true?

   A) The system could have no solution, one solution, or infinitely many solutions.

   B) The system has no solution because two equations with the same slope never intersect.

   C) The system has either no solution or infinitely many solutions, depending on the y-intercepts.

   D) The system has infinitely many solutions because two equations with the same slope represent the same line.

$$\begin{cases} hx - 4y = -10 \\ kx + 3y = -15 \end{cases}$$

4. If the graphs of the lines in the system of equations above intersect at $(-3, 1)$, what is the value of $\dfrac{k}{h}$?

   A) $\dfrac{3}{2}$

   B) 2

   C) 3

   D) 6

5. A sofa costs $50 less than three times the cost of a chair. If the sofa and chair together cost $650, how much more does the sofa cost than the chair?

   A) $175

   B) $225

   C) $300

   D) $475

$$\begin{cases} \dfrac{1}{2}x - \dfrac{2}{3}y = 7 \\ ax - 8y = -1 \end{cases}$$

6. If the system of linear equations above has no solution, and a is a constant, then what is the value of a?

   A) -2

   B) $-\dfrac{1}{2}$

   C) 2

   D) 6

7. A party store has 54 packs of plates in stock. The packs are either sets of 8 or sets of 12. If the store has 496 total plates in stock, how many plates would a customer buy if he or she buys all of the packs of 12 that the store has in stock?

   A)   16

   B)   38

   C)   192

   D)   304

$$\begin{cases} 3x - 9y = -6 \\ \dfrac{1}{2}x - \dfrac{3}{2}y = c \end{cases}$$

8. If the system of linear equations above has infinitely many solutions, and c is a constant, what is the value of c?

   A) -6

   B) -3

   C) -2

   D) -1

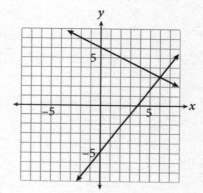

9. What is the y-coordinate of the solution to the system shown above?

   A) -5

   B) 3

   C) 5

   D) 6

10. If $2x - 3y = 14$ and $5x + 3y = 21$, then what is the value of x?

    A) -1

    B) 0

    C) $\dfrac{7}{3}$

    D) 5

11. At a certain movie theater, there are 16 rows and each row has either 20 or 24 seats. If the total number of seats in all 16 rows is 348, how many rows have 24 seats?

    A) 7

    B) 9

    C) 11

    D) 13

Equation 1	
x	*y*
−2	6
0	4
2	2
4	0

Equation 2	
x	*y*
−8	−8
−4	−7
0	−6
4	−5

12. The tables above represent data points for two linear equations. If the two equations form a system, what is the *x*-coordinate of the solution to that system?

CHAPTER 4

Linear Inequalities and Systems of Inequalities

CHAPTER OBJECTIVES

By the end of this chapter, you will be able to:

1. Identify the key differences between solving inequalities and equations
2. Efficiently solve systems of inequalities

SMARTPOINTS

Point Value	SmartPoint Category
40 Points	Inequalities

LINEAR INEQUALITIES & SYSTEMS OF INEQUALITIES

Chapter 4

Homework

Extra Practice: #1-13

Key

📖 Book Assignment

🎥 Online Video Assignment

Online Quiz Assignment

RULES FOR SOLVING INEQUALITIES

There's more to algebra than just equations, and inequalities will show up rather frequently on the SAT. Fortunately, many of the same strategies that apply to solving equations also apply to inequalities. There are a few key exceptions to keep in mind, but don't worry—these will be explained throughout this chapter.

First, the language used to describe inequalities tends to be more complex than the language used to describe equations. You "solve" an equation for x, but with an inequality, you might be asked to "describe all possible values of x" or provide an answer that "includes the entire set of solutions for x." This difference in wording exists because an equation describes a specific value of a variable, whereas an inequality describes a range of values. Regardless of the language, your task is the same: Isolate x on one side.

> ✔ **Note**
>
> If the variable ends up on the right-hand side of the symbol when you solve an inequality, be careful when matching it to an answer choice. For instance, $3 > x$ can be rewritten as $x < 3$. Notice that the small end of the symbol stays pointed at x.

The following question tests your basic inequality-solving skills.

1. A bowling alley charges a flat $6.50 fee for shoe and ball rental plus $3.75 per game and 6.325% sales tax. If each person in a group of seven people has $20 to spend on a bowling outing, which inequality represents the maximum number of shoe and ball rentals (r) and games (g) that can be purchased by the group?

A) $1.06325(6.5r + 3.75g) \leq 140$

B) $1.06325(6.5r + 3.75g) \leq 20$

C) $1.06325\left(\dfrac{6.5}{r} + \dfrac{3.75}{g}\right) \leq 140$

D) $0.06325(6.5r + 3.75g) \leq 20$

Work through the Kaplan Method for Math step-by-step to solve this question. The following table shows Kaplan's strategic thinking on the left, along with suggested math scratchwork on the right.

Strategic Thinking	Math Scratchwork
Step 1: Read the question, identifying and organizing important information as you go The question asks for an inequality that represents the situation described.	

Math

Strategic Thinking	Math Scratchwork
Step 2: Choose the best strategy to answer the question Use the Kaplan Strategy for Translating English into Math. The variables are already defined, so you only need to correctly piece them together with the given numbers. The question states that a shoe and ball rental costs $6.50 and that a game costs $3.75. Combine these with the correct variables, remembering to incorporate sales tax. Be careful when writing the right side of the inequality; the question asks for an inequality that represents the entire group, not just one person.	$r \rightarrow$ rentals, $6.5r$ $g \rightarrow$ games, $3.75g$ including tax: 1.06325 total $\$: 7 \times 20 = 140$ $1.06325(6.5r + 3.75g) \leq 140$
Step 3: Check that you answered the *right* question Choice (A) contains the inequality you derived.	

Notice B is a trap answer. If you write the inequality to reflect the cost for just one person, you'll be led right to it.

> ✔ **Note**
>
> Choice D is a trap waiting for students who improperly incorporate the sales tax component. Using 0.06325 calculates the amount spent on sales tax, not the total amount spent on the bowling outing.

Inequalities can also be presented graphically in one or two dimensions. In one dimension, inequalities are graphed on a number line with a shaded region. For example, $x > 1$ could be graphed like this:

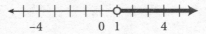

Notice the open dot at $x = 1$, indicating that 1 is not a solution to the inequality. This is called a **strict** inequality. By contrast, the graph of $x \leq 0$ looks like this:

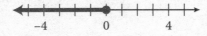

Notice the closed dot, indicating that 0 should be included in the solution set for the inequality.

> ✔ **Note**
>
> To help remember which way to shade, read the $<$ symbol as "less than," which tells you to shade to the left of the dot. Note the *L*s: *L*ess than means shade *L*eft.

In two dimensions, things get a bit more complicated. While linear equations graph as simple lines, inequalities graph as lines called **boundary lines** with shaded regions known as **half planes**. Solid lines involve inequalities that have $\leq$ or $\geq$ because the line itself is included in the solution set. Dashed lines involve strict inequalities that have $>$ or $<$ because, in these cases, the line itself is not included in the solution set. The shaded region represents all points that make up the solution set for the inequality.

SOLVING SYSTEMS OF INEQUALITIES

Multiple inequalities can be combined to create a system of inequalities. This system can involve multiple variables, or it can be used to provide more detailed bounds for a range of solutions for a single variable. You'll get to try both in questions shortly.

Systems of inequalities can also be presented graphically with multiple boundary lines and multiple shaded regions. Follow the same rules for graphing single inequalities, but keep in mind that the solution set is the region where the shading overlaps. Shading in different directions (e.g., parallel lines slanted up for one inequality and down for the other) makes the overlap easier to see. This is illustrated in an upcoming question.

2. Which of the following graphs represents the solution set for $5x - 10y > 6$?

A)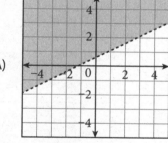

C)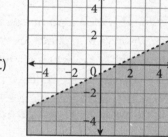

B)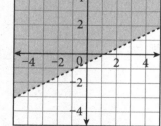

D)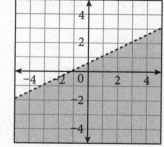

Prepare

Work through the Kaplan Method for Math step-by-step to solve this question. The following table shows Kaplan's strategic thinking on the left, along with suggested math scratchwork on the right.

Strategic Thinking	Math Scratchwork
Step 1: Read the question, identifying and organizing important information as you go The question is asking for the graph that matches the inequality given.	
Step 2: Choose the best strategy to answer the question It's risky to eliminate choices now, as the inequality is not in slope-intercept form. Rearrange the inequality so that it's in this form, remembering to flip the inequality symbol in the final step because you're dividing by −10. The inequality in slope-intercept form indicates a negative y-intercept, so you can eliminate A and D. The "less than" symbol indicates that the shading should be below the dashed line, meaning (C) must be correct. Alternatively, you can plug a point (such as the origin) into the inequality. When plugged into the inequality, you'll see that the origin should not be in the solution set because 0 is not greater than $0 + \dfrac{3}{5}$. This means (C) is correct.	$5x - 10y > 6$ $-10y > -5x + 6$ $\dfrac{-10y}{-10} > \dfrac{-5x}{-10} + \dfrac{6}{-10}$ $y < \dfrac{1}{2}x - \dfrac{3}{5}$
Step 3: Check that you answered the *right* question Choice (C) matches the inequality.	

3. If $\frac{1}{2}x + \frac{2}{3}y \leq 1$ and $\frac{1}{2}x + \frac{1}{3}y \leq \frac{2}{3}$ form a system of inequalities, what is one possible value of $x + y$?

Work through the Kaplan Method for Math step-by-step to solve this question. The following table shows Kaplan's strategic thinking on the left, along with suggested math scratchwork on the right.

Strategic Thinking	Math Scratchwork
Step 1: Read the question, identifying and organizing important information as you go The question asks for a possible value of $x + y$.	
Step 2: Choose the best strategy to answer the question The question asks for an unusual quantity, $x + y$, so look for a shortcut. Examine the coefficients of the variables. If you write one equation under the other, you'll see that the coefficients of the x terms sum to 1, as do the coefficients of the y terms. You can add the inequalities together (because they have the same symbol) and get $x + y$ on one side.	$\frac{1}{2}x + \frac{1}{3}y \leq \frac{2}{3}$ $+\ \frac{1}{2}x + \frac{2}{3}y \leq 1$ $\overline{\qquad\qquad\qquad}$ $x + y \leq \frac{5}{3}$
Step 3: Check that you answered the *right* question This is a grid-in question, so pick a number between 0 and $\frac{5}{3}$, inclusive, such as 0, 1, or $\frac{5}{3}$.	$0 \leq x + y \leq \frac{5}{3}$

✔ **Note**

You can add two inequalities ONLY if they have the same symbol.

Math

4. If $12x - 4y > 8$ and $\frac{2}{3}x + 6y \geq 14$ form a system of inequalities, which of the fol-

lowing graphs shows the solution set for the system?

A)

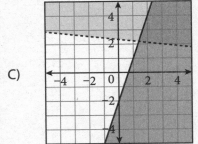

C)

B)

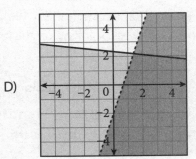

D)

Work through the Kaplan Method for Math step-by-step to solve this question. The following table shows Kaplan's strategic thinking on the left, along with suggested math scratchwork on the right.

Strategic Thinking	Math Scratchwork
Step 1: Read the question, identifying and organizing important information as you go You need to identify the graph that shows the solution to the system of inequalities.	
Step 2: Choose the best strategy to answer the question Start by rewriting each inequality in slope-intercept form. Once finished, determine what the correct graphs will look like. The boundary line for $y < 3x - 2$ should be a dashed line, and the boundary line for $y \geq -\dfrac{1}{9}x + \dfrac{7}{3}$ should be a solid line. You can eliminate C based on this. The half-plane below $y < 3x - 2$ should be shaded, and the half-plane above $y \geq -\dfrac{1}{9}x + \dfrac{7}{3}$ should be shaded; of the remaining choices, only (B) satisfies this requirement.	$12x - 4y > 8$ $\qquad -4y > -12x + 8$ $\qquad \dfrac{-4y}{-4} > \dfrac{-12x}{-4} + \dfrac{8}{-4}$ $\qquad y < 3x - 2$ $\dfrac{2}{3}x + 6y \geq 14$ $\qquad 6y \geq -\dfrac{2}{3}x + 14$ $\qquad \dfrac{6y}{6} \geq \dfrac{1}{6} \times \left(-\dfrac{2}{3}x\right) + \dfrac{14}{6}$ $\qquad y \geq -\dfrac{1}{9}x + \dfrac{7}{3}$
Step 3: Check that you answered the *right* question Choice (B) correctly depicts the solution to the system. You can check your answer by plugging a point from (B)'s solution set, such as (4, 4), into both inequalities given in the question and verifying that each results in a true statement.	

Math

Now you'll have a chance to try a test-like problem in a scaffolded way. We've provided some guidance, but you'll need to fill in the missing parts of the explanation or the step-by-step math to get to the correct answer. Don't worry—after going through the worked examples at the beginning of this section, this problem should be completely doable.

5. A network of hotels across the United States normally charges $180 for an overnight stay at any of its properties. This network also offers a deal for longer trips: A traveler who purchases a hotel discount card for $720 will pay only $120 per night at any of the network's properties for the duration of the traveler's trip. Which of the following inequalities represents the number of nights n a traveler must stay in any combination of the network's hotels during a trip in order to make the discount card a better deal?

A) $n > 12$

B) $n < 12$

C) $n > 9$

D) $n < 9$

Use the following scaffolding as your map through the question. If you aren't sure where to start, fill in the blanks in the table as you work from top to bottom.

Strategic Thinking	Math Scratchwork
Step 1: Read the question, identifying and organizing important information as you go You need to identify the inequality that gives the number of nights a traveler must stay during a trip in order to make the discount card a better deal.	
Step 2: Choose the best strategy to answer the question Use the Kaplan Strategy for Translating English into Math. You're told n is the number of overnight stays. The cost of travel with the card is $720 + 120n$. Without the card, a traveler would pay $180n$. Combine these expressions in an inequality and solve for n. Keep in mind that a "better deal" means the total cost is *less*.	____ < ____ ____ < ____ ____ < ____
Step 3: Check that you answered the *right* question If you got (A), you're right!	_____

Now that you've seen the variety of ways in which the SAT can test you on linear inequalities, try the following questions to check your understanding. Give yourself 2 minutes to tackle these two questions.

6. If $-3 < \frac{4}{3}h + \frac{1}{6} < 1$, then what is one possible value of $12h - 4$?

7. Sarah and Zena are head sales associates at a dance apparel shop. In addition to their annual raises, the two will be eligible for holiday bonuses if their dance tops and pants sales meet the following criteria in December: Between the two of them, the girls must sell an average of at least 75 items each, and their combined generated revenue must be at least $6,000. Each top costs $35, and each pair of pants costs $60. If Sarah sells t_S tops and p_S pairs of pants and Zena sells t_Z tops and p_Z pairs of pants, which of the following systems of inequalities correctly depicts the minimum quantities the two must sell to earn a holiday bonus?

A) $t_S + p_S + t_Z + p_Z \geq 75$
   $35(t_S + t_Z) + 60(p_S + p_Z) \geq 3,000$

B) $t_S + p_S + t_Z + p_Z \geq 150$
   $90(t_S + p_S + t_Z + p_Z) \geq 6,000$

C) $t_S + p_S + t_Z + p_Z \geq 150$
   $35(t_S + t_Z) + 60(p_S + p_Z) \geq 6,000$

D) $t_S + p_S + t_Z + p_Z \geq 150$
   $35(t_S + p_S) + 60(t_Z + p_Z) \geq 6,000$

Answers and Explanations for this chapter begin on page 896.

Math

EXTRA PRACTICE

$$\frac{1}{5}(7 - 3b) > 2$$

1. Which of the following gives all values of b that satisfy the inequality above?

   A) $b < -1$

   B) $b > -1$

   C) $b < 1$

   D) $b > 1$

2. If $n - 3 > 8$ and $n + 1 < 14$, then which of the following could be a value for n?

   A) 11

   B) 12

   C) 13

   D) 14

$$15 - x \boxed{} 9$$

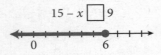

3. The number line above shows the solution to the inequality. Which of the following symbols would make the statement true?

   A) $<$

   B) $>$

   C) $\leq$

   D) $\geq$

Electric Company	Price (cents per kWh)
Company A	15.2
Company B	17.4
Company C	16.5
Company D	14.8

4. A kilowatt-hour is a unit of measure for consumable energy. A kilowatt-hour, written kWh, is equivalent to using 1,000 watts of power in 1 hour. The table above shows the per-kWh rates charged by several electric companies in New England. According to the United States Energy Information Administration, an average household in New England uses between 530 and 730 kWh of energy per month. Which inequality represents how much less in energy costs a household would pay per month if it uses Company D as its energy supplier, than if it uses Company B?

   A) $x \leq 0.026$

   B) $0.148 \leq x \leq 0.174$

   C) $13.78 \leq x \leq 18.98$

   D) $29.60 \leq x \leq 34.80$

5. A shipping company employee is in charge of packing cargo containers for shipment. He knows a certain cargo container can hold a maximum of 50 microwaves or a maximum of 15 refrigerators. Each microwave takes up 6 cubic feet of space, and each refrigerator takes up 20 cubic feet. The cargo container can hold a maximum of 300 cubic feet. The employee is trying to figure out how to pack a container containing both microwaves and refrigerators. Which of the following systems of inequalities can the employee use to determine how many of each item (microwaves, m, and refrigerators, r) he can pack into one cargo container?

A) $\begin{cases} m \leq 6 \\ r \leq 20 \\ 50m + 15r \leq 300 \end{cases}$

B) $\begin{cases} m \leq 50 \\ r \leq 15 \\ m + r \leq 300 \end{cases}$

C) $\begin{cases} m \leq 50 \\ r \leq 15 \\ 6m + 20r \leq 300 \end{cases}$

D) $\begin{cases} m \leq 50 \\ r \leq 15 \\ 50m + 15r \leq 300 \end{cases}$

6. If $-\dfrac{2}{5} < 3k - 4 < \dfrac{6}{7}$, then which of the following is not a possible value for $-6k + 8$?

A) $-\dfrac{5}{7}$

B) $\dfrac{1}{7}$

C) $\dfrac{1}{3}$

D) $\dfrac{4}{3}$

$\begin{cases} y \leq \dfrac{2}{3}x + 1 \\ 2x - 3y \leq 12 \end{cases}$

7. Which of the following best describes the solution set for the system of inequalities above?

A) The system has no solution.

B) The solution set consists of a single point.

C) The solution set consists of all real numbers.

D) The solution set consists of all points that lie between the boundary lines.

8. Marco is paid $80 per day plus $15 per hour for overtime. If he works five days per week and wants to make a minimum of $520 this week, what is the fewest number of hours of overtime he must work?

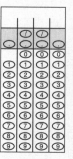

Math

9. Which of the following represents the solution to the inequality $2(4x - 1) > 5x + 13$?

A)

B)

C)

D)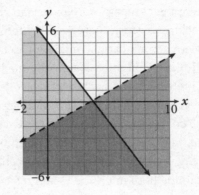

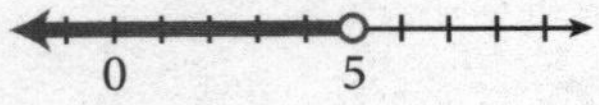

10. Which of the following best describes the graphical solution to the inequality $y < -2x + 3$?

   A) A dashed boundary line that rises from left to right, with shading in the half-plane below the boundary line

   B) A dashed boundary line that falls from left to right, with shading in the half-plane below the boundary line

   C) A dashed boundary line that falls from left to right, with shading in the half-plane above the boundary line

   D) A solid boundary line that falls from left to right, with shading in the half-plane below the boundary line

11. The figure above shows the solution set for the system $\begin{cases} y < \dfrac{3}{5}x - 2 \\ y \le -\dfrac{4}{3}x + 5 \end{cases}$. Which of the following is not a solution to this system?

   A) $(-1, -4)$

   B) $(1, -1)$

   C) $(4, -1)$

   D) $(6, -3)$

$$\begin{cases} y < 2x - 3 \\ y \boxed{?} mx + 3 \end{cases}$$

12. Which value of m and which symbol result in the system of inequalities shown above as having no solution?

   A) $m = -2; >$

   B) $m = -\dfrac{1}{2}; <$

   C) $m = 2; >$

   D) $m = 2; <$

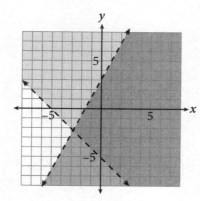

13. The figure above shows the solution for the system of inequalities $\begin{cases} y > -x - 5 \\ y < 2x + 3 \end{cases}$.
Suppose (a, b) is a solution to the system.

If $a = 0$, what is the greatest possible integer value of b?

Problem Solving & Data Analysis

BY THE END OF THIS UNIT, YOU WILL BE ABLE TO:

1. Apply the Kaplan Method for Multi-Part Math Questions

2. Use rates, ratios, proportions, and percentages

3. Interpret and extract information from scatterplots and two-way tables

4. Analyze simple and complex data sets using descriptive statistics

CHAPTER 5

Rates, Ratios, Proportions, and Percentages

CHAPTER OBJECTIVES

By the end of this chapter, you will be able to:

1. Use the Kaplan Method for Multi-Part Math Questions to answer Problem Solving and Data Analysis questions effectively

2. Solve multi-part question sets involving rates, ratios, and proportions

3. Use appropriate formulas to find percentages and single or multiple percent changes

SMARTPOINTS

Point Value	SmartPoint Category
Point Builder	Kaplan Method for Multi-Part Math Questions
80 Points	Rates, Ratios, Proportions & Percentages

Math

RATES, RATIOS, PROPORTIONS, AND PERCENTAGES

Chapter 5

Homework

Extra Practice: #1-20

Even More

The Kaplan Method for
Multi-Part Math

Math Quiz 2

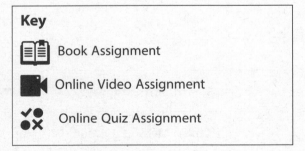

Key

Book Assignment

Online Video Assignment

Online Quiz Assignment

Math

The new SAT contains multiple-choice and grid-in questions, as well as multi-part math question sets. These question sets have multiple parts that are based on the same scenario and may require more analysis and planning than a typical multiple-choice question. To help you answer these questions effectively, use the Kaplan Method for Multi-Part Math Questions.

KAPLAN METHOD FOR MULTI-PART MATH QUESTIONS

Step 1: Read the first question in the set, looking for clues

Step 2: Identify and organize the information you need

Step 3: Based on what you know, plan your steps to navigate the first question

Step 4: Solve, step-by-step, checking units as you go

Step 5: Did I answer the *right* question?

Step 6: Repeat for remaining questions, incorporating results from the previous question if possible

The next few pages will walk you through each step in more detail.

Step 1: Read the first question in the set, looking for clues

- **Focus all your energy here** instead of diluting it over the whole set of questions; solving a multi-part question in pieces is far simpler than trying to solve all the questions in the set at once. Further, you may be able to use the results from earlier parts to solve subsequent ones. Don't even consider the later parts of the question set until you've solved the first part.

- **Watch for hints** about what information you'll actually need to use to answer the questions. Underlining key quantities is often helpful to separate what's important from extraneous information.

Step 2: Identify and organize the information you need

If you think this sounds like the Kaplan Method for Math, you're absolutely correct. You'll use some of those same skills. The difference: A multi-part math question is just more involved with multiple pieces.

- **What information am I given?** Jot down key notes, and group related quantities to develop your strategy.

- **What am I solving for?** This is your target. As you work your way through subsequent steps, keep your target at the front of your mind. This will help you avoid unnecessary work (and subsequent time loss). You'll sometimes need to tackle these problems from both ends, so always keep your goal in mind.

> ✔ **Expert Tip**
>
> Many students freeze when they encounter a problem with multiple steps and seemingly massive amounts of information. Don't worry! Take each piece one at a time, and you won't be intimidated.

Step 3: Based on what you know, plan your steps to navigate the first question

- **What pieces am I missing?** Many students become frustrated when faced with a roadblock such as missing information, but it's an easy fix. Sometimes you'll need to do an intermediate calculation to reveal the missing piece or pieces of the puzzle.

Step 4: Solve, step-by-step, checking units as you go

- **Work quickly but carefully**, just as you've done on other SAT math questions.

Step 5: Did I answer the *right* question?

- As is the case with the Kaplan Method for Math, **make sure your final answer is the requested answer**.
- Review the first question in the set.
- Double-check your units and your work.

Step 6: Repeat for remaining questions, incorporating results from the previous question if possible

- Now take your results from the first question and think critically about whether they fit into the subsequent questions in the set. Previous results won't always be applicable, but when they are, they often lead to huge time savings. But be careful—don't round results from the first question in your calculations for the second question—only the final answer should be rounded.

When you've finished, congratulate yourself for persevering through such a challenging task. A multi-part math question is likely to be one of the toughest on the SAT. If you can ace these questions, you'll be poised for a great score on Test Day. Don't worry if the Kaplan Method seems complicated; we'll walk through an example shortly.

> ✔ **Expert Tip**
>
> Because these question sets take substantially more time, consider saving multi-part math questions for last.

RATES, MEASUREMENT, AND UNIT CONVERSIONS

By now, you've become adept at using algebra to answer many SAT math questions, which is great, because you'll need those algebra skills to answer questions involving rates. You're likely already familiar with many different rates—kilometers per hour, meters per second, and even miles per gallon are all considered rates.

A fundamental equation related to rates is "Distance = rate × time" (a.k.a. the DIRT equation—**D**istance **I**s **R**ate × **T**ime). If you have two of the three components of the equation, you can easily find the third. An upcoming multi-part math example demonstrates this nicely.

You'll notice units of measurement are important for rate questions (and others that require a unit conversion) and, therefore, also an opportunity to fall for trap answers if you're not careful. How can you avoid this? Use the factor-label method (also known as dimensional analysis). The factor-label method is a simple yet powerful way to ensure you're doing your calculations correctly and getting an answer with the requested units.

For example, suppose you're asked to find the number of cups there are in two gallons. First, identify your starting quantity's units (gallons) and then identify the end quantity's units (cups). The next step is to piece together a path of relationships that will convert gallons into cups, canceling out units as you go. Keep in mind that you will often have multiple stepping stones between your starting and ending quantities, so don't panic if you can't get directly from gallons to cups.

The test makers won't expect you to know English measurements by heart. Instead, they'll provide conversion factors when needed. For example, a gallon is the same as 4 quarts, every quart contains 2 pints, and a pint equals 2 cups. And there you have it! Your map from gallons to cups is complete. The last step is to put it together as a giant multiplication problem. Each relationship, called a conversion factor, is written as a fraction. The basic rules of fraction multiplication apply, so you can cancel a unit that appears in both the numerator and denominator.

> ✔ **Note**
>
> The SAT will not require you to memorize conversions for conventional units. If the test asks you to convert miles into inches, for example, you will be provided with enough conversion factors to solve the problem.

Follow along as we convert from gallons to quarts to pints to cups using the factor-label method:

$$2 \text{ gallons} \times \frac{4 \text{ quarts}}{1 \text{ gallon}} \times \frac{2 \text{ pints}}{1 \text{ quart}} \times \frac{2 \text{ cups}}{1 \text{ pint}} = (2 \times 4 \times 2 \times 2) \text{ cups} = 32 \text{ cups}$$

The DIRT equation is actually a variation of this process. Suppose you travel at 60 mph for 5 hours. You would calculate the distance traveled using the equation $d = rt = \frac{60 \text{ mi}}{1 \text{ hr}} \times 5 \text{ hr} = 300$ miles.

The units for hours cancel out, leaving only miles, which is precisely what you're looking for, a distance. This built-in check is a great way to ensure your path to the answer is correct. If your units are off, check your steps for mistakes along the way. The SAT will never ask you for a quantity such as miles^4 or gallons^3, so if you end up with funky units like that, you've made an error somewhere in your work.

> ✔ **Note**
>
> When using the factor-label method, don't be afraid to flip fractions and rates to make the units cancel out as needed.

The following question demonstrates the factor-label method in a test-like question.

1. Quinn wants to rent a self-storage unit for her college dorm room furniture for the summer. She estimates that she will need 700 cubic feet of storage space, but the self-storage provider measures its units in cubic meters. If 1 meter is approximately 3.28 feet, about how many cubic meters of space will Quinn need?

    A) 19.84

    B) 25.93

    C) 65.07

    D) 213.41

Work through the Kaplan Method for Math to solve this question step-by-step. The following table shows Kaplan's strategic thinking on the left, along with suggested math scratchwork on the right.

Strategic Thinking	Math Scratchwork
Step 1: Read the question, identifying and organizing important information as you go You need to determine how many cubic meters of space Quinn needs for her belongings.	$700 \text{ ft}^3 \text{ space needed } = ? \text{ m}^3$
Step 2: Choose the best strategy to answer the question The factor-label method will be the quickest path to the correct answer. You're starting in cubic feet and need to convert to cubic meters. You know that 1 m = 3.28 ft, but be careful: 1 m^3 is not the same as 3.28 ft^3! Consider each feet-to-meters conversion separately.	starting qty: 700 ft^3 end qty: $? \text{ m}^3$ $\dfrac{700 \text{ ft}^3}{1} \times \dfrac{1 \text{ m}}{3.28 \text{ ft}} \times \dfrac{1 \text{ m}}{3.28 \text{ ft}} \times \dfrac{1 \text{ m}}{3.28 \text{ ft}}$ $= \dfrac{700}{(3.28)^3} \text{m} \sim 19.84 \text{ m}^3$
Step 3: Check that you answered the *right* question You've correctly converted cubic feet to cubic meters to get the correct answer, which is (A).	19.84 m^3

✔ Note

The conversion from feet to meters is not the same as the conversion from cubic feet to cubic meters (or square feet to square meters). Trap answers will often use incorrect conversion factors. Be particularly careful when dealing with area or volume conversions that have multiple dimensions.

Next, you'll walk through a test-like multi-part question that involves rates. Follow along with the Kaplan Method and think about how knowledge of rates and conversion factors is used to get to the answer.

Remember, even though these questions have multiple parts, you'll rely on the same math skills you'd use in a simple multiple-choice question to solve each part. If you find that there are missing pieces or missing quantities, use techniques such as the factor-label method to bridge the gap. Also keep in mind that you may be able to use the answer from one part as a shortcut to answering the next part. If you do, don't round until the final answer, especially on grid-in questions.

Questions 2 and 3 refer to the following information.

Dismantling fraud rings, intercepting enemy communications, and protecting national infrastructure are just a few tasks for which Special Agents in the FBI's Cyber Division utilize state-of-the-art computers and other technology. The New Haven field office recently seized a hard drive with 2.43 terabytes (TB) of encrypted information during a raid on an infrastructure-hacking operations base, which agents believe contains information on a planned attack.

2. The cyber team's decryption software can decrypt 4.5 MB per second. How many hours will it take to decrypt the entire hard drive? (One TB is equal to 10^6 megabytes (MB).)

3. Newly gathered intelligence indicates a high likelihood of an infrastructure attack occurring before the hard drive is fully decrypted. Consequently, the New York and Boston field offices have been asked to divert resources to the decryption task. New York's decryption software is 40% faster than New Haven's, but Boston's is 20% slower than New Haven's. By how many hours will the decryption time be reduced with the three cyber teams working together? Round your answer to the nearest hour.

Work through the Kaplan Method for Multi-Part Math Questions step-by-step to solve this set of questions. The following table shows Kaplan's strategic thinking on the left, along with suggested math scratchwork on the right.

Strategic Thinking	Math Scratchwork
Step 1: Read the first question in the set, looking for clues You're told the size of the seized hard drive and the speed at which it will be decrypted.	2.43 TB drive 4.5 MB/s decryption
Step 2: Identify and organize the information you need The first part of the question set asks for the time required to decrypt the hard drive. The given rate will help you determine this amount.	hours to decrypt: ?
Step 3: Based on what you know, plan your steps to navigate the first question The hard drive's capacity is in TB, but the rate is in MB/s (and you're asked for time in hours), so the DIRT equation requires a couple of extra calculations before you can use it. The factor-label method will be faster. Map your conversion steps.	starting qty: 2.43 TB desired qty: ? h TB → MB → s → min → h
Step 4: Solve, step-by-step, checking units as you go Plug in the appropriate conversion factors. When properly set up, all units except hours will cancel, and you'll have the time needed for the decryption.	$2.43 \text{ TB} \times \dfrac{10^6 \text{ MB}}{1 \text{ TB}} \times \dfrac{1 \text{ s}}{4.5 \text{ MB}} \times \dfrac{1 \text{ min}}{60 \text{ s}}$ $\times \dfrac{1 \text{ h}}{60 \text{ min}} = 150 \text{ h}$
Step 5: Did I answer the *right* question? It will take 150 hours to fully decrypt the hard drive.	

 Note

You might be given extra information on questions like these. If you don't need it to get to the answer, then don't worry about it.

Now on to Step 6: Repeat for remaining questions in the set. Kaplan's strategic thinking is on the left, along with suggested math scratchwork on the right.

Strategic Thinking	Math Scratchwork
Step 1: Read the second question in the set, looking for clues This part of the question set provides a relative description of New York and Boston's decryption software speeds.	NY: 40% faster than NH B: 20% slower than NH
Step 2: Identify and organize the information you need You need to determine the reduction in decryption time (in hours) if all three systems work together.	new decryption time: ? difference between old and new times: ?
Step 3: Based on what you know, plan your steps to navigate the second question You must calculate the decryption speeds of the New York and Boston systems; you can't simply use the given percents to directly get the final answer. With the speeds in hand, you can find the total rate and the adjusted decryption time.	% → MB/s TB → MB → s → min → h
Step 4: Solve, step-by-step, checking units as you go Use the given percents to determine the speeds of the New York and Boston systems, being mindful when picking which decimal to plug in for what percent. Apply the factor-label method to calculate the required decryption time with all three systems working, and then find the difference in times.	NY: $1.4 \times 4.5 = 6.3$ MB/s B: $0.8 \times 4.5 = 3.6$ MB/s total rate $= 4.5 + 6.3 + 3.6$ $\qquad\qquad = 14.4$ MB/s $2.43 \text{ TB} \times \dfrac{10^6 \text{MB}}{1 \text{ TB}} \times \dfrac{1 \text{ s}}{14.4 \text{ MB}} \times \dfrac{1 \text{ min}}{60 \text{ s}}$ $\qquad \times \dfrac{1 \text{ h}}{60 \text{ min}} = 46.875 \text{ h}$ $150 - 46.875 = 103.125$
Step 5: Did I answer the *right* question? Round per the question stem's instructions, and you're done.	103

Prepare

RATIOS AND PROPORTIONS

Ratios and proportions are quite common in everyday life. Whether it's making a double batch of meatballs or calculating the odds of winning the lottery, you'll find that ratios and proportions are invaluable in myriad situations.

A ratio is a comparison of one quantity to another. When writing ratios, you can compare part of a group to another part of that group, or you can compare a part of the group to the whole group. Suppose you have a bowl of apples and oranges. You can write ratios that compare apples to oranges (part to part), apples to total fruit (part to whole), and oranges to total fruit (part to whole).

You can also combine ratios. If you have two ratios, $a{:}b$ and $b{:}c$, you can derive $a{:}c$ by finding a common multiple of the b terms. Take a look at the following table to see this in action.

a	:	b	:	c
3	:	4		
		3	:	5
9	:	12		
		12	:	20
9	:			20

What's a common multiple of the b terms? The number 12 is a good choice because it's the least common multiple of 3 and 4 which will reduce the need to simplify later. Where do you go from there? Multiply each ratio by the factor (use 3 for $a{:}b$ and 4 for $b{:}c$) that will get you to $b = 12$.

The ratio $a{:}c$ equals 9:20. Notice we didn't merely say $a{:}c$ is 3:5; this would be incorrect on Test Day (and likely a wrong-answer trap!).

A proportion is simply two ratios set equal to each other. Proportions are an efficient way to solve certain problems, but you must exercise caution when setting them up. Watching the units of each piece of the proportion will help you with this. Sometimes the SAT will ask you to determine whether certain proportions are equivalent—check this by cross-multiplying. You'll get results that are much easier to compare.

If $\dfrac{a}{b} = \dfrac{c}{d}$, then: $ad = bc$, $\dfrac{a}{c} = \dfrac{b}{d}$, $\dfrac{d}{b} = \dfrac{c}{a}$, $\dfrac{b}{a} = \dfrac{d}{c}$, BUT $\dfrac{a}{d} \neq \dfrac{c}{b}$

Each derived ratio shown except the last one is simply a manipulation of the first, so all except the last are correct. You can verify this via cross-multiplication ($ad = bc$).

Alternatively, pick numerical values for a, b, c, and d; then simplify and confirm the two sides of the equation are equal. For example, take the two equivalent fractions $\frac{2}{3}$ and $\frac{6}{9}$ ($a = 2$, $b = 3$, $c = 6$, $d = 9$).

Cross-multiplication gives $2 \times 9 = 3 \times 6$, which is a true statement. Dividing a and b by c and d gives $\frac{2}{6} = \frac{3}{9}$, also true, and so on. However, attempting to equate $\frac{a}{d}\left(\frac{2}{9}\right)$ and $\frac{b}{c}\left(\frac{3}{6}\right)$ will not work.

Let's take a look at a test-like question that involves ratios:

4. Neil is preparing two cans of paint for a client. The first is 25 parts red paint and 60 parts blue paint; the second is 30 parts yellow paint, 70 parts blue paint, and 15 parts white paint. The client has also asked Neil to prepare a third can containing only white and red paint per the ratios of the first two cans. What ratio of white to red paint should Neil use for the third can?

   A) 35:18

   B) 18:35

   C) 5:3

   D) 3:5

Work through the Kaplan Method for Math step-by-step to solve this question. The following table shows Kaplan's strategic thinking on the left, along with suggested math scratchwork on the right.

Strategic Thinking	Math Scratchwork
Step 1: Read the question, identifying and organizing important information as you go You're asked for the ratio of white to red paint in the third can. Two ratios are given.	R:B = 25:60 Y:B:W = 30:70:15
Step 2: Choose the best strategy to answer the question The ratio terms are rather large, so reduce the first ratio with a common factor, and then repeat with the second ratio. To combine two ratios, they must share a common term. Both ratios contain blue paint, but the blue paint terms aren't identical. Find a common multiple of 12 and 14. Once you've found one, merge the two ratios to directly compare white and red paint.	R:B = 25:60 → 5:12 Y:B:W = 30:70:15 → 6:14:3 common multiple of 12 & 14: 84 R:B = (5:12) × 7 = 35:84 Y:B:W = (6:14:3) × 6 = 36:84:18 R:B:Y:W = 35:84:36:18 R:W = 35:18
Step 3: Check that you answered the *right* question The question asks for the ratio of white paint to red paint, so flip your ratio, and you're done. Choice (B) is correct.	W:R = 18:35

> ✔ **Note**
>
> Beware of trap answers that contain incorrect ratios. Always confirm that you've found the ratio requested.

PERCENTAGES

Percentages aren't just for test grades; you'll find them frequently throughout life—discount pricing in stores, income tax brackets, and stock price trackers all use percents in some form. It's critical that you know how to use them correctly, especially on Test Day.

Suppose you have a bag containing 10 blue marbles and 15 pink marbles, and you're asked what percent of the marbles are pink. You can determine this easily by using the formula Percent $= \dfrac{\text{part}}{\text{whole}} \times 100\%$.

Plug 15 in for the part and 10 + 15 (= 25) for the whole to get $\dfrac{15}{25} \times 100\% = 60\%$ pink marbles.

Another easy way to solve many percent problems is to use the following statement: (blank) percent of (blank) is (blank). Translating from English into math, you obtain (blank)% × (blank) = (blank). As you saw with the DIRT equation in the rates section, knowledge of any two quantities will unlock the third.

> ✔ **Note**
>
> The percent formula requires the percent component to be in decimal form. Remember to move the decimal point appropriately before using this formula.

You might also be asked to determine the **percent change** in a given situation. Fortunately, you can find this easily using a variant of the percent formula:

$$\text{Percent increase or decrease} = \frac{\text{amount of increase or decrease}}{\text{original amount}} \times 100\%$$

Sometimes more than one change will occur. Be especially careful here, as it can be tempting to take a "shortcut" by just adding two percent changes together (which will almost always lead to an incorrect answer). Instead you'll need to find the total amount of the increase or decrease and calculate accordingly. We'll demonstrate this in an upcoming problem.

The following is a test-like question involving percentages.

5. Some people like to dilute 100% juice drinks with water to lessen the flavor intensity and reduce caloric intake. Kristina, a personal trainer, is preparing several blends of varying juice concentrations to see which ratio her fitness club's clients prefer. She plans to make 240 ounces each of 80% juice, 60% juice, 50% juice, 40% juice, and 20% juice blends. If the 100% juice Kristina plans to buy comes in 32-ounce bottles and partial bottles cannot be bought, how many bottles will Kristina need to make her blends?

    A)   8

    B)   18

    C)   19

    D)   60

Work through the Kaplan Method for Math step-by-step to solve this question. The following table shows Kaplan's strategic thinking on the left, along with suggested math scratchwork on the right.

Strategic Thinking	Math Scratchwork
Step 1: Read the question, identifying and organizing important information as you go You're asked how many bottles of 100% juice Kristina needs to buy to make her five blends. You're given the percent juice content of each.	five blends: 80%, 60%, 50%, 40%, 20% juice
Step 2: Choose the best strategy to answer the question Although this looks like calculator busywork, there's a faster (but less obvious) route to the answer. Notice that each percentage is a multiple of 10. Therefore, all you need to do is find 10% of 240 and multiply by the appropriate number to get the ounces of juice in each blend.	$0.1 \times 240\,oz = 24\,oz$ $\times 2: 20\% = 48\,oz\ juice$ $\times 4: 40\% = 96\,oz\ juice$ $\times 5: 50\% = 120\,oz\ juice$ $\times 6: 60\% = 144\,oz\ juice$ $\times 8: 80\% = 192\,oz\ juice$ sum: 600 oz. $\dfrac{600}{32} = 18.75 \rightarrow 19$
Step 3: Check that you answered the *right* question You've found the number of juice bottles required; the correct answer is (C).	19

An example of a multi-part question that tests your percentage expertise follows on the next page.

Questions 6 and 7 refer to the following information.

Projected Undergraduate Costs at the University of California

2014-15	2015-16	2016-17	2017-18	2018-19	2019-20
$12,192	$12,804	$13,446	$14,118	$14,820	$15,564

Source: regents.universityofcalifornia.edu

Over the last decade, colleges have come under fire for significant tuition and fee increases. In 2014, the University of California approved a series of tuition and fee increases over the course of five years. The table above summarizes the total cost per undergraduate per year through the 2019-20 academic year.

6. If fees account for 8.75% of one year's total expenses, what is the average fee increase per academic year? Round your answer to the nearest dollar.

7. Suppose the University of California system wants to extend these increases through the 2022-23 academic year. Assuming the average yearly increase for this extension remains the same as it was from 2014-15 through 2019-20, by what percentage will total tuition and fees have increased at the end of the 2022-23 academic year since their implementation? Round your answer to the nearest whole percent.

Work through the Kaplan Method for Multi-Part Math Questions step-by-step to solve this question. The following table shows Kaplan's strategic thinking on the left, along with suggested math scratchwork on the right.

Strategic Thinking	Math Scratchwork
Step 1: Read the first question in the set, looking for clues You are given a table with total costs for several academic years. The first question in the set states that fees account for 8.75% of one year's expenses.	
Step 2: Identify and organize the information you need This question asks for the portion of the total cost increase that is comprised of fees.	*fees (in $): ?*
Step 3: Based on what you know, plan your steps to navigate the first question Find the total cost increase in dollars and the average annual increase. From there, determine the portion of the increase that fees make up. The percent given in the first question indicates you should use the three-part percent formula.	*8.75% is fees* *(blank)% of (blank) is (blank)*

Math

Strategic Thinking	Math Scratchwork
Step 4: Solve, step-by-step, checking units as you go Instead of finding each year-to-year increase, find the total increase from 2014-15 through 2019-20. Once there, determine the average increase for each year. Use the three-part percent formula to find the fee portion of the average increase.	$\$15,564 - \$12,192 = \$3,372$ $avg = \dfrac{\$3372}{5}$ $\quad = \$674.40$ $0.0875 \times \$674.40 = \$59.01$
Step 5: Did I answer the *right* question? You found the average fee increase per year. Once you round appropriately, the first question is complete.	59

✔ **Note**

By finding the total increase instead of each individual increase, you saved yourself a substantial amount of time.

The first part of the question set is finished! Now on to Step 6: Repeat for the other questions in the set.

The following table shows Kaplan's strategic thinking on the left, along with suggested math scratchwork on the right.

Strategic Thinking	Math Scratchwork
Step 1: Read the second question in the set, looking for clues There's a proposal to extend the tuition/fee hikes through 2022-23.	
Step 2: Identify and organize the information you need The second part of the question set asks for the percent increase in total tuition/fee cost between 2014-15 and 2022-23.	% increase: ?
Step 3: Based on what you know, plan your steps to navigate the second question You know the average yearly increase from the first question. Use this to determine what the cost for the 2022-23 year will be, and then calculate the total increase. Use this result to calculate the percent increase.	2014-15 thru 2019-20: $3,372 avg. yearly incr.: $674.40
Step 4: Solve, step-by-step, checking units as you go Extending the increases past 2019-20 means increases for 2020-21, 2021-22, and 2022-23, which is 3 years total. Multiply the average yearly increase by 3 to determine the additional increase. Add this to the increase you found in the first question to find the total increase from 2014-15 through 2022-23.	$674.40 \times 3 = \$2,023.20$ $\$2,023.20 + \$3,372 = \$5,395.20$
To calculate the percent change, divide the total increase by the original cost from 2014-15, and multiply the result by 100.	$\dfrac{\$5,395.20}{\$12,192} \times 100 = 44.252\%$
Step 5: Did I answer the *right* question? Round the percent change per the instructions, and you're done.	44

Now you'll have a chance to try a few test-like problems in a scaffolded way. We've provided some guidance, but you'll need to fill in the missing parts of explanations or the step-by-step math to get to the correct answer. Don't worry—after going through the worked examples at the beginning of this section, these problems should be completely doable.

8. Ramp meters are often used in and around metropolitan areas to reduce freeway congestion during AM and PM rush hours. Depending on freeway volume, ramp meters in Milwaukee allow one car onto the freeway every 5-9 seconds. Assuming a constant ramp car queue, between the hours of 3:30 PM and 6:30 PM, how many more cars can move through a ramp meter with a 5-second interval than one with an 8-second interval?

A) 270

B) 320

C) 810

D) 960

The following table can help you structure your thinking as you go about solving this problem. Kaplan's strategic thinking is provided, as are bits of structured scratchwork. If you're not sure how to approach a question like this, start at the top and work your way down.

Strategic Thinking	Math Scratchwork
Step 1: Read the question, identifying and organizing important information as you go You must determine how many more cars pass through a ramp meter with a 5-second interval.	
Step 2: Choose the best strategy to answer the question One car every 5 (or 8) seconds is a rate, so turn to the DIRT equation. Be careful here; you need to manipulate the given form of the rate before you can use it. The 3:30 PM to 6:30 PM window translates to 3 hours, which is your time. Your rate, however, involves seconds, so you'll need to convert time to seconds. Finding d will give you the number of cars; do this for both intervals. Watch your units! Almost finished. Subtract the 8-second car count from the 5-second car count to find the difference.	5-second interval: $r_5 = 1$ car per 5 s = ____ cars/s 8-second interval: $r_8 = 1$ car per 8 s = ____ cars/s $3\,h \times$ ____ $\times$ ____ = ____ s 5 seconds $d_5 =$ ____ $\times$ ____ $d_5 =$ ____ 8 seconds $d_8 =$ ____ $\times$ ____ $d_8 =$ ____ ____ – ____ = ____

Strategic Thinking	Math Scratchwork
Step 3: Check that you answered the _right_ question If your answer is (C), you're correct!	_____

✔ **Expert Tip**

Sometimes distance or time units won't look like those you're used to (e.g., miles, minutes, etc.). Don't let this deter you. If you have a rate, you can use the DIRT equation.

Here's another test-like example to try using this method:

Murray's Annual Income Tax Liability

Federal ($0-$9,225)	Federal ($9,226-$37,450)	Federal ($37,451-$90,750)	State (flat rate)
10%	15%	25%	4.5%

9. Murray has an annual salary of $75,400. He contributes 20% of his pre-tax income to his 401(k), and he pays $150 per month for health insurance (pre-tax, deducted after 401(k)). The table above summarizes Murray's tax liability; all taxes are calculated based on Murray's adjusted gross income (pay remaining after 401(k) and insurance payments). He must pay 10% on the first $9,225 in income, 15% on any income between $9,226 and $37,450, 25% on income between $37,451 and $90,750, and a 4.5% state-tax on all of his adjusted gross income. All taxes are deducted simultaneously. What is Murray's biweekly take-home pay after all deductions have been made?

A) $1,537.98

B) $1,586.79

C) $1,699.78

D) $1,748.57

The following table can help you structure your thinking as you go about solving this problem. Kaplan's strategic thinking is provided, as are bits of structured scratchwork. If you're not sure how to approach a question like this, start at the top and work your way down.

Math

Strategic Thinking	Math Scratchwork

Step 1: Read the question, identifying and organizing important information as you go
 	
You need to find Murray's income after deductions. You have information about each deduction, as well as the order in which they're taken.
	start (\$ _____) – _____ 401(k)
	       – _____ insurance
	       – taxes
	       = take-home pay

Step 2: Choose the best strategy to answer the question The table provides tax information for annual income, so don't convert to biweekly yet. Follow the order you extracted in Step 1 to calculate each deduction first. To find the amount Murray deducts before taxes, use the three-part percent formula to find his 401(k) contribution, then subtract his health insurance cost. The question states that all taxes are deducted simultaneously; that is, don't deduct state tax and then take federal tax on what's left and vice versa. Use the quantity left after the insurance deduction for all tax calculations, and then subtract Murray's total tax liability from the remaining quantity post-insurance. The question asks for Murray's biweekly take-home pay. Divide by the number of pay periods in one year to get the final answer.	401(k): _____ × _____ = \$ _____ annually insurance: \$ _____ × _____ = \$ _____ annually \$ _____ – \$ _____ – \$ _____ = \$ _____ annual pre-tax taxes: state _____ × _____ = _____ M. owes \$ _____ for state fed 10% bracket _____ × _____ = _____ M. owes \$ _____ for 10% bracket fed 15% bracket _____ × _____ = _____ M. owes \$ _____ for 15% bracket fed 25% bracket _____ × _____ = _____ M. owes \$ _____ for 25% bracket total tax: \$ _____ take-home: \$ _____ – \$ _____ = \$ _____ annually $\dfrac{\$\ \_\_\_\_\_}{wks}$ = \$ _____ biweekly
Step 3: Check that you answered the *right* question If you chose (D), you're right.	_____

Now try your hand at a multi-part question.

Questions 10 and 11 refer to the following information.

Shuang has a set of square ceramic plates she'd like to glaze. She wants to create evenly spaced concentric squares on the plates with gray and black glaze as shown in the diagram above. The squares' edges are each 0.5 inches apart, and the area of the innermost square is 1 square inch.

10. What fraction of one plate will Shuang cover with gray glaze?

11. Shuang also plans to glaze smaller square plates with the same type of pattern as the plate in the figure. The smaller plates' squares are the same size and distance apart as those of the larger plates. If a small plate has four concentric squares, then the fraction of a small plate that Shuang will cover with black glaze is how many times as great as that of a large plate?

The following table can help you structure your thinking as you go about solving this problem. Kaplan's strategic thinking is provided, as are bits of structured scratchwork. If you're not sure how to approach a question like this, start at the top and work your way down.

Strategic Thinking	Math Scratchwork
Step 1: Read the first question in the set, looking for clues You're given a picture of one of Shuang's plates and told that she will use two colors to create the design.	
Step 2: Identify and organize the information you need You need to find the fraction of the plate that will be gray.	gray/total: ?
Step 3: Based on what you know, plan your steps to navigate the first question To get started, you need to find the side length of the innermost square. Then, you can find the side lengths of the other squares based on that. Label the squares to help keep your calculations clear.	 1 2 3 4 5 6 7 8
Step 4: Solve, step-by-step, checking units as you go You're given that the area of the innermost square is 1 square inch, which means the side length is the square root of that, or 1 inch. Remember how far apart the square edges are; this will help you find the side lengths and areas of the other squares. Also keep in mind you'll need to account for the fact that each square outside the first is not actually a full square. To find the ratio of gray glaze to total glaze, divide the gray glaze area by the total glaze area.	sq. 1 = ____ in.^{2} sq. 2 = ____^{2} − ____ = ____ in.^{2} sq. 3 = ____^{2} − ____ = ____ in.^{2} sq. 4 = ____^{2} − ____ = ____ in.^{2} sq. 5 = ____^{2} − ____ = ____ in.^{2} sq. 6 = ____^{2} − ____ = ____ in.^{2} sq. 7 = ____^{2} − ____ = ____ in.^{2} sq. 8 = ____^{2} − ____ = ____ in.^{2} gray: ____ + ____ + ____ + ____ = ____ in.^{2} black: ____ + ____ + ____ + ____ = ____ in.^{2} gray/total = _____
Step 5: Did I answer the *right* question? If you got 7/16, great job! You're correct.	_____

Fantastic! Now repeat for the other question in the set. Once again, Kaplan's strategic thinking is provided, as are bits of structured scratchwork. If you're not sure how to approach the second part, start at the top and work your way down.

Strategic Thinking	Math Scratchwork
Step 1: Read the second question in the set, looking for clues You're told a smaller plate has four concentric squares with edges 0.5 inches apart as in a larger plate.	4 squares in a small plate
Step 2: Identify and organize the information you need You'll need to find the fraction of black glaze on one small plate and one large plate.	sm. black: ? lg. black: ?
Step 3: Based on what you know, plan your steps to navigate the second question You'll need to find the black fraction of the two plates. Fortunately, the black fraction for the larger plate is easy to find because you found its gray counterpart in the previous question.	large black = 1 – _____ = _____
Step 4: Solve, step-by-step, checking units as you go Good news! To find the black fraction for the small plate, you already did most of the work in the previous question. Just use the same numbers.	square 1 (gray) = ____ in.² square 2 (black) = ____ in.² square 3 (gray) = ____ in.² square 4 (black) = ____ in.² small gray: ____ + ____ = ____ in.² small black: ____ + ____ = ____ in.² small black vs. large black: ____ ÷ ____ = ____ × ____ = ____
Step 5: Did I answer the *right* question? Did you get 10/9? If so, congrats! You're correct.	_____

Now that you've seen the variety of ways in which the SAT can test you on ratios, rates, proportions, and percentages, try the following questions to check your understanding. Give yourself 5 minutes to answer the following four questions. Make sure you use the Kaplan Method for Math as often as you can (as well as the Kaplan Method for Multi-Part Math Questions when necessary). Remember, you want to emphasize speed and efficiency in addition to simply getting the correct answer.

12. Grocery stores often differ in how they price fruit; some charge by weight, and others charge per piece. FoodCo sells bananas for $0.60 a pound, Bob's charges $0.29 per banana, Acme charges $1.50 for a two-pound banana bunch, and Stu's offers a special: buying three pounds of bananas at $0.65 per pound gets you a fourth pound free. If one banana weighs $\frac{1}{3}$ lb, which of the following correctly lists the four grocers in order of decreasing cost per banana (assuming all purchases are made in 4-lb increments)?

A) Bob's, Acme, FoodCo, Stu's

B) Bob's, FoodCo, Acme, Stu's

C) Stu's, FoodCo, Acme, Bob's

D) Stu's, Acme, FoodCo, Bob's

13. The owner of an aerial adventure park wants to construct a zipline for kids who aren't tall enough to ride the regular zipline, which starts at a platform in a tree 10 meters above the ground and is 26 meters in length. The desired platform height for the new zipline is 3 meters. If the owner wants the kids' zipline length and platform height to be proportional to those of the regular zipline, what will be the difference in length of the two ziplines?

Questions 14 and 15 refer to the following information.

Gas stations in the United States sell gasoline by the gallon, whereas those in Great Britain sell it by the liter. Mark is assembling a budget for a trip to Great Britain. He plans to drive from London to Edinburgh and back with various excursions along the way; he estimates his total mileage to be 960 miles. The Great Britain pound (GBP) to U.S. dollar (USD) exchange rate is currently 1:1.52, and 1 gallon (gal) is approximately 3.785 liters (L).

14. If Mark rents a car that averages 40 miles per gallon throughout the trip and estimates an average gas cost of 1.20 GBP per liter, how much money (in USD) should Mark budget for fuel? Round your answer to the nearest dollar.

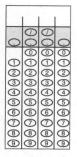

15. The rental car company Mark is using has a special offer: For an extra 30 GBP, Mark can lock in a subsidized fuel cost of 0.75 GBP per liter for the duration of his trip. How much, in USD, would Mark save with this offer? Round your answer to the nearest dollar.

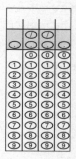

Answers and Explanations for this chapter begin on page 900.

EXTRA PRACTICE

 You may use your calculator for all questions in this section.

1. At all trials and hearings, a court reporter types every word spoken during the proceedings so that there is a written record of what transpired. Because they must type every word, the average court reporter must be able to type at a minimum rate of 3.75 words per second in order to be certified. Suppose a trial transcript contains 25 pages with an average of 675 words per page. Assuming the court reporter typed the transcript at the minimum rate, how long was she actively typing?

   A) 1 hour, 15 minutes

   B) 1 hour, 45 minutes

   C) 2 hours, 30 minutes

   D) 3 hours

2. In 1912, the original candidates for United States President were Woodrow Wilson and William H. Taft. Because of party disagreements, former President Theodore Roosevelt also decided to run and ended up splitting the vote with his fellow Republican and incumbent, Taft. In a certain state, the ratio of the popular vote of Taft to Roosevelt to Wilson was approximately 35:41:63. If approximately 208,500 votes were cast in that state for the three candidates altogether, how many were cast for Taft?

   A) 15,000

   B) 45,000

   C) 52,500

   D) 69,500

3. Political canvassers polled voters in two locations on whether they viewed a particular candidate for governor favorably. At the first location, they asked 125 people and of those, 22.4% responded favorably. At the second location, 37.5% of 272 people responded favorably. What percent of all the people surveyed responded favorably?

   A) 25.7%

   B) 30.0%

   C) 31.5%

   D) 32.7%

4. At 350°F, an oven can cook approximately 3 pounds of turkey per hour. At 450°F, it can cook approximately 4.5 pounds per hour. How many more ounces of turkey can the oven cook at 450° than at 350° in 10 minutes? (1 pound = 16 ounces)

   A) 4

   B) 6

   C) 8

   D) 12

5. A company specializes in converting people's VHS movies and DVDs to digital formats, which, once converted, are approximately 4.5 gigabytes in size. Once converted, the company uploads the videos to a secure cloud drive, where the customers can retrieve their files. The company uploads the videos every day, from closing time at 5:00 PM until 9:00 PM. Their internet service provider has an upload speed of 12 megabytes per second. What is the maximum number of videos the company can upload each evening? (1 gigabyte = 1,024 megabytes)

A)   2

B)   37

C)   242

D)   682

6. A museum is building a scale model of Sue, the largest *Tyrannosaurus rex* skeleton ever found. Sue was 13 feet tall and 40 feet long, and her skull had a length of 5 feet. If the length of the museum's scale model skull is 3 feet, 1.5 inches, what is the difference between the scale model's length and its height?

A)   8 feet, 1.5 inches

B)   16 feet, 10.5 inches

C)   22 feet, 6.5 inches

D)   27 feet, 4 inches

Extra Practice

Questions 7 and 8 refer to the following information.

Mia is planning to work as a hostess at a restaurant. Two restaurants in her area have offered her jobs, both of which utilize "tip share," which means that the hostess gets a portion of all tips left by all customers. Restaurant A has a tip share for hostesses of 7%, while Restaurant B has a tip share of only 4%.

7. Mia does some research and finds that, on average, restaurants in her area bring in approximately $1,100 in tips for the evening shift. Based on this information, how much more in dollars would Mia make in tips at Restaurant A than at Restaurant B if she worked 5 evenings a week for 4 weeks?

8. Upon further research, Mia discovers that Restaurant B is making some improvements to become a more upscale establishment, which will result in an increase in meal prices and, consequently, should also increase tips. Assuming both restaurants originally brought in the average tips given in the previous question, what percent increase would Restaurant B need to experience in tips in order for Mia to make the same amount of money in one evening at both restaurants from the hostess tip share? Assume that Restaurant B doesn't increase its tip share percentage. Enter your answer as a whole number and ignore the percent sign.

116   Unit Three: Problem Solving & Data Analysis

9. While reviewing for exams, a teacher knows that the number of topics he can cover is directly proportional to the length of time he has to review. If he can cover 9 topics in a single 45-minute period, how many topics can he cover in a 1-hour period?

   A) 5

   B) 7

   C) 10

   D) 12

10. Weight is dependent on the gravitational force exerted on an object. In other words, in space, you would weigh nothing because there is no gravity. Likewise, because the moon's gravitational pull is less than Earth's, objects weigh less on the moon. In general, 1 pound on Earth is equal to approximately 0.166 pounds on the moon. If a man weighs 29 pounds on the moon, about how much, in pounds, does he weigh on Earth?

   A) 21

   B) 48

   C) 175

   D) 196

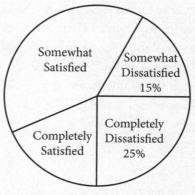

11. A company conducts a customer satisfaction survey. The results are summarized in the pie graph. If 240 customers responded to the survey, how many customers were either completely or somewhat satisfied?

   A) 60

   B) 96

   C) 144

   D) 204

12. When medical tests are conducted, there is always the possibility that the test will return a false positive or a false negative. A false positive means the test shows that a patient has the condition being studied, when the patient actually does not; a false negative indicates that a patient does not have the condition, when the patient actually does. Suppose a certain medical test has a false positive rate of 6 out of 3,500. How many people were tested during a period when 27 false positives came back?

   A) 14,000

   B) 15,750

   C) 17,500

   D) 21,000

13. A tutoring service offers a free one-hour tutoring session. After a client signs up, the next 10 hours of tutoring are billed at a rate of $30 per hour. For all hours after that, the client receives a discounted rate. If a client pays $664 for 25 hours of tutoring, what is the service's discounted hourly rate?

    A) $24.50

    B) $25.54

    C) $26.00

    D) $26.56

14. In a week, a light bulb factory produces 12,500 light bulbs. The ratio of light emitting diodes (LED bulbs) to compact fluorescent lamps (CFL bulbs) is 2:3. Of the LED bulbs produced, 3% were defective. How many LED bulbs were not defective?

    A)   150

    B)   2,425

    C)   4,850

    D)   7,275

15. In 1950, scientists estimated a certain animal population in a particular geographical area to be 6,400. In 2000, the population had risen to 7,200. If this animal population experiences the same percent increase over the next 50 years, what will the approximate population be?

    A)   8,000

    B)   8,100

    C)   8,400

    D)   8,600

16. On average, Betsy reads 1 page of her book every 1.5 minutes. Her book has 116 pages. Raymond starts a 94-page book on Saturday morning at 8:30 AM and reads straight through until he finishes it at 11:38 AM. How many more minutes does it take Raymond to read his book than Betsy to read hers?

17. An emergency room doctor prescribes a certain pain medication to be delivered through an IV drip. She prescribes 800 mL of the medication to be delivered over the course of 8 hours. The IV delivers 1 mL of medication over the course of 30 drips. How many drips per minute are needed to deliver the prescribed dosage?

18. A power company divides the geographic regions it serves into grids. The company is able to allocate the power it generates based on the usage and needs of a particular grid. Certain grids use more power at certain times of the day, so companies often shift power around to different grids at various times. On any given day, the company makes several changes in the power allocation to Grid 1. First, it increases the power by 20%. Then, it decreases it by 10%. Finally, it increases it by 30%. What is the net percent increase in this grid's power allocation? Round to the nearest whole percent and ignore the percent sign when entering your answer.

Math

Questions 19 and 20 refer to the following information.

Every Saturday morning, three friends meet for breakfast at 9:00 AM. Andrea walks, Kellan bikes, and Joelle drives.

19. Last Saturday, all three friends were exactly on time. Andrea left her house at 8:30 AM and walked at a rate of 3 miles per hour. Kellan left his house at 8:15 AM and biked at a rate of 14 miles per hour. Joelle left her house at 8:45 AM and drove an average speed of 35 miles per hour. How many miles from the restaurant does the person who traveled the farthest live?

20. Kellan lives 12 miles away from Andrea. On a different Saturday, Kellan biked at a rate of 15 miles per hour to Andrea's house. The two then walked to the restaurant at a rate of 2.5 miles per hour, and they arrived five minutes early. What time did Kellan leave his house? Enter your answer as three digits and ignore the colon. For example, if your answer is 5:30 AM, enter 530.

21. An expert on car depreciation determines that a certain car that costs $35,000 new will immediately depreciate by $12,000 once it is driven off the lot. After that, for the first 50,000 miles, the car will depreciate approximately $0.15 per mile driven. For every mile after that, it will depreciate by $0.10 per mile driven until the car reaches its scrap value. How much would this car be worth after being driven 92,000 miles?

    A) $11,300

    B) $13,800

    C) $17,000

    D) $27,700

22. A general contractor is building an addition onto a home. He budgets 20% for materials, 55% for labor, 10% for equipment rental, and the rest is his fee. If the estimate the contractor gives to the homeowners says he will spend $5,200 on materials, then how much is his fee?

    A) $2,600

    B) $3,900

    C) $5,200

    D) $6,500

23. In extreme climates, temperatures can vary as much as 20° Celsius in a single day. How many degrees Fahrenheit can these climates vary if the relation between Fahrenheit degrees and Celsius degrees is given by the equation $F = \dfrac{9}{5} C + 32$?

    A) 20°F

    B) 36°F

    C) 62°F

    D) 68°F

24. An architect is designing a new stadium-seating movie theater. The theater company has given the architect the following guidelines for designing the rows:

    • The length of each row must be at least 20 feet long, but no longer than 90 feet.

    • Each row should be at least 20% longer than the row in front of it.

    • Each row length must be evenly divisible by the width needed for each seat, 2.5 feet.

    Which list of row lengths meets the theater company's guidelines and includes as many row lengths as possible?

    A) 24, 30, 36, 45, 54, 66, 81

    B) 20, 32.5, 45, 57.5, 72.5, 85

    C) 20, 30, 40, 50, 60, 70, 80, 90

    D) 25, 30, 37.5, 45, 55, 67.5, 82.5

25. An online movie subscription service charges a dollars for the first month of membership and b dollars per month after that. If a customer has paid $108.60 so far for the service, which of the following expressions represents the number of months he has subscribed to the service?

    A) $\dfrac{108.60}{a + b}$

    B) $\dfrac{108.60 - a}{b}$

    C) $\dfrac{108.60 - a - b}{b}$

    D) $\dfrac{108.60 - a + b}{b}$

26. A certain real estate agent uses what he calls a *step-strategy* to sell houses. He puts a house on the market at a higher-than-expected selling price and if it hasn't sold in two weeks, he drops the price by 5%. If it still hasn't sold in another 2 weeks, he drops the price by another 5%. After that, he continues to drop the price by 3% every two weeks until it reaches a cut-off amount assigned by the homeowner, or the house sells, whichever comes first. If a house is originally listed at $200,000 and the homeowner sets a cut-off amount of $166,000, what is the final selling price given that the house sells after being on the market for 9 weeks?

    A) $162,901.25

    B) $164,737.48

    C) $166,000.00

    D) $169,832.45

27. A company reimburses employees for a portion of their gas costs for commuting to and from work based on mileage. Based on the following data, what is the rate in dollars per gallon that the company uses to reimburse employees?

    - The company has 126 employees who commute.

    - The average employee traveled 12,250 miles to and from work over the course of the year.

    - The average gas mileage reported by all employees was 22.5 miles per gallon.

    - The company paid out a total of $96,040.00 in gas reimbursements.

    A) $0.44

    B) $0.71

    C) $1.40

    D) $1.60

28. Mikal has two saltwater fish tanks in his home. One has eels and lionfish in a ratio of 5 to 2. The second tank has eels and seahorses in a ratio of 2 to 3. Mikal wants to put a tank in his office with seahorses and lionfish, using the same ratio he has at home to make it easier to buy food for them in bulk. What ratio of lionfish to seahorses should he use?

    A) 2:3

    B) 5:2

    C) 7:8

    D) 4:15

29. Katrina is working on a school project and determines that she needs 576 square inches of cardboard, but the craft store only sells cardboard by the square foot. How many square feet of cardboard does she need?

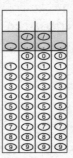

30. A county employee is collecting water samples from all the houses in a subdivision where trace amounts of lead were found in the water. There are 45 houses in the subdivision. If he starts the first house at 9:00 AM and starts the sixth house at 10:00 AM, how many minutes will it take the employee to collect samples from all the houses in the subdivision, assuming it takes the same amount of time at each house?

32. A bank offers a long-term savings account with a 1.0% annual interest rate. At the end of each year, the interest is rounded down to the nearest cent and added to the principal. If the initial deposit was $1,500, how much interest has the account earned at the end of 5 years?

31. On a map, the scale is the ratio of the distance shown on the map to the actual distance. A geography teacher has a map on her wall with a scale of 1 inch:100 miles. She uses the school's copier to shrink the large wall map down to the size of a piece of paper to hand out to each of her students. To do this, she makes the map $\frac{1}{4}$ of its original size. Suppose on the students' maps, the distance between two cities is 2.5 inches. How many actual miles apart are those cities?

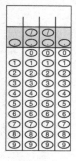

Math

Questions 33 and 34 refer to the following information.

Bridget is starting a tutoring business to help adults get their GEDs. She already has five clients and decides they can share a single textbook, which will be kept at her office, and that she also needs one notebook and four pencils for each of them. She records her supply budget, which includes tax, in the table shown.

Supply	Total Number Needed	Cost Each
Textbook	1	$24.99
Notebooks	5	$3.78
Pencils	20	$0.55

33. The textbook makes up what percent of Bridget's total supply budget? Round to the nearest tenth of a percent and ignore the percent sign when entering your answer.

34. Bridget's business does very well, and she needs more supplies. She always orders them according to the table above, for five clients at a time. At the beginning of this year, she orders the supplies for the whole year, which cost $988.02. Halfway through the year, she decides to take inventory of the supplies. She has used $713.57 worth of the supplies. How many pencils should be left, assuming the supplies were used at the rate for which she originally planned?

Questions 35 and 36 refer to the following information.

A restaurant offers a 20% discount to students and to members of the military. The restaurant is also currently participating in a charity drive. If patrons donate a gently used item of clothing, they get an additional 5% off their bill, which is applied before any other discounts, such as student or military discounts.

35. A student brings in an item of clothing and has a total bill, before any discounts, of $13.00. How much does she pay, once all applicable discounts are applied, not including tax?

36. Sharon is a member of the military. She dines with her friend, Damien. Damien brings an item of clothing, but Sharon forgot to bring one. If Sharon's meal before discounts is $16.25 and Damien's is $12.80 before discounts, how much did the discounts save them altogether?

Math

Questions 37 and 38 refer to the following information.

Jordan is beginning a marathon-training program. During his first day of training, he wears a pedometer to get an idea of how far he can currently run. At the end of the run, the pedometer indicates that he took 24,288 steps.

37. Jordan knows from experience that his average stride (step) is 2.5 feet. How many miles did he run on his first day of training? (1 mile = 5,280 feet)

38. Jordan was telling his friend Alexa, who is from Europe, about his training and told her how far he ran. Alexa wasn't sure whether that distance was long or short because she is familiar with the metric system, which uses kilometers, instead of miles. Jordan wants to convert the distance for her. If 1 kilometer equals approximately 0.62 miles, what number should he tell Alexa? Round your answer to the nearest tenth of a kilometer.

CHAPTER 6

Scatterplots

 CHAPTER OBJECTIVES

By the end of this chapter, you will be able to:

1. Decide whether a linear, quadratic, or exponential model describes the data presented in a scatterplot

2. Use an equation for a line of best fit to describe trends between variables in a scatterplot

3. Use a line of best fit to determine an average rate of change and to extrapolate values from given data

SMARTPOINTS

Point Value	SmartPoint Category
40 Points	Scatterplots

Math

SCATTERPLOTS

Chapter 6

Homework

Extra Practice: #1-20

Key

 Book Assignment

 Online Video Assignment

 Online Quiz Assignment

SCATTERPLOT BASICS

Some students tend to associate scatterplots with nasty-looking statistical analyses and consequently become nervous when they hear they'll likely encounter a few scatterplots on Test Day. However, these seemingly difficult plots are usually straightforward—if you know what to look for. We'll go over the foundational concepts of scatterplots, growth and decay examples, and modeling with scatterplots over the next several pages.

First, let's look at the anatomy of a scatterplot.

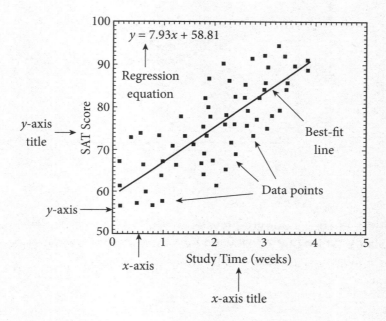

- You're already familiar with the **x- and y-axes**, but something that might be new is their **units**. Most scatterplots that use real data have units on the axes; these are important when trying to draw conclusions and inferences based on data (more on this later).

- The **domain** of a set of data points is the set of inputs, which corresponds to the *x*-values of the data points when plotted on a graph. The set of values that make up the **range** corresponds to the *y*-values.

- The **line of best fit** is drawn through the **data points** to describe the relationship between the two variables as an equation. This line does not need to go through most or all data points, but it should accurately reflect the trend shown by the data with about half the points above the line and half below. As in "plain" equations, *x* is the independent variable, and *y* is the dependent variable.

- The **equation of the line of best fit** (also called the **regression equation**) is the equation that describes the line of best fit algebraically. On Test Day, you'll most likely encounter this equation as linear, quadratic, or exponential, though it can also be other types of equations.

Prepare

Below is a test-like question that involves a scatterplot.

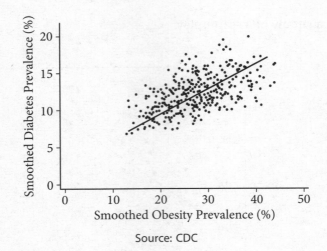

Source: CDC

1. The scatterplot shows obesity prevalence plotted against diabetes prevalence in the United States. Which of the following best estimates the average rate of change in the diabetes prevalence compared to the obesity prevalence?

   A) 0.25

   B) 0.87

   C) 1.5

   D) 4

Work through the Kaplan Method for Math step-by-step to solve this question. The following table shows Kaplan's strategic thinking on the left, along with suggested math scratchwork on the right.

Strategic Thinking	Math Scratchwork
Step 1: Read the question, identifying and organizing important information as you go You need to determine the average rate of change in diabetes prevalence vs. obesity prevalence. An info-graphic is provided.	
Step 2: Choose the best strategy to answer the question Examine the infographic. Look for units, labels, variables, and trends. Obesity prevalence is plotted along the *x*-axis, and diabetes prevalence along the *y*-axis. As the former increases, so does the latter. A rate of change corresponds to the slope of the line of best fit, so estimate a pair of points and find the slope between them.	$(16, 9)$ and $(44, 16)$ $m = \dfrac{y_2 - y_1}{x_2 - x_1} = \dfrac{16 - 9}{44 - 16} = \dfrac{7}{28} = \dfrac{1}{4}$ $slope = 0.25$
Step 3: Check that you answered the *right* question You found the rate of change, also known as the slope. The correct answer is (A).	

Remember that you don't need to understand fully what "diabetes prevalence" is to correctly answer this question. As long as you can interpret and use a scatterplot, you'll be in good shape.

  Note

Make a note of the scales along the axes. Misreading them is an easy way to fall for a trap answer.

GROWTH AND DECAY

The real world is full of examples of growth and decay, and you're bound to see some examples on Test Day. The two most common types are linear and exponential. Following is the model for a linear equation:

$$y = kx + x_0$$

If this equation looks familiar, it would be for good reason: It's a linear equation in slope-intercept form with different variables standing in for the ones you've seen in the past. You should be able to match each piece to a quantity in the slope-intercept form of an equation. Take a look at the following table for a translation of the new components.

Linear Growth/ Decay Variable	What It Represents	Slope-Intercept Counterpart
x_0	y-intercept or initial quantity in a word problem	b
k	rate of change, slope	m

Recognizing that the previous equation, which might look weird at first glance, is really something you've seen before, will go a long way on Test Day.

 ✔ Note

You might also see this expressed in function notation. We've included several homework problems in this format for you to try. For an overview of functions, see chapter 9.

A more complex model is the exponential equation:

$$y = x_0(1 + r)^x$$

You'll notice most of the terms, such as y, x_0 (pronounced "x-naught"), and x are in both linear and exponential equations, which makes exponential equations a bit easier to understand. The new variable, r, is the rate of change, akin to k in a linear equation. Also note that x is now an exponent.

What happens if you have a negative exponential rate of change?

Suppose $r = -\dfrac{3}{4}$ and $x_0 = 100$. Substituting these values into the exponential model gives $y = 100\left(1 - \dfrac{3}{4}\right)^x = 100\left(\dfrac{1}{4}\right)^x$. Use exponent rules to distribute the x, which yields $y = 100 \times \dfrac{1^x}{4^x}$. Because 1^x will always be 1, you can drop it and move 100 to the numerator to give the final equation, $y = \dfrac{100}{4^x}$. This can also be written as $y = 100 \times 0.25^x$, so be ready for both fraction and decimal forms. Here's an easy way to remember whether you have exponential growth or decay: If r is positive, you're looking at growth; if r is negative, decay is occurring. An r of 0 will give you 1^x, which drops out and leaves *y* equal to a constant (and therefore a horizontal line instead of an exponential curve).

Another key difference to note: The rate of change in linear growth and decay is constant, but it is variable for exponential growth or decay. Graphically, linear growth/decay is a straight line, whereas exponential growth/decay has a curve. This will often help you identify which is occurring in a given situation.

Now let's look at a test-like question that involves growth. It's up to you to figure out whether it is linear or exponential.

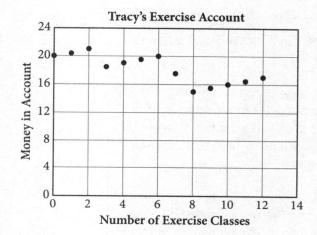

2. Tracy recently joined a workout group in which each member commits to attending three exercise classes per week. To increase accountability, each member sets aside $20 in an account. If a member misses a class, that individual will lose $2.50, which is then equally distributed among the members who attended that class. After missing three classes, Tracy vows to hold herself more accountable and not miss any more. The scatterplot above shows Tracy's account balance over time. Assuming exactly one person is absent from any given class and no one else has joined or left the group since its inception, which of the following equations could represent Tracy's account balance after she resolves not to miss any further classes?

A) $y = 20(1.5)^x$

B) $y = x^{1.5} + 11$

C) $y = 0.5x + 11$

D) $y = 0.5x + 20$

Math

Work through the Kaplan Method for Math step-by-step to solve this question. The following table shows Kaplan's strategic thinking on the left, along with suggested math scratchwork on the right.

Strategic Thinking	Math Scratchwork
Step 1: Read the question, identifying and organizing important information as you go You need to determine which equation correctly represents Tracy's account balance after her second missed class, assuming she does not miss any after that. You're given some information about the account's behavior.	$20 @ start present: $+x$ no-show: $-\$2.50$
Step 2: Choose the best strategy to answer the question Find the relevant data points on the scatterplot. The last class Tracy missed corresponds to the third (and final) decrease on the scatterplot. You need the equation that represents Tracy's account balance after that class, so you can disregard her attendance prior to that. Because the no-show count and group size do not change, you can assume Tracy's account balance will increase at a constant rate, indicating a linear equation. You can therefore eliminate A and B. To determine which of the remaining answer choices is correct, draw a line of best fit through the appropriate points. The y-intercept is 11, meaning (C) must be correct.	**Tracy's Exercise Account** (scatterplot: Money in Account vs. Number of Exercise Classes, with circled points near x=8–12) **Tracy's Exercise Account** (scatterplot with line of best fit: Money in Account vs. Number of Exercise Classes)
Step 3: Check that you answered the *right* question Only choice (C) contains a linear equation with the correct y-intercept.	$y = 0.5x + 11$

Nice job! Let's continue our exploration of scatterplots with a section on modeling.

SCATTERPLOT MODELING

As you've seen, the SAT can ask a variety of questions related to scatterplots. In addition, you might be asked to do some more advanced tasks, such as drawing conclusions and making predictions. This task sounds daunting, but it's not as challenging as you might think.

Look at the following graphs for a preview of the types of models you might see.

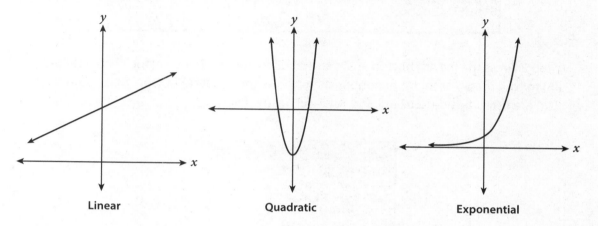

Linear   Quadratic   Exponential

A **linear model** will always increase (when its slope is positive) or always decrease (when its slope is negative) at a constant rate, making it easy to spot.

A **quadratic model** is U-shaped and the trend of the data changes from decreasing to increasing, or vice versa. The graph of a quadratic equation takes the shape of a parabola, which has either a minimum or a maximum called the vertex (although it is sometimes not shown on the graph). A parabola opens upward when the coefficient of the x^2 term is positive, and it opens downward when the coefficient of the x^2 term is negative.

An **exponential model** typically starts with a gradual rate of change, which increases significantly over time. Unlike a quadratic model, the trend of the data does not change direction, and the graph does not have a vertex.

Using a Graphing Calculator to Model Data

There are times when using a graphing calculator on Test Day can speed things up considerably; deriving an equation that fits a data set is one of those times. These equations are called **regression equations** and can take several shapes depending on the data's behavior. The **correlation coefficient**, *r*, indicates how well a regression equation fits the data; the closer *r* is to 1 for an increasing equation (or −1 for a decreasing equation), the better the fit. To find the equation for the line of best fit and the correlation coefficient, follow the steps on the next page (for a TI-83/84 calculator).

Math

Step 1: Press the [STAT] button. Choose [EDIT], then enter your data for [L₁] and [L₂].

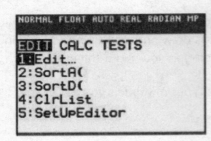

Step 2: Press the [STAT] button again and scroll to [CALC]. Select [4] for a linear regression, [5] for quadratic, or [0] for exponential and press the [ENTER] button. Make sure [L₁] and [L₂] are listed beside [XList] and [YList], respectively.

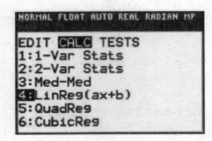

Step 3: Scroll down to [Calculate], then press the [ENTER] button. The variable values are listed, as is the correlation coefficient. If r is not close to 1/−1, try another regression type.

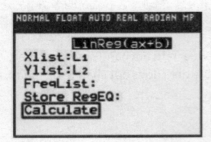 

Note: If r is not displayed, go to the [CATALOG] menu (press [2nd] then [0]), scroll to the Ds, then select [DiagnosticOn].

✔ Note

If you have a calculator other than the TI-83/84, make sure you read its manual prior to Test Day so you're familiar with how to use this function.

Below is a test-like example that asks you to extrapolate data from a scatterplot.

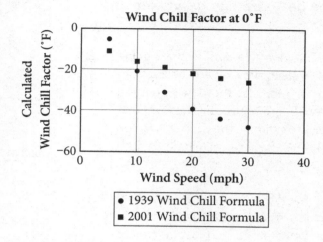

3. Inhabitants of colder climates are often concerned about frostbite in the winter months and use the wind chill factor to gauge how much time they can safely spend outside. Wind chill reflects the temperature that one feels when outside based on the actual temperature and the wind speed. Wind chill was first introduced in 1939, and the formula was revised in 2001. If the outside temperature is 0°F, what is the approximate wind chill at 40 mph based on the 2001 formula, and what wind speed would produce the same wind chill using the 1939 formula?

    A)   −30°F, 10 mph

    B)   −30°F, 15 mph

    C)   −50°F, 15 mph

    D)   −50°F, 40 mph

Work through the Kaplan Method for Math step-by-step to solve this question. The following table shows Kaplan's strategic thinking on the left, along with suggested math scratchwork on the right.

Strategic Thinking	Math Scratchwork
Step 1: Read the question, identifying and organizing important information as you go You are asked to identify a wind chill value and a wind speed. Although the question stem is lengthy, most of the information is irrelevant. Pay attention to both the title and axis labels on the scatterplot when solving.	

Math

Strategic Thinking	Math Scratchwork
Step 2: Choose the best strategy to answer the question Use the trend of the 2001 formula data to draw a line that extends to 40 mph. Next, draw a vertical line from 40 mph on the *x*-axis to intersect the data extension that you drew, and then draw a horizontal line from that intersection to the *y*-axis to estimate the wind chill factor, which is approximately −30°F. You can eliminate C and D based on this finding. The second part asks for the temperature that would yield the same wind chill (−30°F) using the 1939 formula. The horizontal line that you drew for the first part crosses right through a point on the 1939 curve. Draw another line down to the *x*-axis from that point to find that the wind speed is approximately 15 mph.	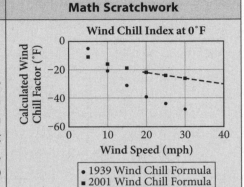 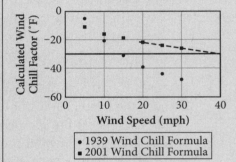 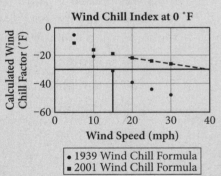
Step 3: Check that you answered the *right* question Choice (B) is the only answer choice that contains both findings.	

✔ **Note**

Watch the axis labels. Don't assume each grid-line always represents one unit.

Now you'll have a chance to try a couple test-like problems in a scaffolded way. We've provided some guidance, but you'll need to fill in the missing parts of explanations or the step-by-step math in order to get to the correct answer. Don't worry—after going through the worked examples at the beginning of this section, these problems should be completely doable.

4. Which of the following plots could be modeled by the equation $y = 3^x + 4$?

A)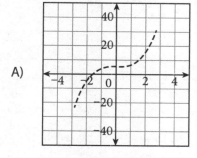

C)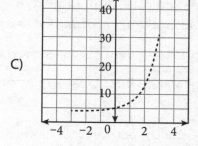

B)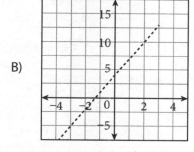

D)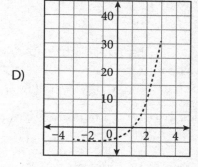

This question is different from the previous ones, but don't worry. The following table can help you structure your thinking as you go about solving this problem. Kaplan's strategic thinking is provided, as are bits of structured scratchwork. If you're not sure how to approach a question like this, start at the top and work your way down.

Strategic Thinking	Math Scratchwork
Step 1: Read the question, identifying and organizing important information as you go You need to match the given equation to the correct plot.	
Step 2: Choose the best strategy to answer the question The x in the exponent position indicates that you have a certain type of graph; there are two choices you can eliminate based on this. To choose between the remaining graphs, plug in a manageable value for x, and see what y is at that point. Determine which graph contains this point.	need a(n) _____ graph; eliminate _____ when $x =$ _____, $y =$ _____ _____ matches
Step 3: Check that you answered the *right* question If you chose (C), you'd be correct!	_____

✔ **Note**

Remember that 3^x is very different from $3x$ and x^3.

Coming up next, you'll get a chance to try a multi-part question involving a scatterplot.

Questions 5 and 6 refer to the following information.

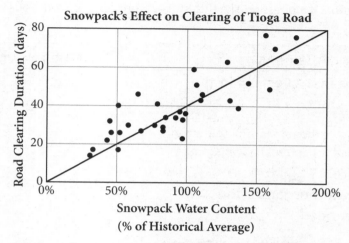

(Data source: www.nps.gov/yose/planyourvisit/tiogaopen.htm)

Tioga (pronounced tie-OH-ga) Road is a mountain pass that crosses the Sierra Nevada through northern Yosemite National Park. Due to its high elevation and the unpredictability of Sierra weather in the winter and early spring, the road is closed from about November through late May. This time period can change depending on the quantity and nature of the season's snowfall, as well as unforeseen obstacles like fallen trees and/or rocks. The scatterplot above compares the snowpack water content on April 1 (for years 1981-2014) as a percent of the historical average to the time it takes the National Park Service to fully clear the road and open it to traffic.

5. For every 5% increase in snowpack water content, how many more days does it take the National Park Service to clear Tioga Road?

6. Assuming no unforeseen obstacles or machinery issues, if the road's snowpack water content on April 1 is 248% of the historical average, how many days will it take to fully clear Tioga Road?

The following tables can help you structure your thinking as you go about solving this more involved question set. Kaplan's strategic thinking is provided, as are bits of structured scratchwork. If you're not sure how to approach a question like this, start at the top and work your way down.

Strategic Thinking	Math Scratchwork
Step 1: Read the first question in the set, looking for clues The infographic shows the relationship between snowpack water content and road clearing duration. A line of best fit is also drawn.	
Step 2: Identify and organize the information you need You are asked to find how much the road clearing time increases with each 5% increase in snowpack water content.	
Step 3: Based on what you know, plan your steps to navigate the first question You need a rate, which means you need to find the slope of the line of best fit. Pick a pair of points to use (look for places where the line passes through a grid-line intersection to minimize error). Read the axes carefully when writing the coordinates!	(——, ——) (——, ——)
Step 4: Solve, step-by-step, checking units as you go Use the slope formula to determine the change in clearing time per 1% increase in snowpack water content.	$m = \dfrac{y_2 - y_1}{x_2 - x_1} =$ ———— = ———— = ————
Step 5: Did I answer the *right* question? Be careful; you're not done yet! The slope represents the clearing duration increase for a 1% increase in snowpack water content. Multiply *m* by 5 to get the requested change. If you got 2, you'd be correct!	—— × —— = ——

Great job! Repeat this for the second question in the set. Kaplan's strategic thinking is on the left, and bits of scratchwork guidance are on the right.

Strategic Thinking	Math Scratchwork
Step 1: Read the second question in the set, looking for clues Not a whole lot of new information, just a bit on the snowpack water content during a particularly snowy winter.	
Step 2: Identify and organize the information you need This question asks for the road clearing duration if snowpack water content is 248% of the historical average. The slope you found in the previous question could be useful here.	$m =$ ___
Step 3: Based on what you know, plan your steps to navigate the second question 248% snowpack water content is not on the graph, and you can easily make an error if you try to extend the line of best fit to estimate at 248%. You can use the slope to write the equation of the line and extrapolate from there.	$y = mx + b$
Step 4: Solve, step-by-step, checking units as you go Determine where the line of best fit intersects the y-axis to identify the value of b. Once there, plug 248 into the equation for the line of best fit, and then solve for y.	eqn: _____ = _____ + _____ $x = 248$: _____ = _____ × _____ + _____ _____ = _____ + _____ = _____
Step 5: Did I answer the *right* question? You needed to find the number of days to clear Tioga Road at 248% snowpack water content. Did you get 99.2? If so, you'd be right!	_____

Nicely done! Now test what you've learned by taking a brief quiz.

Now that you've seen the variety of ways in which the SAT can test you on scatterplots, try the following questions to check your understanding. Give yourself 4 minutes to tackle the following three questions. Make sure you use the Kaplan Method for Math as often as you can. Remember, you want to emphasize speed and efficiency in addition to simply getting the correct answer.

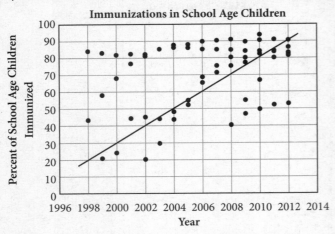

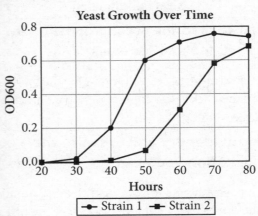

7. The graph above shows the percent of school age children in the United States who received immunizations for various illnesses between 1996 and 2012. What was the average rate of increase in the percent of children immunized over the given time period?

A) 5%

B) 10%

C) 25%

D) 70%

8. A marketing team is conducting a study on the use of smartphones. In a certain metropolitan area, there were 1.6 million smartphone users at the end of 2014. The marketing team predicts that the number of smartphone users will increase by 35% each year. If y represents the number of smartphone users in this metropolitan area after x years, then which of the following equations best models the number of smartphone users in this area over time?

A) $y = 1,600,000(1.35)^x$

B) $y = 1,600,000(35)^x$

C) $y = 35x + 1,600,000$

D) $y = 1.35x + 1,600,000$

9. A microbiologist is comparing the growth rates of two different yeast strains. She indirectly measures the number of yeast cells by recording the optical density (OD600) of each strain every ten hours. The measurements are presented in the graph above. Based on the data, which of the following is NOT a true statement?

A) Strain 1 had a higher OD600 reading than Strain 2 throughout the monitored period.

B) The growth rate of Strain 2 was less than the growth rate of Strain 1 until hour 50, at which point Strain 1's growth rate became the lesser one.

C) Between hours 50 and 70, Strain 2's OD600 reading increased by approximately 0.03 every hour.

D) The growth rate of Strain 1 was greater than the growth rate of Strain 2 throughout the monitored period.

Answers and Explanations for this chapter begin on page 912.

EXTRA PRACTICE

 You may use your calculator for all questions in this section.

1. Which of the following is best modeled using a linear regression equation, $y = ax + b$, where $a < 0$?

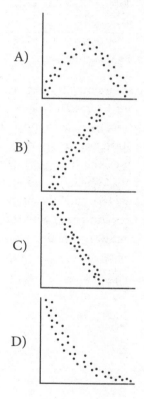

A)

B)

C)

D)

2. Adriana used the data from a scatterplot she found on the U.S. Census Bureau's website to determine a regression model showing the relationship between the population in the area where she lived and the number of years, x, after she was born. The result was an exponential growth equation of the form $y = x_0(1 + r)^x$. Which of the following does x_0 most likely represent in the equation?

A) The population in the year that she was born

B) The rate of change of the population over time

C) The maximum population reached during her lifetime

D) The number of years after her birth when the population reached its maximum

Math

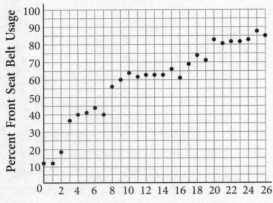

Seatbelt Use in England (1983-2009)

Percent Front Seat Belt Usage

Years After Seatbelt Law Enacted

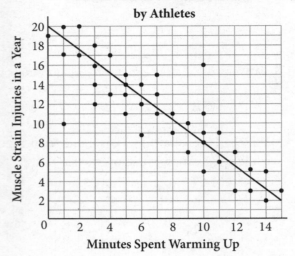

Minor Muscle Strains Sustained by Athletes

Muscle Strain Injuries in a Year

Minutes Spent Warming Up

3. In 1983, the British Parliament enacted a mandatory seat belt law. The scatterplot above shows data collected each year after the law was enacted regarding the percent of drivers and front seat passengers who wore seat belts. Which of the following equations best represents the trend of the data shown in the figure?

   A) $y = 0.4x + 25$

   B) $y = 1.8x + 15$

   C) $y = 2.1x + 35$

   D) $y = 2.6x + 25$

4. The scatterplot above shows the number of minor muscle strain injuries sustained in a year by athletes, plotted against their self-reported amount of time spent stretching and doing other "warm up" activities before engaging in rigorous physical activity. Which of the following best estimates the average rate of change in the number of injuries compared with the number of minutes spent warming up?

   A) -1.2

   B) -0.8

   C) 2

   D) 20

5. The Federal Reserve controls certain interest rates in the United States. Investors often try to speculate as to whether the Federal Reserve will raise or lower rates and by how much. Suppose a company conducts extensive interviews with financial analysts, and as a result, predicts that "the Fed" will increase rates by an average of 0.25 percentage points every six months for the foreseeable future. Which type of equation could be used to model the predicted interest rates over the next several years, assuming no other significant changes?

A)   A linear equation

B)   A quadratic equation

C)   A polynomial equation

D)   An exponential equation

6. A physics class is doing an experiment in order to write a function that models the height of a new super bouncy ball after each time that it bounces off the parking lot. The ball is thrown from the roof of the gym straight down to the parking lot pavement. The ball bounces to a height of 80 feet. The ball is allowed to bounce again, without anyone touching it, this time reaching a maximum height of 40 feet. It bounces again, reaching a height of 20 feet, and continues until it eventually stops bouncing. Which of the following functions could be used to model the height (H) of the ball after each time that it hits the pavement (b), until the ball stops bouncing?

A) $H(b) = \dfrac{80}{2^b}$

B) $H(b) = \dfrac{80}{2^{b-1}}$

C) $H(b) = 80 - 2b$

D) $H(b) = 80 - 2(b - 1)$

Math

Questions 7 and 8 refer to the following information.

Most chickens reach maturity and begin laying eggs at around 20 weeks of age. From this point forward, however, as the chicken ages, its egg production decreases. A farmer was given a flock of 100 chickens (all of which are the same age) and asked to measure daily egg output for the entire flock at random intervals starting at maturity until the chickens were 70 weeks old. The data is recorded in the scatterplot below and the line of best fit has been drawn.

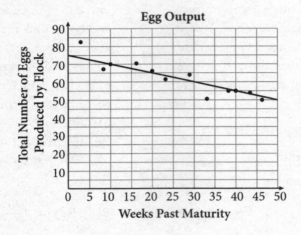

7. How many times did the farmer's data differ by at least 5 eggs from the number of eggs predicted by the line of best fit?

8. Based on the line of best fit, what is the predicted number of eggs that will be produced by the flock when it is 36 weeks past maturity?

9. If a scatterplot shows a strong positive linear correlation, then which of the following best describes the trend of the data points?

   A) Points in a perfectly straight line that rises from left to right

   B) Points in a perfectly straight line that falls from left to right

   C) Points that fit fairly close to a straight line that rises from left to right

   D) Points that fit fairly close to a straight line that falls from left to right

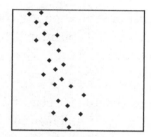

10. Which of the following is the best estimate for the slope of the line that best fits the data shown in the figure above? (Assume that the black bordered area is a square and that the scale of measurement is the same on every side.)

    A) -3

    B) $-\dfrac{1}{3}$

    C) $\dfrac{1}{3}$

    D) 3

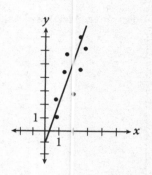

11. Which of the equations best models the data shown above?

    A) $y = 0.5x - 1$

    B) $y = 0.5x + 1$

    C) $y = 1.5x + 1$

    D) $y = 1.5x - 1$

12. Suppose a scatterplot shows a weak negative linear correlation. Which of the following statements is true?

    A) The slope of the line of best fit will be a number less than -1.

    B) The slope of the line of best fit will be a number between -1 and 0.

    C) The data points will follow, but not closely, the line of best fit, which has a negative slope.

    D) The data points will be closely gathered around the line of best fit, which has a negative slope.

Math

Employee Sick Day Usage

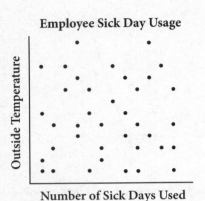

13. The Human Resources department of a company tracks employee sick day usage to see if there are patterns. One of the HR representatives decides to check employee sick day usage against outside temperature. He compiles the information for the employees' sick day usage and temperature in the scatterplot above. Which of the following conclusions can he draw based on this data?

A) There is no relationship between the number of sick days used by employees in general and outside temperature.

B) There is no relationship between the number of sick days used by this company's employees and outside temperature.

C) No conclusions can be drawn about the number of sick days used by this company's employees and outside temperature.

D) There is a relationship between, but not causation by, the number of sick days used by this company's employees and outside temperature.

14. Scientists plotted data for two animal populations on a scatterplot: Population A, which they graphed along the x-axis, and Population B, which they graphed along the y-axis. The data showed a strong negative correlation. Which of the following statements is justified?

A) The rise in Population A caused the decline in Population B.

B) The decline in Population B caused the rise in Population A.

C) Because the correlation is negative, there cannot be causation between the two populations.

D) The rise in Population A is correlated to the decline in Population B, but causation is unknown.

15. If a scatterplot shows data points in the first quadrant of a coordinate plane that decrease very quickly at first, and then continue to decrease but at a much slower rate, then which of the following functions is the best model for the data?

A) $f(x) = ax^2 + bx + c$, where $a > 0$

B) $f(x) = ax^2 + bx + c$, where $a < 0$

C) $f(x) = a(1 + r)^x$, where $r > 0$

D) $f(x) = a(1 + r)^x$, where $r < 0$

16. When a baby is born, it has a small stomach and therefore only needs small amounts of breast milk or formula at a time. As the baby gets older, it needs more calories to grow, so it starts consuming more milk. At about 6 months, babies are able to eat solid foods and will get some of their calories from that. Accordingly, the child's need for milk starts to decrease, until it is no longer even necessary, which occurs at about one year of age. If data is collected on a typical infant's milk intake over the first year and plotted on a scatterplot, what kind of model would most likely match the data?

    A) Positive linear

    B) Negative linear

    C) Positive quadratic

    D) Negative quadratic

17. Genji is compiling data relating snowfall to temperature where he lives. He records his data points in the form (temperature in degrees Fahrenheit, snowfall in inches). He plots the data on a scatterplot and draws a line of best fit, which indicates a strong negative correlation. He then remembers that his temperature gauge reads 10 degrees colder than it actually is. This means all of his data points are correct for the amount of snowfall, but the temperature readings are all lower than they should be. To correct the problem, he adds 10 degrees to all of his temperature readings and re-plots the data. What does this mean for his data?

    A) The data is no longer necessarily correlated.

    B) There is no change in the strength of correlation.

    C) The rate of change for the line of best fit is less now.

    D) The rate of change for the line of best fit is greater now.

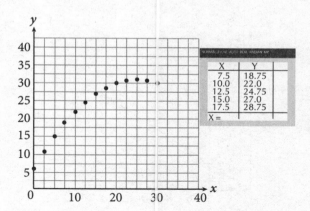

18. The maximum value of the data shown in the scatterplot above occurs at $x = 25$. If the data is modeled using a quadratic regression and the correlation coefficient is 1.0 (the fit is exact), then what is the y-value when $x = 35$?

    A) 10

    B) 15

    C) 22

    D) 27

Math

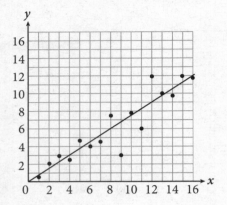

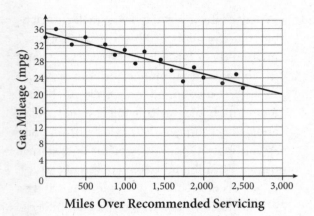

Miles Over Recommended Servicing

19. What is the *y*-value of the data point that has the highest percent error from the mean of the data shown in the scatterplot above?

20. Research suggests that for any given make and model of car, the more miles the car is driven over the recommended miles between servicing, the worse gas mileage the car gets. Suppose a car dealership compiles data on a specific make and model of car and creates the scatterplot shown above. They then use the equation $y = -\dfrac{1}{200}x + 35$ to model the data. Based on the information, how many miles per gallon could be expected if this particular car is driven 3,400 miles over the recommended miles between servicing?

CHAPTER 7

Two-way Tables, Statistics, and Probability

 ## CHAPTER OBJECTIVES

By the end of this chapter, you will be able to:

1. Use two-way tables to summarize data and calculate basic probabilities

2. Make inferences about population parameters based on sample data

3. Evaluate scenarios and reports to make inferences, justify conclusions, and determine appropriateness of data collection methods

4. Use statistics to investigate measures of center of data and analyze shape, center, and spread

SMARTPOINTS

Point Value	SmartPoint Category	
50 Points	Statistics and Probability	

TWO-WAY TABLES, STATISTICS, AND PROBABILITY

Chapter 7

Homework

Extra Practice: #1-20

Even More

Math Quiz 3

Key

  Book Assignment

  Online Video Assignment

  Online Quiz Assignment

TWO-WAY TABLES AND CHARTS/GRAPHS

Data can be represented in a multitude of ways. In this chapter, we'll focus on a numerical approach (two-way table) and a pictorial one (chart or graph).

A two-way table is a table that contains data on two variables. This type of table can be used to make comparisons and determine whether relationships exist between the variables. You might see this data referred to as bivariate (two-variable) data.

If you're worried about having to learn a new topic, you need not be. You've likely encountered two-way tables in the past and just not known their formal name—if you've ever generated a spreadsheet, two-way tables should look familiar. Take a look at the following example that contains data on several antique book stores' sales to see what we mean.

	Bob's Books	Nalia's Novels	Tumiko's Tomes	Vladimir's Volumes	Total
Monday	14	7	15	12	48
Tuesday	8	13	15	13	49
Wednesday	10	13	12	14	49
Thursday	8	15	14	10	47
Friday	13	7	10	9	39
Total	53	55	66	58	232

Two-way tables contain a wealth of information: You can quickly determine how many books Nalia's Novels sold on Friday just by finding the appropriate cell in the table. You can also find quantities that are not explicitly written. For instance, you can determine numerous ratios: total books sold on Wednesday to total books sold on Thursday, Tumiko's Monday sales to Tumiko's total sales, and so on. You can also calculate percentages and probabilities.

> ✔ **Note**
>
> Although two-way tables are generally easy to follow, they're also easy to misinterpret when you're in a rush. Take time to ensure that you've extracted the correct information for a given question.

Ratios and the like aside, you could be asked to make a prediction based on given data; that is, you'll need to extrapolate data to derive an answer. For instance, let's say the community in which these four shops are located has an annual antique appreciation week, and Nalia anticipates that her antique book sales will increase by 40% from the week for which the data is shown in the table. She sold 55 books that week, and 40% of 55 is 22. This means that if Nalia's prediction is true, she can expect to sell 55 + 22 = 77 books during antique appreciation week.

Math

In addition to two-way tables, the SAT can also ask questions about charts and graphs, whether about the data itself or a prediction based on the data. Take a look at the next few pages for sample questions involving two-way tables, charts, and graphs.

Use the table introduced at the beginning of this section to answer the following question.

1. Which of the four shops made the greatest fraction of its total sales on Tuesday?

   A) Bob's Books

   B) Nalia's Novels

   C) Tumiko's Tomes

   D) Vladimir's Volumes

Work through the Kaplan Method for Math step-by-step to solve this question. The following table shows Kaplan's strategic thinking on the left, along with suggested math scratchwork on the right.

Strategic Thinking	Math Scratchwork
Step 1: Read the question, identifying and organizing important information as you go Understanding what's being asked is the trickiest part of this question. You *do not* want the shop that sold the most books on Tuesday. Rather, you are looking for the shop whose Tuesday sales, as a fraction of the shop's total sales, were the greatest.	need $\dfrac{\text{Tuesday}}{\text{Total}}$
Step 2: Choose the best strategy to answer the question Only two rows matter for this question: the Tuesday row and the Total row (*not* the Total column). Divide each shop's Tuesday sales by its total sales. The shop with the largest result is the correct answer. Because the fractions involve less manageable numbers, using a calculator to simplify the arithmetic is reasonable here. Nalia's Tuesday sales as a fraction of her total sales were the highest of the four shops.	B: $\dfrac{8}{53} \approx 0.1509$ N: $\dfrac{13}{55} \approx 0.2364$ T: $\dfrac{15}{66} \approx 0.2273$ V: $\dfrac{13}{58} \approx 0.2241$
Step 3: Check that you answered the *right* question You've identified the shop that had the highest fraction of its sales on Tuesday, so you're done. Choice (B) is correct.	

✔ **Expert Tip**

If you're adept at quantitative comparison of fractions, you can omit the decimal conversion calculations (and save some time).

The following question requires the table used for question 1.

2. What fraction of all the books sold on Monday, Wednesday, and Friday were sold at Tumiko's Tomes and Vladimir's Volumes?

A) $\dfrac{9}{29}$

B) $\dfrac{11}{32}$

C) $\dfrac{9}{17}$

D) $\dfrac{18}{31}$

Work through the Kaplan Method for Math step-by-step to solve this question. The following table shows Kaplan's strategic thinking on the left, along with suggested math scratchwork on the right.

Strategic Thinking	Math Scratchwork
Step 1: Read the question, identifying and organizing important information as you go You need to find how many books Tumiko and Vladimir sold on Monday, Wednesday, and Friday as a fraction of the total number of books all four shops sold on those days.	
Step 2: Choose the best strategy to answer the question Use the Monday, Wednesday, and Friday rows and the Tumiko, Vladimir, and Total columns (*not* the Total row). Add the number of books Tumiko and Vladimir sold on these three days, and then repeat the process with the total number of books all four shops sold on these days. Combine these values into a fraction.	Mon + Wed + Fri for T & V: $(15 + 12) +$ $(12 + 14) + (10 + 9) = 72$ Mon + Wed + Fri total: $48 + 49 + 39 = 136$ $\dfrac{72}{136}$
Step 3: Check that you answered the *right* question You'll need to simplify the fraction. The GCF of 72 and 136 is 8, so the most simplified form of the fraction is $\dfrac{9}{17}$. Select (C) and you're done.	$\dfrac{72}{136} = \dfrac{9}{17}$

STATISTICS AND PROBABILITY

While there are entire high school and college courses devoted to the study of statistics, the SAT will (fortunately) only test you on a few basic statistical concepts. If you aren't a statistics fan, now is a great time to rethink your position: Statistics is a part of almost every major in college and can be used in a variety of careers. Using an example from high school, let's take a look at the sort of concepts the SAT expects you to be familiar with.

Suppose you took five tests in a world history class and earned scores of 85, 92, 85, 80, and 96. Descriptions of six fundamental statistics figures you can find for this data set follow:

- **Mean (also called average):** The sum of the values divided by the number of values. For your history class, the mean of your test scores is $\dfrac{85 + 92 + 85 + 80 + 96}{5} = \dfrac{438}{5} = 87.6$. At most schools, that's a B or B+.

- **Median:** The value that is in the middle of the set *when the values are arranged in ascending order.* The test scores in ascending order are 80, 85, 85, 92, and 96, making the median 85. Be careful: The SAT could give you a set of numbers that is not in order. Make sure you properly arrange them before determining the median.

- **Mode:** The value that occurs most frequently. The score that appears more than any other is 85 (twice vs. once), so it is the mode. If more than one value appears the most often, that's okay: A set of data can have multiple modes.

- **Range:** The difference between the highest and lowest values. From finding the median, you know the highest and lowest scores are 96 and 80, respectively; so the range is $96 - 80 = 16$.

- **Standard deviation:** A measure of how far a typical data point is from the mean. A low standard deviation means most values in the set are fairly close to the mean; a high standard deviation means there is much more spread in the data set. On the SAT, **you will need to know what standard deviation is and what it tells you about a set of data, but you won't have to calculate it.**

- **Margin of error:** A description of the maximum expected difference between a true value for a data pool (e.g., mean) and a random sampling from the data pool. A lower margin of error is achieved by increasing the size of the data pool. **As with standard deviation, you will need to know what a margin of error is on the SAT, but you won't be asked to calculate one.**

Mean, median, and mode are referred to as measures of central tendency because they can be used to represent a typical value in the data set. Range, standard deviation, and margin of error are measures of spread because they show how much the data in a set vary.

> ✔ **Note**
>
> To find the median of a data set that contains an even number of terms, arrange the terms in ascending order, then find the average of the two middle terms.

On Test Day, you might also be asked to analyze the shape of data. The shape of a data set can be either symmetric (also referred to as a *normal* distribution) or skewed (asymmetric). Many data sets have a head, where many data points are clustered in one area, and tails, where the number of data points slowly decreases to 0. Examining the tails will help you describe the shape of a data set. A data set is skewed in the direction of its longer tail.

Symmetric

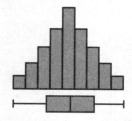

The data are evenly spread out.
mean ≈ median

Skewed to the Left

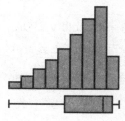

The tail is longer on the left.
mean < median

Skewed to the Right

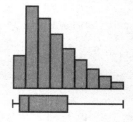

The tail is longer on the right.
mean > median

> ✔ **Expert Tip**
>
> When you have a group of evenly spaced terms (e.g., 2, 4, 6, 8, 10, 12), the mean and median will be identical. With this data set, the mean is
>
> $$\frac{2 + 4 + 6 + 8 + 10 + 12}{6} = \frac{42}{6} = 7,$$ and
>
> the median is $\frac{6 + 8}{2} = \frac{14}{2} = 7$. In
>
> addition, you can find the mean of a group of evenly spaced terms by taking the mean of the highest and lowest:
>
> $$\frac{12 + 2}{2} = \frac{14}{2} = 7.$$

It is possible to determine the mean of a data set from a bar graph (also called a histogram). Suppose a teacher made a bar graph, such as the one shown here, of student performance on a recent test.

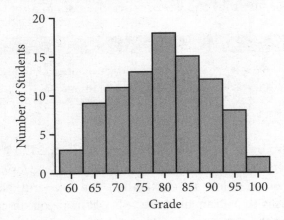

To find the mean test score, first determine the sum of the scores and then divide by the number of scores. From the graph, 3 students scored 60, 9 scored 65, 11 scored 70, and so on. Add these values to find the sum of the scores; then divide by the total number of scores.

$$\frac{3(60) + 9(65) + 11(70) + 13(75) + 18(80) + 15(85) + 12(90) + 8(95) + 2(100)}{3 + 9 + 11 + 13 + 18 + 15 + 12 + 8 + 2} = \frac{7,265}{91} = 79.8$$

The mean score on this test was 79.8.

A concept closely linked to statistics is probability. **Probability** is a fraction or decimal comparing the number of desired outcomes to the number of total possible outcomes. The formula is:

$$\text{Probability} = \frac{\text{\# desired outcomes}}{\text{\# total possible outcomes}}$$

For instance, if you have a full deck of playing cards and want to know the probability of drawing an ace, you would compute $\frac{\text{\# aces}}{\text{\# cards}} = \frac{4}{52} = \frac{1}{13} \approx 0.077$. To find the probability that an event will *not* happen, subtract the probability that the event will happen from 1. In the ace example, this would be:

$$1 - \frac{\text{\# aces}}{\text{\# cards}} = 1 - \frac{4}{52} = \frac{48}{52} = \frac{12}{13} \approx 0.923$$

You can also find the probability for a series of events. If you're asked for the probability of drawing an ace without replacement (the card does not go back in the deck) followed by a red nine, multiply the probability of the first event by that of the second:

$$\frac{\text{\# aces}}{\text{\# cards}} \times \frac{\text{\# red nines}}{\text{\# cards} - 1} = \frac{4}{52} \times \frac{2}{51} = \frac{8}{2,652} \approx 0.003$$

> ✔ **Note**
>
> "With replacement" means the item chosen, in this case a card, is returned to the original group (here, the deck). The number of possible outcomes in the denominator will stay constant. "Without replacement" indicates the item is not returned; the number of possible outcomes will change to reflect the new possible outcome count.

Using a two-way table, you can find the probability that a randomly selected data value (be it a person, object, etc.) will fit a certain profile. In addition, you might be asked to calculate a conditional probability. Conditional probability questions are easy to spot, as the word *given* is often present.

The following is a two-way table summarizing a survey on water preference.

	Bottled	**Carbonated**	**Tap**	**Total**
Female	325	267	295	887
Male	304	210	289	803
Total	629	477	584	1,690

If asked for the probability of randomly selecting a female who prefers bottled water from all the participants of the original survey for a follow-up survey, you would calculate it using the same general formula as before: $\dfrac{\text{\# female, bottled}}{\text{\# total}} = \dfrac{325}{1{,}690} = \dfrac{5}{26} \approx 0.192$.

If asked for the probability of randomly selecting a female for the follow-up survey, given that the chosen participant prefers bottled water, the setup is a little different. The clause starting with "given" indicates the number of possible outcomes is the total participants who prefer bottled water, which is 629, not the grand total of 1,690. The calculation is now $\dfrac{\text{\# female, bottled}}{\text{\# total, bottled}} = \dfrac{325}{629} \approx 0.517$.

Conversely, if you need to find the probability of selecting someone who prefers bottled water for the follow-up survey, given that the chosen participant is female, the new number of possible outcomes is the female participant total (887). The calculation becomes $\dfrac{\text{\# bottled}}{\text{\# total, females}} = \dfrac{325}{887} \approx 0.366$.

Take a look at the next few pages for some test-like questions involving two-way tables and probability.

Math

Questions 3 and 4 refer to the following information.

The table below summarizes the results of a survey about favorite video game genres for a group of high school students. Assume that every student had a favorite video game genre and that each student could only select one favorite.

	Freshmen	Sophomores	Juniors	Seniors	Total
First-person shooters	144	122	134	115	515
Strategy games	126	140	152	148	566
Role-playing games	120	117	153	148	538
Indie games	110	114	63	98	385
Total	500	493	502	509	2004

3. The research group that conducted the survey wants to select one sophomore and one senior at random for a follow-up survey. What is the probability that both students selected will prefer a type of video game other than strategy games?

A) $\dfrac{140}{493} + \dfrac{148}{509}$

B) $\dfrac{140}{493} \times \dfrac{148}{509}$

C) $\dfrac{353}{493} + \dfrac{361}{509}$

D) $\dfrac{353}{493} \times \dfrac{361}{509}$

There's no scratchwork for this question, but Kaplan's strategic thinking is provided in the table on the next page. Follow along as we reason through the question to get the correct answer.

Strategic Thinking
Step 1: Read the question, identifying and organizing important information as you go You need to determine the probability that a sophomore and a senior selected at random will both prefer a video game genre other than strategy games.
Step 2: Choose the best strategy to answer the question The answer choices are unsimplified expressions, which means that you don't need to find the actual probability—you just need to set up the correct expression. The word "both" in the question stem signals that you need to find the probability that one event AND another will both happen. To find the probability that more than one event will occur, multiply the individual probabilities together. This means that A and C, which feature addition rather than multiplication, are incorrect. You can determine which of the remaining answer choices is correct without any number crunching. Of the 493 sophomores, 140 prefer strategy games. Choice B contains the probability $\frac{140}{493}$, which means it's incorrect—you want the probability of picking students who *don't* prefer strategy games.
Step 3: Check that you answered the *right* question By process of elimination, you know that (D) must be correct.

4. The research group that conducted the survey wishes to see if there is a connection between the time a student spends playing video games and that student's grade point average (GPA). The school at which the initial survey was conducted was in Dallas, Texas; the group decides to include three additional Dallas high schools in the follow-up study. Data produced from the follow-up study showed a moderately strong negative correlation between time spent playing video games and GPA. Based on these findings, which of the following is a valid conclusion?

   A) There is an association between the amount of time a high school student in Dallas spends playing video games and his/her GPA.

   B) There is an association between the amount of time a high school student anywhere in Texas spends playing video games and his/her GPA.

   C) An increase in the amount of time a high school student in Dallas spends playing video games causes a decrease in his/her GPA.

   D) An increase in the amount of time a high school student anywhere in Texas spends playing video games causes a decrease in his/her GPA.

There's no scratchwork for this question, but Kaplan's strategic thinking is provided in the table. Follow along as we reason through the question to get the correct answer.

Strategic Thinking
Step 1: Read the question, identifying and organizing important information as you go
You're asked to identify the valid conclusion (in other words, the true statement).
Step 2: Choose the best strategy to answer the question
Carefully examine each answer choice. You're told that there is a moderately strong correlation between time spent playing video games and GPA. However, because the study involved students in Dallas only, no conclusions about the entire Texas high school population can be drawn. Eliminate B and D.
To determine which of the two remaining answer choices is correct, carefully read each choice and compare it to the question stem. Although there is a correlation between time spent playing video games and GPA, the study did not conclude that one causes the other. Eliminate C.
Step 3: Check that you answered the *right* question
Choice (A) matches your analysis.

✔ Expert Tip

Look for key details—such as the study's population, location, and any results derived—in questions like this one. These details will help you quickly solve for the correct answer.

On the next few pages, we'll work through another multi-part question set involving the concepts you've learned in this chapter. Remember to answer the questions one step at a time, and follow the Kaplan Method for Multi-Part Math Questions.

Questions 5 and 6 refer to the following information.

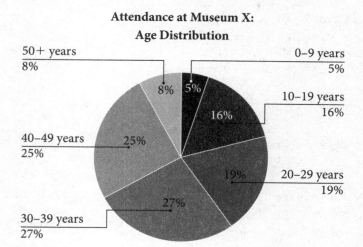

Attendance at Museum X:
Age Distribution

The pie graph above shows the age distribution of visitors to Museum X in 2014. Visitors aged 0-9 years get into Museum X for free, visitors aged 50 and older pay $5 for admission, and everyone else pays $10.

5.   If 553 people aged 20 years and older visited Museum X in 2014, then approximately how many people visited Museum X in 2014 ?

6.   Based on the pie graph and the result from the previous question, how much revenue did Museum X collect from tickets sold to people aged 40 and older in 2014 ?

Work through the Kaplan Method for Multi-Part Math Questions step-by-step to solve this question (for a review of this Method, see chapter 5). The following table shows Kaplan's strategic thinking on the left, along with suggested math scratchwork on the right.

Strategic Thinking	Math Scratchwork
Step 1: Read the first question in the set, looking for clues The infographic shows the age distribution of visitors to Museum X in 2014. From the accompanying text you also learn the ticket prices based on age.	0–9: free 10–49: $10 50+: $5
Step 2: Identify and organize the information you need You're asked to find the total number of visitors to Museum X in 2014, given that 553 of the visitors were aged 20 and up.	need total # attendees

Strategic Thinking	Math Scratchwork
Step 3: Based on what you know, plan your steps to navigate the first question You know the *number* of visitors aged 20 and up. If you find the accompanying percent, you can figure out the total using the three-part percent formula you learned previously.	_____ % of total is 553
Step 4: Solve, step-by-step, checking units as you go You could add the percentages for the 20-29, 30-39, 40-49, and 50+ categories, but there's a faster route. Look at the sections of the pie graph for the two groups that are *not* 20 or older: 0-9 and 10-19. Those two groups represent 5% and 16% of the total, respectively. Subtract these values from 100% to find what percent of visitors were aged 20 and up. To find the total number of visitors, plug what you know into the three-part percent formula.	% not aged 20+: 5% + 16% = 21% % aged 20+: 100% − 21% = 79% total × 0.79 = 553 $total = \dfrac{553}{0.79} = 700$
Step 5: Did I answer the *right* question? The question asks for the total number of visitors in 2014, which is 700.	

The first question is complete. Now on to Step 6: Repeat for the second question in the set. Kaplan's strategic thinking is on the left, along with suggested math scratchwork on the right.

Strategic Thinking	Math Scratchwork
Step 1: Read the second question in the set, looking for clues From the previous question, you know the total number of visitors in 2014; nothing new is given in this question.	700 total attendees
Step 2: Identify and organize the information you need This question asks for the revenue from tickets sold to people aged 40 and older. The total number of visitors, which you learned in the previous question, will help calculate this figure.	$ from aged 40+: ?

Strategic Thinking	Math Scratchwork
Step 3: Based on what you know, plan your steps to navigate the second question Because you already know the total number of visitors, you can calculate the number of visitors aged 40-49 and 50+ using the percentages given in the pie graph.	find # of 40–49, 50+
Step 4: Solve, step-by-step, checking units as you go Calculate the number of attendees in the 40-49 and 50+ age groups by taking 25% of 700 and 8% of 700, respectively. The 40-49 group paid $10 per ticket, and the 50+ group paid $5 per ticket. Use these facts to determine the revenue generated from these groups.	# aged 40–49: $700 \times 0.25 = 175$ # aged 50+: $700 \times 0.08 = 56$ 175 ppl paid $10/ticket 56 ppl paid $5/ticket $175 \times \$10 = \$1{,}750$ $56 \times \$5 = \$280$ $\$1{,}750 + \$280 = \$2{,}030$
Step 5: Did I answer the *right* question? $2,030 was collected from the 40-49 and 50+ age groups; grid in 2030.	

✔ **Note**

It's easy to misread questions like #6 and use a part of the infographic other than the one you need. Take time to ensure that you know what you need to find.

WORD PROBLEMS

You're already well versed in deciphering SAT word problems, but word problems involving probability sometimes require you to use different skills. You'll need to use your analytical abilities to develop inferences and predictions, draw and justify logical conclusions, and evaluate the appropriateness of data collection techniques. Sometimes you'll need to consult a provided two-way table as you did for some earlier questions, and in other cases you'll just study the question stem to gather pertinent information. Perhaps the best part of these questions is the fact that they often require little or no actual mathematical calculation!

Here is a test-like question.

7. A local softball league has male and female members. If m is the average age of the males, f is the average age of the females, a is the overall average age, and 65 percent of the league's members are male, then which one of the following statements must be true about m, f, and a ?

A)   If $m < f$, then $a > \dfrac{m + f}{2}$.

B)   If $m > f$, then $a < \dfrac{m + f}{2}$.

C)   If $m < f$, then $a < \dfrac{m + f}{2}$.

D) $a = \dfrac{m + f}{2}$

There's no scratchwork for this question, but Kaplan's strategic thinking is provided in the table. Follow along as we reason through the question to get the correct answer.

Strategic Thinking
Step 1: Read the question, identifying and organizing important information as you go
The question asks you to identify the statement that is true. You're told that 65% of the league's members are male, and you're given the definition of three variables: m, f, and a.
Step 2: Choose the best strategy to answer the question
Don't panic over the limited amount of information. Examine the answer choices to see if you can spot any useful patterns. Each answer choice makes a comparison between a (the overall average age) and $\frac{m+f}{2}$. If the male and female member counts were equal, then the overall average age would simply be the average of the male and female average ages, or $\frac{m+f}{2}$. However, because there are more males than females in the group, the overall average must be closer to the average male age than to the average female age. You don't know which of m or f is greater, so use a number line to visualize this information. There are two ways to do so: The first assumes that $m < f$; the second assumes that $m > f$. 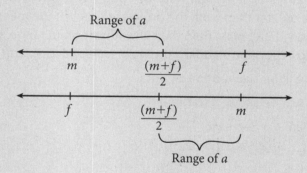 The only choice consistent with the visualization is (C): Based on the top number line, when m is less than f, the value of a is less than the average age of both groups.
Step 3: Check that you answered the *right* question
Choice (C) matches your analysis.

✔ **Note**

For questions like this, think about what information is given or not given, the conclusion(s) you can draw from either, and answers you can eliminate based on those conclusion(s).

Practice

Now you'll have a chance to try a few more test-like problems in a scaffolded way. We've provided some guidance, but you'll need to fill in the missing parts of explanations or the step-by-step math in order to get to the correct answer. Don't worry—after going through the worked examples at the beginning of this section, these problems should be completely doable.

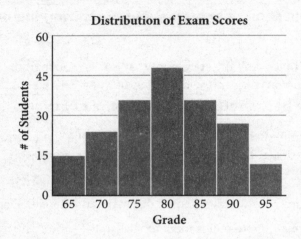

Distribution of Exam Scores

8. A history professor observes that the scores of a recent 20-question multiple choice exam are normally distributed as shown in the histogram above. However, she later discovers that 25% of the results were omitted from the distribution. Of the omitted scores, 80% are greater than what the professor thought the mean was; the rest are less. Assuming all new data points fit in the current histogram range, which of the following is most likely to occur upon adding the new scores to the data?

A) The data will be skewed to the right.

B) The data will be skewed to the left.

C) The median will decrease.

D) The range will decrease.

The following table can help you structure your thinking as you go about solving this more involved problem. Kaplan's strategic thinking is provided, as are bits of structured scratchwork. If you're not sure how to approach a question like this, start at the top and work your way down.

Strategic Thinking	Math Scratchwork
Step 1: Read the question, identifying and organizing important information as you go You need to determine the effect of adding extra data points, most of which are above the mean, to what was previously a normal (symmetric) distribution.	

Strategic Thinking	Math Scratchwork
Step 2: Choose the best strategy to answer the question The question states that most of the new scores are above the mean. Draw a rough sketch of what the new distribution will look like. The choices mention skew, median, and range. Think about the effect the additions to the data set will have on each of these.	post-addition: direction of skew: _____ median shift: _____ range shift: _____
Step 3: Check that you answered the *right* question If you chose (B), congrats! You're correct.	_____

Now try a multi-part question set.

Questions 9 and 10 refer to the following information.

	1	2	3	4	5	Total
Worker Placement	5	17	24	10	5	61
Bidding	3	12	28	8	3	54
Area Control	3	10	30	14	2	59

A small boutique sells board games online. The boutique specializes in worker placement, bidding, and area control board games. Any customer who purchases a game is invited to rate the game on a scale of 1 to 5. A rating of 1 or 2 is considered "bad," a rating of 3 is considered "average," and a rating of 4 or 5 is considered "good." The table above shows the distribution of average customer ratings of the board games sold by the boutique. For example, 24 of the worker placement games sold by the boutique have an average rating of 3.

9. According to the table, what percent of all the board games sold by the boutique received a rating of "bad"? Round to the nearest tenth of a percent and ignore the percent sign when entering your answer.

10. The boutique decides to stop selling 50% of the board games that received a rating of "bad" to make room for promising new stock. Assuming no significant changes in ratings in the foreseeable future, what should the difference be between the percentages of board games with a rating of "bad" before and after this change? Round to the nearest tenth of a percent and ignore the percent sign when entering your answer.

Practice

The following table can help you structure your thinking as you go about solving this more involved problem. Kaplan's strategic thinking is provided, as are bits of structured scratchwork. If you're not sure how to approach a question like this, start at the top and work your way down.

Strategic Thinking	Math Scratchwork
Step 1: Read the first question in the set, looking for clues You're provided a chart with data on the average ratings of board games sold by a boutique.	
Step 2: Identify and organize the information you need You're asked to find the percent of games that received a rating of "bad", meaning a rating of 1 or 2.	find % of games with "bad" rating
Step 3: Based on what you know, plan your steps to navigate the first question Examine the chart carefully, identifying the necessary data from each type of game. You need to determine how many games received a rating of 1 or 2. Add the figures to get the total number of games that received a rating of "bad."	worker placement 1: _____ games 2: _____ games bidding 1: _____ games 2: _____ games area control 1: _____ games 2: _____ games total: _____
Step 4: Solve, step-by-step, checking units as you go Use the values in the table to find the total number of games in these groups. Write the "bad" *part* over the *total* game count, and then convert to a percent.	_____ × 100% = _____%
Step 5: Did I answer the *right* question? If you got 28.7, you're correct!	_____

Great job! Repeat for the second question. Kaplan's strategic thinking is on the left, and bits of scratchwork guidance are on the right.

Strategic Thinking	Math Scratchwork
Step 1: Read the second question in the set, looking for clues From the previous question, you know the number (and percent) of games that received a rating of "bad."	# games with "bad" rating: _____ ; = _____%
Step 2: Identify and organize the information you need You're asked for the difference between the percentages of games that received a "bad" rating before and after 50% of such games are removed from the store's inventory. Your answer from the previous question is key to this calculation.	"bad" % pre-removal: _____% "bad" % post-removal: ?
Step 3: Based on what you know, plan your steps to navigate the second question You know the store wants to get rid of 50% of the games that received a "bad" rating. You already know the current number with a "bad" rating, so finding the new "bad" game count is straightforward. Once there, determine the new "bad" percentage and subtract that from the original.	_____ × old "bad" count = new "bad" count → convert to % old "bad" % − new "bad" % = answer
Step 4: Solve, step-by-step, checking units as you go After the 50% reduction in "bad" games, how many games should have a "bad" rating? Reduce the original "bad" game count by 50%. Divide your new "bad" count by the total game count. Remember that when the number of "bad" games decreases, the total count decreases by the same amount. Write your results using a couple of decimal points to minimize rounding errors. Subtract the new "bad" percent from the old "bad" percent.	_____% × old "bad" count = new "bad" count _____ × _____ = _____ new "bad" %: _____ × 100 = _____% old "bad" % − new "bad" %: _____% − _____% = _____%
Step 5: Did I answer the *right* question? Did you get 12? If so, you're absolutely correct!	% change: _____

Nice work! Now test what you've learned by taking a brief quiz.

Now that you've seen the variety of ways in which the SAT can test you on two-way tables, statistics, and probability, try the following questions to check your understanding. Give yourself 5 minutes to tackle the following four questions. Make sure you use the Kaplan Method for Math (and the Kaplan Method for Multi-Part Math Questions where appropriate) as often as you can. Remember, you want to emphasize speed and efficiency in addition to simply getting the correct answer.

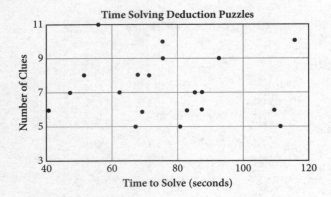

Time Solving Deduction Puzzles

	Ceren	Han	Billy
Run 1	8.3	8.5	8.4
Run 2	7.7	8.0	8.0
Run 3	7.1	8.5	7.5
Run 4	6.6	7.8	9.0
Run 5	8.0	8.1	7.5
Run 6	6.6	7.5	7.2
Mean Score	7.38	8.07	7.93
Standard Deviation	0.73	0.39	0.67

11. Randolph recently completed a book of 20 deduction puzzles. The scatterplot above shows the time it took Randolph to solve a puzzle versus the number of clues it had. If a puzzle is selected at random from the book, what is the probability that it had fewer than six clues, took Randolph fewer than 100 seconds to solve, or both?

A) 10%

B) 15%

C) 85%

D) 90%

12. Ceren, Han, and Billy participated in a snowboarding competition. The scores for each of their six qualifying runs are in the table above. According to the data, which of the following is a valid conclusion?

A) Ceren had the smallest mean score, so her performance was the least consistent.

B) Han had the smallest standard deviation, so his performance was the most consistent.

C) Ceren had the largest standard deviation, so her performance was the most consistent.

D) Billy had the highest score on any one run, so his performance was the most consistent.

Questions 13 and 14 refer to the following information.

	Scarves	Pairs of Mittens	Hats	Pairs of Socks	Total
Wilhelmina	7	2	24	19	52
Emanuel	8	2	9	14	33
Jose Raul	3	4	18	10	35
Alexandra	15	1	9	9	34
Total	33	9	60	52	154

Wilhelmina, Emanuel, Jose Raul, and Alexandra are in a knitting club. The table above shows the quantity of several different items each person has knitted over the lifetime of the club.

13. The four club members plan to knit hats to sell for Spirit Week at their college. They surveyed a group of students regarding their hat pattern preferences and found that 60% of those surveyed prefer solid-colored hats, 22% prefer stripes, and 18% prefer stars. The club anticipates that 1,800 students will each buy one hat. If the ratios in the table remain constant for Spirit Week hat production, how many solid-colored hats will Wilhelmina and Alexandra be responsible for knitting?

14. The knitting club plans to embroider a small, hidden emblem on the interior of 20% of the hats they make for Spirit Week; anyone who finds this emblem on their hat will win a free scarf. The four members will split up the making of the free scarves according to the ratios in the table. For how many winning hats and scarf prizes will Emanuel and Jose Raul be responsible?

Answers and Explanations for this chapter begin on page 918.

EXTRA PRACTICE

 You may use your calculator for all questions in this section.

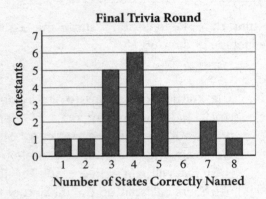

Final Trivia Round

Number of States Correctly Named

1. In the final round of a trivia competition, contestants were asked to name as many states that begin with the letter M as they could in 15 seconds. The bar graph shows the number of states the contestants were able to name. How many contestants participated in the final round of this competition?

   A) 6

   B) 8

   C) 14

   D) 20

2. An electronics manufacturer wants to know if customers would be interested in a detachable keyboard for their tablets and if so, what the most important features would be. The manufacturer partners with an electronics store to include copies of the survey with every purchase at that store for one week. Which of the following best explains why this random sample is unlikely to be a good representative sample of tablet owners' preferences for a detachable keyboard?

   A) One week is likely not enough time to get a large enough sample.

   B) Most people won't bother to send in the survey, which is likely to skew the results.

   C) There is no way to verify whether the responders to the survey actually own a tablet.

   D) The survey is biased because it was conducted through an electronics store, not the general population.

Appliance Sales

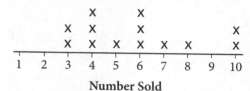

Number Sold

Distribution of Fish Breeds

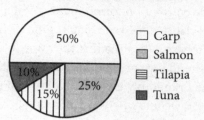

3. An appliance salesman sets a goal to sell an average of 6 appliances per day for the first two weeks of his new job. The dot plot shows the number he sold each day during the first 13 days. What is the minimum number of appliances he must sell on the 14th day in order to reach his goal?

A) 5

B) 6

C) 7

D) 8

4. Muscles, a membership-only gym, is hoping to open a new branch in a small city in Pennsylvania that currently has no fitness centers. According to their research, approximately 12,600 residents live within driving distance of the gym. Muscles sends out surveys to a sample of 300 randomly selected residents in this area (all of whom respond) and finds that 40 residents say they would visit a gym if one was located in their area. Based on past survey research, Muscles estimates that approximately 30% of these respondents would actually join the gym if they opened one in the area. Based on this information and the results of the sample survey, about how many residents should Muscles expect to join its new branch?

A) 134

B) 504

C) 1,680

D) 3,780

5. Mercury poisoning is a dangerous overload of mercury within the body. A major source of mercury poisoning is consuming fish that contain mercury. Certain fish are more prone to having higher levels of mercury than others. The pie chart shows the distribution of four breeds of fish at a hatchery. The hatchery has approximately 6,000 fish. A biologist from the Centers for Disease Control and Prevention randomly tests 5% of each breed of fish for mercury content. Her findings are shown in the following table.

Mercury Content Test Results

Breed	Number of Fish with Dangerous Mercury Levels
Carp	11
Salmon	6
Tilapia	5
Tuna	8

Based on the biologist's findings, if a single salmon is randomly selected from those that were tested, what is the probability that this particular fish would have a dangerous mercury level?

A) 0.001

B) 0.004

C) 0.02

D) 0.08

6. A Writer's Association sponsored a nation-wide convention for nonfiction writers. The association received 1,650 responses from members indicating that they were planning to attend the convention. The association sent a randomly generated follow-up email to 250 writers who were planning to attend and asked them about lunch preferences. Seventy-four said salads, 22 said pizza, 30 said pasta salad, 29 said grilled chicken, and the rest said sandwiches. Out of all of the writers planning to attend, about how many could the association expect to want sandwiches for lunch at the convention?

Questions 7 and 8 refer to the following information.

The amount of glucose, or sugar, in a person's blood is the primary indicator of diabetes. When a person fasts (doesn't eat) for eight hours prior to taking a blood sugar test, his/her glucose level should be below 100 mg/dL. A person is considered at risk for diabetes, but is not diagnosed as diabetic, when fasting glucose levels are between 100 and 125. If the level is above 125, the person is considered to have diabetes. The following table shows the ages and glucose levels of a group of diabetes study participants.

Diabetes Study Results

Age Group	<100 mg/dL	100-125 mg/dL	>125	Total
18-25	9	22	17	48
26-35	16	48	34	98
36-45	19	35	40	94
Older than 45	12	27	21	60
Total	56	132	112	300

7. According to the data, which age group had the smallest percentage of people with a healthy blood sugar level?

A) 18-25

B) 26-35

C) 36-45

D) Older than 45

8. Based on the table, if a single participant is selected at random from all the participants, what is the probability that he or she will be at risk for diabetes and be at least 36 years old?

A) $\dfrac{7}{60}$

B) $\dfrac{11}{25}$

C) $\dfrac{31}{77}$

D) $\dfrac{31}{150}$

Math

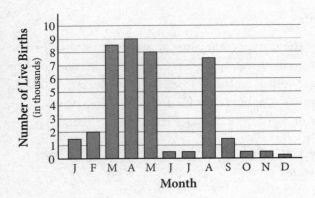

Cookies Baked

	Chocolate Chip	Oatmeal Raisin	Total
With Nuts		40	
Without Nuts			104
Total			186

9. Most animals give birth during a general time of year. This is because animals naturally breed so that their young will be born at the time of year when there will be an adequate food supply. The bar graph shows the number of live births of a jackrabbit native to California over the course of Year X. Based on the data, which of the following would be an appropriate conclusion?

A) In general, rabbits give birth during the spring months.

B) In general, rabbits give birth during the summer months.

C) In general, Californian jackrabbits give birth during the spring months.

D) In general, Californian jackrabbits give birth during the summer months.

10. A baker makes 186 cookies. Some are chocolate chip and some are oatmeal raisin, and both kinds are made with and without nuts, as shown in the table above. Because they are more popular, the baker made $\frac{2}{3}$ of the cookies chocolate chip. If a chocolate chip cookie is chosen at random, what is the probability that it will have nuts?

A) $\frac{21}{93}$

B) $\frac{21}{62}$

C) $\frac{41}{93}$

D) $\frac{21}{41}$

11. A bottled water company conducts a survey to find out how many bottles of water people consume per day. If a representative sample of 500 people is chosen without bias from a population estimated to be 50,000, which of the following accurately describes how the mean of the sample data relates to the estimated mean of the entire population?

A) The mean of the sample data is equal to the estimated mean of the population.

B) The mean of the sample data cannot be used to estimate the mean of the much larger population.

C) The mean of the sample data should be multiplied by 100 to get the estimated mean of the population.

D) The mean of the sample data should be multiplied by 1,000 to get the estimated mean of the population.

12. A fertilizer company conducted an experimental study to determine which of five compounds is most effective relative to helping soil retain nutrients. If, after application of the compounds, the fertilizer company only tested for nitrogen and potassium, which of the following is a valid conclusion?

   A) The compound that is found to be the most effective will work for all nutrients in the soil.

   B) The compound that is found to be the most effective will work only for nitrogen and potassium.

   C) The study is clearly biased and therefore not significantly relevant to determining which compound is most effective.

   D) The study will only be able to produce results concerning the effects of the compounds on nitrogen and potassium.

History Majors Declared at College X

Year	Number of History Majors
2010	225
2011	287
2012	162
2013	240
2014	s

13. The table above shows the number of history majors declared each year at a certain college from 2010 to 2014. If the median number of history majors declared for the five years was 225, what is the greatest possible value of s ?

   A) 161

   B) 225

   C) 239

   D) 288

Country Music Festival Attendees

	Attendees
Entertainer A (Day 1)	1,280
Entertainer B (Day 2)	1,120
Entertainer C (Day 3)	1,600

14. Three well-known entertainers performed at a country music festival, one on each day. Tickets sold were valid for the full three-day period, and ticket holders were permitted to enter and leave as desired. The table above shows the number of people who attended each day of the festival. The host of the festival wants to know which performer was the most popular. If the host defines a performer's popularity rating as the ratio of the number of attendees on that performer's day to the combined number of attendees across all three days, then what was the most popular performer's popularity rating?

Math

Questions 15 and 16 refer to the following information.

Numerous health studies have found that people who eat breakfast are generally healthier and weigh less than people who skip it. Although scientists are not certain as to the reason, it is generally believed that breakfast jumpstarts the metabolism and encourages a more regular consumption of calories throughout the day, instead of the calories being consumed in two big meals at lunch and dinner. The following table shows the results of a study related to this topic.

Breakfast Study Results

	Breakfast ≤1 time per week	Breakfast 2-4 times per week	Breakfast 5-7 times per week	Total
Within Healthy Weight Range	6	15	36	57
Outside Healthy Weight Range	38	27	9	74
Total	44	42	45	131

15. What percent of the participants who were outside a healthy weight range ate breakfast one or fewer times per week?

   A) 29.00%

   B) 51.35%

   C) 56.49%

   D) 86.36%

16. A large company that provides breakfast for all its employees wants to determine how many of them are likely to be within a healthy weight range, given that all the employees take advantage of the free breakfast all 5 weekdays. If the company has 3,000 employees, and assuming the participants in the study were a good representative sample, about how many of the employees are likely to be within a healthy weight range?

   A) 825

   B) 1,030

   C) 1,900

   D) 2,400

Questions 17 and 18 refer to the following information.

When people sleep, they experience various types of brain activity. Scientists have classified these types of activity into four sleep stages: 1, 2, 3, and 4 (also known as REM). Stage 3 is the only stage considered to be deep sleep. Suppose a person went to a sleep clinic to have his/her sleeping brainwaves analyzed. A technician monitored the person's brainwaves in 15-minute intervals, for 8 continuous hours, and categorized them into one of the four stages. The bar graph below shows the results of the one-night study.

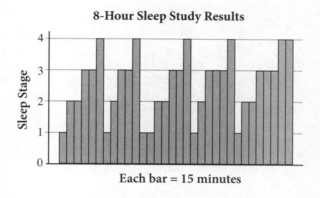

8-Hour Sleep Study Results

Each bar = 15 minutes

17. Based on the graph, how many minutes did the patient spend in non-deep sleep over the course of the entire night?

18. If one 15-minute time period is chosen at random, what is the probability that the patient was in deep sleep during that time?

Math

Questions 19 and 20 refer to the following information.

As part of its market research, a company sent out a survey to see how much consumers would be willing to pay for a certain product. The survey distinguished between a store brand version of the product and a brand name version, and people participating in the survey only received questions about one of the versions. A summary of the survey results is shown in the following bar graph.

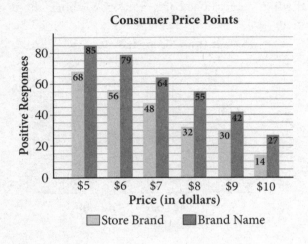

19. On average, how many more cents are consumers willing to pay for the brand name version of the product than the store brand version? Round your answer to the nearest cent.

20. If a consumer is chosen at random from all of the respondents, what is the probability that the consumer is willing to pay at least $8 for the product?

21. A shoe manufacturing company is thinking about introducing a new product designed to help athletes jump higher. The company conducts a marketing study by asking people outside community gymnasiums and sporting goods stores whether they would purchase such a product. Approximately 40% of 3,000 respondents said they would purchase these shoes over regular tennis shoes. Based on the study, the company concludes that 40% of shoe store customers shopping for tennis shoes would purchase their new product. Why is this not a valid conclusion?

A) The study was too small to draw any conclusions about the larger population.

B) The data from the survey does not represent the whole population because it was not conducted across the whole country.

C) The data from the survey likely underestimates the number of people interested in the new product because it only compared the new product to tennis shoes, not all types of shoes.

D) The data from the survey likely overestimates the number of people interested in the new product because the survey targeted respondents already interested in athletics.

22. On a used vehicle lot, 50% of the vehicles are cars, $\frac{3}{4}$ of which have automatic transmissions. Of the cars with automatic transmissions, $\frac{1}{3}$ have leather interiors. If a vehicle is chosen from the lot at random, what is the probability that it will be a car with an automatic transmission and a leather interior?

A) $\frac{1}{8}$

B) $\frac{1}{6}$

C) $\frac{1}{4}$

D) $\frac{1}{3}$

23. A United States senator is running for reelection and wants to know what the most important issue to the greatest number of people who might vote for him is. If his campaign hires a company to collect data by conducting a survey, which of the following samples should the company use?

A) United States voters

B) United States citizens

C) Voters in the senator's district

D) Citizens in the senator's district

Reduction of Debt Schedule

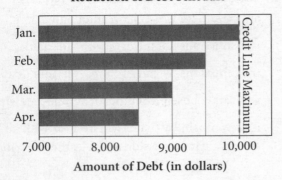

Amount of Debt (in dollars)

Quarterly Profits

	Branch A	Branch B	Branch C	Branch D
Q1	4.1	7.4	8.0	5.4
Q2	3.6	5.2	3.7	6.2
Q3	5.0	4.5	4.9	4.8
Q4	4.9	6.3	5.9	5.6
$\bar{x}$	4.4	5.85	5.625	5.5
s	0.67	1.27	1.82	0.58

24. A credit score is a number used by financial institutions to determine a person's financial health. One of the factors that affects a person's credit score is the percentage of credit available that he or she is currently utilizing. For example, a person with a credit line of $1,000 who has debt of $900 is utilizing 90% of his or her available credit. Ideally, a person should use no more than 25% of available credit. Charlie has been trying to pay down his debt to increase his credit score. Suppose Charlie has a credit line of $10,000. The graph above shows the amount of debt he is currently carrying on that credit line each month. If he continues to pay down this debt at the same rate, how many months from when Charlie reached his credit line maximum will it take him to reach 25% utilization?

A)   8

B)   15

C)   20

D)   24

25. A company affected by a downturn in the economy decides to close one of its four branches. The table shows each branch's quarterly profits in millions of dollars for 2014, along with the mean ($\bar{x}$) and the standard deviation (s) of the data. The accounting department recommends that the company's Board of Directors close either the store with the lowest average quarterly profits or the store that performs the least consistently. According to the data in the table, which branches will the accounting department recommend for closure to the board?

A)   Branches A or C

B)   Branches A or D

C)   Branches B or C

D)   Branches B or D

Questions 26 and 27 refer to the following information.

At most colleges, students receive letter grades, which correspond to a GPA score, rather than a numerical grade, such as 92. The following figure shows the distribution of grades and corresponding GPA scores among students in a history class.

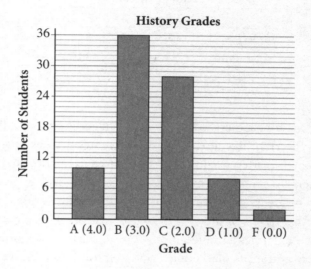

26. What is the approximate mean history GPA for this class of students?

    A) 2.0

    B) 2.5

    C) 2.6

    D) 3.0

27. College professors sometimes use statistics to summarize class performance so that students will have an idea of how they are doing relative to the rest of the class. If this professor wants to report that at least half of the grades were a 3.0 or above, which measure of center should she use to describe the results?

    A) Mean

    B) Mode

    C) Mode or median

    D) Standard deviation

Math

Questions 28 and 29 refer to the following information.

The following table shows the number of houses in a development. The table categorizes the houses by type (single-family or townhouse) and by the number of bedrooms.

Development Houses

	2 Br	3 Br	4 Br	Total
Single-Family	5	19	34	58
Townhouse	24	42	30	96
Total	29	61	64	154

28. The homeowner's association partners with a local daycare center. The HOA has agreed to allow the daycare center to advertise in the development using flyers. In general, families with children typically reside in single-family homes or townhouses that have 3 or more bedrooms. The daycare center has a limited budget and plans to concentrate its marketing efforts on only those homes and townhouses. What percent of the dwellings in the development should receive the flyer? Round to the nearest whole percent and ignore the percent sign when entering your answer.

29. In addition to sending out flyers, the daycare center decides to send out invitations for a free day of daycare, but determines that it would be too expensive to do this for all of the family residences in the development. Instead, it decides to market this benefit only to the two categories in the table with the most dwellings. If a dwelling that already received a flyer is chosen at random to receive the second stage of the marketing, what is the probability that the dwelling belongs to one of these two groups? Enter your answer as a decimal.

Passport to Advanced Math

BY THE END OF THIS UNIT, YOU WILL BE ABLE TO:

1. Simplify, solve, and rewrite expressions and equations involving polynomials, radicals, and exponents

2. Solve a formula for a given variable

3. Solve function questions graphically and algebraically

4. Combine multiple functions

5. Solve quadratic equations with and without a calculator

6. Connect quadratic equations to features of a parabola

CHAPTER 8

Exponents, Radicals, Polynomials, and Rational Expressions and Equations

CHAPTER OBJECTIVES

By the end of this chapter, you will be able to:

1. Simplify and solve expressions and equations involving exponents and/or radicals
2. Perform arithmetic operations on polynomials
3. Simplify expressions using polynomial long division and find polynomial remainders
4. Simplify and solve rational expressions and equations
5. Solve a formula for a given variable

SMARTPOINTS

Point Value	SmartPoint Category
80 Points	Exponents

Math

EXPONENTS, RADICALS, POLYNOMIALS, AND RATIONAL EXPRESSIONS AND EQUATIONS

Chapter 8

Homework

Extra Practice: #1-20

Even More

Math Quiz 5

Key

   Book Assignment

   Online Video Assignment

   Online Quiz Assignment

INTRODUCTION TO EXPONENTS AND RADICALS

We often turn to our calculators to solve difficult radical and exponent problems, especially in math-intensive classes. However, being too calculator dependent can cost you time and points on the SAT. Further, on the SAT, many radical and exponent problems are structured in such a way that your calculator can't help you, even if it is allowed.

This chapter will review algebra and arithmetic rules that you may have learned at some point but likely haven't used in a while. This chapter will reacquaint you with the formulas and procedures you'll need to simplify even the toughest expressions and equations on the SAT. We'll start with exponents.

Questions involving exponents often look intimidating, but when you know the rules governing them, you'll see that there are plenty of shortcuts. First, it's important to understand the anatomy of a term that has an exponent. This term is comprised of two pieces: a base and an exponent (also called a power). The base is the number in larger type and is the value being multiplied by itself. The exponent, written as a superscript, shows you how many times the base is being multiplied by itself.

$$Base \Rightarrow 3^4 \Leftarrow Exponent \text{ is the same as } 3 \times 3 \times 3 \times 3$$

The following table lists the rules you'll need to handle any exponent question you'll see on the SAT.

Rule	Example
When multiplying two terms with the same base, add the exponents.	$a^b \times a^c = a^{(b + c)} \rightarrow 4^2 \times 4^3 = 4^{2 + 3} = 4^5$
When dividing two terms with the same base, subtract the exponents.	$\dfrac{a^b}{a^c} = a^{(b - c)} \rightarrow \dfrac{4^3}{4^2} = 4^{3 - 2} = 4$
When raising a power to another power, multiply the exponents.	$(a^b)^c = a^{(bc)} \rightarrow (4^3)^2 = 4^{3 \times 2} = 4^6;$ $(2x^2)^3 = 2^{1 \times 3} x^{2 \times 3} = 8x^6$
When raising a product to a power, apply the power to all factors in the product.	$(ab)^c = a^c \times b^c \rightarrow (2m)^3 = 2^3 \times m^3 = 8m^3$
Any term raised to the zero power equals 1.	$a^0 = 1 \rightarrow 4^0 = 1$
A base raised to a negative exponent can be rewritten as the reciprocal raised to the positive of the original exponent.	$a^{-b} = \dfrac{1}{a^b}; \dfrac{1}{a^{-b}} = a^b \rightarrow 4^{-2} = \dfrac{1}{4^2}; \dfrac{1}{4^{-2}} = 4^2$

✔ **Note**

Raising an expression involving addition or subtraction to a power, such as $(a + b)^2$, requires a special process called FOIL, which you'll learn about in chapter 10. You *cannot* merely distribute the exponent; this will certainly lead you to a trap answer.

Different things happen to different kinds of numbers when they are raised to powers. Compare the locations and values of the variables and numbers on the following number line to the results in the table for a summary.

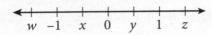

$$w \quad -1 \quad x \quad 0 \quad y \quad 1 \quad z$$

Quantity	Even Exponent Result	Odd Exponent Result	Example
w	positive, absolute value increases	negative, absolute value increases	$(-5)^2 = 25; (-5)^3 = -125$
-1	always 1	always -1	n/a
x	positive, absolute value decreases	negative, absolute value decreases	$\left(-\dfrac{1}{2}\right)^2 = \dfrac{1}{4}; \left(-\dfrac{1}{2}\right)^3 = -\dfrac{1}{8}$
0	always 0	always 0	n/a
y	positive, absolute value decreases	positive, absolute value decreases	$\left(\dfrac{1}{4}\right)^2 = \dfrac{1}{16}; \left(\dfrac{1}{4}\right)^3 = \dfrac{1}{64}$
1	always 1	always 1	n/a
z	positive, absolute value increases	positive, absolute value increases	$3^2 = 9; 3^3 = 27$

Give this exponent question a try:

1. Which expression is equivalent to $2(-4j^3k^{-4})^{-3}$?

A) $\quad -\dfrac{k^{12}}{512j^9}$

B) $\quad -\dfrac{k^{12}}{32j^9}$

C) $\quad -\dfrac{j^9}{32k^{12}}$

D) $\quad -\dfrac{k^{12}}{128j^9}$

Use the Kaplan Method for Math to solve this question, working through it step-by-step. The following table shows Kaplan's strategic thinking on the left, along with suggested math scratchwork on the right.

Strategic Thinking	Math Scratchwork
Step 1: Read the question, identifying and organizing important information as you go You're asked to find the equivalent expression.	
Step 2: Choose the best strategy to answer the question Use exponent rules to quickly find the answer. Move the expression in parentheses to the denominator to make the exponent outside the parentheses positive. Then distribute the exponent to each term it contains. You're not done yet. Look for terms you can cancel, and eliminate any remaining negative exponents by appropriately moving their respective terms.	$2(-4j^3k^{-4})^{-3}$ $= \dfrac{2}{(-4j^3k^{-4})^3}$ $= \dfrac{2}{(-4)^3(j^3)^3(k^{-4})^3}$ $= \dfrac{2}{-64\,j^9k^{-12}}$ $= -\dfrac{k^{12}}{32j^9}$
Step 3: Check that you answered the _right_ question Choice (B) matches the simplified expression.	

Let's try one more before moving on.

2. What is the value of $\dfrac{3^5 \times 27^3}{81^3}$?

Work through the Kaplan Method for Math step-by-step to solve this question. The following table shows Kaplan's strategic thinking on the left, along with suggested math scratchwork on the right.

Strategic Thinking	Math Scratchwork
Step 1: Read the question, identifying and organizing important information as you go You're asked to find the value of the expression presented, which means you'll need to simplify it.	
Step 2: Choose the best strategy to answer the question Simplify the expression using exponent rules. You can't combine the bases or the exponents of the expression as written. However, $27 = 3^3$ and $81 = 3^4$, so rewrite the numerator and denominator to reflect these relationships. Add the exponents of the numbers in the numerator. Once finished, subtract the exponent of the number in the denominator.	$$\frac{3^5 \times 27^3}{81^3} = \frac{3^5 \times (3^3)^3}{(3^4)^3}$$ $$= \frac{3^5 \times 3^9}{3^{12}} = \frac{3^{14}}{3^{12}} = 3^2$$
Step 3: Check that you answered the *right* question After simplification is complete, you'll get 9 as the correct answer.	9

> ✔ **Note**
>
> A calculator could probably handle numbers the size of those in the previous question, but what if the question is in the no-calculator section? Knowing exponent rules for Test Day is critical.

RADICALS

A radical can be written using a fractional exponent. You can think of addition and subtraction (and multiplication and division) as opposites; similarly, raising a number to a power and taking the root of the number are another opposite pair. Specifically, when you raise a term to the nth power, taking the nth root will return the original term. Consider for example $3^4 = 3 \times 3 \times 3 \times 3 = 81$. If you take the fourth root of 81 (that is, determine the number that can be multiplied by itself four times to get 81), you will arrive at the original term: $\sqrt[4]{81} = \sqrt[4]{3 \times 3 \times 3 \times 3} = 3$.

Radicals can be intimidating at first, but remembering the basic rules for radicals can make them much easier to tackle. The following table contains all the formulas you'll need to know to achieve "radical" success on the SAT.

Rule	Example
When a fraction is under a radical, you can rewrite it using two radicals: one containing the numerator and the other containing the denominator.	$\sqrt{\dfrac{a}{b}} = \dfrac{\sqrt{a}}{\sqrt{b}} \rightarrow \sqrt{\dfrac{4}{9}} = \dfrac{\sqrt{4}}{\sqrt{9}} = \dfrac{2}{3}$
Two factors under a single radical can be rewritten as separate radicals multiplied together.	$\sqrt{ab} = \sqrt{a} \times \sqrt{b} \rightarrow \sqrt{75} = \sqrt{25} \times \sqrt{3} = 5\sqrt{3}$
A radical can be written using a fractional exponent.	$\sqrt{a} = a^{\frac{1}{2}}, \sqrt[3]{a} = a^{\frac{1}{3}} \rightarrow \sqrt{289} = 289^{\frac{1}{2}}$
When you have a fractional exponent, the numerator is the power to which the base is raised, and the denominator is the root to be taken.	$a^{\frac{b}{c}} = \sqrt[c]{a^b} \rightarrow 5^{\frac{2}{3}} = \sqrt[3]{5^2}$
When a number is squared, the original number can be positive or negative, but the square root of a number can only be positive.	If $a^2 = 81$, then $a = \pm 9$, BUT $\sqrt{81} = 9$ only.

> **✔ Note**
>
> Note this difference: By definition, the square root of a number is positive. However, when you take the square root to solve for a variable, you get two solutions, one that is positive and one that is negative. For instance, by definition $\sqrt{4} = 2$. However, if you are solving $x^2 = 4$, x will have two solutions: $x = \pm 2$.

It is not considered proper notation to leave a radical in the denominator of a fraction. However, it's sometimes better to keep them through intermediate steps to make the math easier (and sometimes the radical is eliminated along the way). Once all manipulations are complete, the denominator can be rationalized to remove a remaining radical by multiplying both the numerator and denominator by that same radical.

1. Original Fraction	2. Rationalization	3. Intermediate Math	4. Resulting Fraction
$\dfrac{x}{\sqrt{5}}$	$\dfrac{x}{\sqrt{5}} \times \dfrac{\sqrt{5}}{\sqrt{5}}$	$\dfrac{x\sqrt{5}}{\sqrt{5 \times 5}} = \dfrac{x\sqrt{5}}{\sqrt{25}} = \dfrac{x\sqrt{5}}{5}$	$\dfrac{x\sqrt{5}}{5}$
$\dfrac{14}{\sqrt{x^2+2}}$	$\dfrac{14}{\sqrt{x^2+2}} \times \dfrac{\sqrt{x^2+2}}{\sqrt{x^2+2}}$	$\dfrac{14\sqrt{x^2+2}}{\sqrt{(x^2+2)(x^2+2)}} = \dfrac{14\sqrt{x^2+2}}{\sqrt{(x^2+2)^2}}$	$\dfrac{14\sqrt{x^2+2}}{x^2+2}$

Sometimes, you'll have an expression such as $2 + \sqrt{5}$ in the denominator. To rationalize this, multiply by its conjugate, which is found by negating the second term; in this case, the conjugate is $2 - \sqrt{5}$.

As a general rule of thumb, you are not likely to see a radical in the denominator of the answer choices on the SAT, so you'll need to be comfortable with rationalizing expressions that contain radicals.

> ✔ **Note**
>
> When you rationalize a denominator, you are not changing the value of the expression; you're only changing the expression's appearance. This is because the numerator and the denominator of the fraction that you multiply by are the same, which means you're simply multiplying by 1.

Ready to take on a test-like question that involves radicals? Take a look at the following:

3. Which of the following represents $\dfrac{\sqrt[6]{x^{10}y^{12}}}{\sqrt[3]{x^5y^6}}$ written in simplest form, given that $x > 0$?

    A) 1

    B) 2

    C) $x^2y^3\sqrt{x}$

    D) $xy^2\sqrt[3]{x^2}$

Work through the Kaplan Method for Math step-by-step to solve this question. The following table shows Kaplan's strategic thinking on the left, along with suggested math scratchwork on the right.

Strategic Thinking	Math Scratchwork
Step 1: Read the question, identifying and organizing important information as you go You must simplify the given expression.	
Step 2: Choose the best strategy to answer the question Attempting to combine the radicals as written is incorrect and will lead you to a trap answer. Rewrite each variable with a fractional exponent instead. When simplifying fractional exponents, remember "power over root." Once you have simplified, subtract the exponents for the x terms, and then repeat for the y terms.	$\dfrac{\sqrt[6]{x^{10}y^{12}}}{\sqrt[3]{x^5y^6}} = \dfrac{x^{\frac{10}{6}}y^{\frac{12}{6}}}{x^{\frac{5}{3}}y^{\frac{6}{3}}}$ $x^{\frac{10}{6}-\frac{5}{3}}y^{\frac{12}{6}-\frac{6}{3}} = x^{\frac{10}{6}-\frac{10}{6}}y^{\frac{12}{6}-\frac{12}{6}}$ $= x^0y^0$
Step 3: Check that you answered the _right_ question Any quantity raised to the zero power is equal to 1, which means (A) is correct.	$x^0y^0 = 1 \times 1 = 1$

POLYNOMIALS

By now you're used to seeing equations, exponents, and variables; another important topic you are sure to see on the SAT is polynomials. A **polynomial** is an expression comprised of variables, exponents, and coefficients, and the only operations involved are addition, subtraction, multiplication, division (by constants *only*), and non-negative integer exponents. A polynomial can have one or multiple terms. The following table contains examples of polynomial expressions and non-polynomial expressions.

Polynomial	$23x^2$	$\dfrac{x}{5} - 6$	$y^{11} - 2y^6 + \dfrac{2}{3}xy^3 - 4x^2$	47
Not a **Polynomial**	$\dfrac{10}{z} + 13$	x^3y^{-6}	$x^{\frac{1}{2}}$	$\dfrac{4}{y-3}$

> ✔ **Note**
>
> Remember that a constant, such as 47, is considered a polynomial; this is the same as $47x^0$. Also, keep in mind that for an expression to be a polynomial, division by a constant is allowed, but division by a variable is not.

Identifying **like terms** is an important skill that will serve you well on Test Day. To simplify polynomial expressions, you combine like terms just as you did with linear expressions and equations (x terms with x terms, constants with constants). To have like terms, the types of variables present and their exponents must match. For example, $2xy$ and $-4xy$ are like terms; x and y are present in both, and their corresponding exponents are identical. However, $2x^2y$ and $3xy$ are not like terms because the exponents on x do not match. A few more examples follow:

Like terms	$7x, 3x, 5x$	$3, 15, 900$	$xy^2, 7xy^2, -2xy^2$
Not **like terms**	$3, x, x^2$	$4x, 4y, 4z$	$xy^2, x^{2y}, 2xy$

You can also **evaluate** a polynomial expression (just like any other expression) for given values in its domain. For example, suppose you're given the polynomial expression $x^3 + 5x^2 + 1$. At $x = -1$, the value of the expression is $(-1)^3 + 5(-1)^2 + 1$, which simplifies to $-1 + 5 + 1 = 5$.

A polynomial can be named based on its **degree**. For a single-variable polynomial, the degree is the highest power on the variable. For example, the degree of $3x^4 - 2x^3 + x^2 - 5x + 2$ is 4 because the highest power of x is 4. For a multi-variable polynomial, the degree is the highest sum of the exponents on any one term. For example, the degree of $3x^2y^2 - 5x^2y + x^3$ is 4 because the sum of the exponents in the term $3x^2y^2$ equals 4.

On Test Day you might be asked about the nature of the **zeros** or **roots** of a polynomial. Simply put, zeros are the x-intercepts of a polynomial's graph, which can be found by setting each factor of the polynomial equal to 0. For example, in the polynomial equation $y = (x + 6)(x - 2)^2$, you would have three equations: $x + 6 = 0$, $x - 2 = 0$, and $x - 2 = 0$ (because $x - 2$ is squared, that binomial appears twice in the equation). Solving for x in each yields -6, 2, and 2; we say that the equation has two zeros: -6 and 2. Zeros can have varying levels of **multiplicity**, which is the number of times that a factor appears in the polynomial equation. In the preceding example, $x + 6$ appears once in the equation, so its corresponding zero (-6) is called a **simple zero**. Because $x - 2$ appears twice in the equation, its corresponding zero (2) is called a **double zero**.

You can recognize the multiplicity of a zero from the polynomial's graph as well. Following is the graph of $y = (x + 6)(x - 2)^2$.

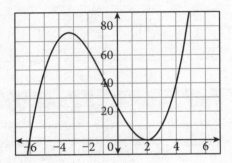

When a polynomial has a simple zero (multiplicity 1) or any zero with an odd multiplicity, its graph will cross the x-axis (as it does at $x = -6$ in the graph above). When a polynomial has a double zero (multiplicity 2) or any zero with an even multiplicity, it just touches the x-axis (as it does at $x = 2$ in the graph above).

Use your knowledge of polynomials to answer the following test-like question.

4. If y is a polynomial equation that has a simple zero at $x = 4$ and a triple zero at $x = -4$, which of the following could be the factored form of y?

   A) $y = (x + 4)(2x - 8)^3$

   B) $y = (x - 4)(3x + 12)$

   C) $y = 3(x + 4)(2x - 8)$

   D) $y = (2x + 8)^3(x - 4)$

There's no scratchwork for this question, but Kaplan's strategic thinking is provided in the table. Follow along as we reason through the question to get the correct answer.

Strategic Thinking
Step 1: Read the question, identifying and organizing important information as you go
You need to determine which equation could be the factored form of the equation that contains the zeros described.

Step 2: Choose the best strategy to answer the question

Adjectives such as "simple" and "triple" indicate how many times a zero's corresponding binomial is repeated in its polynomial equation. This means that you need one binomial raised to the first power and one raised to the third power. You can eliminate B and C, both of which lack the third power exponent.

The remaining answer choices each contain two binomial expressions: one with an exponent of 1 (remember, if no exponent is written, it is assumed to be 1) and one with an exponent of 3. Quick mental math reveals that both have 4 and -4 as zeros. You need the equation that has an exponent of 3 on the binomial that gives $x = -4$ and an exponent of 1 on the binomial that gives $x = 4$. Only (D) meets this requirement.

Step 3: Check that you answered the *right* question

Choice (D) is the only answer choice that satisfies the criteria in the question.

Adding and subtracting polynomials are straightforward operations, but what about multiplying and dividing them? These operations are a little tougher but (fortunately) far from impossible.

Multiplying polynomials is just like multiplying ordinary numbers except you want to pay special attention to distributing and combining like terms. Take the expression $(3x^3 + 5x)(2x^2 + x - 17)$ as an example. All you need to do is distribute each term in the first set of parentheses to each term in the second set. Distribute the $3x^3$ first, then repeat with $5x$:

$$
\begin{array}{cc}
\overset{1 \quad 2 \quad 3}{(3x^3 + 5x) \; (2x^2 + x - 17)} & \overset{4 \quad 5 \quad 6}{(3x^3 + 5x) \; (2x^2 + x - 17)}
\end{array}
$$

The following table shows the product for each step:

1	2	3
$3x^3 \cdot 2x^2 = 6x^5$	$3x^3 \cdot x = 3x^4$	$3x^3 \cdot (-17) = -51x^3$

4	5	6
$5x \cdot 2x^2 = 10x^3$	$5x \cdot x = 5x^2$	$5x \cdot (-17) = -85x$

All that's left to do now is write out the expression and combine any like terms.

$$6x^5 + 3x^4 - 51x^3 + 10x^3 + 5x^2 - 85x$$

$$= 6x^5 + 3x^4 - 41x^3 + 5x^2 - 85x$$

Although it is relatively straightforward to add, subtract, and multiply polynomials, dividing polynomial expressions requires a different, more involved process called **polynomial long division**. Polynomial long division is just like regular long division except, as the name suggests, you use polynomials in place of numbers.

Suppose you want to divide $x^3 + 3x + 7$ by $x + 4$. You can set this up as a long division problem:

$$x + 4 \overline{)x^3 + 0x^2 + 3x + 7}$$

Notice that even though the dividend does not have an x^2 term, a placeholder is used to keep the terms organized. Because $0x^2$ is equal to 0, adding this placeholder term doesn't change the value of the polynomial. Start by dividing the first term of the dividend by the first term of the divisor to get x^2. Multiply the entire divisor by x^2 and subtract this product from the dividend.

$$
\begin{array}{r}
x^2 \\
x + 4 \overline{)x^3 + 0x^2 + 3x + 7} \\
-(x^3 + 4x^2) \\
\hline
-4x^2 + 3x + 7
\end{array}
$$

Continue by dividing the next term, $-4x^2$, by the first term of the divisor. Bring down leftover terms as needed. Multiply the quotient, $-4x$, by the entire divisor and then subtract.

$$
\begin{array}{r}
x^2 - 4x \\
x + 4 \overline{)x^3 + 0x^2 + 3x + 7} \\
-(x^3 + 4x^2) \\
\hline
-4x^2 + 3x + 7 \\
-(-4x^2 - 16x) \\
\hline
19x + 7
\end{array}
$$

Finally, repeat this process with the $19x + 7$.

$$
\require{enclose}
\begin{array}{r}
x^2 - 4x + 19 \\
x + 4 \enclose{longdiv}{x^3 + 0x^2 + 3x + 7} \\
\end{array}
$$

$$
\begin{array}{r}
-(x^3 + 4x^2) \\
\hline
-4x^2 + 3x + 7 \\
-(-4x^2 - 16x) \\
\hline
19x + 7 \\
-(19x + 76) \\
\hline
-69
\end{array}
$$

When all is said and done, the quotient is $x^2 - 4x + 19$ with a remainder of -69; the remainder is written over the divisor in a separate term. Thus, the final answer is $x^2 - 4x + 19 - \dfrac{69}{x+4}$.

This is a topic many students tend to forget soon after it's tested in math class, so make sure you spend sufficient time brushing up on it.

> ✔ **Note**
>
> You can use polynomial long division to determine whether a binomial is a factor of a polynomial. If the remainder in the previous example had been 0, then $x + 4$ would have been a factor of the polynomial $x^3 + 3x + 7$.

Let's try a polynomial long division question.

5. What is the remainder when $16a^2 + 3$ is divided by $4a + 2$?

    A) -7

    B) -1

    C) 1

    D) 7

Work through the Kaplan Method for Math step-by-step to solve this question. The following table shows Kaplan's strategic thinking on the left, along with suggested math scratchwork on the right.

Strategic Thinking	Math Scratchwork
Step 1: Read the question, identifying and organizing important information as you go You must find the remainder when $16a^2 + 3$ is divided by $4a + 2$.	
Step 2: Choose the best strategy to answer the question Write as a polynomial long division problem. Once it's set up, work carefully through each step until you get to the end.	$$\begin{array}{r} 4a - 2 \\ 4a+2\overline{)16a^2 + 0a + 3} \\ -(16a^2 + 8a) \\ \hline -8a + 3 \\ -(-8a - 4) \\ \hline 7 \end{array}$$
Step 3: Check that you answered the *right* question You get 7 for the remainder, which is (D).	

RATIONAL EXPRESSIONS

A **rational expression** is simply a ratio (or fraction) of polynomials. In other words, it is a fraction with a polynomial as the numerator and another polynomial as the denominator. The rules that govern fractions and polynomials also govern rational expressions, so if you know these well, you'll be in good shape when you encounter one on Test Day.

There are a few important tidbits to remember about rational expressions; these are summarized here. They are also true for rational equations.

- For an expression to be rational, the numerator and denominator must both be polynomials.

- Like polynomials, rational expressions are also designated certain degrees based on the term with the highest variable exponent sum. For instance, the expression $\frac{1 - 2x}{3x^2 + 3}$ has a first-degree numerator and a second-degree denominator.

- Because rational expressions by definition can have polynomial denominators, they will often be undefined for certain values. For example, the expression $\frac{x - 4}{x + 2}$ is defined for all values of

x except -2. This is because when $x = -2$, the denominator of the expression is 0, which would make the expression undefined.

- Factors in a rational expression can be cancelled when simplifying, but under no circumstances can you do the same with individual terms. Consider, for instance, the expression $\dfrac{x^2 - x - 6}{x^2 + 5x + 6}$.

  Many students will attempt to cancel the x^2, x, and 6 terms to give $\dfrac{1 - 1 - 1}{1 + 5 + 1} = \dfrac{-1}{7}$, which is *never* correct. Don't even think about trying this on Test Day.

- Like fractions, rational expressions can be proper or improper. A proper rational expression has a lower-degree numerator than denominator $\left(\text{e.g., } \dfrac{1 - x}{x^2 + 3}\right)$, and an improper one has a higher-degree numerator than denominator $\left(\text{e.g., } \dfrac{x^2 + 3}{1 - x}\right)$. The latter can be simplified using polynomial long division.

✔ **Note**

For those who are curious, the correct way to simplify $\dfrac{x^2 - x - 6}{x^2 + 5x + 6}$ is to factor, which you'll learn about in chapter 10. For now, know that this equals $\dfrac{(x + 2)(x - 3)}{(x + 2)(x + 3)}$. Cancel the $x + 2$ factors to get $\dfrac{x - 3}{x + 3}$.

SOLVING RATIONAL EQUATIONS

Rational equations are just like rational expressions except for one difference: They have an equal sign. They follow the same rules as rational expressions. The steps you take to solve the more friendly looking linear equations apply to rational equations as well.

When solving rational equations, beware of **extraneous solutions**—solutions derived that don't satisfy the original equation. This happens when the derived solution causes 0 in the denominator of *any* of the terms in the equation (because division by 0 is not possible). Take the equation $\dfrac{1}{x + 4} + \dfrac{1}{x - 4} = \dfrac{8}{(x + 4)(x - 4)}$, for instance. After multiplying both sides by the common denominator $(x + 4)(x - 4)$, you have $(x - 4) + (x + 4) = 8$. Solving for x yields $2x = 8$ which simplifies to $x = 4$. However, when 4 is substituted for x, you get 0 in the denominator of both the second and third terms of the equation, so 4 is an extraneous solution. Therefore, this equation is said to have no solution.

✔ **Note**

Whenever you encounter an equation with variables in a denominator or under a radical, make sure you check the solutions by plugging the values back into the original equation.

---

6. $\dfrac{x}{x+2} + \dfrac{2}{x+6} = \dfrac{-8}{(x+2)(x+6)}$

What are the solution(s) to the equation shown above?

A) -2

B) 2

C) -2 and -6

D) No solution

Work through the Kaplan Method for Math step-by-step to solve this question. The following table shows Kaplan's strategic thinking on the left, along with suggested math scratchwork on the right.

Strategic Thinking	Math Scratchwork
Step 1: Read the question, identifying and organizing important information as you go You're asked for the solution(s) to the equation.	
Step 2: Choose the best strategy to answer the question The first order of business is to eliminate the fractions. Do this by multiplying both sides of the equation by the least common denominator for the whole equation, $(x+2)(x+6)$.	Left side: $(x+2)(x+6)\left(\dfrac{x}{x+2} + \dfrac{2}{x+6}\right)$ $= x(x+6) + 2(x+2)$ $= x^2 + 6x + 2x + 4$ $= x^2 + 8x + 4$ Right side: denominator cancels and you just get -8. Set the sides equal.
You've created a quadratic equation, so move all the terms to one side so that it is equal to 0, and then factor to solve it. Look for a pair of integers with a sum of 8 and a product of 12; the magic picks are 2 and 6. Split the two binomials into separate equations, set them equal to 0, and then solve.	$x^2 + 8x + 4 = -8$ $x^2 + 8x + 12 = 0$ $(x+2)(x+6) = 0$ $x + 2 = 0 \rightarrow x = -2$ and $x + 6 = 0 \rightarrow x = -6$
Be careful here. The question asks for the solutions, but you must plug them back into the equation (at least mentally) to make sure they're not extraneous: -2 causes $x+2$ to be 0, and -6 causes $x+6$ to be 0, so both solutions are extraneous. Therefore, the equation actually has no solution.	

Strategic Thinking	Math Scratchwork
Step 3: Check that you answered the *right* question You've solved for x and determined that both solutions are extraneous. Choice (D) is the correct answer.	

✔ **Note**

Extraneous solutions are solutions that cause the entire expression to become undefined. Look out for zeros in denominators and negatives under square roots.

MODELING REAL-WORLD APPLICATIONS USING POLYNOMIAL, RADICAL, AND RATIONAL EQUATIONS

A typical rational equation that models a real-world scenario (and that you're likely to see on Test Day) involves rates. Recall from chapter 5 that distance is the product of rate and time ($d = rt$); this equation will serve you well when solving rational equations involving rates. In some cases, you may want to change d to W (for work), as some questions ask how long it will take to complete some kind of work or a specific task. The good news is that the math doesn't change. For example, you can calculate a combined rate by rewriting $W = rt$ as $r = \dfrac{W}{t}$ for each person (or machine) working on a job and then adding the rates together.

Here's an example: Suppose machine A can complete a job in 2 hours and machine B can do the same job in 4 hours. You want to know how long it will take to do this job if both machines work together. Their rates would be $r_A = \dfrac{W_A}{t_A} = \dfrac{1}{2}$ job per hour and $r_B = \dfrac{W_B}{t_B} = \dfrac{1}{4}$ job per hour, respectively. The combined rate would be $\dfrac{3}{4}$ job per hour, which means $t_{total} = \dfrac{W_{total}}{r_{total}} = \dfrac{1}{\frac{3}{4}} = \dfrac{4}{3}$. Thus, it will take $\dfrac{4}{3}$ hours to complete the job if A and B work together.

Ready for a real-world example? Check out the next couple of pages.

7. Johanna, Elizabeth, and Dan are preparing a chemical solution for a research project. When working alone, either Johanna or Elizabeth can prepare the solution in six minutes. Dan can prepare the solution in four minutes if he works alone. How many minutes will it take the three of them to prepare the solution if they work together?

A) $\dfrac{5}{12}$

B) $\dfrac{7}{12}$

C) $\dfrac{12}{7}$

D) $\dfrac{12}{5}$

Work through the Kaplan Method for Math step-by-step to solve this question. The following table shows Kaplan's strategic thinking on the left, along with suggested math scratchwork on the right.

Strategic Thinking	Math Scratchwork
Step 1: Read the question, identifying and organizing important information as you go You're asked how long it will take the three colleagues to prepare the solution if they work together. A rate for each colleague is given.	
Step 2: Choose the best strategy to answer the question The question asks for a total time, so start by determining individual rates. Once you've done that, add them together to find the combined rate in terms of time. There is one solution to prepare (or one job to do), so use 1 for W.	$W = rt \rightarrow r = \dfrac{W}{t}$ J: 6 min to complete $\rightarrow \dfrac{1}{6}$ completed per minute E: 6 min to complete $\rightarrow \dfrac{1}{6}$ completed per minute D: 4 min to complete $\rightarrow \dfrac{1}{4}$ completed per minute t = time working together $\dfrac{1}{6} + \dfrac{1}{6} + \dfrac{1}{4} = \dfrac{1}{t}$

Strategic Thinking	Math Scratchwork
Once you have an equation, isolate t. Start by combining the fractions on the left side (by first writing them over the same denominator), then cross-multiply to solve for t.	$\dfrac{2}{12} + \dfrac{2}{12} + \dfrac{3}{12} = \dfrac{1}{t}$ $\dfrac{7}{12} = \dfrac{1}{t}$ $7t = 12$ $t = \dfrac{12}{7}$
Step 3: Check that you answered the _right_ question Working together, Johanna, Elizabeth, and Dan will need $\dfrac{12}{7}$ minutes to prepare the solution, which is (C).	

SOLVING A FORMULA OR EQUATION FOR A GIVEN VARIABLE

If you've ever taken a chemistry or physics course, you've probably noticed that many real-world situations can't be represented by simple linear equations. There are frequently radicals, exponents, and fractions galore. For example, the root-mean-square velocity for particles in a gas can be described by the following equation:

$$v = \sqrt{\frac{3kT}{m}}$$

In this equation, v represents the root-mean-square velocity, k is the Boltzmann constant, T is the temperature in degrees Kelvin, and m is the mass of one molecule of the gas. It's a great equation if you have k, T, and m and are looking for v. However, if you're looking for a different quantity, having that unknown buried among others (and under a radical to boot) can be unnerving, but unearthing it is easier than it appears. Let's say you're given v, k, and m but need to find T. First, square both sides to eliminate the radical to yield $v^2 = \dfrac{3kT}{m}$. Next, isolate T by multiplying both sides by m and dividing by $3k$; the result is $\dfrac{mv^2}{3k} = T$.

At this point, you can plug in the values of m, v, and k to solve for T. Sometimes the SAT will have you do just that: Solve for the numerical value of a variable of interest. In other situations, you'll need to rearrange an equation so that a different variable is isolated. The same rules of algebra you've used all along apply. The difference: You're manipulating solely variables.

Now you'll have a chance to try a few more test-like questions. Some guidance is provided, but you'll need to fill in the missing parts of explanations or the step-by-step math to get to the correct answer. Don't worry—after going through the examples at the beginning of this chapter, these questions should be completely doable. If you're still struggling, review the worked examples in this chapter.

8. Special relativity is a branch of physics that deals with the relationship between space and time. The Lorentz term, a term that relates the change in time, length, and relativistic mass of a moving object, is given by the following formula:

$$\gamma = \frac{1}{\sqrt{1 - \dfrac{v^2}{c^2}}}$$

In the formula, v is the relative velocity of the object and c is the speed of light in a vacuum. Which of the following equations correctly represents the relative velocity in terms of the other variables?

A) $v = c\sqrt{\dfrac{1}{\gamma^2} - 1}$

B) $v = c\sqrt{1 - \gamma^2}$

C) $v = c\left(1 - \dfrac{1}{\gamma^2}\right)$

D) $v = c\sqrt{1 - \dfrac{1}{\gamma^2}}$

Use the scaffolding that follows as your map through the question. Strategic thinking is on the left, and bits of scratchwork are on the right. If you aren't sure where to start, fill in the blanks in the table as you work from top to bottom.

Strategic Thinking	Math Scratchwork
Step 1: Read the question, identifying and organizing important information as you go You need to identify the expression that equals relative velocity. Translation: Solve the given equation for *v*.	$\gamma = \dfrac{1}{\sqrt{1 - \dfrac{v^2}{c^2}}}$
Step 2: Choose the best strategy to answer the question Don't let the multiple variables intimidate you; just treat them as you would when manipulating a "friendlier" equation. Start by undoing the radical so you can get to what's underneath, and then isolate the correct variable.	___ = ___ ___ = ___ ___ = ___ ___ = ___ ___ = ___ ___ = ___
Step 3: Check that you answered the *right* question Did you get (D)? If so, you're absolutely correct!	___

> ✔ **Note**
>
> Don't panic over the unfamiliarity of the physics terms or symbols; just identify what you need to do (in this case, isolate *v* on one side of the equation).

Math

Now try simplifying a fairly complicated-looking radical expression:

9. Given that g and h are both positive, which of the following is equivalent to the expression $\sqrt[3]{g^6h^3 - 27g^4h^3}$?

A) $\dfrac{1}{3}gh\sqrt[3]{g^2 - 27}$

B) $gh\sqrt[3]{g^3 - 27g}$

C) $g^2h - 3gh\sqrt[3]{g}$

D) $g^2h - 3\sqrt[3]{g}$

Use the scaffolding that follows as your map through the question. Strategic thinking is on the left, and bits of scratchwork are on the right. If you aren't sure where to start, fill in the blanks in the table as you work from top to bottom.

Strategic Thinking	Math Scratchwork
Step 1: Read the question, identifying and organizing important information as you go	
You need to simplify the given expression.	
Step 2: Choose the best strategy to answer the question	
Identifying the GCF should be your first step. Once this is complete, check to see whether any part of it can be "cube rooted" and placed outside the radical.	GCF:_____ $\sqrt[3]{\underline{}(\underline{} - \underline{})}$
Double check to make sure no factoring was missed, and then look for a match in the answer choices. If you can't find one, try rewriting the expression.	$= \underline{}\sqrt[3]{\underline{}(\underline{} - \underline{})}$ $= \underline{}\sqrt[3]{\underline{} - \underline{}}$
Step 3: Check that you answered the _right_ question	
If your answer is (B), congrats! You're correct.	_____

Ready to try an exponent question?

10. Human blood contains three primary cell types: red blood cells (RBC), white blood cells (WBC), and platelets. In an adult male, a single microliter (1×10^{-3} milliliters) of blood contains approximately 5.4×10^6 RBC, 7.5×10^3 WBC, and 3.5×10^5 platelets on average. What percentage of an adult male's total blood cell count is comprised of red blood cells?

A) 1.30%

B) 6.21%

C) 60.79%

D) 93.79%

Use the scaffolding that follows as your map through the question. Strategic thinking is on the left, and bits of scratchwork are on the right. If you aren't sure where to start, fill in the blanks in the table as you work from top to bottom.

Strategic Thinking	Math Scratchwork
Step 1: Read the question, identifying and organizing important information as you go You need to calculate the percent of an adult male's blood that is comprised of red blood cells.	
Step 2: Choose the best strategy to answer the question Remember that a percentage is derived from a ratio that compares a partial quantity to a total quantity. Write an equation that compares the RBC count to the total blood cell count and simplify. You can save time by using exponent rules instead of punching everything into your calculator. Note that the answer choices are fairly far apart. Compare the numerator and denominator of your simplified expression; you can estimate the resulting quantity and eliminate incorrect answers accordingly. Multiply the RBC fraction you found by 100 to convert it to a percent.	$RBC\% =$ _____ $\dfrac{}{\_\_ + \_\_ + \_\_}$ $= $ _____ $= $ _____ $= $ _____ _____ $\times\ 100 = $ _____%
Step 3: Check that you answered the *right* question Did you get (D)? If so, you're absolutely correct!	____

✔ **Expert Tip**

You can do this question almost entirely without a calculator. Just use what you know about exponents and scientific notation.

It's time to try a question involving rational expressions.

11.   A botanical garden is draining its lily pad pools for the winter using three pumps. The second pump is two times faster than the first pump, and the first pump is three times faster than the third. Let x be the number of hours that it takes the third pump to drain the pools by itself. If the three pumps work together, which expression represents the fraction of all the lily pad pools that the second pump can drain in 1 hour?

A) $\dfrac{6}{x}$

B) $\dfrac{3}{x}$

C) $\dfrac{2}{x}$

D) $\dfrac{1}{x}$

Use the scaffolding that follows as your map through the question. Strategic thinking is on the left, and bits of scratchwork are on the right.

Strategic Thinking	Math Scratchwork
Step 1: Read the question, identifying and organizing important information as you go You need to identify the expression that could represent the portion of the draining done by the second pump in one hour.	
Step 2: Choose the best strategy to answer the question Don't assume that the terms related to the pumps are ordered 1-2-3 in the equation. Start by ordering the pumps in order of increasing drain speed. Write the pump speeds as a ratio based on the information in the question stem. Use the second pump component of the ratio to derive an expression that represents the portion of the draining it could complete in one hour.	*speed:* ___ < ___ < ___ ___ : ___ : ___ *2nd pump completes* ___
Step 3: Check that you answered the *right* question Did you get (A)? If so, congrats! You're right.	___

Now that you've seen the variety of ways in which the SAT can test you on the topics in this chapter, try the following questions to check your understanding. Give yourself 3.5 minutes to tackle the following three questions. Make sure you use the Kaplan Method for Math as often as you can. Remember, you want to emphasize speed and efficiency in addition to simply getting the correct answer.

12. An object launched straight up into the air is said to have parabolic motion (because it goes up, reaches a maximum height, and then comes back down). The height (h) of a projectile at time t is given by the equation $h = \frac{1}{2}at^2 + v_0t + h_0$, where a is the acceleration due to gravity and v_0 and h_0 are the object's initial velocity and initial height, respectively. Which of the following equations correctly represents the object's acceleration due to gravity in terms of the other variables?

A) $a = \dfrac{h - v_0t - h_0}{t}$

B) $a = \dfrac{h - v_0t - h_0}{2t^2}$

C) $a = \dfrac{2(h - v_0t - h_0)}{t^2}$

D) $a = t\sqrt{2(h - v_0t - h_0)}$

13. Which of the following expressions is equivalent to $\dfrac{3 + \sqrt{72}}{3 - \sqrt{72}}$?

A) $\dfrac{9 + 4\sqrt{2}}{-7}$

B) $\dfrac{9 + 2\sqrt{2}}{-7}$

C) $\dfrac{9}{-7}$

D) $1 + \dfrac{4\sqrt{2}}{9}$

14. Car dealerships often require car buyers to provide a down payment (money paid up front), which is a percent of a car's price. The down payment is deducted from the purchase price, and the buyer usually takes out a loan to pay for what is left. Teri is buying a car that costs $19,560. Her monthly car payment is given by $m = \dfrac{Pr}{1 - (1 + r)^{-N}}$, where P is the initial loan balance, r is the monthly interest rate expressed as a decimal, and N is the number of payments to be made over the duration of the loan. If Teri wants to fully pay off the loan in five years at 1.5% annual interest and wishes to have a monthly payment of $200, what percent of the purchase price will she need for her down payment? Round to the nearest whole percent and ignore the percent sign when entering your answer.

Answers and Explanations for this chapter begin on page 925.

EXTRA PRACTICE

1. If $-2x^2 + 5x - 8$ is multiplied by $4x - 9$, what is the coefficient of x in the resulting polynomial?

   A) -77

   B) -45

   C) -32

   D) -13

2. If $p(x)$ is a polynomial that has a simple zero at $x = -3$ and a double zero at $x = \dfrac{5}{4}$, then which of the following could be the factored form of $p(x)$?

   A) $p(x) = 2(x + 3)(5x - 4)$

   B) $p(x) = (x + 3)(5x - 4)^2$

   C) $p(x) = 2(x + 3)(4x - 5)$

   D) $p(x) = (x + 3)(4x - 5)^2$

$$v = \frac{2\pi r}{T}$$

3. Uniform circular motion is used in physics to describe the motion of an object traveling at a constant speed in a circle. The speed of the object is called tangential velocity, and it can be calculated using the formula above, where r is the radius of the circle and T is the time is takes for the object to make one complete circle, called a period. Which of the following formulas could be used to find the length of one period if you know the tangential velocity and the radius of the circle?

   A) $T = \dfrac{v}{2\pi r}$

   B) $T = \dfrac{2\pi r}{v}$

   C) $T = 2\pi r v$

   D) $T = \dfrac{1}{2\pi r v}$

$$\frac{8x}{3(x - 5)} + \frac{2x}{3x - 15} = \frac{50}{3(x - 5)}$$

4. What value(s) of x satisfy the equation above?

   A) 0

   B) 5

   C) No solution

   D) Any value such that $x \neq 5$

5. Given the equation $\dfrac{6}{x} = \dfrac{3}{k + 2}$, and the constraints $x \neq 0$ and $k \neq -2$, what is x in terms of k?

   A) $x = 2k + 4$

   B) $x = 2k + 12$

   C) $x = 2k - \dfrac{1}{4}$

   D) $x = \dfrac{1}{4}k + 12$

6. If $A = 4x^2 + 7x - 1$ and $B = -x^2 - 5x + 3$, then what is $\dfrac{3}{2}A - 2B$?

   A) $4x^2 + \dfrac{31}{2}x - \dfrac{9}{2}$

   B) $4x^2 + \dfrac{41}{2}x - \dfrac{15}{2}$

   C) $8x^2 + \dfrac{31}{2}x - \dfrac{9}{2}$

   D) $8x^2 + \dfrac{41}{2}x - \dfrac{15}{2}$

$$\frac{\sqrt[3]{x} \cdot x^{\frac{5}{2}} \cdot x}{\sqrt{x}}$$

7. If x^n is the simplified form of the expression above, what is the value of n?

8. If $\dfrac{16}{7x + 4} + A$ is equivalent to $\dfrac{49x^2}{7x + 4}$, what is A in terms of x?

   A) $7x + 4$

   B) $7x - 4$

   C) $49x^2$

   D) $49x^2 + 4$

9. Which of the following expressions is equivalent to $-x^{\frac{1}{4}}$?

   A) $-\dfrac{1}{4x}$

   B) $-\dfrac{1}{x^4}$

   C) $-\sqrt[4]{x}$

   D) $\dfrac{1}{\sqrt[4]{-x}}$

10. What is the difference when $\dfrac{3x + 7}{x - 1}$ is subtracted from $\dfrac{8x - 5}{x - 1}$?

   A) $\dfrac{5x + 2}{x - 1}$

   B) $\dfrac{5x + 2}{2x - 1}$

   C) $\dfrac{5x - 12}{x - 1}$

   D) $\dfrac{-5x + 12}{x - 1}$

11. What is the sum of the polynomials $6a^2 - 17a - 9$ and $-5a^2 + 8a - 2$?

   A) $a^2 - 9a - 11$

   B) $a^2 - 25a - 7$

   C) $11a^2 - 9a - 11$

   D) $11a^2 - 25a - 7$

$$\frac{18x^4 + 27x^3 - 36x^2}{9x^2}$$

12. Which of the following is equivalent to the expression above?

   A) $2x^2 + 3x - 4$

   B) $2x^2 + 3x - 6$

   C) $2x^4 + 3x^3 - 4x^2$

   D) $2x^6 + 3x^5 - 4x^4$

$$8 + \frac{\sqrt{2x + 29}}{3} = 9$$

13. For what value of x is the equation above true?

   A) -10

   B) -2

   C) 19

   D) No solution

$$\frac{6x^2 + 19x + 10}{2x + 5}$$

14. If $ax + b$ represents the simplified form of the expression above, then what is the value of $a + b$?

   A) 2

   B) 3

   C) 5

   D) 6

15. Which of the following expressions is equivalent to $25x^2y^4 - 1$?

   A) $5(x^2y^4 - 1)$

   B) $-5(xy^2 + 1)$

   C) $(5xy - 1)(5xy + 1)$

   D) $(5xy^2 - 1)(5xy^2 + 1)$

16. For all a and b, what is the sum of $(a - b)^2$ and $(a + b)^2$?

   A) $2a^2$

   B) $2a^2 - 2b^2$

   C) $2a^2 + 2b^2$

   D) $2a^2 + 4ab + 2b^2$

$$T = 2\pi\sqrt{\frac{L}{g}}$$

17. The formula above was created by Italian scientist Galileo Galilei in the early 1600s to demonstrate that the time it takes for a pendulum to complete a swing, called its period (T), can be found using only the length of the pendulum, L, and the force of gravity, g. He proved that the mass of the pendulum did not affect its period. Based on the equation above, which of the following equations could be used to find the length of the pendulum given its period?

   A) $L = \dfrac{gT}{2\pi}$

   B) $L = \dfrac{gT^2}{4\pi^2}$

   C) $L = \dfrac{T^2}{4\pi^2 g}$

   D) $L = \dfrac{g}{4\pi^2 T^2}$

18. Mail-order pharmacies typically use machines to count pills and dispense them into bottles, particularly pills that are prescribed on a regular basis by physicians, such as blood pressure medicine, cholesterol medicine, and diabetes medicine. Suppose a pharmacy has two pill counters that work in tandem (together). The first counter can finish separating a typical batch of blood pressure pills in 1 hour, and the second counter can finish the same batch in 40 minutes. How many minutes should it take to finish a typical batch if both pill counters work together?

   A) 18

   B) 24

   C) 36

   D) 50

19. When simplified, $8^{\frac{4}{3}}$ is what number?

$$\frac{2x^4 + 16x^3 + 34x^2 + 10x + k}{x + 4}$$

20. For what value of k, where k is a constant, will the expression above have no remainder?

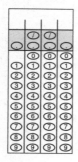

21. If $\dfrac{7\sqrt{x}}{2} = 14$, then what is the value of x?

A) 2

B) 4

C) 16

D) 49

$$\frac{4x + 8y}{24x - 12}$$

22. Which of the following is the simplified form of the rational expression above?

A) $\dfrac{1}{6} - \dfrac{2y}{3}$

B) $\dfrac{x + 2y}{6x - 3}$

C) $\dfrac{x + 2y}{2x - 1}$

D) $\dfrac{x + 8y}{6x - 12}$

23. What is the resulting coefficient of x when $-x + 6$ is multiplied by $2x - 3$?

A) -15

B) -2

C) 9

D) 15

24. Which of the following is equivalent to the expression $4\sqrt[3]{ab^9}$?

A) $4a^{\frac{1}{3}}b^3$

B) $4a^3b^{\frac{1}{3}}$

C) $4a^3b^{27}$

D) $\dfrac{4}{a^{\frac{1}{3}}b^3}$

$$\sqrt{0.75} \times \sqrt{0.8}$$

25. Which of the following has the same value as the expression above?

A) $\dfrac{3}{5}$

B) $\dfrac{\sqrt{15}}{5}$

C) $\sqrt[4]{0.6}$

D) $\sqrt{1.55}$

26. Which of the following expressions is equivalent to $(27x^6 y^{12})^{\frac{1}{3}}$?

    A) $3x^2 y^4$

    B) $9x^2 y^4$

    C) $\dfrac{27x^6 y^{12}}{3}$

    D) $(27x^6 y^{12})^{-3}$

$$\dfrac{12x^3 y^2 - 9x^2 y}{6x^4 y + 18x^3 y^3}$$

27. Which of the following is equivalent to the expression above?

    A) $\dfrac{4xy - 3}{x + 3y^2}$

    B) $\dfrac{3x^2 y - 3xy}{x + 3y^2}$

    C) $\dfrac{4xy - 3}{2x^2 + 6xy^2}$

    D) $\dfrac{4xy - 9}{2x^2 + 18xy^3}$

28. If $30x^3 + 45x^2 - 10x$ is divided by $5x$, what is the resulting coefficient of x?

    A) 6

    B) 9

    C) 25

    D) 40

$$\sqrt{9m^5 n^2 - m^4 n^2}$$

29. Which of the following is equivalent to the expression above, given that m and n are positive?

    A) $3\sqrt{m}$

    B) $3mn$

    C) $3n\sqrt{m}$

    D) $m^2 n\sqrt{9m - 1}$

30. An online business card printer charges a setup fee of \$15 plus \$0.02 per card, based on a minimum order of at least 100 cards. Assuming a customer orders x cards, and $x \geq 100$, which of the following represents the average cost per card, $C(\text{ave})$, including the setup fee, before taxes and shipping costs?

    A) $C_{\text{ave}} = \dfrac{15 + 0.02}{x}$

    B) $C_{\text{ave}} = \dfrac{15}{x} + 0.02$

    C) $C_{\text{ave}} = 0.02x + 15$

    D) $C_{\text{ave}} = \dfrac{15}{x} + 0.02x$

31. When $18x^2 + 24x - 10$ is divided by $3x + 5$, there is no remainder. What is the constant in the resulting quotient?

    A) -2

    B) $-\dfrac{1}{2}$

    C) 0

    D) 2

$$\sqrt{2} \times \sqrt[4]{2}$$

32. Which of the following is equivalent to the product given above?

A) $\sqrt[4]{8}$

B) $\sqrt[6]{2}$

C) $\sqrt[8]{2}$

D) $\sqrt[8]{4}$

33. Which of the following best describes the solutions to the rational equation
$$\frac{3}{x-2} - \frac{12}{x^2-4} = 1?$$

A) No solution

B) Two valid solutions

C) Two extraneous solutions

D) One valid solution and one extraneous solution

34. Which of the following is a factor of the polynomial $15x^4 + 107x^3 + 193x^2 + 17x - 12$?

A) $3x - 5$

B) $3x - 1$

C) $3x + 1$

D) $3x + 5$

35. What is the remainder when $x^3 + 12$ is divided by $x + 2$?

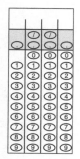

36. If $12 + \dfrac{3\sqrt{x-5}}{2} = 18$, then what is the value of x?

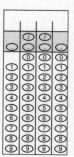

37. Marcia has two window air-conditioning units, one in each bedroom of her townhouse. Both bedrooms are upstairs and can be closed off from the rest of the townhouse by shutting a door at the top of the stairs. The first AC unit, an older model, can lower the temperature of the 260-square foot guest bedroom by 15 degrees Fahrenheit in 3 hours and 15 minutes. The second, a new energy-efficient model, can lower the temperature of the 300-square foot master bedroom by 15 degrees Fahrenheit in 2.5 hours. If Marcia closes the door at the top of the stairs, opens the bedroom doors, and lets both air conditioners work together to cool the two bedrooms, how many hours should it take to lower the temperature of both rooms by 15 degrees Fahrenheit? Do not round your answer.

CHAPTER 9

Functions

CHAPTER OBJECTIVES

By the end of this chapter, you will be able to:

1. Use function notation to answer questions containing equations, tables, and/or graphs

2. Interpret functions and functional statements that represent real-world scenarios

3. Combine functions using basic operations and compute compositions of functions

4. Determine when a function is increasing, decreasing, or constant and apply transformations to a given function or functions

SMARTPOINTS

Point Value	SmartPoint Category
50 points	Functions

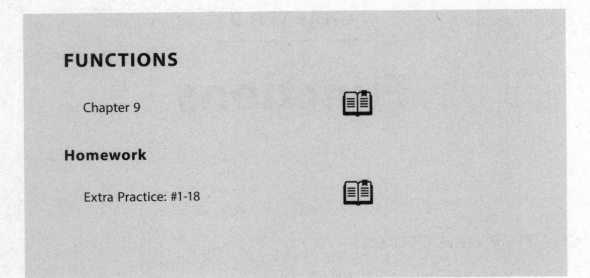

FUNCTIONS

Chapter 9

Homework

Extra Practice: #1-18

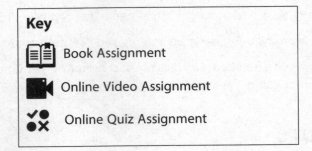

Key

Book Assignment

Online Video Assignment

Online Quiz Assignment

FUNCTIONS

Functions act as rules that transform inputs into outputs, and they differ from equations in that each input must have only one corresponding output. For example, imagine a robot: Every time you give it an apple, it promptly cuts that apple into three slices. The following table summarizes the first few inputs and their corresponding outputs.

Domain, x: # apples given to robot	Range, f(x): # slices returned by robot
0	0
1	3
2	6
3	9

From the table you see that the output will always be triple the input, and you can express that relationship as the function $f(x) = 3x$ (read "f of x equals three x").

SAT questions, especially those involving real-world situations, might ask you to derive the equation of a function, so you'll need to be familiar with the standard forms. Following is the standard form of a linear function:

$$f(x) = kx + f(0)$$

The input, or **domain**, is the value represented by x. Sometimes the domain will be constrained by the question (e.g., x must be an integer). Other times, the domain could be defined by real-world conditions. For example, if x represents the time elapsed since the start of a race, the domain would need to exclude negative numbers. The output, or **range**, is what results from substituting a domain value into the function and is represented by f(x). The initial amount, or **y-intercept**, is represented by f(0)—the value of the function at the very beginning. If you think this looks familiar, you're absolutely right. It's just a dressed-up version of the standard $y = mx + b$ equation you've already seen. Take a look at the following table for a translation:

Function Notation	What It Represents	Slope-Intercept Counterpart
f(x)	dependent variable or output	y
k	rate of change, slope	m
f(0)	y-intercept or initial quantity in a word problem	b

As you might have guessed, an exponential equation has a standard function notation as well. Here we've used g in place of f for visual clarity. Know that the letter used to represent a function (f, g, h, etc.) is sometimes arbitrarily chosen.

$$g(x) = g(0)(1 + r)^x$$

Just as before, $g(0)$ represents the initial amount and r represents the growth (or decay) rate. Recognizing that function notation is a variation of something you already know will go a long way toward reducing nerves on Test Day. You should also note that graphing functions is a straightforward process: In the examples above, just replace $f(x)$ or $g(x)$ with y and enter into your graphing calculator.

> ✔ **Note**
>
> A quick way to determine whether an equation is a function is to conduct the vertical line test: If a vertical line passes through the graph of the equation more than once for any given value of x, the equation is not a function.

Below is an example of a test-like question about functions.

1. The cube of x subtracted from the fourth root of the sum of three and the square of the product of two and x is less than $f(x)$. Which of the following correctly depicts the function described?

   A) $f(x) < \sqrt[4]{3 + 4x^2} - x^3$

   B) $f(x) > x^3 - \sqrt[4]{3 + 4x^2}$

   C) $f(x) > \sqrt[4]{3 + 4x^2} - x^3$

   D) $f(x) > \sqrt[4]{3 + 2x^2} - x^3$

Because there isn't any scratchwork required for a question like this, only the column containing Kaplan's strategic thinking is included. Follow along as we reason our way through this question.

Strategic Thinking
Step 1: Read the question, identifying and organizing important information as you go
The question asks for the function that correctly describes the situation presented.
Step 2: Choose the best strategy to answer the question
This is an exercise in translating English into math, so utilize tactics from that Kaplan Strategy. Take each piece one at a time. "The cube of x" becomes x^3." The fourth root of the sum of three and the square of the product of two and x" becomes $\sqrt[4]{3 + (2x)^2}$; don't forget the parentheses around $2x$.

Strategic Thinking
Read carefully when deciding how to combine these two pieces. "The cube of x" is being sub-tracted from "the fourth root … ," so the expression should now read $\sqrt[4]{3 + (2x)^2} - x^3$. According-ing to the question, this entire quantity is less than $f(x)$ (in other words, $f(x)$ is greater than the quantity). The inequality should read $f(x) > \sqrt[4]{3 + (2x)^2} - x^3$. Simplify $(2x)^2$ as $4x^2$ and you should see a match.
Step 3: Check that you answered the *right* question
Choice (C) is the correct answer.

Once broken into simpler pieces, this function question became much easier. Read on for more information about other ways the SAT can test your knowledge of functions.

FUNCTIONS DEFINED BY TABLES AND GRAPHS

The ability to interpret the graph of a function will serve you well on Test Day. To interpret graphs of functions, you'll need to utilize the same skills you use to interpret "regular" equations on the coordinate plane, so this material shouldn't be completely foreign.

You know from the first part of this chapter that a function is merely a dressed-up equation, so translating from function to "regular" notation or vice versa is a straightforward process. Consider the following brief example.

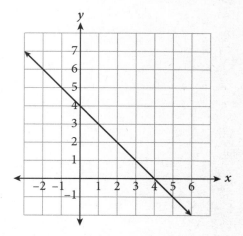

Suppose you're asked to find the value of x for which $f(x) = 6$. Because $f(x)$ represents the output value, or range, translate this as "When does the y value equal 6?" To answer the question, find 6 on the y-axis, then trace over to the function (the line). Read the corresponding x value: It's -2, so when $f(x) = 6$, x must be -2.

The SAT might also present functions in the form of tables. These may or may not have an equation associated with them, but regardless, you'll need to be adept at extracting the information necessary to answer questions. Most of the time the table will have just two columns, one for the domain and another for the range.

> ✔ **Note**
>
> Remember: A value of *f*(*x*) corresponds to a location along the *y*-axis. A value of *x* corresponds to a location on the *x*-axis.

Now let's try a test-like example.

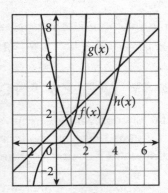

2. In the figure above, what is the value of $h(0) - 3(g(2) - f(2))$?

   A) −23

   B) −11

   C) $-\dfrac{11}{2}$

   D) $-\dfrac{3}{2}$

Work through the Kaplan Method for Math step-by-step to solve this question. The following table shows Kaplan's strategic thinking on the left, along with suggested math scratchwork on the right.

Strategic Thinking	Math Scratchwork
Step 1: Read the question, identifying and organizing important information as you go You're asked to determine the value of $h(0) - 3(g(2) - f(2))$. In other words, you need to find the y-value of function h when $x = 0$, the y-value of function g when $x = 2$, and the y-value of function f when $x = 2$. You then need to manipulate them as dictated by the given expression.	
Step 2: Choose the best strategy to answer the question Consider each value in the expression one at a time. Study the graph to determine the value of each function at the specified x-values. Plug each value into the original expression, and then follow the order of operations to simplify. Be careful as you do this, as it's easy to make careless mistakes, especially with negative signs.	 $h(0) - 3(g(2) - f(2))$ $4 - 3(8 - 3) = 4 - 3(5) = -11$
Step 3: Check that you answered the *right* question You found that the expression equals -11, which is (B).	

✔ **Note**

Watch your axis scales; just like scatterplot questions, questions involving graphs of functions often contain trap answers for students who misread the axes.

Although this question would have been much simpler if the graph had labeled the points or given you an equation to plug values into, it wouldn't have tested your knowledge of functions. Your ability to figure out what questions about functions are actually asking is key to solving them correctly on Test Day.

Try out a question in which a function is presented in the form of a table.

Day	Vote Count
3	21
4	35
5	53
6	75
7	101

3. Clara is one of five contest finalists in the running for a year's worth of college book expenses. The winner is the finalist with the highest number of votes on the contest host's website. Clara recorded her vote total each day of the contest; data for five days are in the table above. Which of the following represents Clara's vote count, v, as a function of time, t, in days?

A) $v(t) = 2t^2 + 3$

B) $v(t) = \dfrac{t^2}{2} + 3$

C) $v(t) = 2t^2 + 21$

D) $v(t) = \dfrac{t^2}{2} + 21$

Work through the Kaplan Method for Math step-by-step to solve this question. The following table shows Kaplan's strategic thinking on the left, along with suggested math scratchwork on the right.

Strategic Thinking	Math Scratchwork
Step 1: Read the question, identifying and organizing important information as you go The question is asking which function accurately depicts the relationship between time (t) and Clara's vote count (v). A table with data for selected days is given.	

Strategic Thinking	Math Scratchwork
Step 2: Choose the best strategy to answer the question Look for answer choices you can easily eliminate. From the table, you can tell that the rate of change of $v(t)$ is not constant and therefore not linear, but none of the choices are linear. However, the first table entry indicates Clara has 21 votes on day 3, and two choices have 21 as a y-intercept. The y-intercept is where $t = 0$; according to the table, $v(t) = 21$ at $t = 3$, not 0. Therefore, you can eliminate C and D. To evaluate the remaining choices, try plugging in a pair of data points. The point (4, 35) validates (A). To ensure (A) is the correct answer, you can repeat this process with B.	$v(3) = 21, v(0) \neq 21$ use $(4, 35)$ A: $35 = 2 \times 4^2 + 3$ $35 = 2 \times 16 + 3$ $35 = 32 + 3$ $35 = 35$ B: $35 = \dfrac{1}{2} \times 4^2 + 3$ $35 = \dfrac{1}{2} \times 16 + 3$ $35 = 8 + 3$ $35 \neq 11$
Step 3: Check that you answered the *right* question The only function that fits the data is (A).	

As you saw, you won't always have to plug points into each answer choice; you can often reduce your work by eliminating blatantly incorrect answers first. This is crucial for saving time on the SAT and quickly getting to the correct answer.

> ✔ **Note**
>
> When you have only one answer choice remaining, it isn't necessary to evaluate it. If you've done your math correctly up until that point, you know the remaining answer choice *has* to be correct. However, if you're at all worried that you made a mistake earlier, check the remaining answer choice to validate your math.

REAL-WORLD APPLICATION OF FUNCTIONS

Because functions are equations, you have a great deal of flexibility in working with them. For example, order of operations (PEMDAS) and the basic rules of algebra apply to functions just as they do to equations. You learned in Unit 1 that equations can represent real-world situations in convenient ways, and the same is true for functions.

Math

For example, suppose a homeowner wants to determine the cost of installing a certain amount of carpet in her living room. In prose, this would quickly become awkward to handle, as a description would need to account for the cost per square foot, fixed installation fee, and sales tax to get the final cost. However, you can easily express this as a function.

Suppose that, in the homeowner example, carpet costs $0.86 per square foot, the installer charges a $29 installation fee, and sales tax on the total cost is 7%. Using your algebra and function knowledge, you can describe this situation in which the cost, c, is a function of square footage, f. The equation would be $c = 1.07(0.86f + 29)$. In function notation, this becomes $c(f) = 1.07(0.86f + 29)$, where $c(f)$ is shorthand for "cost as a function of square footage." The following table summarizes what each piece of the function represents in the scenario.

English	Overall cost	Square footage	Material cost	Installation fee	Sales tax
Math	c	f	$0.86f$	29	1.07

> ✔ **Note**
>
> Why does a 7% tax translate to 1.07? Using 0.07 would only provide the sales tax due. Because the function is meant to express the total cost, 1.07 is used to retain the carpet cost and installation fee while introducing the sales tax. Think of it as 100% (the original price) + the 7% sales tax on top. In decimal form, $1 + 0.07 = 1.07$.

This test-like question will test your ability to write a function.

4. Each calendar year, a certain credit card gives cardholders 5% cash back on gasoline purchases up to $1,500 and 2% cash back on any amount spent on gasoline thereafter. If $g(x)$ and $e(x)$ represent cash back earned on gasoline purchases up to $1,500 and in excess of $1,500, respectively, which of the following sets of functions could be used to determine the amount of cash back earned at each tier?

A) $g(x) = 0.05x, 0 \leq x < 1{,}500; e(x) = 0.02(x - 1{,}500), x \geq 1{,}500$

B) $g(x) = 0.05x, 0 < x \leq 1{,}500; e(x) = 0.02x, x > 1{,}500$

C) $g(x) = 0.05x, 0 \leq x \leq 1{,}500; e(x) = 0.02(x - 1{,}500), x > 1{,}500$

D) $g(x) = 0.05x, 0 \leq x \leq 1{,}500; e(x) = 0.02(1{,}500 - x), x > 1{,}500$

A word problem like this is a great time to reach for the Kaplan Strategy for Translating English into Math. The following table shows Kaplan's strategic thinking on the left, along with suggested math scratchwork on the right.

Strategic Thinking	Math Scratchwork
Step 1: Read the question, identifying and organizing important information as you go You're asked to find the functions that describe the situation given.	
Step 2: Choose the best strategy to answer the question Use the Kaplan Strategy for Translating English into Math to extract what you need. The question has already defined the variables for you. The function $g(x)$ represents cash back on gasoline purchases up to \$1,500, which the question states is 5%. Therefore, a cardholder earns $0.05x$ on this portion of gasoline purchases. Because this rate applies only to the first \$1,500, there is a restriction on the function domain: $0 \le x \le 1,500$. Eliminate A and B. The function $e(x)$ is used for cash back on gasoline purchases over \$1,500. To account for this \$1,500, you must subtract it from x. The difference is then multiplied by 0.02 to calculate the additional cash back for gasoline purchases beyond \$1,500. Like $g(x)$, $e(x)$ has a domain restriction.	$g(x) = 5\%$ on gas up to \$1,500 $g(x) = 0.05x, 0 \le x \le 1,500$ $e(x) = 2\%$ above \$1,500 $e(x) = 0.02(x - 1,500), x > 1,500$
Step 3: Check that you answered the *right* question Choice (C) is the only choice with both of the functions you built. Watch out for choice A, which lacks the correct inequality symbols in the domain restrictions.	

✔ Note

On Test Day it would take considerable time to write out everything in this scratchwork column verbatim; use good judgment when doing scratchwork, and abbreviate when you can. For clarity, we've included more than the average student would write.

Notice that even with a more difficult word problem, the Kaplan Strategy for Translating English into Math gets the job done. You also should have noticed how function notation can help keep your scratchwork clear and organized.

MULTIPLE FUNCTIONS

There are several ways in which the SAT might ask you to juggle multiple functions simultaneously. Fortunately, the rules governing what to do are easy to understand. To start, we'll look at how to combine functions. This technique simply involves adding, subtracting, multiplying, and/or dividing the functions in play. Check out the following table for a synopsis of how to combine functions with the four basic operations (and make them look less intimidating).

When you see . . .	. . . convert it to:
$(f+g)(x)$	$f(x)+g(x)$
$(f-g)(x)$	$f(x)-g(x)$
$(fg)(x)$	$f(x)\times g(x)$
$\left(\dfrac{f}{g}\right)(x)$	$\dfrac{f(x)}{g(x)}$

You'll have a chance to solve a problem involving combined functions shortly.

A more challenging type of function question that you're likely to see is a **composition of functions** or **nested functions**. Questions involving a composition of functions require that you find an output value for one function and use the result as the input for another function to get the final solution. A composition of functions can be written as $f(g(x))$ or $(f \circ g)(x)$. The first is read as *f of g of x*, and the second, *f composed with g of x*. To answer these questions, start with the innermost parentheses and work your way out.

> ✔ **Note**
>
> You might see a composition of functions written as $(f \circ g)(x)$. Just remember that it's the same as $f(g(x))$, and solve as you would normally, working from the inside outward.

Suppose $f(x) = 8x$ and $g(x) = x + 3$. To find the value of $f(g(1))$, your steps would be as follows:

1. Determine $g(1)$, the innermost function when $x = 1$.

2. By substituting 1 for x in $g(x)$, you find that $g(1) = 1 + 3 = 4$. Now rewrite $f(g(1))$ as $f(4)$.

3. Find $f(4)$, the outer function when $x = 4$. Substituting 4 for x in function f, the final answer is $8(4) = 32$.

> ✔ **Note**
>
> Note that $f(g(x))$ does *not* equal $g(f(x))$. Not only is interchanging these incorrect, but this practice might also lead to a trap answer on Test Day.

On Test Day, you might see **piecewise functions**. A piecewise function is a function that is defined, literally, by multiple pieces. What breaks a function into pieces are different rules that govern different parts of the function's domain. Here's an example:

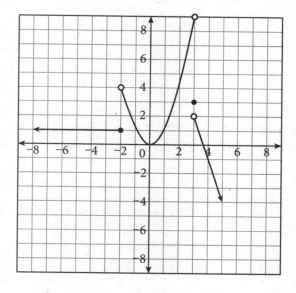

$$f(x) = \begin{cases} 1, & \text{if } x \leq -2 \\ x^2, & \text{if } -2 < x < 3 \\ 3, & \text{if } x = 3 \\ -3x + 11, & \text{if } x > 3 \end{cases}$$

In the function shown, the behavior of the graph depends on the domain. Linear, quadratic, and even a single point interval make up this function. Each "rule" is written inside the open bracket in "pieces." To the right is the domain interval for which each "rule" applies. On the graph, an open dot indicates that a point is not included in the interval; a closed dot indicates one that is. Note that the different inequality signs used in the domain constraints dictate whether a dot is open or closed on the graph. For a single-point interval, an equal sign is used.

To evaluate a piecewise function, first determine to which piece of the domain the input value belongs, and then substitute the value into the corresponding rule. For example, in the function above, $f(2) = (2)^2 = 4$, because the input value 2 is between -2 and 3 (the second piece of the domain). Similarly, $f(5) = -3(5) + 11 = -4$ because the input value 5 is greater than 3 (the last piece of the domain). You can confirm these values by looking at the graph. At $x = 2$, the point on the graph is $(2, 4)$, and at $x = 5$, the point on the graph is $(5, -4)$.

Math

Give this function question a try:

5. If $p(x) = x^2 - 4x + 8$ and $q(x) = x - 3$, what is the value of $\dfrac{q(p(5))}{p(q(5))}$?

    A) 0

    B) 0.4

    C) 1

    D) 2.5

Appearances can be deceiving. At first glance, this question looks tough, but the following table will clarify anything confusing. Kaplan's strategic thinking is on the left, along with suggested math scratchwork on the right.

Strategic Thinking	Math Scratchwork
Step 1: Read the question, identifying and organizing important information as you go You're asked for the value of $\dfrac{q(p(5))}{p(q(5))}$.	
Step 2: Choose the best strategy to answer the question The numerator and denominator look quite similar, so keep track of your calculations. Start with the numerator: Compute the innermost set of parentheses first, and then work your way outward. Repeat this process with the denominator. Once finished, combine the final values in the original expression.	$p(5) = 5^2 - 4 \times 5 + 8 = 13$ $q(13) = 13 - 3 = 10$ $q(p(5)) = 10$ $q(5) = 5 - 3 = 2$ $p(2) = 2^2 - 4 \times 2 + 8 = 4$ $p(q(5)) = 4$ $\dfrac{q(p(5))}{p(q(5))} = \dfrac{10}{4} = 2.5$
Step 3: Check that you answered the *right* question You've correctly calculated the expression. The correct answer is (D).	

Following is another example of a real-world scenario involving functions. Recall that the notation $(f \circ g)(x)$ means that f and g are functions of x such that $f(x)$ is computed based on $g(x)$.

6. Everett works at an electronics store. His base salary is $1,000 per week, and he earns a 10% commission on any sales over his $4,000 per week goal. If Everett's commission (c) and sales in excess of $4,000 ($e$) are both functions of his overall sales (s), which of the following correctly describes Everett's total weekly pre-tax pay?

    A) $(c \circ e)(s + 1,000)$

    B) $(e \circ c)(s + 1,000)$

    C) $(e \circ c)(s) + 1,000$

    D) $(c \circ e)(s) + 1,000$

Because there isn't any scratchwork required for a question like this, only the column containing Kaplan's strategic thinking is included. Follow along as we reason our way through this question.

Strategic Thinking
Step 1: Read the question, identifying and organizing important information as you go
You need to identify the expression that correctly depicts Everett's total weekly pay.
Step 2: Choose the best strategy to answer the question
Consider each part of Everett's pay separately. To find Everett's commission, you must first determine the portion of his sales to use for the commission calculation. In other words, commission (c) depends on sales in excess of $4,000 ($e$). This means you'll have a composition of functions with c computed based on e, which translates to c of e of s, or using composition notation, $(c \circ e)(s)$. Everett earns $1,000 regardless of sales, so this figure is independent of functions c and e. It should be added outside the composition of the functions. You can eliminate incorrect answer choices based on this information and the previous information.
Step 3: Check that you answered the right question
The only match for your function is (D).

Handling multiple functions in the same question or equation is only slightly more involved than manipulating a single function. Be sure to read particularly carefully when the question is embedded in a real-world scenario.

Math

DESCRIBING FUNCTION BEHAVIOR AND PERFORMING TRANSFORMATIONS

When describing the graph of a function or an interval (a specific segment) of a function, the trend of the relationship between the x- and y-values while reading the graph from left to right is often important. Three terms you are sure to see in more difficult function questions are **increasing**, **decreasing**, and **constant**. Let's look at what these terms mean and how they apply to SAT questions.

- **Increasing** functions have y-values that *increase* as the corresponding x-values increase.

- **Decreasing** functions have y-values that *decrease* as the corresponding x-values increase.

- **Constant** functions have y-values that *stay the same* as the x-values increase.

The SAT can ask about function trends in a variety of ways. The most basic would be to examine a function's behavior and determine whether (and where) the function is increasing, decreasing, or constant. Tougher questions might ask you to identify the trend and then explain what it means in the context of a real-life situation presented in the question, or to identify the effect a transformation would have on the trend of a function.

A function **transformation** occurs when a change is made to the function's equation or graph. Transformations include translations (moving a graph up/down, left/right), reflections (flips about an axis or other line), and expansions/compressions (stretching or squashing horizontally or vertically). How do you know which is occurring? The following table provides some rules for guidance when altering a hypothetical function $f(x)$.

Algebraic Change	Corresponding Graphical Change	Graph	Algebraic Change	Corresponding Graphical Change	Graph
$f(x)$	N/A—original function		$f(x + a)$	$f(x)$ moves left a units	
$f(x) + a$	$f(x)$ moves up a units		$f(x - a)$	$f(x)$ moves right a units	

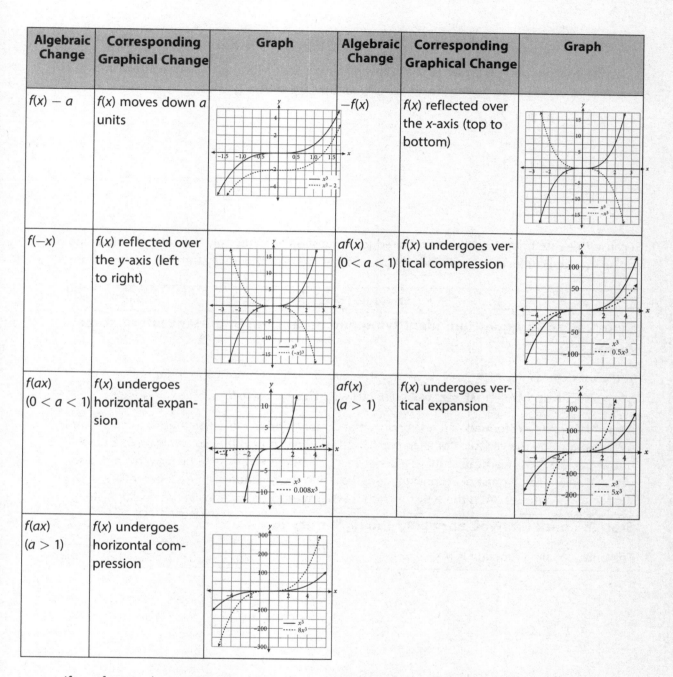

Algebraic Change	Corresponding Graphical Change	Graph	Algebraic Change	Corresponding Graphical Change	Graph
$f(x) - a$	$f(x)$ moves down a units		$-f(x)$	$f(x)$ reflected over the x-axis (top to bottom)	
$f(-x)$	$f(x)$ reflected over the y-axis (left to right)		$af(x)$ $(0 < a < 1)$	$f(x)$ undergoes vertical compression	
$f(ax)$ $(0 < a < 1)$	$f(x)$ undergoes horizontal expansion		$af(x)$ $(a > 1)$	$f(x)$ undergoes vertical expansion	
$f(ax)$ $(a > 1)$	$f(x)$ undergoes horizontal compression				

If you forget what a particular transformation looks like, you can always plug in a few values for x and plot the points to determine the effect on the function's graph.

✔ Expert Tip

Adding or subtracting inside the parentheses of a function will always cause a horizontal change (e.g., shift left/right, horizontal reflection); if the alteration is outside the parentheses, the result is a vertical change.

A function transformation question for you to try follows.

7. Given function $j(x)$, which of the following choices corresponds to a horizontal compression, a reflection about the x-axis, and an upward shift?

A) $-j(2x) + 2$

B) $-j(2x + 2)$

C) $j(-2x) + 2$

D) $-j\left(\dfrac{1}{2}x\right) + 2$

Because there isn't any scratchwork required for a question like this, only the column containing Kaplan's strategic thinking is included. Follow along as we reason our way through this question.

Strategic Thinking
Step 1: Read the question, identifying and organizing important information as you go
You must determine which function shows the transformations specified in the question stem.
Step 2: Choose the best strategy to answer the question
Remember your transformation rules. A horizontal compression results when there is a coefficient greater than 1 on the variable (for example, $f(3x)$); D doesn't contain this, so eliminate it. A reflection about the x-axis (vertical) requires a negative sign before j. Eliminate C. An upward shift (also vertical) means there must be a constant added outside the function argument parentheses. Of the remaining choices, (A) is the only function that satisfies the conditions in the question stem.
Step 3: Check that you answered the *right* question
The only matching function is (A).

Now you'll have a chance to try a couple test-like problems in a scaffolded way. We've provided some guidance, but you'll need to fill in the missing parts of explanations or the step-by-step math in order to get to the correct answer. Don't worry—after going through the worked examples at the beginning of this section, these problems should be completely doable.

8. Joan is an entomologist (a scientist who studies insects) researching possible causes of honeybee disappearance. At the start of a recent study, she estimated the number of honeybees in a 50 square mile area to be 4.23×10^8 distributed among 7,050 hives. Joan discovered that the honeybee population in this area decreases by 35% every month. Assuming the rate of disappearance remains 35% every month, approximately how many honeybees will remain after one year?

   A)   340

   B)   1,430

   C)   2,406,000

   D) 116,166,000

The following table can help you structure your thinking as you go about solving this question. Kaplan's strategic thinking is provided, as are bits of structured scratchwork. If you're not sure how to approach a question like this, start at the top and work your way down.

Strategic Thinking	Math Scratchwork
Step 1: Read the question, identifying and organizing important information as you go You need to determine the approximate number of honeybees remaining in Joan's study area after one year.	
Step 2: Choose the best strategy to answer the question You're asked about the honeybee population, so focus on information on the honeybee count and any rates of change. A reduction of 35% each month means the exact number of honeybees lost will change over time, so the best model is an exponential decay function. Add the values you know to create a function. The question wants a value, so plug in the correct duration into your function to find the number of remaining honeybees. Watch your time units.	exponential change: $y = x_0(1 + r)^x$ $p(t) =$ honeybee population $t =$ time in _____ $p(t) = ($_____$)(1 +$ _____$)^t$ $p($__$) = ($____$)($____$) -$ $=$ ____
Step 3: Check that you answered the *right* question If you picked (C), you'd be correct.	_____

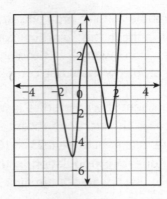

9. The graph of the function $a(x)$ is shown above. If $b(x) = \dfrac{1}{x}$, which of the following is a true statement about $(b \circ a)(x)$?

A) $(b \circ a)(x)$ is defined for all real numbers.

B) $(b \circ a)(x)$ is undefined for three real values of x.

C) $(b \circ a)(x)$ is undefined for four real values of x.

D) $(b \circ a)(x)$ is undefined for all real numbers.

The following table can help you structure your thinking as you go about solving this problem. Kaplan's strategic thinking is provided, as are bits of structured scratchwork.

Strategic Thinking	Math Scratchwork
Step 1: Read the question, identifying and organizing important information as you go You need to figure out when the composition of the functions is undefined (if it is).	
Step 2: Choose the best strategy to answer the question Think about what a composition means. The output of one function becomes the input for the other. You'll notice there's an x in the denominator of $b(x)$; think about what restriction this places on $b(x)$ and when this would make $(b \circ a)(x)$ undefined. Examine the graph of $a(x)$ to determine how many times this value occurs.	$(b \circ a)(x) \rightarrow b(a(x))$ output of _____ = input of _____ If $b(x) = \dfrac{1}{x}$, then $x \neq$ _____ . $\rightarrow a(x) \neq$ _____ in $(b \circ a)(x)$ $a(x) =$ _____ at _____ places
Step 3: Check that you answered the *right* question If you got (C), you're absolutely correct!	_____

Now that you've seen the variety of ways in which the SAT can test you on functions, try the following questions to check your understanding. Give yourself 3.5 minutes to tackle the following three questions. Make sure you use the Kaplan Method for Math as often as you can. Remember, you want to emphasize speed and efficiency in addition to simply getting the correct answer.

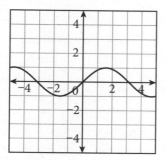

10. The graph of a trigonometric function, $h(x) = \sin x$, is shown above. Which of the following correctly depicts the transformations affected in $\dfrac{h(2x)}{3} - 4$?

A)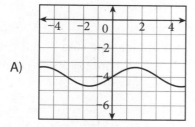

B)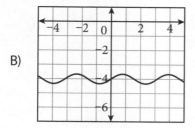

C)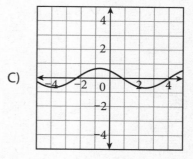

D)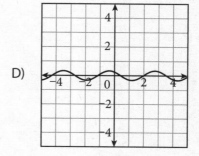

11. Briana is writing a 60-page paper for a law school class; she has completed a full outline of the paper and needs to convert it to prose. She estimates that she will average 45 words per minute while typing. If one page of prose contains approximately 500 words, which of the following correctly estimates the number of prose pages, p, remaining as a function of the number of minutes, m, that Briana types?

A) $p(m) = 60 - \dfrac{9m}{100}$

B) $p(m) = \dfrac{60 - 100}{9m}$

C) $p(m) = 60 - \dfrac{100}{9m}$

D) $p(m) = \dfrac{60 - 9m}{100}$

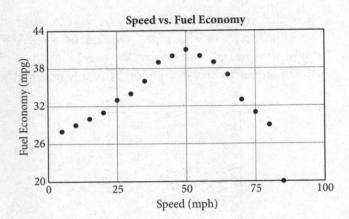

Speed vs. Fuel Economy

12. The graph above shows a compact car's fuel economy as a function of speed. Which of the following is true?

A) The rate of increase in fuel economy below 50 mph is greater than the rate of decrease in fuel economy above 50 mph.

B) The rate of increase in fuel economy below 50 mph is equal to the rate of decrease in fuel economy above 50 mph.

C) Fuel economy peaks at 50 mph, but nothing can be said about the rates of change in fuel economy above and below 50 mph.

D) The rate of increase in fuel economy below 50 mph is less than the rate of decrease in fuel economy above 50 mph.

Answers and Explanations for this chapter begin on page 935.

EXTRA PRACTICE

1. If $k(x) = 5x + 2$, then what is the value of $k(4) - k(1)$?

   A) 15

   B) 17

   C) 19

   D) 21

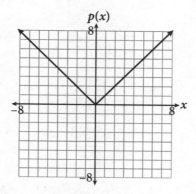

2. The figure shows the function $p(x) = |x|$. Which statement about the function is not true?

   A) $p(0) = 0$

   B) $p(-4) = 4$

   C) $p(4) = -4$

   D) The domain of $p(x)$ is all real numbers.

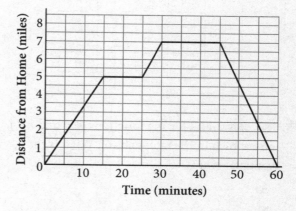

3. The graph above shows Carmel's distance from home over a one-hour period, during which time he first went to the library, then went to the grocery store, and then returned home. Which of the following statements could be true?

   A) The grocery store is about 5 miles from Carmel's house.

   B) Carmel traveled a total of 7 miles from the time he left home until he returned.

   C) The grocery store is 7 miles farther from Carmel's house than the library is.

   D) Carmel spent 10 minutes at the library and 15 minutes at the grocery store.

4. If the graph of a function $g(x)$ passes through the point (5, 3), and $h(x)$ is defined as $h(x) = -g(x - 2) + 8$, through which point does the graph of $h(x)$ pass?

   A) $(-3, 11)$

   B) $(3, 5)$

   C) $(7, 5)$

   D) $(7, 11)$

x	g(x)
−6	−3
−3	−2
0	−1
3	0
6	1

x	h(x)
0	6
1	−4
2	2
3	0
4	−2

5. Several values for the functions $g(x)$ and $h(x)$ are shown in the tables above. What is the value of $g(h(3))$?

A)   −1

B)   0

C)   3

D)   6

6. If p is a function defined over the set of all real numbers and $p(x + 2) = 3x^2 + 4x + 1$, then which of the following defines $p(x)$?

A) $p(x) = 3x^2 - 7x + 3$

B) $p(x) = 3x^2 - 8x + 5$

C) $p(x) = 3x^2 + 16x + 9$

D) $p(x) = 3x^2 + 16x + 21$

7. A company uses the function $P(x) = 150x - x^2$ to determine how much profit the company will make when it sells 150 units of a certain product that sells for x dollars per unit. How much more profit per unit will the company make if it charges $25 for the product than if it charges $20 ?

8. The customer service department of a wireless cellular provider has found that on Wednesdays, the polynomial function $C(t) = -0.0815t^4 + t^3 + 12t$ approximates the number of calls received by any given time, where t represents the number of hours that have passed since the department opened at 7 AM. Based on this function, how many calls can be expected by 5 PM ?

9. If $g(x) = -2x^2 + 7x - 3$, what is the value of $g(-2)$?

A)   −25

B)   −9

C)   −1

D)   3

10. Which of the following does not represent the graph of a function?

A)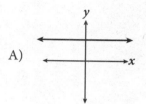

B)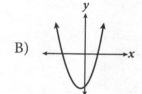

C)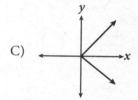

D)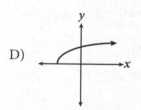

11. A biologist is studying the effect of pollution on the reproduction of a specific plant. She uses the function $n(p)$ to represent these effects, where p is the number of seeds germinated by the test group of the plant over a given period of time. Which of the following lists could represent a portion of the domain for the biologist's function?

A) $\{\ldots-150, -100, -50, 0, 50, 100, 150\ldots\}$

B) $\{-150, -100, -50, 0, 50, 100, 150\}$

C) $\{0, 0.25, 0.5, 0.75, 1, 1.25, 1.5\ldots\}$

D) $\{0, 20, 40, 60, 80\ldots\}$

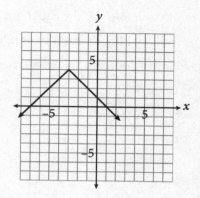

12. The graph of $f(x)$ is shown above. Which of the following represents the domain and range of the function?

A) Domain: $f(x) \geq 4$; Range: all real numbers

B) Domain: $f(x) \leq 4$; Range: all real numbers

C) Domain: all real numbers; Range: $f(x) \geq 4$

D) Domain: all real numbers; Range: $f(x) \leq 4$

13. If $g(x) = (x - 2)^2 - 5$, which of the following statements is true?

A) The function $g(x)$ is increasing over the entire domain.

B) The function $g(x)$ is decreasing over the entire domain.

C) The function $g(x)$ is increasing for $x < 2$ and decreasing for $x > 2$.

D) The function $g(x)$ is decreasing for $x < 2$ and increasing for $x > 2$.

14. A function is defined by the equation $f(x) = \dfrac{x^2}{4} - 11$. For this function, which of the following domain values corresponds to a range value of 14 ?

A) −4

B) 10

C) 38

D) 100

$$f(x) = \begin{cases} x^2 + 1, & \text{if } x \leq 0 \\ \dfrac{2x}{3} - 1, & \text{if } 0 < x \leq 3 \\ 4 - x, & \text{if } x > 3 \end{cases}$$

15. For the piecewise function $f(x)$ defined above, what is the value of $f(-3)$?

A) −3

B) 7

C) 10

D) −3, 7, and 10

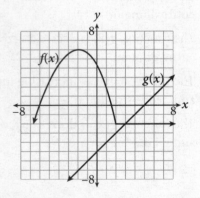

16. Based on the figure above, what is the value of $f(-2) + g(2)$?

A) −3

B) 0

C) 3

D) 6

17. If $f(x) = 3 - x$ and $g(x) = \dfrac{x^2}{2}$, which of the following is not in the range of $f(g(x))$?

A) −3

B) 0

C) 2

D) 4

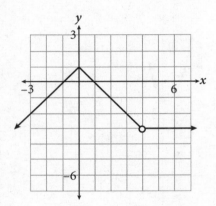

18. Which of the following piecewise functions could have been used to generate the graph above?

A) $g(x) = \begin{cases} -|x|, & \text{if } x \leq 4 \\ -3, & \text{if } x > 4 \end{cases}$

B) $g(x) = \begin{cases} -|x|, & \text{if } x < 4 \\ x - 3, & \text{if } x > 4 \end{cases}$

C) $g(x) = \begin{cases} -|x| + 1, & \text{if } x < 4 \\ -3x, & \text{if } x > 4 \end{cases}$

D) $g(x) = \begin{cases} -|x| + 1, & \text{if } x < 4 \\ -3, & \text{if } x > 4 \end{cases}$

CHAPTER 10

Quadratic Equations

CHAPTER OBJECTIVES

By the end of this chapter, you will be able to:

1. Solve quadratic equations via algebra, graphing, or the quadratic formula

2. Sketch the graph of a given quadratic equation

3. Identify how various components of a quadratic equation are significant to its graph or a real-world scenario

SMARTPOINTS

Point Value	SmartPoint Category
40 Points	Quadratics

Math

QUADRATIC EQUATIONS

Chapter 10

Homework

Extra Practice: #1-20

Even More

Math Quiz 4

Key

 Book Assignment

 Online Video Assignment

 Online Quiz Assignment

INTRODUCTION TO QUADRATIC EQUATIONS

A quadratic equation or expression is simply one that contains a squared variable (x^2) as the highest-order term (also called highest-powered term). In standard form, a quadratic equation is written as $ax^2 + bx + c = 0$, where a, b, and c are constants. However, quadratics can be written in a variety of other forms as well, such as these:

$$x^2 - 9 = 0 \qquad 2r^2 - 8r + 10 = 4 \qquad 2(x - 3)^2 = 8 \qquad (x - 2)(x + 3) = 6$$

✔ **Note**

At first glance, the last equation might not look quadratic, but it is; it's merely masquerading as a product of binomials. You'll learn a strategy for unveiling its x^2 term shortly.

All quadratic equations have 0, 1, or 2 real solutions. When you are asked to find the solutions of a quadratic equation, all you need to do is equate the variable to a constant. Solutions might also be called roots, x-intercepts, or zeros.

Before you can solve, however, there is a step you must always complete: **Set the equation equal to 0**. In other words, move everything to one side of the equation so that 0 is the only thing left on the other side. Once the quadratic equation is equal to 0, you can take one of three routes to determine how many solutions it has: **algebra**, **graphing**, or the **quadratic formula**. Read on for more information about these three techniques.

SOLVING QUADRATICS ALGEBRAICALLY

Using algebra is often necessary when working with quadratic equations, so getting comfortable with it is critical. We'll start with a technique that is highly useful for manipulating quadratics: FOIL. **FOIL is essential for putting a quadratic into standard form.**

✔ **Expert Tip**

If you get stuck on the algebra in a question about a quadratic equation, Picking Numbers can often help. Just remember that it might take more time than the algebraic route, so use good judgment if you're in a bind—and remember that you can always skip the question and revisit it later.

FOIL

Whenever you see a pair of binomials on the SAT, your default algebra strategy should be FOIL, which stands for **F**irst, **O**uter, **I**nner, **L**ast. This acronym helps ensure that you don't forget any terms when distributing. Multiply the first terms in each binomial together, then repeat with the outer, inner, and last terms. Then add the four products together, combining like terms as needed. Here is a generic scheme for the FOIL procedure:

$$(a + b)(c + d) = ac + ad + bc + bd$$
$$\text{(Binomial 1)(Binomial 2)} = \textbf{F}\text{irst} + \textbf{O}\text{uter} + \textbf{I}\text{nner} + \textbf{L}\text{ast}$$

It is often tempting to FOIL in your head, but this is risky: It is very easy to lose a negative sign or switch a pair of coefficients (and arrive at a trap answer). Show *all* of your work when using FOIL.

Factoring

Factoring, also known as reverse-FOILing, allows you to go from a quadratic to a product of two binomials. This is a very powerful tool; once you have a binomial pair, you're a few short algebraic steps away from finding the solution(s). The factoring process for a quadratic equation that is written in standard form ($ax^2 + bx + c$) is demonstrated in the following table:

Step	Scratchwork
Starting point: Notice a, the coefficient in front of x^2, is equal to 1, a great condition for factoring.	$x^2 + 5x + 6 = 0 \rightarrow (x \pm ?)(x \pm ?) = 0$
1. What are the factors of c? Remember to include negatives.	factors of 6: 1 & 6, −1 & −6, 2 & 3, −2 & −3
2. Which factor pair, when added, equals b, the coefficient in front of x?	$2 + 3 = 5$
3. Write as a product of binomials.	$(x + 2)(x + 3) = 0$
4. Split the product of binomials into two equations set equal to 0.	$x + 2 = 0, x + 3 = 0$
5. Solve each equation.	$x = -2, x = -3$

Factoring is easiest when a is 1, so whenever possible, try to simplify the expression so that is the case. In addition, if you see nice-looking numbers (integers, simple fractions) in the answer choices, this is a clue that factoring is possible. If you're ever not sure that you've done your factoring correctly, go ahead and FOIL to check your work. You should get the expression you started with.

> ✔ **Note**
>
> Sometimes, the two binomials factors will be identical. In this case, the quadratic equation will have only one real solution (because the two solutions are identical).

Completing the Square

For more difficult quadratics, you'll need to turn to a more advanced strategy: **completing the square**. In this process you'll create a perfect square trinomial, which has the form $(x + h)^2 = k$, where h and k are constants. This route takes some practice to master but will pay dividends when you sail through the most challenging quadratic equation questions on Test Day. The following table illustrates the procedure along with a corresponding example (even though the equation could have been factored).

Step	Scratchwork
Starting point.	$x^2 + 6x - 7 = 0$
1. Move the constant to the opposite side.	$x^2 + 6x = 7$
2. Divide b by 2, then square the quotient.	$b = 6; \left(\dfrac{b}{2}\right)^2 = \left(\dfrac{6}{2}\right)^2 = (3)^2 = 9$
3. Add the number from the previous step to both sides of the equation, then factor.	$x^2 + 6x + 9 = 7 + 9 \rightarrow (x+3)(x+3) = 16 \rightarrow (x+3)^2 = 16$
4. Take the square root of both sides.	$\sqrt{(x+3)^2} = \pm\sqrt{16} \rightarrow x + 3 = \pm 4$
5. Split the product into two equations and solve each one.	$x + 3 = 4, x + 3 = -4 \rightarrow x = 1, x = -7$

A note about completing the square: a needs to be 1 to use this process. You can divide the first term by a to convert the coefficient to 1, but if you start getting strange-looking fractions, it may be easier to use the quadratic formula instead.

Grouping

Although less commonly seen than other strategies, **grouping** is useful with more challenging quadratics, especially when the leading coefficient (the value of a) is not 1. You'll need two x terms to use this route. The goal of grouping is to identify the greatest common factor (GCF) of the first two terms, repeat for the second two terms, then finally combine the two GCFs into a separate binomial. Check out the following example.

Step	Scratchwork
Starting point.	$2x^2 - 7x - 15 = 0$
1. You need to split the x term in two; the sum of the new terms' coefficients must equal b, and their product must equal ac.	$a \times c = 2 \times (-15) = -30, b = -7$ new x term coefficients: 3 and -10 $2x^2 - 10x + 3x - 15 = 0$

Step	Scratchwork
2. What's the GCF of the first pair of terms? How about the second pair of terms?	GCF of $2x^2$ and $-10x$ is $2x$ GCF of $3x$ and -15 is 3
3. Factor out the GCFs for each pair of terms.	$2x^2 - 10x + 3x - 15 = 0$ $2x(x-5) + 3(x-5) = 0$
4. Factor out the newly formed binomial and combine the GCFs into another factor.	$2x(x-5) + 3(x-5) = 0$ $(2x+3)(x-5) = 0$
5. Split into two equations and solve as usual.	$2x + 3 = 0, x - 5 = 0 \rightarrow x = -\dfrac{3}{2}, x = 5$

Straightforward Math

Sometimes you can get away with not having to FOIL or factor extensively, but you need to be able to spot patterns or trends. Don't resort to complex techniques when some easy simplification will get the job done. Equations similar to the following examples are highly likely to appear on the SAT.

No Middle Term	No Last Term	Squared Binomial
$x^2 - 9 = 0$	$x^2 - 9x = 0$	$(x-3)^2 = 9$
$x^2 = 9$	$x(x-9) = 0$	$(x-3) = \pm\sqrt{9}$
$x = \pm\sqrt{9}$	$x = 0, x - 9 = 0$	$(x-3) = \pm 3$
$x = \pm 3$	$x = 0, x = 9$	$x - 3 = 3 \rightarrow x = 6$ $x - 3 = -3 \rightarrow x = 0$

> ✔ **Expert Tip**
>
> You can also factor $x^2 - 9$ to get $(x+3)(x-3)$; this is called a difference of squares. Note that this only works when the terms are being subtracted.

Quadratic Formula

The quadratic formula can be used to solve any quadratic equation. However, because the math can often get complicated, use this as a last resort or when you need to find exact (e.g., not rounded, fractions, and/or radicals) solutions. If you see square roots in the answer choices, this is a clue to use the quadratic formula.

The quadratic formula that follows yields solutions to a quadratic equation that is written in standard form, $ax^2 + bx + c = 0$:

$$x = \frac{-b \pm \sqrt{b^2 - 4ac}}{2a}$$

The $\pm$ sign that follows $-b$ indicates that you will have two solutions, so remember to find both.

The expression under the radical ($b^2 - 4ac$) is called the discriminant, and its value determines the number of real solutions. If this quantity is positive, the equation has two distinct real solutions; if it is equal to 0, there is only one distinct real solution; and if it's negative, there are no real solutions.

> ✔ **Note**
>
> Being flexible and familiar with your strengths on Test Day is essential. By doing so, you can identify the path to the answer to a quadratics question that is the most efficient for you.

On the next few pages, you'll get to try applying some of these strategies to test-like SAT problems.

1. Which of the following is an equivalent form of the expression $(6 - 5x)(15x - 11)$?

    A) $-75x^2 + 35x - 66$

    B) $-75x^2 + 145x - 66$

    C) $90x^2 - 141x + 55$

    D) $90x^2 + 9x + 55$

Work through the Kaplan Method for Math step-by-step to solve this question. The following table shows Kaplan's strategic thinking on the left, along with suggested math scratchwork on the right.

Strategic Thinking	Math Scratchwork
Step 1: Read the question, identifying and organizing important information as you go You're asked to identify the quadratic expression equivalent to $(6 - 5x)(15x - 11)$.	
Step 2: Choose the best strategy to answer the question You have a product of two binomials in the question stem and quadratics written in standard form in the answer choices, so FOIL is the quickest route. Follow the standard FOIL procedure, and then simplify.	$(6 - 5x)(15x - 11)$ $= (6)(15x) + (6)(-11)$ $\quad + (-5x)(15x) + (-5x)(-11)$ $= 90x - 66 - 75x^2 + 55x$ $= -75x^2 + 145x - 66$
Step 3: Check that you answered the *right* question You correctly expanded the quadratic using FOIL and got an exact match for (B), the correct answer.	$-75x^2 + 145x - 66$

Use the strategies you've learned in this section to simplify the rational expression that follows.

2. Which of the following is equivalent to $\dfrac{x^2 - 10x + 25}{3x^2 - 75}$?

A) $\dfrac{3(x - 5)}{(x + 5)}$

B) $\dfrac{3(x + 5)}{(x - 5)}$

C) $\dfrac{(x - 5)}{3(x + 5)}$

D) $\dfrac{(x + 5)}{3(x - 5)}$

Work through the Kaplan Method for Math step-by-step to solve this question. The following table shows Kaplan's strategic thinking on the left, along with suggested math scratchwork on the right.

Strategic Thinking	Math Scratchwork
Step 1: Read the question, identifying and organizing important information as you go You need to identify which answer choice contains an expression equivalent to the one in the question stem.	
Step 2: Choose the best strategy to answer the question There are a few x^2 terms, so you should be thinking about quadratics and factoring. Also, whenever you're given a fraction, think about ways to cancel terms. Examine the numerator first: You can use the quadratic shortcut $a^2 - 2ab + b^2 = (a - b)^2$ to rewrite it. The denominator is more involved. Factor out a 3 first, and then factor the quadratic, which is a difference of squares. Lastly, cancel any factors that the numerator and denominator share.	$\dfrac{x^2 - 10x + 25}{3x^2 - 75}$ $= \dfrac{(x - 5)(x - 5)}{3(x^2 - 25)}$ $= \dfrac{(x - 5)\cancel{(x - 5)}}{3(x + 5)\cancel{(x - 5)}}$
Step 3: Check that you answered the *right* question The expression is now in simplest form, so you're done. Choice (C) is correct.	$\dfrac{x - 5}{3(x + 5)}$

> ✔ **Expert Tip**
>
> Recognizing special quadratics, such as difference of squares, will eliminate factoring tasks and save time on Test Day.

3. Which of the following is a value of x that satisfies the equation $x^2 + 2x - 5 = 0$?

    A) -1

    B) $1 - \sqrt{6}$

    C) $1 + \sqrt{6}$

    D) $-1 - \sqrt{6}$

This question is full of radicals, but don't panic. You can use the Kaplan Method for Math to efficiently tackle this kind of question on Test Day. The following table shows Kaplan's strategic thinking on the left, along with suggested math scratchwork on the right.

Strategic Thinking	Math Scratchwork
Step 1: Read the question, identifying and organizing important information as you go The question asks for a solution to the given equation.	
Step 2: Choose the best strategy to answer the question The equation is a quadratic, so you have a few potential options. Because -5 does not have factors that add up to 2, you cannot factor or group. However, because the coefficient of x^2 is 1, completing the square is doable. We'll use that method here, but you could also use the quadratic formula if you prefer.	$x^2 + 2x - 5 = 0$ $x^2 + 2x = 5$ $\left(\dfrac{b}{2}\right)^2 = \left(\dfrac{2}{2}\right)^2 = 1^2 = 1$ $x^2 + 2x + 1 = 5 + 1$ $(x + 1)^2 = 6$ $x + 1 = \pm\sqrt{6}$ $x = -1 \pm \sqrt{6}$
Step 3: Check that you answered the *right* question The question asks for one possible value of x, so you should expect to see one (but not both) of the values in the choices. Choice (D) contains one of these values.	$x = -1 + \sqrt{6}$ or $x = -1 - \sqrt{6}$

CONNECTIONS BETWEEN QUADRATICS AND PARABOLAS

A quadratic function is simply a quadratic equation set equal to y or $f(x)$ instead of 0. To solve one of these, you would follow the same procedure as before: Substitute 0 for y, or $f(x)$, then solve using one of the three methods demonstrated (algebra, graphing, quadratic formula). Consider the graphical connection: When you set y equal to 0, you're really finding the x-intercepts.

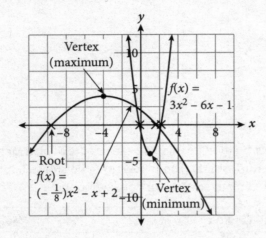

The graph of every quadratic equation (or function) is a parabola, which is a symmetric U-shaped graph that opens either up or down. To determine whether a parabola will open up or down, examine the value of a in the equation. If a is positive, the parabola will open up; if a is negative, it will open down. Take a look at the examples below to see this graphically.

Like quadratic equations, quadratic functions will have zero, one, or two real solutions, corresponding to the number of times the parabola crosses the x-axis. As you saw with previous examples, graphing is a powerful way to determine the number of solutions a quadratic function has.

Two Real Solutions	One Real Solution	No Real Solutions

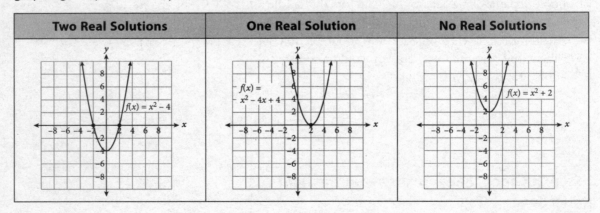

There are three algebraic forms that a quadratic equation can take: standard, factored, and vertex. Each is provided in the following table along with some features that are revealed by writing the equation in that particular form.

Standard	Factored	Vertex
$y = ax^2 + bx + c$	$y = a(x - m)(x - n)$	$y = a(x - h)^2 + k$
y-intercept is c	Solutions are m and n	Vertex is (h, k)
In real-world contexts, starting quantity is c	x-intercepts are m and n	Minimum/maximum of function is k
Format used to solve via quadratic formula	Vertex is halfway between m and n	Axis of symmetry is given by $x = h$

You've already seen standard and factored forms earlier in this chapter, but vertex form might be new to you. In vertex form, a is the same as the a from standard form, and h and k are the coordinates of the **vertex** (h, k). If a quadratic function is not in vertex form, you can still find the x-coordinate of the vertex by plugging the appropriate values into the equation $h = \dfrac{-b}{2a}$, which is also the equation for the axis of symmetry (see graph that follows). Once you determine h, plug this value into the quadratic function and solve for y to determine k, the y-coordinate of the vertex.

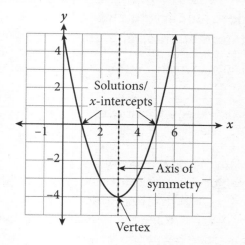

In addition to familiarity with the various forms a quadratic equation/function can take, you should have a foundational knowledge of the structure of a parabola. Some of the basic pieces you could be asked about on Test Day are shown above. You already know how to determine the solutions and the vertex, and finding the axis of symmetry is straightforward. The **equation of the axis of symmetry** of a parabola is $x = h$, where h is the x-coordinate of the vertex.

> ✔ **Note**
>
> The formula for a parabola's axis of symmetry is easy to remember: It's the quadratic formula without the radical component. If the x-intercepts are rational numbers, you can also determine the axis of symmetry by finding the midpoint, the point exactly halfway between.

Prepare

Take some time to explore the questions on the next several pages to test your new wealth of quadratic knowledge.

A question like this next one could arise in either the calculator or the no-calculator section. Think critically about how you'd solve it in either case.

4. What are the x-intercepts of the parabolic function $f(x) = 3x^2 - 2x - 8 = 0$?

A) $\dfrac{1}{3}$ and -25

B) $\dfrac{4}{3}$ and -2

C) $-\dfrac{4}{3}$ and 2

D) $-\dfrac{4}{3}$ and -2

Work through the Kaplan Method for Math step-by-step to solve this question. The following table shows Kaplan's strategic thinking on the left, along with suggested math scratchwork on the right.

Strategic Thinking	Math Scratchwork
Step 1: Read the question, identifying and organizing important information as you go You're given a quadratic equation in standard form and asked to find its x-intercepts.	
Step 2: Choose the best strategy to answer the question Because the coefficient of x^2 isn't 1, you can't easily factor. However, the grouping method will work. You'll need two numbers whose product is ac (-24) and whose sum is b (-2); the two magic numbers are -6 and 4. Rewrite the middle term using these numbers before you group, then factor and solve for x.	$f(x) = 3x^2 - 2x - 8 = 0$ $ac = 3 \times (-8) = -24$ $b = -2$ $3x^2 - 6x + 4x - 8 = 0$ $3x(x-2) + 4(x-2) = 0$ $(3x+4)(x-2) = 0$ $(3x+4) = 0$ or $(x-2) = 0$
Step 3: Check that you answered the *right* question The question asks for the x-intercepts of the equation, which is what you calculated. Select (C) and move on.	$x = -\dfrac{4}{3}$ and $x = 2$

✔ **Note**

If a question like this were in the calculator section, you could also solve it by graphing.

260 Unit Four: Passport to Advanced Math

In one final type of quadratic-related problem, you may be asked to match a function to a graph or vice-versa. An example of this follows; unfortunately, it is not likely to appear in the calculator section of the test.

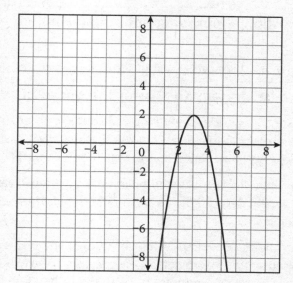

5. If the function shown in the graph is represented by $f(x) = a(x - h)^2 + k$, which of the following statements is not true?

    A) The value of a is negative.

    B) $f(x)$ is symmetrical across the line $y = 3$.

    C) The function $g(x) = \dfrac{2x}{3}$ intersects $f(x)$ at its vertex.

    D) The value of h is positive.

Because there isn't any scratchwork required for a question like this, only the column containing Kaplan's strategic thinking is included.

Strategic Thinking
Step 1: Read the question, identifying and organizing important information as you go The equation given is in vertex form. You must pick the answer choice that is *not* true.
Step 2: Choose the best strategy to answer the question Take control of this question—consider everything in a strategic order. Choices A and D contain the simplest statements, so check them first. Choice A says that a is negative. For parabolas that open downward, a will always be negative, so this statement is true. Eliminate it. Choice D says that h is positive. Recall that when a parabola is written in vertex form, h represents the x-coordinate of the vertex. Because the vertex is (3, 2), h must indeed be positive. Choice D is therefore true, so eliminate it. Of the remaining answer choices, B is simpler: It involves the parabola's axis of symmetry, which you can quickly find. Because the x-coordinate of the vertex is 3, the axis of symmetry is the line $x = 3$. Choice B says that the axis of symmetry is $y = 3$ and is therefore false.
Step 3: Check that you answered the *right* question Remember that you're looking for a false statement, not a true statement. Choice (B) is false, so you can select it confidently without even bothering to evaluate C.

> ✔ **Note**
>
> Stay on the lookout for words such as "not" that are easily missed if you don't read the question stem carefully. This is especially true of questions testing more involved topics.

GRAPHING QUADRATIC EQUATIONS ON A CALCULATOR

At this point, you've become quite an expert at working with quadratics on paper. In this part, we'll explore how you can use your calculator to efficiently graph quadratics. Calculators can be great time-savers *when you're allowed to use them*.

Graphing

All quadratic equations can be solved by graphing, unless they happen to have imaginary solutions which are covered in chapter 12. That said, you might ask why you need to learn all the algebra techniques. There are a few reasons why graphing shouldn't be the first option you turn to:

- Remember, there's a no-calculator section on the SAT; graphing isn't an option here.

- Graphing is often slower because entering complex equations and then zooming to find points of interest can be tedious.

- It is easy to accidentally mistype when you're being timed—a misplaced parenthesis or negative sign will likely lead to a trap answer choice.

However, if you have complicated algebra ahead (e.g., fractional coefficients), decimals in the answer choices, or time-consuming obstacles to overcome, graphing can be a viable alternative to solving quadratic equations algebraically. Steps for graphing on a calculator follows:

1. Manipulate the equation so that it equals 0.

2. Substitute $y =$ for the 0.

3. Enter the equation into your calculator.

4. Trace the graph to approximate the x-intercepts (usually the answer choices will be sufficiently different to warrant an approximation over an exact value) or use your calculator's built-in capability to find the x-intercepts exactly.

Graphing on the TI-83/84

While on the home screen, press [Y=]. Then enter the function to be graphed. Press [GRAPH] and allow the function to plot. If you can't see everything or want to make sure there isn't something hiding, consider pressing [WINDOW] to set your own manual parameters or hitting [ZOOM] to quickly zoom in and out. If you want to simply investigate your graph, press [TRACE] and use the right and left arrow keys to move around on the graph. If you type in any x-value and press [ENTER], the y-value will be returned on screen.

Determining Solutions on the TI-83/84

Once you have your graph on screen, you're ready to find solutions. Press [2ND] [TRACE] to pull up the CALC menu, which has options for finding points of interest. Select option 2:ZERO by highlighting and pressing [ENTER]. You will be taken back to the graph. Use the arrow keys to move to the left of the x-intercept (zero) that you want to calculate. Once you are just to the left of only the zero you are interested in, press [ENTER]—this is called the Left Bound. Next, move to the right of that zero only, careful not to go past any others, and press [ENTER]—this is called the Right Bound. Finally, the calculator will ask you to "Guess," so move left or right to approximate this zero, and press [ENTER].

Because you've already set the quadratic equation equal to zero, you know the zeros that your calculator returns will be the solutions to the overall equation.

 Note

Take the time to get comfortable with your calculator functions regardless of what calculator you have. You can find great instructions and even video demonstrations on the Internet.

Next, you'll get to try a sample test-like problem that could be solved via graphing or the quadratic formula. Choose wisely. In almost every case, graphing will be faster, but familiarize yourself with the quadratic formula approach in case you encounter a problem like this in the no-calculator section.

6. Which of the following are the real values of x that satisfy the equation $2x^2 - 5x - 2 = 0$?

A) 1 and 4

B) $-\dfrac{5}{4} + \dfrac{\sqrt{41}}{4}$ and $-\dfrac{5}{4} - \dfrac{\sqrt{41}}{4}$

C) $\dfrac{5}{4} + \dfrac{\sqrt{41}}{4}$ and $\dfrac{5}{4} - \dfrac{\sqrt{41}}{4}$

D) No real solutions

Work through the Kaplan Method for Math step-by-step to solve this question. The following table shows Kaplan's strategic thinking on the left, along with suggested math scratchwork on the right.

Strategic Thinking	Math Scratchwork
Step 1: Read the question, identifying and organizing important information as you go You need to solve the given equation for x.	
Step 2: Choose the best strategy to answer the question Attempting to factor is not wise, as the coefficients aren't factoring-friendly. Using a calculator would work, but it's likely to be messy: Two answer choices contain radicals, so you'd have to plug both solutions into the calculator and use the [TRACE] feature to see which ones approximately match the values you find. The quadratic formula, although a longer route, is actually the most efficient option for this question. Plug in the coefficients and the constant carefully. Labeling the equation will help keep the values of a, b, and c straight.	$\overset{a}{}\ \overset{b}{}\ \overset{c}{}$ $2x^2 - 5x - 2 = 0$ $x = \dfrac{-b \pm \sqrt{b^2 - 4ac}}{2a}$ $x = \dfrac{-(-5) \pm \sqrt{(-5)^2 - 4(2)(-2)}}{2(2)}$ $= \dfrac{5 \pm \sqrt{25 - (-16)}}{4}$ $= \dfrac{5 \pm \sqrt{41}}{4}$ $x = \dfrac{5}{4} \pm \dfrac{\sqrt{41}}{4}$
Step 3: Check that you answered the *right* question The question asks for the solutions to the equation, so you're finished. Your match is (C).	$\dfrac{5}{4} + \dfrac{\sqrt{41}}{4}$ and $\dfrac{5}{4} - \dfrac{\sqrt{41}}{4}$

> ✔ **Note**
>
> Note that in the previous question, the quadratic formula was the most efficient approach. Be prepared to use any of the quadratic equation tools at your disposal on Test Day.

Nicely done! Take a look at another example.

7. The equation $\frac{1}{4}(4x^2 - 8x - k) = 30$ is satisfied when $x = -5$ and when $x = 7$. What is the value of $2k$?

   A)   40

   B)   20

   C)   0

   D)   −20

Although this question seems more complicated than others you've seen in this chapter, if you use the Kaplan Method for Math, you'll arrive at the correct answer. The following table shows Kaplan's strategic thinking on the left, along with suggested math scratchwork on the right.

Strategic Thinking	Math Scratchwork
Step 1: Read the question, identifying and organizing important information as you go You're asked to find the value of $2k$.	
Step 2: Choose the best strategy to answer the question Notice that the equation in the question stem is not in standard form. Distributing the $\frac{1}{4}$ won't result in unmanageable fractions, so doing so won't cost you a lot of time. After distributing, set the equation equal to 0. The "normal" routes to the solutions (factoring, etc.) would be difficult to take here because of the presence of k. Instead, use the given solutions to construct and FOIL two binomials. The quadratic expressions must be equal because they share the same solutions. Set them equal to each other, and then use algebra to solve for k.	$\frac{1}{4}(4x^2 - 8x - k) = 30$ $x^2 - 2x - \frac{k}{4} = 30$ $x^2 - 2x - \frac{k}{4} - 30 = 0$ $(x - 7)(x + 5) = 0$ $x^2 - 2x - 35 = 0$ so $x^2 - 2x - \frac{k}{4} - 30 = x^2 - 2x - 35$ $-\frac{k}{4} = -5$ $-k = -20$ $k = 20$
Step 3: Check that you answered the *right* question Be careful! Many students will select B, but you're asked for the value of $2k$. Multiply the value of k by 2, and select (A).	$k = 20$ $2k = 40$

As demonstrated, even the most daunting quadratic equation questions are made more straightforward by using the Kaplan Method for Math.

Now you'll have a chance to try a few test-like problems in a scaffolded way. We've provided some guidance, but you'll need to fill in the missing parts of explanations or the step-by-step math in order to get to the correct answer. Don't worry—after going through the worked examples at the beginning of this section, these problems should be completely doable.

8. The height of a potato launched from a potato gun can be described as a function of elapsed time according to the following quadratic equation: $f(t) = -16t^2 + 224t + 240$. What is the sum of the potato's maximum height and the time it takes the potato to reach the ground?

    A)   15

    B)   240

    C)   1,024

    D)   1,039

Use the scaffolding in the table that follows as your map through the question. If you aren't sure where to start, fill in the blanks in the table as you work from top to bottom.

Math

Strategic Thinking	Math Scratchwork
Step 1: Read the question, identifying and organizing important information as you go You're asked to find the sum of the maximum height and the time it takes the potato to hit the ground. The t^2 indicates a quadratic (and therefore a parabolic trajectory).	
Step 2: Choose the best strategy to answer the question Because a (the t^2 coefficient) is negative, this parabola opens down, which means the maximum height will be at the vertex. First, find the x-coordinate of the vertex, h, and then use it to find the maximum height.	$h = \dfrac{-b}{2a} = \underline{\hspace{2cm}}$ $k = f(h)$ $k = -16(\underline{\ \ })^2 + 224(\underline{\ \ }) + 240$ $k = \underline{\hspace{1.5cm}}$
Next, find the amount of time it takes the potato to hit the ground. (Hint: Its height will be zero.) Translation: Factor!	$0 = \underline{\hspace{2cm}}$ $0 = (\underline{\hspace{1.5cm}})(\underline{\hspace{1.5cm}})$ $t = \underline{\hspace{1.5cm}}, t = \underline{\hspace{1.5cm}}$
Step 3: Check that you answered the *right* question Remember, the question asks you for the sum of the potato's maximum height and the time it takes the potato to hit the ground. If you came up with (D), you're absolutely correct.	$\text{sum} = \underline{\hspace{1cm}} + \underline{\hspace{1cm}}$ $= \underline{\hspace{1.5cm}}$

If you're up for a challenge, try the next question.

9. If $ab > 0$, $b^2ac < 0$, a is a constant, and b and c are distinct x-intercepts of the function $f(x)$, then $f(x)$ could equal which of the following?

   A) $f(x) = 5x^2 + 1$

   B) $f(x) = (x - \sqrt{17})(x + \sqrt{24})$

   C) $f(x) = (x - \sqrt{17})(x - \sqrt{24})$

   D) $f(x) = (x + \sqrt{17})(x + \sqrt{24})$

Use the scaffolding that follows as your map through the question. If you aren't sure where to start, fill in the blanks in the table as you work from top to bottom.

Strategic Thinking	Math Scratchwork
Step 1: Read the question, identifying and organizing important information as you go You need to select the equation that satisfies the given properties of $f(x)$.	
Step 2: Choose the best strategy to answer the question If $ab > 0$, then a and b are either both positive or both negative.	$ab > 0$ a and b have _____ sign
In the inequality $b^2 ac < 0$, b^2 will be positive regardless of the sign of b. Therefore, either a or c is positive, and the other must be negative.	$b^2 ac < 0$ a and c have _____ signs
The x-intercepts are b and c. Since b has the same sign as a, while c has the opposite sign as a, it follows that b and c also have opposite signs.	b and c are roots of $f(x)$ $f(x)$ has one _____ root and one _____ root
The correct answer must be a function with one negative root and one positive root. Scan the functions to find the correct one. Ignore the complicated-looking numbers; all that matters are the signs!	A's roots are _____ B's roots are _____ C's roots are _____ D's roots are _____
Step 3: Check that you answered the *right* question If you picked (B), then you got it!	_____

Now that you've seen the variety of ways in which the SAT can test you on quadratics, try the following questions to check your understanding. Give yourself 5 minutes to tackle the following four questions. Make sure you use the Kaplan Method for Math as often as you can. Remember, you want to emphasize speed and efficiency in addition to simply getting the correct answer.

$$4x - 12\sqrt{x} + 9 = 16$$

10. If the equation above is true, then what is the positive value of the expression $10\sqrt{x} - 15$?

    A) 20

    B) 25

    C) 30

    D) 35

11. How many times do the parabolas given by the equations $f(x) = 3(x - 4)^2 + 4$ and $g(x) = (x + 5)^2 + 2x - 135$ intersect?

    A) Never

    B) Once

    C) Twice

    D) More than twice

12. What is the positive difference between the x-intercepts of the parabola given by the equation $g(x) = -2.5x^2 + 10x - 7.5$?

13. Which equation represents the axis of symmetry for the graph of the quadratic function $f(x) = -\dfrac{11}{3}x^2 + 17x - \dfrac{43}{13}$?

    A) $x = -\dfrac{102}{11}$

    B) $x = -\dfrac{51}{22}$

    C) $x = \dfrac{51}{22}$

    D) $x = \dfrac{102}{11}$

Answers and Explanations for this chapter begin on page 940.

EXTRA PRACTICE

1. The factored form of a quadratic equation is $y = (2x + 1)(x - 5)$, and the standard form is $y = 2x^2 - 9x - 5$. Which of the following statements accurately describes the graph of y?

   A) The x-intercepts are -1 and 5, and the y-intercept is -5.

   B) The x-intercepts are $-\dfrac{1}{2}$ and 5, and the y-intercept is -5.

   C) The x-intercepts are $-\dfrac{1}{2}$ and 5, and the y-intercept is 5.

   D) The x-intercepts are 1 and -5, and the y-intercept is -5.

2. Taylor fires a toy rocket from ground level. The height of the rocket with respect to time can be represented by a quadratic function. If the toy rocket reaches a maximum height of 34 feet, 3 seconds after it was fired, which of the following functions could represent the height, h, of the rocket t seconds after it was fired?

   A) $h(t) = -16(t - 3)^2 + 34$

   B) $h(t) = -16(t + 3)^2 + 34$

   C) $h(t) = 16(t - 3)^2 + 34$

   D) $h(t) = 16(t + 3)^2 + 34$

3. If $x^2 - 7x = 30$ and $x > 0$, what is the value of $x - 5$?

   A) 5

   B) 6

   C) 10

   D) 25

4. Which of the following linear expressions divides evenly into $6x^2 + 7x - 20$?

   A) $3x - 10$

   B) $3x - 5$

   C) $3x - 4$

   D) $3x - 2$

$$\begin{cases} y = 2x \\ 2x^2 + 2y^2 = 240 \end{cases}$$

5. If (x, y) is a solution to the system of equations above, what is the value of x^2?

   A) 24

   B) 40

   C) 120

   D) 576

Tyree's Punt

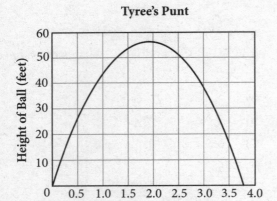

6. Tyree punts a football into the air. The equation $h = -16t^2 + 60t$ represents the height of the ball in feet, t seconds after it was punted. The graph of part of the equation is shown in the figure above. If Craig punts a ball higher than Tyree did, which of the following equations could be used to find the height of Craig's punt?

A) $h = -16(t^2 - 3t)$

B) $h = -8t(2t - 9)$

C) $h = -4(2t - 5)^2 + 48$

D) $h = -4(2t - 6)^2 + 52$

7. If $x = -5$ when $x^2 + 2xk + k^2 = 0$, what is the value of k?

8. If the graph of $y = ax^2 + bx + c$ passes through the points $(-2, -10)$, $(0, 2)$, and $(4, 14)$, what is the value of $a + b + c$?

9. Which of the following is equivalent to $(2a + 5b)(a - 3b)$?

A) $2a^2 - 2ab - 15b^2$

B) $2a^2 - ab - 15b^2$

C) $2a^2 + 2ab - 15b^2$

D) $2a^2 + 11ab - 15b^2$

10. Which of the following are roots of the quadratic equation $(x + 3)^2 = 49$?

A) $x = -10, x = 4$

B) $x = -10, x = 10$

C) $x = -4, x = 10$

D) $x = 3 \pm 2\sqrt{13}$

11. What information does the value of c reveal when a quadratic equation is written in the form $y = ax^2 + bx + c$, assuming $a \neq 0$, $b \neq 0$, and $c \neq 0$?

A) The solution (zero) of the equation

B) The location of the graph's axis of symmetry

C) The y-intercept of the graph of the equation

D) The maximum or minimum value of the equation

272   Unit Four: Passport to Advanced Math

Math

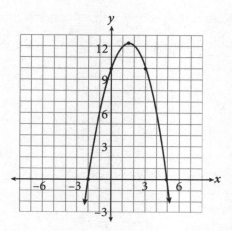

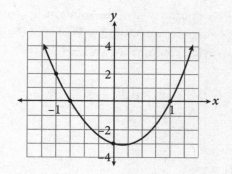

12. Which of the following could be the equation of the graph shown?

A) $y = 2x + 10$

B) $y = -x^2 + \dfrac{3}{2}x + 10$

C) $y = -(x - 2)(x + 5)$

D) $y = -(x + 2)(x - 5)$

13. Which of the following equations has the same solutions as the equation $40 - 6x = x^2$?

A) $y = (x - 6)^2 - 40$

B) $y = (x - 6)^2 + 40$

C) $y = (x + 3)^2 - 49$

D) $y = (x + 3)^2 + 49$

14. The following quadratic equations are all representations of the graph above. Which equation reveals the exact values of the x-intercepts of the graph?

A) $y = 4x^2 - x - 3$

B) $y = (4x + 3)(x - 1)$

C) $y = 4(x - 0.125)^2 - 3.0625$

D) $y + 3.0625 = 4(x - 0.125)^2$

15. Given the equation $y = -(2x - 4)^2 + 7$, which of the following statements is not true?

A) The vertex is $(4, 7)$.

B) The y-intercept is $(0, -9)$.

C) The parabola opens downward.

D) The graph crosses the x-axis at least one time.

Math

16. The x-coordinates of the solutions to a system of equations are 3.5 and 6. Which of the following could be the system?

A) $\begin{cases} y = x + 3.5 \\ y = x^2 + 6 \end{cases}$

B) $\begin{cases} y = 2x - 7 \\ y = -(x - 6)^2 \end{cases}$

C) $\begin{cases} y = \dfrac{1}{2}x + 3 \\ y = -(x - 5)^2 + 7 \end{cases}$

D) $\begin{cases} y = \dfrac{1}{2}x + 7 \\ y = -(x - 6)^2 + 3.5 \end{cases}$

17. What is the positive difference between the roots of the equation $y = \dfrac{1}{3}x^2 - 2x + 3$?

Questions 18-20 refer to the following information.

The following graph shows the paths of two bottle rockets that were fired straight up at the same time. The functions $h_1(t)$ and $h_2(t)$ represent the heights in feet of the rockets t seconds after they were fired off.

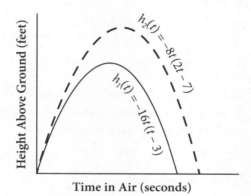

Height Above Ground (feet)

$h_2(t) = -8t(2t - 7)$

$h_1(t) = -16t(t - 3)$

Time in Air (seconds)

18. After 1 second in the air, how many feet higher was the second bottle rocket than the first?

19. How many seconds longer did it take the second rocket to reach its maximum height than the first rocket?

20. When the functions are written in the form $h(t) = -16t^2 + v_o t + h_o$, the variable quantities v_o and h_o represent the initial velocity in feet per second of the rocket and the initial height in feet of the rocket, respectively. How much greater was the initial velocity in feet per second of the second rocket than the first?

21. The factored form of a quadratic equation is $y = (2x - 3)(x + 5)$. What are the solutions to the equation?

A) $x = -5, x = \dfrac{2}{3}$

B) $x = -5, x = \dfrac{3}{2}$

C) $x = 5, x = -\dfrac{2}{3}$

D) $x = 5, x = -\dfrac{3}{2}$

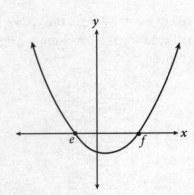

22. If e is half as far from the origin as f in the figure above, which of the following could be the factored form of the graph's equation?

   A) $y = \left(x - \dfrac{1}{2}\right)(x + 1)$

   B) $y = (x - 1)(x + 2)$

   C) $y = (x - 1)(2x + 1)$

   D) $y = \left(x + \dfrac{1}{2}\right)(2x + 1)$

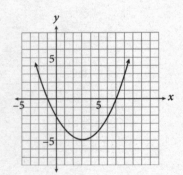

23. If $f(x) = ax^2 + bx + c$ represents the quadratic function whose graph is shown in the figure above, which of the following statements is not true?

   A) $a > 0$

   B) $b > 0$

   C) $c < 0$

   D) All of the statements are true.

24. Which of the following equations could represent a parabola that has a minimum value of 5 and whose axis of symmetry is the line $x = -3$?

   A) $y = (x - 3)^2 + 5$

   B) $y = (x + 3)^2 + 5$

   C) $y = (x - 5)^2 + 3$

   D) $y = (x + 5)^2 - 3$

$$\begin{cases} x + y = 4 \\ y = x^2 - 2x - 15 \end{cases}$$

25. If (a, b) and (c, d) represent the solutions to the system of equations above, and $a < c$, then which of the following statements is true?

   A) $a > 0$ and $c > 0$

   B) $a < 0$ and $c < 0$

   C) $a > 0$ and $c < 0$

   D) $a < 0$ and $c > 0$

26. If the equation of the axis of symmetry of the parabola given by $y = 3x^2 + 12x - 8$ is $x = m$, then what is the value of m?

   A) -8

   B) -4

   C) -2

   D) 0

27. Given that a, b, and c are all positive integers such that $ac > \dfrac{b^2}{4}$, how many times does the graph of the equation $y = ax^2 + bx + c$ cross the x-axis?

A) 0

B) 1

C) 2

D) There is not enough information to determine how many times the graph crosses the x-axis.

28. If the quadratic equation $y = 3(x + 5)^2 + 12$ is rewritten in standard form, $y = ax^2 + bx + c$, what is the value of c?

29. If m and n are positive integers where n is 2 less than three times m, and the product of m and n is 176, what is the smaller of the two integers?

x	$p(x)$
-2	3
0	-3
2	-5
4	-3
6	3
8	13

30. The table above shows several points that lie on the graph of quadratic function $p(x)$. Based on the data in the table, what is $p(-4)$?

UNIT FIVE

Additional Topics in Math

BY THE END OF THIS UNIT, YOU WILL BE ABLE TO:

1. Solve geometry questions involving lines, angles, triangles, and other complex shapes

2. Use special right triangles and Pythagorean triplets to save time on Test Day

3. Solve for unknown parts of circles

4. Interpret 3-D figures and solve problems using formulas for volume

5. Solve problems involving imaginary and complex numbers

6. Interpret basic trigonometric functions and use them to solve problems involving right triangles

CHAPTER 11

Geometry

CHAPTER OBJECTIVES

By the end of this chapter, you will be able to:

1. Apply the properties of lines and angles to solve geometry questions

2. Use the Pythagorean theorem, Pythagorean triplets, and special right triangles to answer questions involving triangles

3. Use concepts and theorems about congruence and similarity to solve problems about lines, angles, and triangles

4. Identify simple shapes within complex figures and use them to solve questions

5. Apply theorems about circles to find arc lengths, angle measures, chord lengths, and areas of sectors

6. Create or use an equation with two variables to solve a problem about a circle in the coordinate plane

7. Solve problems using volume formulas

SMARTPOINTS

Point Value	SmartPoint Category
40 Points	Geometry

Math

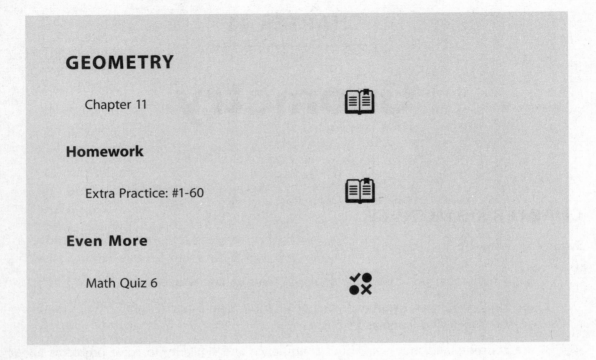

GEOMETRY

Chapter 11

Homework

Extra Practice: #1-60

Even More

Math Quiz 6

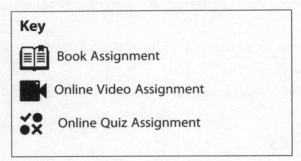

Key

Book Assignment

Online Video Assignment

Online Quiz Assignment

LINES AND ANGLES

Lines and angles are the foundation of SAT geometry. Therefore, mastering their basic rules will make solving these questions, as well as related geometry questions, easier. With the knowledge you'll gain from this chapter, you can quickly identify geometric relationships, build upon the information given in the question, and often bypass complex algebra.

Familiarity with angle types will often unlock information that is not explicitly given in a question. This makes getting to the answer much easier for even the toughest geometry questions. First, let's take a look at the types of angles you should be able to recognize.

Angle Type	Angle Measurement	Example
Acute	Less than 90°	
Right	90°	
Obtuse	Between 90° and 180°	
Straight	180°	

More often than not, you'll work with multiple angles in a single question. Therefore, it's worth noting two likely familiar terms that involve working with two or more angles: complementary and supplementary angles. Two angles are **complementary** if their measures add up to 90°; if their measures add up to 180°, the angles are **supplementary**.

✔ **Note**

Two angles need *not* be adjacent to be complementary or supplementary.

Intersecting lines create angles with special relationships you'll need to know as well. When two lines intersect, adjacent angles are supplementary, and **vertical** angles (two angles opposite a vertex) are equal, or **congruent**. Take a look at the following figure for an example.

The angles marked $a°$ and $b°$ are supplementary; therefore, $a + b = 180$. The angle marked $a°$ is vertical (and thus equal) to the one marked 60°, so $a = 60$. With this new information, you can find b: $a + b = 60 + b = 180$, so $b = 120$.

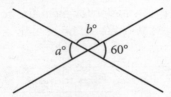

✔ **Note**

Unless otherwise noted, figures on the SAT are drawn to scale. Be especially careful when you see "<u>Note:</u> Figure not drawn to scale."

When two parallel lines are intersected by another line (called a **transversal**), all acute angles are equal, and all obtuse angles are equal. Additionally, **corresponding angles** are angles that are in the same position but on different parallel lines/transversal intersections; they are also equal. Furthermore, **alternate interior angles** and **alternate exterior angles** are equal. Alternate interior angles are angles that are positioned between the two parallel lines on opposite sides of the transversal, whereas alternate exterior angles are positioned on the outside of the parallel lines on opposite sides of the transversal. Consider the following figure:

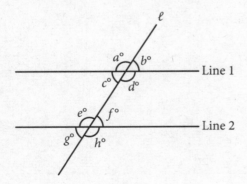

- Line 1 and Line 2 are parallel and cut by transversal ℓ.
- Angles a, d, e, and h are obtuse and equal.
- Angles b, c, f, and g are acute and equal.
- Angle pairs (b and f), (c and g), (a and e), and (d and h) are corresponding angles.
- Angle pairs (a and h) and (b and g) are alternate exterior angles.
- Angle pairs (d and e) and (c and f) are alternate interior angles.

Below is a summary of the essential theorems related to parallel lines that you'll need to know. Notice that the converse of most of these theorems is also true.

Angle Theorem	Definition
Alternate Interior Angles	• If two parallel lines are cut by a transversal, the alternate interior angles are congruent. • If two lines are cut by a transversal and the alternate interior angles are congruent, the lines are parallel.
Alternate Exterior Angles	• If two parallel lines are cut by a transversal, the alternate exterior angles are congruent. • If two lines are cut by a transversal and the alternate exterior angles are congruent, the lines are parallel.
Corresponding Angles	• If two parallel lines are cut by a transversal, the corresponding angles are congruent. • If two lines are cut by a transversal and the corresponding angles are congruent, the lines are parallel.
Vertical Angles	• If two parallel lines are cut by a transversal, the vertical angles are congruent.

 Note

Parallel lines cut by a transversal are powerful: Even if you know only one angle measure, you can get the other seven in mere seconds by knowing these rules.

TRIANGLES

Lines and angles form the basis of triangles—some of the most commonly occurring shapes on the SAT. Luckily, triangle questions usually don't involve a lot of complex algebra and are a great way to earn a few quick points on Test Day. Having a good command of triangle properties will help you recognize and solve these questions quickly. Many seemingly difficult questions will become easier once you can confidently speak the language of triangles.

All triangles follow the rules listed here, regardless of the type of triangle, so take the time now to get comfortable with these rules.

Triangle Theorem	Definition
Triangle Sum and Exterior Angle Theorems	• Interior angles add up to 180°. • An exterior angle equals the sum of the two opposite interior angles.
Isosceles Triangle Theorems	• If two sides of a triangle are congruent, the angles opposite them are congruent. • If two angles of a triangle are congruent, the sides opposite them are congruent.
Triangle Inequality Theorem	• The sum of the lengths of any two sides of a triangle must be greater than the length of the third side. • The difference of the lengths of any two sides of a triangle must be less than the length of the third side.
Side-Angle Relationship	• In a triangle, the longest side is across from the largest angle. • In a triangle, the largest angle is across from the longest side.
Mid-Segment Theorem	• A triangle mid-segment (or midline) is parallel to one side of the triangle and joins the midpoints of the other two sides. • The mid-segment's length is half the length of the side to which it is parallel.

The corresponding angles and side lengths of **congruent triangles** are equal. **Similar triangles** have the same angle measurements and proportional sides. In the figure below, $\triangle ABC$ and $\triangle DEF$ have the same angle measurements, so the side lengths can be set up as the following proportion: $\frac{A}{D} = \frac{B}{E} = \frac{C}{F}$.

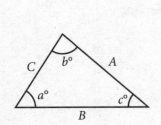
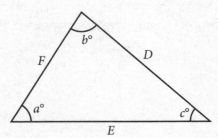

Drawing multiple heights in one triangle creates similar triangles, as shown in the diagram below. When you encounter a question like this, redrawing the similar triangles with their angles and sides in the same positions will help keep information in order.

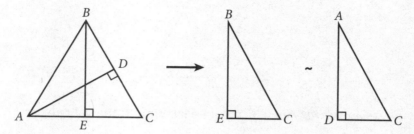

COMPLEX FIGURES

Complex figures are also a recurring SAT geometry topic, particularly ones that involve triangles. A complex figure is not a shape such as a dodecahedron. Instead, a complex figure is usually a larger shape that is composed of multiple (familiar) shapes; these can be obvious or cleverly hidden. These figures can always be broken down into squares, rectangles, triangles, and/or circles. Although this chapter emphasizes triangles, you'll get plenty of practice with other figures over the next few questions. No matter how convoluted the figure, following the guidelines here will lead you to the correct answer on Test Day.

- Transfer information from the question stem to the figure. If a figure isn't provided, draw one!

- Break the figure into familiar shapes.

- Determine how one line segment can play multiple roles in a figure. For example, if a circle and triangle overlap correctly, the circle's radius might be the triangle's hypotenuse.

- Work from the shape with the most information to the shape with the least information.

Now use your knowledge of lines, angles, triangles, and complex figures to answer a couple of test-like questions.

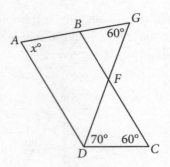

1. In the figure above, $\overline{AD}$ and $\overline{BC}$ are parallel. What is the value of x?

   A) 60

   B) 70

   C) 80

   D) 110

Work through the Kaplan Method for Math step-by-step to solve this question. The following table shows Kaplan's strategic thinking on the left, along with suggested math scratchwork on the right.

Strategic Thinking	Math Scratchwork
Step 1: Read the question, identifying and organizing important information as you go You're asked for the value of x.	
Step 2: Choose the best strategy to answer the question Look for familiar shapes within the given figure. There are three triangles present. Because $\overline{AD}$ and $\overline{BC}$ are parallel, $BFDA$ is a trapezoid. Although x might seem far removed from the known angles, you can find it. It will just take more than one step. In $\triangle FDC$, only one angle is missing, so you can solve for it and fill it in easily. Note that $\angle DFC$ and $\angle BFG$ are vertical angles, so $m\angle BFG$ is also 50°. At this point, you have two of the three angles in $\triangle BFG$, so you can solve for the third. $\angle FBG$ and $\angle BAD$ are corresponding angles (and are therefore congruent). You can now conclude that $x = 70$.	$m\angle DFC = 180° - 70° - 60° = 50°$ $m\angle BFG = m\angle DFC = 50°$ $m\angle FBG = 180° - 50° - 60° = 70°$ $m\angle BAD = x = m\angle FBG = 70°$ *(figure showing triangle with angles labeled: B 70° 60° G, A $x°$, 50° at F, 50° below F, D 70° 60° C)*
Step 3: Check that you answered the *right* question You're asked for x, so select (B), and you're done.	$x = 70$

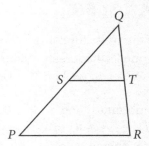

2. In the figure above, $\overline{ST}$ is a mid-segment of $\triangle PQR$. If $ST = 4x + 9$ and $PR = 16x + 6$, what is the length of $\overline{PR}$?

    A)   0.25

    B)   1.5

    C)   15

    D)   30

Work through the Kaplan Method for Math step-by-step to solve this question. The following table shows Kaplan's strategic thinking on the left, along with suggested math scratchwork on the right.

Strategic Thinking	Math Scratchwork
Step 1: Read the question, identifying and organizing important information as you go You must find the length of $\overline{PR}$.	
Step 2: Choose the best strategy to answer the question A triangle's mid-segment has a length that is half that of the side to which it is parallel. In other words, $ST = \frac{1}{2}PR$. You're given an expression for each segment, so plug in the expressions and solve for x.	$ST = \frac{1}{2}PR$ $4x + 9 = \frac{1}{2}(16x + 6)$ $-4x = -6$ $x = \frac{3}{2}$
The question asks for the length of $\overline{PR}$. Substitute the value you got for x back into the expression for PR and simplify.	$16 \times \frac{3}{2} + 6 = 30$
Step 3: Check that you answered the *right* question The correct choice is (D).	

Math

THE PYTHAGOREAN THEOREM, PYTHAGOREAN TRIPLETS, & SPECIAL RIGHT TRIANGLES

The Pythagorean theorem is one of the most fundamental equations in geometry, and it will be of great use to you on the SAT. Common Pythagorean triplets and special right triangle ratios that originate from this formula will also serve you well on Test Day.

The **Pythagorean theorem** is an important triangle topic that you are probably familiar with already. If you know the lengths of any two sides of a right triangle, you can use the Pythagorean theorem equation to find the missing side. The equation is expressed as $a^2 + b^2 = c^2$, where a and b are the shorter sides of the triangle (called legs) and c is the hypotenuse, which is always across from the right angle of the triangle.

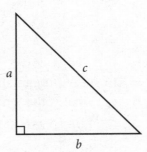

✔ **Note**

The Pythagorean theorem can only be applied to right triangles.

Consider an example: A right triangle has a leg of length 9 and a hypotenuse of length 14. To find the missing leg, plug the known values into the Pythagorean theorem: $9^2 + b^2 = 14^2$. This simplifies to $81 + b^2 = 196$, which becomes $b^2 = 115$. Take the square root of both sides to get $b = \sqrt{115}$. Because no factors of 115 are perfect squares, $b = \sqrt{115}$ is the answer.

✔ **Note**

Wait to simplify radicals until you have your final answer. Leave answers in radical form unless a question says otherwise or the answer choices are written as decimals.

Because time is at such a premium on the SAT, time-saving strategies are invaluable, and there are two that will come in handy on triangle questions. The first is knowing common **Pythagorean triplets**, which are right triangles that happen to have integer sides. These triangles show up *very* frequently on the SAT. The two most common are 3-4-5 and 5-12-13. Multiples of these (e.g., 6-8-10 and 10-24-26) can also pop up, so watch out for them as well. The beauty of these triplets is that if you see any two sides, you can automatically fill in the third without having to resort to the time-consuming Pythagorean theorem.

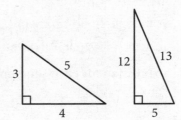

The second time-saving strategy involves recognizing **special right triangles**. Like Pythagorean triplets, special right triangles involve a ratio comparing the lengths of a right triangle's legs and hypotenuse, but with these triangles, you only need to know the length of one side in order to calculate the other two. These triangles are defined by their angles.

The ratio of the sides of a **45-45-90** triangle is $x : x : x\sqrt{2}$, where x is the length of each leg and $x\sqrt{2}$ is the length of the hypotenuse.

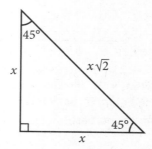

The ratio of the sides of a **30-60-90** triangle is $x : x\sqrt{3} : 2x$, where x is the shorter leg, $x\sqrt{3}$ is the longer leg, and $2x$ is the hypotenuse.

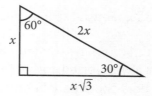

While the Pythagorean theorem can always be used to solve right triangle questions, it is not always the most efficient way to proceed. Further, many students make errors when simplifying radicals and exponents. The Pythagorean triplets and special right triangles allow you to save time and avoid those mistakes. Use them whenever possible!

> ✔ **Note**
>
> Although you will be given the special right triangle ratios on Test Day, you can save yourself some time by memorizing them. That way you won't have to keep flipping back to the formula page! You should also commit Pythagorean triplets to memory to bypass the Pythagorean theorem on Test Day.

Math

AREA OF A TRIANGLE

On Test Day, you might also be asked to find the area of a triangle or use the area of a triangle to find something else. The area of a triangle can be determined using $A = \frac{1}{2}bh$, where b is the triangle base and h is the triangle height.

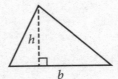

When you have a right triangle, you can use the legs as the base and the height. If the triangle isn't a right triangle, you'll need to draw the height in, as demonstrated in the figure shown. Remember that the height *must* be perpendicular to the base.

A final note about triangles: You are likely to see triangle questions involving real-world situations. But don't fret: All you need to do is follow the Kaplan Strategy for Translating English into Math. Extract the geometry information you need, then solve.

Take a look at the next example for another test-like triangle question.

3.   When Ted earned his driver's license, he wanted his first solo drive to be to a friend's house. Previously, Ted had always biked to his friend's house and was able to cut through the yards of neighbors and a park in order to bike there in a straight line. In his car, however, Ted had no choice but to follow the streets. As a result, he traveled 6 miles east, 6 miles south, and 2 more miles east. How much shorter, in miles, is Ted's bike route than his car route?

Work through the Kaplan Method for Math step-by-step to solve this question. The following table shows Kaplan's strategic thinking on the left, along with suggested math scratchwork on the right.

Strategic Thinking	Math Scratchwork
Step 1: Read the question, identifying and organizing important information as you go You're given the lengths of various sections of streets. If only there were some way to arrange this information visually.	
Step 2: Choose the best strategy to answer the question To translate this question into a geometry problem, draw a figure. Sketch the streets, label the distances, and add a direct line between the start and destination. Based on the diagram, Ted's car route is $6 + 6 + 2 = 14$ miles. Two triangles are now visible, but you'll notice the current information is insufficient because you don't know exactly where the dashed line intersects the vertical line.	
Drawing in extra lines reveals a third triangle, and you already know its dimensions. The new triangle has legs measuring 6 miles and 8 miles. Do you see the Pythagorean triplet? It's a 6-8-10 triangle, meaning Ted's bike route (the hypotenuse) is 10 miles.	 Car: 14 mi Bike: 10 mi
Step 3: Check that you answered the *right* question The difference is $14 - 10 = 4$ miles. Grid in 4, and you're done!	

TRIANGLE CONGRUENCE THEOREMS

Many students ask why they need to learn how to do proofs when they take geometry. Although you will likely not need them in college (unless you're a math or computer science major), there is a fundamental skill that comes with constructing proofs: the ability to construct an argument effectively for a statement or position. This skill is critical in numerous situations and fields—for criminal cases in law, research proposals in science, treatment plans in medicine, and others—so it's a powerful tool to have in your skill set.

That being said, there's no question that proofs can be unnerving. The good news: You will *not* need to construct a complete proof on the SAT. The language of certain questions might still be slightly intimidating, but it will be far more manageable than a full-blown proof.

There are several theorems that can be used to prove two triangles are congruent; these are summarized in the following table. Make sure you are comfortable with all of them—you may need to determine that two triangles are congruent in order to find a side length or an angle measure in one or both of the triangles.

Triangle Congruence Theorem	Notation	Diagram
If three sides of one triangle are congruent to the corresponding sides of another triangle, then the two triangles are congruent.	SSS (side-side-side)	
If two sides and the included angle of one triangle are congruent to the corresponding parts of another triangle, then the two triangles are congruent.	SAS (side-angle-side)	
If two angles and the non-included side of one triangle are congruent to the corresponding parts of another triangle, then the two triangles are congruent.	AAS (angle-angle-side)	
If two angles and the included side of one triangle are congruent to the corresponding parts of another triangle, then the two triangles are congruent.	ASA (angle-side-angle)	
If the hypotenuse and leg of one right triangle are congruent to the corresponding parts of another right triangle, then the two triangles are congruent.	HL (hypotenuse-leg)	
An angle or line segment is congruent to itself.	Reflexive Property	
Corresponding parts of congruent triangles are congruent.	CPCTC	

✔ **Note**

There are two bogus congruence "theorems" to watch out for: AAA and SSA. Two triangles with identical angles are always similar, but they aren't necessarily congruent. If you have two triangles with two adjacent congruent sides and a congruent angle outside them, the third side can be two different lengths. SSA is valid only with right triangles, in which case you call it HL. Never use AAA.

QUADRILATERAL THEOREMS

Quadrilaterals are four-sided figures, with interior angles that add up to 360°. You will likely not see a question solely about quadrilaterals; if a quadrilateral appears at all, it will likely contain hidden triangles. However, the properties of the quadrilateral will allow you to deduce information about the triangles present, so make sure you know the basic properties of the most common quadrilaterals.

Given the high likelihood of a Test Day geometry problem containing hidden triangles, you should familiarize yourself with the types of quadrilaterals that are most likely to have useful triangles within.

Parallelogram Theorems	Properties
Parallelogram	• Both pairs of sides are parallel. • Both pairs of sides are congruent. • Both pairs of opposite angles are congruent. • An angle is supplementary to both angles adjacent to it. • The diagonals bisect each other.
Rhombus	• It has all the properties of a parallelogram. • All four sides are congruent. • Diagonals bisect angles and are perpendicular.
Rectangle	• It has all the properties of a parallelogram. • All angles are right angles. • Diagonals are congruent.
Square	• It has all the properties of a parallelogram, rhombus, and rectangle. • All sides are congruent.

A word of caution: Do not make any assumptions about a test figure that go beyond the information provided in the question. It's tempting to assume a quadrilateral is a rectangle or other more "friendly" shape, but unless this is proven or stated in the question (or indicated in the figure), don't do it!

INTRODUCTION TO CIRCLES

You already know the SAT can ask a variety of questions about lines, angles, and triangles; it can also test you on your knowledge of circles. Keep reading for a refresher on these ubiquitous shapes.

Circle Anatomy & Basic Formulas

There are a number of circle traits you should know for Test Day. The good news: Most will already be familiar to you if you've taken geometry.

- **Radius (*r*):** The distance from the center of a circle to its edge
- **Chord:** A line segment that connects two points on a circle
- **Diameter (*d*):** A chord that passes through the center of a circle. The diameter is always the longest chord a circle can have and is twice the length of the radius.
- **Circumference (*C*):** The distance around a circle; the equivalent of a polygon's perimeter. Find this using the formula $C = 2\pi r = \pi d$.
- **Area:** The space a circle takes up, just like a polygon. A circle's area is found by computing $A = \pi r^2$.
- Every circle contains 360°. You'll find out more about this fact's utility shortly.

As the formulas demonstrate, the radius is often the key to unlocking several other components of a circle. Therefore, your first step for many circle questions will be to find the radius.

Circles on the Coordinate Plane and Their Equations

When you have a circle on the coordinate plane, you can describe it with an equation. The equation of a circle in **standard form** is as follows:

$$(x - h)^2 + (y - k)^2 = r^2$$

In this equation, *r* is the radius of the circle, and *h* and *k* are the *x*- and *y*-coordinates of the circle's center, respectively: (*h*, *k*).

> ✔ **Note**
>
> A circle is one of the four conic sections, which are made by slicing a double cone with a plane. The parabola is another conic section that you read about in chapter 10. The ellipse and hyperbola (with standard forms $\frac{(x - h)^2}{a^2} + \frac{(y - k)^2}{b^2} = 1$ and $\frac{(x - h)^2}{a^2} - \frac{(y - k)^2}{b^2} = 1$, respectively) will not be tested on the SAT. Watch out for them in trap answer choices, however!

You might also see what is referred to as **general form**:

$$x^2 + y^2 + Cx + Dy + E = 0$$

At first glance, this probably doesn't resemble the equation of a circle, but the fact that you have an x^2 term and a y^2 term with coefficients of 1 is your indicator that the equation does indeed graph as a circle. To convert to standard form, complete the square for the x terms, then repeat for the y terms. Refer to chapter 10 for a review of completing the square.

> ✔ **Note**
>
> The x^2 and y^2 terms in the equation of a circle occasionally have coefficients other than 1 (but the coefficients must be equal). If this is the case, simply divide all terms in the equation by the coefficient to eliminate them.

Ready to try a circle question?

$$x^2 + 6x + y^2 - 8y = 171$$

4.   The equation of a circle in the xy-plane is shown above. What is the positive difference between the x- and y-coordinates of the center of the circle?

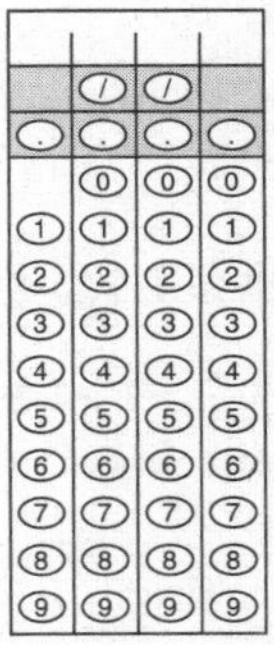

Work through the Kaplan Method for Math step-by-step to solve this question. The following table shows Kaplan's strategic thinking on the left, along with suggested math scratchwork on the right.

Strategic Thinking	Math Scratchwork
Step 1: Read the question, identifying and organizing important information as you go You need to determine the positive difference between the x- and y-coordinates of the center of the circle.	
Step 2: Choose the best strategy to answer the question You'll need to rewrite the equation in standard form to find what you need. The coefficients of the x and y terms are even, so consider completing the square for x and y. Divide b (from the x term) by 2 and square the result. Repeat for y. Then add the resulting amounts to both sides of the equation. Factor to write the equation in standard form. The center of the circle is $(-3, 4)$; subtract -3 from 4 to get the positive difference.	$(x - h)^2 + (y - k)^2 = r^2$ $x^2 + 6x + y^2 - 8y = 171$ x term: $\dfrac{b}{2} = \dfrac{6}{2} = 3 \rightarrow 9$ y term: $\dfrac{b}{2} = \dfrac{-8}{2} = -4 \rightarrow 16$ $x^2 + 6x + 9 + y^2 - 8y + 16 = 171 + 9 + 16$ $(x + 3)^2 + (y - 4)^2 = 196$ center: $(-3, 4)$
Step 3: Check that you answered the _right_ question The positive difference between the two coordinates is 7.	$4 - (-3) = 7$

Circle Ratios: Arcs, Central Angles, & Sectors

The SAT can ask you about parts of circles as well. There are three partial components that can be made in a circle: arcs, central angles, and sectors. These circle pieces are frequently used in proportions with their whole counterparts, so the ability to set up ratios and proportions correctly is of utmost importance for these questions.

- An **arc** is part of a circle's circumference. Both chords and radii can cut a circle into arcs. The number of arcs present depends on how many chords and/or radii are present. If only two arcs are present, the smaller arc is called the **minor arc**, and the larger one is the **major arc**. If a diameter cuts the circle in half, the two formed arcs are called **semicircles**. An arc length can never be greater than the circle's circumference.

- When radii cut a circle into multiple (but not necessarily equal) pieces, the angle at the center of the circle contained by the radii is the **central angle**. Because a full circle contains 360°, a central angle measure cannot be greater than this.

- Radii splitting a circle into pieces can also create **sectors**, which are parts of the circle's area. The area of a sector cannot be greater than its circle's total area.

Here's a summary of the ratios formed by these three parts and their whole counterparts.

$$\frac{\text{arc length}}{\text{circumference}} = \frac{\text{central angle}}{360°} = \frac{\text{sector area}}{\text{circle area}}$$

Notice that all of these ratios are equal. Intuitively, this should make sense: When you slice a pizza into four equal slices, each piece should have $\frac{1}{4}$ of the cheese, sauce, crust, and toppings. If you slice a circle into four equal pieces, the same principle applies: Each piece should have $\frac{1}{4}$ of the degrees, circumference, and area.

Inscribed Angle Theorem

An angle whose vertex is on the edge of the circle is called an **inscribed angle**. As this vertex moves along the edge, the measure of the inscribed angle remains constant as long as the minor arc created (in other words, isolated or **subtended** by the chords) does not change. When the chords that create an inscribed angle subtend the same minor arc that a pair of radii do, a special relationship appears: The central angle measure is twice that of the inscribed angle.

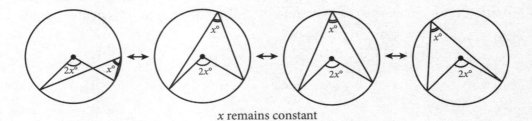

x remains constant

Arcs Formed Between Parallel Chords

Another theorem states that two parallel chords will intercept two congruent arcs; see the following diagram for an example. The congruent arcs will be between the chords.

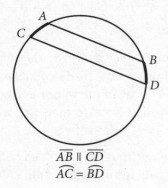

$$\overline{AB} \parallel \overline{CD}$$
$$\overset{\frown}{AC} = \overset{\frown}{BD}$$

Tangent Lines

A **tangent line** touches a circle at exactly one point and is perpendicular to a circle's radius at the point of contact. The following diagram demonstrates what this looks like.

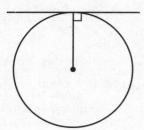

The presence of a right angle opens up the opportunity to draw otherwise hidden shapes, so pay special attention to tangents when they're mentioned. They often come up in complex figure questions.

The next question will give you a chance to see how these properties of circles can be tested on the SAT.

5. An orange with a diameter of 2 inches is sitting on a counter. If the distance from the center of the orange to the edge of the counter is 10 inches, how many inches is it between the point where the orange sits on the counter to the counter edge?

   A) $4\sqrt{6}$

   B) $3\sqrt{11}$

   C) 10

   D) $\sqrt{101}$

Work through the Kaplan Method for Math step-by-step to solve this question. The following table shows Kaplan's strategic thinking on the left, along with suggested math scratchwork on the right.

Strategic Thinking	Math Scratchwork
Step 1: Read the question, identifying and organizing important information as you go You must calculate the distance between where the orange sits and the edge of the counter.	
Step 2: Choose the best strategy to answer the question Draw a cross section of the orange on the counter; you'll see this is a circle with a tangent line. Draw in a perpendicular radius and a line from the center of the orange to the edge of the counter to reveal a right triangle. Use the Pythagorean theorem to calculate the distance requested.	 1 in., 10 in., x $1^2 + x^2 = 10^2$ $x^2 = 99$ $x = \sqrt{99}$
Step 3: Check that you answered the *right* question Simplify the radical; (B) is correct.	$\sqrt{99} = \sqrt{9 \times 11} = 3\sqrt{11}$

INTRODUCTION TO 3-D SHAPES

Over the last several pages, you learned about two-dimensional (2-D) shapes and how to tackle SAT questions involving them. Now you'll learn how to do the same for questions containing three-dimensional (3-D) shapes, also called solids. There are several different types of solids that might appear on Test Day—rectangular solids, cubes, cylinders, prisms, spheres, cones, pyramids—so it is critical that you be familiar with them. The following is a diagram showing the basic anatomy of a 3-D shape.

A **face** (or **surface**) is a 2-D shape that acts as one of the sides of the solid. Two faces meet at a line segment called an **edge**, and three faces meet at a single point called a **vertex**.

Keep reading for more on types of 3-D shapes and questions you could be asked about them.

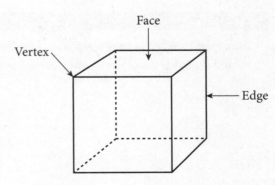

Volume

Volume is the amount of 3-D space occupied by a solid. This is analogous to the area of a 2-D shape like a triangle or circle. You can find the volume of many 3-D shapes by finding the area of the base and multiplying it by the height. We've highlighted the base area components of the formulas in the following table using parentheses.

Rectangular Solid	Cube	Right Cylinder
$(l \times w) \times h$	$(s \times s) \times s = s^3$	$(\pi \times r^2) \times h$

> ✔ **Note**
>
> Recall that a square is a special type of rectangle that has four equal sides. Likewise, a cube is a special type of rectangular solid whose edges (and faces) are all equal.

These three 3-D shapes are prisms. Almost all prisms on the SAT are right prisms; that is, all faces are perpendicular to those with which they share edges.

Following are some examples of less commonly seen prisms.

Triangular Prism	Hexagonal Prism	Decagonal Prism

Like the rectangular solids, cubes, and cylinders you saw earlier, these right prisms use the same general volume formula ($V = A_{\text{base}} \times h$).

> ✔ **Note**
>
> You might not be told explicitly the area of the base of a prism, in which case you'll need to rely on your two-dimensional geometry expertise to find it before calculating the volume.

More complicated 3-D shapes include the right pyramid, right cone, and sphere. The vertex of a right pyramid or right cone will always be centered above the middle of the base. Their volume formulas are similar to those of prisms, albeit with different coefficients.

> ✔ **Note**
>
> Some of these formulas might look daunting, but don't fret—you won't have to memorize them for Test Day. They'll be provided on the reference page at the beginning of each math section.

Right Rectangular Pyramid	Right Cone	Sphere
$\frac{1}{3} \times (l \times w) \times h$	$\frac{1}{3} \times (\pi \times r^2) \times h$	$\frac{4}{3} \times \pi \times r^3$

> ✔ **Note**
>
> A right pyramid can have any polygon as its base; the square variety is the one you're most likely to see. Also note that the vertex above the base of a right pyramid or cone is not necessarily formed by an intersection of exactly three faces, as in prisms, but it is still a single point and is still called a vertex.

Surface Area

Surface area is the sum of the areas of all faces of a solid. You might liken this to determining the amount of wrapping paper needed to cover all faces of a solid.

To calculate the surface area of a solid, simply find the area of each face using your 2-D geometry skills, then add them all together.

> ✔ **Note**
>
> You won't be expected to know the surface area formulas for right pyramids, right cones, and spheres; they'll be provided if you need them. However, you could be asked to find the surface area of a prism, in which case you'll be given enough information to find the area of each surface of the solid.

You might think that finding the surface area of a solid with many sides, such as a 10-sided right octagonal prism, is a tall order. However, you can save time by noticing a vital trait: This prism has two identical octagonal faces and eight identical rectangular faces. Don't waste time finding the area of each of the 10 sides; find the area of one octagonal face and one rectangular face instead. Once complete, multiply the area of the octagonal face by 2 and the area of the rectangular face by 8, add the products together, and you're done! The same is true for other 3-D shapes such as rectangular solids (including cubes), other right prisms, and certain pyramids.

If you're ready to test your knowledge of 3-D shapes, check out the next question.

6. Desiree is making apple juice from concentrate. The cylindrical container of concentrate has a diameter of 7 centimeters and a height of 12 centimeters. To make the juice, the concentrate must be diluted with water so that the mix is 75% water and 25% concentrate. If Desiree wishes to store all of the prepared juice in one cylindrical pitcher that has a diameter of 10 centimeters, what must its minimum height in centimeters be (rounded to the nearest centimeter)?

Work through the Kaplan Method for Math step-by-step to solve this question. The following table shows Kaplan's strategic thinking on the left, along with suggested math scratchwork on the right.

Strategic Thinking	Math Scratchwork
Step 1: Read the question, identifying and organizing important information as you go You need to find the minimum height of a pitcher with a diameter of 10 centimeters that can hold the entire amount of juice after it has been properly mixed.	
Step 2: Choose the best strategy to answer the question Before finding the height of the pitcher, you'll need to determine the volume of the juice after it has been mixed with the water. Determine the volume of concentrate Desiree has, then multiply this amount by 4 (because the concentrate only makes up 25% of the new juice volume) to calculate the post-dilution volume. Use the volume formula again to find the minimum height of the juice pitcher.	$d_{conc} = 7 \rightarrow r_{conc} = 3.5$ $V_{conc} = \pi r^2 h$ $\quad = \pi \times 3.5^2 \times 12$ $\quad = 147\pi$ $V_{dil} = 4 \times 147\pi = 588\pi$ $d_{pitcher} = 10 \rightarrow r_{pitcher} = 5$ $588\pi = \pi \times 5^2 \times h$ $\quad h = \dfrac{588\pi}{25\pi} \approx 23.52$
Step 3: Check that you answered the _right_ question Round to the nearest centimeter, and you're done!	24

✔ **Note**

Double-check your rounding on questions like this: Make sure you've rounded to the correct place _and_ done so correctly.

Now you'll have a chance to try a few more test-like geometry problems in a scaffolded way. We've provided some guidance, but you'll need to fill in the missing parts of explanations or the step-by-step math in order to get to the correct answer. Don't worry—after going through the worked examples at the beginning of this section, these problems should be completely doable.

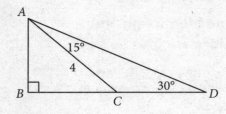

7. Given $\triangle ABC$ and $\triangle ABD$ above, what is the perimeter of $\triangle ACD$?

A) $2\sqrt{6} - 2\sqrt{2}$

B) $4\sqrt{3}$

C) $4 + 2\sqrt{6} + 2\sqrt{2}$

D) $2\sqrt{6} + 6\sqrt{2}$

Use the following scaffolding as your map through the question. Fill in the blanks in the table as you work from top to bottom.

Strategic Thinking	Math Scratchwork
Step 1: Read the question, identifying and organizing important information as you go You need to find the perimeter of $\triangle ACD$.	
Step 2: Choose the best strategy to answer the question Look for unknown values that you can derive from the information in the question stem. For instance, you can find the measure of $\angle ACD$ from the two given angles. From there you can easily determine the measures of the angles in $\triangle ABC$. Fill in the blanks on the right as you go. Notice that both $\triangle ABC$ and $\triangle ABD$ have special characteristics. Use these to determine the length of each missing side. Once again, update the figure on the right as you work. $\overline{BD}$ is the sum of $\overline{BC}$ and $\overline{CD}$. Subtract $\overline{BC}$ from $\overline{BD}$ to find $\overline{CD}$. Once you find all three sides of $\triangle ACD$, add them together to find its perimeter.	$m\angle ACD = \underline{\quad}° - \underline{\quad}° - \underline{\quad}°$ 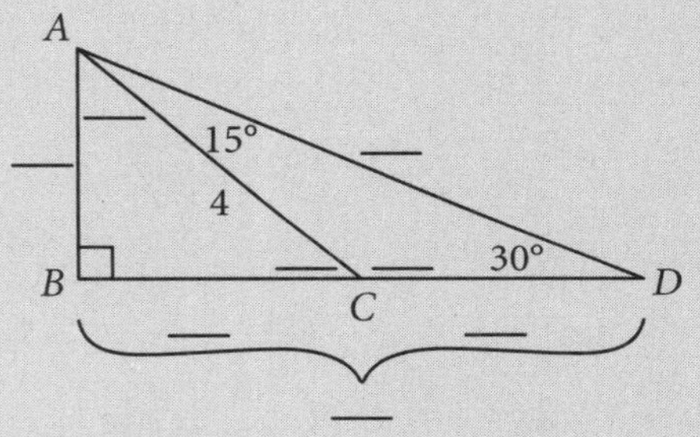 $= \underline{\quad}°$ (figure: triangle with vertices A, B, C, D; angle $15°$ at A, length 4, angle $30°$ at D, right angle at B) $ABC: \underline{\quad} - \underline{\quad} - \underline{\quad}$ $ABD: \underline{\quad} - \underline{\quad} - \underline{\quad}$ $\overline{CD} = \underline{\quad} - \underline{\quad} = \underline{\quad}$ $P_{ACD} = \underline{\quad} + (\underline{\quad}) + \underline{\quad}$ $= \underline{\quad}$
Step 3: Check that you answered the *right* question If you got (C), you are correct!	$\underline{\qquad}$

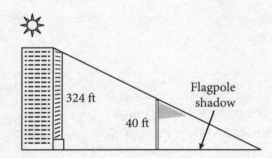

8. The diagram above shows a 40-foot flagpole and its shadow in relation to a nearby building that is 324 feet tall. If the flagpole's shadow is 50% longer than the flagpole itself, how far is the building from the flagpole?

The following table can help you structure your thinking as you go about solving this problem. Kaplan's strategic thinking is provided, as are bits of structured scratchwork. If you're not sure how to approach a question like this, start at the top and work your way down.

Strategic Thinking	Math Scratchwork
Step 1: Read the question, identifying and organizing important information as you go You're asked to find the distance between the building and the flagpole.	
Step 2: Choose the best strategy to answer the question You have a pair of similar triangles. Once you find the length of the flagpole's shadow using the percentage given, you can use a proportion to find the distance between the building and the flagpole. There are a couple of different ways you can write your proportion. Follow the rules for assembling a proportion (see chapter 5 for a refresher), and you'll be in good shape. Don't forget to subtract the length of the shadow from the horizontal leg of the large triangle after solving the proportion!	flagpole shadow: ____ × ____ = ____ $\frac{\quad}{\quad} = \frac{\quad}{\quad}$ $\frac{\quad}{\quad} = \frac{\quad}{\quad}$ $\frac{\quad}{\quad} = \frac{\quad}{\quad}$ ____ − ____ = ____
Step 3: Check that you answered the *right* question If you got 426 feet, congrats! You're correct.	____

Math

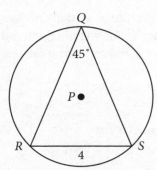

Note: Figure not drawn to scale.

9. In circle *P* above, *RS* = 4 and ∠*RQS* measures 45°. What is the circumference of circle *P*?

    A) 4π

    B) $4\pi\sqrt{2}$

    C) 8π

    D) $8\pi\sqrt{2}$

Use the scaffolding that follows as your map through the question. Fill in the blanks in the table as you work from top to bottom.

Strategic Thinking	Math Scratchwork
Step 1: Read the question, identifying and organizing important information as you go You need to find the circumference of circle *P*.	
Step 2: Choose the best strategy to answer the question Pay attention to the note below the figure. The shapes are not drawn to scale, and although it looks like it, all the angles in the triangle are not 45° (they can't be because the sum wouldn't be 180°). You'll need to draw in a couple of additional lines to reveal a more useful triangle. Once done, use your knowledge of subtended arcs to determine a special property of your new triangle. The legs of your new triangle are radii of the circle, so they are congruent. Use this and the fact that *RS* = 4 to determine the radius and then the circumference of the circle.	 *(figure: circle P with inscribed triangle QRS, 45° angle at Q, center P marked, RS = 4)* △ _____ is a _____-_____-_____ triangle
Step 3: Check that you answered the *right* question Did you get (B)? If so, you're absolutely right!	 _____

10. Brian wants to inflate several beach balls for a pool party. Each ball has a diameter of 66 centimeters, and Brian can exhale 6 liters (L) of air per full breath into a ball. Given that 1 L = 1,000 cm^3, approximately how many full breaths will Brian use to fully inflate three of these beach balls?

A) 25

B) 75

C) 151

D) 201

Work through the Kaplan Method for Math step-by-step to solve this question. The following table shows Kaplan's strategic thinking on the left, along with suggested math scratchwork on the right.

Strategic Thinking	Math Scratchwork
Step 1: Read the question, identifying and organizing important information as you go You must find the number of full breaths Brian will need to inflate three beach balls. You're given some useful facts and an equation. Also note the word "approximately"; you'll eventually need to round π.	
Step 2: Choose the best strategy to answer the question Start by finding the volume of one beach ball. Take care to find the radius and avoid the trap of using the diameter in your calculations. Use the given relationship, 1 L = 1,000 cm^3 = 6 full breaths, to convert to the desired units. Be careful; you're asked for the number of breaths for three beach balls, not one. Triple the number of breaths from the last calculation.	$V_{sphere} = \underline{\quad}$ $d = \underline{\quad} \rightarrow r = \underline{\quad}$ $V = \underline{\quad} \times (\underline{\quad})^3 = \underline{\quad}$ cm^3 $\underline{\quad}$ cm$^3 \times \dfrac{1\,L}{1,000\ cm^3} \times \dfrac{1\,breath}{\underline{\quad}\ L}$ $= \underline{\quad}$ breaths $\underline{\quad} \times 3 = \underline{\quad}$ breaths
Step 3: Check that you answered the *right* question Did you get (B)? If so, you're absolutely right.	$\underline{\quad}$

Now that you've seen the variety of ways in which the SAT can test your geometry skills, try the following questions to check your understanding. Give yourself 5 minutes to answer the following four questions. Make sure you use the Kaplan Method for Math as often as you can. Remember, you want to emphasize speed and efficiency in addition to simply getting the correct answer.

11. During a camping trip, Aundria and Annette decide to climb a mountain using two different routes to the top. Aundria takes the hiking route that travels 5 miles south, 6 miles east, 7 miles south, and 2 miles west to the summit; Annette uses the climbing route that starts at the same point as the hiking route but goes directly from there to the summit. Assuming vertical travel distance is not considered, about how many miles in all will the two travel?

   A) 32.65

   B) 33.42

   C) 34.00

   D) 34.42

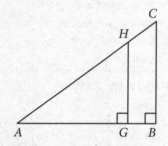

Note: Figure not drawn to scale.

12. $\triangle ABC$ above has an area of 150 square units. If $\overline{AB} = \overline{AH} = 20$, then what is the length of $\overline{HG}$?

   A)   5

   B) 12

   C) 16

   D) 20

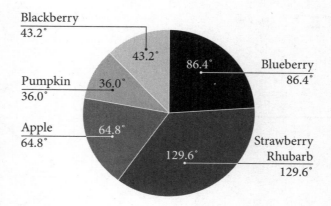

13. After the local Pie-Athon, John brought home several different kinds of pie in a single 10-inch diameter pie tin. The portion that each type of pie takes up in the tin is shown above. What is the area, in square inches, of the portion of leftover pie that is not strawberry rhubarb?

    A) 9π

    B) 16π

    C) 36π

    D) 64π

14. Marcus has a square sandbox measuring 24 feet across that is currently one-third full of sand from the bottom up. He purchases 96 cubic feet of sand, which, when added to the box, will completely fill it. How many inches deep is the sandbox?

    A) 2

    B) 3

    C) 4

    D) 5

Answers & Explanations for this chapter begin on page 949.

EXTRA PRACTICE

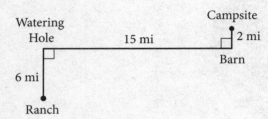

1. A tourist ranch built the horse-riding trail shown in the figure. The trail takes a rider from the ranch to an old watering hole, then to a historic barn, and finally to a campsite where riders can spend the night. If a rider took a horse on a direct path from the ranch to the campsite, how much shorter, in miles, would the trip be?

   A)   6

   B)   8

   C) 17

   D) 23

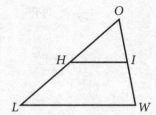

Note: Figure not drawn to scale.

2. Triangle *LOW* is shown in the figure above, where $\overline{HI}$ is the bisector of both $\overline{LO}$ and $\overline{OW}$. Given that $\overline{LW} = 30$ and $\overline{HI} = 4x - 1$, what is the value of x?

   A) 3.5

   B) 4

   C) 7.75

   D) 8

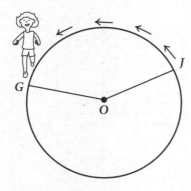

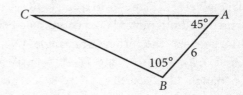

3. Cherie is jogging around a circular track. She started at point *J* and has jogged 200 yards to point *G*. If the radius of the track is 120 yards, what is the measure to the nearest tenth of a degree of minor angle *JOG*?

A) 95.5

B) 98.2

C) 102.1

D) 105.4

4. Alma pours water into a small cylindrical glass with a height of 6 inches and a diameter of 3 inches. The water fills the glass to the very top, so she decides to pour it into a bigger glass that is 8 inches tall and 4 inches in diameter. Assuming Alma doesn't spill any when she pours, how many inches high will the water reach in the bigger glass?

A) 1.5

B) 2.25

C) 3.375

D) 6.0

5. What is the area of the triangle shown in the figure?

A) $18\sqrt{3}$

B) $9 + 9\sqrt{3}$

C) $9 + 18\sqrt{3}$

D) $18 + 18\sqrt{3}$

$$x^2 + y^2 + 8x - 20y = 28$$

6. What is the diameter of the circle given by the equation above?

A) 12

B) 24

C) 28

D) 56

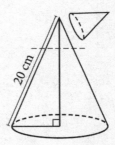

7. The height of the cone shown above is 16 centimeters. If the top quarter of the cone's height is cut off and discarded, what will be the volume in cubic centimeters of the remaining solid?

A) 192π

B) 576π

C) 756π

D) 768π

8. Triangle *ANT* is similar to triangle *BUG*, which are both plotted on a coordinate plane (not shown). The vertices of triangle *ANT* are $A(3, 2)$, $N(3, -1)$, and $T(-1, -1)$. Two of triangle *BUG*'s vertices are $(-8, -3)$ and $(8, -3)$. If vertex B is in the same quadrant of the coordinate plane as vertex A, what is the y-coordinate of vertex B?

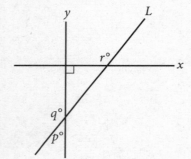

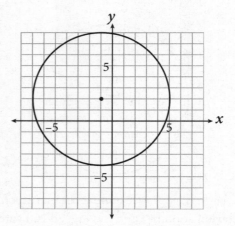

10. Which of the following represents the equation of the circle shown above?

    A) $(x - 1)^2 + (y + 2)^2 = 6$

    B) $(x + 1)^2 + (y - 2)^2 = 6$

    C) $(x - 1)^2 + (y + 2)^2 = 36$

    D) $(x + 1)^2 + (y - 2)^2 = 36$

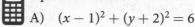

9. In the figure above, if $q = 140$, what is the value of $r - p$?

    A) 0

    B) 10

    C) 90

    D) 130

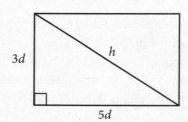

11. In the figure above, the diagonal of the rectangle has length h. What is the value of h in terms of d?

    A) d

    B) $4d$

    C) $\sqrt{34d}$

    D) $d\sqrt{34}$

12. If △*OLD* is similar to △*NEW*, and the ratio of the length of $\overline{OL}$ to $\overline{NE}$ is 7:4, which of the following ratios must also be equal to 7:4 ?

A) $\overline{OD}:\overline{EW}$

B) $m\angle D:m\angle W$

C) area of △*OLD* : area of △*NEW*

D) perimeter of △*OLD* : perimeter of △*NEW*

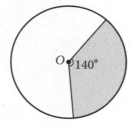

13. If the area of the shaded sector in circle *O* is 14π square units, what is the radius of the circle?

A) 6

B) 8

C) 9

D) 12

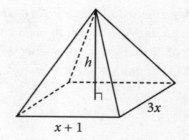

14. If the volume of the pyramid shown in the figure above can be represented by the function $V(x) = x^3 - x$, which of the following expressions represents the height?

A) x

B) $2x$

C) $x - 1$

D) $x - 3$

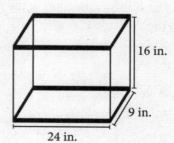

15. A pet store just decided to sell fish, so the manager purchased 50 of the fish tanks shown above to hold the fish. The staff need to fill the bottom two inches of each tank with sand, which comes in bags of 40 pounds. If 1 cubic inch of sand weighs about 2 ounces, how many bags of sand does the pet store need to buy? (There are 16 ounces in 1 pound.)

A) 45

B) 68

C) 84

D) 125

16. Two rectangles, *LION* and *PUMA*, are similar. Rectangle *LION* has a length of 86 units and a width of 52 units. If the perimeter of rectangle *PUMA* is 69 units, what is its width?

    A) 13

    B) 17.25

    C) 26

    D) 34.5

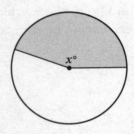

17. In the figure above, the ratio of the shaded area to the unshaded area is 4 to 5. What is the value of *x*?

    A) 135

    B) 145

    C) 160

    D) 170

18. The area of a right triangle is 35 square inches. If the longer leg is 3 inches longer than the shorter leg, what is the length of the hypotenuse in inches?

    A) 10

    B) $\dfrac{\sqrt{35}}{2}$

    C) $7\sqrt{10}$

    D) $\sqrt{149}$

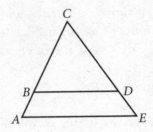

Note: Figure not drawn to scale.

19. In the figure above, $\overline{BD} \parallel \overline{AE}$ and $AB = 5$. If *BC* is three times *AB* and *CD* is 2 more than half *AC*, then what is the length of segment *DE*?

    A) 3

    B) 4

    C) 5

    D) 6

20. A yogurt factory fills cylindrical containers 80% of the way to the top, putting 6 ounces of yogurt in each cup. The containers are 4 inches tall and 2.5 inches wide. Approximately how many cubic inches of space does one ounce of yogurt take up?

    A) 2.1

    B) 2.6

    C) 3.3

    D) 4.2

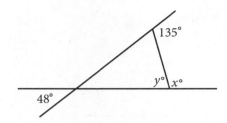

21. The sides of the triangle above have been extended as shown. What is the value in degrees of $x - y$?

    A) 3

    B) 6

    C) 87

    D) 180

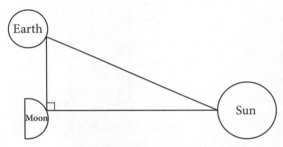

Note: Figure not drawn to scale.

22. The moon goes through several phases, such as new, crescent, quarter, and full. During the quarter phase, we see half the moon. During this phase, the sun (relative to Earth) forms a right angle with the moon, as shown in the figure above. If the distance from Earth to the moon is approximately 240,000 miles, and the distance from the moon to the sun is approximately 91,674,000 miles, how many miles are between Earth and the sun?

    A) 84,042,000

    B) 88,434,000

    C) 91,674,000

    D) 8,404,180,000

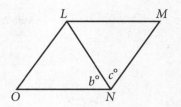

23. In the figure above, $\overline{LM} = \overline{MN} = \overline{NO} = \overline{OL} = \overline{LN}$. What is the value of $b - c$?

    A) −30

    B) 0

    C) 10

    D) 30

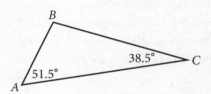

24. If the length of side $\overline{AB}$ in the triangle above is 28 centimeters and the length of $\overline{BC}$ is 45 centimeters, what is the length in centimeters of $\overline{AC}$?

    A) 35

    B) 45

    C) 53

    D) 64

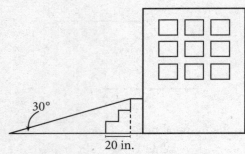

30°

20 in.

Note: Figure not drawn to scale.

25. A company designs removable handicapped-access ramps as temporary measures for buildings to become compliant with the Americans with Disabilities Act (ADA). The particular ramp shown in the figure must be placed at a 30° angle, eight feet from the bottom step. About how long, in inches, is the ramp? (There are 12 inches in 1 foot.)

A) 67

B) 116

C) 128

D) 134

26. The longer leg of a right triangle is three times the length of the shorter leg. Given that the length of each leg is a whole number, which of the following could be the length of the hypotenuse?

A) $\sqrt{40}$

B) $\sqrt{47}$

C) $\sqrt{55}$

D) $\sqrt{63}$

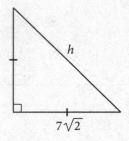

h

$7\sqrt{2}$

27. What is the value of h in the figure above?

A) 3.5

B) 7

C) 12.5

D) 14

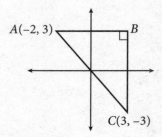

$A(-2, 3)$ B

$C(3, -3)$

28. Which angle has the smallest measure in the figure above?

A) Angle A

B) Angle B

C) Angle C

D) All three angles have equal measures.

29. If the vertices of a right triangle have coordinates $(-6, 4)$, $(1, 4)$, and $(1, -2)$, what is the length of the hypotenuse of the triangle?

A) 7

B) 8

C) $\sqrt{85}$

D) $5\sqrt{17}$

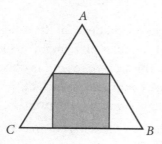

30. In the figure above, the shaded region is a square with an area of 12 square units, inscribed inside equilateral triangle ABC. What is the perimeter of triangle ABC?

A) $18\sqrt{3}$

B) $4 + \sqrt{3}$

C) $4 + 6\sqrt{3}$

D) $12 + 6\sqrt{3}$

31. What is the measure in degrees of the smallest angle of a triangle that has sides of length 1.5, $\dfrac{3\sqrt{3}}{2}$, and 3?

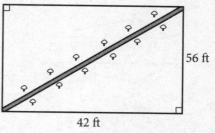

Note: Figure not drawn to scale.

32. A college has a sidewalk that cuts through a block of greenspace on the campus. To ensure student safety, the college decides to put lights along both sides of the sidewalk. If the lights should be placed 5 feet apart, as shown in the figure, how many lights does the college need?

33. Given that triangle DOG is congruent to triangle CAT, and that triangle CAT is congruent to triangle HEN, $\overline{OG}$ must be congruent to which of the following sides?

A) $\overline{CA}$

B) $\overline{CT}$

C) $\overline{EN}$

D) $\overline{HE}$

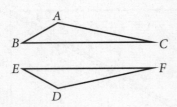

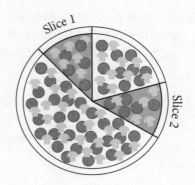

34. If $\angle A \cong \angle D$ and $\overline{AB} \cong \overline{DE}$ in the diagram above, what additional information is needed to prove $ABC \cong DEF$ by the ASA theorem?

   A) $\angle B \cong \angle E$

   B) $\angle C \cong \angle F$

   C) $\overline{AC} \cong \overline{DF}$

   D) $\overline{BC} \cong \overline{EF}$

35. Triangle BED is similar to triangle COT. Triangle COT has side lengths of 8, 15, and 17. Which of the following could be the side lengths of triangle BED?

   A) 3, 4, 5

   B) 5, 12, 13

   C) 10, 17, 19

   D) 24, 45, 51

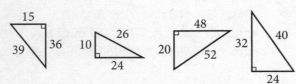

Note: Figure not drawn to scale.

36. What is the area, in square units, of the triangle that is not similar to the other three?

   A) 120

   B) 270

   C) 288

   D) 384

37. Four cuts are made from the center of a perfectly circular pizza to form Slice 1 and Slice 2. The arc lengths of the crusts of both slices are congruent. Which of the following statements regarding the two slices is true?

   A) The two slices may or may not be congruent, depending on the length of each side of each slice.

   B) The two slices may or may not be congruent, depending on the angle created by the cuts that were made.

   C) The two slices cannot be congruent because the side lengths of each slice cannot be the same length.

   D) The two slices must be congruent because the arc lengths are congruent and the side lengths of each slice are congruent.

Math

38. If $\triangle TIM \sim \triangle JOE$, $m\angle T = 40°$, and $m\angle I = 65°$, what is the measure of $\angle E$?

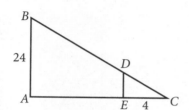

39. In the figure above, $\overline{DE} \parallel \overline{AB}$ and $\overline{DE} \perp \overline{AC}$. If $AE = 28$, what is the length of BD ?

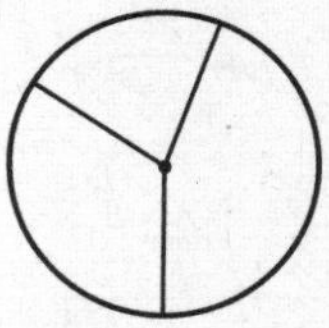

40. If the central angles in the circle shown above are in the ratio 4:3:2, what is the measure in degrees of the smallest angle?

A) 40

B) 60

C) 72

D) 80

41. What is the length, to the nearest inch, of an arc intercepted by a central angle of 135 degrees in a circle that has a radius of 12 inches?

A) 9

B) 16

C) 21

D) 28

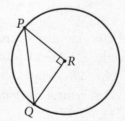

42. What is the length of chord PQ in the figure above if the radius of the circle is 4 centimeters?

A) 4

B) $4\sqrt{2}$

C) 8

D) $8\sqrt{2}$

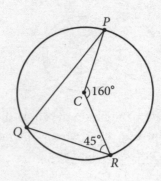

43. What is the measure of ∠QPC in the figure above?

   A) 25°

   B) 30°

   C) 35°

   D) 40°

44. At 2:15, the short hand of an analog clock lines up exactly with the 11-minute tick mark, and the long hand lines up with the 15-minute tick mark. What central angle do the hands form at 2:15?

   A) 18°

   B) 20°

   C) 24°

   D) 28°

45. Which system of equations has no solution?

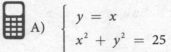

   A) $\begin{cases} y = x \\ x^2 + y^2 = 25 \end{cases}$

   B) $\begin{cases} y = x + 6 \\ x^2 + y^2 = 9 \end{cases}$

   C) $\begin{cases} y = x - 4 \\ x^2 + y^2 = 16 \end{cases}$

   D) $\begin{cases} y = x + 8 \\ x^2 + y^2 = 100 \end{cases}$

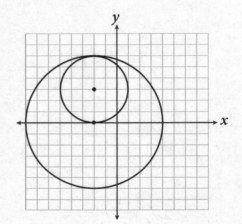

46. If the area of the smaller circle shown above is 144π square units, then what is the equation of the larger circle?

   A) $(x + 2)^2 + y^2 = 36$

   B) $(x + 2)^2 + (y - 3)^2 = 9$

   C) $(x + 8)^2 + (y - 12)^2 = 144$

   D) $(x + 8)^2 + y^2 = 576$

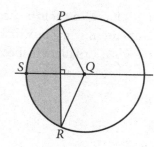

47. If the measure of $\angle PQR$ in the figure above is 120°, and the radius of the circle is 4 units, what is the area in square units of the shaded portion of the circle?

A) $\dfrac{4\pi}{3} - 8\sqrt{3}$

B) $\dfrac{5\pi}{3} - 4\sqrt{3}$

C) $\dfrac{8\pi}{3} - 4\sqrt{3}$

D) $\dfrac{16\pi}{3} - 4\sqrt{3}$

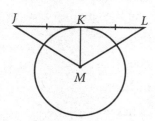

48. In the figure above, $\overline{JL}$ is tangent to circle M at point K. If the area of the circle is 36π, and $JL = 16$, what is the length of $\overline{LM}$?

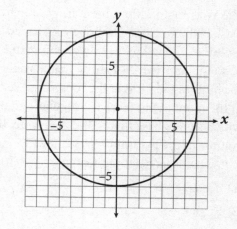

49. If the equation of the circle shown above is written in the form $x^2 + y^2 + ax + by = c$, what is the value of $a + b + c$?

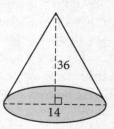

50. What is the volume in cubic units of the solid shown above?

A) 252π

B) 588π

C) $1,764\pi$

D) $2,352\pi$

51. The Washington Monument in Washington, D.C., is the world's tallest obelisk-shaped building. The tall part of the monument is a rectangular prism-like shape that is wider at the bottom than it is at the top. At the very top of the monument, there is a regular pyramid with a square base that is 34.5 feet wide. If the volume of the pyramid top is 21,821.25 cubic feet, what is its height in feet?

A)   6.1

B)   18.3

C)   55.0

D)   210

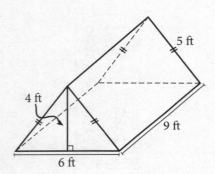

52. The figure above represents a camping tent that will be sprayed using a waterproofing agent. If it takes 1 ounce of the agent to cover 3 square feet, how many ounces will it take to spray the entire tent, inside and outside, including the tent bottom and its front door flaps?

A)   56

B)   112

C)   168

D)   336

53. What is the volume, in cubic inches, of a cubical cardboard moving box that has a surface area of 1,176 square inches?

A)   84

B)   196

C)   1,176

D)   2,744

54. One of the three most expensive cheeses in the world is a Swedish cheese made from moose milk, which sells for about $500 a pound. Suppose a moose cheesemaker produces his cheese in rectangular blocks, each with a volume of 576 cubic inches. Customers or restaurants can buy this cheese in increments of $\frac{1}{8}$ blocks. One day, a customer buys $\frac{1}{8}$ of a block and a restaurant buys $\frac{1}{2}$ of a block. If the height of a cheese block is always 8 inches and the width is always 6 inches, what is the difference in the lengths of the two purchases?

A)   4.5 inches

B)   6 inches

C)   7.6 inches

D)   12 inches

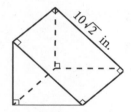

55. A solid wood cube is cut perfectly in half diagonally from corner to corner, as shown above, to be used as chocks, which are wedges placed behind wheels of vehicles to prevent them from rolling. What is the volume in cubic inches of one of these chocks?

A)   10

B)   100

C)   500

D)   1,000

56. Rupert has a collection of Blu-ray discs he wants to store in a cubical box with edges of length 10 inches. If each Blu-ray has dimensions of 5 inches by 5 inches by $\frac{1}{4}$ inch, what is the maximum number of discs that can fit into the box?

A)   60

B)   80

C)   120

D)   160

57. A medical test tube is made up of a cylinder with a half-sphere on the bottom. The volume in square inches of the tube is $\frac{19}{12}\pi$. The diameter of the cylinder (and the half-sphere) is 1 inch. How tall in inches is the test tube?

A)   4.75

B)   5

C)   6

D)   6.5

58. The roof of a certain bell tower is in the shape of a square pyramid with a length and width of 20 feet and a slant height of 18 feet. The roof needs new shingles, which are 72 square inches in size. The shingles must overlap so that water doesn't leak between the seams. What is the minimum number of shingles needed to cover the roof, assuming 20% extra to account for the overlap?

A)   432

B)   518

C)   1,440

D)   1,728

59. The opening of a perfectly circular sewer tunnel has a circumference of 8π. The tunnel has a volume of $2,048\pi$ cubic feet. How many feet long is the tunnel?

60. The length, width, and height of a rectangular prism are in the ratio 4:2:1 (in that order). If the volume of the prism is 216 cubic inches, how many inches wide is the prism?

CHAPTER 12

Imaginary Numbers and Trigonometry

CHAPTER OBJECTIVES

By the end of this chapter, you will be able to:

1. Perform arithmetic operations on imaginary and complex numbers

2. Solve equations that have imaginary solutions

3. Use trigonometric ratios to calculate sides of right triangles

4. Convert between degrees and radians

SMARTPOINTS

Point Value	SmartPoint Category
10 Points	Imaginary Numbers
10 Points	Trigonometry

Math

IMAGINARY NUMBERS AND TRIGONOMETRY

Chapter 12

Homework

Extra Practice: #1-16

Key

  Book Assignment

  Online Video Assignment

  Online Quiz Assignment

INTRODUCTION TO IMAGINARY NUMBERS

Until you reached more advanced math classes like Algebra 2 and Trigonometry, you were likely taught that it is impossible to take the square root of a negative number. There is some truth to this, as the result isn't a **real number**. What you get instead is an **imaginary number**.

To take the square root of a negative number, it is necessary to use i, which is defined in math as the square root of -1. Take $\sqrt{-49}$ as an example. To simplify this expression, rewrite $\sqrt{-49}$ as $\sqrt{-1 \times 49}$, take the square root of -1 (which is by definition i), and then take the square root of 49, which is 7. The end result is $7i$.

> ✔ **Expert Tip**
>
> The simplification $i^2 = \left(\sqrt{-1}\right)^2 \rightarrow i^2 = -1$ also comes in handy when working with imaginary numbers.

> ✔ **Note**
>
> Be particularly careful when multiplying two radicals that contain negative numbers. The first step is *always* to rewrite each quantity as the square root of the product of -1 and a positive number. Take the square root of -1 and then multiply the resulting expressions. For example, if you're asked to simplify $\sqrt{-16} \times \sqrt{-25}$, you must first rewrite the expression as $i\sqrt{16} \times i\sqrt{25}$, which becomes $4i \times 5i = 20i^2 = -20$. Combining the two radicals into one and canceling the negative signs to give $\sqrt{16 \times 25}$ is incorrect and will likely lead to a trap answer.

When a number is written in the form $a + bi$, where a is the real component and b is the imaginary component (and i is $\sqrt{-1}$), it is referred to as a **complex number**. The realm of complex numbers encompasses all numbers, including those that do not have an imaginary component (such as 5, π, and $\sqrt{2}$), in which case $b = 0$, and those that do not have a real component (such as $3i$), in which case $a = 0$. When writing complex numbers, the real part is typically written first, followed by the imaginary part.

Operations on Complex Numbers

You can add, subtract, multiply, and divide complex numbers just as you do real numbers.

- To add (or subtract) complex numbers, simply add (or subtract) the real parts and then add (or subtract) the imaginary parts.

- To multiply complex numbers, treat them as binomials and use FOIL. To simplify the product, use the simplification $i^2 = -1$ and combine like terms.

- To divide complex numbers, write them in fraction form and then rationalize the denominator (just as you would a fraction with a radical in the denominator) by multiplying top and bottom by the conjugate of the complex number in the denominator.

Math

Rationalizing the Denominator of a Complex Number

In chapter 8, you learned how to use the conjugate of an expression to rationalize a denominator; you can do this with complex numbers as well. Suppose you're asked to simplify the expression $\frac{21}{3 + 5i}$. The conjugate of $3 + 5i$ is $3 - 5i$, so you would multiply the expression by $\frac{3 - 5i}{3 - 5i}$. This is the same as multiplying by 1, so you're not changing the value of the expression. The result is this:

$$\frac{21}{3 + 5i} \times \frac{3 - 5i}{3 - 5i} = \frac{21(3 - 5i)}{(3 + 5i)(3 - 5i)} = \frac{63 - 105i}{9 - 25i^2}$$

You know $i^2 = -1$, so the expression simplifies to $\frac{63 - 105i}{9 - (25)(-1)} = \frac{63 - 105i}{34}$. To separate the complex expression into its real and imaginary components, you can write each of the terms in the numerator over the denominator in separate fractions, yielding $\frac{63}{34} - \frac{105}{34}i$.

Powers of *i*

When an imaginary number is raised to a power, you can use the pattern shown below to determine what the resulting term will be. Knowing the cycles of *i* will save you time on Test Day.

When you have ...	i^1	i^2	i^3	i^4
... it becomes:	i	$\sqrt{-1} \times \sqrt{-1} = -1$	$i^2 \times i = -i$	$i^2 \times i^2 = -1 \times -1 = 1$

When you have an imaginary number with *i* raised to an exponent greater than 4, divide the exponent by 4. The remainder will dictate what the *i* component will become. For example, if you're asked to simplify $-3i^{44}$, start by dividing 44 by 4. The quotient is 11 with a remainder of 0, meaning $i^{44} = (i^4)^{11} = 1^{11}$. Therefore, the expression $-3i^{44}$ becomes -3. Take $15i^{63}$ as another example. Divide 63 by 4 to get 15 with a remainder of 3. This means that $i^{63} = (i^4)^{15} \times i^3 = 1^{15}i^3$. Because $i^3 = -i$, $15i^{63}$ becomes $-15i$.

Math

Ready to try some test-like questions involving imaginary numbers? Check out the next few pages.

1. Which of the following is the correct simplification of the expression $(2i - 3) - (6 + 4i)$?

    A) $-9 - 2i$

    B) $-9 + 6i$

    C) $-7 - 4i$

    D) $3 + 6i$

Work through the Kaplan Method for Math step-by-step to solve this question. The following table shows Kaplan's strategic thinking on the left, along with suggested math scratchwork on the right.

Strategic Thinking	Math Scratchwork
Step 1: Read the question, identifying and organizing important information as you go You must correctly simplify the expression given.	
Step 2: Choose the best strategy to answer the question Use straightforward math to simplify. Distribute the negative sign and then combine like terms.	$(2i-3)-(6+4i)$ $2i-3-6-4i$ $-9-2i$
Step 3: Check that you answered the *right* question Choice (A) contains the correct simplification.	

✔ **Note**

Read carefully! Don't trust that both expressions in the parentheses have the real and imaginary components in the same order. Not checking the order means you risk falling for a trap answer.

Math

2. Which of the following is equal to $(17 + 7i)(3 - 5i)$? (Note: $i = \sqrt{-1}$)

   A) 16

   B) 86

   C) $16 - 64i$

   D) $86 - 64i$

Work through the Kaplan Method for Math step-by-step to solve this question. The following table shows Kaplan's strategic thinking on the left, along with suggested math scratchwork on the right.

Strategic Thinking	Math Scratchwork
Step 1: Read the question, identifying and organizing important information as you go You need to correctly simplify the given expression.	
Step 2: Choose the best strategy to answer the question Use FOIL as you did when multiplying regular binomials in chapter 10. Be careful when multiplying the two imaginary components together; i^2 will become -1.	$(17+7i)(3-5i)$ $=(17)(3)+(17)(-5i)+(7i)(3)+(7i)(-5i)$ $=51-85i+21i-35i^2$ $=51-64i-(35)(-1)$ $=51-64i+35$ $=86-64i$
Step 3: Check that you answered the _right_ question Choice (D) is equal to the original expression.	

3. Which of the following is equivalent to $\dfrac{6 + \sqrt{-8}}{3 + \sqrt{-18}}$?

   A) $\dfrac{10}{9}$

   B) $\dfrac{8}{3}$

   C) $\dfrac{2}{9} - \dfrac{4\sqrt{2}}{9}i$

   D) $\dfrac{10}{9} - \dfrac{4\sqrt{2}}{9}i$

Work through the Kaplan Method for Math step-by-step to solve this question. The following table shows Kaplan's strategic thinking on the left, along with suggested math scratchwork on the right.

Strategic Thinking	Math Scratchwork
Step 1: Read the question, identifying and organizing important information as you go You need to simplify the expression.	
Step 2: Choose the best strategy to answer the question Use caution in the first couple of steps. There's a negative under the radical in the denominator, as well as under the one in the numerator. Rewrite the expression with the negatives properly removed before rationalizing the denominator. No match in the answer choices? Look for a way to simplify your expression. Separate the real and imaginary components and then reduce the fractions.	$$\frac{6 + \sqrt{-8}}{3 + \sqrt{-18}} = \frac{6 + i\sqrt{8}}{3 + i\sqrt{18}}$$ conjugate of denominator: $3 - i\sqrt{18}$ $$\frac{6 + i\sqrt{8}}{3 + i\sqrt{18}} \times \frac{3 - i\sqrt{18}}{3 - i\sqrt{18}}$$ $$= \frac{6(3) + (6)(-i\sqrt{18}) + (i\sqrt{8})(3) + (i\sqrt{8})(-i\sqrt{18})}{3(3) + (3)(-i\sqrt{18}) + (i\sqrt{18})(3) + (i\sqrt{18})(-i\sqrt{18})}$$ $$= \frac{18 - 6i\sqrt{18} + 3i\sqrt{8} - i^2\sqrt{144}}{9 - 18i^2}$$ $$= \frac{18 - 6i\sqrt{9 \times 2} + 3i\sqrt{4 \times 2} - (-1)(12)}{9 - (18)(-1)}$$ $$= \frac{18 - 18i\sqrt{2} + 6i\sqrt{2} + 12}{9 + 18}$$ $$= \frac{30 - 12i\sqrt{2}}{27}$$ $$= \frac{30}{27} - \frac{12\sqrt{2}}{27}i = \frac{10}{9} - \frac{4\sqrt{2}}{9}i$$
Step 3: Check that you answered the *right* question You've correctly simplified the expression. Choice (D) is correct.	

Math

Great job persevering through that challenging question! As you saw, complex numbers follow the same rules of arithmetic that real numbers do.

Quadratic Equations That Have Imaginary Solutions

Chapter 10 showed you how to find the real solutions of a quadratic equation using a variety of techniques, including factoring, completing the square, using the quadratic formula, and graphing. This chapter will expand on that by showing you how to find imaginary solutions.

Recall that the quadratic formula is $x = \dfrac{-b \pm \sqrt{b^2 - 4ac}}{2a}$ and that the sign of the discriminant, $b^2 - 4ac$, dictates the nature of the solutions. When $b^2 - 4ac < 0$, the equation will have two imaginary solutions because you are taking the square root of a negative quantity.

Graphically, a quadratic equation has imaginary solutions when its vertex is above the x-axis and the parabola opens upward, or when its vertex is below the x-axis and the parabola opens downward. In either case, the graph does not cross the x-axis and therefore has no real solutions.

Let's try another test-like question.

4. What are the solutions to the equation $x^2 - 4x + 5 = 0$?

    A) 5, −1

    B) $2 \pm i$

    C) $2 \pm 3i$

    D) $-2 \pm i$

Work through the Kaplan Method for Math step-by-step to solve this question. The following table shows Kaplan's strategic thinking on the left, along with suggested math scratchwork on the right.

Strategic Thinking	Math Scratchwork
Step 1: Read the question, identifying and organizing important information as you go You're asked to identify the solutions (a.k.a. the *x*-intercepts) of the given equation.	
Step 2: Choose the best strategy to answer the question The x^2 term indicates a quadratic equation. Attempts to factor will reveal no pair of numbers that yields a product of 5 and a sum of -4. Because the numbers are fairly small, try completing the square. Start by subtracting 5 from each side of the equation. Divide b (the coefficient of the x term) by 2, square that result, and then add it to both sides. Rewrite the left side as the square of a binomial and take the square root of both sides. Don't fret about the negative sign; this equation just has imaginary solutions. Replace $\sqrt{-1}$ with i and solve for x.	*factors of* 5: 1, 5; $-1, -5$ $x^2 - 4x + 5 = 0$ $x^2 - 4x = -5$ $b = -4 \rightarrow \dfrac{-4}{2} = -2 \rightarrow (-2)^2 = 4$ $x^2 - 4x + 4 = -5 + 4$ $(x-2)^2 = -1$ $x - 2 = \pm\sqrt{-1}$ $x = 2 \pm i$
Step 3: Check that you answered the *right* question You've found the (imaginary) solutions to the equation, so you're done! Choice (B) is correct.	

✔ Note

You can also answer this question using the quadratic formula, but it might take more time, especially if a question like this is in the no-calculator section. Additionally, if it's in the calculator section, you can graph the equation to make sure the solutions really are imaginary (the graph will not touch or intersect the *x*-axis).

Working with Complex Numbers Using a Calculator

You can use your TI-83/84 to simplify challenging complex number expressions more quickly than you can by hand (if a question happens to be in the calculator section of the test).

Step 1: Press [MODE] and then scroll down to the row that starts with REAL. Highlight $a + bi$ and press [ENTER]. If you miss this step, you'll get an error message when you try to compute a complex expression.

```
NORMAL  SCI  ENG
FLOAT  0123456789
RADIAN  DEGREE
FUNC  PAR  POL  SEQ
CONNECTED  DOT
SEQUENTIAL  SIMUL
REAL  a+bi  re^θi
FULL  HORIZ  G-T
SET CLOCK 01/01/01 12:04AM
```

Step 2: Exit the mode screen and enter the expression you wish to simplify. Press [ENTER] when done. If you wish to convert decimal coefficients into fractions, press [MATH][ENTER][ENTER].

```
√(-4)
                        2i
(4-2i)/(4+2i)
                     .6-.8i
Ans▶Frac
              3/5-4/5i
```

> ✔ **Note**
>
> If you have an expression containing a fraction with imaginary components in the numerator and/or denominator, such as $\dfrac{4 - 2i}{4 + 2i}$, you need to be very careful. Enter the expression using parentheses: $(4 - 2i)/(4 + 2i)$.

INTRODUCTION TO TRIGONOMETRY

Although the word *trigonometry* comes from Greek words meaning "triangle" and "measure," some students fear the subject enough that they believe the word came from the Greek roots *trig*, meaning "designed," and *onometry*, meaning "to give high school students nightmares." Fortunately, any SAT trig questions you encounter won't be ludicrously difficult, and investing just a little time in studying this topic will give you a slight edge over your competition.

Trigonometric Ratios

You probably remember learning the acronym SOH CAH TOA, a mnemonic device for the sine, cosine, and tangent ratios. Check out the triangle and the table beneath for a summary of the ratios and what each equals for angle *A* in triangle *CAB*.

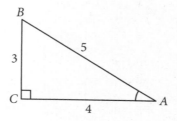

Sine (sin)	Cosine (cos)	Tangent (tan)
$\dfrac{\text{opposite}}{\text{hypotenuse}}$	$\dfrac{\text{adjacent}}{\text{hypotenuse}}$	$\dfrac{\text{opposite}}{\text{adjacent}}$
$\dfrac{3}{5}$	$\dfrac{4}{5}$	$\dfrac{3}{4}$

✔ **Note**

Related note: $\tan A = \dfrac{\sin A}{\cos A}$.

✔ **Note**

Alternate mnemonic: Some Old Hag Cracked All Her Teeth On Asparagus.

The Unit Circle

Up until now, you've likely been told that the trigonometric ratios are only applicable to right triangles; however, you can expand their utility to include angles greater than 90° by using the **unit circle**. The unit circle is a circle with a radius of 1 centered around the origin in the *xy*-plane. Below is such a circle containing an example triangle.

> ✔ **Note**
>
> An angle in the unit circle always begins with its radius on the positive side of the *x*-axis. As the angle measure increases, the radius moves counterclockwise through each quadrant. If you have a negative angle, the radius starts in the same spot but moves clockwise as the absolute value of the angle measure increases.

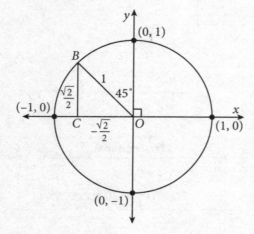

Suppose you were asked to determine sin 135° and cos 135°. Draw a radius at 135° (which is 45° past the *y*-axis in the second quadrant) and then add a vertical line from where the radius intersects the circle down to the *x*-axis. Because this radius ($\overline{OB}$) is within the unit circle, its length is 1. Triangle

OBC is a 45-45-90 triangle, so each of its legs has a length of $\frac{\sqrt{2}}{2}$. This means $\sin 135° = \dfrac{\frac{\sqrt{2}}{2}}{1} = \dfrac{\sqrt{2}}{2}$.

Note that because $\overline{OC}$ lies on the negative part of the *x*-axis, you should use $-\dfrac{\sqrt{2}}{2}$ as the "measure"

of the adjacent side. Therefore, $\cos 135° = \dfrac{-\frac{\sqrt{2}}{2}}{1} = -\dfrac{\sqrt{2}}{2}$. Notice that if you were to label point *B*

on the unit circle, its (*x, y*) coordinates would correspond to (cos 135°, sin 135°).

Radians

Most geometry questions present angle measures in degrees. In trigonometry, however, you will encounter a different unit: the radian. The prospect of learning a new unit shouldn't scare you, though; just remember that $180° = \pi$ radians. For instance, if you're asked to convert $90°$ into radians, use this relationship as a conversion factor with the factor-label method (refer to chapter 5 to brush up): $90° \times \dfrac{\pi}{180°} = \dfrac{\pi}{2}$. Note that there isn't a symbol for radians, so $\dfrac{\pi}{2}$ in trigonometry is read as "$\dfrac{\pi}{2}$ radians." This conversion works in the opposite direction as well: To convert radians to degrees, multiply by $\dfrac{180°}{\pi}$.

✔ **Note**

Most graphing calculators have both degree and radian modes. Make sure you're in the correct mode when working on trigonometry questions!

Here is a handy unit circle diagram with common degree and radian measures (and the coordinates of the ends of their respective radii) that you're likely to see on Test Day.

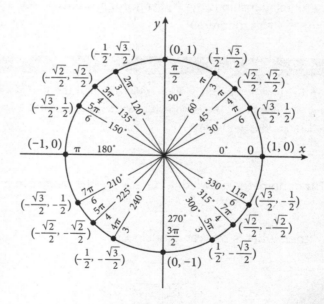

✔ **Note**

The coordinates at a particular angle measure translate into the leg lengths of the triangle created when a vertical line is drawn from the end of the radius down (or up if you're in quadrant III or IV) to the x-axis. For example, at $60°$, the horizontal leg has a length of $\dfrac{1}{2}$, and the vertical leg has a length of $\dfrac{\sqrt{3}}{2}$.

Benchmark Angles

Knowing the trig functions for the most commonly tested "benchmark" angles (multiples of 30° and 45°) will save time on Test Day. You will not be asked to evaluate trig functions for angles that require a calculator.

Other Trig Relationships

Complementary angles have a special relationship relative to sine and cosine.

- $\sin x = \cos\left(\dfrac{\pi}{2} - x\right)$ or $\sin x = \cos(90° - x)$

- $\cos x = \sin\left(\dfrac{\pi}{2} - x\right)$ or $\cos x = \sin(90° - x)$

In plain English, this translates as: The sine of an acute angle is equal to the cosine of the angle's complement and vice versa. To see some examples, look at the first quadrant of the unit circle: $\cos 30° = \sin 60°$, $\cos 45° = \sin 45°$, and $\cos 60° = \sin 30°$. Understanding how trig functions of complementary angles work can help you learn the unit circle and answer trig questions on Test Day.

Another particularly useful relationship is the **Pythagorean identity**: $\sin^2 x + \cos^2 x = 1$. (Notice that it resembles the Pythagorean theorem.)

✔ **Note**

Note that $\sin^2 x$ is *not* the same as $\sin x^2$. The former dictates that the sine of x is squared, but the latter indicates finding the sine of x^2. The exponent is written between the trigonometric function and the variable to eliminate this ambiguity.

Ready to test your SAT trigonometry knowledge? Check out the next several pages for some test-like questions.

5.   If $\tan x = \dfrac{7}{24}$, then what is the value of $\sin x$?

Work through the Kaplan Method for Math step-by-step to solve this question. The following table shows Kaplan's strategic thinking on the left, along with suggested math scratchwork on the right.

Strategic Thinking	Math Scratchwork
Step 1: Read the question, identifying and organizing important information as you go You need to find the value of sin x.	
Step 2: Choose the best strategy to answer the question If $\tan x = \dfrac{7}{24}$, then the sides that are opposite and adjacent to angle x must be 7 and 24, respectively. Draw a diagram to reflect this. Because $\sin x = \dfrac{opp}{hyp}$, you'll need to find the length of the hypotenuse using the Pythagorean theorem. Once you calculate this, plug that value into the sine ratio.	$\tan x = \dfrac{opp}{adj}, \sin x = \dfrac{opp}{hyp}$ $7^2 + 24^2 = hyp^2$ $49 + 576 = hyp^2$ $625 = hyp^2$ $25 = hyp$
Step 3: Check that you answered the *right* question The value of sin x is $\dfrac{7}{25}$. Grid in $\dfrac{7}{25}$ or .28.	$\sin x = \dfrac{7}{25}$

✔ Expert Tip

The triangle in this question is another Pythagorean triplet (7-24-25). Although the 7-24-25 is not as common as the 3-4-5 and 5-12-13, knowing it means you can skip a Pythagorean theorem calculation (and save a few seconds).

Math

6. If cos x = sin y, then which of the following pairs of angle measures could not be the values of x and y?

A) $\dfrac{\pi}{4}, \dfrac{\pi}{4}$

B) $\dfrac{\pi}{6}, \dfrac{\pi}{3}$

C) $\dfrac{\pi}{8}, \dfrac{3\pi}{8}$

D) $\dfrac{\pi}{2}, \dfrac{\pi}{2}$

Work through the Kaplan Method for Math step-by-step to solve this question. The following table shows Kaplan's strategic thinking on the left, along with suggested math scratchwork on the right.

Strategic Thinking	Math Scratchwork
Step 1: Read the question, identifying and organizing important information as you go You need to determine which pair of angle measures do not satisfy the equation cos x = sin y.	
Step 2: Choose the best strategy to answer the question Complementary angles have a special relationship relative to trig values: The cosine of an acute angle is equal to the sine of the angle's complement and vice versa. The question states that cos x = sin x, and all the angles in the answer choices are acute angles, so you are looking for the pair that are *not* complementary angles. In degrees, complementary angles add up to 90, so in radians they must add up to $90° \times \dfrac{\pi}{180°} = \dfrac{\pi}{2}$. Add each pair of angles to see which one does not give the correct sum.	A: $\dfrac{\pi}{4} + \dfrac{\pi}{4} = \dfrac{2\pi}{4} = \dfrac{\pi}{2}$ B: $\dfrac{\pi}{6} + \dfrac{\pi}{3} = \dfrac{\pi}{6} + \dfrac{2\pi}{6} = \dfrac{3\pi}{6} = \dfrac{\pi}{2}$ C: $\dfrac{\pi}{8} + \dfrac{3\pi}{8} = \dfrac{4\pi}{8} = \dfrac{\pi}{2}$ (D): $\dfrac{\pi}{2} + \dfrac{\pi}{2} = \dfrac{2\pi}{2} = \pi$
Step 3: Check that you answered the *right* question The only pair of angles that are not complementary is (D).	

Now let's try a question that tests both your geometry skills and what you've learned about trig ratios. Remember, trig ratios apply to right triangles.

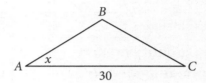

7. If the area of △ABC is 225 and $AB = 17$, then what is the value of cos x?

    A) $\dfrac{8}{17}$

    B) $\dfrac{8}{15}$

    C) $\dfrac{17}{30}$

    D) $\dfrac{15}{17}$

Work through the Kaplan Method for Math step-by-step to solve this question. The following table shows Kaplan's strategic thinking on the left, along with suggested math scratchwork on the right.

Strategic Thinking	Math Scratchwork
Step 1: Read the question, identifying and organizing important information as you go You're asked to calculate the value of cos *x*. You're given that $AB = 17$.	
Step 2: Choose the best strategy to answer the question The area of a triangle is half the product of the base and height, so draw in a height. Label the point at which the base and height intersect *D* to help keep things clear. Use the triangle area formula to find the height; you'll find that $BD = 15$. You now have two sides of a right triangle ($\triangle ABD$), but not necessarily the two sides you need. To find the value of cos *x*, you need the side adjacent to *x* and the hypotenuse. Here, you have the opposite side (*BD*) and the hypotenuse (*AB*), so you need to find the length of the third side (*AD*). You might recognize $\triangle ABD$ as an 8-15-17 Pythagorean triplet, but if not, use the Pythagorean theorem.	(triangle diagram: vertices A, B, C with height BD, $AB = 17$, angle x at A, $D\ 30$ along base) $A = \dfrac{1}{2}bh$ $225 = \dfrac{1}{2} \times 30h$ $225 = 15h$ $h = \dfrac{225}{15} = 15 = BD$ $AD^2 + 15^2 = 17^2$ $AD^2 = 17^2 - 15^2$ $AD^2 = 289 - 225$ $AD = \sqrt{64} = 8$
Step 3: Check that you answered the *right* question The question asks for cos *x*. Recall that $\cos x = \dfrac{\text{adjacent}}{\text{hypotenuse}}$. Thus, $\cos x = \dfrac{AD}{AB} = \dfrac{8}{17}$, (A).	$\cos x = \dfrac{\text{adj}}{\text{hyp}} = \dfrac{8}{17}$

Now you'll have a chance to try a couple of test-like questions. Some guidance is provided, but you'll need to fill in the missing parts of explanations or the step-by-step math in order to get to the correct answer. Don't worry—after going through the examples at the beginning of this chapter, these questions should be completely doable. If you're still struggling, review the worked examples in this chapter.

Many students ask when they'd need to use imaginary numbers in the real world. One field that commonly uses them is electrical engineering, as demonstrated below. Note that electrical engineers use j to represent $\sqrt{-1}$, as i is used to represent a different quantity in their field.

8. The voltage of an alternating current circuit is given by the formula $E = I \times Z$, where E is voltage in volts, I is current in amps, and Z is impedance (a type of resistance encountered with alternating current) in ohms. If a certain circuit has a voltage of $38 + 18j$ volts and an impedance of $4 + 6j$ ohms, what is the current, in amps, that passes through the circuit? (Note: $j = \sqrt{-1}$)

A) $\dfrac{11}{13} - 3j$

B) $5 - 3j$

C) $\dfrac{19}{2} + 3j$

D) $44 + 300j$

Use the following scaffolding as your map through the question, filling in the blanks in the table as you work from top to bottom.

Strategic Thinking	Math Scratchwork
Step 1: Read the question, identifying and organizing important information as you go You're asked to calculate the current of an alternating current circuit. The question provides an equation and the values of two of the variables in it.	
Step 2: Choose the best strategy to answer the question You know the voltage and impedance, so all you need to do is plug those values into the given equation and solve for current (I). Once there, determine the conjugate of the denominator and use it to eliminate the imaginary component from the denominator. If your answer isn't among the choices, remember that complex numbers can be broken into their real and imaginary components. Do this with your fraction and simplify.	$E = I \times Z$ $\underline{\hspace{2cm}} = I \times \underline{\hspace{2cm}}$ $I = \underline{\hspace{2cm}} \times \underline{\hspace{2cm}}$ $I = \underline{\hspace{3cm}}$ $I = \underline{\hspace{2.5cm}}$ $I = \underline{\hspace{2.5cm}}$ $I = \underline{\hspace{1.5cm}}$ $I = \underline{\hspace{1.5cm}} - \underline{\hspace{1.5cm}} j$ $I = \underline{\hspace{1.5cm}}$
Step 3: Check that you answered the *right* question Did you get (B)? If so, you're right!	$\underline{\hspace{2cm}}$

9. If the measure, in radians, of one acute angle in a right triangle is $\frac{\pi}{3}$, what is the measure of the other acute angle?

A) $\frac{\pi}{12}$

B) $\frac{\pi}{6}$

C) $\frac{\pi}{3}$

D) $\frac{2\pi}{3}$

Use the following scaffolding as your map through the question, filling in the blanks in the table as you work from top to bottom.

Strategic Thinking	Math Scratchwork
Step 1: Read the question, identifying and organizing important information as you go You're given the measure of one acute angle in a right triangle, and you need to find the measure of the other acute angle.	right triangle one acute angle has measure $\frac{\pi}{3}$ answers in radians
Step 2: Choose the best strategy to answer the question One angle in a right triangle has a measure of 90°, so the missing acute angle must have a measure of $90° - \frac{\pi}{3}$. The answer choices are all given in radians, so convert 90° to radians and then subtract. You'll need to find a common denominator to subtract.	$90° \times$ _____ = _____ in radians _____ $- \frac{\pi}{3}$ = ? _____ $-$ _____ = _____
Step 3: Check that you answered the *right* question Did you get (B)? If so, you're right.	_____

Now that you've seen the variety of ways in which the SAT can test you on imaginary numbers and trigonometry, try the following questions to check your understanding. Give yourself 4 minutes to answer the
following three questions. Make sure you use the Kaplan Method for Math as often as you can. Remember,
you want to emphasize speed and efficiency in addition to simply getting the correct answer.

10. When the complex number $(11 + 14i)^3$ is
expanded, simplified, and written in the
form $a + bi$ where a is the real component, b is the imaginary component, and
$i = \sqrt{-1}$, what is the value of b?

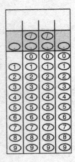

$$(x^4 + 84x^2 + 243)(x^2 + 5x - 36) = 0$$

11. Which of the following is not a solution
to the equation shown above?

A) $-9i$

B) $-\sqrt{3}i$

C) $3i$

D) $9i$

12. If $\sin x = \cos\left(\dfrac{13\pi}{6}\right)$, then which of the
following could be the value of x? (Assume
this question is in the no-calculator section
of the test.)

A) $\dfrac{\pi}{6}$

B) $\dfrac{\pi}{4}$

C) $\dfrac{\pi}{3}$

D) $\dfrac{\pi}{2}$

Answers and Explanations for this chapter begin
on page 966.

EXTRA PRACTICE

1. Which of the following is equivalent to $4i(5 - 7i)$? (Note: $i = \sqrt{-1}$)

   A) $-8i$

   B) $48i$

   C) $-28 + 20i$

   D) $28 + 20i$

2. Which of the following represents $\dfrac{1}{3-i}$ written in the form $a + bi$? (Note: $i = \sqrt{-1}$)

   A) $\dfrac{3}{10} + \dfrac{1}{10}i$

   B) $\dfrac{1}{3} - \dfrac{1}{i}$

   C) $\dfrac{3}{8} + \dfrac{1}{8}i$

   D) $3 + i$

3. Which of the following is equivalent to $(3 + 2i)^4$? (Note: $i = \sqrt{-1}$)

   A) 97

   B) $-119 + 120i$

   C) $5 + 12i$

   D) $81 - 16i$

4. Which of the following has the same value as $i^{14} + i^{122}$? (Note: $i = \sqrt{-1}$)

   A) i^{136}

   B) $2i^2$

   C) $2i^{136}$

   D) $(1 + i)(1 - i)$

5. What are the solutions over the complex number system to the equation $x^2 + 13 = 4x$? (Note: $i = \sqrt{-1}$)

   A) $-4 \pm 3i$

   B) $2 \pm 3i$

   C) $2 \pm 6i$

   D) $4 \pm 3i$

6. Which of the following shows the product $\left(2 + \sqrt{-9}\right)\left(-1 + \sqrt{-4}\right)$ written in the form $a + bi$? (Note: $i = \sqrt{-1}$)

   A) $-8 + i$

   B) $-8 - i$

   C) $4 + i$

   D) $4 - i$

7. Which of the following is equivalent to the complex number $\dfrac{1}{4 - 2i} + (3 + i)$? (Note: $i = \sqrt{-1}$)

   A) $\dfrac{4 + i}{4 - 2i}$

   B) $\dfrac{4 - i}{4 + 2i}$

   C) $\dfrac{15 - 2i}{4 - 2i}$

   D) $\dfrac{15 + 2i}{4 + 2i}$

8. The absolute value of a complex number
   $a + bi$ is defined as $\sqrt{a^2 + b^2}$. What is
   $|15 + 8i|$? (Note: $i = \sqrt{-1}$)

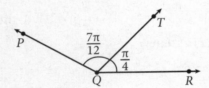

9. What is the measure in degrees of $\angle PQR$ shown above?

   A) 105

   B) 120

   C) 135

   D) 150

10. Which of the following angles has the same trigonometric values as 450°?

    A) 30°

    B) 45°

    C) 60°

    D) 90°

11. The cosine of which of the following angles is not equal to the cosine of the other three?

    A) −120

    B) −60

    C) 120

    D) 240

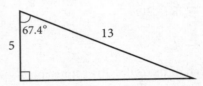

12. Based on the figure above, which of the following is true?

    A) $\sin 22.6° = \dfrac{5}{12}$

    B) $\sin 67.4° = \dfrac{5}{13}$

    C) $\cos 22.6° = \dfrac{5}{13}$

    D) $\cos 67.4° = \dfrac{5}{13}$

13. If $\sin x = \cos\left(\dfrac{\pi}{6}\right)$, then which of the following could not be the value of x?

    A) $\dfrac{\pi}{3}$

    B) $\dfrac{2\pi}{3}$

    C) $\dfrac{5\pi}{3}$

    D) $\dfrac{7\pi}{3}$

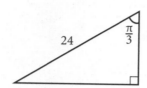

14. If the hypotenuse of the triangle shown above has length 24 units, what is the area in square units of the triangle?

    A) $72\sqrt{3}$

    B) $144\sqrt{3}$

    C) 288

    D) $288\sqrt{3}$

 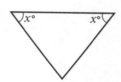

15. The triangle shown above is a cross section of a feeding trough that is 24 inches deep and whose top is 36 inches across. If $\cos x = B$, what is the value of B?

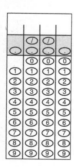

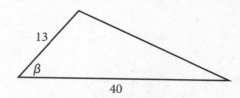

Note: Figure not drawn to scale.

16. If the area of the triangle shown above is 240 square inches, what is $\tan \beta$?

PART TWO

Evidence-Based Reading and Writing

UNIT SIX

Reading

BY THE END OF THIS UNIT, YOU WILL BE ABLE TO:

1. Apply the Kaplan Method for Reading Comprehension

2. Identify Reading Test question types and apply the appropriate strategies to correctly answer them

CHAPTER 13

The Kaplan Method for Reading Comprehension and Reading Test Passage Types

CHAPTER OBJECTIVES

By the end of this chapter, you will be able to:

1. Identify the three types of passages on the SAT Reading Test

2. Passage Map passages using the Kaplan Method for Reading Comprehension, identifying keywords and central ideas across passage types

3. Predict an answer and find its match among the answer choices using a Passage Map

SMARTPOINTS

Point Value	SmartPoint Category
Point Builder	The Kaplan Method for Reading Comprehension
Point Builder	Passage Mapping
Point Builder	U.S. and World Literature Passages
Point Builder	History/Social Studies Passages
Point Builder	Science Passages

THE KAPLAN METHOD FOR READING COMPREHENSION & READING TEST PASSAGE TYPES

Chapter 13

Homework

Extra Practice: #1-10

Even More

The Kaplan Method for Reading Comprehension

History/Social Studies Passages

Reading Quiz 1

Key

 Book Assignment

 Online Video Assignment

 Online Quiz Assignment

OVERVIEW OF THE SAT READING TEST PASSAGE TYPES

SAT Reading Test Passage Distribution	
U.S. and World Literature	1 passage; 10–11 questions
History/Social Studies	2 passages OR 1 passage and 1 paired-passage set; 10–11 questions each
Science	2 passages OR 1 passage and 1 paired-passage set; 10–11 questions each

It is imperative that you use the Kaplan Method for Reading Comprehension for every passage on the SAT Reading Test. Doing so ensures that you spend your time efficiently and maximize your opportunity to earn points.

THE KAPLAN METHOD FOR READING COMPREHENSION

The Kaplan Method for Reading Comprehension consists of three steps:

Step 1: Read actively

Step 2: Examine the question stem

Step 3: Predict and answer

Let's take a closer look at each step.

Step 1: Read actively

Active reading means:

• Ask questions and take notes *as* you read the passage. Asking questions about the passage and taking notes are integral parts of your approach to acing the SAT Reading Test.

You should ask questions such as:

• Why did the author write this word/detail/sentence/paragraph?

• Is the author taking a side? If so, what side is he or she taking?

• What are the tone and purpose of the passage?

Make sure you remember to:

- Identify the passage type.

- Take notes, circle keywords, and underline key phrases.

> ✔ **Expert Tip**
>
> Questions will range from general to specific. By using clues in the question stem to identify what the question is looking for, you will be better able to complete Step 3 of the Kaplan Method for Reading Comprehension.

Step 2: Examine the question stem

This means you should:

- Identify keywords and line references in the question stem.

- Apply question type strategies as necessary.

Step 3: Predict and answer

This means you should:

- Predict an answer before looking at the answer choices, also known as "predict before you peek."

- Select the best match.

Predicting before you peek helps you:

- Eliminate the possibility of falling into wrong answer traps.

PASSAGE MAPPING

Step 1 of the Kaplan Method for Reading Comprehension dictates that you must take notes as you read the passage. We call these notes a Passage Map because they guide you through the passage and will lead you to the correct answers.

> ✔ **On Test Day**
>
> A Passage Map should not replace the occasional underline or circle—it is important that you underline, circle, *and* take notes to create the most effective Passage Map.

Make sure you pay attention and take note of the following when you map the passage:

- The "why" or the central idea of the passage—in other words, the thesis statement

- Transitions or changes in direction in a passage's logic

- The author's opinions and other opinions the author cites

- The author's tone and purpose

While Passage Mapping may seem time-consuming at first, with practice it will become second nature by Test Day, and your overall SAT Reading Test timing will greatly improve because you'll spend less time searching the passage for answers to the questions.

Just as the passages span different genres, your approaches will also vary from subject to subject. The approach for each type of SAT Reading Test passage will be addressed in this chapter.

Now, let's look at the specific passage types individually.

U.S. AND WORLD LITERATURE PASSAGES

There will be a single U.S. and World Literature passage on the SAT. It is different from the other passages because:

- There will be multiple characters and, therefore, multiple opinions.
- The tone will be nuanced and emotion-based, rather than informative or explanatory.

As you read a U.S. and World Literature passage, you should:

1. Identify the characters and evaluate how the author describes them
   - What do the characters want?
   - What are the characters doing?
   - What adjectives describe each character?

2. Assess the characters' opinions of each other and themselves
   - Do they like each other? Dislike each other?
   - Why does each character make a particular decision or take a particular course of action?
   - What do these decisions or actions tell you about a character?

3. Identify the themes of the story
   - What are the "turning points" in the passage?
   - Is there a moral to the story?

Let's look at the following example of an abbreviated U.S. and World Literature passage and question set. After the mapped passage, the left column contains questions similar to those you'll see on the SAT Reading Test on Test Day. The column on the right features the strategic thinking a test expert employs when approaching the passage and questions presented. Note how a test expert can quickly condense the entire passage into a few words, and use his or her Passage Map to ask questions that build a prediction for the correct answer.

Strategic Thinking
Step 1: Read actively
Read the passage and the notes provided. Remember, a well-crafted Passage Map should summarize the central idea of each paragraph as well as important topics or themes. Your notes for U.S. and World Literature passages should focus on characters. Use your Passage Map to help you answer each question.

Questions 1-2 are based on the following passage.

The following passage is an excerpt from English novelist and poet Thomas Hardy's *Tess of the D'Urbervilles*, published in 1891.

The women—or rather girls, for they were mostly young—wore drawn cotton bonnets with great flapping curtains to keep off the sun, and
Line gloves to prevent their hands being wounded by
(5) the stubble. There was one wearing a pale pink jacket, another in a cream-coloured, tight-sleeved gown, another in a petticoat as red as the arms of a reaping-machine; and others, older in the brown-rough "wropper," or over-all—the old-established
(10) and most appropriate dress of the field-woman, which the young ones were abandoning. This morning, the eye returns involuntarily to the girl in the pink cotton jacket, she being the most flexuous and finely-drawn figure of them all. But her bonnet
(15) is pulled so far over her brow that none of her face is disclosed while she binds, though her complexion may be guessed from a stray twine or two of dark brown hair which extends below the curtain of her bonnet. Perhaps one reason why she seduces
(20) casual attention is that she never courts it, though the other women often gaze around them.

Her binding proceeds with clock-like monotony. From the sheaf last finished she draws a handful of ears, patting their tips with her left palm to bring
(25) them even. Then, stooping low, she moves forward, gathering the corn with both hands against her knees and pushing her left gloved hand under the bundle to meet the right on the other side, holding the corn in an embrace like that of a lover. She
(30) brings the ends of the bond together and kneels on the sheaf while she ties it, beating back her skirts now and then when lifted by the breeze. A bit of her naked arm is visible between the buff leather of the gauntlet and the sleeve of her gown; and as
(35) the day wears on, its feminine smoothness becomes scarified by the stubble and bleeds.

At intervals she stands up to rest, and to retie her disarranged apron, or to pull her bonnet straight. Then one can see the oval face of a handsome
(40) young woman with deep, dark eyes and long, heavy, clinging tresses, which seem to clasp in a beseeching way anything they fall against. The cheeks are paler, the teeth more regular, the red lips thinner than is usual in a country-bred girl.

¶1: girls work in fields; one stands out

¶2: girl's system for work

¶3: girl is pretty; not usual country girl (theme)

Questions	Strategic Thinking
1. The passage is best described as A) a psychological study of a character's personality. B) a sweeping portrait of nature in autumn. C) a drab rendering of a farmland routine. D) a gradual focusing on a single individual.	**Step 2: Examine the question stem** Identify the key words and phrases in the question stem. The phrase "passage is best described as" implies that you are looking for a description of the passage as a whole. Use your Passage Map notes to find the author's central theme. **Step 3: Predict and answer** Although the passage begins with a general description of many women doing agricultural labor, the majority of the passage focuses on the features and actions of one young woman. Choice (D) is correct.
2. The activity described in lines 22-29 ("Her binding ... of a lover") seems indicative of A) routine. B) memory. C) necessity. D) optimism.	**Step 2: Examine the question stem** Identify the key words and phrases in the question stem. The word "activity" and the line reference indicate you should look at your Passage Map notes surrounding those lines. **Step 3: Predict and answer** Lines 22-29 include the phrase "clock-like monotony" (line 22) and the Passage Map note says, "girl's system for work." In this context, "system" is synonymous with "routine." Choice (A) is correct.

HISTORY/SOCIAL STUDIES PASSAGES

The History/Social Studies portion of the SAT Reading Test will consist of either two single History/Social Studies passages or one single History/Social Studies passage and one History/Social Studies paired-passage set. History/Social Studies passages are different from other passage types because:

- The passage will have a clearly stated topic, a well-defined scope, and a specific purpose.

- There will be at least one primary source passage that uses antiquated language.

> ✔ **Expert Tip**
>
> Some paragraphs are longer than others. If you are mapping a very long paragraph, you can write two or three short notes rather than trying to fit everything into just one long note.

Because History/Social Studies passages can be densely written, you should:

1. Identify the topic and scope of the passage

   - You can usually find the topic and scope in the first paragraph.

2. Identify the topic sentence of each succeeding paragraph

   - What does this paragraph accomplish? Does it provide evidence to support a previous statement? Or does it introduce questions about an earlier claim?

3. Summarize the purpose of the passage

   - Some common purposes include: to inform, to refute, to promote, to explore.

> ✔ **Note**
>
> Resist the temptation to reread large portions of the passage. Your Passage Map can help you predict and answer questions correctly without having to dive completely back into the text. Doing so will save you time on Test Day!

Let's look at the following example of an abbreviated History/Social Studies passage and question set. After the mapped passage, the left column contains questions similar to those you'll see on the SAT Reading Test on Test Day. The column on the right features the strategic thinking a test expert employs when approaching the passage and questions presented. Note how a test expert can quickly condense the entire passage into a few words and use his or her Passage Map to ask questions that build a prediction for the correct answer.

Reading & Writing

Strategic Thinking

Step 1: Read actively

Read the passage and the notes provided. Remember, a well-crafted Passage Map should summarize the central idea of each paragraph as well as important topics or themes. Use your Passage Map to help you answer each question.

Questions 3-4 are based on the following passage.

The following passage is an excerpt from a speech by Canassatego, an Iroquois, as printed by Benjamin Franklin in the 1740s.

We know that you highly esteem the kind of learning taught in those colleges, and that the maintenance of our young men, while with you,
Line would be very expensive to you. We are convinced,
(5) therefore, that you mean to do us good by your proposal, and we thank you heartily. But you who are wise must know that different nations have different conceptions of things; and you will therefore not take it amiss if our ideas of this
(10) kind of education happen not to be the same with yours. We have had some experience of it: several of our young people were formerly brought up at the colleges of the northern provinces; they were instructed in all your sciences; but
(15) when they came back to us, they were bad runners; ignorant of every means of living in the woods; unable to bear either cold or hunger; knew neither how to build a cabin, take a deer, or kill an enemy; spoke our language imperfectly; were therefore
(20) neither fit for hunters, warriors, or counselors; they were totally good for nothing. We are, however, not the less obliged by your kind offer, though we decline accepting it: and to show our grateful sense of it, if the gentlemen of Virginia will send us a
(25) dozen of their sons, we will take great care of their education, instruct them in all we know, and make men of them.

*1: Iro.
thank BF for
d offer*

*1, cont.:
iff groups =
iff ed*

*¶1, cont.:
decline
BF's offer
(purpose)*

Reading & Writing

Questions	Strategic Thinking
3. In lines 6-11 ("But . . . yours"), what general idea is the author most likely conveying? A) It can be a mistake to disagree on the purpose of education. B) What constitutes a useful education for one group of people may not be useful for another group of people. C) Although grateful for the opportunity to attend college, the author wishes to pursue a more practical course of study. D) Challenging wise men on their concept of education is best done on a national basis.	**Step 2: Examine the question stem** The key phrases in this question stem are the line reference, "general idea," and "most likely conveying." **Step 3: Predict and answer** The Passage Map notes that different people have different ideas about what constitutes an appropriate and complete education. Choice (B) is correct.
4. The passage can best be described as A) an attempt to explain why the Iroquois could not accept such a generous offer. B) a desire to describe the benefits of promoting multiple points of view on a subject. C) an examination of the similarities and differences between two viable options. D) an argument that the Iroquois' concept of education was better suited to tribal needs.	**Step 2: Examine the question stem** There are no key words or phrases in this question stem; the fact that there are no specific keywords indicates this is a general question about the passage as a whole. Use the entire Passage Map to answer this question and particularly focus on the author's purpose for writing. **Step 3: Predict and answer** The purpose of the passage is to decline Benjamin Franklin's education proposal by providing information about how the Iroquois' own system of education is better for their nation than Benjamin Franklin's offered system. Choice (D) is correct.

SCIENCE PASSAGES

The SAT Reading Test will contain either two single Science passages or one single Science passage and one set of paired Science passages. Science passages differ from other passage types because:

- They often contain a lot of jargon and technical terms.

- They can utilize unfamiliar terms and concepts.

While Science passages can be tricky due to unfamiliar language, you will never need to employ knowledge outside of the passage when answering questions. Use the following strategy when approaching Science passages on the SAT:

1. Locate the central idea in the first paragraph

2. Note how each paragraph relates to the central idea. Does the paragraph…

   - Explain?

   - Support?

   - Refute?

   - Summarize?

3. Don't be distracted by jargon or technical terms.

   - Unfamiliar terms will generally be defined within the passage or in a footnote.

Let's look at the following example of an abbreviated Science passage and question set. After the mapped passage, the left column contains questions similar to those you'll see on the SAT Reading Test on Test Day. The column on the right features the strategic thinking a test expert employs when approaching the passage and questions presented. Note how a test expert can quickly condense the entire passage into a few words and use his or her Passage Map to ask questions that build a prediction for the correct answer.

✔ Remember

When you encounter more than one theory or idea, paraphrase each in as few words as possible in your Passage Map.

Strategic Thinking

Step 1: Read actively

Read the passage and the notes provided. Remember, a well-crafted Passage Map should summarize the central idea of each paragraph as well as important topics or themes. Your notes for Science passages should focus on the passage's central idea and how each paragraph relates to that idea. Use your Passage Map to help you answer each question.

Questions 5-6 are based on the following passage.

This passage details the regular journey of a group of green sea turtles from their feeding to breeding grounds.

Green sea turtles, shelled reptiles that traversed the oceans eons before mammals evolved, are known for their prodigious migrations. One group
Line of green sea turtles makes a regular journey from
(5) feeding grounds near the Brazilian Coast to breed-ing beaches on Ascension Island, a barren, rela-tively predator-free island in the central equatorial Atlantic. Proverbially slow on land, these turtles cover the distance of more than 2,000 kilometers
(10) in as little as two weeks. But how is this navigation of deep, featureless ocean accomplished? The sun's movements seem to provide the turtles with a navi-gational aid, but this is only part of the answer.

In addition to possessing good eyesight, green
(15) turtles appear to have an excellent sense of smell. In fact, the turtles may orient themselves by detecting traces of substances released from Ascension Island itself. Because Ascension Island lies in the midst of a major west-flowing ocean current, scientists
(20) believe that chemical substances picked up from the islands would tend to flow westward toward the feeding grounds of the turtle. As a result, these substances may provide a scented chemical trail that the turtles are able to follow. A mathematical
(25) model has been used to show that a concentration of substances delivered from Ascension Island to the turtles' feeding grounds, though diluted, would probably be sufficient to be sensed by the turtles.

The turtles' eyesight, meanwhile, may help direct
(30) the turtles from their feeding grounds into the path of this chemical trail. It is an established fact that turtles are capable of distinguishing between different light densities. Turtles recognize at least four colors and are especially attuned to the color
(35) red, because it often appears in their shell color-ation. Researchers believe that these turtles swim east toward the rising sun at the beginning of their migration, changing course toward Ascension Island's beaches as soon as their route intersects the
(40) scented path.

¶1: long-dist. turtle migration: how? (cen-tral idea)

¶2: use smell to navigate

¶3: use sight (swim east) & then smell (to beach)

Questions	Strategic Thinking
5. The main purpose of the last paragraph, lines 29-40, is to A) connect two partial explanations for the turtles' navigational ability. B) describe how color perception depends upon the eye's ability to recognize different light densities. C) establish that color sensitivity and shell coloration are closely linked but not explained. D) argue that color perception is the main reason that sea turtles can navigate to Ascension Island.	**Step 2: Examine the question stem** The key words and phrases in the question stem are "main purpose" and the paragraph/line reference. The Passage Map notes from the last paragraph will help you answer this question. **Step 3: Predict and answer** The Passage Map notes for the last paragraph state that the turtles' eyesight helps them find the scented path discussed in paragraph 2. Choice (A) is correct.
6. According to the passage, turtles' eyesight is especially sensitive to A) patterns of stars. B) the sun's movements. C) the color red. D) the chemical trail.	**Step 2: Examine the question stem** The key words and phrases of this question stem are "according to the passage" and "turtles' eyesight." Your Passage Map notes will help you identify which paragraph contains the information to answer this question. **Step 3: Predict and answer** The turtles' eyesight is discussed in the third paragraph. The author says that turtles are sensitive to the color red: "Turtles recognize at least four colors and are especially attuned to the color red" (lines 33-35). Choice (C) is correct.

You have seen the ways in which the SAT presents Reading passages and the way an SAT expert approaches these types of questions.

You will use the Kaplan Method for Reading Comprehension to complete this section. Part of the test-like passage has been mapped already. Your first step is to complete the Passage Map. Then, you will continue to use the Kaplan Method for Reading Comprehension and the strategies discussed in this chapter to answer the questions. Strategic thinking questions have been included to guide you—some of the answers have been filled in, but you will have to fill in the answers to others.

Use your answers to the strategic thinking questions to select the correct answer, just as you will on Test Day.

Strategic Thinking
Step 1: Read actively
The passage below is partially mapped. Read the passage and the first part of the Passage Map. Then, complete the Passage Map on your own. Remember to focus on the central ideas of each paragraph as well as the central idea of the overall passage. Use your Passage Map as a reference when you're answering questions.

Questions 7-8 are based on the following passage.

The following passage explains the forces of flight.

¶1: 4 forces of flight (central idea)

What do paper airplanes and large commercial airliners such as the Boeing 747 have in common?
Plenty. Despite differences in size and weight, both
Line must make use of the same physical forces in order
(5) to fly. The flight of any airplane results from the interaction of four different forces: thrust, drag, gravity, and lift.

¶2: #1 - thrust

All of the forces acting on the airplane must balance each other in order for the plane to travel
(10) along in steady horizontal flight. Thrust supplied by jet engines or propellers (or by a person's hand for a paper airplane) is the force that drives the airplane forward. The airplane cannot actually move any distance forward, however, unless the amount of
(15) thrust is enough to overcome the force of drag.

¶2, cont.: #2 - drag, impact on aircraft design

Drag is the air resistance that the plane encounters in flight. Just as the name indicates, air resistance has the effect of dragging the airplane backward as it moves through the air. Jet engines are designed
(20) so that the airplane has the necessary thrust to overcome air resistance. Drag can be reduced if the

airplane is streamlined—that is, constructed in such a way that air flows smoothly around it so that there is little friction at the airplane's surface.

(25) To rise into the air, an airplane has to overcome the force of gravity, the downward pull that the Earth exerts on everything on or near its surface. The airplane accomplishes this feat with lift force, which acts in an upward direction opposite to
(30) gravity. Lift is provided by the airplane's wings. The wings and wing flaps are shaped and angled so that air will flow more rapidly over them than under them. When air flows more rapidly over the wing tops, air pressure above the wings drops
(35) in comparison with the air pressure below the wings. (This phenomenon is known to engineers as Bernoulli's principle.) When an airplane taxis down the runway (or when a paper airplane is released from a person's hand), the greater air pressure
(40) below the wings pushes the wings upward, allowing the airplane to rise despite the pull of gravity. Once the plane is safely in the air, all four of the basic aerodynamic forces figure into the flight as well, whether it is the flight of a big jet or a paper
(45) airplane.

Don't get distracted by less important details. While there is a lot going on in this passage, your additions to the Passage Map should have noted the final two forces (gravity and lift) as well as how planes take off. If you're stuck, review the example Passage Map in the Answers & Explanations for this chapter on page 971.

review the example Passage Map in the Answers & Explanations for this chapter on page 971.

Questions	Strategic Thinking
7. As used in line 29, "acts" most nearly means A) behaves. B) works. C) portrays. D) pretends.	**Step 2: Examine the question stem** *What are the keywords in the question stem?* The line reference, cited word, and "most nearly means." **Step 3: Predict and answer** *Read around the cited word. What synonym can you predict to replace "acts" in this context?* "Functions" or "works." *What answer choice matches this prediction?* _____
8. Which of the following does the passage imply about drag force? A) Drag is the most important physical force needed for flight. B) Drag increases when surface friction increases. C) Drag decreases as a function of increased thrust. D) Drag reduces wind speed and direction.	**Step 2: Examine the question stem** *What are the keywords in the question stem?* "Drag force." *What parts of the passage are relevant?* Paragraph 2, which is where drag force is introduced. **Step 3: Predict and answer** *What does the second paragraph state about drag and drag force?* _____ _____ _____ *Which answer choice correctly reflects the passage's discussion of drag force?* _____

Now, try a test-like SAT Reading passage and question set on your own. Give yourself 6 minutes to read the passage and answer the questions.

Questions 9-12 are based on the following passage.

The following passage is an excerpt from Abraham Lincoln's second autobiography, published in a Pennsylvania newspaper in 1860.

I was born February 12, 1809, in Hardin County, Kentucky. My parents were both born in Virginia, of undistinguished families—second families,
Line perhaps I should say. My mother, who died in my
(5) tenth year, was of a family of the name of Hanks, some of whom now reside in Adams, and others in Macon County, Illinois. My paternal grandfather, Abraham Lincoln, emigrated from Rockingham County, Virginia, to Kentucky about 1781 or 1782,
(10) where a year or two later he was killed by the Indians, not in battle, but by stealth, when he was laboring to open a farm in the forest. His ancestors, who were Quakers, went to Virginia from Berks County, Pennsylvania. An effort to identify them with the
(15) New England family of the same name ended in nothing more definite than a similarity of Christian names in both families, such as Enoch, Levi, Mordecai, Solomon, Abraham, and the like.

My father, at the death of his father, was but
(20) six years of age, and he grew up literally without education. He removed from Kentucky to what is now Spencer County, Indiana in my eighth year. We reached our new home about the time the state came into the Union. It was a wild region,
(25) with many bears and other wild animals still in the woods. There I grew up. There were some schools, so called, but no qualification was ever required of a teacher beyond "readin', writin', and cipherin'" to the rule of three. If a straggler supposed to understand
(30) Latin happened to sojourn in the neighborhood, he was looked upon as a wizard. There was absolutely nothing to excite ambition for education. Of course, when I came of age I did not know much. Still, somehow I could read, write, and cipher to the rule

(35) of three, but that was all. I have not been to school since. The little advance I now have upon this store of education I have picked up from time to time under the pressure of necessity.

I was raised to farm work, which I continued till
(40) I was twenty-two. At twenty-one I came to Illinois, Macon County. Then I got to New Salem, at that time in Sangamon, now in Menard County, where I remained a year as a sort of clerk in a store.

Then came the Black Hawk War, and I was
(45) elected a captain of volunteers, a success which gave me more pleasure than any I have had since. I went the campaign, was elated, ran for the legislature the same year (1832), and was beaten—the only time I have ever been beaten by the people. The next and
(50) three succeeding biennial elections I was elected to the legislature. I was not a candidate afterward. During this legislative period I had studied law, and removed to Springfield to practice it. In 1846 I was once elected to the lower house of Congress.
(55) I was not a candidate for reelection. From 1849 to 1854, both inclusive, practiced law more assiduously than ever before. Always a Whig in politics; and generally on the Whig electoral tickets, making active canvasses. I was losing interest in politics
(60) when the repeal of the Missouri Compromise aroused me again. What I have done since then is pretty well known.

If any personal description of me is thought desirable, it may be said I am, in height, six feet four
(65) inches, nearly; lean in flesh, weighing on an average one hundred and eighty pounds; dark complexion, with coarse black hair and gray eyes. No other marks or brands recollected.

9. The author's stance is most similar to that of

   A) an ambitious politician campaigning for office.

   B) an education activist arguing for school reform.

   C) an accomplished storyteller spinning fanciful yarns.

   D) a common man describing his humble beginnings.

10. The author's central purpose for writing this passage is most likely to

    A) emphasize the influence his early education had on his later accomplishments.

    B) recount the important events that shaped his political philosophy.

    C) describe his life prior to his rise to national prominence.

    D) convey the idea that early hardship can strengthen an individual's character.

11. As used in line 38, "under the pressure of necessity" most nearly means

    A) when most convenient.

    B) when he needed to.

    C) whenever he could.

    D) when he was interested.

12. Based on the passage, which answer choice best describes the effect of the Black Hawk War on the author's life?

    A) It gave him an understanding of military tactics.

    B) It allowed him to escape the drudgery of working as a clerk.

    C) It launched his career into electoral politics.

    D) It informed his opinions on the necessity of the Civil War.

Answers & Explanations for this chapter begin on page 971.

EXTRA PRACTICE

Questions 1-10 are based on the following passage.

This passage is adapted from Guy de Maupassant's short story, "The False Gems," from *The Entire Original Maupassant Short Stories*.

Monsieur Lantin had met the young girl at a reception at the house of the second head of his department and had fallen head over heels in love
Line with her.
(5)   Her simple beauty had the charm of angelic modesty, and the imperceptible smile which constantly hovered about the lips seemed to be the reflection of a pure and lovely soul.

Monsieur Lantin, then chief clerk in the
(10) Department of the Interior, enjoyed a snug little salary of three thousand five hundred francs, and he proposed to this model young girl, and was accepted. He was unspeakably happy with her. She governed his household with such clever economy
(15) that they seemed to live in luxury.

He found fault with only two of her tastes: her love for the theatre and her taste for imitation jewelry.

After a time, Monsieur Lantin begged his wife to
(20) request some lady of her acquaintance to accompany her, and to bring her home after the theatre. She opposed this arrangement, at first; but, after much persuasion, finally consented, to the infinite delight of her husband.
(25)   Now, with her love for the theatre, came also the desire for ornaments. Her costumes remained as before, simple, in good taste, and always modest; but she soon began to adorn her ears with huge rhinestones, which glittered and sparkled like real
(30) diamonds. Around her neck she wore strings of false pearls, on her arms bracelets of imitation gold, and combs set with glass jewels.

Her husband frequently remonstrated with her, saying:
(35)   "My dear, as you cannot afford to buy real jewelry, you ought to appear adorned with your beauty and modesty alone, which are the rarest ornaments of your sex."

But she would smile sweetly, and say:
(40)   "Look! are they not lovely? One would swear they were real."

One evening, in winter, she had been to the opera, and returned home chilled through and through. The next morning she coughed, and
(45) eight days later she died of inflammation of the lungs.

He wept unceasingly; his heart was broken as he remembered her smile, her voice, every charm of his dead wife.
(50)   Time did not assuage his grief. Everything in his wife's room remained as it was during her lifetime; all her furniture, even her clothing, being left as it was on the day of her death. Here he was wont to seclude himself daily and think of her who had
(55) been his treasure—the joy of his existence.

But life soon became a struggle.

One morning, finding himself without a cent in his pocket, he resolved to sell something, and immediately the thought occurred to him of disposing
(60) of his wife's paste jewels, for he cherished in his heart a sort of rancor against these "deceptions," which had always irritated him in the past. The very sight of them spoiled, somewhat, the memory of his lost darling.
(65)   To the last days of her life she had continued to make purchases, bringing home new gems almost every evening, and he turned them over some time before finally deciding to sell the heavy necklace, which she seemed to prefer, and which, he thought,
(70) ought to be worth about six or seven francs; for it was of very fine workmanship, though only imitation.

He put it in his pocket, and started out in search of what seemed a reliable jeweler's shop. At length
(75) he found one, and went in, feeling a little ashamed to expose his misery, and also to offer such a worthless article for sale.

"Sir," said he to the merchant, "I would like to know what this is worth."

(80) The man took the necklace, examined it, called his clerk, and made some remarks in an undertone; he then put the ornament back on the counter, and looked at it from a distance to judge of the effect.

Monsieur Lantin, annoyed at all these ceremo-
(85) nies, was on the point of saying: "Oh! I know well enough it is not worth anything," when the jeweler said: "Sir, that necklace is worth from twelve to fifteen thousand francs; but I could not buy it, unless you can tell me exactly where it came from."

(90) The widower opened his eyes wide and remained gaping, not comprehending the merchant's meaning. Finally he stammered: "You say—are you sure?"

Monsieur Lantin, beside himself with astonish-
(95) ment, took up the necklace and left the store.

1. As used in line 5, "angelic" most nearly means

   A) invisible.

   B) generous.

   C) religious.

   D) innocent.

2. The author describes Monsieur Lantin's wife early in their marriage as

   A) wealthy.

   B) artistic.

   C) frugal.

   D) flighty.

3. The passage suggests that Lantin believed the jewels to be false because

   A) they did not have enough money to buy real jewels of this size.

   B) the theatregoers all wore elaborate costume jewelry.

   C) his wife preferred costume jewelry to real jewels.

   D) Madame Lantin was too concerned with modesty to wear real jewels.

4. Which choice provides the best evidence for the answer to the previous question?

   A) Lines 16-18 ("He found fault . . . jewelry")

   B) Lines 19-24 ("After a time . . . of her husband")

   C) Lines 25-30 ("Now, with her love . . . real diamonds")

   D) Lines 33-38 ("Her husband frequently . . . your sex")

5. Lines 47-55 ("He wept . . . joy of his existence") suggest that which of the following is true of Lantin?

   A) He holds a grudge due to his wife's spending.

   B) He is profoundly depressed after his wife's death.

   C) He idealized his wife and overlooked her flaws.

   D) He is resilient and will find happiness in the future.

6. Which choice provides the best evidence for the answer to the previous question?

   A) Lines 19-24 ("After a time ... her husband")

   B) Lines 47-49 ("He wept unceasingly ... his dead wife")

   C) Lines 65-72 ("To the last ... only imitation")

   D) Lines 90-95 ("The widower opened ... left the store")

7. As used in line 61, "rancor" most nearly means

   A) passion.

   B) prejudice.

   C) warning.

   D) bitterness.

8. The main purpose of lines 87-89 ("'Sir, that necklace is worth . . . where it came from'") is to

   A) offer a resolution to Lantin's crisis.

   B) foreshadow future happiness for Lantin.

   C) create a plot twist by suggesting a conflict.

   D) develop an antagonist character in the story.

9. The end of the passage suggests that which of the following was true of Madame Lantin?

   A) She was a notorious jewel thief.

   B) She accrued massive debts to purchase her jewels.

   C) She hid a substantial inheritance from her husband.

   D) She was not as virtuous as her husband believed.

10. What central theme does the excerpt communicate through Lantin's experiences?

    A) Appearances can be deceiving.

    B) People never appreciate what they have until it is gone.

    C) Beautiful things make for a rich life.

    D) A good reputation is easily damaged.

Questions 11-21 are based on the following passage.

The following passage details the antibody that produces peanut allergies and how scientists are using this information to develop a peanut that does not cause allergic reactions.

Peanuts can cause deadly allergic reactions in some people, and there is no real cure for peanut allergies. However, scientists may be working on
Line the next best thing to a cure: peanuts that do not
(5) cause allergic reactions.

  Allergic reactions start with the immune system, which normally works to keep us healthy. The immune system recognizes dangerous materials, such as poisons and viruses, and reacts to keep
(10) the materials from harming the rest of the body. Some of these reactions, such as swelling of nose and throat tissues, keep the materials from moving farther through the body. Other reactions, such as producing mucus and coughing, help expel the
(15) foreign materials. Unfortunately, too much swelling, mucus, or coughing make it hard to breathe and can even be life-threatening.

  People who are allergic to peanuts produce an antibody called IgE that combines with a specific
(20) part of the peanut protein. The IgE-protein complex then alerts the immune system and the reactions begin. Once the allergic person's throat starts swelling, that person will need immediate medical treatment to reduce the risk of injury or death.

(25) People who are allergic to peanuts must avoid them, and avoiding peanuts can be very hard to do. Many popular fast foods contain peanuts or peanut oil, or have been made using machines that also handle peanuts. Some very sensitive people cannot
(30) even be in the same room where peanuts are being eaten. This can be very difficult for children, and many allergic children cannot safely eat lunch in their own school cafeteria.

  Some scientists wondered if they could find a
(35) way to change the allergen, the part of the peanut protein that causes the allergic reaction, to keep IgE from combining with it. They first needed to measure the amount of reaction caused by untreated peanuts. Measuring how much of an allergic
(40) reaction the peanuts caused in people would not be safe, so they instead measured how much IgE combined with the peanut protein in a laboratory test. They found that frying and boiling peanuts reduced the amount of reaction, as compared to
(45) raw peanuts. However, frying and boiling do not reduce the amount of antibody reaction to a safe

amount, so scientists tried other treatments. Some of the treatments, such as high heat for long periods of time, changed the taste of the peanuts too much.

(50)   One treatment that showed promise was exposing the peanuts to very strong light. The light used by the scientists is similar to normal sunlight, but thousands of times stronger. By "pulsing" the light, or producing the light in short bursts, the scientists
(55) hoped to avoid heating the peanuts to the point where the taste changed while still deactivating the allergens in the peanuts.

In one experiment, the scientists exposed the peanuts to 3 pulses of light per second for
(60) different amounts of time. They then extracted the protein from the peanuts. To measure the amount of allergens left in the peanut protein, they coated a special plastic plate with the extracted protein. Next, they added blood plasma that contained the
(65) IgE antibodies. When they washed the plasma off the plate, the IgE antibodies that combined with the allergen part of the protein remained stuck to the plate. They then added other chemicals that combined with the IgE antibodies and produced
(70) a dark blue color; the darker the blue, the more IgE antibodies remained. Blood also contains very small amounts of other antibodies that will stick to the plate, so the same test on blood from a non-allergic person would still produce a small amount
(75) of blue color. To account for this, the scientists used blood plasma that did not have any IgE antibodies as a negative control. They then compared the darkness of all of the samples to the darkness of the negative control.
(80)   From the results, it appears that the scientists can change the peanut allergens so that the reaction in an allergic person is about the same as in a non-allergic person. The next steps will be to test the peanuts on humans: first by testing for reactions
(85) on the skin of allergic people, and then by having allergic people eat the peanuts while being monitored for any reaction. Eventually, the scientists hope, they will have a treatment that will make a safe peanut, which will make eating a much safer
(90) and simpler experience for many.

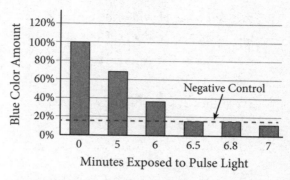

Results of allergen measurements for peanuts exposed to pulsed light for different amounts of time.

Adapted from Xingyu Zhao, "Effect of Pulsed Light on Allergenic Proteins of Shelled Whole Peanuts." ©2013.

11. As used in line 14, "expel" most nearly means

A) dismiss.

B) eject.

C) emit.

D) separate.

12. The passage most strongly suggests that

A) exposure to peanut proteins can be potentially fatal for almost anyone.

B) a peanut allergy is caused by a compromised or weakened immune system.

C) anyone who wishes to avoid developing a peanut allergy should avoid all peanut products.

D) the body of a person allergic to peanuts sees the peanut protein as a dangerous invader.

13. Which choice provides the best evidence for the answer to the previous question?

    A) Lines 6-10 ("Allergic reactions . . . body")

    B) Lines 25-26 ("People who are . . . hard to do")

    C) Lines 34-37 ("Some scientists . . . combining with it")

    D) Lines 87-90 ("Eventually . . . for many")

14. Based on the information in the passage, how does an allergic reaction compare to a normal immune system response to a dangerous material?

    A) An allergic reaction is milder than a normal immune system response and is usually shorter in duration.

    B) A normal immune system response is characterized by the body's producing mucus and coughing, while an allergic reaction makes it difficult to breathe.

    C) A normal immune system response is milder than an allergic response, but the allergic response is triggered by a material that is dangerous.

    D) An allergic reaction is similar to a normal immune system response, but the response can be stronger and cause life-threatening symptoms.

15. According to paragraph 4, people with peanut allergies

    A) will likely encounter peanut allergens on a daily basis.

    B) are more likely to have other allergies than people without a peanut allergy.

    C) will prefer the taste of peanuts with deactivated allergens.

    D) have a difficult time avoiding peanut allergens.

16. Which choice provides the best evidence for the answer to the previous question?

    A) Lines 3-5 ("However, scientists . . . allergic reactions")

    B) Lines 31-33 ("This can be . . . school cafeteria")

    C) Lines 47-49 ("Some of the treatments . . . too much")

    D) Lines 80-83 ("From the results . . . a non-allergic person")

17. As used in line 56, "deactivating" most nearly means

    A) restricting.

    B) hindering.

    C) disabling.

    D) arresting.

18. It can be reasonably inferred from both the evidence in the passage and the data in the graph that

    A) of the peanuts tested, those exposed to pulses of light for the shortest periods of time contained the lowest amounts of the protein that acts as an allergen.

    B) of the peanuts tested, those exposed to pulses of light for the longest periods of time contained the lowest amounts of the protein that acts as an allergen.

    C) of the peanuts tested, those exposed to pulses of light for the longest periods of time contained the highest amounts of the protein that acts as an allergen.

    D) the amount of time a peanut was exposed to pulses of light had little to no effect on the amounts of the protein that acts an allergen.

19. According to the passage, why did scientists measure how much IgE combined with peanut protein in a lab test instead of measuring the allergic reaction in people?

    A) They could not find enough people allergic to peanuts to create a large enough sample.

    B) The lab tests gave more accurate and reliable data than experiments with people.

    C) It would be unsafe to provoke a potentially fatal allergic response in a person.

    D) The scientists conducted tests on people before the lab tests began.

20. Paragraphs 6 and 7 can best be described as

    A) a suggestion for how scientists can more productively study how people who are allergic to peanuts are affected by the IgE antibodies.

    B) a description of how some treatments of peanuts aimed at deactivating the allergens in peanuts affect the taste of the peanut.

    C) a summary of one method of treating peanuts scientists hope can reduce the allergic response in people who are allergic to peanuts.

    D) an explanation of how the chemical structure of peanuts can be altered by small genetic changes to the plant.

21. The purpose of the last paragraph is to

    A) describe the next steps scientists might take toward creating a safer environment for peanut allergy sufferers.

    B) persuade the reader to learn more about peanut allergies and how scientists are working to help those who suffer from allergies.

    C) explain how future experiments on peanut proteins could provide clues to helping people who suffer from other food allergies.

    D) summarize the results of the experiments on peanuts described in detail throughout the passage.

CHAPTER 14

Synthesis Questions and the Kaplan Method for Infographics

 ## CHAPTER OBJECTIVES

By the end of this chapter, you will be able to:

1. Apply the Kaplan Strategy for Paired Passages to History/Social Studies and Science paired passages and question sets

2. Synthesize, compare, and contrast information from two different but related passages

3. Use the Kaplan Method for Infographics to analyze quantitative information and infographics

4. Combine information from infographics and text to answer questions about charts and graphs

SMARTPOINTS

Point Value	SmartPoint Category
Point Builder	The Kaplan Method for Infographics
35 Points	Quantitative Synthesis
25 Points	Paired Passage Synthesis

Reading & Writing

SYNTHESIS QUESTIONS AND THE KAPLAN METHOD FOR INFOGRAPHICS

Chapter 14

Homework

Extra Practice: #1-11

Even More

The Kaplan Method for Infographics

Paired Passages

Reading Quiz 3

Key

 Book Assignment

 Online Video Assignment

 Online Quiz Assignment

SYNTHESIS QUESTIONS

There are two types of Synthesis questions on the SAT:

- Questions asking you to synthesize information from both passages of a Paired Passage set

- Questions associated with an infographic

Synthesis questions require you to analyze information from separate sources and then understand how those sources relate to each other.

Let's take a closer look at the two types of Synthesis questions.

PAIRED PASSAGES

There will be exactly one set of Paired Passages on the SAT Reading Test. These passages will be either History/Social Studies passages or Science passages.

The Kaplan Strategy for Paired Passages helps you attack each pair you face by dividing and conquering, rather than processing two different passages and 10–11 questions all at once:

- Read Passage 1, then answer its questions

- Read Passage 2, then answer its questions

- Answer questions about both passages

By reading Passage 1 and answering its questions before moving on to Passage 2, you avoid falling into wrong answer traps that reference the text of Passage 2. Furthermore, by addressing each passage individually, you will have a better sense of the central idea and purpose of each passage. This will help you answer questions that ask you to synthesize information about both passages.

> ✔ **Remember**
>
> Even though the individual passages are shorter in a Paired Passage set, you should still map both of them. Overall, there is still too much information to remember effectively in your head. Your Passage Maps will save you time by helping you locate key details.

Fortunately, questions in a Paired Passage set that ask about only one of the passages will be no different from questions you've seen and answered about single passages. Use the same methods and strategies you've been using to answer these questions.

Other questions in a Paired Passage set are Synthesis questions. These questions will ask you about both passages. You may be asked to identify similarities or differences between the passages or how the author of one passage may respond to a point made by the author of the other passage.

THE KAPLAN METHOD FOR INFOGRAPHICS

The SAT Reading Test will contain two passages that include infographics. One History/Social Studies passage (or Paired Passage set) and one Science passage (or Paired Passage set) will include infographics. Infographics will convey or expand on information related to the passages. Questions about infographics may ask you to read data, to draw conclusions from the data, or to combine information from the infographic and the passage text.

The Kaplan Method for Infographics consists of three steps:

> Step 1: Read the question
>
> Step 2: Examine the infographic
>
> Step 3: Predict and answer

Let's take a closer look at each step.

> ✔ **Expert Tip**
>
> Expert test takers consider infographics as part of the corresponding passages, so they make sure to take notes on the infographic as part of their Passage Map.

Step 1: Read the question

Assess the question stem for information that will help you zero in on the specific parts of the infographic that apply to the question.

Step 2: Examine the infographic

Make sure to:

- Identify units of measurement, labels, and titles
- Circle parts of the infographic that relate directly to the question

> ✔ **Expert Tip**
>
> For more data-heavy infographics, you should also make note of any trends in the data or relationships between variables.

Step 3: Predict and answer

Just as in Step 3 of the Kaplan Method for Reading Comprehension, do not look at the answer choices until you've used the infographic to make a prediction.

Let's look at the following example of a test-like passage and question set. After the mapped passage, the left column contains questions similar to those you'll see on the SAT Reading Test on Test Day. The column on the right features the strategic thinking a test expert employs when approaching the passage and questions presented. Pay attention to how test experts vary the approach to answer different question types.

Strategic Thinking

Step 1: Read actively

Read the paired passages and the notes provided. Remember, a well-crafted Passage Map should summarize the central idea of each paragraph as well as important topics or themes. Use your Passage Map to help you answer each question.

✔ **Remember**

When answering Paired Passage questions, first read and answer questions about Passage 1. Then read and answer questions about Passage 2. Finally, answer the questions about both passages.

Questions 1-3 are based on the following passages and supplementary material.

Passage 1 warns against society becoming preoccupied with the rehabilitation of criminals. Passage 2 discusses the merits of said rehabilitation.

Passage 1

Nowadays, you hear quite a bit of mealy-mouthed hogwash about diversion and reha-bilitation of criminals. If we were to listen to the
Line so-called experts, we would conclude as a society
(5) that criminals are simply misunderstood, and that the only thing that separates good, law-abiding citizens from the worst scofflaws is an accident of birth. These pundits can quote all sorts of statistics and studies, but they seem to do so at the expense
(10) of one simple fact: as a society, we must uphold the standards of right and wrong. If we lose track of this obligation to reward the just and punish the guilty, then it is not just the criminals who have lost their moral compass, but society itself.

Passage 2

(15) When a crime is committed in our society, we are always quick to cast blame. The politicians and pundits who profit from fear and anger will be quick to promote newer and harsher penalties nearly every time that a violent crime appears in the
(20) national news, locking up the criminals for longer at greater expense to the taxpayers and society it-self, and yet nothing changes. The root cause of the crime has not been addressed, and in the rush to blame, nothing has been done to prevent the next

(25) violent crime from occurring. For only a fraction of the money it takes to lock up an offender, we could intercede earlier on, mentoring at-risk kids and making sure that they have the educational opportunities that will steer them away from
(30) crime. Instead of locking up criminals forever, we can give them the counseling and job training they need to become productive members of society. It is easy to blame, but changing things for the better requires more.

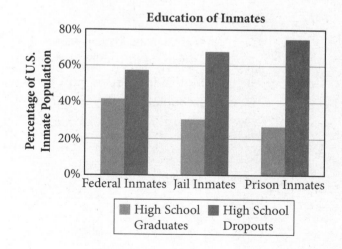

Margin notes:

¶1: author: criminal rehab foolish; punish = moral

¶1: society/ pol. want harsher punish-ments; not root cause; author: prevention better

Questions	Strategic Thinking

1. The authors of both passages agree that
 	
  A) the root causes of crime need to be addressed.
 	
  B) society must uphold standards of right and wrong.
 	
  C) it is important for society to confront the problem of crime.
 	
  D) diversion and rehabilitation can help criminals become productive members of society.
	Step 2: Examine the question stem
	
	Identify the keywords in the question stem: "authors of both passages agree." The correct answer will describe a point on which the authors of both passages agree.
	
	Step 3: Predict and answer
	
	Review your Passage Maps to find each author's main idea. The authors have very different purposes for writing, but both are writing about the same topic: the importance of addressing crime.
	
	Choice (C) is correct.

2. One difference between the conclusions reached in the two passages is that, unlike the author of Passage 1, the author of Passage 2
 	
  A) recommends lighter sentences for violent criminals.
 	
  B) argues that increasing educational opportunities can help reduce crime.
 	
  C) blames politicians instead of pundits for the increase in criminal behavior.
 	
  D) believes that individuals must be held accountable for their actions.
	Step 2: Examine the question stem
	
	The keywords in this question stem are "one difference between the conclusions" and "unlike the author of Passage 1, the author of Passage 2." The correct answer will focus on how the conclusion of Passage 2 differs from that of Passage 1.
	
	Step 3: Predict and answer
	
	The author of Passage 1 concludes, "we must uphold the standards of right and wrong" (lines 10-11) by punishing criminals. The author of Passage 2 concludes that addressing the root causes of crime will provide better societal outcomes. Predict that prevention efforts like education can help reduce crime.
	
	Choice (B) is correct.

Questions	Strategic Thinking
3. How would author 2 describe the graph's data about high school dropouts? A) Evidence that education could be an effective crime prevention measure B) Evidence that criminals should have longer sentences C) Evidence that there is no relationship between education and crime D) Evidence that imprisoning inmates is expensive for taxpayers	**Step 1: Read the question** Assess the question for information on what part of the infographic to focus on: the bars that represent the percentage of high school dropouts in inmate populations. The bars that represent the percentage of high school graduates can be ignored for the sake of this question. **Step 2: Examine the infographic** The unit of measurement on the *y*-axis is the percentage of the inmate population. The labels on the *x*-axis are different kinds of inmates: federal, jail, and prison. The key also provides labels for the two different categories: high school graduates and high school dropouts. The title of the graph is "Education of Inmates." **Step 3: Predict and answer** Since the graph concerns inmates and education, review what author 2 thinks about education. Use your Passage Map to find the part of the passage about prevention. Here, author 2 considers education a way to keep "at-risk kids" out of trouble (lines 27-30). Predict that author 2 would think the statistics in the graph showing numerous high school dropouts indicate greater education opportunities would help prevent crime. Choice (A) is correct.

You have seen the ways in which the SAT tests you on Synthesis in Reading passages and the way an SAT expert approaches these types of questions.

You will use the Kaplan Method for Reading Comprehension to complete this section. Part of the test-like passage has been mapped already. Your first step is to complete the Passage Map. Then, you will continue to use the Kaplan Method for Reading Comprehension and the strategies discussed in this chapter to answer the questions. Strategic thinking questions have been included to guide you—some of the answers have been filled in, but you will have to fill in the answers to others.

Use your answers to the strategic thinking questions to select the correct answer, just as you will on Test Day.

When answering Paired Passage questions, remember to first read and answer questions about Passage 1. Then read and answer questions about Passage 2. Finally, answer the questions about both passages.

Strategic Thinking
Step 1: Read actively
The paired passage set below is partially mapped. Read the first passage and its Passage Map. Then, complete the Passage Map for the second passage on your own. Remember to focus on the central ideas of each paragraph as well as the central idea of the overall passage. Use your Passage Map as a reference when you're answering questions.

Questions 4-6 are based on the following passages and supplementary material.

Passage 1 describes how scientists study stem cells and possible uses. Passage 2 discusses the potential risks of stem cell research.

Passage 1

¶1: author: SC = "miracle cure;" how SC work

Stem cells truly are science's miracle cure. These undifferentiated cells have not yet chosen what type of cell to become, and can be nudged into becom-
Line ing whatever type of cell is needed to help a sick
(5) patient. Stem cells can be used to replace damaged cells in a person who has a degenerative disease or a serious injury.

¶2: embryonic > adult SCs; help diseases; help research

Scientists obtain stem cells primarily from discarded embryos. True, they can also be obtained
(10) from the blood or organs from healthy adults, but these stem cells, while showing some usefulness, are not as adaptable as embryonic stem cells. Embryonic stem cells are incredibly helpful and can mean

a revolutionary change in quality of life for patients
(15) suffering from debilitating diseases such as Parkinson's or Alzheimer's. Someday, stem cells could even eliminate the need for human test subjects in drug tests. Without the use of embryonic stem cells, though, that could take an immeasurably longer
(20) amount of time to become a reality.

With stem cell research, the benefits for living, breathing, sentient people outweigh any debate regarding the origins of the cells themselves. In this age of scientific enlightenment, we must always ask
(25) ourselves: What action can best benefit humanity? By answering, we see clearly that stem cell research must continue.

¶3: author: SC research must go on

Passage 2

We stand at an important crossroads in scientific progress. We have the capability now to improve
(30) humanity in ways never thought possible, but at what cost? At what point must progress bow before conscience? Just because we can, is it true that we should?

Stem cell research has the potential to be an
(35) enormous boon to the medical industry. The advance of diseases can be assuaged or halted completely through this remarkable new medicine. But scientists assault the dignity of life when they use embryonic stem cells for their work. By taking
(40) cells from discarded embryos, we begin treading on a slippery slope. It is all too easy to transition from using discarded embryos to creating embryos solely for the purpose of stem cell medicine.

Since stem cells can be obtained from healthy
(45) adults with no cost to life, this is the path on which we should be progressing. These stem cells, safely obtained, can have a significant positive impact on the lives of patients.

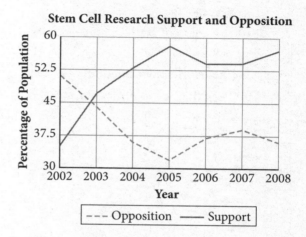

Stem Cell Research Support and Opposition

Don't get distracted by less important details. Your Passage Map for Passage 2 should note the author's views on the ethics surrounding embryonic stem cell research. If you're stuck, review the example Passage Map in the Answers & Explanations for this chapter on page 975.

Questions	Strategic Thinking
4. Which assumption do the authors of both passages share? A) Embryonic stem cells have greater potential than adult stem cells. B) The medical benefits of stem cell research outweigh any ethical concerns. C) Stem cell research could provide enormous benefits to humanity. D) The medical benefits of stem cell research must be weighed against ethical concerns.	**Step 2: Examine the question stem** *What are the keywords in this question stem?* The keywords in this question stem are "assumption" and "both passages share." The correct answer will describe an assumption both authors make. **Step 3: Predict and answer** *Although the authors have very different arguments, what can you predict they share in common about their central ideas?* The authors of both passages claim that stem cell research is potentially beneficial. *Which answer choice matches this prediction?* _____

Reading & Writing

Questions	Strategic Thinking
5. The authors of the passages disagree most strongly on which issue? A) The benefit of stem cells for treating diseases B) The value of stem cell research to medical science C) The adaptability of adult stem cells D) The ethics of using embryonic stem cells	**Step 2: Examine the question stem** *What are the keywords in this question stem?* The keywords in this question stem are "disagree most strongly." You will find the correct answer by finding the biggest difference between the two different opinions. **Step 3: Predict and answer** *What is the central idea of Passage 1?* _____ _____ *What is the central idea of Passage 2?* _____ _____ *What is the biggest difference between these central ideas?* _____ _____ *Which answer choice matches this prediction?* _____

Questions	Strategic Thinking
6. What claim about stem cell research is supported by the graph? A) Between 2003 and 2005, support for stem cell research increased more than opposition to stem cell research decreased. B) Between 2004 and 2006, support for stem cell research decreased and then increased. C) Between 2005 and 2007, opposition to stem cell research increased more than support for stem cell research decreased. D) Between 2006 and 2008, opposition to stem cell research decreased and then increased.	**Step 1: Read the question** *What are the keywords in this question stem?* The question stem does not offer any information about what part of the infographic will provide the answer. **Step 2: Examine the infographic** *What are the units of measurement, labels, or titles of the infographic? What trends do you see in the data?* _____ _____ _____ _____ _____ **Step 3: Predict and answer** *What can you predict?* Because this question stem is general, it is difficult to make a prediction. While keeping in mind the trends on the graph, evaluate each answer choice. *Is choice A supported by the graph? How do you know?* No, because the increase of support and the decrease of opposition are equal, according to the graph. (You can determine they're equal by counting the number of boxes each line spans on the y-axis.)

Reading & Writing

Reading & Writing

Questions	Strategic Thinking
	Is choice B supported by the graph? How do you know? _____ _____ *Is choice C supported by the graph? How do you know?* _____ _____ *Is choice D supported by the graph? How do you know?* _____ _____ *What is the correct answer?* _____

Now, try a test-like SAT Reading passage on your own. Give yourself 6 minutes to read the passage and answer the questions.

Remember to first read and answer questions about Passage 1. Then read and answer questions about Passage 2. Finally, answer the questions about both passages.

Questions 7-9 are based on the following passages and supplementary material.

The following passages reflect on the Machnovschina, an anarchist peasant uprising in the Ukraine active from approximately 1917 to 1922. During their brief and turbulent history, the Makhnovshchina (also known as Makhnovists) fought against the Central Powers, the White Army, and the Red Army, their sometimes ally that eventually turned on them and defeated them. During this time period, Ukraine alternated between rule by Russia (later the Soviet Union) and brief periods of independence.

The first passage discusses the relationship between the Makhnovists and their supporters, while the second discusses the differences between the Makhnovists on the outskirts of the emerging Soviet Union and the Bolsheviks who controlled the Soviet Union.

Passage 1

Even had the Ukrainian civilians wanted to ignore the sectarianism of their time and remain neutral, they did not have that luxury—the tur-
Line moil was too absolute, the excitement and terror of
(5) revolutionary upheaval too absolutely compelling. Even for the most isolated of peasants, political impartiality was impossible. From the beginning, there was a bond among revolutionary intellectuals, civilians, and military leaders.
(10)   The causes of civil unrest compounded. Adding to the burden of uncounted years of economic and political subjugation under a quasi-feudal system[1] was the added pressure of an invading Austro-Hungarian army. Meanwhile, Russia was in a state of
(15) chaos, and the Bolsheviks[2] were rapidly consolidating power in a system that promised equality and the rule of the proletariat[3]. There was no central authority to organize them (Russia had all but given up the Ukraine to the invading Central Powers[4]),
(20) and the traditional power of the rich landlords had collapsed with the Czarist government. There was no status quo and no safe choice.

Faced with this state of affairs, many Ukrainian peasants chose to organize themselves within the
(25) Makhnovshchina. Educated in the field and trained behind the plow, they were now charged with the task of organizing and defending a new society under conditions of tremendous adversity. Although the Makhnovshchina was an anarchist, revolution-
(30) ary movement, it was one that emerged out of necessity. It was a way for peasants to join together for mutual aid, revolutionary intellectuals to explore the possibility of a society without central authority, and generals to attempt to secure the rights of the
(35) Ukrainian people to self-determination.

Passage 2

The revolutionary period in Russian history is a classic example of the conflicts between the programs of dogmatic, rigid leaders and the desires and needs of ordinary people. One of the
(40) best examples of this is the struggle between the Bolsheviks and the Makhnovshchina. Not only did the word "revolution" mean very different things to the Kremlin[5] bureaucrats and the Ukrainian partisans, but the reality of the revolution was
(45) very different as well. This fact was noted by one anonymous soldier who, beginning his career as a Kremlin guard, eventually became a member of the Makhnovist army. He noted that "conditions could not have been more different between the
(50) two camps. In the one, decisions were based on the political theories of Marx[6] and Lenin,[7] theories which were never doubted or questioned in the least. In the other, theories were even more important—debated vigorously and openly—but

Reading & Writing

(55) only after the day's work had been done and the important decisions had been made based on the needs of the community for food, freedom, and self-defense."

Although the Kremlin's approach might seem
(60) like harmless intellectualism, it had disastrous con sequences that the anonymous soldier couldn't have forseen. As the Bolshevik Party gained increasing power, it began to control the official view of events with a systematic paranoia unprecedented in
(65) history. If the events differed from the official view, the events themselves (and those who participated in them) were deemed the enemy.

The wartime writings of Leon Trotsky[8] are the best indication of this trend. He alternately char-
(70) acterized the Makhnovists as heroes and traitors depending on the current needs of the Bolsheviks. When he required Makhnovists to fight alongside the Red Army,[9] he portrayed them as courageous heroes and valiant fighters, but when he did not,
(75) they suddenly became traitors and enemies of the revolution. In 1920, as the Makhnovshchina and the Red Army united to fight against a powerful White Army[10] campaign, Trotsky wrote:

"The working class of the Ukraine can never,
(80) and especially not in conditions of tremendous military danger, allow particular units sometimes to fight in our ranks and sometimes to stab us in the back.[11] Waging war against the world's exploiters, the workers' and peasants' Red Army says: 'Who is not
(85) with me is against me, and whoever is with me is to remain in my ranks and not leave them till the end.'"

The Ukranian partisans, even as peasants and workmen, were painted as the servants of foreign aristocrats bent on undermining the revolution.
(90) Even though Bolshevik presence had been weak in the Ukraine, Trotsky still saw fit to portray himself as the representative of "the working class of the Ukraine" and the Makhnovists as loyal to the work-ing class only to the degree that they recognized
(95) Red Army authority.

[1] Serfdom had only been abolished in 1861, and many traces of it remained.
[2] The Bolsheviks were the Communist party that established the Soviet Union.
[3] Working class
[4] The Central Powers fought the Allies during World War I (which took place from 1914 to 1918). During the period in question, the Austro-Hungarian Army was occupying much of the Ukraine.
[5] The Russian capital building which, at the time, was occupied by the Bolshevik Party
[6] Karl Marx, the ideological founder of Communism
[7] Vladimir Ilyich Lenin, the leader of the Bolsheviks
[8] Leon Trotsky, one of the leaders of the Bolsheviks
[9] The Bolshevik Army
[10] A conservative army opposed to the revolutionary movements in Russia
[11] The previous alliance between the Makhnovshchina and the Red Army had been broken when the Bolsheviks attacked and devas-tated the unsuspecting anarchists in a surprise attack.

Proportion of Seats in the Russian Constituent Assembly, 1918

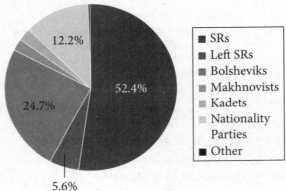

7. The author of Passage 2 would most likely characterize the Bolsheviks' promise described in Passage 1 as

A) the reason the Makhnovischina fought alongside the Red Army.

B) based on theories that had been openly debated.

C) an example of the Bolsheviks' attempt to control the official view of events.

D) inspired by Trotsky's wartime writings.

8. The authors of both passages would most likely agree that

   A) the Bolshevik and Makhnovischina leaders shared many fundamental principles.

   B) the Austro-Hungarian army posed the greatest threat to the Ukranian peasants.

   C) the Makhnovischina were servants of foreign aristocrats.

   D) the Makhnovischina was composed of peasants, intellectuals, and soldiers.

9. It can be reasonably inferred from Passage 2 and the graphic that the Bolsheviks

   A) wielded political power disproportionate to their voting power.

   B) must have had supporters in the Nationality Parties.

   C) represented a loyal opposition to the ruling SR group.

   D) allied with the Makhnovischina only when necessary to form a majority.

Answers & Explanations for this chapter begin on page 975.

Reading & Writing

EXTRA PRACTICE

The following questions provide an opportunity to practice the concepts and strategic thinking covered in this chapter. While many of the questions pertain to Synthesis, some touch on other concepts tested on the Reading Test to ensure that your practice is test-like, with a variety of question types per passage.

Questions 1-11 are based on the following passages.

Passage 1 tells the story behind the writing of the United States' national anthem. Passage 2 discusses how the prevalence, use, and value of the United States' national anthem have changed over time.

Passage 1

The story behind "The Star-Spangled Banner," America's national anthem, begins with the War of 1812. This war, which began just three decades after
Line the Revolution, was again waged between American
(5) and British forces for various reasons, including trade interference. Stakes were high: this was one of America's earliest opportunities to solidify its status as a sovereign nation equal to other world powers. Moreover, many Americans feared that the
(10) nation might forfeit its hard-earned liberty were the British to defeat them.

Britain's involvement was limited in the war's first two years due to conflict at home, where Napoleon's army had attacked. But in the summer
(15) of 1814, after the conflict with France had mostly subsided, Britain's focus turned to the American theater, which up to this point had been merely a distraction. In August of that year, the British sent an invading force that quickly defeated a smaller
(20) American force was ill-equipped and poorly trained. Later that night, the British Army invaded Washington, setting fire to several buildings, including the president's home and the Capitol. A few weeks later, on September 12th, British infantry
(25) troops tried to overtake Baltimore, but America's defenses prevailed. The next morning, Britain's navy began a heavy bombardment of Baltimore's Fort McHenry, located at the mouth of Baltimore's harbor.
(30) Some American men, including lawyer Francis Scott Key, happened to be aboard a British ship

in the harbor that same day. These men had come to peacefully request a captive friend's release—a request that, to their fortune, was granted. But
(35) the British detained them on the ship until the attack on McHenry had run its course. From this vantage point, Key and his companions witnessed Fort McHenry's bombardment: twenty-five rain-drenched hours of rockets, explosions, and gunfire.

(40) Through the night, Key waited in grim expectation that the morning would reveal a white flag raised over the fort, symbolizing McHenry's surrender. But instead, by dawn's light he saw the American flag. McHenry had endured; British
(45) forces were already retreating. Moved by the sight, Key began to write, on the back of a letter he was carrying, the words that would become America's national anthem.

This event marked a turning point in America's
(50) favor; within months, the war would be over. The War of 1812 would list among the less significant wars in United States history, by many accounts. But Francis Scott Key's eloquent description of the flag—and the brave victory it represented—would
(55) become a lasting emblem of American patriotism.

Passage 2

America's National Anthem began as a poem titled "The Defence of Fort McHenry." Its melody came from the British tune, "Anacreon in Heaven." Written on September 14, 1814, and distributed
(60) shortly thereafter, the song enjoyed almost instant popularity. A Baltimore theater housed its first public performance about a month after its writing. Following this, a music shop printed the song under the enduring title "The Star-Spangled Banner."
(65) Over the next century, the song gained increas-

ing value in the hearts of Americans, growing especially popular during the Civil War. Around the 1890s, the military began playing the song for ceremonial uses. At the time of World War I, when
(70) patriotic music again served as a crucial ideological refuge for America's people, "The Star-Spangled Banner" began to be treated by the military as the national anthem. Also around this time, the anthem was played in its first baseball game: a Cubs
(75) versus Red Sox game in which the song surprised and moved the crowds during the seventh-inning stretch. This effect made national headlines, and, in each game to follow during that series, the anthem was played, meeting an equally enthusiastic recep-
(80) tion. This launched the tradition of the national anthem's now near-ubiquitous presence at major American sporting events.

    In 1931, Congress and President Hoover passed the bill to officially designate the song as America's
(85) national anthem. It had long since distinguished itself from other patriotic songs and held special significance in American hearts, but now it would remain the nation's staple celebratory score. Today, the song is taught to children in schools, used in
(90) various ceremonies, printed in many church hymnals and community songbooks, and sung collectively at sporting events, including those featuring American participation internationally, such as World Cup Soccer or the opening ceremonies of
(95) the Olympics. The anthem's final words about those over whom the flag waves ("O'er the land of the free / and the home of the brave") remind Americans of the liberty for which the country was established and the courage of those who fought for it.

1. What is the author of Passage 1's overall purpose?
    A) Analyzing the impact of the War of 1812
    B) Describing the reasons for the War of 1812
    C) Explaining the origins of the national anthem
    D) Evaluating the legacy of the national anthem

2. The author of Passage 1 most likely includes the information in lines 6-11 ("Stakes were high . . . defeat them") in order to
    A) call attention to the reasons for going to war.
    B) emphasize the role of Francis Scott Key in defending the nation.
    C) explain the symbolism featured in the anthem.
    D) show the significance of the outcome of the war.

3. As used in line 26, "prevailed" most nearly means
    A) entrenched.
    B) floundered.
    C) persuaded.
    D) succeeded.

4. The information in paragraph 4 of Passage 1 most clearly suggests that Francis Scott Key wrote the national anthem to
    A) call public attention to the bombardment of American forces.
    B) honor the act of American fortitude that he witnessed.
    C) denounce critics of the War of 1812.
    D) inspire the defenders of Fort McHenry.

5. Which choice provides the best evidence for the answer to the previous question?

A) Lines 40-41 ("Through the night . . . expectation")

B) Lines 41-42 ("morning . . . the fort")

C) Lines 44-45 ("British forces . . . retreating")

D) Lines 45-46 ("Moved by . . . to write")

6. The author of Passage 1 would most likely agree with which of the following statements?

A) The national anthem grew out of an incidental war but gained importance as a result of government propaganda during later wars.

B) The national anthem captured the triumph of the United States in defending its sovereignty and might during the War of 1812.

C) The national anthem would have gone unnoticed if it were not for its popular resonance with an American people steeped in British musical tradition.

D) The national anthem rallied support for the defense of Fort McHenry and helped sustain American forces through the War of 1812.

7. Why does the author of Passage 2 most likely begin with lines 56-58 ("America's National Anthem . . . 'Anacreon in Heaven'")?

A) To show that Key did not set out to write the national anthem

B) To give credit to the influence of British tradition in American culture

C) To highlight the poetic devices that Key used in the writing of the national anthem

D) To demonstrate that the national anthem describes a specific event, not American patriotism

8. As used in line 81, "near-ubiquitous" most nearly means

A) commonplace.

B) controversial.

C) intermittent.

D) offensive.

9. In lines 96-97, the author quotes "The Star-Spangled Banner" primarily to

A) demonstrate the lyrical mastery of Francis Scott Key.

B) explain the symbolism of the American flag in the national anthem.

C) recall the specific events of the War of 1812.

D) show how the lyrics of the national anthem reflect American patriotism.

10. How does the information in Passage 2 most enhance the content of Passage 1?

A) It describes the immediate popularity of the original poem.

B) It emphasizes the patriotic nature of the national anthem.

C) It explores the origins of the national anthem in the War of 1812.

D) It explains how Key's words became the national anthem.

11. Which choice provides the best evidence for the answer to the previous question?

A) Lines 59-61 ("Written . . . popularity")

B) Lines 69-73 ("At the time . . . anthem")

C) Lines 88-92 ("Today . . . events")

D) Lines 95-98 ("The anthem's . . . established")

Questions 12-22 are based on the following passages and supplementary material.

Passage 1 is about how scientists use radioisotopes to date artifacts and remains. Passage 2 discusses the varying problems with radioactive contaminants.

Passage 1

Archaeologists often rely on measuring the amounts of different atoms present in an item from a site to determine its age. The identity of an atom
Line depends on how many protons it has in its nucleus;
(5) for example, all carbon atoms have 6 protons. Each atom of an element, however, can have a different number of neutrons, so there can be several versions, or isotopes, of each element. Scientists name the isotopes by the total number of protons
(10) plus neutrons. For example, a carbon atom with 6 neutrons is carbon-12 while a carbon atom with 7 neutrons is carbon-13.

Some combinations of protons and neutrons are not stable and will change over time. For example,
(15) carbon-14, which has 6 protons and 8 neutrons, will slowly change into nitrogen-14, with 7 protons and 7 neutrons. Scientists can directly measure the amount of carbon-12 and carbon-14 in a sample or they can use radiation measurements to calcu-
(20) late these amounts. Each atom of carbon-14 that changes to nitrogen-14 emits radiation. Scientists can measure the rate of emission and use that to calculate the total amount of carbon-14 present in a sample.

(25) Carbon-14 atoms are formed in the atmosphere at the same rate at which they decay. Therefore, the ratio of carbon-12 to carbon-14 atoms in the atmosphere is constant. Living plants and animals have the same ratio of carbon-12 to carbon-14 in
(30) their tissues because they are constantly taking in carbon in the form of food or carbon dioxide. After the plant or animal dies, however, it stops taking in carbon and so the amount of carbon-14 atoms in its tissues starts to decrease at a predictable rate.

(35) By measuring the ratio of carbon-12 to carbon-14 in a bone, for example, a scientist can determine how long the animal the bone came

from has been dead. To determine an object's age this way is called "carbon-14 dating." Carbon-14
(40) dating can be performed on any material made by a living organism, such as wood or paper from trees or bones and skin from animals. Materials with ages up to about 50,000 years old can be dated. By finding the age of several objects found at different
(45) depths at an archeological dig, the archeologists can then make a timeline for the layers of the site. Objects in the same layer will be about the same age. By using carbon dating for a few objects in a layer, archeologists know the age of other objects in that
(50) layer, even if the layer itself cannot be carbon dated.

Passage 2

Radioactive materials contain unstable atoms that decay, releasing energy in the form of radiation. The radiation can be harmful to living tissue because it can penetrate into cells and damage their
(55) DNA. If an explosion or a leak at a nuclear power plant releases large amounts of radioactive materials, the surrounding area could be hazardous until the amount of radioactive material drops back to normal levels. The amount of danger from the
(60) radiation and the amount of time until the areas are safe again depends on how fast the materials emit radiation.

Scientists use the "half-life" of a material to indicate how quickly it decays. The half-life of a
(65) material is the amount of time it takes for half of a sample of that material to decay. A material with a short half-life decays more quickly than a material with a long half-life. For example, iodine-131 and cesium-137 can both be released
(70) as a result of an accident at a nuclear power plant. Iodine-131 decays rapidly, with a half-life of 8 days. Cesium-137, however, decays more slowly, with a half-life of 30 years.

If an accident releases iodine-131, therefore, it
(75) is a short-term concern. The amount of radiation emitted will be high but will drop rapidly. After two months, less than one percent of the original

iodine-131 will remain. An accidental release of cesium-137, however, is a long-term concern. The
(80) amount of radiation emitted at first will be low but will drop slowly. It will take about 200 years for the amount of cesium-137 remaining to drop below one percent. The total amount of radiation emitted in both cases will be the same, for the same amount
(85) of initial material. The difference lies in whether the radiation is all released rapidly at high levels in a short time, or is released slowly at low levels, over a long time span.

Decay of Carbon-14

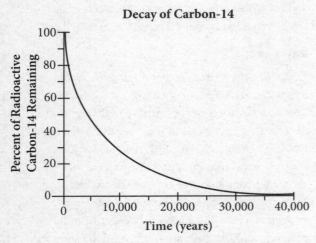

This data is from the *Journal of Research of the National Bureau of Standards*, Vol. 64, No. 4, April 1951, pp. 328 – 333.

12. Based on the information in Passage 1, which of the following could be dated using carbon-14 dating?

    A) An iron pot found in a cave

    B) A rock at the bottom of a quarry

    C) An arrowhead made from bone

    D) The remains of a house made from stone

13. Which choice provides the best evidence for the answer to the previous question?

    A) Lines 10-12 ("For example . . . carbon-13")

    B) Lines 28-31 ("Living plants . . . dioxide")

    C) Lines 31-34 ("After the plant . . . rate")

    D) Lines 39-42 ("Carbon-14 dating . . . animals")

14. As used in line 26, "decay" most nearly means

    A) yield.

    B) deteriorate.

    C) discharge.

    D) circulated.

15. Which statement best describes the relationship between carbon-12 and carbon-14 in living tissue?

    A) There is more carbon-14 than carbon-12.

    B) There is more carbon-12 than carbon-14.

    C) The ratio of carbon-12 to carbon-14 is constant.

    D) The ratio of carbon-12 to carbon-14 fluctuates greatly.

16. Which choice provides the best evidence for the answer to the previous question?

    A) Lines 13-14 ("Some combinations … time")

    B) Lines 25-26 ("Carbon-14 atoms … decay")

    C) Lines 28-31 ("Living plants … carbon dioxide")

    D) Lines 31-34 ("After the plant … rate")

17. In Passage 2, the author refers to an accident that results in the release of iodine-131 as a "short-term concern" (line 75) because the initial amount of radiation released is

    A) low but will drop slowly.

    B) high but will drop quickly.

    C) low and will drop quickly.

    D) high and will drop slowly.

18. Based on the information in Passage 2, living tissue exposed to radioactive material can

    A) be destroyed by high levels of heat caused by the radiation.

    B) become radioactive itself and damage surrounding tissue.

    C) suffer injury when the cells' components are damaged.

    D) be killed by extra protons released by the radioactive material.

19. As used in line 77, "original" most nearly means

    A) earliest.

    B) unique.

    C) unusual.

    D) critical.

20. According to Passage 2, scientists use the half-life of radioactive material to determine the

    A) amount of danger posed by radiation immediately following a nuclear accident.

    B) likelihood of a nuclear accident involving the release of radioactive material at any given location.

    C) amount of radiation contained in a sample of iodine-131 or cesium-137 used in nuclear reactions.

    D) length of time that must pass until an area is safe after the release of radioactive material.

21. Which generalization about the study of physics is supported by both passages?

    A) The study of atomic and nuclear physics can have many applications in a variety of fields.

    B) The study of physics has helped revolutionize how archaeologists study artifacts.

    C) Scientists use physics to keep people and wildlife safe following a nuclear accident.

    D) Scientists use different concepts to date ancient items and assess danger from nuclear accidents.

22. Based on the graph and the information in the passages, which statement is accurate?

    A) Carbon-14 has a half-life of about 5,400 years.

    B) The half-life of carbon-14 is similar to that of cesium-137.

    C) The half-life of iodine-131 is greater than that of cesium-137.

    D) All radioactive materials have a half-life of 30 to 5,400 years.

Reading & Writing

CHAPTER 15

Global and Command of Evidence Questions

 ## CHAPTER OBJECTIVES

By the end of this chapter, you will be able to:

1. Locate appropriate textual evidence to support the answer to a previous question

2. Summarize the passage or key information and ideas within the passage

3. Identify central ideas and themes of a passage to answer questions about central ideas and themes

SMARTPOINTS

Point Value	SmartPoint Category
10 Points	Global
60 Points	Command of Evidence

Reading & Writing

GLOBAL AND COMMAND OF EVIDENCE QUESTIONS

Chapter 15

Homework

Extra Practice: #1-11

Even More

Science Passages

Command of Evidence

Reading Quiz 2

Key

 Book Assignment

 Online Video Assignment

 Online Quiz Assignment

GLOBAL QUESTIONS

Global questions require you to both identify explicit and determine implicit central ideas or themes in a text. If you pay attention to the big picture—the author's central idea and purpose—while reading SAT Reading passages, you will be able to answer Global questions with little to no rereading of the passage. To fully understand the central ideas and themes of a passage, you must synthesize the different points the author makes with his or her thesis statement, which you should underline when Passage Mapping.

Global questions may also ask you to choose a correct summary of the passage as a whole or identify key information and ideas within the passage. When presented with this type of Global question, you can use your Passage Map, which is essentially a brief summary of what you have read.

> ✔ **On Test Day**
>
> The introductory portion at the beginning of an SAT Reading passage can be very helpful in determining the author's central ideas and themes. Make sure you take the time on Test Day to read this information—it orients you to the passage.

You can recognize Global questions because they typically do not reference line numbers or even individual paragraphs. To confidently answer Global questions, you need to not only identify the central idea or theme of the passage but also avoid choosing answers that summarize secondary or supplementary points.

Note that there is a slight difference between nonfiction and fiction passages. Science and History/Social Studies passages are nonfiction and will have a definite central idea and thesis statement; U.S. and World Literature passages are fiction and will have a central theme but no thesis statement.

> ✔ **Remember**
>
> History/Social Studies and Science passages on the SAT Reading Test are just well-written essays or article excerpts. You can normally find the thesis statement of a well-written piece at the end of the introductory paragraph.

COMMAND OF EVIDENCE QUESTIONS

A Command of Evidence question relies on your answer to the question that precedes it. These questions require you to identify the portion of the text that provides the best evidence for the conclusion you reached when selecting your answer to the previous question.

Kaplan's Strategy for Command of Evidence questions involves retracing your steps; that is, you must return to the previous question to ensure you answer the Command of Evidence question correctly.

To answer Command of Evidence questions efficiently and correctly, employ the following Kaplan Strategy:

- When you see a question asking you to choose the best evidence to support your answer to the previous question, review how you selected that answer.
- Avoid answers that provide evidence for incorrect answers to the previous question.
- The correct answer will support why the previous question's answer is correct.

✔ Expert Tip

You can recognize Command of Evidence questions easily. The question stem usually reads, "Which choice provides the best evidence for the answer to the previous question?" Furthermore, the answer choices are always line numbers with parentheses containing the first and last word of the intended selection. Answer choices are listed in the order they appear in the passage.

Command of Evidence questions ask that you cite the textual evidence that best supports, disputes, strengthens, or weakens a given claim or point. Whether the argument is supported or not, the use of textual evidence is the same. The evidence can be personal stories, scientific facts, tone, writing style, and infographics. It is important to identify the appropriate aspect of the text used for Command of Evidence questions and not to make assumptions beyond what is written.

The first step to approaching a Command of Evidence question is to make sure you answered the previous question—no matter its type—correctly. If you answer the question preceding a Command of Evidence question incorrectly, you have a smaller chance of selecting the correct answer.

✔ Remember

There is no wrong answer penalty on the SAT, so even if you have no idea of how to approach a question, take your best guess and move on.

Let's look at the following example of a test-like passage and question set. After the mapped passage, the left column contains questions similar to those you'll see on the SAT Reading Test on Test Day. The column on the right features the strategic thinking test experts employ when approaching the passage and questions presented. Pay attention to how test experts vary the approach to answer different question types.

Strategic Thinking
Step 1: Read actively
Read the passage and the notes provided. Remember, a well-crafted Passage Map should summarize the central idea of each paragraph as well as important topics or themes. Use your Passage Map to help you answer each question.

Questions 1-3 are based on the following passage.

The following is excerpted from Frederick Douglass's autobiographical *Narrative of the Life of Frederick Douglass, An American Slave.*

¶1:Mrs. helped FD read; Mr. thought "slaves not human"

His mistress had been severely reprimanded by
her husband for helping Frederick Douglass learn
to read. After all, the husband admonished, giving a
Line slave the knowledge to read was like giving the slave
(5) access to thinking he or she was human. If you give
the slaves an inch, they will take the ell.

¶2: Mrs. = kind at first

My mistress was, as I have said, a kind and
tender-hearted woman; and in the simplicity of her
soul she commenced, when I first went to live with
(10) her, to treat me as she supposed one human being
ought to treat another. In entering upon the
duties of a slaveholder, she did not seem to perceive
that I sustained to her the relation of a mere chat-
tel, and that for her to treat me as a human being
(15) was not only wrong, but dangerously so. Slavery
proved as injurious to her as it did to me. When
I went there, she was a pious, warm, and tender-
hearted woman. There was no sorrow or suffering
for which she had not a tear. She had bread for

¶2, cont.: being a slave owner turned Mrs. hard and mean

(20) the hungry, clothes for the naked, and comfort for
every mourner that came within her reach. Slavery
soon proved its ability to divest her of these heav-
enly qualities. Under its influence, the tender heart
became stone, and the lamblike disposition gave
(25) way to one of tiger-like fierceness. The first step in
her downward course was in her ceasing to instruct
me. She now commenced to practice her husband's
precepts. She finally became even more violent in
her opposition [to my learning to read] than her
(30) husband himself. She was not satisfied with simply
doing as well as he had commanded; she seemed
anxious to do better. Nothing seemed to make her

more angry than to see me with a newspaper. She
seemed to think that here lay the danger. I have
(35) had her rush at me with a face made all up of fury,
and snatch from me a newspaper, in a manner that
fully revealed her apprehension. She was an apt
woman; and a little experience soon demonstrated,
to her satisfaction, that education and slavery were
(40) incompatible with each other.

From this time I was most narrowly watched. If
I was in a separate room any considerable length of
time, I was sure to be suspected of having a book,
and was at once called to give an account of myself.

¶3: FD no longer allowed to learn to read

(45) All this, however, was too late. The first step had
been taken. Mistress, in teaching me the alphabet,
had given me the inch, and no precaution could
prevent me from taking the ell.

The plan which I adopted, and the one by which

¶4: FD got children to teach him

(50) I was most successful, was that of making friends
of all the white children whom I met in the street.
As many of these as I could, I converted into teachers. With their kindly aid, obtained at different
times and in different places, I finally succeeded in
(55) learning to read. When I was sent on errands, I always took my book with me, and by going one part
of my errand quickly, I found time to get a lesson
before my return. I used also to carry bread with
me, enough of which was always in the house, and
(60) to which I was always welcome, for I was much
better off in this regard than many of the poor
white children in our neighborhood. This bread
I used to bestow upon the hungry little urchins,
who, in return, would give me that more valuable
(65) bread of knowledge. I am strongly tempted to give
the names of two or three of those children, as
a testimonial of the gratitude and affection I bear

them; but prudence forbids—not that it would injure me, but it might embarrass them; for it is al-
(70) most an unpardonable offense to teach slaves to read in this Christian country. I used to talk this matter of slavery over with them. I would sometimes say to them, I wished I could be as free as they would be when they got to be men. This used to trouble
(75) them; they would express for me the liveliest sympathy, and console me with the hope that something would occur by which I might be free.

¶4, cont.: FD hopes for change

Questions	Strategic Thinking
1. The main purpose of the passage is to A) emphasize the cruelty of slavery. B) refute the idea that education and slavery are incompatible. C) offer historical background to provide context for positions Douglass later espoused. D) describe the risks Douglass willingly took to learn to read.	**Step 2: Examine the question stem** Identify the keywords in the question stem. The phrase "main purpose" indicates that you will find the answer by using the entire Passage Map to summarize the central idea and purpose of the passage. **Step 3: Predict and answer** While the beginning of the passage discusses Douglass's relationship with his mistress, it is primarily about how Douglass learned to read despite his slave status. Choice (D) matches this prediction.
2. The statement in lines 15-16 ("Slavery proved . . . to me") suggests that A) the mistress and Douglass suffered equally from the institution of slavery. B) owning slaves destroyed the mistress's admirable human qualities. C) the mistress regretted the actions she was forced to take as a slave owner. D) Douglass pitied the mistress for the sacrifices she made.	**Step 2: Examine the question stem** Identify the keywords in the question stem: the line references and parenthetical quotation, as well as the phrase "suggests that." You can find your answer by using your Passage Map notes near lines 15-16, particularly those about the mistress, to answer the question. **Step 3: Predict and answer** In this section, the Passage Map notes about the mistress say that she was kind at first but slavery was eventually harmful to her as well because she became hard and mean. Choice (B) matches this prediction.

Questions	Strategic Thinking
3. Which choice provides the best evidence for the answer to the previous question? A) Lines 11-15 ("In entering . . . dangerously so") B) Lines 23-25 ("Under its . . . fierceness") C) Lines 41-44 ("If I . . . of myself") D) Lines 53-55 ("With their . . . to read")	**Step 2: Examine the question stem** This question stem indicates that you will need to choose the answer choice featuring the lines from the passage that best support your answer to the previous question. Use the Kaplan Strategy for Command of Evidence questions when you encounter this question stem. **Step 3: Predict and answer** You found the answer to the previous question—that owning slaves destroyed the mistress's admirable human qualities—by using the Passage Map notes surrounding the cited sentence in lines 15-16. The Passage Map says that the mistress became hard and mean. This is supported from line 21 through the end of the paragraph (line 40). Choice (B) is the only answer choice that falls within these lines and is therefore correct.

✔ **Note**

Remember the Kaplan Strategy for Command of Evidence questions: Review how you selected the answer to the previous question and avoid answer choices that provide evidence for incorrect answer choices to it. The correct answer will support why the previous question's answer is correct.

You have seen the ways in which the SAT tests you on Citing Textual Evidence and Global Questions in Reading passages and the way an SAT expert approaches these types of questions.

You will use the Kaplan Method for Reading Comprehension to complete this section. Part of the test-like passage has been mapped already. Your first step is to complete the Passage Map. Then, you will continue to use the Kaplan Method for Reading Comprehension and the strategies discussed in this chapter to answer the questions. Strategic thinking questions have been included to guide you—some of the answers have been filled in, but you will have to fill in the answers to others.

Use your answers to the strategic thinking questions to select the correct answer, just as you will on Test Day.

Strategic Thinking
Step 1: Read actively
The passage below is partially mapped. Read the passage and the first part of the Passage Map. Then, complete the Passage Map on your own. Remember to focus on the central ideas of each paragraph as well as the central idea of the overall passage. Use your Passage Map as a reference when you're answering questions.

Questions 4-6 are based on the following passage.

The following passage explains the challenges facing a population of trees and possible solutions.

Today, oaks are plagued with problems. There is lack of regeneration in populations of certain species. Pests such as the acorn weevil and the
Line filbert worm eat away at acorns and prevent
(5) germination. By undermining the root systems of seedlings and saplings, ground squirrels, gophers, and other small mammals often prevent these young plants from reaching tree size. Severe diseases, such as sudden oak death, kill many
(10) adult oaks. Many mature oaks are having a tough time with fire suppression. In the past, with light surface fires, the oaks had been able to maintain a stronghold where other plants were not able to compete and died out. Now oaks are being toppled
(15) by trees that have a higher tolerance for shade and are not fire-resistant; earlier such trees would have been killed when Native Americans set fires.

Given all of these challenges, the "old-growth" oaks—the large old valley oaks, Garry oaks, coast
(20) live oaks, and canyon live oaks that have huge girth and large canopies—may become a thing of the past. These oaks in particular are important because there are often more terrestrial vertebrates living in mature oak stands than in seedling and
(25) sapling areas. This prevalence of animals occurs because the large crowns of such oaks provide cover and feeding sites for a large variety of wildlife.

The University of California has embarked
(30) on an ambitious and necessary research program called the Integrated Hardwood Range Management Program to explore the significant causes of oak decline and offer varied solutions. These include investigating the use of grassing
(35) regimes that are compatible with oak seedling establishment, revegetating sites with native grasses to facilitate better germination of oak seedlings, documenting insects and pathogens that attack oaks, and exploring the ways that native
(40) people managed oaks in the past. Scientists at the Pacific Northwest Research Station in Olympia, Washington, and at Redwood National Park in northern California are reintroducing the burning practices of Native Americans. When used in

¶1: oak problems: pests & disease, other trees

¶2: oaks in danger

¶3: research into problems & solutions

¶3:
various
solutions
include
Native
American
approach
of using
fire

(45) Garry oak ecosystems, fires keep Douglas firs from encroaching on the oaks and promote the growth of wildflowers that are important food plants. Further investigations about these fire practices may be essential in figuring out how to maintain (50) oaks in the western landscape today, given that the fires address many of the factors that are now causing oak decline, from how to eliminate insect pests of acorns to how to maintain an open structure in oak groves.

(55)   Ecological restoration, the traditional approach to woodland maintenance, refers to humans intervening on a very limited time scale to bring back plants and animals known to have historically existed in an area. The decline of oaks, one of the (60) most significant plants to Native Americans, shows us that humans may play an integral part in the restoration of oak areas. While animals such as jays have been recognized as crucial partners in oak well-being, human actions through the eons may (65) also have been key to the oaks' flourishing.

Sudden oak death, for example, although of exotic origin, may be curtailed locally by thinning around coastal oaks and tan oaks and setting light surface fires, simulating ancient fire management (70) practices of Native Americans. Indigenous shrubs and trees that grow in association with oaks are hosts to the sudden oak death pathogen. By limiting the growth of these shrubs, burning that mimics earlier Native American ways may reduce (75) opportunities for disease agents to jump from other plants to oak trees. With a more open environment, it may be harder for sudden oak death to spread.

The oak landscapes that we inherited, which still bear the marks of former Native American (80) interactions, demand a new kind of restoration that complements other forms of ecological restoration. This new kind of restoration could be called ethnobotanical restoration, defined as reestablishing the historic plant communities of (85) a given area and restoring indigenous harvesting, vegetation management, and cultivation practices (seedbearing, burning, pruning, sowing, tilling, and weeding) necessary to maintain these communities in the long term.

(90)   Thus, this kind of restoration is not only about restoring plants but also about restoring the human place within nature. Ethnobotanical restoration is viewed not as a process that can be completed but rather as a continuous interaction (95) between people and plants, as both of their fates are intertwined in a region. Using oaks (through harvesting acorns and making products from all parts of the tree) and human intervention (by thinning tree populations and lighting light fires) (100) may offer us ways to beneficially coexist while improving the long-term health and well-being of the remarkable oak.

Don't get distracted by less important details. While there is a lot going on in this passage, your additions to the Passage Map should note the views regarding human involvement in ecological restoration as well as the definitions of unfamiliar terms like "ecological restoration" and "ethnobotanical restoration." If you're stuck, review the Suggested Passage Map Notes in the Answers & Explanations for this chapter on page 980.

Questions	Strategic Thinking

4. Throughout the passage, the author emphasizes that a key element in the restoration of the oak tree is
 	
  A) protecting the wildlife diversity found in the oaks' large crowns.
 	
  B) preventing Douglas firs from encroaching on oak tree habitats.
 	
  C) utilizing a continuous restoration process focused on human and oak interactions.
 	
  D) curtailing sudden oak death by eliminating exotic pathogens.
	Step 2: Examine the question stem
	
	What are the keywords in the question stem?
	
	The keywords in this question stem are "throughout the passage" and "a key element in the restoration of the oak tree."
	
	What parts of your Passage Map are relevant?
	
	The author begins to focus on the restoration of the oak tree in line 55. Look at your Passage Map notes from this point through the end of the passage to determine what the "key element" is.
	
	Step 3: Predict and answer
	
	What can you predict?
	
	The Passage Map notes from this point on focus on how humans can affect ecological restoration.
	
	Which answer choice matches this prediction?
	
	_____

5. According to the passage, an important distinction between "ecological restoration" in line 55 and "ethnobotanical restoration" in line 83 is that the latter
 	
  A) recreates ecosystems that accurately reflect historical uses of an area.
 	
  B) aspires to reintegrate humans into the continuous maintenance of plant communities.
 	
  C) intervenes for a limited time to restore an area to an earlier condition.
 	
  D) uses fire suppression more effectively to reduce risks from a variety of factors.
	Step 2: Examine the question stem
	
	What are the keywords in the question stem?
	
	The keywords in this question stem are "according to the passage," which implies the answer will be directly stated in the text, as well as the two quoted phrases and the lines in which they appear.
	
	What parts of your Passage Map are relevant?
	
	Use your Passage Map near these lines to compare the two types of restoration.
	
	Step 3: Predict and answer
	
	What is the primary difference between ecological restoration and ethnobotanical restoration?
	
	_____
	
	_____
	
	_____
	
	_____
	
	Which answer choice matches this prediction?
	
	_____

Questions	Strategic Thinking
6. Which choice provides the best evidence for the answer to the previous question? A) Lines 11-14 ("In the . . . died out") B) Lines 44-47 ("When used . . . plants") C) Lines 72-76 ("By limiting . . . trees") D) Lines 90-92 ("Thus, this . . . nature")	**Step 2: Examine the question stem** *What are the keywords in the question stem?* _____ _____ _____ _____ _____ *What parts of your Passage Map are relevant?* _____ _____ _____ _____ **Step 3: Predict and answer** *What part of the passage supports your answer to the previous question?* _____ _____ _____ *Which answer choice matches this prediction?* _____

Now, try a test-like SAT Reading passage on your own. Give yourself 6 minutes to read the passage and answer the questions.

Questions 7-11 are based on the following passage.

The following passage details findings from different eras of prenatal screening and the methods and experiments those findings prompted.

Screening newborns for rare genetic diseases is a relatively new practice that began in the mid-20th century. Prior to the advent of screening,
Line biomedical researchers and health professionals
(5) were preoccupied with the most prominent causes of newborn mortality, such as diarrheal diseases, influenza, and other infectious diseases. By 1960, however, the infant mortality rate had dropped to less than three percent of live births from over
(10) ten percent fifty years earlier. The declining rate was due, in part, to the widespread use of antibiotics; the development of vaccines, particularly the Salk and Sabin polio vaccines; improved nutrition; better education; and generally improved sanitary
(15) practices. As infant mortality rates dropped, attention shifted to the etiology of rare diseases. The first major milestone in this focus shift occurred in 1962, when President Kennedy announced that the federal government would begin exploring the
(20) problem of mental disability—until then, a largely ignored issue. He created the President's Panel on Mental Retardation to lead this exploration.

During roughly the same time period, a major scientific breakthrough in the study of
(25) phenylketonuria, or PKU, was underway. In 1934, Dr. Asbjorn Folling of Norway first described the condition when he observed that some of his mentally disabled patients had phenylpyruvic acid in their urine, a finding indicative of a deficiency in
(30) the enzyme that converts phenylalanine to tyrosine, a necessary component for protein synthesis. When this transformation does not occur, phenylalanine accumulates in the blood. High levels of phenylalanine are toxic to the developing brain of
(35) an infant and cause mental retardation. At the time,

the preventive strategy was to reduce phenylalanine levels in the patient's diet. This approach had one serious drawback, though. Phenylalanine is an essential amino acid necessary for proper growth,
(40) so deficiencies in it may also lead to mental retardation.

Despite this risk, the younger siblings of children with PKU were given diets low in phenylalanine from a very early age. The results were somewhat
(45) encouraging and, in light of the beneficial evidence from this special diet, two therapeutically promising research initiatives were launched. One was to devise a source of protein free of phenylalanine. The outcome was the infant formula Lofenalac,
(50) which is still in use today. The other initiative was aimed at developing a method for detecting high phenylalanine levels before damage to the developing brain could occur.

Dr. Robert Guthrie led the second initiative,
(55) which yielded a breakthrough in the early 1960s. He developed a test to detect PKU before it became clinically symptomatic. The test consisted of a culture of *Bacillus subtilis* and B-2-thienylalanine, which inhibits the growth of the bacteria. Once a
(60) blood sample from the newborn was added to this culture, the bacteria would leach the phenylalanine from the blood spot, overcome the inhibition caused by the B-2-thienylalanine, and grow. Bacterial growth beyond a normal range indicated
(65) elevated levels of phenylalanine and thus the presence of PKU in the newborn.

The test was not perfect. Over the next few years, it produced quite a few false positives, and some children unnecessarily received low phenyl-
(70) alanine diets. To compound the problem, there was uncertainty about the amount of phenylalanine to cut from the diet; as a result, some healthy children developed mental disabilities because of the treat-

ment. Nevertheless, PKU screening was generally con-
(75) sidered a success, and spurred questions about whether
other diseases might be prevented through early detec-
tion. After further study, it became clear that they could.
By the late 1960s, newborn screening for rare genetic
diseases had become a permanent part of infant health
(80) care in the United States.

7. The passage most strongly suggests that prior
    to the research initiatives described in lines
    42-53,

    A) little research had been conducted on the
        causes of newborn mortality.

    B) influenza research had yielded the most
        effective treatments.

    C) a treatment for PKU was implemented,
        despite its inherent risks.

    D) screening newborns for genetic diseases
        was a well-established practice.

8. Which choice provides the best evidence for
    the answer to the previous question?

    A) Lines 1-3 ("Screening newborns . . . mid-
        20th century")

    B) Lines 6-7 ("such as . . . diseases")

    C) Lines 31-33 ("When this . . . blood")

    D) Lines 39-41 ("Phenylalanine . . . retarda-
        tion")

9. This passage can best be described as

    A) a brief history of biomedical research in
        the 20th century.

    B) a description of how an important diag-
        nostic tool grew out of an attempt to treat
        a specific disease.

    C) an argument in support of genetic
        screening for rare diseases.

    D) an essay questioning the ethical nature of
        using untested medical treatments.

10. According to the passage, which of the
    following contributed to the practice of
    screening newborns for rare genetic diseases?

    A) Increased use of antibiotics

    B) The development of Lofenalac

    C) The false positives produced by Dr.
        Guthrie's test

    D) The success of PKU screening

11. Which choice provides the best evidence for
    the answer to the previous question?

    A) Lines 10-15 ("The declining . . .
        practices")

    B) Lines 49-50 ("The outcome . . . today")

    C) Lines 67-70 ("Over the . . . diets")

    D) Lines 74-77 ("Nevertheless, PKU . . .
        detection")

Answers & Explanations for this chapter begin on
page 980.

EXTRA PRACTICE

The following questions provide an opportunity to practice the concepts and strategic thinking covered in this chapter. While many of the questions pertain to Citing Textual Evidence and Global questions, some touch on other concepts tested on the Reading Test to ensure that your practice is test-like, with a variety of question types per passage.

Questions 1-11 are based on the following passage and supplementary material.

This passage describes how tree farms, widely thought to offer little support to wildlife, became home to a rare species of birds.

As our environment changes over time, certain species thrive while others become rarer. One such species is the small, difficult-to-find Swainson's
Line warbler. Scientists struggle to estimate the
(5) population of this songbird because it is challenging to track. America's foremost wildlife artist, John James Audubon, attempted to describe the bird in the 1830s. Even then, it was considered uncommon. Some of the other birds studied by Audubon
(10) have already become extinct, including the ivory-billed woodpecker. Others, such as the Allen's hummingbird, the spotted owl, and the osprey, are at increased risk of extinction due to their habitats disappearing. Against all odds, the Swainson's
(15) warbler has held on by changing where it spends its summer seasons.

The Swainson's warbler has been at risk for extinction due to the specificity of its needs. During breeding season, summer, the bird traditionally
(20) spends time in the southeastern United States forests and lowlands. It then migrates to subtropical locations in the winter, seeking the dry forests of Jamaica or other evergreen forests in Mexico and Cuba. The low population has been attributed to the
(25) loss of these habitats due to the gradual conversion of hardwood forests into farmland, reservoirs, and urban or suburban areas. With numbers as low as 90,000 worldwide, the prognosis for the continued survival of the bird has been bleak.
(30) Scientists have been studying the birds across the southern United States for more than two decades, but attempts to conserve the species have fallen

short due to a lack of understanding of their true habitat needs. Scientists tried to shift the Swainson's
(35) warbler to national forests, public refuges, and private sanctuaries, but success was limited. Recently, though, researchers found that the population is increasing. Since the 1990s, Swainson's warblers have been doing what scientists attempted to do for
(40) them: the birds have created new breeding grounds for themselves by moving into industrial pine plantations that have been planted in ten different states.

Millions of acres of industrial pine forests have been planted since the 1920s. Some of these planta-
(45) tions are even located in the same areas that Swainson's warblers used to use for breeding grounds before the area's natural forests disappeared. With trees cut every 25 to 35 years, these plantations support a $200 billion industry that produces wood-
(50) based goods from housing lumber to notebook paper. The pine plantations were once thought by scientists to offer little support to any wildlife. They do not make ideal habitats due to the even spacing of planted rows and the lack of diversity in tree
(55) species. These plantations, though, happen to offer the Swainson's warbler two of the things they most require from their habitats.

When the pines at these tree farms reach about twenty feet high, they hit the one specific stage of
(60) growth that appeals to the birds. This height creates high-density undergrowth that the birds rely on for protection during their breeding season. This point of the pine development best mimics the bird's traditional habitat. Before deforestation occurred in
(65) the Southeastern United States, Swainson's warblers lived in thickets of cane or areas with dense vines and tangled undergrowth. At the pine plantations,

the habitat lasts for about seven to eight years before the trees grow too tall to provide the birds
(70) the coverage that they seek. The birds move on once the tangled undergrowth they prefer disappears.

The Swainson's warbler's secondary requirement that pine plantations can easily provide is space. A single breeding pair of the species requires between
(75) 10 and 20 acres of land. This large amount of space is one of the reasons why the species was so vulnerable to deforestation.

Today, pine plantations occupy some 40 million acres in the southern United States. Not all of these
(80) acres are usable to the birds, though. When the cutting cycles and the amount of time the trees offer the type of undergrowth desirable to the Swainson's warblers are considered, it is estimated that approximately 10 million acres of pine plantations
(85) are available to the birds at one time.

These numbers suggest that pine plantations will become the Swainson's warbler's primary habitat over time. The species owes its continued existence to its ability to adapt. While other species of war-
(90) bler have disappeared entirely due to the clearing of natural forests, the Swainson's warbler has remained flexible, shifting its behavior to ensure its own preservation.

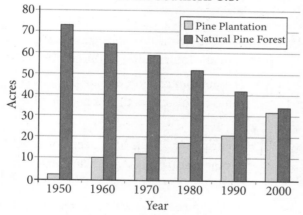

Planted vs. Natural Pine Forests in the Southern U.S.

Adapted from *United States Geological Survey, Land Cover Trends Project.*

1. The central idea of the passage is primarily concerned with

   A) the impact of deforestation on endangered birds throughout North America and the Caribbean.

   B) how industrial pine plantations have affected the manufacturing of wood-based commercial goods.

   C) how the population of the Swainson's warbler is recovering despite the destruction of the bird's natural habitat.

   D) the ways in which scientists have struggled to increase populations of the Swainson's warbler.

2. The author refers to the Allen's hummingbird, spotted owl, and osprey in lines 11-12 to

   A) contrast the habitat needs of the Swainson's warbler with that of other bird species.

   B) illustrate the difficulties faced by conservationists attempting to protect threatened birds.

   C) provide examples of other birds threatened by the disappearance of their habitats.

   D) imply that more species of birds will find alternative habitats as deforestation continues.

3. Based on the information in the passage, conservation efforts to protect the Swainson's warbler have been unsuccessful because scientists have

   A) been unable to track the Swainson's warbler population.

   B) not had the resources to move the birds to new habitats.

   C) not understood the bird's habitat needs.

   D) been unable to get the birds to breed in captivity.

4. Which choice provides the best evidence for the answer to the previous question?

A) Lines 4-6 ("Scientists struggle . . . track")

B) Lines 18-21 ("During breeding . . . lowlands")

C) Lines 30-34 ("Scientists have . . . habitat needs")

D) Lines 58-60 ("When the pines . . . birds")

5. As used in line 25, "conversion" most nearly means

A) translation.

B) destruction.

C) variation.

D) transformation.

6. Based on the information in the passage, the reader can infer that

A) bird populations will continue to decrease if their natural habitats are destroyed.

B) the Swainson's warbler's population will decrease again if more pine forests are not planted.

C) the profitability of the pine forests is increased by the presence of the Swainson's warbler.

D) populations of other endangered birds would increase if they moved to private sanctuaries.

7. Which choice provides the best evidence for the answer to the previous question?

A) Lines 1-4 ("As our environment . . . warbler")

B) Lines 11-14 ("Others, such as . . . disappearing")

C) Lines 43-44 ("Millions of acres . . . 1920s")

D) Lines 51-52 ("The pine plantations . . . wildlife")

8. The primary purpose of this passage is to

A) argue that more must be done to protect endangered bird species.

B) persuade readers to learn more about how they can help protect birds.

C) summarize the ways that conservation groups have failed to protect endangered birds.

D) explain how one threatened species of bird has adapted to its disappearing habitat.

9. The migration of the Swainson's warbler to industrial pine forests is most similar to which of the following?

A) Beavers building dams using sticks and logs

B) Spiders creating cobwebs in bushes and trees

C) Aquatic animals creating artificial reefs from shipwrecks

D) Raccoons foraging for food in garbage bins

10. As used in line 62, "point" most nearly means

A) stage.

B) purpose.

C) detail.

D) level.

11. Which of the following conclusions is supported by the information in the graph?

A) The number of acres of pine plantation could soon surpass that of natural pine forests.

B) Natural pine forests have been converted to pine plantations to provide habitats for birds.

C) Natural pine forests will be completely replaced by pine plantations by the year 2050.

D) Pine plantations produce more usable lumber per acre than natural pine forests.

Questions 12-21 are based on the following passage.

The following passage is adapted from Lucy Maud Montgomery's 1908 novel *Anne of Green Gables*. This excerpt details a conversation between Anne, the young protagonist, and Marilla, Anne's guardian.

"And what are your eyes popping out of your head about now?" asked Marilla, when Anne had just come in from a run to the post office. "Have
Line you discovered another kindred spirit?" Excite-
(5) ment hung around Anne like a garment, shone in her eyes, kindled in every feature. She had come dancing up the lane, like a wind-blown sprite, through the mellow sunshine and lazy shadows of the August evening.

(10) "No, Marilla, but oh, what do you think? I am invited to tea at the manse tomorrow afternoon! Mrs. Allan left the letter for me at the post office. Just look at it, Marilla. 'Miss Anne Shirley, Green Gables.' That is the first time I was ever called 'Miss.'
(15) Such a thrill as it gave me! I shall cherish it forever among my choicest treasures."

"Mrs. Allan told me she meant to have all the members of her Sunday-school class to tea in turn," said Marilla, regarding the wonderful event very
(20) coolly. "You needn't get in such a fever over it. Do learn to take things calmly, child."

For Anne to take things calmly would have been to change her nature. All "spirit and fire and dew," as she was, the pleasures and pains of life came to
(25) her with trebled intensity. Marilla felt this and was vaguely troubled over it, realizing that the ups and downs of existence would probably bear hardly on this impulsive soul and not sufficiently understanding that the equally great capacity for delight might
(30) more than compensate. Therefore Marilla conceived it to be her duty to drill Anne into a tranquil uniformity of disposition as impossible and alien to her as to a dancing sunbeam in one of the brook shallows. She did not make much headway, as she
(35) sorrowfully admitted to herself. The downfall of some dear hope or plan plunged Anne into "deeps of affliction." The fulfillment thereof exalted her to dizzy realms of delight. Marilla had almost begun to despair of ever fashioning this waif of the world

(40) into her model little girl of demure manners and prim deportment. Neither would she have believed that she really liked Anne much better as she was.

Anne went to bed that night speechless with misery because Matthew had said the wind was
(45) round northeast and he feared it would be a rainy day tomorrow. The rustle of the poplar leaves about the house worried her, it sounded so like pattering raindrops, and the full, faraway roar of the gulf, to which she listened delightedly at other times,
(50) loving its strange, sonorous, haunting rhythm, now seemed like a prophecy of storm and disaster to a small maiden who particularly wanted a fine day. Anne thought that the morning would never come.

But all things have an end, even nights before
(55) the day on which you are invited to take tea at the manse. The morning, in spite of Matthew's predictions, was fine and Anne's spirits soared to their highest. "Oh, Marilla, there is something in me today that makes me just love everybody I see,"
(60) she exclaimed as she washed the breakfast dishes. "You don't know how good I feel! Wouldn't it be nice if it could last? I believe I could be a model child if I were just invited out to tea every day. But oh, Marilla, it's a solemn occasion too. I feel so
(65) anxious. What if I shouldn't behave properly? You know I never had tea at a manse before, and I'm not sure that I know all the rules of etiquette, although I've been studying the rules given in the Etiquette Department of the Family Herald ever since I came
(70) here. I'm so afraid I'll do something silly or forget to do something I should do. Would it be good manners to take a second helping of anything if you wanted to VERY much?"

"The trouble with you, Anne, is that you're
(75) thinking too much about yourself. You should just think of Mrs. Allan and what would be nicest and most agreeable to her," said Marilla, hitting for once in her life on a very sound and pithy piece of advice. Anne instantly realized this.
(80) "You are right, Marilla. I'll try not to think about myself at all."

12. In lines 3-4, what is implied by Marilla's question, "'Have you discovered another kindred spirit?'"

    A) Anne is deeply spiritual.

    B) Anne is a sociable person.

    C) Anne seeks out adventures.

    D) Anne has a fear of strangers.

13. The author's use of words such as "dancing" and "wind-blown" in line 7 implies that Anne is

    A) graceful and rhythmic.

    B) messy and disorganized.

    C) energetic and active.

    D) scatterbrained and confused.

14. As used in line 39, "fashioning" most nearly means

    A) preparing.

    B) constructing.

    C) styling.

    D) devising.

15. Which choice best describes the relationship between Anne and Matthew?

    A) Anne does not trust Matthew's predictions.

    B) Anne is worried about Matthew's safety.

    C) Anne takes Matthew's statements seriously.

    D) Anne is uncertain about Matthew's intentions.

16. According to the passage, what does Marilla think is Anne's greatest challenge in life?

    A) Anne thinks about herself too much.

    B) Anne must learn to take things calmly.

    C) Anne needs to master the rules of etiquette.

    D) Anne worries too much about things she cannot control.

17. The fourth paragraph is important to the passage's progression of ideas because it

    A) explains the antagonistic relationship between Anne and Marilla.

    B) offers background information about Marilla's concerns about Anne.

    C) explains how Marilla has systematically changed Anne into a model child.

    D) provides a transition from Anne reading the letter to the following morning.

18. As used in line 78, "sound" most nearly means

    A) practical.

    B) clamor.

    C) ethical.

    D) secure.

19. It can be inferred that the author

    A) is an omniscient third-person observer.

    B) allows the reader to know only Anne's inner thoughts.

    C) offers an objective perspective from within the story.

    D) is unaware of actions that take place elsewhere in the story.

20. The passage most strongly suggests that which of the following is true of Marilla?

   A) She hopes Anne will soon learn to admire Mrs. Allen.

   B) She believes Anne's "deeps of affliction" are dangerous.

   C) She has come to dislike Anne's overly excitable nature.

   D) She values calm and even-keeled responses to all situations.

21. Which choice provides the best evidence for the answer to the previous question?

   A) Lines 20-21 ("'You needn't . . . child'")

   B) Lines 25-30 ("Marilla felt . . . compensate")

   C) Lines 41-42 ("Neither would . . . as she was")

   D) Lines 74-79 ("The trouble . . . advice")

CHAPTER 16

Connections and Vocab-in-Context Questions

 ## CHAPTER OBJECTIVES

By the end of this chapter, you will be able to:

1. Identify and answer Connections questions that ask about explicitly stated cause-and-effect, compare-and-contrast, and sequenced relationships in a passage

2. Identify and answer Connections questions that ask about implicit cause-and-effect, compare-and-contrast, and sequenced relationships in a passage

3. Interpret words and phrases in context to answer test-like questions

SMARTPOINTS

Point Value	SmartPoint Category
10 Points	Connections
60 Points	Vocab-in-Context

Reading & Writing

CONNECTIONS & VOCAB-IN-CONTEXT QUESTIONS

Chapter 16

Homework

Extra Practice: #1-10

Even More

The Kaplan Method for Vocab-in-Context

Reading Quiz 4

Key

 Book Assignment

 Online Video Assignment

 Online Quiz Assignment

CONNECTIONS QUESTIONS

Before we jump into the specifics about inferring connections—explicit and implicit—let's look at different kinds of connections that can exist in an SAT Reading passage.

Connections questions ask about how two events, characters, or ideas are related. The three most common connection types are:

1. **Cause-and-Effect** connections require you to identify an action or condition that brings about a predictable result. You can identify cause-and-effect relationships by the keywords *caused by*, *results in*, *because*, and *therefore*.

2. **Compare-and-Contrast** connections highlight the similarities or differences between two items. Common compare-and-contrast keywords are *similar*, *different*, *despite*, and *like*.

3. **Sequential** connections describe the chronology, or order, in which the items are arranged or occur. Keywords include *first*, *second*, *following*, and *after*.

EXPLICIT CONNECTIONS QUESTIONS

Some Connections questions will ask about explicit information; the question stem will provide one part of the relationship and ask you to find the other part. In an explicit Connections question, the wording of the correct answer will be very similar to the wording of the passage.

> ✔ **Remember**
>
> Don't forget Step 2 of the Kaplan Method for Reading Comprehension: Examine the question stem.

IMPLICIT CONNECTIONS QUESTIONS

Questions about implicit connections, like those about explicit connections, ask you to identify how items are related. However, unlike explicit Connections questions, an implicit Connections question requires you to find a relationship that may not be directly stated in the passage.

When answering implicit Connections questions, describe the relationship being tested in your own words by using keywords like *because*, *although*, and *in order to*.

> ✔ **Expert Tip**
>
> Eliminating answer choices that are clearly wrong will help you answer even the toughest implicit Connections questions correctly.

Reading & Writing

Reading & Writing

VOCAB-IN-CONTEXT QUESTIONS

Vocab-in-Context questions require you to deduce the meaning of a word or phrase by using the context in which the word or phrase appears. You can recognize Vocab-in-Context questions because the wording of the question stem is often like this: "As used in line 7, 'clairvoyant' most nearly means . . . "

> ✔ **Expert Tip**
>
> Some Vocab-in-Context questions ask about infrequently used words that you don't know or that may not have a common meaning. Approach these questions exactly the same way you would any other Vocab-in-Context question—by using the Kaplan Strategy.

Kaplan's Strategy for Vocab-in-Context questions relies heavily on Step 3 of the Kaplan Method for Reading Comprehension: Predict and answer.

To answer Vocab-in-Context questions efficiently and correctly, employ the following Kaplan Strategy:

- Pretend the word is a blank in the sentence
- Predict what word could be substituted for the blank
- Select the answer choice that best matches your prediction

> ✔ **Real-World Application**
>
> You can use the Kaplan Strategy for Vocab-in-Context questions outside of the test preparation context. It works for texts you read for school and in your free time.

Let's look at the following example of a test-like passage and question set. After the mapped passage, the left column contains questions similar to those you'll see on SAT Reading Test on Test Day. The column on the right features the strategic thinking test experts employ when approaching the passage and questions presented. Pay attention to how test experts vary the approach to answer different question types.

> ✔ **Note**
>
> SAT passages often use primary source material, which means the language can seem antiquated to modern readers. In some instances, we have modified this language. Don't let that distract you from making a Passage Map focusing on the central ideas.

Strategic Thinking

Step 1: Read actively

Read the passage and the notes provided. Remember, a well-crafted Passage Map should summarize the central idea of each paragraph, as well as important topics or themes. Use your Passage Map to help you answer each question.

Questions 1-3 are based on the following passage.

The following passage is adapted from President Abraham Lincoln's Second Inaugural Address, delivered on March 4, 1865.

At this second appearing to take the oath of the Presidential office there is less occasion for an extended address than there was at the first. Then,
Line a statement somewhat in detail of a course to be
(5) pursued seemed fitting and proper. Now, at the expiration of four years, during which public declarations have been constantly called forth on every point and phase of the great contest which still absorbs the attention and engrosses the energies
(10) of the nation, little that is new would be presented. The progress of our arms, upon which all else chiefly depends, is as well known to the public as to myself, and it is, I trust, reasonably satisfactory and encouraging to all. With high hope for the future,
(15) no prediction in regard to it is ventured.

On the occasion corresponding to this four years ago all thoughts were anxiously directed to an impending civil war. All dreaded it, all sought to avert it. While the inaugural address was being delivered
(20) from this place, devoted altogether to *saving* the Union without war, urgent agents were in the city seeking to *destroy* it without war—seeking to dissolve the Union and divide effects by negotiation. Both parties deprecated war, but one of them would
(25) *make* war rather than let the nation survive, and the other would *accept* war rather than let it perish, and the war came.

One-eighth of the whole population were black slaves, not distributed generally over the Union,
(30) but localized in the southern part of it. These slaves constituted a peculiar and powerful interest. All

knew that this interest was somehow the cause of the war. To strengthen, perpetuate, and extend this interest was the object for which the insurgents
(35) would rend the Union, even by war; while the Government claimed no right to do more than to restrict the territorial enlargement of it. Neither party expected for the war the magnitude or the duration which it has already attained. Neither an-
(40) ticipated that the cause of the conflict might cease with or even before the conflict itself should cease. Each looked for an easier triumph, and a result less fundamental and astounding.

¶1: 1st vs 2nd AL inauguration address

1, cont.: progress good; public knows too

2: before: war about to happen but no one wanted it

2, cont.: bad guys made war to destroy Union; good guys accepted to have it

3: before: most slaves South

¶3, cont.: slavery = cause of war

¶3, cont.: no one knew how big or how long war would be

Questions	Strategic Thinking
1. Which choice best describes the differing attitudes of the insurgents and the government toward slavery? A) The insurgents wanted to preserve slavery's reach, while the government wanted to reduce it. B) The insurgents wanted to extend slavery's reach, while the government wanted to abolish the institution. C) The insurgents wanted to extend slavery's reach, while the government wanted to limit the expansion of slavery. D) The insurgents wanted to reduce slavery's reach, while the government wanted to preserve it.	**Step 2: Examine the question stem** Identify the key words and phrases in the question stem: "differing attitudes of the insurgents and the government toward slavery." Information about different attitudes be found in the third paragraph. **Step 3: Predict and answer** According to the third paragraph, the insurgents wanted "to strengthen, perpetuate, and extend" slavery (line 33) and the government wanted to "restrict the territorial enlargement" of slavery (line 37). Choice (C) matches this prediction.
2. As used in line 34, "interest" most nearly means A) involvement. B) attention. C) claim. D) return.	**Step 2: Examine the question stem** The keywords in this question stem are the cited word and "most nearly means." Use the Kaplan Strategy for Vocab-in-Context questions to answer question stems with this phrasing. **Step 3: Predict and answer** "Interest" is used three times in lines 31-34, but this question is asking about its third appearance. The context of "interest" in this sentence is related to the goals of the insurgents, who wanted to extend slavery. "Interest" could be replaced by *ownership* or *privilege*. Choice (C) matches this prediction.

Questions	Strategic Thinking
3. The result referred to in lines 42-43 ("a result . . . astounding") was most likely caused by the A) magnitude of the war. B) limitation of slavery. C) duration of the war. D) dissolution of the Union.	**Step 2: Examine the question stem** The key words and phrases in the question stem are the cited phrase and "most likely caused by." The Passage Map notes for paragraph 3 will point toward the correct answer. **Step 3: Predict and answer** The Passage Map notes for this paragraph cite slavery as the cause of the war. Choice (B) matches this prediction.

You have seen the ways in which the SAT tests you on Connections and Vocab-in-Context questions in Reading passages and the way an SAT expert approaches these types of questions.

You will use the Kaplan Method for Reading Comprehension to complete this section. Part of the test-like passage has been mapped already. Your first step is to complete the Passage Map. Then, you will continue to use the Kaplan Method for Reading Comprehension and the strategies discussed in this chapter to answer the questions. Strategic thinking questions have been included to guide you—some of the answers have been filled in, but you will have to fill in the answers to others.

Use your answers to the strategic thinking questions to select the correct answer, just as you will on Test Day.

Strategic Thinking
Step 1: Read actively The passage below is partially mapped. Read the passage and the first part of the Passage Map. Then, complete the Passage Map on your own. Remember to focus on the central ideas of each paragraph as well as the central idea of the overall passage. Use your Passage Map as a reference when you're answering questions.

Questions 4-6 are based on the following passage.

The following passage is an excerpt from the preface of *Moll Flanders* (1722) by Daniel Defoe.

¶1: book is not fiction

The world is so taken up of late with novels and romances, that it will be hard for a private history to be taken for genuine, where the names and other
Line circumstances of the person are concealed, and on
(5) this account we must be content to leave the reader to pass his own opinion upon the ensuing sheet, and take it just as he pleases.

¶2: MF conceals name

The author is here supposed to be writing her own history, and in the very beginning of her
(10) account she gives the reasons why she thinks fit to conceal her true name, after which there is no occasion to say any more about that.

¶3: MF uses modest tone

It is true that the original of this story is put into new words, and the style of the famous lady we here
(15) speak of is a little altered; particularly she is made to tell her own tale in modester words than she told it at first, the copy which came first to hand having been written in language more like one still in Newgate than one grown penitent and humble, as
(20) she afterwards pretends to be.

The pen employed in finishing her story, and making it what you now see it to be, has had no little difficulty to put it into a dress fit to be seen, and to make it speak language fit to be read. When
(25) a woman debauched from her youth, nay, even being the offspring of debauchery and vice, comes to give an account of all her vicious practices, and even to descend to the particular occasions and circumstances by which she ran through in
(30) threescore years, an author must be hard put to wrap it up so clean as not to give room, especially for vicious readers, to turn it to his disadvantage.

¶4: MF's story is dark

All possible care, however, has been taken to give no lewd ideas, no immodest turns in the
(35) new dressing up of this story; no, not to the worst parts of her expressions. To this purpose some of the vicious part of her life, which could not be modestly told, is quite left out, and several other parts are very much shortened. What is left 'tis
(40) hoped will not offend the chastest reader or the modest hearer; and as the best use is made even of the worst story, the moral 'tis hoped will keep the

reader serious, even where the story might incline
him to be otherwise. To give the history of a wicked
(45) life repented of, necessarily requires that the wicked
part should be make as wicked as the real history
of it will bear, to illustrate and give a beauty to
the penitent part, which is certainly the best and
brightest, if related with equal spirit and life.

(50)   But as this work is chiefly recommended to
those who know how to read it, and how to make
the good uses of it which the story all along recommends to them, so it is to be hoped that such readers will be more pleased with the moral than the
(55) fable, with the application than with the relation,
and with the end of the writer than with the life of
the person written of.

There is in this story abundance of delightful
incidents, and all of them usefully applied. There
(60) is an agreeable turn artfully given them in the

relating, that naturally instructs the reader, either
one way or other. The first part of her lewd life
with the young gentleman at Colchester has so
many happy turns given it to expose the crime,
(65) and warn all whose circumstances are adapted to
it, of the ruinous end of such things, and the foolish, thoughtless, and abhorred conduct of both the
parties, that it abundantly atones for all the lively
description she gives of her folly and wickedness.

(70)   Upon this foundation this book is recommended to the reader as a work from every part
of which something may be learned, and some
just and religious inference is drawn, by which the
reader will have something of instruction, if he
(75) pleases to make use of it.

Don't get distracted by less important details. While there is a lot going on in this passage, your
additions to the Passage Map should show that Moll Flanders did eventually change and how the
author thinks the reader should respond to the story. If you're stuck, review the Suggested Passage
Map Notes in the Answers & Explanations for this chapter on page 984.

Questions	Strategic Thinking
4. According to the passage, the narrator is concerned that readers may not believe the story because A) each reader is entitled to form his or her own opinion about the story. B) some parts of the story have been omitted. C) different readers will interpret the story in different ways. D) readers will assume that the story is a novel.	**Step 2: Examine the question stem** *What are the keywords in this question stem?* The keywords in this question stem are "According to the passage" and "readers may not believe the story because . . . " The answer will be found in the passage. *What parts of your Passage Map are relevant?* The Passage Map notes for the first paragraph say that the story might not seem true, which corresponds to the question stem. The answer will be in the first paragraph. **Step 3: Predict and answer** *What can you predict?* The author is concerned that the readers might not believe the story because "the world is so taken up of late with novels and romances," which may cause many readers to believe that the story is fictional (lines 1-2). *Which answer choice matches this prediction?* _____
5. Based on the passage, the narrator hopes that readers of the story will A) understand the reasons for omitting certain parts of the story. B) recognize the harm that a misguided reading might cause. C) use the moral of the story to improve their own lives. D) enjoy the story for the vividness of the characterizations.	**Step 2: Examine the question stem** *What are the keywords in this question stem?* The keywords in this question stem are the phrase "Based on the passage," which implies that the correct answer is not explicitly stated, and "narrator hopes." *What parts of the passage are relevant?* The narrator discusses his hopes for the reader in the final paragraph, where you will find the answer. **Step 3: Predict and answer** *What does the narrator specifically want the reader to take away from the story?* _____ _____ _____ _____ *Which answer choice matches this prediction?* _____

434 Unit Six: Reading

Questions	Strategic Thinking

6. As used in line 59, "usefully applied" most nearly means
 	
  A) well written.
  B) consistent with the author's purpose.
  C) useful in the proper context.
  D) humorously recounted.
	Step 2: Examine the question stem
	
	What are the keywords in this question stem?
	_____
	_____
	_____
	_____
	
	How can you find the answer?
	_____
	_____
	_____
	_____
	
	Step 3: Predict and answer
	
	What word or phrase can you substitute for the phrase in question?
	_____
	_____
	_____
	
	Which answer choice matches this prediction?
	_____

Perform

Now, try a test-like SAT Reading passage on your own. Give yourself 6 minutes to read the passage and answer the questions.

Questions 7-10 are based on the following passage.

The following passage is about the role chemistry plays in archaeology.

Demonstrating that chemistry sometimes can inform history, researchers from the National Institute of Standards and Technology (NIST), Colorado
Line College and Mount Saint Mary's University in
(5) Emmitsburg, Maryland, have shown that sensitive nondestructive evaluation (NDE) techniques can be used to determine the elemental composition of ancient coins, even coins that generally have been considered too corroded for such methods. Along
(10) the way, the researchers' analysis of coins minted in ancient Judea has both raised new questions about who ruled the area while giving insight into trading patterns and industry in the region.

Elemental and isotope analysis of the metals in
(15) ancient artifacts sometimes can pinpoint the places where the metal was mined because ores in a given region often have a unique composition. This can be combined with historical records of when mines in the area were operating to determine when the
(20) coin was likely struck. The results not only help date the coin, but also offer insight into trade and power relationships in the region.

To compare the effectiveness of various nondestructive analytical methods with destructive
(25) methods often used to determine the age and origin of ancient coins, the group studied coins minted by Kings Herod Agrippa I and Herod Agrippa II, in what is modern day Palestine and Israel, during a biblically and historically significant period.

(30) The vast numbers of a particular coin, the *prutah*, found in the archaeological record has led scholars to disagree about when they were struck and by whom. The provenance of the coin is important because it is used to establish dates for places
(35) and events in the early years of Christianity and the onset of the Jewish War (66-70 CE) against the Romans and the Diaspora that followed.

To better establish whether the coins were minted by Agrippa I (41-45 CE) or Agrippa II (after
(40) 61 CE), the team performed X-ray fluorescence and lead isotope analysis to fingerprint the ores used in the production of the coins. These NDE methods are not commonly used on corroded coins because the corrosion can affect the results—in some cases
(45) making it difficult to get a result at all. The team showed that these problems could be overcome using polarizing optics and powerful new software for X-ray fluorescence analysis, combined with careful calibration of the mass spectrometer using
(50) Standard Reference Materials from NIST.

The lead isotope analysis, performed at NIST, showed that the coins that had been attributed to Agrippa I were indeed from that era. More interestingly, however, the group found that the
(55) copper from which the coins were made most likely came from mines that scholars thought hadn't been opened until a century later.

"All the archaeological evidence has thus far suggested that the Romans had moved into Arabia
(60) in the second century CE," says Nathan Bower of Colorado College. "What this analysis shows is that the Romans may have reached the region earlier or found that these mines had already been opened. Either way, our findings suggest that the Romans
(65) had a much closer relationship with this particular region than scholars had previously thought."

To follow up on their research, the group is planning to perform more tests to determine if the mines in question may have been operating even
(70) earlier than their recent findings suggest.

Reading & Writing

7. As used in line 32, "struck" most nearly means

   A) made.

   B) hit.

   C) ignited.

   D) discovered.

8. The passage strongly suggests that the results of the lead isotope analysis on the ancient coins

   A) proved the value of an experimental method of analysis.

   B) offered a definitive analysis regarding the strength of ancient regimes.

   C) showed how the ability to mine coins affects trading practices.

   D) answered old questions and raised new ones.

9. According to the passage, the researchers chose to analyze a particular coin because

   A) it was less corroded than other coins of the same era.

   B) historians knew very little about the era during which it was minted.

   C) the metal used to mint the coin came from mines in Arabia.

   D) scholars disagreed about the origin of the coin.

10. As used in line 38, "establish" most nearly means

   A) ascertain.

   B) install.

   C) build.

   D) begin.

Answers & Explanations for this chapter begin on page 984.

Reading & Writing

EXTRA PRACTICE

The following questions provide an opportunity to practice the concepts and strategic thinking covered in this chapter. While many of the questions pertain to Connections and Vocab-in-Context questions, some touch on other concepts tested on the Reading Test to ensure that your practice is test-like, with a variety of question types per passage.

Questions 1-10 are based on the following passage.

The following passage is adapted from *Around the World in Eighty Days* by Jules Verne.

Phileas Fogg, having shut the door of his house at half-past eleven, and having put his right foot before his left five hundred and seventy-five times, and his left foot before his right five hundred and
(5) seventy-six times, reached the Reform Club. He repaired at once to the dining-room and took his place at the habitual table, the cover of which had already been laid for him. A flunkey handed him an uncut Times, which he proceeded to cut with
(10) a skill which betrayed familiarity with this delicate operation. The perusal of this paper absorbed Phileas Fogg until a quarter before four, whilst the Standard, his next task, occupied him till the dinner hour. Dinner passed as breakfast had done, and
(15) Mr. Fogg re-appeared in the reading-room and sat down to the *Pall Mall*[1] at twenty minutes before six. Half an hour later several members of the Reform came in and drew up to the fireplace. They were Mr. Fogg's usual partners at whist:[2] Andrew Stuart,
(20) an engineer; John Sullivan and Samuel Fallentin, bankers; Thomas Flanagan, a brewer; and Gauthier Ralph, one of the Directors of the Bank of England.

"Well, Ralph," said Thomas Flanagan, "what about that robbery?"

(25) "Oh," replied Stuart, "the Bank will lose the money."

"On the contrary," broke in Ralph, "I hope we may put our hands on the robber. Skillful detectives have been sent to all the principal ports of America
(30) and the Continent, and he'll be a clever fellow if he slips through their fingers."

"But have you got the robber's description?" asked Stuart.

"In the first place, he is no robber at all,"
(35) returned Ralph, positively.

"What! a fellow who makes off with fifty-five thousand pounds, no robber?"

"No."

"Perhaps he's a manufacturer, then."

(40) "The Daily Telegraph says that he is a gentleman."

It was Phileas Fogg, whose head now emerged from behind his newspapers, who made this remark. A package of banknotes, to the value of
(45) fifty-five thousand pounds, had been taken from the principal cashier's table, that functionary being at the moment engaged in registering the receipt of three shillings and sixpence. Let it be observed that the Bank of England reposes a touching confidence
(50) in the honesty of the public. There are neither guards nor gratings to protect its treasures; gold, silver, banknotes are freely exposed, at the mercy of the first comer. A keen observer of English customs relates that, being in one of the rooms of the Bank
(55) one day, he had the curiosity to examine a gold ingot weighing some seven or eight pounds. He took it up, scrutinised it, passed it to his neighbour, he to the next man, and so on until the ingot, going from hand to hand, was transferred to the end of a
(60) dark entry; nor did it return to its place for half an hour. Meanwhile, the cashier had not so much as raised his head. But in the present instance things had not gone so smoothly. The package of notes not being found when five o'clock sounded from the
(65) ponderous clock in the "drawing office," the amount was passed to the account of profit and loss.

There were real grounds for supposing, as the Daily Telegraph said, that the thief did not belong

to a professional band. On the day of the robbery a
(70) well-dressed gentleman of polished manners, and with
a well-to-do air, had been observed going to and fro in
the paying room where the crime was committed. A
description of him was easily procured and sent to the
detectives; and some hopeful spirits, of whom Ralph
(75) was one, did not despair of his apprehension. The papers
and clubs were full of the affair, and everywhere people
were discussing the probabilities of a successful pursuit;
and the Reform Club was especially agitated, several of
its members being Bank officials.

(80)   Ralph would not concede that the work of the
detectives was likely to be in vain, for he thought that
the prize offered would greatly stimulate their zeal and
activity. But Stuart was far from sharing this confidence;
and, as they placed themselves at the whist-table, they
(85) continued to argue the matter.

"I maintain," said Stuart, "that the chances are in
favour of the thief, who must be a shrewd fellow."

"Well, but where can he fly to?" asked Ralph. "No
country is safe for him."

(90)   "Pshaw!"

"Where could he go, then?"

"Oh, I don't know that. The world is big enough."

"It was once," said Phileas Fogg, in a low tone.

[1] *Pall Mall*: an evening newspaper (the *Pall Mall
Gazette*) founded in London in 1865
[2] whist: a trick-taking card game; modern derivatives
include hearts and spades

1. As used in line 6, "repaired" most nearly
    means

    A) fixed.

    B) returned.

    C) stormed.

    D) proceeded.

2. The passage suggests that Phileas Fogg is a
    man who

    A) focuses on cultural activities.

    B) lives beyond his means.

    C) enjoys routine.

    D) keeps to himself.

3. Which choice provides the best evidence for
    the answer to the previous question?

    A) Lines 5-8 ("He repaired . . . for him")

    B) Lines 8-11 ("A flunkey . . . delicate opera-
    tion")

    C) Lines 14-16 ("Dinner passed . . . before
    six")

    D) Lines 28-31 ("Skillful detectives . . . their
    fingers")

4. The passage suggests that Fogg

    A) keeps abreast of current events.

    B) is a political reformer.

    C) has strong opinions about crime.

    D) makes his living as a banker.

5. Which choice provides the best evidence for
    the answer to the previous question?

    A) Lines 8-11 ("A flunkey . . . delicate opera-
    tion")

    B) Lines 17-18 ("Half an hour . . . the fire-
    place")

    C) Lines 28-31 ("Skillful detectives . . . their
    fingers")

    D) Lines 42-44 ("It was . . . this remark")

6. According to the passage, which statement
    about the Bank of England is true?

    A) The public has faith in the integrity of the
    Bank.

    B) The Bank has taken few precautions to
    guard against theft.

    C) The Bank has a history of money being
    stolen.

    D) The Bank has carefully managed public
    relations.

7. As used in line 46, "functionary" most nearly means

A) official.

B) money.

C) servant.

D) criminal.

8. The passage suggests that the thief was not part of a professional crime ring because

A) the suspect acted alone.

B) the Bank had never been burglarized before.

C) the suspect was described as a gentleman.

D) the Bank carefully screened the customers.

9. The purpose of line 93 ("'It was once,' ... a low tone") is to

A) create an ominous atmosphere at the table.

B) foreshadow Fogg's ideas about the world.

C) illustrate Fogg's proper demeanor and social skills.

D) introduce the conflict of the plot.

10. What is the primary purpose of the passage?

A) To illustrate the problems with theft at the Bank of England

B) To examine the lives of wealthy men in England

C) To introduce Phileas Fogg and his social circle at the Reform Club

D) To parody the social customs of the upper class

Questions 11-21 are based on the following passages.

Passage 1 discusses possible uses of video games in designing educational materials. Passage 2 explores how elements of video games can be used in combating deteriorating cognition in older adults.

Passage 1

Many teenagers have heard from their parents that playing too many video games can negatively affect their learning and socialization. Studies performed in
Line the 1990s supported this claim. Scientists evaluated the
(5) content of popular video games and the amount of time children and teenagers were allowed to spend playing them. They eventually connected video games to anger issues, obesity, and addiction.

Studies showed that violent video games played for
(10) long periods of time inadvertently mimic a the same type of repetition used by teachers to reinforce subject matter. The method of advancement in many violent video games involves winning a contest of some kind. This is also an approach used in the classroom and other
(15) settings familiar to children and teenagers. This method makes the content of the video games, including overall aggressive themes, easy to absorb.

Until recently, the only positive effect of playing video games seemed to be an improvement in manual
(20) dexterity and computer literacy. These important upsides didn't seem to outweigh the negatives. A 2013 study by the National Academy of Sciences shows that the playing of fast-paced video games can actually improve performance in many areas, such as attention
(25) span, spatial navigation, cognition, reasoning, and memory. Researchers tested small pools of gamers and found that those who had a history of playing action-packed video games were better at tasks such as pattern discrimination. They also found that the gamers
(30) excelled at conceptualizing 3-D objects.

This new information could change the form that educational materials take. Content developers hope that the new materials may inspire interest in the fields of engineering, math, and technology. Educators can
(35) transform this data into classroom experiences that will not only cater to the current interests of students, but also use old patterns of teaching in a new and more modern way.

Passage 2

As adults age, certain brain functions deteriorate.
(40) Two of these important functions are cognition and
memory. This kind of decline can lead to an associated
loss of well-being. The number of adults affected by
Alzheimer's disease or dementia is also on the rise. Researchers are racing to find ways for people to maintain
(45) brain health while aging. A recent study examined the
effects of non-action video-game training on people
experiencing cognitive decline.

The study worked with small sample sizes of aging
participants. Researchers found that that the use of
(50) video games can allow the adult brain to maintain some
plasticity. Test subjects trained their memories with
games that featured patterned blocks, jigsaw puzzles,
facial recognition, and other iterations requiring the
recall of patterns. Test subjects who completed as few as
(55) twenty training sessions with these video games showed
an increase in attention span, alertness, and visual
memory. They also showed a decrease in distraction.
These results are encouraging, as they suggest that there
may be ways to stave off mental decline and to help the
(60) elderly maintain functions needed for safe driving and
other activities of daily living.

More tests need to be done in order to understand
the full potential of video games in the anti-aging market. There are several companies currently capitalizing
(65) on the success of these studies, and increasingly more
games that promise increased cognitive function are
sure to find their way to retailers soon.

11. The central idea of Passage 1 is primarily
concerned with

A) the effects of video games on teenagers
who play popular violent video games.

B) outdated methods used by teachers and
content developers to interest students in
science and engineering.

C) how research about the effects of video
games on gamers is being used to develop
new teaching methods.

D) how the impact that video games have
had on children and teenagers has
changed over the past few decades.

12. Which choice provides the best evidence for
the answer to the previous question?

A) Lines 4-7 ("Scientists evaluated . . .
them")

B) Lines 15-17 ("This method . . . absorb")

C) Lines 18-20 ("Until recently . . . literacy")

D) Lines 34-38 ("Educators . . . modern
way")

13. Based on the information in the passage,
studies performed in the 1990s support the
claim that

A) excessive video game playing can have a
negative effect on teenagers.

B) children who play video games are
more likely to be interested in math and
science.

C) video games can improve performance
in many areas related to success in
education.

D) teenagers who spend too much time
playing violent video games become
violent criminals.

14. As used in line 10, "inadvertently" most nearly
means

A) hastily.

B) impulsively.

C) unintentionally.

D) imprudently.

15. According to the information presented in Passage 1, the content of video games is easily absorbed by teenagers because

A) games are played for many hours a day on a daily basis.

B) the games utilize methods used in the classroom to encourage retention.

C) playing video games improves memory and increases cognitive functions.

D) teenagers are predisposed to absorb material to which they are repeatedly exposed.

16. Based on the information in Passage 2, the reader can infer that

A) elderly people who are able to ward off or reverse dementia may be able to live longer independently.

B) video games could completely cure dementia and other age-related cognitive problems.

C) playing board games for extended periods of time could have the same effect as playing video games.

D) too much time spent playing video games would likely have a negative effect on cognition in aging populations.

17. Which choice provides the best evidence for the answer to the previous question?

A) Lines 42-43 ("The number of . . . rise")

B) Lines 45-47 ("A recent study . . . decline")

C) Lines 58-61 ("These results . . . living")

D) Lines 62-64 ("More tests . . . market")

18. As used in line 39, "deteriorate" most nearly means

A) adapt.

B) restrict.

C) transform.

D) diminish.

19. The author of Passage 2 supports the central claim of the passage in paragraph 2 by

A) explaining the results of preliminary research involving the elderly and video games.

B) describing the physiological causes of memory loss and declining cognitive functions.

C) listing ways that the elderly can reduce the cognitive effects of aging and Alzheimer's disease.

D) giving details about the research methods used to study dementia in elderly populations.

20. The purpose of Passage 2 is to

A) describe the potential of video games to help combat the deterioration of brain function in aging populations.

B) explain how companies are reaching out to the elderly to increase video game markets.

C) encourage the reader to play video games as a way to increase memory and attention span.

D) support research that will increase the quality of life of people as they age and lose brain function.

21. Which generalization about video games does the evidence presented in both passages support?

    A) People who have trouble with memory loss and are easily distracted should avoid video games.

    B) Initial research conducted in the 1990s failed to uncover some of the benefits of playing video games.

    C) Video games could be part of a comprehensive approach to helping people cope with the effects of aging.

    D) Researchers in a diverse range of fields are looking to video games for solutions to problems.

Reading & Writing

CHAPTER 17

Rhetoric

CHAPTER OBJECTIVES

By the end of this chapter, you will be able to:

1. Determine the author's purpose and point of view in a given passage

2. Determine why the author uses a certain word or phrase in a given passage

3. Evaluate both the overall and part-to-whole text structure of a given test-like passage

4. Distinguish between claims and counterclaims and evaluate the use of evidence to support the author's reasoning

SMARTPOINTS

Point Value	SmartPoint Category
50 Points	Rhetoric

Reading & Writing

RHETORIC QUESTIONS

Chapter 17

Homework

Extra Practice: #1-11

Even More

US and World Literature Passages

Reading Quiz 5

Key

 Book Assignment

 Online Video Assignment

 Online Quiz Assignment

RHETORIC QUESTIONS: ANALYZING PURPOSE

Overall, rhetoric refers to the language the author uses, especially in order to persuade or influence the reader.

Some Analyzing Purpose questions ask about the purpose of the passage as a whole. Every author has a reason for writing. To identify that reason—or purpose—ask these two questions:

- Why did the author write this passage?

- What does the author want the reader to think about this topic?

Other Analyzing Purpose questions will ask you to identify the purpose of part of a passage, usually one or more paragraphs. To answer this type of question, read around the cited portion, review your Passage Map, and ask these two questions:

- What is the function of this section?

- How does this section help achieve the author's purpose?

RHETORIC QUESTIONS: ANALYZING POINT OF VIEW

The author's point of view is closely tied to the purpose of the passage. Though some authors are neutral, most authors have an opinion, or point of view. Questions that ask you to analyze point of view require you to establish the author's perspective and how that perspective affects the content and the style of the passage. That is, you need to figure out not only what the author says, but also how the author says it. Mapping the passage will help you determine the author's point of view.

As you map a passage, ask:

- Is the author's tone positive, negative, or neutral?

- Does the author want things to change or stay the same?

- Is the author addressing supporters or opponents?

RHETORIC QUESTIONS: ANALYZING WORD CHOICE

Rhetoric questions about word choice ask about how a particular word or phrase affects your understanding of the author's purpose and point of view.

Don't confuse analyzing word choice questions with Vocab-in-Context questions, which ask about the meaning of a word or phrase. Analyzing Word Choice questions ask about the function of a word or phrase within the passage; that is, why did the author use this word or phrase?

To answer Analyzing Word Choice questions, ask what the function of the cited word or phrase is. Common functions of words or phrases include:

- Setting a mood

- Conveying an emotion

- Building to a conclusion

- Calling to action

- Stating an opinion

> ✔ **Remember**
>
> Correct answers to Analyzing Word Choice questions will always be in line with the author's overall purpose.

RHETORIC QUESTIONS: ANALYZING TEXT STRUCTURE

Some Rhetoric questions will require you to analyze the structure of the passage. The SAT Reading Test will ask about two kinds of text structures:

1. **Overall text structure** refers to how the information within a passage is organized. Some common text structures are cause-and-effect, compare-and-contrast, sequence, problem-and-solution, and description.

2. **Part-whole relationships** describe how a particular part of the passage (e.g., a sentence, quotation, or paragraph) relates to the overall text. When asked about a part-whole relationship, make sure you determine what function the part plays in the passage.

> ✔ **Expert Tip**
>
> Include the structure of the passage in your Passage Map. Identifying the structure of the text will make it easier to understand and analyze its content.

RHETORIC QUESTIONS: ANALYZING ARGUMENTS

Other Rhetoric questions will ask you to analyze arguments within the text for both their form and content.

Questions that ask you to analyze a text's arguments vary in scope. There are three types of Analyzing Arguments questions. You may be asked to:

1. **Analyze claims and counterclaims.** A claim is not an opinion but rather the main point or thesis of a passage the author promotes. A counterclaim is the opposite of a claim—it will negate or disagree with the thesis or central idea of the passage.

2. **Assess reasoning.** The reasoning of a passage is composed of the statements offering support for claims and counterclaims. On the SAT Reading test, you may be asked whether an author's or character's reasoning is *sound*—that is, whether the argument is valid and the reasoning for the argument is true.

3. **Analyze evidence.** Evidence can be facts, reasons, statistics, and other information the author employs to *support* a claim or counterclaim. You will have to assess how and why this evidence is used.

Let's look at the following example of a test-like passage and question set. After the mapped passage, the left column contains questions similar to those you'll see on the Reading Test on Test Day. The column on the right features the strategic thinking test experts employ when approaching the passage and questions presented. Pay attention to how test experts vary the approach to answer different question types.

Strategic Thinking
Step 1: Read actively
Read the passage and the notes provided. Remember, a well-crafted Passage Map should summarize the central idea of each paragraph as well as important topics or themes. Use your Passage Map to help you answer each question.

Questions 1-3 are based on the following passage.

This passage details the varying and changing scientific theories surrounding sunspots.

Astronomers noted more than 150 years ago that sunspots wax and wane in number in an 11-year cycle. Ever since, people have speculated that the solar
Line cycle might exert some influence on the Earth's
(5) weather. In this century, for example, scientists have linked the solar cycle to droughts in the American Midwest. Until recently, however, none of these correlations has held up under close scrutiny.

One problem is that sunspots themselves are so
(10) poorly understood. Observations have revealed that the swirly smudges represent areas of intense magnetic activity where the sun's radiative energy has been blocked and that they are considerably cooler than bright regions of the sun. Scientists have not
(15) been able, however, to determine just how sunspots are created or what effect they have on the solar constant (a misnomer that refers to the sun's total radiance at any instant).

The latter question, at least, now seems to have
(20) been resolved by data from the *Solar Maximum*
Mission satellite, which has monitored the solar constant since 1980, the peak of the last solar cycle. As the number of sunspots decreased through 1986, the satellite recorded a gradual dimming
(25) of the sun. Over the past year, as sunspots have proliferated, the sun has brightened. The data suggest that the sun is 0.1 percent more luminous at the peak of the solar cycle, when the number of sunspots is greatest, than at its nadir, according to
(30) Richard C. Willson of the Jet Propulsion Laboratory and Hugh S. Hudson of the University of California at San Diego.

The data show that sunspots do not themselves make the sun shine brighter. Quite the contrary.
(35) When a sunspot appears, it initially causes the sun to dim slightly, but then after a period of weeks or months islands of brilliance called faculas usually emerge near the sunspot and more than compensate for its dimming effect. Willson says faculas
(40) may represent regions where energy that initially was blocked beneath a sunspot has finally breached the surface.

Note annotations (margin):

¶1: sunspot cycle & weather

¶2: sunspots = poorly understood

¶3: SMM = effects of spots on solar constant

¶4: not sunspots, but faculas that brighten

Does the subtle fluctuation in the solar constant manifest itself in the Earth's weather? Some recent
(45) reports offer statistical evidence that it does, albeit rather indirectly. The link seems to be mediated by a phenomenon known as the quasi-biennial oscillation (QBO), a 180-degree shift in the direction of stratospheric winds above the Tropics that occurs
(50) about every two years.

¶5: spots indirectly affect weather (QBO)

Karin Labitzke of the Free University of Berlin and Harry van Loon of the National Center for Atmospheric Research in Boulder, Colorado, were the first to uncover the QBO link. They gathered
(55) temperature and air-pressure readings from various latitudes and altitudes over the past three solar cycles. They found no correlation between the solar cycle and their data until they sorted the data into two categories: those gathered during the QBO's
(60) west phase (when the stratospheric winds blow west) and those gathered during its east phase. A remarkable correlation appeared: temperatures and pressures coincident with the QBO's west phase rose and fell in accordance with the solar cycle.

¶6: KL & HvL found link to temp & pressure

(65) Building on this finding, Brian A. Tinsley of the National Science Foundation discovered a statistical correlation between the solar cycle and the position of storms in the North Atlantic. The latitude of storms during the west phase of the QBO, Tinsley
(70) found, varied with the solar cycle: storms occurring toward the peak of a solar cycle traveled at latitudes about six degrees nearer the Equator than storms during the cycle's nadir.

¶7: BT found link b/t solar cycle & storms

Labitzke, van Loon, and Tinsley acknowledge
(75) that their findings are still rather mysterious. Why does the solar cycle seem to exert more of an influence during the west phase of the QBO than it does during the east phase? How does the 0.1 percent variance in solar radiation trigger the much
(80) larger changes—up to six degrees Celsius in polar regions—observed by Labitzke and van Loon? Van Loon says simply, "We can't explain it."

¶8: sci. can't explain links

John A. Eddy of the National Center for Atmospheric Research, nonetheless, thinks these QBO
(85) findings as well as the *Solar Maximum Mission* data "look like breakthroughs" in the search for a link between the solar cycle and weather. With further research into how the oceans damp the effects of solar flux, for example, these findings may lead to
(90) models that have some predictive value. The next few years may be particularly rich in solar flux.

¶9: break-throughs, but more research to be done

Questions	Strategic Thinking
1. The author's point of view can best be described as that of A) a meteorologist voicing optimism that the findings of recent solar research will improve weather forecasting. B) an astronomer presenting a digest of current findings to a review board of other astronomers. C) a science writer explaining the possible influence of a solar phenomenon on terrestrial weather patterns. D) a historian detailing the contributions to climate science made by the *Solar Maximum Mission*.	**Step 2: Examine the question stem** Identify the keywords in the question stem: "The author's point of view." Any Passage Map notes about the author's viewpoint will help answer this question. However, the Passage Map doesn't note any specific view or opinion the author offers. **Step 3: Predict and answer** Because the author doesn't express his or her own opinions regarding the topic, the correct answer will accurately reflect the informative style and neutral tone of the passage, as well as the passage's central idea. Choice (C) is correct.
2. The main purpose of the questions in paragraph 8 (lines 74-82) is to A) emphasize how little scientists know about the solar constant. B) explain more fully the mysterious nature of the scientists' findings. C) question the basis upon which these scientists built their hypotheses. D) express doubts about the scientists' interpretations of their findings.	**Step 2: Examine the question stem** Identify the keywords in the question stem: "main purpose of the questions" and "paragraph 8." Look at the Passage Map notes for paragraph 8 to answer this question. **Step 3: Predict and answer** The notes next to paragraph 8 say, "sci. can't explain links." The correct answer will allude to the uncertainty that surrounds Labitzke, van Loon, and Tinsley's findings. Choice (B) is correct.
3. The use of the quoted phrase "look like breakthroughs" in line 86 is primarily meant to convey the idea that A) information about the solar cycle has allowed scientists to predict changes in Earth's complex climate system. B) additional analysis of the link between the solar cycle and Earth's weather may yield useful models. C) despite the associated costs, space missions can lead to important discoveries. D) an alternative interpretation of the data may contradict the initial findings.	**Step 2: Examine the question stem** Identify the keywords in the question stem. The key words include not only the cited phrase and its line number, but also the phrase, "primarily meant to convey the idea." The correct answer will not restate the meaning of the cited phrase but its purpose within the passage. Look at the Passage Map notes surrounding "look like breakthroughs" in line 86. **Step 3: Predict and answer** The cited phrase is a quotation from an official at the National Center for Atmospheric Research. The note next to this part of the passage says that more research is required to fully comprehend any possible link between the solar cycle and weather. Choice (B) is correct.

Reading & Writing

You have seen the ways in which the SAT tests you on Rhetoric in Reading passages and the way an SAT expert approaches these types of questions.

You will use the Kaplan Method for Reading Comprehension to complete this section. Part of the test-like passage has been mapped already. Your first step is to complete the Passage Map. Then, you will continue to use the Kaplan Method for Reading Comprehension and the strategies discussed in this chapter to answer the questions. Strategic thinking questions have been included to guide you—some of the answers have been filled in, but you will have to fill in the answers to others.

Use your answers to the strategic thinking questions to select the correct answer, just as you will on Test Day.

Strategic Thinking

Step 1: Read actively

The passage below is partially mapped. Read the passage and the first part of the Passage Map. Then, complete the Passage Map on your own. Remember to focus on the central ideas of each paragraph as well as the central idea of the overall passage. Use your Passage Map as a reference when you're answering questions.

Questions 4-6 are based on the following passage.

The following passage was written (on the last night of 1849) by Florence Nightingale. She was not only a pioneer in the profession of nursing but also one of the first European women to travel to Egypt (1849-1850) and keep a detailed journal of her letters and reflections of her journey.

My Dear People,

Yes, I think your imagination has hardly followed me through the place where I have been
Line spending the last night of the old year. Did you
(5) listen to it passing away and think of me? Where
do you think I heard it sigh out its soul? In the
dim unearthly colonnades of Karnak, which stood
and watched it, motionless, silent, and awful, as
they had done for thousands of years, to whom, no
(10) doubt, thousands of years seem but as a day. Would
that I could call up Karnak before your eyes for one
moment, but it "is beyond expression."

No one could trust themselves with their
imagination alone there. Gigantic shadows spring
(15) upon every side; "the dead are stirred up for thee to
meet thee at thy coming, even the chief ones of the
earth," and they look out from among the columns,

and you feel as terror-stricken to be there, miser-
able intruder, among these mighty dead, as if you
(20) had awakened the angel of the Last Day. Imagine
six columns on either side, of which the last is
almost out of sight, though they stand very near
each other, while you look up to the stars from
between them, as you would from a deep narrow
(25) gorge in the Alps, and then, passing through 160
of these, ranged in eight aisles on either side, the
end choked up with heaps of rubbish, this rubbish consisting of stones twenty and thirty feet
long, so that it looks like a mountain fallen to ruin,
(30) not a temple. How art thou fallen from heaven,
oh Lucifer, son of the morning! He did exalt his
throne above the stars of God; for I looked through
a colonnade, and under the roof saw the deep
blue sky and star shining brightly; and as you look
(35) upon these mighty ruins, a voice seems continually
saying to you, And seekest thou good things for
thyself? Seek them not, for is there ought like this
ruin? One wonders that people come back from
Egypt and live lives as they did before.

¶1: impossible to describe Karnak

¶2: details of K temple ruins

(40)   Yet Karnak by starlight is not to me painful: we had seen Luxor in the sunshine. I had expected the temples of Thebes to be solemn, but Luxor was fearful. Rows of painted columns, propylae, colossi, and—built up in the Holy Place—mud [not even huts, (45) but] unroofed enclosures chalked out, or rather mudded out, for families, with their one oven and broken earthen vessel; and, squatting on the ground among the painted hieroglyphs, creatures with large nose-rings, the children's eyes streaming with matter, on (50) which the mothers let the flies rest, because "it is good for them," without an attempt to drive them off; tattooed men on the ground, with camels feeding out of their laps, and nothing but a few doura stalks strewed for their beds;—I can-not describe the impression it (55) makes: it is as if one were steering towards the sun, the glorious Eastern sun, arrayed in its golden clouds, and were to find, on nearing it, that it were full—instead of glorified beings as one expect-ed—of a race of dwarf cannibals, stained with (60) blood and dressed in bones. The contrast could not be more terrible than the savages of the Present in the temples of the Past at Luxor.

But Karnak by starlight is peace; not peace and joy, but peace—solemn peace. You feel like (65) spirits revisiting your former world, strange and fallen to ruins; but it has done its work, and there is nothing agonizing about it. Egypt should have no sun and no day, no human beings. It should always be seen in solitude (70) and by night; one eternal night it should have, like Job's, and let the stars of the twilight be its lamps; neither let it see the dawning of the day.

Don't get distracted by less important details. While there is a lot going on in this passage, your additions to the Passage Map should continue to note how the author perceives and describes what she experienced on her trip to Egypt. If you're stuck, review the suggested Passage Map notes in the Answers & Explanations for this chapter on page 988.

Questions	Strategic Thinking
4. The statement in lines 38-39 ("One wonders . . . before") is primarily included to A) suggest that many people who visit Egypt overlook many of its important temples. B) express how profoundly Egypt has affected the author. C) emphasize how difficult it can be to understand someone else's experience. D) criticize travelers who do not experience Egypt in the same way the author did.	**Step 2: Examine the question stem** *What are the keywords in this question stem?* The keywords in this question stem are the cited statement and "primarily included to." *What parts of your Passage Map are relevant?* Looking at how the Passage Map notes surrounding the cited lines serve the passage as a whole will help you find the answer. **Step 3: Predict and answer** *What can you predict?* The Passage Map note next to the cited phrase should reveal that the author believes traveling to Egypt is a life-changing experience. *Which answer choice matches this prediction?*

Reading & Writing

Questions	Strategic Thinking
5. What is the most likely reason the author draws a distinction between the two cities in lines 40-41 ("Yet Karnak . . . sunshine")? A) To show that some ancient ruins have retained special relevance while others have reverted to everyday use B) To argue that Egyptian authorities should do more to protect Luxor C) To communicate how dreadful it was to find mundane activities in a place meant to hold great spiritual significance D) To demonstrate how much more difficult it is to describe Karnak than it is to describe Luxor	**Step 2: Examine the question stem** *What are the keywords in this question stem?* The keywords in this question stem are "the most likely reason," "distinction between the two cities," and the cited lines. **Step 3: Predict and answer** *What parts of your Passage Map are relevant?* Look at your Passage Map for notes about the author's contrast of the two cities. The author has a generally positive attitude toward Karnak and a generally negative attitude toward Luxor. *What purpose does providing this contrast serve in the passage as a whole?* _____ _____ *Which answer choice matches this prediction?* _____
6. Throughout the passage, the author employs which of the following techniques to convey her meaning? A) Physical descriptions interspersed with lyrical portrayals B) A series of analogies emphasizing the difference between past and present C) An extended metaphor evoking eternal truths D) Expository prose describing a journey to Egypt	**Step 2: Examine the question stem** *What are the keywords in this question stem?* The keywords in the question stem are "throughout the passage" and "techniques." The answer to the question will be found by analyzing how the author conveys her meaning rather than what that meaning is. *What parts of your Passage Map are relevant?* Your Passage Map probably will not contain the answer, but it can guide you to the more important parts of the passage. **Step 3: Predict and answer** *What are the consistencies in the author's style and tone throughout the passage?* _____ _____ *Which answer choice matches this prediction?* _____

Now, try a test-like Reading passage on your own. Give yourself 6 minutes to read the passage and answer the questions.

Questions 7-10 are based on the following passage.

This passage explores the differences in perception between humans and owls.

It's not difficult to believe that humans and animals perceive the world in different ways. As humans, sight is the sense with which we primarily in-
Line terpret the information around us, and other senses
(5) are generally subordinate. Our sense of survival is fortunately not dependent on our acute senses, or we would surely starve to death or be hunted into extinction. Owls, however, are masters of their senses, making such optimal use of their biologi-
(10) cal strengths that we, by comparison, can best be described as wearing blindfolds and earplugs. Were an owl to attempt to hunt with our limited senses, it would most likely call us the lesser species, and possibly initiate attempts to label us as endangered.

(15) As evidenced by our expression "owl-eyed," owls are known for their acute vision and all-seeing nature. Surprisingly, however, owls have a more limited range of view than humans. Whereas a human can see 180 degrees without turning his or
(20) her head, an owl can only see 110 degrees under the same conditions. Owls have extremely well-developed eyes, but their structure is such that they are fixed in one position: an owl can look nowhere but straight ahead. They are farsighted, prevented
(25) from seeing clearly anything within a few inches of their eyes; the popular image of a cartoon owl with reading glasses is not far removed from truth. Despite these limitations, however, owls maximize their advantages. Their sensitive eyes are very
(30) effective at collecting and processing light, making them efficient night hunters. They can turn their heads almost completely around and nearly upside down, capitalizing on this range of movement to see over their own shoulders and directly
(35) beneath themselves. They optimize their farsight-edness to spot the minute movements of prey at

great distances. With regard to auditory efficiency, owls, like humans, hear a limited range of audible sounds. Within that range, however, they have
(40) acute hearing at certain frequencies, helping them detect diminutive movements in the undergrowth. Some nocturnal species, such as the barn owl, have asymmetrical ear openings and disc-like facial feathers to facilitate the channeling and interpreta-
(45) tion of sounds. They aggregate sensory information instantaneously to produce a mental map of their surroundings and location of possible prey.

Like owls, we use our senses to map the world around us, but the similarities end there. We cannot
(50) understand the complex means by which the owl's hearing and sight work concurrently to detect the subtle shifting of snow or leaves that signals food. The comparison itself is ludicrous, in fact, because our means for survival are so different; humans do
(55) not live solitary lives, constantly alert to the movement of prey that determines whether we live or die. We do not think in the same way, if thought is even the right concept: we interpret information using extremely different cerebral processes, and
(60) we can't know whether owls are even consciously aware of the complex workings of their brains. When I sit in the forest and study my environment, my world is interpreted with language. The owl's world is—well, it's impossible to tell, isn't it?

(65) The owl may see the same forest we see, but he is aware of it in a completely different way. I admire the foliage and the rustling leaves, and listen to birdsong. He hears the soft rustle of a leaf and knows that a chipmunk moves thirty feet off to our
(70) right, directly underneath the poplar tree. I can say that the owl thinks about the chipmunk, but not how, for I don't have the correct mental processes to describe the complex interpretations of sensory detail into impulse and action; I am governed by
(75) words instead of instinct.

7. Which of the following statements supports the author's central argument?

   A) Owls are better adapted to survive than humans because owls are masters of their senses.

   B) Owls, as opposed to humans, overcome limitations by maximizing their advantages.

   C) Humans and owls evolved in differing environments, resulting in a variety of adaptations.

   D) Human brains and owl brains share few, if any, similarities in how sensory input is interpreted.

8. The author provides support for which of the following claims about owls?

   A) Their survival is not dependent on their acute senses.

   B) They do not live solitary lives.

   C) They maximize their advantages.

   D) They have a greater range of view than humans.

9. In line 42, the author refers to the barn owl in order to

   A) contrast the barn owl's hearing to human hearing.

   B) illustrate the range of evolutionary adaptations displayed by various species.

   C) imply that feathers are uniquely suited to channeling sound.

   D) provide an example of adaptation that improves the owl's ability to locate prey.

10. The structure of the passage can best be described as a

    A) comparison between humans and other animals using specific examples to illustrate similarities and differences.

    B) discussion of the evolutionary advantages afforded by differing adaptations to various environmental stimuli.

    C) philosophical discourse on the role of language and its limitations when discussing the acquisition of knowledge.

    D) hypothetical situation presented in the context of adaptive strategies employed by various species in response to environmental stress.

Answers & Explanations for this chapter begin on page 988.

Reading & Writing

EXTRA PRACTICE

The following questions provide an opportunity to practice the concepts and strategic thinking covered in this chapter. While many of the questions pertain to Rhetoric questions, some touch on other concepts tested on the Reading Test to ensure that your practice is test-like, with a variety of question types per passage.

Questions 1-11 are based on the following passage.

The following passage explores the history and impact of public higher education in the United States.

Every year, hundreds of thousands of students graduate from U.S. public universities. Many of the largest and most elite schools in the nation fall into
Line the category of public, or state, institutions. Unlike
(5) private universities, which generally operate independently from any government influence, public higher education was established through government legislation and is sustained through state and federal involvement in various ways. A look into
(10) the history of U.S. public higher education can shed light on the changing ideals of the American story over the past century and a half.

America's earliest higher-education institutions, like Harvard, were initially developed by and for
(15) clergy, or church workers. For 17th-century Puritans in America, church leadership was of utmost importance. At that time, clergy was the main profession for which college degrees were offered. Later, during the 18th and 19th centuries, parallel-
(20) ing the onset of secular (and increasingly scientifically inclined) modern thought, the nation and government acknowledged the need for broader higher education opportunities. Philosophers and politicians alike were aware that well-educated
(25) citizens were a vital element of a functional democracy. A better-informed voting population could secure a better political future. Moreover, with aims to advance the fields of technology and agriculture through higher education, legislators anticipated
(30) potential economic improvements nationwide as well. It was in the nation's best interest to make college more accessible.

In 1862, President Lincoln signed the Morill Land-Grant Act. This was, in many ways, the force
(35) behind the public university system. The Morill Act ensured that public land would be set aside for the establishment of universities across the country. The coming decades saw a massive increase in the opening of universities in the nation. Hundreds
(40) of U.S. public universities began to operate. These schools received federal and state support, offered practical, accessible education, and sought, originally, to advance the fields of agriculture and mechanics. Soon these schools offered wide varieties
(45) of subjects and specialties. These universities would be operated by their respective states, but all would adhere to certain broad federal regulations.

At the time, the government was seeking to mend racial injustices through legislation. To this
(50) effect, a second land act was passed in 1890 in hopes of inhibiting discrimination in public universities. While at the time this did not accomplish the intended openness and diversity, it paved the way for the culture of diversity the American university
(55) system enjoys today. Many public universities are now richly diverse, with regulations in place to accept students of any race, ethnicity, or socioeconomic status. In a similar vein, women, who were once a minority in colleges, increasingly gained a
(60) strong presence in U.S. universities over the past 150 years. Women actually surpassed men in overall U.S. college attendance around the turn of the 21st century.

Since the legislation of the 19th century, public
(65) universities have undergone momentous growth. The system has evolved to address and accommodate the nuances of 20th- and 21st-century Ameri-

can culture and development. Offering in-state students some of the most affordable degree programs in higher
(70) education, these schools have now graduated millions of undergraduate and graduate students. Public universities also manage the majority of the nation's government-funded academic research initiatives. Featuring some of the most competitive athletic programs in the
(75) world, as well as elite scholarship and arts programs, the U.S. public universities' accomplishments seem boundless. With schools in Alaska, Hawaii, and even U.S. territories like Puerto Rico and Guam, public university impact reaches the farthest corners and populations of
(80) the nation. The state school system has been formative for American culture, philosophy, economics, medicine, politics, and much more.

The eminence of the U.S. public university network stretches beyond the United States. Students travel from
(85) across the globe to study at top programs. Cutting-edge schools like the University of Virginia (UVA) and University of California at Los Angeles (UCLA) receive continual international attention for their accomplishments in scholarship and research. Programs, faculty,
(90) and students from these schools participate in the global conversation in significant ways, working toward a better future for the planet.

Given those early visions for a more robustly educated voting population, the enormity of the system
(95) that the Morrill Act launched is remarkable. U.S. public universities have both shaped and employed many of America's greatest thinkers. Considering their timeline and their accomplishments, these schools seem to reflect the post–Civil War history of diversity, liberty,
(100) creativity, and equal opportunity that in many ways distinguishes the American cultural identity.

1. In the second paragraph, the author uses the idea that educated citizens are necessary for a functioning democracy to

   A) show why an educated work force increased agricultural production.

   B) demonstrate the continued role of the clergy in American public life.

   C) explain why the government was playing a larger role in public education.

   D) emphasize the importance of technological innovation for the economy.

2. Which choice provides the best evidence for the answer to the previous question?

   A) Lines 17-18 ("At that time . . . were offered")

   B) Lines 19-23 ("Later, during . . . opportunities")

   C) Lines 26-27 ("A better-informed . . . political future")

   D) Lines 27-31 ("Moreover, with aims . . . nationwide as well")

3. The purpose of the third paragraph is to

   A) highlight an example of the government increasing access to public education.

   B) discuss initial technological advances in agriculture and mechanics.

   C) outline the effects of the Morrill Land-Grant Act on the U.S. economy.

   D) explain the relationship between federal and state control of public universities.

4. In line 42, the author's use of the word "accessible" implies that

   A) public universities would expand course offerings to encompass a range of subjects.

   B) the likelihood that people with limited means could attend a university was increasing.

   C) agriculture and mechanics would receive the most federal and state support.

   D) President Lincoln supported passage of the Morill Land-Grant Act to expand education.

5. As used in line 47, "adhere" most nearly means

   A) resist.

   B) notice.

   C) acquiesce.

   D) comply.

6. Which of the following pieces of evidence would most strengthen the author's line of reasoning throughout the passage?

   A) Information about the ways in which private and public universities differ in paragraph 1

   B) An example of how the 17th-century clergy benefited from higher education in paragraph 2

   C) Statistics showing increased enrollment numbers of minority students in paragraph 4

   D) An example of a competitive public university athletic program in paragraph 5

7. In the fourth paragraph, the author uses the fact that more women than men now attend college to

   A) contrast the advances of women's rights with racial injustice in public universities.

   B) provide an example of how the land acts initially failed to stop discrimination.

   C) show that public universities have grown increasingly diverse over time.

   D) illustrate the challenges many people still face to attend public universities.

8. Which choice provides the best evidence for the answer to the previous question?

   A) Lines 49-52 ("To this effect . . . public universities")

   B) Lines 52-55 ("While at the time . . . enjoys today")

   C) Lines 55-58 ("Many public universities . . . status")

   D) Lines 58-61 ("In a similar vein . . . 150 years")

9. As used in line 67, "nuances" most nearly means

   A) eras.

   B) categories.

   C) circumstances.

   D) variations.

10. The passage's primary purpose is to

   A) summarize the accomplishments of U.S. public universities since the 19th century.

   B) explain the historical influence of religion on the development of the university system.

   C) discuss the relationship between U.S. higher education and the cultural values of the nation.

   D) summarize the historical effect of the Morill Land-Grant Act on United States public universities.

11. The fifth paragraph supports the central idea of the passage by

   A) discussing how public university athletic programs have grown increasingly competitive.

   B) providing evidence of the success of federal legislation meant to invest in public universities.

   C) explaining that in-state tuition rates have increased enrollment in United States public universities.

   D) noting that the U.S. public university system has expanded into U.S. territories.

Questions 12-21 are based on the following passage.

Adapted from "The Red House Mystery" by A.A. Milne, first published in 1922.

Whether Mark Ablett was a bore or not depended on the point of view, but it may be said at once that he never bored his company on the subject of
Line his early life. However, stories get about. There is
(5) always somebody who knows. It was understood—and this, anyhow, on Mark's own authority—that his father had been a country clergyman. It was said that, as a boy, Mark had attracted the notice, and patronage, of some rich old spinster of the neigh-
(10) bourhood, who had paid for his education, both at school and university. At about the time when he was coming down from Cambridge, his father had died; leaving behind him a few debts, as a warning to his family, and a reputation for short sermons, as
(15) an example to his successor. Neither warning nor example seems to have been effective. Mark went to London, with an allowance from his patron, and (it is generally agreed) made acquaintance with the money-lenders. He was supposed, by his patron and
(20) any others who inquired, to be "writing"; but what he wrote, other than letters asking for more time to pay, has never been discovered. However, he attended the theatres and music halls very regularly—no doubt with a view to some serious articles in the
(25) "Spectator" on the decadence of the English stage.

Fortunately (from Mark's point of view) his patron died during his third year in London, and left him all the money he wanted. From that moment his life loses its legendary character, and becomes
(30) more a matter of history. He settled accounts with the money-lenders, abandoned his crop of wild oats to the harvesting of others, and became in his turn a patron. He patronized the Arts. It was not only usurers who discovered that Mark Ablett no
(35) longer wrote for money; editors were now offered free contributions as well as free lunches; publishers were given agreements for an occasional slender volume, in which the author paid all expenses and waived all royalties; promising young painters and

(40) poets dined with him; and he even took a theatrical company on tour, playing host and "lead" with equal lavishness.

He was not what most people call a snob. A snob has been defined carelessly as a man who loves a
(45) lord; and, more carefully, as a mean lover of mean things—which would be a little unkind to the peerage if the first definition were true. Mark had his vanities undoubtedly, but he would sooner have met an actor-manager than an earl; he would have
(50) spoken of his friendship with Dante—had that been possible—more glibly than of his friendship with the Duke. Call him a snob if you like, but not the worst kind of snob; a hanger-on, but to the skirts of Art, not Society; a climber, but in the neighbour-
(55) hood of Parnassus, not Hay Hill.

His patronage did not stop at the Arts. It also included Matthew Cayley, a small cousin of thirteen, whose circumstances were as limited as had been Mark's own before his patron had rescued him. He
(60) sent the Cayley cousin to school and Cambridge. His motives, no doubt, were unworldly enough at first; a mere repaying to his account in the Recording Angel's book of the generosity which had been lavished on himself; a laying-up of treasure in
(65) heaven. But it is probable that, as the boy grew up, Mark's designs for his future were based on his own interests as much as those of his cousin, and that a suitably educated Matthew Cayley of twenty-three was felt by him to be a useful property for a man in
(70) his position; a man, that is to say, whose vanities left him so little time for his affairs.

Cayley, then, at twenty-three, looked after his cousin's affairs. By this time Mark had bought the Red House and the considerable amount of land
(75) which went with it. Cayley superintended the necessary staff. His duties, indeed, were many. He was not quite secretary, not quite land-agent, not quite business-adviser, not quite companion, but something of all four. Mark leant upon him and
(80) called him "Cay," objecting quite rightly in the

circumstances to the name of Matthew. Cay, he felt was, above all, dependable; a big, heavy-jawed, solid fellow, who didn't bother you with unnecessary talk—a boon to a man who liked to do most of the
(85) talking himself.

12. What is most likely true about Mark's father's successor?

    A) He made more money than Mark's father had.

    B) He was more popular than Mark's father.

    C) His sermons were long and boring.

    D) He took a great deal of interest in Mark's life.

13. Which choice provides the best evidence for the answer to the previous question?

    A) Lines 4-7 ("There is . . . clergyman")

    B) Lines 5-11 ("It was . . . university")

    C) Lines 11-15 ("At about the time . . . successor")

    D) Lines 15-16 ("Neither . . . been effective")

14. What can be inferred from the author's choice to place the word "writing" in quotation marks in line 20?

    A) People doubted that Mark was actually writing.

    B) Mark's writing was understood by many to be terrible.

    C) Mark's writing more closely resembled philosophy than entertainment.

    D) Mark was writing in secret but his acquaintances knew about his talent.

15. Why is the death of Mark's patron "fortunate" for him (line 26)?

    A) Mark becomes wealthy as a result.

    B) Mark and his patron do not like each other.

    C) Mark's patron disapproved of his writing.

    D) Mark felt pressure from his patron to start a career.

16. As used in line 34, "usurer" most nearly means

    A) employer.

    B) lender.

    C) relative.

    D) supporter.

17. As used in line 42, "lavishness" most nearly means

    A) diplomacy.

    B) enthusiasm.

    C) melodrama.

    D) skill.

18. Mark's acquaintances probably consider stories of his later life

    A) less respectable than when he had to work for his money.

    B) more interesting because of the lessons he has learned.

    C) less exciting than those of his earlier life in London.

    D) more scandalous than he is willing to admit.

19. Which choice provides the best evidence for the answer to the previous question?

    A) Lines 19-22 ("He was . . . discovered")

    B) Lines 28-30 ("From that . . . of history")

    C) Lines 47-52 ("Mark had . . . the Duke")

    D) Lines 52-55 ("Call him . . . Hay Hill")

20. "Parnassus" (line 55) is included in the passage to illustrate the idea of

    A) a place where the wealthy gather.

    B) an artistic community.

    C) a myth to which Mark can be compared.

    D) a place that does not really exist.

21. The tone of the last paragraph serves to

    A) suggest parallels between Matthew and Mark.

    B) surprise the reader with Matthew's capabilities.

    C) demonstrate the dramatic changes in Mark's character.

    D) mock Mark for the way he sees Matthew.

Detail and Inference Questions

CHAPTER OBJECTIVES

By the end of this chapter, you will be able to:

1. Identify and answer Detail questions that ask about explicit meanings within the passage

2. Identify and answer Inference questions that ask about implicit meanings within the passage

3. Identify and answer Inference questions that require analogical reasoning

SMARTPOINTS

Point Value	SmartPoint Category
15 Points	Detail
35 Points	Inference

Reading & Writing

DETAIL AND INFERENCE QUESTIONS

Chapter 18

Homework

Extra Practice: #1-11

Even More

Reading Quiz 6

Key

  Book Assignment

  Online Video Assignment

  Online Quiz Assignment

DETAIL QUESTIONS

Detail questions ask about a specific part of the passage. Because your Passage Map should note only the *location* of key details rather than the details themselves, you will have to refer to the passage to answer these questions.

You can recognize Detail questions because they normally include line references or phrasing that directs you to a particular part of the passage.

When answering Detail questions:

- Read around the cited text to understand the context.

- Predict by rephrasing the relevant section in your own words.

- Eliminate any answer choices that do not match your prediction.

Also, make sure to read answer choices carefully. Watch out for negatives such as *not* and *no* that change an otherwise correct answer choice into the opposite of what you are looking for.

> ✔ **Expert Tip**
>
> Watch out for misused details—details that are in the passage but do not answer the question.

INFERENCE QUESTIONS: IMPLICIT MEANING

Implicit Meaning Inference questions ask you to find something that must be true based on the passage but is not directly stated in the passage. The answer will be in the text, but you will need to read between the lines to find it.

To answer these questions efficiently and effectively, you must not only use your Passage Map but also fully utilize Step 3 of the Kaplan Method for Reading Comprehension: Predict and answer. If you need to review the Kaplan Method for Reading Comprehension, please turn to chapter 13.

There are two types of inferences that can be derived from questions asking about implicit meanings:

1. **Narrow Inferences** refer to specific parts of the passage. To answer these questions, find the relevant details and look for clues indicating how the author connects these details. Then, make a general prediction based on how the details are connected.

These questions will use phrasing such as:

- In lines xx-xx, the author implies that . . .

- The author strongly suggests that . . .

- It can be reasonably inferred that . . .

2. **Broad Inferences** ask about what can be inferred from the passage as a whole or what the author would generally agree with. To answer these questions, consider how the author's point of view limits the range of what could be true.

These questions will use phrasing such as:

- The passage indicates that . . .

- It can be inferred from the passage . . .

> ✔ **Expert Tip**
>
> An inference is NOT an opinion. It is a conclusion drawn from facts in the passage.

INFERENCE QUESTIONS: ANALOGICAL REASONING

Analogical Reasoning Inference questions ask you to take ideas and information found in the passage and use an analogy to describe a new and parallel situation. In every Analogical Reasoning Inference question, there is a strong connection between the two ideas. Identify that relationship and describe it in a short sentence.

You can recognize Analogical Reasoning Inference questions because they normally include line references or phrasing such as "The situation described in line x is most comparable to . . ."

When answering Analogical Reasoning Inference questions:

- Go to the cited lines and read around them to understand the context.

- Identify the relationship between the characters, the information, or the ideas cited in the question stem.

- Describe the relationship through characteristics (qualities that each idea possesses) and functions (roles played by each part).

- Look for the answer choice that describes a situation that is similar to the one in the passage.

Also, make sure to read answer choices carefully. Eliminate answer choices that include only one of the parts or have the parts in reverse order.

> ✔ **Remember**
>
> The question stem will describe the situation and tell you where to look for it in the passage. Always go back to the passage and find it.

Let's look at the following example of a test-like passage and question set. After the mapped passage, the left column contains questions similar to those you'll see on the Reading Test on Test Day. The column on the right features the strategic thinking test experts employ when approaching the passage and questions presented. Pay attention to how test experts vary the approach to answer different question types.

Strategic Thinking

Step 1: Read actively

Read the passage and the notes provided. Remember, a well-crafted Passage Map should summarize the central idea of each paragraph as well as important topics or themes. Use your Passage Map to help you answer each question.

Questions 1-3 are based on the following passage.

This passage looks into the effects of and interactions between light and color and the resulting types of luminescence.

Atoms can be excited in many ways other than by absorbing a photon. The element phosphorous spontaneously combines with oxygen when
Line exposed to air. There is a transfer of energy to
(5) the phosphorous electrons during this chemical reaction, which excites them to sufficiently high energy states so that they can subsequently emit light when dropping into a lower state. This is an example of what is termed chemiluminescence, the
(10) emission of light as a result of chemical reaction.

A related effect is bioluminescence, when light is produced by chemical reactions associated with biological activity. Bioluminescence occurs in a variety of life forms and is more common in marine
(15) organisms than in terrestrial or freshwater life. Examples include certain bacteria, jellyfish, clams, fungi, worms, ants, and fireflies. There is considerable diversity in how light is produced. Most processes involve the reaction of a protein with oxygen,
(20) catalyzed by an enzyme. The protein varies from one organism to another, but all are grouped under the generic name luciferin. The enzymes are known as luciferase. Both words stem from the Latin *lucifer* meaning light-bearing. The various chemical steps
(25) leading to bioluminescence are yet to be explained in detail, but in some higher organisms the process is known to be activated by the nervous system.

The firefly is best understood. Its light organ is located near the end of the abdomen. Within it
(30) luciferin is combined with other atomic groups in a series of processes in which oxygen is converted

into carbon dioxide. The sequence culminates when the luciferin is split off from the rest, leaving it in an excited state. The excess energy is released
(35) as a photon. The peak in the emission spectrum lies between 550 and 600 nm depending on the type of luciferase. This flash produced by the simultaneous emission of many photons serves to attract mates, and females also use it to attract
(40) males of other species, which they devour.

Certain bacteria also produce light when stimulated by motion. This is why the breaking sea or a passing boat generates the greenish light seen in some bodies of water such as Phosphorescent
(45) Bay in Puerto Rico. Some fish have a symbiotic relationship with bacteria. The "flashlight fish" takes advantage of the light created by bacteria lodged beneath each eye. Certain other fish produce their own bioluminescence, which
(50) serves as identification. However, the biological advantage, if any, of bioluminescence in some other organisms such as fungi remains a mystery.

Triboluminescence is the emission of light when one hard object is sharply struck against
(55) another. This contact, when atom scrapes against atom, excites electrons and disrupts electrical bonds. Light is then created when the electrons find their way to lower states. Triboluminescence is not to be confused with the glow of small
(60) particles that may be broken off by the impact. Such "sparks" are seen as a result of their high temperature. Light given off by hot objects is known as thermoluminescence, or incandescence.

¶1: intro chemilumin

¶2: intro biolumin, how produces light, intro luciferin

¶3: how fireflies use biolumin

¶4: light producing bacteria in sea, advantages not known for all organisms

¶5: tribolum. vs thermolum.

¶6: ther-
molum.
used for
dating

(65) Another form of thermoluminescence is the basis for dating ancient ceramic objects. Quartz and other constituents of clay are continually irradiated by naturally occurring radioactive elements (e.g., uranium and thorium) and by cosmic rays. This produces defects in the material where electrons (70) may be trapped. Heating pottery to 500°C releases the trapped electrons, which can then migrate back to their original atoms, where on returning to an atomic orbit they then emit a photon. The intensity of thermoluminescence is therefore a measure of (75) the duration of irradiation since the time when the pottery had been previously fired.

Excitation is also possible by other means. The passage of an electrical current (electroluminescence) is one. The impact of high-(80) energy particles is another. The *aurora borealis* and its southern counterpart the *aurora australis,* arise when a stream of high-energy particles from the sun enters the Earth's upper atmosphere and literally shatters some of the molecules in the air. (85) This leaves their atoms in excited states, and the light subsequently given off is characteristic of the atoms. Although the oxygen molecule, a major constituent of our atmosphere, has no emission in the visible spectrum, the oxygen atom can emit (90) photons in either the red or green portions of the spectrum. Other atoms contribute to light at other wavelengths.

¶7: aurora
borealis

Questions	Strategic Thinking
1. The statement "the emission spectrum lies between 550 and 600 nm" in lines 35-36 most strongly suggests that the spectrum A) contains mostly ultraviolet light. B) requires special equipment to detect. C) is produced only by fireflies. D) is visible to a variety of insects.	**Step 2: Examine the question stem** The key words and phrases in this question stem are the cited phrase and "most strongly suggests." The cited lines are from paragraph 3, which your Passage Map notes details the example of the firefly. **Step 3: Predict and answer** The emission spectrum in the cited phrase refers to light produced by fireflies. This light is used to attract mates and prey. Therefore, you can infer that if insects are attracted to the spectrum, they must be able to see it. Choice (D) is correct.
2. According to the passage, "biolumines-cence," line 11, is more often found A) with oxygen when exposed to the air. B) among terrestrial creatures. C) in marine life. D) in light given off by hot objects.	**Step 2: Examine the question stem** The key words and phrases in the question stem are "according to the passage," the quoted word, and its line reference. The Passage Map notes for the second paragraph, where the quoted word in the question stem ("bioluminescence") is first mentioned, will help you answer the question. **Step 3: Predict and answer** The Passage Map note for paragraph 2 says that bioluminescence is common in marine life. Choice (C) is correct.
3. Which of the following situations most closely parallels the description of the excitation caused by the impact of high-energy particles in lines 77-87? A) A bowling ball striking bowling pins B) A snowflake hitting the pavement C) A prism reflecting light D) A goalie stopping a shot	**Step 2: Examine the question stem** The key words and phrases in the question stem are "most closely parallels" and the line numbers of the cited description. The Passage Map for the last paragraph will help you answer this question. **Step 3: Predict and answer** The last paragraph is about the excitation caused by the impact of high-energy particles. According to the passage, the "stream of high-energy particles … literally shatters some of the molecules in the air" (lines 82-84). Choice (A) is correct.

Reading & Writing

Reading & Writing

You have seen the ways in which the SAT tests you on Detail and Inference questions in Reading passages and the way an SAT expert approaches these types of questions.

You will use the Kaplan Method for Reading Comprehension to complete this section. Part of the test-like passage has been mapped already. Your first step is to complete the Passage Map. Then, you will continue to use the Kaplan Method for Reading Comprehension and the strategies discussed in this chapter to answer the questions. Strategic thinking questions have been included to guide you—some of the answers have been filled in, but you will have to fill in the answers to others.

Use your answers to the strategic thinking questions to select the correct answer, just as you will on Test Day.

Strategic Thinking
Step 1: Read actively
The passage below is partially mapped. Read the passage and the first part of the Passage Map. Then, complete the Passage Map on your own. Remember to focus on the central ideas of each paragraph as well as the central idea of the overall passage. Use your Passage Map as a reference when you're answering questions.

Questions 4-6 are based on the following passage.

The following passage describes findings regarding American colonists based on archaeological explorations at Jamestown, Virginia.

¶1: artifacts show how colonists lived

Archaeological explorations at Jamestown, Virginia, have brought to light thousands of colonial period artifacts that were used by the
Line Virginia settlers from 1607 until 1699. A study of
(5) these objects, which were buried under the soil at Jamestown for decades, reveals in many ways how the English colonists lived on a small wilderness island over 300 years ago. Artifacts unearthed include building materials and handwrought
(10) hardware, kitchen utensils and fireplace accessories, furniture hardware, and many items relating to household and town industries.

¶2: clues about life

These artifacts provide valuable information concerning the everyday life and manners of the
(15) first Virginia settlers. Excavated artifacts reveal that the Jamestown colonists built their houses in the same style as those they knew in England, insofar as local materials permitted. There were differences, however, for the settlers were in a land replete with

(20) vast forests and untapped natural resources close at hand that they used to their advantage.

¶3: settlers used woodworking skills

The Virginia known to the first settlers was a carpenter's paradise, and consequently the early buildings were the work of artisans in wood. The
(25) first rude shelter, split-wood fencing, clapboard roof, puncheon floors, cupboards, benches, stools, and wood plows are all examples of skilled working with wood.

¶4: early structures primitive, focus on survival

Timber at Jamestown was plentiful, so many
(30) houses, especially in the early years, were of frame construction. During the first decade or two, house construction reflected a primitive use of materials found ready at hand, such as saplings for a sort of framing, and use of branches, leafage, bark, and
(35) animal skins. During these early years, when the settlers were having such a difficult time staying alive, mud walls, wattle-and-daub, and coarse marsh-grass thatch were used. Out of these years of improvising, construction with squatted posts,
(40) and later with studs, came into practice. There

was probably little thought of plastering walls during the first two decades. When plastering was adopted, clay, either by itself or mixed with oyster-shell lime, was first used. The early floors were of clay, and such
(45) floors continued to be used in the humbler dwellings throughout the 1600s. It can be assumed that most of the dwellings, or shelters, of the early Jamestown settlers had a rough and primitive appearance.

After Jamestown had attained some degree of
(50) permanency, many houses were built of brick. It is quite clear from documentary records and archaeological remains that the colonists not only made their own brick but also that the process, as well as the finished products, followed closely the
(55) English method. Four brick kilns were discovered on Jamestown Island during archaeological explorations.

While some of the handwrought hardware found at Jamestown was made in the colony, most of it was imported from England. Types of building hardware
(60) unearthed include an excellent assortment of nails, spikes, staples, locks, keys, hinges, pintles, shutter fasteners, bolts, hasps, latches, door knockers, door pulls, bootscrapes, gutter supports, wall anchors, and ornamental hardware. In many instances, each type
(65) is represented by several varieties. It is believed that wooden hardware was used on many of the early houses.

A few glass windowpanes may have been made in the Jamestown glass factory, which
(70) was built in 1608. Most of the window glass used in the colony, however, was shipped from England. Many of the early panes used were diamond-shaped pieces known as "quarrels" and were held in place by means of slotted lead
(75) strips known as "cames." The window frames used in a few of the Jamestown houses were handwrought iron casements. Most of the humbler dwellings had no glass panes in the windows. The window openings were closed
(80) by batten shutters, operated by hinges of wood, and fitted with wooden fastening devices.

Busy conquering a stubborn wilderness, the first Jamestown settlers had only a few things to make their homes cozy and cheerful. In
(85) most cases, their worldly goods consisted of a few cooking utensils, a change of clothing, a weapon or two, and a few pieces of handmade furniture. After the early years of hardship had passed, the colonists began to acquire pos-
(90) sessions for more pleasant living; by 1650 the better houses were equipped with most of the necessities of life of those times, as well as a few luxuries of comfortable living.

Don't get distracted by less important details. While there is a lot going on in this passage, your additions to the Passage Map should have noted the evolution of building practices, bricks, furniture, and glass. If you're stuck, review the example Passage Map in the Answers & Explanations for this chapter on page 993.

Questions	Strategic Thinking
4. The statement in lines 40-42 ("There was . . . decades") suggests that the Jamestown colonists A) followed London fashions. B) lacked the resources to import the raw materials from England. C) focused their energies on survival, not on decoration. D) hesitated to build more permanent homes until bricks were available.	**Step 2: Examine the question stem** The key words and phrases in this question stem are the cited statement with its corresponding line numbers and the word "suggests." **Step 3: Predict and answer** *Read around the cited lines. Why was there "little thought of plastering walls during the first two decades" (lines 41-42)?* _____ _____ _____ *Which answer choice matches this prediction?* _____
5. All of the following are true about the Jamestown colonists EXCEPT A) some of them were skilled woodworkers. B) they struggled to survive in the early decades. C) they made floors out of clay. D) they constructed most of their own hardware.	**Step 2: Examine the question stem** *What are the key words and phrases in this question stem?* _____ *What parts of your Passage Map are relevant?* _____ **Step 3: Predict and answer** *Is A mentioned in the passage? If so, where?* _____ *Is B mentioned in the passage? If so, where?* _____ *Is C mentioned in the passage? If so, where?* _____ *Is D mentioned in the passage? If so, where?* _____ *Which answer choice is not mentioned in the passage and is therefore correct?* _____

Questions	Strategic Thinking
6. The description of the Jamestown colonists' brick industry, as discussed in lines 49-56, is most comparable to A) traditional weavers making cloth with imported cotton. B) mountain climbers carrying all of their food and shelter on their expedition. C) pioneer farmers bringing seeds and agricultural techniques to new lands. D) an immigrant chef using local ingredients to make recipes from her homeland.	**Step 2: Examine the question stem** *What are the key words and phrases in this question stem?* _____ *What parts of your Passage Map are relevant?* _____ **Step 3: Predict and answer** *How do the cited lines describe the brick industry?* _____ *Which answer choice is most similar to this process?* _____

Now, try a test-like SAT Reading passage on your own. Give yourself 6 minutes to read the passage and answer the questions.

Questions 7-10 are based on the following passage.

The following passage is an excerpt from "The Murders in the Rue Morgue," a short story by Edgar Allan Poe published in 1841.

Our first meeting was at an obscure library in the Rue Montmartre, where the accident of our both being in search of the same very rare and very remarkable volume, brought us into closer
(5) communion. We saw each other again and again. I was deeply interested in the little family history which he detailed to me with all that candor which a Frenchman indulges whenever mere self is the theme. I was astonished too, at the vast
(10) extent of his reading; and, above all, I felt my soul enkindled within me by the wild fervor, and the vivid freshness of his imagination. Seeking in Paris the objects I then sought, I felt that the society of such a man would be to me a treasure beyond
(15) price; and this feeling I frankly confided to him. It was at length arranged that we should live together during my stay in the city; and as my worldly circumstances were somewhat less embarrassed than his own, I was permitted to be at the expense
(20) of renting, and furnishing in a style which suited the rather fantastic gloom of our common temper, a time-eaten and grotesque mansion, long deserted through superstitions into which we did not inquire, and tottering to its fall in a retired and
(25) desolate portion of the Faubourg St. Germain.

Had the routine of our life at this place been known to the world, we should have been regarded as madmen—although, perhaps, as madmen of a harmless nature. Our seclusion was perfect. We
(30) admitted no visitors. Indeed the locality of our retirement had been carefully kept a secret from my own former associates; and it had been many years since Dupin had ceased to know or be known in Paris. We existed within ourselves alone.

(35) It was a freak of fancy in my friend (for what else shall I call it?) to be enamored of the Night for her own sake; and into this bizarrerie, as into all his others, I quietly fell; giving myself up to his wild whims with a perfect abandon. The sable divin-
(40) ity would not herself dwell with us always; but we could counterfeit her presence. At the first dawn of the morning we closed all the massy shutters of our old building; lighted a couple of tapers which, strongly perfumed, threw out only the ghastliest
(45) and feeblest of rays. By the aid of these we then busied our souls in dreams—reading, writing, or conversing, until warned by the clock of the advent of the true Darkness. Then we sallied forth into the streets, arm in arm, continuing the topics of
(50) the day, or roaming far and wide until a late hour, seeking, amid the wild lights and shadows of the populous city that infinity of mental excitement which quiet observation can afford.

At such times I could not help remarking and
(55) admiring (although from his rich ideality I had been prepared to expect it) a peculiar analytic ability in Dupin. He seemed, too, to take an eager delight in its exercise—if not exactly in its display—and did not hesitate to confess the
(60) pleasure thus derived. He boasted to me, with a low chuckling laugh, that most men, in respect to himself, wore windows in their bosoms, and was wont to follow up such assertions by direct and very startling proofs of his intimate knowledge of
(65) my own. His manner at these moments was frigid and abstract; his eyes were vacant in expression; while his voice, usually a rich tenor, rose into a treble which would have sounded petulantly but for the deliberateness and entire distinctness of the
(70) enunciation. Observing him in these moods, I often dwelt meditatively upon the old philosophy of the Bi-Part soul, and amused myself with the fancy of a double Dupin—the creative and the resolvent.

7. The statement in lines 17-19 ("my worldly . . . his own") suggests that

    A) Dupin wishes his family history were different.

    B) the narrator was more self-confident about his own wealth.

    C) Dupin was less well-off than the narrator.

    D) the narrator led an exemplary life.

8. In the third paragraph, the relationship between the narrator and Dupin most closely parallels which of the following situations?

    A) Two scientists collaborating on a research project

    B) A professor instructing a new student

    C) An art student adapting a teacher's techniques in a new way

    D) A fan dressing and acting like a pop star

9. According to the passage, the narrator and Dupin met because they

    A) lived in the Rue Montmartre.

    B) wanted to find the same book.

    C) preferred the night to the day.

    D) enjoyed solitude.

10. The narrator would most likely agree with which of the following statements?

    A) Dupin understood other people's inner thoughts in ways the narrator could not comprehend.

    B) Dupin was a humorously eccentric character given to flights of fancy.

    C) Dupin enjoyed entertaining groups of other fashionable Parisians.

    D) Dupin represented an obscure aspect of French society that the narrator wished to study.

Answers & Explanations for this chapter begin on page 993.

EXTRA PRACTICE

The following questions provide an opportunity to practice the concepts and strategic thinking covered in this chapter. While many of the questions pertain to Inference and Detail questions, some touch on other concepts tested on the Reading Test to ensure that your practice is test-like, with a variety of question types per passage.

Questions 1-11 are based on the following passages and supplementary material.

The following passages detail different aspects of the United States National Parks System.

Passage 1

In the mid- to late-nineteenth century, America legislated an idea that would come to be emulated worldwide: the National Parks System. Starting
Line with Yellowstone National Park in 1872, the
(5) United States government sparked a national and international trend of setting aside treasured spaces for preservation, protection, and public enjoyment. Since then, over 400 national parks have been established in American states and territories, and
(10) globally over a thousand parks are now protected by similar systems in their respective nations.

The United States National Park Service (NPS) is responsible for managing and protecting these parks. Set up by President Wilson in 1916, this
(15) federal organization oversees budgeting, care, advocacy, and education for the country's parks. As a piece of legislation enacted in 1933, the NPS includes landmarks of historic and scientific significance in addition to those significant for their
(20) sheer natural beauty or unique wildlife populations. There are now 84 million acres of United States national parkland (and water). Thousands of employees and millions of volunteers work with the NPS to accomplish its vast responsibilities. From
(25) national monuments and battlegrounds, to the breathtaking vistas of the Great Smoky Mountains, Alaska's Glacier Bay, and even underwater snorkeling trails in the U.S. Virgin Islands, spaces marked with awe and meaning are preserved for
(30) the enjoyment of generations to come.

Today, more than 275 million people visit America's national parks yearly. They come prepared to be amazed; the stunning beauty, powerful history, and inspiring intricacies of nature
(35) they encounter never disappoint. And America's great idea, in which over a hundred countries now participate, enables that amazement to be spread and shared across nations and generations. The National Park System teaches and invites people
(40) worldwide to practice preservation in their daily lives by making choices to protect the earth's wonders and treasures.

Passage 2

John Muir, often called "Father of the National Park System," was America's most famous and
(45) influential naturalist. Born in 1838, he bore witness to the establishment of the first national parks and the many visions, debates, and victories of the early environmentalist movement. Muir was a man of many talents. He began his career working
(50) in carriage production but soon chose a life of exploring the nation's spectacular wilderness, traveling thousands of miles by foot and across oceans. From relative anonymity as a wayfarer, shepherd, and mill laborer, Muir would soon
(55) become a national hero whose widely read writings would drive government policy makers to action.

When Muir encountered California's Yosemite Valley and the greater Sierra Nevada mountains, he immediately recognized their worth. He saw in
(60) them not only astounding scenic beauty, but also crucial ecological significance. Over the rest of his life, he would advocate for their protection. Yet his interest would stretch far beyond the Sierras. Muir regularly traversed California's forested mountains
(65) and made a home in Yosemite Valley, but his activism and wanderlust also drew him to other

picturesque locations, such as Washington's Mount Rainier and Alaska's coast and glaciers. He published hundreds of articles documenting his travels. These invoked the (70) wonder of the natural beauty he witnessed, channeling that marvel into the hearts of readers nationwide.

The political impact of Muir's life was immense. His publications were elemental in persuading the United States government to establish Yosemite, Sequoia, (75) the Grand Canyon, and Mount Rainier as national parks. His relationship with Theodore Roosevelt was foundational to the environmental policies and gains made during Roosevelt's presidency; Muir's relentless advocacy for protecting the Sierras catalyzed and (80) empowered a movement that would carry through the coming centuries. Much of this advocacy manifested itself in Muir's founding of a political activist organization called the Sierra Club. Internationally this group was one of the first of its kind, and it remains one (85) of the nation's leading environmental organizations.

However, perhaps even greater than Muir's political accomplishments was his ideological impact. His unforgettable philosophies about the importance of nature reminded Americans that the wild was worth (90) cherishing and saving, even at the expense of short-lived material gains for which it might be exchanged. Muir's legacy has invited and inspired billions of people worldwide to guard the global ecosystem and to go out and enjoy it all.

Average Yearly Visitation to Popular National Parks in America

Yearly Visitors (in millions)

Years of Park Operation

Key
Grand Canyon National Park
Great Smoky Mountains National Park
Olympic National Park

1. As used in line 2, "emulated" most nearly means

   A) admired.

   B) feared.

   C) imitated.

   D) invented.

2. What is the most likely purpose of the second paragraph of Passage 1?

   A) To describe the impressive scale of the National Parks System

   B) To show that national parks have become popular despite early setbacks

   C) To argue that national parks are valuable because of their aesthetic value

   D) To defend the existence of national parks against critics of their economic cost

3. What can be most strongly concluded about the United States National Parks System from Passage 1?

   A) It is more popular with visitors today than it was initially.

   B) Its accomplishments have historically been controversial.

   C) It is the most popular service provided by the American government.

   D) Its ideas about conservation have been influential internationally.

4. Which choice provides the best evidence for the answer to the previous question?

   A) Lines 14-16 ("Set up . . . country's parks")

   B) Lines 22-24 ("Thousands of . . . vast responsibilities")

   C) Lines 31-32 ("Today, more than . . . yearly")

   D) Lines 35-38 ("And America's . . . and generations")

5. As used in line 66, "wanderlust" most likely means

   A) an interest in travel.

   B) an inability to concentrate.

   C) a love of diversity.

   D) a desire for the countryside.

6. What does the use of the word "channeling" in line 70 suggest about Muir's writings?

   A) They were focused on his spiritual connection with nature.

   B) They were emotionally moving to his readers.

   C) They were entertaining in a manner similar to television.

   D) They were strident and opinionated.

7. With which statement would the author of Passage 2 most likely agree?

   A) The preservation of the wilderness came at an economic cost.

   B) John Muir's contributions were largely unrecognized during his life.

   C) Many naturalists were important in creating the national parks system.

   D) The most important work John Muir did was in helping create government policy.

8. Which choice provides the best evidence for the answer to the previous question?

   A) Lines 72-76 ("His publications . . . national parks")

   B) Lines 76-81 ("His relationship . . . coming centuries")

   C) Lines 86-87 ("However . . . ideological impact")

   D) Lines 87-91 ("His unforgettable . . . exchanged")

9. How do the central ideas of the two passages primarily differ?

   A) Passage 1 describes the parks system generally, while Passage 2 focuses on its founding.

   B) Passage 1 argues that the parks system is underappreciated, while Passage 2 celebrates it as a national treasure beloved by many.

   C) Passage 1 focuses on the parks system's creation, while Passage 2 focuses on its structure.

   D) Passage 1 describes the idea of national parks, while Passage 2 focuses specifically on how the idea was applied in the United States.

10. The authors of both passages would most likely agree that the most important role of national parks is to

    A) preserve natural beauty so it can inspire visitors.

    B) allow city residents to escape polluted environments.

    C) instill a sense of patriotism in those who spend time there.

    D) help foster economic development through the use of public lands.

11. What conclusion can be drawn from the graph?

    A) The population of the United States has doubled since 1930.

    B) Olympic National Park is in a location difficult for most visitors to access.

    C) The Great Smoky Mountains National Park has become less popular since its inception.

    D) The Grand Canyon has consistently been a more popular destination than the Olympic National Park.

Questions 12-21 are based on the following passage.

This passage is adapted from Jane Austen's *Sense and Sensibility*.

Before the house-maid had lit their fire the
next day, or the sun gained any power over a cold,
gloomy morning in January, Marianne, only half
Line dressed, was kneeling against one of the window-
(5) seats for the sake of all the little light she could
command from it, and writing as fast as a continual
flow of tears would permit her. In this situation,
Elinor, roused from sleep by her agitation and sobs,
first perceived her; and after observing her for a few
(10) moments with silent anxiety, said, in a tone of the
most considerate gentleness,

"Marianne, may I ask-?"

"No, Elinor," she replied, "ask nothing; you will
soon know all."

(15) The sort of desperate calmness with which this
was said, lasted no longer than while she spoke, and
was immediately followed by a return of the same
excessive affliction. It was some minutes before she
could go on with her letter, and the frequent bursts
(20) of grief which still obliged her, at intervals, to with-
hold her pen, were proofs enough of her feeling
how more than probable it was that she was writing
for the last time to Willoughby.

At breakfast she neither ate, nor attempted to
(25) eat any thing; and Elinor's attention was then all
employed, not in urging her, not in pitying her, nor
in appearing to regard her, but in endeavouring to
engage Mrs. Jennings's notice entirely to herself.

As this was a favourite meal with Mrs. Jennings,
(30) it lasted a considerable time, and they were just setting themselves, after it, round the common working table, when a letter was delivered to Marianne,
which she eagerly caught from the servant, and,
turning of a death-like paleness, instantly ran out
(35) of the room. Elinor, who saw as plainly by this, as if
she had seen the direction, that it must come from
Willoughby, felt immediately such a sickness at
heart as made her hardly able to hold up her head,
and sat in such a general tremour as made her fear

(40) it impossible to escape Mrs. Jennings's notice. That
good lady, however, saw only that Marianne had received a letter from Willoughby, which appeared to
her a very good joke, and which she treated accordingly, by hoping, with a laugh, that she would find it
(45) to her liking. Of Elinor's distress, she was too busily
employed in measuring lengths of worsted for her
rug, to see any thing at all; and calmly continuing
her talk, as soon as Marianne disappeared, she said,

"Upon my word, I never saw a young woman so
(50) desperately in love in my life! MY girls were nothing to her, and yet they used to be foolish enough;
but as for Miss Marianne, she is quite an altered
creature. I hope, from the bottom of my heart, he
won't keep her waiting much longer, for it is quite
(55) grievous to see her look so ill and forlorn. Pray,
when are they to be married?"

Elinor, though never less disposed to speak than
at that moment, obliged herself to answer such an
attack as this, and, therefore, trying to smile, re-
(60) plied, "And have you really, Ma'am, talked yourself
into a persuasion of my sister's being engaged to
Mr. Willoughby? I thought it had been only a joke,
but so serious a question seems to imply more;
and I must beg, therefore, that you will not deceive
(65) yourself any longer. I do assure you that nothing
would surprise me more than to hear of their being
going to be married."

"For shame, for shame, Miss Dashwood! how
can you talk so? Don't we all know that it must be
(70) a match, that they were over head and ears in love
with each other from the first moment they met?
Did not I see them together in Devonshire every
day, and all day long; and did not I know that your
sister came to town with me on purpose to buy wed-
(75) ding clothes? Come, come, this won't do. Because
you are so sly about it yourself, you think nobody
else has any senses; but it is no such thing, I can tell
you, for it has been known all over town this ever so
long. I tell every body of it and so does Charlotte."

(80) "Indeed, Ma'am," said Elinor, very seriously, "you
are mistaken. Indeed, you are doing a very unkind
thing in spreading the report, and you will find that
you have though you will not believe me now."

Reading & Writing

12. As used in line 57, "disposed" most nearly means

    A) capable.

    B) inclined.

    C) shed.

    D) permitted.

13. In line 34, the author describes Marianne as "turning of a death-like paleness" in order to emphasize

    A) her comical overreaction to an everyday event.

    B) the anxiety she feels about the letter's contents.

    C) the supernatural elements that surround the house.

    D) her knowledge that the letter contains news of illness.

14. The passage most strongly suggests which of the following about Elinor's feelings toward Marianne?

    A) Elinor feels protective of Marianne.

    B) Elinor is sad that they are not closer.

    C) Elinor is jealous of Marianne's success in life.

    D) Elinor considers them to be rivals in matters of love.

15. Which choice provides the best evidence for the answer to the previous question?

    A) Lines 15-18 ("The sort . . . excessive affliction")

    B) Lines 24-28 ("At breakfast . . . entirely to herself")

    C) Lines 53-55 ("I hope . . . ill and forlorn")

    D) Lines 62-65 ("'I thought . . . any longer'")

16. Which statement does the passage most strongly suggest is true of Mrs. Jennings?

    A) She does not have many people with whom to talk.

    B) She knows the intimate details of Marianne's feelings.

    C) She is not very perceptive about the events around her.

    D) She has spoken to Willoughby more recently than Marianne.

17. Which choice provides the best evidence for the answer to the previous question?

    A) Lines 24-28 ("At breakfast . . . to herself")

    B) Lines 29-35 ("As this was . . . of the room")

    C) Lines 45-47 ("Of Elinor's . . . any thing at all")

    D) Lines 49-50 ("Upon my word . . . in my life")

18. As used in line 61, "persuasion" most nearly means

    A) argument.

    B) belief.

    C) excitement.

    D) joke.

19. According to the passage, Mrs. Jennings believes that

    A) Willoughby intends to marry Marianne.

    B) Elinor is overreacting to Willoughby's letter.

    C) Marianne loves someone other than Willoughby.

    D) Elinor is mistaken about why Marianne is upset.

20. Based on the information in the passage, Marianne's situation can most directly be compared to that of

A) a stray cat who shows affection to strangers in hopes of being fed.

B) a person who cultivates charm in order to compensate for a lack of physical beauty.

C) a scientist working on an ambitious project in which only she has faith.

D) a worker who has not been hired for a job she was certain she would get.

21. What is the author's most likely purpose in providing the last paragraph of dialogue?

A) To help readers understand why Marianne is so upset

B) To demonstrate the degree of Elinor's concern about Marianne

C) To argue that Mrs. Jennings's understanding of the situation may be accurate

D) To persuade readers that Marianne is not entirely innocent

Expression of Ideas

BY THE END OF THIS UNIT, YOU WILL BE ABLE TO:

1. Apply the Kaplan Method for Writing & Language

2. Evaluate the effectiveness and clarity of a given passage

3. Identify proper and effective language use

4. Utilize the standard conventions of usage in written English

The Kaplan Methods for Writing & Language and Infographics

CHAPTER OBJECTIVES

By the end of this chapter, you will be able to:

1. Distinguish among the three different Writing and Language text types
2. Identify issues in a passage and select the correct answer by applying the Kaplan Method for Writing & Language
3. Identify and analyze quantitative information and infographics
4. Synthesize information from infographics and text

SMARTPOINTS

Point Value	SmartPoint Category
Point Builder	The Kaplan Method for Writing & Language
Point Builder	The Kaplan Method for Infographics
10 Points	Quantitative

Reading & Writing

THE KAPLAN METHOD FOR WRITING & LANGUAGE & INFOGRAPHICS

Chapter 19

Homework

Extra Practice: #1-11

Even More

Writing & Language Text Types

The Kaplan Method for Writing
& Language

Key

 Book Assignment

 Online Video Assignment

 Online Quiz Assignment

OVERVIEW OF THE WRITING & LANGUAGE PASSAGE TYPES

You will see four Writing & Language passages on Test Day, each of which will have 11 questions. Recognizing the text type of a Writing & Language passage helps you focus on the questions as they relate to the passage's general purpose. Knowing the overarching aim of the passage will help you answer questions more efficiently and accurately.

Writing & Language Passage Types	
1–2 Argumentative texts	Author will advocate a point, idea, or proposal
1–2 Informative/Explanatory texts	Author will explain, describe, or analyze a topic in order to impart information without necessarily advocating
1 Nonfiction Narrative text	Author will use a story-like approach to convey information or ideas

✔ **Remember**

The SAT rewards critical thinking in context. Pay attention to the text type to answer Writing & Language questions more efficiently.

Let's look at three short Writing & Language passage excerpts (without errors) and see how an SAT expert identifies the text type of each. The left column features the passage excerpt, while the right column demonstrates the strategic thinking a test expert employs when identifying Writing & Language text types.

Passages	Strategic Thinking
As if malpractice suits and unnecessary bankruptcies were not enough of a problem, lawyers have chosen to increase the burden that they place on society by engineering an excess of increasingly ridiculous product warnings. Why else would a box of sleeping pills be marketed with the cautionary note that consumers may experience drowsiness? Or a cup of coffee be emblazoned with a notice that "THIS PRODUCT MAY BE HOT"? Anyone with common sense will not need to be warned about these possibilities, and anyone WITHOUT common sense is probably not going to be stopped from undertaking a foolish course of action by a warning label anyway. So honestly, in the long run, the only ones who benefit from these warnings are the lawyers who are paid hundreds of dollars an hour to compose them.	The phrases "ridiculous product warnings," "anyone with common sense," and "foolish course of action," in addition to the rhetorical questions in the passage, indicate that the tone of the passage is incredulous, cynical, and mocking. The author is mocking the "excess of increasingly ridiculous product warnings." The author states that "the only ones who benefit from these warnings are the lawyers who are paid hundreds of dollars an hour to compose them." The text type of this passage excerpt is therefore **Argumentative.**
It is amazing how little the structure of the American public school system has changed since its inception. Students still change classes according to bells, even though the bell system originated during the days of factories. School is still not in session during the summer, although most students will not use that time to work on farms. Although class and school sizes have varied widely and the curriculum has certainly become varied, the actual system remains surprisingly similar to the way it once was. Despite these idiosyncrasies, however, the American public school system continues to educate the children of this country in a fair and equitable fashion. Without the established structure, the chaotic nature of school would severely inhibit learning.	In the first sentence of the passage, the author establishes the topic of the passage. The keywords "although" and "despite" later in the passage suggest that the author is reporting on various aspects of the public school system. The text type of this passage excerpt is **Informative/Explanatory.**

Passages	Strategic Thinking
I still remember the magic of walking home under the cold, brittle blue sky, watching the sun strike the glittering blanket laid down by that first snowfall. The world dripped with frosting, and everything was pure and silent. I breathed deeply, enjoying the sting of the icy air in my nostrils, and set off through the trees, listening to the muffled crunch of my footsteps and the chirps of the waking birds. Later, the cars and schoolchildren and mundane lives would turn the wonderland back into dingy slush; the hush would be interrupted by horns and shouts. Indeed for now, the sparkling, cloistered world was mine alone. I smiled, and for a moment, my mind was still.	This passage is explicitly different from the previous two passages because it is written in the first person, as evidenced by the author's use of personal pronouns such as "I." The text type of this passage is **Nonfiction Narrative**.

THE KAPLAN METHOD FOR WRITING & LANGUAGE

The Kaplan Method for Writing & Language is the method you will use to boost your score on the Writing & Language Test. By understanding what the question is looking for, how it relates to the passage, and the questions you should ask yourself on Test Day, you will maximize the number of points you earn. Use the Kaplan Method for Writing & Language for every SAT Writing & Language Test passage and question you encounter, whether practicing, completing your homework, working on a Practice Test, or taking the actual exam on Test Day.

The Kaplan Method for Writing & Language has three steps:

Step 1: Read the passage and identify the issue

- If there's an infographic, apply the Kaplan Method for Infographics

Step 2: Eliminate answer choices that do not address the issue

Step 3: Plug in the remaining answer choices and select the most correct, concise, and relevant one

✔ On Test Day

The SAT will expect you to be able to recognize errors in organization, pronouns, agreement, comparisons, development, sentence structure, modifiers, verbs, wordiness, style, tone, and syntax.

Let's take a closer look at each step.

Step 1: Read the passage and identify the issue

This means:

- Rather than reading the whole passage and then answering all of the questions, you can answer questions as you read because they are mostly embedded in the text itself.

- When you see a number, stop reading and look at the question. If you can answer it with what you've read so far, do so. If you need more information, keep reading until you have enough context to answer the question.

Step 2: Eliminate answer choices that do not address the issue

Eliminating answer choices that do not address the issue:

- Increases your odds of getting the correct answer by removing obviously incorrect answer choices

Step 3: Plug in the remaining answer choices and select the most correct, concise, and relevant one

Correct, concise, and relevant means that the answer choice you select:

- Makes sense when read with the correction
- Is as short as possible while retaining the information in the text
- Relates well to the passage overall

> **✔ Remember**
>
> There is no wrong answer penalty on the SAT. When in doubt, eliminate what you can and then guess. You won't lose points for guessing.

Answer choices should not:

- Change the intended meaning of the original sentence, paragraph, or passage
- Introduce new grammatical errors

> **✔ On Test Day**
>
> If you have to guess, eliminate answer choices that are clearly wrong and then choose the shortest one—the SAT rewards students who know how to be concise.

When you encounter a Writing & Language question, use the Kaplan Method, asking yourself a series of strategic thinking questions. By asking these strategic thinking questions, you will be able to select the correct answer choice more easily and efficiently. Pausing to ask yourself questions before answering each question may seem like it takes a lot of time, but it actually saves you time by preventing you from weighing the four answer choices against each other; it's better to ask questions that lead you directly to the correct answer than to debate which of four answers seems the least incorrect.

Let's look at the following Writing & Language passage and questions. After the passage, there are two columns. The left column contains test-like questions. The column on the right features the strategic thinking a test expert employs when approaching the passage and questions presented.

Child Expenditures

    A 2005 report from the United States Department of Agriculture estimates that the cost of raising a child from birth until age seventeen is approximately $500,000. This cost includes housing, food, clothing, transportation, health care, child care, and education and does, of course, vary considerably. However, with the average cost of having and raising a child set at half a million dollars, and with additional children in the family raising that financial expenditure accordingly, it becomes clear that parenthood should not be entered into lightly. Even for families that plan for children, there may be costs for which they are unprepared. For instance, if a woman chooses to spend the first years of her child's life as a full-time mother and homemaker, she can lose career momentum and end up making a substantially lower salary than a woman with the same background who maintains consistent employment. While these factors should in no way be construed as a recommendation against having children, **1** <u>if you're planning a family, be ready.</u>

Questions	Strategic Thinking
1. A) NO CHANGE B) but think about the problems it might cause. C) they speak to the need for responsible family planning and financial preparation. D) make sure you understand what you're getting into.	**Step 1: Read the passage and identify the issue** The underlined phrase is grammatically correct. When there is no apparent grammatical issue, check style, tone, and syntax. The tone of the underlined portion is much more informal than the tone of the overall passage, as evidenced by the use of the second person ("you"). **Step 2: Eliminate answer choices that do not address the issue** Eliminate A because there is a tone issue in the underlined portion. Eliminate B and D because they still use the second person (it's implied in B with the imperative mood of the verb "think"). **Step 3: Plug in the remaining answer choices and select the most correct, concise, and relevant one** Choice (C) is correct.

Reading & Writing

THE KAPLAN METHOD FOR INFOGRAPHICS

The SAT Writing & Language Test will contain one or more passages that include infographics. Each infographic will convey or expand on information related to the passage.

The Kaplan Method for Infographics has three steps:

> Step 1: Read the question
>
> Step 2: Examine the infographic
>
> Step 3: Predict and answer

Let's examine these steps a bit more closely.

Step 1: Read the question

Analyze the question stem for information that will help you zero in on the specific parts of the infographic that apply to the question.

Step 2: Examine the infographic

Make sure to:

- Identify units of measurement, labels, and titles
- Circle parts of the infographic that relate directly to the question

> ✔ **Expert Tip**
>
> For more data-heavy infographics, you should also make note of any trends in the data or relationships between variables.

Step 3: Predict and answer

Just as in Step 3 of the Kaplan Method for Reading Comprehension, do not look at the answer choices until you've used the infographic to make a prediction. Asking questions and taking time to assess the given information before answering the test question will increase your chances of selecting the correct answer. Infographics vary in format—there can be tables, graphs, charts, and so on—so be flexible when you ask yourself these critical-thinking questions.

When you apply the Kaplan Method for Infographics, keep in mind that infographics will either represent data described in the passage or present new data that expand on what the passage is about.

Let's look at the following Writing & Language infographic and questions. After the infographic, there are two columns. The left column contains test-like questions. The column on the right features the strategic thinking a test expert employs when approaching the infographic and questions presented.

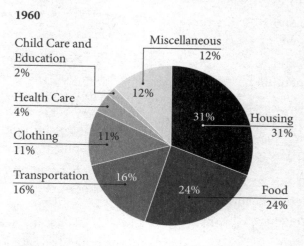

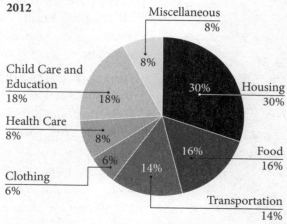

Expenditures on a Child from Birth Through Age 17: Budgetary Component Shares, 1960 versus 2012

Prepare

Reading & Writing

Questions	Strategic Thinking
2. Which claim about the cost of raising children is supported by the two pie charts? A) Between 1960 and 2012, the percent of a budget spent on food increased. B) Between 1960 and 2012, the percent of a budget spent on health care decreased. C) Between 1960 and 2012, the percent of a budget spent on transportation experienced the greatest decrease. D) Between 1960 and 2012, the percent of a budget spent on child care and education experienced the greatest increase.	**Step 1: Read the question** The question is asking you to evaluate which answer choice is correct when compared to the two pie charts. **Step 2: Examine the infographic** It is unclear which parts of the infographic relate directly to the question because the question stem is very general. You'll have to look at the answer choices for guidance on what part of the infographic to examine closely. The title of the infographic is "Expenditures on a Child from Birth Through Age 17: Budgetary Component Shares, 1960 versus 2012." The labels are "1960" for one pie chart and "2012" for the other. The categories in both pie charts are Housing, Food, Transportation, Clothing, Health Care, Child Care and Education, and Miscellaneous. **Step 3: Predict and answer** Choice A claims that the percent of a budget spent on food increased from 1960 to 2012; however, it decreased from 24% to 16%. Eliminate A. Choice B claims that the percent of a budget spent on health care decreased from 1960 to 2012; however, it increased from 4% to 8%. Eliminate B. Choice C claims that the greatest cost decrease occurred in transportation. However, the percent of a budget spent on transportation decreased from 16% in 1960 to 14% in 2012, while the percent of a budget spent on food decreased from 24% in 1960 to 16% in 2012. Eliminate C. The percent of a budget spent on child care and education increased from 2% in 1960 to 18% in 2012. This is the greatest increase, as choice (D) claims. Choice (D) is correct.

496 **Unit Seven: Expression of Ideas**

You have seen the ways in which the SAT tests you on Infographics in Writing & Language passages and the way an SAT expert approaches these types of questions.

Use the Kaplan Method for Writing & Language to answer the three questions that accompany the following Writing & Language passage excerpt. Remember to look at the strategic thinking questions that have been laid out for you—some of the answers have been filled in, but you will have to complete the answers to others.

Use your answers to the strategic thinking questions to select the correct answer, just as you will on Test Day.

Questions 3–5 are based on the following passage.

Industrial Progress

Is industrial progress a mixed blessing? **3** <u>Hundred years</u> ago, this question was seldom asked. Science and industry were flooding the world with products that made life easier. But today we know that many industrial processes create pollution that can destroy our environment. Industries produce toxic waste, discharging harmful chemicals directly into lakes, rivers, and the air. One of the results of this pollution that must be managed in order to protect our ecosystems is acid rain.

Air, clouds, and rain containing acids caused by industrial pollution can have terrible effects. Acid droplets in the air can be inhaled, causing illness. From clouds, these acid droplets fall as rain. If natural chemical processes in soils do not deactivate the acids, these acids can accumulate and kill both plant and animal life. In some parts of the Northeast and Midwest, 10 percent of all lakes show dangerous acid levels. In eastern mountains in the United States, large forest tracts have disappeared at elevations where trees are regularly bathed in acid rain.

Acid rain is caused by industrial processes that release compounds of nitrogen and sulfur. **4** <u>These pollutants</u> combine with clean air, the results are nitric and sulfuric acids. The main components of acid rain **5** <u>is</u> oxides of nitrogen and sulfur dioxide, which are emitted by oil- and coal-burning power plants. To reduce acid rain, emissions from these plants, particularly sulfur dioxide, must be reduced. One way to do this is to install machines that remove sulfur dioxide from a plant's emissions. Another is to build new plants modeled on currently experimental designs that produce less sulfur dioxide.

Practice

Questions	Strategic Thinking
3. A) NO CHANGE B) A hundred years, give or take, C) One hundred years D) Hundred years or so	**Step 1: Read the passage and identify the issue** *What is the issue?* As written, the underlined portion uses the incorrect form of a number, which is an error in idiom construction. **Step 2: Eliminate answer choices that do not address the issue** *What answer choice(s) can you eliminate?* _____ _____ _____ **Step 3: Plug in the remaining answer choices and select the most correct, concise, and relevant one** *What is the correct answer?*_____
4. A) NO CHANGE B) Because these pollutants C) When these pollutants D) Where these pollutants	**Step 1: Read the passage and identify the issue** *What is the issue?* While there is nothing obviously incorrect about the underlined portion, if you keep reading the entire sentence, you'll see that it is a run-on. **Step 2: Eliminate answer choices that do not address the issue** *What answer choice(s) can you eliminate?* _____ _____ _____ **Step 3: Plug in the remaining answer choices and select the most correct, concise, and relevant one** *What is the correct answer?* _____

Reading & Writing

Questions	Strategic Thinking

5. A) NO CHANGE
     B) are
     C) was
     D) were
	Step 1: Read the passage and identify the issue
	
	What is the issue?
	
	The singular verb "is" does not agree with its subject, "the main components." You need a plural verb in the present tense.
	
	Step 2: Eliminate answer choices that do not address the issue
	
	What answer choice(s) can you eliminate?
	
	_____
	_____
	_____
	
	Step 3: Plug in the remaining answer choices and select the most correct, concise, and relevant one
	
	What is the correct answer? _____

Now, try a test-like Writing & Language passage and infographic on your own. Give yourself 5 minutes to read the passage and answer the questions.

Questions 6-13 are based on the following passage and supplementary material.

Jupiter

As the fifth planet from the Sun, and by far the most massive in our solar system at 318 times the mass of Earth, Jupiter has **6** fascinated and intrigued scientists for centuries. In fact, it was the initial discovery of this massive, gaseous planet that marked the first time astronomers considered the possibility that the movement of other planets was not centered around the Earth. More specifically, when Jupiter was first viewed from Earth by the Italian astronomer Galileo in 1610, four large moons were also spotted in orbit around this enormous planet. It was these moons, now known as the Galilean moons, that provided important evidence for Galileo's outspoken support of Copernicus's heliocentric theory of planetary **7** movement. Because these moons seemed to revolve around a planet other than Earth.

The first close look at Jupiter came in 1973, when the unmanned NASA probe *Pioneer 10* completed a successful **8** flyby, and it collected important data regarding the planet's chemical composition and interior structure. **9** After completing its mission to Jupiter, *Pioneer 10* became the first spacecraft to leave the solar system. Designated as one of the gas planets—along with Saturn, Uranus, and Neptune—Jupiter is composed of about 90 percent hydrogen and 10 percent helium

6. A) NO CHANGE
    B) fascinated
    C) intrigued, and fascinated
    D) fascinated intriguing

7. A) NO CHANGE
    B) movement. These
    C) movement. Although
    D) movement because

8. A) NO CHANGE
    B) flyby and it collected
    C) flyby, and collecting
    D) flyby and collected

9. The writer is considering deleting the underlined sentence. Should the writer do this?

    A) No, because it adds an interesting detail about the *Pioneer 10* mission.

    B) No, because it provides support for the claim that the mission was successful.

    C) Yes, because it shifts the focus of the passage from Jupiter to the *Pioneer 10* mission.

    D) Yes, because it does not include information about when *Pioneer 10* left the solar system.

and has no solid surface, only varying densities of gas. In fact, very little is known about the interior of Jupiter. When looking at a gas planet like Jupiter, it is really only possible to see the tops of the clouds making up the outermost atmosphere, and probes have been able to penetrate only about 90 miles below this layer. However, after analyzing traces of water and minerals collected from Jupiter's atmosphere, scientists believe that the planet has a core of rocky material amounting to a mass perhaps as much as 15 times that of Earth.

10 Jupiter is like other gaseous planets. Jupiter has high-velocity winds that blow in wide bands of latitude, each moving in an alternate direction. Slight chemical and temperature changes between these bands, and the resulting chemical reactions, are probably responsible for the array of vibrant colors that dominate the planet's appearance. **11** Measurement taken by a number of probes indicate that the powerful winds moving these bands can reach speeds exceeding 400 miles per hour and likely extend thousands of miles below Jupiter's outer atmosphere.

Yet perhaps the most fascinating characteristic of this planet is the rotational speed of the entire globe of gas itself. While Earth takes 24 hours to make a full rotation, Jupiter completes a full rotation **12** in less time, an amazingly short period of time for a planet with a diameter roughly 11 times **13** ours. How Jupiter is able to rotate so fast is just one of many mysteries that scientists continue to explore in their efforts to understand our largest neighbor.

10. A) NO CHANGE
    B) Like other gaseous planets,
    C) Jupiter is like other gaseous planets,
    D) Jupiter, like other gaseous planets,

11. A) NO CHANGE
    B) A measurement
    C) The measurement
    D) Measurements

12. Which choice most accurately reflects the data in the table on the following page?
    A) NO CHANGE
    B) in half that time,
    C) in fewer than 10 Earth hours,
    D) in more time than all the other planets,

13. A) NO CHANGE
    B) our planet.
    C) our own.
    D) our planet's diameter.

Planets in Our Solar System				
Planet	Period of Revolution Around the Sun (1 planetary year)	Period of Rotation (1 planetary day)	Mass (kg)	Diameter (miles)
Mercury	87.96 Earth days	58.7 Earth days	3.3×10^{23}	3,031 miles
Venus	224.68 Earth days	243 Earth days	4.87×10^{24}	7,521 miles
Earth	365.26 days	24 hours	5.98×10^{24}	7,926 miles
Mars	686.98 Earth days	24.6 Earth hours	6.42×10^{23}	4,222 miles
Jupiter	11.862 Earth years	9.84 Earth hours	1.90×10^{27}	88,729 miles
Saturn	29.456 Earth years	10.2 Earth hours	5.69×10^{26}	74,600 miles
Uranus	84.07 Earth years	17.9 Earth hours	8.68×10^{25}	32,600 miles
Neptune	164.81 Earth years	19.1 Earth hours	1.02×10^{26}	30,200 miles

Answers & Explanations for this chapter begin on page 998.

EXTRA PRACTICE

Questions 1-11 are based on the following passage.

Physical Therapy Careers: Health Care in Motion

Physical therapy is a health care field that is **[1]** concurrently rated by the U.S. Bureau of Labor Statistics as one of today's best career choices. Featuring considerable variety in work environments, patient relationships, and job activity levels, the work of a physical therapist has the potential to be both highly motivating and satisfying. **[2]** And current projections indicate that this particular field of physical therapy should grow significantly over the next decade and continue to be one of the more flexible—not to mention enjoyable and fun—jobs in health care.

[3] A license is required to practice as a physical therapist, even in a foreign country. After completing a bachelor's degree (and specific science-related prerequisites), students must obtain a Doctor of Physical Therapy (DPT) degree. This program typically lasts three years. All graduates of DPT programs must then pass the National Physical Therapy Examination. After the exam, they must complete any additional requirements for licensure in the state in which they intend to practice. Once licensed by the state, physical therapists (PTs) are equipped to begin their careers.

1. A) NO CHANGE
    B) consistently
    C) unusually
    D) finally

2. A) NO CHANGE
    B) And current projections indicate that the field should grow significantly over the next several years and the next decade and remain one of the more flexible—not to mention enjoyable—jobs in health care.
    C) Current projections and predictions by the Bureau of Labor indicate that the field should grow significantly over the next decade and remain one of the more flexible and even enjoyable—jobs in the health care industry.
    D) Current projections indicate that the field should grow significantly over the next decade and remain one of the more flexible and enjoyable jobs in health care.

3. Which choice most effectively establishes the main topic of the second paragraph?
    A) NO CHANGE
    B) Those pursuing careers in physical therapy must undergo the appropriate education and licensure processes.
    C) Requirements vary from state to state to practice physical therapy, just as they do for physicians and physicians' assistants.
    D) Physical therapists must pass a national exam that covers a wide range of material.

4 PTs work with a broad range of patients in a wide variety of settings such as hospitals or private clinics. Some clientele, for example, are elderly or ill. Other patients include athletes ranging from elite professionals and college sports stars to middle school sports players. **5** **6** And some kinds of PTs have personal, long-term patient relationships, while others focus on research or testing most of the time and occasionally interact with patients only minimally.

4. A) NO CHANGE
    B) PTs work with a broad range of patients, in a wide variety of settings some work in hospitals, while others work in private clinics.
    C) PTs work with a broad range of patients; in a wide variety of settings. Some work in hospitals; others in private clinics.
    D) PTs work with a broad range of patients: the variety of settings, includes hospitals and private clinics.

5. At this point, the writer is considering adding a sentence to support the main topic of the paragraph. Which choice best supports the main topic of paragraph 3?
    A) PTs must demonstrate their willingness to spend long hours on the job.
    B) Still others include people who have been injured at work.
    C) The clientele pay for their physical therapy services according to their ability, so some PTs earn more than others.
    D) No special license is required to work with patients who are professional athletes, but some states may require additional courses to work with students.

6. A) NO CHANGE
    B) Some PTs have personal, long-term patient relationships, while others, who focus on research or testing, have minimal interaction with patients.
    C) Some PTs have personal, long-term patient relationships; others interact with patients only minimal and focus on research or testing.
    D) And some kinds of PTs have personal, long-term patient relationships. Others focus on research or testing and interact with patients only minimally.

[1] **7** A physical therapist primarily works with patients who have suffered motion loss from illness or injury. The goal is to restore mobility while managing and limiting pain. [2] **8** This job often involves long-term planning, creatively personalized application, and patience, in addition to highly refined medical knowledge. [3] In many cases, physical therapists invite and rely on patients to participate actively in their own recovery. [4] This interpersonal and **9** collaborative aspect of physical therapy is often essential to the medical work itself. [5] For example, recovering athletes must often commit to long-term conditioning programs before returning to their sports. [6] Surgery or medication alone isn't always enough to restore full mobility; many PT patients must relearn their muscle use and work hard to increase flexibility. [7] PTs determine the course of action and coach their patients through the steps to recovery. **10**

7. A) NO CHANGE

   B) A physical therapist primarily works with patients. They have suffered motion loss from illness or injury. And the therapist's goal is to restore mobility. While managing and limiting pain.

   C) A physical therapist, whose goal is to restore mobility and manage pain primarily works with patients who have suffered motion loss or illness or injury.

   D) A physical therapist primarily works with patients who have suffered motion loss from illness or injury to restore mobility while managing and limiting pain.

8. A) NO CHANGE

   B) This job often involves long-term planning, creatively personalized application, patience, and highly refined medical knowledge.

   C) This job often involves long-term planning, creative personalized application and patience, in addition to highly refined medical knowledge.

   D) This job often involves long-term planning, creatively personal application and patience, as well as highly refined medical knowledge.

9. A) NO CHANGE

   B) concentrated

   C) planned

   D) consolidated

10. To make this paragraph most logical, sentence 2 should be placed

    A) before sentence 1.

    B) after sentence 3.

    C) after sentence 5.

    D) after sentence 7.

[1] The horizon for employment rates in physical therapy is exceptionally bright. [2] The Bureau of Labor Statistics predicts that the coming decade will see a 36% growth in PT jobs. [3] This means that there should be a need for over 70,000 new PTs nationwide. [4] Physical therapist assistants (PTAs) will also be needed. [5] For those willing to commit the time and effort to become experts in physical therapy, the possibilities and quality of the PT work environment are among the most desirable in health care, and considering projected employment rates, such a career seems to be an especially prudent choice. **11**

11. Which sentence should be removed in order to improve the focus of this paragraph?

A) Sentence 1

B) Sentence 2

C) Sentence 3

D) Sentence 4

Questions 12-22 are based on the following passage and supplementary material.

The Pony Express: Not a Tame Ride

The 19th century saw the Civil War, the California Gold Rush, and the migration of thousands of people to the West along the Oregon Trail. With these events came **12** the really great and strong need for communication between the original colonies and the new state of California.

13 William H. Russell, Alexander Majors, and William B. Waddell brought about the solution to this need by creating Leavenworth & Pike's Peak Express Company, which later became known as the Pony Express.

The Pony Express was a system of riders that ran 2,000 miles from St. Joseph, Missouri, to Sacramento, California. Riders, who carried mail in leather satchels, changed every 75 to 100 miles. They changed horses every 10 to 15 miles. **14** When the Pony Express was at its largest, it had a lot of riders who were paid for their services.

Riders changed horses or took a short break at relay posts, or stations: small, simple cabins, with dirt floors and a few stalls for the horses. Riders could get small meals at the **15** stations, these meals usually consisted of dried fruit, cured meats, pickles, coffee, and cornmeal. At some bigger stations, known as "home stations," riders were able to enjoy a more relaxed meal, perhaps chat with other riders, and get some sleep.

12. A) NO CHANGE
    B) the very strong and real need
    C) the need
    D) the strong and real need

13. A) NO CHANGE
    B) William H. Russell Alexander Majors and William B. Waddell
    C) William H. Russell Alexander Majors, and William B. Waddell
    D) William H. Russell, Alexander Majors, and, William B. Waddell

14. Which choice most effectively revises the underlined sentence?
    A) When the Pony Express was at its largest, it was a very glamorous job.
    B) At its largest, the Pony Express had over 150 riders of all ages and they were paid.
    C) When the Pony Express peaked, it employed a lot of riders and the youngest one was named Bronco Charlie Miller.
    D) At its peak, the Pony Express employed over 180 riders who ranged in age from 11 to 50 years old and earned $50 a month.

15. A) NO CHANGE
    B) stations these meals usually consisted
    C) stations. These meals usually consisted
    D) stations yet these meals usually consisted

The relay posts were also a source of employment. Each housed a station keeper who was responsible for having horses saddled and ready when a rider arrived, as well as for logging **16** accurate records of arrival and departure times. The job of a station keeper was not an easy one. The **17** stations were located in remote areas, had little access to resources, and were being unprotected from attacks by Native Americans.

18 The riders' routes were fraught with danger of many kinds. Riders often rode through rough, unfamiliar terrain; were exposed to harsh weather; and were susceptible to attack by hostile Native Americans. **19** As a result of these challenges, only one mail delivery was

16. A) NO CHANGE
    B) lengthy
    C) sorrowful
    D) agreeable

17. A) NO CHANGE
    B) stations were located in remote areas, had little access to resources, and were unprotected
    C) stations were being located in remote areas, had little access to resources, and were unprotected
    D) stations were located in remote areas, having little access to resources, and were unprotected

18. Which choice most effectively establishes the main topic of the paragraph?
    A) NO CHANGE
    B) The Pony Express helped tie California with the rest of the country.
    C) The Pony Express was not successful financially.
    D) Some of the riders died while trying to deliver the mail.

19. A) NO CHANGE
    B) Despite
    C) However
    D) For instance

lost during the Pony Express's 19 months of operation.

Shortly after the first riders of the Pony Express set out on April 3, 1860, Congress approved a bill [20] funding the construction of a transcontinental telegraph line on March 5, 1860. The result of this bill was the creation of the Overland Telegraph Company of California and the Pacific Telegraph Company of Nevada. Once they were fully [21] invented on October 24, 1861, the Pony Express was no longer needed. Two days later, the Pony Express announced its closure.

Although its existence was a short one, the Pony Express played an important role in the development of [22] the Pacific Coast. It remains an icon of the Wild West.

History of the Pony Express

January–March 1860 ➤	Russell, Majors, and Waddell establish Pony Express mail service.
April 3, 1860 ➤	First riders leave St. Joseph, Missouri, and Sacramento, California.
June 8, 1860 ➤	Congress authorizes building of transcontinental telegraph line.
October 24, 1861 ➤	East and West coasts connected by telegraph line.
October 26, 1861 ➤	Pony Express discontinued.

20. Which choice completes the sentence with accurate data based on the timeline?
    A) NO CHANGE
    B) funding the construction of a transcontinental telegraph line on June 8, 1860.
    C) funding the construction of a transcontinental telegraph line on October 24, 1861.
    D) funding the construction of a transcontinental telegraph line on January, 1860.

21. A) NO CHANGE
    B) breached
    C) operational
    D) contrasted

22. Which choice most effectively combines the sentences at the underlined portion?
    A) the Pacific Coast, since it remains
    B) the Pacific Coast, however, it remains
    C) the Pacific Coast, that it remains
    D) the Pacific Coast and remains

CHAPTER 20

Organization

CHAPTER OBJECTIVES

By the end of this chapter, you will be able to:

1. Organize a text's information and ideas into the most logical order

2. Evaluate whether transition words, phrases, or sentences are used effectively to introduce, conclude, or connect information and ideas, and revise the text to improve these transitions when necessary

SMARTPOINTS

Point Value	SmartPoint Category
50 Points	Organization

Reading & Writing

ORGANIZATION

Chapter 20

Homework

Extra Practice: #1-11

Even More

Writing & Language Quiz 1

Key

 Book Assignment

Online Video Assignment

 Online Quiz Assignment

ORGANIZATION

Organization questions require you to assess the logic and coherence of a Writing & Language passage. These questions differ in scope; you might be asked to organize the writing at the level of the sentence, the paragraph, or even the entire passage.

There are two kinds of Organization questions:

1. Logical Sequence

- These questions ask you to reorder the sentences in a paragraph or paragraphs in a passage to ensure that information and ideas are logically conveyed.

- When rearranging sentences or paragraphs, begin by determining which sentence or paragraph most logically introduces the paragraph or the passage, respectively.

2. Introductions, Conclusions, and Transitions

- These questions task you with improving the beginning or ending of a passage or paragraph, making sure that the transition words, phrases, or sentences are being used effectively not only to connect information and ideas but also to maintain logical structure.

- While introductions and conclusions focus on the beginning and ending of a passage or paragraph, respectively, transitions are a bit more complicated. It's important to identify what two ideas the transition is linking and how it is doing so. Common types and examples of transitions are listed in the following chart.

Contrast Transitions	Cause-and-Effect Transitions	Continuation Transitions
although	as a result	**Providing an example**
but	because	for example
despite	consequently	for instance
even though	since	**Showing emphasis**
however	so	certainly
in contrast	therefore	in fact
nonetheless	thus	indeed
on the other hand		that is
rather than		**Showing a parallel relationship**
though		also
unlike		furthermore
while		in addition
yet		and
		moreover

> ✔ **Remember**
>
> Organization questions require you not only to improve grammar and style but also to ensure that these elements accurately express the author's logic and reasoning.

Let's look at the following Writing & Language passage and questions. After the passage, there are two columns. The left column contains test-like questions. The column on the right features the strategic thinking a test expert employs when approaching the passage and questions presented.

Reading & Writing

Product Warnings

1 <u>As if malpractice suits and unnecessary bankruptcies were not enough of a problem, lawyers have chosen to increase the burden that they place on society by engineering an excess of increasingly ridiculous product warnings.</u> Why else would a box of sleeping pills be marketed with the cautionary note that consumers may experience drowsiness? Or a cup of coffee be emblazoned with a notice that "THIS PRODUCT MAY BE HOT"? Anyone with common sense will not need to be warned about these possibilities, and anyone WITHOUT common sense is probably not going to be stopped by a warning label from undertaking a foolish course of action anyway. So honestly, in the long run, the only ones who benefit from these warnings are the lawyers who are paid hundreds of dollars an hour to compose them.

Passages & Questions	Strategic Thinking
1. Which choice most effectively establishes the main topic of the paragraph? A) NO CHANGE B) Each year, effective product warning labels help countless people avoid serious injuries resulting from their use of consumer products. C) In recent years, a coalition of lawyers and consumer safety advocates has successfully campaigned to require companies to include safety warnings on product labels. D) Product safety warnings are necessary to protect consumers who thoughtlessly use products without first thinking about the possible risks involved.	**Step 1: Read the passage and identify the issue** The underlined segment contains the introductory sentence, which introduces the passage's topic of the ridiculousness of product warnings. The author concludes that lawyers are the only people who benefit from product warnings because they are paid to write them. **Step 2: Eliminate answer choices that do not address the issue** Eliminate B because the author does not believe the product warnings are "effective." Eliminate C because the author mentions the lawyers only in a negative light. Eliminate D because the author does not believe product safety warnings are "necessary." **Step 3: Plug in the remaining answer choices and select the most correct, concise, and relevant one** Choice (A) is correct.

Reading & Writing

Public Schools

[1] It is amazing how little the structure of the American public school system has changed since its inception. [2] Students still change classes according to bells, even though the bell system originated during the days of factories. [3] School is still not in session during the summer, although most students will not use that time to work on farms. [4] Although class and school sizes have varied widely and the curriculum has certainly become varied, the actual system remains surprisingly similar to the way it once was. [5] Despite these idiosyncrasies, however, the American public school system continues to educate the children of this country in a fair and equitable fashion. [6] Without the established structure, the chaotic nature of school would severely inhibit learning. **2**

Passages & Questions	Strategic Thinking
2. To make this paragraph most logical, sentence 4 should be placed A) where it is now. B) before sentence 1. C) after sentence 1. D) after sentence 6.	**Step 1: Read the passage and identify the issue** Sentence 4 is about the fact that even though there have been educational changes over the years, the school system itself has actually not changed that much. It is not properly placed within the paragraph. **Step 2: Eliminate answer choices that do not address the issue** Eliminate A because sentence 4's location is incorrect as is. Eliminate B because sentence 4 is not an appropriate introduction to the paragraph. Eliminate D because sentence 4 is not an appropriate conclusion to the paragraph. **Step 3: Plug in the remaining answer choices and select the most correct, concise, and relevant one** Choice (C) is correct.

First Snowfall

I still remember the magic of walking home under the cold, brittle blue sky, watching the sun strike the glittering blanket laid down by that first snowfall. The world dripped with frosting, and everything was pure and silent. I breathed deeply, enjoying the sting of the icy air in my nostrils, and set off through the trees, listening to the muffled crunch of my footsteps and the chirps of the waking birds. Later, the cars and schoolchildren and mundane lives would turn the wonderland back into dingy slush; the hush would be interrupted by horns and shouts. **3** <u>Indeed</u> for now, the sparkling, cloistered world was mine alone. I smiled, and for a moment, my mind was still.

Passages & Questions	Strategic Thinking
3. A) NO CHANGE B) But C) Consequently D) In fact	**Step 1: Read the passage and identify the issue** The underlined word is a continuation transition showing emphasis. It is incorrect as written because the sentence preceding it discusses what will happen to the snow while this sentence discusses what the snow is like now. A contrast transition would be more appropriate in this context. **Step 2: Eliminate answer choices that do not address the issue** Eliminate C and D because they are not contrast transitions. **Step 3: Plug in the remaining answer choices and select the most correct, concise, and relevant one** Choice (B) is correct.

You have seen the ways in which the SAT tests you on Organization in Writing & Language passages and the way an SAT expert approaches these types of questions.

Use the Kaplan Method for Writing & Language to answer the three questions that accompany the following Writing & Language passage excerpt. Remember to look at the strategic thinking questions that have been laid out for you—some of the answers have been filled in, but you will have to complete the answers to others.

Use your answers to the strategic thinking questions to select the correct answer, just as you will on Test Day.

Questions 4-6 are based on the following passage.

Earthquakes

[1]

The recent devastating earthquakes in China, Haiti, Chile, Mexico, and elsewhere have caused many to wonder if this earthquake activity is unusual.

[2]

"While the number of earthquakes is within the normal range, this does not diminish the fact that there has been extreme devastation and loss of life in heavily populated areas," says USGS Associate Coordinator for Earthquake Hazards, Dr. Michael Blanpied. **4**

[3]

Scientists say 2010 is not showing signs of unusually high earthquake activity. Since 1900, an average of 16 magnitude 7 or greater earthquakes—the size that seismologists define as major—have occurred worldwide each year. Some years have had as few as 6, as in 1986 and 1989, while 1943 had 32, with considerable variability from year to year.

[4]

With six major earthquakes striking in the first four months of this year, 2010 is well within the normal range. From April 15, 2009, to April 14, 2010, there have been 18 major earthquakes, a number also well within the expected variation.

---

[5]

[1] What will happen next? [2] It is unlikely that any of these aftershocks will be stronger than the earthquakes experienced so far, but structures damaged in the previous events could be further damaged and should be treated with caution. [3] Beyond the ongoing aftershock sequences, earthquakes in recent months have not raised the likelihood of future major earthquakes; that likelihood has not decreased, either. [4] Aftershocks will continue in the regions around each of this year's major earthquakes sites. [5] Large earthquakes will continue to occur just as they have in the past. **5**

[6]

Though the recent earthquakes are not unusual, they are a stark reminder that earthquakes can produce disasters when they strike populated areas, especially areas where the buildings have not been designed to withstand strong shaking. What can be done to prepare? Scientists cannot predict the timing of specific earthquakes. **6** <u>However, families and communities can improve their safety and reduce their losses by taking actions to make their homes, places of work, schools, and businesses as earthquake-safe as possible.</u>

Questions	Strategic Thinking

4. To make the passage most logical, paragraph 2 should be placed
 	
  A) where it is now.
 	
  B) after paragraph 3.
 	
  C) after paragraph 4.
 	
  D) after paragraph 5.
	Step 1: Read the passage and identify the issue
	
	What is the issue?
	
	Paragraph 2 is not properly placed within the passage.
	
	What is the content of paragraph 2?
	
	A quotation from a USGS official about how, despite the fact that the number of earthquakes is normal for the area, the loss and devastation suffered in populated regions is still profound.
	
	What two topics does this paragraph connect?
	
	The frequency of earthquakes and the damage caused by earthquakes.
	
	Step 2: Eliminate answer choices that do not address the issue
	
	What answer choice(s) can you eliminate?
	_____
	_____
	_____
	
	Step 3: Plug in the remaining answer choices and select the most correct, concise, and relevant one
	
	What is the correct answer? _____

Questions	Strategic Thinking
5. To make this paragraph most logical, sentence 4 should be placed A) where it is now. B) before sentence 1. C) before sentence 2. D) after sentence 2.	**Step 1: Read the passage and identify the issue** *What is the issue?* Sentence 4 is not properly placed within the paragraph. *What is the content of sentence 4?* It explains what will happen next in the regions that have suffered earthquakes. *Where in the paragraph does this sentence belong (beginning, middle, end)? Why?* In the beginning, because the sentence discusses the immediate future while the paragraph ends with a reference to the far future. **Step 2: Eliminate answer choices that do not address the issue** *What answer choice(s) can you eliminate?* _____ _____ _____ **Step 3: Plug in the remaining answer choices and select the most correct, concise, and relevant one** *What is the correct answer?* _____

Reading & Writing

Questions	Strategic Thinking
6. Which choice most effectively concludes the paragraph? A) NO CHANGE B) However, earthquake forecasting employs methods to assess the general earthquake hazard in a particular area. C) However, researchers have studied dogs to determine their ability to sense an impending earthquake. D) However, undersea earthquakes produce low-frequency sound waves that can arrive minutes before the associated tsunami wave.	**Step 1: Read the passage and identify the issue** *What is the issue?* The question is asking whether the underlined sentence is an appropriate conclusion for the paragraph. *What is the content of the paragraph?* Earthquakes are normal, yet unpredictable. *All of the answer choices begin with the transition "however." What does this transition indicate?* _____ _____ **Step 2: Eliminate answer choices that do not address the issue** *What answer choice(s) can you eliminate?* _____ _____ _____ **Step 3: Plug in the remaining answer choices and select the most correct, concise, and relevant one** *What is the correct answer?* _____

Now try a test-like Writing & Language passage on your own. Give yourself 5 minutes to read the passage and answer the questions.

Questions 7-14 are based on the following passage.

The Internet and Conversation

[1]

Internet speak is often maligned as vacuous in its reliance on acronyms and abbreviations, but **7** this is far from universal. On certain discussion boards, you can witness opinions stated and arguments debated with an eloquence that people rarely use when speaking, freely sharing knowledge just for the joy of it. I participate in an online Renaissance music discussion group that has a library of original articles that are the product of a master's thesis. The author gained no monetary reward for the information (which he made available for free) and receives little praise for it outside the community that shares his interest. He posts because he is passionate about the music, and that inspires him to share what he knows with anyone who wants to learn.

[2]

[1] In part, this has to do with my habit of observing the world from my bedroom. [2] As a child, I was frequently ill and forced to stay inside. [3] Although my health is much better now, **8** I still go out much less than most people. [4] After all, I have everything I need inside. [5] Everyone can be everywhere they want when they want, and every social situation feels completely comfortable and natural. [6] From my room,

7. A) NO CHANGE
   B) these are
   C) this reliance is
   D) empty chatter is

8. Which choice provides the best transition within the paragraph?
   A) NO CHANGE
   B) I still remember those long afternoons cooped up inside.
   C) I am still careful to eat well and get plenty of rest.
   D) I regret not being able to play outdoors with other children.

I have access to people all over the world. [7] I can talk about medieval literature with a friend in China and later collaborate on a piece of music with a synthesizer virtuoso in Spain. [8] There is no need for awkward introductions or a graceful exit—people feel free to launch right into what they want to talk about and, when they are done, just sign off with a "g2g," or "got to go." [9] Everything is **9** <u>succinct and to the point</u>. **10**

[3]

For as long as I can remember, conversation **11** <u>had</u> always struck me as a strange chimera, something that is half two minds exchanging sophisticated ideas and **12** <u>at the same time</u> two dogs barking at each other. I do not find the banalities of small talk comforting, but boring and idiotic. **13** <u>When</u> I can dispense with it altogether and proceed right to substantive dialogue, it is almost like flying. I can be talking with the closest of friends or a mere acquaintance with a shared interest. Either way, the kinship is there. I don't feel myself included by smiles, pats on the back, or eye contact so much as by the willingness of a partner to share my ideas or gift me with thoughts of his own. There is nothing more ingratiating than intellectual passion. **14**

9. A) NO CHANGE
    B) succinct
    C) succinctly stated and to the point
    D) succinct, brief, and to the point

10. To make this paragraph most logical, sentence 5 should be placed
    A) where it is now.
    B) before sentence 4.
    C) after sentence 7.
    D) after sentence 8.

11. A) NO CHANGE
    B) has
    C) would have
    D) have

12. A) NO CHANGE
    B) similar to
    C) frequently like
    D) half

13. A) NO CHANGE
    B) Now
    C) Later
    D) Where

14. Which choice places the paragraphs of this passage in the most logical order?
    A) NO CHANGE
    B) 1, 3, 2
    C) 3, 1, 2
    D) 3, 2, 1

Answers & Explanations for this chapter begin on page 1002.

EXTRA PRACTICE

The following questions provide an opportunity to practice the concepts and strategic thinking covered in this chapter. While many of the questions pertain to Organization, some touch on other concepts tested on the Writing & Language Test to ensure that your practice is test-like, with a variety of question types per passage.

Questions 1-11 are based on the following passage.

Inside Looking Out: Post-Impressionism

Post-Impressionism was an artistic movement that took place between 1886 and 1892 and **1** produces some of the world's foremost artists. Post-Impressionism emerged as one of the many different artistic styles created in response to the Impressionist movement, which focused on creating realistic representations of human perceptions. **2** Next, Impressionists sought to **3** restate nature in their work. They used small, controlled brush strokes in an effort to capture how the human eye sees light. Post-Impressionism was radically different. Artists of this time focused more on self-discovery than anything else. Instead of looking out on a landscape and **4** attempt to paint exactly what they saw, they turned their eyes inward. They interpreted subjects through their own **5** unique vision, which included their personal experiences and emotions. This change influenced the course of all art created since.

1. A) NO CHANGE
   B) produced
   C) was producing
   D) will produce

2. A) NO CHANGE
   B) For example,
   C) Consequently,
   D) However,

3. A) NO CHANGE
   B) obscure
   C) photocopy
   D) replicate

4. A) NO CHANGE
   B) attempting
   C) was attempted
   D) is attempting

5. A) NO CHANGE
   B) single
   C) cautious
   D) acceptable

Reading & Writing

6 <u>Among the Impressionist artists were Claude Monet, Pierre-Auguste Renoir, and Edgar Degas.</u> Paul Cezanne and Georges Seurat used shape and color to describe their worlds rather than mimic them. Their work acted as a bridge between Impressionist art and the more abstract subcategories of Post-Impressionism. Two such subcategories were Cubism and Abstract Expressionism. **7** <u>Cubism was created by Spanish painter Pablo Picasso and French painter Georges Braque. It featured geometric shapes used to construct conceptual portraits.</u> Both of these artists rejected traditional views on modeling nature and people, as well as classical techniques. Abstract Expressionism used color instead of geometric figures, and artists like Jackson Pollock and Willem de Kooning covered their canvases with color and indistinct forms. Abstract Expressionists aimed to express deep emotional themes. Paul Gauguin and Vincent van Gogh are also considered Abstract Expressionists, as **8** <u>they</u> both prioritized the depiction of their memories and emotions over

6. Which choice most effectively establishes the central idea of the paragraph?

A) NO CHANGE

B) Modern artists are well versed in many different kinds of styles thanks to the many artists of the past.

C) Artists in the Post-Impressionist era employed a wide range of methods when creating their art.

D) Prior to the Impressionist and Post-Impressionist eras, artists painted in a much more realistic style.

7. Which choice most effectively combines the sentences at the underlined portion?

A) NO CHANGE

B) Created by Spanish painter Pablo Picasso and French painter Georges Braque, Cubism featured geometric shapes used to construct conceptual portraits.

C) Cubism was created by Spanish painter Pablo Picasso and French painter Georges Braque so it featured geometric shapes.

D) Cubism was created by Spanish painter Pablo Picasso and French painter Georges Braque, but it featured geometric shapes.

8. A) NO CHANGE

B) it

C) you

D) we

observations that could be made with the eye. **9** Never before had such an emphasis on individualism taken precedence over classical technique, a change that laid the foundation for art in the 20th century and beyond.

[1] These artists worked and created during the same time period and movement. [2] However, they had varying world views and techniques. [3] Today, we can get to know the souls of some of the world's greatest artists by visiting **10** <u>they're</u> Post-Impressionist work in museums around the world. [4] These differences cumulatively succeeded in breaking from the natural guidelines of Impressionism to create something entirely new that dramatically influenced all artists who came after them. [5] In the words of Edvard Munch, another Post-Impressionist painter, "Nature is not only all that is visible to the eye . . . it also includes the inner pictures of the soul." **11**

9. Which choice, if added here, most effectively supports the central idea of the paragraph?

   A) Some Impressionist artists, such as Renoir, painted images of children, flowers, and social gatherings.

   B) Degas often painted ballet dancers at the barre as well as molding sculptures of them.

   C) Art is often viewed as a window into the minds and experiences of artists as they lived their lives.

   D) To transfer their emotions to their canvases, Post-Impressionist artists sometimes used violent gestures to apply paint.

10. A) NO CHANGE

    B) their

    C) they are

    D) there

11. To make this paragraph most logical, sentence 3 should be placed

    A) where it is now.

    B) after sentence 1.

    C) before sentence 5.

    D) after sentence 5.

Questions 12-22 are based on the following passage and supplementary material.

Putting Microbes to Work for Us

[1]

The decline of the world's supply of fossil fuels is a growing concern. With increasingly more countries becoming dependent on fossil fuels for transportation, heating homes, and powering engines, the **12** failing of this finite resource has the potential to cause major disruption around the globe. To combat this issue, scientists are researching alternative energy sources. **13** Used to produce biofuel are living things or the waste of living things, and biofuel is one such alternative.

[2]

14 Until recently, the primary focus of biofuel development has been ethanol. Ethanol is created from plants such as corn, sugarcane, soybeans, and rice. While ethanol is a viable energy **15** source, its use has been met with several challenges. These have limited its development as a quality alternative to traditional fossil fuels. One roadblock is that ethanol is expensive to produce. The plant must be first broken down into sugars and then fermented by microbes into a final useable product. It cannot be distributed by pipeline because it can pick up impurities along the way, so it must be transported by truck, train, or barge. Additionally, very large areas of cropland must be dedicated to growing these plants in order to produce enough ethanol to be designated for commercial use.

12. A) NO CHANGE
    B) wilting
    C) depletion
    D) obstruction

13. A) NO CHANGE
    B) Biofuel is produced from living things or the waste of living things, and is one such alternative.
    C) Living things or the waste of living things are used in producing the one such alternative known as biofuel.
    D) One such alternative is biofuel, produced from living things or from the waste of living things.

14. Which choice most effectively establishes the central idea of this paragraph?
    A) NO CHANGE
    B) A variety of food crops can be used to produce ethanol.
    C) Many farmers have begun to grow corn for ethanol rather than food.
    D) Converting corn to ethanol is a complicated and expensive process.

15. A) NO CHANGE
    B) source, its'
    C) source, it's
    D) source, it is

This raises ethical questions because it means farmers are growing food sources earmarked solely for fuel when there are many people around the world in **16** horrible need of food. **17** In recent years, the price of corn has increased as the percentage of corn produced for ethanol has stayed the same. In addition, countries such as Brazil are decimating rain forests in order to grow sugarcane for ethanol production.

[3]

Once ethanol is produced, it is limited in its use as a commercial fuel. Therefore, it must be heavily refined and then blended with petroleum-based fuels in order to be used. **18** Standard internal combustion engines, such as those in cars, cannot run on ethanol alone.

16. A) NO CHANGE
     B) dire
     C) grim
     D) grieving

17. Which choice best supports the paragraph with relevant and accurate information based on the graph?
     A) NO CHANGE
     B) In recent years, the price of corn has stayed the same as the percentage of corn produced for ethanol has decreased.
     C) In recent years, the price of corn has increased as the percentage of corn produced for ethanol has increased.
     D) In recent years, the price of corn has decreased as the percentage of corn produced for ethanol has increased.

18. Which choice best supports the central idea of the paragraph?
     A) NO CHANGE
     B) Most fuel sold for automobiles in the United States contains a blend of ethanol and gasoline.
     C) Ethanol has been used as an energy source in the United States for over 200 years.
     D) Although most often used to power automobiles, ethanol can also be used to power other engines.

[4]

The fossil fuels we rely on today for energy are finite. By researching alternate energy resources, including fuel produced by bacteria and other microbes, we can become less dependent on nonrenewable sources. **19**

[5]

Researchers in the United Kingdom **20** had been developing a new kind of biofuel that addresses several of the issues hindering ethanol use. They have extracted genes from different species of bacteria and inserted them into *E. coli* bacteria. Once this process is complete, the *E. coli* can then perform the same metabolic functions as the donor **21** bacteria, this enables it to absorb fat molecules, convert these molecules to hydrocarbons, and then excrete the hydrocarbons as a waste product. The hydrocarbons produced by the genetically modified *E. coli* are the same as those found in commercial fossil fuels. **22** Finally, the newly created hydrocarbon molecules are interchangeable with the hydrocarbon molecules found in petroleum-based diesel fuels. This allows them to be used in a typical diesel engine, without any blending or refining.

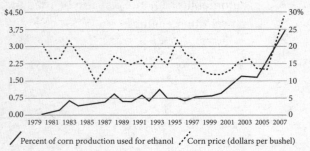

Percentage of U.S. Corn Used to Produce Ethanol and Price per Bushel, 1980-2007

Percent of corn production used for ethanol ⋯ Corn price (dollars per bushel)

Adapted from United States Department of Agriculture–Economic Research Service and United States Energy Information Administration, "Percentage of U.S. Corn Used to Produce Ethanol and Price per Bushel, 1980-2007."

19. To make the passage most logical, paragraph 4 should be placed

  A) where it is now.
  B) before paragraph 2.
  C) before paragraph 3.
  D) after paragraph 5.

20. A) NO CHANGE
  B) have developed
  C) had developed
  D) were developing

21. A) NO CHANGE
  B) bacteria; and this enables it
  C) bacteria. This enables it
  D) bacteria this enables it

22. A) NO CHANGE
  B) Therefore,
  C) For example,
  D) Also,

Reading & Writing

CHAPTER 21

Development

CHAPTER OBJECTIVES

By the end of this chapter, you will be able to:

1. Evaluate the effectiveness and clarity of a passage's arguments, information, and ideas and determine whether a revision is necessary for the passage to be clear and effective

2. Evaluate information and ideas intended to support claims or points in the passage

3. Identify elements in the passage that are not relevant to the passage's topic and purpose

SMARTPOINTS

Point Value	SmartPoint Category
40 Points	Development

Reading & Writing

DEVELOPMENT

Chapter 21

Homework

Extra Practice: #1-11

Even More

Writing & Language Quiz 2

Key

 Book Assignment

 Online Video Assignment

 Online Quiz Assignment

PROPOSITION

Proposition questions ask about how well a writer uses language—arguments, information, and ideas—to express the central purpose of a passage or part of a passage.

You will be asked to add, revise, or retain portions of the passage to communicate key ideas, claims, counterclaims, and topic sentences most clearly and effectively.

To answer Proposition questions, you need to identify the topic and purpose of the passage and focus on the writer's point of view. Ask questions such as:

- What is the central idea of the passage?
- Why did the author write the passage?
- What does the author think about the subject?
- What is the author's tone?

SUPPORT

Support questions test issues related to information and ideas presented by the writer. You will be asked to evaluate the effectiveness of the facts and details employed by the writer to support claims made in the passage.

Support questions may ask you to keep, change, or add a detail or example. A Support question could ask about an example used to support a central argument or simply a minor detail used to weaken a point made by the author.

To answer Support questions, look around the underlined portion for a clue indicating what kind of support is required. If the example supports a central idea or claim, ask if the example strengthens the author's central idea. Eliminate answer choices that don't fit the context or have a negative or trivial effect on the central idea.

FOCUS

Focus questions require you to assess whether portions of the passage include only the information and ideas relevant to the author's topic and purpose. You may be asked to add, change, or omit text.

When answering Focus questions, identify whether the text in question fits the topic, scope, and purpose of the entire passage.

> ✔ **Remember**
>
> *Topic* is what the passage is about. *Scope* is the aspect of the broader topic that is the center of the author's focus. *Purpose* is the author's reason for writing.

Let's look at the following Writing & Language passage and questions. After the passage, there are two columns. The left column contains test-like questions. The column on the right features the strategic thinking a test expert employs when approaching the passage and questions presented.

Questions 1-4 are based on the following passage.

Dr. Barry Marshall

For hundreds of years, the medical community and conventional wisdom held that ulcers were caused by stress. Strong gastric juices would sometimes burn sores through the lining of the stomach or intestines, causing widely varied symptoms, including internal bleeding, inflammation, and stomach pain. Doctors reasoned that if patients with ulcers changed their daily habits to reduce the level of tension in their lives, altered their diets to avoid foods that would irritate the stomach, and took medicine to moderate the amount of stomach acid, these ulcers would heal. Although the problem often recurred, no one seriously questioned why. **1** <u>This medical advice remained standard for generations, until Dr. Barry Marshall came along.</u>

Beginning in the 1980s, Marshall, an Australian physician, hypothesized that at least some ulcers were caused by bacteria that often lie dormant in the human stomach. The international medical community scoffed. It was common knowledge, or so Marshall's colleagues believed, that no microbes could survive for long in the highly acidic environment of the stomach. **2** <u>At medical conferences, the veteran, well-known Marshall was regarded as at best, a maverick, and at worst, a quack.</u> Over several years, he and his fellow researcher, Dr. J. Robin Warren, attempted to isolate and identify the bacteria that caused ulcers. As is the case with many medical discoveries, their breakthrough came about partly by accident, when they left a culture growing in the lab overnight. **3**

After this, to further prove his point, Dr. Marshall took a bold step. Although hospitals frown on such potentially dangerous actions, the doctor experimented on himself by deliberately drinking a flask of the bacteria. Over a two-week period, Marshall developed vague, though not disabling, symptoms, and medical tests showed evidence of ulcers and infection. Other researchers' studies later confirmed that Marshall's and Warren's findings apply to about 90% of all ulcers, which can now be cured by a short course of antibiotics instead of being temporarily managed by antacids.

In 2005, Marshall's bold move earned him and Warren the Nobel Prize in Medicine. **4** <u>Dr. Marshall brought his wife to the Nobel Prize ceremony, and she was very proud to witness the public celebration of his work.</u>

Questions	Strategic Thinking
1. A) NO CHANGE B) This medical advice remains the standard today, despite Dr. Barry Marshall's recent efforts. C) This medical advice remained the standard for generations, until Dr. Barry Marshall developed a cure for the stomach ulcer. D) This medical advice remained standard for generations despite a lack of evidence. That is, until Dr. Barry Marshall proved it with scientific experiments.	**Step 1: Read the passage and identify the issue** The underlined portion is the concluding sentence of the first paragraph and should therefore provide a claim central to the passage as a whole. **Step 2: Eliminate answer choices that do not address the issue** Eliminate B because it is untrue according to the rest of the passage. Eliminate C and D because they distort the supporting details provided in the remainder of the passage. **Step 3: Plug in the remaining answer choices and select the most correct, concise, and relevant one** Choice (A) is correct.
2. A) NO CHANGE B) At medical conferences, the young, unknown Marshall was regarded as at best, a maverick, and at worst, a quack. C) At medical conferences, the young, unknown Marshall was regarded as friendly and sociable at after-hours networking events. D) Dr. Marshall mostly avoided medical conferences and symposia.	**Step 1: Read the passage and identify the issue** The underlined sentence provides details about Dr. Marshall's character that you need to make sure fit the tone, scope, and purpose of the passage. **Step 2: Eliminate answer choices that do not address the issue** Eliminate A because the surrounding text does not support that Marshall was "veteran" and "well-known." Eliminate C and D because they are irrelevant to the passage as a whole. **Step 3: Plug in the remaining answer choices and select the most correct, concise, and relevant one** Choice (B) is correct.

Questions	Strategic Thinking
3. Which additional detail is most appropriate to include at this point in the passage? A) Dr. Marshall was a well-organized man and valued a neat workspace; the misplaced petri dish was almost certainly Dr. Warren's fault. B) The following morning, Marshall and Warren found a vibrant culture of a theretofore overlooked bacteria that they soon realized was an important suspect in the formation of ulcers. C) Marshall's and Warren's research was supported by grants, and by that point they were nearing the exhaustion of their funds. D) What Marshall and Warren discovered in their lab the next day brought them closer to finding the link between bacteria, ulcers, and stress.	**Step 1: Read the passage and identify the issue** The question stem asks for the answer choice that includes an "appropriate" detail for this point in the passage. Details should support the passage's central idea. **Step 2: Eliminate answer choices that do not address the issue** The preceding paragraph is about Dr. Marshall's first hypothesis, his career and partnership, and the fact that his and Dr. Warren's breakthrough was an accident. Eliminate A and C because they do not describe the discovery. Eliminate D because it is too general. **Step 3: Plug in the remaining answer choices and select the most correct, concise, and relevant one** Choice (B) is correct.

Questions	Strategic Thinking
4. Which choice most effectively concludes the passage? A) NO CHANGE B) Both of their careers flourished from this point forward, with each earning a tenured, endowed faculty position at a prestigious university. C) Sadly, since 2005, Marshall's and Warren's work has been neglected by the medical and scientific communities, and our understanding of ulcers has not progressed since that time. D) Their important advance, like many other scientific discoveries in history, was a combination of experimentation, persistence, and luck.	**Step 1: Read the passage and identify the issue** The question asks for an effective conclusion for the overall passage. An effective conclusion should contain a summary of the author's central idea and argument. **Step 2: Eliminate answer choices that do not address the issue** Eliminate A and B because they are only details. Eliminate C because it goes beyond the scope of the passage by describing events since 2005 and contradicts the passage's mention of "other researchers' studies." **Step 3: Plug in the remaining answer choices and select the most correct, concise, and relevant one** Choice (D) is correct.

Reading & Writing

You have seen the ways in which the SAT tests you on Development in Writing & Language passages and the way an SAT expert approaches these types of questions.

Use the Kaplan Method for Writing & Language to answer the four questions that accompany the following Writing & Language passage excerpt. Remember to look at the strategic thinking questions that have been laid out for you—some of the answers have been filled in, but you will have to complete the answers to others.

Use your answers to the strategic thinking questions to select the correct answer, just as you will on Test Day.

Questions 5-8 are based on the following passage.

Human Skin

The skin is the human body's largest organ. An adult's skin comprises between 15 and 20 percent of the total body weight. Each square centimeter has 6 million cells, 5,000 sensory points, 100 sweat glands, and 15 sebaceous glands. The outer layer, the epidermis, consists of rows of cells about 12 to 15 deep and is between .07 and .12 millimeters thick (the thickness of a piece of paper). This top layer **5** has already been studied by countless scientists, and few new discoveries or insights are likely to occur. One square inch of skin contains up to 4.5 m of blood vessels, which regulate body temperature. The skin varies in thickness from .5 mm on the eyelids to 4 mm or more on the palms and the soles.

The skin forms a protective barrier against the action of physical, chemical, and bacterial agents on the deeper tissues and contains the special nerve organs for the various sensations commonly grouped as the sense of touch. The body replaces its skin every month, and because the skin constitutes the first line of defense against dehydration, infection, injuries, and extreme temperatures, **6** the skin detoxifies harmful substances with many of the same enzymatic processes the liver uses.

Skin is constantly being regenerated. A cell is born in the lower layer of the skin, called the dermis, which is supplied with blood vessels and nerve endings. For the next two weeks, the cell migrates upward until it reaches the bottom portion of the epidermis, which is the outermost skin layer. The cell then flattens out and continues moving toward the surface until it dies and is shed.

The most important property of the skin is that it provides our sense of touch. All other senses have a definite key organ that can be studied, but the skin is spread over the entire body and cannot be as easily studied. Receptors located at the ends of nerve fibers are used to detect stimuli and convert them into neural impulses to be sent to the brain through the peripheral and central nervous systems. The sense of touch is actually recorded in the dermis (skin) and passed on to the central nervous system.

The most important job of the skin is to protect the inside of the body; it acts like a "shock absorber." If a body falls, the skin protects all of the internal organs. When the skin is broken, **7** there is an elaborate repair system that relies primarily on blood cells, which clot the breach, fight infection, and initiate healing. The skin also acts as a thermostat to regulate body temperature. **8** It is no exaggeration to say that skin is among the most important organs; without it, a body simply cannot continue living.

Questions	Strategic Thinking
5. A) NO CHANGE B) has already been studied by countless scientists. C) is mainly composed of dead cells and thus is not of great interest to scientists. D) is mainly composed of dead cells and these are constantly being replaced by newer cells.	**Step 1: Read the passage and identify the issue** *What is the issue?* Focus. The underlined portion consists of details in the middle of a paragraph that are unrelated to the main idea. **Step 2: Eliminate answer choices that do not address the issue** *What is this paragraph about?* It introduces the topic of the passage—human skin—and contains many details about said organ. *What answer choice(s) can you eliminate?* _____ _____ _____ **Step 3: Plug in the remaining answer choices and select the most correct, concise, and relevant one** *What is the correct answer?* _____

Questions	Strategic Thinking
6. Which choice most effectively concludes the sentence and paragraph? A) NO CHANGE B) the skin detoxifies harmful substances in a way scientists are still trying to understand. C) the skin relies on other organs, such as the liver, to detoxify harmful substances with special enzymatic processes. D) the skin requires careful and upkeep and care.	**Step 1: Read the passage and identify the issue** *What is the issue?* Focus. The underlined portion belongs to the last sentence of a body paragraph, which should tie back into the passage's central idea. **Step 2: Eliminate answer choices that do not address the issue** *What is the central idea of the passage?* _____ _____ _____ *What answer choice(s) can you eliminate?* _____ _____ _____ **Step 3: Plug in the remaining answer choices and select the most correct, concise, and relevant one** *What is the correct answer?* _____

Questions	Strategic Thinking
7. Which choice results in a sentence that best supports the central idea of the paragraph and passage? A) NO CHANGE B) immediate medical attention is necessary to protect the internal organs. C) it has its own defense system that immediately goes into repair mode. D) there is an elaborate repair system that relies primarily on red and white blood cells, which clot the breach, fight infection, and initiate healing.	**Step 1: Read the passage and identify the issue** *What is the issue?* Support. *How do you know?* _____ _____ _____ **Step 2: Eliminate answer choices that do not address the issue** *What is this paragraph about?* _____ _____ _____ *What answer choice(s) can you eliminate?* _____ _____ _____ **Step 3: Plug in the remaining answer choices and select the most correct, concise, and relevant one** *What is the correct answer?* _____

Questions	Strategic Thinking
8. Which choice most effectively concludes the passage? A) NO CHANGE B) Since skin covers the body and is easily visible, it is no wonder that its color and decoration have important cultural meanings. C) However, more important organs do indeed exist and likely deserve more scientific attention than the skin. D) Without the skin's properties, most importantly the sense of touch, life would hardly be worth living.	**Step 1: Read the passage and identify the issue** *What is the issue?* _____ *How do you know?* _____ _____ _____ **Step 2: Eliminate answer choices that do not address the issue** *What would effectively conclude the passage?* _____ _____ _____ *What answer choice(s) can you eliminate?* _____ _____ _____ **Step 3: Plug in the remaining answer choices and select the most correct, concise, and relevant one** *What is the correct answer?* _____

Now, try a test-like Writing & Language passage on your own. Give yourself 5 minutes to read the passage and answer the questions.

Questions 9-16 are based on the following passage.

James Polk

For much of his distinguished career, James Knox Polk followed in the footsteps of Andrew Jackson.[1] **9** In fact, "Young Hickory's" policies were very similar to Jackson's: **10** both men favored lower taxes; championed the frontiersmen, farmers, and workers; and neither was afraid to indulge in Tennessee whiskey. Polk, however, did not share Jackson's rather fierce temperament; he was instead known for remaining soft-spoken even as he worked energetically toward his goals. Although history will likely always remember the frontier persona of Andrew Jackson, it was Polk who did much more to shape the course of American history.

9. Which choice, if added here, would provide the most relevant detail?

   A) Like the fiery Jackson, Polk was born in North Carolina and moved to Tennessee to begin a political career.

   B) Both men were fiery, aggressive personalities who hailed from North Carolina and later moved to Tennessee to begin their political careers.

   C) Like the fiery Jackson, Polk was born in North Carolina and moved to Tennessee, but unlike Jackson, he did not fight in the War of 1812.

   D) Polk, like Jackson, had antipathy toward the Native Americans of the southeastern United States, and his efforts to remove them defined his career.

10. A) NO CHANGE

    B) while they agreed on little regarding taxes or the suffrage of frontiersmen, farmers, and workers, both men were known to indulge in Tennessee whiskey.

    C) both men favored lower taxes; championed the frontiersmen, farmers, and workers; and opposed the controversial Bank of the United States.

    D) both men favored lower taxes; championed the frontiersmen, farmers, and workers; and yet they could not agree on the controversial Bank of the United States.

[1] U.S. President from 1829 to 1837 and War of 1812 hero often referred to as "Old Hickory."

11 The Polk family was poor—James's father had emigrated from Scotland and arrived in the U.S. South penniless. From an early age, Polk suffered ill health that would turn out to be a lifelong affliction. Despite his physical shortcomings, he was an able student and graduated from the University of North Carolina with honors in 1818. Two years later, Polk was admitted to the bar to practice law, and in 1823, **12** he married Sarah Childress, the daughter of a prominent planter and merchant from Murfreesboro. From there, he was elected to the U.S. House of Representatives in 1825, serving until 1839. **13** Polk was also Speaker of the House from 1835 to 1839.

11. Which choice most effectively introduces this paragraph?

A) NO CHANGE

B) James Polk's parents tried to discourage the draw of politics and law, instead urging their eldest son to become a farmer.

C) Polk married his wife, Sarah Childress, in 1823.

D) Polk was born in Mecklenburg, North Carolina, in 1795 as the oldest of ten children.

12. Which choice results in a sentence that best supports the point developed in the paragraph and is consistent with the information in the rest of the passage?

A) NO CHANGE

B) he married Sarah Childress.

C) he was elected as governor of Tennessee.

D) he was elected to the Tennessee House of Representatives.

13. Which choice most effectively concludes the paragraph and transitions to the following paragraph?

A) NO CHANGE

B) Polk was also Speaker of the House from 1835 to 1839, an experience that made him wary of wading deeper into national politics.

C) Polk was also Speaker of the House from 1835 to 1839, a post that catapulted him to a position of prominence in politics.

D) Polk was also Speaker of the House from 1835 to 1839, an experience that left his already strained constitution exhausted and forced him into a temporary retirement.

After he left Congress to serve as governor of Tennessee in 1839, it became clear that Polk's political aspirations were high indeed. During the 1844 presidential campaign, **14** a young Abraham Lincoln threw his support behind Whig Henry Clay instead of the Democratic ex-President Martin van Buren. Both men, as part of their platforms, opposed expansionist policies, and neither intended to annex the independent state of Texas or the Oregon Territory. **15** Polk, spurred on by Jackson's advice, recognized that neither candidate had correctly surmised the feelings of the people, so he publicly announced that, as president, he would do his utmost to acquire Texas and Oregon. Polk was the first political "dark horse" in American politics, coming out of nowhere to win the Democratic nomination and the election.

As the eleventh President of the United States, **16** Polk pursued an agenda of diverse issues. First, he reached an agreement with England that divided the Oregon Territory, carving out the present-day states of Washington and Oregon. Polk also quickly annexed Texas and provoked war with Mexico to acquire California and the New Mexico territory. While these triumphs were somewhat diminished by controversy from abolitionists who opposed the spread of slavery into new territories, under Polk's leadership the dream of "manifest destiny" became a reality, and the United States fully extended its borders from the Atlantic to the Pacific.

14. Which choice provides the most relevant detail?

A) NO CHANGE

B) the leading Democratic candidate was ex-President Martin van Buren and the Whig candidate was Henry Clay.

C) the issue of slavery's expansion into new territories began its long stint as the most divisive issue to plague national politics.

D) both the leading Democratic candidate, ex-President Martin van Buren, and the Whig candidate, Henry Clay, sought to campaign under the banner of "Manifest Destiny" and territorial expansion.

15. A) NO CHANGE

B) Polk, against Jackson's advice, recognized

C) Polk recognized

D) Polk, against the wishes of his advisors, recognized

16. Which choice provides the most appropriate introduction to the paragraph?

A) NO CHANGE

B) Polk worked tirelessly to expand the borders of the nation.

C) Polk worked to reign in unchecked expansion of the frontiers.

D) Polk stopped at nothing short of war to expand the borders of the nation.

Answers & Explanations for this chapter begin on page 1006.

EXTRA PRACTICE

Questions 1-11 are based on the following passage and supplementary material.

Reefs at Risk

[1] **1** Coral reefs contain more than one quarter of all marine life and help reduce storm damage to coastal lands. [2] **2** Ultimately, about ten percent of the world's coral reefs have been destroyed and **3** about sixty percent of the remaining reefs are in danger. [3] Many people enjoy snorkeling and fishing near coral reefs. [4] **4** A coral reef is formed by a community of very small plants and animals; these plants and animals are known as algae and polyps. [5] The algae use sunlight to produce their own food for energy and growth. [6] The polyps eat other small animals that come to feed on the algae. [7] They also make a hard substance, called limestone, which eventually builds up to form a reef.

1. Which sentence should be removed in order to improve the focus of this paragraph?
   A) Sentence 1
   B) Sentence 3
   C) Sentence 6
   D) Sentence 7

2. A) NO CHANGE
   B) Unfortunately,
   C) Consequently,
   D) Inevitably,

3. Which choice most accurately represents the information in the pie charts?
   A) NO CHANGE
   B) threats have been made to sixty percent of remaining reefs.
   C) more than 6 in 10 reefs have faced threats of some kind or another.
   D) about sixty percent of the remaining reefs have experienced danger.

4. A) NO CHANGE
   B) Very small plants and animals, known as algae and polyps, make up the community that forms a coral reef.
   C) A coral reef is formed by a community of very small plants and animals called algae and polyps.
   D) Known as algae and polyps, very small plants and animals form a community that is called a coral reef.

The health of a coral reef depends on having clean water and sunlight, but human activities can threaten these **5** basic resources. Oil or chemical spills in the water near the reefs can harm the polyps, and chemical runoff into streams from mines and farms can also destroy the polyps and algae.

6 Fishing and boating are popular sports near coral reefs. People who fish for a living often use explosives to catch the many fish that are attracted to coral reefs, causing significant damage. Boats also destroy reefs with their anchors, and tourists who swim in coral reefs often break coral off to keep as a souvenir.

Development along a coast, such as cutting down trees and building roads or parking lots, **7** increased the amount of dirt and sand that washes into the ocean and settles on the bottom. This covers the coral and blocks sunlight. Without sunlight, the algae cannot grow, and in turn, the polyps lack the energy needed to produce limestone and build up the reef.

5. A) NO CHANGE
   B) elusive
   C) committed
   D) vital

6. Which choice most effectively establishes the paragraph's central idea?
   A) NO CHANGE
   B) People who participate in activities near coral reefs often cause damage.
   C) Boats are dangerous to the health of coral reefs.
   D) Coral reefs are fragile, and people should be careful around them.

7. A) NO CHANGE
   B) increases
   C) increasing
   D) increase

[1] Marine biologists have found that small crabs living in coral reefs can help prevent the damage caused by coastal development. [2] They remove particles of dirt and sand that settle on the coral and **8** <u>stop</u> sunlight. [3] The crabs also eat some of the polyps, which **9** <u>would probably suggest</u> that the crabs might also be a threat to the coral. [4] The crabs help the coral survive **10** <u>but benefit from the relationship as well.</u> [5] The crabs living on the coral have a steady source of food, and the reef provides the crabs with shelter from predators. [6] However, when the biologists removed crabs from sections of coral, less coral survived than in the sections where the crabs remained. **11**

The destruction of coral reefs does not have to continue. Recognizing the part that local animals, such as crabs, can play to reduce the amount of damage will help to slow the loss of coral reefs and may provide better ways to protect them.

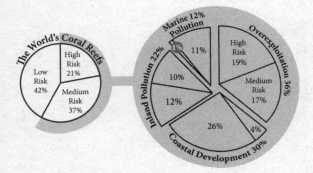

Almost 60% of the world's coral reefs are at high or medium risk of destruction.

Adapted from Wheeling Jesuit University/NASA-supported Classroom of the Future, "Exploring the Environment: Coral Reefs."

8. A) NO CHANGE
    B) hinder
    C) obstruct
    D) cover

9. A) NO CHANGE
    B) would suggest
    C) maybe suggests
    D) almost certainly suggests

10. Which choice results in a sentence that best supports the central idea of the paragraph?
    A) NO CHANGE
    B) but are one of millions of animals that live in coral reefs.
    C) and can be very large or very small in size.
    D) and are found on coral reefs all over the world.

11. To make this paragraph most logical, sentence 6 should be placed
    A) where it is now.
    B) before sentence 1.
    C) after sentence 2.
    D) after sentence 3.

Questions 12-22 are based on the following passage.

The Power of the PA

12 Today, physician assistants are vital members of any health care system, but it hasn't always been that way. In 1960s America, there were not enough doctors to meet the primary care needs of patients nationwide. Due to the shortage, and in hopes of improving health care and its accessibility, educators sought to establish alternatives to medical school that would effectively equip other health care workers to share more of the physicians' workload. Their project altered health care history: the physician assistant (PA) was born. In 1967, the first PA program **13** launched at Duke University, notable for its education degrees and sports teams. The coming decades saw the field develop into what is considered today to be one of the most desirable and quickly growing careers in the country.

12. Which choice most effectively establishes the main topic of the paragraph?

A) NO CHANGE

B) For many years, doctors and educators struggled to find a role for the high number of incoming medical students.

C) The difference between physician assistants and nurse practitioners was often hard to quantify, but then came a shift in health care needs.

D) Physician assistants had long played a vital role in the medical field, but the PA career didn't become popular until the mid-20th century.

13. A) NO CHANGE

B) launched at Duke University, noted for its education degrees.

C) launched at the renowned Duke University.

D) launched at Duke University.

[1] Becoming a PA is simpler than becoming a physician, which usually takes over nine years of higher education and training. [2] Those seeking acceptance into PA programs typically study science or health as undergraduates. [3] Once practicing, PAs are required to maintain proficiency through continued education and a recertification exam every ten years. [4] They also usually **14** <u>obtain</u> some health-related work experience before applying. [5] **15** <u>Once accepted to a program</u>, most students will be in their programs for about twenty-seven months. [6] Schooling involves both classroom and field study, and students undergo hundreds of hours in clinical training rotations in order to gain a breadth of supervised experience. [7] Today there are over one hundred and seventy accredited PA programs, most of which award masters degrees to graduates. [8] After graduation, **16** <u>graduates</u> must complete one final step: passing the national licensure exam. **17**

While physicians can work **18** <u>anonymously</u>, PAs always work under the supervision of physicians. But like nurse practitioners, another primary care alternative that emerged in the 1960s, PAs can do much of the work commonly expected of a physician. PAs are trained and qualified to meet with, examine, treat, diagnose, and counsel patients. They can prescribe medication, interpret lab data, and help physicians with surgical procedures. **19** <u>In many ways</u>, PAs lighten the workload for physicians on their teams. This enables clinics, hospitals, and other health care systems to run more

14. A) NO CHANGE
    B) accrue
    C) perceive
    D) formulate

15. A) NO CHANGE
    B) Once accepted,
    C) Once they begin,
    D) Once programs accept them,

16. A) NO CHANGE
    B) physicians
    C) PAs
    D) candidates

17. To make this paragraph most logical, sentence 3 should be placed
    A) where it is now.
    B) after sentence 5.
    C) after sentence 6.
    D) after sentence 8.

18. A) NO CHANGE
    B) defensively,
    C) autonomously,
    D) fundamentally,

19. A) NO CHANGE
    B) On the other hand,
    C) For example,
    D) First of all,

efficiently and meet patient needs with greater accuracy and timeliness.

Physician assistants enjoy various options in terms of where they can practice. Almost every field of medicine has positions for those PAs who specialize accordingly. Also, depending on the needs of the physicians **20** under which PAs work, as well as the particular limitations that might be imposed by a specific state, the requirements and responsibilities of the job can vary.

The past half-century saw the career of physician assistant rise from nascence to become a highly sought-after and still rapidly growing addition to American health care. Projections indicate that within the next decade, the number of employed PAs should increase significantly. **21** I believe PAs are an ever-increasing presence in health care and a powerful influence on the medical world for the better. **22**

20. A) NO CHANGE
    B) where PAs work,
    C) under whom PAs work,
    D) who work under PAs,

21. A) NO CHANGE
    B) PAs are an ever-increasing presence
    C) Doctors believe PAs are an ever-increasing presence
    D) You can believe that PAs are an ever-increasing presence

22. Which detail, if added to the paragraph, would best support the writer's claims?

    A) The number of PAs hired over the last half-century
    B) The expected PA-to-patient ratio over the next decade
    C) The number of PA positions compared to the number of nurse practitioner positions
    D) The specific rate at which PAs will be employed over the next decade

Effective Language Use

CHAPTER OBJECTIVES

By the end of this chapter, you will be able to:

1. Revise the text as needed to improve the exactness or content appropriateness of word choice or eliminate wordiness and redundancy

2. Improve the consistency of style and tone with the passage's purpose as necessary

3. Evaluate the use of sentence structure to accomplish the intended rhetorical purpose of a passage

SMARTPOINTS

Point Value	SmartPoint Category
60 Points	Effective Language Use

Reading & Writing

EFFECTIVE LANGUAGE USE

Chapter 22

Homework

Extra Practice: #1-11

Even More

Writing & Language Quiz 3

Key

 Book Assignment

 Online Video Assignment

 Online Quiz Assignment

PRECISION

On the SAT, precision refers to the exactness and accuracy of the author's choice of words, also known as diction. Precision questions will ask you to revise a text as needed to make a vague word more precise or to change a word or phrase so that it makes sense with the rest of the content.

Word choice is important because being precise in language use allows an author to effectively and clearly convey his or her thoughts, including the thesis and central arguments.

SAT Precision questions mostly test your knowledge of correct word choice in context. Though these questions are similar to the Reading test's Vocab-in-Context questions, Precision questions do not ask about the definition or implication of a word, but about the correctness of it—is it the right word to convey the author's meaning?

CONCISION

Remember the third step of the Kaplan Method for Writing & Language: Plug in the remaining answer choices and select the most clear, *concise*, and relevant one. You must use not only the correct words to convey your ideas but also as few words as possible.

Concision questions will require you to revise text to improve the economy of word choice by eliminating wordiness and redundancy. The SAT tests concision by presenting you with unnecessarily long and complex structures or redundant usage—or sometimes both.

> ✔ **On Test Day**
>
> The shortest answer is often but not always the correct one; the portion of the passage in question needs to also be grammatically correct and retain the intended meaning.

Unnecessarily long and complex structure implies that a sentence uses more words than necessary to make its point, even though it may be grammatically correct. Not every long, underlined segment will include a concision issue; sometimes it takes a lot of words to convey meaning. Nevertheless, when a long selection is underlined, you should ask, "Are all of these words necessary? Is there a more concise way to say the same thing?"

Another aspect of concision is redundancy. Redundancy errors occur when two words in the sentence have essentially the same meaning in context or when the meaning of one word is implicit in the meaning of another.

Reading & Writing

STYLE AND TONE

Elements of an author's style and tone include his or her choices of words, rhetorical devices, and sentence structure. The author might write informally, as if for a friendly, general audience; academically, as if for an expert audience; or forcefully, as if expounding his or her point of view. SAT Style and Tone questions ask you to revise a text to ensure consistency of style and tone or to reflect the author's purpose. You must also confirm that the text's style and tone match the subject and format.

Some Style and Tone questions will have question stems, while others will not. In the case of the latter, you must determine if the underlined segment matches the general tone of the passage or if one of the other choices is more appropriate in context.

> ✔ **Expert Tip**
>
> If you spot a Style and Tone question at the beginning of a passage, read the rest of the passage before answering it so you can first determine the overall tone.

SYNTAX

Syntax refers to the arrangement of words and phrases within a sentence. Questions about syntax will ask you to assess whether different sentence structures accomplish an author's intended rhetorical purpose. In narratives or prose, syntax can enhance the intended meaning and contribute toward tone.

Academic texts, such as the passages you'll see on the SAT, employ varied kinds of syntax. One way in which syntax is categorized is by sentence type. The following table describes four sentence types that are classified by the clauses they contain.

> ✔ **Definition**
>
> A clause is a part of a sentence containing a subject and a predicate verb.

Sentence Type	Description	Example
Simple	Contains a single, independent clause	*I applied for a summer job.*
Compound	Contains two independent clauses that are joined by a coordinating conjunction (e.g., *but, or, and, so*)	*I applied for a summer job, and the human resources manager hired me.*
Complex	Contains an independent clause plus one or more dependent clauses (a dependent clause starts with a coordinating conjunction such as *that, because, while, although, where, if*)	*I applied for a summer job at the local hospital because I am interested in gaining experience in the medical field.*
Compound-Complex	Contains three or more clauses (of which at least two are independent and one is dependent)	*I applied for a summer job at the local hospital, and the human resources manager hired me because I am interested in gaining experience in the medical field.*

Let's look at the following Writing & Language passage and questions. After the passage, there are two columns. The left column contains test-like questions. The column on the right features the strategic thinking a test expert employs when approaching the passage and questions presented.

Questions 1-4 are based on the following passage.

Modern Readers

Judging by the types of novels that typically receive the top rankings on contemporary "best seller" lists, one would be wise to conclude that the modern book consumer does not enjoy reading ancient mythology. Seemingly, such antiquated stories hold little relevance to the concerns of the modern age. It is a literature not for the **1** distracted reader immersed in his "everyday" cares, but for a more imaginative audience with more universal tastes.

To even begin **2** to understand or comprehend this issue, we must understand what it is that most readers seek out in the works they read. What is it in a book—a novel, for example—that causes them to continue turning the pages? The answer can be a bit slippery. Is it the psychological realism of the characters? Is it the drama of the events they encounter? Is it the modern author's consciousness of his position as author and the relationship—distant or intimate, serious or playful—that he develops with his readers?

The obvious answer is that it is all of these things. The defining features of the modern story are its complexity and ambivalence. Narrators are not always reliable. Loyalties are often fleeting, and even a character's central motives may undergo a transformation before the story is done. There is no neat conclusion, no definitive redemption or damnation, and not always even a clear message. In this confusion and dislocation, the modern reader sees his own life reflected, complete with all of its **3** <u>complexity and ambivalence</u>.

In a complex world where the disparate lives of alienated individuals still manage to affect each other on a daily basis, there is a paradoxical credulity extended towards anything murky and unclear. Far from the cosmopolitan savant he would like us to believe he is (to say nothing of the author who writes for him), the modern reader is only able to take comfort in his own confusion. When, for example, George and Jane finish their fairy-tale courtship and suddenly find themselves unable to live together, the contemporary pop intellectual will **4** <u>nod his head sagely, and he will think about</u> the relationships in his own life that he didn't understand either.

What escapes the minds of the masses is that, taken past a certain point, realism is not art. Neither unsatisfying conclusions, nor irritating characters, nor obscure motives are indications of the literary talents of the author. The older, mythic characters may be drawn with a broad brush, and may possess a simplicity and singularity of purpose that finds no parallel in day-to-day life, but that simplicity is not a sign of an author lacking in subtlety. Rather, a purposeful author will have purposeful characters. Whether the story is meant to illustrate moral principles, explore character types, or simply entertain, a quality work of art must have a purpose.

Questions	Strategic Thinking
1. A) NO CHANGE B) prosaic C) voracious D) modern	**Step 1: Read the passage and identify the issue** The underlined word, "distracted," does not directly contrast with the "more imaginative audience with more universal tastes," as indicated by the use of the word "but." A better word choice will describe readers who are less imaginative and more selective in their reading. **Step 2: Eliminate answer choices that do not address the issue** Eliminate A because the underlined word is not precise enough. Eliminate C because a "voracious" reader is one who reads an enormous amount, not a less imaginative reader. Eliminate D because the reader's era has nothing to do with the sentence. **Step 3: Plug in the remaining answer choices and select the most correct, concise, and relevant one** Since "prosaic" means ordinary, (B) is correct.

Questions	Strategic Thinking
2. A) NO CHANGE B) to understand or to comprehend C) to understand and comprehend D) to understand	**Step 1: Read the passage and identify the issue** The underlined portion is redundant as written; "understand" and "comprehend" have the same meaning. The underlined portion needs to be more concise. **Step 2: Eliminate answer choices that do not address the issue** Eliminate A because the underlined portion is incorrect as written and needs to be changed. Eliminate B and C because they do not correct the redundancy issue. **Step 3: Plug in the remaining answer choices and select the most correct, concise, and relevant one** Choice (D) is correct.

Reading & Writing

Questions	Strategic Thinking
3. A) NO CHANGE B) ambivalence C) complexity D) ambivalent complexity	**Step 1: Read the passage and identify the issue** The style and tone of the passage are authoritative and academic. Check to see if the underlined portion reflects this style and tone appropriately. **Step 2: Eliminate answer choices that do not address the issue** The author uses the underlined phrase previously in the second sentence of the paragraph: "The defining features of the modern story are its complexity and ambivalence." Eliminate B and C because they both remove one of the previously used words. Eliminate D because even though it is more concise, it alters the intended meaning. **Step 3: Plug in the remaining answer choices and select the most correct, concise, and relevant one** Choice (A) is correct.

Prepare

Questions	Strategic Thinking
4. Which choice most effectively combines the sentences at the underlined portion? A) NO CHANGE B) nod his head sagely. He will think about C) nod his head sagely, thinking about D) nod his head sagely, be thinking about	**Step 1: Read the passage and identify the issue** Although the two independent clauses are correctly combined with a comma and the conjunction "and," the sentence is wordy as written and unnecessarily repeats the subject "he." The syntax of the sentence needs to be corrected. **Step 2: Eliminate answer choices that do not address the issue** Eliminate A because the sentence is incorrect as written. Eliminate B because it separates the underlined portion into two sentences, which, while grammatically correct, is not the most effective combination; the separated sentences place unnecessary distance between the two parts. Eliminate D because it is grammatically incorrect. **Step 3: Plug in the remaining answer choices and select the most correct, concise, and relevant one** Choice (C) is correct.

Reading & Writing

You have seen the ways in which the SAT tests you on Effective Language Use in Writing & Language passages and the way an SAT expert approaches these types of questions.

Use the Kaplan Method for Writing & Language to answer the four questions that accompany the following Writing & Language passage excerpt. Remember to look at the strategic thinking questions that have been laid out for you—some of the answers have been filled in, but you will have to complete the answers to others.

Use your answers to the strategic thinking questions to select the correct answer, just as you will on Test Day.

Questions 5-8 are based on the following passage.

Military Nurses

During the American Civil War, Miss Dorothea Dix was in charge of organizing the volunteer nurses who assisted the Union Army. The nurses chosen by Dix were all women, preferably plain ones, and had to dress simply in order to serve. Dorothea Dix's volunteers were the first famous nurses in United States history, but on both the Union and Confederate sides, **5** other health care professionals there that few people knew about were male nurses. As the nineteenth century progressed, nursing became increasingly considered "women's work," until, at the turn of the 20th century, female nurses began to organize, unofficially excluding men. The American Nursing Association was formed in 1917, and men were not officially permitted to join until 1930.

One of the **6** major victories of the female-dominated nursing community was to have men **7** denied admission to and excluded from military nursing. Traditionally, non-volunteer military nurses had been exclusively male, but in 1901, the United States Army Nurse Corps was formed exclusively for women. **8** It is amazing to even think that men couldn't work as military nurses until after the Korean War. Today, depending on the branch of service, anywhere between 35% and 70% of military nurses are men; this is in sharp contrast to the civilian world, where an average of 6% of American nurses are men.

Questions	Strategic Thinking
5. A) NO CHANGE B) few people knew there were other health care professionals about: male nurses. C) some health care professionals were male nurses that few people knew about. D) there were other health care professionals that few people knew about: male nurses.	**Step 1: Read the passage and identify the issue** *What is the issue?* Syntax. As written, the sentence is hard to follow due to the placement of the words. **Step 2: Eliminate answer choices that do not address the issue** *What answer choice(s) can you eliminate?* Eliminate A, B, and C because they all contain a syntax error. **Step 3: Plug in the remaining answer choices and select the most correct, concise, and relevant one** *What is the correct answer?* _____

Reading & Writing

Questions	Strategic Thinking

6.   A) NO CHANGE
 	
    B) first triumphs
 	
    C) undisputed wins
 	
    D) finest achievements
	Step 1: Read the passage and identify the issue
	
	What is the issue?
	
	Word choice, or precision.
	
	What does the underlined phrase indicate? Does it fit the context of the passage? Why or why not?
	
	The passage is concerned with the early years of female nursing. The underlined phrase does not make this connection.
	
	Step 2: Eliminate answer choices that do not address the issue
	
	What answer choice(s) can you eliminate?
	
	_____
	
	_____
	
	_____
	
	Step 3: Plug in the remaining answer choices and select the most correct, concise, and relevant one
	
	What is the correct answer? _____

Reading & Writing

Questions	Strategic Thinking
7. A) NO CHANGE B) denied to and excluded from C) excluded from D) denied and excluded from	**Step 1: Read the passage and identify the issue** *What is the issue?* Redundancy, or concision. *Why is the underlined portion redundant?* _____ _____ **Step 2: Eliminate answer choices that do not address the issue** *What answer choice(s) can you eliminate?* _____ _____ _____ **Step 3: Plug in the remaining answer choices and select the most correct, concise, and relevant one** *What is the correct answer?* _____

Questions	Strategic Thinking
8. A) NO CHANGE B) It was not until after the Korean War that men could once more work as military nurses. C) In this day and age, it is nearly inconceivable that it took until after the Korean War before men could once more exercise their right to work as military nurses. D) Not until after the Korean War could men once more take up the noble calling to serve as military nurses.	**Step 1: Read the passage and identify the issue** *What is the issue?* Style and tone. *What are the style and tone of the passage?* _____ _____ *Does the underlined portion match the style and tone of the passage? Why or why not?* _____ _____ **Step 2: Eliminate answer choices that do not address the issue** *What answer choice(s) can you eliminate?* _____ _____ _____ **Step 3: Plug in the remaining answer choices and select the most correct, concise, and relevant one** *What is the correct answer?* _____

Reading & Writing

Now try a test-like Writing & Language passage on your own. Give yourself 5 minutes to read the passage and answer the questions.

Questions 9-16 are based on the following passage.

Genetically Modified Organisms

Although biotechnology companies and the chronically naïve **9** imagine that there is no danger to be feared from genetically modified foods, they overlook a plethora of evidence indicating that they may be gambling with people's lives by continuing to **10** interfere and tamper with nature to create these "Frankenfoods." Potential problems range from the relatively minor—increased possibilities of allergic reactions to certain foods, for instance—to the potentially devastating—the complete skewing of the balance of an ecosystem. All of these factors should be carefully considered before **11** we choose to risk so much for the possibility of a better tomato.

For example, the cultivation of insect-resistant plants could lead to the reduction or even destruction of certain insect species that naturally feed on those plants. A change in the insect population could have a disastrous impact on **12** certain bird species. They rely on the affected insects as their food source. Also, alterations in the balance of the bird population could have further-reaching consequences, all the way up the food chain. An ecosystem is a delicate thing, and the ripple created by genetically altering one variety of soybean **13** will translate into a shock wave of unforeseen repercussions in the long term.

9. A) NO CHANGE
   B) insist
   C) hope
   D) think

10. A) NO CHANGE
    B) thoughtlessly interfere and casually tamper
    C) interfere by casually tampering
    D) tamper

11. A) NO CHANGE
    B) we as a society
    C) those of us who comprise society
    D) the citizens making up our population

12. Which choice most effectively combines the sentences at the underlined portion?
    A) NO CHANGE
    B) certain bird species that rely on the affected insects
    C) certain bird species relying on the affected insects
    D) certain bird species, and they rely on the affected insects

13. A) NO CHANGE
    B) must
    C) would
    D) could

14 The actual impact on the genetically modified organisms themselves, and on those who consume foods produced from genetically modified organisms, also remains to be seen. Some studies indicate that certain genetically modified foods have negative effects on the digestive systems and cardiac health of rats that consume those foods in high quantities; although human studies have not been performed, the possibility that tampering with an organism's genetic structure could cause far-reaching health consequences for the people who eat genetically modified foods must be confronted.

Arguments about the potential for genetic engineering to end world hunger by maximizing the quantity and quality of food grown around the world are based on **15** an essential fallacy: people do not starve because there is a lack of food. People starve because it is more profitable to let food go to waste than to distribute it to the world's impoverished and famine-stricken regions. We have plenty of farmland sitting fallow and plenty of food rotting in warehouses. Many of the agribusinesses arguing that genetically modified foods can solve world hunger are the same companies that accept government subsidies now to limit their production of crops in order to avoid flooding the market. These companies are primarily concerned with profit, and whatever lip service they pay to global well-being, the driving force behind genetically modified organisms and foods is profit, not people. **16** In conclusion, the benefits and risks of any new technology must be carefully considered before implementing that technology.

14. A) NO CHANGE
    B) What also remains to be seen, on both the genetically modified organisms themselves and on those who consume foods produced from genetically modified organisms, is the actual impact.
    C) Remaining to be seen is the actual impact on genetically modified organisms themselves and those who consume genetically modified organisms.
    D) The actual impact remains to be seen on genetically modified organisms themselves and those who consume genetically modified organisms.

15. A) NO CHANGE
    B) a harmful delusion:
    C) a fanciful illusion:
    D) a fundamental untruth:

16. Which choice most effectively concludes the paragraph and the passage?
    A) NO CHANGE
    B) It would be nice if we could trust the very companies that could benefit most from the creation of genetically modified organisms.
    C) Unfortunately, those companies affect so many aspects of modern life that we have no choice but to trust them.
    D) Why would we trust our own well-being and that of the planet to companies recklessly pursuing money at the risk of Mother Earth?

Answers & Explanations for this chapter begin on page 1010.

EXTRA PRACTICE

The following questions provide an opportunity to practice the concepts and strategic thinking covered in this chapter. While many of the questions pertain to Effective Language Use, some touch on other concepts tested on the Writing & Language Test to ensure that your practice is test-like, with a variety of question types per passage.

Questions 1-11 are based on the following passage.

Long History, Short Poem: The Haiku

[1] Of the many forms poetry can take, triolet, ballad, ode, and epigram, to name a few, none is quite as briefly beautiful as the Japanese haiku. With a [2] complex history and a challenging structure, the haiku is as popular as it is difficult to master. Composed of only three lines and 17 or fewer syllables, haiku have been written by some of the world's most prominent poets.

1. A) NO CHANGE
   B) Of the many forms poetry can take—triolet, ballad, ode, and epigram, to name a few—none is quite as briefly beautiful as the Japanese haiku.
   C) Of the many forms poetry can take, triolet, ballad, ode and epigram to name a few—none is quite as briefly beautiful as the Japanese haiku.
   D) Of the many forms poetry can take: triolet, ballad, ode, and epigram to name a few, none is quite as briefly beautiful as the Japanese haiku.

2. A) NO CHANGE
   B) controversial
   C) brief
   D) difficult

3 [1] Pre-Buddhist and early Shinto ceremonies included narrative poems called "uta," or songs. [2] These songs were written about common activities like planting and prayer. [3] The most popular "uta" were "waka," or songs featuring 31 syllables broken into five different lines. [4] Later, the "waka" format was distilled into the 5-7-5-7-7 syllables-per-line format that is still used and recognized today. [5] During the same time period, writers played word games. [6] The syllabic 5-7-5-7-7 structure would remain throughout the work, adhering to the guidelines used in ceremonies and royal court proceedings. [7] They would compose lines of poetry, alternating turns, until long strings of text called "renga" were created. [8] It was not until the 15th and 16th centuries that writers of "renga" broke with tradition and shortened the form, writing "hokku," meaning "first verse." [9] **4** <u>This name changed into "haiku" over time.</u> **5**

3. Which choice, if added here, would provide the most appropriate introduction to the topic of the paragraph?

   A) Although the format remained unknown to Americans until the 1950s, haiku dates back as early as the seventh century.

   B) The art of haiku includes specific rules about how lines are to be structured, but these rules are difficult to pin down.

   C) Despite its difficult reputation and the years it takes to master, haiku is highly entertaining.

   D) Haiku is a Japanese poetic art form and many poets enjoy the challenge of writing a poem within its rules.

4. A) NO CHANGE

   B) Nobody is quite sure when it became known as "haiku."

   C) These days, we know this word as "haiku."

   D) DELETE the underlined portion.

5. To make this paragraph most logical, sentence 7 should be placed

   A) where it is now.

   B) after sentence 1.

   C) after sentence 5.

   D) after sentence 8.

[6] Previously, hokku master Matsunaga Teitoku began teaching renga in an attempt to ignite a classical renaissance. He founded a writing school where he taught Matsuo Basho, who is now known as one of Japan's most famous writers. Basho traveled throughout Japan writing about nature and his travels.

It is through Basho's many poems that [7] haiku came to be known as being pretty tied up with nature and the seasons. [8] Basho influenced many students of verse over the course of his lifetime and was declared the saint of the haiku in the Shinto religion.

6. A) NO CHANGE

   B) However,

   C) In the next century,

   D) As a result,

7. A) NO CHANGE

   B) haiku transformed into a mode of artistic expression that was irreversibly intertwined with the themes of

   C) haiku became popular because it was seen as having something to do with

   D) haiku developed its common association with

8. Which choice, if added here, would provide the most relevant detail?

   A) However, haiku can be used to communicate many other ideas as well, from love to humor.

   B) His words emphasized contentment and solitary contemplation, ideals linked to Japanese religions.

   C) Basho's poetic influence continues to be felt even now in the work of several modern poets.

   D) For example, a Basho haiku might focus on a frog or on the coming of spring.

It was not until 1827 that hokku was renamed haiku by Masaoka Shiki. **9** Shiki was a poet, and he most famously shrank the structure of the haiku to its current format of 5-7-5. His work **10** helped Western writers like e. e. cummings and Ezra Pound, but haiku did not become the easily recognizable, popular type of poetry that it is today until writers like Allen Ginsberg and Jack Kerouac popularized it.

These writers were taken by **11** the brevity of the form, but it provided them a new, challenging form of expression while enabling them to share full ideas in such a short form. Both Japanese and American poets continue to use the haiku structure to create snapshots of beauty and calm.

9. A) NO CHANGE

   B) Shiki was a poet who also shrank the structure of the haiku to the current 5-7-5 format.

   C) Shiki was the poet who shrank the structure of the haiku to its current 5-7-5 format.

   D) Shiki was the poet who was also known for shrinking the structure of the haiku to its current format of 5-7-5.

10. A) NO CHANGE

    B) inspired

    C) aided

    D) started

11. A) NO CHANGE

    B) the brevity of the form, it

    C) the brevity of the form, and it

    D) the brevity of the form, as it

Questions 12-22 are based on the following passage and supplementary material.

Tesla Lights Up the World

[1] Nikola Tesla, born in 1856, was an Austrian electrical engineer who worked for a telegraph company in Budapest before immigrating to the United States to join Thomas Edison's company in New York. [2] The two engineers did not work well together, and Tesla moved on to work with George Westinghouse, another engineer and inventor, at the Westinghouse Electric & Manufacturing Company in 1885. [3] **12** During his time there, Tesla invented the alternating current system, what we know in our homes as AC power. [4] Several years later, Tesla made the first successful wireless energy transfer. [5] Reportedly, Tesla slept little and often occupied himself with games, such as chess and billiards. **13**

12. A) NO CHANGE
    B) Tesla, while there, invented the AC power system we know in our homes, more formally called the alternating current system.
    C) Tesla invented the alternating current system during his time there, also known in our homes as AC power.
    D) When he worked there, the alternating current system, or what we know in our homes as AC power, was invented by him.

13. Which sentence should be removed in order to improve the focus of this paragraph?
    A) Sentence 1
    B) Sentence 2
    C) Sentence 4
    D) Sentence 5

[1] The Westinghouse Electric Company was quick to put Tesla's invention to work. [2] They **14** <u>implemented</u> the use of alternating current during the World Colombian Exposition in **15** <u>1897</u>, with fantastic results. [3] It was more efficient than Edison's earlier energy transfer system, the direct current (DC) system, as well as more effective. [4] Edison knew that the DC system was difficult to transmit over long distances. [5] He didn't, however, believe that Tesla's AC system was a credible threat to the dominance he and his company held over the electrical market of the time because of his invention of the light bulb. [6] **16** <u>But it is Tesla's system that moves power from a main grid across long distances.</u>

14. A) NO CHANGE
     B) encouraged
     C) invoked
     D) developed

15. Which choice completes the sentence with accurate data based on the timeline at the end of the passage?
     A) NO CHANGE
     B) 1882,
     C) 1890,
     D) 1893,

16. Which choice most effectively conveys the central idea of the paragraph?
     A) NO CHANGE
     B) However, bulbs alone do not light our homes; it is Tesla's system that moves power from one grid across long distances to the fixtures we use every day.
     C) Later, Tesla developed a system that allows us to use light bulbs every day.
     D) We now use Edison's bulbs every day; we can thank Tesla for inventing the system that moves power from one grid across distances to those fixtures.

[1] Tesla went on to develop the technology that is now used in X-rays, as well as radio and remote controls. [2] Some of his inventions even worked together, expanding his influence on the world and history. [3] Tesla paired his AC system with his understanding of physics to invent an electric motor. [4] Developing the AC system was only the beginning for Tesla, though. [5] To do so, he used his knowledge of magnetism to create a closed system in which a motor could turn without disruption or the use of manpower. [6] The motor generated a stable current that had been lacking in earlier attempts to transition industry to AC power. [7] With Tesla's motor, though, AC power systems could be broadly used in manufacturing and beyond. **17** **18**

17. Which sentence provides the best transition from the previous paragraph if placed before sentence 1?

A) Sentence 2

B) Sentence 4

C) Sentence 6

D) Sentence 7

18. Based on the timeline, "In 1883," would be most appropriately added to the beginning of which of the following sentences?

A) Paragraph 1, sentence 2

B) Paragraph 2, sentence 1

C) Paragraph 3, sentence 3

D) Paragraph 4, sentence 3

[1] Tesla's inventions are not only a part of our daily lives, they continue **19** to be expanded upon to create new advances in science and technology. [2] **20** Tesla's approach to energy transmission, as well as his invention of the radio, including antenna and other recognizable aspects, has allowed leaps and bounds to be made in wireless communications, such as radio broadcasting. [3] Edison may have invented the lightbulb, **21** but Tesla was an inventor bent on bringing electricity to the people, seeking no fame or fortune. [4] The reach of his technology goes even as far as the mobile phone. [5] Although long gone, Tesla remains **22** a pathfinder on the edge of miraculous invention.

Tesla's Inventions

1882 ➤	Rotating Magnetic Field—A rotating field that enabled alternating current to power a motor.
1883 ➤	AC Motor—The rotating magnetic field was put into practice in this motor, which spun without a mechanical aid.
1890 ➤	Tesla Coil—A coil that enables transformers to produce extremely high voltages.
1893 ➤	Tesla and Westinghouse display their AC current systems at the Columbian Exposition in Chicago.
1897 ➤	Radio—Tesla invented the radio, including antennae, tuners, and other familiar components.

19. Which of the following provides the most concise revision without altering the writer's intended meaning?
   A) to necessitate
   B) to be developed into
   C) to inspire scientists to make
   D) to lead to

20. Which supporting detail is least essential to sentence 2?
   A) That Tesla invented the radio
   B) That Tesla's invention of the radio included the "antenna and other recognizable aspects"
   C) That Tesla's invention of the radio allowed further innovation in wireless communications
   D) That radio broadcasting is a kind of wireless communication

21. A) NO CHANGE
   B) but Tesla, seeking no fame or fortune, was an inventor bent on bringing electricity to the people.
   C) but seeking no fame or fortune, Tesla was an inventor bent on bringing electricity to the people.
   D) but Tesla was an inventor bent on seeking no fame or fortune, bringing electricity to the people.

22. A) NO CHANGE
   B) an explorer
   C) a champion
   D) a pioneer

Reading & Writing

Standard English Conventions

BY THE END OF THIS UNIT, YOU WILL BE ABLE TO:

1. Recognize correct and incorrect instances of conventions of usage and punctuation

2. Identify and correct errors in sentence structure

3. Identify and correct usage errors

CHAPTER 23

Sentence Structure

CHAPTER OBJECTIVES

By the end of this chapter, you will be able to:

1. Recognize and correct grammatically incomplete or substandard sentences

2. Recognize and correct inappropriate grammatical shifts in the construction of verb and pronoun phrases

SMARTPOINTS

Point Value	SmartPoint Category
60 Points	Sentence Formation

Reading & Writing

SENTENCE STRUCTURE

Chapter 23

Homework

Extra Practice: #1-11

Even More

Writing & Language Quiz 4

Key

 Book Assignment

 Online Video Assignment

 Online Quiz Assignment

RUN-ONS AND FRAGMENTS

Run-ons and fragments create grammatically incorrect sentences. The SAT requires that you know the specific rules governing sentence construction.

A complete sentence must have a subject and a predicate verb in an independent clause that expresses a complete thought. If any one of these elements is missing, the sentence is a fragment. You can recognize a fragment because the sentence will not make sense as written. A fragment lacks one of the three components.

- *Seth running down the street.* (The fragment lacks a predicate verb.)

- *Because Michaela led the team in assists.* (The fragment is a dependent clause and does not express a complete thought.)

- *Practiced the piano every day.* (The fragment needs a subject.)

✔ Definition

A **predicate** is the part of the sentence that describes what the **subject** *does* (action), *is* (being), or *has* (condition); the **predicate verb** is the main verb in the sentence.

If a sentence has more than one independent clause, the clauses must be properly joined. Otherwise, the sentence is a run-on.

- *My friends and I usually walk home from school together, we ride the bus if the weather isn't nice.*

To Correct a Run-On	Example
Use a semicolon.	*My friends and I usually walk home from school together; we ride the bus if the weather isn't nice.*
Make one clause dependent.	***Although** my friends and I usually walk home from school together, we ride the bus if the weather isn't nice.*
Add a FANBOYS conjunction: *For, And, Nor, But, Or, Yet, So.*	*My friends and I usually walk home from school together, **but** we ride the bus if the weather isn't nice.*

Reading & Writing

COORDINATION AND SUBORDINATION

Coordination and subordination questions focus on the relationship between clauses. On the SAT, you will be asked to determine the best way to link clauses to most effectively express the writer's intent.

Coordinate Clauses

Coordinate clauses are independent clauses that can stand on their own and express a complete thought. When two or more independent clauses are properly joined, they form a compound sentence.

Two independent clauses are coordinated by using a comma and the conjunction and:

- *The class was interesting, and we prepared thoroughly for each session.* (Equal emphasis on the two ideas suggests that the class would have been interesting whether or not we prepared, and it suggests that we would have prepared whether or not the class was interesting.)

Subordinate Clauses

A subordinate clause cannot stand on its own and still make sense. Combining a subordinate clause with an independent clause by using a connecting word forms a complex sentence in which the independent clause expresses the central idea of the sentence and the subordinate clause provides additional support that modifies or clarifies the central idea.

The central idea of the sentence is changed depending upon which clause is subordinated:

- *Because the class was interesting,* we prepared thoroughly for each session. (The main emphasis is on our preparation. The subordinate clause gives the reason for our thoroughness.)

- The class was interesting *because we prepared thoroughly for each session.* (The main emphasis is on the class. The subordinate clause explains why it was interesting.)

PARALLELISM

Parallelism questions on the SAT test your ability to revise sentences to create parallel structure. Items in a series, list, or compound must be parallel in form. Series, lists, and compounds may contain nouns, adjectives, adverbs, or verb forms.

Check for parallelism if the sentence contains:

Feature	Example	Parallel Form
A list	*Before you leave, you should* **charge your phone**, **clean your room**, *and* **find your bus pass**.	3 verb phrases
A compound	**Swimming** *and* **biking** *provide aerobic exercise.*	2 gerund verb forms
A correlative	*The debate coach encouraged the students* **to listen** *carefully and* **to speak** *clearly.*	2 infinitive verb forms
A comparison	*Your* **practice test sessions** *are just as important as your* **class sessions**.	2 nouns
Related nouns	**Students** *who complete all of their* **homework assignments** *are more likely to earn* **higher test scores**.	3 related plural nouns

MODIFIERS

A modifier is a word or a group of words that describes, clarifies, or provides additional information about another part of the sentence. Modifier questions on the SAT Writing & Language Test require you to identify the part of a sentence being modified and use the appropriate modifier in the proper place.

> ✔ **Expert Tip**
>
> On the SAT, modifiers should be close to the words they modify.

Modifier	Function	Example
Adjective	An adjective is a single word modifier that describes a noun or pronoun.	*Asara bought a* **blue** *backpack from the* **thrift** *shop.*
Adverb	An adverb is a single word modifier that describes a verb, an adjective, or another adverb.	*Ian* **carefully** *walked over the* **rapidly** *melting ice.*
Modifying phrase	Modifying phrases and clauses must be properly placed to correctly modify another part of the sentence.	**Wanting to do well at the competition**, *Sasha devoted extra time to her practice sessions.*

Reading & Writing

Use context clues in the passage to identify the correct placement of a modifier; a misplaced modifier can cause confusion:

- *The restaurant provides carryout meals to its diners **in recyclable containers**.*

Who or what is in the containers? The context of the sentence suggests that the meals are in the containers; however, since modifiers should be placed near what they modify, the sentence can be grammatically interpreted to suggest that the diners are in the containers! When the modifier is correctly placed near what it modifies, the meaning is clarified:

- *The restaurant provides carryout meals **in recyclable containers** to its diners.*

Modifier placement can change the meaning of a sentence:

- *The waiter **just** described the dinner specials.* (The sentence is about **when** the action took place.)
- ***Just** the waiter described the dinner specials.* (The sentence is about **who** completed the action.)
- *The waiter described **just** the dinner specials.* (The sentence is about **what** was acted upon.)

VERB TENSE, MOOD, AND VOICE

On the SAT Writing & Language Test, you will be asked to identify and replace unnecessary shifts in verb tense, mood, and voice. Because these shifts may occur within a single sentence or among different sentences, you will need to read around the underlined portion to identify the error.

In questions about shifts in construction, the underlined segment must logically match the tense, mood, and voice in other parts of the sentence.

Verb tense places the action or state of being described by the verb into a place in time: **present**, **past**, or **future**. Each tense has three forms: **simple**, **progressive**, and **perfect**.

> ✔ **On Test Day**
>
> Shifts in verb tense are grammatically incorrect unless warranted by the context of the sentence or passage.

	Present	Past	Future
Simple: Actions that simply occur at some point in time	*She studies diligently every day.*	*She studied two extra hours before her math test.*	*She will study tomorrow for her French test.*
Progressive: Actions that are ongoing at some point in time	*She is studying today for her math test tomorrow.*	*She was studying yesterday for a French test today.*	*She will be studying tomorrow for her physics test next week.*
Perfect: Actions that are completed at some point in time	*She has studied diligently every day this semester.*	*She had studied two extra hours before her math test yesterday.*	*She will have studied each chapter before her physics test next week.*

Grammatical **moods** are classifications that indicate the attitude of the speaker.

	Description	Example
Indicative Mood	Used to make a statement or ask a question	*Snow **covered** the moonlit field.*
Imperative Mood	Used to give a command or make a request	*Please **drive** carefully in the snow.*
Subjunctive Mood	Used to express hypothetical outcomes	*If I **were** at the library, I could find the book I need.*

The **voice** of a verb describes the relationship between the action expressed by the verb and the subject.

	Description	Example
Active	The subject is the agent or doer of the action.	*The carpenter **hammered** the nail.*
Passive	The subject is the target of the action.	*The nail **was hammered** by the carpenter.*

> ✔ **Expert Tip**
>
> On the SAT, the active voice is preferred over the passive voice.

PRONOUN PERSON AND NUMBER

Pronouns replace nouns in sentences. They must agree with the noun they are replacing in person and number. The SAT will test your ability to recognize and correct inappropriate shifts in pronoun usage. To learn more about pronoun clarity and pronoun-antecedent agreement on the SAT, turn to chapter 24.

Pronoun Person and Number			
Person	**Refers to**	**Singular Pronouns**	**Plural Pronouns**
First person	the person speaking	I, me, my	we, us, our
Second person	the person spoken to	you, your	you, your
Third person	the person or thing spoken about	he, she, it, him, her, his, hers, its	they, them, theirs
Indefinite	a nonspecific person or group	anybody, anyone, each, either, everyone, someone, one	both, few, many, several

Reading & Writing

> ✔ **Remember**
>
> Do not shift between "you" and "one" unnecessarily. "You" refers to a specific person or group. "One" refers to an indefinite individual or group.

Let's look at the following Writing & Language passage and questions. After the passage, there are two columns. The left column contains test-like questions. The column on the right features the strategic thinking a test expert employs when approaching the passage and questions presented.

Questions 1-3 are based on the following passage.

SMOM

At 69 Condotti Street in Rome sits what is believed by many to be the smallest country in the world, a country that is not known by many. The Sovereign Military and Hospitaller Order of St. John of Jerusalem of Rhodes and of Malta, or SMOM, is an ancient order of knights well known for its humanitarian activities. The order's headquarters in Rome—a mere 6,000 square meters, or about one acre—is considered an independent state by at least 75 nations. How SMOM got to Rome is a story almost a millennium old, spanning as many places as the order's official name suggests.

SMOM began in 1099, during the First Crusade, as a large-scale military conflict pitting Christian armies against the Muslim rulers of what is now Israel. The order's task was to protect and defend Christian pilgrims traveling to Jerusalem as well as **1** providing a hospital for their care. Though it began as a religious order, SMOM developed into a military knighthood as a result of the volatile political situation.

Because of the ongoing conflict between Muslims and Christians, the order was forced to move a number of times. The Muslims overran Jerusalem in the 1170s, forcing SMOM to relocate first to the Mediterranean island of Cyprus and then to the nearby island of Rhodes. The Ottoman Turks seized Rhodes in 1522, forcing SMOM to move again, this time to Malta. **2** Then Napoleon drives the order from Malta in 1798, and the island fell into British hands soon after. SMOM wandered from city to city in Italy, finally establishing its current headquarters in 1834.

Today, SMOM is a knighthood and a religious order but no longer actively combats Muslims, as it did in the past. Instead, SMOM concentrates on caring for humanitarian needs regardless of **3** creed. Establishing hospitals and charities in all corners of the world. Its many activities include vaccination programs, refugee relief, and philanthropic works to combat deadly diseases, such as leprosy and malnutrition.

Because of the order's dual role, the Vatican, the central governing body of the Catholic Church, has always recognized—and continues to recognize—SMOM as an independent nation and its headquarters in Rome as the sovereignty of SMOM. Seventy-five countries recognize the order as a country, although the United States and Great Britain do not. SMOM coins its own money, mints its own stamps, and issues its own passports. The order is a Permanent Observer in the United Nations and enjoys membership in other international organizations as well. Although not physically important anymore, SMOM continues its more than 90-year mission of helping the sick of every nation from its base in the smallest country on Earth.

Questions	Strategic Thinking
1. A) NO CHANGE B) to provide C) providing them D) ensuring availability of	**Step 1: Read the passage and identify the issue** The underlined verb ("providing") is not parallel to the verbs used earlier in the sentence ("to protect and defend"). **Step 2: Eliminate answer choices that do not address the issue** Eliminate A, C, and D because they do not correct the parallelism error. **Step 3: Plug in the remaining answer choices and select the most correct, concise, and relevant one** Choice (B) is correct.
2. A) NO CHANGE B) Then Napoleon is driving C) Napoleon drove D) Napoleon drives	**Step 1: Read the passage and identify the issue** The verb in the underlined portion is in a different tense from the other verbs in this paragraph. A writer can shift verb tense only when there is a logical reason to do so. In this instance, the writer does not have a reason to switch tenses; the earlier verbs are in the simple past tense, which indicates that the action occurred at some point in the past. **Step 2: Eliminate answer choices that do not address the issue** Eliminate A, B, and D because they are not in the simple past tense. **Step 3: Plug in the remaining answer choices and select the most correct, concise, and relevant one** Choice (C) is correct.

Reading & Writing

Questions	Strategic Thinking

3. A) NO CHANGE
 	
  B) creed, establishing
 	
  C) creed establishing
 	
  D) creed; establishing
	Step 1: Read the passage and identify the issue
	
	The second sentence in the underlined portion is a fragment because it is missing a predicate verb. Eliminate A.
	
	Step 2: Eliminate answer choices that do not address the issue
	
	Eliminate C because it creates a run-on sentence. Eliminate D because it does not correct the sentence fragment.
	
	Step 3: Plug in the remaining answer choices and select the most correct, concise, and relevant one
	
	Choice (B) is correct.

You have seen the ways in which the SAT tests you on Sentence Structure in Writing & Language passages and the way an SAT expert approaches these types of questions.

Use the Kaplan Method for Writing & Language to answer the three questions that accompany the following Writing & Language passage excerpt. Remember to look at the strategic thinking questions that have been laid out for you—some of the answers have been filled in, but you will have to complete the answers to others.

Use your answers to the strategic thinking questions to select the correct answer, just as you will on Test Day.

Questions 4-6 are based on the following passage.

The Sun

It is perhaps impossible to overestimate the impact of the Sun on our planet Earth. Functioning like a great thermonuclear reactor situated roughly 100 million miles away, the Sun provides essentially all of Earth's heat in the form of radiant energy, without which there would be no light, warmth, plants, or animals. In addition, with a core temperature of nearly 30 million degrees Fahrenheit, the Sun affects all of Earth's natural phenomena, including all weather and atmospheric movement. Even the energy sources we use daily to fuel our cars and heat our homes, resources like oil and coal harvested from deep within the Earth's crust, were produced by the power of the Sun acting upon living organisms millions of years ago. Yet, **4** while its ability to provide heat and light can be easily felt by simply lying out on a beach or gazing up into a brilliant blue sky, closer inspection of the Sun's dynamic surface through special telescopes has revealed activity capable of affecting Earth in less obvious ways.

Technically classified by scientists as a yellow dwarf star and thought to be approximately 4 billion years old, the Sun has a constantly changing surface that is actually quite stormy. However, it is not the visually dramatic gas particle eruptions that constitute the Sun's most volatile surface activity. Instead, **5** they are the seemingly static black spots that pepper the surface, referred to by scientists as sunspots, that are the true storms. At roughly half the Sun's surface temperature of 10,300 degrees Fahrenheit, sunspots are by far the coolest areas of the Sun, which is why they appear darker than the hotter plasma that surrounds them. And, although in telescopic images these spots appear as little more than tiny black specks, they can be more than 19,000 miles across—wide enough to fit two Earths with orbiting moons.

Historical records show that these spots were first viewed by telescope as early as 1610, but scientists today still know relatively little about them. Almost always seen in pairs, sunspots are thought to be **6** powerfully created by magnetic fields that keep heat from flowing up to the Sun's surface. Scientists have also noticed that these spots seem to erupt and fade in 11-year cycles, manifesting incessant change that is thought to affect the Sun's luminosity and, in turn, Earth's climate. In addition, studies have shown that the charged particles released by sunspots can react with Earth's magnetic field and disrupt satellite communications, radio broadcasts, and even cell phone calls. As scientists continue to carefully observe such occurrences, referred to as space weather, they gain a greater understanding of the powerful ability of the Sun to impact our lives.

Questions	Strategic Thinking
4. A) NO CHANGE B) when C) with D) because	**Step 1: Read the passage and identify the issue** *What part of speech is underlined?* A subordinating conjunction. *What does a subordinating conjunction do?* It helps to join an independent clause with a dependent clause. **Step 2: Eliminate answer choices that do not address the issue** *What answer choice(s) can you eliminate?* _____ _____ _____ **Step 3: Plug in the remaining answer choices and select the most correct, concise, and relevant one** *What is the correct answer?* _____

Questions	Strategic Thinking
5. A) NO CHANGE B) they are not C) we are D) it is	**Step 1: Read the passage and identify the issue** *What is the issue?* Pronoun consistency. *What pronoun is used in the sentence before the one to which the underlined portion belongs?* "It." *To what does the underlined pronoun refer?* _____ _____ **Step 2: Eliminate answer choices that do not address the issue** *What answer choice(s) can you eliminate?* _____ _____ _____ **Step 3: Plug in the remaining answer choices and select the most correct, concise, and relevant one** *What is the correct answer?*_____

Reading & Writing

Questions	Strategic Thinking
6. A) NO CHANGE B) created by powerful magnetic C) powerful created by magnetic D) strongly created by magnetic	**Step 1: Read the passage and identify the issue** *What is the issue?* Modifier placement and form. *What type of modifier is included in the underlined segment?* _____ *What should the adverb ("powerfully") logically modify?* _____ *Based on what the adverb ("powerfully") should logically modify, what part of speech should it be?* _____ **Step 2: Eliminate answer choices that do not address the issue** *What answer choice(s) can you eliminate?* _____ _____ _____ **Step 3: Plug in the remaining answer choices and select the most correct, concise, and relevant one** *What is the correct answer?*_____

Reading & Writing

Now try a test-like Writing & Language passage on your own. Give yourself 5 minutes to read the passage and answer the questions.

Questions 7-14 are based on the following passage.

Sergei Eisenstein

Considered the father of the montage, a popular cinematic technique that involves a rapid succession of shots, often superimposed, [7] one of the principal architects of the modern movie was the Russian director Sergei Eisenstein. Although his career was not particularly prolific—he completed only seven feature-length films—Eisenstein's work contains a clarity and sharpness of composition that make the depth of his plots and the powerful complexity of his juxtaposed images easily accessible to most [8] viewers, in fact, few filmmakers were more instrumental in pushing the envelope of the established, conservative nineteenth-century Victorian theatre than Eisenstein, whose films helped to usher in a new era of abstract thought and expression in art.

Born in 1898 in what is now the independent nation of Latvia, Eisenstein grew up in affluence as the son of a successful architect. Following in his father's footsteps, he studied at the Institute of Civil Engineering in Petrograd. After the Bolshevik Revolution of 1917, however, Eisenstein was pushed out of academics [9] and into the service of the Red Army as an engineer. When the Russian Civil War ended, Eisenstein sought to leave his work for the new Soviet state behind him. He quickly found employment in show business as a set

7. A) NO CHANGE
   B) Sergei Eisenstein, the Russian director, was one of the principal architects of the modern movie.
   C) the Russian director Sergei Eisenstein was one of the principal architects of the modern movie.
   D) one of the principal architects of the modern movie was Sergei Eisenstein, the Russian director.

8. A) NO CHANGE
   B) viewers. In fact,
   C) viewers—in fact,
   D) viewers in fact,

9. A) NO CHANGE
   B) nor
   C) or
   D) as far as

designer for a prominent Moscow theatre, but the new communist government [10] <u>was likely to remain</u> a heavy influence throughout his career.

It was with [11] <u>Eisenstein's</u> feature debut, a film entitled *Statchka* released in 1924, that Eisenstein introduced moviegoers to the montage. Expanding upon a complex theory of biomechanics, the study of the mechanical forces at work within a particular body or organ, Eisenstein's first montage consisted of a powerful sequence of conflicting images that were able to abbreviate time spans in the film while introducing new metaphors and allusions to the storyline. Essentially, Eisenstein sought to use the montage to create a [12] <u>regressive emotional ef-</u><u>fect that was greater than the sum of the individual shots.</u> It was with this enormously successful technique that Eisenstein's work caught the eye of the new Communist Party leaders in Moscow, who saw in his cinematic style a film for the [13] <u>"common man." And</u> a chance to use his skills as a propaganda tool for the state.

Eisenstein's second and third films, [14] <u>the enor-</u><u>mously famous 1925 hit *Battleship Potemkin* and the</u> <u>1927 celebration of the October Revolution, *Oktibr*,</u> still widely considered to be masterpieces, were commissioned by party officials in an attempt to use Eisenstein's mass appeal to disseminate Soviet propaganda. As a result, these achievements have been frequently criticized for their lack of artistic integrity. Yet, in the end, regardless of politics, Eisenstein's films continue to have an undeniably significant and lasting impact on filmmakers.

10. A) NO CHANGE
    B) remained
    C) did likely remain
    D) remains

11. A) NO CHANGE
    B) Sergei Eisenstein's
    C) its
    D) his

12. A) NO CHANGE
    B) regressive that was greater than the sum of the individual shots.
    C) detrimental emotional effect that was greater than the sum of the individual shots.
    D) cumulative emotional effect that was greater than the sum of the individual shots.

13. A) NO CHANGE
    B) "common man," and
    C) "common man" and
    D) "common man" and,

14. A) NO CHANGE
    B) the enormously famous 1925 hit and the 1927 celebration of the October Revolution, *Battleship Potemkin* and *Oktibr*,
    C) the famously enormous 1925 hit *Battleship Potemkin* and the 1927 celebration of the October Revolution, *Oktibr*,
    D) the 1925 film *Battleship Potemkin* and the 1927 film *Oktibr*,

Answers & Explanations for this chapter begin on page 1015.

EXTRA PRACTICE

The following questions provide an opportunity to practice the concepts and strategic thinking covered in this chapter. While many of the questions pertain to Sentence Structure, some touch on other concepts tested on the Writing & Language Test to ensure that your practice is test-like, with a variety of question types per passage.

Questions 1-11 are based on the following passage.

The Experts of Visual Communication

[1] The digital explosion of the past two decades has resulted in decreased costs of devices for the average consumer. From early cave painters and the intricate craftspeople of ancient worlds to the vast, magnificent artwork that has emerged across countless generations and cultures, art accomplishes fascinating measures of human communication. In today's world, the [2] prominent arena in which art and communication meet is graphic design. The digital age has seen an explosion of media and connectivity. This offers an ever-growing platform for art, through graphic design, to deliver ideas and messages.

Incorporating creativity, communication knowledge, and technological expertise, graphic designers fashion messages for the public eye. Their work is peppered throughout Western life. [3] Business logos; billboard advertisements; website layouts, T-shirt designs; and even the decorated cardboard of cereal boxes and coffee cups feature graphic design. In a culture increasingly wired for visual communication, graphic designers

1. Which choice provides the most appropriate introduction to the passage?
   A) NO CHANGE
   B) Throughout history, visual art has contested verbal communication in its power to convey meaning.
   C) In recent times, cell phone and tablet use have rendered the desktop computer nearly obsolete.
   D) Because of the increasing use of wireless communication, new laws will be needed to regulate usage.

2. A) NO CHANGE
   B) obscure
   C) inconspicuous
   D) distinguished

3. A) NO CHANGE
   B) Business logos, billboard advertisements—website layouts, T-shirt designs, and even the decorated cardboard of cereal boxes and coffee cups feature graphic design.
   C) Business logos and billboard advertisements and website layouts, T-shirt designs, and even the decorated cardboard of cereal boxes and coffee cups feature graphic design.
   D) Business logos, billboard advertisements, website layouts, T-shirt designs, and even the decorated cardboard of cereal boxes and coffee cups feature graphic design.

are the artists of today's media. **4** <u>They create and craft the medium and formats, visual images, and symbols that add vibrancy and color to this world and shape the way information is passed, transmitted, and received.</u>

[1] How do these powerful innovators navigate a career path? [2] Most begin by studying graphic design in a bachelor's degree program. [3] Here they build skills through highly interactive class settings to **5** <u>teach</u> expertise. [4] These programs are heavily project-based, mirroring the sort of experience professional work will entail. [5] Once students have graduated, these portfolios are essential for the job search, revealing an artist's excellence and creative potential. [6] Students gradually compile design portfolios to showcase their best work. **6**

Job competition for graphic designers is rigorous, but graphic design features a variety of professional options. Some work in design studios. **7** <u>There they team with other graphic designers, taking on projects for external clients.</u> Others work "in-house"

4. A) NO CHANGE

   B) They create and craft the medium and formats, visual images, and symbols that add color to this world and shape the way information is passed, transmitted, and received.

   C) They craft the formats, images, and symbols that color this world and shape the way information is passed and received.

   D) They create the formats, visual images, and symbols that add color to this world and shape the way information is passed, transmitted, and received.

5. A) NO CHANGE

   B) hone

   C) fulfill

   D) discipline

6. To make this paragraph most logical, sentence 6 should be placed

   A) where it is now.

   B) after sentence 2.

   C) after sentence 3.

   D) after sentence 4.

7. A) NO CHANGE

   B) There they team with other graphic designers; taking on projects for external clients.

   C) There they team with other graphic designers. Taking on projects for external clients.

   D) There they team with other graphic designers—taking on projects for external clients.

for businesses that staff their own graphic designers to create media on a more consistent basis. Those with more entrepreneurial inclinations can work as freelance graphic designers, doing their own networking and contracting. **8**

8. At this point, the writer wants to add information that supports the main topic of the paragraph. Which choice provides the most relevant detail?

A) Often, graphic designers are encouraged by employers to obtain a master's degree.

B) Some graphic designers return to the university to pursue business administration degrees.

C) Increasingly, graphic designers are taking their skills online and transferring them to website and web application design, which is another growing field for tech-minded artists.

D) Graphic designers often earn less as freelancers than their counterparts who are employed by design studios.

Reading & Writing

[9] Because the demand for graphic designers continues, the highly competitive job market gives some prospective artists pause. The trope of the "struggling artist" holds true, it seems, even in this visually dominant generation. [10] Most graphic designers find their careers not only satisfying, but also one of invigoration. Perhaps, for those brave artists who follow this career path, the thrill and beauty of the work yields enough motivation and inspiration to persevere and succeed. [11]

9. A) NO CHANGE
   B) Although
   C) Since
   D) Consequently,

10. A) NO CHANGE
    B) Most graphic designers find their careers satisfying, in addition to being vigorous.
    C) Most graphic designers find their careers not only satisfying, but also invigorating.
    D) Most graphic designers find their careers to be not only one of satisfaction, but also invigorating.

11. Which choice, if added here, would provide the most relevant detail to this paragraph?
    A) Graphic designers experience creative opportunities not offered by other careers.
    B) This visually dominant generation spends more on entertainment than any previous age group.
    C) Perseverance is vital to a successful career, but luck plays an important factor, too.
    D) Graphic designers, along with physical therapists, experience the most competitive job markets.

Questions 12-22 are based on the following passage.

Musical Enjoyment: Better in Numbers?

Music is many things to many 12 people: a mode of expression, an escape, or a way to understand life experiences. Although its prominence in global culture has stayed the same, music has changed considerably since its prehistoric invention. 13 Music has evolved from a primarily group-enjoyed art form into one consumed mostly on an individual basis.

Researchers have no way of knowing who first invented music, 14 but educated guesses can be made about the purposes it served. It is hypothesized that in the Prehistoric Era, early humans used sounds like hand clapping and foot stomping to create rhythmic repetition. 15 For instance, art in both Stone Age cave paintings and later Persian cave paintings shows examples of people using handmade instruments to create music in a group setting. The sounds produced were an early form of communication. The use of music as a tool opened early humans 16 up to one another. Advancing social bonding even in an age before common languages.

12. A) NO CHANGE

B) people, a mode of expression, an escape, or a way

C) people; a mode of expression; an escape; or a way

D) people: a mode of expression or an escape or a way

13. A) NO CHANGE

B) Music has evolved from an art form that has been primarily enjoyed by groups

C) Music has evolved from a group art form

D) Primarily, music as a group art form has evolved

14. A) NO CHANGE

B) but they can make educated guesses about the purposes it served

C) but educated guesses of the purposes it served have been made

D) but educated guesses are made about the purposes it served

15. A) NO CHANGE

B) Similarly

C) For example

D) In other words

16. Which choice most effectively combines the sentences at the underlined portion?

A) up to one another while advancing

B) up to one another; this advanced

C) up to one another, advancing

D) up to one another, a tool advancing

17 In ancient Egypt, musicians were appointed to play for specific gods. In addition to enhancing religious ceremonies, music was used in the royal court. Gifted musicians were hired to honor the pharaoh and impress guests of the royal family. In American history, music has been used as a vehicle for storytelling. At the time of the Underground Railroad, music was used to deliver messages to groups of people trying to escape slavery. Directions were embedded 18 <u>in lyrics that were well-known to many.</u> Although these examples are very different, they highlight how music was used to encourage social bonding.

[1] With the 19 <u>advent</u> of headphones in 1910, music was changed from an inherently social experience to a personal one. [2] Based on Thomas Edison's discovery of sound created by electrical signals, Nathaniel Baldwin created the first headset that could amplify sound. [3] This invention has been greatly improved upon since. [4] Instead of music being primarily used in group settings, it became a highly individual form of entertainment. [5] While this is seen as a positive departure, studies link the use of headphones to feelings of isolation and decreased personal satisfaction. [6] With music becoming more portable than ever, headphones have enabled people to listen to music in almost any situation, including on their way to work, at the workplace, and at home while their families listen to their own choice of music. 20

17. Which choice creates the most cohesive transition from the previous paragraph?

A) More recent examples show music primarily becoming a source of entertainment.

B) Music became a notable social bonding tool among wealthy and aristocratic circles.

C) Music from Egypt traveled to America and helped convey the importance of social bonding.

D) Further examples throughout history show the development of music as a social bonding tool.

18. A) NO CHANGE

B) in lyrics that included references to famous abolitionists

C) in popular lyrics, hiding helpful instructions in plain sight

D) in lyrics that were typically banned by plantation owners

19. A) NO CHANGE

B) enhancement

C) prevalence

D) prohibition

20. To make this paragraph most logical, sentence 5 should be placed

A) where it is now.

B) after sentence 2.

C) before sentence 4.

D) after sentence 6.

Reading & Writing

21 Psychologists' and sociologists' hypothesize that the shift in music from a social to an individual enjoyment contributes to a high number of people reporting feelings of loneliness in recent studies. While the long-term psychological effects of this shift will take time to analyze, it is already apparent that humans are less connected in their enjoyment of something we have shared throughout history. **22**

21. A)   NO CHANGE

    B)   Psychologists and sociologists'

    C)   Psychologist's and sociologist's

    D)   Psychologists and sociologists

22. Which choice, if added to this paragraph, would best support the author's claims?

    A)   The number of people reporting feelings of loneliness in recent studies

    B)   Which psychologists and sociologists are making these claims

    C)   The specific differences in the ways humans have shared music over time

    D)   Which long-term psychological effects may be related to using headphones

Reading & Writing

Conventions of Usage

CHAPTER OBJECTIVES

By the end of this chapter, you will be able to:

1. Recognize and correct errors in pronoun clarity, grammatical agreement, and logical comparison

2. Distinguish among commonly confused possessive determiners, contractions, and adverbs

3. Recognize and correct incorrectly constructed idioms and frequently misused words

SMARTPOINTS

Point Value	SmartPoint Category
40 Points	Usage

CONVENTIONS OF USAGE

Chapter 24

Homework

Extra Practice: #1-11

Even More

Writing & Language Quiz 5

Key

 Book Assignment

 Online Video Assignment

 Online Quiz Assignment

Reading & Writing

PRONOUNS

A pronoun is ambiguous if the noun to which it refers (its antecedent) is either missing or unclear. On the SAT, you must be able to recognize either situation and make the appropriate correction. When you see an underlined pronoun, make sure you can find the specific noun to which it refers.

Missing Antecedent

- *When the flight arrived, **they** told the passengers to stay seated until the plane reached the gate.* (The pronoun "they" does not have an antecedent in this sentence.)

- *When the flight arrived, **the flight crew** told the passengers to stay seated until the plane reached the gate.* (Replacing the pronoun with a specific noun clarifies the meaning.)

Unclear Antecedent

- *Kayla asked Mia to drive Sree to the airport because **she** was running late.* (The pronoun "she" could refer to any of the three people mentioned in the sentence.)

- *Because Kayla was running late, **she** asked Mia to drive Sree to the airport.* (The pronoun "she" now unambiguously refers to Kayla.)

> ✔ **Definition**
>
> The **antecedent** is the noun that the pronoun replaces or stands in for elsewhere in the sentence. To identify the **antecedent** of a pronoun, check the nouns near the pronoun. Substitute those nouns for the pronoun to see which one makes sense.

AGREEMENT

Pronoun-Antecedent Agreement

Pronouns must agree with their antecedents not only in person and number, but also in gender. Only third-person pronouns make distinctions based on gender.

Gender	Example
Feminine	*Because Yvonne had a question, **she** raised her hand.*
Masculine	*Since **he** had lots of homework, Rico started working right away.*
Neutral	*The rain started slowly, but then **it** became a downpour.*
Unspecified	*If a traveler is lost, **he or she** should ask for directions.*

Pronoun-Case Agreement

There are three pronoun cases:

1. Subjective case: The pronoun is used as the subject

2. Objective case: The pronoun is used as the object of a verb or a preposition

3. Possessive case: The pronoun expresses ownership

Subjective Case	I, you, she, he, it, we, you, they, who
Objective Case	me, you, her, him, it, us, you, them, whom
Possessive Case	my, mine, your, yours, his, her, hers, its, our, ours, their, theirs, whose

✔ Expert Tip

When there are two pronouns or a noun and a pronoun in a compound structure, drop the other noun to confirm which pronoun case to use. For example: *Leo and me walk into town.* Would you say, "Me walk into town"? No, you would say, "I walk into town." Therefore, the correct case is subjective and the original sentence should read *Leo and I walk into town.*

✔ Remember

Use "who" when a sentence refers to "she," "he," or "I." (*Quynh was the person **who** provided the best answer.*) Use "whom" when a sentence refers to "her," "him," or "me." (*With **whom** did Aaron attend the event?*)

Subject-Verb Agreement

A verb must agree with its subject in person and number:

- Singular: *The **apple tastes** delicious.*
- Plural: ***Apples taste** delicious.*

The noun closest to a verb may not be its subject: *The **chair** with the cabriole legs **is** an antique.* The noun closest to the verb in this sentence ("is," which is singular) is "legs," which is plural. However, the verb's subject is "chair," so the sentence is correct as written.

Only the conjunction *and* forms a compound subject requiring a plural verb form:

- *Saliyah **and** Taylor **are** in the running club.*
- ***Either** Saliyah **or** Taylor **is** in the running club.*
- ***Neither** Saliyah **nor** Taylor **is** in the running club.*

Noun-Number Agreement

Related nouns must be consistent in number:

- **Students** *applying for college must submit their* **applications** *on time.* (The sentence refers to multiple students, and they all must submit applications.)

FREQUENTLY CONFUSED WORDS

English contains many pairs of words that sound alike but are spelled differently and have different meanings.

ACCEPT/EXCEPT: To *accept* is to take or receive something that is offered: *My neighbor said he would accept my apology for trampling over his rose beds as long as I helped weed them in the spring.* To *except* is to leave out or exclude: *The soldier was excepted from combat duty because he had poor field vision. Except* is usually used as a preposition that signifies "with the exception of, excluding:" *When the receptionist found out that everyone except him had received a raise, he demanded a salary increase as well.*

AFFECT/EFFECT: To *affect* is to have an influence on something: *Eli refused to let the rain affect his plans for a picnic, so he sat under an umbrella and ate his sandwich.* An *affect* is an emotion or behavior: *The guidance counselor noticed that more outdoor time resulted in improved student affect.* To *effect* is to bring something about or cause something to happen: *The young activist received an award for effecting a change in her community.* An *effect* is an influence or a result: *The newspaper article about homeless animals had such an effect on Zarak that he brought home three kittens from the shelter. Affect* is most often used in its verb form, and *effect* is most often used in its noun form.

AFFLICT/INFLICT: To *afflict* is to torment or distress someone or something. It usually appears as a passive verb: *Jeff is afflicted with frequent migraine headaches.* To *inflict* is to impose punishment or suffering on someone or something: *No one dared displease the king, for he was known to inflict severe punishments on those who upset him.*

ALLUSION/ILLUSION: An *allusion* is an indirect reference to something, a hint: *The teacher's comment about the most enigmatic smile in art history was not lost on Sophie; this allusion could only be a reference to Leonardo da Vinci's* Mona Lisa. An *illusion* is a false, misleading, or deceptive appearance: *A magician creates the illusion that something has disappeared by hiding it faster than the eye can follow it.*

EMIGRATE/IMMIGRATE: To *emigrate* is to leave one country for another country. It is usually used with the preposition *from: Many people emigrated from Europe in search of better living conditions.* To *immigrate* is to enter a country to take up permanent residence there. It is usually used with the preposition *to: They immigrated to North America because land was plentiful.*

EMINENT/IMMINENT: Someone who is *eminent* is prominent or outstanding: *The eminent archeologist Dr. Wong has identified the artifact as prehistoric in origin.* Something that is *imminent* is likely to happen soon or is impending: *After being warned that the hurricane's arrival was imminent, beachfront residents left their homes immediately.*

LAY/LIE: To *lay* is to place or put something down and is usually followed by a "something"—a direct object: *Before she begins to paint, Emily lays all of her pencils, brushes, and paints on her worktable to avoid interruptions while she draws and paints.* One form, *laid*, serves as the simple past and the past participle of *lay*: *I laid my necklace on the counter, just where Rebecca had put hers.* To *lie* is to recline, to be in a lying position or at rest. This verb never takes a direct object: you do not lie anything down. The simple past form of *lie* is *lay*; the past participle is *lain*. Notice that the past form of *lie* is identical with the present form of *lay*. This coincidence complicates the task of distinguishing the related meanings of *lay* and *lie*: *Having laid the picnic cloth under the sycamore, they lay in the shady grass all last Sunday afternoon.*

RAISE/RISE: *Raise* means to lift up, or to cause to rise or grow, and it is paired with a direct object: you *raise* weights, roof beams, tomato plants, or children. *Raise* is a regular verb. *The trade tariff on imported leather goods raised the prices of Italian shoes.* To *rise* is to get up, to go up, or to be built up. This verb is never paired with a direct object: you do not *rise* something. The past and past participle forms are irregular; *rose* is the simple past tense, while *risen* is the past participle. *Long-distance commuters must rise early and return home late.*

SET/SIT: The difference between *set* and *sit* is very similar to the difference between *lay* and *lie* and between *raise* and *rise*. To *set* is to put or place, settle or arrange something. However, *set* takes on other specific meanings when it is combined with several different prepositions, so always think carefully about the meaning of the word in the sentence. *Set* is an irregular verb because it has one form that serves as present tense, past tense, and past participle. *Set* usually has a direct object: you *set* a ladder against the fence, a value on family heirlooms, or a date for the family reunion: *The professor set the students' chairs in a semicircle to promote open discussion.* To *sit* is to take a seat or to be in a seated position, to rest somewhere, or to occupy a place. This verb does not usually have a direct object: *The beach house sits on a hill at some distance from the shoreline.* When *sit* doesn't make sense, consider the word *sat*: *The usher sat us in the center seats of the third row from the stage.*

Other pairs of words do not sound alike but have similar meanings that are often confused:

AMONG/BETWEEN: The preposition *among* refers to collective arrangements; use it when referring to three or more people or items. *The soccer team shared dozens of oranges among themselves.* *Between* is also a preposition, but it refers to only two people or items: *Amy and Tonia split the tasks between them.*

AMOUNT/NUMBER: *Amount* is used in reference to mass nouns (also known as uncountable nouns): *The amount of bravery displayed was awe-inspiring.* *Number* is used in reference to countable nouns: *The recipe calls for a specific number of eggs.*

LESS/FEWER: *Less* should be used only with mass nouns, which are grammatically singular: *Diana's yard has less wildlife than mine.* One common misuse of *less* is a sign you probably encounter frequently at the supermarket: The *10 items or less* sign should actually be *10 items or fewer*, because the items are countable. *Fewer* should be used when referring to countable objects and concepts: *Diana's yard has fewer squirrels than mine.*

MUCH/MANY: *Much* modifies things that cannot be counted, often singular nouns: *Jim has much more money than I do. Many,* on the other hand, modifies things that can be counted, such as plural nouns. *Samantha has many awards in her collection.*

The SAT will also test your ability to correctly use and identify possessive pronouns, contractions, and adverbs that sound the same:

ITS/IT'S: *Its* is a possessive pronoun like *his* and *hers: The rare book would be worth more if its cover weren't ripped. It's* is a contraction that can mean *it is, it has,* or *it was: It's been a long time since I last saw you.*

THEIR/THEY'RE/THERE: *Their* is a possessive form of the pronoun *they: The players respected their coach. They're* is a contraction of *they are: The students say they're planning to attend college. There* is used to introduce a sentence or indicate a location: *There was plenty of water in the well when we arrived there.*

THEIRS/THERE'S: *Theirs* is the possessive plural form of the pronoun *they: The team was ecstatic when it was announced that the prize was theirs. There's* is a contraction of *there is* or *there has: There's been a lot of rain this summer.*

WHOSE/WHO'S: *Whose* is a possessive pronoun used to refer to people or things: *Whose phone is ringing? Who's* is a contraction of *who is* or *who has: Who's planning to join us for dinner?*

COMPARISONS

The SAT will test your ability to recognize and correct improper comparisons. There are three rules governing correct comparisons:

1. Compare Logical Things

   The **price of tea** has risen sharply, while **coffee** has remained the same.

   This sentence incorrectly compares *the price of tea* to *coffee*. The sentence should read: *The* **price of tea** *has risen sharply, while the* **price of coffee** *has remained the same.*

2. Use Parallel Structure

   On a sunny day, I enjoy **hiking** *and* **to read** *outside.*

   This sentence incorrectly uses the gerund verb form (*hiking*) and then switches to the infinitive verb form (*to read*). To correct the sentence, make sure the verb forms are consistent: *On a sunny day, I enjoy* **hiking** *and* **reading** *outside.*

3. Structure Comparisons Correctly

*Some animals are **better** at endurance running **than** they are at sprinting.*
*Others are **as** good at endurance running **as** they are at sprinting.*
Both of these sentences are correctly structured: the first with the use of *better . . . than,* and
the second with the use of *as . . . as.*

When comparing like things, use adjectives that match the number of items being compared. When
comparing two items or people, use the comparative form of the adjective. When comparing three
or more items or people, use the superlative form.

Comparative	Superlative
Use when comparing two items.	Use when comparing three or more items.
better	best
more	most
newer	newest
older	oldest
shorter	shortest
taller	tallest
worse	worst
younger	youngest

IDIOMS

An **idiom** is a combination of words that must be used together to convey either a figurative or
literal meaning. Idioms are tested in four ways on the SAT:

1. Proper Preposition Usage in Context

*The three finalists will compete **for** the grand prize: an all-inclusive cruise to Bali.*
*Roger will compete **against** Rafael in the final round of the tournament.*
*I will compete **with** Deborah in the synchronized swimming competition.*

2. Verb Forms

*The architect likes **to draft** floor plans.*
*The architect enjoys **drafting** floor plans.*

3. Idiomatic Expressions

Idiomatic expressions refer to words or phrases that must be used together to be correct.

*Simone will **either** continue sleeping **or** get up and get ready for school.*
***Neither** the principal **nor** the teachers will tolerate tardiness.*
*This fall, Shari is playing **not only** soccer **but also** field hockey.*

4. Implicit Double Negatives

Some words imply a negative and therefore cannot be paired with an explicit negative.

*Janie **cannot hardly** wait for summer vacation.*

This sentence is incorrect as written. It should read: *Janie **can hardly** wait for summer vacation.*

Frequently Tested Prepositions	Idiomatic Expressions	Words That Can't Be Paired with Negative Words
at	as . . . as	barely
by	between . . . and	hardly
for	both . . . and	scarcely
from	either . . . or	
of	neither . . . nor	
on	just as . . . so too	
to	not only . . . but also	
with	prefer . . . to	

Let's look at the following Writing & Language passage and questions. After the passage, there are two columns. The left column contains test-like questions. The column on the right features the strategic thinking a test expert employs when approaching the passage and questions presented.

Questions 1-4 are based on the following passage.

Akira Kurosawa

What do samurai,[1] cowboys, shogun,[2] gangsters, peasants, and William Shakespeare all have in common? These are just some of the varied influences on the work of Akira Kurosawa (1910–1998), a Japanese film director considered by movie critic Leonard Maltin to be "one of the undisputed giants of cinema." Over his career, Kurosawa's unique blend of Western themes and Eastern settings made him arguably the **1** more important Japanese filmmaker in history.

Kurosawa's style reflects his own experiences. As a young man, he studied Western art and literature, deciding to be a painter. However, World War II led Kurosawa to film; he acted as an assistant director of wartime propaganda films in Tokyo. After Japan's surrender in 1945, he took the lessons he learned in Tokyo and began making his own films— **2** work that took the values and traditions of the West and reinterpreted them with a Japanese sensibility, using distinctly Japanese settings and characters.

The most famous example of Kurosawa's style is his 1954 film *Seven Samurai*. Although the setting is medieval Japan, with peasants and samurai, its story is influenced by Western films: a group of villagers, terrorized by local bandits, turn to seven down-on-their-luck yet good-hearted samurai for their protection. Like movie cowboys, the samurai are romantic heroes, sure of their morals and battling clear forces of evil. This contrasts with the traditional Japanese version of a samurai as a noble and often distant symbol of Japan's imperial heritage. To **3** him, the film's samurai were distinctly human characters, with both a conscience and the will to act to correct the wrongs around them.

Although Kurosawa's films enjoyed—and still enjoy—a lofty reputation in the West, Japanese audiences have regarded his work with suspicion. By using Western ideals and themes—even reinterpreting Western authors such as William Shakespeare and Fyodor Dostoyevsky—Kurosawa is viewed by many critics and moviegoers in his home country as **4** neither original nor particularly Japanese. They see his using Japanese culture as mere "window dressing" applied to what were essentially foreign stories. Ironically, it was Kurosawa's success that opened the door for other, more "Japanese" directors, such as Yasujiro Ozu and Kenji Mizoguchi, to gain a wider audience.

Regardless of the criticism, Kurosawa's effect on Western filmmaking is beyond dispute. Ironically, Kurosawa's films have influenced the very same American movie genres that Kurosawa admired so much. *Seven Samurai* became the basis for the American Western epic *The Magnificent Seven. Yojimbo,* another story of a samurai for hire, strongly influenced the film *A Fistful of Dollars.* Other genres benefited from Kurosawa's work as well; *Rashomon,* a crime story told from different points of view, has influenced almost every crime movie since. Finally, *The Hidden Fortress,* about two peasants escorting a princess during a war, became George Lucas's expressed basis for the science fiction masterpiece *Star Wars.*

[1] samurai: noble warriors of medieval Japan, similar to European knights
[2] shogun: military dictators of Japan from 1603 to 1868

Questions	Strategic Thinking
1. A) NO CHANGE B) important C) most important D) least important	**Step 1: Read the passage and identify the issue** The underlined portion contains the word "more," which is an adjective used to compare two items. In this instance, the author is comparing Kurosawa to all other Japanese filmmakers. **Step 2: Eliminate answer choices that do not address the issue** Eliminate A because more than two items are being compared. Eliminate B because it removes the comparison. Eliminate D because it changes the meaning of the sentence. **Step 3: Plug in the remaining answer choices and select the most correct, concise, and relevant one** Choice (C) is correct.
2. A) NO CHANGE B) works C) working D) idea	**Step 1: Read the passage and identify the issue** The underlined word is used as a synonym for the word that precedes the dash; however, the singular noun, "work," does not match the plural noun, "films." **Step 2: Eliminate answer choices that do not address the issue** Eliminate A because the singular "work" does not agree with the plural "films." Eliminate C because "working" is a verb, not a noun. Eliminate D because it changes the author's meaning. **Step 3: Plug in the remaining answer choices and select the most correct, concise, and relevant one** Choice (B) is correct.

Questions	Strategic Thinking
3. A) NO CHANGE B) them C) Kurosawa D) the samurai	**Step 1: Read the passage and identify the issue** The underlined pronoun's antecedent is unclear. **Step 2: Eliminate answer choices that do not address the issue** The most logical antecedent of the underlined pronoun "him" is Akira Kurosawa. Eliminate A because it is ambiguous as written. Eliminate B because it is also ambiguous. Eliminate D because the pronoun does not refer to "the samurai." **Step 3: Plug in the remaining answer choices and select the most correct, concise, and relevant one** Choice (C) is correct.
4. A) NO CHANGE B) either C) never D) both	**Step 1: Read the passage and identify the issue** The underlined word is part of an idiomatic expression. "Neither . . . nor" is a common idiomatic expression; both "neither" and "nor" must be used for the idiom to be used correctly. **Step 2: Eliminate answer choices that do not address the issue** Eliminate B, C, and D because the sentence later uses the word "nor," which means "neither" must precede it. **Step 3: Plug in the remaining answer choices and select the most correct, concise, and relevant one** Choice (A) is correct.

You have seen the ways in which the SAT tests you on Conventions of Usage in Writing & Language passages and the way an SAT expert approaches these types of questions.

Use the Kaplan Method for Writing & Language to answer the four questions that accompany the following Writing & Language passage excerpt. Remember to look at the strategic-thinking questions that have been laid out for you—some of the answers have been filled in, but you will have to complete the answers to others.

Use your answers to the strategic thinking questions to select the correct answer, just as you will on Test Day.

Questions 5-8 are based on the following passage.

Opossum

Commonly seen rooting through the trash or slipping down a sewer grate, the opossum is actually one of North America's **5** best animals. While its rodent-like body seems unremarkable at first glance, the opossum is actually closely related to the kangaroo and is the only marsupial native to this continent. Like all female marsupials, the female opossum has a pouch for carrying and nursing her young. After a 12-day gestation period, thought to be the shortest of any marsupial, between 5 and 25 blind and hairless babies instinctively crawl the two inches from the birth canal to the pouch. Upon arrival, they quickly attach themselves to a nipple, drawing constant nourishment from the mother for more than two months.

The distinctive features of the opossum go beyond its surprising relation to the kangaroo. **6** It boasts an incredible array of 50 razor-sharp teeth, the most of any mammal in the world. The opossum is also among the most primitive of animals, having lived during the time of the dinosaurs. It has survived for millions of years by adapting to diverse habitats—including dense urban areas—and food supplies. Opossums eat beetles and even earthworms as well as tree roots, eggs, vegetables, and fruit. Today, many opossums that live in areas densely populated by humans survive on garbage and small mice. Opossums thrive in fields and woodlands, but they can also survive by digging a nest under a building or deck.

Of course, the opossum does have vulnerabilities. Its average three-year life span is not unusual for its size, typically between two and three feet long. What is unusual is that opossums continue growing throughout their lifetimes. Such a state of constant development is linked with metabolic limitations **7** in the amount of food and energy that can be stored within the opossum's body, requiring that ready food sources be available year-round. In addition, opossums are highly susceptible to the cold, making it rather common to see opossums with frostbitten ears and tails. Nevertheless, opossums have displayed amazing resilience over the years, often surviving attacks from intimidating predators like dogs and even hawks. While the opossum's first reaction when threatened is to begin running to the nearest tree, **8** their primary defense is a nervous system reaction that, when sensing danger, throws the opossum's body into a catatonic state that dramatically slows its heart rate. The opossum will then begin to drool and appear dead, another trait that only adds to the fascinating nature of these animals.

Questions	Strategic Thinking

5. A) NO CHANGE
   B) most unusual
   C) better
   D) abnormal
	Step 1: Read the passage and identify the issue
	
	What is the issue?
	Comparisons. The underlined word is a superlative adjective, used to compare three or more items.
	
	Step 2: Eliminate answer choices that do not address the issue
	
	What answer choice(s) can you eliminate?
	_____
	_____
	_____
	
	Step 3: Plug in the remaining answer choices and select the most correct, concise, and relevant one
	
	*What is the correct answer?*_____

6. A) NO CHANGE
   B) They
   C) The kangaroo
   D) The opossum
	Step 1: Read the passage and identify the issue
	
	What is the issue?
	Pronoun clarity. The underlined word is a pronoun that begins a sentence.
	
	To what does the underlined pronoun refer?
	_____
	_____
	
	Step 2: Eliminate answer choices that do not address the issue
	
	What answer choice(s) can you eliminate?
	_____
	_____
	_____
	
	Step 3: Plug in the remaining answer choices and select the most correct, concise, and relevant one
	
	*What is the correct answer?*_____

Reading & Writing

Questions	Strategic Thinking
7. A) NO CHANGE B) with C) on D) for	**Step 1: Read the passage and identify the issue** *What is the issue?* Idioms. The underlined word is a preposition, so the question is likely testing proper preposition usage in context. **Step 2: Eliminate answer choices that do not address the issue** *What answer choice(s) can you eliminate?* _____ _____ _____ **Step 3: Plug in the remaining answer choices and select the most correct, concise, and relevant one** *What is the correct answer?*_____
8. A) NO CHANGE B) there C) its D) his	**Step 1: Read the passage and identify the issue** *What is the issue?* Pronoun-antecedent agreement. The underlined word is a pronoun in the middle of a sentence. *What is the underlined pronoun's antecedent?* _____ _____ **Step 2: Eliminate answer choices that do not address the issue** *What answer choice(s) can you eliminate?* _____ _____ _____ **Step 3: Plug in the remaining answer choices and select the most correct, concise, and relevant one** *What is the correct answer?*_____

Now try a test-like Writing & Language passage on your own. Give yourself 5 minutes to read the passage and answer the questions.

Questions 9-16 are based on the following passage.

The Hindenburg

Today, airships are seen mostly as advertisements hovering in the sky over sporting events. Such companies as Goodyear®, Metropolitan Life®, and Fuji Film® have all made use of "blimps" in this way. But before World War II, **9** airships—as well as other lighter-than-air vehicles—were used as modes of transportation. One in particular, the German airship *Hindenburg*, changed the fate of airships forever. In spectacular fashion, the *Hindenburg* revealed the downside of the use of airships in transportation.

Airships enjoyed many advantages in the early twentieth century, and the *Hindenburg* was considered one of a kind. When the 804-foot *Hindenburg* was launched in 1936, it was the **10** large airship in the world. Like most airships of the period, the *Hindenburg* was built with a solid frame that encased a simple balloon filled with a light gas—in this case, hydrogen. In an age when airplanes could not carry more than 10 passengers at a time, **11** they could initially carry 50 passengers, a capacity that was later upgraded to 72.

Despite these advantages, the *Hindenburg* was hampered by many of the same drawbacks as other airships. Tickets to fly in the *Hindenburg* were not affordable for most people. The massive amount of fuel needed not only to fill the balloon **12** and to power **13** it's propellers

9. A) NO CHANGE
   B) the blimp
   C) the airship
   D) airplanes

10. A) NO CHANGE
    B) largest
    C) big
    D) larger

11. A) NO CHANGE
    B) it
    C) the *Hindenburg*
    D) he

12. A) NO CHANGE
    B) but also
    C) and also
    D) nor

13. A) NO CHANGE
    B) its
    C) it is
    D) their

made this airship very expensive to operate. Even with all of that fuel, the *Hindenburg* flew at a mere 76 miles per hour—a snail's pace considering that it was used for transatlantic passenger service. Because an airship is essentially a balloon with an engine, it is extremely vulnerable to air currents and stormy weather, and the *Hindenburg* was no different.

The *Hindenburg's* fate, however, rested **14** by the most dangerous characteristic of these airships: hydrogen gas is extremely flammable. Any spark or flame that came near the gas could cause a horrific explosion, which is exactly what happened. On May 6, 1937, as the *Hindenburg* was landing in Lakehurst, New Jersey, it suddenly burst into flames, killing 36 of the 97 passengers and crew on board. This explosion, which ultimately destroyed the airship, was believed to have been caused by a discharge of electricity in the air, which reacted with a small leak in the **15** balloons.

However, when the disaster occurred, the airship was already obsolete as a mode of transportation. By the 1940s, commercial airplanes had advanced in development far beyond the airship's capacity. Today, airplanes cost much less to operate and fly at more than seven times the speed of the *Hindenburg*, and airline tickets are far more affordable. The airship thus became outdated as a mode of passenger service and acquired **16** their modern-day role as an advertising platform.

14. A) NO CHANGE
    B) in
    C) on
    D) with

15. A) NO CHANGE
    B) blimps
    C) hydrogen
    D) balloon

16. A) NO CHANGE
    B) its
    C) it's
    D) they're

Answers & Explanations for this chapter begin on page 1019.

EXTRA PRACTICE

The following questions provide an opportunity to practice the concepts and strategic thinking covered in this chapter. While many of the questions pertain to Conventions of Usage, some touch on other concepts tested on the Writing & Language Test to ensure that your practice is test-like, with a variety of question types per passage.

Questions 1-11 are based on the following passage and supplementary material.

Batteries Out in the Cold

Many people have trouble starting their cars on a cold winter morning. In a cold car, the engine turns over more slowly, **1** since it sometimes does not turn over at all. Car owners may **2** credit their cold engines, but the real problem is a cold battery.

[1] A motor is generally connected to its circuit through a battery. [2] When a motor is hooked up in a circuit with a battery, electrons move through the circuit, creating a current. [3] Likewise, decreasing the number of electrons moving decreases the current, which then decreases the amount of power available. [4] Increasing the number of electrons moving increases the current, which then increases the amount of power available to the motor. **3**

1. A) NO CHANGE
   B) and
   C) but
   D) yet

2. A) NO CHANGE
   B) criticize
   C) accuse
   D) blame

3. To make this paragraph most logical, sentence 3 should be placed
   A) where it is now.
   B) before sentence 1.
   C) before sentence 2.
   D) after sentence 4.

[4] Electrons move through a battery as a result of two chemical reactions occurring within the battery, one at each pole. [5] A typical car battery, uses lead, and sulfuric acid. At the negative pole, lead reacts with sulfate ions in the solution around it to form lead sulfate, giving off electrons. At the positive pole, lead oxide [6] would have reacted with sulfate ions, hydrogen ions, and electrons in the same solution to also form lead sulfate, taking in electrons. The electrons produced at the negative pole flow through the [7] boundary to the positive pole, providing an electric current in the circuit.

4. Which choice most effectively establishes the main topic of the paragraph?
   A) NO CHANGE
   B) Sulfuric acid can cause burns to the skin, eyes, lungs, and digestive tract, and severe exposure can result in death.
   C) In a direct current circuit, one pole is always negative, the other pole is always positive, and the electrons flow in one direction only.
   D) Lead sulfate is toxic by inhalation, ingestion, and skin contact; repeated exposure may lead to anemia, kidney damage, and other serious health issues.

5. A) NO CHANGE
   B) A typical car battery uses lead, and sulfuric acid.
   C) A typical car battery, uses lead and sulfuric acid.
   D) A typical car battery uses lead and sulfuric acid.

6. A) NO CHANGE
   B) did react
   C) reacts
   D) reacted

7. A) NO CHANGE
   B) cycle
   C) circuit
   D) path

Reading & Writing

A battery charger uses the same reactions, but in reverse. As the current flows in the opposite direction, supplied by house current or a generator, the lead sulfate at the positive pole reacts to change back to lead oxide. **8**

Temperature affects the speed of chemical reactions in two ways. For a chemical reaction to happen, the reactants must collide with enough energy to get the reaction going. As the temperature increases, the motion of the reactants increases. The increased motion of the reactants increases the **9** practicality that they will collide and therefore increases the rate of reaction. The amount of energy in the reactants also increases as temperature increases.

This makes it more likely that any two colliding reactants in a battery will have enough energy to react, and so **10** its rate of reaction increases.

8. At this point, the writer wants to add information that supports the main topic of the paragraph. Which choice most effectively accomplishes this goal?

A) Lead oxide, sometimes called litharge, is an inorganic compound with a formula including lead and oxygen.

B) At the same time, the lead sulfate at the negative pole reacts to change back to lead metal.

C) The difference between a house current and a generator is that the generator converts mechanical energy to electrical energy for use in an external circuit.

D) Using a battery charger incorrectly can be dangerous since a car battery contains chemicals that produce hydrogen, a potentially volatile gas.

9. A) NO CHANGE
    B) way
    C) question
    D) probability

10. A) NO CHANGE
     B) it's
     C) their
     D) they're

Low temperatures have the opposite effect from high temperatures. The chemicals in the battery react more slowly at low temperatures, due both to fewer collisions and less energetic collisions, so fewer electrons move through the circuit. A cold battery takes longer to charge and often cannot provide enough energy to start a car. A cold car that will not start will need either additional power from another car to get the motor moving or a source of heat to warm up the battery and speed up the chemical reactions. Research conducted by FleetCarma in Waterloo, Ontario, demonstrates that **11** <u>colder temperatures negatively affect the distance electric cars can travel.</u>

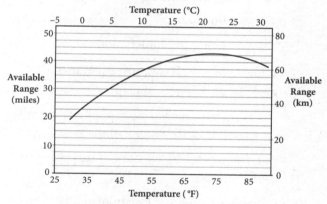

Average Range of Electric Cars as a Function of Temperature

Adapted from research published by FleetCarma, Waterloo, Ontario.

11. Which choice most accurately represents the information in the graph?

A) NO CHANGE

B) the number of kilometers an electric car can travel declines as the outside temperature increases.

C) temperatures below 15°C make it extremely difficult to start an electric car.

D) once the electric car's battery has an alternate heat source by which to start, the distance the car can travel is greatly increased.

Reading & Writing

Questions 12-22 are based on the following passage
and supplementary material.

Pearl Harbor

On December 7, 1941, Japanese fighter planes attacked the American naval base at Pearl Harbor near
Honolulu, Hawaii, sinking or damaging 19 ships and
destroying 169 planes. More than 2,400 soldiers, sailors,
and marines died in the attack, and another 1,178 were
wounded. The next day President Franklin D. Roosevelt
12 hinted the United States' entrance into World War II
by asking Congress to declare war on Japan.

Japan and the U.S. had been in a standoff for years.
In 1937, Japan had declared war on China, seeking to
expand into Chinese territory and secure its import
markets. The U.S. had responded by placing bans on
Japanese exports and imposing other trade embargoes.
13 But Japan had not capitulated; fortunately, it had
strengthened its expansionist aims.

Although the conflict with Japan **14** was being understood to be dangerous, the great distance across the
Pacific Ocean made it seem unlikely that Japan would
attack the United States. American intelligence officials
thought that if Japan did attack, it would hit a European
colony in the South Pacific, such as Singapore. **15** Nearly
the entire Pacific Fleet was moored around Ford Island
in the harbor, and hundreds of airplanes were grounded
at nearby airfields. Pearl Harbor was a large open target.

12. A) NO CHANGE
    B) signaled
    C) mimicked
    D) communicated

13. A) NO CHANGE
    B) But Japan had not capitulated; rather,
    C) And Japan had not capitulated; in fact,
    D) However, Japan had not capitulated;
       furthermore,

14. A) NO CHANGE
    B) was understanding
    C) was understood
    D) was being and understood

15. Which choice best supports the statement
    made in the previous sentence?
    A) This had been true in multiple previous
       conflicts with other nations as well.
    B) But Japan had a history of surprising its
       enemies.
    C) After decades of isolationism, the Ameri-
       can navy was impressive.
    D) Therefore, Pearl Harbor was not heavily
       defended.

The Japanese plan was **16** <u>simple; destroy</u> the Pacific Fleet. That way, the Americans would not be able to fight back as Japan's armed forces spread across the South Pacific. **17** <u>On December 7, after they had been making plans and practicing for months and months, the Japanese launched their attack.</u>

The attack began around **18** <u>8:00 o'clock AM</u>, with Japanese planes dropping bombs and raining bullets. Torpedoes and huge **19** <u>bombs, some weighing</u> over a ton and a half, destroyed the battleships USS *Arizona* and USS *Oklahoma*, each of which had hundreds of sailors trapped inside. In all, eight battleships **20** <u>put up with</u> heavy damage. Dry docks and airfields were likewise destroyed.

16. A) NO CHANGE
    B) simple: destroy
    C) simple destroy
    D) simple, destroy

17. A) NO CHANGE
    B) On December 7, after months of planning and practice, the Japanese launched their attack.
    C) On December 7, after they had for months and months been practicing, the Japanese launched their attack.
    D) On December 7, after months of planning as well as a voluminous amount of practice, the Japanese launched their attack.

18. A) NO CHANGE
    B) 8:00 o'clock AM in the morning
    C) 8:00 AM in the morning,
    D) 8:00 AM

19. A) NO CHANGE
    B) bombs, some weighed
    C) bombs, some were weighing
    D) bombs, some weigh

20. A) NO CHANGE
    B) lost
    C) sustained
    D) tolerated

21 The Pearl Harbor attack united the American people around the long-contentious issue of Japanese aggression: there was widespread determination to go to war. In a December 8 radio address, President Roosevelt said, "I believe I interpret the will of the Congress and of the people when I assert that we will not only defend ourselves to the uttermost, but will make very certain that this form of treachery shall never endanger us again." In a sense, the Japanese plan had backfired. Japanese hopes had been to get trade sanctions lifted; instead, the U.S. entered a war that would **22** end in Japan's defeat by a foreign power.

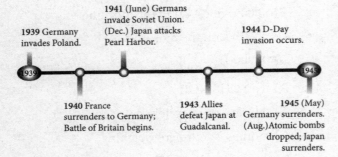

Timeline of WWII Events

1939 Germany invades Poland.

1941 (June) Germans invade Soviet Union. (Dec.) Japan attacks Pearl Harbor.

1944 D-Day invasion occurs.

1940 France surrenders to Germany; Battle of Britain begins.

1943 Allies defeat Japan at Guadalcanal.

1945 (May) Germany surrenders. (Aug.) Atomic bombs dropped; Japan surrenders.

21. Which choice most effectively establishes the main topic of this paragraph?

A) NO CHANGE

B) The United States had been very reluctant to go to war; in fact, it had long been considered an isolationist nation.

C) President Roosevelt had been an extremely popular president so far; he had implemented new programs to pull the United States out of the Great Depression.

D) Japan and the United States might have avoided war if their leaders had managed to come to a diplomatic solution; instead, the conflict had simmered for years.

22. Which choice completes the sentence most accurately, based on the timeline?

A) NO CHANGE

B) end two years later after a long and brutal battle on Guadalcanal.

C) prove to be Japan's last military battle for four long years.

D) cost it millions of lives before Germany's surrender allowed an American victory.

CHAPTER 25

Conventions of Punctuation

CHAPTER OBJECTIVES

By the end of this chapter, you will be able to:

1. Recognize and correct inappropriate uses of punctuation within and at the end of sentences

2. Identify and correct inappropriate uses of possessive nouns

3. Recognize and omit unnecessary punctuation

SMARTPOINTS

Point Value	SmartPoint Category
40 Points	Punctuation

Reading & Writing

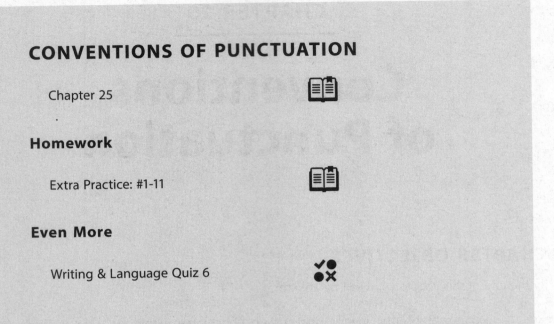

CONVENTIONS OF PUNCTUATION

Chapter 25

Homework

Extra Practice: #1-11

Even More

Writing & Language Quiz 6

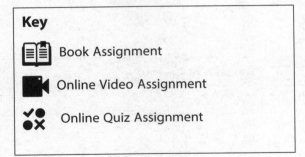

Key

Book Assignment

Online Video Assignment

Online Quiz Assignment

END-OF-SENTENCE AND WITHIN-SENTENCE PUNCTUATION

The SAT Writing & Language Test will require you to identify and correct inappropriate use of ending punctuation that deviates from the intent implied by the context. You will also have to identify and correct inappropriate colons, semicolons, and dashes when used to indicate breaks in thought within a sentence.

You can recognize Punctuation questions because the underlined portion of the text will include a punctuation mark. The answer choices will move that punctuation mark around or replace it with another punctuation mark.

Use **commas** to:

- Separate independent clauses connected by a FANBOYS conjunction (*For, And, Nor, But, Or, Yet, So*)
  Jess finished her homework earlier than expected, so she started on a project that was due the following week.

- Separate an introductory or modifying phrase from the rest of the sentence
  Knowing that soccer practice would be especially strenuous, Tia filled up three water bottles and spent extra time stretching beforehand.

- Set off three or more items in a series or list
  Jeremiah packed a sleeping bag, a raincoat, and a lantern for his upcoming camping trip.

- Separate nonessential information from the rest of the sentence
  Professor Mann, who was the head of the English department, was known for including a wide variety of reading materials in the curriculum.

- Separate an independent and dependent clause
  Tyson arrived at school a few minutes early, which gave him time to clean his locker before class.

> ✔ **Expert Tip**
>
> When you see an underlined comma, ask yourself, "Can the comma be replaced by a period or a semicolon?" If yes, the comma is grammatically incorrect and needs to be changed.

Use **semicolons** to:

- Join two independent clauses that are not connected by a FANBOYS conjunction
  Gaby knew that her term paper would take at least four more hours to write; she got started in study hall and then finished it at home.

- Separate items in a series or list if those items already include commas
  The team needed to bring uniforms, helmets, and gloves; oranges, almonds, and water; and hockey sticks, pucks, and skates.

Reading & Writing

Use **colons** to:

- Introduce and/or emphasize a short phrase, quotation, explanation, example, or list
  Sanjay had two important projects to complete: a science experiment and an expository essay.

Use **dashes** to:

- Indicate a hesitation or a break in thought
  Going to a history museum is a good way to begin researching prehistoric creatures—on second thought, heading to the library will likely be much more efficient.

Let's look at the following Writing & Language passage and questions. After the passage, there are two columns. The left column contains test-like questions. The column on the right features the strategic thinking a test expert employs when approaching the passage and questions presented.

Questions 1-2 are based on the following passage.

Sir Edmund Hilary

In the late spring of 1953, New Zealand mountaineer Sir Edmund Hillary and Nepalese Sherpa Tenzing Norgay became the first men to walk on the top of the world. After a grueling expedition that spanned several **1** months. They had finally reached the summit of Mount Everest. This was the mountain the Tibetan people called "Mother of the Universe," but despite its maternal nomenclature, it had already claimed the lives of George Mallory and Andrew Irvine before Hillary and Norgay finally conquered its icy peak. The mountain's siren call continues to lure mountaineers to this day. But climbing Mount Everest may be easier than answering the question posed by decades of non-climbers: Why? Perhaps Mallory said it best in 1923 before his ill-fated **2** climb; "Because it is there."

Questions	Strategic Thinking
1. A) NO CHANGE B) months, and they C) months; they D) months, they	**Step 1: Read the passage and identify the issue** The underlined segment includes a period, but the sentence before the period is a fragment. **Step 2: Eliminate answer choices that do not address the issue** Eliminate A because, as written, the sentence before the period is a fragment. Eliminate B because it creates a run-on. Eliminate C because it does not correct the original error. **Step 3: Plug in the remaining answer choices and select the most correct, concise, and relevant one** Choice (D) is correct.

Questions	Strategic Thinking
2. A) NO CHANGE B) climb: "Because it is there." C) climb. "Because it is there." D) climb "Because it is there."	**Step 1: Read the passage and identify the issue** The underlined segment includes a semicolon that is used incorrectly because it neither joins two independent clauses nor separates items containing commas in a series or list. The underlined segment here is intended to provide emphasis. **Step 2: Eliminate answer choices that do not address the issue** Eliminate C because it creates two separate sentences that change the author's intended meaning. Eliminate D because it removes punctuation altogether, creating a new error. **Step 3: Plug in the remaining answer choices and select the most correct, concise, and relevant one** Choice (B) is correct.

POSSESSIVE NOUNS AND PRONOUNS

Possessive nouns and pronouns indicate who or what possesses another noun or pronoun. Each follows different rules, and the SAT will test both. These questions require you to identify both the singular and plural forms.

You can spot errors in possessive noun and pronoun construction by looking for:

- Two nouns in a row

- Context clues

- Pronouns with apostrophes

- Words that sound alike

Possessive Nouns		
Singular	sister's	*My oldest **sister's** soccer game is on Saturday.*
Plural	sisters'	*My two older **sisters'** soccer games are on Saturday.*

Questions about possessive pronouns often require you to watch out for contractions and sound-alike words.

Possessive Pronouns and Words to Watch Out For	
its = possessive	it's = it is
their = possessive	there = location/place
whose = possessive	who's = who is/who has

Let's look at the following Writing & Language passage and questions. After the passage, there are two columns. The left column contains test-like questions. The column on the right features the strategic thinking a test expert employs when approaching the passage and questions presented.

Questions 3-4 are based on the following passage.

Literary Theory

Sometimes, being overeducated about literary theory and criticism can have detrimental effects on one's reading. In some cases, before one even opens a book, one might have certain expectations as to **3** <u>it's</u> literary genre, its cultural and historical significance, its symbolism, its author's life and times, and other matters. One can therefore lose out on the experience of entering a world for the first time, where every **4** <u>sight, sound, and taste</u> is eternally new, where the book is forever in the process of forming itself. When one brings preconceived notions and generalizations to a book, the book is petrified in time and space.

Reading & Writing

Questions	Strategic Thinking
3. A) NO CHANGE B) its C) it is D) the	**Step 1: Read the passage and identify the issue** The underlined apostrophe suggests there is a grammatical issue. "It's" is a contraction meaning "it is," but the sentence requires a possessive pronoun. **Step 2: Eliminate answer choices that do not address the issue** Eliminate A, C, and D because they are not possessive pronouns. **Step 3: Plug in the remaining answer choices and select the most correct, concise, and relevant one** Choice (B) is correct.
4. A) NO CHANGE B) sight, sound, taste C) sight, and sound, and taste D) sight sound and taste	**Step 1: Read the passage and identify the issue** The underlined portion contains a series. Commas should be used to set off three or more items in a series or list. These commas should be placed after every item in the series preceding the "and." A series or list should include the word "and" following the comma before the last item. **Step 2: Eliminate answer choices that do not address the issue** Eliminate B, C, and D because they do not feature proper series or list construction. **Step 3: Plug in the remaining answer choices and select the most correct, concise, and relevant one** Choice (A) is correct.

PARENTHETICAL/NONRESTRICTIVE ELEMENTS AND UNNECESSARY PUNCTUATION

Use **commas**, **dashes**, or **parentheses** to set off parenthetical or nonrestrictive information in a sentence.

✔ **Definition**

Parenthetical or nonrestrictive information includes words or phrases that aren't essential to the sentence structure or content. Sometimes, however, this information is explanatory.

The SAT will also ask you to recognize instances of unnecessary punctuation, particularly **commas**.

Do not use a comma to:

- Separate a subject from its predicate
- Separate a verb from its object or its subject, or a preposition from its object
- Set off restrictive elements
- Precede a dependent clause that comes after an independent clause
- Separate adjectives that work together to modify a noun

✔ **Expert Tip**

To determine if information is nonessential, read the sentence without the information. If the sentence still makes sense without the omitted words, then those words need to be set off with punctuation.

Let's look at the following Writing & Language passage and questions. After the passage, there are two columns. The left column contains test-like questions. The column on the right features the strategic thinking a test expert employs when approaching the passage and questions presented.

Questions 5-6 are based on the following passage.

Chimpanzees and Language

Many linguistic researchers are excited about the possibility of humans using language to communicate with chimpanzees, our close cousins in the animal world. Some scientists believe that chimpanzees, and in particular Bonobo chimpanzees, may have the comprehension skills of two-and-a-half-year-old children. With dedicated **5** training, the scientists claim these chimpanzees are able to understand complicated **6** sentences, and to communicate on an advanced level with human beings. In a recent and rather astonishing episode, for example, a Bonobo chimpanzee pressed symbols on a special keyboard in order to tell her trainers about a fight between two chimpanzees in a separate facility.

Reading & Writing

Reading & Writing

Questions	Strategic Thinking
5. A) NO CHANGE B) training, the scientists claim, these C) training the scientists claim these D) training the scientists claim, these	**Step 1: Read the passage and identify the issue** The underlined segment includes a comma that precedes nonessential information that the scientists claim the content of the sentence to be true. The nonessential information ("the scientists claim") is separated from the rest of the sentence by only one comma before "the" rather than one comma before "the" and one after "claim." **Step 2: Eliminate answer choices that do not address the issue** Eliminate A because the sentence is incorrect as written. Eliminate C because it removes all punctuation. Eliminate D because it makes the sentence grammatically incorrect. **Step 3: Plug in the remaining answer choices and select the most correct, concise, and relevant one** Choice (B) is correct.
6. A) NO CHANGE B) sentences and to communicate C) sentences: to communicate D) sentences and communicating	**Step 1: Read the passage and identify the issue** The comma used in the underlined portion is incorrect. The phrase "and to communicate" placed after the comma forms a compound with "to understand complicated sentences," which precedes it. No punctuation is necessary when two phrases are joined by "and," thus forming a compound. **Step 2: Eliminate answer choices that do not address the issue** Eliminate A because the sentence is incorrect as written. Eliminate C because it incorrectly replaces the comma with a colon. Eliminate D because it introduces a parallelism error. **Step 3: Plug in the remaining answer choices and select the most correct, concise, and relevant one** Choice (B) is correct.

You have seen the ways in which the SAT tests you on Punctuation in Writing & Language passages and the way an SAT expert approaches these types of questions.

Use the Kaplan Method for Writing & Language to answer the four questions that accompany the following Writing & Language passage excerpt. Remember to look at the strategic thinking questions that have been laid out for you—some of the answers have been filled in, but you will have to complete the answers to others.

Use your answers to the strategic thinking questions to select the correct answer, just as you will on Test Day.

Questions 7-10 are based on the following passage.

Bebop Jazz

For a jazz musician in New York City in the early 1940s, the most interesting place to spend the hours between midnight and dawn was probably a Harlem nightclub called Minton's. After finishing their jobs at other clubs, young musicians like **7** Charlie Parker, Dizzy Gillespie, Kenny Clarke, Thelonious Monk would gather at Minton's and have jam sessions, informal performances featuring lengthy group and solo improvisations. The all-night sessions resulted in the birth of modern jazz as these African-American artists together forged a new sound, known as bebop.

Unlike swing, the enormously popular jazz played in the 1930s, bebop was not dance music. It was often blindingly fast, incorporating tricky, irregular rhythms and discordant sounds that jazz audiences had never heard before. Earlier jazz, like practically all of Western music up to that time, used an eight-note scale. Bebop, in contrast, was based on a 12-note **8** scale. Thereby, it opened up vast new harmonic opportunities for musicians.

The musicians who pioneered bebop shared two common elements: a vision of the new music's possibilities and astonishing improvisational skill—the ability to play or compose a musical line on the spur of the moment. After all, **9** improvisation, within the context of a group setting, is the essence of jazz, which has been described as the musical experience of the passing moment. Parker, perhaps the greatest instrumental genius jazz has known, was an especially brilliant improviser. He often played twice as fast as the rest of the band, but his solos were always in rhythm and exquisitely shaped, revealing a harmonic imagination that enthralled his listeners.

Like many revolutions, unfortunately, the bebop movement encountered heavy resistance. Opposition came from older jazz musicians initially, but also, later and more lastingly, from a general public alienated by the **10** music's complexity and sophistication. Furthermore, due to the government ban on recording that was in effect during the early years of World War II (records were made of vinyl, a petroleum product that was essential to the war effort), the creative ferment that first produced bebop remains largely undocumented today.

Questions	Strategic Thinking
7. A) NO CHANGE B) Charlie Parker; Dizzy Gillespie; Kenny Clarke; and Thelonious Monk C) Charlie Parker and Dizzy Gillespie, and Kenny Clarke and Thelonious Monk D) Charlie Parker, Dizzy Gillespie, Kenny Clarke, and Thelonious Monk	**Step 1: Read the passage and identify the issue** *Are there any clues suggesting a grammatical issue?* Yes, the underlined portion contains a series. *What kind of punctuation is used to set off three or more items in a series or list?* Commas. *Where should these punctuation marks be placed?* After every item that precedes the word "and." *Is there anything else a series or list should include? If so, what?* A series or list should include the word "and" following the comma before the last item. **Step 2: Eliminate answer choices that do not address the issue** *What answer choice(s) can you eliminate?* _____ _____ _____ **Step 3: Plug in the remaining answer choices and select the most correct, concise, and relevant one** *What is the correct answer?* _____

Questions	Strategic Thinking
8. A) NO CHANGE B) scale, and thereby opening up C) scale, opening up D) scale, thereby opening up	**Step 1: Read the passage and identify the issue** *What punctuation does the underlined segment include?* A period. *What is the issue?* _____ _____ **Step 2: Eliminate answer choices that do not address the issue** *What answer choice(s) can you eliminate?* _____ _____ _____ **Step 3: Plug in the remaining answer choices and select the most correct, concise, and relevant one** *What is the correct answer?*_____

Reading & Writing

Questions	Strategic Thinking
9. A) NO CHANGE B) improvisation within the context of a group setting is the essence C) improvisation within the context of a group setting, is the essence D) improvisation, within the context of a group setting is the essence	**Step 1: Read the passage and identify the issue** *What punctuation does the underlined segment include?* Two commas surrounding the phrase "within the context of a group setting." *What purpose do two commas surrounding a phrase within a sentence serve?* _____ _____ *Is the information set off by the commas in the underlined portion nonessential? Why or why not?* _____ _____ **Step 2: Eliminate answer choices that do not address the issue** *What answer choice(s) can you eliminate?* _____ _____ _____ **Step 3: Plug in the remaining answer choices and select the most correct, concise, and relevant one** *What is the correct answer?* _____

Reading & Writing

Questions	Strategic Thinking
10. A) NO CHANGE B) musics C) musics' D) music	**Step 1: Read the passage and identify the issue** *What punctuation does the underlined segment include?* _____ *What is this type of punctuation used for?* _____ _____ **Step 2: Eliminate answer choices that do not address the issue** *What answer choice(s) can you eliminate?* _____ _____ _____ **Step 3: Plug in the remaining answer choices and select the most correct, concise, and relevant one** *What is the correct answer?* _____

Reading & Writing

Now try a test-like Writing & Language passage on your own. Give yourself 5 minutes to read the passage and answer the questions.

Questions 11-18 are based on the following passage.

Mauritius

[11] Although, most of the products we buy today are made abroad in well-known places like Mexico and China, a quick check of many clothing labels will reveal the name of a country that might not be so [12] familiar. It's Mauritius. Named in honor of Prince Maurice of Nassau by the Dutch who colonized it in 1638, this small island in the Indian Ocean has a complicated history influenced by several international powers. Since gaining independence in 1968, Mauritius has emerged as a stable democracy with one of Africa's highest per capita [13] incomes. Mauritius is considered a significant player in the modern global economy of the Southern Hemisphere.

Yet, Mauritius was not always so conspicuous. The island itself, situated 1,200 miles off the east coast of Africa, covers only about 450 square miles. As recently as the tenth century, it was completely uninhabited by humans, although it was likely known to Arab and Malay sailors of this period. The Portuguese landed in 1511, and with this initial visit, Mauritius gained its first taste of distinction through the discovery of an unlikely creature: the dodo bird. Early Portuguese accounts of encounters with this large, slow-moving bird on the island suggest that the dodo did not recognize humans as [14] predators, making the dodo even easier to catch

11. A) NO CHANGE
    B) Although most
    C) Although; most
    D) Most

12. A) NO CHANGE
    B) familiar, and it's Mauritius.
    C) familiar: Mauritius.
    D) familiar named Mauritius.

13. A) NO CHANGE
    B) incomes; Mauritius is
    C) incomes, and is
    D) incomes and is

14. A) NO CHANGE
    B) predators and made
    C) predators by making
    D) predators making

for food. As a result, by the mid-1600s, the entire dodo population had been wiped out.

Soon after the disappearance of the dodo, the Portuguese presence was replaced by that of the Dutch. Roughly 80 years of Dutch control brought waves of [15] traders, planters, and slaves; indentured laborers, merchants, and artisans, [16] who's collective arrival brought international recognition to Mauritius.

In 1715, the island again changed hands, this time to the French, and in 1810, with a successful invasion during the Napoleonic Wars, the British became the fourth European power to rule the island. Yet it was during this period of changing [17] colonial powers—Mauritius was traded like a commodity, that the demographics of the island began to experience important changes with great political ramifications.

By the time slavery was abolished in 1835, for example, the growing Indian population, the Creoles who could trace their roots back to island's sugarcane plantations, and the Muslim community originating from present-day Pakistan far outnumbered the remaining Franco-Mauritian elites. And with these demographic changes came political change. The first step toward self-rule came with the legislative elections of 1947, and in March of 1968, an official constitution was adopted. Today, Mauritius peacefully balances the diversity of its multicultural society and flourishes in international [18] trade through its advantageous geographic location and large labor force.

15. A) NO CHANGE
     B) traders, planters and slaves, indentured laborers, merchants and artisans,
     C) traders, planters, slaves, indentured laborers, merchants, artisans,
     D) traders, planters, slaves, indentured laborers, merchants, and artisans,

16. A) NO CHANGE
     B) whose collective arrival
     C) their collective arrival
     D) the collective arrival of whom

17. A) NO CHANGE
     B) colonial powers—Mauritius was traded like a commodity that
     C) colonial powers—Mauritius was traded like a commodity—that
     D) colonial powers, Mauritius was traded like a commodity that

18. A) NO CHANGE
     B) trade, through
     C) trade through,
     D) trade; through

Answers & Explanations for this chapter begin on page 1024.

EXTRA PRACTICE

The following questions provide an opportunity to practice the concepts and strategic thinking covered in this chapter. While many of the questions pertain to Conventions of Punctuation, some touch on other concepts tested on the Writing & Language Test to ensure that your practice is test-like, with a variety of question types per passage.

Questions 1-11 are based on the following passage and supplementary material.

Feeling the Burn of Lactic Acid

As a person works a muscle excessively or for a long period of time, that person will most likely feel a burning sensation. Coaches and trainers often encourage **1** they're athletes to exercise until they "feel the burn" because that is an indication that the muscle is working hard. Some people **2** bond the burning feeling with "burning" calories, but the burning sensation has nothing to do with the energy released during exercise; **3** first, it is caused by chemicals that form when muscles use more oxygen than they have available.

4 Blood brings the energy muscles need to move in the form of glucose. The muscles cannot use the glucose directly, however; they can use only adenosine triphosphate (ATP), which is a molecule formed when cells break down glucose. First, the muscle cells break the six-carbon glucose into two three-carbon molecules of pyruvic acid. This makes two ATP molecules available for the muscle cells to use. When enough oxygen is available, the cells **5** then continues to break the pyruvic acid down in a series of steps, each of which produces more ATP. The full cycle releases another 34 ATP molecules, as well as carbon dioxide and water, from one molecule of glucose.

When a cell breaks down glucose without oxygen present, however, it can only accomplish the first step. Even

1. A) NO CHANGE
   B) their
   C) it's
   D) its

2. A) NO CHANGE
   B) equate
   C) acquaint
   D) observe

3. A) NO CHANGE
   B) instead,
   C) although,
   D) consequently,

4. Which choice most effectively establishes the central idea of this paragraph?
   A) NO CHANGE
   B) Adenosine triphosphate (ATP) is a molecule that is found in all living cells.
   C) Glucose is a carbohydrate that is absorbed into the blood during digestion.
   D) Muscles are made of soft tissue and require an external energy source to move.

5. A) NO CHANGE
   B) did continue
   C) continue
   D) continued

the first step will halt, unless the cell converts the pyruvic acid formed into lactic acid. The longer we exercise without enough oxygen, the more lactic acid we build up in our muscle tissues. You are probably familiar with the discomfort acetic **6** acid found in vinegar, causes when it comes in contact with a cut; lactic acid **7** annoys muscle tissues in a similar way, causing a burning sensation.

8 [1] Lactic acid does not form during normal daily activities because our muscles have a small store of ATP available, which is easily replenished as it is used. [2] More intense activity, however, quickly uses up that **9** store once the store is used up, and if the level of oxygen needed for the activity is greater than the amount reaching the muscles, lactic acid starts to build up. [3] The buildup of lactic acid occurs most quickly while engaging in so-called power sports, such as sprinting. [4] After we stop exercising, **10** you continue to breathe harder in order to get enough oxygen to convert the lactic acid back to pyruvic acid, to be used in the normal cycle once again. [5] As a result, lactic acid does not return to normal immediately after we stop exercising. **11**

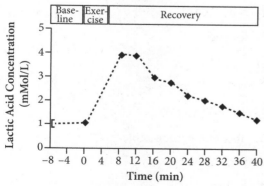

Concentration of Lactic Acid in Blood
Before, During, and After Exercise
(5-minute fast run)

Based on data from Journal of Sport Sciences, 28(9) pp. 975-982.

6. A) NO CHANGE
   B) acid, found in vinegar, causes
   C) acid found, in vinegar, causes
   D) acid found in vinegar causes

7. A) NO CHANGE
   B) rubs
   C) hurts
   D) irritates

8. Which choice provides the least support for the central idea of this paragraph?
   A) Sentence 1
   B) Sentence 2
   C) Sentence 3
   D) Sentence 4

9. A) NO CHANGE
   B) store once, the store
   C) store; once the store
   D) store: once the store

10. A) NO CHANGE
    B) we
    C) they
    D) them

11. Based on the information in the graph, which choice, if added here, would provide the most effective conclusion to the passage?
    A) Lactic acid concentration peaks at eight minutes then begins to drop.
    B) At 28 minutes, lactic acid concentration is half of what it is during exercise.
    C) We continue to "feel the burn" for nearly 40 minutes after we stop.
    D) Lactic acid concentration declines steadily when exercise stops.

Reading & Writing

Questions 12-22 are based on the following passage and supplementary material.

The Brooklyn Bridge: The Eighth Wonder of the World

As one of New York City's most iconic landmarks, the Brooklyn Bridge spans 5,989 feet across the East River. Connecting the boroughs of Brooklyn (Kings County) and Manhattan, this bridge was a fantastic marvel of engineering **12** <u>when it was completed in 1883, just years after the Golden Gate Bridge</u>. The Brooklyn Bridge was the longest suspension bridge of **13** <u>its time. It was dubbed</u> the "8th Wonder of the World." Its construction, **14** <u>consequently</u>, was riddled with problems from the very start.

Residents of Brooklyn had **15** <u>watched</u> for a bridge to connect them with Manhattan, as the frozen East River was **16** <u>absolutely so impossible</u> to cross during the winter. The dream would finally come to fruition, when New York legislators approved John Augustus Roebling's plan for a suspension bridge over the East River.

12. Which choice most accurately completes the sentence based on the table?
   A) NO CHANGE
   B) when it was completed in 1883, several years before the Tower Bridge in London, England, was built.
   C) when it was completed in 1883, two years after the Tower Bridge in London, England, was built.
   D) when it was completed in 1883, the same year that the Golden Gate Bridge was built.

13. Which choice most effectively combines the sentences at the underlined portion?
   A) its time, however, it was dubbed
   B) its time, and it was dubbed
   C) its time, was dubbed
   D) its time, it was dubbed

14. A) NO CHANGE
   B) as a result
   C) for example
   D) however

15. A) NO CHANGE
   B) longed
   C) fought
   D) went

16. A) NO CHANGE
   B) absolutely impossible
   C) impossible
   D) so impossible

Roebling had a successful reputation as a designer of suspension bridges, and the Brooklyn Bridge would be **17** their biggest feat yet, as both the suspension bridge with the longest span (1,600 feet from tower to tower) and as the first steel-cabled suspension bridge.

Roebling would never see his design completed; in fact, he would never even see construction begin. Just before construction was about to start in 1867, Roebling was the victim of **18** a special accident; a boat **19** was smashing into his foot, and he succumbed to tetanus. His son, Washington Roebling, took over the project.

20 Designs for the Brooklyn Bridge included a promenade above the traffic. The first task was for workers to excavate the riverbed in order to anchor the two towers of the bridge to the bedrock below. To accomplish this, bottomless wooden boxes called caissons were sunk into the depths of the river. Once inside, workers would begin the laborious task of removing mud and boulders. To get down into the caissons, workers traveled in airlocks filled with compressed air, which prevented water **21** from entering, if the workers ascended to the surface and left the compressed air too quickly, they would suffer from the debilitating condition known as "caisson disease," or "the bends." Over 100 workers experienced caisson disease, and many others died or were injured from construction-related accidents. The cement-filled caissons remain under the towers of the bridge today.

17. A) NO CHANGE
    B) its
    C) her
    D) his

18. A) NO CHANGE
    B) an exceptional
    C) a common
    D) a freak

19. A) NO CHANGE
    B) smashing
    C) smashed
    D) was smashed

20. Which choice most effectively establishes the central idea of the paragraph?
    A) NO CHANGE
    B) The conditions inside the caissons were so terrible that workmen could stay there only for two hours.
    C) The towers were built of limestone, granite, and cement that came from a village called Rosendale in upstate New York.
    D) The building of the bridge was a monumental and often dangerous undertaking.

21. A) NO CHANGE
    B) from entering. If the workers ascended
    C) from entering if the workers ascended
    D) from entering, since if the workers ascended

Washington Roebling himself suffered from the bends and was partially paralyzed for the rest of his life. Determined to remain part of the project now supervised by his wife, Emily, he watched the construction continue with a telescope. **22** <u>In May, 1883, more than a dozen years after construction began, Emily Roebling was given the first ride over the completed Brooklyn Bridge.</u> She was followed by 150,300 people on that opening day. Despite the setbacks, Manhattan and Brooklyn were finally connected.

22. Which choice most effectively revises the underlined sentence?

A) In 1883, many years after construction began, Emily Roebling was given a ride over the completed Brooklyn Bridge.

B) In May 1883, many years after construction began, Emily Roebling was given the first ride over the completed Brooklyn Bridge.

C) On May 24, 1883, 14 years after construction began, Emily Roebling was given the first ride over the completed Brooklyn Bridge.

D) In 1883, 14 years after construction began, Emily Roebling was given a ride over the completed Brooklyn Bridge.

Bridges of the World			
Bridge Name & Location	**Date Completed**	**Length**	**Largest Single Span**
Akashi Kaikyo Bridge, Japan	1998	12,828 feet	6,527 feet
Brooklyn Bridge, New York	1883	5,989 feet	1,595 feet
Golden Gate Bridge, San Francisco	1937	8,981 feet	4,200 feet
Tower Bridge, London	1894	880 feet	200 feet

Reading & Writing

PART THREE

The Essay

The Essay

BY THE END OF THIS UNIT, YOU WILL BE ABLE TO:

1. Apply the Kaplan Method for the SAT Essay

2. Use the Kaplan Template for the SAT Essay to create an effective outline

The Kaplan Method for the SAT Essay

CHAPTER OBJECTIVES

By the end of this chapter, you will be able to:

1. Apply the Kaplan Method for the SAT Essay to produce a clear analysis of a source text

SMARTPOINTS

Point Value	SmartPoint Category
Point Builder	The Kaplan Method for the SAT Essay

THE KAPLAN METHOD FOR THE SAT ESSAY

Chapter 26

Homework

Extra Practice: Essay Prompt

Even More

The Kaplan Method for Essays

Key

 Book Assignment

 Online Video Assignment

 Online Quiz Assignment

THE SAT ESSAY IS OPTIONAL. SHOULD YOU WRITE IT?

The SAT Essay is optional, so if you don't want to spend 50 minutes writing an essay, you certainly don't have to. You are free to leave after the final multiple choice section of the test.

However, just because you can leave without completing the SAT Essay doesn't mean that you should. If you can state with 100 percent certainty that the colleges to which you are applying do not require the essay component of the SAT, feel free to omit it on Test Day. However, if you are unsure, or don't yet have a finalized list of colleges, Kaplan recommends you complete the SAT Essay for the following reasons:

First, consider the fact that the SAT is not an exam you can take in bits and pieces. If you want to take the SAT Essay at a later date, you'll have to sit through the entire SAT again. That can translate to a lot of unnecessary stress during your senior year.

Second, if the colleges you apply to don't require you to take the SAT Essay, they won't negatively judge you if you do. There is nothing to lose by completing the essay. You might get a great score and add a few more possibilities to your list of potential schools.

Finally, while the SAT Essay question on the new SAT will be challenging, it is also standardized. That means you can learn how to write a high-scoring essay by putting in some time, effort, and willingness to practice. This chapter is a great place to start.

THE KAPLAN METHOD FOR THE SAT ESSAY

The SAT Essay, while optional, presents you with a challenge: to read and understand a high-quality source text and write an essay analyzing the author's argument in 50 minutes. By using the Kaplan Method for the SAT Essay, you will be able to make the most out of those 50 minutes and produce a high-scoring written response to a previously published, sophisticated source.

The Kaplan Method for the SAT Essay consists of four steps:

Step 1: Read the source text, taking notes on how the author uses:

- Evidence to support claims

- Reasoning to develop ideas and to connect claims and evidence

- Stylistic or persuasive elements to add power to the ideas expressed

Step 2: Use the Kaplan Template to create an outline

Step 3: Write your essay

Step 4: Check your essay for mistakes in grammar, spelling, and clarity

Let's take a closer look at each step.

Step 1: Read the source text, taking notes on how the author uses:

- **Evidence to support claims**

- **Reasoning to develop ideas and to connect claims and evidence**

- **Stylistic or persuasive elements to add power to the ideas expressed**

What is the source text?

The source text for the SAT Essay will consist of a passage that is very similar to the passages you'll see in the Reading Test. It will typically be 500–750 words and will deal with topics of general interest in the arts, sciences, and public life. In many cases, the passages will be biased in favor of the author's argument.

While the source text changes from test to test, the directions and essay prompt remain similar. Spend more time reading and understanding the text—the prompt will likely be very similar to other prompts that you've encountered.

What kinds of notes should I take?

The notes you take while reading the source text are similar to those you would take when creating a Passage Map on the SAT Reading Test (see chapter 13). However, these notes will focus on how the author connects central ideas and important details.

Your notes should focus on:

- Evidence to support claims (e.g., cited data or statistics, or authoritative sources that support the author's argument)

- Reasoning to develop ideas and make connections (e.g., the author explains his logic for using a specific piece of evidence to support a specific claim)

- Stylistic or persuasive elements to add power to the ideas expressed (e.g., using figurative language, irony, metaphor, and other elements to appeal to emotions)

In addition to taking notes in the margins of the passage, it is also helpful to underline and circle the following:

- Central ideas

- Important details

- Facts and opinions

- Textual evidence (quotations, paraphrases, or both)

Your goal is to identify three features such as juxtaposition, imagery, and symbolism that the author uses to build his or her argument.

> ✔ **Definition**
>
> Features are the key elements of the essay that you marked in your notes. They could include stylistic techniques (such as irony) or data (such as statistics) used to bolster a claim.

You should spend approximately 10 minutes on Step 1.

Step 2: Use the Kaplan Template to create an outline

Why do I need an outline?

Creating an outline before you write your essay is a huge time-saver, which is essential when you have only 50 minutes to complete the SAT Essay. Spending the first part of the allotted time effectively (i.e., reading and taking notes on the source text and creating an outline) will lead to a well-organized, more convincing essay. You'll also find that organizing your thoughts ahead of time will enable you to write much more quickly!

What should I put in my outline?

Kaplan has created an efficient and effective template to outline the SAT Essay. Using the template will prevent you from encountering a writing or thinking block. With the template and the Kaplan Method, you will know what you want to write about the source text and not waste any time.

You should spend approximately 8 minutes on Step 2.

> ✔ **On Test Day**
>
> You will not be able to bring this template with you to Test Day. Therefore, it is important that you memorize the gist and logical flow of the template well before Test Day so that creating an outline is second nature to you when you sit down to write your essay.

Step 3: Write your essay

After you have read and analyzed the source text, your next goal is to write a cohesive essay that demonstrates your use and command of standard written English. To demonstrate your proficiency, you must:

- Provide your own precise central claim
- Use a variety of sentence structures
- Employ precise word choice
- Maintain a constant and appropriate style and tone

You should spend approximately 30 minutes on Step 3.

Step 4: Check your essay for mistakes in grammar, spelling, and clarity

While a few grammar and spelling mistakes won't drastically harm your SAT Essay score, setting aside some time to proofread can help you catch careless errors that you can easily correct, thereby increasing your Writing score on the SAT Essay.

You should spend the remaining 2 minutes on Step 4.

THE SAT ESSAY PROMPT

As mentioned previously in this chapter, the SAT Essay source text will change from administration to administration, but the prompt will remain largely the same in both format and wording.

Become familiar with the idea behind the prompt and assignment as soon as you can so that on Test Day, you will be able to focus on reading, analyzing, and writing, rather than figuring out what the prompt is asking you to accomplish.

The generic SAT Essay prompt is as follows:

As you read the passage below, consider how [the author] uses

- evidence, such as facts or examples, to support claims.

- reasoning to develop ideas and to connect claims and evidence.

- stylistic or persuasive elements, such as word choice or appeals to emotion, to add power to the ideas expressed.

Source Text Will Appear Here

Write an essay in which you explain how [the author] builds an argument to persuade [his/her] audience that [author's claim]. In your essay, analyze how [the author] uses one or more of the features listed above (or features of your own choice) to strengthen the logic and persuasiveness of [his/her] argument. Be sure that your analysis focuses on the most relevant features of the passage.

Your essay should not explain whether you agree with [the author's] claims, but rather explain how [the author] builds an argument to persuade [his/her] audience.

SAT ESSAY SCORING RUBRIC

There are three different scores for the SAT Essay: Reading, Analysis, and Writing. Each category will be scored on a scale of 1 to 4. The scores you receive will range from 2 to 8, as they will be the scores of two raters.

The raters will use the following rubric to determine each area score.

	1	2
Reading	• Demonstrates **little or no comprehension** of the source text • Fails to show an understanding of the text's central idea(s), and may include only details without reference to central idea(s) • May contain numerous errors of fact and/or interpretation with regard to the text • Makes little or no use of textual evidence	• Demonstrates **some comprehension** of the source text • Shows an understanding of the text's central idea(s) but not of important details • May contain errors of fact and/or interpretation with regard to the text • Makes limited and/or haphazard use of textual evidence
Analysis	• Offers **little or no analysis or ineffective analysis** of the source text and demonstrates **little to no understanding** of the analytical task • Identifies without explanation some aspects of the author's use of evidence, reasoning, and/or stylistic and persuasive elements, and/or feature(s) of the student's own choosing • Numerous aspects of analysis are unwarranted based on the text • Contains little or no support for claim(s) or point(s) made, or support is largely irrelevant • May not focus on features of the text that are relevant to addressing the task • Offers no discernible analysis (e.g., is largely or exclusively summary)	• Offers **limited analysis** of the source text and demonstrates only **partial understanding** of the analytical task • Identifies and attempts to describe the author's use of evidence, reasoning, and/or stylistic and persuasive elements, and/or feature(s) of the student's own choosing, but merely asserts rather than explains their importance • One or more aspects of analysis are unwarranted based on the text • Contains little or no support for claim(s) or point(s) made • May lack a clear focus on those features of the text that are most relevant to addressing the task
Writing	• Demonstrates **little or no cohesion** and **inadequate skill** in the use and control of language • May lack a clear central claim or controlling idea • Lacks a recognizable introduction and conclusion; does not have a discernible progression of ideas • Lacks variety in sentence structures; sentence structures may be repetitive; demonstrates general and vague word choice; word choice may be poor or inaccurate; may lack a formal style and objective tone • Shows a weak control of the conventions of standard written English and may contain numerous errors that undermine the quality of writing	• Demonstrates **little or no cohesion** and **limited skill** in the use and control of language • May lack a clear central claim or controlling idea or may deviate from the claim or idea • May include an ineffective introduction and/or conclusion; may demonstrate some progression of ideas within paragraphs but not throughout • Has limited variety in sentence structures; sentence structures may be repetitive; demonstrates general or vague word choice; word choice may be repetitive; may deviate noticeably from a formal style and objective tone • Shows a limited control of the conventions of standard written English and contains errors that detract from the quality of writing and may impede understanding

	3	4
Reading	• Demonstrates **effective comprehension** of the source text • Shows an understanding of the text's central idea(s) and important details • Is free of substantive errors of fact and interpretation with regard to the text • Makes appropriate use of textual evidence	• Demonstrates **thorough comprehension** of the source text • Shows an understanding of the text's central idea(s) and most important details and how they interrelate • Is free of errors of fact or interpretation with regard to the text • Makes skillful use of textual evidence
Analysis	• Offers an **effective analysis** of the source text and demonstrates an **understanding** of the analytical task • Competently evaluates the author's use of evidence, reasoning, and/or stylistic and persuasive elements, and/or feature(s) of the student's own choosing • Contains relevant and sufficient support for claim(s) or point(s) made • Focuses primarily on those features of the text that are most relevant to addressing the task	• Offers an **insightful analysis** of the source text and demonstrates a **sophisticated understanding** of the analytical task • Offers a thorough, well-considered evaluation of the author's use of evidence, reasoning, and/or stylistic and persuasive elements, and/or feature(s) of the student's own choosing • Contains relevant, sufficient, and strategically chosen support for claim(s) or point(s) made • Focuses consistently on those features of the text that are most relevant to addressing the task
Writing	• Is **mostly cohesive** and demonstrates **effective use and control** of language • Includes a central claim or implicit controlling idea • Includes an effective introduction and conclusion; demonstrates a clear progression of ideas both within paragraphs and throughout the essay • Has variety in sentence structures; demonstrates some precise word choice; maintains a formal style and objective tone • Shows a good control of the conventions of standard written English and is free of significant errors that detract from the quality of writing	• Is **cohesive** and demonstrates a **highly effective use and command** of language • Includes a precise central claim • Includes a skillful introduction and conclusion; demonstrates a deliberate and highly effective progression of ideas both within paragraphs and throughout the essay • Has a wide variety of sentence structures; demonstrates a consistent use of precise word choice; maintains a formal style and objective tone • Shows a strong command of the conventions of standard written English and is free or virtually free of errors

THE KAPLAN TEMPLATE FOR THE SAT ESSAY

To maximize your essay score, organize your notes using Kaplan's SAT Essay Template.

¶1: Introductory paragraph

- Introductory statement
- Paraphrase the author's central idea or claim
- Specifically state the features the author uses to support the central idea or claim

¶2: First body paragraph

- Introduce Feature 1 and provide a quote or paraphrase of the feature
- Specifically state how Feature 1 provides evidence to support the author's reasoning
- Discuss how Feature 1 reflects the author's thinking and the way the author ties his or her claim and evidence together
- Analyze the effect Feature 1 is likely to have on the audience

¶3: Second body paragraph

- Introduce Feature 2 and provide a quote or paraphrase of the feature
- Specifically state how Feature 2 provides evidence to support the author's reasoning
- Discuss how Feature 2 reflects the author's thinking and the way the author ties his or her claim and evidence together
- Analyze the effect Feature 2 is likely to have on the audience

——Time valve: If you are running out of time, don't write a 3rd body paragraph. Instead, take the time to write a thorough conclusion paragraph and proofread your essay. ——

¶4: Third body paragraph

- Introduce Feature 3 and provide a quote or paraphrase of the feature
- Specifically state how Feature 3 provides evidence to support the author's reasoning
- Discuss how Feature 3 reflects the author's thinking and the way the author ties his or her claim and evidence together
- Analyze the effect Feature 3 is likely to have on the audience

¶5: Conclusion paragraph

- Recap author's central idea or claim
- Recap what features the author used to build his or her argument
- Recap how effective the features are on the audience

> ✔ **Expert Tip**
>
> Use the time valve option to your advantage. If you are running out of time, focusing on two strong body paragraphs and a complete conclusion is much better than rushing through a third body paragraph or leaving your essay unfinished.

Look at the test-like source text and prompt that follows. Notice what kinds of notes an SAT expert takes in the margins of the passage. Then, look at how the SAT expert creates an outline using the Kaplan template.

As you read the passage below, consider how Tony Blair uses

- evidence, such as facts or examples, to support claims.

- reasoning to develop ideas and to connect claims and evidence.

- stylistic or persuasive elements, such as word choice or appeals to emotion, to add power to the ideas expressed.

Adapted from British Prime Minister Tony Blair's speech to American citizens following 9/11/2001.

1   The only purpose of being in politics is to strive for the values and ideals we believe in: freedom, justice, what we Europeans call solidarity but you might call respect for and help for others. These are the decent democratic values we all avow. But alongside the values we know we <u>need a hard-headed pragmatism</u>— a (realpolitik)— required to give us any chance of translating those values into the practical world we live in.

juxt. btwn. Euro & aud. (U.S.)

2   The same tension exists in the two views of international affairs. One is utilitarian: each nation maximizes its own self-interest. The other is utopian: we try to create a better world. Today I want to suggest that more than ever before those two views are merging.

ev: util. vs utop. views

3   I advocate an enlightened self-interest that puts fighting for our values right at the heart of the policies necessary to protect our nations. (Engagement) in the world on the basis of these values, not isolationism from it, is the <u>hard-headed pragmatism</u> for the 21st century.

4   Why? In part it is because the countries and people of the world today <u>are more interdependent than ever.</u> In truth, it is very rare today that trouble in one part of the globe remains limited in its effect. Not just in security, but in trade and finance—witness the <u>crisis of 1998</u> which began in Thailand and ended in Brazil—the world is interlocked.

rhet. ?

ev: 1998 crisis

5   This is heightened by mass communications and technology. In Queen Victoria's time, reports of battles came back weeks or months after they were won or lost. Today we see them enacted live on the BBC, Sky or CNN. Their very visibility, immediate and in Technicolor, inflames feelings that can spread worldwide across different ethnic, religious, and cultural communities.

ev: Queen Vic. time's reports vs today's

6   So today, more than ever, "their" problem becomes "our" problem. Instability is contagious and, again today, more than ever, nations, at least most of them, crave stability. That's for a simple reason. Our people want it, because without it, they can't do business and prosper. What brings nations together—what brought them together post–September 11—is the international recognition that the world needs order. Disorder is the enemy of progress.

quotes → irony

7   The struggle is for stability, for the security within which progress can be made. Of course, countries want to protect their territorial integrity but few are into empire-building. This is especially true of democracies whose people vote for higher living standards and punish governments who don't deliver them. For 2,000 years Europe fought over territory.

ex: 2000 year Eur. fight

8   Today boundaries are virtually fixed. Governments and people know that any territorial ambition threatens stability, and instability threatens prosperity.

9   And of course the surest way to stability is through the very values of freedom, democracy and justice. Where these are strong, the people push for moderation and order. Where they are absent, regimes act unchecked by popular accountability and pose a threat; and the threat spreads.

logic & results

10 So the promotion of these values becomes not just right in itself but part of our long-term security and prosperity. We can't intervene in every case. Not all the wrongs of the world can be put right, but where disorder threatens us all, we should act.

11 Like it or not, whether you are a utilitarian or a utopian, the world is interdependent. One consequence of this is that foreign and domestic policy are ever more closely interwoven.

12 It was September 11 that brought these thoughts into sharper focus. Watching the horror unfold, imagining the almost unimaginable suffering of the thousands of innocent victims of the terror and carnage, the dominant emotion after the obvious feelings of revulsion, sympathy, and anger was determination.

what prompted speech
juxt. "imagining... unimaginable"

13 The guts and spirit of the people of New York and America in the aftermath of that terrible day were not just admirable, they were awesome. They were the best riposte to the terrorists that humanity could give and you should be very proud of that. I want you to know too

praising aud.

that the British people were with you from the first moment, and we will always be with you at times like those. We are not half-hearted friends and we never will be. But the determination must be not just to pursue those responsible and bring them to justice but to <u>learn from September 11</u>. There is a real danger we forget the lessons of September 11. Human beings recover from tragedy and the memory becomes less fraught. That is a healthy part of living. But <u>we should learn from our experience</u>.

promises

14   The <u>most obvious lesson is indeed our</u> (interdependence.) For a time our world stood still. Quite apart from our security, the shock impacted on economic confidence, on business, on trade, and it is only now, with the terrorist network on the run, that confidence is really returning. <u>Every nation in the world</u> felt the reverberation of that fateful day. And that <u>has been well illustrated</u> by the role which the United Nations—under Kofi Annan's excellent leadership—has played since September 11.

ex: U.N. & Kofi A. global effects of 9/11

15   So if we didn't know it before, we know now: these events and our re-sponse to them shape the fate <u>not of one nation but of one world</u>.

For America, it has laid bare the reality. American power affects the world fundamentally. It is there. It is real. It is never irrelevant. It can affect the world for good, or for bad. Stand aside or engage; it never fails to affect.

short sentences

16   You know I want it engaged. Under President Bush, I am confident it will be and for good. But if that's what I and many others want, it comes at a price for us too. It means we don't shirk our responsibility. It means that when America is fighting for those values, then, however tough, we fight with her. No grandstanding, no offering implausible but impracti-cal advice from the comfort of the touchline, no wishing away the hard not the easy choices, but working together, side by side.

personification of America

> Write an essay in which you explain how Tony Blair builds an argument to persuade his audience that imbuing the world with values must be approached pragmatically and universally. In your essay, analyze how Blair uses one or more of the features listed above (or features of your own choice) to strengthen the logic and persuasiveness of his argument. Be sure your analysis focuses on the most relevant features of the passage.
>
> Your essay should not explain whether you agree with Blair's claims, but rather explain how Blair builds an argument to persuade his audience

Now that you've seen what kinds of notes a test expert takes for the SAT Essay source text, look at how he or she does some analysis by using the Kaplan Template to create an outline.

While the following example includes full sentences and quotations from the source text, please know that you should use shorthand and ellipses on Test Day; it's not your outline that's evaluated, but your actual essay.

¶1: Introductory paragraph

- **Introductory statement:** *In his speech to American citizens after September 11, 2001, British Prime Minister Tony Blair discusses how the world should respond.*

- **Paraphrase the author's central idea or claim:** *All nations must join together to fight for freedom, democracy, and justice.*

- **Specifically state the features the author uses to support the central idea or claim**

  - *Feature 1: Historical evidence*

  - *Feature 2: Juxtaposition*

  - *Feature 3: Emphatic rhetoric*

¶2: First body paragraph

- **Introduce Feature 1 and provide a quote or paraphrase of the feature**

  - Feature 1: Historical Evidence

    - *¶4: Crisis of 1998, evidence of world's interdependence: ". . . which began in Thailand and ended in Brazil."*

    - *¶15: 9/11: "So if we didn't know it before, we know now: these events and our response to them shape the fate not of one nation but of one world."*

- **Specifically state how Feature 1 provides evidence to support the author's reasoning:** *Provides evidence for author's reasoning by taking his claim from a personal point of view into reality with specific, actual historical events.*

- **Discuss how Feature 1 reflects the author's thinking and the way the author ties his or her claim and evidence together:** *Reflects the author's thinking by providing specific examples to support his claim that the world is interdependent. The evidence and claim are tied together by making a statement and supporting it with historical events.*

- **Analyze the effect Feature 1 is likely to have on the audience:** *Emphasizes and makes the claim concrete by providing examples which are clearly understood by the audience, whose members may well have been affected by 9/11 and the 1998 financial crisis. The intent is to elicit audience agreement with the author.*

Now, look at how these notes translate into the first two paragraphs of a high-scoring student response to the SAT Essay.

In his speech to American citizens after the events of September 11, 2001, British Prime Minister Tony Blair discusses how the interdependent state of the world in the 21st century should influence the way countries respond to this tragedy. Blair emphatically asserts that all nations must band together in the fight for the values of freedom, democracy, and justice. Blair effectively conveys this argument by using historical examples, juxtaposition, and emphatic rhetoric.

Throughout the passage, Blair refers to specific historical events that have changed our perception of the world from separate nations with their own agendas, to a world so interdependent that events in one country echo through all countries. In the fourth paragraph, he reminds the audience of the trade and financial crisis of 1998, stating that it "began in Thailand and ended in Brazil," and uses this example to support his previous sentence that ""In truth, it is very rare today that trouble in one part of the globe remains limited in its effect." The author introduces the events of 9/11 in paragraph 12, stating that "It was September 11 that brought these thoughts into sharper focus," and emphasizing that we should "learn from September 11," and that "the most obvious lesson is indeed our interdependence." The author's blanket statement that "the countries and people of the world today are more interdependent than ever" is strongly supported by these historical examples, which prove that his thesis is not just rhetoric but fact. An audience, faced with the factual events, cannot help but be persuaded of the need for nations to work together toward common goals with common resources.

¶3: Second body paragraph

Introduce Feature 2 and provide a quote or paraphrase of the feature

_____

_____

_____

_____

Specifically state how Feature 2 provides evidence to support the author's reasoning

_____

_____

_____

Discuss how Feature 2 reflects the author's thinking and the way the author ties his or her claim and evidence together

_____

_____

_____

Analyze the effect Feature 2 is likely to have on the audience

_____

_____

_____

You have seen the kinds of notes SAT experts take and the strategic thinking questions they ask while planning their responses to the SAT Essay source text.

Based on the prompt on pages 664-666, use the Kaplan Template to plan an additional body paragraph for the response essay. You may use one of the other two features mentioned on page 667 (Juxtaposition and Emphatic Rhetoric) or come up with one of your own.

Now, use your ¶3 (the second body paragraph) notes on page 669 to write a full body paragraph on the lines that follow. Give yourself 8 minutes to write the paragraph.

_____

_____

_____

_____

_____

_____

_____

_____

_____

_____

_____

_____

_____

_____

_____

_____

_____

_____

_____

_____

_____

_____

_____

_____

_____

_____

_____

_____

Answers & Explanations for this chapter begin on page 1028.

Essay

EXTRA PRACTICE

As you read the passage below, consider how Emmeline Pankhurst uses

- evidence, such as facts or examples, to support claims.

- reasoning to develop ideas and to connect claims and evidence.

- stylistic or persuasive elements, such as word choice or appeals to emotion, to add power to the ideas expressed.

Adapted from "Freedom or Death," a speech delivered by Emmeline Pankhurst on November 13, 1913, in Hartford, Connecticut

1   Mrs. Hepburn, ladies, and gentlemen:

2   Tonight I am not here to advocate woman suffrage. American suffragists can do that very well for themselves. I am here as a soldier who has temporarily left the field of battle in order to explain what civil war is like when civil war is waged by women. I am here as a person who, according to the law courts of my country, it has been decided, is of no value to the community at all: and I am adjudged because of my life to be a dangerous person.

3   Now, first of all I want to make you understand the inevitableness of revolution and civil war, even on the part of women, when you reach a certain stage in the development of a community's life. . . It is quite easy for you to understand the desirability of revolution if I were a man. If an Irish revolutionary had addressed this meeting, and many have addressed meetings all over the United States during the last twenty or thirty years, it would not be necessary for that revolutionary to explain the need of revolution beyond saying that the people of his country were denied—and by people, meaning men—were denied the right of self-government. That would explain the whole situation. If I were a man and I said to you, "I come from a country which professes to have representative institutions and yet denies me, a taxpayer, an inhabitant of the country, representative rights," you would at once understand that that human being, being a man, was justified in the adoption of revolutionary methods to get representative institutions. But since I am a woman it is necessary in the twentieth century to explain why women have adopted revolutionary methods in order to win the rights of citizenship.

4   You see, in spite of a good deal that we hear about revolutionary methods not being necessary for American women, we women, in trying to make our case clear, always have to make as part of our argument, and urge upon men in our audience the fact—a very simple fact—that women are human beings. I want to put a few political arguments before you—not arguments

for the suffrage, because I said when I opened, I didn't mean to do that—but arguments for the adoption of militant methods in order to win political rights.

5 Suppose the men of Hartford had a grievance, and they laid that grievance before their legislature, and the legislature obstinately refused to listen to them, or to remove their grievance, what would be the proper and the constitutional and the practical way of getting their grievance removed? Well, it is perfectly obvious at the next general election, when the legislature is elected, the men of Hartford would turn out that legislature and elect a new one: entirely change the personnel of an obstinate legislature.

6 But let the men of Hartford imagine that they were not in the position of being voters at all, that they were governed without their consent being obtained, that the legislature turned an absolutely deaf ear to their demands, what would the men of Hartford do then? They couldn't vote the legislature out. They would have to make a choice of two evils: they would either have to submit indefinitely to an unjust state of affairs, or they would have to rise up and adopt some of the antiquated means by which men in the past got their grievances remedied. We know what happened when your forefathers decided that they must have representation for taxation, many, many years ago. When they felt they couldn't wait any longer, when they laid all the arguments before an obstinate British government that they could think of, and when their arguments were absolutely disregarded, when every other means had failed, they began by the tea party at Boston, and they went on until they had won the independence of the United States of America. That is what happened in the old days.

7 It is perfectly evident to any logical mind that when you have got the vote, you can get out of any legislature whatever you want, or, if you cannot get it, you can send them about their business and choose other people who will be more attentive to your demands. But, it is clear to the meanest intelligence that if you have not got the vote, you must either submit to laws just or unjust, administration just or unjust, or the time inevitably comes when you will revolt against that injustice and use violent means to put an end to it.

Write an essay in which you explain how Emmeline Pankhurst builds an argument to persuade her audience that violent as well as nonviolent protest tactics are necessary and justifiable to gain political rights for women. In your essay, analyze how Pankhurst uses one or more of the features listed above (or features of your own choice) to strengthen the logic and persuasiveness of her argument. Be sure that your analysis focuses on the most relevant features of the passage.

Your essay should not explain whether you agree with Pankhurst's claims, but rather explain how Pankhurst builds an argument to persuade her audience.

Reading, Analyzing, and Writing the SAT Essay

CHAPTER OBJECTIVES

By the end of this chapter you will be able to:

1. Identify the source text's central ideas and important details and how they interrelate

2. Evaluate the author's use of evidence, reasoning, and/or stylistic and persuasive elements

3. Understand the standards by which the technical aspects of your written response will be evaluated

SMARTPOINTS

Point Value	SmartPoint Category
4 Points	Reading
4 Points	Analysis
4 Points	Writing

READING, ANALYZING, AND WRITING THE SAY ESSAY

Chapter 27

Homework

Extra Practice: Essay Prompt

Key

    Book Assignment

    Online Video Assignment

    Online Quiz Assignment

THE SAT ESSAY: READING

One of the three scores you'll receive on the SAT Essay is the Reading score. Graded on a scale of 1 to 4 by two different readers for a total score of 2 to 8, the Reading score is based on:

- Your understanding of the source text
- Your comprehension of the source text's central ideas, important details, and their interrelationship
- The accuracy of your interpretation of the source text
- Your use of textual evidence to demonstrate your understanding of the source text

Your ability to achieve a high Reading score depends on how well you accomplish Step 1 of the Kaplan Method for the SAT Essay:

Step 1: Read the source text, taking notes on how the author uses:
- **Evidence to support claims**
- **Reasoning to develop ideas and to connect claims and evidence**
- **Stylistic or persuasive elements to add power to the ideas expressed**

For an in-depth review of the Kaplan Method for the SAT Essay, please read chapter 26.

Central Ideas

The **central idea** of a text is the key point the author wants to make. The central idea is also often referred to as the text's theme or thesis. Here are some questions to help you pinpoint a text's central idea:

- What is the author's central idea or claim?
- Why did the author write this passage?
- What is the tone of the passage?
- What is this passage primarily about?

✔ **Expert Tip**

Do not confuse a text's topic and its central idea. The topic is what the author is writing about, such as ecology, politics, or literary criticism. The central idea is the author's opinion about the topic. The topic can usually be summarized in one sentence; the central idea often requires several sentences to describe the author's point of view and why he or she takes that position.

Essay

Important Details

While a source text will inevitably be full of details, the important details are those that support or explain the author's central idea. Authors often use certain structural clues or keywords to highlight important details. The following chart lists common categories of keywords and examples.

List	to begin with, first, secondly, next, then, finally, most important, also, for instance, in fact, for example, another
Chronology	on (date), not long after, now, as, before, after, when
Compare-and-Contrast	however, but, as well as, on the other hand, not only . . . but also, either . . . or, while, although, unless, similarly, yet, neither . . . nor
Cause-and-Effect	because, since, therefore, consequently, as a result, this led to, so that, nevertheless, accordingly, if . . . then, thus

If you're unsure if a detail is important when reading a source text, it probably isn't. Always ask: "Does this detail support or enhance the author's central idea? How?"

Let's look at the following test-like source text excerpt. Notice what kinds of notes an SAT expert takes in the margins of the passage. After the annotated passage, there is a series of questions and answers an SAT expert would ask to determine the text's central idea and important details.

Adapted from Hayakawa, S.I. Language in *Thought and Action* (Fifth Edition). New York: Harcourt Brace & Company, 1991.

The following passage is excerpted from a book that examines language and its necessity in ensuring survival in society.

central idea: names lead to behavior

1   Names that are "loaded" tend to influence behavior toward those to whom they are applied. Currently the shop doorways and freeway underpasses of American cities are sheltering tens of thousands of people who have no work and no homes. These people used to be referred to as "bums"—a word that suggests not only a lack of employment but a lack of desire to work, people who are lazy, satisfied with little, and who have no desire to enter the mainstream of the American middle class or subscribe to its values. Thus, to think of these people as "bums" is to think that they are only getting what they deserve. With the search for new names for such people—"street people," "homeless," "displaced persons"—we may find new ways of helping these individuals.

ex. of "bums" connotation

if rename, better help?

2   . . . One other curious fact needs to be recorded about the words we apply to such hotly debated issues as race, religion, political heresy, and economic dissent. Every reader is acquainted with people who, according

Essay

to their own flattering descriptions of themselves, "believe in being frank" and like to "tell it like it is." By "telling it like it is," such people usually mean calling anything or anyone by the term which has the strongest and most disagreeable affective connotations. Why people should pin medals on themselves for "candor" for performing this nasty feat has often puzzled me. Sometimes it is necessary to violate verbal taboos as an aid to clearer thinking, but more often, to insist upon "telling it like it is" is to provide our minds with a greased runway down which we may slide back into unexamined and reactive patterns of evaluation and behavior.

"candor" does not = being mean but many think it does

What is the author's central idea or claim? Names or labels, especially those with negative connotations, can lead to negative behavior or beliefs.

Why did the author write this passage? To demonstrate how language, even on the level of word or name choice, can affect society and influence people's attitudes toward others.

What is the tone of this passage? Appalled or indignant.

What is this passage mostly about? How negative names can affect our actions and the excuses people use to continue to be politically incorrect.

What is the most important detail in the first paragraph? The example of the connotations of the word "bums."

How does this detail serve the author's central idea? The example supports the idea that the connotation of a word used to label a group of people can color how most of society views that group and how that view may be skewed.

What is the most important detail in the second paragraph? The author's assertion that when most people "tell it like it is," they call "anything or anyone by the term which has the strongest and most disagreeable affective connotations," thereby allowing society to "slide back into unexamined and reactive patterns of evaluation and behavior."

How does this detail serve the author's central idea? It discusses how the more generalized theory behind why people use derogatory labels causes negative societal behavior.

THE SAT ESSAY: ANALYSIS

One of the three scores you'll receive on the SAT Essay is the Analysis score. Graded on a scale of 1 to 4 by two different readers for a total score of 2 to 8, the Analysis score is based on:

- Your analysis of the source text and understanding of the analytical task
- Your evaluation of the author's use of evidence, reasoning, and/or stylistic and persuasive elements, and/or features of your own choosing
- Your support for the claims or points you make in your response
- Your focus on features of the text that are most relevant to addressing the task

The SAT Essay prompt dictates that you analyze one or more features the author uses to strengthen the logic and persuasiveness of his or her argument. The Kaplan Template for the SAT Essay detailed in chapter 26 suggests that you pick three features to discuss in your response. Because the source text is different for every administration of the SAT, the three features you pick to analyze will depend on the source text.

Commonly Used Features and Styles

Feature	Defintion	Example
Allusion	A literary, historical, religious or mythological reference	*Eli's weakness for sugary drinks is his Achilles' heel.*
Appeals to authority, emotion, and/or logic	Rhetorical arguments in which the speaker claims to be an authority or expert in a field, attempts to play upon the emotions, or appeals to the use of reason	*As the eminent scientist Dr. Carl Sagan suggested, though the world is dependent on science and technology, few understand either. Sound reasoning, then, requires that we expose children to both from their earliest cognitive years.*
Claim	The assertion of something as fact	*It is very clear that the pursuit of riches is the driving force in society today; morality has given way to greed.*
Compare/contrast	A discussion in which two or more things are compared, contrasted, or both	*For years, people have debated the benefits of running for exercise. On one hand, running puts stress on your joints. On the other hand, running can strengthen tissues and tendons if you include moderation, rest, and recovery as part of your approach.*

Feature	Defintion	Example
Diction	The author's word choice, which often reveals an author's attitude and point of view	*It was quite a surprise when the timid Mr. Patel jumped to his feet, pounded the table, and roared his opposition.*
Hyperbole	Overstatement characterized by exaggerated language, usually to make a point or draw attention	*I told my sister that because she made me wait for an eternity to get a table at her favorite restaurant, I was now dying of hunger.*
Irony	A contrast between what is stated and what is really meant, or between what is expected and what actually happens	*As Petros walked into the classroom and glanced at what his teacher had written on the board, he grimaced and muttered, "A pop quiz in my first class—what a great way to start the day."*
Juxtaposition	Placing two things or ideas together to contrast them	*As Charles Dickens wrote in* A Tale of Two Cities, *"It was the best of times, it was the worst of times, it was the age of wisdom, it was the age of foolishness, it was the epoch of belief, it was the epoch of incredulity . . . "*
Rebuttal/refutation	An argument technique wherein opposing arguments are anticipated and countered	*To formulate a convincing rebuttal to the claim that technology is detrimental to positive social interaction, I compiled information and statistics that show how technology enhances social communication and expression.*
Rhetorical question	A question that is asked simply for the sake of stylistic effect and is not expected to be answered	*Who would not want to have a great satisfying job that allows you to do what you love every day? And what is more satisfying than fulfilling one's dreams?*
Symbolism	Use of a person, place, thing, event, or pattern that figuratively represents or "stands for" something else; often the thing or idea represented is more abstract or general than the symbol, which is concrete	*In William Blake's poem "Ah Sunflower," the sunflower refers to humankind and the sun represents life: "Ah Sunflower, weary of time, Who countest the steps of the sun."*

You can choose to analyze any of these features in your SAT Essay response; however, make sure to select features that are easily found within the source text and that the author uses to further his or her argument. If you cannot answer the questions posed in the Kaplan Template for the SAT Essay, pick another feature.

Let's look at the following test-like source text excerpt. After the annotated passage, the left column contains the features used in the excerpt. The column on the right describes how those features are used.

Adapted from Jonathan Swift's *A Modest Proposal*, written in 1729.

In the following passage, the narrator is proposing an idea "For Preventing the Children of Poor People From Being a [Burden] to Their Parents."

1 I shall now therefore (humbly) propose my own thoughts, which I hope will not be liable to the least objection.

2 I have been assured <u>by a very knowing American</u> of my acquaintance in London that a young healthy child well nursed is at a year old <u>a most delicious, nourishing, and wholesome food,</u> whether stewed, roasted, baked, or boiled; and I make no doubt that it will equally serve in a fricassee or a ragout.*

appeal to authority

3 I do therefore (humbly) <u>offer it to public consideration</u> that of the hundred and twenty thousand children already computed[†], twenty thousand may be reserved for breed, whereof only one-fourth part be males; <u>which is more than we allow to sheep, black cattle, or swine;</u> and my reason is that these children are seldom the fruits of marriage, a circumstance not much regarded by our savages; therefore one male will be sufficient to serve four females. That the remaining hundred thousand may, at a year old, be offered in sale to the persons of quality and fortune through the kingdom; always advising the mother to let them suck plentifully in the last month, so as to render them plump and fat for a good table. A child will make two dishes at an entertainment for friends; and when the family dines alone, the fore or hind quarter will make a reasonable dish, and seasoned with a little pepper or salt will be very good boiled on the fourth day, especially in winter.

audience = public

compare boys to livestock

children as food!!

4 <u>I have reckoned upon</u> a medium that a child just born will weigh twelve pounds, and in a solar year, if tolerably nursed, will increase to twenty-eight pounds.

stats/logic/math

5 I grant this food will be somewhat dear, and therefore very proper for landlords, who, as they have already devoured most of the parents, seem to have the best title to the children.

---

* a spicy meat stew
† that is, the number of children annually born to Irish parents who cannot support them

Feature	How It's Used
Appeal to authority	The author cites his "very knowing American" acquaintance in London who claims that "a young healthy child well nursed is at a year old a most delicious, nourishing, and wholesome food."
Diction	The author's repetitive use of the word "humbly" in the first and third paragraphs implies that his proposal is a modest one (thereby reinforcing the title of the essay).
Irony	The author presents a completely unacceptable solution to hunger and asks the audience to take seriously a preposterous suggestion.

THE SAT ESSAY: WRITING

Just as the SAT Writing & Language Test assesses your knowledge of expression of ideas and conformity to the conventions of standard written English grammar, usage, and punctuation by having you revise and edit texts, so too does the SAT Essay Test by having you craft an original response. Therefore, the stronger your mastery of the writing and grammar concepts outlined in Unit 7: Expression of Ideas and Unit 8: Standard English Conventions, the better able you will be to earn a high Writing score on the SAT Essay.

One of the three scores you'll receive on the SAT Essay is the Writing score. Graded on a scale of 1 to 4 by two different readers for a total score of 2 to 8, the Writing score is based on:

- Your use of a central claim
- Your use of effective organization and progression of ideas
- Your use of varied sentence structures
- Your employment of precise word choice
- Your ability to maintain a consistent and appropriate style and tone
- Your command of the conventions of standard written English

Grammar Tips for the SAT Essay

1. **Avoid Sentence Fragments and Run-On Sentences.** Technically, a sentence fragment has no independent clause. A run-on sentence has two or more independent clauses that are improperly connected.

2. **Use Commas Correctly.** When using the comma, follow these guidelines:

- Use commas to separate items in a series. If more than two items are listed in a series, they should be separated by commas.

- Do not place commas before the first element of a series or after the last element.

- Use commas to separate two or more adjectives before a noun; do not use a comma after the last adjective in the series.

- Use commas to set off parenthetical clauses and phrases. A parenthetical expression is one that is not necessary to the central idea of the sentence.

- Use commas after most introductory phrases.

- Use commas to separate independent clauses (clauses that could stand alone as complete sentences) connected by coordinating conjunctions such as *and*, *but*, *not*, and *yet*.

3. **Use Semicolons Correctly.** Follow these guidelines for correct semicolon usage:

- A semicolon may be used instead of a coordinating conjunction such as *and*, *or*, or *but* to link two closely related independent clauses.

- A semicolon may also be used between independent clauses connected by words like *therefore*, *nevertheless*, and *moreover*.

4. **Use Colons Correctly.** When you see a colon, it means "something's coming." Follow these rules for correct colon usage:

- In formal writing, the colon is used only as a means of signaling that what follows is a list, definition, explanation, or concise summary of what has gone before. The colon usually follows an independent clause, and it will frequently be accompanied by a reinforcing expression like *the following*, *as follows*, or *namely*, or by an explicit demonstrative like *this*.

- Be careful not to put a colon between a verb and its direct object.

- Context will occasionally make clear that a second independent clause is closely linked to its predecessor, even without an explicit expression. Here, too, a colon is appropriate, although a period will always be correct too.

5. **Use Apostrophes Correctly.** Follow these guidelines for correct apostrophe usage:

- Use the apostrophe with contracted forms of verbs to indicate that one or more letters have been eliminated in writing. Generally, though, you should try to avoid contractions when writing your SAT Essay response.

- Use the apostrophe to indicate the possessive form of a noun.

- The apostrophe is used to indicate possession only with nouns; in the case of pronouns, there are separate possessives for each person and number, with the exception of the neutral *one*, which forms its possessive by adding an apostrophe and an *s*.

6. **Pay Attention to Subject-Verb Agreement.** Singular subjects and plural subjects take different forms of the verb in the present tense. Usually, the difference lies in the presence or absence of a final *s*, but sometimes the difference is more radical. You can usually trust your ear to give you the correct verb form. However, certain situations may cause difficulty, such as:

   • When the subject and verb are separated by a number of words

   • When the subject is an indefinite pronoun

   • When the subject consists of more than one noun

7. **Use Modifiers Correctly.** In English, the position of a word within a sentence often establishes the word's relationship to other words in the sentence. This is especially true with modifying phrases. Modifiers, like pronouns, are generally connected to the nearest word that agrees with the modifier in person and number. If a modifier is placed too far from the word it modifies (the referent), the meaning may be lost or obscured. Avoid ambiguity by placing modifiers as close as possible to the words they are intended to modify.

8. **Use Pronouns Correctly.** A pronoun is a word that replaces a noun in a sentence. Every time you write a pronoun—*he, him, his, she, her, it, its, they, their, that*, or *which*—be sure there can be absolutely no doubt what its antecedent is. The antecedent is the particular noun a pronoun refers to or stands for. Careless use of pronouns can obscure your intended meaning.

9. **Pay Attention to Parallelism.** Matching constructions must be expressed in parallel form. It is often rhetorically effective to use a particular construction several times in succession in order to provide emphasis. The technique is called parallel construction, and it is effective only when used sparingly. If your sentences are varied, a parallel construction will stand out. If your sentences are already repetitive, a parallel structure will further obscure your meaning.

Style Tips For The SAT Essay

1. **Write succinctly.**

   • Do not use several words when one word will do.

   • If you have something to say, just say it.

2. **Write assertively.**

   • Avoid overuse of qualifiers.

   • You don't need to overly clarify your statements.

   • Put verbs in the active voice whenever possible.

3. **Write clearly.**

   • Try not to begin sentences with *there is, there are, it would be, it could be, it can be*, or *it is*.

   • Avoid vague references, indirect language, and general wordiness. Choose specific, descriptive words.

   • Avoid clichés, which are overused expressions. Always substitute more specific language for a cliché.

- Limit your use of jargon.
- Avoid using slang and colloquialisms.

Let's look at examples of how to correct common style issues.

The left column contains the issue. The column in the middle features a sample sentence. The column on the right demonstrates how to improve the sample sentence.

Issue	Incorrect	Correct
Needless qualification	This rather serious breach of etiquette may possibly shake the very foundations of the diplomatic community.	This serious breach of etiquette may shake the foundations of the diplomatic community.
Filling up space	Which idea of the author's is more in line with what I believe? This is a very interesting question. . . .	The author's beliefs are similar to mine.
Needless self-reference	I am of the opinion that air pollution is a more serious problem than the government has led us to believe.	Air pollution is a more serious problem than the government has led us to believe.
Weak openings	There are several reasons why Andre and his brother will not share an apartment.	Andre and his brother will not share an apartment for several reasons.
Vagueness	Chantal is highly educated.	Chantal has a master's degree in business administration.

Remember Step 1 of the Kaplan Method for the SAT Essay: Read the source text, taking notes on how the author uses:

- evidence to support claims

- reasoning to develop ideas and to connect claims and evidence

- stylistic or persuasive elements to add power to the ideas expressed

Read the following test-like source text excerpt and accompanying notes. Then, use the Kaplan Template for the SAT Essay to plan your introduction and first body paragraph.

Adapted from David Foster Wallace's "Tense Present: Democracy, English, and the Wars over Usage." *Harper's Magazine*, April 2001.

The following passage is excerpted from a monthly journal of literature, politics, culture, and the arts.

1   My own humble opinion is that some of the cultural and <u>political realities of American life are themselves racially insensitive and elitist and offensive and unfair</u>, and that tiptoeing around these realities with <u>euphemistic doublespeak</u> is not only hypocritical but toxic to the project of ever actually changing them. Such tiptoeing has of course now achieved the status of a dialect—one powerful enough to have turned the normal politics of the Usage Wars sort of inside out.

varied diction

juxt. of colloquial & academic

2   I refer here to <u>Politically Correct English (PCE)</u>. Although it's common to make jokes about PCE, be advised that Politically Correct English's various pre- and proscriptions are <u>taken very seriously *indeed* by colleges and corporations and government agencies,</u> whose own institutional dialects now evolve under the beady scrutiny of a whole new kind of Language Police.

some think PCE = joke

others think PCE = serious

appeal to authority

3   From one perspective, the history of PCE evinces a kind of irony. That is, the same ideological principles that informed the original sixties-era rejections of <u>traditional</u> authority and <u>traditional</u> inequality have now actually produced a far more inflexible <u>tradition</u> or complexity backed by the threat of real-world sanctions (termination, litigation) for those who fail to conform. <u>This is sort of funny in a dark way, maybe,</u> and most criticism of PCE seems to consist in making fun of its trendiness or vapidity. This reviewer's <u>own opinion is that prescriptive PCE is not just silly but confused and dangerous.</u>

explains irony of PCE

use of colloquial makes his opinion clear

4   <u>Usage is always political,</u> of course, but it's complexly political. With respect, for instance, to political change, usage conventions can function in two ways: on the one hand <u>they can be a *reflection* of</u> political

Essay

change, and on the other they can be <u>an *instrument* of political change.</u> These two functions are different and have to be kept straight. Confusing them—in particular, mistaking for political efficacy what is really just a (language's political) symbolism—enables the bizarre conviction that America ceases to be elitist or unfair simply because Americans stop using certain vocabulary that is <u>historically associated with elitism and unfairness.</u> This is PCE's central fallacy—that a society's mode of expression is productive of its attitudes rather than a product of those attitudes.

instrument vs reflection of pol. change

central argument

¶1: Introductory paragraph

Introductory statement

_____

_____

Paraphrase the author's central idea or claim

_____

_____

Specifically state the features the author uses to support the central idea or claim

_____

_____

_____

¶2: First body paragraph

Introduce Feature 1 and provide a quote or paraphrase of the feature

_____

_____

_____

Specifically state how Feature 1 provides evidence to support the author's reasoning

_____

_____

_____

Discuss how Feature 1 reflects the author's thinking and the way the author ties his or her claim and evidence together

_____

_____

_____

Analyze the effect Feature 1 is likely to have on the audience

_____

_____

_____

Essay

Now, use the Kaplan Template notes you wrote on page 688 to complete Steps 3 and 4 of the Kaplan Method for the SAT Essay: Write your essay and check your essay for mistakes in grammar, spelling, and clarity. Give yourself 8 minutes to write the introduction and first body paragraph.

_____

_____

_____

_____

_____

_____

_____

_____

_____

_____

_____

_____

_____

_____

_____

_____

_____

_____

_____

_____

_____

_____

_____

_____

_____

_____

_____

_____

_____

Essay

Essay

Answers & Explanations for this chapter begin on page 1034.

EXTRA PRACTICE

As you read the passage below, consider how Vice President Agnew uses

- evidence, such as facts or examples, to support claims.

- reasoning to develop ideas and to connect claims and evidence.

- stylistic or persuasive elements, such as word choice or appeals to emotion, to add power to the ideas expressed.

Adapted from Vice President Spiro Agnew's 1969 speech "Television News Coverage."

1   Tonight I want to discuss the importance of the television news medium to the American people. No nation depends more on the intelligent judgment of its citizens. No medium has a more profound influence over public opinion. So, nowhere should there be more conscientious responsibility exercised than by the news media.

2   Monday night a week ago, President Nixon delivered the most important address of his Administration, one of the most important of our decade. His subject was Vietnam. My hope, as his at that time, was to rally the American people to see the conflict through to a lasting and just peace in the Pacific. For 32 minutes, he reasoned with a nation that has suffered almost a third of a million casualties in the longest war in its history.

3   When the President completed his address—an address, incidentally, that he spent weeks in the preparation of—his words and policies were subjected to instant analysis and querulous criticism. The audience of 70 million Americans was inherited by a small band of network commentators and self-appointed analysts, the majority of whom expressed in one way or another their hostility to what he had to say.

4   It was obvious that their minds were made up in advance. Those who recall the fumbling and groping that followed President Johnson's dramatic disclosure of his intention not to seek another term have seen these men in a genuine state of nonpreparedness. This was not it.

5   One commentator twice contradicted the President's statement about the exchange of correspondence with Ho Chi Minh.[1] Another challenged the President's abilities as a politician. A third asserted that the President was following a Pentagon line. Others, by the expressions on their faces, the tone of their questions, and the sarcasm of their responses, made clear their sharp disapproval.

6   To guarantee in advance that the President's plea for national unity would be challenged, one network trotted out Averell Harriman for the occasion.

7   All in all, Mr. Harriman offered a broad range of gratuitous advice challenging and contradicting the policies outlined by the President of the United States. Where the President had issued a call for unity, Mr. Harriman was encouraging the country not to listen to him.

8   Now every American has a right to disagree with the President of the United States and
to express publicly that disagreement. But the President of the United States has a right
to communicate directly with the people who elected him, and the people of this country
have the right to make up their own minds.

9   When Winston Churchill rallied public opinion to stay the course against Hitler's
Germany, he didn't have to contend with a gaggle of commentators raising doubts about
whether he was reading public opinion right, or whether Britain had the stamina to see
the war through. When President Kennedy rallied the nation in the Cuban missile crisis,
his address to the people was not chewed over by a roundtable of critics who disparaged
the course of action he'd asked America to follow.

10 At least 40 million Americans every night, it's estimated, watch the network news. Seven
million of them view ABC, the remainder being divided between NBC and CBS. According to Harris polls and other studies, for millions of Americans the networks are the sole
source of national and world news.

11 Now how is this network news determined? A small group of anchormen, commentators,
and executive producers settle upon the 20 minutes or so of film and commentary that's to
reach the public. This selection is made from the 90 to 180 minutes that may be available.
Their powers of choice are broad.

12 They decide what 40 to 50 million Americans will learn of the day's events in the nation
and in the world. These men can create national issues overnight. They can make or break
by their coverage and commentary a moratorium on the war. They can elevate men from
obscurity to national prominence within a week. They can reward some politicians with
national exposure and ignore others.

13 The views of the majority of this fraternity do *not*—and I repeat, not—represent the views
of America. Not only did the country receive the President's speech more warmly than the
networks, but so also did the Congress of the United States.

14 Yesterday, the President was notified that 300 individual Congressmen and 50 Senators
of both parties had endorsed his efforts for peace. As with other American institutions,
perhaps it is time that the networks were made more responsive to the views of the nation
and more responsible to the people they serve.

> Write an essay in which you explain how Vice President Agnew builds an argument to persuade his
> audience that the way in which network news covered a presidential address was inappropriate. In your
> essay, analyze how Agnew uses one or more of the features listed above (or features of your own choice)
> to strengthen the logic and persuasiveness of his argument. Be sure that your analysis focuses on the
> most relevant features of the passage.
>
> Your essay should not explain whether you agree with Agnew's claims, but rather explain how he builds
> an argument to persuade his audience.

Essay

Essay

Essay

Essay

PART FOUR

Review

CHAPTER 28

Putting It All Together

KAPLAN METHOD FOR MATH

Step 1: Read the question, identifying and organizing important information as you go

Step 2: Choose the best strategy to answer the question

Step 3: Check that you answered the *right* question

Step 1: Read the question, identifying and organizing important information as you go

- **What information am I given?** Take a few seconds to jot down the information you are given and try to group similar items together.

- **Separate the question from the context.** Word problems may include information that is unnecessary to solve the question. Feel free to discard any unnecessary information.

- **How are the answer choices different?** Reading answer choices carefully can help you spot the most efficient way to solve a multiple-choice math question. If the answer choices are decimals, then painstakingly rewriting your final answer as a simplified fraction is a waste of time; you can just use your calculator instead.

- **Should I label or draw a diagram?** If the question describes a shape or figure but doesn't provide one, sketch a diagram so you can see the shape or figure and add notes to it. If a figure is provided, take a few seconds to label it with information from the question.

Step 2: Choose the best strategy to answer the question

- **Look for patterns.** Every SAT math question can be solved in a variety of ways, but not all strategies are created equally. To finish all of the questions, you'll need to solve questions as *efficiently* as possible. If you find yourself about to do time-consuming math, take a moment to look for time-saving shortcuts.

- **Pick numbers or use straightforward math.** While you can always solve an SAT math question with what you've learned in school, doing so won't always be the fastest way. On questions that describe relationships between numbers (such as percentages) but don't actually use numbers, you can often save time on Test Day by using techniques such as Picking Numbers instead of straightforward math.

Step 3: Check that you answered the *right* question

- When you get the final answer, **resist the urge to immediately bubble in the answer.** Take a moment to:

    - Review the question stem.

    - Check units of measurement.

    - Double-check your work.

- The SAT will often ask you for quantities such as $x + 1$ or the product of x and y. **Be careful on these questions!** They often include tempting answer choices that correspond to the values of x or y individually. There's no partial credit on the SAT, so take a moment at the end of every question to make sure you're answering the right question.

KAPLAN METHOD FOR MULTI-PART MATH QUESTIONS

Step 1: Read the first question in the set, looking for clues

Step 2: Identify and organize the information you need

Step 3: Based on what you know, plan your steps to navigate the first question

Step 4: Solve, step-by-step, checking units as you go

Step 5: Did I answer the *right* question?

Step 6: Repeat for remaining questions, incorporating results from the previous question if possible

Step 1: Read the first question in the set, looking for clues

- **Focus all your energy here** instead of diluting it over the whole set of questions; solving a multi-part question in pieces is far simpler than trying to solve all the questions in the set at once. Furthermore, you may be able to use the results from earlier parts to solve subsequent ones. Don't even consider the later parts of the question set until you've solved the first part.

- **Watch for hints** about what information you'll actually need to use to answer the questions. Underlining key quantities is often helpful to separate what's important from extraneous information.

Step 2: Identify and organize the information you need

- **What information am I given?** Jot down key notes, and group-related quantities to develop your strategy.

- **What am I solving for?** This is your target. As you work your way through subsequent steps, keep your target at the front of your mind. This will help you avoid unnecessary work (and subsequent time loss). You'll sometimes need to tackle these problems from both ends, so always keep your goal in mind.

Step 3: Based on what you know, plan your steps to navigate the first question

- **What pieces am I missing?** Many students become frustrated when faced with a roadblock such as missing information, but it's an easy fix. Sometimes you'll need to do an intermediate calculation to reveal the missing piece or pieces of the puzzle.

Step 4: Solve, step-by-step, checking units as you go

- **Work quickly but carefully**, just as you've done on other SAT math questions.

Step 5: Did I answer the *right* question?

- As is the case with the Kaplan Method for Math, **make sure your final answer is the requested answer.**

- Review the first question in the set.

- Double-check your units and your work.

Step 6: Repeat for remaining questions, incorporating results from the previous question if possible

Now take your results from the first question and think critically about whether they fit into the subsequent questions in the set. Previous results won't always be applicable, but when they are, they often lead to huge time savings. But be careful—don't round results from the first question in your calculations for the second question—only the final answer should be rounded.

KAPLAN METHOD FOR READING COMPREHENSION

Step 1: Read actively

Step 2: Examine the question stem

Step 3: Predict and answer

Step 1: Read actively

Active reading means:

- Ask questions and take notes *as* you read the passage. Asking questions about the passage and taking notes are integral parts of your approach to acing the SAT Reading Test.

Some of the questions you might want to ask are:

- Why did the author write this word/detail/sentence/paragraph?

- Is the author taking a side? If so, what side is he or she taking?

- What are the tone and purpose of the passage?

Make sure you remember to:

- Identify the passage type.

- Take notes, circle keywords, and underline key phrases.

Step 2: Examine the question stem

This means you should:

- Identify keywords and line references in the question stem.

- Apply question-type strategies as necessary.

Step 3: Predict and answer

This means you should:

- Predict an answer before looking at the answer choices, also known as "predict before you peek."

- Select the best match.

Predicting before you peek helps you:

- Eliminate the possibility of falling into wrong answer traps.

KAPLAN METHOD FOR INFOGRAPHICS

Step 1: Read the question

Step 2: Examine the infographic

Step 3: Predict and answer

Step 1: Read the question

- Analyze the question stem for information that will help you zero in on the specific parts of the infographic that apply to the question.

Step 2: Examine the infographic

- Circle parts of the infographic that relate directly to the question.

- Identify units of measurement, labels, and titles.

Step 3: Predict and answer

- Do not look at the answer choices until you've used the infographic to make a prediction.

KAPLAN METHOD FOR WRITING & LANGUAGE

Step 1: Read the passage and identify the issue

- If there's an infographic, apply the Kaplan Method for Infographics.

Step 2: Eliminate answer choices that do not address the issue

Step 3: Plug in the remaining answer choices and select the most correct, concise, and relevant one

Step 1: Read the passage and identify the issue

This means:

- Rather than reading the whole passage and then answering all of the questions, you can answer questions as you read because they are mostly embedded in the text itself.

- When you see a number, stop reading and look at the question. If you can answer it with what you've read so far, do so. If you need more information, keep reading for context until you can answer the question.

Step 2: Eliminate answer choices that do not address the issue

Eliminating answer choices that do not address the issue:

- Increases your odds of getting the correct answer by removing obviously incorrect answer choices

Step 3: Plug in the remaining answer choices and select the most correct, concise, and relevant one

Correct, concise, and relevant means that the answer choice you select:

- Makes sense when read with the correction
- Is as short as possible while retaining the information in the text
- Relates well to the passage overall

Answer choices should not:

- Change the intended meaning of the original sentence, paragraph, or passage
- Introduce new grammatical errors

KAPLAN METHOD FOR THE SAT ESSAY

Step 1: Read the source text, taking notes on how the author uses:

- Evidence to support claims
- Reasoning to develop ideas and to connect claims and evidence
- Stylistic or persuasive elements to add power to the ideas expressed

Step 2: Use the Kaplan Template to create an outline

Step 3: Write your essay

Step 4: Check your essay for mistakes in grammar, spelling, and clarity

Step 1: Read the source text, taking notes on how the author uses:

- **Evidence to support claims**
- **Reasoning to develop ideas and to connect claims and evidence**
- **Stylistic or persuasive elements to add power to the ideas expressed**

Your notes should focus on:

- Evidence to support claims (e.g., cited data or statistics, or authoritative sources that support the author's argument)
- Reasoning to develop ideas and make connections (e.g., the author explains his logic for using a specific piece of evidence to support a specific claim)
- Stylistic or persuasive elements to add power to the ideas expressed (e.g., using figurative language, irony, metaphor, and other elements to appeal to emotions)

In addition to taking notes in the margins of the passage, it is also helpful to underline and circle the following:

- Central ideas
- Important details
- Errors of fact or interpretation
- Textual evidence (quotations, paraphrases, or both)

You should spend approximately 10 minutes on Step 1.

Step 2: Use the Kaplan Template to create an outline

Using the Kaplan Template to create an outline before you write your essay is a huge time-saver, which is essential when you have only 50 minutes to complete the SAT Essay Test. Spending the first part of the allotted time effectively (i.e., reading and taking notes on the source text and creating an outline) will lead to a well-organized, more convincing essay. You'll also find that organizing your thoughts ahead of time will enable you to write much more quickly!

You should spend approximately 8 minutes on Step 2.

Step 3: Write your essay

After you have read and analyzed the source text, your next goal is to write a cohesive essay that demonstrates your use and command of standard written English. To demonstrate your proficiency, you must:

- Provide your own precise central claim.
- Use a variety of sentence structures.
- Employ precise word choice.
- Maintain a constant and appropriate style and tone.

You should spend approximately 30 minutes on Step 3.

Step 4: Check your essay for mistakes in grammar, spelling, and clarity

While a few grammar and spelling mistakes won't drastically harm your SAT Essay score, setting aside some time to proofread can help you catch careless errors that you can easily correct, thereby increasing your Writing score on the SAT Essay.

You should spend the remaining 2 minutes on Step 4.

KAPLAN STRATEGY FOR TRANSLATING ENGLISH INTO MATH

- Define any variables, choosing letters that make sense.
- Break sentences into short phrases.
- Translate each phrase into a mathematical expression.
- Put the expressions together to form an equation.

KAPLAN STRATEGY FOR COMMAND OF EVIDENCE QUESTIONS

- When you see a question asking you to choose the best evidence to support your answer to the previous question, review how you selected that answer.
- Avoid answers that provide evidence for incorrect answers to the previous question.
- The correct answer will support why the previous question's answer is correct.

KAPLAN STRATEGY FOR VOCAB-IN-CONTEXT QUESTIONS

- Pretend the word is a blank in the sentence.
- Predict what word could be substituted for the blank.
- Select the answer choice that best matches your prediction.

KAPLAN STRATEGY FOR PAIRED PASSAGES

- Read Passage 1, then answer its questions.
- Read Passage 2, then answer its questions.
- Answer questions about both passages.

COUNTDOWN TO TEST DAY

The Week Before the Test

- Finish up any required homework assignments, including online quizzes.

- Focus your additional practice on the question types and/or subject areas in which you usually score highest. Now is the time to sharpen your best skills, not cram new information.

- Make sure you are registered for the test. Remember, Kaplan cannot register you. If you missed the registration deadlines, you can request Waitlist Status on the test maker's website, collegeboard.org.

- Confirm the location of your test site. Never been there before? Make a practice run to make sure you know exactly how long it will take to get from your home to your test site. Build in extra time in case you hit traffic on the morning of the test.

- Get a great night's sleep the two days before the test.

The Day Before the Test

- Review the Kaplan Methods and Strategies, as well as the ReKap pages.

- Put new batteries in your calculator.

- Pack your backpack or bag for Test Day with the following items:
  - Photo ID
  - Registration slip or printout
  - Directions to your test site location
  - Five or more sharpened no. 2 pencils (no mechanical pencils)
  - Pencil sharpener
  - Eraser
  - Calculator
  - Extra batteries
  - Non-prohibited timepiece
  - Tissues
  - Prepackaged snacks, like granola bars
  - Bottled water, juice, or sports drink
  - Sweatshirt, sweater, or jacket

The Night Before the Test

- No studying!

- Do something relaxing that will take your mind off the test, such as watching a movie or playing video games with friends.

- Set your alarm to wake up early enough so that you won't feel rushed.

- Go to bed early, but not too much earlier than you usually do. You want to fall asleep quickly, not spend hours tossing and turning.

The Morning of the Test

- Dress comfortably and in layers. You need to be prepared for any temperature.

- Eat a filling breakfast, but don't stray too far from your usual routine. If you normally aren't a breakfast eater, don't eat a huge meal, but make sure you have something substantial.

- Read something over breakfast. You need to warm up your brain so you don't go into the test cold. Read a few pages of a newspaper, magazine, or novel.

- Get to your test site early. There is likely to be some confusion about where to go and how to sign in, so allow yourself plenty of time, even if you are taking the test at your own school.

- Leave your cell phone at home or in your car's glovebox. Many test sites do not allow them in the building.

- While you're waiting to sign in or be seated, read more of what you read over breakfast to stay in reading mode.

During the Test

- Be calm and confident. You're ready for this!

- Remember that while the SAT is a three-hour marathon (or four if you opt to do the essay), it is also a series of shorter sections. Focus on the section you're working on at that moment; don't think about previous or upcoming sections.

- Use the Kaplan Methods and Strategies as often as you can.

- Don't linger too long on any one question. Mark it and come back to it later.

- Can't figure out an answer? Try to eliminate some choices and guess strategically. Remember, there is no penalty for an incorrect answer, so even if you can't eliminate any choices, you should take a guess.

- There will be plenty of questions you CAN answer, so spend your time on those first!

- Maintain good posture throughout the test. It will help you stay alert.

- If you find yourself losing concentration, getting frustrated, or stressing about the time, stop for 30 seconds. Close your eyes, put your pencil down, take a few deep breaths, and relax your shoulders. You'll be much more productive after taking a few moments to relax.

- Use your breaks effectively. During the five-minute breaks, go to the restroom, eat your snacks, and get your energy up for the next section.

After the Test

- Congratulate yourself! Also, reward yourself by doing something fun. You've earned it.

- If you got sick during the test or if something else happened that might have negatively affected your score, you can cancel your scores by the Wednesday following your test date. Request a score cancellation form from your test proctor, or visit the test maker's website for more information. If you have questions about whether you should cancel your scores, call 1-800-KAP-TEST.

- Your scores will be available online approximately three to four weeks after your test and will be mailed to you in approximately six weeks.

- Email your instructor or tutor with your SAT scores. We want to hear how you did!

PART FIVE

Practice Tests

HOW TO SCORE YOUR PRACTICE TESTS

For each subject area in the practice test, convert your raw score, or the number of questions you answered correctly, to a scaled score using the table below. To get your raw score for Evidence-Based Reading & Writing, add the total number of Reading questions you answered correctly to the total number of Writing questions you answered correctly; for Math, add the number of questions you answered correctly for the Math—No Calculator and Math—Calculator sections.

Evidence-Based Reading and Writing		Math		Evidence-Based Reading and Writing		Math	
TOTAL Raw Score	Scaled Score	Raw Score	Scaled Score	TOTAL Raw Score	Scaled Score	Raw Score	Scaled Score
0	200	0	200	49	490	49	700
1	200	1	220	50	500	50	710
2	210	2	240	51	500	51	720
3	220	3	260	52	510	52	740
4	240	4	290	53	510	53	750
5	260	5	310	54	520	54	760
6	270	6	320	55	520	55	770
7	270	7	330	56	530	56	780
8	290	8	340	57	530	57	790
9	290	9	360	58	540	58	800
10	300	10	370	59	540		
11	300	11	380	60	550		
12	310	12	390	61	550		
13	320	13	400	62	560		
14	320	14	410	63	560		
15	330	15	420	64	570		
16	330	16	430	65	570		
17	340	17	430	66	580		
18	340	18	440	67	580		
19	350	19	450	68	590		
20	350	20	450	69	590		
21	360	21	460	70	600		
22	360	22	470	71	600		
23	370	23	480	72	610		
24	370	24	490	73	610		
25	370	25	500	74	610		
26	380	26	510	75	620		
27	380	27	520	76	620		
28	380	28	530	77	630		
29	380	29	540	78	630		
30	390	30	540	79	640		
31	390	31	550	80	640		
32	400	32	560	81	660		
33	400	33	560	82	660		
34	410	34	570	83	670		
35	410	35	580	84	680		
36	420	36	590	85	690		
37	430	37	600	86	700		
38	430	38	600	87	700		
39	440	39	610	88	710		
40	440	40	620	89	710		
41	450	41	630	90	730		
42	450	42	640	91	740		
43	460	43	640	92	750		
44	460	44	660	93	760		
45	470	45	670	94	780		
46	480	46	670	95	790		
47	480	47	680	96	800		
48	490	48	690				

SAT PRACTICE TEST 1 ANSWER SHEET

Remove (or photocopy) this answer sheet and use it to complete the test. See the answer key following the test when finished.

Start with number 1 for each section. If a section has fewer questions than answer spaces, leave the extra spaces blank.

SECTION 1

1. Ⓐ Ⓑ Ⓒ Ⓓ
2. Ⓐ Ⓑ Ⓒ Ⓓ
3. Ⓐ Ⓑ Ⓒ Ⓓ
4. Ⓐ Ⓑ Ⓒ Ⓓ
5. Ⓐ Ⓑ Ⓒ Ⓓ
6. Ⓐ Ⓑ Ⓒ Ⓓ
7. Ⓐ Ⓑ Ⓒ Ⓓ
8. Ⓐ Ⓑ Ⓒ Ⓓ
9. Ⓐ Ⓑ Ⓒ Ⓓ
10. Ⓐ Ⓑ Ⓒ Ⓓ
11. Ⓐ Ⓑ Ⓒ Ⓓ
12. Ⓐ Ⓑ Ⓒ Ⓓ
13. Ⓐ Ⓑ Ⓒ Ⓓ

14. Ⓐ Ⓑ Ⓒ Ⓓ
15. Ⓐ Ⓑ Ⓒ Ⓓ
16. Ⓐ Ⓑ Ⓒ Ⓓ
17. Ⓐ Ⓑ Ⓒ Ⓓ
18. Ⓐ Ⓑ Ⓒ Ⓓ
19. Ⓐ Ⓑ Ⓒ Ⓓ
20. Ⓐ Ⓑ Ⓒ Ⓓ
21. Ⓐ Ⓑ Ⓒ Ⓓ
22. Ⓐ Ⓑ Ⓒ Ⓓ
23. Ⓐ Ⓑ Ⓒ Ⓓ
24. Ⓐ Ⓑ Ⓒ Ⓓ
25. Ⓐ Ⓑ Ⓒ Ⓓ
26. Ⓐ Ⓑ Ⓒ Ⓓ

27. Ⓐ Ⓑ Ⓒ Ⓓ
28. Ⓐ Ⓑ Ⓒ Ⓓ
29. Ⓐ Ⓑ Ⓒ Ⓓ
30. Ⓐ Ⓑ Ⓒ Ⓓ
31. Ⓐ Ⓑ Ⓒ Ⓓ
32. Ⓐ Ⓑ Ⓒ Ⓓ
33. Ⓐ Ⓑ Ⓒ Ⓓ
34. Ⓐ Ⓑ Ⓒ Ⓓ
35. Ⓐ Ⓑ Ⓒ Ⓓ
36. Ⓐ Ⓑ Ⓒ Ⓓ
37. Ⓐ Ⓑ Ⓒ Ⓓ
38. Ⓐ Ⓑ Ⓒ Ⓓ
39. Ⓐ Ⓑ Ⓒ Ⓓ

40. Ⓐ Ⓑ Ⓒ Ⓓ
41. Ⓐ Ⓑ Ⓒ Ⓓ
42. Ⓐ Ⓑ Ⓒ Ⓓ
43. Ⓐ Ⓑ Ⓒ Ⓓ
44. Ⓐ Ⓑ Ⓒ Ⓓ
45. Ⓐ Ⓑ Ⓒ Ⓓ
46. Ⓐ Ⓑ Ⓒ Ⓓ
47. Ⓐ Ⓑ Ⓒ Ⓓ
48. Ⓐ Ⓑ Ⓒ Ⓓ
49. Ⓐ Ⓑ Ⓒ Ⓓ
50. Ⓐ Ⓑ Ⓒ Ⓓ
51. Ⓐ Ⓑ Ⓒ Ⓓ
52. Ⓐ Ⓑ Ⓒ Ⓓ

[ ] # correct in Section 1

[ ] # incorrect in Section 1

SECTION 2

1. Ⓐ Ⓑ Ⓒ Ⓓ
2. Ⓐ Ⓑ Ⓒ Ⓓ
3. Ⓐ Ⓑ Ⓒ Ⓓ
4. Ⓐ Ⓑ Ⓒ Ⓓ
5. Ⓐ Ⓑ Ⓒ Ⓓ
6. Ⓐ Ⓑ Ⓒ Ⓓ
7. Ⓐ Ⓑ Ⓒ Ⓓ
8. Ⓐ Ⓑ Ⓒ Ⓓ
9. Ⓐ Ⓑ Ⓒ Ⓓ
10. Ⓐ Ⓑ Ⓒ Ⓓ
11. Ⓐ Ⓑ Ⓒ Ⓓ

12. Ⓐ Ⓑ Ⓒ Ⓓ
13. Ⓐ Ⓑ Ⓒ Ⓓ
14. Ⓐ Ⓑ Ⓒ Ⓓ
15. Ⓐ Ⓑ Ⓒ Ⓓ
16. Ⓐ Ⓑ Ⓒ Ⓓ
17. Ⓐ Ⓑ Ⓒ Ⓓ
18. Ⓐ Ⓑ Ⓒ Ⓓ
19. Ⓐ Ⓑ Ⓒ Ⓓ
20. Ⓐ Ⓑ Ⓒ Ⓓ
21. Ⓐ Ⓑ Ⓒ Ⓓ
22. Ⓐ Ⓑ Ⓒ Ⓓ

23. Ⓐ Ⓑ Ⓒ Ⓓ
24. Ⓐ Ⓑ Ⓒ Ⓓ
25. Ⓐ Ⓑ Ⓒ Ⓓ
26. Ⓐ Ⓑ Ⓒ Ⓓ
27. Ⓐ Ⓑ Ⓒ Ⓓ
28. Ⓐ Ⓑ Ⓒ Ⓓ
29. Ⓐ Ⓑ Ⓒ Ⓓ
30. Ⓐ Ⓑ Ⓒ Ⓓ
31. Ⓐ Ⓑ Ⓒ Ⓓ
32. Ⓐ Ⓑ Ⓒ Ⓓ
33. Ⓐ Ⓑ Ⓒ Ⓓ

34. Ⓐ Ⓑ Ⓒ Ⓓ
35. Ⓐ Ⓑ Ⓒ Ⓓ
36. Ⓐ Ⓑ Ⓒ Ⓓ
37. Ⓐ Ⓑ Ⓒ Ⓓ
38. Ⓐ Ⓑ Ⓒ Ⓓ
39. Ⓐ Ⓑ Ⓒ Ⓓ
40. Ⓐ Ⓑ Ⓒ Ⓓ
41. Ⓐ Ⓑ Ⓒ Ⓓ
42. Ⓐ Ⓑ Ⓒ Ⓓ
43. Ⓐ Ⓑ Ⓒ Ⓓ
44. Ⓐ Ⓑ Ⓒ Ⓓ

[ ] # correct in Section 2

[ ] # incorrect in Section 2

Practice Tests

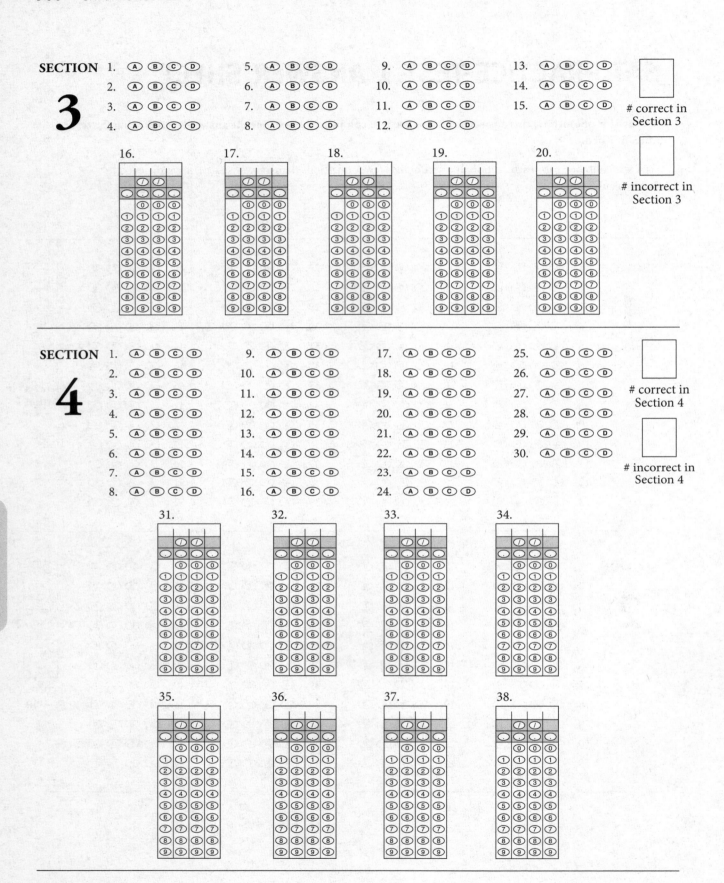

SECTION

3

correct in Section 3

incorrect in Section 3

SECTION

4

correct in Section 4

incorrect in Section 4

READING TEST

65 Minutes—52 Questions

Turn to Section 1 of your answer sheet to answer the questions in this section.

Directions: Each passage or pair of passages below is followed by a number of questions. After reading each passage or pair, choose the best answer to each question based on what is stated or implied in the passage or passages and in any accompanying graphics (such as a table or graph).

Questions 1-10 are based on the following passage.

The following passage is adapted from Henry David Thoreau's *Walden*, a mid-19th-century philosophical and personal reflection on the writer's experience living in nature and simplicity. This excerpt is from the chapter titled "Where I Lived, and What I Lived For."

It matters not what the clocks say or the attitudes and labors of men. Morning is when I am awake and there is a dawn in me. Moral reform is the
Line effort to throw off sleep. Why is it that men give so
(5) poor an account of their day if they have not been slumbering? They are not such poor calculators. If they had not been overcome with drowsiness, they would have performed something. The millions are awake enough for physical labor; but only one in a
(10) million is awake enough for effective intellectual exertion, only one in a hundred millions to a poetic or divine life. To be awake is to be alive. I have never yet met a man who was quite awake. How could I have looked him in the face?
(15) We must learn to reawaken and keep ourselves awake, not by mechanical aids, but by an infinite expectation of the dawn, which does not forsake us in our soundest sleep. I know of no more encouraging fact than the unquestionable ability of man to
(20) elevate his life by a conscious endeavor. It is something to be able to paint a particular picture, or to carve a statue, and so to make a few objects beautiful; but it is far more glorious to carve and paint the very atmosphere and medium through which we
(25) look, which morally we can do. To affect the quality of the day, that is the highest of arts. Every man is tasked to make his life, even in its details, worthy of

the contemplation of his most elevated and critical hour. If we refused, or rather used up, such paltry
(30) information as we get, the oracles would distinctly inform us how this might be done.

I went to the woods because I wished to live deliberately, to front only the essential facts of life, and see if I could not learn what it had to teach,
(35) and not, when I came to die, discover that I had not lived. I did not wish to live what was not life, living is so dear; nor did I wish to practice resignation, unless it was quite necessary. I wanted to live deep and suck out all the marrow of life, to live so
(40) sturdily and Spartan-like as to put to rout all that was not life, to cut a broad swath and shave close, to drive life into a corner, and reduce it to its lowest terms, and, if it proved to be mean, why then to get the whole and genuine meanness of it, and publish
(45) its meanness to the world; or if it were sublime, to know it by experience, and be able to give a true account of it in my next excursion. For most men, it appears to me, are in a strange uncertainty about it, whether it is of the devil or of God, and have
(50) somewhat hastily concluded that it is the chief end of man here to "glorify God and enjoy him forever."

Still we live meanly, like ants; though the fable tells us that we were long ago changed into men; like pygmies we fight with cranes; it is error upon
(55) error, and clout upon clout, and our best virtue has for its occasion a superfluous and evitable wretchedness. Our life is frittered away by detail. An honest man has hardly need to count more than his ten fingers, or in extreme cases he may
(60) add his ten toes, and lump the rest. Simplicity, simplicity, simplicity! I say, let your affairs be as two

GO ON TO THE NEXT PAGE

or three, and not a hundred or a thousand; instead of a million count half a dozen, and keep your accounts on your thumb-nail. In the midst of this
(65) chopping sea of civilized life, such are the clouds and storms and quicksands and thousand-and-one items to be allowed for, that a man has to live, if he would not founder and go to the bottom and not make his port at all, by dead reckoning, and he
(70) must be a great calculator indeed who succeeds. Simplify, simplify. Instead of three meals a day, if it be necessary eat but one; instead of a hundred dishes, five; and reduce other things in proportion.

1. The activities described in lines 20-25 ("It is something . . . morally we can do") explain how people can

    A) develop a satisfying and morally upright career.

    B) give an elevated and proper account of their day.

    C) learn to reawaken and live by conscious endeavor.

    D) awaken enough for effective intellectual exhaustion.

2. As used in lines 37-38, "resignation" most nearly means

    A) complacency.

    B) departure.

    C) quitting.

    D) revival.

3. The first paragraph of the passage most strongly suggests that which of the following is true of the author?

    A) He believes that to affect the quality of the day is the highest form of art.

    B) He feels that people perform poorly at work because they sleep too much.

    C) He is determined to spend as many waking hours as possible working.

    D) He believes that most people have yet to realize their fullest potential in life.

4. Which choice provides the best evidence for the answer to the previous question?

    A) Lines 4-6 ("Why is . . . slumbering")

    B) Lines 8-12 ("The millions . . . life")

    C) Line 12 ("To be . . . alive")

    D) Lines 12-13 ("I have . . . awake")

5. What central claim does the author make about our society as a whole?

    A) The few artists in our society do not receive the recognition they deserve.

    B) Our society willingly focuses too much on drudgery and insignificant details.

    C) Too many people hastily choose to dedicate their lives to religion.

    D) People should move to the woods to find their own conscious endeavor.

6. What can reasonably be inferred about the author's views on religion?

    A) He believes too few people critically examine their religious beliefs.

    B) He thinks that his studies in the woods will prove that God is sublime.

    C) He thinks that meanness and the sublime are the same in nature.

    D) He believes that oracles give us clues about how to live a sublime life.

GO ON TO THE NEXT PAGE

7. Which choice provides the best evidence for the answer to the previous question?

   A) Lines 26-29 ("Every man . . . hour")

   B) Lines 32-36 ("I went . . . not lived")

   C) Lines 38-47 ("I wanted . . . excursion")

   D) Line 47-51 ("For most . . . forever")

8. As used in line 40, "Spartan-like" most nearly means

   A) indulgent.

   B) rigid.

   C) pioneering.

   D) austere.

9. The author uses such words as "meanly" and "wretchedness" in lines 52-57 in order to imply that

   A) people are cruel to one another.

   B) society will destroy itself in time.

   C) many people's lives are harsh and mundane.

   D) negative tendencies ruin our intelligence.

10. Which of the following describes an approach to life that is similar to the one Thoreau promotes in this passage?

    A) Taking courses and acquiring books on how to simplify your life

    B) Hiring people to help you do your chores so you can live more simply

    C) Cleaning out your closet so that you are left with only the most essential items of clothing

    D) Traveling to a cabin without cell phone service to get away from life's complications for a weekend

Questions 11-20 are based on the following passage.

This passage is adapted from "The Opening of the Library" by W.E.B. DuBois, professor of Economics and History at Atlanta University, published in the *Atlanta Independent* on April 3, 1902.

"With simple and appropriate exercises the beautiful new Carnegie Library was thrown open to the public yesterday." So says the morning paper
Line of Atlanta, Georgia . . . .
(5)   The white marble building, the gift of Andrew Carnegie, is indeed fair to look upon. The site was given the city by a private library association, and the City Council appropriates $5,000 annually of the city moneys for its support. If you will climb
(10) the hill where the building sits, you may look down upon the rambling city. Northward and southward are 53,905 whites, eastward and westward are 35,912 blacks.
        And so in behalf of these 36,000 people my
(15) companions and I called upon the trustees of the Library on this opening day, for we had heard that black folk were to have no part in this "free public library," and we thought it well to go ask why. It was not pleasant going in, for people stared and won-
(20) dered what business we had there; but the trustees, after some waiting, received us courteously and gave us seats—some eight of us in all. To me, had fallen the lot to begin the talking. I said, briefly:
        "Gentlemen, we are a committee come to ask
(25) that you do justice to the black people of Atlanta by giving them the same free library privileges that you propose giving the whites. Every argument which can be adduced to show the need of librar-ies for whites applies with redoubled force to the
(30) blacks. More than any other part of our population, they need instruction, inspiration and proper di-version; they need to be lured from the temptations of the streets and saved from evil influences, and they need a growing acquaintance with what the
(35) best of the world's souls have thought and done and said. It seems hardly necessary in the 20th century to argue before men like you on the necessity and propriety of placing the best means of human uplifting into the hands of the poorest and lowest
(40) and blackest. . . .

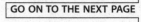
GO ON TO THE NEXT PAGE

I then pointed out the illegality of using public money collected from all for the exclusive benefit of a part of the population, or of distributing public utilities in accordance with the amount of
(45) taxes paid by any class or individual, and finally I concluded by saying:

"The spirit of this great gift to the city was not the spirit of caste or exclusion, but rather the catholic spirit which recognizes no artificial differ-
(50) ences of rank or birth or race, but seeks to give all men equal opportunity to make the most of themselves. It is our sincere hope that this city will prove itself broad enough and just enough to administer this trust in the true spirit in which it was given."

(55) Then I sat down. There was a little pause, and the chairman, leaning forward, said: "I should like to ask you a question: Do you not think that allowing whites and blacks to use this library would be fatal to its usefulness?"

(60) There come at times words linked together which seem to chord in strange recurring resonance with words of other ages and one hears the voice of many centuries and wonders which century is speaking . . . .

(65) I said simply, "I will express no opinion on that point."

Then from among us darker ones another arose. He was an excellent and adroit speaker. He thanked the trustees for the privilege of being there, and
(70) reminded them that but a short time ago even this privilege would have been impossible. He said we did not ask to use this library, we did not ask equal privileges, we only wanted some privileges somewhere. And he assured the trustees that he had
(75) perfect faith in their justice.

The president of the Trustee Board then arose, gray-haired and courteous. He congratulated the last speaker and expressed pleasure at our call. He then gave us to understand four things:
(80) 1. Blacks would not be permitted to use the Carnegie Library in Atlanta.
2. That some library facilities would be provided for them in the future.

3. That to this end the City Council would be
(85) asked to appropriate a sum proportionate to the amount of taxes paid by blacks in the city.
4. That an effort would be made, and had been made, to induce Northern philanthropists
(90) to aid such a library, and he concluded by assuring us that in this way we might eventually have a better library than the whites.

Then he bade us adieu politely and we walked home wondering.

11. Which choice best explains why DuBois wrote this passage?

A) To encourage philanthropists such as Andrew Carnegie to fund new libraries

B) To present the trustees' explanation of why African Americans could not use the library

C) To contrast his position on public access to libraries with that of the trustees

D) To state his support for construction of a new library for just African Americans

12. Which choice provides the best evidence for the answer to the previous question?

A) Lines 14-18 ("And so . . . ask why")

B) Lines 41-45 ("I then . . . or individual")

C) Lines 68-71 ("He thanked . . . impossible")

D) Lines 88-92 ("That an effort . . . than the whites")

13. As used in line 23, "lot" most nearly means

A) a predictable result.

B) a random decision.

C) an unaccepted consequence.

D) an agreed-upon responsibility.

GO ON TO THE NEXT PAGE ⟹

14. It can reasonably be inferred from the passage that

   A) the trustees would consider the construction of segregated public library facilities.

   B) the trustees agreed with DuBois's arguments in favor of expanding access to public libraries.

   C) the trustees were open to the idea of integrating Atlanta's public library system.

   D) the trustees proposed concrete plans to provide public library facilities for African Americans.

15. Which choice provides the best evidence for the answer to the previous question?

   A) Lines 55-59 ("There was a little . . . to its usefulness")

   B) Lines 76-78 ("The president . . . at our call")

   C) Lines 80-81 ("Blacks . . . in Atlanta")

   D) Lines 82-83 ("That some . . . in the future")

16. As used in line 34, "growing acquaintance" most nearly means

   A) a friendly relationship.

   B) an increasing comprehension.

   C) an active involvement.

   D) a brief initiation.

17. Which claim does DuBois make to the trustees?

   A) Allowing all of Atlanta's residents to use the new library would render it useless.

   B) Blacks will benefit less from access to public libraries than white residents.

   C) Poor blacks have greater need for a public library than other residents.

   D) Atlanta should invest in public libraries and schools for all of its residents.

18. DuBois uses the example of a "catholic spirit" (line 49) to support the argument that

   A) the city's neighborhoods continue to be segregated by race and economic class.

   B) Atlanta has an obligation to provide equal opportunity for all its residents to better themselves.

   C) access to public libraries should be based on the amount of taxes one pays.

   D) Northern philanthropists should provide private money to help pay for a public library.

19. The author's reflections expressed in lines 60-64 most likely indicate that he

   A) wishes he lived in a different century.

   B) is frustrated that people's attitudes have not changed over time.

   C) is thinking about a time when another person said the exact same words to him.

   D) is planning a detailed response to the chairman's question.

20. The four-point list in the passage can be described as

   A) a summary of the author's supporting points.

   B) an acknowledgement of a counterargument.

   C) an introduction to a counterargument.

   D) a response to the author's main argument.

Questions 21-31 are based on the following passage and supplementary material.

The following passage is adapted from an essay about Denis Diderot, an 18th century French philosopher.

Over a thirty-year period, Denis Diderot tirelessly undertook a bold endeavor; the philosopher and writer furthered technology education by
Line creating one of the most important books of the
(5) 18th century. He documented the Western world's collective knowledge through a massive set of

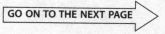

volumes called the *Encyclopédie*. Today, Diderot's *Encyclopédie* remains one of the most accessible primary sources for the study of technology during
(10) the Enlightenment, having received exposure in recent times through the Internet.

Since Diderot didn't know all there was to know, he sought contributors, more than 150, and organized their 72,000 articles into entries on politics,
(15) economics, technology, and other topics. His goal was to create an intellectual work instructionally useful to all, but soon, his *Encyclopédie* became mired in controversy, and this precursor to the modern encyclopedia was seized after its inception,
(20) its publication banned by the French government. The encyclopedia, however, had already sparked mass interest in the secrets of manufacturing and more, and so this "how-to" compendium was widely circulated underground after eventually be-
(25) ing published in 1765 by a Swedish printer.

Undoubtedly, the *Encyclopédie* served then as a beacon of free thought, and questions about control of its content caused critics to boil over. For in building a compilation of human knowledge, Diderot
(30) made a direct political statement. Essentially, the political statement was: You, the average person, can now know what only kings knew before.

In particular, Diderot created an "encyclopedic revolution" by integrating scientific discover-
(35) ies with the liberal arts. He linked technology to culture when he divided the *Encyclopédie* into three categories: history, philosophy, and poetry. Diderot then assigned subjects to these three groupings such as industry, political theory, theology,
(40) agriculture, and the arts and sciences.

The execution was deceptively simple enough because Diderot pursued everyday trade topics such as cloth dying, for example, accompanying his explanations with diagrams and illustrations. Thus,
(45) Diderot elevated "unacademic" craft knowledge to a scholarly status, challenging viewpoints about erudition held by the aristocratic ruling class of the time. More important, Diderot suggested that everyone could have access to the rational, down-to-earth truth,
(50) since he believed that knowledge about reality could be obtained by reason alone, rather than through authority or other means.

Not surprisingly, such rationalist philosophy was considered radical. The new idea of showing
(55) in amazing detail how the production techniques used in tanning and metalwork were accomplished displeased those in power. Trade guilds held control of such knowledge, and so Diderot's *Encyclopédie* was viewed as a threat to the establishment.
(60) Diderot's ideology of progress by way of better quality materials, technical research, and greater production speed was unprecedented in printed books.

Royal authorities did not want the masses
(65) exposed to Diderot's liberal views such as this one: "The good of the people must be the great purpose of government. By the laws of nature and of reason, the governors are invested with power to that end. And the greatest good of the people is liberty."
(70) But the opposition was too late. Despite an official ban, the *Encyclopédie's* beautiful bookplates survived, recording production techniques dating to the Middle Ages. Ironically, with the advent of both the English Industrial Revolution and the
(75) French Revolution, the trades shown in Diderot's work changed significantly after the encyclopedia's publication. Therefore, instead of becoming a technical dictionary, the *Encyclopédie* rather serves today as a history of technology, showing us what
(80) trades were like before machines swept in to transform industry.

GO ON TO THE NEXT PAGE ⟩

1500-1800 Scientific Revolution

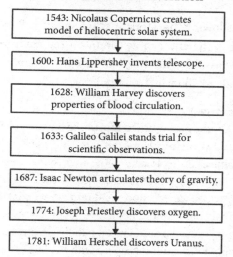

1543: Nicolaus Copernicus creates model of heliocentric solar system.

↓

1600: Hans Lippershey invents telescope.

↓

1628: William Harvey discovers properties of blood circulation.

↓

1633: Galileo Galilei stands trial for scientific observations.

↓

1687: Isaac Newton articulates theory of gravity.

↓

1774: Joseph Priestley discovers oxygen.

↓

1781: William Herschel discovers Uranus.

21. Which choice expresses a central idea of the passage?

A) Diderot crafted a revolutionary guide for the development of industrial technology.

B) Diderot provided students with a superb reference for the study of scientific principles.

C) Diderot's *Encyclopédie* continues to serve as a valuable technical resource.

D) Diderot's *Encyclopédie* helped promote the liberalization and expansion of knowledge.

22. The passage most clearly reflects the author's

A) devotion to the study of science.

B) disdain for intellectualism.

C) interest in early printing methods.

D) respect for individual innovation.

23. Which choice provides the best evidence for the answer to the previous question?

A) Lines 33-35 ("In particular . . . liberal arts")

B) Lines 54-57 ("The new idea . . . in power")

C) Lines 64-67 ("Royal . . . of government")

D) Lines 73-77 ("Ironically . . . publication")

24. According to the passage, Diderot's main goal in developing the *Encyclopédie* was to

A) express his views.

B) challenge political authority.

C) provide information and instruction.

D) create a historical record of technology.

25. As used in line 24, "underground" most nearly means

A) cautiously.

B) secretly.

C) perilously.

D) privately.

26. In lines 26-27, the function of the phrase "a beacon of free thought" is to suggest that Diderot's work

A) attracted more people to the pursuit of knowledge.

B) provided information for people most likely to use it.

C) encouraged revolutionary thinking.

D) spread scientific theory among intellectual circles.

27. The passage most strongly suggests that during this time period

A) access to information was limited to select demographics.

B) advances in printing resulted in comparable advances in other fields.

C) demands for political and social reform were severely punished.

D) intellectuals were widely respected and elevated to elite status.

Practice Tests

GO ON TO THE NEXT PAGE ⇨

28. Which choice provides the best evidence for the answer to the previous question?

    A) Lines 12-15 ("Since Diderot . . . topics")

    B) Lines 41-44 ("The execution . . . illustrations")

    C) Lines 57-59 ("Trade guilds . . . establishment")

    D) Lines 70-73 ("Despite . . . Middle Ages")

29. As used in lines 46-47, "erudition" most nearly means

    A) hierarchy.

    B) sophistication.

    C) skill.

    D) learning.

30. Which choice best describes how the impact of the *Encyclopédie* changed over time?

    A) Advances in science and industry made the *Encyclopédie* obsolete.

    B) Advances in science and industry changed the *Encyclopédie* from a "how-to" source into a history of technology.

    C) Advances in science and industry turned the *Encyclopédie* into an affordable, mass-produced publication used by millions.

    D) Advances in science and industry led to an expansion of the number of *Encyclopédie* volumes in each set.

31. Based on the passage and the graphic, which of the following is most likely to be true?

    A) Diderot would not have included information about Galileo's scientific observations.

    B) Diderot would have included information on the production techniques used to create the first telescope.

    C) Diderot would not have included information about the discovery of Uranus.

    D) Diderot would have included information about Einstein's theory of relativity.

Questions 32-42 are based on the following passages.

The following passages discuss acidity. Passage 1 describes the effect of acid rain on the environment, while Passage 2 focuses on how the human body responds to abnormal acidity levels.

Passage 1

In the past century, due to the burning of fossil fuels in energy plants and cars, acid rain has become a cause of harm to the environment. How-
Line ever, rain would still be slightly acidic even if these
(5) activities were to stop. Acid rain would continue to fall, but it would not cause the problems we see now. The environment can handle slightly acidic rain; it just cannot keep up with the level of acid rain caused by burning fossil fuels.

(10) A pH of 7 is considered neutral, while pH below 7 is acidic and pH above 7 is alkaline, or basic. Pure rain water can have a pH as low as 5.5. Rain water is acidic because carbon dioxide gas in the air reacts with the water to make carbonic acid.
(15) Since it is a weak acid, even a large amount of it will not lower the pH of water much.

Soil, lakes, and streams can tolerate slightly acidic rain. The water and soil contain alkaline materials that will neutralize acids. These include
(20) some types of rocks, plant and animal waste, and ashes from forest fires. Altogether, these materials can easily handle the slightly acidic rain that occurs naturally. The alkaline waste and ashes will slowly be used up, but more will be made to replace it.

(25) Anthropomorphic causes of acid rain, such as the burning of fossil fuels, release nitrogen oxide and sulfur oxide gases. These gases react with water to make nitric acid and sulfuric acid. Since these are both strong acids, small amounts can lower
(30) the pH of rain water to 3 or less. Such a low pH requires much more alkaline material to neutralize it. Acid rain with a lower pH uses up alkaline materials faster, and more cannot be made quickly enough to replace what is used up. Soil and water
(35) become more acidic and remain that way, as they are unable to neutralize the strong acid.

GO ON TO THE NEXT PAGE

Passage 2

In humans, keeping a constant balance between acidity and alkalinity in the blood is essential. If blood pH drops below 7.35 or rises above 7.45, (40) all of the functions in the body are impaired and life-threatening conditions can soon develop. Many processes in the body produce acid wastes, which would lower the pH of blood below the safe level unless neutralized. Several systems are in place (45) to keep pH constant within the necessary range. Certain conditions, however, can cause acids to be made faster than these systems can react.

Most of the pH control involves three related substances: carbon dioxide, carbonic acid, and (50) bicarbonate ions. Carbonic acid is formed when carbon dioxide reacts with water. Bicarbonate ions are formed when the carbonic acid releases a hydrogen ion. Excess carbonic acid lowers the pH, while excess bicarbonate ions raise it.

(55) The kidneys store bicarbonate ions and will release or absorb them to help adjust the pH of the blood. Breathing faster removes more carbon dioxide from the blood, which reduces the amount of carbonic acid; in contrast, breathing more slowly has (60) the opposite effect. In a healthy body, these systems automatically neutralize normal amounts of acid wastes and maintain blood pH within the very small range necessary for the body to function normally.

In some cases, these systems can be overwhelmed. (65) This can happen to people with diabetes if their blood sugar drops too low for too long. People with type 1 diabetes do not make enough insulin, which allows the body's cells to absorb sugar from the blood to supply the body with energy. If a (70) person's insulin level gets too low for too long, the body breaks down fats to use for energy. The waste produced from breaking down fats is acidic, so the blood pH drops. If the kidneys exhaust their supply of bicarbonate ions, and the lungs cannot remove (75) carbon dioxide fast enough to raise pH, other functions in the body begin to fail as well. The person will need medical treatment to support these functions until the pH balancing system can catch up. The system will then keep the blood pH constant, (80) as long as the production of acid wastes does not exceed the body's capacity to neutralize them.

32. Passage 1 most strongly suggests that

A) the environment will be damaged seriously if people do not reduce the burning of fossil fuels.

B) scientists must find a way to introduce more alkaline materials into the water supply to combat acid rain.

C) acid rain will not be a problem in the future as we move away from fossil fuels and toward alternative energy sources.

D) acidic rain water is more of a problem than acidic soil because soil contains more alkaline materials.

33. Which choice provides the best evidence for the answer to the previous question?

A) Lines 7-9 ("The environment . . . fuels")

B) Lines 13-14 ("Rain water . . . acid")

C) Lines 17-18 ("Soil, lakes . . . rain")

D) Lines 25-27 ("Anthropomorphic . . . gases")

34. According to the information in Passage 1, which pH level for rain water would cause the most damage to the environment?

A) 2.25

B) 4

C) 5

D) 9.1

35. As used in line 17, "tolerate" most nearly means

A) accept.

B) endure.

C) acknowledge.

D) distribute.

GO ON TO THE NEXT PAGE

36. Passage 2 most strongly suggests that

    A) a pH of 7.35 is ideal for blood in the human body.

    B) acid wastes in the blood multiply if not neutralized.

    C) the normal range of blood pH narrows as a person ages.

    D) small amounts of acid wastes in the blood are a normal condition.

37. Which choice provides the best evidence for the answer to the previous question?

    A) Lines 38-41 ("If blood pH . . . develop")

    B) Lines 46-47 ("Certain conditions . . . react")

    C) Lines 60-63 ("In a healthy . . . normally")

    D) Lines 66-69 ("People with . . . energy")

38. As used in line 73, "exhaust" most nearly means

    A) fatigue.

    B) consume.

    C) deplete.

    D) dissolve.

39. Which of the following plays a role in the environment most similar to the role played by excess bicarbonate ions in the blood?

    A) Acid rain

    B) Ashes from a forest fire

    C) Sulfur oxide gases

    D) Fossil fuels

40. Based on the information in Passage 2, which of the following can cause the body to break down fats to use for energy?

    A) An excess of carbonic acid

    B) Low blood pH

    C) A drop in blood sugar

    D) Not enough insulin

41. Which of the following best describes a shared purpose of the authors of both passages?

    A) To encourage readers to care for delicate systems such as the environment and human body

    B) To explain how the human body neutralizes acid wastes that it produces and deposits in the blood

    C) To describe systems that can neutralize small amounts of acids but become over-whelmed by large amounts

    D) To persuade readers to work toward reducing acid rain by cutting consumption of fossil fuels

42. Both passages support which of the following generalizations?

    A) The human body and environment are delicate systems that require balance to function properly.

    B) There are many similarities between the systems that make up the human body and the water cycle.

    C) Acid rain is an important issue that will continue to impact the environment until we reduce the use of fossil fuels.

    D) Medical treatment is necessary when the pH of a person's blood drops below 7.35 or rises above 7.45.

Questions 43-52 are based on the following passage and supplementary material.

The following passage discusses the benefits of using hydrogen as a renewable energy source.

Scientists worldwide have been working diligently to advance hydrogen as a renewable energy source. Hydrogen, the most abundant
Line element in the universe, is found primarily with
(5) oxygen in water. Because it can be safely used as fuel, it is a candidate for gasoline replacement in passenger vehicles.

GO ON TO THE NEXT PAGE

The potential benefits to moving away from petroleum-based fuel are plentiful. Since hydro-
(10) gen can be produced within the United States, discovering ways to safely and economically switch to hydrogen fuel would drastically reduce our dependency on other petroleum-producing nations. In addition to making us more independent, hydro-
(15) gen produces no pollution, including greenhouse gasses, when used as fuel. For this reason alone, forward-thinking scientists have made it a priority to invent new ways to use hydrogen.

Until now, there have been several challenges
(20) preventing hydrogen from becoming a mainstream form of clean energy. In the United States, engines that run on hydrogen are much more expensive than gasoline. Additionally, it is difficult to store enough hydrogen to get comparable mileage to a
(25) gasoline vehicle. However, these factors have not been the biggest drawback in producing hydro-gen for use in fuel cells; the biggest drawback has been that fossil fuels were needed to generate large amounts of hydrogen. Relying on fossil
(30) fuels to produce this element nearly negates the environmental benefit behind the concept.

Recently, a new method has been discovered, allowing scientists to create large quantities of the element using lower amounts of energy derived
(35) from renewable sources. As in traditional methods, scientists employ electrolysis, a process during which electricity is used to break the bonds between the atoms found in water by passing a current through the water via a semiconductor. Once the water mol-
(40) ecules are broken into separate hydrogen and oxygen atoms, both are released as individual gasses and the hydrogen can be harvested.

When people think of solar power, huge panels usually come to mind, the type of panels that
(45) could not be used to power consumer vehicles in a way equivalent to gasoline. However, scientists have recently been successful at employing solar power as the catalyst in electrolysis, harvesting energy from the sun and using it to break apart
(50) water molecules. The same scientists who made this achievement then built a semiconductor out of affordable, oxide-based materials. When these two advances are coupled, they also reduce the

economic and environmental cost of generating
(55) and processing hydrogen.

Another bonus to this new method of production is that it is significantly more efficient than older production methods. The team of researchers attained the most efficient solar-to-fuel conversion to date, and
(60) they did it without using cost-prohibitive materials.

There are still several challenges to be overcome before hydrogen is a viable gasoline replacement. This new method of production, though, is a huge
(65) step in the right direction. There are many ongo-ing research initiatives that aim to make hydrogen extraction even more cost-effective, as well as easy to store. When these issues are solved, hydrogen will become a fuel that works for humanity and the
(70) earth at the same time.

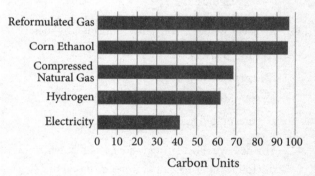

Alternative Fuel Emissions in California Passenger Cars

Adapted from U.S. Department of Energy Alternative Fuels Data Center.

43. With which of the following statements would the author most likely agree?

A) Scientists should consider the final cost to consumers when exploring alternatives to petroleum-based fuels.

B) The development of hydrogen fuel for auto-mobiles will give a boost to the economy in the United States.

C) Safety concerns surrounding hydrogen used as fuel pose the biggest problem for scien-tists studying alternative energy.

D) Gasoline must be eliminated as a source of fuel for automobiles within the next decade.

GO ON TO THE NEXT PAGE →

44. Which choice provides the best evidence for the answer to the previous question?

    A) Lines 5-7 ("Because it . . . vehicles")

    B) Lines 9-13 ("Since hydrogen . . . nations")

    C) Lines 21-23 ("In the United States . . . gasoline")

    D) Lines 52-70 ("When these . . . time")

45. According to the passage, which of the following is true of hydrogen?

    A) It exists mostly with oxygen in water molecules in its natural state.

    B) It is more efficient than solar power as an energy source.

    C) It can be used as fuel in most types of engines.

    D) It can be easily harvested from water molecules.

46. As used in line 2, "diligently" most nearly means

    A) impulsively.

    B) persistently.

    C) rapidly.

    D) perpetually.

47. The passage most strongly suggests that which of the following is true of petroleum-based fuel?

    A) Its cost is higher than most alternative fuels.

    B) Its use has a negative effect on the environment.

    C) It cannot be produced in the United States.

    D) It is more efficient than other types of fuel.

48. Which choice provides the best evidence for the answer to the previous question?

    A) Lines 1-3 ("Scientists . . . source")

    B) Lines 14-16 ("In addition . . . as fuel")

    C) Lines 56-58 ("Another bonus . . . methods")

    D) Lines 58-61 ("The team . . . materials")

49. In paragraph 2, why does the author explain that hydrogen energy will reduce our dependency on petroleum-producing nations?

    A) To illustrate why scientists in other countries are not working to develop hydrogen energy

    B) To highlight how hydrogen energy is superior to other forms of alternative energy

    C) To suggest how hydrogen energy can help protect the environment

    D) To clarify why the development of hydrogen as a fuel source is important

50. As used in line 34, "derived" most nearly means

    A) gained.

    B) received.

    C) obtained.

    D) copied.

51. The passage most strongly suggests that which of the following is true about methods of extracting hydrogen from water?

    A) Much additional research is needed to perfect hydrogen extraction.

    B) Scientific breakthroughs will soon make hydrogen extraction unnecessary.

    C) Scientists are on course to develop a safe way to extract hydrogen within one year.

    D) It is unlikely that hydrogen extraction will ever be done in an environmentally friendly way.

52. Information from both the passage and the graphic support the conclusion that

    A) compressed natural gas is the most environmentally friendly form of automobile fuel.

    B) scientists are making great advances in the development of hydrogen as a fuel for automobiles.

    C) electricity produces less air pollution than hydrogen and compressed natural gas.

    D) switching from gasoline to hydrogen to fuel automobiles would significantly reduce air pollution.

Practice Tests

WRITING AND LANGUAGE TEST

35 Minutes—44 Questions

Turn to Section 2 of your answer sheet to answer the questions in this section.

Directions: Each passage below is accompanied by a number of questions. For some questions, you will consider how the passage might be revised to improve the expression of ideas. For other questions, you will consider how the passage might be edited to correct errors in sentence structure, usage, or punctuation. A passage or a question may be accompanied by one or more graphics (such as a table or graph) that you will consider as you make revising and editing decisions.

Some questions will direct you to an underlined portion of a passage. Other questions will direct you to a location in a passage or ask you to think about the passage as a whole.

After reading each passage, choose the answer to each question that most effectively improves the quality of writing in the passage or that makes the passage conform to the conventions of standard written English. Many questions include a "NO CHANGE" option. Choose that option if you think the best choice is to leave the relevant portion of the passage as it is.

Questions 1-11 are based on the following passage and supplementary material.

Sorting Recyclables for Best Re-Use

From the time a plastic container is thrown into a recycling bin to the time the plastic **1** are actually recycled, it passes through several sorting cycles. In addition to being separated from the non-plastic items, the plastics themselves must be **2** detached, because not all plastics are alike, making some easier to recycle than others.

3 Special machines have been developed to assist in sorting plastics. During manual sorting, people

1. A) NO CHANGE
   B) is
   C) has been
   D) will be

2. A) NO CHANGE
   B) demolished,
   C) flanked,
   D) categorized,

3. Which choice most effectively sets up the information that follows?
   A) NO CHANGE
   B) Sorting by hand is less efficient than using machines to sort plastics.
   C) Classifying plastics can be done manually or by machines.
   D) Plastics are widely used today, so they need to be recycled.

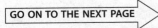
GO ON TO THE NEXT PAGE

[4] very thoroughly check the numbers on the bottom of each plastic item. The numbers indicate the type of plastic each is made from. Some sorting can be automated by using machines that can detect the composition of the plastic. The detectors in these machines use infrared light to characterize and sort the plastics, similar to how a human might use visible light to sort materials by their color. By either method, the plastics can eventually be arranged into bins or piles corresponding to the recycling code numbers running from one to seven.

In some cases, plastics are further sorted by the method by which they were manufactured. [5] However, [6] bottles, tubs and, trays are typically [7] made from either PET (polyethylene terephthalate) or HDPE (high density polyethylene), two of the least recovered plastics. Bottles are produced by a process called blow-molding, in which the plastic is heated until soft, then blown up, much like a balloon, while being pushed against a mold. Tubs and trays are usually made by a process called injection molding, in which the plastic is heated until it can be pushed through nozzles into a mold. Different additives are added to the plastics before [8] molding. It depends on the method. Since the additives for injection molding might not be suitable for blow-molding of the recycled plastic, PET and HDPE bottles are often separated out from the other PET and HDPE plastics.

4. A) NO CHANGE
    B) completely and thoroughly check
    C) thoroughly check
    D) make sure to thoroughly check

5. A) NO CHANGE
    B) For example,
    C) Consequently,
    D) Similarly,

6. A) NO CHANGE
    B) bottles, tubs, and trays
    C) bottles tubs, and trays,
    D) bottles, tubs, and, trays

7. Which choice completes the sentence with accurate data based on the graphic?
    A) NO CHANGE
    B) made from PET (polyethylene terephthalate) or HDPE (high density polyethylene), the two most recovered plastics after the leading type, LDPE.
    C) made from PP (polypropene) or PS (polystyrene), the two most recovered plastics after the leading type, PVC.
    D) made from PP (polypropene) or PS (polystyrene), the two most recovered plastics after the leading type, EPS.

8. Which choice most effectively combines the sentences at the underlined portion?
    A) molding, however, it depends
    B) molding, depending
    C) molding despite depending
    D) molding, it depends

Practice Tests

While the numbers 1 through 6 indicate a ⑨ specific plastic, number 7 indicates that the plastic is either one of many other plastics, or that it is a blend of plastics. These plastics are more difficult to recycle, as different amounts of the various types of number 7 plastics will be sent to recycling each day. They are typically used for products in which the plastic will be mixed with other materials.

Although there are many types of plastics to be found in a typical recycling bin, each one can play a part in a recycled ⑩ product, the many cycles of sorting guarantee that each piece can be correctly processed and sent off for re-use. ⑪

9. A) NO CHANGE
   B) vague
   C) common
   D) pending

10. A) NO CHANGE
    B) product the many
    C) product. The many
    D) product, so the many

11. Which choice most effectively establishes a concluding sentence for the paragraph?
    A) Sorting ensures that plastics will not linger in the landfills, but continue to be of use.
    B) Sorting different types of plastics is done in many ways, either by hand or machine.
    C) Oftentimes, people are required to sort their own plastics by type.
    D) There are many different kinds of plastics, and each one is useful.

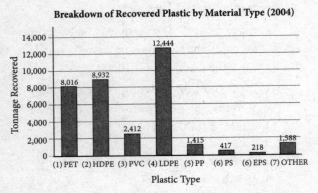

Breakdown of Recovered Plastic by Material Type (2004)

Tonnage Recovered vs. Plastic Type

(1) PET: 8,016
(2) HDPE: 8,932
(3) PVC: 2,412
(4) LDPE: 12,444
(5) PP: 1,415
(6) PS: 417
(6) EPS: 218
(7) OTHER: 1,588

Original graph at http://www.recycle.co.nz/symbols.php.

Questions 12-22 are based on the following passage.

Interpreter at America's Immigrant Gateway

[12] Among the many diverse and fascinating possibilities for a career, David Kaufman chose language interpretation. Throughout his career as an interpreter at America's largest immigrant processing station, Kaufman has spent many ferry rides mentally preparing himself for the vivid realities of his job. Although some of his contemporaries might consider his work menial or inconsequential, he cherishes his opportunity to witness and contribute to the unfolding stories of countless immigrants. These immigrant stories, Kaufman knows, hold [13] great significance for his and American history. Most of the brave, sea-worn travelers who disembark at Ellis Island will soon depart as new Americans, [14] lugging all there courage, hope, and worldly possessions into New York City. Many [15] will remain in the city and some other people will disperse across the nation.

12. Which choice provides the most appropriate introduction to the passage?
    A) NO CHANGE
    B) Many people never consider language interpretation as a job, but David Kaufman knows all about it.
    C) All jobs come with difficulties, and David Kaufman believes language interpretation is no different.
    D) A pale horizon meets the early-morning sky as David Kaufman's commuter ferry crosses the New York Harbor, bound for Ellis Island.

13. A) NO CHANGE
    B) great significance for his—and America's—history.
    C) great significance for his: and America's history.
    D) great significance for his, and America's, history.

14. A) NO CHANGE
    B) lugging all they're courage,
    C) lugging all their courage,
    D) lugging all there are courage,

15. A) NO CHANGE
    B) will remain in the city, but other people will nonetheless disperse across the
    C) will remain in the city; many others will disperse across the
    D) will remain in the city, though yet others will disperse across the

[1] The year is 1907: the busiest year Kaufman, or Ellis Island, has seen. [2] One and a quarter million immigrants have been admitted to the U.S. this year. [3] Only about 2 percent of Ellis Island's immigrants are denied, typically for perceived potential criminal or public health threats. [4] The rest will establish life in America, although not without difficulty and perseverance. [5] At the immigration station, Kaufman regularly sees the range of raw human emotion, from deep, exhausted grief to powerful hope. [6] He has witnessed it all. **16**

17 Many Ellis Island interpreters were born to European immigrants. **18** His heritage, and surrounding community, enabled him to learn six languages. Fluency in six languages is typical for Ellis Island interpreters, although Kaufman knows some who speak as many as twelve or thirteen. Kaufman knows that in some ways, his ability to listen and translate effectively can impact the course of an immigrant's future. For this reason, he constantly hones his language skills, picking up various **19** shades and dialects in hopes to better help those he serves.

16. Sentence 1 should be placed
A) where it is now.
B) after sentence 2.
C) after sentence 3.
D) after sentence 4.

17. Which sentence most effectively establishes the central idea of the paragraph?
A) NO CHANGE
B) Like many Ellis Island interpreters, Kaufman was born to European immigrants.
C) Language ability was especially important among Ellis Island interpreters.
D) Some accused children of European immigrants of having an unfair advantage in getting jobs at Ellis Island.

18. A) NO CHANGE
B) His heritage, and surrounding community enabled him to learn six languages.
C) His heritage and surrounding community, enabled him to learn six languages.
D) His heritage and surrounding community enabled him to learn six languages.

19. A) NO CHANGE
B) meanings
C) tricks
D) nuances

GO ON TO THE NEXT PAGE

Kaufman assists colleagues at every checkpoint. Ellis Island is equipped with a hospital, dining room, and boarding room, in addition to the more central processing facilities. [20] <u>Kaufman is one of an army of Ellis Island employees spread around the enormous compound.</u> This morning, he helps an Italian family discuss their child's health with nurses. Later, he translates for a Polish woman who expects to meet her brother soon. When Kaufman meets immigrants whose language he cannot speak, he finds another interpreter [21] <u>to help speak to them instead of him doing it.</u>

To some extent, Kaufman sees himself distinctly in the shoes of these immigrants. He intimately knows the reality that almost all Americans, somewhere in their ancestry, were not native to this nation. With every encounter, Kaufman hopes that these immigrants will soon find whatever they crossed oceans to seek. He hopes, as he still does for his own family, that life in America will someday render the [22] <u>advantages</u> of leaving home worthwhile.

20. Which sentence best supports the central idea of the paragraph?

   A) NO CHANGE

   B) From medical screening to records confirmation to inspection, Kaufman interprets as needs arise.

   C) Sometimes, Kaufman feels the stress of being pulled in many different directions, but ultimately he finds his job worthwhile.

   D) Kaufman and his colleagues work, eat, and practically live together, making them feel closer than typical coworkers.

21. A) NO CHANGE

   B) to help speak instead of him.

   C) helping him out with speaking.

   D) to help.

22. A) NO CHANGE

   B) journeys

   C) difficulties

   D) penalties

GO ON TO THE NEXT PAGE →

Questions 23-33 are based on the following passage.

Software Sales: A Gratifying Career

Ever since she was a young girl, Stephanie Morales took on the role of family problem-solver. [23] She remembers her brother never being able to find his favorite movie when he wanted to watch it: So, she alphabetized the family DVD collection. [24] "They're about efficiency and what makes sense to a user," Morales says, "and putting systems in place so that using something becomes effortless."

Growing up, Morales became notorious amongst her friends as the one to plan parties and trips, and she was always voted team captain because everyone knew she could see the big picture and enact a plan. [25] After college, she tried a career in interior design, but homes and offices didn't excite her. "I didn't have a passion for furniture or architecture. I knew there must be a field out there that really tapped into my particular skill set," Morales says.

23. A) NO CHANGE
    B) She remembers her brother never being able to find his favorite movie, when he wanted to watch it so she alphabetized the family DVD collection.
    C) She remembers her brother never being able to find his favorite movie; when he wanted to watch it, so she alphabetized the family DVD collection.
    D) She remembers her brother never being able to find his favorite movie when he wanted to watch it, so she alphabetized the family DVD collection.

24. A) NO CHANGE
    B) It's
    C) Their
    D) Its

25. A) NO CHANGE
    B) After college, she tried a career in interior design,—but homes and offices; didn't excite her.
    C) After college, she tried a career in interior design but homes, and offices didn't excite her.
    D) After college she tried a career, in interior design; but homes and offices didn't excite her.

Practice Tests

[1]To her surprise, that career turned out to be software consulting. [2] Morales returned from a backpacking trip around Europe to her parents' New Hampshire home, needing income. [3] New Hampshire also has many fine backpacking trails. [4] **26** Although she had no direct experience in the field, Morales convinced a family friend to hire her as a software consultant to work with new clients. **27** **28** She had helped many of her friends with their computers. Knowing her interpersonal skills were strong.

26. A) NO CHANGE
    B) Although she had no direct experience in the field, Morales convinces
    C) Although she has no direct experience in the field, Morales convinced
    D) Although she will have no direct experience in the field, Morales convinces

27. Which sentence does not support the paragraph's topic and purpose?
    A) Sentence 1
    B) Sentence 2
    C) Sentence 3
    D) Sentence 4

28. A) NO CHANGE
    B) She had helped many of her friends; with their computers and she knew her interpersonal skills were strong.
    C) She had helped many of her friends with their computers; knowing her interpersonal skills were strong.
    D) She had helped many of her friends with their computers, and she knew her interpersonal skills were strong.

[29] Because she was willing to work in a factory, she was able to achieve success as a consultant. For example, Morales worked with a manufacturing company that was growing quickly but had trouble [30] maintaining employees. The company's human resources department could not keep up with regular payroll and billing, plus running advertisements and interviewing potential replacement employees. Morales used staff management software to gather data about employee satisfaction. Analysis showed that employees found the shift work too challenging for their schedules. The company changed the hours of the morning and evening shifts to meet employees' needs, which led to fewer workers leaving the company.

Nowadays, Morales works with what she calls "big data," such as information about consumer habits gathered through a supermarket membership card. These stores of information are a treasure trove to Morales, because they tell the story of how people interact with the world around them. She uses the data to make changes—just like alphabetizing a DVD collection. Her goal is to [31] vacillate into the health care field, where

29. Which choice most logically introduces the paragraph?

A) NO CHANGE

B) Morales's management of data led to the success of the company's advertising campaign.

C) Where the job really matched up with her strengths was in problem-solving and finding creative solutions.

D) Morales's advice to the human resources department resulted in higher wages for employees.

30. A) NO CHANGE

B) retaining

C) containing

D) detaining

31. A) NO CHANGE

B) convert

C) transition

D) fluctuate

GO ON TO THE NEXT PAGE

she wants to bring the benefits of technology to people's physical and mental well-being. **32** For example, Morales is also interested in whether people pay for their medications with credit or debit cards.

Morales knows that people's health is extremely important, and every time someone fills a prescription online or has a follow-up visit with their doctor, that information helps medical experts better determine the efficacy of the medication. The technological revolution has the power **33** to quicken doctor's visits, improve the care we get, and even save lives.

Questions 34-44 are based on the following passage.

The Art of Collecting

At an art exhibition for artist Henri Matisse, enthusiasts can also view a black and white photograph of two siblings. These sisters, wearing Victorian-style dresses and top hats, are the renowned art collectors Claribel and Etta Cone. When Etta passed away in 1949, she **34** bequeathed some 3,000 objects to the Baltimore Museum of Art (BMA). Now, works from the Cone Collection, internationally renowned and consisting of masterpieces by early 20th century artists, travel on loan from BMA so that people can experience the Cone sisters' visionary passion for and dedication to modern art.

32. Which choice best supports the topic sentence of the paragraph?

A) NO CHANGE

B) For example, Morales spends countless hours walking through discount stores surveying the customers.

C) For example, Morales still gets great satisfaction from organizing her friends' and family's DVD collections.

D) For example, Morales can use "big data" to determine how many patients from a particular clinic use online automated refills.

33. A) NO CHANGE

B) to quicken doctor's visits improve the care we get, and even save lives.

C) to quicken doctor's visits, improve the care we get, and even, save lives.

D) to quicken doctor's visits; improve the care we get, and even save lives.

34. A) NO CHANGE

B) liquidated

C) delivered

D) allotted

[35] Henri Matisse was a well-known supporter of female artists and art patrons, and he revealed these unconventional attitudes in his work. What made the Cone sisters innovative was their recognition of the value of art pieces by virtually unknown avant-garde artists of their time, such as Pablo Picasso. Critics failed to understand the Cones' [36] tastes and such opinions did not squelch the sisters' passion for collecting. According to Katy Rothkopf, senior curator at the BMA, Matisse's use of vibrant color, for example, was initially shocking. "At first the Cones . . . really found [the art] quite scary," states Rothkopf. However, the siblings befriended Matisse and other artists, gaining respect for the painters' unorthodox experimentation. As the Cones began buying and collecting art, [37] there selections improved.

"It took a lot of gall—guts—to paint it," Matisse once said about a controversial painting, "but much

35. Which choice best establishes the central idea of the paragraph?

A) NO CHANGE

B) Together the Cones, supported by the wealth from their family's textile business, gathered one of the finest collections of French art in the United States.

C) The Cones became great contributors to the Baltimore Museum of Art, and their renowned exhibition was praised by artists around the globe.

D) During this time period, only the wealthy could afford to purchase original artworks, and the Cones became famous for spending their entire fortune on art.

36. A) NO CHANGE

B) tastes, so such opinions

C) tastes therefore such opinions

D) tastes, but such opinions

37. A) NO CHANGE

B) they're

C) their

D) her

more to buy it." Claribel and Etta had that kind of gall. **38** Each had took risks by not purchasing traditional landscape paintings and instead amassing works that at the time were considered contemptuous and wild.

[1] A further legacy of the Cone Collection was its documentation of post-World War I Europe. [2] The art the Cones collected **39** suggested changes in Europe, such as the increasing use of machines in contemporary life and the emergence of modern thinking. [3] Traditional limitations in art were overcome by experimental forms and new media, allowing artists to explore their creativity. [4] Today, there are even more experimental forms of art than there were after World War I. **40**

41 Additionally in visiting Paris, Budapest, Athens, Cairo, and Shanghai, the Cones represented the beginning of the new woman at the turn of the century. **42** Though their unconventional lifestyle, the far-seeing Cone sisters experienced freedom from narrower roles.

38. A) NO CHANGE
    B) They took risks
    C) They have taken risks
    D) Each will take risks

39. A) NO CHANGE
    B) depicted
    C) referenced
    D) divulged

40. Which sentence should be deleted to best maintain the theme of the paragraph?
    A) Sentence 1
    B) Sentence 2
    C) Sentence 3
    D) Sentence 4

41. A) NO CHANGE
    B) Additionally, in visiting: Paris,
    C) Additionally, in visiting Paris,
    D) Additionally in visiting Paris

42. A) NO CHANGE
    B) Therefore
    C) Thorough
    D) Through

They avoided the gross inequalities between genders by becoming connoisseurs of radical art. **43**

Public acceptance of the **44** Cone's avant-garde collection testifies to their accomplishments. While the estimated value of their artwork is one billion dollars, their larger contribution is inestimable. As bold patrons, the Cones advanced appreciation for modern art for generations to come.

43. What changes to the paragraph would best strengthen the author's claims?

A) The author should define the terms "new woman" and "narrower roles."

B) The author should list more nations and cities visited by the Cone sisters.

C) The precise centuries referenced by "turn of the century" should be included.

D) The author should add reactions from contemporary critics to the Cones' travels.

44. A) NO CHANGE
    B) Cones'
    C) Cones
    D) Cones's

MATH TEST

25 Minutes—20 Questions

NO-CALCULATOR SECTION

Turn to Section 3 of your answer sheet to answer the questions in this section.

Directions: For this section, solve each problem and decide which is the best of the choices given. Fill in the corresponding oval on the answer sheet. You may use any available space for scratch work.

Notes:

1. Calculator use is NOT permitted.
2. All numbers used are real numbers.
3. All figures used are necessary to solving the problems that they accompany. All figures are drawn to scale EXCEPT when it is stated that a specific figure is not drawn to scale.
4. Unless stated otherwise, the domain of any function f is assumed to be the set of all real numbers x, for which $f(x)$ is a real number.

Information:

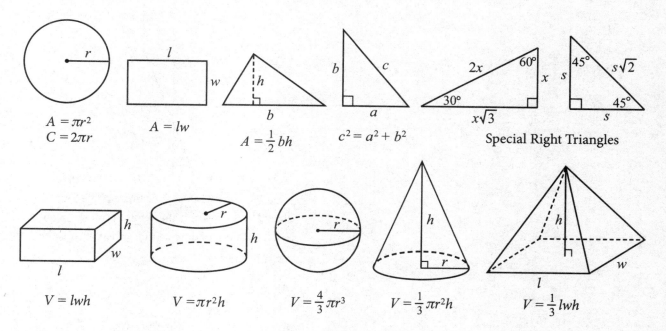

$A = \pi r^2$
$C = 2\pi r$

$A = lw$

$A = \frac{1}{2}bh$

$c^2 = a^2 + b^2$

Special Right Triangles

$V = lwh$

$V = \pi r^2 h$

$V = \frac{4}{3}\pi r^3$

$V = \frac{1}{3}\pi r^2 h$

$V = \frac{1}{3}lwh$

The sum of the degree measures of the angles in a triangle is 180.

The number of degrees of arc in a circle is 360.

The number of radians of arc in a circle is 2π.

GO ON TO THE NEXT PAGE

1. A biologist develops the equation $y = 20.942x + 127$ to predict the regrowth of a certain species of plant x months after a natural disaster occurred. Which of the following describes what the number 20.942 represents in this equation?

   A) The estimated number of the plants after x months

   B) The estimated monthly increase in the number of the plants

   C) The estimated monthly decrease in the number of the plants

   D) The estimated number of the plants that survived the natural disaster

2. Which of the following expressions is equivalent to $25x^2 - \dfrac{4}{9}$?

   A) $\sqrt{5x - \dfrac{2}{3}}$

   B) $x\left(5x - \dfrac{2}{3}\right)$

   C) $\left(5x + \dfrac{2}{3}\right)\left(5x - \dfrac{2}{3}\right)$

   D) $\left(25x + \dfrac{2}{3}\right)\left(25x - \dfrac{2}{3}\right)$

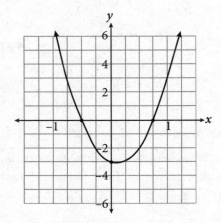

3. Which of the following could be the factored form of the equation graphed in the figure shown?

   A) $y = (2x + 1)(4x - 3)$

   B) $y = (x + 2)(x - 3)$

   C) $y = \left(x - \dfrac{1}{2}\right)\left(x + \dfrac{3}{4}\right)$

   D) $y = \dfrac{1}{2}(x + 1)(x - 3)$

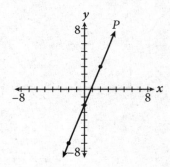

4. Line P is shown in the coordinate plane here. If line Q (not shown) is the result of translating line P left 4 units and down 3 units, then what is the slope of line Q?

   A) $-\dfrac{4}{3}$

   B) -1

   C) $\dfrac{4}{3}$

   D) $\dfrac{5}{2}$

GO ON TO THE NEXT PAGE

$$a = \frac{v_f - v_i}{t}$$

5. Acceleration is the rate at which the velocity of an object changes with respect to time, or in other words, how much an object is speeding up or slowing down. The average acceleration of an object can be found using the formula shown above, where t is the time over which the acceleration is being measured, v_f is the final velocity, and v_i is the initial velocity. Which of the following represents t in terms of the other variables?

    A) $t = \dfrac{a}{v_f - v_i}$

    B) $t = \dfrac{v_f - v_i}{a}$

    C) $t = a(v_f - v_i)$

    D) $t = \dfrac{1}{a(v_f - v_i)}$

6. Which of the following equations could represent a parabola that has a minimum value of -5 and whose axis of symmetry is the line $x = 1$?

    A) $y = (x - 5)^2 + 1$

    B) $y = (x + 5)^2 + 1$

    C) $y = (x - 1)^2 - 5$

    D) $y = (x + 1)^2 - 5$

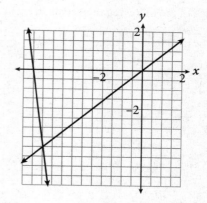

7. If (A, B) is the solution to the system of equations shown in the graph above, what is the value of $A + B$?

    A) -18

    B) -9

    C) 1

    D) 5.5

8. If $A = x^2 + 4x + 9$ and $B = x^3 + 6x - 2$, what is $3A + B$?

    A) $4x^2 + 18x + 25$

    B) $x^3 + x^2 + 10x + 7$

    C) $x^3 + 3x^2 + 18x + 25$

    D) $3x^3 + 3x^2 + 30x + 29$

9. How many real values of x satisfy the quadratic equation $9x^2 - 12x + 4 = 0$?

    A) 0

    B) 1

    C) 2

    D) 4

Practice Tests

GO ON TO THE NEXT PAGE

10. Which of the following represents the solution set for the inequality $\frac{3}{5}\left(x + \frac{2}{7}\right) > -6$?

A) $x > -\frac{72}{7}$

B) $x > -\frac{216}{35}$

C) $x > -\frac{136}{35}$

D) $x > -\frac{18}{7}$

11. Acetaminophen is one of the most common drugs given to children and one of the most difficult to give correctly because it's sold in several different forms and different concentrations. For example, the old concentration given by dropper was 90 milligrams of acetaminophen per 1 milliliter of liquid, while the new concentration given by syringe is 160 milligrams per 5 milliliters. Several dosages are shown in the table below.

Infant Acetaminophen Dosages			
Age	0–3 mo	4–11 mo	12–23 mo
Dropper	0.5 ml	1.0 ml	1.5 ml
Syringe	1.25 ml	2.5 ml	3.75 ml

Which linear function represents the relationship between the amount of liquid in the dropper, d, and the amount of liquid in the syringe, s?

A) $s = 0.4d$

B) $s = 1.25d$

C) $s = 2d$

D) $s = 2.5d$

12. Which of the following equations, when graphed on a coordinate plane, will not cross the y-axis?

A) $0.5(4x + y) = y - 9$

B) $2(x + 7) - x = 4(y + 3)$

C) $0.25(8y + 4x) - 7 = -2(-y + 1)$

D) $6x - 2(3y + x) = 10 - 3y$

$$\begin{cases} Hx + 2y = -8 \\ Kx - 5y = -13 \end{cases}$$

13. If the solution to the system of equations shown above is $(2, -1)$, what is the value of $\frac{K}{H}$?

A) -3

B) $-\frac{1}{3}$

C) $\frac{1}{3}$

D) 3

14. It is given that $\sin A = k$, where A is an angle measured in radians and $\pi < A < \frac{3\pi}{2}$. If $\sin B = k$, which of the following could be the value of B?

A) $A - \pi$

B) $\pi + A$

C) $2\pi - A$

D) $3\pi - A$

15. Which of the following is equivalent to the expression $\left(\dfrac{x^{\frac{1}{2}}}{x^{-2}}\right)^2$?

A) x^2

B) $\left(\dfrac{x^2}{x}\right)^{\frac{1}{2}}$

C) $\left(\dfrac{(x^2)(x^{\frac{1}{3}})}{x^4}\right)^3$

D) $\left(\dfrac{(x^3)(x^4)}{x^{-3}}\right)^{\frac{1}{2}}$

Directions: For questions 16-20, solve the problem and enter your answer in the grid, as described below, on the answer sheet.

1. Although not required, it is suggested that you write your answer in the boxes at the top of the columns to help you fill in the circles accurately. You will receive credit only if the circles are filled in correctly.

2. Mark no more than one circle in any column.

3. No question has a negative answer.

4. Some problems may have more than one correct answer. In such cases, grid only one answer.

5. **Mixed numbers** such as $3\frac{1}{2}$ must be gridded as 3.5 or $\frac{7}{2}$.

   (If $3\frac{1}{2}$ is entered into the grid as $\boxed{3\;1\;/\;2}$, it will be interpreted as $\frac{31}{2}$, not $3\frac{1}{2}$.)

6. **Decimal answers:** If you obtain a decimal answer with more digits than the grid can accommodate, it may be either rounded or truncated, but it must fill the entire grid.

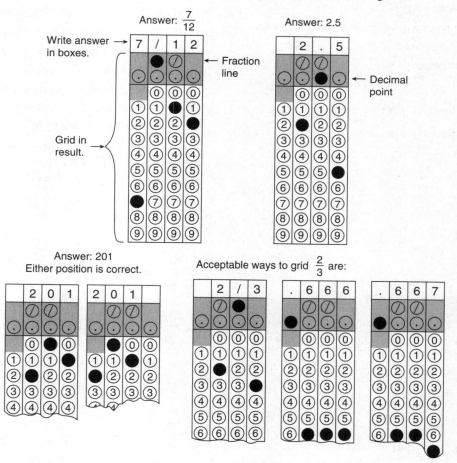

GO ON TO THE NEXT PAGE

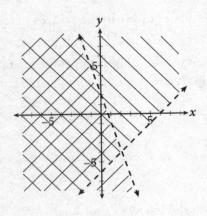

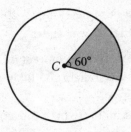

$$\begin{cases} y < -3x + 2 \\ y > x - 6 \end{cases}$$

16. The figure above shows the solution set for the given system of inequalities. Suppose (a, b) is a solution to the system. If $a = 0$, what is the greatest possible integer value of b?

17. Given the function $f(x) = \dfrac{2}{3}x - 5$, what input value corresponds to an output of 3?

18. If the area of the shaded sector in circle C shown above is 6π square units, what is the diameter of the circle?

19. What is the diameter of the circle given by the equation $x^2 + y^2 + 10x - 4y = 20$?

20. In economics, the law of demand states that as the price of a commodity rises, the demand for that commodity goes down. A company determines that the monthly demand for a certain item that it sells can be modeled by the function $q(p) = -2p + 34$, where q represents the quantity sold in hundreds and p represents the selling price in dollars. It costs $7 to produce this item. How much more per month in profits can the company expect to earn by selling the item at $12 instead of $10? (Profit = sales − costs)

Practice Tests

MATH TEST

55 Minutes—38 Questions

CALCULATOR SECTION

Turn to Section 4 of your answer sheet to answer the questions in this section.

Directions: For this section, solve each problem and decide which is the best of the choices given. Fill in the corresponding oval on the answer sheet. You may use any available space for scratch work.

Notes:

1. Calculator use is permitted.
2. All numbers used are real numbers.
3. All figures used are necessary to solving the problems that they accompany. All figures are drawn to scale EXCEPT when it is stated that a specific figure is not drawn to scale.
4. Unless stated otherwise, the domain of any function f is assumed to be the set of all real numbers x, for which $f(x)$ is a real number.

Information:

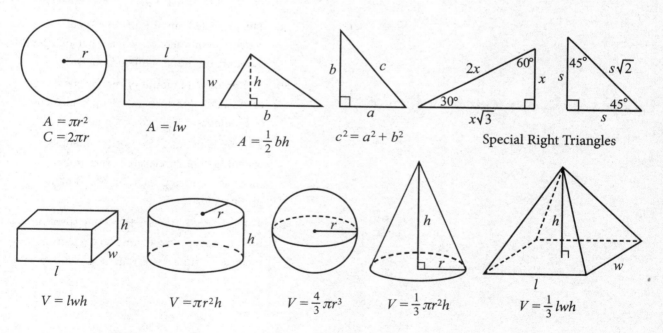

$A = \pi r^2$
$C = 2\pi r$

$A = lw$

$A = \frac{1}{2}bh$

$c^2 = a^2 + b^2$

Special Right Triangles

$V = lwh$

$V = \pi r^2 h$

$V = \frac{4}{3}\pi r^3$

$V = \frac{1}{3}\pi r^2 h$

$V = \frac{1}{3}lwh$

The sum of the degree measures of the angles in a triangle is 180.

The number of degrees of arc in a circle is 360.

The number of radians of arc in a circle is 2π.

GO ON TO THE NEXT PAGE

1. The USDA recommends that adult females consume 75 milligrams of ascorbic acid, also known as vitamin C, each day. Because smoking inhibits vitamin absorption, smokers are encouraged to consume an additional 35 milligrams daily. If one grapefruit contains 40 mg of vitamin C and one serving of spinach contains 10 milligrams, which of the following inequalities represents the possible intake of grapefruit, g, and spinach, s, that a smoking female could consume to meet or surpass the USDA's recommended amount of vitamin C?

   A) $40g + 10s \geq 75$

   B) $40g + 10s \geq 110$

   C) $40g + 10s > 110$

   D) $\dfrac{40}{g} + \dfrac{10}{s} \geq 110$

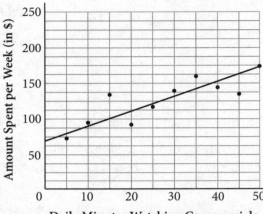

Daily Minutes Watching Commercials

2. The scatterplot above shows the relationship between the amount of time spent watching commercials each day and the amount of money spent each week on brand name grocery products for 10 consumers. The line of best fit for the data is also shown. Which of the following best represents the meaning of the slope of the line of best fit in the context of this question?

   A) The predicted amount of time spent watching commercials when a person spends 0 dollars on brand name products

   B) The predicted amount of money spent on brand name products when a person spends 0 minutes watching commercials

   C) The predicted increase in time spent watching commercials for every dollar increase in money spent on brand name products

   D) The predicted increase in money spent on brand name products for every one-minute increase in time spent watching commercials

GO ON TO THE NEXT PAGE

3. There are very few states in the United States that require public schools to pay sales tax on their purchases. For this reason, many schools pay for student portraits and then the parents reimburse the school. Parents can choose between the basic package for $29.50 and the deluxe package for $44.50. If 182 parents ordered packages and the school's total bill was $6,509, which of the following systems of equations could be used to find the number of parents who ordered a basic package, b, and the number who ordered a deluxe package, d, assuming no parent ordered more than one package?

A) $\begin{cases} b + d = 6{,}509 \\ 29.5b + 44.5d = 182 \end{cases}$

B) $\begin{cases} b + d = 182 \\ 29.5b + 44.5d = 6{,}509 \end{cases}$

C) $\begin{cases} 2(b + d) = 182 \\ 29.5b + 44.5d = 6{,}509 \end{cases}$

D) $\begin{cases} b + d = 182 \\ 29.5b + 44.5d = \dfrac{6{,}509}{2} \end{cases}$

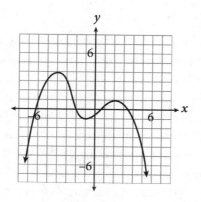

4. The graph of a polynomial function $p(x)$ is shown above. For what value(s) of x does $p(x) = -4$?

A) -1

B) 4

C) -7 and 5

D) -7, 4, and 5

5. If $4x + 3 = 19$, what is the value of $4x - 3$?

A) -19

B) 4

C) 13

D) 19

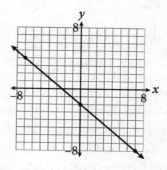

6. What is the slope of the line shown in the graph?

A) -2

B) $-\dfrac{7}{6}$

C) $-\dfrac{6}{7}$

D) 2

Practice Tests

Legislation Impact

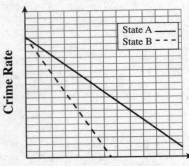

State A ——
State B - - -

Crime Rate

Years After Legislation

7. Most crimes in the United States are governed by state law rather than federal. Suppose two states passed laws that raised the penalty for committing armed robbery. The figure above represents the crime rate for armed robbery in both states after the laws were passed. Based on the graph, which of the following statements is true?

A) State A's law had a more positive impact on the crime rate for armed robbery.

B) State B's law had a more positive impact on the crime rate for armed robbery.

C) The laws in both states had the same impact on the crime rate for armed robbery.

D) Without axis labels, it is not possible to determine which state's law had a bigger impact.

8. On average, for every 2,500 cans of colored paint a home improvement chain mixes, exactly 40 are the wrong color (defective). At this rate, how many cans of paint were mixed during a period in which exactly 128 were defective?

A) 5,200

B) 7,500

C) 8,000

D) 10,200

9. According to the American Association of University Women, the mean age of men who have a college degree at their first marriage is 29.9 years. The mean age of women with a college degree at their first marriage is 28.4 years. Which of the following must be true about the combined mean age m of all people with college degrees at their first marriage?

A) $m = 29.15$

B) $m > 29.15$

C) $m < 29.15$

D) $28.4 < m < 29.9$

10. When scuba divers ascend from deep water, they must either rise slowly or take safety breaks to avoid nitrogen buildup in their lungs. The length of time a diver should take to ascend is directly proportional to how many feet she needs to ascend. If a scuba diver can safely ascend 165 feet in 5.5 minutes, then how many feet can she ascend in 90 seconds?

A) 45

B) 60

C) 75

D) 90

11. The chief financial officer of a shoe company calculates that the cost C of producing p pairs of a certain shoe is $C = 17p + 1,890$. The marketing department wants to sell the shoe for \$35 per pair. The shoe company will make a profit only if the total revenue from selling p pairs is greater than the total cost of producing p pairs. Which of the following inequalities gives the number of pairs of shoes p that the company needs to sell in order to make a profit?

A) $p < 54$

B) $p > 54$

C) $p < 105$

D) $p > 105$

GO ON TO THE NEXT PAGE ⇒

12. The human body has a very limited ability to store carbohydrates, which is why it is important for athletes to consume them during long training sessions or competitions. It is recommended that athletes consume approximately 3 calories per minute in situations like these. How many calories would an athlete biking a 74-mile race need to consume, assuming he bikes at an average speed of 9.25 miles per hour during the race?

A) 480

B) 1,440

C) 1,665

D) 2,053.5

x	3	−1	−5	−7
y	0	14	28	?

13. If the values in the table represent a linear relationship, what is the missing value?

A) 21

B) 30

C) 35

D) 42

Questions 14 and 15 refer to the following information.

The figure shows the age distribution of homebuyers and the percent of the market each age range makes up in a particular geographic region.

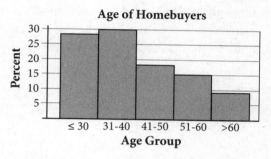

Age of Homebuyers

14. A new real estate agent is deciding which age group she should market toward in order to get the most clients. Which of the following measures of the data would be best for her to use when making this decision?

A) Mean

B) Mode

C) Range

D) Median

15. Based on the information in the figure, which of the following statements is true?

A) The shape of the data is skewed to the right, so the mean age of homebuyers is greater than the median.

B) The shape of the data is skewed to the left, so the median age of homebuyers is greater than the mean.

C) The shape of the data is fairly symmetric, so the mean age of homebuyers is approximately equal to the median.

D) The data has no clear shape, so it is impossible to make a reliable statement comparing the mean and the median.

Practice Tests

GO ON TO THE NEXT PAGE

16. A railway company normally charges $35 round trip from the suburbs of a city into downtown. The company also offers a deal for commuters who use the train frequently to commute from their homes in the suburbs to their jobs in the city. Commuters can purchase a discount card for $900, after which they only have to pay $12.50 per round trip. How many round trips, t, must a commuter make in order for the discount card to be a better deal?

A) $t < 40$

B) $t > 40$

C) $t < 72$

D) $t > 72$

17. Most people save money before going on vacation. Suppose Etienne saved $800 to spend during vacation, 20 percent of which he uses to pay for gas. If he budgets 25 percent of the remaining money for food, allots $300 for the hotel, and spends the rest of the money on entertainment, what percentage of the original $800 did he spend on entertainment?

A) 14.5%

B) 17.5%

C) 22.5%

D) 28.5%

18. A microbiologist placed a bacteria sample containing approximately 2,000 microbes in a petri dish. For the first 7 days, the number of microbes in the dish tripled every 24 hours. If n represents the number of microbes after h hours, then which of the following equations is the best model for the data during the 7-day period?

A) $n = 2,000(3)^{\frac{h}{24}}$

B) $n = 2,000(3)^{24h}$

C) $n = \dfrac{h}{24} \times 2,000$

D) $n = 24h \times 2,000$

	For	Against	Undecided	Total
1L	32	16	10	58
2L	24	12	28	64
3L	17	25	13	55
Total	73	53	51	177

19. A survey is conducted regarding a proposed change in the attendance policy at a law school. The table above categorizes the results of the survey by year of the student (1L, 2L, or 3L) and whether they are for, against, or undecided about the new policy. What fraction of all 1Ls and 2Ls are against the new policy?

A) $\dfrac{14}{61}$

B) $\dfrac{24}{61}$

C) $\dfrac{28}{53}$

D) $\dfrac{28}{177}$

20. Which of the following expressions is equivalent to $(6 + 5i)^3$? (Note: $i = \sqrt{-1}$)

A) $11 + 60i$

B) $216 - 125i$

C) $-234 + 415i$

D) $-3,479 + 1,320i$

GO ON TO THE NEXT PAGE

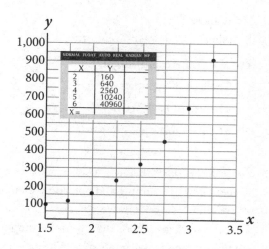

21. If an exponential function is used to model the data shown in the figure, and it is written in the form $f(x) = f(0)(1 + r)^x$, what would be the value of r?

A) 2

B) 3

C) 4

D) 5

22. The Great Pyramid of Giza, built in the 26th century BC just outside of Cairo, Egypt, had an original height of 480 feet, 8 inches, before some of the stones in which it was encased fell away. Inside the pyramid is a 53.75-foot passage, called the Dead End Shaft, which archeologists have yet to discover the purpose of. Suppose a museum is building a scale model of the pyramid for patrons to explore. Because of the museum's ceiling height, they can only make the pyramid 71 feet, 6 inches tall. About how many feet long should the museum's Dead End Shaft be?

A) 8

B) 12

C) 30

D) 96

$$\frac{-x^2 - 10x + 24}{2 - x}$$

23. Which of the following is equivalent to the expression above, given that $x \neq 2$?

A) $-x - 12$

B) $x - 12$

C) $12 - x$

D) $x + 12$

24. Ethanol is an alcohol commonly added to gasoline to reduce the use of fossil fuels. A commonly used ratio of ethanol to gasoline is 1:4. Another less common and more experimental additive is methanol, with a typical ratio of methanol to gasoline being 1:9. A fuel producer wants to see what happens to cost and fuel efficiency when a combination of ethanol and methanol are used. In order to keep the ratio of gasoline to total additive the same, what ratio of ethanol to methanol should the company use?

A) 1:1

B) 4:9

C) 9:4

D) 36:9

Practice Tests

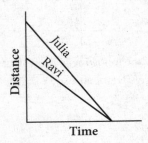

Time

25. Julia and Ravi are meeting at a museum. The figure above represents the drives from their homes to the museum. Based on the figure, which of the following statements is true?

A) Julia drove to the museum at a faster speed than Ravi.

B) Julia and Ravi drove to the museum at about the same speed.

C) It took Ravi longer to arrive at the museum because his home is farther away.

D) It took Julia longer to arrive at the museum because her home is farther away.

26. If the graph of the function $g(x)$ passes through the point $(8, -3)$, then through which point does the graph of $-g(x - 4) - 6$ pass?

A) $(-12, -9)$

B) $(-12, -3)$

C) $(4, -3)$

D) $(12, -3)$

27. If $f(x) = x - 1$, $g(x) = x^3$, and $x \leq 0$, which of the following could not be in the range of $f(g(x))$?

A) -27

B) -3

C) -1

D) 1

28. Given the equation $y = -3(x - 5)^2 + 8$, which of the following statements is not true?

A) The y-intercept is $(0, 8)$.

B) The axis of symmetry is $x = 5$.

C) The vertex is $(5, 8)$.

D) The parabola opens downward.

29. Every weekend for 48 hours, a law firm backs up all client files by scanning and uploading them to a secure remote server. On average, the size of each client file is 2.5 gigabytes. The law firm's computer can upload the scans at a rate of 5.25 megabytes per second. What is the maximum number of client files the law firm can back up each weekend? (1 gigabyte = 1,000 megabytes)

A) 362

B) 363

C) 476

D) 477

30. Main Street and 2nd Street run parallel to each other. Both are one-way streets. Main Street runs north, and 2nd Street runs south. The city is planning to build a new road, also one-way, that runs toward the southeast and cuts through both streets at an angle. Traffic turning off of Main Street would have to make a 125° turn onto the new road. What angle would traffic turning off of 2nd Street have to make turning onto the new road?

A) 55°

B) 65°

C) 125°

D) 235°

GO ON TO THE NEXT PAGE ⇒

Directions: For questions 31-38, solve the problem and enter your answer in the grid, as described below, on the answer sheet.

1. Although not required, it is suggested that you write your answer in the boxes at the top of the columns to help you fill in the circles accurately. You will receive credit only if the circles are filled in correctly.

2. Mark no more than one circle in any column.

3. No question has a negative answer.

4. Some problems may have more than one correct answer. In such cases, grid only one answer.

5. **Mixed numbers** such as $3\frac{1}{2}$ must be gridded as 3.5 or $\frac{7}{2}$.

   (If $3\frac{1}{2}$ is entered into the grid as $\boxed{3\ 1\ /\ 2}$, it will be interpreted as $\frac{31}{2}$, not $3\frac{1}{2}$.)

6. **Decimal answers:** If you obtain a decimal answer with more digits than the grid can accommodate, it may be either rounded or truncated, but it must fill the entire grid.

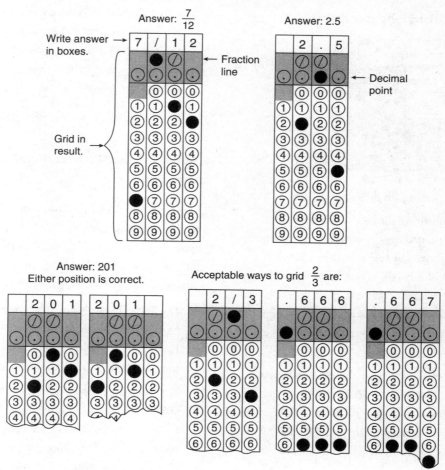

GO ON TO THE NEXT PAGE

$$\frac{4h - (21 - 8h)}{3} = \frac{15 + 6(h - 1)}{2}$$

31. What is the value of h in the equation above?

32. A company is buying two warehouses near their production plants in two states, New York and Georgia. As is always the case in the real estate market, the geographic location plays a major role in the price of the property. Consequently, the warehouse in New York costs $30,000 less than four times the Georgia warehouse. Together, the two warehouses cost the company $445,000. How many more thousand dollars does the New York property cost than the Georgia property?

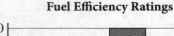
Fuel Efficiency Ratings

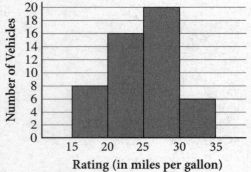

33. The histogram above shows the number of vehicles that a car rental agency currently has available to rent, categorized by fuel efficiency ratings. If a customer randomly selects one of the available cars, what is the probability that he will get a car that has a fuel efficiency rating of at least 25 miles per gallon? Enter your answer as a decimal number.

34. The volume of a rectangular shipping crate being loaded onto a barge for international shipment across the Panama Canal is 10,290 cubic feet. If the length to width to height ratio of the crate is 3:5:2 (in that order), what is the length of the crate in feet?

Regional Manager Job Performance

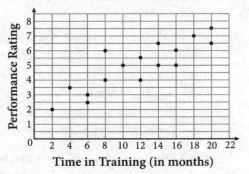

35. A company conducted a study comparing the overall job performance of its regional managers with the length of time each one spent in the company's management-training program. The scatterplot above shows the results of the study. What is the length of the time spent in training, in months, of the manager represented by the data point that is the greatest distance from the line of best fit (not shown)?

36. If $(2^{32})^{(2^{32})} = 2^{(2^x)}$, what is the value of x?

Questions 37 and 38 refer to the following information.

Three cars all arrive at the same destination at 4:00 PM. The first car traveled 144 miles mostly by highway. The second car traveled 85 miles mainly on rural two-lane roads. The third car traveled 25 miles primarily on busy city streets.

37. The first car traveled at an average speed of 64 mph. The second car started its drive at 2:18 PM. How many minutes had the first car already been traveling before the second car started its drive?

38. The third car encountered heavy traffic for the first 60% of its trip and only averaged 15 mph. Then traffic stopped due to an accident, and the car did not move for 20 minutes. After the accident was cleared, the car averaged 30 mph for the remainder of the trip. At what time in the afternoon did the third car start its trip? Use only digits for your answer. (For example, enter 1:25 PM as 125.)

ESSAY TEST

50 Minutes

The essay gives you an opportunity to show how effectively you can read and comprehend a passage and write an essay analyzing the passage. In your essay, you should demonstrate that you have read the passage carefully, present a clear and logical analysis, and use language precisely.

Your essay must be written on the lines provided in your answer booklet; except for the planning page of the answer booklet, you will receive no other paper on which to write. You will have enough space if you write on every line, avoid wide margins, and keep your handwriting to a reasonable size. Remember that people who are not familiar with your handwriting will read what you write. Try to write or print so that what you are writing is legible to those readers.

You have 50 minutes to read the passage and write an essay in response to the prompt provided inside this booklet.

1. Do not write your essay in this booklet. Only what you write on the lined pages of your answer booklet will be evaluated.
2. An off-topic essay will not be evaluated.

As you read the passage below, consider how William Faulkner uses

- evidence, such as facts or examples, to support claims.

- reasoning to develop ideas and to connect claims and evidence.

- stylistic or persuasive elements, such as word choice or appeals to emotion, to add power to the ideas expressed.

Adapted from William Faulkner's Nobel Prize Acceptance Speech, delivered in Stockholm on December 10, 1950.

1   I feel that this award was not made to me as a man, but to my work—a life's work in the agony and sweat of the human spirit, not for glory and least of all for profit, but to create out of the materials of the human spirit something which did not exist before. So this award is only mine in trust. It will not be difficult to find a dedication for the money part of it commensurate with the purpose and significance of its origin. But I would like to do the same with the acclaim too, by using this moment as a pinnacle from which I might be listened to by the young men and women already dedicated to the same anguish and travail, among whom is already that one who will some day stand where I am standing.

2   Our tragedy today is a general and universal physical fear so long sustained by now that we can even bear it. There are no longer problems of the spirit. There is only the question: When will I be blown up? Because of this, the young man or woman writing today has forgotten the problems of the human heart in conflict with itself which alone can make good writing because only that is worth writing about, worth the agony and the sweat.

3   He must learn them again. He must teach himself that the basest of all things is to be afraid: and, teaching himself that, forget it forever, leaving no room in his workshop for anything but the old verities and truths of the heart, the universal truths lacking which any story is ephemeral and doomed—love and honor and pity and pride and compassion and sacrifice. Until he does so, he labors under a curse. He writes not of love but of … defeats in

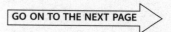

GO ON TO THE NEXT PAGE

Practice Tests

which nobody loses anything of value, of victories without hope and, worst of all, without pity or compassion. His griefs grieve on no universal bones, leaving no scars …

4   Until he learns these things, he will write as though he stood among and watched the end of man. I decline to accept the end of man. It is easy enough to say that man is immortal because he will endure: that when the last ding-dong of doom has clanged and faded from the last worthless rock hanging tideless in the last red and dying evening, that even then there will still be one more sound: that of his puny inexhaustible voice, still talking. I refuse to accept this. I believe that man will not merely endure: he will prevail. He is immortal, not because he alone among creatures has an inexhaustible voice, but because he has a soul, a spirit capable of compassion and sacrifice and endurance. The poet's, the writer's, duty is to write about these things. It is his privilege to help man endure by lifting his heart, by reminding him of the courage and honor and hope and pride and compassion and pity and sacrifice which have been the glory of his past. The poet's voice need not merely be the record of man, it can be one of the props, the pillars to help him endure and prevail.

Write an essay in which you explain how William Faulkner builds an argument to persuade his audience that authors must write from the heart to ensure that mankind prevails. In your essay, analyze how Faulkner uses one or more of the features listed in the box that precedes the passage (or features of your own choice) to strengthen the logic and persuasiveness of his argument. Be sure that your analysis focuses on the most relevant aspects of the passage.

Your essay should not explain whether you agree with Faulkner's claims, but rather explain how Faulkner builds an argument to persuade his audience.

ANSWER KEY
READING TEST

1. C	14. A	27. A	40. D
2. A	15. D	28. C	41. C
3. D	16. B	29. D	42. A
4. B	17. C	30. B	43. A
5. B	18. B	31. C	44. C
6. A	19. B	32. A	45. A
7. D	20. D	33. A	46. B
8. D	21. D	34. A	47. B
9. C	22. D	35. B	48. B
10. C	23. A	36. D	49. D
11. C	24. C	37. C	50. C
12. A	25. B	38. C	51. A
13. D	26. A	39. B	52. D

WRITING AND LANGUAGE TEST

1. B	12. D	23. D	34. A
2. D	13. B	24. B	35. C
3. C	14. C	25. A	36. D
4. C	15. C	26. A	37. C
5. B	16. A	27. C	38. B
6. B	17. B	28. D	39. B
7. B	18. D	29. C	40. D
8. B	19. D	30. B	41. C
9. A	20. B	31. C	42. D
10. C	21. D	32. D	43. A
11. A	22. C	33. A	44. B

Practice Tests

MATH—NO CALCULATOR TEST

1. B	6. C	11. D	16. 1
2. C	7. B	12. C	17. 12
3. A	8. C	13. D	18. 12
4. D	9. B	14. D	19. 14
5. B	10. A	15. D	20. 800

MATH—CALCULATOR TEST

1. B	11. D	21. B	31. 11.5 or **23/2** or **69/6**
2. D	12. B	22. A	32. 255
3. B	13. C	23. D	33. .52
4. C	14. B	24. C	34. 21
5. C	15. A	25. A	35. 8
6. C	16. B	26. D	36. 37
7. B	17. C	27. D	37. 33
8. C	18. A	28. A	38. 220
9. D	19. A	29. A	
10. A	20. C	30. A	

ANSWERS AND EXPLANATIONS

READING TEST

Walden

Suggested Passage Map notes:

¶1: sleep more do better
¶2: man is responsible for being present in life
¶3: HDT wanted to live fully, used nature to achieve it
¶4: let go of small things
¶5: keep life simple

1. C   Difficulty: Medium

Category: Detail

Getting to the Answer: Reread the entire paragraph to assess the intention of the sentence in question, and determine which answer choice best shows the author's reason for including this sentence. The author's previous statements in the paragraph directly relate to the idea that the conscious endeavors described are the very activities that will reawaken people; therefore, (C) is correct.

2. A   Difficulty: Hard

Category: Vocab-in-Context

Getting to the Answer: Read the complete sentence for context clues, and determine which answer choice's definition best serves the idea presented. The sentence suggests the author wants to live actively and "suck out all the marrow of life" (line 39) rather than live in a resigned, accepting manner; thus, (A) is correct because it best describes how the author does not wish to live.

3. D   Difficulty: Medium

Category: Inference

Getting to the Answer: Read the first paragraph expressly for the purpose of determining the author's

views. The author suggests that most people are only awake enough for physical labor, some for intellectual discussions, and very few for a higher calling. This implies that he feels most people are not working toward their fullest potential, so (D) is correct.

4. B   Difficulty: Hard

Category: Command of Evidence

Getting to the Answer: Choose the quote from the passage that best supports the correct answer to the previous question. Choice (B) is the correct answer not just because it shows the author's belief that most people are not truly awake, but also because it shows that the author thinks most people spend their lives pursuing goals beneath their human potential.

5. B   Difficulty: Easy

Category: Global

Getting to the Answer: Consider the entire passage to determine the author's central claim about society. Then choose the answer choice that correctly reflects this. Throughout the passage, the author frequently mentions that our society focuses on mundane labor and details and that we shun a life of conscious endeavors; therefore, (B) is the correct answer.

6. A   Difficulty: Medium

Category: Inference

Getting to the Answer: Because the author's views on religion are not explicitly stated, you must make inferences by examining details in the entire passage. Throughout the third paragraph, the author explains that he is going to the woods to determine the sublime or mean qualities of nature and God, and he states that far too many people hastily agree to preconceived ideas on these topics. Choice (A) is correct.

7. D   Difficulty: Easy

Category: Command of Evidence

Getting to the Answer: Choose the quote from the passage that best supports the correct answer to the previous question. Choice (D) is the correct answer, because it offers the most direct evidence that the author believes a person should critically examine his or her religious beliefs before dedicating a life to them.

8. D   Difficulty: Medium

Category: Vocab-in-Context

Getting to the Answer: Read the sentence for context clues, and determine which answer choice comes closest to reflecting the author's intent. The sentence and paragraph as a whole describe the author's indifference to the harshness of life for the sake of accomplishing a goal; therefore, (D), "austere," is correct.

9. C   Difficulty: Medium

Category: Rhetoric

Getting to the Answer: Carefully read the paragraph and ask yourself how these particular words help Thoreau convey his message. The author touches on many broad, negative aspects of human nature and existence in the paragraph, and the use of "meanly" and "wretchedness" strengthen the negative tone of the message. Choice (C) is correct.

10. C   Difficulty: Medium

Category: Inference

Getting to the Answer: Think about the author's intention in this passage when he discusses his views on how life should be lived. Identify the types of actions he promotes and review the answer choices to find the one that is most similar. The author urges readers to "simplify," and as an example he urges them to eat one meal a day instead of three and to reduce the number of dishes from 100 to 5. You can infer from this that Thoreau would advocate paring

down one's clothing to the bare essentials. Choice (C) is correct.

"The Opening of the Library"

Suggested Passage Map notes:

¶1: new library

¶2: library still segregated

¶3: African Am excluded from using library

¶4: WEB wants African Am to be allowed to use it: education will keep them off the streets

¶5-6: public money means it should be used by all

¶7: chairman says integration will kill library

¶8: segregation should be in the past

¶9-10: African Am in crowd spoke, thanked the trustees for listening

¶11-12: trustees gave response: said no

11. C   Difficulty: Medium

Category: Rhetoric

Getting to the Answer: Consider which answer choice describes an idea that is supported throughout the text. The passage begins with DuBois's arguments in favor of expanding access to public libraries and ends with the trustees' response to his arguments, highlighting the difference between the two positions. Therefore, (C) is correct.

12. A   Difficulty: Medium

Category: Command of Evidence

Getting to the Answer: The correct answer will support your response to the previous question. Choice (A) indicates that DuBois would present an argument "in behalf" (line 14) of others while asking the trustees to explain their side.

13. D   Difficulty: Medium

Category: Vocab-in-Context

Getting to the Answer: Make sure that your answer choice does not alter the meaning of the sentence in the passage. The paragraph in which the word appears indicates that speaking on behalf of so many others was not a responsibility DuBois took lightly, and the decision about who would speak had been previously decided. Choice (D) is correct.

14. A   Difficulty: Medium

Category: Inference

Getting to the Answer: Eliminate answer choices that are not suggested in the passage. Choice (A) is correct. The president of the Trustee Board did not make assurances, but he detailed a course of action that would potentially result in a new library for African Americans if the city council approved funding.

15. D   Difficulty: Hard

Category: Command of Evidence

Getting to the Answer: Review your answer to the previous question. Read each choice and figure out which one provides specific support for that answer. Choice (D) indicates the trustees' support for separate library facilities with approved funding. It best supports the idea that segregated library facilities would at least be considered.

16. B   Difficulty: Medium

Category: Vocab-in-Context

Getting to the Answer: Look for context clues in the sentence to help you determine the correct meaning. Choice (B) reflects the meaning of the phrase in the sentence; DuBois was arguing for the necessity of literacy and a strong comprehension of the books that a library offers.

17. C   Difficulty: Hard

Category: Detail

Getting to the Answer: Pay close attention to the reasons DuBois presents that support his argument for expanding access to public libraries. Avoid choices that sound plausible but take the ideas too far.

Choice (C) is correct. DuBois specifically argues that the reason whites need public libraries "applies with redoubled force" (line 29) to poor African Americans.

18. B   Difficulty: Medium

Category: Rhetoric

Getting to the Answer: Look for the argument in the passage that this particular example supports. Choice (B) is correct. Note that DuBois's mention of the "catholic spirit" (line 49) is used to remind the trustees that we create differences between us, and what we have in common should inspire us to ensure that everyone has equal opportunity to improve themselves.

19. B   Difficulty: Medium

Category: Inference

Getting to the Answer: Read the cited lines, and then read them in the context of the paragraphs that come before and after. Think about how the chairman's words are affecting the author at this point in the passage. The chairman has just suggested that integrating the library "would be fatal to its usefulness" (lines 58-59), implying that African Americans and whites would be unable to use the library alongside each other without violence or chaos. Because DuBois's aim is to integrate the library, he is frustrated by the chairman's words, which echo the assumptions of past centuries. Choice (B) is correct.

20. D   Difficulty: Medium

Category: Rhetoric

Getting to the Answer: Keep in mind that the question is asking how this portion of the passage functions in relation to the passage as a whole. DuBois argued in favor of expanding access to public libraries for all citizens. The Trustee Board's president then responded to DuBois's persuasive argument. Therefore, (D) is correct.

Practice Tests

Diderot Passage

Suggested Passage Map notes:

¶1: DD created volumes of documented tech advances during his time

¶2: DD found people to contribute, volumes were controversial

¶3: encyclopedie was progressive

¶4: science merged with liberal arts

¶5: made mundane crafts scholarly

¶6: angered people who protected trade secrets

¶7: upper society was angry

¶8: opposition too late, encyclo eventually became historical book

21. D   **Difficulty:** Medium

Category: Global

Getting to the Answer: Keep in mind that the correct answer will reflect the central purpose and opinion of the author as expressed in the passage. The passage explores the impact and influence of Diderot's *Encyclopédie*. The author states that the value of the work is not in its merit as a lasting technical reference or dictionary, but as a repository of historical knowledge and as an early attempt to extend the knowledge of the day to the masses. Choice (D) is correct.

22. D   **Difficulty:** Medium

Category: Rhetoric

Getting to the Answer: Choose the answer that reflects that author's overall point of view, or perspective, suggested by the passage. The passage examines the individual achievements of Diderot, specifically his efforts to extend the access to knowledge to a greater segment of European society. Choice (D) is correct, because it speaks to the author's obvious respect for Diderot as an innovator.

23. A   **Difficulty:** Medium

Category: Command of Evidence

Getting to the Answer: Reread each quote in the context of the passage. This will help you decide the correct answer. The correct answer to the previous question asserts that the author admires the individual accomplishments of innovators such as Diderot. Choice (A) is correct, because it calls attention to Diderot's contributions as revolutionizing encyclopedic thought.

24. C   **Difficulty:** Medium

Category: Detail

Getting to the Answer: Scan the passage for statements about Diderot's intentions and goals. Be sure not to confuse the results of his efforts with his goals. The passage states that Diderot's goal "was to create an intellectual work instructionally useful to all" (lines 16-17). While the work did create political controversy and also became part of the historical record, neither of these was his main goal. Choice (C) is correct.

25. B   **Difficulty:** Easy

Category: Vocab-in-Context

Getting to the Answer: Decide which answer choice could be substituted for the word without changing the meaning of the sentence. The paragraph states that Diderot's work was banned by the French government; therefore, the work's circulation, once published, was done secretly. Choice (B) is correct.

26. A   **Difficulty:** Medium

Category: Rhetoric

Getting to the Answer: The correct answer will reflect the meaning and intention behind the excerpted phrase as well as the surrounding text. The term "beacon" means a light that can be seen far away, usually with the purpose of guiding or attracting people to it. The phrase "free thought" in this context refers to the right of people to pursue knowledge. The surrounding text describes Diderot's work as having political purpose in expanding access to knowledge beyond the established elite to the masses. Therefore, (A) is correct.

27. A   Difficulty: Medium

Category: Inference

Getting to the Answer: Eliminate answer choices that don't represent the author's ideas. The passage refers repeatedly to the impact of Diderot's work in making information accessible to more people. The author states that political, economic, and intellectual elites opposed the publication of his encyclopedia because it lessened their control on trades and other valuable information. Choice (A) is correct.

28. C   Difficulty: Medium

Category: Command of Evidence

Getting to the Answer: Avoid answers that provide evidence for incorrect answers to the previous question. The correct answer to the previous question asserts that information was limited to a specific demographic, or segment of the population, at that time. Choice (C) is correct because it states clearly that the trade guilds, a select demographic, controlled certain knowledge and opposed the expansion of access to such knowledge.

29. D   Difficulty: Medium

Category: Vocab-in-Context

Getting to the Answer: Remember that you're looking for the answer that will make the most sense when substituted for the original word. The sentence discusses the way in which Diderot changed the perception and exploration of knowledge, making (D) correct. The word "erudition" refers to learning acquired by reading and study.

30. B   Difficulty: Medium

Category: Connections

Getting to the Answer: Remember that the correct answer must be based on information in the passage, not on speculation. Based on the last sentence of the passage and the information in paragraph 4, (B) is correct. It's the only answer choice directly supported by information in the passage.

31. C   Difficulty: Medium

Category: Synthesis

Getting to the Answer: Eliminate answer choices that cannot be inferred from the information in the passage and graphic. Choice (C) is the correct answer; Uranus was discovered after Diderot's *Encyclopédie* was published. Other answer choices are either impossible, as in the case of D, or cannot be inferred from the information provided.

Paired Passages—Acidity

Suggested Passage Map notes:

Passage 1
¶1: acid rain is a problem
¶2: explain pH scale
¶3: slightly acidic rain ok
¶4: human-made problems make bad acid rain

Passage 2
¶1: human blood needs controlled pH
¶2: pH controlled in body
¶3: kidneys aid in maintaining pH
¶4: uncontrolled pH causes problems - ex: diabetes

32. A   Difficulty: Medium

Category: Inference

Getting to the Answer: Consider what the author of Passage 1 is saying in the first paragraph about the causes and consequences of acid rain. Avoid answers like C that go too far and are not directly supported by the evidence in the passage. The author clearly states that acid rain, largely caused by the burning of fossil fuels, is bad for the environment. It is reasonable to conclude that if the burning of fossil fuels is not reduced, the environment will be damaged. Therefore, (A) is correct.

33. A   Difficulty: Medium

Category: Command of Evidence

Getting to the Answer: Look back at your answer to the previous question. Think about the information you found in the passage that helped you choose this answer. The last sentence in the first paragraph provides the strongest evidence for the idea that burning fossil fuels will seriously damage the environment. Therefore, (A) is correct.

34. A   Difficulty: Easy

Category: Detail

Getting to the Answer: Find where Passage 1 discusses the pH of rain water. Determine whether lower or higher pH levels indicate that rain water is dangerously acidic. The passage states that the pH of pure rain water can be as low as 5.5, and a pH level of 3 can cause soil and water to become too acidic. A pH level of 2.25 is less than 3, meaning it is even more dangerously acidic; therefore, the correct answer is (A).

35. B   Difficulty: Easy

Category: Vocab-in-Context

Getting to the Answer: Remember that some answer choices might be synonyms for "tolerate" but do not reflect the meaning of the word in this context. In this context, "tolerate" most nearly means "endure." Choice (B) is the correct answer.

36. D   Difficulty: Hard

Category: Inference

Getting to the Answer: Reread the text, looking for evidence to support each of the answer choices. The first paragraph of Passage 2 states: "Many processes in the body produce acid wastes" (lines 41-42), from which you can infer that it's normal to have acid wastes in the blood. Choice (D), therefore, is the correct answer.

37. C   Difficulty: Medium

Category: Command of Evidence

Getting to the Answer: Look for evidence that supports the inference you made in the previous question. In lines 60-63, the author explains how normal amounts of acid are neutralized in the blood. Choice (C) is correct.

38. C   Difficulty: Medium

Category: Vocab-in-Context

Getting to the Answer: Eliminate any answer choices that don't make sense in the context of the sentence. In this context, "exhaust" means "to use up" or "deplete." Therefore, (C) is the correct answer.

39. B   Difficulty: Hard

Category: Inference

Getting to the Answer: Read paragraph 2 of Passage 2 again, and determine the role of excess bicarbonate ions in the blood. Each answer choice is mentioned in Passage 1. Determine how each acts in the environment. Choice (B) is the correct answer. In Passage 2, the author explains that excess bicarbonate ions raise the pH of the blood, neutralizing acid wastes. In paragraph 3 of Passage 1, the author explains that alkaline materials in the environment, such as ashes from a forest fire, neutralize acid in the water supply.

40. D   Difficulty: Medium

Category: Connections

Getting to the Answer: You are looking for a cause-and-effect relationship to answer this question. Skim Passage 2, looking for an explanation of what causes the body to break down fats for energy. In paragraph 4 of Passage 2, the author explains that low insulin will cause the body to break down fats for energy. Therefore, (D) is the correct answer.

41. C   Difficulty: Medium

Category: Synthesis

Getting to the Answer: Consider the main topic and purpose of each passage. Decide what the passages have in common. Each passage describes a different system, the environment and the human body respectively, and how each system deals with acid. In each passage, the author describes how acid can be introduced into the system and neutralized in small amounts but also describes the ways in which large amounts of acid can damage or overwhelm each system, making (C) the correct answer.

42. A   Difficulty: Easy

Category: Synthesis

Getting to the Answer: The question is asking you about both passages. Eliminate answers that only address the information found in one of the passages. Although Passage 1 is about the environment and Passage 2 is about the human body, both passages are about delicate systems that need balance to remain healthy, so (A) is correct.

Hydrogen Passage

Suggested Passage Map notes:

¶1: hydrogen next renewable resource

¶2: looking for safe, low cost hydrogen fuel

¶3: challenges to hydrogen fuel production

¶4: new method for harvesting hydrogen

¶5: using solar power to harvest hydrogen, reduces cost of harvesting

¶6: more efficient way to harvest

¶7: more research to be done

43. A   Difficulty: Medium

Category: Inference

Getting to the Answer: Avoid answers like B, which are related to details presented but take the ideas too far. Think about the arguments presented by the author throughout the passage. In paragraph 3, the author lists drawbacks to hydrogen fuel as a replacement for gasoline. In this paragraph, the author notes that engines that run on hydrogen are more expensive than those that use gasoline. Choice (A) is the correct answer.

44. C   Difficulty: Medium

Category: Command of Evidence

Getting to the Answer: Read the previous question again. Look at each quote from the passage and decide which provides the strongest evidence. Choice (C) is the correct answer, as it provides the strongest evidence that the author is concerned with the cost to consumers of using hydrogen fuel.

45. A   Difficulty: Medium

Category: Detail

Getting to the Answer: Eliminate answer choices that contain details that are not stated directly in the text. In paragraph 1, the author states that hydrogen is found primarily with oxygen in water; therefore, (A) is correct.

46. B   Difficulty: Easy

Category: Vocab-in-Context

Getting to the Answer: Read the sentence again and replace "diligently" with each of the answer choices. Look for the answer that does not change the meaning of the sentence. When you consider the overall meaning of the sentence, (B) is the best choice. In this context, "persistently" means nearly the same thing as "diligently."

47. B   Difficulty: Medium

Category: Inference

Getting to the Answer: Pay attention to the parts of the passage that refer to petroleum-based fuels and the reasons scientists are seeking alternatives. Though the author does not explicitly state that petroleum-based fuels are bad for the environment, he or she does give the fact that hydrogen produces no pollution as a reason to look toward hydrogen and away from petroleum products. You can infer, then, that (B) is the correct answer.

48. B   Difficulty: Medium

Category: Command of Evidence

Getting to the Answer: Read the previous question again. Look at each quote from the passage and decide which most clearly supports the idea stated in the correct answer for that question. In paragraph 2, the author lists potential benefits for using hydrogen energy over petroleum-based energy sources. No pollution is one of the potential benefits, which leads to the conclusion that petroleum products are bad for the environment. Choice (B) is therefore the correct answer.

49. D   Difficulty: Medium

Category: Rhetoric

Getting to the Answer: Think about the purpose that paragraph 2 serves in creating the author's overall argument. In paragraph 2, the author asserts that decreasing dependence on other petroleum-producing countries is a potential benefit to the development of hydrogen as a fuel. The inclusion of this point helps clarify why hydrogen fuel is important. Choice (D) is correct.

50. C   Difficulty: Medium

Category: Vocab-in-Context

Getting to the Answer: Keep in mind that although all answer choices might be synonyms of "derived," only one fits the context of the sentence in which the word appears. In this context, "derived" most nearly means (C), "obtained."

51. A   Difficulty: Medium

Category: Inference

Getting to the Answer: Locate the parts of the passage that discuss advances in extracting hydrogen molecules from water. Then, find the answer choice that makes the most sense in the context of the passage. In lines 65-70, the author discusses research initiatives that focus on hydrogen extraction. You can infer from the fact that there are "many ongoing research initiatives" (lines 65-66) that much more research will be needed before hydrogen extraction is perfected. Choice (A) is correct.

52. D   Difficulty: Medium

Category: Synthesis

Getting to the Answer: Avoid answer choices that are supported only by the information in one of the sources. Look for the answer that is supported by both the passage and the graphic. The data presented in the graphic supports the author's argument that hydrogen fuel produces less greenhouse gas than gasoline. Choice (D) is correct.

WRITING AND LANGUAGE TEST

Sorting Recyclables for Best Re-Use

1. B   Difficulty: Easy

Category: Usage

Getting to the Answer: Read the sentence and check to see whether the verb agrees with the subject. The verb "are" is in a plural form, but the subject is singular. Choice (B) is correct because it is the singular form of the verb "to be."

2. D   Difficulty: Medium

Category: Effective Language Use

Getting to the Answer: Read the sentences surrounding the word to better understand the context in which the word appears. Then substitute each answer choice into the sentence to see which fits into the context best. The passage states that the plastics are sorted by types. Only (D) has the correct connotation and fits within the context of the sentence.

3. C   Difficulty: Hard

Category: Development

Getting to the Answer: Read the entire paragraph and write down the central idea. Then review the answer choices and look for a close match with your prediction. The paragraph discusses the two methods used to sort plastics. Choice (C) is closest to this summation.

4. C   Difficulty: Easy

Category: Effective Language Use

Getting to the Answer: Watch out for choices like A and B, which use extra words that do not add meaning to the sentence. It is better to be as direct and simple as possible. The word "thoroughly" indicates that the people doing the job are paying attention to every detail. Additional words such as "very" or "completely" do not add more meaning to this sentence. Choice (C) is the most concise and effective way of stating the information.

5. B   Difficulty: Medium

Category: Organization

Getting to the Answer: Look for the relationship between this sentence and the previous one. This will help you choose the appropriate transition word. Read the sentence using the word you chose to ensure that it makes sense. Choice (B) shows the relationship between the two sentences by giving an example of how the products are manufactured.

6. B   Difficulty: Medium

Category: Punctuation

Getting to the Answer: Study the words in a series to see where a comma might need to be placed or eliminated. Only one answer choice will include the correct punctuation. Choice (B) is correct.

7. B   Difficulty: Hard

Category: Quantitative

Getting to the Answer: The graphic gives specific information about how much of each type of plastic was recovered. Study the graphic in order to select the correct answer choice. Choice (B) accurately reflects the information in the graphic.

8. B   Difficulty: Medium

Category: Effective Language Use

Getting to the Answer: Watch out for choices that may include incorrect transition words. Choice (B) uses the present participle "depending" to join the sentences concisely and correctly.

9. A   Difficulty: Easy

Category: Effective Language Use

Getting to the Answer: Check each answer choice for its connotations, and be sure to pick one that fits with the context of the sentence. Substitute each answer choice for the word to see which works best. Notice that the sentence sets up a contrast between plastics numbered 1 through 6 and plastics with the number 7, which may consist of one of many other plastics or a blend of plastics. Choice (A) is correct because the word "specific" indicates that each of the numbers 1 through 6 is used for only one type of plastic.

10. C   Difficulty: Medium

Category: Sentence Formation

Getting to the Answer: Two complete thoughts should be two separate sentences. Be careful of inappropriate transition words. Choice (C) divides the two thoughts into two complete sentences by adding a period and capitalizing the first word of the second sentence.

11. A   Difficulty: Medium

Category: Development

Getting to the Answer: Read the entire paragraph and then read each of the choices. Decide which one sums up the paragraph best by stating the overall central idea. Choice (A) is the correct answer. It concludes the paragraph by stating the overall central idea of the paragraph and passage.

Interpreter at America's Immigrant Gateway

12. D   **Difficulty:** Hard

Category: Development

Getting to the Answer: Read the entire first paragraph. The correct answer should offer descriptive details and introduce David Kaufman as a character. The first paragraph discusses David Kaufman specifically and his relationship to his job. While A, B, and C are informative, they do not add beauty or descriptive interest to the paragraph. Only (D) sparks the reader's interest with descriptive language and relates directly to the following sentences.

13. B   **Difficulty:** Medium

Category: Punctuation

Getting to the Answer: Determine whether the information is all one thought or whether the sentence suggests that some part of it is an aside. The sentence is mainly discussing Kaufman, but it also introduces the idea of America's history almost as an afterthought. By setting this aside within dashes, the sentence will draw attention to its parenthetical relationship to the rest of the sentence. Choice (B) is correct.

14. C   **Difficulty:** Easy

Category: Usage

Getting to the Answer: Determine whether the underlined word is being used as a place or a possessive. Then consider which answer choice would be most appropriate here. In this sentence, "there" is describing "baggage" belonging to these new Americans. It should therefore be changed to the correct possessive form "their," making (C) correct.

15. C   **Difficulty:** Medium

Category: Effective Language Use

Getting to the Answer: Eliminate unnecessary words. Then reorder the nouns and verbs to achieve

the most concise language possible. Choice (C) contains no unnecessary words. It concisely explains the actions taken by the two different groups of people and is the correct answer.

16. A   **Difficulty:** Medium

Category: Organization

Getting to the Answer: Consider the function of this sentence. At what point in the paragraph should this function be employed? The sentence is setting a scene, so it should be placed where it is now, at the beginning of the paragraph. To place it later would cause confusion in the following sentences, as the reader does not have all the information he or she needs. Choice (A), leaving it in its current position, is the correct answer.

17. B   **Difficulty:** Medium

Category: Development

Getting to the Answer: The correct answer should introduce an idea that is supported by the sentences that follow. Consider whether the current sentence should be revised to do this. The rest of the paragraph discusses the relationship between immigrant communities and language ability, as well as information about Kaufman's position. Therefore, the introductory sentence to this paragraph should tie together these thoughts. Choice (B) is the correct answer, as it ties Kaufman to his background in an immigrant community.

18. D   **Difficulty:** Easy

Category: Punctuation

Getting to the Answer: Determine whether the information enclosed in commas is separate or should be integrated into the rest of the sentence. The subject of the sentence is a compound noun: "his heritage and surrounding community." Therefore, the nouns making up this compound noun should not be separated by commas. Choice (D) punctuates this sentence correctly.

19. D   Difficulty: Hard

Category: Effective Language Use

Getting to the Answer: Consider the tone of this sentence as well as its meaning. Then review the answer choices to determine which one best matches both the tone and the meaning. The sentence suggests that Kaufman is trying to make his language abilities more refined and precise in order to help the immigrants. While C, "tricks," is tempting, it does not match the more formal tone of the passage. Choice (D), "nuances," conveys the fact that Kaufman is trying to understand the subtleties of language; this answer maintains the passage's formal tone.

20. B   Difficulty: Medium

Category: Development

Getting to the Answer: Reread the rest of the paragraph to determine which answer choice would most effectively add specific, relevant detail to this section of the passage. The paragraph notes that Kaufman helps "at every checkpoint," then mentions the variety of facilities Ellis Island possesses. Choice (B) adds detail about the variety of ways Kaufman helps at Ellis Island and is therefore the correct answer.

21. D   Difficulty: Medium

Category: Effective Language Use

Getting to the Answer: Consider whether the sentence's intended meaning can be conveyed in fewer words. All that is really needed in this sentence is "to help." The reader will still understand what is happening. The other options are wordy and awkward. Choice (D) is the correct answer.

22. C   Difficulty: Medium

Category: Effective Language Use

Getting to the Answer: Before looking at the answer choices, identify a word on your own that will convey the correct meaning for the context. The context of the sentence makes clear that the correct

word is something that is "rendered . . . worthwhile." In other words, it is a challenging situation that will be made worthwhile by living in America. While both (C) and D are negative words, (C), "difficulties," specifically connotes something hard or troubling, so it is the correct answer.

Software Sales: A Gratifying Career

23. D   Difficulty: Medium

Category: Punctuation

Getting to the Answer: Determine the relationship between the two different parts of the sentence. Then choose the punctuation that fits best. In this sentence, two independent clauses are joined by the coordinating conjunction "so." When two independent clauses are joined in this manner, a comma is needed before the conjunction. Only (D) combines the two independent clauses correctly.

24. B   Difficulty: Easy

Category: Usage

Getting to the Answer: Substitute the phrases for their contractions, such as "It is," for "It's" to determine the correct usage. "They're" and "Their" are inappropriate because when the subject is not clear (such as "It is raining"), it is grammatically correct to use "it" instead of "they." Choice (B) is correct.

25. A   Difficulty: Medium

Category: Punctuation

Getting to the Answer: Commas should be used sparingly to help the reader understand the passage. Only one comma is needed to successfully combine two independent clauses with a conjunction. Choice (A) is the correct answer.

26. A   Difficulty: Hard

Category: Usage

Getting to the Answer: Read the entire paragraph

to establish the verb tense. Identify the key verbs in the paragraph and their tenses. Both "turned" and "returned" are past tense, making (A) the correct choice.

27. C   Difficulty: Medium

Category: Development

Getting to the Answer: Determine the focus of the paragraph by identifying its topic and purpose. Then read the answer choices, looking for the choice that is least relevant. The paragraph has an informational purpose and is about the unusual route Morales took to a career in software sales. The opinion that "New Hampshire also has many fine backpacking trails" is extraneous to this topic and purpose. Choice (C) is correct.

28. D   Difficulty: Medium

Category: Sentence Formation

Getting to the Answer: Identify whether the underlined portion contains sentences or fragments, or a combination of both. Then determine the best way to join them. The underlined portion contains a sentence and a fragment. Only (D) correctly rewords the fragment to make it an independent clause and then uses a conjunction to join the two parts of the sentence.

29. C   Difficulty: Medium

Category: Development

Getting to the Answer: Read the entire paragraph and summarize the supporting details to help you determine the appropriate topic sentence. The supporting details of the paragraph all relate to Morales's ability to come up with a creative solution to a company's problem. Choice (C) is the correct topic sentence of the paragraph.

30. B   Difficulty: Medium

Category: Effective Language Use

Getting to the Answer: Notice the prefixes used in

the answer choices and think about what they mean. Then choose the word that best fits into the context of the sentence. The prefix "re-" means "back," as in "return" or "replace." "Retaining" means to keep or hold back. This fits into the context of the sentence, so (B) is correct.

31. C   Difficulty: Medium

Category: Effective Language Use

Getting to the Answer: Read the sentence to determine which word provides the correct meaning in context. "Vacillate" means to be indecisive, "convert" means to change into a different form, and "fluctuate" means to change continually. Choice (C), "transition," means to move from one thing to another. Morales's goal is to move from one field to another, so (C) is the correct answer.

32. D   Difficulty: Medium

Category: Development

Getting to the Answer: Identify the topic sentence in the paragraph. Then review the answer choices to find the one that best supports it. The topic sentence of the paragraph is about "big data." Morales's use of "big data" to gather information regarding health care supports the topic sentence. The other choices do not involve capturing data from outside sources. Choice (D) is correct.

33. A   Difficulty: Medium

Category: Punctuation

Getting to the Answer: When a sentence contains a series of actions, make sure the elements are parallel and punctuated correctly. Then, determine whether you should eliminate or insert any commas. Choice (A) is correct, because there are three identifiable actions in the series: "quicken," "improve," and "save."

The Art of Collecting

34. A   **Difficulty:** Medium

Category: Effective Language Use

Getting to the Answer: Read for context clues and determine which answer offers the most appropriate word choice. The sentence states that Etta "passed away" before her art was given to the BMA. Because this was a gift after death, "bequeathed" is the most appropriate word choice in this sentence. Choice (A) is correct.

35. C   **Difficulty:** Hard

Category: Development

Getting to the Answer: After reading the paragraph, reread each sentence to determine which one summarizes the overall message of the paragraph. Aside from (C), all other sentences offer details and ideas that are not supported by the rest of the paragraph. Only (C) encapsulates the central idea that the Cones contributed their art to the BMA.

36. D   **Difficulty:** Medium

Category: Sentence Formation

Getting to the Answer: Reread the sentence to figure out what is meant. Then choose the coordinating conjunction that creates the most logical and grammatically correct sentence. Choice (D) is correct. Because the second independent clause discusses what the sisters did despite the statement in the first independent clause, the coordinating conjunction "but" is most appropriate here.

37. C   **Difficulty:** Easy

Category: Usage

Getting to the Answer: Read for context clues and determine which answer choice is most logical and grammatically correct. The possessive determiner "their" is grammatically correct and correctly explains the sisters' ownership of the selections, so (C) is the correct answer.

38. B   **Difficulty:** Medium

Category: Usage

Getting to the Answer: Read the surrounding sentences for context clues to determine which pronoun and verb combination creates the clearest and most effective sentence. The pronoun must be "they," as it refers to both Etta and Claribel. The rest of the paragraph is written in the past tense, making "took" the correct verb. Choice (B) is correct.

39. B   **Difficulty:** Medium

Category: Effective Language Use

Getting to the Answer: Read the sentence for context clues, and determine which answer offers the most appropriate word choice. The sentence describes what the art collected by the Cones showed, or "depicted." The other answer choices are less precise, making (B) the correct answer.

40. D   **Difficulty:** Hard

Category: Development

Getting to the Answer: Read the entire paragraph and determine the central idea. Then read the answer choices, looking for the choice that distracts from the paragraph's focus. The central idea of the paragraph is that the Cone collection documented the changes in post-World War I Europe. The statement "Today, there are more experimental forms of art than there were after World War I" may be accurate, but it does not relate to the central idea. Choice (D) is the correct answer.

41. C   **Difficulty:** Medium

Category: Punctuation

Getting to the Answer: Reread the sentence to determine which set of punctuation marks creates a grammatically correct sentence. Introductory words such as "additionally" are followed by a comma when they begin a sentence. The word "Paris" is the beginning of a list and also should be followed by a comma. No other punctuation is required in this portion of the sentence, so (C) is correct.

42. D   **Difficulty:** Medium

Category: Usage

Getting to the Answer: Reread the sentence for context clues to determine which answer choice provides the correct meaning. The current underlined word, "though," means "despite," creating an illogical contrast between the two parts of the sentence. The definitions for B, "therefore" (for that reason), and C, "thorough" (completed with exacting detail), likewise do not create logical sentences. The definition of "through" best expresses the idea that the sisters experienced freedom "by means of" their lifestyle. Choice (D) is the correct answer.

43. A   **Difficulty:** Hard

Category: Development

Getting to the Answer: Determine the central idea of the paragraph, and decide which additional facts noted in the answer choices would have the greatest benefit to the reader. Because the paragraph is about how the Cones challenged traditional views of women, and because the author uses several undefined but important terms, (A) is the correct answer.

44. B   **Difficulty:** Medium

Category: Punctuation

Getting to the Answer: Review the sentence to assess which answer choice offers the correct use of plural punctuation to convey the proper sense of possession. The possessive plural of "Cones" refers to both sisters owning something, and requires an apostrophe after the "s" with no additional letters or punctuation. Choice (B) is correct.

MATH—NO CALCULATOR TEST

1. B   **Difficulty:** Easy

Category: Heart of Algebra / Linear Equations

Getting to the Answer: Look at the structure of the equation. It is written in the form $y = mx + b$. The question is asking about 20.942, which is m in the equation, and therefore represents a rate of change. The variable x represents number of months. The value of m is positive, so it represents the estimated monthly increase in the number of the plants after the natural disaster occurred, (B).

2. C   **Difficulty:** Easy

Category: Passport to Advanced Math / Quadratics

Getting to the Answer: The expression is a difference of two squares, so write each term as a quantity squared and then use the difference of squares rule $a^2 - b^2 = (a + b)(a - b)$.

$$25x^2 - \frac{4}{9}$$
$$= (5x)^2 - \left(\frac{2}{3}\right)^2$$
$$= \left(5x + \frac{2}{3}\right)\left(5x - \frac{2}{3}\right)$$

Choice (C) is correct.

3. A   **Difficulty:** Medium

Category: Passport to Advanced Math / Quadratics

Getting to the Answer: Factored form of a quadratic equation reveals the roots, or x-intercepts, of the equation, so start by identifying the x-intercepts on the graph. An x-intercept is an x-value that corresponds to a y-value of 0. Read the axis labels carefully—each grid-line represents $\frac{1}{4}$, so the x-intercepts of the graph, and therefore the roots of the equation, are $x = -\frac{1}{2}$ and $x = \frac{3}{4}$. This means you are looking for factors that when solved result in these values of x. Choice (A) is correct because $2x + 1$ gives you $x = -\frac{1}{2}$ and $4x - 3$ gives you $x = \frac{3}{4}$.

4. D   **Difficulty:** Easy

Category: Heart of Algebra / Linear Equations

Getting to the Answer: Don't jump right into translating the line. Think about how the translation would affect the slope—it wouldn't. Translating the line moves all the points by the same amount, so the slope doesn't change. Find the slope of line *P* by counting the rise and the run from one point to the next, and you'll have your answer. From the *y*-intercept $(0, -2)$, the line rises 5 units and runs 2 units to the point $(2, 3)$, so the slope is $\frac{5}{2}$, (D).

5. B **Difficulty:** Easy

Category: Passport to Advanced Math / Exponents

Getting to the Answer: Solve the equation for *t*. Multiply both sides of the equation by *t* to get it out of the denominator, and then divide both sides by *a*.

$$a = \frac{v_f - v_i}{t}$$
$$t\left(a = \frac{v_f - v_i}{t}\right)t$$
$$ta = v_f - v_i$$
$$t = \frac{v_f - v_i}{a}$$

This matches (B).

6. C **Difficulty:** Medium

Category: Passport to Advanced Math / Quadratics

Getting to the Answer: Imagine the graph of a parabola. The minimum value is the *y*-coordinate of its vertex, and the axis of symmetry also passes through the vertex. Use these properties to identify the vertex, and then use it to write the equation of the parabola in vertex form, $y = a(x - h)^2 + k$, where (h, k) is the vertex. If the minimum of the parabola is -5, then the vertex of the parabola looks like $(x, -5)$. The axis of symmetry, $x = 1$, tells you the *x*-coordinate—it's 1. That means (h, k) is $(1, -5)$, and the equation of the parabola looks like $y = a(x - 1)^2 - 5$. The value of *a* in each of the answer choices is 1, so (C) is correct.

7. B **Difficulty:** Medium

Category: Heart of Algebra / Systems of Linear Equations

Getting to the Answer: The solution to a system of linear equations shown graphically is the point where the lines intersect. Read the axis labels carefully. Each grid-line represents $\frac{1}{2}$. The two lines intersect at $(-5, -4)$, so $A + B = -5 + (-4) = -9$, (B).

8. C **Difficulty:** Easy

Category: Passport to Advanced Math / Exponents

Getting to the Answer: When adding or subtracting polynomial expressions, simply combine like terms (terms that have the same variable part). Pay careful attention to the exponents. To keep things organized, arrange the terms in descending order before you combine them. Substitute the given expressions for *A* and *B* into $3A + B$. Distribute the 3 to each term of *A* and then combine like terms. Be careful—the first term of *B* is x^3, not x^2, so these cannot be combined.

$$3\left(x^2 + 4x + 9\right) + \left(x^3 + 6x - 2\right)$$
$$= 3x^2 + 12x + 27 + x^3 + 6x - 2$$
$$= x^3 + 3x^2 + 12x + 6x + 27 - 2$$
$$= x^3 + 3x^2 + 18x + 25$$

This matches (C).

9. B **Difficulty:** Medium

Category: Passport to Advanced Math / Quadratics

Getting to the Answer: A quadratic equation can have zero, one, or two real solutions. There are several ways to determine exactly how many. You could graph the equation and see how many times it crosses the *x*-axis; you could calculate the discriminant (the value under the square root in the quadratic formula); or you could try to factor the equation. Use whichever method gets you to the answer the quickest. Notice that the first and last terms in the equation are perfect squares—this is a hint that it could be a perfect square trinomial, which it is. The factored form of the equation is $(3x - 2)(3x - 2)$. Both factors are the same, so there is only one real value, $x = \dfrac{2}{3}$, that satisfies the equation, so (B) is correct.

10. A   Difficulty: Medium

Category: Heart of Algebra / Inequalities

Getting to the Answer: When an equation or an inequality involves fractions, there are a number of ways to approach it. You could distribute the fractions or you could clear the fractions by multiplying both sides by the lowest common denominator. In this question, clearing one fraction at a time will prevent having to work with messy fractions and large numbers. First, multiply everything by 5, and then divide by 3—this will clear the first fraction:

$$\cancel{5} \cdot \left[\frac{3}{\cancel{5}}\left(x + \frac{2}{7}\right)\right] > [-6] \cdot 5$$

$$3\left(x + \frac{2}{7}\right) > -30$$

$$\frac{\cancel{3}\left(x + \frac{2}{7}\right)}{\cancel{3}} > \frac{-30}{3}$$

$$x + \frac{2}{7} > -10$$

Now, multiply everything by 7 and go from there:

$$7 \cdot \left[x + \frac{2}{7}\right] > [-10] \cdot 7$$

$$7x + 2 > -70$$

$$7x > -72$$

$$x > -\frac{72}{7}$$

Choice (A) is correct.

11. D   Difficulty: Medium

Category: Heart of Algebra / Linear Equations

Getting to the Answer: Don't let all the contextual information confuse you. The question at the end tells you that you are looking for the linear

relationship between the pairs of numbers in the last two rows of the table. This amounts to writing an equation in the form $y = mx + b$. Take a peek at the answers—none of the equations have a y-intercept, so all you need to do is write the equation $y = mx$, or here, $s = md$. To find m, use any two ordered pairs from the table and the slope formula. Be careful—d represents x in the equation, so the dropper amounts should be written first in the ordered pairs. Using (0.5, 1.25) and (1.0, 2.5), the slope is:

$$m = \frac{y_2 - y_1}{x_2 - x_1}$$

$$= \frac{2.5 - 1.25}{1.0 - 0.5}$$

$$= \frac{1.25}{0.5}$$

$$= 2.5$$

This means the equation is $s = 2.5d$, which matches (D).

12. C   Difficulty: Medium

Category: Heart of Algebra / Linear Equations

Getting to the Answer: Think conceptually before you start simplifying the equations. The only type of line that does not cross the y-axis is a vertical line (because it runs parallel to the axis). All vertical lines take the form $x = a$. In other words, a vertical line does not have a y term. Eliminate equations that will clearly have a y term once simplified. You don't need to worry about the x terms or the constants.

Choice A: Although it may appear that the y terms will cancel, you must first distribute 0.5. The result is $0.5y$ on the left side of the equation and y on the right, which do not cancel, so eliminate A.

Choice B: No y terms on the left, but $4y$ on the right, so eliminate B.

Choice (C): $0.25(8y) = 2y$ on the left and $-2(-y) = 2y$ on the right, which do indeed cancel, so (C) is correct.

You don't need to waste time checking D—just move on to the next question. (*Choice D:* $-6y$ on the left and $-3y$ on the right, which do not cancel.)

13. D   **Difficulty:** Medium

Category: Heart of Algebra / Systems of Linear Equations

Getting to the Answer: Typically, solving a system of equations means finding the values of x and y that satisfy both equations simultaneously. Because the solution to the system satisfies both equations, you can substitute 2 and -1, for x and y respectively, and then solve for H and K. Before selecting your answer, check that you found what the question was asking for (the value of $\frac{K}{H}$).

$$Hx + 2y = -8$$
$$H(2) + 2(-1) = -8$$
$$2H - 2 = -8$$
$$2H = -6$$
$$H = -3$$

$$Kx - 5y = -13$$
$$K(2) - 5(-1) = -13$$
$$2K + 5 = -13$$
$$2K = -18$$
$$K = -9$$

So, $\frac{K}{H} = \frac{-9}{-3} = 3$, (D).

14. D   **Difficulty:** Hard

Category: Additional Topics in Math / Trigonometry

Getting to the Answer: If an angle with measure A such that $\pi < A < \frac{3\pi}{2}$ is drawn on a unit circle, its terminal side will fall in Quadrant III, and $\sin A = k$ will be a negative value (because sine represents the y-value of the point that intersects the unit circle). If $\sin B = k$ also (and k is negative), then the terminal side of B must land in either of Quadrants III or IV (because sine is negative in those quadrants). Choose an easy radian measure (in Quadrant III) for angle A, such as $\frac{5\pi}{4}$. Try each answer choice to see which one results in an angle that lies in the third or

fourth quadrant:

Choice A: $\frac{5\pi}{4} - \pi = \frac{5\pi}{4} - \frac{4\pi}{4} = \frac{\pi}{4}$, which is in Quadrant I, so eliminate A.

Choice B: $\pi + \frac{5\pi}{4} = \frac{4\pi}{4} + \frac{5\pi}{4} = \frac{9\pi}{4}$, which is in Quadrant I (because it is the same as $\frac{\pi}{4}$ rotated one full circle), so eliminate B.

Choice C: $2\pi - \frac{5\pi}{4} = \frac{8\pi}{4} - \frac{5\pi}{4} = \frac{3\pi}{4}$, which is in Quadrant II, so eliminate C.

Choice (D): $3\pi - \frac{5\pi}{4} = \frac{12\pi}{4} - \frac{5\pi}{4} = \frac{7\pi}{4}$, which is in Quadrant IV, so (D) is correct.

15. D   **Difficulty:** Hard

Category: Passport to Advanced Math / Exponents

Getting to the Answer: For this question, use the following rules of exponents: When you raise a power to a power, you multiply the exponents, and when you divide with exponents, you subtract them. Distribute the 2 outside the parentheses to the exponent in the numerator and in the denominator:

$$\left(\frac{x^{\frac{1}{2}}}{x^{-2}} \right)^2 = \frac{x^{\frac{1}{2} \times 2}}{x^{-2 \times 2}} = \frac{x^1}{x^{-4}}$$

Now, subtract the exponents:

$$\frac{x}{x^{-4}} = x^{1-(-4)} = x^{1+4} = x^5$$

Unfortunately, x^5 is not one of the answer choices, so look for an answer choice that is also equivalent to x^5. You can eliminate A right away, and the exponents in B look too small, so start with C, which simplifies to $\frac{x^7}{x^{12}} = \frac{1}{x^5}$ and is therefore not correct. Choice (D) is correct because:

$$\left(\frac{\left(x^3\right)\left(x^4\right)}{x^{-3}}\right)^{\frac{1}{2}} = \left(\frac{x^7}{x^{-3}}\right)^{\frac{1}{2}}$$

$$= \left(x^{7-(-3)}\right)^{\frac{1}{2}}$$

$$= \left(x^{10}\right)^{\frac{1}{2}}$$

$$= x^5$$

16. 1   Difficulty: Medium

Category: Heart of Algebra / Inequalities

Getting to the Answer: If (a, b) is a solution to the system, then a is the x-coordinate of any point in the region where the shading overlaps and b is the corresponding y-coordinate. When $a = 0$ (or $x = 0$), the maximum possible value for b lies on the upper boundary line, $y < -3x + 2$. (You can tell which boundary line is the upper line by looking at the y-intercept.) The point on the boundary line is $(0, 2)$, but the boundary line is dashed (because the inequality is strictly less than), so you cannot include $(0, 2)$ in the solution set. This means 1 is the greatest possible integer value for b when $a = 0$.

17. 12   Difficulty: Medium

Category: Passport to Advanced Math / Functions

Getting to the Answer: For any function $f(x)$, the x is the input value, and the output is the result after plugging in the input and simplifying. The question tells you that the *output* is 3 (not the input), so set the equation equal to 3 and solve for x.

$$3 = \frac{2}{3}x - 5$$

$$8 = \frac{2}{3}x$$

$$3 \times 8 = \cancel{3} \times \frac{2}{\cancel{3}}x$$

$$24 = 2x$$

$$12 = x$$

18. 12   Difficulty: Medium

Category: Additional Topics in Math / Geometry

Getting to the Answer: Use the relationship $\dfrac{\text{area of sector}}{\text{area of circle}} = \dfrac{\text{central angle}}{360°}$. To help you remember this relationship, just think $\dfrac{\text{partial area}}{\text{whole area}} = \dfrac{\text{partial angle}}{\text{whole angle}}$. The unknown in this question is the diameter of the circle, which is twice the radius. You can find the radius of the circle by first finding the area of the whole circle, and then by using the area equation, $A = \pi r^2$. You have everything you need to find the area of the circle. Because this is a no-calculator question, you can bet that numbers will simplify nicely.

$$\frac{\text{area of sector}}{\text{area of circle}} = \frac{\text{central angle}}{360°}$$

$$\frac{6\pi}{A} = \frac{60}{360}$$

$$\frac{6\pi}{A} = \frac{1}{6}$$

$$A = 36\pi$$

Now, solve for r using $A = \pi r^2$:

$$36\pi = \pi r^2$$

$$36 = r^2$$

$$\pm 6 = r$$

The radius can't be negative, so it must be 6, which means the diameter of the circle is twice that, or 12.

19. 14   Difficulty: Hard

Category: Additional Topics in Math / Geometry

Getting to the Answer: When the equation of a circle is in the form $(x - h)^2 + (y - k)^2 = r^2$, the r represents the length of the radius. To get the equation into this form, complete the squares. You already have an x^2 and a y^2 in the given equation and the coefficients of x and y are even, so completing the square is fairly straightforward—there are just a lot of steps. Start by grouping the xs and ys together. Then, take the coefficient of the x term and divide it by 2, square it, and add it to the two terms with x variables. Do the same with the y term. Don't forget to add these amounts to the other side of the equation as well. This creates a perfect square of *x* terms and *y* terms, so take the square root of each.

$$x^2 + y^2 + 10x - 4y = 20$$
$$x^2 + 10x + y^2 - 4y = 20$$
$$\left(x^2 + 10x + 25\right) + \left(y^2 - 4y + 4\right) = 20 + 25 + 4$$
$$(x + 5)^2 + (y - 2)^2 = 49$$

The equation tells you that $r^2 = 49$, which means that the radius is 7 and the diameter is twice that, or 14.

20. 800   Difficulty: Hard

Domain: Passport to Advanced Math / Functions

Getting to the Answer: Think about the question logically and in terms of function notation. Find the quantity that the company can expect to sell at each price using the demand function. Don't forget that the quantity is given in hundreds. Then, find the total sales, the total costs, and the total profits using multiplication.

Price	$12	$10
Quantity	q(12) = −2(12) + 34 = −24 + 34 = 10	q(10) = −2(10) + 34 = −20 + 34 = 14
In hundreds	10(100) = 1,000	14(100) = 1,400
Sales	1,000(12) = $12,000	1,400(10) = $14,000
Costs	1,000(7) = $7,000	1,400(7) = $9,800
Profits	$5,000	$4,200

The company will earn $5,000 − $4,200 = $800 more per month.

MATH—CALCULATOR TEST

1. B   Difficulty: Easy

Category: Heart of Algebra / Inequalities

Getting to the Answer: When trying to match an inequality to a real-world scenario, you need to examine the numbers, the variables, and the inequality symbol. The question asks how much is needed to *meet or surpass* the recommended amount, which is another way of saying *greater than or equal to*, so you can eliminate C. Adult females should consume 75 milligrams of vitamin C, and smokers should consume an additional 35 mg, so the total amount that a smoking female should consume is 75 + 35 = 110 milligrams. This means the right-hand side of the equation should be ≥ 110, and you can eliminate A. To choose between (B) and D, think in concrete terms. *Multiplying* (not dividing) the number of milligrams in each grapefruit or serving of spinach yields the total amount of vitamin C in each, so (B) is correct.

2. D   Difficulty: Easy

Category: Problem Solving and Data Analysis / Scatterplots

Getting to the Answer: You don't need to know the slope of the line of best fit to answer the question, so don't waste valuable time trying to find it. Instead, use the labels on the axes to determine the meaning of the slope. On a graph, slope means the change in the *y*-values (rise) compared to the change in the *x*-values (run). In a real-world scenario, this is the same as the unit rate. In this context, the rise is the amount of money spent, and the run is the number of minutes watching commercials. Thus, the unit rate, or slope, represents the predicted increase in money spent on brand name products for every one-minute increase in time spent watching commercials, (D).

3. B   Difficulty: Easy

Category: Heart of Algebra / Systems of Linear Equations

Getting to the Answer: Whenever a question gives you information about a total number of items and a total cost of those items, you should write one equation that represents the total number (here, the number of packages) and a second equation that represents the total cost (here, the cost of the portraits). The number of parents who ordered basic packages plus the number who ordered deluxe packages equals the total number of parents (182), so one equation is $b + d = 182$. This means you can eliminate A and C. Now write the cost equation: cost per basic package (29.5) times number ordered (b) plus cost per deluxe package (44.5) times number ordered (d) equals the total bill ($6,509). The cost equation is $29.5b + 44.5d = 6,509$. Together, these two equations form the system in (B). Don't let D fool you—there are two choices of packages, but this does not impact the total amount of the school's bill.

4. C   Difficulty: Easy

Category: Passport to Advanced Math / Functions

Getting to the Answer: Understanding the language of functions will make answering this question very simple. Another way of saying "For what values of x does $f(x) = -4$?" is "What is the x-value when $y = -4$?" Draw a horizontal line across the graph at $y = -4$ and find the x-coordinates of any points that hit your line.

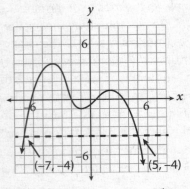

The line hits the graph at $x = -7$ and at $x = 5$, (C).

5. C   Difficulty: Easy

Category: Heart of Algebra / Linear Equations

Getting to the Answer: Don't let this fairly simple question fool you. Just because 3 and −3 are opposites, this does not mean the value on the right-hand side of the equals sign will be the opposite of 19. Solve for x, then substitute that value into the second equation for x and simplify.

$$4x + 3 = 19$$
$$4x = 16$$
$$x = 4$$

Thus, $4x - 3 = 4(4) - 3 = 16 - 3 = 13$, (C).

You might also recognize that $4x - 3$ is 6 less than $4x + 3$, so you can simply subtract 6 from 19 to arrive at 13. This is a great shortcut, but only works when the variable terms are identical.

6. C   Difficulty: Easy

Category: Heart of Algebra / Linear Equations

Getting to the Answer: To find the slope of a line from its graph, either count the rise and the run from one point to the next, or choose two points that lie on the line and substitute them into the slope formula, $m = \dfrac{y_2 - y_1}{x_2 - x_1}$. Use whichever method gets you to the answer the quickest. Pay careful attention to negative signs. Using the points $(0, -2)$ and $(7, -8)$, the slope is:

$$m = \frac{-8 - (-2)}{7 - 0}$$
$$= \frac{-6}{7}$$
$$= -\frac{6}{7}$$

Choice (C) is correct.

7. B   Difficulty: Easy

Category: Heart of Algebra / Linear Equations

Getting to the Answer: Compare the differences in the two lines to the statements in the answer choices. Pay careful attention to which line represents each state. Be careful—this is a real-world scenario, and the word "positive" does not refer to the slope of the lines. The key difference between the lines in the graph is their slopes. The dashed line (State B) has a steeper negative slope, while the solid line (State A) has a more gradual slope. This means that the crime rate for armed robbery in State B decreased at a faster rate than in State A. Because, in the real world, a positive impact means fewer crimes, State B's law had a more positive impact on the crime rate for armed robbery. This matches (B).

8. C   Difficulty: Easy

Category: Problem Solving and Data Analysis / Rates, Ratios, Proportions, and Percentages

Getting to the Answer: When ratios involve large numbers, simplify if possible to make the calculations easier. Let p equal the number of cans of paint mixed. Set up a proportion and solve for p. Try writing the proportion in words first.

$$\frac{4\cancel{0}\ \text{defective}}{2,50\cancel{0}\ \text{mixed}} = \frac{128\ \text{defective}}{p\ \text{mixed}}$$

$$\frac{4}{250} = \frac{128}{p}$$

$$4p = 32,000$$

$$p = 8,000$$

Choice (C) is correct.

9. D   Difficulty: Medium

Category: Problem Solving and Data Analysis / Statistics and Probability

Getting to the Answer: Because the mean ages are different and you do not know how many men or women have college degrees and get married, you need to reason logically to arrive at the correct answer. The mean age of the women is lower than that of the men, so the combined mean cannot be greater than or equal to that of the men. Similarly, the mean age of the men is greater than that of the women, so the combined mean cannot be less than or equal to the mean age of the women. In other words, the combined mean age must fall somewhere between the two means, making (D) correct.

10. A   Difficulty: Easy

Category: Problem Solving and Data Analysis / Rates, Ratios, Proportions, and Percentages

Getting to the Answer: To answer a question that says "directly proportional," set two ratios equal to

each other and solve for the missing amount. Don't forget—match the units in the numerators and in the denominators on both sides. Let f equal the number of feet that the diver can safely ascend in 90 seconds. Set up a proportion and solve for f. Because the first rate is given in terms of minutes, write 90 seconds as 1.5 minutes.

$$\frac{165\ \text{feet}}{5.5\ \text{minutes}} = \frac{f\ \text{feet}}{1.5\ \text{minutes}}$$

$$1.5(165) = 5.5(f)$$

$$247.5 = 5.5f$$

$$45 = f$$

Choice (A) is correct.

11. D   Difficulty: Medium

Category: Heart of Algebra / Inequalities

Getting to the Answer: You could graph the cost function ($y = 17p + 1,890$) and the revenue function ($y = 35x$) and try to determine where the revenue function is greater (higher on the graph). However, the numbers are quite large and this may prove to be very time-consuming. Instead, create and solve an inequality comparing revenue and cost. If the revenue from a single pair of shoes is $35, then the total revenue from p pairs is 35p. If revenue must be greater than cost, then the inequality should be $35p > 17p + 1,890$. Now, solve for p using inverse operations:

$$35p > 17p + 1,890$$

$$18p > 1,890$$

$$p > 105$$

This matches (D).

12. B   Difficulty: Easy

Category: Problem Solving and Data Analysis / Rates, Ratios, Proportions, and Percentages

Getting to the Answer: This is a question about rates, so pay careful attention to the units. As you read the question, decide how and when you will need to convert units. First, determine how long it will take the athlete to complete the race. Set up a proportion.

$$\frac{9.25 \text{ miles}}{1 \text{ hour}} = \frac{74 \text{ miles}}{x \text{ hours}}$$
$$9.25x = 74$$
$$x = 8$$

The question asks for the total number of calories needed. The recommended rate of consumption is given in calories per minute, and you now know the number of hours that it will take the athlete to complete the race. You could convert the number of hours to minutes (8×60 minutes = 480 minutes) and then multiply this by 3 (the calorie per minute rate given) to find that the athlete should consume $480 \times 3 = 1,440$ calories, (B). Or, you could also convert the given rate (3 calories per minute) to a per-hour rate ($3 \times 60 = 180$ calories per hour) and then multiply this by the number of hours it will take the athlete to finish the race ($180 \times 8 = 1,440$ calories).

13. C   Difficulty: Medium

Category: Heart of Algebra / Linear Equations

Getting to the Answer: The rate of change (or slope) of a linear relationship is constant, so find the rate and apply it to the missing value. You could also look for a pattern in the table. Choose any two points (preferably ones with the nicest numbers) from the table, and substitute them into the slope formula. Using the points (3, 0) and (−1, 14), the slope is $\frac{14 - 0}{-1 - 3} = \frac{14}{-4} = \frac{7}{-2}$. This means that for every 2 units the *x*-value decreases, the *y*-value increases by 7, and the decrease from $x = -5$ to $x = -7$ happens to be −2. So, increase the *y*-value by 7 one time: $28 + 7 = 35$, (C).

14. B   Difficulty: Medium

Category: Problem Solving and Data Analysis / Statistics and Probability

Getting to the Answer: Think about what the question is asking. The real estate agent wants to figure out which measure of the data (mean, mode, range,

or median) is going to be most useful. The *mode* of a data set tells you the data point, or in this case the age range, that occurs most often. If the real estate agent markets to the age range that represents the mode, (B), she will be marketing to the largest group of clients possible.

15. A   Difficulty: Hard

Category: Problem Solving and Data Analysis / Statistics and Probability

Getting to the Answer: Some data sets have a *head*, where many data points are clustered in one area, and one or two *tails*, where the number of data points slowly decreases to 0. Examining the tail will help you describe the shape of the data set. A data set is *skewed* in the direction of its longest tail. The graph in this question has its tail on the right side, so the data is skewed to the right. When data is skewed to the right, the mean is greater than the median because the mean is more sensitive to the higher data values in the tail than is the median, so (A) is correct. If you're not sure about the mean/median part, read the rest of the answer choices—none of them describes the data as skewed to the right, so you can eliminate all of them.

16. B   Difficulty: Medium

Category: Heart of Algebra / Inequalities

Getting to the Answer: The question states that *t* represents the number of round trips. The cost of one round trip without the discount card is $35 per trip, or 35*t*. If a commuter purchases the discount card, round trips would equal the cost of the card plus $12.50 per trip, or 900 + 12.5*t*. Combine these into an inequality, remembering which way the inequality symbol should be oriented. You want the cost with the discount card to be less than (<) the cost without the card, so the inequality should be 900 + 12.5*t* < 35*t*. Now, solve for *t*:

$$900 + 12.5t < 35t$$
$$900 < 22.5t$$
$$40 < t$$

Turn the inequality around to find that $t > 40$, which means a commuter must make more than 40 trips for the discount card to be a better deal, which is (B).

17. C   Difficulty: Medium

Category: Problem Solving and Data Analysis / Rates, Ratios, Proportions, and Percentages

Getting to the Answer: Etienne starts with $800. He spends 20% of $800, or 0.2(800) = $160, on gas. He has $800 − $160 = $640 left over. He budgets 25% of $640, or 0.25(640) = $160, for food and allots $300 for the hotel. He spends all the remaining money on entertainment, which is $640 − $160 − $300 = $180. Divide this amount by the original amount to find the percent he spent on entertainment: $\frac{180}{800} = 0.225 = 22.5\%$, (C).

18. A   Difficulty: Medium

Category: Passport to Advanced Math / Scatterplots

Getting to the Answer: When the dependent variable in a relationship increases by a scale factor, like doubling, tripling, etc., there is an exponential relationship between the variables which can be written in the form $y = a(b)^x$, where a is the initial amount, b is the scale factor, and x is time. The question states that the number of microbes tripled every 24 hours, so the relationship is exponential. This means you can eliminate C and D right away. Choices (A) and B are written in the form $y = a(b)^x$, with the initial amount equal to 2,000 and the scale factor equal to 3, so you can't eliminate either one at first glance. To choose between them, try an easy number for h (like 24) in each equation to see which one matches the information given in the question. In the first equation, $n = 2,000(3)^{\frac{24}{24}} = 2,000 \times (3)^1 = 6,000$, which is 2,000 tripled, so (A) is correct.

19. A   Difficulty: Medium

Category: Problem Solving and Data Analysis / Statistics and Probability

Getting to the Answer: When working with two-way tables, always read the question carefully, identifying which pieces of information you need. Here, you need to focus on the "Against" column and the "1L" and "2L" rows. To stay organized, it may help to circle these pieces of information in the table. There are 58 1Ls and 64 2Ls in the survey sample, for a total of 58 + 64 = 122 1Ls and 2Ls. There are 16 1Ls and 12 2Ls against the policy, for a total of 16 + 12 = 28. This means that 28 out of the 122 1Ls and 2Ls are against the new policy. Written as a fraction, this is $\frac{28}{122}$, which reduces to $\frac{14}{61}$, (A).

20. C   Difficulty: Medium

Category: Additional Topics in Math / Imaginary Numbers

Getting to the Answer: You will not be expected to raise a complex number like the one in this question to the third power by hand. That's a clue that you should be able to use your calculator. The definition of i has been programmed into all graphing calculators, so you can perform basic operations on complex numbers using the calculator (in the Calculator Section of the test). Enter the expression as follows: $(6 + 5i)^3$. On the TI83/84 calculators, you can find i on the button with the decimal point. After entering the expression and pressing Enter, the calculator should return $-234 + 415i$, which is (C).

You could, however, expand the number by hand, by writing it as $(6 + 5i)(6 + 5i)(6 + 5i)$ and carefully multiplying it all out.

21. B   Difficulty: Hard

Category: Problem Solving and Data Analysis / Scatterplots

Getting to the Answer: When an exponential function is written in the form $f(x) = f(0)(1 + r)^x$, the quantity $(1 + r)$ represents the growth rate or the decay rate depending on whether the y-values are increasing or decreasing. The y-values are increasing in this graph, so r represents a growth rate. Because the data is modeled using an exponential function (not a linear function), the rate is not the same as the slope. Look at the y-values in the calculator screenshot—they are quadrupling as the x-values increase by 1. In the equation, this means that $(1 + r) = 4$. Solve this equation to find that $r = 3$, (B).

22. A   Difficulty: Medium

Category: Problem Solving and Data Analysis / Rates, Ratios, Proportions, and Percentages

Getting to the Answer: Pay careful attention to the units. You need to convert all of the dimensions to inches and then set up and solve a proportion. There are 12 inches in one foot, so the real pyramid's height was $(480 \times 12) + 8 = 5,760 + 8 = 5,768$ inches; the length of the passage in the real pyramid was $53.75 \times 12 = 645$ inches; the museum's pyramid height will be 71 feet, 6 inches, or 858 inches; and the length of the museum's passage is unknown. Set up a proportion and solve for the unknown. Use words first to help you keep the measurements in the right places:

$$\frac{\text{real passage length}}{\text{real height}} = \frac{\text{museum passage length}}{\text{museum height}}$$

$$\frac{645}{5,768} = \frac{x}{858}$$

$$553,410 = 5,768x$$

$$95.94 = x$$

The museum should make the length of its passage about 96 inches, or $96 \div 12 = 8$ feet, (A).

23. D   Difficulty: Medium

Category: Passport to Advanced Math / Exponents

Getting to the Answer: You could use polynomial long division to answer this question, or you could try to factor the numerator and see if any terms cancel. It is very tricky to factor a quadratic equation with a negative coefficient on x^2, so start by factoring -1 out of both the numerator and the denominator. To factor the resulting quadratic in the numerator, you need to find two numbers whose product is -24 and whose sum is 10. The numbers are -2 and $+12$.

$$\frac{-x^2 - 10x + 24}{2 - x} = \frac{\cancel{-1}\left(x^2 + 10x - 24\right)}{\cancel{-1}(x - 2)}$$

$$= \frac{\cancel{(x - 2)}(x + 12)}{\cancel{x - 2}}$$

$$= x + 12$$

This matches (D).

24. C   Difficulty: Hard

Category: Problem Solving and Data Analysis / Rates, Ratios, Proportions, and Percentages

Getting to the Answer: You're given two ratios: ethanol to gasoline and methanol to gasoline. Your job is to "merge" them so you can directly compare ethanol to methanol. Both of the given ratios contain gasoline, but the gasoline amounts (4 and 9) are not identical. To directly compare them, find a common multiple (36). Multiply each ratio by the factor that will make the number of parts of gasoline equal to 36 in each:

Ethanol to Gasoline: $(1:4) \times (9:9) = 9:36$

Methanol to Gasoline: $(1:9) \times (4:4) = 4:36$

Now that the number of parts of gasoline needed is the same in both ratios, you can merge the two ratios to compare ethanol to methanol directly: $9:36:4$. So the proper ratio of ethanol to methanol is $9:4$, which is (C).

25. A   Difficulty: Medium

Category: Heart of Algebra / Linear Equations

Getting to the Answer: Add reasonable numbers to the graph such as the ones shown in the following example:

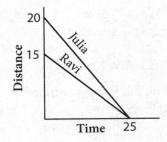

Use the numbers to help you evaluate each statement. It took Julia and Ravi each 25 minutes to drive to the museum, so you can eliminate C and D. Julia drove 20 miles in 25 minutes, while Ravi only drove 15 miles in 25 minutes; their rates are not the same, so B is not correct. This means (A) must be correct. Julia starts out farther away than Ravi, so Julia must have driven at a faster speed than Ravi to arrive at the museum in the same amount of time.

26. D   Difficulty: Hard

Category: Passport to Advanced Math / Functions

Getting to the Answer: Transformations that are grouped with the x in a function shift the graph horizontally and therefore affect the x-coordinates of points on the graph. Transformations that are not grouped with the x shift the graph vertically and therefore affect the y-coordinates of points on the graph. Remember, horizontal shifts are always backward of what they look like.

Perform each transformation on the coordinates of the point, one at a time, following the same order of operations that you use when simplifying arithmetic expressions. Start with $(x - 4)$. This shifts the graph right 4 units, so add 4 to the x-coordinate of the given point: $(8, -3) \rightarrow (8 + 4, -3) = (12, -3)$. Next, apply the negative in front of g, which is not grouped with the x, so it makes the y-coordinate the opposite of what it was: $(12, -3) \rightarrow (12, 3)$. Finally, the -6 is not grouped with x, so subtract 6 from the y-coordinate: $(12, 3) \rightarrow (12, 3 - 6) = (12, -3)$. Therefore, (D) is correct. You could also plot the point on a coordinate plane, perform the transformations (right 4, reflect vertically over the x-axis, and then down 6), and find the resulting point.

27. D   Difficulty: Medium

Category: Passport to Advanced Math / Functions

Getting to the Answer: Sometimes, a question requires thought rather than brute force. Here, you need to understand that when dealing with compositions, the range of the inner function becomes the domain of the outer function, which in turn produces the range of the composition. In the composition $f(g(x))$, the function $g(x) = x^3$ is the inner function. Because the question states that x is either zero or a negative number ($x \leq 0$), every value of x, when substituted into this function, will result in zero or a negative number (because a negative number raised to an odd power is always negative). This means that the largest possible range value for $g(x)$ is 0, and consequently that the largest possible domain value for $f(x)$ is also 0. Substituting 0 for x in $f(x)$ results in -1, which is the largest possible range value for the composition. Because $1 > -1$, it is not in the range of $f(g(x))$, so (D) is correct.

28. A   Difficulty: Hard

Category: Passport to Advanced Math / Quadratics

Getting to the Answer: To answer this question, you need to recall nearly everything you've learned about quadratic graphs. The equation is given in vertex form ($y = a(x - h)^2 + k$), which reveals the vertex (h, k), the direction in which the parabola opens (upward when $a > 0$ and downward when $a < 0$), the axis of symmetry ($x = h$), and the minimum/maximum value of the function (k).

Start by comparing each answer choice to the equation, $y = -3(x - 5)^2 + 8$. The only choice that you cannot immediately compare is (A), because vertex form does not readily reveal the y-intercept, so start with B. Don't forget, you are looking for the statement that is not true. *Choice B*: The axis of symmetry is given by $x = h$, and h is 5, so this statement is true and therefore not correct. *Choice C*: The vertex is given by (h, k), so the vertex is indeed (5, 8) and this choice is not correct. *Choice D*: The value of a is -3, which indicates that the parabola opens downward, so this choice is also incorrect. That means (A) must be the correct answer. To confirm, you could substitute 0 for x in the equation to find the y-intercept.

$$y = -3(x - 5)^2 + 8$$
$$= -3(0 - 5)^2 + 8$$
$$= -3(-5)^2 + 8$$
$$= -3(25) + 8$$
$$= -75 + 8$$
$$= -67$$

The y-intercept is $(0, -67)$, not $(0, 8)$, so the statement is not true and therefore the correct answer.

29. A   Difficulty: Hard

Category: Problem Solving and Data Analysis / Rates, Ratios, Proportions, and Percentages

Getting to the Answer: Don't let all the technical words in this question overwhelm you. Solve it step-by-step, examining the units as you go. Notice that some of the numbers in the answer choices are just 1 apart, so think carefully before selecting your answer.

Step 1: Determine the number of megabytes the computer can upload in 1 weekend (48 hours):

$$\frac{5.25 \text{ megabytes}}{1 \text{ sec}} \times \frac{60 \text{ sec}}{1 \text{ min}} \times \frac{60 \text{ min}}{1 \text{ hr}} \times 48 \text{ hr}$$

$$= 907,200 \text{ megabytes}$$

Step 2: Convert this amount to gigabytes (because the information about the scans is given in gigabytes, not megabytes):

$$907,200 \text{ megabytes} \times \frac{1 \text{ gigabyte}}{1,000 \text{ megabytes}}$$

$$= 907.2 \text{ gigabytes}$$

Step 3: Each client file is about 2.5 gigabytes in size, so divide this number by 2.5 to determine how many client files the computer can upload to the remote server: $907.2 \div 2.5 = 362.88$ files. Remember, you should round this number down to 362, because the question asks for the maximum number the computer can upload, and it cannot complete the 363rd scan in the time allowed. Choice (A) is correct.

30. A   Difficulty: Medium

Category: Additional Topics in Math / Geometry

Getting to the Answer: This question does not provide a graphic, so sketch a quick diagram of the information presented. Be sure to show the direction of traffic for each street. The question describes two parallel streets, cut by a transversal. Start with that, and then add all the details.

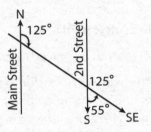

Traffic traveling north on Main Street must make a 125° turn onto the new road. This is the angle between where the traffic was originally headed and where it is headed after it makes the turn. Traffic on 2nd Street is traveling south, the opposite direction. As shown in the diagram, the angle that the southbound traffic would make is supplementary to the corresponding angle made by the northbound traffic. When two parallel lines are cut by a transversal, corresponding angles are congruent, which means that cars turning off of 2nd Street will make a $180 - 125 = 55°$ turn onto the new road. Choice (A) is correct.

31. 11.5 or 23/2 or 69/6   Difficulty: Easy

Category: Heart of Algebra / Linear Equations

Getting to the Answer: Simplify each numerator. Then, cross-multiply. Finally, isolate the variable using inverse operations.

$$\frac{4h - (21 - 8h)}{3} = \frac{15 + 6(h - 1)}{2}$$

$$\frac{4h - 21 + 8h}{3} = \frac{15 + 6h - 6}{2}$$

$$\frac{12h - 21}{3} = \frac{6h + 9}{2}$$

$$2(12h - 21) = 3(6h + 9)$$

$$24h - 42 = 18h + 27$$

$$6h = 69$$

$$h = \frac{69}{6} = \frac{23}{2} = 11.5$$

32. 255   Difficulty: Medium

Category: Heart of Algebra / Systems of Linear Equations

Getting to the Answer: Translate English into math to write the two equations: The New York property costs 30 thousand dollars less than four times the cost of the Georgia property, so $N = 4G - 30$; together, the two properties cost 445 thousand dollars, so $N + G = 445$.

The system of equations is:

$$\begin{cases} N = 4G - 30 \\ N + G = 445 \end{cases}$$

The top equation is already solved for N, so substitute $4G - 30$ into the second equation for N and solve for G:

$$4G - 30 + G = 445$$

$$5G - 30 = 445$$

$$5G = 475$$

$$G = 95$$

The Georgia property costs 95 thousand dollars, so the New York property costs $4(95) - 30 = 350$ thousand dollars. This means the New York property costs $350 - 95 = 255$ thousand more dollars than the Georgia property.

33. .52   Difficulty: Medium

Category: Problem Solving and Data Analysis / Statistics and Probability

Getting to the Answer: The probability that an event will occur is the number of desired outcomes (number of available cars that have a rating of at least 25 mpg) divided by the number of total possible outcomes (total number of cars). "At least" means that much or greater, so find the number of cars represented by the two bars to the right of 25 in the histogram: $20 + 6 = 26$ cars. Now find the total number of available cars: $8 + 16 + 20 + 6 = 50$. Finally, divide to find the indicated probability: $\frac{26}{50} = 0.52$.

34. 21   Difficulty: Medium

Category: Additional Topics in Math / Geometry

Getting to the Answer: Use the formula for finding the volume of a rectangular solid, $V = lwh$, to write an equation. Because the dimensions are given as the ratio 3:5:2, let the length, width, and height be represented by $3x$, $5x$, and $2x$. Substitute the expressions into the formula and solve for x:

$$10{,}290 = (3x)(5x)(2x)$$

$$10{,}290 = 30x^3$$

$$343 = x^3$$

$$7 = x$$

The length was represented by $3x$, so multiply to find that the length is $3(7) = 21$ feet.

35. 8   Difficulty: Medium

Category: Problem Solving and Data Analysis / Scatterplots

Getting to the Answer: Draw the line of best fit so that approximately half the data points fall above the line and half fall below it:

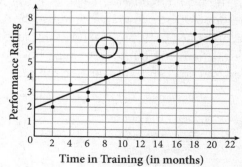

Regional Manager Job Performance

Look for the point that is farthest from the line you drew, which is (8, 6). Because time is plotted along the horizontal axis, this point represents a manager who spent 8 months in the training program.

36. 37   Difficulty: Hard

Category: Passport to Advanced Math / Exponents

Getting to the Answer: Although this question is in the calculator portion of the test, you get an overflow error if you try to use your calculator. This is because the numbers are simply too large. You'll need to rely on the rules of exponents to answer this question. When a power is raised to a power, multiply the exponents. You want to be able to add the exponents later, so the bases need to be the same, and you'll need to recognize that 32 is the same as 2 raised to the 5th power.

$$\left(2^{32}\right)^{\left(2^{32}\right)}$$
$$= 2^{\left(32 \times 2^{32}\right)}$$
$$= 2^{\left(2^{5} \times 2^{32}\right)}$$

Now that the two bases in the exponent are the same, you can add their exponents.

$$= 2^{\left(2^{5+32}\right)}$$
$$= 2^{\left(2^{37}\right)}$$

Therefore, $x = 37$.

37. 33   Difficulty: Medium

Category: Problem Solving and Data Analysis / Rates, Ratios, Proportions, and Percentages

Getting to the Answer: Questions that involve distance, rate, and time can almost always be solved using the formula Distance = rate × time. Use the speed, or rate, of the first car (64 mph) and its distance from the destination (144 mi) to determine how long it traveled. You don't know the time, so call it t.

$$\text{Distance} = \text{rate} \times \text{time}$$
$$144 = 64t$$
$$2.25 = t$$

This means it took 2.25 hours for the first car to arrive. You need the number of minutes, so multiply 2.25 by 60 to get $60 \times 2.25 = 135$ minutes. Now determine how long it took the second car. It started its drive at 2:18 PM and arrived at 4:00 PM, so it took 1 hour and 42 minutes, or 102 minutes. This means that the first car had been traveling for $135 - 102 = 33$ minutes before the second car started its drive.

38. 220   Difficulty: Hard

Category: Problem Solving and Data Analysis / Rates, Ratios, Proportions, and Percentages

Getting to the Answer: To get started, you'll need to find the distance for each part of the third car's trip—the question only tells you the total distance (25 miles). Then, use the formula Distance = rate × time to find how long the car traveled at 15 mph and then how long it traveled at 30 mph.

First part of trip: (60% of the drive)

$$0.6 \times 25\,\text{mi} = 15\,\text{mi}$$
$$15 = 15t$$
$$1 = t$$

So the first part of the trip took 1 hour. Then the car did not move for 20 minutes due to the accident.

Last part of trip: (40% of the drive remained)

$$0.4 \times 25\,\text{mi} = 10\,\text{mi}$$
$$10 = 30t$$
$$\frac{10}{30} = t$$
$$t = \frac{1}{3}$$

So the last part of the trip took one-third of an hour, or 20 minutes. This means it took the third car a total of 1 hour and 40 minutes to arrive at the destination. Because the car arrived at 4:00 PM, it must have left at 2:20 PM. Enter the answer as 220.

ESSAY TEST RUBRIC

The Essay Demonstrates ...

4—Advanced	• **(Reading)** A strong ability to comprehend the source text, including its central ideas and important details and how they interrelate; and effectively use evidence (quotations, paraphrases, or both) from the source text. • **(Analysis)** A strong ability to evaluate the author's use of evidence, reasoning, and/or stylistic and persuasive elements, and/or other features of the student's own choosing; make good use of relevant, sufficient, and strategically chosen support for the claims or points made in the student's essay; and focus consistently on features of the source text that are most relevant to addressing the task. • **(Writing)** A strong ability to provide a precise central claim; create an effective organization that includes an introduction and conclusion, as well as a clear progression of ideas; successfully employ a variety of sentence structures; use precise word choice; maintain a formal style and objective tone; and show command of the conventions of standard written English so that the essay is free of errors.
3—Proficient	• **(Reading)** Satisfactory ability to comprehend the source text, including its central ideas and important details and how they interrelate; and use evidence (quotations, paraphrases, or both) from the source text. • **(Analysis)** Satisfactory ability to evaluate the author's use of evidence, reasoning, and/or stylistic and persuasive elements, and/or other features of the student's own choosing; make use of relevant and sufficient support for the claims or points made in the student's essay; and focus primarily on features of the source text that are most relevant to addressing the task. • **(Writing)** Satisfactory ability to provide a central claim; create an organization that includes an introduction and conclusion, as well as a clear progression of ideas; employ a variety of sentence structures; use precise word choice; maintain an appropriate formal style and objective tone; and show control of the conventions of standard written English so that the essay is free of significant errors.
2—Partial	• **(Reading)** Limited ability to comprehend the source text, including its central ideas and important details and how they interrelate; and use evidence (quotations, paraphrases, or both) from the source text. • **(Analysis)** Limited ability to evaluate the author's use of evidence, reasoning, and/or stylistic and persuasive elements, and/or other features of the student's own choosing; make use of support for the claims or points made in the student's essay; and focus on relevant features of the source text. • **(Writing)** Limited ability to provide a central claim; create an effective organization for ideas; employ a variety of sentence structures; use precise word choice; maintain an appropriate style and tone; or show control of the conventions of standard written English, resulting in certain errors that detract from the quality of the writing.

Practice Tests

1—Inadequate	• **(Reading)** Little or no ability to comprehend the source text or use evidence from the source text.
	• **(Analysis)** Little or no ability to evaluate the author's use of evidence, reasoning, and/or stylistic and persuasive elements; choose support for claims or points; or focus on relevant features of the source text.
	• **(Writing)** Little or no ability to provide a central claim, organization, or progression of ideas; employ a variety of sentence structures; use precise word choice; maintain an appropriate style and tone; or show control of the conventions of standard written English, resulting in numerous errors that undermine the quality of the writing.

ESSAY RESPONSE #1 (ADVANCED SCORE)

When William Faulkner made his Nobel Prize Acceptance Speech in 1950, he was speaking at the height of the Cold War. The memory of the devastation of the atomic bombs dropped on Japan was still fresh in people's minds, and it's clear from Faulkner's speech that people were afraid more destruction was to come. Faulkner felt strongly that in order for mankind to prevail, writers must write from the heart, rather than writing from fear. In this speech, he uses several techniques to persuade his audience of his claim: he establishes his authority, uses vivid language and imagery, and appeals to his audience's sense of duty.

At the ceremony, Faulkner was speaking from a position of strength and expertise, having just been awarded the Nobel Prize for Literature. In a subtle way, he reminds his audience of this expertise throughout the speech, lending credibility to his claims. In the first paragraph, he redefines the award as an honor for his life's work in mining the human spirit to create great literature. He then reminds the audience of his position as an elder statesman by directing his speech to the "young men and women" who are also engaged in this great work, and goes on to tell them what they must "learn" and "teach themselves" about life and writing. By framing the speech as a lesson for younger writers based on his career-long exploration of the human spirit, Faulkner establishes his authority and commands respect for his ideas.

Faulkner also uses vivid language and imagery to create a vision of a higher purpose to which he would like his audience to aspire. In paragraphs 2 and 3, he paints a picture of the writer as an artist involved in a great struggle, which he characterizes with words like "agony" and "sweat." According to Faulkner, a writer will never succeed if he avoids universal truths, and until the writer realizes this, "he labors under a curse." To Faulkner, a writer who writes from a place of fear instead of compassion creates meaningless work that touches upon "no universal bones, leaving no scars." On the other hand, a writer who writes with pity and compassion lifts the reader's heart and reminds him of his "immortal" nature. This type of vivid language, which is clearly written from Faulkner's heart, helps to support his argument that writing from the heart is the way to create great literature that inspires mankind to prevail.

Finally, in speaking to his audience of younger writers, he calls upon their sense of duty. It's clear earlier in the speech that Faulkner is concerned that younger writers are being defeated by fear, and are failing to explore the rich material of the human heart. He asserts that rather than writing about defeat, they should elevate humans by reminding them of their great capacity for courage, compassion, sacrifice, and other noble qualities. These characteristics are unique to humans and are the "glory" of their past, which Faulkner exhorts them to carry into the future. In the final line, Faulkner calls upon writers to be more than just record-keepers—rather, they should actively inspire humankind to prevail.

In a time of great fear, William Faulkner used his Nobel Prize acceptance speech to express his belief that writers must write from the heart in order to ensure the success of mankind. To convince his audience that they should accept his claim, he first establishes his authority, then uses vivid language and imagery to illustrate the value of writing from the heart, and finally calls upon his audience's sense of duty to elevate the human race. Through skillful use of these features, he constructs a persuasive argument.

ESSAY RESPONSE #2 (PROFICIENT SCORE)

William Faulkner believed that authors must write from their hearts to make sure that humans prevail on Earth. In his Nobel Prize Acceptance Speech, Faulkner uses his expertise, vivid language, and calls to his audience's sense of responsibility to make his case.

In this speech, Faulkner speaks as both a writer and a teacher. He acknowledges that young writers are listening to him; and he has lessons to give to them. Since he just won the Nobel Prize his listeners believe him to be an expert and this makes them more willing to accept his message. He tells his young listeners that they have lost their way, and they must relearn the "problems of the human heart," which are what make good writing. Faulkner tells his listeners that being afraid is the lowest of human feelings, and they need to put their fears aside and instead explore the higher truths of the human heart. Faulkner knows that his young audience is looking up to him, and so he uses his position of authority to guide them to strive for something greater than their fear.

Faulkner also uses vivid language to enhance his argument. Twice he uses the phrase "agony and sweat" to describe the struggle of the writer who writes from the heart. This type of vivid language makes the writer's struggle seem like a goal worth fighting for. Faulkner describes writing that avoids the problems of the human heart as having no "bones" or "scars." By using words that evoke the human body, Faulkner implies that this type of writing has no weight or depth. Faulkner uses very vivid language to paint a picture of a world after a nuclear apacalypse, which is what his audience fears. In this picture, the evening is "red and dying," the rocks are "worthless" and man's voice is "puny" but still talking. Faulkner then tells his audience he refuses to accept this bleak image—that man will do more than just exist, he will prevail. By using vivid language to describe the defeatist view of mankind, Faulkner makes his audience feel revulsion at this image, and makes the alternative seem much more appealing.

Faulkner wanted writers to write about courage, hope, love, compassion, and pity because these things uplift the human spirit. Faulkner calls upon his listeners' sense of responsibility by telling them that they have a duty to write about these subjects. His implication is that if they don't, mankind will fall back into the bleakness he described previously. He also says that the writer has a responsibility to be a "pillar" holding up mankind. By making his audience feel that they have a responsibility to help mankind, Faulkner strengthens his position.

In this speech, Faulkner makes an effective argument that writers must write from the heart to save mankind and help it prevail. To strengthen his argument, he uses the features of expertise, vivid language, and calls to responsibility.

SAT PRACTICE TEST 2 ANSWER SHEET

Remove (or photocopy) this answer sheet and use it to complete the test. See the answer key following the test when finished.

Start with number 1 for each section. If a section has fewer questions than answer spaces, leave the extra spaces blank.

SECTION

1

1. Ⓐ Ⓑ Ⓒ Ⓓ	14. Ⓐ Ⓑ Ⓒ Ⓓ	27. Ⓐ Ⓑ Ⓒ Ⓓ	40. Ⓐ Ⓑ Ⓒ Ⓓ
2. Ⓐ Ⓑ Ⓒ Ⓓ	15. Ⓐ Ⓑ Ⓒ Ⓓ	28. Ⓐ Ⓑ Ⓒ Ⓓ	41. Ⓐ Ⓑ Ⓒ Ⓓ
3. Ⓐ Ⓑ Ⓒ Ⓓ	16. Ⓐ Ⓑ Ⓒ Ⓓ	29. Ⓐ Ⓑ Ⓒ Ⓓ	42. Ⓐ Ⓑ Ⓒ Ⓓ
4. Ⓐ Ⓑ Ⓒ Ⓓ	17. Ⓐ Ⓑ Ⓒ Ⓓ	30. Ⓐ Ⓑ Ⓒ Ⓓ	43. Ⓐ Ⓑ Ⓒ Ⓓ
5. Ⓐ Ⓑ Ⓒ Ⓓ	18. Ⓐ Ⓑ Ⓒ Ⓓ	31. Ⓐ Ⓑ Ⓒ Ⓓ	44. Ⓐ Ⓑ Ⓒ Ⓓ
6. Ⓐ Ⓑ Ⓒ Ⓓ	19. Ⓐ Ⓑ Ⓒ Ⓓ	32. Ⓐ Ⓑ Ⓒ Ⓓ	45. Ⓐ Ⓑ Ⓒ Ⓓ
7. Ⓐ Ⓑ Ⓒ Ⓓ	20. Ⓐ Ⓑ Ⓒ Ⓓ	33. Ⓐ Ⓑ Ⓒ Ⓓ	46. Ⓐ Ⓑ Ⓒ Ⓓ
8. Ⓐ Ⓑ Ⓒ Ⓓ	21. Ⓐ Ⓑ Ⓒ Ⓓ	34. Ⓐ Ⓑ Ⓒ Ⓓ	47. Ⓐ Ⓑ Ⓒ Ⓓ
9. Ⓐ Ⓑ Ⓒ Ⓓ	22. Ⓐ Ⓑ Ⓒ Ⓓ	35. Ⓐ Ⓑ Ⓒ Ⓓ	48. Ⓐ Ⓑ Ⓒ Ⓓ
10. Ⓐ Ⓑ Ⓒ Ⓓ	23. Ⓐ Ⓑ Ⓒ Ⓓ	36. Ⓐ Ⓑ Ⓒ Ⓓ	49. Ⓐ Ⓑ Ⓒ Ⓓ
11. Ⓐ Ⓑ Ⓒ Ⓓ	24. Ⓐ Ⓑ Ⓒ Ⓓ	37. Ⓐ Ⓑ Ⓒ Ⓓ	50. Ⓐ Ⓑ Ⓒ Ⓓ
12. Ⓐ Ⓑ Ⓒ Ⓓ	25. Ⓐ Ⓑ Ⓒ Ⓓ	38. Ⓐ Ⓑ Ⓒ Ⓓ	51. Ⓐ Ⓑ Ⓒ Ⓓ
13. Ⓐ Ⓑ Ⓒ Ⓓ	26. Ⓐ Ⓑ Ⓒ Ⓓ	39. Ⓐ Ⓑ Ⓒ Ⓓ	52. Ⓐ Ⓑ Ⓒ Ⓓ

☐ # correct in Section 1

☐ # incorrect in Section 1

SECTION

2

1. Ⓐ Ⓑ Ⓒ Ⓓ	12. Ⓐ Ⓑ Ⓒ Ⓓ	23. Ⓐ Ⓑ Ⓒ Ⓓ	34. Ⓐ Ⓑ Ⓒ Ⓓ
2. Ⓐ Ⓑ Ⓒ Ⓓ	13. Ⓐ Ⓑ Ⓒ Ⓓ	24. Ⓐ Ⓑ Ⓒ Ⓓ	35. Ⓐ Ⓑ Ⓒ Ⓓ
3. Ⓐ Ⓑ Ⓒ Ⓓ	14. Ⓐ Ⓑ Ⓒ Ⓓ	25. Ⓐ Ⓑ Ⓒ Ⓓ	36. Ⓐ Ⓑ Ⓒ Ⓓ
4. Ⓐ Ⓑ Ⓒ Ⓓ	15. Ⓐ Ⓑ Ⓒ Ⓓ	26. Ⓐ Ⓑ Ⓒ Ⓓ	37. Ⓐ Ⓑ Ⓒ Ⓓ
5. Ⓐ Ⓑ Ⓒ Ⓓ	16. Ⓐ Ⓑ Ⓒ Ⓓ	27. Ⓐ Ⓑ Ⓒ Ⓓ	38. Ⓐ Ⓑ Ⓒ Ⓓ
6. Ⓐ Ⓑ Ⓒ Ⓓ	17. Ⓐ Ⓑ Ⓒ Ⓓ	28. Ⓐ Ⓑ Ⓒ Ⓓ	39. Ⓐ Ⓑ Ⓒ Ⓓ
7. Ⓐ Ⓑ Ⓒ Ⓓ	18. Ⓐ Ⓑ Ⓒ Ⓓ	29. Ⓐ Ⓑ Ⓒ Ⓓ	40. Ⓐ Ⓑ Ⓒ Ⓓ
8. Ⓐ Ⓑ Ⓒ Ⓓ	19. Ⓐ Ⓑ Ⓒ Ⓓ	30. Ⓐ Ⓑ Ⓒ Ⓓ	41. Ⓐ Ⓑ Ⓒ Ⓓ
9. Ⓐ Ⓑ Ⓒ Ⓓ	20. Ⓐ Ⓑ Ⓒ Ⓓ	31. Ⓐ Ⓑ Ⓒ Ⓓ	42. Ⓐ Ⓑ Ⓒ Ⓓ
10. Ⓐ Ⓑ Ⓒ Ⓓ	21. Ⓐ Ⓑ Ⓒ Ⓓ	32. Ⓐ Ⓑ Ⓒ Ⓓ	43. Ⓐ Ⓑ Ⓒ Ⓓ
11. Ⓐ Ⓑ Ⓒ Ⓓ	22. Ⓐ Ⓑ Ⓒ Ⓓ	33. Ⓐ Ⓑ Ⓒ Ⓓ	44. Ⓐ Ⓑ Ⓒ Ⓓ

☐ # correct in Section 2

☐ # incorrect in Section 2

Practice Tests

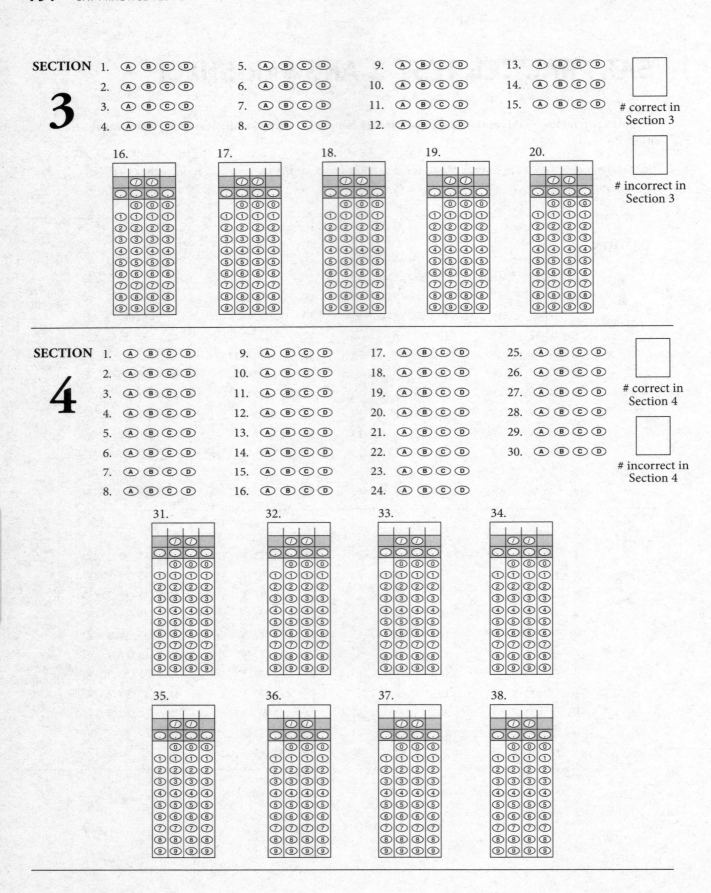

READING TEST

65 Minutes—52 Questions

Turn to Section 1 of your answer sheet to answer the questions in this section.

Directions: Each passage or pair of passages below is followed by a number of questions. After reading each passage or pair, choose the best answer to each question based on what is stated or implied in the passage or passages and in any accompanying graphics (such as a table or graph).

Questions 1-10 are based on the following passage.

The following passage is adapted from Charles Dickens's 1860 novel *Great Expectations*. In this scene, the narrator, a boy named Pip, eats breakfast with his older sister's acquaintance, Mr. Pumblechook. Pumblechook has agreed to take Pip to see Miss Havisham, a wealthy woman who has requested this visit, although Pip has never met her.

Mr. Pumblechook and I breakfasted at eight o'clock in the parlor behind the shop, while the shopman took his mug of tea and hunch of bread and butter
Line on a sack of peas in the front premises. I considered
(5) Mr. Pumblechook wretched company. Besides being possessed by my sister's idea that a mortifying and penitential character ought to be imparted to my diet,[1]—besides giving me as much crumb as possible in combination with as little butter, and putting
(10) such a quantity of warm water into my milk that it would have been more candid to have left the milk out altogether,—his conversation consisted of nothing but arithmetic. On my politely bidding him Good morning, he said, pompously, "Seven times nine,
(15) boy?" And how should I be able to answer, dodged in that way, in a strange place, on an empty stomach! I was hungry, but before I had swallowed a morsel, he began a running sum that lasted all through the breakfast. "Seven?" "And four?" "And eight?" . . . And
(20) so on. And after each figure was disposed of, it was as much as I could do to get a bite or a sup, before the next came; while he sat at his ease guessing nothing, and eating bacon and hot roll, in (if I may be allowed the expression) a gorging and gormandizing manner.

(25) For such reasons, I was very glad when ten o'clock came and we started for Miss Havisham's; though I was not at all at my ease regarding the manner in which I should acquit myself under that lady's roof. Within a quarter of an hour we came to Miss
(30) Havisham's house, which was of old brick, and dismal, and had a great many iron bars to it. Some of the windows had been walled up; of those that remained, all the lower were rustily barred. There was a courtyard in front, and that was barred; so we
(35) had to wait, after ringing the bell, until some one should come to open it. While we waited at the gate, I peeped in (even then Mr. Pumblechook said, "And fourteen?" but I pretended not to hear him), and saw that at the side of the house there was a large
(40) brewery. No brewing was going on in it, and none seemed to have gone on for a long long time.

A window was raised, and a clear voice demanded "What name?" To which my conductor replied, "Pumblechook." The voice returned, "Quite right,"
(45) and the window was shut again, and a young lady came across the courtyard, with keys in her hand.

"This," said Mr. Pumblechook, "is Pip."

"This is Pip, is it?" returned the young lady, who was very pretty and seemed very proud; "come in, Pip."

(50) Mr. Pumblechook was coming in also, when she stopped him with the gate.

"Oh!" she said. "Did you wish to see Miss Havisham?"

"If Miss Havisham wished to see me," returned
(55) Mr. Pumblechook, discomfited.

"Ah!" said the girl; "but you see she don't."

She said it so finally, and in such an

[1]Pip's sister indicated to Pumblechook that Pip should be grateful, even penitent (unreasonably so) for his help.

GO ON TO THE NEXT PAGE

undiscussible way, that Mr. Pumblechook, though in a condition of ruffled dignity, could not
(60) protest. But he eyed me severely,—as if I had done anything to him!—and departed with the words reproachfully delivered: "Boy! Let your behavior here be a credit unto them which brought you up by hand!"[2] I was not free from apprehension that
(65) he would come back to propound through the gate, "And sixteen?" But he didn't.

[2]Pumblechook is speaking of Pip's sister, who often boasts that she raised him "by hand."

1. According to the first paragraph, Pip's breakfast with Mr. Pumblechook is

   A) eaten on the run.

   B) small and of poor quality.

   C) better than Pip usually receives.

   D) carefully cooked and served.

2. As used in line 5, "wretched" most nearly means

   A) shameful.

   B) deprived.

   C) distressing.

   D) heartbroken.

3. Based on the passage, it can be inferred that Mr. Pumblechook

   A) has looked forward to his morning with Pip.

   B) is as uncomfortable as Pip is during breakfast.

   C) has known Pip and his sister for a very long time.

   D) is indifferent to Pip's discomfort during breakfast.

4. Which choice provides the best support for the answer to the previous question?

   A) Lines 1-4 ("Mr. Pumblechook and I . . . premises")

   B) Lines 5-13 ("Besides . . . arithmetic")

   C) Lines 43-44 ("To which my . . . Pumblechook")

   D) Lines 57-60 ("She said . . . not protest")

5. What theme is communicated through the experiences of Pip, the narrator?

   A) The world can be a puzzling and sometimes cruel place.

   B) Young people are misunderstood by their elders.

   C) Mean-spirited people deserve to be treated harshly.

   D) The favors one receives in life should be reciprocated.

6. Which word best describes the young lady's demeanor when she approaches Pip and Mr. Pumblechook?

   A) Rude

   B) Timid

   C) Self-centered

   D) Authoritative

7. Which of the following is true when Mr. Pumblechook leaves Pip at Miss Havisham's house?

   A) Pip is excited to finally meet Miss Havisham.

   B) Pip is nervous about being away from his sister for so long.

   C) Pip is relieved to be away from Mr. Pumblechook.

   D) Pip is anxious about spending time with the young lady who greets them.

8. Which choice provides the best support for the answer to the previous question?

   A) Lines 1-4 ("Mr. Pumblechook . . . premises")

   B) Lines 42-43 ("A window . . . name")

   C) Lines 57-60 ("She said it . . . protest")

   D) Lines 64-66 ("I was not . . . he didn't")

GO ON TO THE NEXT PAGE ▷

Practice Tests

9. As used in line 59, "condition" most nearly means

   A) illness.

   B) prerequisite.

   C) state.

   D) limitation.

10. The function of the parenthetical comment in lines 23-24 is to reveal that

   A) Pip is usually more polite in his references to others.

   B) Mr. Pumblechook appreciates gourmet food.

   C) Pip is very angered that his own breakfast is so meager.

   D) Mr. Pumblechook has no qualms about overeating in public.

Questions 11-20 are based on the following passage.

This passage is adapted from Martin Luther King, Jr.'s "Letter from Birmingham Jail."

. . .I think I should give the reason for my being in Birmingham, since you have been influenced by the argument of "outsiders coming in." I have
Line the honor of serving as president of the Southern
(5) Christian Leadership Conference, an organization operating in every Southern state with headquarters in Atlanta, Georgia. We have some eighty-five affiliate organizations all across the South, one being the Alabama Christian Movement for
(10) Human Rights. Whenever necessary and possible we share staff, educational, and financial resources with our affiliates. Several months ago our local af-filiate here in Birmingham invited us to be on call to engage in a nonviolent direct action program if such
(15) were deemed necessary. We readily consented and when the hour came we lived up to our promises. So I am here, along with several members of my staff, because we were invited here. I am here because I have basic organizational ties here. Beyond this, I
(20) am in Birmingham because injustice is here. . . .

Moreover, I am cognizant of the interrelatedness of all communities and states. I cannot sit idly by in Atlanta and not be concerned about what happens in Birmingham. Injustice anywhere is a
(25) threat to justice everywhere. We are caught in an inescapable network of mutuality, tied in a single garment of destiny. Whatever affects one directly affects all indirectly. Never again can we afford to live with the narrow, provincial "outside agitator"
(30) idea. Anyone who lives inside the United States can never be considered an outsider anywhere in this country. . . .

You may well ask, "Why direct action? Why sit-ins, marches, etc.? Isn't negotiation a better path?" You
(35) are exactly right in your call for negotiation. Indeed, this is the purpose of direct action. Nonviolent direct action seeks to create such a crisis and establish such creative tension that a community that has constantly refused to negotiate is forced to confront the issue. It
(40) seeks so to dramatize the issue that it can no longer be ignored. I just referred to the creation of tension as a part of the work of the nonviolent resister. This may sound rather shocking. But I must confess that I am not afraid of the word tension. I have earnestly
(45) worked and preached against violent tension, but there is a type of constructive nonviolent tension that is necessary for growth. Just as Socrates felt that it was necessary to create a tension in the mind so that individuals could rise from the bondage of myths and
(50) half-truths to the unfettered realm of creative analysis and objective appraisal, we must see the need of having nonviolent gadflies to create the kind of tension in society that will help men rise from the dark depths of prejudice and racism to the majestic
(55) heights of understanding and brotherhood. So the purpose of the direct action is to create a situation so crisis-packed that it will inevitably open the door to negotiation. We, therefore, concur with you in your call for negotiation. Too long has our beloved
(60) Southland been bogged down in the tragic attempt to live in monologue rather than dialogue. . . .

My friends, I must say to you that we have not made a single gain in civil rights without determined legal and nonviolent pressure.
(65) History is the long and tragic story of the fact that privileged groups seldom give up their privileges voluntarily. Individuals may see the moral light and voluntarily give up their unjust posture; but as Reinhold Niebuhr has reminded us, groups are
(70) more immoral than individuals.

We know through painful experience that freedom is never voluntarily given by the oppressor; it must be demanded by the oppressed. . . . For years now I have heard the word "Wait!" It rings in
(75) the ear of every African American with a piercing familiarity. This "wait" has almost always meant "never." It has been a tranquilizing thalidomide, relieving the emotional stress for a moment, only to give birth to an ill-formed infant of frustra-
(80) tion. We must come to see with the distinguished jurist of yesterday that "justice too long delayed is justice denied." We have waited for more than three hundred and forty years for our constitutional and God-given rights. The nations of Asia and Africa
(85) are moving with jet-like speed toward the goal of political independence, and we still creep at horse and buggy pace toward the gaining of a cup of coffee at a lunch counter. . . .

11. King's purpose for writing this letter is

A) to explain why he came to Birmingham to protest.

B) to launch a nonviolent protest movement in Birmingham.

C) to open an affiliate of the Southern Christian Leadership Conference in Birmingham.

D) to support fellow civil rights activists in Birmingham.

12. Which choice provides the best evidence for the answer to the previous question?

A) Lines 1-2 ("I think . . . in Birmingham")

B) Lines 3-7 ("I have . . . Atlanta, Georgia")

C) Lines 7-10 ("We have some . . . Rights")

D) Lines 24-25 ("Injustice anywhere . . . everywhere")

13. The passage most strongly suggests that which of the following statements is true?

A) King was warmly welcomed when he arrived in Birmingham.

B) King received criticism for his decision to come to Birmingham.

C) King did not want to cause a disruption by coming to Birmingham.

D) King was abandoned by his supporters when he arrived in Birmingham.

14. As used in lines 21-22, "interrelatedness of all communities and states" most nearly means that

A) King has personal connections to people in the town.

B) the Southern Christian Leadership Conference needs national support.

C) events in one part of the country affect everyone in the nation.

D) local civil rights groups operate independently of one another.

15. Based on paragraph 3, it can be reasonably inferred that King believed circumstances in Birmingham at the time

A) were unfair and wrong.

B) constituted an isolated event.

C) justified his arrest.

D) required federal intervention.

GO ON TO THE NEXT PAGE

16. Which choice provides the best evidence for the answer to the previous question?

    A) Lines 21-22 ("Moreover, . . . states")

    B) Lines 24-25 ("Injustice anywhere . . . everywhere")

    C) Lines 25-27 ("We are caught . . . destiny")

    D) Lines 28-30 ("Never again . . . idea")

17. As used in line 40, "dramatize" most nearly means

    A) cast events in an appealing light.

    B) draw attention to significant events.

    C) exaggerate events to seem more important.

    D) turn events into a popular performance.

18. Which choice most clearly paraphrases a claim made by King in paragraph 4?

    A) A failure to negotiate in the South has provoked secret action by civil rights activists.

    B) A focus on dialogue blinds reformers to the necessity for direct action to promote change.

    C) Direct action is necessary to motivate people to talk about prejudice and racism.

    D) Nonviolent protest encourages a sense of brotherhood and understanding among citizens.

19. Paragraph 4 best supports the claims made in paragraph 3 by

    A) arguing that nonviolent pressure is most likely to spur just action by individuals.

    B) clarifying that throughout history, privileged classes have been reluctant to let go of privilege.

    C) drawing a distinction between the morality of individuals and of groups.

    D) pointing out that few gains in civil rights have been made without nonviolent pressure.

20. King refers to "the gaining of a cup of coffee at a lunch counter" (lines 87-88) primarily to

    A) call attention to the sedative effect of delaying civil rights reform in the United States.

    B) emphasize that white Americans will not willingly end oppression against black Americans.

    C) describe the progress made toward the winning of equal rights in other countries.

    D) underscore the contrast between progress made in other countries and the United States.

Questions 21-31 are based on the following passages and supplementary material.

The idea of a World Bank became a reality in 1944, when delegates to the Bretton Woods Conference pledged to "outlaw practices which are agreed to be harmful to world prosperity." Passage 1 discusses the benefits of the World Bank, while Passage 2 focuses on the limited lifespan of the Bretton Woods system.

Passage 1

In 1944, 730 delegates from forty-four Allied nations met in Bretton Woods, New Hampshire, just as World War II was ending. They were attend-
Line ing an important conference. This mostly forgotten
(5) event shaped our modern world because delegates at the Bretton Woods Conference agreed on the establishment of an international banking system.

To ensure that all nations would prosper, the United States and other allied nations set rules
(10) for a postwar international economy. The Bretton Woods system created the International Monetary Fund (IMF). The IMF was founded as a kind of global central bank from which member countries could borrow money. The countries needed money
(15) to pay for their war costs. Today, the IMF facilitates international trade by ensuring the stability of the international monetary and financial system.

The Bretton Woods system also established the World Bank. Although the World Bank shares

Practice Tests

(20) similarities with the IMF, the two institutions remain distinct. While the IMF maintains an orderly system of payments and receipts between nations, the World Bank is mainly a development institution. The World Bank initially gave loans to European countries dev-
(25) astated by World War II, and today it lends money and technical assistance specifically to economic projects in developing countries. For example, the World Bank might provide a low-interest loan to a country attempting to improve education or
(30) health. The goal of the World Bank is to "bridge the economic divide between poor and rich countries." In short, the organizations differ in their purposes. The Bank promotes economic and social progress so people can live better lives, while the IMF represents
(35) the entire world in its goal to foster global monetary cooperation and financial stability.

These two specific accomplishments of the Bretton Woods Conference were major. However, the Bretton Woods system particularly benefited
(40) the United States. It effectively established the U.S. dollar as a global currency. A global currency is one that countries worldwide accept for all trade, or international transactions of buying and selling. Because only the U.S. could print dollars, the United
(45) States became the primary power behind both the IMF and the World Bank. Today, global currencies include the U.S. dollar, the euro (European Union countries), and the yen (Japan).

The years after Bretton Woods have been
(50) considered the golden age of the U.S. dollar. More importantly, the conference profoundly shaped foreign trade for decades to come.

Passage 2

The financial system established at the 1944 Bretton Woods Conference endured for many years. Even
(55) after the United States abrogated agreements made at the conference, the nation continued to experience a powerful position in international trade by having other countries tie their currencies to the U.S. dollar. The world, however, is changing.
(60) In reality, the Bretton Woods system lasted only three decades. Then, in 1971, President Richard Nixon introduced a new economic policy by ending the convertibility of the dollar to gold. It marked the end of the Bretton Woods international monetary

(65) framework, and the action resulted in worldwide financial crisis. Two cornerstones of Bretton Woods, however, endured: the International Monetary Fund (IMF) and the World Bank.

Since the collapse of the Bretton Woods system,
(70) IMF members have been trading using a flexible exchange system. Namely, countries allow their exchange rates to fluctuate in response to changing conditions. The exchange rate between two currencies, such as the Japanese yen and the U.S.
(75) dollar, for example, specifies how much one currency is worth in terms of the other. An exchange rate of 120 yen to dollars means that 120 yen are worth the same as one dollar.

Even so, the U.S. dollar has remained the most
(80) widely used money for international trade, and having one currency for all trade may be better than using a flexible exchange system.

This seems to be the thinking of a powerful group of countries. The Group of Twenty (G20), which has
(85) called for a new Bretton Woods, consists of governments and leaders from 20 of the world's largest economies including China, the United States, and the European Union. In 2009, for example, the G20 announced plans to create a new global currency
(90) to replace the U.S. dollar's role as the anchor currency. Many believe that China's yuan, quickly climbing the financial ranks, is well on its way to becoming a major world reserve currency.

In fact, an earlier 1988 article in *The Economist*
(95) stated, "30 years from now, Americans, Japanese, Europeans, and people in many other rich countries and some relatively poor ones will probably be paying for their shopping with the same currency."

The article predicted that the world supply of
(100) currency would be set by a new central bank of the IMF. This prediction seems to be coming to fruition since the G20 indicated that a "world currency is in waiting." For an international construct such as the original Bretton Woods to last some 26
(105) years is nothing less than amazing. But move over Bretton Woods; a new world order in finance could be on the fast track.

GO ON TO THE NEXT PAGE

Top 10 International Currencies						
(Percent Shares of Average Daily Currency Trading)						
	2007		2010		2013	
	Share	*Rank*	*Share*	*Rank*	*Share*	*Rank*
U.S. Dollar (USD)	85.6%	1	84.9%	1	87.0%	1
Euro (EUR)	37.0%	2	39.1%	2	33.4%	2
Japanese Yen (JPY)	17.2%	3	19.0%	3	23.0%	3
UK Pound (GBP)	14.9%	4	12.9%	4	11.8%	4
Australian Dollar (AUD)	6.6%	6	7.6%	5	8.6%	5
Swiss Franc (CHF)	6.8%	5	6.3%	6	5.2%	6
Canadian Dollar (CAD)	4.3%	7	5.3%	7	4.6%	7
Mexican Peso (MXN)	1.3%	12	1.3%	14	2.5%	8
Chinese Yuan (CNY)	0.5%	20	0.9%	17	2.2%	9
New Zealand Dollar	1.9%	11	1.6%	10	2.0%	10

Adapted from Mauldin Economics; Bank for International Settlements, September 2013 Triennial Central Bank Survey.

21. Based on Passage 1, it can reasonably be inferred that

A) world leaders recognized the need for markets to function independently.

B) Bretton Woods increased U.S. economic influence around the world.

C) the IMF and the World Bank work closely together to ensure prosperity.

D) the conclusion of World War II had little influence on events at Bretton Woods.

22. Which choice provides the best evidence for the answer to the previous question?

A) Lines 8-10 ("To ensure . . . economy")

B) Lines 10-12 ("The Bretton . . . Fund")

C) Lines 44-46 ("Because only . . . World Bank")

D) Lines 50-52 ("More importantly . . . to come")

23. As used in line 35, "foster" most nearly means

A) publicize.

B) rear.

C) stabilize.

D) encourage.

GO ON TO THE NEXT PAGE

24. Which statement best explains the difference between the purposes of the IMF and the World Bank?

    A) The IMF provides money to pay for war costs, while the World Bank offers assistance to rebuild countries recovering from war across the globe.

    B) The IMF encourages stability in the global financial system, while the World Bank promotes economic development in relatively poor nations.

    C) The IMF supports the U.S. dollar in international markets, while the World Bank provides low-interest loans to many nations around the world.

    D) The IMF offers governments advice about participation in global markets, while the World Bank encourages monetary cooperation between nations.

25. Based on the second paragraph in Passage 2, it can be reasonably inferred that

    A) the United States did not support the goals of the IMF and the World Bank.

    B) Bretton Woods was originally intended to last for three decades.

    C) President Nixon acted to reinforce the decisions made at Bretton Woods.

    D) some U.S. policy decisions differed from international consensus over Bretton Woods.

26. Which choice provides the best evidence for the answer to the previous question?

    A) Lines 60-61 ("In reality . . . three decades")

    B) Lines 61-63 ("Then, in 1971 . . . to gold")

    C) Lines 66-68 ("Two cornerstones . . . World Bank")

    D) Lines 69-71 ("Since the collapse . . . exchange system")

27. As used in line 90, "anchor" most nearly means

    A) key.

    B) fastening.

    C) rigid.

    D) supporting.

28. It can reasonably be inferred from both Passage 2 and the graphic that

    A) international markets are increasingly comfortable using the yuan as trade currency.

    B) the United States favors using the yuan as one of the world's reserve currencies.

    C) the G20 wants to replace the yuan and other currencies with a new global currency.

    D) the IMF continues to support the yuan and other currencies in a flexible exchange system.

29. The last paragraph of Passage 2 can be described as

    A) a refutation of opponents' criticisms.

    B) an indication of the author's opinion.

    C) a summary of the author's main points.

    D) an introduction of a contradictory position.

GO ON TO THE NEXT PAGE

30. Which statement most effectively compares the authors' purposes in both passages?

    A) Passage 1's purpose is to contrast the functions of the IMF and World Bank, while Passage 2's purpose is to outline the benefits of a flexible trade system to the United States.

    B) Passage 1's purpose is to describe the history of international trade in the 20th century, while Passage 2's purpose is to explain why the Bretton Woods system collapsed.

    C) Passage 1's purpose is to describe Bretton Woods' effect on the global economy, while Passage 2's purpose is to suggest that a new currency for global trade may soon be implemented.

    D) Passage 1's purpose is to promote the economic benefits of the IMF and World Bank, while Passage 2's purpose is to encourage the reestablishment of the Bretton Woods system.

31. Both passages support which generalization about the global economy?

    A) U.S. influence on global trade has continued under a flexible exchange system.

    B) The purposes of the International Monetary Fund and the World Bank are indirectly related.

    C) The Group of Twenty represents the financial interests of the world's largest economies.

    D) International institutions such as the IMF continue to influence economic trade and development.

Questions 32-42 are based on the following passage.

This passage is adapted from an article about treating paralysis.

According to a study conducted by the Christopher and Dana Reeve Foundation, more than six million people in the United States suffer from debilitating
Line paralysis. That's close to one person in every fifty
(5) who suffers from a loss of the ability to move or feel in areas of his or her body. Paralysis is often caused by illnesses, such as stroke or multiple sclerosis, or injuries to the spinal cord. Research scientists have made advances in the treatment of paralysis, which
(10) means retraining affected individuals to become as independent as possible. Patients learn how to use wheelchairs and prevent complications that are caused by restricted movement. This retraining is key in maintaining paralytics' quality of life; however, an actual
(15) cure for paralysis has remained elusive—until now.
In 2014, surgeons in Poland collaborated with the University College London's Institute of Neurology to treat a Polish man who was paralyzed from the chest down as a result of a spinal cord in-
(20) jury. The scientists chose this patient for their study because of the countless hours of physical therapy he had undergone with no signs of progress. Twenty-one months after their test subject's initial spinal cord injury, his condition was considered
(25) complete as defined by the American Spinal Injury Association (ASIA)'s Impairment Scale. This meant that he experienced no sensory or motor function in the segments of his spinal cord nearest to his injury.
(30) The doctors used a technique refined during forty years of spinal cord research on rats. They removed one of two of the patient's olfactory bulbs, which are structures found at the top of the human nose. From this structure, samples of olfactory ensheath-
(35) ing cells, responsible for a portion of the sense of smell, were harvested. These cells allow the olfactory system to renew its cells over the course of a human life. It is because of this constant regeneration that scientists chose these particular cells to implant into

GO ON TO THE NEXT PAGE

(40) the patient's spinal cord. After being harvested, the cells were reproduced in a culture. Then, the cells were injected into the patient's spinal cord in 100 mini-injections above and below the location of his injury. Four strips of nerve tissue were then placed
(45) across a small gap in the spinal cord.

After surgery, the patient underwent a tailor-made neurorehabilitation program. In the nineteen months following the operation, not only did the patient experience no adverse effects, but his condi-
(50) tion improved from ASIA's class A to class C. Class C is considered an incomplete spinal cord injury, meaning that motor function is preserved to a certain extent and there is some muscle activity. The patient experienced increased stability in the trunk
(55) of his body, as well as partial recovery of voluntary movements in his lower extremities. As a result, he was able to increase the muscle mass in his thighs and regain sensation in those areas. In late 2014, he took his first steps with the support of only a walker.
(60) These exciting improvements suggest that the nerve grafts doctors placed in the patient's spinal cord bridged the injured area and prompted the regeneration of fibers. This was the first-ever clinical study that showed beneficial effects of cells transplanted into the
(65) spinal cord. The same team of scientists plans to treat ten more patients using this "smell cell" transplant technique. If they have continued success, patients around the world can have both their mobility and their hope restored.

32. The passage is primarily concerned with

A) how various diseases and injuries can cause permanent paralysis.

B) ways in which doctors and therapists work to improve patients' quality of life.

C) one treatment being developed to return mobility to patients suffering paralysis.

D) methods of physical therapy that can help patients with spinal cord injuries.

33. The author includes a description of retraining paralytics in lines 8-13 primarily to

A) describe how people with paralysis cope with everyday tasks.

B) appeal to the reader's sympathies for people with paralysis.

C) show that most research scientists do not believe a cure can be found.

D) help readers appreciate the significance of research that may lead to a cure.

34. Based on the information in the passage, it can be inferred that the author

A) believes more research should be done before patients with paralysis are subjected to the treatment described in the passage.

B) feels that increased mobility will have a positive impact on patients suffering from all levels of paralysis.

C) thinks that more scientists should study paralysis and ways to improve the quality of life for patients with limited mobility.

D) was part of the research team that developed the new method of treating paralysis described in the passage.

35. Which choice provides the best support for the answer to the previous question?

A) Lines 6-8 ("Paralysis is . . . spinal cord")

B) Lines 16-20 ("In 2014 . . . injury")

C) Lines 53-56 ("The patient . . . extremities")

D) Lines 67-69 ("If they . . . restored")

36. As used in line 13, "restricted" most nearly means

A) confidential.

B) dependent.

C) increased.

D) limited.

GO ON TO THE NEXT PAGE

37. In lines 46-47, the author's use of the word "tailor-made" helps reinforce the idea that

    A) the injected cells were from the patient and were therefore well-suited to work in his own body.

    B) spinal cord cells were replaced during the transplant portion of the individualized treatment.

    C) olfactory bulbs were removed from rats and placed in the patient's spinal cord during surgery.

    D) the method used by doctors to locate the damaged area required expertise and precision.

38. It can reasonably be inferred from the passage that

    A) the patient's treatment would have been more successful if scientists had used cells from another area of his body instead of from his olfactory bulbs.

    B) cells from olfactory bulbs will be used to cure diseases that affect areas of the body other than the spinal cord.

    C) the patient who received the experimental treatment using cells from olfactory bulbs would not have regained mobility without this treatment.

    D) soon doctors will be able to treat spinal injuries without time-consuming and demanding physical therapy.

39. Which choice provides the best evidence for the answer to the previous question?

    A) Lines 8-11 ("Research scientists . . . possible")

    B) Lines 20-22 ("The scientists . . . progress")

    C) Lines 31-33 ("They removed . . . nose")

    D) Lines 60-63 ("These exciting . . . fibers")

40. As used in line 30, "refined" most nearly means

    A) advanced.

    B) improved.

    C) experienced.

    D) treated.

41. The success of the patient's treatment was due in large part to

    A) studies done on other patients.

    B) research conducted by other doctors in Poland.

    C) many experiments performed on rats.

    D) multiple attempts on various types of animals.

42. The procedure described in which cells from olfactory bulbs are injected into a damaged area of the spinal cord is most analogous to which of the following?

    A) Replacing a diseased organ in a patient with an organ from a donor who has the same tissue type

    B) Giving a patient with a high fever an injection of medication to bring the core body temperature down

    C) Placing a cast on a limb to hold the bone in place to encourage healing after suffering a break

    D) Grafting skin from a healthy area of the body and transplanting it to an area that has suffered severe burns

Practice Tests

GO ON TO THE NEXT PAGE

Questions 43-52 are based on the following passage and supplementary material.

The following passage is adapted from an essay about mercury in fish.

Mercury is an unusual element; it is a metal but is liquid at room temperature. It is also a neurotoxin and a teratogen, as it causes nerve damage
Line and birth defects. Mercury can be found just about
(5) everywhere; it is in soil, in air, in household items, and even in our food. Everyday objects, such as thermometers, light switches, and fluorescent lightbulbs, contain mercury in its elemental form. Batteries can also contain mercury, but they contain
(10) it in the form of the inorganic compound mercury chloride. Mercury can also exist as an organic compound, the most common of which is methylmercury. While we can take steps to avoid both elemental and inorganic mercury, it is much harder
(15) to avoid methylmercury.

Most of the mercury in the environment comes from the emissions of coal-burning power plants; coal contains small amounts of mercury, which are released into the air when coal burns. The concen-
(20) tration of mercury in the air from power plants is very low, so it is not immediately dangerous. However, the mercury is then washed out of the air by rainstorms and eventually ends up in lakes and oceans.

The mercury deposited in the water does not in-
(25) stantaneously get absorbed by fish, as elemental mercury does not easily diffuse through cell membranes. However, methylmercury diffuses into cells easily, and certain anaerobic bacteria in the water convert the elemental mercury to methylmercury as a by-
(30) product of their metabolic processes. Methylmercury released into the water by the bacteria diffuses into small single-celled organisms called plankton. Small shrimp and other small animals eat the plankton and absorb the methylmercury in the plankton
(35) during digestion. Small fish eat the shrimp and then larger fish eat the smaller fish; each time an animal preys on another animal, the predator absorbs the

methylmercury. Because each animal excretes the methylmercury much more slowly than it absorbs
(40) it, methylmercury builds up in the animal over time and is passed on to whatever animal eats it, resulting in a process called bioaccumulation.

As people became aware of the bioaccumulation of mercury in fish, many reacted by eliminating
(45) seafood from their diet. However, seafood contains certain omega-3 fatty acids that are important for good health. People who do not eat enough of these fatty acids, especially eicosapentaenoic acid (EPA) and docosahexaenoic acid (DHA), are more likely
(50) to have heart attacks than people who have enough EPA and DHA in their diet. Because fish and shellfish, along with some algae, are the only sources of these fatty acids, eliminating them from our diet might have worse health effects than consuming
(55) small amounts of mercury.

Scientists have studied the effects of mercury by conducting tests on animals and by studying various human populations and recording the amount of mercury in their blood. By determining the lev-
(60) els of mercury consumption that cause any of the known symptoms of mercury poisoning, they were able to identify a safe level of mercury consumption. The current recommendation is for humans to take in less than 0.1 microgram of mercury for
(65) every kilogram of weight per day. This means that a 70-kilogram person (about 155 pounds) could safely consume 7 micrograms of mercury per day. Because haddock averages about 0.055 micrograms of mercury per gram, that person could safely eat
(70) 127 grams (about 4.5 ounces) of haddock per day. On the other hand, swordfish averages about 0.995 micrograms of mercury per gram of fish, so the 70-kilogram person could safely eat only about 7 grams (about one-quarter of an ounce) of swordfish
(75) per day.

Nutritionists recommend that, rather than eliminate fish from our diet, we try to eat more of the low-mercury fish and less of the high-mercury fish. Low-mercury species tend to be smaller
(80) omnivorous fish while high-mercury species tend

GO ON TO THE NEXT PAGE

to be the largest carnivorous fish. Awareness of the particulars of this problem, accompanied by mindful eating habits, will keep us on the best course for healthy eating.

Species	Average Weight Range (grams)	Average Mercury Concentration (parts per billion)
Alaskan Pollock	227–1,000	31
Atlantic Haddock	900–1,800	55
Atlantic Herring	100–600	84
Chub Mackerel	100–750	88
Cod	800–4,000	111
Skipjack Tuna	2,000–10,000	144
Black-Striped Bass	6,820–15,900	152
Albacore Tuna	4,540–21,364	358
Marlin	180,000	485

43. The author of the passage would most likely agree with which of the following statements?

    A) Mercury poisoning is only one of many concerns that should be considered when choosing which fish to add to one's diet.

    B) More should be done by scientists and nutritionists to inform people about the dangers of mercury poisoning.

    C) Fish is an essential part of a healthy diet and can be eaten safely if recommendations for mercury consumption are kept in mind.

    D) The mercury present in the air is more dangerous to people than the mercury consumed by eating fish with high mercury levels.

44. Which choice provides the best evidence for the answer to the previous question?

    A) Lines 16-17 ("Most of . . . plants")

    B) Lines 30-32 ("Methylmercury released . . . plankton")

    C) Lines 56-59 ("Scientists . . . their blood")

    D) Lines 81-84 ("Awareness . . . eating")

45. In addition to the levels of mercury in a specific species of fish, people should also consider which of the following when determining a safe level of consumption?

    A) Their own body weight

    B) Where the fish was caught

    C) The other meats they are eating

    D) What they ate the day before

46. As used in lines 19-20, "concentration" most nearly means

    A) focus.

    B) application.

    C) density.

    D) awareness.

47. The passage most strongly suggests which of the following statements is accurate?

    A) It is not possible to completely avoid environmental exposure to mercury.

    B) Inorganic mercury is more dangerous to humans than organic mercury.

    C) Most of the exposure to mercury experienced by humans comes from fish consumption.

    D) Mercury is one of the most abundant elements found in nature.

GO ON TO THE NEXT PAGE

48. Which choice provides the best evidence for the answer to the previous question?

    A) Lines 1-2 ("Mercury is an unusual . . . temperature")

    B) Lines 4-6 ("Mercury . . . our food")

    C) Lines 19-21 ("The concentration . . . dangerous")

    D) Lines 27-30 ("However, methylmercury . . . processes")

49. The main purpose of paragraph 3 is to explain

    A) the reasons why mercury deposited in water is not harmful to fish.

    B) the relationships between predators and prey in aquatic animals.

    C) how the largest fish accumulate the greatest amounts of mercury.

    D) the difference between methylmercury and other types of mercury.

50. Which of the following pieces of evidence would most strengthen the author's line of reasoning?

    A) More examples in paragraph 1 of places mercury is found

    B) Details in paragraph 2 about the levels of mercury found in the air

    C) An explanation in paragraph 4 of how to treat mercury poisoning

    D) More examples in paragraph 5 of how many micrograms of mercury people of different weights could eat

51. As used in line 82, "particulars" most nearly means

    A) data.

    B) specifics.

    C) points.

    D) evidence.

52. Based on the information in the passage and the graphic, which of the following statements is true?

    A) The fish with the lowest average weight is the safest to eat.

    B) A person can safely eat more marlin than albacore tuna in one day.

    C) Eating large fish carries a lower risk of mercury poisoning than eating small fish.

    D) A person can safely eat more Alaskan pollock than black striped bass in one day.

IF YOU FINISH BEFORE TIME IS CALLED, YOU MAY CHECK YOUR WORK ON THIS SECTION ONLY. DO NOT TURN TO ANY OTHER SECTION IN THE TEST. STOP

WRITING AND LANGUAGE TEST

35 Minutes—44 Questions

Turn to Section 2 of your answer sheet to answer the questions in this section.

Directions: Each passage below is accompanied by a number of questions. For some questions, you will consider how the passage might be revised to improve the expression of ideas. For other questions, you will consider how the passage might be edited to correct errors in sentence structure, usage, or punctuation. A passage or a question may be accompanied by one or more graphics (such as a table or graph) that you will consider as you make revising and editing decisions.

Some questions will direct you to an underlined portion of a passage. Other questions will direct you to a location in a passage or ask you to think about the passage as a whole.

After reading each passage, choose the answer to each question that most effectively improves the quality of writing in the passage or that makes the passage conform to the conventions of standard written English. Many questions include a "NO CHANGE" option. Choose that option if you think the best choice is to leave the relevant portion of the passage as it is.

Questions 1-11 are based on the following passage and supplementary material.

The UN: Promoting World Peace

The United Nations (UN) is perhaps the most important political contribution of the 20th century. Some may argue that the work of the UN **1** ; an international peacekeeping organization—has proven futile, given persisting global conflict. But the UN's worldwide influence demands a closer look. This organization's

1. A) NO CHANGE
   B) —an international peacekeeping organization;
   C) —an international peacekeeping organization—
   D) ; an international peacekeeping organization,

Practice Tests

global impact is undeniable. The UN is a strong political organization determined to create opportunities for its member nations to enjoy a peaceful and productive world. **2**

　　3 <u>Decades ago,</u> provoked by the events of World Wars I and II, world leaders began imagining a politically neutral force for international peace. The UN was born in 1945 with 51 participating nations. It was to be a collective political authority for global peace and security. Today, 193 nations are UN members. **4** <u>In keeping with the original hope, the UN still strives toward peaceful international relations.</u>

　　Understandably, no single organization can perfectly solve the world's countless, complex problems. But the UN has offered consistent relief for many of the past half-century's most difficult disasters and conflicts. It also provides a safe space for international conversation.

2. Which choice would most clearly end the paragraph with a restatement of the author's claim?

A) The UN is an organization dedicated to advancing social and political justice around the world.

B) Those who argue otherwise are not well educated about geopolitical issues in the 20th century or today.

C) The UN has had its share of corruption over the years, but it has a well-earned reputation of effectively settling international disputes.

D) A better understanding of the UN suggests that the UN enables far greater peace in today's world than could have been possible otherwise.

3. A) NO CHANGE

B) Recently,

C) Consequently,

D) In other words,

4. A) NO CHANGE

B) In having kept with the original hope, the UN still strives toward peaceful international relations.

C) In keeping with the original hope, the UN still strived toward peaceful international relations.

D) In keeping with the original hope, the UN still strove toward peaceful international relations.

GO ON TO THE NEXT PAGE

Moreover, it advocates for issues such as justice, trade, hunger relief, human rights, health, and gender **5** equality, the UN also coordinates care for those displaced by disaster and conflict, **6** dictates environmental protection, and works toward conflict reconciliation.

7 The UN's budget, goals, and personnel count have significantly expanded to meet more needs. **8** The year 2014 witnessed the UN peacekeeping force grow to over 100,000 strong. These uniformed, volunteer, civilian personnel represent 128 nations. The UN's budget has also grown over the years to support an international court system, as well as countless agencies, committees, and centers addressing sociopolitical

5. A) NO CHANGE
    B) equality. The UN
    C) equality: the UN
    D) equality, The UN

6. A) NO CHANGE
    B) prefers
    C) promotes
    D) celebrates

7. Which choice provides the most logical introduction to the paragraph?

    A) NO CHANGE
    B) The UN has developed over the years, but critics charge it has met with limited success.
    C) The responsibilities of the UN have expanded in recent years in response to challenging events.
    D) The UN has maintained a quiet but effective voice on the world stage in spite of criticism.

8. Which choice best completes the sentence with accurate data based on the graphic?

    A) NO CHANGE
    B) The year 2010 led to an increase of approximately 100,000 in the UN peacekeeping force.
    C) The year 2010 saw the UN peacekeeping force grow to approximately 100,000 strong.
    D) The year 2010 saw the UN peacekeeping force decrease to just over 100,000 strong.

Practice Tests

GO ON TO THE NEXT PAGE

topics. Today's UN does big things, and it functions with remarkable organization and efficiency. Critics highlight shortcomings to discount the UN's effectiveness. But considering the countless disasters to which the UN has responded over its six decades of existence, today's world might enjoy [9] far less peace, freedom, and safety without the UN.

[1] From promoting overarching sociopolitical change to offering food and care for displaced groups, the UN serves to protect human rights. [2] Equally [10] quotable are its initiatives to foster international collaboration, justice, and peace. [3] The UN provided aid to the Philippines after the disastrous 2013 typhoon. [4]Certainly, this work is not finished. [5] But no other organization compares with the work and influence of the UN. [6] This brave endeavor to insist on and strive for peace, whatever the obstacles, has indeed united hundreds of once-divided nations. [7] Today, with eleven Nobel Peace Prizes to its name, the UN is undoubtedly an irreplaceable and profoundly successful force for peace. [11]

9. A) NO CHANGE
    B) considerably less peace, less freedom, and less safety
    C) much less peace, less freedom, and less safety
    D) significantly less peace and freedom, and less safety

10. A) NO CHANGE
    B) luminous
    C) noteworthy
    D) repeatable

11. Which sentence should be removed to improve the focus of the concluding paragraph?
    A) Sentence 1
    B) Sentence 3
    C) Sentence 5
    D) Sentence 6

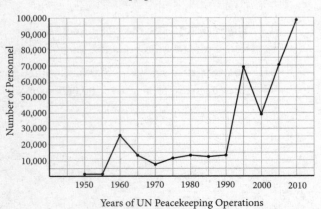

UN Peacekeeping Personnel Numbers Since 1950

Years of UN Peacekeeping Operations

Questions 12-22 are based on the following passage.

DNA Analysis in a Day

Jane Saunders, a forensic DNA specialist, arrives at work and finds a request waiting for her: She needs to determine if the DNA of a fingernail with a few skin cells on it **12** match any records in the criminal database.

"Human DNA is a long, double-stranded **13** molecule; each strand consists of a complementary set of nucleotides," she explains. "DNA has four nucleotides: **14** adenine (A), thymine (T), guanine (G), and, cytosine (C). On each strand is a sequence of nucleotides that 'match,' or pair up with the nucleotides on the other, or complementary, strand. **15** On the other hand, when there is an adenine on one strand, there is a thymine on the complementary strand, and where there is guanine on one strand, there is cytosine on the complementary strand."

She begins by **16** moving the DNA from the rest of the sample, transferring it to a **17** reaction tube. She adds a solution of primers, DNA polymerase, and nucleotides. Her goal is to separate the two strands of the DNA molecules and then make complementary copies of each strand.

12. A) NO CHANGE
     B) matches
     C) has matched
     D) will be matching

13. A) NO CHANGE
     B) molecule, each strand consists
     C) molecule each strand consists
     D) molecule but each strand consists

14. A) NO CHANGE
     B) adenine (A), thymine (T), guanine (G), and cytosine (C).
     C) adenine (A), thymine (T) guanine (G) and cytosine (C).
     D) adenine (A) thymine (T), guanine (G) and cytosine (C).

15. A) NO CHANGE
     B) Specifically,
     C) However,
     D) Similarly,

16. A) NO CHANGE
     B) reviewing
     C) changing
     D) detaching

17. Which choice most effectively combines the sentences at the underlined portion?
     A) reaction tube since she adds
     B) reaction tube, however, she adds
     C) reaction tube, and adding
     D) reaction tube, she adds

GO ON TO THE NEXT PAGE

18 The process of testing the DNA includes several steps and many changes in temperature. After mixing the primers, DNA polymerase, and nucleotides with the evidence DNA, Saunders closes the reaction tube and puts it in a thermocycler. It is programmed to raise the temperature to 94°C to separate the double strands into single strands, and then lower the temperature to 59°C to attach the primers to the single strands. Finally, it raises the temperature to 72°C for the DNA polymerase to build the complementary strands. The thermocycler holds each temperature for one minute and repeats the cycle of three temperatures for at least 30 cycles. At the end of each cycle, the number of DNA segments containing the sequence marked by the primers doubles. If the original sample contains only 100 DNA strands, **19** the absolute final sample will have billions of segments.

18. Which sentence most effectively establishes the central idea?

A) NO CHANGE

B) The object of testing the DNA is to recreate many strands of the DNA in question.

C) Saunders uses a variety of machines in order to analyze the DNA.

D) Saunders would be unable to identify the DNA without the thermocycler.

19. A) NO CHANGE

B) absolutely the final sample

C) the final sample

D) the most final sample

GO ON TO THE NEXT PAGE ▷

[1] After a short lunch break, Saunders needs to separate and identify the copied DNA segments. [2] She had used primers that bind to 13 specific sites in human DNA called short tandem repeats, or STRs. [3] The 13 STRs are segments of four nucleotides that repeat, such as GATAGATAGATA. [4] "Now here's where the real magic happens!" Saunders says excitedly. [5] "Most DNA is identical for all humans. [6] But STRs vary greatly. [7] The chances of any two humans—other than identical twins—having the same set of 13 STRs is less than one in one trillion." **20**

Saunders knows that the detectives will be **21** prepared to hear her findings, so she sits down at her desk to compare her results with the criminal database in the hopes of finding a match. **22** Is it possible that too much time is spent identifying DNA in cases that are relatively easy to solve?

20. Where should sentence 1 be placed to make the paragraph feel cohesive?

A) Where it is now

B) After sentence 2

C) After sentence 3

D) After sentence 4

21. A) NO CHANGE

B) eager

C) impatient

D) conditioned

22. At this point, the writer wants to add a conclusion that best reflects Jane's feelings conveyed in the passage. Which choice accomplishes that?

A) NO CHANGE

B) It takes a good deal of work and expense to identify DNA in the world of modern forensics.

C) She takes pride in the fact that her scientific expertise plays such a key role in bringing criminals to justice.

D) She marvels at how far science has come in DNA analysis.

Practice Tests

Questions 23-33 are based on the following passage.

Will Your Start-Up Succeed?

According to research from Harvard Business School, the majority of small businesses **23** fail in fact the success rate for a first-time company owner is a meager 18 percent. With odds so dismal, why would anyone become a business entrepreneur?

24 Many people desire the freedom of being their own boss, but to be successful, an entrepreneur must also be productive, persistent, and creative. Veteran entrepreneurs achieve a higher 30 percent success rate, so the most predictive factor for success appears to be the number of innovations that a person has "pushed out." More specifically, the people who succeed at building a robust start-up are the ones who have previously tried. Finally, many entrepreneurs **25** grab the idea for their business by solving practical problems, and it's more than luck; 320 new entrepreneurs out of 100,000 *do* succeed by starting a company at the right time in the right industry.

23. A) NO CHANGE
    B) fail, in fact,
    C) fail; in fact,
    D) fail: in fact

24. Which sentence most effectively establishes the central idea?
    A) NO CHANGE
    B) The Small Business Administration defines a small business as one with fewer than 500 employees and less than $7 million in sales annually.
    C) Many small businesses fail because company founders are not realistic about the amount of time it takes for a company to become profitable.
    D) Running a small business can take up a lot more time than punching a clock for someone else and might not be enjoyable for everyone.

25. A) NO CHANGE
    B) derive
    C) achieve
    D) grasp

GO ON TO THE NEXT PAGE

Mitch Gomez is evidence of this data. He 26 did graduate from college with a degree in accounting. "I quickly realized that I have too big of a personality to be content practicing accounting," he laughs. He first built a successful insurance claims 27 service, and next founded his own independent insurance agency. "I continually employ my accounting skills, but I've ascertained that I'm an even more effective salesperson."

Similarly, Barbara Vital, the woman behind Vital Studio, explains, "I love spending as much time with my family as possible." Vital saw an opportunity to 28 launch a monogramming business when her two young sons started school, so she founded a company that offers monogrammed backpacks and water bottles for kids, as well as 29 totes, rain boots; and baseball caps for college students. What is the secret to Vital's success? "I'm always learning how to incorporate social media and add functionality to my product website to keep customers happy," she says.

Finally, Chris Roth is an entrepreneur who can step out of his comfort zone. Always seeking a new 30 challenge his company designed and manufactured technology to keep the nozzles of water misting systems clean. Roth has also established a corporate travel agency and

26. A) NO CHANGE
    B) has graduated
    C) graduated
    D) would have graduated

27. A) NO CHANGE
    B) service. And next
    C) service and next
    D) service; and next

28. A) NO CHANGE
    B) present
    C) propel
    D) impact

29. A) NO CHANGE
    B) totes; rain boots; and
    C) totes, rain boots, and,
    D) totes, rain boots, and

30. A) NO CHANGE
    B) challenge: his company
    C) challenge; his company
    D) challenge, his company

GO ON TO THE NEXT PAGE →

a truck customization company, most recently claiming he has become an innovator who beat the odds by "striving to serve customers better than my competition." **31** Large companies often employ corporate travel agencies to arrange travel for their employees and clients.

Gomez, Vital, and Roth **32** agrees that although being an entrepreneur can be a formidable challenge, exceptionally skillful entrepreneurs have important strategies for success, including stretching **33** his personal boundaries and recovering from failures. "And nothing beats being your own boss," adds Gomez.

31. Which sentence would best support the central idea?
A) NO CHANGE
B) Savvy entrepreneurs know which risks are worth taking and which risks can tank their business before their doors open.
C) Now Roth's small business installs water misters on restaurant patios and even sets up misting stations at outdoor music festivals.
D) Many new small businesses fail because company founders fail to do market research and identify the needs of their community.

32. A) NO CHANGE
B) agree
C) should agree
D) had agreed

33. A) NO CHANGE
B) their
C) our
D) her

Questions 34-44 are based on the following passage and supplementary material.

Edgard Varèse's Influence

Today's music, from rock to jazz, has many [34] influences. And perhaps none is as unique as the ideas from French composer Edgard Varèse. Called "the father of electronic music," he approached compositions from a different theoretical perspective than classical composers such as Bartók and Debussy. He called his [35] works "organized sound"; they did not [36] endear melodies but waged assaults of percussion, piano, and human voices. He thought of sounds as having intelligence and treated music spatially, as "sound objects floating in space."

His unique vision can be credited to his education in science. Born in 1883 in France, Varèse was raised by a great-uncle and grandfather in the Burgundy region. He was interested in classical music and composed his first opera as a teenager. While the family lived [37] in Italy he studied engineering in Turin, where he learned math and science and was inspired by the work of the artist Leonardo da Vinci.

In 1903, he returned to France to study music at the Paris Conservatory. There, he composed the radical percussion performance piece *Ionisation*, which featured cymbals, snares, bass drum, xylophone, and sirens wailing. Later compositions were scored for the theremin, a new electronic instrument controlled by [38] the player's hands waving over its antennae, which sense their posi-

34. A) NO CHANGE
B) influences, and perhaps none is as
C) influences, but perhaps none is as
D) influences. Or perhaps none is as

35. A) NO CHANGE
B) works "organized sound": They
C) works "organized sound", they
D) works—"organized sound"— they

36. A) NO CHANGE
B) amplify
C) deprive
D) employ

37. A) NO CHANGE
B) in Italy, he studied engineering in Turin, where he
C) in Italy he studied engineering in Turin where he
D) in Italy, he studied engineering in Turin; where he

38. A) NO CHANGE
B) the players' hands
C) the players hands
D) the player's hands'

GO ON TO THE NEXT PAGE

tion. No composer had ever scored any music for the theremin before.

In his thirties, Varèse moved to New York City, where he played piano in a café and conducted other composers' works until his own compositions gained success. His piece *Amériques* was performed in Philadelphia in 1926. Varèse went on to travel to the western United States, where he recorded, lectured, and collaborated with other musicians. By the 1950s, he was using tape recordings in **39** contention with symphonic performance. His piece *Déserts* was aired on a radio program amid selections by Mozart and Tchaikovsky but was received by listeners with hostility. **40**

Varèse's ideas were more forward-thinking than could be realized. One of his most ambitious scores, called *Espace*, was a choral symphony with multilingual lyrics, which was to be sung simultaneously by choirs in Paris, Moscow, Peking, and New York. He wanted the timing to be orchestrated by radio, but radio technology did not support worldwide transmission. If only Varèse **41** had had the Internet!

39. A) NO CHANGE
    B) conjunction
    C) appropriation
    D) supplication

40. If added to the paragraph, which fact would best support the author's claims?
    A) The critical response to his 1926 performance in Philadelphia
    B) The selections by Mozart and Tchaikovsky that were played on the radio
    C) Which specific states he traveled to in the western United States
    D) The cities in which the radio program was aired

41. A) NO CHANGE
    B) would have had
    C) would have
    D) have had

Although many of [42] their written compositions were lost in a fire in 1918, many modern musicians and composers have been influenced by Varèse, including Frank Zappa, John Luther Adams, and John Cage, who wrote that Varèse is "more relevant to present musical necessity than even the Viennese masters." [43] Despite being less famous than Stravinsky or Shostakovich, his impact is undeniable. [44] Varèse's love of science and mathematics is shown in his later compositions, but less so in his early works.

Composer	Number of Surviving Works
Edgard Varèse	14
Benjamin Britten	84
Charles Ives	106
Igor Stravinsky	129
Arnold Schoenberg	290
Dmitri Shostakovich	320

42. A) NO CHANGE
    B) its
    C) our
    D) his

43. Which choice most accurately and effectively represents the information in the graph?

    A) NO CHANGE
    B) Despite having fewer surviving works than his contemporaries, his impact is undeniable.
    C) Even though he wrote pieces using a wider range of instruments than other composers, his impact is undeniable.
    D) Even though far fewer of his works are now performed compared with those of his contemporaries, his impact is undeniable.

44. Which sentence best summarizes the central idea?

    A) NO CHANGE
    B) In contrast with his newfound popularity, Varèse's early works have long been ignored due to increasing critical hostility.
    C) Varèse and his innovative compositions became an inspiration for artists seeking to challenge traditional musical beliefs.
    D) Though Varèse's contemporary critics failed to call him a "Viennese master," this distinction is changing.

IF YOU FINISH BEFORE TIME IS CALLED, YOU MAY CHECK YOUR WORK ON THIS SECTION ONLY. DO NOT TURN TO ANY OTHER SECTION IN THE TEST. STOP

Practice Tests

MATH TEST

25 Minutes—20 Questions

NO-CALCULATOR SECTION

Turn to Section 3 of your answer sheet to answer the questions in this section.

Directions: For this section, solve each problem and decide which is the best of the choices given. Fill in the corresponding oval on the answer sheet. You may use any available space for scratch work.

Notes:

1. Calculator use is NOT permitted.
2. All numbers used are real numbers.
3. All figures used are necessary to solving the problems that they accompany. All figures are drawn to scale EXCEPT when it is stated that a specific figure is not drawn to scale.
4. Unless stated otherwise, the domain of any function f is assumed to be the set of all real numbers x, for which $f(x)$ is a real number.

Information:

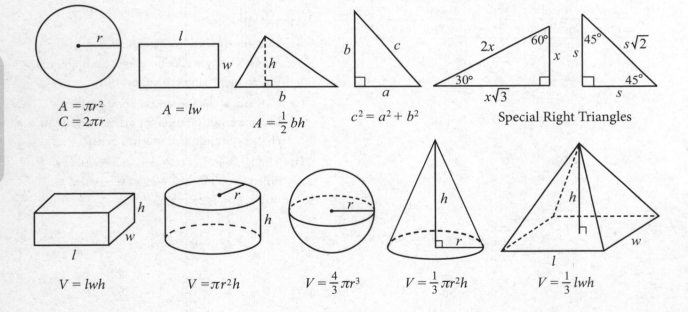

$A = \pi r^2$
$C = 2\pi r$

$A = lw$

$A = \frac{1}{2}bh$

$c^2 = a^2 + b^2$

Special Right Triangles

$V = lwh$

$V = \pi r^2 h$

$V = \frac{4}{3}\pi r^3$

$V = \frac{1}{3}\pi r^2 h$

$V = \frac{1}{3}lwh$

The sum of the degree measures of the angles in a triangle is 180.

The number of degrees of arc in a circle is 360.

The number of radians of arc in a circle is 2π.

GO ON TO THE NEXT PAGE

$$\frac{4(n-2)+5}{2} = \frac{13-(9+4n)}{4}$$

1. In the equation above, what is the value of n ?

    A) $\dfrac{5}{6}$

    B) $\dfrac{5}{2}$

    C) There is no value of n that satisfies the equation.

    D) There are infinitely many values of n that satisfy the equation.

$$\frac{18x^3 + 9x^2 - 36x}{9x^2}$$

2. Which of the following is equivalent to the expression above?

    A) $2x - \dfrac{4}{x}$

    B) $18x^3 - 36x$

    C) $2x + 1 - \dfrac{4}{x}$

    D) $18x^3 - 36x + 1$

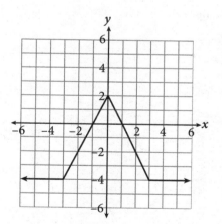

3. The figure above shows the graph of $f(x)$. For which value(s) of x does $f(x)$ equal 0 ?

    A) -3 and 3

    B) -1 and 1

    C) -1, 1, and 2

    D) 2 only

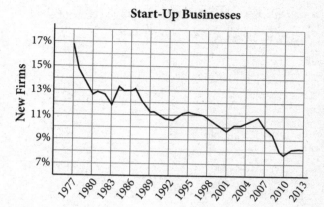

Start-Up Businesses

4. A start-up business is typically one that offers a "new" type of service or produces a "new" product. Start-ups are designed to search for a sustainable business model. The function shown in the graph represents new business start-up rates in the United States from 1977 to 2013 as reported by the U.S. Census Bureau. If t represents the year, then which of the following statements correctly describes the function?

    A) The function is increasing overall.

    B) The function is decreasing overall.

    C) The function is increasing for all t such that $1977 < t < 2013$.

    D) The function is decreasing for all t such that $1977 < t < 2013$.

5. Which of the following systems of inequalities has no solution?

    A) $\begin{cases} y \geq x \\ y \leq 2x \end{cases}$

    B) $\begin{cases} y \geq x \\ y \leq -x \end{cases}$

    C) $\begin{cases} y \geq x+1 \\ y \leq x-1 \end{cases}$

    D) $\begin{cases} y \geq -x+1 \\ y \leq x-1 \end{cases}$

Practice Tests

GO ON TO THE NEXT PAGE

6. At what value(s) of x do the graphs of $y = -2x + 1$ and $y = 2x^2 + 5x + 4$ intersect?

A) -8 and $\dfrac{1}{2}$

B) -3 and $-\dfrac{1}{2}$

C) -3 and 3

D) $-\dfrac{1}{2}$ and 3

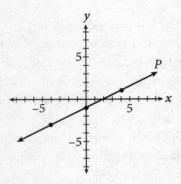

7. If line P shown in the graph is reflected over the x-axis and shifted up 3 units, what is the new y-intercept?

A) $(0, -4)$

B) $(0, -2)$

C) $(0, 2)$

D) $(0, 4)$

8. Which of the following are roots of the equation $3x^2 - 6x - 5 = 0$?

A) $1 \pm 2\sqrt{6}$

B) $\dfrac{1 \pm 2\sqrt{2}}{3}$

C) $\dfrac{3 \pm 2\sqrt{2}}{3}$

D) $\dfrac{3 \pm 2\sqrt{6}}{3}$

9. If $m = \dfrac{1}{n^{-\frac{1}{4}}}$, where both $m > 0$ and $n > 0$, which of the following gives n in terms of m?

A) $n = m^4$

B) $n = \dfrac{1}{m^4}$

C) $n = \dfrac{1}{\sqrt[4]{m}}$

D) $n = m^{\frac{1}{4}}$

$$\begin{cases} y = 3x - 1 \\ y = \dfrac{5x + 8}{2} \end{cases}$$

10. If (x, y) represents the solution to the system of equations shown above, what is the value of y?

A) 10

B) 19

C) 29

D) 31

11. If $0 < \dfrac{d}{2} + 1 \leq \dfrac{8}{5}$, which of the following is not a possible value of d?

A) -2

B) $-\dfrac{6}{5}$

C) 0

D) $\dfrac{6}{5}$

12. The value of cos 40° is the same as which of the following?

   A) sin 50°

   B) sin(−40°)

   C) cos(−50°)

   D) cos 140°

13. A business's "break-even point" is the point at which revenue (sales) equals expenses. When a company breaks even, no profit is being made, but the company is not losing any money either. Suppose a manufacturer buys materials for producing a particular item at a cost of $4.85 per unit and has fixed monthly expenses of $11,625 related to this item. The manufacturer sells this particular item to several retailers for $9.50 per unit. How many units must the manufacturer sell per month to reach the break-even point for this item?

   A)   810

   B) 1,225

   C) 2,100

   D) 2,500

14. If $\frac{1}{2}y - \frac{3}{5}x = -16$, what is the value of $6x - 5y$?

   A)   32

   B)   80

   C)   96

   D) 160

15. If $f(g(2)) = -1$ and $f(x) = x + 1$, then which of the following could define $g(x)$?

   A) $g(x) = x - 6$

   B) $g(x) = x - 4$

   C) $g(x) = x - 2$

   D) $g(x) = x - 1$

Practice Tests

GO ON TO THE NEXT PAGE

Directions: For questions 16-20, solve the problem and enter your answer in the grid, as described below, on the answer sheet.

1. Although not required, it is suggested that you write your answer in the boxes at the top of the columns to help you fill in the circles accurately. You will receive credit only if the circles are filled in correctly.

2. Mark no more than one circle in any column.

3. No question has a negative answer.

4. Some problems may have more than one correct answer. In such cases, grid only one answer.

5. **Mixed numbers** such as $3\frac{1}{2}$ must be gridded as 3.5 or $\frac{7}{2}$.

   (If $3\frac{1}{2}$ is entered into the grid as $\boxed{3\,1\,/\,2}$, it will be interpreted as $\frac{31}{2}$, not $3\frac{1}{2}$.)

6. **Decimal answers:** If you obtain a decimal answer with more digits than the grid can accommodate, it may be either rounded or truncated, but it must fill the entire grid.

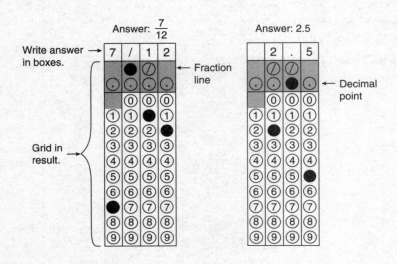

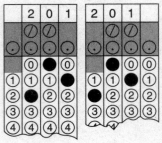

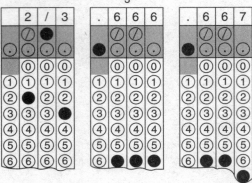

GO ON TO THE NEXT PAGE ⟶

Practice Tests

$$k(10x - 5) = 2(3 + x) - 7$$

16. If the equation above has infinitely many solutions and k is a constant, what is the value of k?

17. A right triangle has leg lengths of 18 and 24 and a hypotenuse of $15n$. What is the value of n?

$$\frac{\sqrt{x} \cdot x^{\frac{5}{4}} \cdot x^2}{\sqrt[4]{x^3}}$$

18. If the expression above is combined into a single power of x with a positive exponent, what is that exponent?

19. If the product of $\left(3 + \sqrt{-16}\right)\left(1 - \sqrt{-36}\right)$ is written as a complex number in the form $a + bi$, what is the value of a? (Note: $\sqrt{-1} = i$)

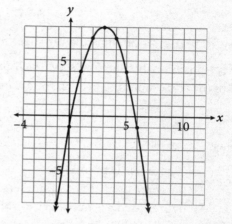

20. If the equation of the parabola shown in the graph is written in standard quadratic form, $y = ax^2 + bx + c$, and $a = -1$, then what is the value of b?

IF YOU FINISH BEFORE TIME IS CALLED, YOU MAY CHECK YOUR WORK ON THIS SECTION ONLY. DO NOT TURN TO ANY OTHER SECTION IN THE TEST.   STOP

MATH TEST

55 Minutes—38 Questions

CALCULATOR SECTION

Turn to Section 4 of your answer sheet to answer the questions in this section.

Directions: For this section, solve each problem and decide which is the best of the choices given. Fill in the corresponding oval on the answer sheet. You may use any available space for scratch work.

Notes:

1. Calculator use is permitted.

2. All numbers used are real numbers.

3. All figures used are necessary to solving the problems that they accompany. All figures are drawn to scale EXCEPT when it is stated that a specific figure is not drawn to scale.

4. Unless stated otherwise, the domain of any function f is assumed to be the set of all real numbers x, for which $f(x)$ is a real number.

Information:

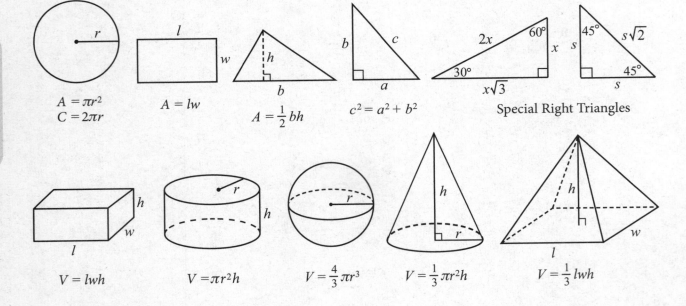

$A = \pi r^2$
$C = 2\pi r$

$A = lw$

$A = \frac{1}{2}bh$

$c^2 = a^2 + b^2$

Special Right Triangles

$V = lwh$

$V = \pi r^2 h$

$V = \frac{4}{3}\pi r^3$

$V = \frac{1}{3}\pi r^2 h$

$V = \frac{1}{3}lwh$

The sum of the degree measures of the angles in a triangle is 180.

The number of degrees of arc in a circle is 360.

The number of radians of arc in a circle is 2π.

GO ON TO THE NEXT PAGE

$$\begin{cases} 4x + y = -5 \\ -4x - 2y = -2 \end{cases}$$

1. What is the y-coordinate of the solution to the system of equations shown above?

   A) -7

   B) -3

   C) 0

   D) 7

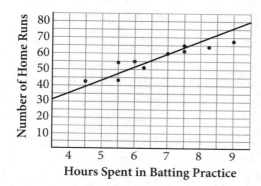

Hours Spent in Batting Practice

2. The scatterplot above shows data collected from 10 major league baseball players comparing the average weekly time each one spent in batting practice and the number of home runs he hit in a single season. The line of best fit for the data is also shown. What does the slope of the line represent in this context?

   A) The estimated time spent in batting practice by a player who hits 0 home runs

   B) The estimated number of single-season home runs hit by a player who spends 0 hours in batting practice

   C) The estimated increase in time that a player spends in batting practice for each home run that he hits in a single season

   D) The estimated increase in the number of single-season home runs hit by a player for each hour he spends in batting practice

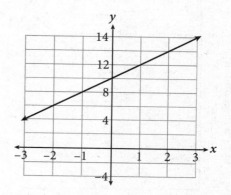

3. Where will the line shown in the graph above intersect the x-axis?

   A) -5.5

   B) -5

   C) -4.5

   D) -4

4. The function $f(x)$ is defined as $f(x) = -3g(x)$, where $g(x) = x + 2$. What is the value of $f(5)$?

   A) -21

   B) -1

   C) 4

   D) 7

5. Sara is grocery shopping. She needs laundry detergent, which is on sale for 30% off its regular price of $8.00. She also needs dog food, which she can buy at three cans for $4.00. Which of the following represents the total cost, before tax, if Sara buys x bottles of laundry detergent and 12 cans of dog food?

   A) $C = 2.4x + 48$

   B) $C = 5.6x + 16$

   C) $C = 5.6x + 48$

   D) $C = 8.4x + 16$

GO ON TO THE NEXT PAGE

Practice Tests

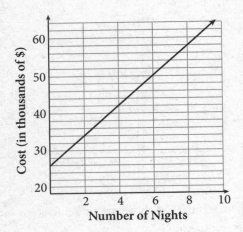

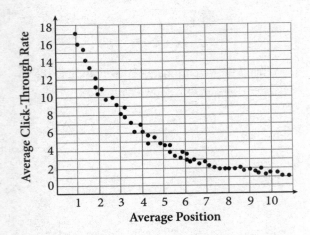

6. The graph above shows the average cost of back surgery followed by a hospital stay in the United States. The hospital charges for the surgery itself plus all the costs associated with recovery care for each night the patient remains in the hospital. Based on the graph, what is the average cost per night spent in the hospital?

A) $2,600

B) $4,000

C) $6,600

D) $8,000

7. The figure above represents a click-through rate curve, which shows the relationship between a search result position in a list of Internet search results and the number of people who clicked on advertisements on that result's page. Which of the following regression types would be the best model for this data?

A) A linear function

B) A quadratic function

C) A polynomial function

D) An exponential function

GO ON TO THE NEXT PAGE

8. Kudzu is a vine-like plant that grows indigenously in Asia. It was brought over to the United States in the early 20th century to help combat soil erosion. As can often happen when foreign species are introduced into a non-native habitat, kudzu growth exploded and it became invasive. In one area of Virginia, kudzu covered approximately 3,200 acres of a farmer's cropland, so he tried a new herbicide. After two weeks of use, 2,800 acres of the farmer's cropland were free of the kudzu. Based on these results, and assuming the same general conditions, how many of the 30,000 acres of kudzu-infested cropland in that region would still be covered if all the farmers in the entire region had used the herbicide?

A) 3,750

B) 4,000

C) 26,000

D) 26,250

x	−2	−1	0	1	2	3
$g(x)$	5	3	1	−1	−3	−5
$h(x)$	−3	−2	−1	0	1	2

9. Several values for the functions $g(x)$ and $h(x)$ are shown in the table. What is the value of $g(h(3))$?

A) −5

B) −3

C) −1

D) 2

10. Mae-Ling made 15 shots during a basketball game. Some were 3-pointers and others were worth 2 points each. If s shots were 3-pointers, which expression represents her total score?

A) $3s$

B) $s + 30$

C) $3s + 2$

D) $5s + 30$

11. Crude oil is sold by the barrel, which refers to both the physical container and a unit of measure, abbreviated as bbl. One barrel holds 42 gallons and, consequently, 1 bbl = 42 gallons. An oil company is filling an order for 2,500 barrels. The machine the company uses to fill the barrels pumps at a rate of 37.5 gallons per minute. If the oil company has 8 machines working simultaneously, how long will it take to fill all the barrels in the order?

A) 5 hours and 50 minutes

B) 12 hours and 45 minutes

C) 28 hours and 30 minutes

D) 46 hours and 40 minutes

Practice Tests

	Jan	Feb	Mar	April
Company A	54	146	238	330
Company B	15	30	60	120

12. Company A and Company B are selling two similar toys. The sales figures for each toy are recorded in the table above. The marketing department at Company A predicts that its monthly sales for this particular toy will continue to be higher than Company B's through the end of the year. Based on the data in the table, and assuming that each company sustains the pattern of growth the data suggests, which company will sell more of this toy in December of that year and how much more?

A) Company A; 182

B) Company A; 978

C) Company B; 29,654

D) Company B; 60,282

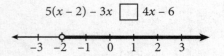

$5(x - 2) - 3x \quad \boxed{} \quad 4x - 6$

13. Which symbol correctly completes the inequality whose solution is shown above?

A) $<$

B) $>$

C) $\leq$

D) $\geq$

Questions 14 and 15 refer to the following information.

A student is drawing the human skeleton to scale for a school assignment. The assignment permits the student to omit all bones under a certain size because they would be too small to draw. The longest bone in the human body is the femur, or thighbone, with an average length of 19.9 inches. The tenth longest bone is the sternum, or breastbone, with an average length of 6.7 inches.

14. If the scale factor of the drawing is one-eighth, about how long in inches should the student draw the femur?

A) 2

B) 2.5

C) 2.8

D) 3

15. The student draws the femur, but then realizes she drew it too long, at 3.5 inches. She doesn't want to erase and start over, so she decides she will adjust the scale factor to match her current drawing instead. Based on the new scale factor, about how long in inches should she draw the sternum?

A) 0.8

B) 1

C) 1.2

D) 1.5

16. If a line that passes through the ordered pairs $(4 - c, 2c)$ and $(-c, -8)$ has a slope of $\frac{1}{2}$, what is the value of c?

A) -5

B) -3

C) -2

D) 2

From	Distance to LHR
DCA	3,718
MIA	4,470

17. Two airplanes departed from different airports at 5:30 AM, both traveling nonstop to London Heathrow Airport (LHR). The distances the planes traveled are recorded in the table. The Washington, D.C. (DCA) flight flew through moderate cloud cover and as a result only averaged 338 mph. The flight from Miami (MIA) had good weather conditions for the first two-thirds of the trip and averaged 596 mph, but then encountered some turbulence and only averaged 447 mph for the last part of the trip. Which plane arrived first and how long was it at the London airport before the other plane arrived?

A) MIA; 2 hours, 40 minutes

B) MIA; 3 hours, 30 minutes

C) DCA; 1 hour, 20 minutes

D) DCA; 3 hours, 40 minutes

18. Which of the following quadratic equations has no solution?

A) $0 = -3(x + 1)(x - 8)$

B) $0 = 3(x + 1)(x - 8)$

C) $0 = -3(x + 1)^2 + 8$

D) $0 = 3(x + 1)^2 + 8$

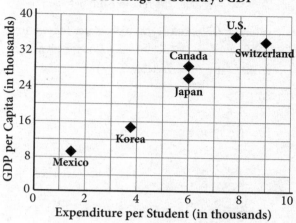

Annual Expenditures per Student as a Percentage of Country's GDP

Adapted from the Organization for Economic Cooperation and Development (OECD), 2003.

19. A student looked at the graph above and determined based on the data that spending more money per student causes the gross domestic product (GDP) to increase. Which of the following statements is true?

A) The student is correct; the data shows that increased spending on students causes an increase in the GDP.

B) The student is incorrect; the data shows that having a higher GDP causes an increase in the amount of money a country spends on students.

C) The student is incorrect; there is no correlation and, therefore, no causation between GDP and expenditures on students.

D) The student is incorrect; the two variables are correlated, but changes in one do not necessarily cause changes in the other.

Practice Tests

GO ON TO THE NEXT PAGE

20. In chemistry, the combined gas law formula

    $\dfrac{p_1 V_1}{T_1} = \dfrac{p_2 V_2}{T_2}$ gives the relationship between the

    volumes, temperatures, and pressures for two fixed
    amounts of gas. Which of the following gives p_2 in
    terms of the other variables?

    A) $p_1 = p_2$

    B) $\dfrac{p_1 T}{V} = p_2$

    C) $\dfrac{p_1 V_1 T_2}{T_1 V_2} = p_2$

    D) $\dfrac{p_1 V_1 V_2}{T_1 T_2} = p_2$

21. An object's weight is dependent upon the gravita-
    tional force being exerted upon the object. This
    is why objects in space are weightless. If 1 pound
    on Earth is equal to 0.377 pounds on Mars and
    2.364 pounds on Jupiter, how many more pounds
    does an object weighing 1.5 tons on Earth weigh
    on Jupiter than on Mars?

    A) 1,131

    B) 4,092

    C) 5,961

    D) 7,092

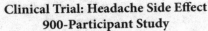

**Clinical Trial: Headache Side Effect
900-Participant Study**

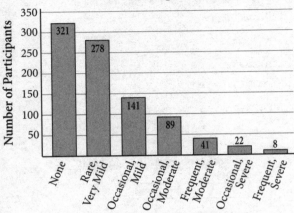

Frequency and Severity of Headaches

22. When a drug company wants to introduce a new
    drug, it must subject the drug to rigorous testing.
    The final stage of this testing is human clinical tri-
    als, in which progressively larger groups of volun-
    teers are given the drug and carefully monitored.
    One aspect of this monitoring is keeping track
    of the frequency and severity of side effects. The
    figure above shows the results for the side effect of
    headaches for a certain drug. According to the trial
    guidelines, all moderate and severe headaches are
    considered to be adverse reactions. Which of the
    following best describes the data?

    A) The data is symmetric with over 50% of
        participants having adverse reactions.

    B) The data is skewed to the right with
        over 50% of participants having adverse
        reactions.

    C) The data is skewed to the right with over
        75% of participants failing to have adverse
        reactions.

    D) The data is skewed to the right with approx-
        imately 50% of participants having no
        reaction at all.

GO ON TO THE NEXT PAGE ⟫

23. In the legal field, "reciprocity" means that an attorney can take and pass a bar exam in one state, and be allowed to practice law in a different state that permits such reciprocity. Each state bar association decides with which other states it will allow reciprocity. For example, Pennsylvania allows reciprocity with the District of Columbia. It costs $25 less than 3 times as much to take the bar in Pennsylvania than in D.C. If both bar exams together cost $775, how much less expensive is it to take the bar exam in D.C. than in Pennsylvania?

A) $200

B) $275

C) $375

D) $575

24. A grain producer is filling a cylindrical silo 20 feet wide and 60 feet tall with wheat. Based on past experience, the producer has established a protocol for leaving the top 5% of the silo empty to allow for air circulation. Assuming the producer follows standard protocol, what is the maximum number of cubic feet of wheat that should be put in the silo?

A) $5,144\pi$

B) $5,700\pi$

C) $20,577\pi$

D) $22,800\pi$

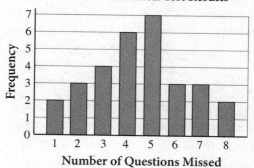

Driver's Education Test Results

25. Mr. Juno took his driver's education class to the Department of Motor Vehicles to take their driver's license test. The number of questions missed by each student in the class is recorded in the bar graph above. Which of the following statements is true?

A) More than half of the students missed 5 or more questions.

B) The mean number of questions missed was between 4 and 5.

C) More students missed 3 questions than any other number of questions.

D) Thirty-six students from Mr. Juno's class took the driver's license test that day.

26. If the graph of the equation $y = ax^2 + bx + c$ passes through the points $(0, 2)$, $(-6, -7)$, and $(8, -14)$, what is the value of $a + b + c$?

A) -19

B) -2

C) 1.75

D) 2.25

GO ON TO THE NEXT PAGE

27. A bakery sells three sizes of muffins—mini, regular, and jumbo. The baker plans daily muffin counts based on the size of his pans and how they fit in the oven, which results in the following ratios: mini to regular equals 5 to 2, and regular to jumbo equals 5 to 4. When the bakery caters events, it usually offers only the regular size, but it recently decided to offer a mix of mini and jumbo instead of regular. If the baker wants to keep the sizes in the same ratio as his daily counts, what ratio of mini to jumbo should he use?

A) 1:1

B) 4:2

C) 5:2

D) 25:8

$$\begin{cases} \frac{1}{3}x + \frac{1}{2}y = 5 \\ kx - 4y = 16 \end{cases}$$

28. If the system of linear equations shown above has no solution, and k is a constant, what is the value of k?

A) $-\frac{8}{3}$

B) -2

C) $\frac{1}{3}$

D) 3

29. What is the value of $3^{90} \times 27^{90} \div \left(\frac{1}{9}\right)^{30}$?

A) 9^{60}

B) 9^{120}

C) 9^{150}

D) 9^{210}

30. If a right cone is three times as wide at its base as it is tall, and the volume of the cone is 384π cubic inches, what is the diameter in inches of the base of the cone?

A) 8

B) 12

C) 16

D) 24

Practice Tests

GO ON TO THE NEXT PAGE

Directions: For questions 31-38, solve the problem and enter your answer in the grid, as described below, on the answer sheet.

1. Although not required, it is suggested that you write your answer in the boxes at the top of the columns to help you fill in the circles accurately. You will receive credit only if the circles are filled in correctly.

2. Mark no more than one circle in any column.

3. No question has a negative answer.

4. Some problems may have more than one correct answer. In such cases, grid only one answer.

5. **Mixed numbers** such as $3\frac{1}{2}$ must be gridded as 3.5 or $\frac{7}{2}$.

   (If $3\frac{1}{2}$ is entered into the grid as [3 1 / 2], it will be interpreted as $\frac{31}{2}$, not $3\frac{1}{2}$.)

6. **Decimal answers:** If you obtain a decimal answer with more digits than the grid can accommodate, it may be either rounded or truncated, but it must fill the entire grid.

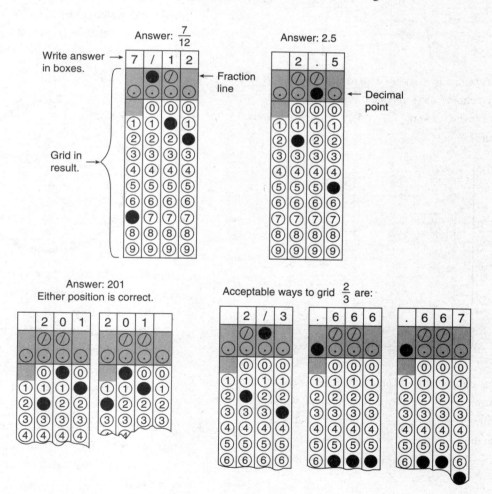

GO ON TO THE NEXT PAGE

31. If $0.004 \leq m \leq 0.4$ and $1.6 \leq n \leq 16$, what is the maximum value of $\frac{m}{n}$?

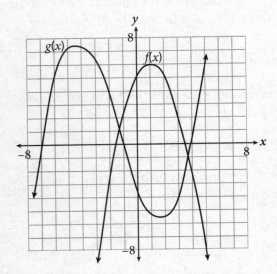

32. The graph above shows a quadratic function $f(x)$ and a cubic function $g(x)$. Based on the graph, what is the value of $(f - g)(3)$, assuming all integer values?

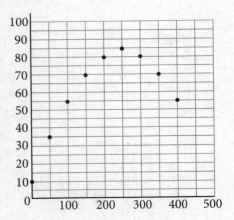

33. Nine data points were used to generate the scatterplot shown above. Assuming all whole number values for the data points, what is the maximum value in the range of the data?

Years at Company	Female	Male
$y < 1$	38	30
$1 \leq y \leq 3$	15	19
$y > 3$	54	48

34. A company conducts a survey among its employees and categorizes the results based on gender and longevity (the number of years the employee has been working for the company). The Director of Human Resources wants to conduct a small follow-up focus group meeting with a few employees to discuss the overall survey results. If the HR Director randomly chooses four employees that participated in the initial survey, what is the probability that all of them will have been with the company for longer than 3 years? Enter your answer as a fraction.

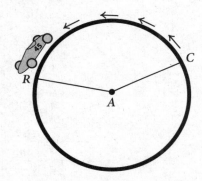

35. Most racetracks are in the shape of an ellipse (an elongated circle similar to an oval), but Langhorne Speedway in Pennsylvania was originally a circular track. If a racecar is traveling around this track, starting at point C and traveling 1,500 feet to point R, and the radius of the track is 840 feet, what is the measure to the nearest degree of minor angle CAR?

36. If $Ax + By = C$ is the standard form of the line that passes through the points $(-4, 1)$ and $(3, -2)$, where A is an integer greater than 1, what is the value of B?

GO ON TO THE NEXT PAGE ⟹

Questions 37 and 38 refer to the following information.

The Great Depression began in 1929 and lasted until 1939. It was a period of extreme poverty, marked by low prices and high unemployment. The main catalytic event to the Great Depression was the Wall Street Crash (stock market crash). The Dow, which measures the health of the stock market, started Black Thursday (October 24, 1929) at approximately 306 points.

37. The stock market had been in steady decline since its record high the month before. If the market had declined by 19.5% between its record high and opening on Black Thursday, what was the approximate value of the Dow at its record high? Round your answer to the nearest whole point.

38. By the end of business on Black Thursday, the Dow had dropped by 2%. Over the course of Friday and the half-day Saturday session, there was no significant change. Unfortunately, the market lost 13% on Black Monday, followed by another 12% on Black Tuesday. What was the total percent decrease from opening on Black Thursday to closing on Black Tuesday? Round your answer to the nearest whole percent and ignore the percent sign when entering your answer.

ESSAY TEST

50 Minutes

The essay gives you an opportunity to show how effectively you can read and comprehend a passage and write an essay analyzing the passage. In your essay, you should demonstrate that you have read the passage carefully, present a clear and logical analysis, and use language precisely.

Your essay must be written on the lines provided in your answer booklet; except for the planning page of the answer booklet, you will receive no other paper on which to write. You will have enough space if you write on every line, avoid wide margins, and keep your handwriting to a reasonable size. Remember that people who are not familiar with your handwriting will read what you write. Try to write or print so that what you are writing is legible to those readers.

You have 50 minutes to read the passage and write an essay in response to the prompt provided inside this booklet.

1. Do not write your essay in this booklet. Only what you write on the lined pages of your answer booklet will be evaluated.

2. An off-topic essay will not be evaluated.

As you read the passage below, consider how Robert F. Kennedy uses

- evidence, such as facts or examples, to support claims.

- reasoning to develop ideas and to connect claims and evidence.

- stylistic or persuasive elements, such as word choice or appeals to emotion, to add power to the ideas expressed.

Adapted from Robert F. Kennedy's address to the National Union of South African Students' Day of Affirmation, 6 June 1966.

1   We stand here in the name of freedom.

2   At the heart of that Western freedom and democracy is the belief that the individual man, the child of God, is the touchstone of value, and all society, groups, the state, exist for his benefit. Therefore the enlargement of liberty for individual human beings must be the supreme goal and the abiding practice of any Western society.

3   The first element of this individual liberty is the freedom of speech.

4   The right to express and communicate ideas, to set oneself apart from the dumb beasts of field and forest; to recall governments to their duties and obligations; above all, the right to affirm one's membership and allegiance to the body politic—to society—to the men with whom we share our land, our heritage and our children's future.

5   Hand in hand with freedom of speech goes the power to be heard—to share the decisions of government which shape men's lives. Everything that makes life worthwhile—family, work, education, a place to rear one's children

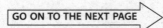

and a place to rest one's head—all this rests on decisions of government; all can be swept away by a government which does not heed the demands of its people. Therefore, the essential humanity of men can be protected and preserved only where government must answer—not just to those of a particular religion, or a particular race; but to all its people.

6   These are the sacred rights of Western society. These are the essential differences between us and Nazi Germany, as they were between Athens and Persia. . . .

7   For two centuries, my own country has struggled to overcome the self-imposed handicap of prejudice and discrimination based on nationality, social class or race—discrimination profoundly repugnant to the theory and command of our Constitution. Even as my father grew up in Boston, signs told him that "No Irish need apply."

8   Two generations later President Kennedy became the first Catholic to head the nation; but how many men of ability had, before 1961, been denied the opportunity to contribute to the nation's progress because they were Catholic, or of Irish extraction.

9   In the last five years, the winds of change have blown as fiercely in the United States as anywhere in the world. But they will not—they cannot—abate.

10   For there are millions of African Americans untrained for the simplest jobs, and thousands every day denied their full equal rights under the law; and the violence of the disinherited, the insulated, the injured, looms over the streets of Harlem and Watts and South Chicago.

11   But an African American trains as an astronaut, one of mankind's first explorers into outer space; another is the chief barrister of the United States Government, and dozens sit on the benches of court; and another, Dr. Martin Luther King, is the second man of African descent to win the Nobel Peace Prize for his nonviolent efforts for social justice between the races.

12   We must recognize the full human equality of all our people before God, before the law, and in the councils of government. We must do this not because it is economically advantageous, although it is; not because the laws of God and man command it, although they do command it; not because people in other lands wish it so. We must do it for the single and fundamental reason that it is the right thing to do.

13   And this must be our commitment outside our borders as well as within.

14   It is your job, the task of the young people of this world, to strip the last remnants of that ancient, cruel belief from the civilization of man. Each nation has different obstacles and different goals, shadowed by the vagaries of history and experience. Yet as I talk to young people around the world I am impressed not by the diversity but by the closeness of their goals, their desires and concerns and hopes for the future. There is discrimination in New York, apartheid in South Africa and serfdom in the mountains of Peru. People stagnate in the streets of India; intellectuals go to jail in Russia; thousands are slaughtered in Indonesia; wealth is lavished on armaments everywhere. These are differing evils. But they are common works of man.

15   And therefore they call upon common qualities of conscience and of indignation, a shared determination to wipe away the unnecessary sufferings of our fellow human beings at home and particularly around the world.

Practice Tests

GO ON TO THE NEXT PAGE ⇨

Write an essay in which you explain how Robert F. Kennedy builds an argument to persuade his audience that the expansion of liberty for all must be the guiding principle of any Western society. In your essay, analyze how Kennedy uses one or more of the features listed in the box that precedes the passage (or features of your own choice) to strengthen the logic and persuasiveness of his argument. Be sure that your analysis focuses on the most relevant aspects of the passage.

Your essay should not explain whether you agree with Kennedy's claims, but rather explain how Kennedy builds an argument to persuade his audience.

ANSWER KEY
READING TEST

1. B	14. C	27. A	40. B
2. C	15. A	28. A	41. C
3. D	16. B	29. B	42. D
4. B	17. B	30. C	43. C
5. A	18. C	31. D	44. D
6. D	19. D	32. C	45. A
7. C	20. D	33. D	46. C
8. D	21. B	34. B	47. A
9. C	22. C	35. D	48. B
10. A	23. D	36. D	49. C
11. A	24. B	37. A	50. D
12. A	25. D	38. C	51. B
13. B	26. B	39. B	52. D

WRITING AND LANGUAGE TEST

1. C	12. B	23. C	34. C
2. D	13. A	24. A	35. A
3. A	14. B	25. B	36. D
4. A	15. B	26. C	37. B
5. B	16. D	27. C	38. A
6. C	17. C	28. A	39. B
7. A	18. A	29. D	40. A
8. C	19. C	30. D	41. A
9. A	20. A	31. C	42. D
10. C	21. B	32. B	43. B
11. B	22. C	33. B	44. C

Practice Tests

MATH—NO CALCULATOR TEST

1. A	6. B	11. A	16. 1/5 or .2
2. C	7. D	12. A	17. 2
3. B	8. D	13. D	18. 3
4. B	9. A	14. D	19. 27
5. C	10. C	15. B	20. 6

MATH—CALCULATOR TEST

1. D	11. A	21. C	31. 1/4 or .25
2. D	12. C	22. C	32. 6
3. B	13. A	23. C	33. 85
4. A	14. B	24. B	34. 1/16
5. B	15. C	25. B	35. 102
6. B	16. B	26. C	36. 7
7. D	17. A	27. D	37. 380
8. A	18. D	28. A	38. 25
9. B	19. D	29. D	
10. B	20. C	30. D	

ANSWERS AND EXPLANATIONS

READING TEST

Great Expectations

Suggested Passage Map notes:

¶1: Pip eating paltry breakfast, Mr. P making him do math while he eats, Pip does not like Mr. P

¶2: Pip visiting Miss H, Miss H's house in disrepair

¶3-9: lady let's in Pip, makes Mr. P go away

¶10: Pip happy to be rid of Mr. P for now

1. B   **Difficulty:** Easy

Category: Detail

Getting to the Answer: Examine the description of breakfast in the first paragraph before choosing the correct answer. In lines 8-9, Pip uses "crumb" and "little butter" to describe what he ate, and he also says that "a quantity of warm water" had been added to his milk. Therefore, it's clear that Pip's breakfast with Mr. Pumblechook is (B), "small and of poor quality."

2. C   **Difficulty:** Medium

Category: Vocab-in-Context

Getting to the Answer: Eliminate answer choices that might be synonyms of "wretched" but don't make sense in the context of the passage. When Pip describes Mr. Pumblechook's company to be "wretched," he means "distressing," or "causing misery." Choice (C) is the correct answer.

3. D   **Difficulty:** Medium

Category: Inference

Getting to the Answer: Review the passage for details that reveal Mr. Pumblechook's attitude. By his actions, you can infer that Mr. Pumblechook is indifferent to Pip's discomfort. Choice (D) is the correct answer.

4. B   **Difficulty:** Medium

Category: Command of Evidence

Getting to the Answer: Find each answer choice in the passage. Think about your answer for the previous question, and determine which lines provide the strongest support for that answer. In the first paragraph, Pip describes how Mr. Pumblechook offers him a meager breakfast and quizzes him on arithmetic during their meal rather than making conversation. Choice (B) is the correct answer.

5. A   **Difficulty:** Hard

Category: Global

Getting to the Answer: Study the answer choices. Eliminate any that go too far in their interpretation of characters and events in the passage. Though B seems to reflect what might be true of Pip and Mr. Pumblechook's relationship, and one might believe that C and D are true, the correct answer is (A). This theme most clearly reflects the message conveyed through Pip's experiences in this passage.

6. D   **Difficulty:** Medium

Category: Detail

Getting to the Answer: Review the section of the passage that describes the young lady's appearance and actions. Select the answer choice that describes her entire demeanor, not just part of it. In line 49, the young lady is described as seeming "very proud." When she tells Mr. Pumblechook that he may not enter, she speaks "finally" (line 57) and in an "undiscussible way" (line 58). This indicates that she is being authoritative. The correct answer is (D).

7. C   **Difficulty:** Medium

Category: Inference

Getting to the Answer: Think about details in the passage that relate to the characters' relationships.

What do they reveal about how Pip probably feels at the end of the passage? It is reasonable to infer that Pip is relieved when he is no longer in Mr. Pumblechook's company. Therefore, (C) is the correct answer.

8. D   **Difficulty:** Hard

Category: Command of Evidence

Getting to the Answer: Locate each answer in the passage and decide which one provides the best support for the answer to the previous question. At the end of the passage, Pip "was not free from apprehension" (line 64) that Mr. Pumblechook would return but then tells the reader that no return took place. Choice (D) best supports the idea that Pip is relieved to be away from Mr. Pumblechook.

9. C   **Difficulty:** Easy

Category: Vocab-in-Context

Getting to the Answer: Substitute each answer choice for "condition." The correct answer will not change the meaning of the sentence. Choice (C) is the correct answer. The narrator says that Mr. Pumblechook is "in a condition of ruffled dignity." In this context, "state" means the same as "condition."

10. A   **Difficulty:** Medium

Category: Rhetoric

Getting to the Answer: Think of what the parenthetical comment by Pip tells you about his personality. In a sense, Pip is apologizing for what he is about to say of Mr. Pumblechook. The parenthetical comment reveals that Pip is usually more polite in his references to others. Choice (A) is the correct answer.

"Letter from Birmingham Jail"

Suggested Passage Map notes:

¶1: MLK states why he is Birmingham, history of SCLC, in Birmingham due to injustice

¶2: MLK cannot let injustice continue, we are one people

¶3: MLK explains why peaceful protests are needed, benefits of tension to open negotiations

¶4: non-violent pressure only way to enact change

¶5: justice must be demanded by the oppressed

11. A   **Difficulty:** Medium

Category: Rhetoric

Getting to the Answer: Avoid answer choices that deal with related issues but do not address the main purpose of the letter. The passage as a whole addresses why King came to Birmingham, and then builds on his explanation for being in Birmingham to explore his cause. Choice (A) is correct.

12. A   **Difficulty:** Easy

Category: Command of Evidence

Getting to the Answer: Choose the answer that relates directly to the purpose you identified in the previous question. King begins the letter by stating "I think I should give the reason for my being in Birmingham," which clearly explains his purpose for writing the letter from the jail. Choice (A) is correct.

13. B   **Difficulty:** Medium

Category: Inference

Getting to the Answer: Determine whether the details in the passage and its title, which relate to how King was treated when he arrived in Birmingham, indicate a positive or negative reception. The title of the passage, "Letter from Birmingham Jail," indicates that King was incarcerated after his arrival in Birmingham. Furthermore, he is writing to an audience that considered him an "[outsider] coming in" (line 3). It is reasonable to infer from these details that King received criticism for his decision to come to Birmingham; therefore, (B) is correct.

14. C   Difficulty: Easy

Category: Vocab-in-Context

Getting to the Answer: Read the complete sentence and the surrounding paragraph to best understand the meaning of the phrase within its greater context. In the paragraph, King goes on to explain that events in Birmingham must necessarily concern him. He states that an injustice in one place threatens justice everywhere, and even writes, "Whatever affects one directly affects all indirectly" (lines 27-28). This suggests that events in Birmingham affect people throughout the nation. Choice (C) is correct, as it explains that the "interrelatedness of all communities and states" refers to the idea that events in one part of the country affect the entire nation.

15. A   Difficulty: Easy

Category: Inference

Getting to the Answer: Predict King's opinions before reviewing the answer choices. The correct answer can be inferred directly from King's views as expressed in the paragraph. In this paragraph, King refers specifically to injustice and how it affects people everywhere. From this, you can most clearly infer that King considered circumstances in Birmingham to be unfair and wrong. Choice (A) is correct.

16. B   Difficulty: Easy

Category: Command of Evidence

Getting to the Answer: Review the answer to the previous question. Read the answer choices to identify the one whose rhetoric provides clear support for the inference. Although the entire paragraph provides general support and context for the inference, only (B) suggests that circumstances in Birmingham were unjust, that is, unfair and wrong.

17. B   Difficulty: Medium

Category: Vocab-in-Context

Getting to the Answer: Before viewing the answer choices, think about the purpose of the word

in the sentence, and form an alternate explanation of the word. Then identify the answer choice that best reflects that meaning and intent. King says that direct action in Birmingham aims to "dramatize the issue that it can no longer be ignored." This suggests that the issue, or events, in Birmingham are of great significance and demand attention that they have not received. Therefore, (B) is correct.

18. C   Difficulty: Hard

Category: Rhetoric

Getting to the Answer: Consider the overall thrust of King's argument in this paragraph. Choose the answer that encapsulates this idea. In paragraph 4, King responds to charges that activists should focus on negotiation, not direct action. He argues that direct action is needed to spur negotiations. King reasons that nonviolent protests create the tension between forces in society needed to bring people to the table to discuss the relevant issues of prejudice and racism. His claim in the paragraph is that direct action is needed to spur negotiation, making choice (C) correct.

19. D   Difficulty: Hard

Category: Rhetoric

Getting to the Answer: Identify an idea in paragraph 4 that provides clear support to the claim made in the previous paragraph. In paragraph 3, King claims that nonviolent direct action is needed to prompt negotiations on civil rights. In paragraph 4, he supports that argument by explaining that no gains have been made in civil rights without such nonviolent action, as choice (D) states.

20. D   Difficulty: Medium

Category: Rhetoric

Getting to the Answer: Read the complete paragraph to best understand the context and purpose of the cited line. The correct answer will identify what the phrase helps achieve in the paragraph. At the start of the paragraph, King argues that oppressors do not willingly give more freedom to the people whom they oppress. He goes on to explain the delay tactics that have kept African Americans from winning equal rights, and concludes that oppressed peoples in other nations are winning independence while African Americans still cannot get a cup of coffee at a lunch counter. The phrase helps King underscore the contrast between these two scenarios, so (D) is the correct answer.

Paired Passages—Bretton Woods

Suggested Passage Map notes:

Passage 1
¶1: background of Bretton Woods
¶2: created IMF to facilitate international trade
¶3: created World Bank to give loans to war affected countries, bridge rich and poor countries
¶4: BW made US dollar global currency
¶5: shaped foreign trade
¶6: BW made US powerful

Passage 2:
¶1: BW only lasted 3 decades, Nixon changed economic policy
¶2: BW collapsed, IMF began flexible exchange system for currency
¶3: US dollar still widely used
¶4: G20 wants to create global currency
¶5-6: predicts worldwide currency, new world order in finance coming

21. B   Difficulty: Medium

Category: Inference

Getting to the Answer: Remember that you are being asked to choose an inference suggested by Passage 1, not a statement of fact. The passage notes that the U.S. dollar became a global currency that nations around the world accept for trade, leaving the United States in a stronger position to influence international markets. Choice (B) is the correct answer.

22. C   Difficulty: Medium

Category: Command of Evidence

Getting to the Answer: The correct choice should support your answer to the previous question. Consider which choice best shows a clear relationship with your answer to the item above. Choice (C) explicitly states the United States became the "primary power" behind the institutions established at Bretton Woods.

23. D   Difficulty: Medium

Category: Vocab-in-Context

Getting to the Answer: Predict an answer based on the context of the passage. The correct answer should not alter the meaning of the sentence in the passage. Then choose the option that best fits your prediction. The passage states that the IMF gives loans to member countries to ensure their continued stability. Choice (D) is correct because it most closely reflects the IMF's goals of proactively promoting global economic growth and stability.

24. B   Difficulty: Medium

Category: Connections

Getting to the Answer: Locate information in the passage that accurately summarizes the purposes of both institutions. Then ask yourself how these purposes differ. Both institutions encourage economic growth. However, Passage 1 notes that the IMF maintains payments and receipts between nations. The World Bank, on the other hand, focuses on "economic and social progress" (line 33) in individual countries. Choice (B) is the correct answer.

25. D   Difficulty: Hard

Category: Inference

Getting to the Answer: Eliminate any answer choices that are not suggested in the passage. Choice (D) is correct. The paragraph states that President Nixon's decision broke with the Bretton Woods framework. It can be reasonably inferred that the decision differed from the consensus of other nations, given the fact that many nations had agreed to Bretton Woods.

26. B   Difficulty: Medium

Category: Command of Evidence

Getting to the Answer: The answer choice should support your answer to the previous question. The paragraph states that President Nixon's decision "marked the end" of the Bretton Woods framework, which best supports the inference that the United States did not have the support of other nations. The correct answer is (B).

27. A   Difficulty: Medium

Category: Vocab-in-Context

Getting to the Answer: Reread the sentence in which the word appears and decide which meaning makes the most sense in context. The sentence is referring to a new global currency that might take the place of the U.S. dollar as the major, or key, currency. Therefore, (A) is the correct definition of "anchor" in this context.

28. A   Difficulty: Hard

Category: Synthesis

Getting to the Answer: Study the yuan's percent share of use in daily trading relative to other currencies in the graphic over time. What does this suggest about global views of the yuan? Passage 2 explicitly states that the yuan is "becoming a major world reserve currency" (lines 92-93). This is supported by the data in the chart, which shows the yuan's percent share of use in daily trading climbing from 0.5% in 2007 to 2.2% in 2013. Choice (A) is correct.

29. B   Difficulty: Medium

Category: Rhetoric

Getting to the Answer: Determine what purpose

the final paragraph of Passage 2 serves in relation to the rest of the passage. Passage 2 is mostly about the changes to the world's financial system since the 1944 Bretton Woods Conference. The last paragraph of Passage 2 discusses a prediction about that system with which the author appears to agree. This is an opinion rather than a fact; therefore, (B) is correct.

30. C   Difficulty: Medium

Category: Synthesis

Getting to the Answer: Identify the overall purpose of each passage. Then consider which answer choice accurately describes these purposes. Choice (C) is the correct answer. Passage 1 focuses on the effects of Bretton Woods, while Passage 2 focuses on the reasons why the international economy may transition to a new global currency.

31. D   Difficulty: Medium

Category: Synthesis

Getting to the Answer: Keep in mind that the correct answer will be a statement that is evident in both passages. The role of the IMF is mentioned prominently in both passages. Therefore, (D) is the correct answer.

Treatment for Paralysis Passage

Suggested Passage Map notes:

¶1: six million US people paralyzed; causes of paralysis
¶2: patient in Poland became subject of study
¶3: spinal cord research on rats, now used to develop treatment
¶4: patient responded well to treatment
¶5: future benefits of treatment

32. C   Difficulty: Easy

Category: Global

Getting to the Answer: Keep in mind that the correct answer will be supported by all of the information in the text rather than just a few details. The passage is concerned with one experimental treatment that doctors are exploring to help paralyzed patients regain mobility. Choice (C) is the correct answer.

33. D   Difficulty: Medium

Category: Rhetoric

Getting to the Answer: Review the cited lines to determine how the information they present affects the reader's perception of the information that follows in the passage. Just after describing how the treatment of paralytics consists of retraining, the author informs the reader that a cure may be in sight. The description of retraining helps the reader understand that finding a cure is a significant leap forward. Choice (D) is correct.

34. B   Difficulty: Medium

Category: Inference

Getting to the Answer: Consider the main points the author makes throughout the passage. The correct answer will be directly related to these points, even if it is not directly stated in the passage. Choice (B) is the correct answer. It can be inferred that the author feels that increased mobility will have a positive impact on patients suffering from all levels of paralysis.

35. D   Difficulty: Easy

Category: Command of Evidence

Getting to the Answer: Locate each answer choice in the passage. Decide which one provides the best support for the answer to the previous question. In the last line of the passage, the author says that paralyzed patients "can have both their mobility and their hope restored" (lines 68-69). This answer, (D), offers the strongest support for the answer to the previous question.

36. D   Difficulty: Easy

Category: Vocab-in-Context

Getting to the Answer: The correct answer will not only be a synonym for "restricted" but will also make sense in the context of the sentence in the passage. Eliminate answers, such as A, that are synonyms for "restricted" but do not make sense in context. Here, the author is explaining that patients in wheelchairs must learn to prevent complications from restricted movement. In this context, "restricted" most nearly means "limited," answer choice (D).

37. A   Difficulty: Hard

Category: Rhetoric

Getting to the Answer: Locate lines 46-47 in the passage, and then read the paragraph that comes before it. This will help you identify why the author chose "tailor-made" to describe the patient's treatment. The patient received his own cells during the treatment, meaning that the treatment was tailored to his own body. Choice (A) fits this situation and is therefore the correct answer.

38. C   Difficulty: Hard

Category: Inference

Getting to the Answer: Remember that when a question is asking you to infer something, the answer is not stated explicitly in the passage. In paragraph 2, the author explains that the patient who received the experimental treatment had not seen an increase in mobility despite "countless hours" (line 21) of physical therapy. Therefore, it is logical to infer that the patient would not have regained mobility without this experimental treatment. Choice (C) is the correct answer.

39. B   Difficulty: Medium

Category: Command of Evidence

Getting to the Answer: Think about how you selected the correct answer for the previous question. Use that information to help you choose the correct answer to this question. In paragraph 2, the author explains that the patient selected for the experimental treatment had not regained mobility despite intensive physical therapy. This provides the strongest support for the answer to the previous question, so (B) is correct.

40. B   Difficulty: Easy

Category: Vocab-in-Context

Getting to the Answer: Substitute each of the answer choices for "refined." Select the one that makes the most sense in context and does not change the meaning of the sentence. In this context, "refined" most nearly means "improved." Choice (B) is the correct answer.

41. C   Difficulty: Easy

Category: Inference

Getting to the Answer: Skim the passage and look for details about how doctors came to use the treatment described. In paragraph 3, the author explains that the doctors used a technique that was developed during years of research on rats. Therefore, (C) is the correct answer.

42. D   Difficulty: Medium

Category: Connections

Getting to the Answer: Compare and contrast each answer choice with the procedure described in the passage. As in the procedure described in the passage, skin transplants for burn victims involve taking tissue containing healthy cells from one area of the body and using it to repair damage done to another area. Choice (D) is the correct answer.

Mercury in Fish Passage

Suggested Passage Map notes:

¶1: what mercury is, uses for mercury
¶2: causes of mercury pollution

¶3: water affected by mercury, issue for many organisms

¶4: consumption of mercury-laden seafood, risks and benefits

¶5: explanation of safe levels of mercury based on bodyweight and fish type

¶6: nutritionists' recommendations

43. C   Difficulty: Medium

Category: Inference

Getting to the Answer: The correct answer will be directly supported by the evidence in the passage. Avoid answers like A and B that go beyond what can logically be inferred about the author. The author explains how mercury gets into the fish that humans eat and goes on to say that it is possible to eat fish that contain mercury without getting mercury poisoning. Choice (C) is the correct answer because it is directly supported by the evidence in the passage.

44. D   Difficulty: Medium

Category: Command of Evidence

Getting to the Answer: The correct answer will provide direct support for the answer to the previous question. Avoid answers like B that include relevant details but do not provide direct support. In the last paragraph, the author says that nutritionists recommend eating low-mercury fish instead of eliminating fish altogether, adding that an awareness of the issues with mercury can help us make healthy eating choices. This statement supports the answer to the previous question, so (D) is the correct answer.

45. A   Difficulty: Easy

Category: Detail

Getting to the Answer: Review the details provided in the passage about how to determine a safe level of mercury consumption. In paragraph 5, the author explains that humans should consume less than 0.1 microgram of mercury for every kilogram of their own weight. Therefore, (A) is the correct answer.

46. C   **Difficulty:** Easy

Category: Vocab-in-Context

Getting to the Answer: Eliminate answer choices that are synonyms for "concentration" but do not make sense in context. In this sentence, the author is describing the amount of mercury in the air from power plants. "Concentration" most nearly means "density" in this context, so (C) is the correct answer.

47. A   **Difficulty:** Medium

Category: Inference

Getting to the Answer: Eliminate any answer choices that are not directly supported by information in the passage. The passage strongly suggests that it is impossible to avoid exposure to mercury completely. Therefore, (A) is the correct answer.

48. B   **Difficulty:** Easy

Category: Command of Evidence

Getting to the Answer: Locate each of the answer choices in the passage. The correct answer should provide support for the answer to the previous question. In paragraph 1, the author explains that mercury can be found in many places. This supports the conclusion that it is impossible to avoid mercury completely. Choice (B) is the correct answer.

49. C   **Difficulty:** Hard

Category: Rhetoric

Getting to the Answer: Think about how the process paragraph 3 describes relates to the rest of the passage. Paragraph 3 describes the process by which larger organisms absorb mercury by eating smaller organisms. This information is necessary to understanding why larger fish have the highest mercury levels. Choice (C) is correct.

50. D   **Difficulty:** Hard

Category: Rhetoric

Getting to the Answer: Consider one of the central ideas of the passage. The correct answer would help provide additional support for this idea. One central idea in the passage is that people can eat fish if they know what mercury levels are safe for human consumption. The author states that scientists have determined safe mercury levels by studying at what point symptoms of mercury poisoning occur. However, the author only provides one example weight of how many micrograms of mercury a person could eat. Therefore, (D) is the correct answer.

51. B   **Difficulty:** Easy

Category: Vocab-in-Context

Getting to the Answer: Reread the sentence and replace "particulars" with each answer choice. Though the answer choices are similar in meaning to a certain degree, one of them makes the most sense when substituted for "particulars." In this context, "particulars" most nearly means "specifics"; therefore, (B) is the correct answer.

52. D   **Difficulty:** Hard

Category: Synthesis

Getting to the Answer: Remember that the correct answer will be supported by information in both the passage and the graphic. Refer to the passage to draw conclusions about the information in the graphic. The passage states that it is safe to eat fish that contain mercury as long as certain guidelines are followed regarding daily consumption. The graphic shows that Alaskan pollock has the lowest concentration of mercury of the fish listed. Therefore, (D) is the correct answer; a person can safely eat more Alaskan pollock than black-striped bass in one day.

WRITING AND LANGUAGE TEST

The UN: Promoting World Peace

1. C   **Difficulty:** Medium

Category: Punctuation

Getting to the Answer: Examine the passage to determine whether the current punctuation is incorrect. Then consider which set of punctuation marks correctly emphasizes the selected part of the sentence. The dashes provide emphasis for the idea that the UN is a peacekeeping organization; the dashes help set off this part of the sentence from the remaining content. The correct answer is (C).

2. D   **Difficulty:** Hard

Category: Development

Getting to the Answer: Review the main points made so far. The correct answer should touch on or summarize previous ideas in the paragraph. Choice (D) is correct. This concluding sentence effectively summarizes the ideas that compose the paragraph's main claim.

3. A   **Difficulty:** Medium

Category: Organization

Getting to the Answer: Read the previous paragraph and identify the word or phrase that is the best transition between the two paragraphs. The previous paragraph describes the UN today, and the paragraph beginning with the phrase in question explains the origins of the UN in the 1940s. Choice (A) indicates the correct shift in time period and provides the most effective transition between paragraphs.

4. A   **Difficulty:** Medium

Category: Usage

Getting to the Answer: Pay close attention to the context of the previous sentence to help you

establish the correct verb tense for this particular sentence. The correct answer is (A). It uses the present tense to logically follow the previous sentence that refers to the UN in the present tense, as well.

5. B   **Difficulty:** Easy

Category: Punctuation

Getting to the Answer: Watch out for choices that may create a run-on sentence. The correct choice is (B), which provides a clear separation between one complete sentence and the next.

6. C   **Difficulty:** Easy

Category: Effective Language Use

Getting to the Answer: Substitute each choice in the complete paragraph. The correct answer will most appropriately fit within the context of the sentence and the paragraph. The correct answer is (C). The UN encourages, or promotes, environmental protection.

7. A   **Difficulty:** Medium

Category: Development

Getting to the Answer: The correct choice should introduce a central idea that is supported by subsequent sentences in the paragraph. The correct answer is (A). The expansion of the UN's budget, goals, and personnel number connects to specific evidence in the rest of the paragraph.

8. C   **Difficulty:** Medium

Category: Quantitative

Getting to the Answer: Notice that the graphic gives specific information about the increases and decreases in the UN peacekeeping force over a period of time. Study the answer choices to find the one that best relates to the paragraph while using accurate information from the graphic. The graphic shows data through the year 2010 and does not indicate that personnel levels rose above 100,000. Choice (C) is the correct answer.

9. A   Difficulty: Medium

Category: Effective Language Use

Getting to the Answer: Watch out for unnecessarily wordy choices like B. The correct answer is (A) because it effectively communicates an idea without additional words that distract from the content.

10. C   Difficulty: Easy

Category: Effective Language Use

Getting to the Answer: Look at the context of the sentence in which the word appears as well as the paragraph itself to choose the answer that works best. Choice (C), "noteworthy," is synonymous with "worth mentioning," which clearly fits within the context of the paragraph and the author's intent to highlight the accomplishments of the UN.

11. B   Difficulty: Medium

Category: Development

Getting to the Answer: Read the entire paragraph. Identify the sentence that is least relevant to the paragraph's topic and purpose. The purpose of this paragraph is to sum up the central ideas of the passage. Choice (B) introduces a detail that, while important, does not summarize the central ideas of the passage and therefore detracts from the paragraph's focus.

DNA Analysis in a Day

12. B   Difficulty: Easy

Category: Usage

Getting to the Answer: Read the sentence and notice that the verb in question is in a clause with intervening prepositional phrases that come between the subject and the verb. Check to see what the subject is and whether the verb agrees with the subject. The verb "match" is in a plural form, but the subject is "DNA," not one of the other nouns in the prepositional phrases. "DNA" is singular. Choice (B) is the correct answer because it is the singular form of the verb "to match."

13. A   Difficulty: Medium

Category: Punctuation

Getting to the Answer: Read the sentence to determine whether the two clauses separated by the semicolon are independent or not. If they are both independent, a semicolon is the appropriate punctuation. Be careful of answer choices with inappropriate transition words. A semicolon is the correct way to separate two independent but related clauses, so (A) is the correct answer.

14. B   Difficulty: Easy

Category: Punctuation

Getting to the Answer: Study the words in a series and see where a comma might need to be inserted or eliminated. Choice (B) is correct.

15. B   Difficulty: Hard

Category: Organization

Getting to the Answer: When you see an underlined transition, identify how the sentence relates to the previous one to determine what kind of transition is appropriate. Choice (B) is correct because the sentence to which the transition belongs provides more detail about a general statement that preceded it.

16. D   Difficulty: Easy

Category: Effective Language Use

Getting to the Answer: Imagine that the sentence has a blank where the word in question is. Read the entire paragraph for context and predict what word could complete the blank. Review the answer choices to find the word closest in meaning to your prediction. The paragraph later states that Jane Saunders's goal is to separate the two strands of DNA. Only answer choice (D) has the correct connotation and fits within the context of the sentence.

17. C   **Difficulty:** Medium

Category: Effective Language Use

Getting to the Answer: It is important to combine sentences in order to vary sentence structures. But the correct choice should not only be the most effective way to combine the two sentences; it must also be in parallel construction with the first sentence. Watch out for choices that may have incorrect transition words as well. Choice (C) is the correct answer. It joins the sentences concisely and correctly because the verb "adding" is in parallel construction with the earlier verbs "detaching" and "transferring." The subject in both sentences is the same, "she," so it can be dropped when combining the two sentences.

18. A   **Difficulty:** Medium

Category: Development

Getting to the Answer: Read the entire paragraph and then put each answer choice at the beginning. Choose the one that makes the most sense and is further explained by subsequent details in the paragraph. The paragraph discusses the process of identifying DNA, which is lengthy and involves changing the temperature of the DNA several times. Choice (A) is closest to this summation of what is to follow and is the correct answer.

19. C   **Difficulty:** Easy

Category: Effective Language Use

Getting to the Answer: Watch out for choices that are wordy or redundant. Choice (C) is the most concise and effective way of stating the information in the passage.

20. A   **Difficulty:** Medium

Category: Organization

Getting to the Answer: Consider the function of this sentence. At what point in the paragraph should this function be employed? The sentence is setting the scene, so it should be placed where it is now, at the beginning of the paragraph. To place it later

would make the meaning of the paragraph unclear. Choice (A) is the correct answer.

21. B   **Difficulty:** Easy

Category: Effective Language Use

Getting to the Answer: Think about the connotations of each answer choice, and be sure to pick the one that fits with the context of the sentence. Substitute each answer choice for the word to see which word works best. "Eager" best reflects how the detectives would be feeling while waiting for important test results. They would be eagerly anticipating this important information and would want it as quickly as possible. Choice (B) is the correct answer.

22. C   **Difficulty:** Hard

Category: Development

Getting to the Answer: Decide which sentence sounds like the most appropriate way to conclude the passage. The rhetorical question currently in the passage (choice A) introduces an opinion that the passage never reveals; there is no sign that Jane Saunders would feel this way. Likewise, there is no indication in the passage of how expensive modern DNA analysis is (choice B), nor that Saunders marvels about how far science has come in DNA analysis (choice D). Choice (C) is the correct answer; it presents a fairly natural way for Saunders to feel given her accomplishments for the day.

Will Your Start-Up Succeed?

23. C   **Difficulty:** Medium

Category: Sentence Formation

Getting to the Answer: Check to see whether there are two independent clauses within this sentence. Two independent clauses without punctuation indicate a run-on sentence. As written, this is a run-on sentence. Choice (C) is the correct answer because it separates the two complete but related thoughts with a semicolon.

24. A   **Difficulty:** Medium

Category: Development

Getting to the Answer: Eliminate answers that might contain details related to the central idea but do not properly express the central idea. This paragraph is mostly about the characteristics of people who are successful entrepreneurs. Choice (A) is the correct answer because it introduces the main idea by summarizing the traits people must have to achieve success as a business owner.

25. B   **Difficulty:** Hard

Category: Effective Language Use

Getting to the Answer: Eliminate answers such as D that mean nearly the same thing as "grab" but do not clarify the meaning of the sentence. In this context, "derive" best clarifies the meaning of the sentence, which explains how entrepreneurs get ideas for their businesses. Choice (B) is the correct answer.

26. C   **Difficulty:** Easy

Category: Usage

Getting to the Answer: Read the rest of the paragraph and pay attention to the verb tense used. The verbs in the rest of this paragraph are in past tense. "Graduated" is the past tense of the verb "to graduate"; therefore, (C) is the correct answer.

27. C   **Difficulty:** Medium

Category: Punctuation

Getting to the Answer: Examine the structure of the whole sentence. Consider whether the punctuation is correct or even necessary. The subject of this sentence is "he," and it is followed by a compound predicate containing the verbs "built" and "founded." When a compound predicate contains only two items, a comma should not separate either verb from the subject. No punctuation is necessary, so (C) is the correct answer.

28. A   **Difficulty:** Medium

Category: Effective Language Use

Getting to the Answer: Replace the underlined word with each answer choice. Consider which word makes the most sense in context and conveys the clearest meaning. The sentence discusses how Vital began her own business. In this context, "launch" conveys the most precise meaning because it connotes the start of a major endeavor. Choice (A) is the correct answer because no change is needed.

29. D   **Difficulty:** Easy

Category: Punctuation

Getting to the Answer: This sentence contains a list of items in a series. Think about the rules of punctuation for items in a series. Items in a series should be separated by commas, with a comma following each word except the last item in the series. The word "and" is not an item in the series and, therefore, should not be followed by a comma. Therefore, (D) is the correct answer.

30. D   **Difficulty:** Easy

Category: Punctuation

Getting to the Answer: Identify the main elements of this sentence, such as the subject, predicate, and any restrictive or nonrestrictive clauses. Remember that a nonrestrictive clause should be set off with a comma. The clause "always seeking a new challenge" is nonrestrictive and should be set off from the rest of the sentence with a comma. Choice (D) is the correct answer.

31. C   **Difficulty:** Hard

Category: Development

Getting to the Answer: Identify the central idea of the paragraph. Read each answer choice and consider which sentence could be added to the paragraph to provide support for the central idea you identified. This paragraph is mostly about Chris Roth, an entrepreneur who now has several companies. (C) is the correct answer because it provides specific details about one of the companies Roth owns.

32. B   Difficulty: Easy

Category: Usage

Getting to the Answer: Read the entire sentence. Identify the subject and determine whether it is plural or singular. Determine the correct verb tense for the sentence. The subject of this sentence is plural (Gomez, Vital, and Roth), so the verb must be plural, as well. (B) is the correct answer because "agree" is the plural present tense of the verb "to agree."

33. B   Difficulty: Easy

Category: Usage

Getting to the Answer: Read the entire sentence and identify the antecedent for the underlined pronoun. The correct answer will be the pronoun that is in agreement with the antecedent. In this sentence, the antecedent is "entrepreneurs," which requires a third-person plural pronoun. Therefore, (B) is the correct answer.

Edgard Varèse's Influence

34. C   Difficulty: Medium

Category: Sentence Formation

Getting to the Answer: Read the two sentences connected by the underlined portion, and decide which answer choice creates a grammatically correct and logical sentence. Choice (C) is correct. Using the coordinating conjunction "but" with a comma to combine the sentences shows that the second portion, which mentions Varèse as being unique, stands in contrast to the first portion, which mentions many influential artists. The other options, featuring "and" and "or," do not show this necessary contrast.

35. A   Difficulty: Hard

Category: Punctuation

Getting to the Answer: Reread the entire sentence to assess how the punctuation in the answer choices affects how each portion of the sentence relates to one another. The correct answer is (A). The semicolon correctly links the two independent clauses that have a direct relationship with one another.

36. D   Difficulty: Medium

Category: Effective Language Use

Getting to the Answer: Read the sentence for context clues, and think about the author's intention. Then determine which answer provides the most appropriate word choice. "Employ" is the only word that matches the meaning of the sentence, which states that Varèse did not use traditional melodies. Thus, choice (D) is correct.

37. B   Difficulty: Medium

Category: Punctuation

Getting to the Answer: Reread the sentence to determine how each portion relates to the others. Then examine how the punctuation in the answer choices affects these relationships. The portion of the sentence discussing the family's move to Italy is an introductory element and needs a comma to offset it from the rest of the sentence. The portion discussing what Varèse learned in Turin is a parenthetical element and also requires a comma. Therefore, choice (B) is correct.

38. A   Difficulty: Medium

Category: Punctuation

Getting to the Answer: Review the sentence for context clues and to assess the subject's ownership of the objects in the sentence. Then determine which form of the possessive noun correctly reflects this ownership. The hands in the sentence belong to a single player using a single theremin; therefore, the correct answer will use the singular possessive noun "player's." Choice (A) is correct.

39. B **Difficulty:** Medium

Category: Effective Language Use

Getting to the Answer: Read the sentence for context clues. Decide on the answer choice that makes the sentence's meaning precise and clear. "Conjunction" is the only word that relates to two things occurring at the same time to create a single outcome, which is the intended meaning of the sentence. Choice (B) is correct.

40. A **Difficulty:** Hard

Category: Development

Getting to the Answer: Assess the central idea of the introductory sentence in the paragraph, and determine which additional fact noted in the answer choices would have the greatest benefit to the reader. The introductory sentence states that Varèse worked in New York until he secured his first success. Describing the critical reaction to the next event mentioned would help strengthen the idea that the Philadelphia performance was a successful event in Varèse's career. Choice (A) is the correct answer.

41. A **Difficulty:** Hard

Category: Usage

Getting to the Answer: Consider what kind of situation the author is presenting here, and decide which tense of the verb "has" creates a grammatically correct sentence that reflects this meaning. Keep in mind the time of the events in the sentence. The sentence imagines a situation in which Varèse had been able to use the Internet, an unrealistic action. The double "had had" is correct; it describes past-tense actions that might have occurred in the past but didn't. Choice (A) is correct.

42. D **Difficulty:** Easy

Category: Usage

Getting to the Answer: Read the entire sentence to figure out who is the owner of the burned compositions. Then select the proper personal pronoun for this antecedent. Choice (D) is the correct singular possessive pronoun because the burned compositions belonged to Varèse, one person, and not a group of artists.

43. B **Difficulty:** Medium

Category: Quantitative

Getting to the Answer: Study the information in the graphic to determine which answer choice most accurately finishes the sentence. Choice (B) is correct because it accurately reflects information included in the graphic.

44. C **Difficulty:** Medium

Category: Development

Getting to the Answer: After reading the final paragraph, examine each answer choice to determine which best summarizes the paragraph's overall message. Choice (C) is correct. It is the one sentence that sets up the idea that Varèse's challenging work has been an inspiration to many later artists, an idea supported by the rest of the paragraph.

MATH—NO CALCULATOR TEST

1. A **Difficulty:** Easy

Category: Heart of Algebra / Linear Equations

Getting to the Answer: You could start by cross-multiplying to get rid of the denominators, but simplifying the numerators first will make the calculations easier. Don't forget to distribute the negative to both terms in the parentheses on the right-hand side of the equation.

$$\frac{4(n-2)+5}{2} = \frac{13-(9+4n)}{4}$$

$$\frac{4n-8+5}{2} = \frac{13-9-4n}{4}$$

$$\frac{4n-3}{2} = \frac{4-4n}{4}$$

$$4(4n-3) = 2(4-4n)$$

$$16n-12 = 8-8n$$

$$16n = 20-8n$$

$$24n = 20$$

$$n = \frac{20}{24} = \frac{5}{6}$$

Choice (A) is correct.

2. C   Difficulty: Easy

Category: Passport to Advanced Math / Exponents

Getting to the Answer: Don't be tempted—you can't simply cancel one term when a polynomial is divided by a monomial. You can, however, split the expression into three terms, each with a denominator of $9x^2$, and simplify. You could also use polynomial long division to answer the question. Use whichever method gets you to the answer more quickly on Test Day.

$$\frac{18x^3+9x^2-36x}{9x^2} = \frac{18x^3}{9x^2} + \frac{9x^2}{9x^2} - \frac{36x}{9x^2}$$

$$= 2x + 1 - \frac{4}{x}$$

Choice (C) is correct.

3. B   Difficulty: Easy

Category: Passport to Advanced Math / Functions

Getting to the Answer: When using function notation, $f(x)$ is simply another way of saying y, so this question is asking you to find the value(s) of x for which $y = 0$, or in other words, where the graph crosses the x-axis. Don't be tempted by the flat parts of the graph—they have a slope of 0, but the function itself does not equal 0 here (it equals -4). The graph crosses the x-axis at the points $(-1, 0)$ and $(1, 0)$, so the values of x for which $f(x) = 0$ are -1 and 1, (B).

4. B   Difficulty: Easy

Category: Passport to Advanced Math / Functions

Getting to the Answer: Your only choice for this question is to compare each statement to the graph. Cross out false statements as you go. A function is decreasing when the slope is negative; it is increasing when the slope is positive. You can see from the graph that the trend is decreasing (going down from left to right), so eliminate A and C. Now, take a closer look to see that there are some time intervals over which the function increases (goes up), so you can't say that the function in decreasing for *all t* such that $1977 < t < 2013$. You can only make a general statement about the nature of the function, like the one in (B). The right-hand side of the graph is lower than the left side, so the function is decreasing overall.

5. C   Difficulty: Medium

Category: Heart of Algebra / Inequalities

Getting to the Answer: You don't need to use algebra to answer this question, and you also don't need to graph each system. Instead, think about how the graphs would look. The only time a system of linear inequalities has no solution is when it consists of two parallel lines shaded in opposite directions. All the inequalities are written in slope-intercept form, so look for parallel lines (two lines that have the same slope but different y-intercepts). The slopes in A are different ($m = 1$ and $m = 2$), so eliminate this choice. The same is true for B ($m = 1$ and $m = -1$) and D ($m = -1$ and $m = 1$). This means (C) must be correct ($m = 1$ and $m = 1$, $b = 1$ and $b = -1$). The graph of the system is shown here:

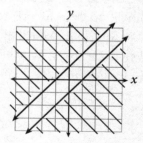

Because the shading never overlaps, the system has no solution.

6. B   **Difficulty:** Medium

Category: Passport to Advanced Math / Quadratics

Getting to the Answer: Although this question asks where the graphs intersect, it is not necessary to actually graph them. The point(s) at which the two graphs intersect are the points where the two equations are equal to each other. So, set the equations equal and use algebra to solve for x. Because the question only asks for the x-values, you don't need to substitute the results back into the equations to solve for y.

$$-2x + 1 = 2x^2 + 5x + 4$$
$$-2x = 2x^2 + 5x + 3$$
$$0 = 2x^2 + 7x + 3$$
$$0 = (2x + 1)(x + 3)$$

Now that the equation is factored, use the Zero-Product Property to solve for x:

$$2x + 1 = 0 \quad \text{and} \quad x + 3 = 0$$
$$2x = -1 \qquad\qquad x = -3$$
$$x = -\frac{1}{2}$$

Choice (B) is correct.

7. D   **Difficulty:** Medium

Category: Heart of Algebra / Linear Equations

Getting to the Answer: You can approach this question conceptually or concretely. When dealing with simple transformations, drawing a quick sketch is most likely the safest approach. You are only concerned about the y-intercept, so keep your focus there. When the graph is reflected over the x-axis, the y-intercept will go from $(0, -1)$ to $(0, 1)$. Next, the line is shifted up 3 units, which adds 3 to the y-coordinates of all the points on the line, making the new y-intercept $(0, 4)$. Choice (D) is correct. A sketch follows:

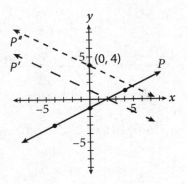

8. D   **Difficulty:** Medium

Category: Passport to Advanced Math / Quadratics

Getting to the Answer: The roots of an equation are the same as its solutions. Take a peek at the answer choices—they contain radicals, which tells you that the equation can't be factored. Instead, either complete the square or solve the equation using the quadratic formula, whichever you are most comfortable with. The equation is already written in the form $y = ax^2 + bx + c$ and the coefficients are fairly small, so using the quadratic formula is probably the quickest method. Jot down the values that you'll need: $a = 3$, $b = -6$, and $c = -5$. Then, substitute these values into the quadratic formula and simplify:

$$x = \frac{-b \pm \sqrt{b^2 - 4ac}}{2a}$$
$$= \frac{-(-6) \pm \sqrt{(-6)^2 - 4(3)(-5)}}{2(3)}$$
$$= \frac{6 \pm \sqrt{36 + 60}}{6}$$
$$= \frac{6 \pm \sqrt{96}}{6}$$

This is not one of the answer choices, so simplify the radical. To do this, look for a perfect square that divides into 96 and take its square root. Then, if possible, cancel any factors that are common to the numerator and the denominator.

$$x = \frac{6 \pm \sqrt{16 \times 6}}{6}$$

$$= \frac{6 \pm 4\sqrt{6}}{6}$$

$$= \frac{\cancel{2}\left(3 \pm 2\sqrt{6}\right)}{\cancel{2}(3)}$$

$$= \frac{3 \pm 2\sqrt{6}}{3}$$

Choice (D) is correct. Be careful—you can't simplify the answer any further because you cannot divide the square root of 6 by 3.

9. A   Difficulty: Medium

Category: Passport to Advanced Math / Exponents

Getting to the Answer: When you write an equation in terms of a specific variable, you are simply solving the equation for that variable. To do this, you'll need to use the property that raising a quantity to the one-fourth power is the same as taking its fourth root and that applying a negative exponent to a quantity is the same as writing its reciprocal. Rewrite the equation using these properties, and then solve for n using inverse operations. Note that the inverse of taking a fourth root of a quantity is raising the quantity to the fourth power.

$$m = \frac{1}{n^{-\frac{1}{4}}}$$

$$m = \frac{\sqrt[4]{n}}{1}$$

$$(m)^4 = \left(\sqrt[4]{n}\right)^4$$

$$m^4 = n$$

Choice (A) is correct.

10. C   Difficulty: Medium

Category: Heart of Algebra / Systems of Linear Equations

Getting to the Answer: When a system consists of two equations already written in terms of y, the quickest way to solve the system is to set the equations equal to each other and then use inverse operations. Don't let the fraction intimidate you—you can write the first equation as a fraction over 1 and use cross-multiplication.

$$\frac{3x - 1}{1} = \frac{5x + 8}{2}$$

$$2(3x - 1) = 5x + 8$$

$$6x - 2 = 5x + 8$$

$$6x = 5x + 10$$

$$x = 10$$

Don't let A fool you—the question is asking for the value of y, not the value of x. To find y, substitute 10 for x in either equation and simplify:

$$y = 3(10) - 1$$

$$= 30 - 1$$

$$= 29$$

Choice (C) is correct.

11. A   Difficulty: Medium

Category: Heart of Algebra / Inequalities

Getting to the Answer: You don't need to separate this compound inequality into pieces. Just remember, whatever you do to one piece, you must do to all three pieces. The fractions in this question make it look more complicated than it really is, so start by clearing them. To do this, multiply everything by the least common denominator, 10.

$$0 < \frac{d}{2} + 1 \le \frac{8}{5}$$

$$10(0) < 10\left(\frac{d}{2} + 1\right) \le \left(\frac{8}{5}\right)10$$

$$0 < 5d + 10 \le 16$$

$$-10 < 5d \le 6$$

$$-2 < d \le \frac{6}{5}$$

Now, read the inequality symbols carefully. The value of d is between -2 and $\frac{6}{5}$, not including -2 because of the < symbol, so (A) is the correct answer. Don't let C fool you—you can't have a 0 *denominator* in a rational expression, but in this expression, the variable is in the numerator, so it *can* equal 0.

12. A   **Difficulty:** Medium

Category: Additional Topics in Math / Trigonometry

Getting to the Answer: The measure of 40° does not appear on the unit circle, which should give you a clue that there must be a property or relationship on which you can rely to help you answer the question. Complementary angles have a special relationship relative to trig values: The cosine of an acute angle is equal to the sine of the angle's complement and vice versa. Because only one of the answers can be correct, look for the simplest relationship (complementary angles): 50° is complementary to 40°, so cos 40° = sin 50°, which means (A) is correct.

13. D   **Difficulty:** Medium

Category: Heart of Algebra / Linear Equations

Getting to the Answer: Assign a variable to the unknown, and then create an equation that represents the scenario. Let n be the number of units the manufacturer sells in a month. Sales must equal expenses for the manufacturer to break even (sales = expenses). The sales are equal to the selling price ($9.50) times the number of units sold (n), so write $9.5n$ on one side of the equal sign. The monthly expenses are the fixed expenses ($11,625) plus the amount paid for the materials needed to produce one unit ($4.85) times the number of units (n), so write $11,625 + 4.85n$ on the other side of the equal sign. Then, solve for n.

$$9.5n = 11,625 + 4.85n$$
$$4.65n = 11,625$$
$$n = 2,500$$

Choice (D) is correct.

14. D   **Difficulty:** Medium

Category: Heart of Algebra / Linear Equations

Getting to the Answer: There is only one equation given, and it has two variables. This means that you don't have enough information to solve for either variable. Instead, look for the relationship between the left side of the equation and the other expression that you are trying to find. The expression you are trying to find ($6x - 5y$) has the x-term first and then the y-term, so start by reversing the order of the terms on the left side of the given equation. Also, notice that the x term in $6x - 5y$ is not negative, so multiply the equation by -1.

$$\frac{1}{2}y - \frac{3}{5}x = -16 \rightarrow -\frac{3}{5}x + \frac{1}{2}y = -16$$
$$-1\left(-\frac{3}{5}x + \frac{1}{2}y = -16\right) \rightarrow \frac{3}{5}x - \frac{1}{2}y = 16$$

Finally, there are no fractions in the desired expression, so clear the fractions by multiplying both sides of the equation by 10. This yields the expression that you are looking for, so no further work is required—just read the value on the right-hand side of the equation, which is 160.

$$10\left(\frac{3}{5}x - \frac{1}{2}y\right) = 16(10)$$
$$6x - 5y = 160$$

Choice (D) is correct.

15. B   **Difficulty:** Medium

Category: Passport to Advanced Math / Functions

Getting to the Answer: Understanding the language of functions will make questions that seem complicated much more doable. When you know the output of a function (or in this question, a composition of two functions), you can work backward to find the input. Because $g(x)$ is the inside function for this composition, its output becomes the input for $f(x)$. Unfortunately, you don't have any information about g yet. You do know however that f of some number, $g(2)$, is -1, so set $f(x)$ equal to -1 and solve for x:

$$-1 = x + 1$$
$$-2 = x$$

You now know that $f(-2) = -1$. In the equation for the composition, $g(2)$ represents x, so you also know that $g(2)$ must be -2. Your only option now is to use brute force to determine which equation for g, when evaluated at 2, results in -2.

Choice A: $g(2) = 2 - 6 = -4$ (not -2), so eliminate.

Choice B: $g(2) = 2 - 4 = -2$

You don't need to go any further; (B) is correct.

You could check your answer by working forward, starting with $g(2)$:

$$g(2) = 2 - 4 = -2$$
$$f(g(2)) = f(-2) = -2 + 1 = -1$$

16. 1/5 or .2   Difficulty: Medium

Category: Heart of Algebra / Linear Equations

Getting to the Answer: There are two variables but only one equation, so you can't actually solve the equation for k. Instead, recall that an equation has infinitely many solutions when the left side is identical to the right side. When this happens, everything cancels out and you get $0 = 0$, which is always true. Start by simplifying the right-hand side of the equation. Don't simplify the left side because k is already in a good position.

$$k(10x - 5) = 2(3 + x) - 7$$
$$k(10x - 5) = 6 + 2x - 7$$
$$k(10x - 5) = 2x - 1$$

Next, compare the left side of the equation to the right side. Rather than distributing the k, notice that $2x$ is a fifth of $10x$ and -1 is a fifth of -5, so if k were $\frac{1}{5}$ (or 0.2), then both sides of the equation would equal $2x - 1$, and it would therefore have infinitely many solutions. Thus, k is $\frac{1}{5}$ or .2.

17. 2   Difficulty: Medium

Category: Additional Topics in Math / Geometry

Getting to the Answer: You could use the Pythago-

rean theorem to solve this, but it will save valuable time on Test Day if you recognize that this question is testing your knowledge of Pythagorean triples. The triangle is a right triangle with leg lengths of 18 and 24, which, when divided by 6, are in the proportion 3:4. This means that the triangle is a scaled up 3:4:5 right triangle with a scale factor of 6. To keep the same proportion, the hypotenuse must be $5 \times 6 = 30$. For $15n$ to equal 30, n must be 2.

18. 3   Difficulty: Hard

Category: Passport to Advanced Math / Exponents

Getting to the Answer: You need to use rules of exponents to simplify the expression. Before you can do that, you must rewrite the radicals as fraction exponents. Use the phrase "power over root" to help you convert the radicals: $\sqrt{x} = {}^{\text{root} \to 2}\sqrt{x^{1 \leftarrow \text{power}}} = x^{\frac{1}{2}}$ and ${}^{\text{root} \to 4}\sqrt{x^{3 \leftarrow \text{power}}} = x^{\frac{3}{4}}$. Then use rules of exponents to simplify the expression. Add the exponents of the factors that are being multiplied and subtract the exponent of the factor that is being divided:

$$\frac{\sqrt{x} \cdot x^{\frac{5}{4}} \cdot x^2}{\sqrt[4]{x^3}} = \frac{x^{\frac{1}{2}} \cdot x^{\frac{5}{4}} \cdot x^{\frac{2}{1}}}{x^{\frac{3}{4}}}$$
$$= x^{\frac{1}{2} + \frac{5}{4} + \frac{2}{1} - \frac{3}{4}}$$
$$= x^{\frac{2}{4} + \frac{5}{4} + \frac{8}{4} - \frac{3}{4}}$$
$$= x^{\frac{12}{4}} = x^3$$

The exponent of the simplified expression is 3.

19. 27   Difficulty: Hard

Category: Additional Topics in Math / Imaginary Numbers

Getting to the Answer: Each of the factors in this product has two terms, so they behave like binomials. This means you can use FOIL to find the product. To avoid messy numbers, simplify the two radicals first using the definition of i. Write each of the numbers under the radicals as a product of -1 and the number, take the square roots, and then FOIL the resulting expressions:

$$\left(3 + \sqrt{-16}\right)\left(1 - \sqrt{-36}\right)$$
$$= \left(3 + \sqrt{16 \times (-1)}\right)\left(1 - \sqrt{36 \times (-1)}\right)$$
$$= (3 + 4i)(1 - 6i)$$
$$= 3 - 18i + 4i - 24i^2$$
$$= 3 - 14i - 24(-1)$$
$$= 3 - 14i + 24$$
$$= 27 - 14i$$

The question asks for the value of a (the real part of the expression), so the correct answer is 27.

20. 6   **Difficulty:** Hard

Category: Passport to Advanced Math / Quadratics

Getting to the Answer: When you are given the graph of a parabola, try to use what you know about intercepts, the vertex, and the axis of symmetry to answer the question. Here, you could try to use points from the graph to find its equation, but this is not necessary because the question only asks for the value of b. As a shortcut, recall that you can find the vertex of a parabola using the formula $x = -\dfrac{b}{2a}$ (the quadratic formula without the radical part). You are given that $a = -1$. Now look at the graph—the vertex of the parabola is (3, 8), so substitute 3 for x, -1 for a, and solve for b.

$$3 = -\frac{b}{2(-1)}$$
$$3 = -\left(\frac{b}{-2}\right)$$
$$3 = \frac{b}{2}$$
$$3(2) = b$$
$$6 = b$$

As an alternate method, you could plug the value of a and the vertex (from the graph) into vertex form of a quadratic equation and simplify:

$$y = a(x - h)^2 + k$$
$$= -1(x - 3)^2 + 8$$
$$= -1(x^2 - 6x + 9) + 8$$
$$= -x^2 + 6x - 9 + 8$$
$$= -x^2 + 6x - 1$$

The coefficient of x is b, so $b = 6$.

MATH—CALCULATOR TEST

1. D   **Difficulty:** Easy

Category: Heart of Algebra / Systems of Linear Equations

Getting to the Answer: A quick examination of the equations in the system will tell you which strategy to use to solve it. Because $4x$ and $-4x$ are opposites of one another, the system is already perfectly set up to solve by elimination (combining the two equations by adding them).

$$\begin{array}{rcl}
\cancel{4x} + y & = & -5 \\
-\cancel{4x} - 2y & = & -2 \\
\hline
-y & = & -7 \\
y & = & 7
\end{array}$$

Choice (D) is correct.

2. D   **Difficulty:** Easy

Category: Problem Solving and Data Analysis / Scatterplots

Getting to the Answer: Graphically, slope is the ratio of the change in the y-values (rise) to the change in the x-values (run). In a real-world scenario, this is the same as the unit rate. In this context, the rise describes the change in the number of home runs hit in a single season, and the run describes the change in the number of hours a player spends in batting practice. Thus, the unit rate, or slope, represents the estimated increase (since the data trends upward) in the number of single-season home runs hit by a player for each hour he spends in batting practice, (D).

3. B   Difficulty: Easy

Category: Heart of Algebra / Linear Equations

Getting to the Answer: Finding an *x*-intercept is easy when you know the equation of the line—it's the value of *x* when *y* is 0. Notice that the answer choices are very close together. This means you shouldn't just estimate visually. Take the time to do the math. Everything you need to write the equation is shown on the graph—just pay careful attention to how the grid-lines are labeled. The *y*-intercept is 10 and the line rises 2 units and runs 1 unit from one point to the next, so the slope is $\frac{2}{1} = 2$. This means the equation of the line, in slope-intercept form, is $y = 2x + 10$. Now, set the equation equal to zero and solve for *x*:

$$0 = 2x + 10$$
$$-10 = 2x$$
$$-5 = x$$

The line will intersect the *x*-axis at −5, which is (B).

4. A   Difficulty: Easy

Category: Passport to Advanced Math / Functions

Getting to the Answer: When you see an expression like $f(x)$, it means to substitute the given value for *x* in the function's equation. When there is more than one function involved, pay careful attention to which function should be evaluated first. You are looking for the value of $f(x)$ at $x = 5$. Because $f(x)$ is defined in terms of $g(x)$, evaluate $g(5)$ first by substituting 5 for *x* in the expression $x + 2$.

$$g(5) = 5 + 2 = 7$$
$$f(5) = -3g(5) = -3(7) = -21$$

This means (A) is correct.

5. B   Difficulty: Medium

Category: Heart of Algebra / Linear Equations

Getting to the Answer: Write an equation in words first, and then translate from English into math. Keep in mind that the laundry detergent is on sale, but

the dog food is not. The detergent is 30% off, which means Sara only pays $100 - 30 = 70\%$ of the price, or $0.7(\$8) = \$5.60$. The dog food is three cans for $4 and she buys 12 cans, which means she buys 4 sets of 3, so she pays $4 \times \$4 = \$16$ for the dog food. The total cost equals the detergent price ($5.60) times how many she buys (*x*) plus the total dog food price ($16). This translates as $C = 5.6x + 16$, which matches (B). Note that there are variables in the answer choices, so you could also use the Picking Numbers strategy to answer this question.

6. B   Difficulty: Medium

Category: Heart of Algebra / Linear Equations

Getting to the Answer: The cost per night in the hospital is the same as the unit rate, which is represented by the slope of the line. Use the grid-lines and the axis labels to count the rise and the run from the *y*-intercept of the line (0, 26,000) to the next point that hits an intersection of two grid-lines, (2, 34,000). Pay careful attention to how the grid-lines are marked (by 2s on the *x*-axis and by 2,000s on the *y*-axis). The line rises 8,000 units and runs 2 units, so the slope is $\frac{8,000}{2}$, which means it costs an average of $4,000 per night to stay in the hospital.

Note that you could also use the slope formula and the two points to find the slope:

$$\frac{34,000 - 26,000}{2 - 0} = \frac{8,000}{2} = 4,000$$

Choice (B) is correct.

7. D   Difficulty: Medium

Category: Problem Solving and Data Analysis / Scatterplots

Getting to the Answer: You aren't given much information to go on except the shape of the graph, so you'll need to think about what the shape means. Remember, linear functions increase at a constant rate, exponential functions increase at either an increasing or decreasing rate, gradually at first and then more quickly or vice versa, and quadratics and polynomials reverse direction one or more times. The graph begins by decreasing extremely quickly, but then it almost (but not quite) levels off. Therefore, it can't be linear and because it doesn't change direction, an exponential function, (D), would be the best model for the data.

8. A   Difficulty: Medium

Category: Problem Solving and Data Analysis / Statistics and Probability

Getting to the Answer: This is a science crossover question. Read the first three sentences quickly—they are simply describing the context. The second half of the paragraph poses the question, so read that more carefully. In the sample, 2,800 out of 3,200 acres were free of kudzu after applying the herbicide. This is $\frac{2,800}{3,200} = 0.875 = 87.5\%$ of the area. For the whole region, assuming the same general conditions, $0.875(30,000) = 26,250$ acres should be free of the kudzu. Be careful—this is not the answer. The question asks how much of the cropland would *still be covered* by kudzu, so subtract to get $30,000 - 26,250 = 3,750$ acres, (A).

9. B   Difficulty: Medium

Category: Passport to Advanced Math / Functions

Getting to the Answer: The notation $g(h(x))$ indicates a composition of two functions, which can be read "g of h of x." It means that the output when x is substituted in $h(x)$ becomes the input for $g(x)$. First, use the top and bottom rows of the table to find that $h(3)$ is 2. This is your new input. Now, use the top and middle rows of the table to find $g(2)$, which is -3, (B).

10. B   Difficulty: Medium

Category: Heart of Algebra / Linear Equations

Getting to the Answer: The key to answering this type of question is determining how many results fit in each category. Here, you need to know how many shots were 3-pointers and how many were 2-pointers. Mae-Ling successfully made 15 shots

total and s were 3-pointers, so the rest, or $15 - s$, must have been 2-pointers. Write the expression in words first: points per 3-pointers (3) times number of shots that were 3-pointers (s), plus points per regular goal (2) times number of regular goals ($15 - s$). Now, translate from English into math: $3s + 2(15 - s)$. This is not one of the answer choices, so simplify the expression by distributing the 2 and then combining like terms: $3s + 2(15 - s) = 3s + 30 - 2s = s + 30$. This matches (B).

11. A   Difficulty: Medium

Category: Problem Solving and Data Analysis / Rates, Ratios, Proportions, and Percentages

Getting to the Answer: Let the units in this question guide you to the answer. You can do one conversion at a time, or all of them at once. Just be sure to line up the units so they'll cancel correctly. The company uses 8 machines, each of which pumps at a rate of 37.5 gallons per minute, so the rate is actually $8 \times 37.5 = 300$ gallons per minute. Find the total number of gallons needed, and then use the rate to find the time.

$$2,500 \text{ bbl} \times \frac{42 \text{ gal}}{1 \text{ bbl}} \times \frac{1 \text{ min}}{300 \text{ gal}} = 350 \text{ min}$$

The answers are given in hours and minutes, so change 350 minutes to $350 \div 60 = 5.833$ hours, which is 5 hours and 50 minutes, (A).

12. C   Difficulty: Medium

Category: Problem Solving and Data Analysis / Functions

Getting to the Answer: Look for a pattern for the sales of each company. Then apply that pattern to see which one will sell more in the last month of the year. Writing a function that represents each pattern will also help, but you have to be careful that you evaluate the function at the correct input value. Company A's sales can be represented by a linear function because each month the company sells 92 more of the toy than the month before, which is a constant difference. The sales can be represented by the function $f(t) = 92t + 54$, where t is the number of months *after January*. December is 11 months (not 12) after January, so during the last month of the year Company A should sell $f(11) = 92(11) + 54 = 1,066$ of the toy. Company B's sales can be represented by an exponential function because the sales are doubling each month, which is a constant ratio (2 for doubling). The function is $g(t) = 15(2)^t$, where t is again the number of months *after January*. In December, Company B should sell $g(11) = 15(2)^{11} = 30,720$. This means that in December, Company B should sell $30,720 - 1,066 = 29,654$ more of the toy than Company A. Choice (C) is correct.

13. A   Difficulty: Medium

Category: Heart of Algebra / Inequalities

Getting to the Answer: Apply logic to this question first, and then algebra. The dot at the beginning of the shaded portion is an open dot, so -2 is not included in the solution set of the inequality. This means you can eliminate C and D because those symbols *would* include the endpoint. Don't immediately choose B just because the arrow is pointing to the right, which typically indicates *greater than*. When dealing with an inequality, if you multiply or divide by a negative number, you must flip the symbol, so the answer is not necessarily what you might think. Because you were able to eliminate two of the choices, the quickest approach is to pick one of the remaining symbols, plug it in, and see if it works. If it does, choose that answer. If it doesn't, then it must be the other symbol. Try (A):

$$5(x - 2) - 3x < 4x - 6$$
$$5x - 10 - 3x < 4x - 6$$
$$2x - 10 < 4x - 6$$
$$-2x < 4$$
$$x > -2$$

The resulting inequality, $x > -2$, means all the values on the number line greater than (or to the right of) -2, so the initial inequality symbol must have been $<$. Choice (A) is correct.

14. B   Difficulty: Easy

Category: Problem Solving and Data Analysis / Rates, Ratios, Proportions, and Percents

Getting to the Answer: When a question involves scale factors, set up a proportion and solve for the missing value.

$$\frac{1}{8} = \frac{x}{19.9}$$
$$8x = 19.9$$
$$x = 2.4875 \approx 2.5$$

Choice (B) is correct.

15. C   Difficulty: Easy

Category: Problem Solving and Data Analysis / Rates, Ratios, Proportions, and Percents

Getting to the Answer: Don't make this question harder than it actually is. You don't need to find the new scale factor. Instead, use the length that the student drew the femur and the actual length to set up and solve a new proportion.

$$\frac{\text{drawing of sternum}}{\text{actual sternum}} = \frac{\text{drawing of femur}}{\text{actual femur}}$$
$$\frac{x}{6.7} = \frac{3.5}{19.9}$$
$$23.45 = 19.9x$$
$$1.1783 = x$$
$$x \approx 1.2$$

Choice (C) is correct.

16. B   Difficulty: Medium

Category: Heart of Algebra / Linear Equations

Getting to the Answer: Given two points (even when the coordinates are variables), the slope of the line between the points can be found using the formula $m = \frac{y_2 - y_1}{x_2 - x_1}$. You are given a numerical value for the slope and a pair of ordered pairs that have variables in them. To find the value of c, plug the points into the slope formula, and then solve for c. Be careful of all the negative signs.

$$m = \frac{y_2 - y_1}{x_2 - x_1}$$

$$\frac{1}{2} = \frac{-8 - 2c}{-c - (4 - c)}$$

$$\frac{1}{2} = \frac{-8 - 2c}{-c - 4 + c}$$

$$\frac{1}{2} = \frac{-8 - 2c}{-4}$$

$$1(-4) = 2(-8 - 2c)$$

$$-4 = -16 - 4c$$

$$12 = -4c$$

$$-3 = c$$

Choice (B) is correct.

17. A   Difficulty: Medium

Category: Problem Solving and Data Analysis / Rates, Ratios, Proportions, and Percents

Getting to the Answer: Questions that involve distance, rate, and time can almost always be solved using the formula Distance = rate × time. Break the question into short steps (first part of trip, second part of trip). Start with the plane from DCA. Use the speed, or rate, of the plane, 338 mph, and its distance from London, 3,718 miles, to determine when it arrived. You don't know the time, so call it t.

$$\text{Distance} = \text{rate} \times \text{time}$$

$$3,718 = 338t$$

$$11 = t$$

It took the DCA flight 11 hours. Now determine how long it took the plane from MIA. You'll need to find the distance for each part of the trip—the question only tells you the total distance. Then, use the formula to find how long the plane flew at 596 mph and how long it flew at 447 mph.

First part of trip:	*Second part of trip:*
$\frac{2}{3} \times 4,470 = 2,980\,\text{mi}$	$\frac{1}{3} \times 4,470 = 1,490\,\text{mi}$
$2,980 = 596t$	$1,490 = 447t$
$5 = t$	$3.\overline{3} = t$

This means it took the MIA flight 5 hours + 3 hours, 20 minutes = 8 hours, 20 minutes. So, the plane from MIA arrived first. It arrived 11 hours − 8 hours, 20 minutes = 2 hours, 40 minutes before the plane from DCA, making (A) correct.

18. D   Difficulty: Medium

Category: Passport to Advanced Math / Quadratics

Getting to the Answer: The graph of every quadratic equation is a parabola, which may or may not cross the x-axis, depending on where its vertex is and which way it opens. When an equation has no solution, its graph does not cross the x-axis, so try to envision the graph of each of the answer choices (or you could graph each one in your graphing calculator, but this will probably take longer). Don't forget—if the equation is written in vertex form, $y = a(x − h)^2 + k$, then the vertex is (h, k) and the value of a tells you which way the parabola opens. When a quadratic equation is written in factored form, the factors tell you the x-intercepts, which means A and B (which are factored) must cross the x-axis, so eliminate them. Now, imagine the graph of the equation in C: The vertex is $(−1, 8)$ and a is negative, so the parabola opens downward and consequently must cross the x-axis. This means (D) must be correct. The vertex is also $(−1, 8)$, but a is positive, so the graph opens up and does not cross the x-axis.

19. D   Difficulty: Medium

Category: Problem Solving and Data Analysis / Statistics and Probability

Getting to the Answer: The two variables are certainly correlated—as one goes up, the other goes up. A linear regression model would fit the data fairly well, so you can eliminate C. The spending is graphed on the x-axis, so it is the independent variable and therefore does not depend on the GDP, graphed on the y-axis, so you can eliminate B as well. The data does show that as spending on students increases, so does the GDP, but this is simply correlation, not causation. Without additional data, no statements can be made about whether spending more on students is the reason for the increased GDP, so (D) is correct.

20. C   Difficulty: Easy

Category: Passport to Advanced Math / Exponents

Getting to the Answer: Focus on the question at the very end—it's just asking you to solve the equation for p_2. Multiply both sides by T_2 to get rid of the denominator on the right-hand side of the equation. Then divide by V_2 to isolate p_2.

$$\frac{p_1 V_1}{T_1} = \frac{p_2 V_2}{T_2}$$

$$\frac{p_1 V_1 T_2}{T_1} = p_2 V_2$$

$$\frac{p_1 V_1 T_2}{T_1 V_2} = p_2$$

Stop here! You cannot cancel the V's and T's because the subscripts indicate that they are not the same variable. In math, subscripts do not behave the same way superscripts (exponents) do. Choice (C) is correct.

21. C   Difficulty: Medium

Category: Problem Solving and Data Analysis / Rates, Ratios, Proportions, and Percents

Getting to the Answer: The factor-label method (cancelling units) is a great strategy for this question. You're starting with tons, so work from that unit, arranging conversions so that units cancel. To keep units straight, use an E for Earth, an M for Mars, and a J for Jupiter.

$$1.5\ \cancel{T} \times \frac{2{,}000\ \text{lb}\cancel{(E)}}{1\ \cancel{T}} \times \frac{0.377\ \text{lb(M)}}{1\ \text{lb}\cancel{(E)}} = 1{,}131\ \text{lb (M)}$$

$$1.5\ \cancel{T} \times \frac{2{,}000\ \text{lb}\cancel{(E)}}{1\ \cancel{T}} \times \frac{2.364\ \text{lb(J)}}{1\ \text{lb}\cancel{(E)}} = 7{,}092\ \text{lb(J)}$$

The object weighs 1,131 pounds on Mars and 7,092 pounds on Jupiter, so it weighs 7,092 − 1,131 = 5,961 more pounds on Jupiter, (C).

22. C   Difficulty: Medium

Category: Problem Solving and Data Analysis / Statistics and Probability

Getting to the Answer: Examine the shape of the data and familiarize yourself with the title and the axis labels on the graph. Data is *symmetric* if it is fairly evenly spread out, and it is *skewed* if it has a long tail on either side. Notice that the data is skewed to the right, so you can immediately eliminate A. Choices B, (C), and D all describe the data as skewed to the right, so you'll need to examine those statements more closely. For B, "adverse reactions" include the last four bars, which represent 89 + 41 + 22 + 8 = 160 participants total, which is not even close to 50% of 900, so eliminate B. Note that you don't need to add all the bar heights to find that there were 900 participants—the title of the graph tells you that. Now look at C—"failed to have adverse reactions" means "None" or "Mild" (the first three bars), which represent 900 − 160 = 740 of the 900 participants. 75% of 900 = 675, and 740 is more than 675, so (C) is correct. For D, the "None" column contains 320 participants, which does not equal approximately 50% of 900, so it too is incorrect.

23. C   Difficulty: Medium

Category: Heart of Algebra / Systems of Linear Equations

Getting to the Answer: Use the Kaplan Method for Translating English into Math. Write a system of equations with p = the cost in dollars of the Pennsylvania bar exam and d = the cost of the D.C. bar exam. The Pennsylvania bar exam (p) costs $25 less ($-25$) than 3 times as much ($3d$) as the D.C. bar exam, or $p = 3d - 25$. Together, both bar exams cost $775, so $d + p = 775$. The system is:

$$\begin{cases} p = 3d - 25 \\ d + p = 775 \end{cases}$$

The top equation is already solved for p, so substitute $3d - 25$ into the second equation for p, and solve for d:

$$d + (3d - 25) = 775$$
$$4d = 800$$
$$d = 200$$

Be careful—that's not the answer. The D.C. bar exam costs $200, which means the Pennsylvania bar exam costs $775 − $200 = $575. This means the D.C. bar exam is $575 − $200 = $375 less expensive than the Pennsylvania bar exam. Choice (C) is correct.

24. B **Difficulty:** Medium

Category: Additional Topics in Math / Geometry

Getting to the Answer: The formula for finding the volume of a cylinder is $V = \pi r^2 h$. Leaving the top 5% of the silo empty is another way of saying that the silo should only be filled to 95% of its total height, so multiply the height (60 feet) by 0.95 to get 57 feet and then find the volume. Don't forget to divide the width of the silo (20 feet) by 2 to find the radius:

$$V = \pi r^2 h$$
$$V = \pi (10)^2 (57)$$
$$V = \pi (100)(57)$$
$$V = 5,700\pi$$

Choice (B) is correct.

25. B **Difficulty:** Medium

Category: Problem Solving and Data Analysis / Statistics and Probability

Getting to the Answer: Always read the axis labels carefully when a question involves a chart or graph. *Frequency*, which is plotted along the vertical axis, tells you how many students missed the number of questions indicated under each bar. Evaluate each statement as quickly as you can.

Choice A: Add the bar heights (frequencies) that represent students that missed 5 or more questions: $7 + 3 + 3 + 2 = 15$. Then, find the total number of students represented, which is the number that missed less than 5 questions plus the 15 you just found: $2 + 3 + 4 + 6 = 15$, plus the 15 you already found, for a total of 30 students. The statement is

not true because 15 is exactly half (not more than half) of 30.

Choice (B): This calculation will take a bit of time so skip it for now.

Choice C: The tallest bar tells you which number of questions was missed most often, which was 5 questions, not 3 questions, so this statement is not true.

Choice D: The number of students from Mr. Juno's class who took the test that day is the sum of the heights of the bars, which you already know is 30, not 36.

This means (B) must be correct. Mark it and move on to the next question. (In case you're curious, find the mean by multiplying each number of questions missed by the corresponding frequency, adding all the products, and dividing by the total number of students, which you already know is 30:

$$\text{mean} = \frac{2 + 6 + 12 + 24 + 35 + 18 + 21 + 16}{30}$$
$$= \frac{134}{30} = 4.4\overline{6}$$

The mean is indeed between 4 and 5.)

26. C **Difficulty:** Hard

Category: Passport to Advanced Math / Quadratics

Getting to the Answer: Writing quadratic equations can be tricky and time-consuming. If you know the roots, you can use factors to write the equation. If you don't know the roots, you need to create a system of equations to find the coefficients of the variable terms. You don't know the roots of this equation, so start with the point that has the nicest values (0, 2) and substitute them into the equation, $y = ax^2 + bx + c$, to get $2 = a(0)^2 + b(0) + c$, or $2 = c$. Now your equation looks like $y = ax^2 + bx + 2$. Next, use the other two points to create a system of two equations in two variables.

$$(-6, -7) \rightarrow -7 = a(-6)^2 + b(-6) + 2 \rightarrow -9 = 36a - 6b$$

$$(8, -14) \rightarrow -14 = a(8)^2 + b(8) + 2 \rightarrow -16 = 64a + 8b$$

You now have a system of equations to solve. If you multiply the top equation by 4 and the bottom equation by 3, and then add the equations, the b terms will eliminate each other.

$$4[-9 = 36a - 6b] \rightarrow -36 = 144a - 24b$$
$$3[-16 = 64a + 8b] \rightarrow \underline{-48 = 192a + 24b}$$
$$-84 = 336a$$
$$-0.25 = a$$

Now, find b by substituting $a = -0.25$ into either of the original equations. Using the top equation, you get:

$$-9 = 36(-0.25) - 6b$$
$$-9 = -9 - 6b$$
$$0 = 6b$$
$$0 = b$$

The value of $a + b + c$ is $(-0.25) + 0 + 2 = 1.75$, (C).

27. D   Difficulty: Hard

Category: Problem Solving and Data Analysis / Rates, Ratios, Proportions, and Percentages

Getting to the Answer: Read the question, organizing important information as you go. You need to find the ratio of mini muffins to jumbo muffins. You're given two ratios: mini to regular and regular to jumbo. Both of the given ratios contain regular muffin size units, but the regular amounts (2 and 5) are not identical. To directly compare them, find a common multiple (10). Multiply each ratio by the factor that will make the number of regular muffins equal to 10.

Mini to regular: $(5:2) \times (5:5) = 25:10$

Regular to jumbo: $(5:4) \times (2:2) = 10:8$

Now that the number of regular muffins is the same in both ratios (10), you can merge the two ratios to compare mini to jumbo directly: 25:10:8. So, the proper ratio of mini muffins to jumbo muffins is 25:8, which is (D).

28. A   Difficulty: Medium

Category: Heart of Algebra / Systems of Linear Equations

Getting to the Answer: Graphically, a system of linear equations that has no solution indicates two parallel lines, or in other words, two lines that have the same slope. So, write each of the equations in slope-intercept form ($y = mx + b$) and set their slopes (m) equal to each other to solve for k. Before finding the slopes, multiply the top equation by 6 to make it easier to manipulate.

$$6\left(\frac{1}{3}x + \frac{1}{2}y = 5\right) \rightarrow 2x + 3y = 30 \rightarrow y = -\frac{2}{3}x + 10$$

$$kx - 4y = 16 \rightarrow -4y = -kx + 16 \rightarrow y = \frac{k}{4}x - 4$$

The slope of the first line is $-\frac{2}{3}$, and the slope of the second line is $\frac{k}{4}$. Set them equal and solve for k:

$$-\frac{2}{3} = \frac{k}{4}$$
$$-8 = 3k$$
$$-\frac{8}{3} = k$$

Choice (A) is correct.

29. D   Difficulty: Hard

Category: Passport to Advanced Math / Exponents

Getting to the Answer: The numbers in some questions are simply too large to use a calculator (you get an "overflow" error message). Instead, you'll have to rely on rules of exponents. Notice that all of the base numbers have 3 as a factor, so rewrite everything in terms of 3. This will allow you to use the rules of exponents. Because 27 is the cube of 3, you can rewrite 27^{90} as a power of 3.

$$27^{90} = \left(3^3\right)^{90}$$
$$= 3^{3 \times 90}$$
$$= 3^{270}$$

Now the product should read: $3^{90} \times 3^{270}$, which is equal to $3^{90 + 270} = 3^{360}$. Repeat this process for the quantity that is being divided:

$$\left(\frac{1}{9}\right)^{30} = \left(\frac{1}{3^2}\right)^{30} = \left(3^{-2}\right)^{30} = 3^{-60}$$

Finally, use rules of exponents one more time to simplify the new expression:

$$\frac{3^{360}}{3^{-60}} = 3^{360 + 60} = 3^{420}$$

All the answer choices are given as powers of 9, so rewrite your answer as a power of 9:

$$3^{420} = 3^{2 \times 210} = \left(3^2\right)^{210} = 9^{210}$$

Choice (D) is correct.

30. D   Difficulty: Hard

Category: Additional Topics in Math / Geometry

Getting to the Answer: If needed, don't forget to check the formulas provided for you at the beginning of each math section. The volume of a right cone is given by $V = \frac{1}{3}\pi r^2 h$. Here, you only know the value of one of the variables, V, so you'll need to use the information in the question to somehow write r and h in terms of just one variable. If the cone is three times as wide at the base as it is tall, then call the diameter $3x$ and the height of the cone one-third of that, or x. The volume formula calls for the radius, which is half the diameter, or $\frac{3x}{2}$. Substitute these values into the formula and solve for x:

$$V = \frac{1}{3}\pi r^2 h$$

$$384\pi = \frac{1}{3}\pi \left(\frac{3}{2}x\right)^2 x$$

$$384 = \left(\frac{1}{3}\right)\left(\frac{9}{4}x^2\right)x$$

$$384 = \frac{3}{4}x^3$$

$$512 = x^3$$

$$\sqrt[3]{512} = x$$

$$8 = x$$

The question asks for the diameter of the base, which is $3x = 3(8) = 24$, choice (D).

31. 1/4 or .25   Difficulty: Medium

Category: Heart of Algebra / Inequalities

Getting to the Answer: The question is asking about $\frac{m}{n}$, so think about how fractions work. Large numerators result in larger values ($\frac{3}{2}$, for example, is larger than $\frac{1}{2}$), and smaller denominators result in larger values ($\frac{1}{2}$, for example, is greater than $\frac{1}{4}$). The largest possible value of $\frac{m}{n}$ is found by choosing the largest possible value of m and the smallest possible value for n: $\frac{0.4}{1.6} = \frac{1}{4} = 0.25$.

32. 6   Difficulty: Medium

Category: Passport to Advanced Math / Functions

Getting to the Answer: The notation $(f - g)(3)$ means $f(3) - g(3)$. You don't know the equations of the functions, so you'll need to read the values from the graph. Graphically, $f(3)$ means the y-value at $x = 3$ on the graph of f, which is 2. Likewise, $g(3)$ means the y-value at $x = 3$ on the graph of g, which is -4. The difference, $f - g$, is $2 - (-4) = 6$.

33. 85   Difficulty: Easy

Category: Problem Solving and Data Analysis / Scatterplots

Getting to the Answer: The *range* of a set of data points is the set of outputs, which correspond to the y-values of the data points on the graph. To find the maximum value in the range of the data, look for the highest point on the graph, which is (250, 85). The y-value is 85, so 85 is the maximum value in the range.

34. 1/16   Difficulty: Medium

Category: Problem Solving and Data Analysis / Statistics and Probability

Getting to the Answer: The probability that the same event (the employee has been there longer than 3 years) will occur 4 times can be found by finding the probability that the event will occur once and then multiplying it by itself 4 times. First, find the probability that if an employee is chosen at random, it will be one who has been with the company for longer than 3 years. The total number of employees who participated in the study is $38 + 30 + 15 + 19 + 54 + 48 = 204$. The total number of both females and males who have been with the company longer (greater) than 3 years is $54 + 48 = 102$. Therefore, the probability of choosing one employee who has been with the company longer than 3 years is: $\frac{102}{204} = \frac{1}{2}$. This means the probability that all 4 employees would have been with the company longer than 3 years is $\frac{1}{2} \times \frac{1}{2} \times \frac{1}{2} \times \frac{1}{2} = \frac{1}{16}$.

35. 102   Difficulty: Medium

Category: Additional Topics in Math / Geometry

Getting to the Answer: The distance around part of a circle is the same as arc length, so use the relationship $\frac{\text{arc length}}{\text{circumference}} = \frac{\text{central angle}}{360°}$ to answer the question. The unknown in the relationship is the central angle, so call it A. Before you can fill in the rest of the equation, you need to find the circumference of the circle: $C = 2\pi r = 2\pi(840) = 1,680\pi$. Now you're ready to solve for A:

$$\frac{\text{arc length}}{\text{circumference}} = \frac{\text{central angle}}{360°}$$

$$\frac{1,500}{1,680\pi} = \frac{A}{360}$$

$$\frac{1,500 \times 360}{1,680\pi} = A$$

$$102.314 \approx A$$

Be careful when you enter this expression into your calculator—you need to put $1,680\pi$ in parentheses so that the calculator doesn't divide by 1,680 and then multiply by π. If entered correctly, the result is about 102 degrees.

36. 7   Difficulty: Hard

Category: Heart of Algebra / Linear Equations

Getting to the Answer: To write the equation of a line, you need two things: the slope and the y-intercept. Start by finding these, substituting them into slope-intercept form of a line ($y = mx + b$), and then manipulate the equation so that it is written in standard form. Use the given points, $(-4, 1)$ and $(3, -2)$, and the slope formula to find m:

$$m = \frac{y_2 - y_1}{x_2 - x_1} = \frac{-2 - 1}{3 - (-4)} = -\frac{3}{7}$$

Next, find the y-intercept, b, using the slope and one of the points:

$$y = -\frac{3}{7}x + b$$

$$1 = -\frac{3}{7}(-4) + b$$

$$1 = \frac{12}{7} + b$$

$$-\frac{5}{7} = b$$

Write the equation in slope-intercept form: $y = -\frac{3}{7}x - \frac{5}{7}$.

Now, rewrite the equation in the form $Ax + By = C$, making sure that A is a positive integer (a whole number greater than 0):

$$y = -\frac{3}{7}x - \frac{5}{7}$$

$$\frac{3}{7}x + y = -\frac{5}{7}$$

$$7\left(\frac{3}{7}x + y = -\frac{5}{7}\right)7$$

$$3x + 7y = -5$$

The question asks for the value of B (the coefficient of y), so the correct answer is 7.

37. 380   Difficulty: Medium

Category: Problem Solving and Data Analysis / Rates, Ratios, Proportions, and Percents

Getting to the Answer: You can use the formula Percent × whole = part to solve this problem, but you will first need to think conceptually about what the question is asking. The question is asking for the Dow value *before* the 19.5% decrease to 306. This means that 306 represents 100 − 19.5 = 80.5% of what the stock market was at its record high. Fill these amounts into the equation and solve for the original whole, the record high Dow value.

$$0.805 \times w = 306$$
$$w = \frac{306}{0.805}$$
$$w = 380.124$$

Rounded to the nearest whole point, the record high was approximately 380 points.

38. 25   Difficulty: Hard

Category: Problem Solving and Data Analysis / Rates, Ratios, Proportions, and Percents

Getting to the Answer: Percent change is given by the ratio $\frac{\text{amount of change}}{\text{original amount}}$. To find the total percent change, you'll need to work your way through each of the days, and then use the ratio. Jot down the Dow value at the end of each day as you go. Do not round until you reach your final answer. First, calculate the value of the Dow at closing on Black Thursday: It opened at 306 and decreased by 2%, which means the value at the end of the day was 100 − 2 = 98% of the starting amount, or 306 × 0.98 = 299.88. Then, it decreased again on Monday by 13% to close at 100 − 13 = 87% of the opening amount, or 299.88 × 0.87 = 260.8956. Finally, it decreased on Tuesday by another 12% to end at 100 − 12 = 88% of the starting amount, or 260.8956 × 0.88 = 229.588. Now use the percent change formula to calculate the percent decrease from opening on Black Thursday (306) to closing on Black Tuesday (229.588):

$$\text{Percent decrease} = \frac{306 - 229.588}{306}$$
$$= \frac{76.412}{306} = 0.2497$$

The Dow had a total percent decrease of approximately 25% between opening on Black Thursday and closing on Black Tuesday.

ESSAY TEST RUBRIC

The Essay Demonstrates ...

4—Advanced	• **(Reading)** A strong ability to comprehend the source text, including its central ideas and important details and how they interrelate; and effectively use evidence (quotations, paraphrases, or both) from the source text.
	• **(Analysis)** A strong ability to evaluate the author's use of evidence, reasoning, and/or stylistic and persuasive elements, and/or other features of the student's own choosing; make good use of relevant, sufficient, and strategically chosen support for the claims or points made in the student's essay; and focus consistently on features of the source text that are most relevant to addressing the task.
	• **(Writing)** A strong ability to provide a precise central claim; create an effective organization that includes an introduction and conclusion, as well as a clear progression of ideas; successfully employ a variety of sentence structures; use precise word choice; maintain a formal style and objective tone; and show command of the conventions of standard written English so that the essay is free of errors.
3—Proficient	• **(Reading)** Satisfactory ability to comprehend the source text, including its central ideas and important details and how they interrelate; and use evidence (quotations, paraphrases, or both) from the source text.
	• **(Analysis)** Satisfactory ability to evaluate the author's use of evidence, reasoning, and/or stylistic and persuasive elements, and/or other features of the student's own choosing; make use of relevant and sufficient support for the claims or points made in the student's essay; and focus primarily on features of the source text that are most relevant to addressing the task.
	• **(Writing)** Satisfactory ability to provide a central claim; create an organization that includes an introduction and conclusion, as well as a clear progression of ideas; employ a variety of sentence structures; use precise word choice; maintain an appropriate formal style and objective tone; and show control of the conventions of standard written English so that the essay is free of significant errors.
2—Partial	• **(Reading)** Limited ability to comprehend the source text, including its central ideas and important details and how they interrelate; and use evidence (quotations, paraphrases, or both) from the source text.
	• **(Analysis)** Limited ability to evaluate the author's use of evidence, reasoning, and/or stylistic and persuasive elements, and/or other features of the student's own choosing; make use of support for the claims or points made in the student's essay; and focus on relevant features of the source text.
	• **(Writing)** Limited ability to provide a central claim; create an effective organization for ideas; employ a variety of sentence structures; use precise word choice; maintain an appropriate style and tone; or show command of the conventions of standard written English, resulting in certain errors that detract from the quality of the writing.

1—Inadequate	• **(Reading)** Little or no ability to comprehend the source text or use evidence from the source text.
	• **(Analysis)** Little or no ability to evaluate the author's use of evidence, reasoning, and/or stylistic and persuasive elements; choose support for claims or points; or focus on relevant features of the source text.
	• **(Writing)** Little or no ability to provide a central claim, organization, or progression of ideas; employ a variety of sentence structures; use precise word choice; maintain an appropriate style and tone; or show command of the conventions of standard written English, resulting in numerous errors that undermine the quality of the writing.

ESSAY RESPONSE #1 (ADVANCED SCORE)

In his speech to the National Union of South African Students in 1966, Robert F. Kennedy makes the claim that the guiding principle of Western societies must be the enhancement of liberty for all individuals. Through appeals to Western values, references to historical evidence, and calls to conscience, Kennedy constructs a powerful and effective argument.

Kennedy begins his speech by praising the core values of Western society—freedom and democracy, and the rights associated with them. In so doing, he both establishes common ground with his South African audience, who viewed themselves as part of Western society, and also highlights the ways in which the repressive government of South Africa in 1966 failed to uphold these values. To Kennedy, the freedom of speech is not merely the right to say whatever one chooses, rather, it allows us to speak up to our governments when they are derelict in their duties, and is a key part of what it means to be an active member of society. Kennedy also insists that the right of individuals to be heard by their government is essential to democracy, because it forces government officials to answer to the people who elected them. Frequently, Kennedy uses heightened language to describe these rights and values, which deepens the impact of his message. The freedom of speech separates us from the "dumb beasts of field and forest." The power to be heard allows people a voice in the decisions that "shape men's lives." Most powerfully, Kennedy states that these rights are "sacred." This kind of elevated language imparts a weight to Kennedy's argument that ordinary language could not.

Kennedy also makes references to historical and current events to bolster his claims. He asserts that the rights he describes are what separate democratic societies from Nazi Germany and Persia, countries known to be extremely repressive. This reference to brutal regimes strengthens his claim that these rights should be the guiding principle of any decent society. He also uses the United States as a model of a society that has been striving for the expansion of liberty and, while failing in some respects, is succeeding overall. Kennedy's father, he says, was barred from many jobs as a young man due to his Irish background, yet several decades later, his son John F. Kennedy became president, proving that conditions can change for the better. Robert Kennedy acknowledges that the United States still has far to go, just like South Africa, yet he cites examples of major progress, such as an African American astronaut and an African American chief justice, as well as Martin Luther King, Jr., who won the Nobel Peace Prize. Kennedy's implication is that the ideals of liberty and justice are worth upholding because they can make a society greater and more inclusive.

Another way Kennedy persuades his audience of the validity of his argument is by making calls to conscience. He states that the most important reason to grant freedom to all is because "it is the right thing to do." He reasons that feelings of compassion are common to all people, as are feelings of outrage when other human beings suffer;

therefore, we should all join together in expanding human rights and lessening the suffering of people everywhere. By calling upon his audience's basic sense of right and wrong, Kennedy gives them a personal lens through which to examine his argument, thus making them more likely to embrace its validity.

Robert F. Kennedy passionately believed in the necessity for all Western societies to make the expansion of liberty their guiding principle. To build and support his argument, Kennedy exalts Western values of democracy and freedom, refers to historical examples in which the promotion of liberty made for a better society, and finally calls upon people's conscience to help them see that the expansion of freedom for all is the right thing to do.

ESSAY RESPONSE #2 (PROFICIENT SCORE)

Robert F. Kennedy's central claim in his speech to the National Union of South African Students is that the guiding principle of Western societies should be the expansion of liberty for all individuals. Kennedy uses several techniques to build his argument, including heightened language, examples of countries that have been improved by the expansion of liberty, and appeals to his audience's sense of right and wrong.

Kennedy was not an ordinary man, nor was he an ordinary writer. His speech contains soaring language that makes his audience feel like they are listening to great literature. When he says that the freedom of speech is what seperates us from "dumb beasts," his vivid language makes that freedom seem even more important. He makes frequent references to God, even calling rights of Western society "sacred." And instead of merely saying that young people must stop racism and injustice, he says that it's there responsibility to "strip the last remnants of that ancient, cruel belief from the civilization of man." This type of language makes the audience feel that they are being called to a higher purpose.

Kennedy also provides examples of ways in which countries that promote liberty fare better than countries that don't. When he contrasts Western societies that value freedom with societies that don't—like Nazi Germany and Persia—he is suggesting that countries that deny people their basic rights eventually fail (in 1966, Nazi Germany and Persia no longer existed, but Western democracies still did). Kennedy then uses America as an example of a country that has been improved by expanding liberties for individuals. He tells a personal anecdote about the prejudice experienced by his Irish father, and acknowledges that the struggle to overcome discrimination can take many years. However he provides evidence that the struggle is worth it as shown by his brother's success in becoming president of the United States, and by the African Americans who at that point had risen to the highest ranks of American society—an astronaut, barristers, and a Nobel Prize winner, Martin Luther King, Jr. These examples support Kennedy's claim that enlarging the liberties of individuals is a worthy goal for Western societies.

Finally, Kennedy appeals to his audience's fundamental sense of right and wrong. He says that expanding liberty is "the right thing to do" and that God commands it. He lists multiple examples of evil in the world—"discrimination in New York, apartheid in South Africa . . ."—and tells his audience of students that they must answer the call to eliminate the suffering of others everywhere in the world. He states that evil is common, therefore it can only be cured by other qualities we all share in common, such as our conscience and determination to make the world a better place.

The argument Kennedy makes in this speech is strengthened by his use of the features mentioned above: heightened language, evidence, and appeals to his audience's sense of what is right and what is wrong.

PART SIX

Answers & Explanations

CHAPTER 2

PRACTICE

8. D   **Difficulty:** Hard
Category: Heart of Algebra / Linear Equations

Getting to the Answer: Pay attention to the order in which the changes to the graph occur. The question states that the downward shift of 2 units occurs first, making the new y-intercept $-\frac{3}{2}$. A reflection over the x-axis follows, which changes the y-intercept to $\frac{3}{2}$ and makes the slope $\frac{7}{4}$. The only graph that correctly depicts these changes is (D). Beware of C; this results from a reflection over the y-axis, not the x-axis. The graphs below visualize each change.

1)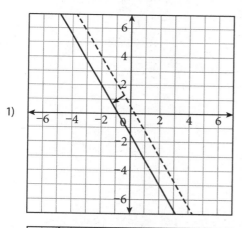

2)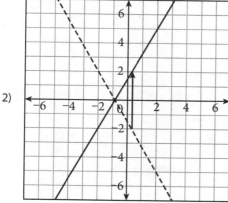

9. C   **Difficulty:** Medium
Category: Heart of Algebra / Linear Equations

Getting to the Answer: Look closely; buried in the text are two sets of coordinates you can use. The question states that admission was $2 when the admission charge was first implemented and increased to $2.50 after 3 years, making your coordinates (0, 2) and (3, 2.5). The slope of the line passing through these is $m = \frac{2.5 - 2}{3 - 0} = \frac{0.5}{3} = \frac{1}{6}$. Eliminate A and D. Because the admission fee started at $2, 2 is the y-intercept, so the full equation is $y = \frac{c}{6} + 2$. Choice (C) is correct.

Because the question says "three years ago," it may be tempting to use $(-3, 2)$ and $(0, 2.5)$ as your coordinates. Think about what that would mean: The first admission charge would be $2.50, as it's impossible to have a negative year. This contradicts the question stem, so B is incorrect.

PERFORM

10. A   **Difficulty:** Easy
Category: Heart of Algebra / Linear Equations

Getting to the Answer: Think about what happens to the slope of a line if you're merely moving the line around the coordinate plane. Any shift of a line, whether it's up, down, left, right, or some combination of these, will not change the line's slope. The slope of the given line is -5 (the coefficient of x), and the slope does not change, so (A) is correct.

11. 36   **Difficulty:** Medium
Category: Heart of Algebra / Linear Equations

Getting to the Answer: That you're asked to find an expression rather than a variable value means there's likely a shortcut. Start by eliminating the fractions. A common multiple of 4 and 3 is 12, so multiply both sides of the equation by that. Once the fractions are gone, move both variable terms to the left side and try to make it look like the desired expression.

$$12\left(\frac{3}{4}y = 6 - \frac{1}{3}c\right)$$
$$9y = 72 - 4c$$
$$4c + 9y = 72$$
$$2c + \frac{9}{2}y = 36$$

The expression on the left side is precisely what you're looking for, so grid in 36.

12. A   Difficulty: Hard

Category: Heart of Algebra / Linear Equations

Getting to the Answer: Don't panic over the presence of *m*. Just solve for *y*, then think about what kind of graph it can have. Start by distributing *m* on the right, then move all terms to the left:

$$x - y = m(2x + y)$$
$$x - y = 2mx + my$$
$$x - 2mx - y - my = 0$$

Continue by factoring out *x* and *y*, then move any terms without *y* back to the right:

$$x(1 - 2m) + y(-1 - m) = 0$$
$$y(-1 - m) = -x(1 - 2m)$$

Divide by $(-1 - m)$, then factor out -1 from the denominator and cancel:

$$y = \frac{-x(1 - 2m)}{(-1 - m)} = \frac{-x(1 - 2m)}{-(1 + m)} = \frac{1 - 2m}{1 + m}x$$

Don't worry about how messy the right side looks yet; for now, you just need to realize that it's merely *x* multiplied by a complicated coefficient. Because the equation is now solved for *y*, you have an equation of a line. The messy coefficient is the slope, and because there's no added (or subtracted) constant, the *y*-intercept is 0. You can eliminate B (not a line) and D ($b \neq 0$) based on this.

Examine the remaining choices more closely: They only differ by the sign of their slope. To determine which is correct, pick a value for *m* between 0 and $\frac{1}{2}$ (but not 0 or $\frac{1}{2}$ themselves), and plug it into the slope expression.

If $m = \frac{1}{4}$, for instance, then the slope would be:

$$\frac{\left(1 - 2 \times \frac{1}{4}\right)}{\left(1 + \frac{1}{4}\right)} = \frac{\left(1 - \frac{1}{2}\right)}{\frac{5}{4}} = \frac{1}{2} \times \frac{4}{5} = \frac{2}{5}$$

Because the slope of this line is positive, (A), which is the only remaining choice with a positive slope, is correct.

EXTRA PRACTICE

1. C   Difficulty: Easy

Category: Heart of Algebra / Linear Equations

Getting to the Answer: Don't let this fairly simple question fool you. Just because 5 and −5 are opposites, this does not mean the value on the right-hand side of the equal sign will be the opposite of 11. Solve for *x*, then substitute that value into the second equation for *x* and simplify.

$$2x + 5 = 11$$
$$2x = 6$$
$$x = 3$$

$$2x - 5 = 2(3) - 5$$
$$= 6 - 5$$
$$= 1$$

Therefore, (C) is correct.

A quicker approach would be to recognize that $2x - 5$ is 10 less than $2x + 5$, so you could find the answer by subtracting 10 from 11. However, this only works when the variable terms are identical.

2. B   Difficulty: Easy

Category: Heart of Algebra / Linear Equations

Getting to the Answer: The *x*-axis represents the number of lightbulbs, so find 1 on the *x*-axis and trace up to where it meets the graph of the line. The *y*-value is somewhere between $1 and $2, so the only possible correct answer choice is $1.80.

You could also find the unit rate by calculating the slope of the line using two of the points shown on the graph: The graph rises 9 units and runs 5 units from one point to the next, so the slope is $\frac{9}{5}$, or 1.80, which means (B) is correct.

3. D **Difficulty:** Medium

Category: Heart of Algebra / Linear Equations

Getting to the Answer: Use the information in the question to write your own expression, and then look for the answer choice that matches. Simplify your expression only if you don't find a match. If a couple earns $50 *per half-hour* that they dance, then they earn $50 \times 2 = $100 *per hour*. Multiply this amount times the number of hours (not including the first 3 hours). This can be expressed as $100(h - 3)$. This is not one of the answer choices, so simplify by distributing to get $100h - 300$, which is (D).

If you're struggling with the algebra, try Picking Numbers. Pick a number of hours a couple might dance, like 5. They don't earn anything for the first 3 hours, but they earn $50 per half-hour for the last 2 hours, which is 50 times 4 half-hours, or $200. Now, find the expression that gives you an answer of $200 when $h = 5$ hours: $100(5) - 300 = 500 - 300 = 200$.

4. D **Difficulty:** Medium

Category: Heart of Algebra / Linear Equations

Getting to the Answer: Take a quick peek at the answer choices. The equations are given in slope-intercept form, so start by finding the slope. Substitute two pairs of values from the table (try to pick easy ones if possible) into the slope formula, $m = \dfrac{y_2 - y_1}{x_2 - x_1}$. Keep in mind that the projected number of pounds sold *depends* on the price, so the price is the independent variable (x) and the projected number is the dependent variable (y). Using the points (1.2, 15,000) and (2, 5,000), the slope is:

$$m = \frac{5,000 - 15,000}{2 - 1.20}$$
$$m = \frac{-10,000}{0.8}$$
$$m = -12,500$$

This means you can eliminate A and B because the slope is not correct. Don't let B fool you—the projected number of pounds sold goes *down* as the price goes *up*, so there is an inverse relationship, which means the slope must be negative. To choose between C and (D), you could find the y-intercept of the line, but this is a fairly time-intensive

process. Instead, choose the easiest pair of values from the table, (2, 5,000), and substitute into C and (D) only. Choice (D) is correct because $5,000 = -12,500(2) + 30,000$ is a true statement.

5. D **Difficulty:** Hard

Category: Heart of Algebra / Linear Equations

Getting to the Answer: If a linear equation has infinitely many solutions, the variable terms will cancel out, leaving a number that is equal to itself (which is always true). Start by simplifying both sides of the equation using the distributive property.

$$2\left(x - \frac{5}{2}\right) = c\left(\frac{4}{5}x - 2\right)$$
$$2x - 5 = \frac{4c}{5}x - 2c$$

Because the constant terms must be equal, set $-5 = -2c$ and solve for c to get $c = \dfrac{5}{2}$, which means (D) is correct. Note that you could also set the variable terms equal to each other and solve for c, but the manipulations would be more difficult.

6. C **Difficulty:** Hard

Category: Heart of Algebra / Linear Equations

Getting to the Answer: As written, the equation doesn't tell you a lot about the graph, but you should notice that there are no exponents on the variables, which means the exponents are all equal to 1. This means the equation is linear and the graph must be a line, so you can eliminate D right away (it is an absolute value equation, not a linear equation). To choose the correct line, rearrange the equation so that it is in slope-intercept form, $y = mx + b$. To do this, first collect the y-terms on the left side of the equation. Rearranging the equation results in the following:

$$y = ay + ax + x + 1$$
$$y - ay = ax + x + 1$$
$$y(1 - a) = x(a + 1) + 1$$
$$y = \frac{a + 1}{1 - a}x + \frac{1}{1 - a}$$

This manipulation reveals a linear equation with a slope of $\dfrac{a + 1}{1 - a}$ and a y-intercept of $\dfrac{1}{1 - a}$. It is given in the question that $a > 1$, so the quantity $a + 1$ is positive, and 1 − *a* is negative, resulting in a negative slope and a negative *y*-intercept. Of the choices given, only the graph in (C) satisfies these conditions.

7. 18   Difficulty: Easy

Category: Heart of Algebra / Linear Equations

Getting to the Answer: Clear the fractions first by multiplying both sides of the equation by 8. Then solve for *x* using inverse operations:

$$\frac{7}{8}(n-6) = \frac{21}{2}$$

$$8\left[\frac{7}{8}(n-6)\right] = 8\left[\frac{21}{2}\right]$$

$$7(n-6) = 4(21)$$

$$7n - 42 = 84$$

$$7n = 126$$

$$n = 18$$

8. 70   Difficulty: Hard

Category: Heart of Algebra / Linear Equations

Getting to the Answer: Because 40 pounds is not shown on the graph, you need more information. In a real-world scenario, the *y*-intercept of a graph usually represents a flat fee or a starting amount. The slope of the line represents a unit rate, such as the cost per pound to airmail the box.

The *y*-intercept of the graph is 10, so the flat fee is $10. To find the cost per pound (the unit rate), substitute two points from the graph into the slope formula. Using the points (0, 10) and (4, 16), the cost per pound is $\frac{16-10}{4-0} = \frac{6}{4} = 1.5$, which means it costs $1.50 per pound to airmail a box. The total cost to airmail a 40-pound box is $10 + 1.50(40) = $10 + $60 = $70. Grid in 70.

9. C   Difficulty: Easy

Category: Heart of Algebra / Linear Equations

Getting to the Answer: Try to picture in your head what "increase in property values starts to slow down" would look like. It doesn't say the values start to decrease, but rather that the increase is not as fast.

An increasing line (one with a positive slope) indicates increasing property values. The steepness of the line (the actual *value* of the slope) indicates how fast the values

are increasing. The second line segment in the graph (between *t* = 8 and *t* = 16) still shows a positive slope, but one that is less steep than the first segment, so the increase in property values starts to slow down at *t* = 8, which is the year 2014 + 8 = 2022, (C).

10. B   Difficulty: Easy

Category: Heart of Algebra / Linear Equations

Getting to the Answer: Read the axis labels carefully. The *y*-intercept is the point at which *x* = 0, which means the number of songs purchased is 0. The *y*-intercept is (0, 20), so the cost is $20 before buying any songs, and therefore most likely represents a flat membership fee for joining the service. Choice (B) is correct.

11. C   Difficulty: Easy

Category: Heart of Algebra / Linear Equations

Getting to the Answer: When writing a linear equation to represent a real-world scenario, a flat rate is a constant while a unit rate is always multiplied by the independent variable. You can identify the unit rate by looking for words like *per* or *for each*.

Because the amount Andrew gets paid daily, $120, is a flat rate that doesn't depend on the number of cruises he books, 120 should be the constant in the equation. This means you can eliminate B and D. The clue "for each cruise" tells you to multiply $25 by the number of cruises he books (*c*), so the equation is *d* = 25*c* + 120, making (C) correct.

12. A   Difficulty: Medium

Category: Heart of Algebra / Linear Equations

Getting to the Answer: This question has multiple fractions, so clear the $\frac{8}{5}$ by multiplying both sides of the equation by its reciprocal, $\frac{5}{8}$. Then, because the answers are given in decimal form, change the other fraction to a decimal by dividing the numerator by the denominator.

$$\frac{8}{5}\left(x + \frac{33}{12}\right) = 16$$

$$\frac{5}{8} \times \left[\frac{8}{5}\left(x + \frac{33}{12}\right)\right] = \frac{5}{8} \times 16$$

$$x + 2.75 = 10$$

$$x = 7.25$$

Choice (A) is correct.

13. C   Difficulty: Medium

Category: Heart of Algebra / Linear Equations

Getting to the Answer: Because the equation represents the balance if Henry deposits his paycheck for x weeks, then his paycheck amount must be multiplied by the number of weeks he works. The only two factors in the equation being multiplied are 360 and x, so 360 must be the amount of his paycheck. This means you can eliminate A and D. The other number in the equation, -126.13, is a constant, which represents a starting amount. Because the constant is negative, Henry must have had a negative balance in his account before setting up the direct deposit, which means he had overdrawn the account. Thus, (C) is correct.

14. C   Difficulty: Medium

Category: Heart of Algebra / Linear Equations

Getting to the Answer: Use the graph to identify the y-intercept and the slope of the line, and then write an equation in slope-intercept form, $y = mx + b$. Once you have your equation, look for the answer choice that matches. The line crosses the y-axis at $(0, -4)$ so the y-intercept (b) is -4. The line rises 1 unit for every 3 units that it runs to the right, so the slope (m) is $\frac{1}{3}$. The equation of the line is $y = \frac{1}{3}x - 4$, which matches (C).

You could also graph each of the answer choices in your calculator to see which one matches the given graph, but this is not the most time-efficient strategy. You also have to be very careful when entering fractions—to graph (C), for example, you would enter $(1/3)x - 4$.

15. A   Difficulty: Hard

Category: Heart of Algebra / Linear Equations

Getting to the Answer: The question tells you that the functions are all linear, so start by finding the rate of change (the slope, m) using any two pairs of values from the table and the slope formula. Next, substitute the slope and any pair of values from the table, such as $(10, 34)$, into the equation $f(x) = mx + b$, and solve for b. Finally, use the value of m and b to write the function.

$$m = \frac{y_2 - y_1}{x_2 - x_1} = \frac{64 - 34}{30 - 10} = \frac{30}{20} = 1.5$$

You can stop right there! Only Choice (A) has a slope of 1.5, so it must be the correct answer.

16. C   Difficulty: Hard

Category: Heart of Algebra / Linear Equations

Getting to the Answer: Let v represent the number of visits. The question asks when the two memberships will cost the same, so write an equation that sets the total membership costs equal to each other. The first membership type costs \$325 for unlimited visits, so write 325 on one side of the equal sign. The second type costs \$8 per visit (not including the first 5 visits), or $8(v - 5)$, plus a flat \$125 enrollment fee, so write $8(v - 5) + 125$ on the other side of the equal sign. Solve for v:

$$325 = 8(v - 5) + 125$$
$$325 = 8v - 40 + 125$$
$$240 = 8v$$
$$30 = v$$

Choice (C) is correct.

17. D   Difficulty: Hard

Category: Heart of Algebra / Linear Equations

Getting to the Answer: If a linear equation has no solution, the variable terms will cancel out, leaving a false statement that consists of two numbers that are not equal to each other. First, check to see if the variables cancel out. In A and B, they don't, so eliminate these choices. To decide between C and (D), check the constant after both sides of the equation have been simplified. If the constants are equal, then the equation has an infinite number of solutions (because a number is always equal to itself). If they are not equal, then the equation has no solution. Choice (D) is correct because:

$$6\left(\frac{2}{3}x + 5\right) = 4x + 5$$
$$4x + 30 = 4x + 5$$
$$30 \neq 5$$

18. B   Difficulty: Hard

Category: Heart of Algebra / Linear Equations

Getting to the Answer: The key to answering this question is determining how many jumps land across each line. If Vera gets 7 jumps total and x jumps land over the farther line, the rest, or $7 - x$, must land over the closer line. Now, write the expression in words: points per farther line (10) times number of jumps landing over the farther line (x), plus points per closer line (5) times number of jumps landing over the closer line $(7 - x)$. Next, translate the words into numbers, variables, and operations: $10x + 5(7 - x)$. This is not one of the answer choices, so simplify the expression by distributing the 5 and then combining like terms: $10x + 5(7 - x) = 10x + 35 - 5x = 5x + 35$, so the function is $f(x) = 5x + 35$, making (B) correct.

19. D   Difficulty: Medium

Category: Heart of Algebra / Linear Equations

Getting to the Answer: Consider each choice systematically, using the numbers on the figure to help you evaluate each statement.

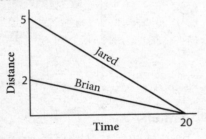

It took Brian and Jared each 20 minutes to bike home so A and B are false. Jared biked 5 miles in 20 minutes, while Brian only biked 2 miles in 20 minutes; their rates are not the same, so C is false. This means (D) must be true. Jared starts out farther away than Brian, so Jared must have biked at a faster rate to arrive home in the same amount of time.

20. B   Difficulty: Hard

Category: Heart of Algebra / Linear Equations

Getting to the Answer: You aren't given any numbers in this question, so make some up. Sketch a quick graph of any simple linear equation that has a positive y-intercept (because it is given that $b > 0$). Then, change the sign of the y-intercept and sketch the new graph on the same coordinate plane. Pick a simple equation that you can sketch quickly, such as $y = x + 3$, and then change the sign of b. The new equation is $y = x - 3$. Sketch both graphs. The second line is shifted down 3 units, twice, or $b \times 2$ units. The graph that follows illustrates this.

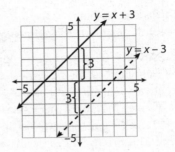

If you're not convinced, try another pair of equations. Choice (B) is correct.

21. C   Difficulty: Easy

Category: Heart of Algebra / Linear Equations

Getting to the Answer: When written in exponent form (no radicals and no variables in the denominator of a fraction), the only exponents on variables in a linear equation should be 1.

You can eliminate D right away because the exponent on x is 2. When written in exponent form, the other equations look like:

Choice A: $y = 3x^{-1}$ (not linear because of the -1 power)

Choice B: $x^{\frac{1}{2}} + y = 0$ (not linear because of the $\frac{1}{2}$ power)

Choice (C): $\frac{1}{2}x - \frac{5}{8}y = 11$ (linear)

22. B   Difficulty: Easy

Category: Heart of Algebra / Linear Equations

Getting to the Answer: For the equations, look at the exponents on the variables. Are they all 1? For the table, check to see if the change in the y-values compared to the change in the x-values is constant for each pair of values.

The table in (B) does not represent a linear relationship because the x-values change by $+4$ each time, while the y-values change by -10 then -8 then $+8$ then $+10$. A linear relationship has a constant rate of change, which means it is either always increasing or always decreasing, and by the same amount. This data clearly changes direction and is therefore not linear, so (B) is correct.

23. A   Difficulty: Easy

Category: Heart of Algebra / Linear Equations

Getting to the Answer: Write the equation in words first and then translate from English into math.

The total cost, *c*, is the weight of the potatoes in pounds, *p*, multiplied by the sale price because the purchase is made on Friday: $0.90 × (100 − 30)% = 0.9 × 0.7= 0.63. This gives the first part of the expression: 0.63*p*. Now, add the cost of two cantaloupes, 3.50 × 2 = 7, to get the equation *c* = 0.63*p* + 7, which is (A).

You could also Pick Numbers to answer this question—pick a number for the weight of the potatoes and calculate how much they would cost (on sale) and add the cost of two cantaloupes. Then find the equation that gives the same amount when you substitute the number you picked.

24. C   Difficulty: Easy

Category: Heart of Algebra / Linear Equations

Getting to the Answer: The total cost of the two kinds of items is the cost of the paintbrushes multiplied by the number purchased plus the cost of the canvases multiplied by the number purchased. Because a canvas cost "6 times" the cost of a paintbrush, a canvas costs 6($1.50) = $9.

Total cost of paintbrushes: 1.50 × *p* or 1.5*p*

Total cost of canvases: 9 × *c* or 9*c*

Sum of both: 9*c* + 1.5*p*

Therefore, (C) is correct.

25. D   Difficulty: Easy

Category: Heart of Algebra / Linear Equations

Getting to the Answer: The total bill consists of a flat tax (the local impact fee) and some part (or percent) of the market value of the volume of gas extracted. The local impact fee is a one-time fee that does not depend on the amount of gas extracted and therefore should not be multiplied by *v*. This means that 50,000 is the local impact fee. The other expression in the equation, 0.004*v*, represents the severance tax times the market value of the volume of gas extracted (which the question tells you is *v*). Therefore, 0.004 could represent the amount of the severance tax as a percentage (0.4%), which is (D).

26. B   Difficulty: Easy

Category: Heart of Algebra / Linear Equations

Getting to the Answer: Don't let questions that involve fractions intimidate you. To make the numbers easier to work with, clear the fraction by multiplying both sides of the equation by the denominator, 2:

$$2 \times \left[\frac{3}{2}(x + 7)\right] = 2 \times 6$$
$$3(x + 7) = 12$$
$$3x + 21 = 12$$
$$3x = -9$$
$$x = -3$$

Choice (B) is correct.

27. A   Difficulty: Easy

Category: Heart of Algebra / Linear Equations

Getting to the Answer: The total amount donated consists of a flat donation and an additional amount per mile. The flat amount is a one-time donation that does not depend on the number of miles walked and therefore should not be multiplied by the number of miles. This means that 250 is the flat donation. The other expression in the equation, 100*x*, represents the amount donated per mile (100) times the number of miles walked (*x*), thus (A) is correct.

28. B   Difficulty: Easy

Category: Heart of Algebra / Linear Equations

Getting to the Answer: Look for two points on the line that hit the intersection of two grid-lines. Then count the rise (or the fall if the line is decreasing) and the run as you move from one point to the next (always left to right). The slope is the change in the *y*-values (rise or fall) over the change in the *x*-values (run). Start at the *y*-intercept, (0, 5), and move to the point (3, 3). The line moves down 2 units and to the right 3 units, so the slope is $-\frac{2}{3}$, making (B) correct.

29. D   Difficulty: Medium

Category: Heart of Algebra / Linear Equations

Getting to the Answer: You could start by cross-multiplying, but there are so many terms and parentheses that you are likely to forget to distribute a factor. Instead, simplify the numerators first. Don't forget to distribute the negative to both terms inside the parentheses on the right-hand side of the equation. Don't try to do steps in your head—writing each step down will keep you organized.

$$\frac{3(n-2)+5}{4} = \frac{11-(7-n)}{6}$$

$$\frac{3n-6+5}{4} = \frac{11-7+n}{6}$$

$$\frac{3n-1}{4} = \frac{4+n}{6}$$

$$6(3n-1) = 4(4+n)$$

$$18n-6 = 16+4n$$

$$14n = 22$$

$$n = \frac{22}{14} = \frac{11}{7}$$

Choice (D) is correct.

30. B   Difficulty: Medium

Category: Heart of Algebra / Linear Equations

Getting to the Answer: There is not a lot of information to go on here, so start by determining the relationship between the number given in the question, 54,000, and the number in the equation, 2,250. Because 54,000 ÷ 2,250 = 24 and there are 24 hours in a day, 2,250 is the number of pages the press can print in 1 hour. If the press can print 2,250 in 1 hour, then it can print 2,250 times x in x hours. This means the function $f(x) = 2,250x$ represents the number of pages the press can print in x hours, which means (B) is correct.

31. D   Difficulty: Medium

Category: Heart of Algebra / Linear Equations

Getting to the Answer: Let x be the number of surfboards Jon sells in a month. Write a linear equation that represents the scenario and then solve for x. Sales must equal expenses for the store to break even. Jon's sales are equal to the selling price ($120) times the number of surfboards he sells (x), so write $120x$ on one side of the equal sign. His monthly expenses are his fixed expenses ($3,600) plus the amount he paid for each surfboard ($80) times the number of surfboards (x), so write $3,600 + 80x$ on the other side of the equal sign. Then, solve for x.

$$120x = 3,600 + 80x$$

$$40x = 3,600$$

$$x = 90$$

Therefore, (D) is correct.

32. A   Difficulty: Medium

Category: Heart of Algebra / Linear Equations

Getting to the Answer: In this scenario, the total cost is the dependent variable and is calculated by multiplying the per person rate by the number of people attending and then adding the flat serving fee. So the total cost is represented by y. Because the flat serving fee and the per person rate are likely to be fixed amounts (determined by the catering company), they should be represented by numbers in the equations, 300 and 11, respectively. The total cost depends on the number of people attending, so the number of people is the independent variable and is most likely represented by x. Therefore, (A) is correct.

33. A   Difficulty: Medium

Category: Heart of Algebra / Linear Equations

Getting to the Answer: A line with an undefined slope is a vertical line (a horizontal line has a slope of 0 because it is flat), so look for an equation that represents a vertical line. Start with the first equation. If $x = 3$ is the only thing you have to go on, choose a few points with an x-coordinate of 3, such as (3, 0), (3, 1), and (3, 2). Plot these points and draw a line through them to see that the graph is a vertical line and therefore has an undefined slope. There is no need to check the other equations. Choice (A) is correct.

34. B   Difficulty: Medium

Category: Heart of Algebra / Linear Equations

Getting to the Answer: When a linear equation is written in the form $y = mx + b$, the variable m represents the slope of the line and b represents the y-intercept of the line. Quickly scan the answer choices—they include inequalities, so you'll need to translate them into something that makes more sense to you. Use the fact that "< 0" means *negative* and "> 0" means *positive*. Now, look at the graph—the line is decreasing (going down from left to right), so the slope is negative ($m < 0$). This means you can eliminate C and D. Finally, look at the y-intercept—it is above the x-axis and is therefore positive ($b > 0$), which means (B) is correct.

35. A   Difficulty: Medium

Category: Heart of Algebra / Linear Equations

Getting to the Answer: Regardless of the scenario presented or the missing axis labels on the graph, the slope of the line tells you the answer. The line is decreasing from left to right, so it has a negative slope. This means there is an inverse relationship between the amount of algae and the number of fish. In other words, as one increases, the other must decrease, so (A) must be correct.

36. A   Difficulty: Medium
Category: Heart of Algebra / Linear Equations

Getting to the Answer: The rate of change (or slope) of a linear relationship is constant, so find the rate and apply it to the missing value. Choose any two points (preferably ones with the nicest numbers) from the table and substitute them into the slope formula. Using the points $(0, 8)$ and $(3, 7)$, the slope is $\frac{7-8}{3-0} = \frac{-1}{3}$. This means that for every 3 units the x-value increases, the y-value decreases by 1, so to get from $x = 3$ to $x = 9$, decrease the y-value by 1, two times: $7 - 1 - 1 = 5$, making (A) correct.

37. A   Difficulty: Hard
Category: Heart of Algebra / Linear Equations

Getting to the Answer: Write an equation in words first, and then translate from English into math. Then, rearrange your equation to find what you're interested in, which is the initial amount of fuel. Call the initial amount A. After you've written your equation, solve for A:

Amount now (x) equals initial amount (A) minus fuel used on last flight (y) plus amount added (18,000).

$$x = A - y + 18{,}000$$
$$x + y - 18{,}000 = A$$

This is the same as $y + x - 18{,}000$. Thus, (A) is correct.

You could also Pick Numbers to answer this question.

38. B   Difficulty: Hard
Category: Heart of Algebra / Linear Equations

Getting to the Answer: Do not automatically assume that an equation has *no solution* or *infinite solutions* just because those choices are given as possible answers. This question can be simplified quite a bit by clearing the fractions first. To do this, multiply both sides of the equation by the least common denominator, 12. Then

solve for h using inverse operations.

$$\frac{1}{4}(10h) - \frac{3}{2}(h + 1) = -\frac{2}{3}\left(\frac{9}{2}h\right) + 6$$

$$12\left[\frac{1}{4}(10h)\right] - 12\left[\frac{3}{2}(h + 1)\right] = 12\left[-\frac{2}{3}\left(\frac{9}{2}h\right)\right] + 12[6]$$

$$3(10h) - 18(h + 1) = -4(9h) + 72$$

$$30h - 18h - 18 = -36h + 72$$

$$12h - 18 = -36h + 72$$

$$48h = 90$$

$$h = \frac{90}{48} = \frac{15}{8}$$

Choice (B) is correct.

39. D   Difficulty: Hard
Category: Heart of Algebra / Linear Equations

Getting to the Answer: Compare the differences in the two lines to the statements in the answer choices. The y-intercept of both lines is the same. The key difference between the lines is their slopes. The solid line (pre-law) has a steeper slope, while the dashed line has a more gradual slope, so you can eliminate C. The slope of each line is negative (falling from left to right), so even after the proposed law is implemented, the population is still expected to decline, which means you can eliminate B. Because the dashed line's slope is more gradual, the decline in the population is slowing down (decelerating, not accelerating), so you can eliminate A. This means (D) is correct.

40. A   Difficulty: Hard
Category: Heart of Algebra / Linear Equations

Getting to the Answer: Try to describe the scenario in words first: If a car is more efficient, it can travel a greater distance on less gas. A less efficient car will use more gas to travel the same distance. In other words, the change in gas compared to the change in distance is greater for a less efficient car. Graphically, this means the slope is steeper for the less efficient car.

Look for the graph where the line representing the less efficient car (i) has a steeper slope (more gas per distance) than the line representing the efficient car (e), which is the graph in (A). Note that C and D don't represent gas mileage at all—in C, the cars aren't traveling anywhere because the distance isn't changing; in D, no gas is being used even though the distance is changing.

41. 6   Difficulty: Medium

Category: Heart of Algebra / Linear Equations

Getting to the Answer: Decimals can be messy, especially without a calculator, so clear the decimals by multiplying each term by 100—this moves the decimal two places to the left, resulting in an equation with only integer values.

$$0.55x - 1.04 = 0.35x + 0.16$$
$$100(0.55x - 1.04) = 100(0.35x + 0.16)$$
$$55x - 104 = 35x + 16$$
$$20x = 120$$
$$x = 6$$

42. 12   Difficulty: Medium

Category: Heart of Algebra / Linear Equations

Getting to the Answer: The place where the line crosses the y-axis is the y-intercept, or b when the equation is written in slope-intercept form ($y = mx + b$), so rewrite the equation in this form. To make the numbers easier to work with, clear the fraction by multiplying each term by 2.

$$\frac{3}{2}y - 2x = 18$$
$$2 \times \left[\frac{3}{2}y - 2x \right] = 2 \times 18$$
$$3y - 4x = 36$$
$$3y = 4x + 36$$
$$y = \frac{4}{3}x + 12$$

The y-intercept is 12.

Because the y-intercept of a graph is always of the form $(0, y)$, you could also substitute 0 for x in the original equation and solve for y.

CHAPTER 3

PRACTICE

7. A   Difficulty: Medium
Category: Heart of Algebra / Systems of Linear Equations

Getting to the Answer: Use the Kaplan Strategy for Translating English into Math to make sense of the situation. First, define your variables: w for wooden and c for crystal are good choices. Breaking apart the question, you know the jewelry artist bought 127 beads total. You're also told each wooden bead costs \$0.20 ($0.2w$) and each crystal bead costs \$0.50 ($0.5c$), as well as the fact that she spent \$41 total. You'll have two equations: one relating the number of wooden beads and crystal beads, and a second relating the costs associated with each.

$$w + c = 127$$
$$0.2w + 0.5c = 41$$

Either combination or substitution is a good choice for solving this system. Both are shown here:

Combination:

$$-0.5(w + c = 127) \rightarrow -0.5w - 0.5c = -63.5$$

$$\begin{array}{r} -0.5w - 0.5c = -63.5 \\ + \ \ 0.2w + 0.5c = 41 \\ \hline -0.3w = -22.5 \\ w = 75 \end{array}$$

Substitution:

$$w + c = 127 \rightarrow c = 127 - w$$

$$0.2w + 0.5(127 - w) = 41$$
$$0.2w + 63.5 - 0.5w = 41$$
$$-0.3w = -22.5$$
$$w = 75$$

$$75 + c = 127 \rightarrow c = 52$$

Be careful here: The question asks for the difference in the amount spent on each type of bead, not the difference in the quantity of each type. Multiply the bead counts by the correct pricing to get \$15 for the wooden beads and \$26 for the crystal beads. Take the difference to get \$11, which is (A).

8. 59   Difficulty: Medium
Category: Heart of Algebra / Systems of Linear Equations

Getting to the Answer: You're asked for the value of an expression rather than the value of one of the variables, so there must be a shortcut. Start by rearranging the two equations so that variables and constants are aligned:

$$x + y = -15$$
$$\frac{x}{2} + \frac{5y}{2} = 37$$

Clear the fractions in the second equation, and then add the equations:

$$2\left(\frac{x}{2} + \frac{5y}{2} = 37\right) \rightarrow x + 5y = 74$$

$$\begin{array}{r} x + y = -15 \\ + \ \ x + 5y = 74 \\ \hline 2x + 6y = 59 \end{array}$$

This is precisely what the question asks for, so you're done! Grid in 59 and move on.

PERFORM

9. B   Difficulty: Hard
Category: Heart of Algebra / Systems of Linear Equations

Getting to the Answer: A system of equations that has infinitely many solutions describes a single line. Therefore, the equations are dependent, and correct manipulation of one will yield the other. Because q is the coefficient of x in the second equation, look for a way to make the coefficient of y equal to that in the first equation. This can be done by multiplying the second equation by -9:

$$-9\left(qx - \frac{y}{3} = -2\right) \rightarrow -9qx + 3y = 18$$

The y terms and constants in the second equation now match those in the first; all that's left is to set the coefficients of x equal to each other and solve for q:

$$-9q = 6 \rightarrow q = -\frac{6}{9} = -\frac{2}{3}.$$ Choice (B) is correct.

10. 3/17 Difficulty: Medium
Category: Heart of Algebra / Systems of Linear Equations

Getting to the Answer: None of the coefficients in either equation is 1, so using combination is the best strategy here.

Examine the coefficients of *x*: They don't share any factors, so multiply each equation by the coefficient from the other equation, remembering to make one of them negative:

$$-5(12x + 15y = 249) \rightarrow -60x - 75y = -1{,}245$$
$$12(5x + 13y = 124) \rightarrow 60x + 156y = 1{,}488$$

Add the resulting equations:

$$-60x - 75y = -1{,}245$$
$$+\ 60x + 156y = 1{,}488$$
$$\overline{81y = 243}$$
$$y = 3$$

Don't stop yet; you need *x* so you can determine the value of $\frac{y}{x}$. Substitute 3 for *y* in one of the original equations:

$$5x + 13(3) = 124$$
$$5x + 39 = 124$$
$$5x = 85$$
$$x = 17$$

Plug your *x*- and *y*-values into $\frac{y}{x}$ to get $\frac{3}{17}$. Grid in 3/17.

11. C   Difficulty: Hard
Category: Heart of Algebra / Systems of Linear Equations

Getting to the Answer: Write equations to represent the profit generated by selling each type of pizza. You're told The Works sells for $17 each and that its ingredients cost the pizzeria $450 per week. This means weekly profit generated by this pizza's sales can be represented by the equation $y = 17x - 450$. Do the same for The Hawaiian: Each one sells for $13, but the pizzeria loses $310 to pay for ingredients each week. Therefore, weekly profits from this pizza can be represented by $y = 13x - 310$. To determine the point at which profits from one pizza overtake the other, set the two equations equal to each other and solve:

$$17x - 450 = 13x - 310$$
$$4x = 140$$
$$x = 35$$

Although ingredients for The Works cost more, the pizza's higher price tag means its profits will eventually surpass those of The Hawaiian. This will occur after the pizzeria sells 35 of each, making (C) correct. Be careful of D; 145 is the *y*-value when *x* = 35.

EXTRA PRACTICE

1. A   Difficulty: Easy
Category: Heart of Algebra / Systems of Linear Equations

Getting to the Answer: The solution to a system of equations shown graphically is the point of intersection. Read the axis labels carefully. Each grid-line represents 2 units. The two lines intersect at the point $(-6, -6)$, so $A + B = -6 + (-6) = -12$, which means (A) is correct.

2. C   Difficulty: Medium
Category: Heart of Algebra / Systems of Linear Equations

Getting to the Answer: Because *x* has a coefficient of 1 in the second equation, solve the system using substitution. Before you select your answer, make sure you found the right quantity (the difference of *x* and *y*).

First, solve the second equation for *x*:

$$x - 5y = 2$$
$$x = 2 + 5y$$
$$4(2 + 5y) + 3y = 14 - y$$
$$8 + 20y + 3y = 14 - y$$
$$8 + 23y = 14 - y$$
$$24y = 6$$
$$y = \frac{6}{24} = \frac{1}{4}$$

Next, substitute this value back into $x = 2 + 5y$ and simplify:

$$x = 2 + 5\left(\frac{1}{4}\right)$$
$$x = \frac{8}{4} + \frac{5}{4}$$
$$x = \frac{13}{4}$$

Finally, subtract $x - y$ to find the difference:

$$\frac{13}{4} - \frac{1}{4} = \frac{12}{4} = 3,\ \text{(C)}$$

3. C   Difficulty: Medium
Category: Heart of Algebra / Systems of Linear Equations

Getting to the Answer: Graphically, a system of linear equations that has no solution consists of two parallel lines that will never intersect. They have the same slope but different *y*-intercepts. A system of linear equations that has infinite solutions is actually the same line, just represented in different ways. Graphically, one line would sit on top of the other, intersecting itself an infinite number of times. These lines would have the same slope *and* the same *y*-intercept. Without additional information, it is not possible to determine whether the system that Charlie graphed has no solutions or an infinite number of solutions. Therefore, the solution to Charlie's system of equations depends on the *y*-intercepts of the lines and (C) is correct.

4. C   **Difficulty:** Medium
Category: Heart of Algebra / Systems of Linear Equations

Getting to the Answer: If the graphs intersect at (−3, 1), then the solution to the system is $x = -3$ and $y = 1$. This means you can substitute these values into both equations and go from there.

$$hx - 4y = -10 \qquad kx + 3y = -15$$
$$h(-3) - 4(1) = -10 \qquad k(-3) + 3(1) = -15$$
$$-3h - 4 = -10 \qquad -3k + 3 = -15$$
$$-3h = -6 \qquad -3k = -18$$
$$h = 2 \qquad k = 6$$

So, $\dfrac{k}{h} = \dfrac{6}{2} = 3$, making (C) correct.

5. C   **Difficulty:** Medium
Category: Heart of Algebra / Systems of Linear Equations

Getting to the Answer: Write a system of equations with c = the cost of the chair in dollars and s = the cost of the sofa in dollars. A sofa costs $50 less than three times the cost of the chair, or $s = 3c - 50$; together, a sofa and a chair cost $650, so $s + c = 650$.

The system is:

$$\begin{cases} s = 3c - 50 \\ s + c = 650 \end{cases}$$

The top equation is already solved for *s*, so substitute $3c - 50$ into the bottom equation for *s* and solve for *c*:

$$3c - 50 + c = 650$$
$$4c - 50 = 650$$
$$4c = 700$$
$$c = 175$$

Be careful—that's not the answer! The chair costs $175 so the sofa costs $3(175) - 50 = 525 - 50 = \$475$. This means the sofa costs $\$475 - \$175 = \$300$ more than the chair. Therefore, (C) is correct.

6. D   **Difficulty:** Hard
Category: Heart of Algebra / Systems of Linear Equations

Getting to the Answer: The easiest way to answer this question is to think about how the graphs of the equations would look. Graphically, a system of linear equations that has no solution indicates two parallel lines, or in other words, two lines that have the same slope but different *y*-intercepts.

To have the same slope, the *x*- and *y*-coefficients must be the same. The two *y*-coefficients are $-\dfrac{2}{3}$ and −8. To make $-\dfrac{2}{3}$ equal −8, multiply by 12. Multiplying $\dfrac{1}{2}x$ by 12 as well gives 6*x*. Because the other *x*-coefficient is *a*, it must be that $a = 6$. Note that you could also write each equation in slope-intercept form and set the slopes equal to each other to solve for *a*.

7. C   **Difficulty:** Hard
Category: Heart of Algebra / Systems of Linear Equations

Getting to the Answer: Create a system of linear equations where *e* represents the number of packs with 8 plates and *t* represents the number of packs with 12 plates.

The first equation should represent the total number of *packs*, each with 8 or 12 plates, or $e + t = 54$. The second equation should represent the total number of *plates*. Because *e* represents packs with 8 plates and *t* represents packs with 12 plates, the second equation is $8e + 12t = 496$. Now solve the system using substitution (or combination if it's faster for you). Solve the first equation for either variable and substitute the result into the second equation:

$$e + t = 54$$
$$e = 54 - t$$
$$- t) + 12t = 496$$
$$- 8t + 12t = 496$$
$$432 + 4t = 496$$
$$4t = 64$$
$$t = 16$$

So, 16 packs have 12 plates. The question asks about packs of 12, so you don't need to find the value of *e*. But you are not done yet. The problem asks how many *plates* a customer would buy if he or she buys all of the packs of 12 the store has, not just the *number of packs*. The customer would buy $16 \times 12 = 192$ plates, which is (C).

8. D   **Difficulty:** Hard
Category: Heart of Algebra / Systems of Linear Equations

Getting to the Answer: A system of linear equations has infinitely many solutions if both lines in the system have the same slope and the same *y*-intercept (in other words, they are the same line).

To have the same slope, the *x*- and *y*-coefficients of the two equations must be the same. Use the *x*-coefficients here: To turn $\frac{1}{2}$ into 3, multiply by 6. So *c* becomes 6*c*, and $6c = -6$, or $c = -1$, (D).

Note that you could also write each equation in slope-intercept form and set the *y*-intercepts equal to each other to solve for *c*.

9. B   **Difficulty:** Easy
Category: Heart of Algebra / Systems of Linear Equations

Getting to the Answer: The solution to a system of linear equations represented graphically is the point of intersection. If the lines do not intersect, the system has no solution.

According to the graph, the lines intersect, or cross each other, at (6, 3). The question asks for the *y*-coordinate of the solution, which is 3, making (B) correct.

10. D   **Difficulty:** Easy
Category: Heart of Algebra / Systems of Linear Equations

Getting to the Answer: The word "and" in this question tells you that you're dealing with a system of equations. Whenever a question involves a system, quickly compare the two equations. Sometimes, writing the equations vertically gives you a clue about how to solve it.

$$\begin{cases} 2x - 3y = 14 \\ 5x + 3y = 21 \end{cases}$$

This system is already set up perfectly to solve using combination because the *y* terms ($-3y$ and $3y$) are opposites.

Add the two equations to cancel $-3y$ and $3y$. Then solve the resulting equation for *x*. Remember, the question only asks for the value of *x*, so you don't need to substitute *x* back into the equation and solve for *y*.

$$\begin{aligned} 2x - 3y &= 14 \\ + 5x + 3y &= 21 \\ \hline 7x &= 35 \\ x &= 5 \end{aligned}$$

Choice (D) is correct.

11. A   **Difficulty:** Hard
Category: Heart of Algebra / Systems of Linear Equations

Getting to the Answer: Create a system of equations where *x* represents the number of rows with 20 seats and *y* represents the number of rows with 24 seats. The first equation should represent the total *number of rows*, each with 20 or 24 seats, or $x + y = 16$. The second equation should represent the total *number of seats*. Because *x* represents rows with 20 seats and *y* represents rows with 24 seats, the second equation in the system should be $20x + 24y = 348$. Now solve the system using substitution. Solve the first equation for either variable and substitute the result into the second equation:

$$\begin{aligned} x + y &= 16 \\ x &= 16 - y \\ 20(16 - y) + 24y &= 348 \\ 320 - 20y + 24y &= 348 \\ 320 + 4y &= 348 \\ 4y &= 28 \\ y &= 7 \end{aligned}$$

So 7 rows have 24 seats, which means (A) is correct. This is all the question asks for, so you don't need to find the value of *x*.

12. 8 **Difficulty:** Medium

Category: Heart of Algebra / Systems of Linear Equations

Getting to the Answer: The solution to the system is the point that both tables will have in common, but the tables, as given, do not share any points. You could use the data to write the equation of each line and then solve the system, but this will use up valuable time on Test Day. Instead, look for patterns that can be extended.

In the table on the left, the x-values increase by 2 each time and the y-values decrease by 2. In the table on the right, the x-values increase by 4 each time and the y-values increase by 1. Use these patterns to continue the tables.

Equation 1		Equation 2	
x	y	x	y
−2	6	−8	−8
0	4	−4	−7
2	2	0	−6
4	0	4	−5
6	−2	**8**	**−4**
8	**−4**	12	−3

The point (8, −4) satisfies both equations, so the x-coordinate of the solution to the system is 8.

CHAPTER 4

PRACTICE

5. A   **Difficulty:** Medium

Category: Heart of Algebra / Inequalities

Getting to the Answer: Use the Kaplan Strategy for Translating English into Math to piece together an inequality. The question states that n represents the number of overnight stays. The cost of hotel accommodations for a trip without the discount card is $180 per night, or $180n$. If a customer purchases the discount card, accommodations would equal the cost of the card plus $120 per night, or $720 + 120n$. Combine these in an inequality, remembering which way the inequality symbol should be oriented. You want the cost with the discount card to be less than the cost without the card, so the inequality is $720 + 120n < 180n$. Solving for n gives $n > 12$; a traveler must stay in hotels in the network more than 12 days for the discount card to be a better deal. Choice (A) is the correct answer.

PERFORM

6. Any value between 0 and 3.5, including 0
Difficulty: Hard

Category: Heart of Algebra / Inequalities

Getting to the Answer: Resist autopilot! Instead of solving two inequalities separately, look for a series of quick manipulations to convert $\frac{4}{3}h + \frac{1}{6}$ to $12h - 4$. Start by multiplying the entire inequality by 9 to yield $-27 < 12h + \frac{3}{2} < 9$. Next, subtract $\frac{3}{2}$ and then 4 more (to get the desired -4) from all parts of the inequality (converting the fraction component to a decimal will make this step easier), which will become $-32.5 < 12h - 4 < 3.5$. Because grid-in answers cannot be negative, pick any value that is greater than or equal to 0 but less than 3.5.

Note that you could also solve the inequality for h and then manipulate the answer so that it looks like the expression in the question, but this strategy is likely to take longer.

7. C   **Difficulty:** Medium

Category: Heart of Algebra / Inequalities

Getting to the Answer: Use the Kaplan Strategy for Translating English into Math to assemble a system of inequalities. The question has defined the variables for you (t_s and p_s, t_z and p_z). You know that tops and pants cost $35 and $60 each, respectively. In addition, the question states that Sarah and Zena must sell an average of at least 75 items each (which means that together they must sell at least 150 items, regardless of who sells more) and that their total sales must be at least $6,000. The sum of the four item counts must meet or exceed 150, so the first inequality is $t_s + p_s + t_z + p_z \geq 150$. Revenue from the sale of tops is $35(t_s + t_z)$, and revenue from the sale of pants is $60(p_s + p_z)$. The minimum revenue required to earn the bonus is $6,000, so the second inequality is $35(t_s + t_z) + 60(p_s + p_z) \geq 6,000$. Choice (C) is the only choice that contains both inequalities.

EXTRA PRACTICE

1. A   **Difficulty:** Easy

Category: Heart of Algebra / Inequalities

Getting to the Answer: You solve an inequality just like an equation. The only difference is that if you multiply or divide both sides by a negative number (usually in the last step of the solution), you must reverse (flip) the inequality symbol. Take a second to study the inequality. Distributing the fraction will yield messy calculations. Instead, multiply both sides of the inequality by 5 to clear the fraction. Then, use inverse operations to isolate the variable:

$$
\begin{aligned}
\cancel{5} \times \frac{1}{\cancel{5}}(7 - 3b) &> 5 \times 2 \\
7 - 3b &> 10 \\
-3b &> 3 \\
b &< -1
\end{aligned}
$$

Notice that the inequality symbol was reversed because the last step in the solution required dividing by -3. The correct answer is (A).

2. B   Difficulty: Easy
Category: Heart of Algebra / Inequalities

Getting to the Answer: There is only one variable here, so solve each inequality for n and then eliminate incorrect choices.

First inequality: $n - 3 > 8$ so $n > 11$. This means you can eliminate A because 11 is not greater than itself.

Second inequality: $n + 1 < 14$ so $n < 13$. This means you can eliminate C and D because neither 13 nor 14 is less than 13. The number 12 is the only answer choice that is both greater than 11 and less than 13, so (B) is correct.

3. D   Difficulty: Medium
Category: Heart of Algebra / Inequalities

Getting to the Answer: You don't have time to try each symbol in the equation. Instead, look at the dot (open or solid?) and the direction of the shading (left or right?). There is a solid dot at 6, which means the sign must be $\geq$ or $\leq$, so you can eliminate A and B. Next, look at the shading. The graph is shaded to the left of the dot. This means the graph shows $x \leq 6$, but be careful—there is a negative coefficient (-1) in front of the x term, so the inequality will be reversed at some point in the solution. This means the original inequality sign, before you reverse it, should be $\geq$, which is (D). You can check your answer by solving the inequality using the sign you chose. If you chose correctly, your answer should match the graph.

4. C   Difficulty: Medium
Category: Heart of Algebra / Inequalities

Getting to the Answer: The best way to answer this question is to pretend you are the person paying for your power. How much less would you pay for *one* kWh of power at Company D than at Company B? If you used 530 kWh, how much would this be? If you used 730 kWh, how much would this be?

Based on the data in the table, a consumer would pay $17.4 - 14.8 = 2.6$ cents (or 0.026) less for one kWh of power at Company D than at Company B. If she used 530 kWh per month, she would pay $530(0.026) = \$13.78$ less at Company D. If she used 730 kWh, she would pay $730(0.026) = \$18.98$ less. So, the consumer would pay somewhere between $13.78 and $18.98 less per month, which can be expressed as the compound inequality $13.78 \leq x \leq 18.98$, which matches (C).

5. C   Difficulty: Medium
Category: Heart of Algebra / Inequalities

Getting to the Answer: Use the Kaplan Method for Translating English into Math. The clue "holds a maximum" means it can hold exactly that much or less, so use the symbol $\leq$ throughout. The cargo container can hold a maximum of 50 microwaves, so the first inequality is $m \leq 50$. This means you can eliminate A. The container can hold a maximum of 15 refrigerators, so the second inequality is $r \leq 15$. The third inequality deals with the size of each appliance. The cargo container can hold m microwaves multiplied by the size of the microwave, 6 cubic feet; it can hold r refrigerators multiplied by the size of the refrigerator, 20 cubic feet; and it can hold a maximum of 300 cubic feet total. Put these together to write the final inequality: $6m + 20r \leq 300$, which is (C).

6. D   Difficulty: Hard
Category: Heart of Algebra / Inequalities

Getting to the Answer: Before immediately trying to solve for k, notice that $-6k + 8$ is simply $3k - 4$ multiplied by -2. So, multiply each of the other parts of the inequality by -2 also. Don't forget to flip the inequality symbols because you are multiplying by a negative number.

$$-2\left[-\frac{2}{5} < 3k - 4 < \frac{6}{7}\right]$$
$$\frac{4}{5} > -6k + 8 > -\frac{12}{7}$$

Now, you don't need to solve for k because the question is asking about $-6k + 8$, but it does help to rewrite the inequality from smallest to largest: $-\frac{12}{7} < -6k + 8 < \frac{4}{5}$. So, any value greater than $-\frac{12}{7}$ but less than $\frac{4}{5}$ is a possible value, but be careful—you are looking for the number that is *not* a possible value. This means you are looking for a number that is *less* than $-\frac{12}{7}$ or *greater* than $\frac{4}{5}$. Choice (D) is correct because $\frac{4}{3} > \frac{4}{5}$.

7. D   **Difficulty:** Hard

Category: Heart of Algebra / Inequalities

Getting to the Answer: The solution to a system of inequalities is where the shading overlaps. The first inequality is ready to graph, but the second is not, so start by rewriting the second inequality in slope intercept form ($y = mx + b$). Don't forget to reverse the inequality symbol when you divide by -3:

$$2x - 3y \leq 12$$
$$-3y \leq -2x + 12$$
$$y \geq \frac{2}{3}x - 4$$

Now, compare the lines. Because the slopes are the same $\left(\frac{2}{3}\right)$ and the y-intercepts are different (1 and -4), the boundary lines are parallel and never intersect. Don't answer too quickly—the answer is *not* "no solution"! The solution set revolves around the shading, not the boundary lines, so draw a quick sketch of the system.

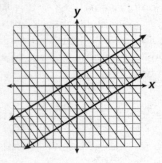

The region between the two boundary lines is shaded in both directions, so (D) is correct.

8. 8   **Difficulty:** Medium

Category: Heart of Algebra / Inequalities

Getting to the Answer: Translate from English into math to create an inequality where h represents the number of hours of overtime Marco must work. Marco gets paid a daily wage plus an hourly rate for overtime, so his weekly pay is his daily rate ($80) times 5 days, plus the number of hours of overtime he works (h) times his overtime rate ($15). If he wants to make *at least* $520, which means that much or more, the inequality is $(80 \times 5) + 15h \geq 520$. Solve for h:

$$400 + 15h \geq 520$$
$$15h \geq 120$$
$$h \geq 8$$

Marco must work at least 8 hours of overtime to make $520 or more this week.

9. C   **Difficulty:** Easy

Category: Heart of Algebra / Inequalities

Getting to the Answer: Solve the inequality by first distributing the 2 and then using inverse operations.

$$2(4x - 1) > 5x + 13$$
$$8x - 2 > 5x + 13$$
$$8x > 5x + 15$$
$$3x > 15$$
$$x > 5$$

Now, find the number line that matches. Because x is greater than (but *not* equal to) 5, the dot should be open, and the graph should be shaded to the right of 5. This is called a *strict* inequality because the numbers in the solution are strictly greater than 5. This means (C) is correct.

10. B   **Difficulty:** Medium

Category: Heart of Algebra / Inequalities

Getting to the Answer: Quickly skim the first answer choice to see that you'll need to decide whether the boundary line is dashed or solid, whether it rises or falls from left to right, and which half-plane should be shaded. The inequality symbol tells you two of these—the symbol does not have an equal sign, so the line should be dashed; the symbol represents *less than*, so the half-plane *below* the line should be shaded. This means either A or B must be correct. To decide which one, recall that when a line is written in the form $y = mx + b$, the variable m represents the slope of the line. Here, $m = -2$, so the line is decreasing, which means it falls from left to right, making (B) correct.

11. B   Difficulty: Medium
Category: Heart of Algebra / Inequalities

Getting to the Answer: The intersection (overlap) of the two shaded regions is the solution to the system of inequalities. Check each point to see whether it lies in the region where the shading overlaps. Be careful—you are looking for the point that is *not* a solution to the system. Choices A and C clearly lie in the overlap so you can eliminate them. Choice D, which is the point (6, −3), lies on a boundary line, and because the line is solid, the point *is* included in the solution region. The only point that does not lie within the overlap is (B). To check this, plug (1, −1) into the first inequality:

$$y < \frac{3}{5}x - 2$$
$$-1 < \frac{3}{5}(1) - 2$$
$$-1 \not< -\frac{7}{5}$$

Choice (B) is correct because −1 is not less than $-\frac{7}{5}$.

12. C   Difficulty: Medium
Category: Heart of Algebra / Inequalities

Getting to the Answer: A question like this is purely conceptual. The only time a system of inequalities has *no solution* (no overlap at all) is when the boundary lines are parallel and the shading is in opposite directions (above the upper boundary line and below the lower boundary line). For the boundary lines to be parallel, the slope of the second line must be equal to the slope of the first line, which is 2. This means you can eliminate A and B. The inequality symbol < (in the first inequality) tells you that the half-plane *below* the boundary line is shaded, which means the half-plane *above* the second boundary line must be shaded. Therefore, the correct symbol is greater than (>). Choice (C) is correct.

13. 2   Difficulty: Medium
Category: Heart of Algebra / Inequalities

Getting to the Answer: If (a, b) is a solution to the system, then a is the x-coordinate of any point in the region where the shading overlaps, and b is the corresponding y-coordinate. When a = 0 (or x = 0), the maximum possible value for b lies on the upper boundary line, y < 2x + 3. It looks like the y-coordinate is 3, but to be sure, substitute x = 0 into the equation and simplify. You can use = in the equation, instead of the inequality symbol, because you are finding a point on the boundary line.

$$y = 2(0) + 3$$
$$y = 3$$

The point on the boundary line is (0, 3). The boundary line is dashed (because the inequality is strictly less than), so (0, 3) is *not* a solution to the system. This means 2 is the greatest possible *integer* value for b when a = 0.

CHAPTER 5

PRACTICE

8. C   **Difficulty**: Medium
Category: Problem Solving and Data Analysis / Rates, Ratios, Proportions, and Percentages

Getting to the Answer: You have a couple rates, but you need to manipulate them slightly before using them in the DIRT equation. Start by changing the given rates to unit rates. For the 5-second interval, $r_5 = 1$ car per 5 s $= 0.2$ cars/s. The 8-second interval becomes $r_8 = 1$ car per 8 s $= 0.125$ cars/s. Next, convert the time window into seconds to match your rates: $3\,h \times \dfrac{60\,min}{1\,h} \times \dfrac{60\,s}{1\,min} = 10{,}800\,s.$

Now you can use the DIRT equation to find the number of cars allowed through at each interval.

5 seconds: $d_5 = 0.2$ cars/s $\times$ 10,800 s $= 2{,}160$ cars

8 seconds: $d_8 = 0.125$ cars/s $\times$ 10,800 s $= 1{,}350$ cars

Subtracting these gives $2{,}160 - 1{,}350 = 810$ more cars, which is (C).

9. D   **Difficulty**: Hard
Category: Problem Solving and Data Analysis / Rates, Ratios, Proportions, and Percentages

Getting to the Answer: Murray starts with $75,400 per year. The first deduction is the 20% 401(k) contribution. Using the three-part percent formula, you'll find Murray has $0.8 \times \$75{,}400 = \$60{,}320$ left. He pays $150 per month for insurance, which is $1,800 per year. This leaves $58,520 pre-tax. Taxes are trickier, so work carefully. State taxes are easy; just take 4.5% of the pre-tax total: $0.045 \times \$58{,}520 = \$2{,}633.40$. Federal taxes involve three separate calculations as follows:

10% bracket: $0.1 \times \$9{,}225 = \$922.50$
15% bracket: $0.15 \times (\$37{,}450 - \$9{,}225) = \$4{,}233.75$
25% bracket: $0.25 \times (\$58{,}520 - \$37{,}450) = \$5{,}267.50$

Adding up all of Murray's tax liability gives $13,057.15. Subtract this from his pre-tax total to get $45,462.85. Don't stop yet! The question asks for Murray's biweekly pay. Divide $45,462.85 by 26, the number of pay periods in one year, to get $1,748.57, which is (D).

10. 7/16   **Difficulty**: Hard
Category: Problem Solving and Data Analysis / Rates, Ratios, Proportions, and Percentages

Getting to the Answer: Start by labeling each square for clarity.

You're given that the area of the innermost square is 1 square inch, which means the side length of this square is 1 inch. If the square edges are 0.5 inches apart, that means square 2 has a side length of $1 + 0.5 + 0.5 = 2$ inches, square 3 has a side length of $2 + 0.5 + 0.5 = 3$ inches, and so on. This translates to areas of 1, 4, 9, 16, 25, 36, 49, and 64 (all in square inches). But don't forget that you need to subtract the square within each to get the true areas! You'll get the following:

$$\text{sq. 1 (gray)} = 1\ \text{in.}^2$$
$$\text{sq. 2 (black)} = 2^2 - 1 = 3\ \text{in.}^2$$
$$\text{sq. 3 (gray)} = 3^2 - 4 = 5\ \text{in.}^2$$
$$\text{sq. 4 (black)} = 4^2 - 9 = 7\ \text{in.}^2$$
$$\text{sq. 5 (gray)} = 5^2 - 16 = 9\ \text{in.}^2$$
$$\text{sq. 6 (black)} = 6^2 - 25 = 11\ \text{in.}^2$$
$$\text{sq. 7 (gray)} = 7^2 - 36 = 13\ \text{in.}^2$$
$$\text{sq. 8 (black)} = 8^2 - 49 = 15\ \text{in.}^2$$

After a few calculations you might start to see a pattern; if so, great! You can shave off a few seconds of number crunching. Now add up the gray squares to get 28, then divide by the area of the whole plate (64) to get $\dfrac{28}{64} = \dfrac{7}{16}$. Grid in 7/16, then move on to the next question in the set.

11. 10/9   Difficulty: Medium

Category: Problem Solving and Data Analysis / Rates, Ratios, Proportions, and Percentages

Getting to the Answer: You've already done most of the work for this part; look closely at your work for the first question to see what you can reuse. Finding the large plate black fraction is easy; just subtract the large plate gray fraction from 1 to get $\frac{9}{16}$. Because the small plate is just a smaller version of the large plate with only four squares, you can use your calculations for squares 1-4 from the first question here. Squares 1 and 3 (gray) comprise 6 square inches, and squares 2 and 4 (black) comprise 10 square inches. This means the small plate black fraction is $\frac{10}{16} = \frac{5}{8}$. To find how many times more black glaze is on the small plate, divide the small plate black fraction by its large plate counterpart: $\frac{5}{8} \div \frac{9}{16} = \frac{5}{8} \times \frac{16}{9} = \frac{10}{9}$. Grid in 10/9, and you're done!

PERFORM

12. A   Difficulty: Easy

Category: Problem Solving and Data Analysis / Rates, Ratios, Proportions, and Percentages

Getting to the Answer: Convert all four rates into the same units before comparing. You might think you should convert each price into cost per banana, but a closer look reveals that all but one price already uses weight. Save time by converting the units into cost per pound; the order will be no different than if you did cost per banana. Use the banana-pound relationship to convert each price into cost per pound. FoodCo's price is already per pound, so no work is needed there. Bob's charges $0.29 per banana, which becomes $\frac{\$0.29}{1\ banana} \times \frac{1\ banana}{\frac{1}{3}\ lb} = \frac{\$0.87}{1\ lb}$.

Acme's price is $1.50 for 2 pounds or $0.75 per pound. The deal at Stu's means you pay $1.95 for 4 pounds, which is $0.4875 per pound. Therefore, the correct order is Bob's, Acme, FoodCo, Stu's. This matches (A).

13. 18.2   Difficulty: Easy

Category: Problem Solving and Data Analysis / Rates, Ratios, Proportions, and Percentages

Getting to the Answer: Start by drawing a diagram to make sense of the situation. Each zipline is the hypotenuse of a right triangle. Because the two zipline setups are proportional, the triangles are similar.

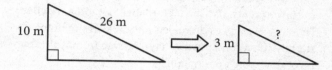

You can use a proportion to solve for the length of the kids' zipline: $\frac{10}{26} = \frac{3}{x}$. Solving for x gives 7.8 meters. But you're not done yet! The question asks for the difference in zipline length, so subtract 7.8 from 26 to get 18.2.

14. 166   Difficulty: Medium

Category: Problem Solving and Data Analysis / Rates, Ratios, Proportions, and Percentages

Getting to the Answer: Identify the units of the start and end quantities, then string together the proper conversion factors. You know Mark will drive 960 miles over the course of his trip, and you need to determine what he should budget for fuel. The full conversion is as follows:

$$960\ mi \times \frac{1\ gal}{40\ mi} \times \frac{3.785\ L}{1\ gal} \times \frac{1.20\ GBP}{1\ L} \times \frac{1.52\ USD}{1\ GBP} =$$

165.69 USD. Round to 166 per the question instructions.

15. 17   Difficulty: Hard

Category: Problem Solving and Data Analysis / Rates, Ratios, Proportions, and Percentages

Getting to the Answer: Determine Mark's fuel cost with the offer, then compare it to the original. If you stopped your calculations in the previous question after the gallon-to-liter conversion, you would find that Mark will use 90.84 L of fuel. At the new fuel price, Mark would pay $90.84 \times 0.75 = 68.13$ GBP for fuel. Add the 30 GBP cost for the rate reduction to get 98.13 GBP. Use the GBP-USD conversion to get 149.16 USD. Subtracting this from 165.69 gives 16.53, which is rounded to 17.

EXTRA PRACTICE

1. A **Difficulty**: Medium
Category: Problem Solving and Data Analysis / Rates, Ratios, Proportions, and Percentages

Getting to the Answer: Whenever multiple rates are given, pay very careful attention to the units. As you read the question, decide how and when you will need to convert units. Use the factor-label method as needed. The answer choices are given in hours and minutes, so start by converting the given typing rate from words per second to words per minute:

$$\frac{3.75 \text{ words}}{1 \text{ second}} \times \frac{60 \text{ seconds}}{1 \text{ minute}} = \frac{225 \text{ words}}{1 \text{ minute}}$$

Next, find the number of words in the 25-page transcript:

$$\frac{675 \text{ words}}{1 \text{ page}} \times 25 \text{ pages} = 16,875 \text{ words}$$

Finally, let m be the number of minutes it takes the court reporter to type the whole transcript. Set up a proportion and solve for m:

$$\frac{225 \text{ words}}{1 \text{ minute}} = \frac{16,875 \text{ words}}{m \text{ minutes}}$$
$$225m = 16,875$$
$$m = 75$$

Because 75 minutes is not an answer choice, convert it to hours and minutes: 75 minutes = 1 hour, 15 minutes, making (A) the correct answer.

2. C **Difficulty**: Medium
Category: Problem Solving and Data Analysis / Rates, Ratios, Proportions, and Percentages

Getting to the Answer: Don't let the three-way ratio scare you. You can solve this problem just like any other ratio question. Set up an equation using *parts*: 35 parts of the vote were for Taft, 41 parts were for Roosevelt, and 63 parts were for Wilson. You don't know how big a part is, so call it x. Now, write and solve an equation:

$$35x + 41x + 63x = 208,500$$
$$139x = 208,500$$
$$x = 1,500$$

Look back at the ratio—35 parts of the vote were for Taft, so the number of votes cast for Taft was 35(1,500) = 52,500, which matches (C).

3. D **Difficulty**: Medium
Category: Problem Solving and Data Analysis / Rates, Ratios, Proportions, and Percentages

Getting to the Answer: Use a variation of the three-part percent formula: Whole × percent = part.

First, find the number of people at each location who responded favorably using the formula. Start with the first location: 125 × 0.224 = 28. Move on to the second location: 272 × 0.375 = 102. Next, find the total number of people that were surveyed at both locations, which was 125 + 272 = 397, and the total number who responded favorably, 28 + 102 = 130. Finally, find the percent of people who responded favorably by using the formula one more time:

$$397 \times \text{percent} = 130 \times 100\%$$
$$\text{percent} = \frac{130}{397} \times 100\%$$
$$= 0.3274 \times 100\%$$
$$= 32.7\%$$

Of all the people surveyed, about 32.7% responded favorably, making (D) the correct answer.

4. A **Difficulty**: Medium
Category: Problem Solving and Data Analysis / Rates, Ratios, Proportions, and Percentages

Getting to the Answer: Let the units in this question guide you to the solution. The cooking rates of the ovens are given in pounds per hour, but the question asks about the number of ounces each oven can cook in 10 minutes, so use the factor-label method to convert pounds per hour to ounces per minute.

Start by converting pounds to ounces. You are given that 1 pound = 16 ounces, so 3 pounds is 48 ounces and 4.5 pounds is 72 ounces. Now convert the hours to minutes:

Oven at 350°:

$$\frac{48 \text{ oz}}{1 \text{ hr}} \times \frac{1 \text{ hr}}{60 \text{ min}} \times 10 \text{ min} = 8 \text{ oz}$$

Answers & Explanations

Oven at 450°:

$$\frac{72\ oz}{1\ hr} \times \frac{1\ hr}{60\ min} \times 10\ min = 12\ oz$$

In 10 minutes, the oven at 450° can cook $12 - 8 = 4$ ounces more than the oven at 350°, making (A) the correct answer.

5. B **Difficulty**: Medium
Category: Problem Solving and Data Analysis / Rates, Ratios, Proportions, and Percentages

Getting to the Answer: Don't let all the technical words in this question overwhelm you. Solve it step-by-step examining the units as you go. Use the factor-label method to help you stay organized.

Step 1: Determine the number of megabytes the company can upload in 1 evening (4 hours):

$$\frac{12\ MB}{1\ sec} \times \frac{60\ sec}{1\ min} \times \frac{60\ min}{1\ hr} \times \frac{4\ hr}{1\ evening} = \frac{172{,}800\ MB}{1\ evening}$$

Step 2: Convert this amount to gigabytes (because the information about the scans is given in gigabytes, not megabytes):

$$172{,}800\ MB \times \frac{1\ GB}{1{,}024\ MB} = 168.75\ GB$$

Step 3: Each video file is about 4.5 gigabytes, so divide by 4.5 to determine how many videos the company can upload to the cloud using its internet service provider: $168.75 \div 4.5 = 37.5$ videos. Remember, you should round this number down to 37, because the question asks for the maximum number the company can upload and it cannot complete the 38th video upload in the time allowed. The correct answer is (B).

6. B **Difficulty**: Medium
Category: Problem Solving and Data Analysis / Rates, Ratios, Proportions, and Percentages

Getting to the Answer: Pay careful attention to the units. You need to convert all of the dimensions to inches, and then find the scale factor. You'll have to start with the skull because it's the only part of the T-rex for which you know both the actual length and the model length.

There are 12 inches in one foot, so Sue's skull length was $12 \times 5 = 60$ inches and the model skull is $3 \times 12 = 36 + 1.5 = 37.5$ inches. Find the scale factor by writing

this as a fraction. Multiply both numbers by 10 to get rid of the decimal and then simplify the ratio to get $\frac{37.5}{60} = \frac{375}{600} = \frac{5}{8}$.

This means the scale factor is $\frac{5}{8}$. You might be tempted to now find the scale model's length and height by multiplying 40 and 13 by $\frac{5}{8}$, but this would waste valuable time. Because the model is a $\frac{5}{8}$-scale model, the difference between the model's length and height will be exactly $\frac{5}{8}$ of the difference between Sue's actual length and height, which is $40 - 13 = 27$ feet. Multiply 27 by $\frac{5}{8}$ to find that the difference between the length and height of the model should be 16.875 feet, or 16 feet, 10.5 inches, which matches (B).

7. 660 **Difficulty:** Easy
Category: Problem Solving and Data Analysis / Rates, Ratios, Proportions, and Percentages

Getting to the Answer: Break this question into short steps. Find the amount of the hostess share for one evening. Multiply this by the number of evenings per week, 5, and then the number of weeks, 4. Do this for each restaurant, and then subtract to find the difference.

Restaurant A:
$0.07 \times \$1{,}100 = \$77$
$\$77 \times 5 = 385$
$\$385 \times 4 = \$1{,}540$

Restaurant B:
$0.04 \times \$1{,}100 = \$44$
$\$44 \times 5 = \$220$
$\$220 \times 4 = \$880$

Mia would make $\$1{,}540 - \$880 = \$660$ more at Restaurant A.

8. 75 **Difficulty**: Hard
Category: Problem Solving and Data Analysis / Rates, Ratios, Proportions, and Percentages

Getting to the Answer: This question requires multiple steps and multiple formulas, so make a plan before you dive in. The formula for percent increase is:

$$\text{Percent increase} = \frac{\text{final amount} - \text{original amount}}{\text{original amount}}$$

This tells you that you need the final amount in tips that Restaurant B needs to bring in to be equal to Restaurant A, which will depend on the amount in tips Restaurant

Answers & Explanations

Answers & Explanations

A brings in. You'll need to use the percent formula (Percent × whole = part) to determine what amount would be required at 4% for the hostess share to be equal.

The hostess tip share for one evening at Restaurant A is $1,100 × 0.07 = $77. Use this amount to find the final amount of tips, t, Restaurant B needs:

$$0.04 \times t = 77$$
$$0.04t = 77$$
$$t = \$1,925$$

Now use the percent increase formula:

$$\text{Percent increase} = \frac{1,925 - 1,100}{1,100}$$
$$= \frac{825}{1,100}$$
$$= 0.75$$

The percent increase needed is 75%. Per the question's instructions, enter this as 75 (not .75).

9. D **Difficulty:** Easy
Category: Problem Solving and Data Analysis / Rates, Ratios, Proportions, and Percentages

Getting to the Answer: To answer a question that says "directly proportional," set two ratios equal to each other and solve for the missing amount. Don't forget—match the units in the numerators and in the denominators on both sides of the proportion.

Because the first rate is given in minutes, write 1 hour as 60 minutes. Let t equal the number of topics the teacher can cover in a 60-minute period. Set up a proportion and solve for t:

$$\frac{9 \text{ topics}}{45 \text{ minutes}} = \frac{t \text{ topics}}{60 \text{ minutes}}$$
$$9(60) = 45(t)$$
$$540 = 45t$$
$$12 = t$$

Choice (D) is correct.

10. C **Difficulty:** Easy
Category: Problem Solving and Data Analysis / Rates, Ratios, Proportions, and Percentages

Getting to the Answer: It can be confusing to decide which operation to perform when dealing with

conversions, especially when the conversions involve decimals. Think about how your answer should look first. A person weighs *less* on the moon, so he or she should weigh *more* on Earth. This means your answer must be greater than 29, so you can eliminate A right away.

The easiest way to convert the units and keep them straight is to set up a proportion.

$$\frac{0.166 \text{ lb on moon}}{1 \text{ lb on Earth}} = \frac{29 \text{ lb on moon}}{p \text{ lb on Earth}}$$
$$29(1) = 0.166p$$
$$174.7 \approx p$$

The man weighs about 175 pounds on Earth. Choice (C) is correct.

11. C **Difficulty:** Easy
Category: Problem Solving and Data Analysis / Rates, Ratios, Proportions, and Percentages

Getting to the Answer: According to the pie graph, 25% of the customers are totally dissatisfied and 15% are somewhat dissatisfied. So, 100% − 25% − 15% = 60% of the customers are totally or somewhat satisfied. Thus, the *number* of customers that are totally or somewhat satisfied is 60% of 240, or 0.6 × 240 = 144 customers, making (C) correct.

12. B **Difficulty:** Medium
Category: Problem Solving and Data Analysis / Rates, Ratios, Proportions, and Percentages

Getting to the Answer: This is a typical proportion question. Use words first to write the proportion. Then translate from English into math. Let n equal the number of people tested. Set up a proportion and solve for n. Be sure to match the units in the numerators and in the denominators on both sides of the proportion.

$$\frac{\text{false positives}}{\text{number tested}} = \frac{\text{false positives}}{\text{number tested}}$$
$$\frac{6}{3,500} = \frac{27}{n}$$
$$6n = 27(3,500)$$
$$6n = 94,500$$
$$n = 15,750$$

This means (B) is correct.

13. C   Difficulty: Medium
Category: Problem Solving and Data Analysis / Rates, Ratios, Proportions, and Percentages

Getting to the Answer: Start with the hours. The client received 25 hours of tutoring, of which 1 hour was free. So, the client paid for 24 hours of tutoring. The first 10 hours were at a different rate than the discounted rate, so subtract these to find that the client paid the discounted rate for 24 − 10 = 14 hours. Now look at the money: The first 10 hours the client was actually billed for cost $30 per hour for a total of $300, so subtract this from the total amount paid to get $664 − $300 = $364. This is the amount charged for the 14 discounted hours. Divide this amount by the number of hours billed at the discounted rate to get $364 ÷ 14 = $26 per hour, making (C) the correct choice.

14. C   Difficulty: Medium
Category: Problem Solving and Data Analysis / Rates, Ratios, Proportions, and Percentages

Getting to the Answer: You are given a lot of numbers in this question. Break the question into short steps. Before you move on, check that you answered the right question (the number of LED bulbs that were *not* defective).

Step 1: Find the number of LED bulbs produced. A total of 12,500 of both kinds of bulbs were produced. The ratio of LED to CFL is 2:3, so two parts LED plus three parts CFL equals 12,500. Write this as $2x + 3x = 12,500$. Simplify and solve this equation to find that $x = 2,500$. Multiply this amount by 2 (because two parts were LED bulbs): $2,500 \times 2 = 5,000$.

Step 2: Use that number to find the number of LED bulbs that were defective: 3% of 5,000 or $0.03 \times 5,000 = 150$ defective LEDs.

Step 3: Find the number of LED bulbs that were *not* defective: $5,000 − 150 = 4,850$. Choice (C) is correct.

15. B   Difficulty: Medium
Category: Problem Solving and Data Analysis / Rates, Ratios, Proportions, and Percentages

Getting to the Answer: Find the percent increase using this formula: $\% \text{ increase} = \dfrac{\text{amount of increase}}{\text{original amount}}$.

Then apply the same percent increase to the animal population in 2000. The amount of increase is $7,200 − 6,400 = 800$, so the percent increase is $\dfrac{800}{6,400} = 0.125 = 12.5\%$ between 1950 and 2000. If the total percent increase over the next 50 years is the same, the animal population should be about $7,200 \times 1.125 = 8,100$. Choose (B) and move on to the next question.

16. 14   Difficulty: Easy
Category: Problem Solving and Data Analysis / Rates, Ratios, Proportions, and Percentages

Getting to the Answer: You know the length of Betsy's book and the rate at which she reads. You need to know how many minutes she reads.

$$116 \text{ p\cancel{g}} \times \frac{1.5 \text{ min}}{1 \text{ p\cancel{g}}} = 174 \text{ min}$$

It takes Betsy 174 minutes to read her book. You know Raymond starts reading at 8:30 AM and reads until 11:38 AM, which is $11:38 − 8:30 = 3$ hours, 8 minutes, or 188 minutes. It takes Raymond $188 − 174 = 14$ minutes longer to read his book.

17. 50   Difficulty: Medium
Category: Problem Solving and Data Analysis / Rates, Ratios, Proportions, and Percentages

Getting to the Answer: Break this problem into short steps.

Step one: Find the total number of drips needed by multiplying the amount of medication prescribed, 800 mL, by the number of drips needed to deliver 1 mL: $800 \times 30 = 24,000$ drips.

Step two: Divide this number by 8 to find how many drips per hour are needed: $24,000 \div 8 = 3,000$ drips per hour.

Step three: Divide this by 60 (because there are 60 minutes in one hour) to convert drips per hour to drips per minute: $3,000 \div 60 = 50$ drips per minute.

18. 40   Difficulty: Hard

Category: Problem Solving and Data Analysis / Rates, Ratios, Proportions, and Percentages

Getting to the Answer: Start by determining what the question is asking. You need to find the net change in the power allocated to Grid 1 over the course of a day. To do this, you need to know how much the grid was allocated at the beginning of the day and how much at the end.

You aren't given a concrete starting point (or units of power), so simply pick a starting number. The best number to use when dealing with percents is 100. First, find how much power the grid was allocated after the first 20% increase: $100 \times 1.2 = 120$. Next, find the amount after the 10% decrease: $120 \times 0.9 = 108$. Finally, find the amount after the last 30% increase: $108 \times 1.3 = 140.4$, which is $140.4 - 100 = 40.4$ more than it started the day with. To find the percent change, use the formula Percent change $= \dfrac{\text{amount of change}}{\text{original amount}}$ to get $\dfrac{40.4}{100} = 0.404$. Rounded to the nearest whole percent, this is 40 percent.

19. 10.5   Difficulty: Medium

Category: Problem Solving and Data Analysis / Rates, Ratios, Proportions, and Percentages

Getting to the Answer: For each of the three friends, you know how long they traveled and their rate. Use the DIRT formula to find the distance for each one. But be careful—the rates are given in miles per hour, which means you must use hours, not minutes, for the times.

Andrea:

30 minutes $=$ 0.5 hours

Distance $= 3 \times 0.5 = 1.5$ miles

Kellan:

45 minutes $=$ 0.75 hours

Distance $= 14 \times 0.75 = 10.5$ miles

Joelle:

15 minutes $=$ 0.25 hours

Distance $= 35 \times 0.25 = 8.75$ miles

Kellan lives the farthest away at 10.5 miles. An important note here—the question did not tell you to round and the entire answer fits in the grid, so you MUST grid the answer in as 10.5. However, had you gotten an answer like 10.57 (which wouldn't fit in the grid), then you could either round to 10.6 or truncate (cut off) the answer at 10.5 because it would still fill the entire grid.

20. 731   Difficulty: Hard

Category: Problem Solving and Data Analysis / Rates, Ratios, Proportions, and Percentages

Getting to the Answer: When answering question sets that share information, you can often save some time by using amounts you found in the first question to answer the second one.

In the previous question, you found that Andrea's house is 1.5 miles from the restaurant. Use the DIRT formula to determine how long Kellan walked with Andrea:

$$1.5 = 2.5 \times \text{time}$$
$$1.5 = 2.5t$$
$$0.6 = t$$

They walked for 0.6 hours, or $60 \times 0.6 = 36$ minutes. Now calculate how long Kellan biked. Again, you have the distance and the rate, so you need to use the formula to find the time:

$$12 = 15 \times \text{time}$$
$$12 = 15t$$
$$0.8 = t$$

Kellan biked for 0.8 hours, or $60 \times 0.8 = 48$ minutes. So Kellan traveled for a total of $36 + 48 = 84$ minutes, or 1 hour, 24 minutes. Don't forget that they arrived 5 minutes early, or at 8:55. So Kellan must have left his house at $8:55 - 1$ hour $= 7:55 - 24$ minutes which is 7:31 AM. Enter this as 731.

21. A   Difficulty: Easy

Category: Problem Solving and Data Analysis / Rates, Ratios, Proportions, and Percentages

Getting to the Answer: When a question involves several rates, break it into separate, manageable pieces and deal with each in turn. When the car is driven off the lot, it immediately loses $12,000 in value, regardless of how far it is driven, so the after-purchase value is $35,000 − $12,000 = $23,000. The first 50,000 miles *reduce* the car's value by $0.15 each, or 50,000(−$0.15) = −$7,500. Now the car's value is $23,000 − $7,500 = $15,500. Any miles driven over 50,000 reduce the value by $0.10 per mile, and the car is driven for 92,000 miles, which is 42,000 over 50,000. This means the car depreciates another 42,000(−0.10) = −$4,200. The value of the car after being driven 92,000 miles is $15,500 − $4,200 = $11,300, which matches (A).

22. B   Difficulty: Easy
Category: Problem Solving and Data Analysis / Rates, Ratios, Proportions, and Percentages

Getting to the Answer: The percent of the budget spent on the contractor's fee is 100% − 20% − 55% − 10% = 15%. You're told that the estimate for materials is $5,200, which represents 20% of the total budget. Let x be the total amount of the budget in dollars. Then 20% of x is $5,200, or 0.2$x$ = 5,200. Solve this equation for x.

$$0.2x = 5,200$$
$$x = 26,000$$

The total budget is $26,000. The contractor's fee represents 15% of this amount, or 0.15 × $26,000 = $3,900, which means (B) is correct.

23. B   Difficulty: Medium
Category: Problem Solving and Data Analysis / Rates, Ratios, Proportions, and Percentages

Getting to the Answer: The question says temperatures can vary by 20°C during a single day. This is not the same as saying the temperature itself is 20°, so you can't just convert the temperature to Fahrenheit. You aren't given exact numbers, just a range, so you'll need to pick some convenient numbers to work with. You might know (or can tell from the formula) that 0°C is equal to 32°F. So pick 0°C and 20°C. Convert each of these to Fahrenheit and then find the difference:

$$F = \frac{9}{5}(C) + 32$$
$$F_{at\,0} = \frac{9}{5}(0) + 32$$
$$= 0 + 32$$
$$= 32$$
$$F_{at\,20} = \frac{9}{5}(20) + 32$$
$$= 36 + 32$$
$$= 68$$

0°C = 32°F and 20°C = 68°F, which means a change in temperature of 20°C is equivalent to a change of 68° − 32° = 36°F, which is (B).

You could also recognize from the formula that Fahrenheit measurements are exactly $\frac{9}{5}$ of Celsius measurements, so you could multiply 20 by $\frac{9}{5}$ to arrive at 36 as well.

24. D   Difficulty: Medium
Category: Problem Solving and Data Analysis / Rates, Ratios, Proportions, and Percentages

Getting to the Answer: Start with the smallest possible row length, 20 feet. The next length must be at least 20% larger, so multiply by 1.2 to get 24 feet. But 24 is not the next row length because each row length must be evenly divisible by the width of each seat, 2.5. The next highest number that is evenly divisible by 2.5 is 25, so 25 is the next row length. You must always use the next highest number up because rounding down would make the subsequent length less than 20% longer than the row in front of it. Now multiply 25 by 1.2 to get 30 feet. This number is evenly divisible by 2.5, so it is the third row length. Continue this process until you reach the maximum length allowed, 90 feet.

$$20 \times 1.2 = 24 \rightarrow 25$$
$$25 \times 1.2 = 30 \rightarrow 30$$
$$30 \times 1.2 = 36 \rightarrow 37.5$$
$$37.5 \times 1.2 = 45 \rightarrow 45$$
$$45 \times 1.2 = 54 \rightarrow 55$$
$$55 \times 1.2 = 66 \rightarrow 67.5$$
$$67.5 \times 1.2 = 81 \rightarrow 82.5$$
$$82.5 \times 1.2 = 99 \rightarrow \text{Too long}$$

The possible row lengths are 25, 30, 37.5, 45, 55, 67.5, and 82.5, which means (D) is correct.

25. D   Difficulty: Hard

Category: Problem Solving and Data Analysis / Rates, Ratios, Proportions, and Percentages

Getting to the Answer: The key to answering this question is translating from English into math. Start by assigning a variable to what you're looking for. Let m be the number of months the customer has subscribed to the service. The first month costs a dollars and the remaining months ($m - 1$) are charged at a rate of b dollars per month. So, the total charge for the subscription so far is $a + b(m - 1)$. Set this equal to the amount the customer has paid and solve for m. Note that you're not going to get a nice numerical answer, because the question doesn't give you the actual rates.

$$a + b(m - 1) = 108.60$$
$$a + bm - b = 108.60$$
$$bm = 108.60 - a + b$$
$$m = \frac{108.60 - a + b}{b}$$

The expression for m matches the one in (D).

26. D   Difficulty: Hard

Category: Problem Solving and Data Analysis / Rates, Ratios, Proportions, and Percentages

Getting to the Answer: Draw a chart or diagram detailing the various price reductions for each two weeks.

Length of Time on Market	% of Most Recent Price	Resulting Price
List Price	–	$200,000.00
After 2 weeks	100% − 5% = 95%	$190,000.00
After 4 weeks	100% − 5% = 95%	$180,500.00
After 6 weeks	100% − 3% = 97%	$175,085.00
After 8 weeks	100% − 3% = 97%	$169,832.45

You can stop here because the item was sold after 9 weeks and the next price reduction would have been at 10 weeks, so the selling price was $169,832.45, which is (D).

27. C   Difficulty: Medium

Category: Problem Solving and Data Analysis / Rates, Ratios, Proportions, and Percentages

Getting to the Answer: This is another question where the units can help you find the answer. Use the number of employees to find the total number of miles driven to find the total number of gallons of gas used. Then you can write an equation, with r equal to the reimbursement rate, and set it equal to the amount of total reimbursements paid.

$$126 \text{ employees} \times \frac{12{,}250 \text{ mi}}{\text{employee}} = 1{,}543{,}500 \text{ mi}$$

$$1{,}543{,}500 \text{ mi} \times \frac{1 \text{ gal of gas}}{22.5 \text{ miles}} = 68{,}600 \text{ gal}$$

$$68{,}600r = \$96{,}040.00$$
$$r = \$1.40$$

The reimbursement rate was $1.40 per gallon, which is (C).

28. D   Difficulty: Hard

Category: Problem Solving and Data Analysis / Rates, Ratios, Proportions, and Percentages

Getting to the Answer: You need to find the ratio of lionfish to seahorses. You're given two ratios: eels to lionfish and eels to seahorses. Both of the given ratios contain eels, but the eel amounts (5 and 2) are not identical. To directly compare them, find a common multiple (10). Multiply each ratio by the factor that will make the number of eels equal to 10:

$$\text{Eels to Lionfish: } (5{:}2) \times (2{:}2) = 10{:}4$$

$$\text{Eels to Seahorses: } (2{:}3) \times (5{:}5) = 10{:}15$$

Now that the number of eels needed are the same in both ratios, you can merge the two ratios to compare lionfish to seahorses directly: 4:10:15. So the proper ratio of lionfish to seahorses is 4:15, which is (D).

29. 4   Difficulty: Easy

Category: Problem Solving and Data Analysis / Rates, Ratios, Proportions, and Percentages

Getting to the Answer: Katrina already knows how much cardboard she needs; she just doesn't have the amount in the proper units. All this question is asking you to do is convert 576 *square* inches to *square* feet.

$$\frac{576 \text{ in.}^2}{1} \times \frac{1 \text{ ft}}{12 \text{ in.}} \times \frac{1 \text{ ft}}{12 \text{ in.}} = \frac{576}{144} \text{ ft}^2 = 4 \text{ ft}^2$$

30. 540 Difficulty: Medium

Category: Problem Solving and Data Analysis / Rates, Ratios, Proportions, and Percentages

Getting to the Answer: Break the question into steps. First, find how long it took the employee to collect samples from one house, and then use that amount to find how long it should take the employee to collect samples from all of the houses.

The employee *started* the 1st house at 9:00 and the 6th house at 10:00, so it took him 1 hour, or 60 minutes, to collect samples from 5 houses. This gives a unit rate of $60 \div 5 = 12$ minutes per house. Multiply the unit rate by the number of houses in the subdivision (45) to get a total of $12 \times 45 = 540$ minutes to collect samples from all the houses.

31. 1000 Difficulty: Medium

Category: Problem Solving and Data Analysis / Rates, Ratios, Proportions, and Percentages

Getting to the Answer: If the student map is $\frac{1}{4}$ the size of the wall map, then 2.5 inches on the student map would be $2.5 \times 4 = 10$ inches on the wall map. Now set up a proportion to find the actual distance between the cities using the scale of the wall map:

$$\frac{1}{100} = \frac{10}{x}$$
$$x = 1{,}000$$

The correct answer is 1000.

32. 76.5 Difficulty: Medium

Category: Problem Solving and Data Analysis / Rates, Ratios, Proportions, and Percentages

Getting to the Answer: This question is tricky. The interest (after being rounded down) is added to the account

at the end of each year. The next year, the new, higher amount is the amount that will earn interest.

Start by multiplying the principal by the interest rate: $1{,}500 \times 0.01 = 15$. Now, add this amount back to the principal: $1{,}500 + 15 = 1{,}515$.

This is the amount that will earn interest in the next year. Repeat this process for 4 more years. Multiply the principal by the interest rate, round the interest down to the nearest cent, and then add it to the principal to use for the next year's calculation.

Year two:
$1{,}515 \times 0.01 = 15.15$
$1{,}515 + 15.15 = 1{,}530.15$

Year three:
$1{,}530.15 \times 0.01 = 15.3015 \rightarrow 15.30$
$1{,}530.15 + 15.30 = 1{,}545.45$

Year four:
$1{,}545.45 \times 0.01 = 15.4545 \rightarrow 15.45$
$1{,}545.45 + 15.45 = 1{,}560.90$

Year five:
$1{,}560.90 \times 0.01 = 15.609 \rightarrow 15.60$
$1{,}560.90 + 15.60 = 1{,}576.50$

Over five years, the account earned $\$1{,}576.50 - \$1{,}500 = \$76.50$ in interest. Enter this as 76.5.

Be careful here—you might be tempted to use the exponential function $f(5) = 1{,}500(1.01)^5$ to arrive at the answer more quickly. However, the question specifically states that the interest is rounded down to the nearest whole cent each year, which changes the answer by just a couple of cents.

33. 45.5 Difficulty: Medium

Category: Problem Solving and Data Analysis / Rates, Ratios, Proportions, and Percentages

Getting to the Answer: Use the three-part percent formula, $\text{Percent} = \frac{\text{part}}{\text{whole}} \times 100\%$. You'll need to do some preliminary calculations to find the *whole*.

The *part* of the budget represented by the textbook is $24.99. The total cost of all the supplies (or the *whole*) is:

1 textbook ($24.99) + 5 notebooks (5 × $3.78 = $18.90) + 20 pencils (20 × $0.55 = $11.00) = $54.89. Now use the formula:

$$\text{Percent} = \frac{24.99}{54.89} \times 100\%$$
$$= 0.45527 \times 100\%$$
$$= 45.527\%$$

Before you grid in your answer, make sure you followed the directions—round to the nearest tenth of a percent and ignore the percent sign, which is 45.5.

34. 100   Difficulty: Hard
Category: Problem Solving and Data Analysis / Rates, Ratios, Proportions, and Percentages

Getting to the Answer: This question contains several steps. Be careful—there are lots of calculations that involve decimals, and you shouldn't round until the very end.

Start with the total cost of the year's supplies: $988.02. After taking inventory, Bridget knows she has used $713.57 worth of supplies, which means she should have $988.02 − $713.57 = $274.45 worth of supplies left. From the previous question, you know that 1 textbook, 5 notebooks, and 20 pencils together cost $54.89, which means Bridget has $274.45 ÷ $54.89 = 5 sets of the initial supplies left. Don't grid in this amount because you're not finished yet! The question asks for the *number of pencils* left. According to the table, each order (set) contains 20 pencils, so there should be 5 × 20 = 100 pencils left.

35. 9.88   Difficulty: Easy
Category: Problem Solving and Data Analysis / Rates, Ratios, Proportions, and Percentages

Getting to the Answer: Make sure you read the question carefully. It says the 5% clothing discount is applied *before* any other discounts, so you much subtract this first.

If the student receives a 5% discount for bringing in the item of clothing, this means she pays 95%, so don't waste time multiplying the amount of her check by 0.05 and then subtracting. Instead, just multiply the amount of her check by 0.95 to get $13.00 × 0.95 = $12.35. Then,

apply the student discount using the same strategy. The student discount is 20% (which means she paid 80%), so she paid $12.35 × 0.8 = $9.88, not including tax.

36. 3.89   Difficulty: Medium
Category: Problem Solving and Data Analysis / Rates, Ratios, Proportions, and Percentages

Getting to the Answer: Calculate the discount for each person. Make sure you answer the right question. The question asks about the *savings*, not about what each person pays, so this time, you *should* multiply by the discount amounts (either 20% or 5%) to save time. Calculate Sharon's military discount first: $16.25 × 0.2 = $3.25 saved. Now, Damien's discount for participating in the clothing drive: $12.80 × 0.05 = $0.64 saved. Add the two amounts to find that together they saved a total of $3.25 + $0.64 = $3.89.

37. 11.5   Difficulty: Medium
Category: Problem Solving and Data Analysis / Rates, Ratios, Proportions, and Percentages

Getting to the Answer: This question involves a proportion and a unit conversion. You may be tempted to divide the number of steps by the number of feet in Jordan's stride (because the number of steps is already very large), but this isn't correct. To be safe, start by writing a proportion comparing feet and steps.

Let f represent the number of feet Jordan ran. There are 2.5 feet to every 1 of Jordan's steps and he took 24,288 steps.

$$\frac{2.5 \text{ feet}}{1 \text{ step}} = \frac{f \text{ feet}}{24{,}288 \text{ steps}}$$
$$f = 2.5(24{,}288)$$
$$f = 60{,}720$$

Jordan ran 60,720 feet. Now convert this to miles. There are 5,280 feet in one mile, so divide to get 60,720 ÷ 5,280 = 11.5 miles. Don't forget—if the question doesn't tell you to round and the answer will fit in the grid, don't round! Enter the answer as 11.5.

You could also use the factor-label method to answer this question:

$$24{,}288 \text{ steps} \times \frac{2.5 \text{ ft}}{1 \text{ step}} \times \frac{1 \text{ mi}}{5{,}280 \text{ ft}} = 11.5 \text{ miles}$$

38. 18.5 Difficulty: Easy

Category: Problem Solving and Data Analysis / Rates, Ratios, Proportions, and Percentages

Getting to the Answer: As in the previous question, don't be tempted to either multiply or divide until you're sure which operation is correct. Let k represent the number of kilometers and set up and solve a proportion:

$$\frac{1 \text{ km}}{0.62 \text{ mi}} = \frac{k \text{ km}}{11.5 \text{ mi}}$$

$$11.5 = 0.62k$$

$$\frac{11.5}{0.62} = k$$

$$18.5483 = k$$

The question tells you to round to the nearest tenth of a kilometer, so enter the answer as 18.5.

CHAPTER 6

PRACTICE

4. C   Difficulty: Easy
Category: Problem Solving and Data Analysis / Scatterplots

Getting to the Answer: Examine the equation to determine the type of plot it will produce. When the exponent in an equation is a variable, the graph of the equation is exponential, so eliminate choices A and B. To distinguish between the remaining choices, pick an easy-to-use value to plug into the given equation for x (e.g., 0). You'll see that when $x = 0$, y should equal 5, which matches the graph in (C).

5. 2   Difficulty: Medium
Category: Problem Solving and Data Analysis / Scatterplots

Getting to the Answer: You're asked for a rate; this means finding the slope of the line of best fit. Start by picking a pair of points, preferably where the line of best fit passes through a grid-line intersection to minimize error. The points (50, 20) and (100, 40) are good choices. Determine the slope:

$$m = \frac{y_2 - y_1}{x_2 - x_1} = \frac{40 - 20}{100 - 50} = \frac{20}{50} = \frac{2}{5}$$

Don't grid in $\frac{2}{5}$, though. Remember what you're being asked: You need the road clearing duration increase for a 5% increase in snowpack water content, not 1%. Multiply $\frac{2}{5}$ by 5, which yields 2.

6. 99.2   Difficulty: Medium
Category: Problem Solving and Data Analysis / Scatterplots

Getting to the Answer: The slope you found in the previous question will save you some time here. The line of best fit on the scatterplot intersects the y-axis at (0, 0). Therefore, the equation of the line of best fit is $y = \frac{2}{5}x$. Plug 248 in for x and simplify:

$$y = \frac{2}{5} \times 248 = \frac{496}{5} = 99.2$$

PERFORM

7. A   Difficulty: Easy
Category: Problem Solving and Data Analysis / Scatterplots

Getting to the Answer: The question asks for a rate of change, which means you'll need the slope of the line of best fit. Pick a pair of points to use in the slope formula, such as (1998, 20) and (2012, 90):

$$m = \frac{y_2 - y_1}{x_2 - x_1} = \frac{90 - 20}{2012 - 1998} = \frac{70}{14} = 5$$

Choice (A) is correct.

8. A   Difficulty: Easy
Category: Problem Solving and Data Analysis / Scatterplots

Getting to the Answer: Identify the type of change described in the question to narrow down your choices. If the number of smartphone users increases by 35% each year, then the amount of the increase is variable (because it's 35% of a bigger number each time), indicating nonlinear (exponential) growth. Eliminate C and D. Recall that when assembling an exponential growth model, r (the rate) must be in decimal form. Therefore, the number raised to the power of x should be $1 + 0.35$ or 1.35. Choice (A) is the only one that fits these criteria.

9. D   Difficulty: Medium
Category: Problem Solving and Data Analysis / Scatterplots

Getting to the Answer: Compare each statement to the infographic one at a time, eliminating true statements as you work. Start with A: It is impossible to tell from the graph which strain has the higher reading at 20 hours, so you cannot say the statement is NOT true. Eliminate A. Choice B states that Strain 2's growth rate (slope) overtook Strain 1's at hour 50, which is consistent with the infographic; eliminate it. Choice C requires math, so skip it for now. Choice (D) states that Strain 1's growth rate was greater than Strain 2's over the entire period. Although Strain 1's growth rate was greater for part of the monitored period, it is not greater for the entire period (because the slope of Strain 1's curve is not steeper than that of Strain 2's curve for every line segment on the graph), which makes (D) false and, therefore, correct.

EXTRA PRACTICE

1. C   Difficulty: Easy
Category: Problem Solving and Data Analysis / Scatterplots

Getting to the Answer: A regression equation is the equation of the line (or curve) that best fits the data. A *linear* regression is used to model data that follows the path of a straight line. In the equation given, *a* represents the slope of the linear regression (the line of best fit), so you are looking for data that is linear (looks like a line) and is decreasing, or falling from left to right ($a < 0$ means a is negative). You can eliminate A and D because the data is not linear (A is quadratic and D is exponential). You can also eliminate B because the data is increasing (rising from left to right). This means (C) is correct.

2. A   Difficulty: Easy
Category: Problem Solving and Data Analysis / Scatterplots

Getting to the Answer: When an exponential equation is written in the form $y = x_0(1 + r)^x$, the value of x_0 gives the *y*-intercept of the equation's graph. To answer this question, you need to think about what the *y*-intercept would represent in the context described.

Whenever time is involved in a relationship that is modeled by an equation or a graph, it is always the independent variable and therefore graphed on the *x*-axis. Therefore, for this question, population would be graphed on the *y*-axis, so x_0 most likely represents the population when the time elapsed was zero, or in other words, in the year that Adriana was born, making (A) correct.

3. D   Difficulty: Medium
Category: Problem Solving and Data Analysis / Scatterplots

Getting to the Answer: A line that "represents the trend of the data" is another way of saying line of best fit. The trend of the data is clearly linear because the path of the dots does not turn around or curve, so draw a line

of best fit on the graph. Remember, about half of the points should be above the line and half below.

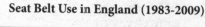
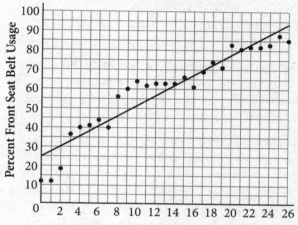

Seat Belt Use in England (1983-2009)

Percent Front Seat Belt Usage (y-axis)
Years After Seat Belt Law Enacted (x-axis)

If you draw the line all the way to the *y*-axis, you'll save a step by finding the *y*-intercept just by looking at the scatterplot. For this graph, it's about 25. This means you can eliminate B and C. To choose between A and (D), find the approximate slope using two points that lie on (or very close to) the line of best fit. You can use the *y*-intercept, (0, 25), as one of the points to save time and estimate the second, such as (21, 80). Use the slope formula to find the slope:

$$m = \frac{y_2 - y_1}{x_2 - x_1} = \frac{80 - 25}{21 - 0} = \frac{55}{21} = 2.62$$

The result is very close to the slope in (D), making it the correct answer.

4. A   Difficulty: Medium
Category: Problem Solving and Data Analysis / Scatterplots

Getting to the Answer: Examine the graph, paying careful attention to units and labels. The average rate of change is the same as the slope of the line of best fit. The data is decreasing (going down from left to right) so you can immediately eliminate C and D. To choose between (A) and B, find the slope of the line of best fit using the slope formula, $m = \dfrac{y_2 - y_1}{x_2 - x_1}$, and any two points that lie on (or very close to) the line. Using the two points

Answers & Explanations

(5, 14) and (10, 8), the average rate of change is about $\frac{8-14}{10-5} = \frac{-6}{5} = -1.2$, which matches (A).

5. A   Difficulty: Medium
Category: Problem Solving and Data Analysis / Scatterplots

Getting to the Answer: Determine whether the predicted change in the interest rate is a common difference (linear function) or a common ratio (exponential function), or if it changes direction (quadratic or polynomial function).

The company predicts that every six months, the Federal Reserve will *raise* rates by 0.25 percentage points. Interest rates are already expressed as percentages, so raising the rates by 0.25 percentage points means *adding* a quarter of a percent every six months. It does not mean it will increase *by* 0.25% every six months. The function therefore involves a common difference, so the best model would be a linear function, which is (A).

6. B   Difficulty: Hard
Category: Problem Solving and Data Analysis / Scatterplots

Getting to the Answer: When presented with a "series" of data, making a chart helps. In this question, the chart should include the number of bounces and the height after the bounce. You can then look for patterns that may tell you which function to pick, or at the very least, which functions to eliminate.

Bounce Number (b)	Height After Bounce (H(b))
1	80
2	40
3	20
4	10

Look for a pattern: the heights are decreasing by a common ratio each time $\left(\frac{1}{2}\right)$, so an exponential function will be the best match. This means you can eliminate C and D (which are linear functions). To choose between A and (B), evaluate each function at $b = 1$ and see what happens.

Choice A: $H(1) = \frac{80}{2^1} = \frac{80}{2} = 40$. The height should be 80 after the first bounce, so eliminate this choice.

Choice B: $H(1) = \frac{80}{2^{1-1}} = \frac{80}{2^0} = \frac{80}{1} = 80$. Choice (B) is correct.

If you're not convinced (or if both results had been 80), move on to $b = 2$ and evaluate each function again, until you are able to eliminate one of them.

7. 2   Difficulty: Easy
Category: Problem Solving and Data Analysis / Scatterplots

Getting to the Answer: Examine the graph, including the axis labels and numbering. Each vertical grid-line represents 5 eggs, so look to see how many data points are more than a complete grid space away from the line of best fit. Only 2 are more than 5 away—the first data point and the one between 30 and 35 weeks, making 2 the correct answer.

8. 57   Difficulty: Hard
Category: Problem Solving and Data Analysis / Scatterplots

Getting to the Answer: This is a Grid-in question, so you can't just use the graph to estimate the y-value when $x = 36$. Instead, you need to find the equation of the line of best fit, and then substitute 36 for x and simplify. Start with the slope—you could pick two points on the line and use the slope formula, or you could count the rise and the run. The latter is easier in this question. Beginning at the point (0, 75), the line falls 5 units and runs 10 units to the first point on the line, so the slope is $\frac{-5}{10} = -\frac{1}{2}$.

This means that the equation looks like $y = -\frac{1}{2}x + b$. Next, find the y-intercept. You can see clearly from the graph that it is approximately 75.

The equation is $y = -\frac{1}{2}x + 75$. Now, substitute 36 for x and simplify to find y:

$$y = -\frac{1}{2}(36) + 75$$
$$y = -18 + 75$$
$$y = 57$$

The correct answer is 57.

9. C **Difficulty:** Easy

Category: Problem Solving and Data Analysis / Scatterplots

Getting to the Answer: Correlation means that there is a discernible relationship between two or more variables. A positive correlation means that as one variable increases, so does the other variable. A negative correlation means that as one variable increases, the other decreases. The closer the relationship is, the stronger the correlation.

Take a quick peek at the answer choices and picture or draw a sketch of each one. *Linear* indicates that the data follows the path of a straight line. *Positive* means rising from left to right. Finally, *strong* means the relationship is a close one, but not perfect, so the data points should be fairly close to, but not exactly on, the line; choice (C) is correct.

10. A **Difficulty:** Easy

Category: Problem Solving and Data Analysis / Scatterplots

Getting to the Answer: A line with a downward slant has a negative slope, so you can immediately eliminate C and D. To choose between (A) and B, recall that slope is a ratio that compares vertical change (rise) to horizontal change (run). Mark the bordered area using equal measures and then estimate the slope of a line drawn through the center of the points as shown.

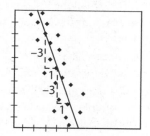

The line appears to fall 3 units and run 1 unit, so a good estimate for the slope is −3, making (A) correct. Note that you could also use what you know about slope to answer the question—lines that have fractional slopes, between −1 and 1, are not steep lines, which means B can't be correct.

11. D **Difficulty:** Easy

Category: Problem Solving and Data Analysis / Scatterplots

Getting to the Answer: Knowing where the y-intercept of the line of best fits falls will help you eliminate answer choices.

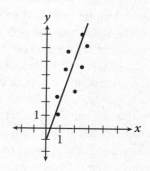

The line of best fit intercepts the y-axis below the x-axis, and is therefore negative, so you can eliminate B and C (the y-intercept is +1 for each of those lines). Now, look at the slope. The line rises along the y-axis slightly faster than it runs along the x-axis, so the slope must be slightly greater than 1, making (D) correct. If you have trouble choosing between A and (D), you could also graph each equation in your calculator to see which one is a better match for the line. Use a viewing window that is approximately the same as in the graph. Here, the viewing window would be $-2 \leq x \leq 5$ and $-2 \leq y \leq 7$.

12. C **Difficulty:** Medium

Category: Problem Solving and Data Analysis / Scatterplots

Getting to the Answer: "Correlation" simply means relationship. The word "weak" refers to the strength of the relationship (how close the data lies to the line of best fit), which has no effect on slope. Be careful not to confuse slope and strength. The fact that a data set shows a weak correlation does not give you any information about the magnitude of the slope. This means you can eliminate A and B. Also, keep in mind that the terms "weak" and "negative" are not related, but rather are two independent descriptors of the correlation. So the fact that the rate of change is negative has nothing to do with the strength of the correlation. In a weak correlation, the data points will loosely follow the line of best fit, making (C) the correct answer.

13. B   **Difficulty:** Medium

Category: Problem Solving and Data Analysis / Scatterplots

Getting to the Answer: There are two things to keep in mind for a question like this: Correlation does not prove causation, and as a general rule, conclusions can only be drawn about the population studied, not about all populations. The data points are scattered and do not form any discernible pattern. This means there is no correlation, which is another way of saying the two variables aren't related, so you can eliminate D. You can also eliminate C because the HR representative *is* able to draw a conclusion—that there is no relationship. To choose between A and (B), recall that when you analyze data from a given population (the employees at that particular company), you can only draw conclusions about that population, not about employee populations in general. Therefore, (B) is correct.

14. D   **Difficulty:** Medium

Category: Problem Solving and Data Analysis / Scatterplots

Getting to the Answer: The fact that the two variables are strongly correlated, whether it be negatively or positively, only shows that there is a relationship between the variables. It does not indicate whether the change in one variable caused the change in the other. For example, Population A might thrive in wet climates, while Population B does not, and in the years studied, rainfall may have increased, which caused the changes in the populations. This means (D) is the correct answer.

15. D   **Difficulty:** Medium

Category: Problem Solving and Data Analysis / Scatterplots

Getting to the Answer: Try drawing a quick graph (or at least visualizing a graph) that matches the description in the question (decreases quickly at first and then at a much slower rate). The shape and direction of the curve should tell you which type of model to choose.

The question doesn't say anything about the data points changing direction at any time, so you can eliminate A and B—they are both quadratic functions, which always turn around at their vertex. To choose between C and (D), skim through the question again. The data is decreasing, or getting smaller. In an exponential function, when the rate

(r) is greater than 0, as in C, the function is an exponential growth model, which increases, not decreases, and therefore cannot be correct. This means (D) is correct. When the rate (r) is less than 0, the function is an exponential decay model, which matches the description of the data.

16. D   **Difficulty:** Medium

Category: Problem Solving and Data Analysis / Scatterplots

Getting to the Answer: According to the question, the amount of milk a typical baby needs starts at 0 ounces and increases until it peaks at about 6 months of age. Then the amount of milk needed decreases until one year of age, when it becomes 0 ounces again. This means the shape of the data would look like an upside down parabola, which would match a negative quadratic model, making (D) correct. (Note: a negative absolute value model could also be used, depending on whether the rates of increase and decrease are constant, but that is not one of the answer choices.)

17. B   **Difficulty:** Medium

Category: Problem Solving and Data Analysis / Scatterplots

Getting to the Answer: Think logically about what happens to the data points and the line of best fit. The amount of snowfall is recorded on the y-axis, so the y-values of the data points stay the same. The x-values of the points all shift to the right 10 units (because Genji adds 10 degrees to each of the temperature readings). This means that all the data points stay in the same place vertically, but shift horizontally, resulting in the same rate of change, so you can eliminate C and D. The line of best fit would also still look the same, just shifted to the right. This means the strength of correlation does not change, as the points will still be the same distance away from the (now moved) line of best fit, making (B) correct.

18. D   **Difficulty:** Hard

Category: Problem Solving and Data Analysis / Scatterplots

Getting to the Answer: When a regression model has a correlation coefficient of 1.0, it means that the model exactly fits the data. This tells you that you can use what you know about quadratic functions to answer the question.

The graph of a quadratic function is symmetric with respect to its axis of symmetry. The axis of symmetry passes through the x-value of the vertex, which also happens to be where the maximum (or minimum) of the function occurs. The question tells you this value—it's $x = 25$. Because 35 is $35 - 25 = 10$ units to the right of the axis of symmetry, you know that the y-value will be the same as the point that is 10 units to the left of the axis of symmetry. This occurs at $x = 25 - 10 = 15$. Read the y-value from the graphing calculator screenshot to find the answer, which is 27. Therefore, (D) is correct.

19. 3   Difficulty: Medium
Category: Problem Solving and Data Analysis / Scatterplots

Getting to the Answer: Percent error gives the deviation of an actual value from an expected value. Graphically, this is determined by how far from the line of best fit the data point is. You don't need to find the percent error of every point (or even a single point) to answer this question. Instead, you just need to understand that the point with the greatest percent error from the mean of the data is the point that is farthest from the line of best fit. Use the grid-lines on the graph to find the point. The point (9, 3) is 4 full grid-lines away from the line of best fit, which is farther than any other data point. The question asks for the y-value of this point, so the correct answer is 3.

20. 18   Difficulty: Medium
Category: Problem Solving and Data Analysis / Scatterplots

Getting to the Answer: Because the y-value of the graph when $x = 3,400$ is not shown, this question requires a mathematical solution; extending the line of best fit will not provide an accurate enough answer. The equation of the model is given as $y = -\dfrac{1}{200}x + 35$. Miles over recommended servicing are graphed along the x-axis, so substitute 3,400 for x to find the answer:

$$y = -\frac{1}{200}(3,400) + 35 = -17 + 35 = 18$$

CHAPTER 7

PRACTICE

8. B   Difficulty: Medium

Category: Problem Solving and Data Analysis / Statistics and Probability

Getting to the Answer: The professor starts with a normal distribution; when the new data are added, the distribution changes:

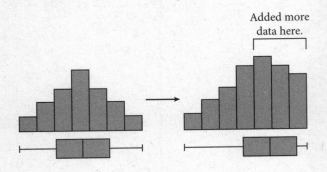

Added more data here.

The new distribution is skewed to the left (in the direction of the graph's tail, not in the direction of its biggest bump), and the median has increased. Although the range of the new data alone might be smaller than the original set, when all data are combined, the range will not have changed from the original data. The correct answer is (B).

9. 28.7   Difficulty: Easy

Category: Problem Solving and Data Analysis / Statistics and Probability

Getting to the Answer: To be considered "bad," a game must have a rating of 1 or 2. Begin by counting the number of "bad" games. There are $5 + 3 + 3 = 11$ games with a rating of 1 and $17 + 12 + 10 = 39$ games with a rating of 2. That's a total of $11 + 39 = 50$ games. Divide this by the total number of games and multiply by 100: $\frac{50}{61 + 54 + 59} \times 100 = 28.7\%$. Grid in 28.7.

10. 12 Difficulty: Medium

Category: Problem Solving and Data Analysis / Statistics and Probability

Getting to the Answer: You know from the previous question that 50 games are "bad." Reducing this number

by 50% is the same as halving it, meaning there will be 25 remaining "bad" games after the removal. Subtract this from the original total game count ($61 + 54 + 59 = 174$) to get the new total, which is 149. Divide the new "bad" count by this total, and then multiply by 100 as you did before: $\frac{25}{149} \times 100 = 16.7785\%$. Subtracting the new percentage from the old one (rounded to a minimum of 4 decimal places just to be safe) gives $28.7356\% - 16.7785\% = 11.9571\%$. This rounds to 12.

PERFORM

11. D   Difficulty: Medium

Category: Problem Solving and Data Analysis / Statistics and Probability

Getting to the Answer: Consider finding the probability of *not* selecting one of the puzzles specified, as there will be fewer dots to count. You can then subtract that probability from 1. There are only three puzzles that *didn't* take Randolph fewer than 100 seconds to solve. Of these, 2 do *not* have fewer than 6 clues. Therefore, the probability that the conditions *won't* be met is $\frac{2}{20} = 0.1$. This isn't what you're asked to find, so don't stop yet. Subtract 0.1 from 1 to get 0.9. Multiply this by 100 to get 90%; (D) is correct.

12. B   Difficulty: Easy

Category: Problem Solving and Data Analysis / Statistics and Probability

Getting to the Answer: Consider the difference between mean and standard deviation: Mean is a measure of center, while standard deviation is a measure of spread. The four answers all involve consistency, which means the explanation should involve standard deviation. Based on this, you can eliminate A and D. Higher consistency means lower standard deviation (and vice versa); the only choice that reflects this—and correctly represents the data in the table—is (B).

13. 594 Difficulty: Medium

Category: Problem Solving and Data Analysis / Statistics and Probability

Getting to the Answer: Identify Wilhelmina and Alexandra's hat contributions from the table, and then extrapolate to find how many solid-colored hats they should knit for Spirit Week. According to the table, Wilhelmina will be responsible for $\frac{24}{60}$ of the hats, and Alexandra will knit $\frac{9}{60}$ of them. The knitting club needs to knit 1,800 hats total, 60% of which should be solid-colored per the survey results, so $0.6 \times 1,080 = 1,080$ hats should be solid-colored. Add together the fractions for Wilhelmina and Alexandra to get $\frac{33}{60}$. Multiplying this by the total number of solid-colored hats will yield the number that Wilhelmina and Alexandra will knit: $\frac{33}{60} \times 1,080 = 594$.

14. 282 Difficulty: Medium

Category: Problem Solving and Data Analysis / Statistics and Probability

Getting to the Answer: Work through this one step at a time. Read carefully; you're asked about the two other club members' Spirit Week production here, and the question is not limited to solid-colored hats. Start with the number of prizes: 20% of 1,800 hats = 360 hats with emblems and therefore 360 prize scarves. The two boys make $\frac{27}{60}$ of the 360 hats = 162 hats. The two boys make $\frac{11}{33} = \frac{1}{3}$ of the 360 scarves = 120 scarves. They are responsible for $162 + 120 = 282$ of these items.

EXTRA PRACTICE

1. D Difficulty: Easy

Category: Problem Solving and Data Analysis / Statistics and Probability

Getting to the Answer: Look carefully at the infographic's axes. Look at the vertical axis—the frequency tells you the number of contestants who named each number of states: 1 contestant named only 1 state, 1 contestant named 2 states, 5 contestants named 3 states, and so on. To answer the question, add all the frequencies to find the total number of contestants: $1 + 1 + 5 + 6 + 4 + 0 + 2 + 1 = 20$, which is (D).

2. C Difficulty: Medium

Category: Problem Solving and Data Analysis / Statistics and Probability

Getting to the Answer: Not everyone who shops at an electronics store owns a tablet. Customers who bought other items, such as laptops, TVs, or MP3 players are likely to make up at least a portion of the surveys distributed with customers' purchases. This means that, despite being randomly selected, the sample is unlikely to be a good representative sample because there is no way to verify whether the responders to the survey actually own a tablet. Therefore, (C) is correct.

3. D Difficulty: Medium

Category: Problem Solving and Data Analysis / Statistics and Probability

Getting to the Answer: Understanding how averages and sums are connected is the key to answering a question like this. If the average of 14 numbers is 6, then the sum of the 14 numbers must be 84 (because $84 \div 14 = 6$). Use the dot plot to find the total number of appliances the salesman has already sold. Then, subtract this amount from 84. The salesman has already sold $3(2) + 4(3) + 5 + 6(3) + 7 + 8 + 10(2) = 76$ appliances, so he needs to sell $84 - 76 = 8$ appliances on the 14th day to reach his goal. This means (D) is correct.

4. B Difficulty: Medium

Category: Problem Solving and Data Analysis / Statistics and Probability

Getting to the Answer: According to the sample survey, $\frac{40}{300}$ say they would join the gym. But the gym estimates that only 30% of these respondents would *actually* join, so multiply 40 by 30% to find that the gym can expect $\frac{12}{300} = 0.04 = 4\%$ of the respondents to join. Multiply this by the total number of residents: $12,600 \times 0.04 = 504$ residents, so (B) is correct.

5. D Difficulty: Hard

Category: Problem Solving and Data Analysis / Statistics and Probability

Getting to the Answer: The probability that one randomly selected salmon from those that were tested would have a dangerous level of mercury is equal to the number of salmon that had dangerous mercury levels divided by the total number of salmon that were tested. This means you only need two numbers to answer this question. One of those numbers is in the table—6 salmon had dangerous mercury levels. Finding the other number is the tricky part. Use information from the question stem and the pie graph. The biologist tested 5% of the total number of each breed of fish, or 5% of 25% of 6,000 fish. Multiply to find that $0.05 \times 0.25 \times 6,000 = 75$ salmon were tested. This means the probability is $\frac{6}{75} = 0.08$, which matches (D).

6. 627   Difficulty: Medium

Category: Problem Solving and Data Analysis / Statistics and Probability

Getting to the Answer: When making inferences about populations based on sample data, find the percent of the sample data that matches the given criteria and multiply by the number in the population. Of the 250 writers in the sample, $250 - 74 - 22 - 30 - 29 = 95$ writers said they would like sandwiches for lunch. This represents $\frac{95}{250} = 0.38$, or 38%. Multiply $0.38 \times 1,650$ to arrive at 627 writers that want sandwiches for lunch.

7. B   Difficulty: Medium

Category: Problem Solving and Data Analysis / Statistics and Probability

Getting to the Answer: To calculate the percentage of people in each age group with a healthy blood sugar level (< 100), divide the number of people in *that* age group with a healthy blood sugar level by the total number of participants in *that* age group. Choice (B) is correct because $16 \div 98 \approx 0.1633 = 16.33\%$, which is a lower percentage than in the other age groups ($18\text{-}25 = 18.75\%$, $36\text{-}45 = 20.21\%$, and Older than $45 = 20\%$).

8. D   Difficulty: Medium

Category: Problem Solving and Data Analysis / Statistics and Probability

Getting to the Answer: This question requires careful reading of the table. The first criterion is fairly straightforward—you're looking for a participant with a blood sugar level in the 100-125 range, so focus on that column in the table. The second criterion is a bit trickier—*at least 36 years old* means 36 years old or older, so you'll need

to use the values in the rows for 36-45, and Older than 45. There were 35 in the 36-45 age group who were considered at risk, and 27 in the Older than 45 age group, resulting in a total of $35 + 27 = 62$ out of 300 participants. The probability of randomly selecting one participant from either of these two groups is $\frac{62}{300}$, which reduces to $\frac{31}{150}$, or (D).

9. C   Difficulty: Easy

Category: Problem Solving and Data Analysis / Statistics and Probability

Getting to the Answer: The question states that the data was collected in California about jackrabbits, so any conclusion drawn can only be generalized to that particular geographic region and to that breed of rabbit. California is in the Northern Hemisphere, so its spring months are March, April, and May. According to the data, the California jackrabbit gives birth mostly during those months, so (C) is correct.

10. B   Difficulty: Medium

Category: Problem Solving and Data Analysis / Statistics and Probability

Getting to the Answer: The table is not complete, so your first step is to fill in the missing values. Start with what you know and work from there. It may not be necessary to complete the entire table, but rather only what you need to answer the question.

You know there are 186 cookies total and that 104 are without nuts, which means $186 - 104 = 82$ have nuts. Because you already know that 40 of those cookies are oatmeal raisin, this mean $82 - 40 = 42$ are chocolate chip. You also know that $\frac{2}{3}$ of the total number of cookies are chocolate chip, which means there are $\frac{2}{3} \times 186 = 124$ chocolate chips cookies, total, so you can fill this number in the "Total" row of that column. You do not need to fill in any more of the table because the question only asks about chocolate chip cookies with nuts. There are 124 chocolate chip cookies total and 42 of them have nuts, so the probability of randomly choosing one with nuts is $\frac{42}{124}$, or $\frac{21}{62}$, which matches (B).

11. A   Difficulty: Medium

Category: Problem Solving and Data Analysis / Statistics and Probability

Getting to the Answer: As long as a sample is both representative and without bias, inferences can be drawn from the sample data to the population from which the sample was taken. In this example, if the mean number of bottles of water consumed per person each day was 2.5, then it can be assumed that the average number consumed in the general population is also 2.5, so the means are equal, and (A) is the correct answer.

12. D   Difficulty: Medium

Category: Problem Solving and Data Analysis / Statistics and Probability

Getting to the Answer: The wording in this question implies that the population for the study includes all nutrients. However, the study only tests for nitrogen and potassium, so the sample was limited. You can eliminate A and B because all nutrients were not included in the sample, so you can't say anything about them, one way or the other. The compounds may or may not help the soil retain other types of nutrients, and you certainly don't know which of the five would produce the best results. You can eliminate C because the question doesn't tell you anything about the data collection methods, so you can't determine whether or not the study was biased. This means that choice (D) is correct—the study will only be able to produce results concerning the effects of the compounds on the soil retaining nitrogen and potassium.

13. B   Difficulty: Medium

Category: Problem Solving and Data Analysis / Statistics and Probability

Getting to the Answer: The median is the middle number in a series of numbers. Arrange the number of history majors from least to greatest, making sure that 225 is in the middle. Use s to balance out the number of history majors on either side of 225. Because there are already two numbers above the median (240 and 287), there must be two numbers below the median, 162 and s:

s, 162, 225, 240, 287

or

162, s, 225, 240, 287

Because s could be on either side of 162, it could be anything less than or equal to 225. Its greatest possible value is therefore 225, which is (B).

14. 2/5 or .4   Difficulty: Medium

Category: Problem Solving and Data Analysis / Statistics and Probability

Getting to the Answer: Take a second to think about the quickest way to answer the question—you're not asked to find the popularity rating of each performer and then compare them. Based on the host's definition, you can pick the most popular performer by simply looking at the numbers in the table. More people attended on Day 3, so you only need to find the popularity rating for Entertainer C: 1,600 people attended on that day out of a total of $1,280 + 1,120 + 1,600 = 4,000$ festival goers, so Entertainer C's popularity rating is $\frac{1,600}{4,000} = \frac{2}{5}$, or .4.

15. B   Difficulty: Easy

Category: Problem Solving and Data Analysis / Statistics and Probability

Getting to the Answer: The question only asks about participants who were outside a healthy weight range, so focus on this row: 38 out of the 74 participants who were outside a healthy weight range ate breakfast one or fewer times per week. This represents $\frac{38}{74} = 0.51351$, or 51.35%, which matches (B).

16. D   Difficulty: Medium

Category: Problem Solving and Data Analysis / Statistics and Probability

Getting to the Answer: The question asks about employees who eat breakfast every weekday, so focus on the "5-7 times per week" column in the table. Assuming the participants in the study were a good representative sample, 36 out of 45, or 80%, of the 3,000 employees are likely to be within a healthy weight range. Multiply $0.8 \times 3,000$ to arrive at 2,400, which is (D).

17. 300 Difficulty: Easy

Category: Problem Solving and Data Analysis / Statistics and Probability

Getting to the Answer: Read the graph carefully, including the key at the bottom indicating that each bar represents 15 minutes. The question states that only stage 3 is considered *deep* sleep, and the question asks how much time was spent in *light* sleep. You could count all of the bars that don't represent stage 3, but it would be faster to count the bars that do and subtract. There are 12 bars that represent stage 3, which means the person spent 12 × 15 = 180 minutes in deep sleep. The study was for 8 hours, or 480 minutes, so the person spent 480 − 180 = 300 minutes in light sleep.

18. 3/8 or .375   Difficulty: Medium
Category: Problem Solving and Data Analysis / Statistics and Probability

Getting to the Answer: Probability compares the number of desired outcomes (here, the number of 15-minute periods with a sleep stage of 3) with the total number of possible outcomes (here, the total number of 15-minute periods over the course of the 8 hours). The opening paragraph tells you that the total amount of sleep over the course of the study is 8 hours. In the previous question, you calculated that 180 minutes, or 3 hours are spent in deep sleep. Therefore, the probability would be $\frac{3}{8}$.

19. 15   Difficulty: Medium
Category: Problem Solving and Data Analysis / Statistics and Probability

Getting to the Answer: The question asks *on average* how many more cents consumers are willing to pay, so you will need to find a weighted average for each version of the product. Start with the store brand. Multiply each dollar amount by the height of the corresponding bar:

$$5 \times 68 = 340$$
$$6 \times 56 = 336$$
$$7 \times 48 = 336$$
$$8 \times 32 = 256$$
$$9 \times 30 = 270$$
$$10 \times 14 = 140$$

Next, add them all together: $1,678. Now, divide this number by the total number of respondents (68 + 56 + 48 + 32 + 30 + 14 = 248): 1,678 ÷ 248 = 6.766, which means *on average* consumers are willing to pay $6.77 for the store brand version of the product. Repeat this process for the brand name version.

$$5 \times 85 = 425$$
$$6 \times 79 = 474$$
$$7 \times 64 = 448$$
$$8 \times 55 = 440$$
$$9 \times 42 = 378$$
$$10 \times 27 = 270$$

Add them all together to get 2,435, and divide by the number of respondents (85 + 79 + 64 + 55 + 42 + 27 = 352) to arrive at 2,435 ÷ 352 = 6.917, or $6.92. *On average*, consumers are willing to pay $6.92 − $6.77 = $0.15, or 15 more cents for the brand name version than the store brand version.

20. 1/3 or .333   Difficulty: Hard
Category: Problem Solving and Data Analysis / Statistics and Probability

Getting to the Answer: First, find the number of respondents willing to pay at least $8 (which means $8 or more). Be careful—the question doesn't specify store brand or brand name, so use both versions of the product:

$$32 + 55 + 30 + 42 + 14 + 27 = 200$$

Now, find the total number of people in the survey. Again, the question doesn't specify store brand or brand name. You know from the previous question that 248 people responded to the store brand survey and 352 responded to the name brand survey, for a total of 600 respondents. This means the probability that a randomly chosen respondent is willing to pay at least $8 is $\frac{200}{600}$, or $\frac{1}{3}$.

21. D   Difficulty: Easy
Category: Problem Solving and Data Analysis / Statistics and Probability

Getting to the Answer: When considering the validity of a study, always look for possible sources of bias. In other words, look for things that might skew the results in either direction. Because the shoe is specifically targeted toward athletes, but is sold in regular shoe stores, conducting the survey outside gyms and sporting goods stores is likely to skew the results. The respondents are already interested in athletics and so are likely to respond more positively than the average shoe store shopper. Therefore, the data from the survey likely overestimates the number of people interested in the new product, making (D) the correct answer.

22. A   Difficulty: Medium

Category: Problem Solving and Data Analysis / Statistics and Probability

Getting to the Answer: Don't neglect the 50% at the beginning of the question just because it is presented in a different form. Instead, convert 50% to a fraction $\left(\dfrac{1}{2}\right)$ and then think logically—the final probability is $\dfrac{1}{3}$ of $\dfrac{3}{4}$ of $\dfrac{1}{2}$. In math, "of" means multiply, so the probability of randomly choosing a vehicle that is a car with an automatic transmission and a leather interior is $\dfrac{1}{2} \times \dfrac{\cancel{3}}{4} \times \dfrac{1}{\cancel{3}} = \dfrac{1}{8}$. This means (A) is correct.

23. C   Difficulty: Medium

Category: Problem Solving and Data Analysis / Statistics and Probability

Getting to the Answer: A good representative sample is not only random, but also a good representation of the population in question. If the senator is only concerned about people who might vote for him, then the survey only needs to focus on people who can vote. Not all citizens can or choose to vote. Additionally, not everyone in the entire country votes for every senator, so he only needs to focus on voters in his district, making (C) correct.

24. B   Difficulty: Medium

Category: Problem Solving and Data Analysis / Statistics and Probability

Getting to the Answer: According to the graph, Charlie has been paying down his debt at a rate of $500 per month. To reach 25% utilization, he needs to get down to $10,000 \times 0.25 = $2,500, which means he needs to pay off $10,000 - $2,500 = $7,500. To do this it would take $7,500 \div $500 = 15 months, making (B) the correct answer.

25. A   Difficulty: Medium

Category: Problem Solving and Data Analysis / Statistics and Probability

Getting to the Answer: The key words in the question are *average* and *consistently*. The average is the mean and the consistency relates to how spread out each branch's profits are. First, find the branch with the lowest mean profit. This is Branch A, so you can eliminate choices C and D. Standard deviation is a measure of spread, so now focus on that row only. Think about what standard deviation tells you. A lower standard deviation indicates that profits are less spread out and therefore more consistent. Likewise, a higher standard deviation indicates that profits are more spread out and therefore less consistent. Notice the opposite nature of this relationship: lower standard deviation = more consistent; higher standard deviation = less consistent. Choice (A) is correct because the standard deviation of Branch C's quarterly profits is the *highest*, which means it performed the *least* consistently.

26. B   Difficulty: Easy

Category: Problem Solving and Data Analysis / Statistics and Probability

Getting to the Answer: The mean of a set of numbers is the same as the average, which is the sum of the numbers divided by the amount of numbers. Use the graph to find the sum of the GPA values, and then calculate the mean. Read the graph carefully—each grid-line represents one student. To save time, multiply the frequency in each category by the GPA value and then divide by the total number of students: $(10 \times 4) + (36 \times 3) + (28 \times 2) + (8 \times 1) + (2 \times 0) = 212 \div 84 = 2.523$, or about 2.5, which is (B).

27. C   Difficulty: Easy

Category: Problem Solving and Data Analysis / Statistics and Probability

Getting to the Answer: You can eliminate D right away because standard deviation is a measure of spread, not a measure of center. You can also eliminate A because you calculated the mean in the previous question, and it was 2.5, which is less than 3.0. To choose between B and (C), you only need to find the median, because the mode is included in both answer choices. You don't have to list out all 84 scores and find the one in the center; instead, think about it logically. There are $10 + 36 = 46$ grades that were a 4.0 or a 3.0, which is more than half of 84, so the median is 3.0. This means either the mode or the median could be used, making (C) correct.

28. 81   Difficulty: Easy

Category: Problem Solving and Data Analysis / Statistics and Probability

Getting to the Answer: There are sixty-one 3-bedroom dwellings and sixty-four 4-bedroom dwellings, so there are $61 + 64 = 125$ total dwellings in the development that have 3 or more bedrooms. There are 154 dwellings in all, which means that $125 \div 154 = 0.8117$ or approximately 81% of all the dwellings should receive flyers.

29. .608   Difficulty: Medium

Category: Problem Solving and Data Analysis / Statistics and Probability

Getting to the Answer: The categories to which the day-care center plans to send an invitation are limited to the 3- and 4-bedroom dwellings (because those are the ones that already received the flyer), so focus on those two columns. The two categories with the most dwellings are Townhouses/3-bedroom and Single-Family/4-bedroom, with a total of $42 + 34 = 76$ dwellings. You determined in the previous question that there were 125 dwellings to which the daycare sent flyers, so the probability of randomly selecting one from the two specified groups is $\dfrac{76}{125} = 0.608$. Grid in .608.

CHAPTER 8

PRACTICE

8. D   **Difficulty:** Hard
Category: Passport to Advanced Math / Exponents

Getting to the Answer: Relative velocity is represented by v, so that's the variable you need to isolate. The manipulation sequence is shown here.

$$\gamma = \frac{1}{\sqrt{1 - \dfrac{v^2}{c^2}}}$$

$$\gamma\sqrt{1 - \frac{v^2}{c^2}} = 1$$

$$\sqrt{1 - \frac{v^2}{c^2}} = \frac{1}{\gamma}$$

$$1 - \frac{v^2}{c^2} = \frac{1}{\gamma^2}$$

$$-\frac{v^2}{c^2} = \frac{1}{\gamma^2} - 1$$

$$v^2 = -c^2\left(\frac{1}{\gamma^2} - 1\right)$$

$$v = c\sqrt{1 - \frac{1}{\gamma^2}}$$

The correct answer is (D).

9. B   **Difficulty:** Medium
Category: Passport to Advanced Math / Exponents

Getting to the Answer: The GCF of the two expressions under the radical is $g^4 h^3$; factoring this out yields $\sqrt[3]{g^4 h^3 (g^2 - 27)}$. You can now pull a g and an h out from under the radical to obtain $gh\sqrt[3]{g(g^2 - 27)}$, which cannot be further simplified except for redistribution of g, which yields $gh\sqrt[3]{g^3 - 27g}$, making (B) correct. Note that $\sqrt[3]{g^3 - 27g}$ does not become $g - 3\sqrt[3]{g}$, as you cannot split the expression into two radicals.

10. D   **Difficulty:** Medium
Category: Passport to Advanced Math / Exponents

Getting to the Answer: Start by setting up a ratio that compares RBC count to total blood cell count. Manipulate the quantities to make all the exponents the same (to convert 7.5×10^3 to a product of 10^6 and another number, move the decimal point in 7.5 three places to the left and write "$\times 10^6$" after it), factor out 10^6, and then add the quantities in parentheses together. Once there, you can use exponent rules to simplify your equation. Divide through and multiply by 100 to get the RBC component as a percentage. Work is shown here:

$$\begin{aligned} \text{RBC} &= \frac{5.4 \times 10^6}{5.4 \times 10^6 + 7.5 \times 10^3 + 3.5 \times 10^5} \\[6pt] &= \frac{5.4 \times 10^6}{5.4 \times 10^6 + 0.0075 \times 10^6 + 0.35 \times 10^6} \\[6pt] &= \frac{5.4 \times \cancel{10^6}}{\cancel{10^6}(5.4 + 0.0075 + 0.35)} \\[6pt] &= \frac{5.4}{5.7575} \end{aligned}$$

Note that the answer choices are, for the most part, far apart. Because 5.4 is relatively close to 5.7575, you can conclude with confidence that the correct answer is likely close to 100%. Therefore, (D) is the correct answer. If this question is in the calculator section, you can plug the numbers into your calculator to check:

$$\% \text{ RBC} = \frac{5.4}{5.7575} \times 100 \approx 93.79\%$$

Choice (D) is still correct.

11. A   **Difficulty:** Medium
Category: Passport to Advanced Math / Exponents

Getting to the Answer: Start by arranging the pumps in order of increasing drain speed; you get P3 < P1 < P2. You're told that the second pump is twice as fast as the first and that the first is three times as fast as the third. You can turn the words into a ratio: If the portion of the draining completed by pump 3 in 1 hour is $\frac{1}{x}$, then the portion completed by pump 1 is $\frac{1}{x} \times 3 = \frac{3}{x}$, and the portion completed by pump 2 is $\frac{3}{x} \times 2 = \frac{6}{x}$. The term $\frac{6}{x}$ matches (A).

PERFORM

12. C Difficulty: Medium
Category: Passport to Advanced Math / Exponents

Getting to the Answer: Begin by moving all terms that don't contain an *a* to one side of the equation. Once there, multiply both sides by 2 to eliminate the fraction, and then divide by t^2 to isolate *a*. The manipulation sequence is shown here.

$$h = \frac{1}{2}at^2 + v_0t + h_0$$

$$h - v_0t - h_0 = \frac{1}{2}at^2$$

$$at^2 = 2(h - v_0t - h_0)$$

$$a = \frac{2(h - v_0t - h_0)}{t^2}$$

Choice (C) is the correct answer.

13. A Difficulty: Hard
Category: Passport to Advanced Math / Exponents

Getting to the Answer: Start by simplifying the radicals: 72 is the product of 2 and 36, so $\sqrt{72} = 6\sqrt{2}$. You can then factor 3 out of the numerator and denominator to yield $\frac{3(1 + 2\sqrt{2})}{3(1 - 2\sqrt{2})}$. Cancel the 3s, and you're left with $\frac{1 + 2\sqrt{2}}{1 - 2\sqrt{2}}$. You can't leave a radical in the denominator, so you'll need to rationalize it. The conjugate of the denominator is $1 + 2\sqrt{2}$, so multiply the entire expression by $\frac{1 + 2\sqrt{2}}{1 + 2\sqrt{2}}$, and then simplify as usual (think FOIL):

$$\frac{1 + 2\sqrt{2}}{1 - 2\sqrt{2}} \times \frac{1 + 2\sqrt{2}}{1 + 2\sqrt{2}}$$

$$= \frac{1 + 2\sqrt{2} + 2\sqrt{2} + 8}{1 + 2\sqrt{2} - 2\sqrt{2} - 8}$$

$$= \frac{1 + 2\sqrt{2} + 2\sqrt{2} + 8}{1 - 8}$$

$$= \frac{9 + 4\sqrt{2}}{-7}$$

This expression matches (A).

14. 41 Difficulty: Hard
Category: Passport to Advanced Math / Exponents

Getting to the Answer: In this question, you're given all the variables you need and an equation that relates them. All you need to do is plug the given values into the correct locations ($m = 200$, $r = \frac{0.015}{12}$, $N = 60$) and solve for what's missing (*P* in this case). Decimals are truncated for brevity here, but no rounding was done until the final step.

$$m = \frac{Pr}{1 - (1 + r)^{-N}}$$

$$200 = \frac{P \times \frac{0.015}{12}}{1 - \left(1 + \frac{0.015}{12}\right)^{-60}}$$

$$200 = \frac{0.00125P}{1 - (1 + 0.00125)^{-60}}$$

$$200 = \frac{0.00125P}{1 - (1.00125)^{-60}}$$

$$200 = \frac{0.00125P}{1 - 0.9278}$$

$$14.4426 = 0.00125P$$

$$P = 11,554.0897$$

Subtract *P* from the total price (19,560) to obtain Teri's down payment. Divide this by 19,560 and multiply by 100 to arrive at 40.93%. Rounded properly, the correct answer is 41.

EXTRA PRACTICE

1. A Difficulty: Easy
Category: Passport to Advanced Math / Exponents

Getting to the Answer: Carefully multiply each term in the first factor by each term in the second factor. Then find the *x* terms and add their coefficients. To save time, you do not need to simplify the other terms in the expression.

$$\left(-2x^2 + 5x - 8\right)\left(4x - 9\right)$$
$$= -2x^2\left(4x - 9\right) + 5x\left(4x - 9\right) - 8\left(4x - 9\right)$$
$$= -8x^3 + 18x^2 + 20x^2 \underline{- 45x - 32x} + 72$$

The coefficient of x in the product is $-45 - 32 = -77$, which means (A) is correct.

2. D   Difficulty: Medium
Category: Passport to Advanced Math / Exponents

Getting to the Answer: A *double zero* occurs in a polynomial when a factor is repeated, or in other words, squared. For example, the factor $(x - a)$ produces a simple zero at $x = a$, while $(x - b)^2$ produces a double zero at $x = b$. The polynomial has a simple zero at $x = -3$, which corresponds to a factor of $(x + 3)$. The double zero at $x = \dfrac{5}{4}$ results from a repeated (squared) factor, so you can eliminate A and C. To choose between B and (D), set each factor equal to 0, and then solve for x (mentally if possible). Choice (D) is correct because:

$$4x - 5 = 0$$
$$4x = 5$$
$$x = \frac{5}{4}$$

3. B   Difficulty: Medium
Category: Passport to Advanced Math / Exponents

Getting to the Answer: The goal here is to solve the equation for T. Start by getting T out of the denominator of the fraction. To do this, multiply both sides of the equation by T, and then divide both sides by v:

$$v = \frac{2\pi r}{T}$$
$$T \times v = \frac{2\pi r}{\cancel{T}} \times \cancel{T}$$
$$Tv = 2\pi r$$
$$T = \frac{2\pi r}{v}$$

Choice (B) is the correct answer.

4. C   Difficulty: Medium
Category: Passport to Advanced Math / Exponents

Getting to the Answer: Because the denominators are the same (just written in different forms), multiplying both sides of the equation by $3x - 15$ will immediately clear all the fractions, the result of which is a much easier equation to solve:

$$8x + 2x = 50$$
$$10x = 50$$
$$x = 5$$

Because there are variables in the denominator, you must check the solution to make sure it is not extraneous. When $x = 5$, each of the denominators is equal to 0, and division by 0 is not possible. Therefore, there is no solution to the equation, making (C) the correct answer.

5. A   Difficulty: Medium
Category: Passport to Advanced Math / Exponents

Getting to the Answer: There are two variables and only one equation, but because you're asked to solve for one of them *in terms of* the other, you solve it the same way you would any other equation. Because there is only one term on each side of the equal sign, cross-multiplying is probably the quickest route to the solution. Don't forget—you want to get x by itself on one side of the equation.

$$\frac{6}{x} = \frac{3}{k + 2}$$
$$6(k + 2) = 3x$$
$$6k + 12 = 3x$$
$$\frac{6k}{3} + \frac{12}{3} = \frac{3x}{3}$$
$$2k + 4 = x$$

Switch x to the left side of the equation and the result matches (A).

6. D   Difficulty: Medium
Category: Passport to Advanced Math / Exponents

Getting to the Answer: Multiply each term in the first expression by $\dfrac{3}{2}$ and each term in the second expression by -2. Then add the two polynomials by writing them vertically and combining like terms.

$$\frac{3}{2}A = \frac{3}{2}(4x^2 + 7x - 1) = 6x^2 + \frac{21}{2}x - \frac{3}{2}$$

$$-2B = -2(-x^2 - 5x + 3) = 2x^2 + 10x - 6$$

$$
\begin{array}{r}
6x^2 + \dfrac{21}{2}x - \dfrac{3}{2} \\[2mm]
+\ 2x^2 + \dfrac{20}{2}x - \dfrac{12}{2} \\[1mm]
\hline
8x^2 + \dfrac{41}{2}x - \dfrac{15}{2}
\end{array}
$$

This means (D) is correct.

7. 10/3   Difficulty: Hard

Category: Passport to Advanced Math / Exponents

Getting to the Answer: Write each factor in the expression in exponential form (using fractional exponents for the radicals). Then use exponent rules to simplify the expression. Add the exponents of the factors that are being multiplied and subtract the exponent of the factor that is being divided:

$$\frac{\sqrt[3]{x} \cdot x^{\frac{5}{2}} \cdot x}{\sqrt{x}} = \frac{x^{\frac{1}{3}} \cdot x^{\frac{5}{2}} \cdot x^1}{x^{\frac{1}{2}}}$$

$$= x^{\frac{1}{3} + \frac{5}{2} + \frac{1}{1} - \frac{1}{2}} = x^{\frac{2}{6} + \frac{15}{6} + \frac{6}{6} - \frac{3}{6}}$$

$$= x^{\frac{20}{6}} = x^{\frac{10}{3}}$$

The question states that n is the power of x, so the value of n is $\frac{10}{3}$.

8. B   Difficulty: Hard

Category: Passport to Advanced Math / Exponents

Getting to the Answer: Because the question states that the expressions are equivalent, set up the equation $\frac{16}{7x + 4} + A = \frac{49x^2}{7x + 4}$ and solve for A. Start by subtracting the first term from both sides of the equation to isolate A. Then, simplify if possible (usually by cancelling common factors). The denominators of the rational terms are the same, so they can be combined.

$$\frac{16}{7x + 4} + A = \frac{49x^2}{7x + 4}$$

$$A = \frac{49x^2}{7x + 4} - \frac{16}{7x + 4}$$

$$A = \frac{49x^2 - 16}{7x + 4}$$

$$A = \frac{(7x + 4)(7x - 4)}{7x + 4}$$

$$A = 7x - 4$$

The correct answer is (B).

9. C   Difficulty: Easy

Category: Passport to Advanced Math / Exponents

Getting to the Answer: Follow the standard order of operations—deal with the exponent first, and then attach the negative sign (because a negative in front of an expression means multiplication by -1). The variable x is being raised to the $\frac{1}{4}$ power, so rewrite the term as a radical expression with 4 as the degree of the root and 1 as the power to which the radicand, x, is being raised.

$$x^{\frac{1}{4}} = \sqrt[4]{x^1} = \sqrt[4]{x}$$

Now attach the negative to arrive at the correct answer, $-\sqrt[4]{x}$, which is (C).

10. C   Difficulty: Easy

Category: Passport to Advanced Math / Exponents

Getting to the Answer: First, write the question as a subtraction problem. Pay careful attention to which expression is being subtracted.

$$\frac{8x - 5}{x - 1} - \frac{3x + 7}{x - 1}$$

The terms in the expression have the same denominator, $x - 1$, so their numerators can be subtracted. Simply combine like terms and keep the denominator the same. Don't forget to distribute the negative to both $3x$ and 7.

$$\frac{8x - 5}{x - 1} - \frac{3x + 7}{x - 1} = \frac{8x - 5 - 3x - 7}{x - 1} = \frac{5x - 12}{x - 1}$$

The reduced expression matches (C).

11. A   **Difficulty:** Easy

Category: Passport to Advanced Math / Exponents

Getting to the Answer: Add polynomial expressions by combining like terms. Be careful of the signs of each term. It may help to write the sum vertically (like you would with big numbers), lining up the like terms.

$$
\begin{array}{r}
6a^2 - 17a - 9 \\
+ \; -5a^2 + 8a - 2 \\
\hline
a^2 - 9a - 11
\end{array}
$$

The correct answer is (A).

12. A   **Difficulty:** Easy

Category: Passport to Advanced Math / Exponents

Getting to the Answer: Find the greatest common factor of both the numerator and the denominator, which in this question happens to be the denominator. Factor out the GCF, $9x^2$, from the numerator and denominator and then cancel what you can.

$$
\frac{18x^4 + 27x^3 - 36x^2}{9x^2} = \frac{9x^2(2x^2 + 3x - 4)}{9x^2}
$$
$$
= 2x^2 + 3x - 4
$$

This matches (A). As an alternate method, you could split the expression up and reduce each term, one at a time.

$$
\frac{18x^4 + 27x^3 - 36x^2}{9x^2} = \frac{18x^4}{9x^2} + \frac{27x^3}{9x^2} - \frac{36x^2}{9x^2}
$$
$$
= 2x^2 + 3x - 4
$$

13. A   **Difficulty:** Medium

Category: Passport to Advanced Math / Exponents

Getting to the Answer: Solve equations containing radical expressions the same way you solve any other equation: Isolate the variable using inverse operations. Start by subtracting 8 from both sides of the equation, and then multiply by 3. Then, square both sides to remove the radical.

$$
8 + \frac{\sqrt{2x + 29}}{3} = 9
$$
$$
\frac{\sqrt{2x + 29}}{3} = 1
$$
$$
\sqrt{2x + 29} = 3
$$
$$
2x + 29 = 9
$$

Now you have a simple linear equation that you can solve using more inverse operations: Subtract 29 and divide by 2 to find that $x = -10$. Be careful—just because the equation started with a radical and the answer is negative, does not mean that *No solution* is the correct answer. If you plug -10 into the expression under the radical, the result is a positive number, which means -10 is a perfectly valid solution. Therefore, (A) is correct.

14. C   **Difficulty:** Medium

Category: Passport to Advanced Math / Exponents

Getting to the Answer: A fraction is the same as division, so you can use polynomial long division to simplify the expression.

$$
\begin{array}{r}
3x + 2 \\
2x + 5 \overline{)\; 6x^2 + 19x + 10} \\
\underline{-(6x^2 + 15x)} \\
4x + 10 \\
\underline{-(4x + 10)} \\
0
\end{array}
$$

The simplified expression is $3x + 2$, so $a + b = 3 + 2 = 5$, which is (C). As an alternate method, you could factor the numerator of the expression, and cancel common factors:

$$
\frac{6x^2 + 19x + 10}{2x + 5} = \frac{(2x + 5)(3x + 2)}{(2x + 5)} = 3x + 2
$$

Use whichever method gets you to the correct answer in the shortest amount of time.

15. D   **Difficulty:** Medium

Category: Passport to Advanced Math / Exponents

Getting to the Answer: Notice that each term is a perfect square and there is a minus sign between the terms, which means you can use the difference of squares rule,

$a^2 - b^2 = (a - b)(a + b)$, to rewrite the expression. If you can't mentally determine what a and b are, write each term as the square of something:

$$25x^2y^4 - 1 = (5xy^2)^2 - 1^2$$
$$= (5xy^2 - 1)(5xy^2 + 1)$$

This matches (D).

16. C Difficulty: Medium
Category: Passport to Advanced Math / Exponents

Getting to the Answer: Whenever a binomial is squared (or raised to any power), you should rewrite it as repeated multiplication and expand it. Do this for both binomials and combine like terms to find the sum.

$$(a - b)^2 + (a + b)^2$$
$$= [(a - b)(a - b)] + [(a + b)(a + b)]$$
$$= (a^2 - ab - ba + b^2) + (a^2 + ab + ba + b^2)$$
$$= (a^2 - 2ab + b^2) + (a^2 + 2ab + b^2)$$
$$= 2a^2 + 2b^2$$

This matches (C).

17. B Difficulty: Medium
Category: Passport to Advanced Math / Exponents

Getting to the Answer: The question asks you to solve the equation for L. Use inverse operations to accomplish the task: Divide both sides of the equation by 2π and then square both sides. You'll need to apply the exponent to all the terms on the left side of the equation, including the π:

$$T = 2\pi\sqrt{\frac{L}{g}}$$

$$\frac{T}{2\pi} = \sqrt{\frac{L}{g}}$$

$$\left(\frac{T}{2\pi}\right)^2 = \left(\sqrt{\frac{L}{g}}\right)^2$$

$$\frac{T^2}{4\pi^2} = \frac{L}{g}$$

Finally, multiply both sides by g to remove g from the denominator and isolate L.

$$L = \frac{gT^2}{4\pi^2}$$

The correct answer is (B).

18. B Difficulty: Hard
Category: Passport to Advanced Math / Exponents

Getting to the Answer: You can solve almost every *work* problem using the formula $W = rt$ or some manipulation of this formula, such as $r = \dfrac{W}{t}$ or $t = \dfrac{W}{r}$. If two or more machines (or people) are working together, start by finding their combined rate and go from there. (Note: W is often 1 because many questions ask about completing *a job*, which is the same as *one job*.)

The first pill counter can complete one batch in 1 hour, so its rate is $r = \dfrac{1}{1} = 1$ batch per hour. The second pill counter can complete one batch in 40 minutes (which is $\dfrac{40}{60} = \dfrac{2}{3}$ hours), so its rate is $r = \dfrac{1}{\frac{2}{3}} = \dfrac{3}{2}$ batches per hour. Working together, the combined rate is $1 + \dfrac{3}{2} = \dfrac{2}{2} + \dfrac{3}{2} = \dfrac{5}{2}$ batches per hour. Use this combined rate in the formula for time to arrive at $t_{combined} = \dfrac{W}{r_{combined}} = \dfrac{1}{\frac{5}{2}} = \dfrac{2}{5}$ hours, which is equivalent to $\dfrac{2}{\cancel{5}} \times \cancel{60}^{12} = 24$ minutes. This means (B) is correct.

19. 16 Difficulty: Hard
Category: Passport to Advanced Math / Exponents

Getting to the Answer: Because this is a no-calculator question, you need to rewrite the exponent in a way that makes it easier to evaluate: Use exponent rules to rewrite $\dfrac{4}{3}$ as a unit fraction raised to a power. Then write the expression in radical form and simplify.

$$8^{\frac{4}{3}} = \left(8^{\frac{1}{3}}\right)^4$$
$$= \left(\sqrt[3]{8}\right)^4$$
$$= 2^4$$
$$= 2 \times 2 \times 2 \times 2$$
$$= 16$$

20. 8   **Difficulty:** Medium

Category: Passport to Advanced Math / Exponents

Getting to the Answer: A fraction bar indicates division, so use polynomial long division and your reasoning skills.

$$
\begin{array}{r}
2x^3 + 8x^2 + 2x + 2 \\
x+4\overline{\smash{)}2x^4 + 16x^3 + 34x^2 + 10x + k} \\
\underline{-(2x^4 + 8x^3)} \\
8x^3 + 34x^2 + 10x + k \\
\underline{-(8x^3 + 32x^2)} \\
2x^2 + 10x + k \\
\underline{-(2x^2 + 8x)} \\
2x + k \\
\underline{-(2x + 8)} \\
k - 8
\end{array}
$$

For there to be no remainder (i.e., a remainder of 0), k must be 8.

21. C   **Difficulty:** Easy

Category: Passport to Advanced Math / Exponents

Getting to the Answer: Solve equations containing radical expressions the same way you solve any other equation: Isolate the variable using inverse operations. To get rid of the fraction, multiply both sides of the equation by 2. Then, divide by 7 to isolate the radical. Finally, square both sides to get rid of the radical and solve for x:

$$
2\left(\frac{7\sqrt{x}}{2}\right) = 2(14)
$$

$$
7\sqrt{x} = 28
$$

$$
\sqrt{x} = 4
$$

$$
\left(\sqrt{x}\right)^2 = 4^2
$$

$$
x = 16
$$

This means (C) is correct. You could also work backward to answer this question, but only if you're comfortable finding square roots without a calculator.

22. B   **Difficulty:** Easy

Category: Passport to Advanced Math / Exponents

Getting to the Answer: To simplify a rational expression, look for common factors that can be divided out

of the numerator and the denominator. If you find any common factors, you can cancel them. Keep in mind that you cannot cancel individual terms. Factor a 4 from the numerator and the denominator, and then cancel the $\frac{4}{4}$.

$$
\frac{4x + 8y}{24x - 12}
$$

$$
= \frac{\cancel{4}(1x + 2y)}{\cancel{4}(6x - 3)}
$$

$$
= \frac{x + 2y}{6x - 3}
$$

This matches (B).

23. D   **Difficulty:** Easy

Category: Passport to Advanced Math / Exponents

Getting to the Answer: Distribute each term in the first factor to each term in the second factor (FOIL). Be careful with the signs.

$$
(-x + 6)(2x - 3) = -x(2x - 3) + 6(2x - 3)
$$

$$
= -2x^2 + 3x + 12x - 18
$$

$$
= -2x^2 + 15x - 18
$$

Be careful—the question asks for the coefficient of x, not x^2, so the answer is 15, which is (D).

24. A   **Difficulty:** Easy

Category: Passport to Advanced Math / Exponents

Getting to the Answer: Write each factor in the expression in exponential form and use exponent rules to simplify the expression. The number 4 is simply being multiplied by the variables. The power of a under the radical is 1 and the root is 3, so the exponent on a is $\frac{1}{3}$ (remember the saying "power over root"). The power of b is 9 and the root is 3, so the exponent on b is $\frac{9}{3} = 3$ (power over root). This means $4\sqrt[3]{ab^9} = 4 \times a^{\frac{1}{3}}b^{\frac{9}{3}} = 4a^{\frac{1}{3}}b^3$, which matches (A).

25. B   Difficulty: Medium
Category: Passport to Advanced Math / Exponents

Getting to the Answer: Chances are that the test makers do not expect you to multiply decimals and then take a square root. Rather, the decimals are likely to have fairly common fraction equivalents that will multiply together nicely. Start with that:

$$\sqrt{0.75} \times \sqrt{0.8} = \sqrt{\frac{3}{4}} \times \sqrt{\frac{4}{5}} = \sqrt{\frac{3}{\cancel{4}} \times \frac{\cancel{4}}{5}}$$

$$= \sqrt{\frac{3}{5}} = \frac{\sqrt{3}}{\sqrt{5}}$$

Don't forget—you're not allowed to leave a radical in the denominator of a fraction, so you need to rationalize the denominator. To do this, multiply the top and bottom of the fraction by the radical in the bottom. The result is $\frac{\sqrt{3}}{\sqrt{5}} \times \frac{\sqrt{5}}{\sqrt{5}} = \frac{\sqrt{15}}{5}$, which matches (B).

26. A   Difficulty: Medium
Category: Passport to Advanced Math / Exponents

Getting to the Answer: Write 27 as 3^3 and then use exponent rules. Don't forget—when you raise an exponent to another exponent, you multiply the exponents.

$$\left(27x^6y^{12}\right)^{\frac{1}{3}}$$

$$= 3^{3 \times \frac{1}{3}} x^{6 \times \frac{1}{3}} y^{12 \times \frac{1}{3}}$$

$$= 3x^2y^4$$

Choice (A) is correct.

27. C   Difficulty: Medium
Category: Passport to Advanced Math / Exponents

Getting to the Answer: Factor out the GCF of *both* the numerator and the denominator. Then cancel what you can. In this expression, the GCF is $3x^2y$.

$$\frac{12x^3y^2 - 9x^2y}{6x^4y + 18x^3y^3}$$

$$= \frac{3x^2y(4xy - 3)}{3x^2y(2x^2 + 6xy^2)}$$

$$= \frac{4xy - 3}{2x^2 + 6xy^2}$$

This matches (C).

28. B   Difficulty: Medium
Category: Passport to Advanced Math / Exponents

Getting to the Answer: Look closely at the dividend and the divisor. The divisor, $5x$, can be divided into each term in the dividend evenly, which means you don't need to use polynomial long division. Just divide each term by $5x$ and leave the signs the same. You could divide each term mentally, but it may be safer to write each term over $5x$, and then use rules of exponents to simplify.

$$\frac{30x^3}{5x} + \frac{45x^2}{5x} - \frac{10x}{5x} = 6x^2 + 9x - 2$$

The question asks for the coefficient of x, so the correct answer is 9, which is (B).

29. D   Difficulty: Medium
Category: Passport to Advanced Math / Exponents

Getting to the Answer: The GCF of the terms under the radical is m^4n^2. Factor this out and see if you can take the square root of anything:

$$\sqrt{9m^5n^2 - m^4n^2} = \sqrt{m^4n^2(9m - 1)}$$

$$= m^2n\sqrt{9m - 1}$$

The result matches (D).

30. B   Difficulty: Easy
Category: Passport to Advanced Math / Exponents

Getting to the Answer: When asked to match an equation to a real-world scenario, Picking Numbers is often the strategy that will get you to the answer the quickest, especially when the answer choices look fairly complicated.

Choose a number of cards to order (at least 100)—let's say 200 cards. Work the scenario out using your calculator: $15 setup fee + 200(0.02) = $19. The question asks about the average cost *per card*, so divide this amount by 200 to get $0.095 per card. Now, plug 200 into each of the equations for x, looking for the same result.

Choice A: $C_{ave} = \frac{15 + 0.02}{200} = 0.0751 \rightarrow$ No match.

Choice (B): $C_{ave} = \frac{15}{200} + 0.02 = 0.095 \rightarrow$ Match!

Check the remaining answer choices for completeness, but you'll see that only (B) is a match for the correct answer.

31. A   Difficulty: Medium

Category: Passport to Advanced Math / Exponents

Getting to the Answer: While you could use long division or factoring to find the quotient and then identify the constant, it is quicker to simply recognize that when a polynomial with a constant is divided by another polynomial with a constant, and there is no remainder, you can simply divide the constants to find the resulting constant of the quotient. Just be careful to use the correct signs. Because $-10 \div 5 = -2$, the constant in the resulting quotient is -2, which is (A).

32. A   Difficulty: Hard

Category: Passport to Advanced Math / Exponents

Getting to the Answer: It is not possible to add, subtract, multiply, or divide radicals that represent roots of different degrees (such as a square root and a cube root) when they are written in radical form. Instead, you must write the radicals using fraction exponents and then use rules of exponents to combine the terms.

Write each radical using a fraction exponent, and then use the rule $a^x \times a^y = a^{x+y}$ to answer the question.

$$\sqrt{2} \times \sqrt[4]{2} = 2^{\frac{1}{2}} \times 2^{\frac{1}{4}}$$
$$= 2^{\frac{1}{2} + \frac{1}{4}}$$
$$= 2^{\frac{2}{4} + \frac{1}{4}}$$
$$= 2^{\frac{3}{4}}$$

The answers are written as radicals, so convert back to radicals using the saying "power over root." The result is $\sqrt[4]{2^3} = \sqrt[4]{8}$, which is (A).

33. D   Difficulty: Hard

Category: Passport to Advanced Math / Exponents

Getting to the Answer: Factor the denominator in the second term to find that the common denominator for all three terms is $(x-2)(x+2)$. Multiply each term in the equation by the common denominator (in factored form or the original form, whichever is more convenient) to clear the fractions. Then solve the resulting equation for x:

$$^{(x+2)}\left(\cancel{x^2-4}\right)\left(\frac{3}{\cancel{x-2}}\right) - \left(\cancel{x^2-4}\right)\left(\frac{12}{\cancel{x^2-4}}\right)$$
$$= 1\left(x^2-4\right)$$

$$3(x+2) - 12 = x^2 - 4$$
$$3x + 6 - 12 = x^2 - 4$$
$$3x - 6 = x^2 - 4$$

$$0 = x^2 - 3x + 2$$
$$0 = (x-1)(x-2)$$

Set each factor equal to 0 to find that the potential solutions are $x = 1$ and $x = 2$. But wait, these are only *potential* solutions because the original equation was a rational equation. When x is 2, the denominators in both terms on the left side are equal to 0, so 2 is an extraneous solution, which means (D) is correct.

34. C   Difficulty: Hard

Category: Passport to Advanced Math / Exponents

Getting to the Answer: Factors of polynomials must divide evenly into the polynomial, which means there is no remainder. This is a *long* polynomial, so think *long* division. In polynomial long division, the only time there is no remainder is when the *constant* in the factor divides evenly into the *constant* in the polynomial. This means you can eliminate A and D (because 5 does not divide evenly into 12). To decide between B and (C), use long division. Start with (C) because it has all positive values, which means faster calculations and fewer potential mistakes:

$$\begin{array}{r} 5x^3 + 34x^2 + 53x - 3 \\ 3x+1{\overline{\smash{\big)}\,15x^4 + 107x^3 + 193x^2 + 17x - 12}} \\ \underline{-(15x^4 + 5x^3)} \\ 102x^3 + 193x^2 + 17x - 12 \\ \underline{-(102x^3 + 34x^2)} \\ 159x^2 + 17x - 12 \\ \underline{-(159x^2 + 53x)} \\ -36x - 12 \\ \underline{-(-36x - 12)} \\ 0 \end{array}$$

Good news! You don't have to check B because $3x + 1$ is indeed a factor of the polynomial, making (C) correct.

35. 4 **Difficulty:** Medium

Category: Passport to Advanced Math / Exponents

Getting to the Answer: To find a remainder, you must use polynomial long division (or synthetic division if you happen to know that nifty technique). Don't forget to set up the dividend with 0 placeholders for all missing terms.

$$
\begin{array}{r}
x^2 - 2x + 4 \\
x+2\overline{)\ x^3 + 0x^2 + 0x + 12} \\
\underline{-(x^3 + 2x^2)} \\
-2x^2 + 0x \\
\underline{-(-2x^2 - 4x)} \\
4x + 12 \\
\underline{-(4x + 8)} \\
4
\end{array}
$$

The remainder is the number left over at the bottom, which is 4.

36. 21 **Difficulty:** Hard

Category: Passport to Advanced Math / Exponents

Getting to the Answer: Solve this radical equation the same way you would solve any other equation: Isolate the variable using inverse operations.

$$12 + \frac{3\sqrt{x-5}}{2} = 18 \qquad \text{Subtract 12.}$$

$$\frac{3\sqrt{x-5}}{2} = 6 \qquad \text{Multiply by 2.}$$

$$3\sqrt{x-5} = 12 \qquad \text{Divide by 3.}$$

$$\sqrt{x-5} = 4 \qquad \text{Square both sides.}$$

$$x - 5 = 16 \qquad \text{Add 5.}$$

$$x = 21$$

The correct answer is 21. This is a Grid-in question, so if you have time it wouldn't hurt to check your answer by plugging 21 back into the original equation.

37. 2.8 **Difficulty:** Hard

Category: Passport to Advanced Math / Exponents

Getting to the Answer: This is a *work* problem, so you'll need to use the formula $W = rt$ or some manipulation of this formula, such as $r = \dfrac{W}{t}$ or $t = \dfrac{W}{r}$. The first unit can cool 260 square feet in 3 hours and 15 minutes, or 3.25 hours. The second unit can cool 300 square feet in 2.5 hours. The question asks how long it would take for both units to cool $260 + 300 = 560$ square feet. So set up a rational expression comparing the square feet (the amount of work) and the corresponding time for each unit and set the sum equal to the combined square feet and corresponding time (which you don't know, so call it h for hours): $\dfrac{260}{3.25} + \dfrac{300}{2.5} = \dfrac{560}{h}$.

Find the unit rate for each term to make the numbers easier to work with. Then cross-multiply and solve for h:

$$\frac{80}{1} + \frac{120}{1} = \frac{560}{h}$$

$$\frac{200}{1} = \frac{560}{h}$$

$$200h = 560$$

$$h = \frac{560}{200} = 2.8$$

The question tells you not to round, so enter 2.8 and you're done.

CHAPTER 9

PRACTICE

8. C   Difficulty: Medium
Category: Passport to Advanced Math / Functions

Getting to the Answer: You're told the honeybee population decreases 35% each month; this means exponential decay is occurring, so use $y = x_0(1 + r)^x$ as your function template. Set p as the honeybee population and t as the time in months; watch the sign of r. Your function should be $p(t) = (4.23 \times 10^8)(0.65)^t$. Now plug in the time in months:

$$p(12) = (4.23 \times 10^8)(0.65)^{12} \approx 2,406,028$$

The correct answer is (C).

9. C   Difficulty: Hard
Category: Passport to Advanced Math / Functions

Getting to the Answer: Translate the composition notation: $(b \circ a)(x)$ means $b(a(x))$ or b of $a(x)$. This tells you to use $a(x)$ as the input for $b(x)$. You can rewrite this as $\frac{1}{a(x)}$, which is the reciprocal of $a(x)$. This new function will be undefined anywhere that $a(x) = 0$. Looking at the graph, you can see that $a(x)$ crosses the x-axis four times, making (C) correct.

PERFORM

10. B   Difficulty: Hard
Category: Passport to Advanced Math / Functions

Getting to the Answer: Don't panic about this involving a trigonometric function; the question is only testing your ability to apply multiple transformations to a graph. The easiest transformation to identify is the -4 downward shift. Eliminate C and D, as neither contains this shift. Both A and (B) contain a vertical compression, but the difference is subtle, so home in on the transformed function's horizontal compression caused by the 2 in parentheses. Choice (B) has a compressed sine graph, so it is correct.

11. A   Difficulty: Medium
Category: Passport to Advanced Math / Functions

Getting to the Answer: Use the two given rates to determine Briana's typing rate in pages per minute. She types 45 words per minute, which becomes:

$$\frac{45 \text{ words}}{1 \text{ min}} \times \frac{1 \text{ page}}{500 \text{ words}} = \frac{45 \text{ pages}}{500 \text{ min}} = \frac{9 \text{ pages}}{100 \text{ min}}$$

Multiplying this rate by m gets you the number of pages typed after m minutes, which can then be subtracted from the starting page count (60) to get the number of pages Briana has left to type. The function should read $p(m) = 60 - \frac{9m}{100}$, which matches (A).

12. D   Difficulty: Medium
Category: Passport to Advanced Math / Functions

Getting to the Answer: Examine the graph. A peak in fuel economy at 50 mph is obvious, but what else can be said? A closer look at the increase below 50 mph (to the left of 50 on the horizontal axis) and the decrease above 50 mph (to the right of 50) reveals a critical detail: The decreasing part of the graph is steeper than the increasing part. This means the rate of decrease is faster than the rate of increase. This corresponds to (D).

EXTRA PRACTICE

1. A   Difficulty: Easy
Category: Passport to Advanced Math / Functions

Getting to the Answer: The notation $k(4)$ means the output value of the function when 4 is substituted for the input (x), and $k(1)$ means the output value of the function when 1 is substituted for the input (x). Substitute 4 and 1 into the function, one at a time, and then subtract the results.

$$k(4) = 5(4) + 2 = 20 + 2 = 22$$
$$k(1) = 5(1) + 2 = 5 + 2 = 7$$
$$k(4) - k(1) = 22 - 7 = 15$$

Choice (A) is correct. Caution—this is not the same as subtracting $4 - 1$ and then substituting 3 into the function.

2. C   **Difficulty:** Easy

Category: Passport to Advanced Math / Functions

Getting to the Answer: The function graphed is the absolute value function, and you can see that all values in its range (the y-values) are positive. That makes the negative value in (C) impossible. Because you're looking for the statement that is NOT true, you can safely conclude that (C) is correct.

3. D   **Difficulty:** Medium

Category: Passport to Advanced Math / Functions

Getting to the Answer: Compare each answer choice to the graph, eliminating false statements as you go.

Choice A: Carmel went to the library first, so the library (not the grocery store) is about 5 miles from his home. Eliminate this choice.

Choice B: Carmel traveled 7 miles away from his home (between $t = 0$ minutes and $t = 30$ minutes), but then also traveled 7 miles back (between $t = 45$ minutes and $t = 60$ minutes), so he traveled a total of 14 miles. Eliminate this choice.

Choice C: When Carmel reached the library, he was 5 miles from home; when he reached the grocery store, he was 7 miles from home. This means the grocery store must be $7 - 5 = 2$ miles farther away. Eliminate this choice.

Choice (D) must be correct. Carmel is the same distance from home (5 miles) between $t = 15$ minutes and $t = 25$ minutes, so he spent 10 minutes at the library. He is stopped once again (at the grocery store) between $t = 30$ minutes and $t = 45$ minutes, so he spent 15 minutes at the grocery store.

4. C   **Difficulty:** Medium

Category: Passport to Advanced Math / Functions

Getting to the Answer: Transformations that are grouped with the x in a function shift the graph horizontally and therefore affect the x-coordinates of points on the graph. Transformations that are not grouped with the x shift the graph vertically and therefore affect the y-coordinates of points on the graph. Remember, horizontal shifts are always the reverse of what they look like. When working with multiple transformations, follow the same order of operations as always—parentheses first, then multiply and divide, then add and subtract.

Start with the parentheses: $(x - 2)$. This shifts the graph right 2 units, so add 2 to the x-coordinate of the given point: $(5, 3) \rightarrow (5 + 2, 3) = (7, 3)$. Next, apply the negative in front of g because it represents multiplication. The negative is not grouped with the x, so multiply the y-coordinate by -1 to get $(7, 3(-1)) \rightarrow (7, -3)$. Finally, the $+ 8$ is not grouped with x, so add 8 to the y-coordinate: $(7, -3) \rightarrow (7, -3 + 8) = (7, 5)$, which matches (C).

You could also plot the point on a coordinate plane, perform the transformations (right 2, reflect vertically over the x-axis, and then up 8), to find the new point. The result will be the same.

5. A   **Difficulty:** Medium

Category: Passport to Advanced Math / Functions

Getting to the Answer: The notation $g(h(x))$ indicates a composition of two functions which can be read "g of h of x." It means that the output when x is substituted in $h(x)$ becomes the input for $g(x)$. First, use the table on the right to find that $h(3)$ is 0. This is your new input. Now, use the table on the left to find $g(0)$, which is -1, making (A) the correct answer.

6. B   **Difficulty:** Hard

Category: Passport to Advanced Math / Functions

Getting to the Answer: The key to answering this question is to have a conceptual understanding of function notation. Here, the input $(x + 2)$ has already been substituted and simplified in the given function. Your job is to determine what the function would have looked like had x been the input instead. To keep things organized, let $u = x + 2$, the old input. This means $x = u - 2$. Substitute this into p and simplify:

$$p(x + 2) = 3x^2 + 4x + 1$$
$$p(u) = 3(u - 2)^2 + 4(u - 2) + 1$$
$$= 3(u^2 - 4u + 4) + 4u - 8 + 1$$
$$= 3u^2 - 12u + 12 + 4u - 8 + 1$$
$$= 3u^2 - 8u + 5$$

When working with function notation, you evaluate the function by substituting a given input value for the variable in the parentheses. Here, if the input value is x, then $p(x) = 3x^2 - 8x + 5$, which means (B) is correct.

7. 3.5 or **3.50**   **Difficulty:** Medium

Category: Passport to Advanced Math / Functions

Getting to the Answer: Start by evaluating the function at $x = 25$ and at $x = 20$. Make sure you follow the correct order of operations as you simplify.

$$P(25) = 150(25) - (25)^2$$
$$= 3,750 - 625$$
$$= 3,125$$
$$P(20) = 150(20) - (20)^2$$
$$= 3,000 - 400$$
$$= 2,600$$

The question asks how much more profit *per unit* the company makes, so find the difference in the amounts of profit and divide by the number of units (150) to get $\frac{3,125 - 2,600}{150} = \frac{525}{150} = \$3.504$, or 3.5.

8. 305   Difficulty: Medium

Category: Passport to Advanced Math / Functions

Getting to the Answer: Always pay careful attention to what the variable in a function represents, especially in questions that deal with real-world scenarios. In this question, t does *not* represent the time, so don't find $C(5)$. Rather, you need to start by finding the number of hours that pass between 7 AM and 5 PM. Because there are 10 hours between 7 AM and 5 PM, evaluate the function at $t = 10$. Make sure you follow the correct order of operations as you simplify.

$$C(t) = -0.0814t^4 + t^3 + 12t$$
$$C(10) = -0.0815(10)^4 + 10^3 + 12(10)$$
$$= -0.0815(10,000) + 1,000 + 120$$
$$= -815 + 1,000 + 120$$
$$= 305$$

9. A   Difficulty: Easy

Category: Passport to Advanced Math / Functions

Getting to the Answer: The notation $g(-2)$ means the value of the function when $x = -2$, so substitute -2 for x and simplify. Don't forget to use the correct order of operations as you work:

$$g(-2) = -2(-2)^2 + 7(-2) - 3$$
$$= -2(4) + (-14) - 3$$
$$= -8 - 14 - 3$$
$$= -25$$

Choice (A) is correct.

10. C   Difficulty: Easy

Category: Passport to Advanced Math / Functions

Getting to the Answer: A function, by definition, only has one output for every input. When you're given graphs to consider, use the vertical line test to see if the graph represents a function. If a vertical line intersects a graph more than one time, then the graph has more than one output for a given input and is therefore *not* a function. The graph in (C) fails the test, so it is not a function.

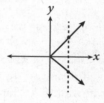

11. D   Difficulty: Easy

Category: Passport to Advanced Math / Functions

Getting to the Answer: The domain of a function represents the possible values of x, or the input values. In this function, x is represented by p, which is the number of seeds germinated by the plants over a given period of time. Because there cannot be a negative number of seeds germinated, or a fraction of a seed germinated, the list in (D) is the only one that could represent a portion of the function's domain.

12. D   Difficulty: Medium

Category: Passport to Advanced Math / Functions

Getting to the Answer: To determine the domain, look at the x-values. To determine the range, look at the y-values. For the domain, the graph is continuous (no holes or gaps in the graph) and has arrows on both sides, so the domain is all real numbers. This means you can eliminate A and B. For the range, the function's maximum (the vertex) is located at $(-3, 4)$, which means the highest possible y-value of $f(x)$ is 4. The graph is continuous and opens downward, so the range of the function is $y \leq 4$, which is the same as $f(x) \leq 4$, making (D) correct.

13. D   Difficulty: Medium

Category: Passport to Advanced Math / Functions

Getting to the Answer: Draw a quick sketch of the equation (or graph it in your graphing calculator).

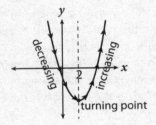

Based on the equation, the graph is a parabola that opens upward with a vertex of $(2, -5)$. A parabola changes direction at the x-coordinate of its vertex. This is all the information you need to answer the question. You can immediately eliminate A and B. To choose between C and (D), take a closer look at the sketch. To the left of 2 (or $x < 2$), the parabola is decreasing, and to the right of 2 (or $x > 2$), it is increasing. This makes (D) correct.

14. B   Difficulty: Medium

Category: Passport to Advanced Math / Functions

Getting to the Answer: In this question, you are given a range value (14), which means $f(x) = 14$, and you are asked for the corresponding domain value (x-value). This means you are solving for x, not substituting for x. Set the function equal to 14 and solve using inverse operations:

$$14 = \frac{x^2}{4} - 11$$
$$25 = \frac{x^2}{4}$$
$$100 = x^2$$
$$\pm 10 = x$$

Negative 10 is not one of the answer choices, so (B) is correct.

15. C   Difficulty: Medium

Category: Passport to Advanced Math / Functions

Getting to the Answer: Piecewise functions look intimidating, but they are usually very simple functions—they're just written in pieces. The right-hand side of each piece of the function tells you what part of the domain (which x-values) goes with that particular expression. In this function, only values of x that are less than or equal to 0 go with the top expression, values of x greater than 0 and less than or equal to 3 go with the middle expression, and values of x that are greater than 3 go with the bottom expression. Because -3 is less than 0, plug it into the top expression and simplify:

$$f(-3) = (-3)^2 + 1$$
$$= 9 + 1$$
$$= 10$$

This matches (C).

16. C   Difficulty: Medium

Category: Passport to Advanced Math / Functions

Getting to the Answer: Graphically, the notation $f(-2)$ means the y-value when x is -2. Pay careful attention to which graph is which. It may help to draw dots on the graph. Find $x = -2$ along the horizontal axis, trace up to the graph of $f(x)$, and draw a dot on the graph. Do the same for $g(2)$, as shown here:

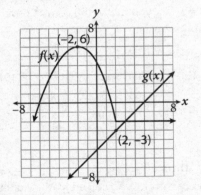

Now, read the y-coordinates from the graph and subtract: $f(-2)$ is 6 and $g(2)$ is -3, so $f(-2) + g(2) = 6 + (-3) = 3$, which is (C).

17. D   Difficulty: Hard

Category: Passport to Advanced Math / Functions

Getting to the Answer: When working with a composition, the range of the inner function becomes the domain of the outer function, which in turn produces the range of the composition. In the composition $f(g(x))$, the function $g(x) = \dfrac{x^2}{2}$ is the inner function. Every value of x, when substituted into this function, will result in a nonnegative value (because the result of squaring a number is always a positive number). This means the smallest possible range value of $g(x)$ is 0. Now look at $f(x)$. Substituting large positive values of x in the function will result in large negative numbers. Consequently, substituting the smallest value from the range of g, which is 0, results in the largest range value for the composition, which is $3 - 0 = 3$. Because $4 > 3$, it is not in the range of $f(g(x))$. Therefore, (D) is correct.

18. D   Difficulty: Hard

Category: Passport to Advanced Math / Functions

Getting to the Answer: Graphing piecewise functions can be tricky. Try describing the graph in words first, and then find the matching function. Use words such as "to the left of" (which translates as *less than*) and "to the right of" (which translates as *greater than*).

First notice that there is a hole in the graph at $x = 4$. This means you can eliminate A right away because the inequality symbol in the top piece would include the endpoint at 4. To choose between the remaining answers, think about parent functions and transformations. To the left of $x = 4$, the graph is an absolute value function that has been reflected vertically across the x-axis and then shifted up one unit. This means either C or (D) must be correct. Now look to the right of $x = 4$: The graph is a horizontal line, which means a line that has a slope of 0. The slope of the line in C is negative 3, so it can't be correct. This means (D) is correct. (The equation of a horizontal line always looks like $y = b$, or in this case, $g(x) = -3$.)

CHAPTER 10

PRACTICE

8. D **Difficulty:** Hard

Category: Passport to Advanced Math / Quadratics

Getting to the Answer: Find the maximum height of the potato, then find the time it takes the potato to hit the ground. The x-coordinate of the vertex is given by $h = \dfrac{-b}{2a} = \dfrac{-224}{2(-16)} = 7$. Plug this into the function to get the y-coordinate: $f(7) = -16(7)^2 + 224(7) + 240 = 1{,}024$. Next, calculate how long it takes for the potato to hit the ground. This will occur when $f(t) = 0$. Plug in and factor to solve:

$$-16t^2 + 224t + 240 = 0$$
$$-16\left(t^2 - 14t - 15\right) = 0$$
$$t^2 - 14t - 15 = 0$$
$$(t - 15)(t + 1) = 0$$
$$t = 15 \ \text{ or } \ t = -1$$

Because time can't be negative, $t = 15$. Don't forget that you were asked for the sum of the height and the time, not for either of the raw values. The sum of 15 and 1,024 is 1,039, choice (D).

9. B **Difficulty:** Medium

Category: Passport to Advanced Math / Quadratics

Getting to the Answer: If $ab > 0$, then a and b are either both positive or both negative. In the second inequality, $b^2ac < 0$, you can ignore the b^2 term because it will be positive regardless of the sign of b. This implies that either a or c is positive, and the other is negative. The x-intercepts are b and c. Because b has the same sign as a, while c has the opposite sign as a, it follows that b and c have opposite signs. The correct answer must therefore be a function with one negative root and one positive root. Scan the functions to find the correct one. Ignore the complicated-looking numbers—all that matter are the signs! Choice (B) is correct.

PERFORM

10. A **Difficulty:** Hard

Category: Passport to Advanced Math / Quadratics

Getting to the Answer: Technically, this isn't a quadratic equation because the highest power on the variable isn't 2. However, it is a "quadratic-type" equation because the square of the variable part of the middle term is equal to the variable in the leading term. This means you can use factoring techniques you learned for quadratics to answer this question as well. The presence of 4, 9, and 16—all perfect squares—is a big clue. Observe that $4x - 12\sqrt{x} + 9$ is an instance of the quadratic shortcut $(a - b)^2 = a^2 - 2ab + b^2$. Use the shortcut to factor the equation and see where that leads you.

$$4x - 12\sqrt{x} + 9 = 16$$
$$(2\sqrt{x} - 3)^2 = 16$$
$$2\sqrt{x} - 3 = \pm 4$$

Now go back to what you're looking for: $10\sqrt{x} - 15$ is 5 times the quantity on the left side of the last equation above, so multiply the positive result, 4, by 5 to get 20. The correct answer is (A).

11. B **Difficulty:** Medium

Category: Passport to Advanced Math / Quadratics

Getting to the Answer: Neither of the functions is presented in standard form, so make this question a little easier by simplifying each one before setting them equal to each other.

$$f(x) = 3(x - 4)^2 + 4 = 3(x^2 - 8x + 16) + 4$$
$$= 3x^2 - 24x + 48 + 4$$
$$= 3x^2 - 24x + 52$$

$$g(x) = (x + 5)^2 + 2x - 135$$
$$= x^2 + 10x + 25 + 2x - 135$$
$$= x^2 + 12x - 110$$

$$f(x) = g(x)$$
$$3x^2 - 24x + 52 = x^2 + 12x - 110$$
$$2x^2 - 36x + 162 = 0$$
$$2(x^2 - 18x + 81) = 0$$
$$x^2 - 18x + 81 = 0$$

Notice that you can now use a quadratic shortcut:

$$x^2 - 18x + 81 = 0$$
$$(x - 9)^2 = 0$$
$$x = 9$$

Note that the question asks how many intersection points there are, *not* what the points are. Since there is only one solution for x, there must be only one point of intersection, which is (B). Don't waste time plugging 9 back in.

12. 2   **Difficulty:** Medium

Category: Passport to Advanced Math / Quadratics

Getting to the Answer: An x-intercept of a function is a point at which the y-coordinate equals 0. Set the equation equal to zero, simplify, and factor.

$$g(x) = -2.5x^2 + 10x - 7.5$$
$$0 = -2.5x^2 + 10x - 7.5$$
$$0 = -2.5(x^2 - 4x + 3)$$
$$0 = x^2 - 4x + 3$$
$$0 = (x - 1)(x - 3)$$
$$x = 1 \text{ or } x = 3$$

Recall that the question asks for the *difference* between the x-intercepts, not for the x-intercepts themselves. The difference between 3 and 1 is 2.

13. C   **Difficulty:** Medium

Category: Passport to Advanced Math / Quadratics

Getting to the Answer: An axis of symmetry splits a parabola in half and travels through the vertex. You have a formula to find h instantly. All you have to do is plug and chug to get your answer—just be careful with the fractions and the negatives.

$$x = -\frac{b}{2a}$$
$$= -17 \div 2\left(\frac{-11}{3}\right)$$
$$= -17 \div \frac{-22}{3}$$
$$= -17 \times \frac{-3}{22}$$
$$= \frac{51}{22}$$

The correct answer is (C).

EXTRA PRACTICE

1. B   **Difficulty:** Easy

Category: Passport to Advanced Math / Quadratics

Getting to the Answer: Using the first equation, set each of the factors equal to 0 and solve for x to find that the x-intercepts are $-\frac{1}{2}$ and 5. This means you can eliminate A and D. From the standard form of the equation, you can see that the y-intercept is -5 (the value of c) because $0^2 - 3(0) - 5 = -5$, so (B) is correct.

2. A   **Difficulty:** Medium

Category: Passport to Advanced Math / Quadratics

Getting to the Answer: The answer choices all look very similar, so think logically to eliminate a couple. A rocket goes *up*, hits a maximum height, and then comes *down*. This tells you that the graph will be an upside-down parabola, which means the equation should have a negative sign in front. Eliminate C and D. To choose between (A) and B, you need to recall what the *vertex form* of a quadratic looks like and what it tells you. When a quadratic equation is written in the form $y = a(x - h)^2 + k$, the vertex of the graph is (h, k). The h tells you *where* the maximum (or minimum) occurs, and the k tells you *what* the maximum (or minimum) value is. Here, the maximum height of 34 feet occurs at 3 seconds, so k is 34 and h is 3. Substitute these values into vertex form to find that the correct equation is $y = -16(x - 3)^2 + 34$. Translate this to function language ($h(t) = y$ and $t = x$) to arrive at the answer: $h(t) = -16(t - 3)^2 + 34$, which is (A).

3. A   **Difficulty:** Medium

Category: Passport to Advanced Math / Quadratics

Getting to the Answer: When finding solutions to a quadratic equation, always start by rewriting the equation to make it equal 0 (unless both sides of the equation are already perfect squares). To make the equation equal 0, subtract 30 from both sides to get $x^2 - 7x - 30 = 0$. The answer choices are all integers, so factor the equation. Look for two numbers whose product is -30 and whose sum is -7. The two numbers are -10 and 3, so the factors are $(x - 10)$ and $(x + 3)$. Set each factor equal to 0 and solve to find that $x = 10$ and $x = -3$. The question states that $x > 0$, so x must equal 10. Before selecting an answer, don't forget to check that you answered the right question—the question asks for the value of $x - 5$, not just x, so the correct answer is $10 - 5 = 5$, which means (A) is correct.

4. C   Difficulty: Medium
Category: Passport to Advanced Math / Quadratics

Getting to the Answer: Understanding that in algebra "divides evenly" means "is a factor" is the key to answering this question. You could use polynomial long division, but in most cases, factoring is quicker. The leading coefficient of the equation is not 1, so you'll need to use the *AC method* and grouping to factor the equation. Multiply a times c (6×-20) and then look for two factors of that product whose sum is equal to the coefficient of the middle term. Break the middle term ($7x$) into two terms using the numbers you found, and then factor by grouping. The product is -120 and the two factors of -120 that add up to 7 are 15 and -8.

$$6x^2 + 7x - 20 = 6x^2 + 15x - 8x - 20$$
$$= (6x^2 + 15x) - (8x + 20)$$
$$= 3x(2x + 5) - 4(2x + 5)$$
$$= (2x + 5)(3x - 4)$$

So, $3x - 4$ divides evenly into the expression, making (C) correct.

5. A   Difficulty: Medium
Category: Passport to Advanced Math / Quadratics

Getting to the Answer: Even though one of the equations in this system isn't linear, you can still solve the system using substitution. You already know that y is equal to $2x$, so substitute $2x$ for y in the second equation. Don't forget that when you square $2x$, you must square both the coefficient and the variable. Also, be careful—there are a lot of 2s floating around, so pay careful attention as you plug in values.

$$2x^2 + 2y^2 = 240$$
$$x^2 + y^2 = 120$$

$$x^2 + (2x)^2 = 120$$
$$x^2 + 4x^2 = 120$$
$$5x^2 = 120$$
$$x^2 = 24$$

The question asks for the value of x^2, not x, so there is no need to take the square root of 24 to find the value of x. Choice (A) is correct.

6. B   Difficulty: Hard
Category: Passport to Advanced Math / Quadratics

Getting to the Answer: The maximum value shown in the graph is about 56 or 57 feet. When a quadratic equation is written in vertex form, $y = a(x - h)^2 + k$, the maximum value is given by k, so check C and D first because they will be the easiest to compare to the graph. In C, k is 48, which is not greater than 56 or 57 and therefore not correct. In D, k is 52, which is also not greater than 56 or 57. This means either A or (B) must be correct. You now have two options—you could expand the equation in each answer choice and then complete the square to find the vertex, or you could expand the equations, find the x-coordinate of the vertex using the formula $x = \dfrac{-b}{2a}$, and then plug in the result to find the y-value. Completing the square usually takes a bit of time, so the second option is probably the quicker route to take. Expanding A, you get $h = -16t^2 + 48t$ with $a = -16$ and $b = 48$. The x-coordinate of the vertex is $\dfrac{-48}{2(-16)} = \dfrac{-48}{-32} = 1.5$. Substituting this back into the equation, the y-value of the vertex (which is the maximum value of the function) is $-16(1.5)^2 + 48(1.5) = 36$, which is not greater than 56 or 57, so (B) must be correct. Don't waste valuable time checking, but if you use the same strategy, you'll find that the maximum height of the equation in (B) is 81 feet.

7. 5   Difficulty: Medium
Category: Passport to Advanced Math / Quadratics

Getting to the Answer: Before you plug -5 in for x, which creates messy numbers, factor the given equation.

$$x^2 + 2xk + k^2 = 0$$
$$(x + k)(x + k) = 0$$
$$(x + k)^2 = 0$$

Now plug in -5 for x and solve for k:

$$(-5 + k)^2 = 0$$
$$\sqrt[2]{(-5 + k)^2} = \pm\sqrt{0}$$
$$-5 + k = 0$$
$$k = 5$$

8. 6.5 or 13/2   **Difficulty:** Hard

Category: Passport to Advanced Math / Quadratics

Getting to the Answer: This is a tough question with no real shortcuts. The highest power of x in the equation is 2, so the equation is quadratic. Writing quadratic equations can be tricky and time-consuming. If you know the roots, you can use factors to write the equation. You don't know the roots of this equation, so start with the point that has the nicest values (0, 2) and substitute them into the equation, $y = ax^2 + bx + c$.

$$2 = a(0)^2 + b(0) + c$$
$$2 = c$$

Now your equation looks like $y = ax^2 + bx + 2$. Next, use the other two points to create a system of two equations in two variables.

$(-2, -10) \rightarrow -10 = a(-2)^2 + b(-2) + 2 \rightarrow -12 = 4a - 2b$

$(4, 14) \rightarrow 14 = a(4)^2 + b(4) + 2 \rightarrow 12 = 16a + 4b$

You now have a system of equations to solve. None of the variables has a coefficient of 1, so use combination to solve the system. If you multiply the top equation by 2, the b terms will eliminate each other.

$$2[4a - 2b = -12] \rightarrow 8a - 4b = -24$$
$$16a + 4b = 12 \rightarrow \underline{16a + 4b = 12}$$
$$24a = -12$$
$$a = -\frac{1}{2}$$

Now, find b by substituting the value of a into either of the original equations. Using the bottom equation, you get this:

$$16\left(-\frac{1}{2}\right) + 4b = 12$$
$$-8 + 4b = 12$$
$$4b = 20$$
$$b = 5$$

The value of $a + b + c = -\frac{1}{2} + 5 + 2 = 6\frac{1}{2}$. You can't enter a mixed number, so grid in your answer as the decimal number 6.5 or the improper fraction 13/2.

9. B   **Difficulty:** Easy

Category: Passport to Advanced Math / Quadratics

Getting to the Answer: To multiply two binomials, distribute each term in the first set of parentheses to each term in the second set. You can also think FOIL. Multiply $2a$ by each term in the second factor and then multiply $5b$ by each term. Combine like terms if possible.

$$(2a + 5b)(a - 3b)$$
$$= 2a(a - 3b) + 5b(a - 3b)$$
$$= 2a(a) + 2a(-3b) + 5b(a) + 5b(-3b)$$
$$= 2a^2 - 6ab + 5ab - 15b^2$$
$$= 2a^2 - ab - 15b^2$$

Choice (B) is correct.

10. A   **Difficulty:** Easy

Category: Passport to Advanced Math / Quadratics

Getting to the Answer: *Roots* are the same as *solutions* to an equation, so you need to solve the equation for x. Taking the square root of a quantity is the inverse operation of squaring it, and both sides of this equation are already perfect squares, so take their square roots. Then solve the resulting equations. Remember, there will be two equations to solve.

$$(x + 3)^2 = 49$$
$$\sqrt[2]{(x + 3)^2} = \pm\sqrt{49}$$
$$x + 3 = \pm7$$

Now simplify each equation: $x + 3 = -7$, or $x = -10$; and $x + 3 = 7$, or $x = 4$, so (A) is correct.

If you didn't recognize that you could use square rooting to solve the equation, you could also expand the left side, then subtract 49, factor the resulting equation, and set the factors equal to 0. This is a perfectly fine way to solve the equation, but it takes considerably longer.

11. C   **Difficulty:** Easy

Category: Passport to Advanced Math / Quadratics

Getting to the Answer: Being able to make connections between equations and graphs is a valuable skill. The pieces of a quadratic equation written in standard form give you lots of information about its graph. For example, finding the value of $\frac{-b}{2a}$ (the quadratic formula without the radical part) tells you where the axis of symmetry occurs.

This question is asking about c, which is the only constant term in the equation. If you substitute 0 for x, the equation becomes $y = a(0)^2 + b(0) + c$, or just $y = c$. This means the point $(0, c)$ will be on the graph, which is the y-intercept, making (C) correct.

12. D   Difficulty: Easy
Category: Passport to Advanced Math / Quadratics

Getting to the Answer: The graph is a parabola, so you can eliminate A right way (the equation is linear, not quadratic). The x-intercepts of the graph are -2 and 5, so the factors of this quadratic must be $(x + 2)$ and $(x - 5)$. The parabola opens downward, so there should be a negative sign in front of the factors. The correct equation is $y = -(x + 2)(x - 5)$. Don't let C fool you—those factors would produce x-intercepts of $+2$ and -5. If you're not convinced, set each factor equal to 0 and solve for x. Therefore, (D) is correct.

13. C   Difficulty: Medium
Category: Passport to Advanced Math / Quadratics

Getting to the Answer: Equations that are equivalent have the same solutions, so you are looking for the equation that is simply written in a different form. You could expand each of the equations in the answer choices, but unless you get lucky, this will use up quite a bit of time. The answer choices are written in vertex form, so use the method of completing the square to convert the equation in the question to the same form. First, write the equation in standard form: $y = x^2 + 6x - 40$. Move the 40 to the other side to temporarily get it out of the way. Then, complete the square on the right-hand side, by finding $\left(\frac{b}{2}\right)^2 = \left(\frac{6}{2}\right)^2 = 3^2 = 9$, and adding the result to both sides of the equation.

$$y = x^2 + 6x - 40$$
$$y + 40 = x^2 + 6x$$
$$y + 40 + 9 = x^2 + 6x + 9$$
$$y + 49 = x^2 + 6x + 9$$

Next, factor the right-hand side of the equation (which should be a perfect square trinomial) and rewrite it as a square.

$$y + 49 = (x + 3)(x + 3)$$
$$y + 49 = (x + 3)^2$$

Finally, solve for y to get $y = (x + 3)^2 - 49$, which makes (C) correct.

14. B   Difficulty: Medium
Category: Passport to Advanced Math / Quadratics

Getting to the Answer: Quadratic equations can be written in several different forms, each of which reveals something special about the graph. For example, the vertex form of a quadratic equation ($y = a(x - h)^2 + k$) gives the minimum or maximum value of the function (it's k), while the standard form ($y = ax^2 + bx + c$) reveals the y-intercept (it's c). The factored form of a quadratic equation reveals the solutions to the equation, which graphically represent the x-intercepts. Choice (B) is the only equation written in factored form and therefore must be correct. You can set each factor equal to 0 and quickly solve to find that the x-intercepts of the graph are $x = -\frac{3}{4}$ and $x = 1$, which agree with the graph.

15. A   Difficulty: Hard
Category: Passport to Advanced Math / Quadratics

Getting to the Answer: To answer this question, you need to recall just about everything you've learned about quadratic graphs. Be careful—the equation looks like vertex form, $y = a(x - h)^2 + k$, but it's not quite there because of the 2 inside the parentheses. You could rewrite the equation in vertex form, but this would involve squaring the quantity in parentheses and then completing the square, which will take quite a bit of time. So, skip A for now and compare each of the other answer choices to the equation. Don't forget, you are looking for the statement that is *not* true.

Choice B: Substitute 0 for x and simplify to find that the y-intercept is indeed $(0, -9)$.

Choice C: There is a negative in front of the equation, so the parabola *does* open downward.

Choice D: Look at the equation as a transformation of the parent function $y = x^2$. The parabola has been shifted to the right, moved up 7 units, and flipped upside down. Picture this in your head—it has to cross the x-axis at least one time.

This means (A) must be correct. As it turns out, the vertex is (2, 7), not (4, 7).

16. C Difficulty: Hard
Category: Passport to Advanced Math / Quadratics

Getting to the Answer: You are not expected to solve each system. Instead, think about it graphically. The solution to a system of equations is the point(s) where their graphs intersect, so graph each pair of equations in your graphing calculator and look for the ones that intersect at $x = 3.5$ and $x = 6$, both of which happen to be positive values and would lie to the right of the x-axis. The graphs of the equations in A and B don't intersect at all, so you can eliminate both answers right away. The graphs in (C) *do* intersect, and both points of intersection are to the right of the x-axis, so (C) could be correct, but check D just in case. The graphs don't intersect at all, so (C) is correct.

A note of caution here—just because the solutions were given as 3.5 and 6, that does *not* mean that either number has to appear in one or both of the equations.

17. 0 Difficulty: Medium
Category: Passport to Advanced Math / Quadratics

Getting to the Answer: To find the roots of an equation, you need to set it equal to 0, factor it, and then solve. Whenever the leading coefficient is a fraction, factoring becomes very messy. Luckily, you can clear the fraction the same way you do when solving equations (multiply both sides of the equation by the denominator of the fraction).

$$0 = \frac{1}{3}x^2 - 2x + 3$$
$$3(0) = 3\left(\frac{1}{3}x^2 - 2x + 3\right)$$
$$0 = x^2 - 6x + 9$$
$$0 = (x - 3)(x - 3)$$

The equation only has one unique solution ($x = 3$), so the positive difference between the roots is actually 0.

18. 8 Difficulty: Easy
Category: Passport to Advanced Math / Quadratics

Getting to the Answer: Whenever you're given the equation for a function, you can evaluate it at any given value by substituting that value for the variable. The variable t

represents the number of seconds after the rockets were fired, so find $h_2(1)$ and $h_1(1)$ and subtract. (Note that the equations are provided in the graphic.) To make the calculations easier, simplify each equation first.

$$h_2(t) = -8t(2t - 7) = -16t^2 + 56t$$
$$h_2(1) = -16(1)^2 + 56(1) = -16 + 56 = 40$$
$$h_1(t) = -16t(t - 3) = -16t^2 + 48t$$
$$h_1(1) = -16(1)^2 + 48(1) = -16 + 48 = 32$$

So, after 1 second the second rocket was $40 - 32 = 8$ feet higher.

19. .25 or 1/4 Difficulty: Hard
Category: Passport to Advanced Math / Quadratics

Getting to the Answer: A quadratic function reaches its maximum (or minimum) value at its vertex. Don't do rework—you've already written each equation in standard form, so use the formula $x = \frac{-b}{2a}$ to find the x-coordinate of the vertex for each function.

$h_2(t)$: $a = -16$ and $b = 56$, so $x = \frac{-56}{2(-16)} = \frac{-56}{-32} = \frac{7}{4}$. This means the second rocket reaches its maximum height at 1.75 seconds.

$h_1(t)$: $a = -16$ and $b = 48$, so $x = \frac{-48}{2(-16)} = \frac{-48}{-32} = \frac{3}{2}$. This means the first rocket reaches its maximum height at 1.5 seconds.

So, it took the second rocket $1.75 - 1.5 = 0.25$ seconds longer to reach its maximum height.

If you are comfortable using your graphing calculator (which could save quite a bit of time), you could graph each equation and use the "maximum" function on the calculator.

20. 8 Difficulty: Medium
Category: Passport to Advanced Math / Quadratics

Getting to the Answer: This question is testing whether you can interpret an equation. If you look carefully, it tells you that the coefficient of the x term from each equation is all you need. Again, don't do rework—you've already written each equation in standard form.

The standard form of the equation for the second rocket is $h_2(t) = -16t^2 + 56t$, so the initial velocity was 56 feet per second. The standard form of the equation for the first rocket is $h_1(t) = -16t^2 + 48t$, so the initial velocity was 48 feet per second. The second rocket's initial velocity was $56 - 48 = 8$ more feet per second than the first rocket's.

21. B   Difficulty: Easy
Category: Passport to Advanced Math / Quadratics

Getting to the Answer: Whenever a quadratic (or any polynomial) equation is given in factored form, to find the solutions set each of the factors equal to 0 and solve for the variable using inverse operations.

The solutions are $x = -5$ and $x = \dfrac{3}{2}$, making (B) correct.

22. C   Difficulty: Medium
Category: Passport to Advanced Math / Quadratics

Getting to the Answer: According to the graph, one x-intercept is to the left of the y-axis, and the other is to the right. This tells you that one value of x is positive, while the other is negative, so you can immediately eliminate D (both factors have the same sign). To choose between the remaining equations, find the x-intercepts by setting each factor equal to 0 and solving for x (mentally if possible). In A, the x-intercepts are $\dfrac{1}{2}$ and -1, but that would mean that e (the negative intercept) is *twice* as far from the origin as f, not *half* as far, so eliminate A. In B, the x-intercepts are 1 and -2. Again, that would mean that e is twice as far from the origin as f, not half as far, so eliminate B. This means (C) must be correct. The x-intercepts are 1 and $-\dfrac{1}{2}$, which fits the criterion that e is half as far from the origin as f.

23. B   Difficulty: Medium
Category: Passport to Advanced Math / Quadratics

Getting to the Answer: Compare each statement to the graph to determine whether it is true, eliminating choices as you go. Remember, you are looking for the statement that is *not* true. The parabola opens upward, so the value of a must be positive, which means you can eliminate A because it *is* true (> 0 means positive). The value of b is the tricky one, so skip it for now, and consider C. When written in standard form, the value of c tells you the y-intercept. According to the graph, the y-intercept

is below the x-axis and is therefore negative, so $c < 0$ is true. Eliminate C. Unfortunately, this means you'll need to consider B. Based on the equation alone, it is not easy to determine whether b is positive or negative, so you'll need to think outside the box. The trick for finding the x-coordinate of the vertex of a parabola is to calculate $\dfrac{-b}{2a}$ (the quadratic formula without the radical part). In the graph, the x-coordinate of the vertex is 3, so set the formula equal to 3, solve for b, and see what happens.

$$\frac{-b}{2a} = \frac{3}{1}$$
$$-b = 6a$$
$$b = -6a$$

You have already determined that a is positive (because the parabola opens upward), so b must be negative. This means b is less than 0, not greater, making (B) correct.

24. B   Difficulty: Medium
Category: Passport to Advanced Math / Quadratics

Getting to the Answer: When a quadratic equation is written in the form $y = a(x - h)^2 + k$, the minimum value (or the maximum value if $a < 0$) is given by k, and the axis of symmetry is given by the equation $x = h$. The question states that the minimum of the parabola is 5, so look for an equation where k is 5. You can eliminate C and D because k is 3 in C and -3 in D. The question also states that the axis of symmetry is $x = -3$, so h must be -3. Be careful—this is tricky. The equation in A is not correct because the vertex form of a parabola has a negative before the h, so $(x - 3)$ would produce an axis of symmetry at $x = 3$, not -3. This means (B) is correct.

You could also graph each equation in your graphing calculator to see which one matches the criteria given in the question, but this is likely to use up valuable time on Test Day.

25. D   Difficulty: Medium
Category: Passport to Advanced Math / Quadratics

Getting to the Answer: Take a peek at the answer choices—they are really just describing the sign of the x-coordinates of the solutions. This means you don't need to find the exact values of the solutions. Instead, draw a quick sketch of the system (or graph it in your calculator), and translate < 0 as *negative* and > 0 as *positive*.

The top equation is a line and the bottom equation is a parabola. Write the linear equation in slope-intercept form and the quadratic equation in factored form to make them easier to sketch: $x + y = 4 \rightarrow y = -x + 4$ and $y = x^2 - 2x - 15 \rightarrow (x - 5)(x + 3)$. A quick sketch is all you need—don't waste valuable time labeling things. The line has a y-intercept of 4 and a negative slope, and the parabola opens upward and crosses the x-axis at 5 and -3. The sketch looks like:

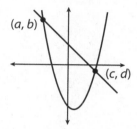

The solutions to the system are the points where the graphs intersect. The question tells you that $a < c$, so (a, b) must be the point on the left and (c, d) is the point on the right. Look at the x-values: a is to the left of the y-axis so it must be negative (or $a < 0$), and c is to the right of the y-axis so it must be positive (or $c > 0$). This means (D) is correct.

26. C   Difficulty: Medium
Category: Passport to Advanced Math / Quadratics

Getting to the Answer: The axis of symmetry of a parabola always passes through the x-coordinate of the parabola's vertex. The trick for finding the x-coordinate of the vertex is to calculate $\frac{-b}{2a}$ (the quadratic formula without the radical part). In the equation, $a = 3$ and $b = 12$, so the equation of the axis of symmetry is $x = \frac{-(12)}{2(3)} = \frac{-12}{6} = -2$. In the question, the equation is $x = m$, so m must be -2, which makes (C) correct.

27. A   Difficulty: Hard
Category: Passport to Advanced Math / Quadratics

Getting to the Answer: The quantity under the radical in the quadratic formula ($b^2 - 4ac$) is called the discriminant because it tells you what kind of solutions to expect. If $b^2 - 4ac = 0$, then the equation has exactly one unique real solution and the graph just touches the x-axis at

that value. If $b^2 - 4ac > 0$, then the equation has two real solutions and the graph crosses the x-axis twice. If $b^2 - 4ac < 0$, then the equation has two imaginary solutions (because the square root of a negative number is imaginary) and does not cross the x-axis at all. Now, take a look at the criteria given in the question: $ac > \frac{b^2}{4}$. Notice that there is an ac, a b^2, and a 4, so try to manipulate the inequality to make it look like the discriminant:

$$ac > \frac{b^2}{4}$$
$$\frac{ac}{1} > \frac{b^2}{4}$$
$$4ac > b^2$$
$$0 > b^2 - 4ac$$
$$b^2 - 4ac < 0$$

This means the solutions are imaginary and the graph does not cross the x-axis at all; therefore (A) is correct.

28. 87   Difficulty: Easy
Category: Passport to Advanced Math / Quadratics

Getting to the Answer: There is no trick to this question. You just need to do the algebra to convert one form to another. Don't forget—when you square a quantity, you can't just square the terms inside the parentheses. Instead, you must multiply the quantity by itself and use FOIL to expand it.

$$\begin{aligned} y &= 3(x + 5)^2 + 12 \\ &= 3(x + 5)(x + 5) + 12 \\ &= 3(x^2 + 5x + 5x + 25) + 12 \\ &= 3(x^2 + 10x + 25) + 12 \\ &= 3x^2 + 30x + 75 + 12 \\ &= 3x^2 + 30x + 87 \end{aligned}$$

The question asks for the value of c, so grid in 87.

29. 8   Difficulty: Medium
Category: Passport to Advanced Math / Quadratics

Getting to the Answer: Start by translating from English into math. You have two statements to translate, so chances are you'll be solving a system of equations. Before you select your answer, make sure you found what the question is asking for (the smaller of the two integers). Translate "n is 2 less than three times m" as $n = 3m - 2$.

Translate "the product of m and n is 176" as $mn = 176$. Use substitution to solve the equations simultaneously:

$$n = 3m - 2$$
$$mn = 176$$

$$m(3m - 2) = 176$$
$$3m^2 - 2m - 176 = 0$$
$$(3m + 22)(m - 8) = 0$$

Setting each factor equal to 0 and solving results in $m = -\dfrac{22}{3}$ and $m = 8$. The question states that m and n are positive integers, so $m = 8$. This means $n = 3(8) - 2 = 22$. The smaller of the two integers is 8.

30. 13   Difficulty: Medium

Category: Passport to Advanced Math / Quadratics

Getting to the Answer: The question states that the function is quadratic, so use what you know about the graphs of parabolas to answer the question. Notice that the x-values in the table increase by two each time. To find $p(-4)$, you just need to imagine adding one extra row to the top of the table. Now, think about symmetry—you can see from the points in the table that $(2, -5)$ is the vertex of the parabola. The points $(0, -3)$ and $(4, -3)$ are equidistant from the vertex, as are the points $(-2, 3)$ and $(6, 3)$. This means the point whose x-value is -4 should have the same y-value as the last point in the table $(8, 13)$. So, $f(-4) = 13$.

CHAPTER 11

PRACTICE

7. C   Difficulty: Hard
Category: Additional Topics in Math / Geometry

Getting to the Answer: Look for hidden special right triangles to help you find the answer, and add new information to your diagram as you find it. Start by finding $m\angle ACD$ from the two given angles: $m\angle ACD = 180° - 15° - 30° = 135°$. Because $\angle ACB$ is supplementary to $\angle ACD$, $\angle ACB$ measures 45°. $\triangle ABC$ is a right triangle, so its missing angle ($\angle BAC$) is also 45°, making $\triangle ABC$ a 45-45-90 triangle. This means $\angle BAD$ is 60°; therefore, $\triangle ABD$ is a 30-60-90 triangle.

Knowing that you have two special right triangles will allow you to unlock the unknown side lengths. $\overline{AC}$ is the hypotenuse of the 45-45-90 triangle (side ratio of $x:x:x\sqrt{2}$), so $\overline{AB}$ and $\overline{BC}$ (the two legs) must be $2\sqrt{2}$ (solve the equation $4 = x\sqrt{2}$ to find this). $\overline{AB}$ is also the shorter leg of the 30-60-90 triangle (side ratio of $x:x\sqrt{3}:2x$), so $\overline{BD}$ (longer leg) is $2\sqrt{6}$, and $\overline{AD}$ (hypotenuse) is $4\sqrt{2}$. Don't stop just yet; remember which perimeter you need. Take the difference of $\overline{BD}$ and $\overline{BC}$ to determine $\overline{CD}$, which is $2\sqrt{6} - 2\sqrt{2}$. You now have all three sides of $\triangle ACD$, so add them together to get your answer:

$$P_{\triangle ACD} = 4 + \left(2\sqrt{6} - 2\sqrt{2}\right) + 4\sqrt{2}$$

This simplifies to $4 + 2\sqrt{6} + 2\sqrt{2}$, making (C) correct.

The completed diagram is shown here:

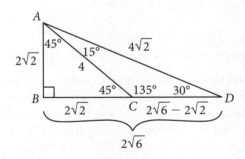

8. 426   Difficulty: Medium
Category: Additional Topics in Math / Geometry

Getting to the Answer: The figure contains a pair of similar triangles. Use the ratio within them to determine the requested length. The shadow cast by the flagpole is 50% longer than the flagpole itself; that is, $1.5 \times 40 = 60$ feet. Use this in conjunction with the lengths provided to determine the distance from the building to the end of the flagpole's shadow.

$$\frac{40}{324} = \frac{60}{x}$$
$$\frac{10}{81} = \frac{60}{x}$$
$$10x = 4,860$$
$$x = 486$$

Subtract the length of the flagpole's shadow, 60, from 486 to obtain 426, the distance from the building to the flagpole. Grid in 426.

9. B   Difficulty: Medium
Category: Additional Topics in Math / Geometry

Getting to the Answer: Start by drawing in $\overline{PR}$ and $\overline{PS}$ as shown here.

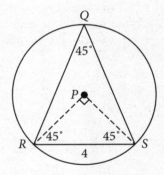

Because the angle formed by $\overline{PR}$ and $\overline{PS}$ subtends the same arc as the angle formed by $\overline{QR}$ and $\overline{QS}$, $\angle RPS$ must be twice $\angle RQS$, which is $45° \times 2 = 90°$. In addition to being legs of $\triangle PRS$, $\overline{PR}$ and $\overline{PS}$ are radii, so they are congruent, which makes $\triangle PRS$ a 45-45-90 triangle. Therefore, the radius of circle P is $\frac{4}{\sqrt{2}} = 2\sqrt{2}$, and the circumference is $2\pi \times 2\sqrt{2} = 4\pi\sqrt{2}$, which makes (B) correct.

10. B   **Difficulty:** Hard

Category: Additional Topics in Math / Geometry

Getting to the Answer: Begin by finding the volume of one beach ball using the volume formula for a sphere, remembering to halve the diameter first:

$$V_{sphere} = \frac{4}{3}\pi r^3 = \frac{4}{3}\pi \left(\frac{66}{2}\right)^3 = 47,916\pi \text{ cm}^3$$

Convert to breaths using the relationships given:

$$47,916\pi \text{ cm}^3 \times \frac{1\,L}{1000 \text{ cm}^3} \times \frac{1 \text{ breath}}{6\,L} \approx 8\pi$$

This is about 25.09, or 25, full breaths. Multiply this by 3 to get 75 full breaths for three beach balls, which is (B).

PERFORM

11. A   **Difficulty:** Medium

Category: Additional Topics in Math / Geometry

Getting to the Answer: Draw a diagram of Aundria and Annette's routes to the summit to visualize the situation. After drawing and labeling the diagram with the information given, look for a way to uncover a right triangle by drawing in additional lines. Once complete, use the rectangle you created to fill in the lengths of the new segments. The completed diagram is shown here:

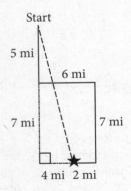

Use the Pythagorean theorem to calculate the distance Annette will travel:

$$c^2 = (5 + 7)^2 + 4^2$$
$$c^2 = 144 + 16$$
$$c^2 = 160$$
$$c = \sqrt{160} = 4\sqrt{10}$$

But you're not done yet! The question asks you to find the total distance the two women will travel. Aundria travels $5 + 6 + 7 + 2 = 20$ miles; together, she and Annette will travel $20 + 4\sqrt{10}$ miles, which is approximately 32.65 miles. Choice (A) is correct.

12. B   **Difficulty:** Medium

Category: Additional Topics in Math / Geometry

Getting to the Answer: Given the area of $\triangle ABC$ and the length of the base AB, you can find its height:

$$150 = \frac{1}{2}(20)(BC)$$
$$150 = 10(BC)$$
$$15 = BC$$

Because $\overline{BC} = 15$ and $\overline{AB} = 20$, $\triangle ABC$ is a 3-4-5 triangle with dimensions scaled up by a factor of 5, so the hypotenuse $(\overline{AC})$ must be $5 \times 5 = 25$. Next, turn your attention to the smaller triangle, $\triangle AGH$. You're told that the hypotenuse of this triangle, $\overline{AH}$, is 20. $\triangle ABC$ and $\triangle AGH$ are similar triangles (because they share an angle at vertex A and they each have a right angle), so their corresponding sides must be proportional.

$$\frac{AH}{AC} = \frac{HG}{CB}$$
$$\frac{20}{25} = \frac{HG}{15}$$
$$300 = 25HG$$
$$\overline{HG} = 12$$

Choice (B) is the correct answer.

13. B   **Difficulty:** Medium

Category: Additional Topics in Math / Geometry

Getting to the Answer: Read carefully; you're asked for information on the portion that is *not* strawberry rhubarb. The diagram includes the measures of central angles, and you're told that the pie tin has a diameter of 10 inches (which means the radius is 5 inches and the area is 25π square inches). Therefore, you can set up a proportion to determine the area of non–strawberry rhubarb pie (which represents 129.6° out of a full 360° circle):

$$\frac{\text{central angle}}{360°} = \frac{\text{sector area}}{\text{circle area}}$$

$$\frac{360 - 129.6}{360} = \frac{x}{25\pi}$$

$$5{,}760\pi = 360x$$

$$x = 16\pi$$

The portion of leftover pie that is not strawberry rhubarb is 16π square inches, which makes (B) correct.

14. B   **Difficulty:** Medium

Category: Additional Topics in Math / Geometry

Getting to the Answer: Adding 96 cubic feet of sand will completely fill the sandbox that starts one-third full, so 96 cubic feet is two-thirds of the total volume. Thus, one-third is $\frac{96}{2} = 48$ cubic feet, and the total volume is $3 \times 48 = 144$ cubic feet. The sandbox described is a rectangular solid, so the volume can be found using the formula $V = lwh$. Because the base of the sandbox is a square, you know the length and width are both 24. With the total volume in hand, you can find the depth (or height) of the sandbox: $144 = 24 \times 24 \times h$, which simplifies to $h = 0.25$. A height of 0.25 feet is the same as 3 inches, so (B) is correct.

EXTRA PRACTICE

1. A   **Difficulty:** Medium

Category: Additional Topics in Math / Geometry

Getting to the Answer: Start by connecting the ranch to the campsite. Then draw in a horizontal line and a vertical line to form a right triangle.

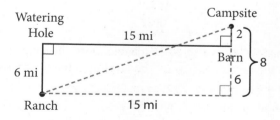

The length of one leg of the triangle is 15 miles, the distance from the watering hole to the barn. The length of the other leg is $6 + 2 = 8$ miles, the distance from the ranch to the watering hole and then from the barn to the campsite. The two legs of the right triangle are 8 and 15. You might recognize the Pythagorean triplet, 8, 15, 17, but if you don't, you can always rely on the Pythagorean theorem:

$$8^2 + 15^2 = c^2$$

$$64 + 225 = c^2$$

$$289 = c^2$$

$$\sqrt{289} = \sqrt{c^2}$$

$$17 = c$$

The actual trail is $6 + 15 + 2 = 23$ miles long. The direct route is 17 miles, so the direct route is $23 - 17 = 6$ miles shorter, making (A) the correct answer.

2. B   **Difficulty:** Medium

Category: Additional Topics in Math / Geometry

Getting to the Answer: You are told that $\overline{HI}$ is the bisector of $\overline{LO}$ and $\overline{OW}$. This tells you two things: 1) The definition of *bisector* tells you that that $\overline{HI}$ divides both $\overline{LO}$ and $\overline{OW}$ exactly in half, and 2) a straight line connecting the midpoints of two sides of a triangle is parallel to the third side, so $\overline{HI}$ is parallel to $\overline{LW}$.

Because $\overline{HI}$ is parallel to $\overline{LW}$, angles L and H must be congruent (they are corresponding angles), and angles W and I must be congruent (they are also corresponding angles). Angle O is shared by both triangles and is equal to itself by the Reflexive Property. This means the side lengths of the two triangles are different, but the corresponding angles are the same, so the triangles are similar. Side lengths of similar triangles are in proportion to one another. You are given the side lengths of $\overline{LW}$ and $\overline{HI}$. Because I is the midpoint of $\overline{OW}$, $\overline{OI}$ is half as long as $\overline{OW}$. The same is true for the other side. So the sides are in the ratio 1:2. Use this ratio to set up a proportion and solve for x:

$$\frac{1}{2} = \frac{4x-1}{30}$$

$$30 = 2(4x-1)$$

$$30 = 8x-2$$

$$32 = 8x$$

$$4 = x$$

The correct answer is (B).

3. A   Difficulty: Medium

Category: Additional Topics in Math / Geometry

Getting to the Answer: Distance around *part* of a circle is the same as arc length, so use the relationship $\frac{\text{arc length}}{\text{circumference}} = \frac{\text{central angle}}{360°}$ to answer the question. The unknown in the relationship is the central angle, so call it *a*. Before you can fill in the rest of the equation, you need to find the circumference of the circle: $C = 2\pi r = 2\pi(120) = 240\pi$. Now you're ready to solve for *a*:

$$\frac{\text{arc length}}{\text{circumference}} = \frac{\text{central angle}}{360°}$$

$$\frac{200}{240\pi} = \frac{a}{360}$$

$$\frac{200(360)}{240\pi} = a$$

$$95.5 \approx a$$

Be careful when you enter this expression into your calculator—you need to put 240π in parentheses so that the calculator doesn't divide by 240 and then multiply by π. If entered correctly, the result is about 95.5 degrees, which matches (A).

4. C   Difficulty: Medium

Category: Additional Topics in Math / Geometry

Getting to the Answer: First, think logically: After it's poured into the larger glass, the volume of the water in the glass will still be the same as the volume when it was in the smaller glass. Find the volume of the water in the smaller glass. Then, substitute this volume into a second equation where the height is unknown and solve for *h*. The volume of a cylinder equals the area of its base times its height, or $V = \pi r^2 h$.

$$V = \pi r^2 h$$

$$V = \pi(1.5)^2(6)$$

$$V = \pi(2.25)(6)$$

$$V = 13.5\pi$$

$$13.5\pi = \pi(2)^2 h$$

$$13.5\pi = 4\pi h$$

$$3.375 = h$$

The water will reach 3.375 inches high in the bigger glass, which is (C).

5. B   Difficulty: Hard

Category: Additional Topics in Math / Geometry

Getting to the Answer: First, find the measure of the missing angle in the triangle: $180 - 105 - 45 = 30°$. Now, draw the height of the triangle up from *B* to a point, *D*, on $\overline{AC}$; this creates two right triangles.

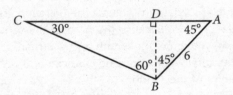

Triangle *ABD* is a 45-45-90 triangle, so its side lengths are in the ratio $x:x:x\sqrt{2}$. Because $\overline{AB}$ is the hypotenuse, set up an equation using the ratio of the sides:

$$6 = x\sqrt{2}$$

$$\frac{6}{\sqrt{2}} = x$$

$$\frac{6}{\sqrt{2}}\left(\frac{\sqrt{2}}{\sqrt{2}}\right) = x$$

$$\frac{6\sqrt{2}}{2} = x$$

$$3\sqrt{2} = x$$

Triangle *BDC* is a 30-60-90 triangle, so its side lengths are in the ratio of $x:x\sqrt{3}:2x$. You just found the dimensions of the shorter leg, $3\sqrt{2}$, so multiply it by $\sqrt{3}$ to find the length of the longer leg ($\sqrt{3} \times 3\sqrt{2} = 3\sqrt{6}$). Now, find the length of *AC*, which is the base of the triangle, by adding $\overline{AD}$ to $\overline{DC}$. The result is $3\sqrt{2} + 3\sqrt{6}$. Finally, use the area formula, $A = \dfrac{1}{2}bh$, to find the area of the whole triangle:

$$A = \frac{1}{2}\left(3\sqrt{2} + 3\sqrt{6}\right)\left(3\sqrt{2}\right)$$
$$= \frac{1}{2}\left(18 + 9\sqrt{12}\right)$$
$$= \frac{1}{2}\left(18 + 9 \cdot 2\sqrt{3}\right)$$
$$= \frac{1}{2}\left(18 + 18\sqrt{3}\right)$$
$$= 9 + 9\sqrt{3}$$

Choice (B) is correct.

6. B   **Difficulty:** Hard

Category: Additional Topics in Math / Geometry

Getting to the Answer: When the equation of a circle is in the form $(x - h)^2 + (y - k)^2 = r^2$, the r represents the length of the radius. To get the equation into this form, complete the square. Then you can double r to find the diameter.

You already have an x^2 and a y^2 in the given equation and the coefficients of x and y are even, so completing the square is fairly straightforward—there are just a lot of steps. Start by grouping the x's and y's together. Then, take the coefficient of the x term and divide it by 2, square it, and add it to the two terms with x variables. Do the same with the y term. Don't forget to add these amounts to the other side of the equation as well. This creates a perfect square of x terms and y terms, so take the square root of each.

$$x^2 + y^2 + 8x - 20y = 28$$
$$x^2 + 8x + y^2 - 20y = 28$$
$$(x + 8x + 16) + (y^2 - 20y + 100) = 28 + 16 + 100$$
$$(x + 4)^2 + (y - 10)^2 = 144$$

The equation tells you that r^2 is 144, which means that the radius is 12 and the diameter is twice that, or 24, which is (B).

7. C   **Difficulty:** Hard

Category: Additional Topics in Math / Geometry

Getting to the Answer: Don't be too quick to answer a question like this. You can't simply find three-fourths of

the volume of the cone because the top is considerably smaller than the bottom. Instead, you'll need to find the volume of the whole cone and subtract the volume of the top piece that is being discarded.

The figure shows a right triangle inside the cone. The height of the cone is the longer leg of the triangle, 16. The hypotenuse is given as 20. You might recognize this as a multiple of a Pythagorean triplet, 3-4-5, or in this case, 12-16-20. This means the radius of the original cone is 12. Substitute this into the formula for volume:

$$V = \frac{1}{3}\pi r^2 h$$
$$V = \frac{1}{3}\pi(12)^2(16)$$
$$V = 768\pi$$

To determine the dimensions of the top piece, use similar triangles.

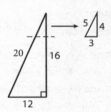

One quarter of the height is $16 \div 4 = 4$, resulting in a 3-4-5 triangle, making the height 4 and the radius 3.

$$V = \frac{1}{3}\pi(3)^2(4) = 12\pi$$

Thus, the volume of the remaining solid is $768\pi - 12\pi = 756\pi$, which is (C).

8. 9   **Difficulty:** Hard

Category: Additional Topics in Math / Geometry

Getting to the Answer: Corresponding sides of similar triangles are proportional. Draw a quick sketch to find as many side lengths as you can, find the ratio of the sides between the two triangles, and use that ratio to find the missing vertex.

Plot all the points given in the question, labeling them as you go so you don't get confused (especially because you won't have graph paper). You know that A and B are in the same quadrant, which means the triangles are both oriented the same way. So make your sketch accordingly.

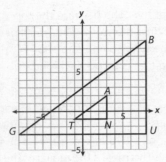

Once you have plotted *ANT* and the base of *BUG*, you can determine that the ratio of the triangles is 1:4 (the base of *ANT* has a length of 4 and the base of *BUG* has a length of 16). To determine where you should put *B*, find the length of side *AN* and then multiply by 4. The length of the vertical side of *BUG* is 12. Because one vertex is at (8, −3), vertex *B* must be 12 vertical units above that point, or (8, 9). The *y*-coordinate of *B* is 9.

9. C   Difficulty: Easy

Category: Additional Topics in Math / Geometry

Getting to the Answer: Line *L* forms a right triangle with the *x*- and *y*-axes, so one of the interior angles of the triangle has a measure of 90°. You know that $q = 140$, and together *p* and *q* form a straight line, which means they are supplementary angles. Thus, *p* must equal $180 - 140 = 40$. One of the interior angles of the triangle is vertical to *p*, so it also equals 40°. Now find the last angle measure inside the triangle by subtracting: $180° - 90° - 40° = 50°$. This angle is supplementary to *r*, so $r = 180 - 50 = 130$. This means that $r - p = 130 - 40 = 90$, making (C) the correct choice.

10. D   Difficulty: Easy

Category: Additional Topics in Math / Geometry

Getting to the Answer: If you're not sure how to start a question with a circle in it, look for the radius. The equation of circle takes the form $(x - h)^2 + (y - k)^2 = r^2$, where (h, k) is the center of the circle and *r* is the length of the radius.

To find the equation of a circle, you need the radius and the *x*- and *y*-coordinates of the center point. Look at the figure—the center has coordinates (−1, 2). From the center, you can count horizontally or vertically to the

edge of the circle to find that its radius is 6. This means the equation is $(x - (-1))^2 + (y - 2)^2 = 6^2$, or $(x + 1)^2 + (y - 2)^2 = 36$, which matches the equation in (D).

11. D   Difficulty: Medium

Category: Additional Topics in Math / Geometry

Getting to the Answer: The sides 3*d*, 5*d*, and *h* form a right triangle, so plug these values into the Pythagorean theorem and then solve for *h*. Be careful—when you square 3*d* and 5*d*, you must square the coefficient and the variable.

$$a^2 + b^2 = c^2$$
$$(3d)^2 + (5d)^2 = h^2$$
$$9d^2 + 25d^2 = h^2$$
$$34d^2 = h^2$$
$$\sqrt{34d^2} = h$$
$$d\sqrt{34} = h$$

Choice (D) is correct.

12. D   Difficulty: Medium

Category: Additional Topics in Math / Geometry

Getting to the Answer: You can eliminate B immediately because corresponding angles of similar triangles are congruent, so they are in a 1:1 ratio. You can also eliminate A, because $\overline{OD}$ would be proportional to $\overline{NW}$, not $\overline{EW}$. Evaluating C might get complicated, so skip it for now. Because the side lengths of the two triangles are proportional, when you find the sum of the side lengths (the perimeter), this number will be in the same proportion. You can check this by assigning numbers that are in the ratio 7:4 and finding the perimeter of each triangle:

$$OL = 7 \text{ and } NE = 4$$
$$LD = 14 \text{ and } EW = 8$$
$$OD = 21 \text{ and } NW = 12$$
$$\text{Perimeter}_{\triangle OLD} = 7 + 14 + 21 = 42$$
$$\text{Perimeter}_{\triangle NEW} = 4 + 8 + 12 = 24$$
$$42:24 = 7:4$$

This means (D) is correct.

13. A   Difficulty: Medium

Category: Additional Topics in Math / Geometry

Getting to the Answer: Use the relationship $\dfrac{\text{area of sector}}{\text{area of circle}} = \dfrac{\text{central angle}}{360°}$ to answer this question. To help remember this relationship, just think $\dfrac{\text{partial area}}{\text{whole area}} = \dfrac{\text{partial angle}}{\text{whole angle}}$.

The unknown in this question is the radius, which you can find by first finding the area of the whole circle and then by using the equation for area of a circle $A = \pi r^2$. You have everything you need to find the area of the circle:

$$\frac{\text{area of sector}}{\text{area of circle}} = \frac{\text{central angle}}{360°}$$

$$\frac{14\pi}{A} = \frac{140}{360}$$

$$5{,}040\pi = 140A$$

$$36\pi = A$$

Now, solve for r using $A = \pi r^2$:

$$36\pi = \pi r^2$$

$$36 = r^2$$

$$\pm 6 = r$$

The radius can't be negative, so the correct answer is 6, which is (A).

14. C   Difficulty: Medium

Category: Additional Topics in Math / Geometry

Getting to the Answer: The formula for finding the volume of a pyramid with a rectangular base is $V = \dfrac{1}{3}lwh$. Start by substituting what you know into the formula. You know the volume is represented by $x^3 - x$. You also know the length is $x + 1$ and the width is $3x$.

$$V = \frac{1}{3}lwh$$

$$x^3 - x = \frac{1}{3}(x+1)(3x)h$$

Multiply both sides of the equation by 3 to clear the fraction, but don't multiply anything else just yet. First, look for a pattern.

$$3x^3 - 3x = (x+1)(3x)h$$

Notice that if you divide both sides of the equation by the width, $3x$, you'll be left with $x^2 - 1$ on the left side and $(x + 1)$ times h on the right side. The difference of squares rule tells you that the factors of $x^2 - 1$ are $x + 1$ and $x - 1$. This means the height of the pyramid must be represented by $x - 1$. Therefore, (C) is correct.

15. B   Difficulty: Medium

Category: Additional Topics in Math / Geometry

Getting to the Answer: Solve this question one step at a time. The volume of sand in one tank (only two inches of the height) will be $V = 24 \times 9 \times 2 = 432$ cubic inches, which means the volume of sand in all 50 tanks will be $50 \times 432 = 21{,}600$ cubic inches. Each cubic inch of sand weighs about 2 ounces, so the weight of all the sand will be $2 \times 21{,}600 = 43{,}200$ ounces. There are 16 ounces in one pound, so the weight of the sand in pounds is $43{,}200 \div 16 = 2{,}700$. Finally, each bag contains 40 pounds of sand, so the pet store needs to buy $2{,}700 \div 40 = 67.5$, or about 68 bags of sand. This means (B) is the correct answer.

16. A   Difficulty: Medium

Category: Additional Topics in Math / Geometry

Getting to the Answer: Just like triangles, corresponding sides of similar quadrilaterals are proportional. This means the perimeters of similar quadrilaterals are also proportional and in the same proportion as each pair of corresponding side lengths.

Find the perimeter of rectangle *LION* and compare it to the perimeter of *PUMA*. *LION* has a perimeter of $86 + 86 + 52 + 52 = 276$. Therefore, the ratio of the perimeter of *LION* to the perimeter of *PUMA* is 276 : 69, which reduces to 4 : 1. This tells you that the width of *LION* is 4 times greater than the width of *PUMA*, which means *PUMA*'s width is $52 \div 4 = 13$ units, making (A) correct.

17. C   Difficulty: Medium

Category: Additional Topics in Math / Geometry

Getting to the Answer: Because the ratio of the shaded area to the unshaded area is 4 : 5, the ratio of the shaded area to the entire circle is $4 : (4 + 5) = 4 : 9$. This ratio is the same as the ratio of the interior angle of the shaded sector to 360°, or $x : 360$. Set up a proportion using these ratios:

$$\frac{4}{9} = \frac{x}{360}$$
$$360(4) = 9x$$
$$1,440 = 9x$$
$$160 = x$$

Choice (C) is correct.

18. D   **Difficulty:** Hard

Category: Additional Topics in Math / Geometry

Getting to the Answer: In a right triangle, one leg is the base and the other is the height. Use x and $x + 3$ to represent the lengths of these two legs (because the question states that one leg is 3 inches longer than the other). Use the area formula and set the equation equal to the given area:

$$35 = \frac{1}{2}(x)(x + 3)$$
$$2(35) = \cancel{2}\left(\frac{1}{\cancel{2}}(x)(x + 3)\right)$$
$$70 = (x)(x + 3)$$
$$70 = x^2 + 3x$$

Now, subtract 70 to make the equation equal 0 and then factor it. The factors are $(x + 10)$ and $(x - 7)$, which means $x = -10$ and $x = 7$. Lengths cannot be negative, so the shorter leg must have a length of 7. This means the longer leg has a length of $7 + 3 = 10$. Now use the Pythagorean theorem to find the length of the hypotenuse.

$$a^2 + b^2 = c^2$$
$$7^2 + 10^2 = c^2$$
$$49 + 100 = c^2$$
$$149 = c^2$$
$$\sqrt{149} = \sqrt{c^2}$$
$$\sqrt{149} = c$$

Choice (D) is correct.

19. B   **Difficulty:** Hard

Category: Additional Topics in Math / Geometry

Getting to the Answer: There are two triangles in this figure, *ACE* and *BCD*. Because $\overline{BD}$ is parallel to $\overline{AE}$, angles *A* and *B* must be congruent (they are corresponding angles), and angles *D* and *E* must be congruent (they are also corresponding angles). Angle *C* is shared by both

triangles and is equal to itself by the Reflexive Property. This means the side lengths of the two triangles are different, but the angles are the same, so the triangles are similar by AAA. Side lengths of similar triangles are in proportion to one another.

You know the two triangles are similar, so set up a proportion using their side lengths. You'll need to translate from English into math as you go: $AB = 5$ and BC is three times that or 15. This means $AC = 5 + 15 = 20$. *CD* is 2 more than half *AC* or $20 \div 2 = 10 + 2 = 12$. Now you know three side lengths, so you can set up and solve a proportion:

$$\frac{BC}{AC} = \frac{DC}{EC}$$
$$\frac{15}{20} = \frac{12}{EC}$$
$$15EC = 240$$
$$EC = 16$$

This is the length of side *EC*, but the question asks for the length of segment *DE*, which is $EC - CD$, or $16 - 12 = 4$. This makes (B) the correct choice.

20. B   **Difficulty:** Hard

Category: Additional Topics in Math / Geometry

Getting to the Answer: Find the volume of the container using the formula for volume of a cylinder, $V = \pi r^2 h$. The question gives you the width, or the diameter of the container, so divide by 2 to get the radius.

$$V = \pi(1.25)^2(4)$$
$$V = \pi(1.5625)(4)$$
$$V = 6.25\pi$$

The factory only fills the cup 80% of the way up, so multiply the container volume by 0.8 to find that the actual volume of the yogurt is $6.25\pi \times 0.8 = 5\pi$, or about 15.708 cubic inches. Divide this by 6 ounces to determine that 1 ounce takes up approximately 2.6 cubic inches of space, which matches (B).

21. B   **Difficulty:** Easy

Category: Additional Topics in Math / Geometry

Getting to the Answer: The sum of the interior angle measures of every triangle is 180°. To figure out the value of x, begin by filling in the angle measures for the triangle. The angle vertical to the 48° angle is also 48°, and the angle supplementary to the 135° angle has a measure of 180° − 135° = 45°. Now that you know two of the angles in the triangle, you can calculate the measure of the third angle, *y*, by subtracting from 180 to get 180 − 48 − 45 = 87°. The angle with measure *x*° is supplementary to angle *y*, so 87 + *x* = 180°. Thus, *x* = 93°, which means that *x* − *y* = 93 − 87 = 6, which is (B).

22. C   Difficulty: Easy
Category: Additional Topics in Math / Geometry

Getting to the Answer: From the question, you know that the triangle formed by Earth, the moon, and the sun is a right triangle. This means you can use the Pythagorean theorem to find the missing side, which is the hypotenuse. You can divide both numbers by 1,000 to reduce the number of zeros and make them more manageable.

$$a^2 + b^2 = c^2$$
$$240^2 + 91{,}674^2 = c^2$$
$$57{,}600 + 8{,}404{,}122{,}276 = c^2$$
$$8{,}404{,}179{,}876 = c^2$$
$$91{,}674.31 = c$$

Don't forget to multiply the result by 1,000 (because you divided by 1,000 earlier). There are approximately 91,674,000 miles between Earth and the sun, which matches (C).

23. B   Difficulty: Easy
Category: Additional Topics in Math / Geometry

Getting to the Answer: Because *LM* = *MN* = *NL*, triangle *LMN* is an equilateral triangle. In an equilateral triangle, each of the three interior angles has a measure of 60 degrees. Thus, *c* = 60. Because *NO* = *OL* = *LN*, triangle *NOL* is also an equilateral triangle, and *b* = 60. Therefore, *b* − *c* = 60 − 60 = 0, which is (B).

24. C   Difficulty: Easy
Category: Additional Topics in Math / Geometry

Getting to the Answer: Don't immediately assume you need to use trig to answer this question (although it is possible). Instead, keep in mind that the SAT is more likely to test your knowledge of right triangles, so start by determining whether triangle *ABC* is a right triangle.

The sum of the angles of every triangle is 180 degrees. Subtract the angle measures given from 180 to find that

angle *B* equals 180 − 51.5 − 38.5 = 90 degrees. This means the triangle is a right triangle. Because *B* is the right angle, side *AC* must be the hypotenuse. Use the Pythagorean theorem to find its length:

$$a^2 + b^2 = c^2$$
$$28^2 + 45^2 = c^2$$
$$784 + 2{,}025 = c^2$$
$$2{,}809 = c^2$$
$$53 = c$$

This makes (C) the correct answer.

25. D   Difficulty: Medium
Category: Additional Topics in Math / Geometry

Getting to the Answer: Two of the angles in the triangle have degree measures 30 and 90, which means the third angle must measure 60 degrees. This means you are dealing with a special right triangle and can use the 30-60-90 shortcut. In a 30-60-90 triangle, the sides are always in the ratio $x : x\sqrt{3} : 2x$ (short leg : long leg : hypotenuse). The only length you know is the long leg—the side represented by the ground and the width of the bottom two steps. The ramp is to be placed 8 feet, or 96 inches, from the bottom step, and the steps themselves account for an additional 20 inches, which means this leg of the triangle is 116 inches long. Use the ratio to determine that you need to divide by $\sqrt{3}$ to find the length of the shorter leg, and then multiply the result by 2 to find the length of the hypotenuse, which represents the ramp.

$$116 \div \sqrt{3} = 66.97$$
$$66.97 \times 2 = 133.95$$

The result is about 134 inches, which matches (D).

26. A   Difficulty: Medium
Category: Additional Topics in Math / Geometry

Getting to the Answer: Start by translating from English into math. Because one leg of the triangle is three times as long as the other, let *x* and 3*x* represent the lengths. Use the Pythagorean theorem to find the hypotenuse.

$$a^2 + b^2 = c^2$$
$$x^2 + (3x)^2 = c^2$$
$$x^2 + 9x^2 = c^2$$
$$10x^2 = c^2$$
$$\sqrt{10x^2} = c$$

Although you can't find a numerical value for c, you do know that the number under the radical must be a multiple of 10, so (A) is correct.

27. D   Difficulty: Medium
Category: Additional Topics in Math / Geometry

Getting to the Answer: Because one angle of the triangle measures 90° and the two legs are congruent (notice the tick marks), this is a 45-45-90 triangle. The side lengths of a 45-45-90 triangle are in the ratio $x:x:x\sqrt{2}$, where x represents the length of a leg and $x\sqrt{2}$ represents the length of the hypotenuse. (Don't forget—the formula page provides this information.) Don't be too hasty in choosing your answer—it's not 7. Set up an equation using the ratio and the length of the side $(7\sqrt{2})$ to find h:

$$h = x\sqrt{2}$$
$$= 7\sqrt{2} \times \sqrt{2}$$
$$= 7\sqrt{4}$$
$$= 7(2)$$
$$= 14$$

The length of the hypotenuse is 14, so (D) is correct.

28. C   Difficulty: Medium
Category: Additional Topics in Math / Geometry

Getting to the Answer: In a triangle, the angle across from the shortest side will have the smallest measure. Use the coordinate grid to figure out which side is the shortest. Point B has the same x-coordinate as C and the same y-coordinate as A, so its coordinates are (3, 3). The length of AB is 5 and the length of BC is 6, so AB is the shortest side. This means the angle opposite it, which is C, has the smallest measure, making (C) correct.

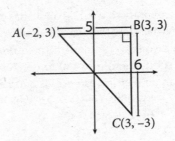

29. C   Difficulty: Medium
Category: Additional Topics in Math / Geometry

Getting to the Answer: Whenever you're given coordinates in a geometry question, start by drawing a quick sketch. You won't have graph paper, so draw carefully and label the coordinates of the points.

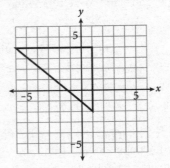

After drawing a sketch, you can see that the triangle is a right triangle. Subtract the coordinates to find the lengths of the legs and use the Pythagorean theorem to find the length of the hypotenuse. To find the length of the horizontal leg, subtract the x-coordinates: $1 - (-6) = 7$. To find the length of the vertical leg, subtract the y-coordinates: $4 - (-2) = 6$. The leg lengths are 6 and 7. Substitute these values into the Pythagorean theorem to find the length of the hypotenuse:

$$a^2 + b^2 = c^2$$
$$6^2 + 7^2 = c^2$$
$$36 + 49 = c^2$$
$$85 = c^2$$
$$\sqrt{85} = \sqrt{c^2}$$
$$\sqrt{85} = c$$

Choice (C) is correct.

30. D   Difficulty: Hard
Category: Additional Topics in Math / Geometry

Getting to the Answer: Start with what you know about the shaded square. Because its area is 12, each side must be $\sqrt{12} = 2\sqrt{3}$. Jot this down because you'll need it later.

Triangle *ABC* is an equilateral triangle, so each of its interior angles measures 60 degrees. This means that the two vertical sides of the square each represent the longer leg of a 30-60-90 triangle (the small white triangles on the sides). This leg has a length of $2\sqrt{3}$, making the short legs 2 each. You now have the length of the base of the large equilateral triangle: $2 + 2\sqrt{3} + 2 = 4 + 2\sqrt{3}$. Therefore, each side of the large equilateral triangle has length $4 + 2\sqrt{3}$. The perimeter is the sum of all three sides, so multiply by 3 to get $12 + 6\sqrt{3}$, making (D) correct.

31. 30   Difficulty: Medium
Category: Additional Topics in Math / Geometry

Getting to the Answer: Write the given lengths of the sides as a ratio (shortest to longest), $1.5 : \dfrac{3\sqrt{3}}{2} : 3$. Try to manipulate this ratio so that it looks like one you're familiar with. Clear the fraction by doubling each part of the ratio to get $3 : 3\sqrt{3} : 6$. Notice that each part of the ratio is divisible by 3, so divide a 3 out. The result is $1 : \sqrt{3} : 2$, which should look very familiar by now. The triangle is a 30-60-90 triangle, which means the measure of the smallest angle is 30 degrees.

32. 28   Difficulty: Medium
Category: Additional Topics in Math / Geometry

Getting to the Answer: Use the Pythagorean theorem to find the length of the diagonal shown in the figure.

$$a^2 + b^2 = c^2$$
$$42^2 + 56^2 = c^2$$
$$1{,}764 + 3{,}136 = c^2$$
$$4{,}900 = c^2$$
$$\sqrt{4{,}900} = \sqrt{c^2}$$
$$70 = c$$

The length of the sidewalk is 70 feet. Now, divide by 5 to get $70 \div 5 = 14$, but be careful—this is not the answer. The college plans to put the lights on *both* sides of the sidewalk, so it actually needs $14 \times 2 = 28$ lights.

33. C   Difficulty: Easy
Category: Additional Topics in Math / Geometry

Getting to the Answer: Corresponding parts of congruent triangles are congruent. The order of the letters in the congruence statements tells you which parts of the triangles are corresponding parts. Because triangle *DOG* is congruent to *CAT* and *CAT* is congruent to *HEN*, then *DOG* must also be congruent to *HEN* by the Transitive Property of Equality. This means the corresponding parts of any of these three triangles are congruent. The corresponding part to $\overline{OG}$ of triangle *CAT* is $\overline{AT}$, and the corresponding part of triangle *HEN* is $\overline{EN}$. Only $\overline{EN}$ is listed as an answer choice, so (C) is correct.

34. A   Difficulty: Easy
Category: Additional Topics in Math / Geometry

Getting to the Answer: The ASA, or Angle Side Angle, theorem states that when two angles and their included side of two triangles are congruent, then the triangles are congruent. Mark the figure so you can see which sides and which angles are congruent to each other.

Your diagram should now look like this:

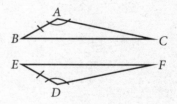

Now, be careful—more than one answer choice might prove that the triangles are congruent, but you are specifically looking for the piece of information that proves congruence using ASA, so you are looking for the *other* angle that makes the side *the included side* given in each triangle, which are angles *B* and *E*. This means (A) is correct.

35. D   Difficulty: Medium

Category: Additional Topics in Math / Geometry

Getting to the Answer: Corresponding sides of similar triangles are proportional. This is the same as saying the larger triangle is a scaled-up version of the smaller triangle. So, you're looking for the same ratio of sides (8:15:17), multiplied by a scale factor. This means (D) is correct because each side length of *COT* has been scaled up by a factor of 3.

36. D   Difficulty: Medium

Category: Additional Topics in Math / Geometry

Getting to the Answer: All four triangles are right triangles, so you can't immediately eliminate any of the choices. Because they are all right triangles, try simplifying the side lengths of the smallest one to look for a Pythagorean triplet. Then see if you can identify scaled-up versions of that one. The second triangle is the smallest with side lengths of 10, 24, and 26. If you divide each of these lengths by 2, you get the common Pythagorean triplet 5, 12, 13. Notice that if you triple these numbers, you get the first triangle; likewise, if you quadruple the numbers, you get the third triangle. The last triangle with side lengths of 24, 32, and 40 is *not* a scaled-up version of a 5, 12, 13 triangle, so it is the one that is not similar. Now, find its area. Remember the area of a triangle is $A = \frac{1}{2}bh$, and in right triangles, the base and height are the leg lengths.

$$A = \frac{1}{2}(24)(32)$$
$$A = \frac{1}{2}(768)$$
$$A = 384$$

This means (D) is correct.

37. D   Difficulty: Medium

Category: Additional Topics in Math / Geometry

Getting to the Answer: Because each cut is made from the center, each side of Slice 1 and Slice 2 is a radius of the circle, and all radii of a circle are congruent. Therefore, both pairs of corresponding sides are congruent. The arc lengths (edges of the crust) are also congruent, which means the central angle that subtends these arcs must be congruent. Now think SAS—the two slices must be congruent, making (D) correct.

38. 75   Difficulty: Easy

Category: Additional Topics in Math / Geometry

Getting to the Answer: Because triangle *TIM* is similar to triangle *JOE*, $m\angle T = m\angle J$, $m\angle I = m\angle O$, and $m\angle M = m\angle E$. This means that if you find the measure of angle *M*, then you'll have your answer. The measure of angle *M* is $180 - 40 - 65 = 75$ degrees, which means the measure of angle *E* is also 75 degrees.

39. 35   Difficulty: Hard

Category: Additional Topics in Math / Geometry

Getting to the Answer: Start by determining whether there is a relationship between triangles *ABC* and *EDC*. The two triangles share a common angle, *C*. It is given that $\overline{DE} \perp \overline{AC}$, so angle *DEC* is a right angle. Because $\overline{DE} \parallel \overline{AB}$, $\overline{BA}$ is also perpendicular to $\overline{AC}$, making angle *BAC* another right angle. Finally, because $\overline{AB}$ and $\overline{DE}$ are parallel lines intersected by a transversal (side *BC*), angles *ABD* and *EDC* are also congruent. This means the two triangles are similar by AAA. Now, start with what you know and find what you can. The length of *AE* is 28, which means the length of *AC* is $28 + 4 = 32$. The length of *EC* is 4, which means that the side lengths of triangle *ABC* are 8 times the side lengths of triangle *EDC*. Now use this to find *DE*: $24 \div 8 = 3$. You might now recognize the Pythagorean triplet 3-4-5, but you could also use the Pythagorean theorem to find that *DC* = 5. Multiply this by 8 to find *BC*: $5 \times 8 = 40$. Be careful—this isn't the answer. The question asks for the length of *BD*, which is $40 - 5 = 35$.

40. D   Difficulty: Easy

Category: Additional Topics in Math / Geometry

Getting to the Answer: Whenever you're given a ratio, you can set up an equation. Sometimes the equation takes the form of a proportion, and sometimes it takes the form of "the sum of the parts equals the whole." In this question, the *whole* is the total number of degrees in a circle, which is 360.

You know the relative size of each of the parts in this question. You don't know the exact size of one part, so call it *x*. Now, set up an equation:

$$4x + 3x + 2x = 360$$
$$9x = 360$$
$$x = 40$$

Beware the trap answer! The question doesn't ask for the value of x but rather for the measure of the smallest angle, which is represented by $2x$. The correct answer is $2(40) = 80$, which is (D).

41. D   Difficulty: Easy
Category: Additional Topics in Math / Geometry

Getting to the Answer: Use the relationship $\dfrac{\text{arc length}}{\text{circumference}} = \dfrac{\text{central angle}}{360°}$ to answer this question. To help you remember this relationship, just think $\dfrac{\text{partial distance}}{\text{whole distance}} = \dfrac{\text{partial angle}}{\text{whole angle}}$.

The unknown in this question is the arc length, so call it l. You need to find the circumference of the circle before you set up the relationship. The question tells you that the radius is 12 inches, so use the formula $C = 2\pi r$ to find that the circumference is $2\pi(12) = 24\pi$. You also know that the central angle has a measure of 135 degrees, so you're ready to set up and solve the relationship:

$$\frac{\text{arc length}}{\text{circumference}} = \frac{\text{central angle}}{360°}$$
$$\frac{l}{24\pi} = \frac{135}{360}$$
$$360l = 3{,}240\pi$$
$$l = \frac{3{,}240}{360}\pi$$
$$l = 9\pi$$

The answer choices are not given in terms of π, so multiply 9 times π to arrive at 28.2743, or about 28 inches, which makes (D) the correct answer.

42. B   Difficulty: Easy
Category: Additional Topics in Math / Geometry

Getting to the Answer: Look carefully at triangle PQR. It is a right triangle that has two congruent legs (because each leg is a radius of the circle), which means it is a 45-45-90 triangle. Recall (or check the formula page at the beginning of the test) that the sides of a 45-45-90 right triangle are always in the ratio $x:x:x\sqrt{2}$. Each leg of the triangle is a radius of the circle, which is given as 4. Side PQ is the hypotenuse of the triangle, so it must have length $4\sqrt{2}$, which is (B).

43. C   Difficulty: Medium
Category: Additional Topics in Math / Geometry

Getting to the Answer: Angle QPC is one angle of a quadrilateral, so you can subtract the measures of the other three angles from 360° to answer the question. However, you're only given one of those angles, so you'll have to use properties of circles to find the other two. Angle PQR is an inscribed angle that intercepts the same arc $\overset{\frown}{(PR)}$ as the 160° central angle, which means the measure of $\angle PQR$ is half that, or 80°. The obtuse angle in the quadrilateral at the center completes a full circle with the 160° central angle, so its measure is $360° - 160° = 200°$. Now you have all the angles you need:

$$m\angle QPR = 360° - (200 + 45 + 80)°$$
$$= 360° - 325°$$
$$= 35°$$

This means (C) is correct.

44. C   Difficulty: Medium
Category: Additional Topics in Math / Geometry

Getting to the Answer: An analog clock has 12 hours marked off, each of which has 5 tick marks representing minutes, for a total of $12 \times 5 = 60$ tick marks. There are 360° in a circle, so the degree measure between each pair of tick marks is $360 \div 60 = 6°$. At 2:15, the hands of the clock are 4 tick marks apart $(15 - 11)$, so the angle between them is $4 \times 6 = 24°$, which is (C).

45. B   Difficulty: Medium
Category: Additional Topics in Math / Geometry

Getting to the Answer: You would not be expected to algebraically solve four systems of equations on Test Day for one question—there simply isn't enough time. This means there must be another way to answer this question. Think graphing!

Take a peek at the answer choices—each one contains a line that is already written in slope-intercept form and a circle that has its center at the origin. Drawing a quick sketch will get you to the answer much quicker than trying to solve the systems algebraically. If the line and the circle don't intersect, then the system has no solution.

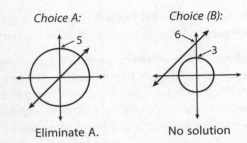

Choice A:
Eliminate A.

Choice (B):
No solution

There is no need to go any further; choice (B) is correct because the graphs do not intersect.

46. D   Difficulty: Hard

Category: Additional Topics in Math / Geometry

Getting to the Answer: To find the equation of a circle, you need the radius and the x- and y-coordinates of the center point. Then, you can use the standard equation: $(x - h)^2 + (y - k)^2 = r^2$, where (h, k) is the center of the circle and r is the length of the radius.

Be careful—choice B is a trap! Sometimes finding the center and the radius from a graph is not as straight forward as you may think. This graph has no number labels on it, so you'll need to use the information given in the question about the smaller circle to determine the value of each grid line:

$$A = \pi r^2$$
$$144\pi = \pi r^2$$
$$144 = r^2$$
$$\pm 12 = r$$

The radius can't be negative, so it must be 12. There are only 3 grid-lines between the center of the smaller circle and its edge, so each grid line must be equal to 4 units. This means the center of the larger circle is $(-8, 0)$ and its radius is $6 \times 4 = 24$. Therefore, the equation must be $(x - (-8))^2 + (y - 0)^2 = 24^2$, or written in simplified form, $(x + 8)^2 + y^2 = 576$, making (D) the correct answer.

47. D   Difficulty: Hard

Category: Additional Topics in Math / Geometry

Getting to the Answer: Don't answer this question too quickly—the shaded portion is *not* the same as the sector because the triangular part at the center is not shaded. However, you'll need to find the area of the sector and then *subtract* the area of the triangle. To find the area

of the sector, you'll need the area of the whole circle: $A = \pi r^2 = \pi(4)^2 = 16\pi$. Now use the formula:

$$\frac{\text{area of sector}}{\text{area of circle}} = \frac{\text{central angle}}{360°}$$
$$\frac{A_{sector}}{16\pi} = \frac{120}{360}$$
$$A_{sector} = \frac{120 \times 16\pi}{360}$$
$$A_{sector} = \frac{16\pi}{3}$$

Time-saving tip: You could actually determine the answer right now—it's (D). The first term in each expression has a π in it, which means it must represent the area of the sector. The second term does not, so it must represent the area of the triangle. Choice (D) is the only one that correctly gives the area of the sector.

In case you really want to know … To find the area of the triangle, notice that triangle *PQR* is formed by two radii and a chord. The height of the triangle represents the shorter leg of each of the smaller triangles inside *PQR*. The small triangles are congruent, and because $\angle PQR$ has a measure of 120°, each of the small triangles is a 30-60-90 triangle. The radius of the circle, which is the hypotenuse of each small triangle, is 4, so the shorter leg (the height) is half that (2), and the longer leg (half the base of *PQR*) is $2\sqrt{3}$, making the base of *PQR* equal to $4\sqrt{3}$. The area of triangle *PQR* is $\frac{1}{2}(4\sqrt{3})(2) = 4\sqrt{3}$.

48. 10   Difficulty: Medium

Category: Additional Topics in Math / Geometry

Getting to the Answer: The key to this question is that the radius of a circle is perpendicular to a tangent line—a line that touches a curve at a point without crossing over—at that point. Once you draw the crucial right angle in, just proceed step-by-step until you have enough information to apply the Pythagorean theorem or (if you've been studying your Kaplan tips) your knowledge of Pythagorean triplets.

$$A = \pi r^2$$
$$36\pi = \pi r^2$$
$$36 = r^2$$
$$6 = r$$

So, $KM = 6$. You also know that $JL = 16$, and the tick marks on the figure indicate congruence, so KL equals half that, or 8.

With $KM = 6$ and $KL = 8$, apply the Pythagorean theorem:

$$c^2 = a^2 + b^2$$
$$c^2 = 36 + 64$$
$$c^2 = 100$$
$$c = 10$$

You may have also noticed that this is a multiple of a 3-4-5 Pythagorean triplet, making it a 6-8-10 triplet, which means 10 is the correct answer.

49. 46   Difficulty: Hard
Category: Additional Topics in Math / Geometry

Getting to the Answer: First, find the center and the radius of the circle: Each grid-line represents one unit on the graph, so the center is (0, 1) and the radius is 7. Substitute these values into the equation for a circle, $(x - h)^2 + (y - k)^2 = r^2$, and then simplify until the equation looks like the one given in the question:

$$(x - 0)^2 + (y - 1)^2 = 7^2$$
$$x^2 + (y - 1)(y - 1) = 49$$
$$x^2 + y^2 - 2y + 1 = 49$$
$$x^2 + y^2 - 2y = 48$$

There is no x term, so $a = 0$. The coefficient of y is -2 and $c = 48$, so $a + b + c = 0 + (-2) + 48 = 46$.

50. B   Difficulty: Easy
Category: Additional Topics in Math / Geometry

Getting to the Answer: This is a straight computation question. The solid is a cone, so check the formula page at the beginning of the test and substitute the values given into the appropriate volume formula, $V = \frac{1}{3}\pi r^2 h$. Be careful—the diagram shows the diameter, but you need to use the radius in the formula, so divide the diameter by 2.

$$V = \frac{1}{3}\pi(7)^2(36)$$
$$V = \pi(49)(12)$$
$$V = 588\pi$$

This makes (B) the correct answer.

51. C   Difficulty: Medium
Category: Additional Topics in Math / Geometry

Getting to the Answer: The volume of a pyramid is given by $V = \frac{1}{3}lwh$. Here, the base is a square, so both the length and the width are equal to 34.5 feet. You're looking for the height of the pyramid, so substitute all the other values into the formula and solve for h:

$$V = \frac{1}{3}lwh$$
$$21,821.25 = \frac{1}{3}(34.5)(34.5)h$$
$$65,463.75 = 1,190.25h$$
$$55 = h$$

Therefore, the height of the pyramid top is 55 feet, which matches (C).

52. B   Difficulty: Medium
Category: Additional Topics in Math / Geometry

Getting to the Answer: In a question like this, you're looking for surface area (not volume) because you would spray the faces of the tent (not the space inside the tent). If you check the formula page, you'll notice that there are no surface area formulas for 3-D shapes. This means you need to decompose the figure into 2-D shapes. Pay careful attention to the dimensions of each shape.

The bottom of the tent is a rectangle: $A = lw = (9)(6) = 54$; the two sides of the tent are also rectangles, but one of the dimensions is different from that of the bottom: $2A = 2(lw) = 2(9)(5) = 90$; the front and back of the tent are triangles:

$$2A_{\text{triangle}} = 2\left(\frac{1}{2}bh\right) = bh = (6)(4) = 24$$

Thus, the total surface area of the tent is $54 + 90 + 24 = 168$ square feet. You're not done: Both the inside and outside of the tent need to be sprayed, so double the surface area to get 336 square feet. And finally, 1 ounce can cover 3 square feet, so divide 336 by 3 to arrive at the final answer, 112 ounces of the waterproofing agent, which is (B).

53. D   **Difficulty:** Easy

Category: Additional Topics in Math / Geometry

Getting to the Answer: To find the volume of a cubical box, you need to know the length of a side. You can find this using the information given about the surface area of the box. The surface area of a cube equals 6 times the area of one face, or $6s^2$, where s is the length of a side. Substitute the given surface area into the formula and solve for s:

$$6s^2 = 1,176$$
$$s^2 = 196$$
$$s = 14$$

Thus, the length of a side of the cube is 14 inches. The volume of a cube is given by $V = lwh$ (or $V = s^3$ because the sides are all equal in length), so the volume of the moving box is 14^3, or 2,744 cubic inches, making (D) correct.

54. A   **Difficulty:** Medium

Category: Additional Topics in Math / Geometry

Getting to the Answer: The cheese block purchases have the same height and width, so the block must be cut according to length. Find the original length of the entire block using the formula for volume of a rectangular solid, $V = lwh$, and then solve for length.

$$V = lwh$$
$$576 = (l)(6)(8)$$
$$12 = l$$

Don't stop here—the question asks for the difference in the two lengths. The customer bought $\frac{1}{8}$ block, which is equal to $(12)\left(\frac{1}{8}\right) = 1.5$ inches. The restaurant bought $\frac{1}{2}$ block, which is equal to $(12)\left(\frac{1}{2}\right) = 6$ inches. The difference in the lengths is $6 - 1.5 = 4.5$ inches, which is (A).

55. C   **Difficulty:** Medium

Category: Additional Topics in Math / Geometry

Getting to the Answer: A wedge shape is an unfamiliar solid, so you shouldn't try to calculate the volume directly. You are told that the solid is half of a cube. Now imagine the other half lying on top of the solid, forming a complete cube.

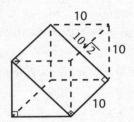

The question tells you that the hypotenuse is $10\sqrt{2}$. Notice that this diagonal with length $10\sqrt{2}$ and two of the cube's edges form an isosceles right triangle, or in other words, a 45-45-90 degree triangle. In a 45-45-90 triangle, the hypotenuse is $\sqrt{2}$ times the length of a leg, so the legs have length 10. Thus, the volume of the whole cube is $10 \times 10 \times 10 = 1,000$, and the volume of the chock is half that, or 500 cubic inches, which is (C).

56. D   **Difficulty:** Medium

Category: Additional Topics in Math / Geometry

Getting to the Answer: There are two ways to approach this question—but only because both shapes (the storage box and the discs) are rectangular prisms and the dimensions match up nicely (two rows of two discs will exactly fill one layer in the box with no extra space left over). One strategy is to find the volume of the storage box and divide by the volume of each disc. Another strategy is to find how many discs Rupert can fit in length, then in width, then in height, and multiply. The second approach must be used when the shapes are different and when the dimensions don't match up just right.

Strategy 1: The volume of a rectangular prism (or a cube) is given by the formula $V = l \times w \times h$, so the volume of the storage box is $10 \times 10 \times 10 = 1,000$ cubic units. The volume of each disc is $5 \times 5 \times \frac{1}{4} = 6.25$. The number of discs that can fit in the box is $1,000 \div 6.25 = 160$ discs, which is (D).

Strategy 2: The box has dimensions of 10 inches by 10 inches by 10 inches. Because each disc is 5 inches in length, he can fit $10 \div 5 = 2$ rows of discs along the length of the box. Each disc is 5 inches in width, so he can fit $10 \div 5 = 2$ rows of discs along the width of the box. Finally, each disc is $\frac{1}{4}$ inch tall, so he can fit $10 \div \frac{1}{4} = 10 \times 4 = 40$ rows of discs along the depth of the box. Multiply to find that Rupert can fit $2 \times 2 \times 40 = 160$ Blu-ray discs in the box.

57. D **Difficulty:** Hard

Category: Additional Topics in Math / Geometry

Getting to the Answer: Try setting this problem up in words first, and then translate from English into Math: The volume of the test tube is equal to the volume of the cylinder plus the volume of the half-sphere. Use the formulas from the formula page to write an equation. Then, solve for the height.

The diameter of the cylinder (and the half-sphere) is 1 inch, so the radius of each is $\frac{1}{2}$ inch .

$$V_{tube} = V_{cylinder} + \frac{1}{2}V_{sphere}$$
$$\frac{19}{12}\pi = \pi r^2 h + \frac{1}{2}\left(\frac{4}{3}\pi r^3\right)$$
$$\frac{19}{12}\pi = \pi\left(\frac{1}{2}\right)^2 h + \frac{2}{3}\pi\left(\frac{1}{2}\right)^3$$
$$\frac{19}{12}\pi = \frac{1}{4}\pi h + \frac{2}{3}\left(\frac{1}{8}\pi\right)$$
$$\frac{19}{12}\pi - \frac{1}{12}\pi = \frac{1}{4}\pi h$$
$$\frac{3}{2}\pi = \frac{1}{4}\pi h$$
$$6 = h$$

Finally, add 6 to the height created by the half sphere (its radius) to get $6 + 0.5 = 6.5$ inches, which matches (D).

58. D **Difficulty:** Hard

Category: Additional Topics in Math / Geometry

Getting to the Answer: Don't let this real-world scenario fool you. You aren't being asked to calculate the surface area or the volume of the pyramid. You only need to calculate the area of the four triangular faces, which is where the shingles will go. Drawing a sketch will help you visualize this and keep the dimensions straight.

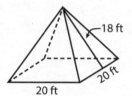

Use the formula for area of a triangle, $A = \frac{1}{2}bh$. The base of each triangular face is 20 feet and the height is

the slant height of the pyramid, 18 feet, so the area of one side of the roof is $\frac{1}{2}(20)(18) = 180$. There are four sides, so the total area to be covered is $4(180) = 720$ square feet. Be careful—this is the area in square *feet* and the shingle size is given in square inches. Convert the square feet to square inches by multiplying 720 by 144 (12 inches × 12 inches). Then, divide the result by 72 to see how many shingles are needed: $720 \times 144 = 103,680 \div 72 = 1,440$. Finally, add 20% to this amount to account for the overlap in the shingles: $1,440 \times 1.2 = 1,728$ shingles, which is (D).

59. 128 **Difficulty:** Medium

Category: Additional Topics in Math / Geometry

Getting to the Answer: The question tells you that the circumference of the opening (which is a circle) is 8π, so substitute this value in the formula for circumference and solve for r.

$$C = 2\pi r$$
$$8\pi = 2\pi r$$
$$4 = r$$

You now have everything you need to find h, which in this case is the length of the tunnel. Use the formula $V = \pi r^2 h$:

$$2,048\pi = \pi(4)^2(h)$$
$$2,048 = 16h$$
$$128 = h$$

The tunnel is 128 feet long.

60. 6 **Difficulty:** Medium

Category: Additional Topics in Math / Geometry

Getting to the Answer: Use the formula for volume of a rectangular solid, $V = lwh$, to write an equation. Because the dimensions are given as the ratio $4:2:1$, let the length, width, and height be represented by $4x$, $2x$, and $1x$. Substitute the expressions into the formula and solve for x.

$$216 = (4x)(2x)(1x)$$
$$216 = 8x^3$$
$$27 = x^3$$
$$3 = x$$

The width was represented by $2x$, so multiply to find that the width is $2(3) = 6$ inches.

CHAPTER 12

PRACTICE

8. B   Difficulty: Hard

Category: Additional Topics in Math / Imaginary Numbers

Getting to the Answer: Substitute $38 + 18j$ for E and $4 + 6j$ for Z. Then rearrange the equation so that I is isolated. Multiply the numerator and denominator by the latter's conjugate and then use FOIL. Combine like terms and reduce fractions as needed. The steps for this sequence are shown below.

$$E = I \times z$$

$$I = \frac{E}{z} = \frac{38 + 18j}{4 + 6j}$$

$$= \frac{38 + 18j}{4 + 6j} \times \frac{4 - 6j}{4 - 6j}$$

$$= \frac{(38 \times 4) + (38 \times -6j) + (18j \times 4) + (18j \times -6j)}{16 - 36j^2}$$

$$= \frac{152 - 228j + 72j - 108j^2}{16 - (-36)}$$

$$= \frac{152 - 156j - (-108)}{52}$$

$$= \frac{260 - 156j}{52}$$

$$= \frac{260}{52} - \frac{156}{52}j$$

$$= 5 - 3j$$

Choice (B) is the correct answer.

9. B   Difficulty: Easy

Category: Additional Topics in Math / Trigonometry

Getting to the Answer: Recall that the sum of the acute angles in a right triangle is $180° - 90° = 90°$. Convert this to radians to find the measure of the missing angle. The sum of the acute angles, in radians, is $90° \times \frac{\pi}{180°} = \frac{90\pi}{180} = \frac{\pi}{2}$. Subtract the known angle to find the other angle: $\frac{\pi}{2} - \frac{\pi}{3} = \frac{3\pi}{6} - \frac{2\pi}{6} = \frac{\pi}{6}$. This matches (B).

PERFORM

10. 2338   Difficulty: Easy

Category: Additional Topics in Math / Imaginary Numbers

Getting to the Answer: Set your TI-83/84 to $a + bi$ mode (or the equivalent if you have a different calculator) and then compute $(11 + 14i)^3$. The result is $-5{,}137 + 2{,}338i$. The question asks for b, the coefficient of the imaginary component, so grid in 2338. Note that you could also expand the expression by writing it as a product and multiplying it all out.

11. C   Difficulty: Medium

Category: Additional Topics in Math / Imaginary Numbers

Getting to the Answer: Factoring the first trinomial yields $(x^2 + 81)(x^2 + 3)$, and factoring the second gives $(x + 9)(x - 4)$. Set each expression equal to 0 and solve for x; you'll find that (C) is the only choice that is not in this list of values, so it is correct.

12. C   Difficulty: Medium

Category: Additional Topics in Math / Trigonometry

Getting to the Answer: Dealing with smaller angles usually makes trig questions easier, so start by reducing the given angle so that it is in the first quadrant. To do this, subtract 2π from $\frac{13\pi}{6}$ to get $\frac{13\pi}{6} - 2\pi = \frac{13\pi}{6} - \frac{12\pi}{6} = \frac{\pi}{6}$. The equation in the question stem becomes $\sin x = \cos \frac{\pi}{6}$. Next, think about complementary angles—they have a special relationship relative to trig values—the cosine of an acute angle is equal to the sine of the angle's complement and vice versa. The angle measures are given in radians, so you're looking for an angle that, when added to $\frac{\pi}{6}$, gives $\frac{\pi}{2}$ (because $\frac{\pi}{2} = 90°$). Because $\frac{\pi}{6} + \frac{2\pi}{6} = \frac{3\pi}{6} = \frac{\pi}{2}$, the two angles, $\frac{\pi}{6}$ and $\frac{\pi}{3}$, are complementary angles, which means (C) is correct.

EXTRA PRACTICE

1. D   Difficulty: Easy

Category: Additional Topics in Math / Imaginary Numbers

Getting to the Answer: The definition of i is given as $i = \sqrt{-1}$. If you square both sides of this definition, you arrive at a more useful form: $i^2 = (\sqrt{-1})^2 = -1$. Distribute the $4i$ and then substitute -1 for i^2:

$$4i(5 - 7i) = 4i(5) - 4i(7i)$$
$$= 20i - 28i^2$$
$$= 20i - 28(-1)$$
$$= 20i + 28$$

Switch the terms so that the real part is first $(28 + 20i)$ to find that (D) is correct.

2. A   Difficulty: Medium

Category: Additional Topics in Math / Imaginary Numbers

Getting to the Answer: Because $i = \sqrt{-1}$, it isn't considered "proper" to leave i in the denominator of a fraction (just as you shouldn't leave a radical in the denominator). Use the same strategy you learned for rationalizing the denominator of a radical expression to rationalize a complex number (by multiplying by the conjugate). The conjugate of $3 - i$ is $3 + i$, so multiply the expression by $\dfrac{3 + i}{3 + i}$:

$$\frac{1}{3 - i} \times \frac{3 + i}{3 + i} = \frac{3 + i}{(3 - i)(3 + i)}$$
$$= \frac{3 + i}{9 + 3i - 3i - i^2}$$
$$= \frac{3 + i}{9 - (-1)}$$
$$= \frac{3 + i}{10}$$

This isn't one of the answer choices, so split the number into its real part and its imaginary part by writing each of the terms in the numerator over 10. The result is $\dfrac{3}{10} + \dfrac{1}{10}i$, which matches (A).

3. B   Difficulty: Medium

Category: Additional Topics in Math / Imaginary Numbers

Getting to the Answer: You will not be expected to raise a complex number like the one in this question to the fourth power by hand. That's a clue that you should be able to use your calculator. The definition of i has been programmed into all graphing calculators, so you can perform basic operations on complex numbers using the calculator (in the calculator section of the test). Enter the expression as follows: $(3 + 2i)^4$. On the TI83/84 calculators, you can find i on the button with the decimal point. After you enter the expression, the calculator should return $-119 + 120i$, which is (B).

4. B   Difficulty: Medium

Category: Additional Topics in Math / Imaginary Numbers

Getting to the Answer: A question like this requires an understanding of how the powers of i cycle. Whenever you're evaluating a high power of i, divide the power by 4 and let the remainder point you to the correct answer. Recall the power pattern for i: i, -1, $-i$, 1, and repeat. Divide 14 by 4, which yields 3 with a remainder of 2. This means $i^{14} = (i^4)^3 \times i^2 = 1 \times -1 = -1$. Repeat this process for i^{122} to get $i^{122} = (i^4)^{30} \times i^2 = 1 \times -1 = -1$. The sum is therefore $-1 + -1 = -2$, which means you're looking for an expression that has the same value. Choices B and C should look tempting (because of the 2), so start with them. In (B), you know $i^2 = -1$ and $2(-1) = -2$, so this is the correct answer.

5. B   Difficulty: Hard

Category: Additional Topics in Math / Imaginary Numbers

Getting to the Answer: Take a peek at the answer choices—they're all complex numbers. This means factoring is out of the question, so think quadratic formula. Before you can use the quadratic formula, the equation must equal 0, so move all the terms to the left side of the equal sign; the quadratic (written in standard form) becomes $x^2 - 4x + 13 = 0$. Now, jot down the values you'll need: $a = 1$, $b = -4$, and $c = 13$.

$$x = \frac{-b \pm \sqrt{b^2 - 4ac}}{2a}$$

$$= \frac{-(-4) \pm \sqrt{(-4)^2 - 4(1)(13)}}{2(1)}$$

$$= \frac{4 \pm \sqrt{16 - 52}}{2}$$

$$= \frac{4 \pm \sqrt{-36}}{2}$$

$$= \frac{4 \pm \sqrt{-1 \times 36}}{2}$$

$$= \frac{4 \pm 6i}{2}$$

$$= \frac{\cancel{2}(2 \pm 3i)}{\cancel{2}}$$

The final answer is $2 \pm 3i$, which matches (B).

6. A   Difficulty: Hard
Category: Additional Topics in Math / Imaginary Numbers

Getting to the Answer: Each of the factors in this product has two terms, so they behave like binomials. This means you can use FOIL to find the product. To avoid messy numbers, simplify the two radicals first using the definition of i. Write each of the numbers under the radicals as a product of -1 and the number, take the square roots, and then FOIL the resulting expressions.

$$\left(2 + \sqrt{-9}\right)\left(-1 + \sqrt{-4}\right)$$

$$= \left(2 + \sqrt{-1 \times 9}\right)\left(-1 + \sqrt{-1 \times 4}\right)$$

$$= (2 + 3i)(-1 + 2i)$$

$$= -2 + 4i - 3i + 6i^2$$

$$= -2 + i + 6(-1)$$

$$= -8 + i$$

Choice (A) is correct.

7. C   Difficulty: Hard
Category: Additional Topics in Math / Imaginary Numbers

Getting to the Answer: Find a common denominator by multiplying the second term by $4 - 2i$. As always, you're given that $\sqrt{-1} = i$, but a more useful fact is that $i^2 = -1$, so be sure to make this substitution as you work. Once you've found the common denominator, you can simply add like terms.

$$\frac{1}{4 - 2i} + (3 + i) = \frac{1}{4 - 2i} + \frac{3 + i}{1}$$

$$= \frac{1}{4 - 2i} + \frac{3 + i}{1}\left(\frac{4 - 2i}{4 - 2i}\right)$$

$$= \frac{1}{4 - 2i} + \frac{12 - 6i + 4i - 2i^2}{4 - 2i}$$

$$= \frac{1}{4 - 2i} + \frac{12 - 2i - 2(-1)}{4 - 2i}$$

$$= \frac{1 + 12 - 2i + 2}{4 - 2i}$$

$$= \frac{15 - 2i}{4 - 2i}$$

This matches (C).

8. 17   Difficulty: Medium
Category: Additional Topics in Math / Imaginary Numbers

Getting to the Answer: Don't let this "new" definition intimidate you. All you're asked to do is to find the square root of the sum of a^2 and b^2. You don't even have to involve the i at all.

$$|15 + 8i| = \sqrt{15^2 + 8^2}$$

$$= \sqrt{225 + 64}$$

$$= \sqrt{289}$$

$$= 17$$

There is nothing else to do—the answer is 17.

9. D   Difficulty: Easy
Category: Additional Topics in Math / Trigonometry

Getting to the Answer: The answers are given in degrees, and it's easier to add degrees than radians, so convert each angle measure to degrees and then find the sum. Use the conversion $180° = \pi$, with π written in the denominator so that it will cancel.

$$\frac{\cancel{\pi}}{4} \times \frac{180°}{\cancel{\pi}} = 45°$$

$$\frac{7\cancel{\pi}}{\cancel{12}^2} \times \frac{\overset{30}{\cancel{180}}°}{\cancel{\pi}} = \frac{210°}{2} = 105°$$

The measure of $\angle PQR$ is $45° + 105° = 150°$, which matches (D).

10. D **Difficulty:** Easy

Category: Additional Topics in Math / Trigonometry

Getting to the Answer: Angles that are coterminal (land in the same place when rotated full circle) have the same trigonometric values. To find coterminal angles, subtract 360° (one full circle) from the given angle: 450° − 360° = 90°. The figure below provides a visual representation of this relationship:

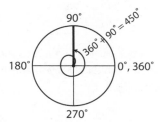

A 90° angle has the same trigonometric values as a 450° angle, making (D) correct.

11. B **Difficulty:** Medium

Category: Additional Topics in Math / Trigonometry

Getting to the Answer: When you're not asked to find a specific value, drawing a quick sketch to determine which quadrant each angle lies in may provide enough information to answer the question. Sketch each angle on a unit circle. It doesn't have to be perfect—you just need to know which quadrant the angle falls in.

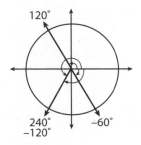

Three of the angles (120°, 240°, and −120°) fall to the left of the *y*-axis (in Quadrants II and III) and therefore have a cosine value that is negative. The angle in (B) falls to the right of the vertical axis (in Quadrant IV) and therefore has a cosine value that is positive. This means (B) is correct because cos(−60°) cannot have the same value as the other three angles.

12. D **Difficulty:** Medium

Category: Additional Topics in Math / Trigonometry

Getting to the Answer: Fill in the missing parts of the triangle. Use the Pythagorean theorem to find the missing leg length and use properties of triangles to find the missing angle.

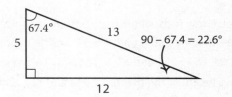

Sine and cosine both involve the hypotenuse (13), so you can eliminate A right away because it doesn't have a 13 in it. Next, quickly compare each answer choice to the trig ratios given by SOH CAH TOA. Sine is opposite over hypotenuse; in B, the side opposite the 67.4° angle has length 5 (not 12), so eliminate B. Cosine is adjacent over hypotenuse; in C, the side adjacent to the 22.6° angle has length 12 (not 5), so eliminate C. This means (D) must be correct. The side adjacent to the 67.4° angle has length 5 and the hypotenuse has length 13, so $\cos 67.4° = \frac{5}{13}$.

13. C **Difficulty:** Medium

Category: Additional Topics in Math / Trigonometry

Getting to the Answer: The angle given $\left(\frac{\pi}{6}\right)$ is in the first quadrant, so its cosine is positive. The question states that sin *x* is equal to the cosine of $\frac{\pi}{6}$, so *x* be must an angle for which the sine is positive, which means it must lie in the first or second quadrant (above the *x*-axis). This means you're looking for the angle that is *not* in one of those quadrants, which is (C): $\frac{5\pi}{3}$ is in the fourth quadrant and therefore has a negative sine value. (The angles in A and B meet this criterion because each one is less than π. The angle in D also meets the criterion because $\frac{7\pi}{3} - 2\pi = \frac{7\pi}{3} - \frac{6\pi}{3} = \frac{\pi}{3}$, which is in the first quadrant.)

14. A   Difficulty: Medium

Category: Additional Topics in Math / Trigonometry

Getting to the Answer: When the measure of an angle in a triangle is given in radians, convert it to degrees so you'll have a better idea of what you're looking at. Use the relationship $180° = \pi$ to convert the angle: $\dfrac{\cancel{\pi}}{3} \times \dfrac{180°}{\cancel{\pi}} = 60°$.

Now you know the triangle is a 30-60-90 triangle, which has sides that are in the ratio $x:x\sqrt{3}:2x$. The hypotenuse is $2x = 24$, so $x = 12$ and $x\sqrt{3} = 12\sqrt{3}$. This means the base and height of the triangle are 12 and $12\sqrt{3}$, and the area of the triangle is $\dfrac{1}{2}(12\sqrt{3})(12) = 72\sqrt{3}$, which is (A).

15. 3/5 or **.6   Difficulty:** Hard

Category: Additional Topics in Math / Trigonometry

Getting to the Answer: Because trig functions typically apply to right triangles, draw in an altitude and label what you know. You know the trough is 24 inches deep and 36 inches across the top. Because the given angles have equal measures ($x°$), the triangle is isosceles and the altitude bisects the top. Your figure should look like this:

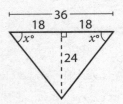

You're given that $B = \cos x$, and the cosine of an angle involves the hypotenuse, so you need to find the length of the hypotenuse using the Pythagorean theorem:

$$18^2 + 24^2 = c^2$$
$$324 + 576 = c^2$$
$$900 = c^2$$
$$30 = c$$

Finally, $\cos x = \dfrac{adj}{hyp} = \dfrac{18}{30} = \dfrac{3}{5}$. Grid in 3/5 or .6.

16. 12/5 or **2.4   Difficulty:** Hard

Category: Additional Topics in Math / Trigonometry

Getting to the Answer: Find the height of the triangle using the information given about the area and add it to the figure.

$$A = \frac{1}{2}bh$$
$$240 = \frac{1}{2}(40)h$$
$$240 = 20h$$
$$12 = h$$

After you find the height, you might recognize the 5-12-13 Pythagorean triplet, which gives you another side of the triangle that contains β.

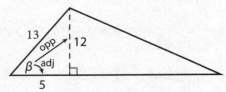

Note: Figure not drawn to scale.

Now use SOH CAH TOA: $\tan\beta = \dfrac{opp}{adj} = \dfrac{12}{5}$. Grid in 12/5 or 2.4.

CHAPTER 13

PRACTICE

Suggested Passage Map notes:

¶1: 4 forces of flight (central idea)

¶2: #1 - thrust

¶2, cont.: #2 - drag, impact on aircraft design

¶3: #3 - gravity

¶3, cont.: #4 - lift

¶3, cont.: Bern. principle = lift

7. B   Difficulty: Medium

Category: Vocab-in-Context

Getting to the Answer: When you see the phrase "most nearly means" and a cited word or phrase, pretend that word or phrase is blank and predict a synonym for it. Read the sentence without "acts" (line 29) and ask what "lift force" (line 28) does. Predict that it "functions" or "works." Choice (B) is correct.

8. B   Difficulty: Medium

Category: Inference

Getting to the Answer: Review your Passage Map notes regarding drag. Remember to be wary of answer choices that are outside the scope of the passage. Paragraph 2 provides details about drag, specifically that it is "the air resistance that the plane encounters in flight" (lines 16-17). At the end of the paragraph, the author writes that drag decreases when "there is little friction at the airplane's surface" (lines 23-24). Choice (B) reflects the relationship between drag and friction and is therefore correct. Choice C may be tempting, but it is incorrect because drag doesn't decrease as thrust increases; instead, thrust must be enough to overcome drag force (line 15).

PERFORM

Suggested Passage Map notes:

¶1: AL humble family background (purpose)

¶2: childhood – "wild" region, little ed

¶3: early jobs

¶4: captain in war, politician, lawyer

¶5: personal description

9. D   Difficulty: Medium

Category: Rhetoric

Getting to the Answer: When a question asks you to identify the author's stance, think about the author's point of view and purpose. The author begins by referring to his parents' families as "undistinguished" (line 3) and keeps the focus of the passage on the simplicity of his life and circumstances. Predict that the author sees himself as an ordinary person who grew up without many advantages. Choice (D) is correct.

10. C   Difficulty: Medium

Category: Global

Getting to the Answer: To summarize the central purpose of the passage, review the key ideas you noted in your Passage Map. Always identify the author's purpose when mapping History/Social Studies passages. While the author does spend a good deal of the passage discussing education, this is not his reason for writing. The overall purpose of the passage is to provide his own history, which shifts from his modest childhood to his national importance. This is underscored by the phrase "What I have done since then is pretty well known" (lines 61-62). Choice (C) is correct.

11. B   Difficulty: Medium

Category: Vocab-in-Context

Getting to the Answer: When you see the phrase "most nearly means" and a cited line, pretend the word or phrase is a blank and predict the meaning of the word or phrase in context. Read the lines surrounding the cited phrase. The author states that he has not been to school since his childhood but "picked up" (line 37) the "little advance . . . upon this store of education . . . under the pressure of necessity" (lines 36-38). Predict that the phrase means that he learned when he had to, or when it was necessary. Choice (B) is correct.

12. C   Difficulty: Hard

Category: Inference

Getting to the Answer: If you are not provided with a line reference, use your Passage Map to locate the part of the passage to which the question stem refers. The question asks about the effect of the Black Hawk War, which is first mentioned in the beginning of paragraph 4. The overall topic of paragraph 4 is the author's campaigns and subsequent elections, suggesting a connection between the war and the author's political career. Choice (C) is correct. The other answer choices may be tempting, but they are all are assumptions that the text itself does not support.

EXTRA PRACTICE

Suggested Passage Map notes:

¶1-2: ML loves girl w/ simple beauty

¶3: ML & girl marry, happy, girl good w/ $

¶4: only 2 faults

¶5: #1 - ML didn't want to go to theater

¶6: #2 - wife wears fake jewelry

¶7-10: ML and wife disagree about jewelry

¶11: wife dies

¶12-14: ML mourns wife

¶15-19: ML is poor, has to sell wife's jewelry

¶20-22: ML is shocked to learn jewelry is real (theme)

1. D   Difficulty: Medium
Category: Vocab-in-Context

Getting to the Answer: Use context clues and tone to help determine the meaning of the word. Create a mental picture of what is being described by using the surrounding text. Finally, make sure the answer choice does not alter the meaning of the sentence when inserted. The paragraph in which the word appears describes the girl as "simple" (line 5) and "pure" (line 8), and as having a "lovely soul" (line 8). Therefore, choice (D) is correct. "Angelic" means "innocent" in this context.

2. C   Difficulty: Medium
Category: Detail

Getting to the Answer: Skim the passage to locate descriptions of Lantin's wife at the beginning of their marriage. Paragraph 3 describes the Lantins' "snug" (line 10) income and attribute their luxurious lifestyle to Lantin's wife's "clever economy" (line 14). Choice (C) is correct. "Frugal" describes someone who is thrifty and economical.

3. A   Difficulty: Medium
Category: Inference

Getting to the Answer: Look for Lantin's thoughts and statements about the jewels. Use this as evidence of his attitude. The Lantins are described as making a "snug" (line 10) salary, and Madame Lantin has to be very economical. Later

in the passage, Lantin mentions that they "cannot afford" (line 35) to buy real jewelry. Choice (A) is correct because Lantin clearly believes they cannot afford real gems.

4. D   Difficulty: Easy
Category: Command of Evidence

Getting to the Answer: Review your answer to the previous question. Decide which lines of text provide evidence that the Lantins did not have enough money to buy large jewels. Choice (D) offers the best support. In these lines, Lantin explicitly states they cannot afford real jewelry.

5. B   Difficulty: Medium
Category: Inference

Getting to the Answer: Reread the text to make a prediction. This section of the passage describes Lantin's intense mourning for his wife, which suggests a deep unhappiness. Choice (B) is correct.

6. B   Difficulty: Medium
Category: Command of Evidence

Getting to the Answer: Review your answer to the previous question. Read each choice and figure out which one provides specific support for that answer. Choice (B) provides the best support. These lines show that Lantin is overcome with grief, as he "wept unceasingly; his heart was broken" (line 47).

7. D   Difficulty: Easy
Category: Vocab-in-Context

Getting to the Answer: Use context clues from the target sentence and surrounding sentences. Predict the meaning of the word and look for a match in the answer choices. Lantin views the jewels as "deceptions" (line 61) and speaks of the irritation her jewels caused him. Looking at the jewels also "spoiled, somewhat" (line 63) the memory of his wife. Choice (D) provides a suitably negative word and makes sense in the context of the rest of the paragraph.

8. C   Difficulty: Medium
Category: Rhetoric

Getting to the Answer: Contrast this sentence with what has already occurred in the passage. Analyze the new information it provides and the response it provokes when you read it. The sentence calls into question the reliability of everything we have learned about Madame

Lantin. Although she and her husband were not wealthy, Madame Lantin has somehow acquired at least one very expensive piece of jewelry. Choice (C) is correct. The author uses this sentence to create an unresolved conflict. Lantin does not know how his wife obtained the jewels, and the sentence suggests the answer might call his wife's virtue into question.

9. D **Difficulty:** Hard
Category: Inference

Getting to the Answer: Review the end of the excerpt. Think about what this text might suggest broadly. Don't speculate by choosing an overly specific answer. The correct answer will provide a logical conclusion about Madame Lantin based on what you have learned about her throughout the passage. Her husband idealized her but has discovered that she has been dishonest and hidden things from him. Choice (D) provides a reasonable conclusion that a reader can make about Madame Lantin. Choices A, B, and C are possible reasons that Madame Lantin had the expensive necklace, but they are not directly supported by the passage.

10. A **Difficulty:** Hard
Category: Global

Getting to the Answer: Ask yourself what the author's theme is in this passage. The events in the passage show that Lantin judges his wife for her love of costume jewelry. After her death, he finds that her jewels are real. Both the "paste" jewels that turn out to be real and Lantin's realization about his wife's jewel collection after her death support the idea that appearances can be deceiving. Choice (A) best describes the central theme the author develops throughout the excerpt.

Suggested Passage Map notes:

¶1: scientists working on peanut that won't cause allergic reaction (central idea)
¶2: why allergic response = immune system; regular v. allergic responses
¶3: peanut allergy antibody IgE
¶4: difficult to avoid peanuts
¶5: change peanut allergen?; experiments
¶6: light tests showed promise
¶7: details of light experiment
¶8: promising results; test people next

11. B **Difficulty: Easy**
Category: Vocab-in-Context

Getting to the Answer: Read the sentence again and predict another word that could substitute for "expel" in context. Predict that "expel" in this context means to get rid of. Choice (B) is correct because in this context, "eject" means almost the same thing as "expel."

12. D **Difficulty:** Medium
Category: Inference

Getting to the Answer: It will be difficult to make predictions for a few questions. In that case, review each answer choice systematically to determine which one is correct. Avoid answers that go too far or are not supported by direct evidence in the passage. In paragraph 2, the author describes how a typical immune system response looks when the body recognizes a dangerous material. The author goes on to explain in paragraph 3 that a particular protein found in peanuts is responsible for triggering the immune system response in people allergic to peanuts. Choice (D) is correct.

13. A **Difficulty:** Hard
Category: Command of Evidence

Getting to the Answer: Find each of the answer choices in the passage. The correct answer should provide direct support for the answer to the previous question. In paragraph 2, the author describes what causes a reaction in the immune system. Choice (A) is correct because this sentence describes what causes the immune system to react—a material it considers dangerous.

14. D **Difficulty:** Medium
Category: Inference

Getting to the Answer: Use your Passage Map to find the paragraph that describes the normal immune system response and an allergic reaction. Summarize each in your head and use those summaries to make a prediction. Paragraph 2 includes information about what a normal immune system response looks like, as well as details about allergic reactions and what makes them dangerous. Choice (D) is correct because it accurately summarizes the differences between a normal immune system response and an allergic reaction. Choices A, B, and C may be tempting, but there are specific reasons why each is incorrect. Choice A is incorrect because an allergic reaction is stronger than a normal reaction. Choice B is incorrect because both a normal immune response and an allergic response could produce mucus and coughing. Choice C is incorrect because the allergic response is triggered by a material that the body incorrectly considers dangerous.

15. D   Difficulty: Medium
Category: Detail

Getting to the Answer: Review your notes for paragraph 4 to predict an answer to the question. In paragraph 4, the author explains that people who have peanut allergies must simply avoid allergens. The author also describes how difficult it is to avoid peanut allergens. Choice (D) is correct. Choice A may be tempting, but while avoidance is difficult, the examples given do not justify A's statement that the allergens will be encountered "daily."

16. B   Difficulty: Medium
Category: Command of Evidence

Getting to the Answer: Locate each quote to determine which provides the best support for the previous answer: people with peanut allergies have a difficult time avoiding the allergens. Choice (B) is correct. This text tells you that allergens are so common that children cannot avoid them, even at school.

17. C   Difficulty: Medium
Category: Vocab-in-Context

Getting to the Answer: Read the sentence again and replace "deactivating" with a prediction based on the sentence's context. Predict that scientists want to stop the allergens. Therefore, choice (C) is correct. In this context, "disabling" means almost the same thing as "deactivating."

18. B   Difficulty: Medium
Category: Synthesis

Getting to the Answer: Carefully evaluate the data in the graph. Use your Passage Map to find where the author discusses the information presented in the graph. In paragraph 7, the author describes the experiment that produced the data presented in the graph. According to lines 70-71, "the darker the blue, the more IgE antibodies remained." Use this information to interpret the graph. The lower the percentage of "Blue Color Amount," the longer the peanuts were

"Exposed to Pulse Light." Choice (B) correctly expresses this relationship.

19. C   Difficulty: Easy
Category: Detail

Getting to the Answer: Use your Passage Map to find the paragraph that describes the lab tests. Eliminate answer choices that are not explicitly stated in the text. In lines 40-41, the author states that it would "not be safe" to measure allergic reactions caused in people. Choice (C) is correct.

20. C   Difficulty: Medium
Category: Rhetoric

Getting to the Answer: Refer to your Passage Map to identify the purposes of paragraphs 6 and 7. Paragraph 6 introduces the method used by scientists to conduct the experiment described in paragraph 7. Paragraphs 6 and 7 are a summary of this method, and therefore choice (C) is correct.

21. A   Difficulty: Medium
Category: Rhetoric

Getting to the Answer: Refer to your Passage Map. Think about the central idea of the paragraph and how it relates to the central idea of the entire passage. In the preceding paragraphs, the author describes experiments that have already taken place. In the final paragraph, the author describes what scientists might do next. Choice (A) is correct.

CHAPTER 14

PRACTICE

Suggested Passage Map notes:

Passage 1

¶1: author: SC = "miracle cure;" how SC work

¶2: embryonic → adult SCs; help diseases; help research

¶3: author: SC research must go on

Passage 2

¶1: ?s of ethics

¶2: SCs useful, but embryo use moral?

¶3: author: use adult SCs

4. C   Difficulty: Medium

Category: Synthesis

Getting to the Answer: Synthesis questions ask you to find similarities and differences between paired passages. Use your Passage Map to compare the different points of view, focusing on how the authors agree and disagree. The author of Passage 1 maintains that stem cell research can provide benefits and recommends using stem cells regardless of the source. The author of Passage 2 agrees that stem cell research can provide benefits but argues that using adult stem cells is the course to follow. Both authors agree that stem cell research has benefits. Choice (C) is correct.

5. D   Difficulty: Hard

Category: Synthesis

Getting to the Answer: To make a strong prediction when faced with a general question, focus on the central idea, topic, and scope of each passage. Harder Synthesis questions will require you to identify not only how the authors agree or disagree but also why they agree or disagree. What these authors disagree on is easy to identify: which type of stem cells should be used in the research. Now, ask why they disagree. The author of Passage 1 thinks that the benefits are defined solely by the physical improvements possible, and the author of Passage 2 thinks that the benefits of stem cell research must be considered in terms of the moral as well as the physical results. Choice (D) is correct.

6. C   Difficulty: Medium

Category: Synthesis

Getting to the Answer: Look for trends in the data. Evaluate the categories and time frames mentioned in the answer choices. Compare the changes on the graph to the changes described in each answer choice and eliminate answer choices that don't match. When you check the time frame of 2005 to 2007, note that opposition to stem cell research increased one full square, and support for stem cell research decreased about one half of a square. This matches the changes in the data described in choice (C).

PERFORM

Suggested Passage Map notes:

Passage 1

¶1: U could not avoid politics; bond among groups

¶2: causes of unrest

¶3: U peasants joined M; M necessary, reasons

Passage 2

¶1: Bol. vs M; soldier quote = difference in theory (accepted vs debated)

¶2: Bol. controlling; if differ = enemy

¶3: ex: T writings view M as good or bad

¶4: T quote: must be loyal to Red Army

¶5: T/Bol. negatively portrays U/M

7. C   Difficulty: Medium

Category: Synthesis

Getting to the Answer: To answer Synthesis questions, focus on the similarities and differences between the passages. This question stem asks what the author of Passage 2 thinks about a promise made by the Bolsheviks. Review your Passage Map of Passage 1 to identify the Bolsheviks' promise: "equality and the rule of the proletariat" (lines 16-17). Now use your Passage Map of Passage 2 to locate what author 2 thinks of the Bolsheviks. Paragraph 2 discusses the extreme control the Bolsheviks held in Russia. Predict that the author of Passage 2 would view the Bolsheviks' promise in a negative light. Choice (C) is correct.

Choices A, B, and D may be tempting, but they do not match your prediction. Choice A is incorrect because lines 56–58 explain that the Makhnovists made decisions based on "the needs of the community for food, freedom, and self-defense," not the Bolsheviks' ideological promises. Choice B is incorrect because in lines 50-52 author 2 claims the theories of the Bolsheviks were "never doubted or questioned." Choice D is incorrect because passage 2 uses the Tolstoy quotes to describe his portrayal of the Makhnovists, not to suggest the writings influenced Bolshevik promises.

8. D   **Difficulty:** Medium
Category: Synthesis

Getting to the Answer: Synthesis questions that ask what the authors agree on require you to identify the similarities in each author's purpose for writing the passage. Since each passage focuses on a different aspect of the Makhnovischina, the correct answer will probably be a general statement about the group. Both describe the Makhnovischina as a group formed to provide mutual aid, intellectual freedom, and military defense (see lines 31-35 in Passage 1 and lines 54-57 in Passage 2). Choice (D) is correct.

Choices A, B, and C may be tempting, but they do not match your prediction. Choice A is incorrect because paragraph 1 of Passage 2 explains the ideological differences between the Bolsheviks and Makhnovischinas. Choice B is incorrect because only Passage 1 even mentions the Austro-Hungarian army, and never claims it was the greatest threat. Choice C is incorrect because it only represents Trotsky's view in Passage 2.

9. A   **Difficulty:** Hard
Category: Synthesis

Getting to the Answer: Read the question stem closely to identify what it asks you to look for. Because the question stem asks what can be inferred by looking at Passage 2 and the data in the pie chart in tandem, base your interpretation of that data on the negative viewpoint that the author of Passage 2 expresses regarding the Bolsheviks. Your Passage Map shows that paragraph 2 discusses the extent of the Bolsheviks' control in Russia, so you can assume they must have been a powerful group. Analyze the chart to see that the Bolsheviks only composed about a quarter of the government. Predict

that the Bolsheviks were stronger than their proportion of seats on the assembly would suggest. Choice (A) is correct.

EXTRA PRACTICE

Suggested Passage Map notes:
Passage 1

¶1: (purpose): describe SSB origin; War of 1812 = high stakes
¶2: Br. involvement low to high; Br. victories; bomb Ft. McH
¶3: Key on Br. ship
¶4: saw flag; inspired to write
¶5: war turning point; song symbol of patriotism

Passage 2

¶1: poem early popularity
¶2: history of use: military, baseball
¶3: law = official anthem; current uses; words = reminder; (purpose): explain history of poem/anthem

1. C   **Difficulty:** Medium
Category: Rhetoric

Getting to the Answer: Review your Passage Map for Passage 1. Paraphrase the purpose before reading the answer choices. The author begins by referencing "the story behind 'The Star-Spangled Banner,' America's national anthem" (lines 1–2). Predict that Passage 1's purpose is to describe the origin of the national anthem. The introduction to the passages also could have provided your prediction for the passage's purpose. Never skip these introductions! Choice (C) is correct.

Remember to answer the questions about Passage 1 immediately after reading it. Choice D reflects the purpose of Passage 2, which could be a tempting answer choice if both passages were read together.

2. D   **Difficulty:** Medium
Category: Rhetoric

Getting to the Answer: Reread around the cited lines and consider their role in the complete paragraph. The reason for including the lines will reflect their role and purpose in relation to the other information. The paragraph introduces the scope of the passage, which is the story behind the national anthem. It then relates the origin of that story in the War of 1812 and provides context for the war. These lines show the significance of the war for the American people and the importance of its outcome, which gives added meaning to the poem that would become the national anthem; however, the lines don't actually "explain" the symbolism as in C. Choice (D) is correct.

3.   D   Difficulty: Easy
Category: Vocab-in-Context

Getting to the Answer: Read the complete sentence in which the cited word appears. Predict a definition before reviewing the answer choices. Compare your prediction with the answer choices and select the one that most nearly reflects the meaning you identified. The line states that "America's defenses prevailed" against an attack by the British. In this context, predict the term most nearly means that America's defenses *hung on*, making choice (D) correct.

4.   B   Difficulty: Medium
Category: Inference

Getting to the Answer: Review your notes and the cited lines. Then, paraphrase their meaning and significance. Select the answer choice that best reflects why and how Key came to write the national anthem. Paragraph 4 demonstrates that Key expected Fort McHenry to fall to British forces. He was surprised by American perseverance and, as a result, was inspired to write the national anthem in response to the Americans' survival during the nightlong British bombardment. Choice (B) is correct.

5.   D   Difficulty: Medium
Category: Command of Evidence

Getting to the Answer: Review your answer to the previous question and your notes on the referenced paragraph. Identify the phrase that most clearly supports the conclusion identified in the previous question: Key wrote to honor the American resistance. Lines 45-46 ("Moved by . . . to write") clearly explain why Key wrote the words that would become the national anthem. In these lines, the author states Key was moved by the "sight." Confirm from the previous sentences that this "sight" is indeed

the American victory he witnessed: "by dawn's light he saw the American flag" (lines 43-44). Choice (D) is correct.

6.   B   Difficulty: Hard
Category: Rhetoric

Getting to the Answer: Using your Passage Map, think about the author's overall tone and purpose to predict what point of view he or she might hold about the national anthem and its origins. Compare your conclusion with the answer choices. The passage begins by explaining the national anthem originated during the War of 1812. The first paragraph goes on to state America was defending its "status as a sovereign nation" (line 8). The last lines of the passage (53–55) describe Key's words as a symbol of America's victory. Taken all together, the passage's purpose is to describe the patriotic origins of "The Star-Spangled Banner." This is best reflected in choice (B) as an accurate description of the entire passage.

7.   A   Difficulty: Easy
Category: Rhetoric

Getting to the Answer: Reread the cited lines and review your notes for Passage 2. Consider the placement of the lines in relation to the rest of the passage and how the lines prepare you to interpret subsequent content. The cited lines lay the foundation for the rest of the passage, which describes how Francis Scott Key's poem came to be the official national anthem known as "The Star-Spangled Banner." Choice (A) is correct because the cited lines state clearly that Key first wrote his words as a poem, not as a song or an anthem.

8.   A   Difficulty: Easy
Category: Vocab-in-Context

Getting to the Answer: Predict a word or phrase that makes sense in context in place of the existing phrase. Lines 73-80 discuss how the national anthem had begun to increase in popularity and appear regularly in sporting events. The implication in the referenced sentence is that the singing of the national anthem has become a "tradition"; predict *very frequent*. Choice (A) is correct.

9.   D   Difficulty: Medium
Category: Inference

Getting to the Answer: Consider how the quotation reflects the specific rhetoric and purpose of the complete sentence. The correct answer will relate the words of the quotation to the rest of the sentence. The text explains that these lyrics "remind Americans of the liberty for which the country was established, and the courage of those who fought for it" (lines 97-99). The author draws a parallel between "land of the free" and "the liberty for which the country was established," and between "home of the brave" and "the courage of those who fought for it." Choice (D) is correct.

10. D   Difficulty: Medium
Category: Synthesis

Getting to the Answer: Review your notes for both passages. Identify what each passage offers to your understanding of the national anthem. The correct answer will reflect the specific contribution of Passage 2. While both passages describe aspects of the history and symbolism of "The Star-Spangled Banner," only Passage 2 traces the events that led to Key's words being officially adopted as the national anthem in 1931. Choice (D) is correct.

Choices A, B, and C may be tempting, but they do not match your prediction. While it is mentioned in Passage 2, choice A only addresses the first paragraph and not the overall contribution of the passage. Choice B is also incorrect. Although Passage 2 does emphasize the national anthem's "patriotic nature," Passage 1 does so as well, so this is not Passage 2's particular enhancement to Passage 1. Choice C is incorrect because the anthem's origins in the War of 1812 are only described at length in Passage 1.

11. B   Difficulty: Medium
Category: Command of Evidence

Getting to the Answer: Predict what type of information would most support your answer to the previous question: something that explains how Key's words became the national anthem. Then, select the answer choice that most closely matches your prediction. Lines 69-73 ("At the time . . . national anthem") demonstrate one way in which the words written by Francis Scott Key gained popularity over time in the United States and even began being thought of as a "national anthem." Choice (B) is correct.

Suggested Passage Map notes:
Passage 1

¶1: (central idea): use atoms to date things; isotopes def. & exs.
¶2: isotopes unstable; measure C-14
¶3: C-14 decay = predictable
¶4: C-14 dating; materials; timeline based on layers

Passage 2

¶1: def. radioactive; why dangerous; danger = radiation rate
¶2: half-life def. = decay rate; exs.
¶3: long half-life = long problem

12. C   Difficulty: Hard

Category: Inference

Getting to the Answer: Use your Passage Map to locate the paragraph that explains carbon-14 dating. This paragraph will contain the description of what materials can be dated using this method. In paragraph 4, the author states that carbon-14 dating can be used on materials made by a living organism. An arrowhead made from a bone is constructed of such material, choice (C).

13. D   Difficulty: Hard
Category: Command of Evidence

Getting to the Answer: Locate each of the answer choices in the passage. The correct answer should provide direct support for the answer to the previous question: the bone arrowhead can be dated using carbon-14 dating. In paragraph 4, the author describes the process for carbon-14 dating. Choice (D) is correct because this sentence provides a direct description of the materials that can be dated using carbon-14 dating.

14. B   Difficulty: Medium
Category: Vocab-in-Context

Getting to the Answer: Pretend that the word "decay" is a blank. Reread around the cited word to predict a word that could substitute for "decay" in context. The previous paragraph discusses how scientists measure the rate of emission to calculate the amount of carbon-14 in a sample. "Emission" means release; therefore, the amount of carbon-14 is becoming smaller if the atoms are releasing it. In this sentence, therefore, predict "decay" means to *decrease*, which matches "deteriorate," choice (B).

15. C   Difficulty: Easy
Category: Inference

Getting to the Answer: Look at your notes for paragraph 3. Summarize the ratio of carbon-12 to carbon-14 in living tissue in your own words. Look for the answer choice that most closely matches your prediction. In paragraph 3, the author explains that the ratio of carbon-12 to carbon-14 for living things is the same as the ratio in the atmosphere: constant. Choice (C) is correct.

16. C   Difficulty: Medium
Category: Command of Evidence

Getting to the Answer: Review what part of the passage you used to predict an answer for the previous question: the ratio is constant for living things. Of the answer choices, only lines 27-30 explain the ratio of carbon-12 to carbon-14 in living things. Choice (C) is correct.

17. B   Difficulty: Medium
Category: Detail

Getting to the Answer: Read around the cited lines. The author directly states why a release of iodine-131 is not cause for long-term concern. In paragraph 3, the author explains that the initial release of radiation from an accident involving iodine-131 will be high, but the level of radiation will drop quickly (lines 74-75). Choice (B) is correct.

18. C   Difficulty: Medium
Category: Detail

Getting to the Answer: Use your Passage Map to find the information about why exposure to radiation is dangerous.

Getting to the Answer: In paragraph 1, lines 53-55, the author explains that radiation is harmful to living tissue because it can cause damage to the cells' DNA, which matches choice (C).

19. A   Difficulty: Easy
Category: Vocab-in-Context

Getting to the Answer: Pretend that the word "original" is a blank. Reread around the cited word to predict a word that could substitute for "original" in context. The previous paragraph explains how scientists use "half-life" to determine how quickly material decays. If the material is decaying, then predict "original" refers to the *first* material. Choice (A) matches your prediction.

20. D   Difficulty: Medium
Category: Detail

Getting to the Answer: Review your notes for Passage 2. Try to put into your own words how scientists use half-life calculations of radioactive materials. Look for the answer that most closely matches your idea. In paragraph 1, the author explains that the level of danger posed by radiation released during a nuclear accident depends on how quickly radiation is released (lines 58-60). In paragraph 2, the author discusses how the half-life of radioactive material is used to determine how long a material will emit radiation. Paragraph 3 then explains how different half-lives translate into short-term or long-term radiation concerns. Choice (D) is correct because it most clearly paraphrases the information in the passage about how scientists use half-life calculations.

21. A   Difficulty: Hard
Category: Synthesis

Getting to the Answer: The central idea will be supported by all of the evidence presented in both passages. Review the central idea you identified for each passage in your Passage Maps. Passage 1 discusses the application of atomic and nuclear physics in archaeology while Passage 2 details how scientists apply atomic and nuclear physics to studies of radioactivity in nuclear power plant accidents. Choice (A) is correct.

22. A   Difficulty: Hard
Category: Synthesis

Getting to the Answer: Analyze the graph to see that it describes the decay of carbon-14 over time. Think about how this data relates to the texts. The graph portrays the decay of carbon-14 as described in Passage 1. The definition of "half-life" is given in Passage 2. The half-life of a material is the amount of time it takes for half of that material to decay. The graph shows that about 50 percent of carbon-14 remains after 5,400 years. Choice (A) is correct.

CHAPTER 15

PRACTICE

Suggested Passage Map notes:

¶ 1: oak problems; pests & disease, other trees

¶2: oaks in danger

¶3: research into problems and solutions; various solutions including fire

¶4: ecological restoration

¶5: more human interaction needed

¶6: go back to Native American ways

¶7: human intervention important

4. C   Difficulty: Medium
Category: Global

Getting to the Answer: Even when you can't make a specific prediction, summarize the author's central idea by reviewing your Passage Map. The author begins by listing the problems plaguing oak trees and continues by describing possible solutions to each of the problems. Common to each of the solutions is the requirement that humans actively participate in an ongoing process. The author concludes the passage by describing this kind of participation as "ethnobotanical restoration" (line 83). Predict that humans need to participate actively in efforts to restore oaks. Choice (C) matches this prediction.

5. B   Difficulty: Medium
Category: Detail

Getting to the Answer: Use your Passage Map to locate cited phrases. Rephrase what each phrase means. The author describes ecological restoration as a process that is completed in a very short time and ethnobotanical restoration as a process that seeks to restore ongoing human interaction with plant communities. Choice (B) is correct.

6. D   Difficulty: Easy
Category: Command of Evidence

Getting to the Answer: To answer this question, use the prediction you made to answer the previous question. To answer the previous question, you needed to recognize that the main difference between the two types of restoration is that while ecological restoration

takes place over a short period of time and can be completed, ethnobotanical restoration requires long-term involvement by humans in the natural process of maintaining historic plant communities. Choice (D) is correct.

PERFORM

Suggested Passage Map notes:

¶1: history of newborn screenings; medical advances meant deaths now from rare issues

¶2: link between PKU and mental retardation

¶3: despite risky, use of low phen diet tried

¶4: new test for PKU done earlier

¶5: test not perfect, but successful

7. C   Difficulty: Medium
Category: Connections

Getting to the Answer: The phrase "most strongly suggests" and the clue word "prior" indicate that this is a Connections question asking about an explicit relationship. Review your Passage Map to understand how the author connects certain ideas to each other. The word "prior" and the cited lines indicate that the relationship is sequential. First, the low phenylalanine diet, which was implemented despite its risks, proved beneficial. Then, the research initiatives began because of the benefits associated with the diet. Predict that the diet was prescribed in spite of those negative outcomes. Choice (C) matches this prediction.

8. D   Difficulty: Medium
Category: Command of Evidence

Getting to the Answer: When answering a Command of Evidence question, find the cited lines that most closely support the prediction you made to answer the previous question. You predicted that the diet was prescribed in spite of the drawbacks. Compare each of the answer choices to your prediction. Only choice (D) describes the drawbacks associated with the special diet.

9. B   Difficulty: Medium
Category: Global

Getting to the Answer: Use your Passage Map to quickly summarize the passage. Maintain focus on the general context of each paragraph. Concentrate on the central ideas in each paragraph, not on specific details. The author introduces the passage by discussing the practice of screening newborns and concludes the passage by describing genetic screening as "a permanent part of infant health care" (lines 79–80). Throughout the passage, the author focuses on the process that brought about the use of genetic screening. Choice (B) is correct.

10. D　**Difficulty:** Easy
Category: Detail

Getting to the Answer: "According to the passage" indicates that this is a Detail question. Use your Passage Map to locate the referenced details. Locate each referenced detail and determine why the author included that detail. Choice A is mentioned as a contributor to the decline in the infant mortality rate and can be eliminated. Eliminate B because Lofenalac was developed to treat PKU. Eliminate C because it discusses problems with the test. Choice (D) is correct because the general success of the test showed the potential of screening tests, as explained in lines 74–77.

11. D　**Difficulty:** Medium
Category: Command of Evidence

Getting to the Answer: To answer a Command of Evidence question, return to the place in the passage that provided the answer to the previous question. Check to see if one of the answer choices to this question includes the detail you found for the previous question. Choice (D) is correct.

EXTRA PRACTICE

Suggested Passage Map notes:
　　¶1: history of S warbler, concern for many birds losing habitats
　　¶2: S warbler declining due to gradual loss of habitats;
　　¶3: hard for scientists to conserve; birds adapting on their own
　　¶4: birds using man made pine plantations
　　¶5: pine plantations good for birds when trees 20 feet high
　　¶6: lots of space on plantations
　　¶7: only some plantations useful
　　¶8: plantations will become new habitat

1. C　**Difficulty:** Medium
Category: Global

Getting to the Answer: Think about the central idea of the passage. Eliminate answer choices such as A and D that contain supporting details for the central idea. The correct answer will be an idea that is supported by all of the details in the passage. This passage is mostly about how the Swainson's warbler population has begun to recover after its natural habitat was reduced by deforestation. Choice (C) is correct.

2. C　**Difficulty:** Medium
Category: Rhetoric

Getting to the Answer: Review your notes for the first paragraph. Consider the central idea of the paragraph and how it relates to the central idea of the passage. Select the answer choice that most accurately describes the purpose this sentence serves in the passage. The author mentions these other species of birds to give examples of other animals that are at risk because their habitats have been destroyed, which matches choice (C).

3. C　**Difficulty:** Medium
Category: Inference

Getting to the Answer: Review your paragraph 3 notes. How did scientists attempt to preserve the population of the Swainson's warbler? The correct answer should paraphrase your own idea. In lines 30–34 of paragraph 3, the author explains that previous attempts at conservation have been unsuccessful because scientists did not understand what the birds need in a habitat. This matches choice (C).

4. C　**Difficulty:** Medium
Category: Command of Evidence

Getting to the Answer: Locate each of the answer choices in the passage. The correct answer should provide direct support for the answer to the previous question. In paragraph 3, the author describes why previous conservation efforts by scientists have failed. Choice (C) is correct.

5. D　**Difficulty:** Medium
Category: Vocab-in-Context

Getting to the Answer: When approaching Vocab-in-Context questions, replace the word in question with a blank and predict a possible synonym. In this sentence, *change* can replace "conversion" without changing the overall meaning. Choice (D) is correct.

6. A   Difficulty: Hard
Category: Inference

Getting to the Answer: This type of open-ended question stem can make it difficult to predict the answer. Instead, look for the answer choice that is directly supported by the evidence in the text. Eliminate answer choices that are related to the main topic but go too far, such as D. In paragraph 1, the author discusses the risk of extinction of other birds due to a decrease in their habitats. Choice (A) is correct because it is most directly supported by the evidence in the passage.

7. B   Difficulty: Medium
Category: Command of Evidence

Getting to the Answer: Use your reasoning for answering the previous question to figure out where in the passage the best evidence for that answer will come from. Lines 9-14 in paragraph 1 provide the most direct support for the idea that more birds will become extinct if their habitats continue to disappear. Choice (B) is correct.

8. D   Difficulty: Easy
Category: Global

Getting to the Answer: Consider the central idea of the passage and the message conveyed by the information included. This passage is mostly about how the Swainson's warbler has adapted after losing much of its natural habitat. Select the answer that most closely explains that the author wants to relate this to the reader. The author's purpose is to explain how this happened, choice (D).

9. C   Difficulty: Hard
Category: Inference

Getting to the Answer: Think about the process undertaken in each of the answer choices and compare it to the Swainson's warbler's migrating to a new, man-made habitat. The migration of the Swainson's warbler to pine forests planted by humans is most similar to aquatic animals making new homes from shipwrecks. In both instances, animals have taken something created by humans and made it into a home. Choice (C) is correct.

10. A   Difficulty: Medium
Category: Vocab-in-Context

Getting to the Answer: In this sentence, the author is describing the stage of development that most closely resembles the bird's natural habitat. Predict that "point" most nearly means *stage*. Eliminate answer choices such as B and D that are synonyms for "point" but do not make sense in context. The prediction is an exact match for choice (A).

11. A   Difficulty: Medium
Category: Synthesis

Getting to the Answer: Consider only the information presented in the graph. The correct answer will be directly supported by the data. The graph shows that over the decade, the number of acres of pine plantations has grown steadily while that of natural pine forests has declined. The conclusion that the number of acres of pine plantations could soon surpass that of natural pine forests is supported by the data presented in the graph. Choice (A) is correct.

Suggested Passage Map notes:

¶1: A excited
¶2: A invited to impt tea
¶3: M not excited for A
¶4: M wants to make A more calm; unsuccessful
¶5: A worried about rain
¶6: A very excited even when doing dishes; but also nervous she might misbehave at the tea
¶7-8: M gives A advice for being proper at the tea

12. B   Difficulty: Easy
Category: Inference

Getting to the Answer: Reread the excerpt for clues that reveal Anne's previous behavior and her personality traits. Marilla specifically asks Anne whether she has found "another" kindred spirit, implying that Anne has previously rushed home excited about having made a new friend. This is a clue that Anne is a sociable, friendly person. Choice (B) is correct.

13. C **Difficulty:** Medium
Category: Rhetoric

Getting to the Answer: Read the sentence and determine how the selected words shape the reader's image of Anne; then, select the answer choice that most accurately reflects this tone and image. The passage states that Anne runs home and implies that she is *excited*. The correct answer, choice (C), supports the image of Anne as energetic.

14. B **Difficulty:** Hard
Category: Vocab-in-Context

Getting to the Answer: Predict a word that could replace the word in the question stem, then find its closest match among the answer choices. The passage states that Marilla hopes to *actively change* Anne from her current state and *mold* her into one of her own designs. Thus, of the various uses of the word "fashioning" used in the answer choices, choice (B) is correct.

15. C **Difficulty:** Medium
Category: Inference

Getting to the Answer: Read the context clues in the passage that relate to Matthew's and Anne's interactions. Examine what these clues suggest about their relationship. Anne goes to bed "speechless with misery" (lines 43-44) because Matthew predicts it will rain the next day. Anne's reaction shows that she takes Matthew's predictions seriously, so choice (C) is correct.

16. B **Difficulty:** Easy
Category: Detail

Getting to the Answer: Marilla explicitly states that Anne's trouble is that she is "thinking too much about [herself]" (line 75), which matches A. However, this advice is intended for the specific situation at hand, the tea party, rather than Anne's greater challenge of learning to take things calmly, which will affect her entire life. This challenge is outlined in lines 22-30; thus, choice (B) is correct.

17. B **Difficulty:** Medium
Category: Rhetoric

Getting to the Answer: Reread the paragraph in question and determine what role it plays in the progression of ideas within the passage. Paragraph 4 explains Marilla's feelings about Anne's personality traits, describes how she hoped to temper them, and states that she failed to do so, while also telling the reader that she likes Anne the way she is. Choice (B) best represents these ideas.

18. A **Difficulty:** Medium
Category: Vocab-in-Context

Getting to the Answer: Read the sentence and paragraph for context clues and determine which usage of the selected word best fits the author's intention. Predict that Marilla's advice is *useful* or *helpful*. Choice (A) is correct.

19. A **Difficulty:** Medium
Category: Rhetoric

Getting to the Answer: Evaluate the depth of the author's participation in the passage and how many perspectives the author introduces. Use this information to determine the correct answer. The author reveals the inner thinking of both Anne and Marilla while taking no active part in the passage, so choice (A) is correct.

20. D **Difficulty:** Easy
Category: Inference

Getting to the Answer: Evaluate how Marilla is presented. Throughout the passage, Marilla asks Anne to remain calm, coolly responds to Anne, and hopes to fashion Anne into a demure model child. Predict that Marilla is calm and collected. Choice (D) is correct.

21. A **Difficulty:** Medium
Category: Command of Evidence

Getting to the Answer: To answer Command of Evidence questions, start by looking at the part of the passage that helped you answer the previous question. Throughout the passage, Marilla asks Anne to remain calm and coolly responds to Anne, and the quotation noted in lines 20–21 shows Marilla doing this; thus, choice (A) is correct.

CHAPTER 16

PRACTICE

Suggested Passage Map notes:

¶1: book is not fiction

¶2: MF conceals name

¶3: MF used modest tone

¶4: MF's story is dark

¶5: author (DD) focuses on MF's repentance

¶6: DD wants readers to focus on moral

¶7: book includes happiness

¶8: readers can learn from MF's life

4. D   Difficulty: Medium

Category: Connections

Getting to the Answer: The phrase "According to the passage" and a relationship clue word indicate that you should ask yourself how items are being related. The clue word "because" suggests that this is a cause-and-effect relationship. Find the reference to the narrator's concern and reread the section. Predict that the recent popularity of novels encourages readers to believe what they read is fictional. This prediction matches choice (D).

5. C   Difficulty: Medium

Category: Connections

Getting to the Answer: Open-ended Connections questions about relationships (explicit or implicit) require you to describe the relationship in your own words and the correct answers can be difficult to predict. Because the question stem is asking about why the narrator wrote the story described in the passage and not the passage itself, focus on what the narrator says about the purpose of the story. By paraphrasing the narrator's intent stated in the final paragraph, you can predict that the narrator thinks readers can learn good things from the story. Choice (C) matches this prediction.

6. B   Difficulty: Medium

Category: Vocab-in-Context

Getting to the Answer: When answering Vocab-in-Context questions, focus on synonyms for the word in question, not on a specific definition. Read the sentence without "usefully applied" and ask what the narrator is trying to convey. Throughout the passage, the narrator

returns to the idea that the story is written not to relate "wicked" tales but to provide readers with an opportunity to learn from the lessons found in the story. Predict that the narrator is reaffirming the purpose for writing such stories. Choice (B) matches your prediction.

PERFORM

Suggested Passage Map notes:

¶1: NDE raises q's about history

¶2: NDE gives date and mine location of coins

¶3: study to compare methods

¶4: scholars disagree about origin

¶5: how problems of corrosion were overcome

¶6: findings contradict previous scholars

¶7: forced scholars to rethink regional politics

¶8: more tests will be done

7. A   Difficulty: Medium

Category: Vocab-in-Context

Getting to the Answer: Remember to avoid common meanings when answering Vocab-in-Context questions. Read the sentence without "struck" and rephrase what the author means. Predict that the author is referring to when the coins were minted. Choice (A) is correct.

8. D   Difficulty: Medium

Category: Connections

Getting to the Answer: To answer Connections questions that are not about specific parts of the passage, find the author's thesis and look for the answer choice that is consistent with it. Use your Passage Map to locate the thesis. The author states in the first sentence that science can help us learn about history. Lead isotope analysis is presented as an example of how science "can inform" (lines 1-2) history. In the first paragraph, the author states that this analysis has raised questions, and in paragraph 6, the author indicates that the analysis answered questions about when the analyzed coins were made. Therefore, choice (D) is correct.

9. D   Difficulty: Medium

Category: Connections

Getting to the Answer: The phrase "according to the passage" and a relationship keyword in the question stem signal a Connections question. The relationship keyword "because" indicates a cause-and-effect relationship, so identify why the researchers chose the coin in question. Predict that if the scientists' technique could help answer historians' questions, then historians would recognize the value of the technique. Choice (D) is correct.

10. A   Difficulty: Easy
Category: Vocab-in-Context

Getting to the Answer: The phrase "most nearly means" and a cited line indicate a Vocab-in-Context question. Read the sentence without "establish" and think of a synonym that can replace it. Predict that because scientists wanted to determine facts through their research, they wanted to determine who made the coins. Choice (A) matches your prediction.

EXTRA PRACTICE

Suggested Passage Map notes:

¶1: F's daily routine

¶1, cont: F's friends

¶2-10: recent robbery

¶11: lack of security at bank

¶12: thief not a professional robber

¶13-19: disagree whether thief will be caught

1. D   Difficulty: Medium
Category: Vocab-in-Context

Getting to the Answer: Locate context clues to help determine the meaning of the word. Predict a meaning for the word and then match it to the closest answer choice. The sentence describes Fogg arriving at the club and going to his usual table. A good prediction might be *went*. Be careful of answer choices that offer alternate meanings for the target word that don't make sense in context. Look for the nearest match in the answers. Choice (D) fits with the tone and context of the sentence.

2. C   Difficulty: Medium
Category: Inference

Getting to the Answer: Review the descriptions of Phileas Fogg and his actions in your Passage Map. Summarize what the beginning of the passage says about Fogg. Paragraph 1 describes Fogg counting out his steps on his way to the club. Upon arriving at the club, Fogg

goes to his "habitual table" (line 7) and performs a routine series of actions. Choice (C) is correct, as the details in paragraph 1 depict a man who likes to keep to a set routine.

3. A   Difficulty: Medium
Category: Command of Evidence

Getting to the Answer: Review your answer to the previous question. Locate the answer choice that directly supports the conclusion you drew. Choice (A) is correct. It provides the best support for the idea that Phileas Fogg is a man of habit and routine. The word "habitual" (line 7) and the fact that his table was prepared ahead of time for him suggest that Fogg followed this routine regularly.

4. A   Difficulty: Medium
Category: Inference

Getting to the answer: This is a very open-ended question stem, so it can be difficult to predict the answer without reviewing the answer choices first. Be sure to return to the passage before choosing an answer; skim your Passage Map for evidence that would prove the answer correct answer choice. Fogg reads the newspaper at the beginning of the passage. He later chimes in with a comment on the robbery the other men are discussing based on the information he learned in the paper. Therefore, choice (A) is correct.

5. D   Difficulty: Easy
Category: Command of Evidence

Getting to the Answer: Review your answer to the previous question. Decide which lines of text show Fogg's knowledge of current events. Choice (D) is correct. In these lines, Fogg interjects with additional information about a crime that is a current event.

6. B   Difficulty: Medium
Category: Detail

Getting to the Answer: Locate the portion of the text that discusses the bank. Your Passage Map for paragraph 11 should note a lack of security at the bank. This paragraph describes the lack of security measures at the bank that led to a theft in broad daylight; lines 51-54 reference a lack of guards or protective gratings. Choice (B) is correct.

7. A   Difficulty: Easy
Category: Vocab-in-Context

Getting to the Answer: Find context clues in the target sentence. Predict the meaning of the word and look for a match in the answer choices. "Functionary" (line 46) refers back to the "principal cashier" (line 46) mentioned earlier in the sentence. When you see two related answer choices, such as "official" and "servant," pay attention to the tone and specific context clues to help you choose. Choice (A) is correct; it provides a suitably neutral word that could substitute for "principal cashier, while C, servant, implies a hierarchy that is not present in the passage.

8. C   Difficulty: Medium
Category: Connections

Getting to the Answer: Find the part of the passage that describes the thief. Locate sentences that focus on a description of the suspect. Summarize the details in a one-sentence description. Lines 69-72 ("On the day . . . crime was committed") describe the suspect as a gentleman. Choice (C) is correct because the passage suggests that the police do not believe the man to be a professional thief due to the description of his appearance and demeanor.

9. B   Difficulty: Hard
Category: Rhetoric

Getting to the Answer: Reread the cited line. Concentrate on how the sentence impacts the text surrounding it. Examining the surrounding text shows that this comment *occurs during a discussion* about the thief being on the run. Fogg has silently listened to the conversation to this point, but now quietly interjects. This suggests that Fogg will have more to say about the topic; choice (B) is correct.

10. C   Difficulty: Medium
Category: Rhetoric

Getting to the Answer: Think about the passage as a whole. Use one sentence to predict the purpose of this passage. Make sure the tone of the answer choice matches the tone of the passage. The excerpt provides a brief character sketch of Phileas Fogg and establishes the dynamics of his friendships at the Reform Club. Choice (C) is correct; it accurately identifies the purpose of the excerpt.

Suggested Passage Map notes:
Passage 1

    ¶1: neg. affects of video games
    ¶2: violent games similar to teaching methods
    ¶3: newer studies show positive effects
    ¶4: can shape future ed. techniques
Passage 2
    ¶1: brain deterioration in old age
    ¶2: studies show video games slow deterioration
    ¶3: need more research

11. C   Difficulty: Medium
Category: Global

Getting to the Answer: Review your notes about the passage's central ideas. The correct answer will include an idea that is supported by all of the evidence presented in the passage. Avoid answer choices like A that refer to only one idea presented in the passage. All of the details presented in the passage are related to the idea that research about the effects of video games on those who play them is being used to develop new educational tools and methods. Choice (C) is correct.

12. D   Difficulty: Medium
Category: Command of Evidence

Getting to the Answer: Locate each answer choice in the passage. Consider which lines from the passage most directly support the central idea of the passage, which you identified in the previous question. The central idea of the passage is related to how research about video games is affecting the development of new methods of teaching. Choice (D) provides the most direct support for the answer to the previous question.

13. A   Difficulty: Easy
Category: Detail

Getting to the Answer: Use your Passage Map to find the paragraph that discusses studies performed in the 1990s. The correct answer will be stated explicitly in the passage. In paragraph 1, the author states that studies performed in the 1990s confirmed what parents had long said: that too many videos games can have a negative impact on learning and socialization in teenagers. Choice (A) is correct.

14. C   Difficulty: Medium
Category: Vocab-in-Context

Getting to the Answer: Treat the tested word as a blank. Replace it with a synonym that makes sense in the context of the sentence, paragraph, and passage. In paragraph 2, the author explains that certain video games simulate a repetition method used in the classroom but indicates that this was *not intentional* on the part of the game developers. Choice (C) is correct because "inadvertently" most nearly means "unintentionally" in this context.

15. B   Difficulty: Medium
Category: Connections

Getting to the Answer: Review your Passage Map notes from paragraph 2. Identify the cause-and-effect relationship the author describes. In paragraph 2, the author explains that when played for extended periods of time, video games mimic methods used in the classroom to teach children information. This is what makes it easier for game players to absorb the content of the games. Choice (B) is correct.

16. A   Difficulty: Hard
Category: Inference

Getting to the Answer: The correct answer will not be stated directly in the text but should be supported by the evidence presented. Avoid answers like B and D that go too far. In paragraph 2, the author asserts that the findings of the research described suggest that those elderly persons who are able to prevent mental decline could better maintain the functions they need to operate independently, such as driving. Choice (A) is correct.

17. C   Difficulty: Medium
Category: Command of Evidence

Getting to the Answer: The answer to the previous question will not be directly stated in the answer choice to this question. Rather, the correct answer to this question will provide the strongest support for your answer to the previous question. In the previous question, you inferred from the information in the passage that people who are able to put off the cognitive effects of aging might be able to live longer independently. Choice (C) provides the strongest support for this connection.

18. D   Difficulty: Medium
Category: Vocab-in-Context

Getting to the Answer: Reread the target sentence and predict your own definition for the cited word. Then, evaluate the answer choices to find the closest match to your prediction. In this context, "deteriorate" most nearly means *get worse* or *weaken*. Choice (D) is correct.

19. A   Difficulty: Medium
Category: Rhetoric

Getting to the Answer: Review your notes from paragraph 2. Consider how the information presented in this paragraph supports the central claim presented by the author in the overall passage. Passage 2 is mostly about how researchers are considering the potential of video games in treating brain deterioration; paragraph 2 focuses on the studies that show video games slow deterioration. Choice (A) is correct.

20. A   Difficulty: Medium
Category: Rhetoric

Getting to the Answer: Consider the overall message the author is conveying through the information presented in the passage. The author's purpose will not be directly stated but will be supported by the evidence presented. You determined the central claim to help you solve the previous question: Passage 2 is mostly about how researchers are considering the potential of video games in treating brain deterioration. Use this claim to help you determine the purpose of the passage: to describe how video games can potentially help elderly people who are experiencing brain deterioration. Choice (A) is correct.

21. D   Difficulty: Medium
Category: Synthesis

Getting to the Answer: The correct answer will be supported by the information in both passages. Think generally to predict what both passages agree on; avoid answers like B and C that refer only to information presented in one of the passages. Both passages discuss how video games are being used by researchers in different fields. Choice (D) is correct.

CHAPTER 17

PRACTICE

Suggested Passage Map notes:

¶1: impossible to describe Karnak

¶2: details of K temple ruins

¶3: description of the people at L ("savages")

¶4: K peaceful, not scary at night

4. B   Difficulty: Easy
Category: Rhetoric

Getting to the Answer: Questions about why an author includes a section in a passage require you to identify how it fits into the passage as a whole. The author concentrates, throughout the passage, on how much Egypt has affected her. The cited section is not so much about the lack of effect Egypt has had on the other people mentioned, but more about the great effect Egypt has had on the author. Choice (B) is correct.

5. C   Difficulty: Medium
Category: Rhetoric

Getting to the Answer: Authors often use contrast to make a point or strengthen an argument. Reread around the cited lines and paraphrase the main points the author makes about the ideas being contrasted. To answer this question, you must compare the author's experiences in Karnak and Luxor. The author describes Karnak in lofty, ethereal language filled with references to the eternal. The author expects to find the same thing in Luxor—"I had expected the temples of Thebes to be solemn . . ." (lines 41–42)—but finds something completely different: "but Luxor was fearful" (lines 42–43). Predict that the comparison between the two cities highlights the author's negative reaction to the conditions at Luxor. Choice (C) matches your prediction.

6. A   Difficulty: Medium
Category: Rhetoric

Getting to the Answer: Questions concerning the overall structure of a text require you to think about how the author presents the central ideas and builds the main argument. Review your Passage Map and look for patterns in how the author expresses the important ideas in

the passage. In the second paragraph, the author shifts between the real and the imagined: "Gigantic shadows spring up on every side; 'the dead are stirred up for thee to meet . . .'" (lines 14–16). This shift between the real and the imagined continues in the third paragraph: "Rows of painted . . . golden clouds" (lines 42–56). Predict that the author mixes real descriptions with imaginative descriptions, which matches choice (A).

PERFORM

Suggested Passage Map notes:

¶1: owls = optimize bio strengths

¶2: maximize vision adv.

¶3: humans map world diff. than owls

¶4: owls = complex sens. detail

7. D   Difficulty: Medium
Category: Rhetoric

Getting to the Answer: Use your Passage Map to answer questions concerning the central argument in a passage. Review the first paragraph to determine the author's thesis. Think about what must be true for the claim to be correct. The author begins with the claim that "humans and animals perceive the world in different ways" (lines 1–2). Predict that the assumption must have to do with how our brains work in different ways, which matches choice (D).

8. C   Difficulty: Medium
Category: Rhetoric

Getting to the Answer: To answer a Rhetoric question that asks about support for a claim, use your Passage Map to locate the claims the author makes and the support the author provides. Make a general prediction about the claims the author supports and then find the answer choice that matches. The author claims that owls and humans have adapted to their environments in different ways. Since this question asks about owls, focus on the claims the author makes about them. Predict that the author provides support for the claim that owls have effectively adapted to their environment. In the second paragraph, the author provides several examples of ways owls successfully adapted. Choice (C) is correct.

9. D   Difficulty: Easy
Category: Rhetoric

Getting to the Answer: When you see the phrase "in order to" and a cited line, identify how the cited detail fits into the overall structure of the passage. Overall, the passage compares the differences between the sensory adaptations of owls and humans. Read around the cited line and paraphrase why the author mentions barn owls. Predict that barn owl hearing is an example of how owls have adapted to improve their ability to hunt. Choice (D) matches your prediction.

10. A   Difficulty: Medium
Category: Rhetoric

Getting to the Answer: Review your Passage Map, focusing on how the author presents the information in the passage. In paragraph 1, the author compares human perception to that of other animals, specifically owls. The author then discusses different ways in which owls and humans use their respective sensory apparatuses. Predict that the passage is structured by comparing the differences between how owls and humans perceive the world. Choice (A) is correct.

EXTRA PRACTICE

Suggested Passage Map notes:

¶1: 2 types of univ. = pub. & private
¶2: pub univ. goal = ↑ higher ed opportunity
¶3: 1862 - gov't gave pub. land for univ.
¶4: history of diversity
¶5: major growth
¶6: US univ. part of global conv.
¶7: univ. reflect diversity, liberty, creativity

1. C   Difficulty: Hard
Category: Rhetoric

Getting to the Answer: The correct answer will reflect a specific position supported in both the second paragraph and the passage as a whole. Predict that the author is citing political and economic reasons to explain why the government "acknowledged the need" (line 22) for educated citizens. Choice (C) is correct.

2. B   Difficulty: Medium
Category: Command of Evidence

Getting to the Answer: Use your support for the previous question to predict the answer. Consider which choice best shows a clear relationship to your answer. In the previous question, line 22 offered support for our answer; Choice (B) is correct because it explicitly states that the government saw the "need for broader higher education opportunities" (lines 22–23).

3. A   Difficulty: Medium
Category: Rhetoric

Getting to the Answer: Summarize the paragraph and think about what the author would want the reader to know after reading it. Be sure to review your Passage Map, which should already state important information about the paragraph. Your Passage Map notes that in 1862, the government gave public land for university development; the paragraph states that the Morill Act was an early example of the federal government's desire to increase enrollment at public universities. Predict that the purpose of the paragraph is to explain how the government supported public higher education. Choice (A) is correct.

4. B   Difficulty: Medium
Category: Rhetoric

Getting to the Answer: The author's choice of words is deliberate. Read the sentence carefully and think about what the author is suggesting when he uses the word "accessible." The passage notes that public universities received federal and state support, which means the universities could then function at a lower cost and could enable more students to attend. Predict that "accessible" was used to describe how higher education was remodeled to be available to more people, especially those with limited means. Choice (B) is correct.

5. D   Difficulty: Easy
Category: Vocab-in-Context

Getting to the Answer: Use context clues to help you predict the meaning of the word as it is used in the sentence. The last sentence in paragraph 3 contrasts the fact that although universities would be operated by states, they would still need to follow, or comply with, federal regulations because they received federal support. Predict that *adhere* most nearly means *follow* or *comply with*. Choice (D) is correct.

6. C   Difficulty: Hard
Category: Rhetoric

Getting to the Answer: It is difficult to predict the exact answer for this type of question, but concisely stating the author's line of reasoning before reviewing the answer choices will help you eliminate the choices that do not strengthen that theme. Throughout the passage, the author discusses how the expansion of public universities has impacted American culture. In paragraph 4, the author describes how public universities have gradually become more diverse, offering educational opportunities to many people who would not have otherwise had them in previous years. This has had a significant impact on American culture. Consider which of these pieces of evidence best supports that theme; choice (C) is correct.

7. C   Difficulty: Medium
Category: Rhetoric

Getting to the Answer: Think about why the author would want to include this fact. The paragraph's central idea is that the student populations of public universities have grown increasingly diverse. Predict that the author is describing an example of how public universities have become more diverse. Look for the answer choice that matches this prediction. Choice (C) is correct.

8. B   Difficulty: Easy
Category: Command of Evidence

Getting to the Answer: There should be a clear relationship between the correct choice and the previous answer. Since you used the fourth paragraph as a whole to predict the last question, look for the choice that offers support for the specific answer to the previous question. Choice (B) clearly states that public universities are diverse today, even though the 1890 land act did not increase diversity when it was passed. This corresponds to the answer to the previous question.

9. D   Difficulty: Easy
Category: Vocab-in-Context

Getting to the Answer: Predict the meaning of the word with context clues from the sentence and paragraph. The second sentence of paragraph 5 states that the public

university system "has evolved," which implies it has done so in response to changes or variations in American culture over time. Predict that "nuances" most nearly means *changes* or *variations*. Always check your answer choice in the sentence to ensure it makes the most sense. Choice (D) is correct.

10. C   Difficulty: Hard
Category: Rhetoric

Getting to the Answer: Consider what the passage is about overall and what the author wants the reader to learn, rather than an idea that is mentioned only in passing or in support of the passage's purpose. Reviewing your whole Passage Map can help you focus on the entirety of the passage. The author has written a brief history of public higher education in the United States; in both the introduction and conclusion, the author connects the evolution of the public university system with the evolution of generally accepted ideals and cultural values, such as diversity and liberty. Predict that the author is discussing the connection between public higher education and generally accepted ideals. Choice (C) is correct.

11. B   Difficulty: Medium
Category: Rhetoric

Getting to the Answer: Consider the central idea of the passage that you identified in a previous question and the central idea in the fifth paragraph. The passage is primarily about the way in which U.S. higher education has reflected American cultural identity. The fifth paragraph summarizes the major growth public higher education has undergone. Predict that as the American culture has grown to value public higher education, public higher education has undergone major growth; the fifth paragraph gives an example that supports the central idea. Choice (B) is correct.

Suggested Passage Map notes:

¶1: Mark = preacher's son; patron paid for school

¶2: M inherited patron's money & became patron

¶3: interested in art, not nobility

¶4: sent cousin to school

¶5: cousin took care of M

12. C   Difficulty: Medium
Category: Inference

Getting to the Answer: The correct answer will be supported directly by the passage. The passage states that Mark's father left behind "a reputation for short sermons, as an example for his successor" (lines 14–15). However, it then states, "neither warning nor example seems to have been effective" (lines 15–16). Predict that his successor gave long sermons. Choice (C) is correct.

13. D   Difficulty: Medium
Category: Command of Evidence

Getting to the Answer: Carefully review the part of the passage that you used to answer the previous question. The passage discusses Mark's father's successor in the context of his father's death; Mark's father has left an "example" of short sermons for his successor, but "neither warning nor example seems to have been effective" (lines 15–16). This suggests that Mark's father's successor did not follow his example of giving short sermons. Choice (D) is correct.

14. A   Difficulty: Hard
Category: Inference

Getting to the Answer: The word "writing" is quoted in order to underscore the fact that it is dialogue. It is Mark who has used the word. The passage goes on to state that "what he wrote . . . has never been discovered" (lines 20–22). Predict that the only reason to believe that writing has taken place is Mark's word; other people have their doubts. Choice (A) is correct.

15. A   Difficulty: Easy
Category: Detail

Getting to the Answer: The correct answer is directly stated in the passage. The passage states, "his patron died

. . . and left him all the money he wanted" (lines 26–28), which directly supports the idea that he is now wealthy. Predict that Mark's patron's death was fortunate for him because it made him wealthy. Choice (A) is correct.

16. B   Difficulty: Medium
Category: Vocab-in-Context

Getting to the Answer: Consider the topic of the paragraph in which the cited word appears. Then, predict a synonym for this word based on the topic and context of the paragraph. Earlier in the paragraph, the passage states, "he settled accounts with the money-lenders" (lines 30–31). The sentence to which the word in question belongs asserts that it was "not only usurers who discovered that Mark Ablett no longer wrote for money" (lines 33–35). "Money-lender," then, seems to be a synonym for "usurer;" predict *money-lender*. Choice (B) is correct.

17. B   Difficulty: Medium
Category: Vocab-in-Context

Getting to the Answer: Consider the usual meaning of "lavish." How might it be applied figuratively here? "Lavish" usually means something like "elaborate" or "sumptuous," depending on the context. Here, it is used to describe how Mark "play[s] host and 'lead'" (line 41). It seems to be used to describe how Mark enjoys his theater company with enthusiasm and relish. Predict that "lavishness" most nearly means *enthusiasm* or *relish*. Choice (B) is correct.

18. C   Difficulty: Medium
Category: Inference

Getting to the Answer: Identify how the passage characterizes Mark's life, then read the answer choices to see how others view it. The passage characterizes Mark's early life in London as an exciting and irresponsible period (lines 16-25). Later, he inherits money, settles his accounts, and becomes financially responsible (lines 26-42). Predict that, compared with his earlier life, his later life (and therefore stories of his later life) was less exciting. Choice (C) is correct.

19. B   Difficulty: Medium

Category: Command of Evidence

Getting to the Answer: Identify the paragraph that most directly supports your answer to the previous question about the different periods of Mark's life. Since lines 26–42 discussed Mark's later life, the best evidence to support your previous answer should come from those lines. The lines quoted in choice (B) make a direct distinction between these two periods of Mark's life: when he inherits money, "his life loses its legendary character, and becomes more a matter of history" (lines 29–30). In other words, his earlier life in London is more like a legend, or myth, and his later life is less exciting. Choice (B) is correct.

20. B   Difficulty: Hard

Category: Inference

Getting to the Answer: Reread the sentence to find the analogy; it will be explicitly stated in the passage. Then, consider why the passage draws the comparison it does. Mark is described as "a hanger-on, but to the skirts of Art, not Society" (lines 53-54). "Art" is being compared with "Parnassus," and "Society" with "Hay Hill." Each appears to be a neighborhood associated with these ideas. Predict that "Parnassus" is an example of Art. Choice (B) is correct.

21. D   Difficulty: Hard

Category: Rhetoric

Getting to the Answer: Identify the narrator's attitude toward Mark in the last paragraph; your Passage Map notes remind you that Matthew took care of Mark. The tone of the last paragraph is one of mock-seriousness. On the surface, it appears to take Mark's ideas about himself and his place in the world seriously. But, when read closely, the final sentence characterizes Mark as a pompous and arrogant man who finds Matthew useful because he doesn't steal attention from himself. Matthew "didn't bother you with unnecessary talk—a boon to a man who liked to do most of the talking himself" (lines 83-85). Predict that the last paragraph serves to subtly make fun of Mark; Choice (D) is correct.

CHAPTER 18

PRACTICE

Suggested Passage Map notes:

¶1: artifacts show how colonists lived

¶2: clues about life

¶3: settlers used woodworking skills

¶4: early structures primitive, focus on survival

¶5: brick processes similar to England

¶6: most hardware from England

¶7: use of glass

¶8: after hardship, gained luxuries

4. C   Difficulty: Easy
Category: Inference

Getting to the Answer: The phrase "the statement . . . suggests" signals that this is an Inference question. Find the relevant details and look for clues indicating how the author connects them. Read around the cited text. In the previous two sentences, the author discusses the hardships the colonists faced in the early years. Focus on the reasons they didn't think about plastering during the early years. Predict that the colonists were too busy trying to stay alive. Choice (C) matches your prediction.

5. D   Difficulty: Easy
Category: Detail

Getting to the Answer: When presented with an EXCEPT question, use your Passage Map to locate the cited details. When you find one of the cited details in the passage, eliminate that answer choice. The third paragraph describes Virginia as a "carpenter's paradise" (line 23) and says the wooden artifacts were skillfully made. Eliminate A. Paragraph 4 describes how the settlers had "a difficult time staying alive" (lines 36-37); eliminate B. In the fourth paragraph, you learn that the colonists made floors from clay, allowing you to eliminate C. The sixth paragraph says that most of the hardware was imported, which directly contradicts choice (D).

6. D   Difficulty: Medium
Category: Inference

Getting to the Answer: The phrase " . . . most comparable to . . . " indicates that this is an Analogical Reasoning Inference question. Identify the relationship between the ideas. The description of the brick industry implies that the colonists made bricks with local materials using techniques they brought with them from England. The relationship is one of local materials formed using imported methods. Choice (D) reflects this relationship.

PERFORM

Suggested Passage Map notes:

¶1: narrator impressed with other's imagination

¶2: secluded life, other character's name revealed: Dupin

¶3: preferred darkness

¶4: narrator admired Dupin's analytic ability

7. C   Difficulty: Medium
Category: Inference

Getting to the Answer: The word "suggests" and the line reference indicate that this is an Inference question. Determine which answer choice can be concluded based on the information in the passage. Read around the cited section. Substituting "because" for "as" clarifies that this is a cause-and-effect relationship. The cause is Dupin's "embarrassed" circumstances (line 18), and the effect is that the narrator paid for everything. Predict that the narrator had more money than Dupin. Choice (C) is correct.

8. D   Difficulty: Hard
Category: Inference

Getting to the Answer: The phrase "closely parallels" is a clue that this is an Analogical Reasoning Inference question. To identify how the ideas are connected, describe the relationship. In the third paragraph, the narrator states that he followed Dupin's lead in everything, indicating that the narrator is subordinate to Dupin. Look for the answer choice that describes a relationship in which one side of the relationship is subordinate to the other. Although C might be tempting, the student acts independently in the second half of the answer choice. Choice (D) is correct.

9. B   **Difficulty:** Medium
Category: Detail

Getting to the Answer: Because this question does not provide a line reference, use your Passage Map to locate the relevant text. Then, paraphrase the detail. Locate the details about how and where the narrator met Dupin. In the first sentence, the narrator mentions first meeting Dupin in a library while searching for a rare book. Predict that they were looking for the same book. Choice (B) is correct.

10. A   **Difficulty:** Hard
Category: Inference

Getting to the Answer: "Most likely agree" signals a broad or open-ended Inference question. Summarize the passage to zero in on statements with which the narrator would most likely agree. The passage focuses on the ways the narrator becomes involved with Dupin. The final paragraph discusses Dupin's ability to see into other people's inner thoughts: "windows in their bosoms" (line 62). The passage ends with the narrator's speculating on how Dupin could do so. Choice (A) is correct.

EXTRA PRACTICE

Suggested Passage Map notes:

> ¶1: U.S. idea of national parks
> ¶2: parks scope and history
> ¶3: millions appreciate parks, parks encourage preservation
> ¶4: JM father of national parks
> ¶5: JM focus on ecology, natural beauty and worth
> ¶6: political impact, started Sierra Club
> ¶7: JM greatest accomplishment importance of nature

1. C   **Difficulty:** Medium
Category: Vocab-in-Context

Getting to the Answer: Look for context clues to help you determine the meaning of unknown words. Read the rest of the paragraph to get a better idea of the relationship between America's national parks and the rest of the world. The last sentence of the paragraph states that "globally over a thousand parks are now protected by similar systems" (lines 10-11). The idea that originated in the United States later became popular worldwide. Choice (C), "imitated," is correct.

2. A   **Difficulty:** Medium
Category: Rhetoric

Getting to the Answer: As you take notes, identify the general idea of each paragraph in the passage in your own words. Compare your notes to each choice to find the correct answer. The second paragraph provides the reader with statistics about the scale of the National Parks System, including the diversity of the parks, the number of employees required to manage the system, and the number of acres the system includes. Choice (A) correctly summarizes the purpose of this paragraph.

3. D   **Difficulty:** Medium
Category: Inference

Getting to the Answer: Look for specific textual evidence in the passage that may support each answer choice. The correct answer will be concluded directly from the passage. The passage mentions the international influence of the United States National Parks System several times. Other answer choices are not supported by evidence. Only choice (D) is directly found within the passage.

4. D   **Difficulty:** Medium
Category: Command of Evidence

Getting to the Answer: Review your answer to the previous question. Then, choose the textual evidence that best supports that conclusion. According to the passage, "over a hundred countries now participate" (lines 36-37) in a national parks system. Choice (D) provides direct evidence for the passage's assertion that America's national parks idea has been influential internationally.

5. A   **Difficulty:** Easy
Category: Vocab-in-Context

Getting to the Answer: Break the word down into its component parts to determine the correct answer. "Wander" suggests travel and "lust" suggests a positive interest. Looking at the context, "his activism and wanderlust also drew him to other picturesque locations" (lines 65-67), an interest in travel is the most logical choice.

6. B   Difficulty: Hard
Category: Rhetoric

Getting to the Answer: Consider why the word "channeling" is used instead of an alternative word. What meaning does it add that a more general word like "communicating" does not? The context of the sentence suggests that Muir's writings were powerful. They seem to have captured the "marvel" (line 71) of the wilderness and transmitted it directly to readers, making them feel it, too. "Channeling" emphasizes the way the power of his writing took the emotion he felt and communicated it directly and powerfully to readers. Choice (B) successfully captures this idea.

7. A   Difficulty: Hard
Category: Inference

Getting to the Answer: Consider the passage as a whole. Are there any answers you can immediately eliminate as being obviously incorrect? The passage consistently states that John Muir was hugely influential during his lifetime, so B can be eliminated. It does acknowledge, however, that the preservation of such vast amounts of wilderness did come at an economic cost, though the passage suggests that this cost was worthwhile. Choice (A) is correct.

8. D   Difficulty: Medium
Category: Command of Evidence

Getting to the Answer: Test each possible answer choice against your selection for the preceding question. Which piece of evidence most directly supports the previous answer choice? The passage states that conserving the wilderness was worthwhile, "even at the expense of short-lived material gains" (lines 90-91). This suggests that there was an economic cost to Muir's preservation goals. Choice (D) is correct, as it directly connects the parks system to ideas of money.

9. A   Difficulty: Hard
Category: Synthesis

Getting to the Answer: Use your Passage Map to summarize each passage. Then, find the answer choice that best matches your ideas. Passage 1 describes the American National Parks System in general, focusing on its creation, its size, and its parks' diversity. Passage

2 focuses specifically on the importance of John Muir and his influence on conservation. Choice (A) correctly summarizes these differences.

10. A   Difficulty: Easy
Category: Synthesis

Getting to the Answer: Evaluate how each passage describes the national parks. What do the word choices suggest about the purpose and value of the parks? Both passages use words like "awe" (line 29) and "wonder" (line 70) to discuss the national parks. Clearly, the authors of both passages agree that the main value of national parks is to preserve natural beauty for visitors. Choice (A) correctly reflects this idea.

11. D   Difficulty: Easy
Category: Synthesis

Getting to the Answer: Carefully study the x- and y-axes to determine what trends can be inferred from the graph. According to the graph, visits to all five parks have increased from 1930 to 2010. No conclusions can be drawn about why parks have been more or less popular destinations during these periods. However, the graph does show that during each period, the Grand Canyon has received more visitors than has Olympic National Park. Choice (D) is the only answer choice that can be definitely concluded from the chart.

Suggested Passage Map notes:
¶ 1-3: M very upset, E concerned
¶4: M having trouble writing to W
¶5: E distracts Mrs. J
¶6: M receives letter from W, W concerned, Mrs. J clueless
¶7: Mrs. J hopes M marries W
¶8: E suggests unlikely
¶9-10: Mrs. J saw love, E says Mrs. J will see she is wrong in time

12. B   Difficulty: Medium
Category: Vocab-in-Context

Getting to the Answer: Consider each word carefully. The most common meaning for a word is not necessarily the correct one. Elinor, "though never less disposed to speak" (line 57), nonetheless speaks in this paragraph. The correct answer should be something like *eager*, since

Elinor is not eager to speak. Plugging in each of the answer choices will reveal which fits best. Choice (B) is similar to *eager*, so it is correct.

13. B   Difficulty: Medium
Category: Rhetoric

Getting to the Answer: Read the lines around this phrase. Look for clues that suggest what is making her react as she does. Marianne is clearly expecting bad news in the letter, as she runs out of the room before even opening it. Choice (B) is correct: she is driven by her anxiety.

14. A   Difficulty: Easy
Category: Inference

Getting to the Answer: Look for clues about Elinor's behavior toward Marianne. What does this suggest about their relationship? Elinor seems almost as upset by what is upsetting Marianne as Marianne herself is. The sisters are clearly very close, and Elinor's words to Mrs. Jennings make clear that Elinor is trying to prevent Mrs. Jennings from doing further damage to Marianne by spreading rumors. Choice (A) is correct, as it reflects the sisters' close relationship.

15. B   Difficulty: Medium
Category: Command of Evidence

Getting to the Answer: Review the answer to the previous question. Consider which of the answer choices provides the clearest sense of Elinor's feelings toward Marianne. Elinor's feelings toward Marianne are protective. This is demonstrated by the lines that show Elinor's trying to distract Mrs. Jennings from noticing Marianne's distress. Choice (B) is correct; it is a clear illustration of Elinor's protective feelings.

16. C   Difficulty: Easy
Category: Inference

Getting to the Answer: Determine what Mrs. Jennings thinks is happening. Does it differ in any way from what is actually happening? Mrs. Jennings appears not to have noticed Marianne's distress over Willoughby. She remarks on how much the two of them seem to be in love, despite Marianne's altered behavior. Choice (C) is correct because it shows that Mrs. Jennings is not perceptive enough to notice what is happening.

17. C   Difficulty: Medium
Category: Command of Evidence

Getting to the Answer: Review the answer to the previous question. Notice what Mrs. Jennings says or does to support your conclusion about her. Mrs. Jennings is not very perceptive. The passage states that she "was too busily employed . . . to see any thing at all" (lines 45-47) and then observes that Marianne and Willoughby are likely to be married. Choice (C) is correct, as it offers an instance of Mrs. Jennings's failure to notice the events around her.

18. B   Difficulty: Medium
Category: Vocab-in-Context

Getting to the Answer: Consider the context of this line. Notice what Elinor is suggesting about Mrs. Jennings. Elinor is surprised that Mrs. Jennings has "talked [herself] into a persuasion" (lines 60-61) that Marianne and Willoughby are to be married. Other context clues make clear that this is what Mrs. Jennings believes will happen, so the correct answer will mean something like *belief*. Choice (B), therefore, is correct.

19. A   Difficulty: Easy
Category: Detail

Getting to the Answer: Read the passage closely to find the answer stated explicitly. Both Elinor and Mrs. Jennings state that Mrs. Jennings believes Willoughby and Marianne are to be married soon. Choice (A) is correct.

20. D   Difficulty: Hard
Category: Inference

Getting to the Answer: In your own words, describe Marianne's situation. Marianne is upset because of a letter that has come from a man everybody believes she will marry. Then, read the answer choices to see what situation is analogous. The correct answer should relate to unexpected disappointment. Choice (D) is correct: it conveys a sense of disappointment after high expectations have not been met.

21. B   Difficulty: Medium
Category: Inference

Getting to the Answer: Consider what would be lost from the passage if this paragraph were not included. Elinor and Mrs. Jennings have argued over the events taking place. The final paragraph shows Elinor trying to convince Mrs. Jennings that she is "doing a very unkind thing" (lines 81-82) by spreading rumors of Marianne's marriage, rumors that will likely humiliate her. Elinor is not simply explaining why she believes Mrs. Jennings is wrong, but trying to stop her from causing Marianne additional pain. Choice (B) is correct because it is the only answer choice that conveys this meaning.

CHAPTER 19

PRACTICE

3. C   **Difficulty:** Medium
Category: Effective Language Use

Getting to the Answer: Consider how you would refer to a number in a different context. Would you say you started school "hundred days" ago? "Hundred" refers to a digit (ones digit, tens digit, hundreds digit, etc.), whereas "one hundred" is an actual number. In order to begin the sentence in an idiomatically correct way, it is necessary to use the full number, "one hundred." Choice (C) matches.

4. C   **Difficulty:** Medium
Category: Sentence Formation

Getting to the Answer: If there is no obvious error in the underlined segment, keep reading until you can identify the issue. The underlined portion is correctly used as the subject of an independent clause. However, because the clause after the comma is also independent, the sentence is a run-on. Since you are not given the option to fix the comma splice, look for the answer choice that makes the first clause dependent without introducing another error. Choice (C) correctly subordinates the first clause by beginning the sentence with "when."

5. B   **Difficulty:** Easy
Category: Usage

Getting to the Answer: Subjects and verbs must agree in person and number. Singular third person subjects need singular third person verbs, and plural third person subjects need plural third person verbs. Keep in mind that the closest noun to an underlined verb may not be its subject. Read around the underlined portion until you can identify the subject of the underlined verb. Remember, a noun that is the object of a preposition cannot be the subject of a sentence. In this sentence, the subject is the plural noun "components" and needs a plural verb. Choice (B) is correct.

PERFORM

6. B   **Difficulty:** Medium
Category: Effective Language Use

Getting to the Answer: Using two words that mean the same thing is redundant. Look for the answer choice that creates the most concise sentence. As written, the sentence uses a compound predicate made up of "fascinated and intrigued." Because both words convey the same idea, namely that scientists found Jupiter to be very interesting, using one is sufficient. Choice (B) concisely conveys the idea.

7. D   **Difficulty:** Medium
Category: Sentence Formation

Getting to the Answer: Read around an underlined period and check to make sure that each clause forms a complete sentence. Because the second clause is a fragment, it needs to be properly connected to the previous sentence with either subordination or punctuation. Choice B provides punctuation that corrects the fragment but does not form an effective sentence. Since the information in the second clause explains why the moons of Jupiter provided evidence for a theory, the second clause needs to be combined with the previous sentence. Choice (D) joins the clause to the sentence.

8. D   **Difficulty:** Easy
Category: Sentence Formation

Getting to the Answer: Compare underlined verbs with related verbs. Related verb forms need to be parallel. The verbs "completed" and "collected" form a compound predicate and need to be parallel in form. As written, the underlined section unnecessarily reintroduces the subject. Join the two verbs without punctuation. Choice (D) is correct.

9. C   **Difficulty:** Easy
Category: Development

Getting to the Answer: If you have the option to omit a sentence, think carefully about the author's topic. If the underlined portion strays from the topic, omit it. The author's topic is Jupiter. The underlined portion adds information about *Pioneer 10* that is irrelevant to the topic. Choice (C) correctly omits the sentence for this reason.

10. B   Difficulty: Medium
Category: Effective Language Use

Getting to the Answer: If an underlined segment does not contain a grammatical error, check for other kinds of errors tested on the SAT. As written, the underlined portion is a complete sentence. Reread that sentence in the context of the following sentence. Together, these two sentences sound choppy and create a wordiness issue. Because the underlined sentence provides information about Jupiter, it can be incorporated into the next sentence. Choice (B) forms a modifying phrase that effectively introduces the subject of the sentence.

11. D   Difficulty: Medium
Category: Usage

Getting to the Answer: Related nouns must be consistent in number. Check other nouns around an underlined noun to make sure they agree. The underlined noun is related to the noun phrase "number of probes." Because there was more than one probe, there was more than one measurement. Choice (D) correctly makes the underlined noun plural.

12. C   Difficulty: Medium
Category: Quantitative

Getting to the Answer: When you see a question with an infographic, remember to use the Kaplan Method for Infographics. The sentence to which the underlined portion belongs is comparing Earth's rotational speed to that of Jupiter's. The relevant information is how much faster Jupiter rotates. Look in the third column of the table for that data. Compare the information you find with the answer choices. Choice (C) provides accurate and relevant information.

13. D   Difficulty: Medium
Category: Usage

Getting to the Answer: A pronoun's antecedent must be clear and unambiguous. Always identify the antecedent of an underlined pronoun. The underlined possessive pronoun could refer to a number of things: our diameter, Earth's diameter, and Earth's rotational speed. Reread the sentence to determine what the author means. The sentence compares the diameter of Jupiter to the diameter of Earth. Look for the answer choice that makes that comparison clear. Choice (D) is correct.

EXTRA PRACTICE

1. B   Difficulty: Medium
Category: Effective Language Use

Getting to the Answer: Read the entire paragraph to determine if a career in physical therapy is rated as a good career choice by the Bureau of Labor Statistics. "Concurrently" means at the same time, and "unusually" means not common. "Finally" implies that physical therapy was not a good career choice in the past. Choice (B) is correct because it means with regularity.

2. D   Difficulty: Medium
Category: Effective Language Use

Getting to the Answer: Read the sentence and determine how it can be more concise. As written, the text begins with a conjunction and uses a dash to indicate an unnecessary break in thought. Choice (D) eliminates both problems, creating a more direct sentence.

3. B   Difficulty: Medium
Category: Development

Getting to the Answer: Read the entire paragraph to identify its focus. Choices A, C, and D each offer only one component of the paragraph. Only choice (B) effectively establishes the main topic of the second paragraph.

4. A   Difficulty: Easy
Category: Punctuation

Getting to the Answer: Read the sentence and determine whether it is grammatically complete. To form a grammatically complete sentence, you must have an independent clause after a semicolon. Choices B, C, and D all have excessive and incorrect punctuation. The sentence is correct as written; choice (A) is correct.

5. B   Difficulty: Hard
Category: Development

Getting to the Answer: Read the entire paragraph to determine the pattern of the evidence. Most sentences include descriptions of the types of patients a PT will encounter. Since (B) is the only sentence that supports the topic sentence, it is the correct answer.

6. B   Difficulty: Medium
Category: Sentence Formation

Getting to the Answer: Read the sentence to determine how to improve its clarity. Consider whether the modifiers are correctly placed near the nouns or verbs they modify. The use of the modifier "minimally" at the end of the sentence is awkward. Choice (B) correctly moves the modifier next to the word it modifies: "interaction." It also removes the conjunction "And" at the beginning of the sentence.

7. D   Difficulty: Medium
Category: Effective Language Use

Getting to the Answer: Read the sentences and determine what words can be eliminated. As written, the text uses short, choppy sentences. Choice (D) combines the two sentences effectively to improve the economy of word choice.

8. B   Difficulty: Hard
Category: Sentence Formation

Getting to the Answer: Read the sentence and examine the order of the details. Reorganize the sentence so that it is clear and smooth. As written, the text contains coordinated ideas without regard to their grammatical form. Choice (B) correctly rearranges the ideas so that the three main ideas are nouns combined with "and" instead of "in addition to."

9. A   Difficulty: Easy
Category: Effective Language Use

Getting to the Answer: Read the sentence and determine the function of the word in the sentence. "Concentrated" means clustered or gathered together, "planned" means to arrange beforehand, and "consolidated" means brought together in a single whole. Only choice (A), "collaborated," means working together intellectually.

10. D   Difficulty: Hard
Category: Organization

Getting to the Answer: Read the paragraph and determine if the sequence of events is logical. For the paragraph to be logical, the examples need to build upon one another. Sentence 7 does not offer a proper conclusion to the paragraph, but sentence 2 gives a good summation.

Choice (D) correctly moves the summative sentence to conclude the paragraph.

11. D   Difficulty: Medium
Category: Development

Getting to the Answer: Closely read the paragraph to find the central idea. Then, determine which sentence does not match the content. The evidence regarding physical therapy assistants does not connect with the main idea of this paragraph, which centers on the benefits of choosing to become a certified physical therapist. Choice (D) is correct.

12. C   Difficulty: Easy
Category: Effective Language Use

Getting to the Answer: Watch out for choices, like B, that are extremely wordy. It is better to be as direct and simple as possible. Additional adjectives do not add more meaning to this content. Choice (C) is the most concise and effective way of stating the information in the passage.

13. A   Difficulty: Medium
Category: Punctuation

Getting to the Answer: Study the words in a series and see where a comma might need to be inserted or eliminated. Recall that the SAT requires lists of three to have commas after the first two items in the list, not just after the first item. Choice (A) is correct.

14. D   Difficulty: Hard
Category: Development

Getting to the Answer: To find the best answer choice, look for the sentence that has the most relevant details presented in a clear and concise way. Choice (D) has the most relevant details about what the Pony Express was like when it was at its peak.

15. C   Difficulty: Medium
Category: Sentence Formation

Getting to the Answer: Be careful of inappropriate transition words when relating sentences to one another. Choice (C) divides the two complete thoughts into two sentences by adding a period and capitalizing the first word of the second sentence.

16. A   Difficulty: Easy
Category: Effective Language Use

Getting to the Answer: The context of the sentence suggests which word would have the correct connotation. Check each word to see how it fits with the context. Only choice (A) fits with the context of the sentence. The other choices are incorrect in context.

17. B   Difficulty: Medium
Category: Sentence Formation

Getting to the Answer: Verbs within a sentence should be parallel. Check to see if this is true here. The correct answer, choice (B), has all the verbs in the same form.

18. A   Difficulty: Hard
Category: Development

Getting to the Answer: To find the central idea of a paragraph, identify important details and summarize them in a sentence. Then, find the choice that is the closest to your summary. Do not choose a detail rather than a central idea. The paragraph mostly discusses the challenges riders faced, so choice (A) most accurately sums up the central idea of the paragraph.

19. B   Difficulty: Medium
Category: Organization

Getting to the Answer: Look for the relationship between this sentence and the previous one to choose the appropriate transition word. Read the word into the sentence to ensure that it makes sense. Choice (B) shows the relationship between the two sentences by emphasizing that the riders could overcome these challenges.

20. B   Difficulty: Medium
Category: Quantitative

Getting to the Answer: The graphic gives specific information about when events relating to the Pony Express took place. Interpret it to choose the correct answer choice. Choice (B) is the only one that accurately reflects the information in the timeline.

21. C   Difficulty: Medium
Category: Effective Language Use

Getting to the Answer: The context of the sentence suggests which word would have the best fit. Check each word to see how it fits with the context. Choice (C) best fits the context of the sentence.

22. D   Difficulty: Medium
Category: Effective Language Use

Getting to the Answer: Watch out for answer choices that may have incorrect transition words. Choice (D) joins the sentences concisely and correctly by using the conjunction "and."

CHAPTER 20

PRACTICE

4. C   **Difficulty:** Hard
Category: Organization

Getting to the Answer: An effective body paragraph can provide evidence to support the author's central idea or introduce a change in the focus of the passage. This paragraph begins with the transition word "while" and establishes a contrast between the number of recent earthquakes and the damage that those earthquakes can cause. The passage also shifts focus from a discussion of earthquake frequency to one of earthquake damage. Therefore, placing this paragraph between the two discussions in paragraph 4 and paragraph 5 makes the most sense. Choice (C) is correct.

5. C   **Difficulty:** Medium
Category: Organization

Getting to the Answer: When reordering a sentence within a paragraph, identify the information in the sentence and locate where in the paragraph that information is discussed. The topic of sentence 4 is aftershocks. Aftershocks are also discussed in sentence 2. However, in sentence 2 the pronoun "these" indicates that aftershocks have been previously discussed in the paragraph. The logical place for sentence 4 is before sentence 2. Choice (C) is correct.

6. A   **Difficulty:** Easy
Category: Organization

Getting to the Answer: Don't answer questions that ask about the conclusion of a paragraph until you have read the entire paragraph. The paragraph focuses on the damage that earthquakes can cause and ways to improve safety in the event of an earthquake. Although the sentence preceding the concluding sentence mentions earthquake predictions, it does so in the context of how to prepare for these natural disasters. Therefore, the final sentence needs to discuss preparations, not predictions. Choice (A) provides a logical conclusion to the paragraph.

PERFORM

7. D   **Difficulty:** Medium
Category: Usage

Getting to the Answer: A pronoun is ambiguous when its antecedent is either missing or unclear. To find the antecedent for the underlined pronoun, read the previous sentence and think about the focus of the paragraph. The previous sentence has more than one possible antecedent—vacuous "Internet speak," "reliance," or "acronyms and abbreviations." However, in the context of the passage, "empty chatter," or choice (D), is the clearest and most relevant antecedent.

8. A   **Difficulty:** Medium
Category: Organization

Getting to the Answer: To answer questions about effective transitions within a paragraph, identify the focus of the paragraph both before and after the transition. The first part of the paragraph discusses the reasons the narrator stayed in his room as a child—because he was ill. After the transition, the narrator discusses why he still stays in his room—because he has access to the world. The transition needs to show how those ideas are linked. Choice (A) provides a logical transition as written.

9. B   **Difficulty:** Easy
Category: Effective Language Use

Getting to the Answer: When two words or phrases in the sentence have the same meaning, the sentence is redundant and contains a concision error. In this sentence, "succinct" and "to the point" have the same meaning, so the correct answer will eliminate one. Choice (B) is correct.

10. C   **Difficulty:** Hard
Category: Organization

Getting to the Answer: To reorder a sentence within a paragraph, identify the information in the sentence and locate what sentence that information should logically precede or follow. As written, sentence 5 summarizes the freedom people experience when connected by the Internet. However, sentence 6 makes a claim about that freedom, and sentence 7 provides examples of that freedom. The summary in sentence 5 should logically follow both the claim and the examples. Choice (C) is correct.

11. B   Difficulty: Easy
Category: Usage

Getting to the Answer: Unless the context in the passage indicates that the time frame has changed, the verb tense should not change. As written, this verb is in the past perfect tense. However, the context of the passage indicates that the action described by the verb continued up until the present moment. Choice (B) correctly uses the present perfect tense.

12. D   Difficulty: Hard
Category: Sentence Formation

Getting to the Answer: Whenever you see a compound, series, or list, check to make sure that all of the items are in parallel form. The underlined phrase is part of a compound formed by the conjunction "and." Reread the sentence and identify the other part of the compound. In this sentence, "half two minds exchanging sophisticated ideas" forms the first part of the compound. The second part must be parallel. Choice (D) is correct.

13. A   Difficulty: Medium
Category: Organization

Getting to the Answer: Introductory transitions must logically connect the information and ideas in the sentences before and after the transition. In the sentence before the underlined transition, the author describes small talk as boring. In the following sentence, he compares a conversation without small talk to flying. The sentence suggests that small talk can be dispensed with only occasionally. This sentence is correct as written, so choice (A) is correct.

14. D   Difficulty: Medium
Category: Organization

Getting to the Answer: Paragraphs in a well-written passage will flow from the general to the specific. To put paragraphs in the most logical order, begin with the paragraph that introduces the central idea in broad terms. As written, paragraph 1 contains a very specific discussion of a particular form of speech. Paragraph 2 introduces the idea of conversation in general terms and outlines the narrator's thoughts about it. Only choice (D) arranges the paragraphs from the general to the specific.

EXTRA PRACTICE

1. B   Difficulty: Easy
Category: Usage

Getting to the Answer: As currently written, this sentence switches verb tense mid-sentence. The other verb in the sentence, "was," indicates that the events happened in the past. The tense of the underlined verb should match and also be in a correct past tense. Choice (B) is correct because it correctly uses the past tense of "produce."

2. B   Difficulty: Medium
Category: Organization

Getting to the Answer: Look for the relationship between this sentence and the previous one. Choice (B) shows the relationship between the two sentences by giving an example of what kind of art the Post-Impressionists were creating.

3. D   Difficulty: Medium
Category: Effective Language Use

Getting to the Answer: Read the complete passage to learn more about the work of Impressionists. The passage states that Impressionists tried to paint exactly what they saw in nature. Only choice (D) has the correct connotation and fits within the context of the sentence.

4. B   Difficulty: Medium
Category: Sentence Formation

Getting to the Answer: The verbs in a sentence have to be parallel. The correct answer is in the same form as the first verb in the sentence, "looking." That means that the gerund, or -ing verb, "attempting" in choice (B) is correct.

5. A   Difficulty: Easy
Category: Effective Language Use

Getting to the Answer: Check each word for its connotations and pick the answer choice that fits the context of the sentence. This sentence describes how Post-Impressionists focused on self-discovery in art by letting their personal experiences and emotions guide their interpretation of their subjects. Therefore, each artist had his or her own distinct, or "unique," vision. The underlined portion is correct as written, and the answer is therefore choice (A).

6. C   **Difficulty:** Hard
Category: Development

Getting to the Answer: Read the entire paragraph and determine the central idea. The paragraph discusses different ways artists in the Post-Impressionism era painted. Choice (C) reflects this summary.

7. B   **Difficulty:** Hard
Category: Effective Language Use

Getting to the Answer: Choice (B) joins the sentences concisely and correctly by changing the verb tense of the first sentence to make it a dependent clause.

8. A   **Difficulty:** Easy
Category: Usage

Getting to the Answer: Read the sentence prior to the pronoun to determine whom the pronoun is referencing. The pronoun "they" refers to Paul Gauguin and Vincent van Gogh, so the pronoun needs to be plural and in the third person. Choice (A) is correct.

9. D   **Difficulty:** Hard
Category: Development

Getting to the Answer: Read the entire paragraph to identify the central idea. Then find the answer choice that provides evidence about this idea. The paragraph concerns the Post-Impressionist period and what kinds of methods Post-Impressionists used to create their art. Choice (D) addresses the central idea by providing additional information about these methods.

10. B   **Difficulty:** Medium
Category: Usage

Getting to the Answer: "They're" is a contraction meaning "they are," which does not make sense in the context of the sentence. What is needed here is a possessive plural pronoun to match the antecedent "artists." Choice (B) is correct.

11. D   **Difficulty:** Medium
Category: Organization

Getting to the Answer: Try inserting this sentence into all of the possible places to figure out where it makes the most sense. Choice (D) is the most logical position for this sentence because it is a comment based on the quotation in sentence 5.

12. C   **Difficulty:** Medium
Category: Effective Language Use

Getting to the Answer: Think about the overall meaning of the sentence. Select the answer choice that makes the most sense in context. "Depletion" is the reduction of a resource, so choice (C) is correct.

13. D   **Difficulty:** Hard
Category: Effective Language Use

Getting to the Answer: The most important element of the sentence is that biofuel is an alternative fuel source. Choice (D) is correct because this sentence places the emphasis on "alternative is biofuel."

14. A   **Difficulty:** Medium
Category: Development

Getting to the Answer: Look for the answer choice that clearly states the main topic of the paragraph and introduces the central idea supported by all of the details presented. Topic sentences or introductory sentences of body paragraphs should generally introduce that paragraph's topic. While other answer choices address details disclosed in the paragraph, choice (A) is the most general and also uses the transition "until recently" to tie this paragraph to the one that precedes it.

15. A   **Difficulty:** Medium
Getting to the Answer: Usage

Getting to the Answer: "It" refers to ethanol and is possessive. The possessive form of "it" is "its," so the sentence is correct as written. Choice (A) is correct.

16. B   **Difficulty:** Medium
Category: Effective Language Use

Getting to the Answer: The underlined word, "horrible," is too casual. Be careful of answer choices that are close in meaning to "horrible" but do not fit the established tone. Replace "horrible" with each of the answer choices. In this context, "dire," which means severe or urgent, best fits the tone and style of the sentence. Choice (B) is correct.

17. C   **Difficulty:** Medium
Category: Quantitative

Getting to the Answer: Look at the most recent data in the graph. Pay attention to the relationship between the two lines: the solid line represents the percentage of corn production used for ethanol, and the dotted line reflects the price of corn. In the most recent years displayed in the graph, the price of corn and the percentage of corn production used for ethanol have both increased. Choice (C) is correct.

18. A   **Difficulty:** Hard
Category: Development

Getting to the Answer: Determine the central idea of the paragraph. In this paragraph, the author explains that ethanol is limited as a commercial fuel. Choice (A) describes one way in which ethanol use is limited and is therefore correct.

19. D   **Difficulty:** Easy
Category: Organization

Getting to the Answer: Read this paragraph in the context of the entire passage to determine its proper placement. This paragraph makes general statements about the central idea of the passage and draws a conclusion. Choice (D) is correct because paragraph 4 is an appropriate concluding paragraph.

20. B   **Difficulty:** Easy
Category: Usage

Getting to the Answer: Read the first few sentences of the paragraph and pay attention to the verb tenses used in the following sentences. As written, the underlined portion is in the past perfect tense. The following sentence, however, uses the present perfect form of the verb "to develop." The underlined portion should also be in the present perfect form; therefore, (B) is correct.

21. C   **Difficulty:** Medium
Category: Sentence Formation

Getting to the Answer: Check to see if this sentence contains two independent clauses that create a run-on sentence without proper punctuation. This sentence contains two complete thoughts with two independent main clauses and should therefore be separated into two sentences with a period. Choice (C) is correct.

22. B   **Difficulty:** Medium
Category: Organization

Getting to the Answer: Read the previous sentence in conjunction with this one. Think about the relationship between the ideas in the two sentences. There is a cause-and-effect relationship between the ideas in the previous sentence and this sentence, but the underlined portion contains a concluding transition. "Therefore" is a cause-and-effect transition, so choice (B) is correct.

CHAPTER 21

PRACTICE

5. D   **Difficulty:** Medium
Category: Development

Getting to the Answer: Scrutinize details of densely factual passages to make sure they are on-topic and do not conflict with other details or the central idea. This passage is concerned with the details of human skin and explaining the properties and purposes of skin. Choice (D) abides by the author's scope and purpose for the passage and is therefore correct.

6. A   **Difficulty:** Medium
Category: Development

Getting to the Answer: Pick the answer choice that is in line with the author's central idea and tone. In this passage, the author explains how the skin is essential to life by listing its various properties and processes for keeping the body in healthy operation. The underlined section is in line with the author's overall effort. Choice (A) is correct.

7. C   **Difficulty:** Medium
Category: Development

Getting to the Answer: Make sure details in the underlined section are relevant to the topic. Even if a detail matches the tone of the passage (in this case, strictly fact-based), it might not be relevant to the central idea. Most of the answer choices for this question sound legitimate and even factually correct. However, only choice (C) keeps the focus on the human skin and its characteristics, so it is correct. Remember, the focus of the paragraph is on the defensive functions of the skin, *not* on how those functions work at a cellular level. You also know that immediate medical attention (choice B) is too extreme for every instance of skin breaking (small cuts, etc.).

8. A   **Difficulty:** Medium
Category: Development

Getting to the Answer: Concluding sentences often reassert or summarize the author's central idea; therefore, they cannot fundamentally conflict with the author's

assertions. In this passage, the author has made clear that the skin is a very important organ that protects the body from a variety of illnesses and disorders, as well as from physical harm. Choice (A) is correct, as it ties preceding points and details together into a coherent conclusion for the author's argument.

PERFORM

9. A   **Difficulty:** Medium
Category: Development

Getting to the Answer: Scrutinize the answer choices for how they relate to the author's central ideas as well as how they potentially conflict with details that come later in the passage. Choice (A) is correct because—without going off-topic or conflicting with later details—it elaborates on the idea that Polk followed in Jackson's footsteps.

10. C   **Difficulty:** Easy
Category: Development

Getting to the Answer: Pay close attention to long lists of evidence to make sure that each component is in line with the central idea and context of the sentence. Choice (C) is correct because it is the only answer choice that both stays focused on matters of policy (as the first part of the sentence mentions) and supports the thesis that Polk and Jackson were in agreement on most points of public policy.

11. D   **Difficulty:** Easy
Category: Development

Getting to the Answer: The first sentence of a paragraph sets the paragraph's tone and purpose. Pay attention to what the other sentences of the paragraph are describing and pick the answer choice that is the best introduction for those details. This paragraph is concerned with explaining the chronology of Polk's early life. Choice (D) is correct because it states the place and date of Polk's birth, making it a logical introduction to the following sentences.

12. D   **Difficulty:** Medium
Category: Development

Getting to the Answer: Supporting details fit the context of the paragraph and do not contradict details found elsewhere in the passage. Select the answer choice that satisfies these guidelines. This paragraph is narrowly concerned with Polk's origins and early political career. Only choice (D) fits the context and does not contradict later details.

13. C   Difficulty: Medium
Category: Development

Getting to the Answer: A paragraph's final sentence ideally guides the paragraph's central idea to a conclusion and remains linked to the central idea of the passage. Choice (C) is correct because it is the most effective conclusion for a paragraph tasked with explaining Polk's early political career. Choice (C) also makes a clear connection to the following paragraph, helping the narrative flow.

14. B   Difficulty: Medium
Category: Development

Getting to the Answer: Remember that supporting evidence needs to focus on and contribute to the central idea. The author's intent is to introduce the two main candidates in the 1844 election, leading to the following sentence that discusses their opinions of expansionism. Choice (B) is correct because it stays focused on the paragraph's topic and contributes to the argument that Polk recognized popular support for expansionism that other candidates overlooked or ignored.

15. A   Difficulty: Medium
Category: Development

Getting to the Answer: Examine details and parenthetical asides for relevance to the central idea. The goal is to make sure that no contradictions are being introduced into the narrative. No change is necessary because the underlined section touches on two central themes of the passage: Polk's support for expansionist policies and his Jacksonian view of America. Choice (A) is correct.

16. B   Difficulty: Hard
Category: Development

Getting to the Answer: Pay close attention to a paragraph's first sentence. It should set the stage for details to follow and also be in line with the passage's central idea. As alluded to in the first paragraph and explained clearly in the final paragraph, Polk did much to expand the borders of the United States. He even supported war with Mexico to gain territory. Choice (B) is correct.

EXTRA PRACTICE

1. B   Difficulty: Medium
Category: Development

Getting to the Answer: Identify the main idea of the paragraph. Eliminate options that do not support the main idea. Although sentence 3 is related to the main topic of the paragraph, coral reefs, the information in this sentence does nothing to support the main idea: the coral reefs' function, threatened status, and composition. Choice (B) is correct.

2. B   Difficulty: Medium
Category: Organization

Getting to the Answer: Read the preceding sentence along with this one and look for a relationship between the ideas in the sentences. The first sentence describes the importance of coral reefs, and this sentence explains how they are in danger of disappearing. "Unfortunately" is the best transition to use here, and choice (B) is the correct answer.

3. A   Difficulty: Medium
Category: Quantitative

Getting to the Answer: Evaluate the data presented in the infographic that accompanies the passage. Read each answer choice and eliminate those not supported by the data in the graph. Choice (A) is correct. As the pie chart shows and the caption confirms, about sixty percent of living reefs are in danger.

4. B   Difficulty: Medium
Category: Effective Language Use

Getting to the Answer: As written, the sentence contains redundant language. Look for the answer choice that retains the meaning of the two original sentences but is less wordy and redundant. Choice (B) is the correct answer because it contains the same information as the original sentences but in a more concise manner. While C is similar, it uses passive voice, which you should avoid using on the SAT.

5. D   Difficulty: Medium
Category: Effective Language Use

Getting to the Answer: Look for the answer that creates the clearest idea within the sentence. The resources referred to in the sentence are clean water and sunlight— things the reef must have to survive. These resources are vital to the coral reefs, so choice (D) is the correct answer.

6. B   Difficulty: Easy
Category: Development

Getting to the Answer: The correct answer will briefly describe the main idea of the paragraph and will be supported by the details in the paragraph. Be careful of answer choices like C that summarize a detail provided in the paragraph rather than the central idea. Choice (B) best describes the main idea of the paragraph. All of the details presented in the paragraph are related to how people engaging in activities near coral reefs often cause damage.

7. B   Difficulty: Easy
Category: Usage

Getting to the Answer: Check the verb tense in the sentences that follow this one. Be sure that the verb tense is consistent. To agree with the sentences in the rest of the paragraph, the verb in this sentence should be written in present tense. Because the noun is singular, choice (B) is the correct answer.

8. C   Difficulty: Medium
Category: Effective Language Use

Getting to the Answer: Look for the answer that creates the clearest idea within the sentence. The word "obstruct" most clearly illustrates how the particles that settle on the coral keep sunlight from reaching the coral. Choice (C) is correct.

9. B   Difficulty: Easy
Category: Effective Language Use

Getting to the Answer: Avoid answers that are grammatically correct but wordy or redundant. The correct answer is the most concise choice. "Would suggest" fits grammatically and is the most concise choice, so choice (B) is the correct answer.

10. A   Difficulty: Medium
Category: Development

Getting to the Answer: Avoid answers that are related to the main topic but do not add relevant details to the

paragraph. The paragraph explains how crabs and coral reefs help each other. Choice (A) is the best addition to this paragraph to support the central idea.

11. D   Difficulty: Medium
Category: Organization

Getting to the Answer: Read the paragraph with the sentence moved to the places suggested by the answer choices. Look for relationships between the ideas in the surrounding sentences. This sentence is a continuation of the idea introduced in sentence 3 (crabs might be damaging the coral) and belongs after sentence 3. Choice (D) is the correct answer.

12. A   Difficulty: Medium
Category: Development

Getting to the Answer: Reread the paragraph to determine which answer choice best introduces the main point. The correct answer, choice (A), is the only one that accurately explains how the career is now popular and helpful but had to develop over time after a shift in health care needs.

13. D   Difficulty:
Category: Development

Getting to the Answer: Reread the sentence and determine which answer choice creates the most focused sentence. The additional comments about the school's quality and features are unnecessary. Choice (D) creates the most focused sentence.

14. B   Difficulty: Medium
Category: Effective Language Use

Getting to the Answer: Look for nearby context clues and use what you know of each answer choice's definition to determine which word most accurately reflects the intention of the sentence. The intention of the sentence is to state that students should acquire hands-on medical knowledge through work experience. The word with the definition that best describes this acquisition is "accrue," choice (B).

15. B   Difficulty: Easy
Category: Effective Language Use

Getting to the Answer: Read the entire sentence for context clues and determine which answer choice creates a logical sentence without wordiness or redundancies. Only choice (B) correctly eliminates wordiness, as the word "programs" is used later in the same sentence.

16. D   Difficulty: Medium
Category: Effective Language Use

Getting to the Answer: Find context clues and determine which answer choice creates a logical sentence without wordiness or redundancies. Because there is still an exam to pass before these individuals become PAs, and because the repetition of the words "graduates" and "graduation" is redundant, choice (D) is the correct answer.

17. D   Difficulty: Medium
Category: Organization

Getting to the Answer: Review the answer choices to determine which creates a paragraph with the best logical progression of ideas. The paragraph discusses the steps a student must take in order to become a PA and should not discuss maintaining one's license until the end, as it is done only after becoming a PA. Choice (D) is correct.

18. C   Difficulty: Medium
Category: Effective Language Use

Getting to the Answer: Use context clues to determine which answer choice best fits the context of the sentence and paragraph while conveying the author's intended meaning. The sentence suggests that doctors work alone while PAs work under supervision. The word with the definition that best describes a doctor's unsupervised work is "autonomously," choice (C).

19. A   Difficulty: Medium
Category: Organization

Getting to the Answer: Decide which answer choice offers the best transition for an accurate flow of ideas. Choice (A) offers the best transition in order to summarize why the previous information is important and to show the positive effects PAs have on the health care team.

20. C   Difficulty: Hard
Category: Usage

Getting to the Answer: Evaluate whether the subject or object of the sentence is referred to by the pronoun and then determine which answer choice creates a logical and grammatically sound sentence. It is the PA who works under a physician, and because the pronoun refers to the object of the sentence, physicians, the appropriate pronoun to use in this situation is "whom." Therefore, choice (C) is correct.

21. B   Difficulty: Medium
Category: Effective Language Use

Getting to the Answer: Reread the paragraph and decide which answer choice maintains the style and tone of the author's voice. The author has not yet referenced him or herself, the reader, or any third party for an opinion in this passage. This makes the consistent tone found in choice (B) correct.

22. D   Difficulty: Medium
Category: Development

Getting to the Answer: Review the paragraph to determine which claim made by the author is lacking details or supporting evidence that would strengthen the author's case. The second sentence in the paragraph is the only one in which the author makes a claim based on projections, but the author fails to use specific figures. Adding these figures would strengthen this claim, thus choice (D) is correct.

CHAPTER 22

PRACTICE

5. D   **Difficulty:** Hard
Category: Effective Language Use

Getting to the Answer: Make sure the order in which words and phrases are written makes sense logically. As written, this sentence is hard to follow. The author is trying to emphasize the information that men also served as nurses during the Civil War. Choice (D) is correct because it is the only answer choice with grammatically and logically correct syntax.

6. B   **Difficulty:** Medium
Category: Effective Language Use

Getting to the Answer: Even if an underlined word or phrase sounds correct, analyze its meaning—both literal and figurative—to ensure it is appropriate in context. While it is easy to interpret a meaning from the underlined phrase "major victories," that meaning does not convey the author's intention. The phrase "major victories" suggests that of all the accomplishments of this organization, excluding men was one of the most important. Reread the sentences before and after the underlined phrase to understand that what the author means to convey is the idea that this exclusion occurred early in the history of the nurses' organization. Choice (B) corrects this error by explaining that this exclusion was one of the early victories within a series of accomplishments.

7. C   **Difficulty:** Easy
Category: Effective Language Use

Getting to the Answer: Avoid the temptation to use more words than necessary. As written, the underlined segment is redundant: "denied admission to" and "excluded from" have the same meaning. Look for the most succinct way to convey the author's intended meaning. Choice (C) is correct.

8. B   **Difficulty:** Medium
Category: Effective Language Use

Getting to the Answer: Style and tone errors are nuanced—pay attention to the details in the sentences surrounding the underlined word or phrase. As written, the underlined portion does not match the style and tone of the passage because it includes the author's opinion while the rest of the passage offers no judgment on any of the situations discussed. Choice (B) correctly maintains the objective tone of the passage by omitting any subjective viewpoints.

PERFORM

9. B   **Difficulty:** Medium
Category: Effective Language Use

Getting to the Answer: Read the sentence to understand the context in which the underlined word, "imagine," is used. The author uses "imagine" to describe how certain groups portray the risks associated with genetically modified organisms. Because the author views these groups as the opposition, the word needs to convey a stronger sense of resistance to the truth. As written, the sentence is too benign. Choice (B) is correct.

10. D   **Difficulty:** Easy
Category: Effective Language Use

Getting to the Answer: "Interfere" and "tamper" have the same meaning and are used to express a single idea about intentionally changing nature. The correct answer will eliminate one of those words. Choice (D) is correct.

11. B   **Difficulty:** Medium
Category: Effective Language Use

Getting to the Answer: Do not automatically select the shortest answer choice when presented with a Concision question. The correct answer choice must fully convey the author's intended meaning. As written, the underlined segment is the shortest answer choice, but it is difficult to determine exactly which group of people the "we" is referencing. Choice (B) is correct because it specifies the people included in "we" most concisely.

12. B   **Difficulty:** Hard
Category: Effective Language Use

Getting to the Answer: Effective Language Use questions focused on syntax often require you to recognize that grammatically correct sentence structure alone may not produce the most effective writing. Although the sentences are grammatically correct as written, the question stem asks which of the answer choices most effectively combines the two sentences. Because the second sentence provides additional information about "certain bird species" mentioned in the first sentence, use the relative pronoun "that" to indicate which species could be affected by the decline in the insect population. Choice (B) is correct.

13. D   Difficulty: Medium
Category: Effective Language Use

Getting to the Answer: Auxiliary verbs, like the underlined "will," add functional or grammatical meaning like expressing tense, voice, or emphasis to the clause in which they appear. When an auxiliary verb is underlined, make sure it fits the context of the paragraph or passage. Throughout the paragraph, the author uses the auxiliary verb "could" to indicate the possibility that certain things could happen—"could lead" and " could have." Nothing in the paragraph suggests that the author has shifted from conjecture (indicated by "could") to either certainty ("will" and "would") or necessity ("must"). Choice (D) is correct.

14. A   Difficulty: Medium
Category: Effective Language Use

Getting to the Answer: When an entire sentence is underlined, check for a syntax error. This sentence is correct as written. The author arranges the parts of the sentence in the most logical order by introducing the topic ("actual impact"), describing what is being impacted, and drawing a conclusion about the topic. Choice (A) is correct.

15. A   Difficulty: Medium
Category: Effective Language Use

Getting to the Answer: To answer Effective Language Use questions focused on word choice, or precision, reread the sentence containing the underlined word or phrase to determine the author's intended meaning. Determine that the underlined phrase "essential fallacy" provides information about the basis for the argument discussed in this sentence. Rephrase the sentence as: the argument is based on a false idea. However, a false idea is not the same as a lie. Choice (A) is correct.

16. D   Difficulty: Medium
Category: Effective Language Use

Getting to the Answer: When answering a question about style and tone, you will sometimes first need to read the entire passage or paragraph. In the first three paragraphs, the author focuses on the negative aspects of genetically modified organisms. In the fourth paragraph, he dismisses the counter argument raised by advocates for genetically modified organisms. The tone in the final paragraph becomes strident and accusatory. The final sentence must match this tone in order to effectively conclude the paragraph and the passage. Choice (D) is correct because it suggests that the stakes for the planet are enormous and our misplaced trust would have dire consequences.

EXTRA PRACTICE

1. B   Difficulty: Medium
Category: Punctuation

Getting to the Answer: Read the sentence to determine how the list within it should be formatted. If it is more of an aside than a direct part of the sentence's main structure, the list should be set off by punctuation. As the sentence is written, its many commas are confusing. Because there is a list in the sentence, the commas within that list should remain. However, the list of poetic forms is not directly related to the rest of the sentence, so this should be clarified with punctuation. Dashes are the best way to mark this as a separate thought. Choice (B) correctly adds dashes to both the beginning and end of the list.

2. A   Difficulty: Easy
Category: Effective Language Use

Getting to the Answer: Determine what the sentence is saying about the history of the haiku. Is "complex" the most accurate way to describe it? The passage describes the many forms and many centuries that comprise the history of haiku. Choice (A), "complex," perfectly describes the long, rich, and detailed history of the poetic form.

3. A   Difficulty: Hard
Category: Development

Getting to the Answer: Consider the purpose of the paragraph, then determine which answer choice makes the most sense as an introduction to the paragraph. The purpose of this paragraph, based on its other sentences, is to explain the history of haiku and how its structure has changed over time. Choice (A) is the only answer choice related to these ideas. While the other answer choices may briefly mention the structure of haiku or its history, they all focus on other aspects of haiku—its entertainment value, the difficulty of understanding its rules, or the challenge of writing it.

4. D   Difficulty: Easy
Category: Development

Getting to the Answer: The sentence's placement in the passage is not optimal. The next sentence returns the discussion to the hokku form and readers encounter another explanation of the name "haiku" later, in paragraph 5. Choice (D) is correct because the sentence should be omitted from paragraph 2.

5. C   Difficulty: Medium
Category: Organization

Getting to the Answer: Consider the information presented by the rest of the paragraph to determine the meaning of the phrase "alternating turns." Sentence 7 describes the specifics of different word games introduced in sentence 5, so it makes sense that it would follow sentence 5. Choice (C) is correct.

6. C   Difficulty: Easy
Category: Organization

Getting to the Answer: Make sure that this sentence clearly and precisely transitions from the topic of the previous paragraph to the topic of this paragraph. As currently written, the first sentence does not make a clear connection to the preceding paragraph. By making the discussion of time more precise, the beginning of this paragraph flows better from the previous one. The reader understands more clearly how the details in each paragraph connect. Choice (C) is correct.

7. D   Difficulty: Medium
Category: Effective Language Use

Getting to the Answer: Determine the purpose of sharing this information with readers. The tone of the sentence should be suited to its purpose. The paragraph is a straightforward piece of informative writing. The original segment and C are both too casual for the rest of the passage, while B is too formal and wordy. Choice (D) correctly communicates the information of this sentence with the right level of formality.

8. D   Difficulty: Hard
Category: Development

Getting to the Answer: Find the answer choice that clearly supports the topic sentence of the paragraph while elegantly tying into the next sentence. The topic sentence of this paragraph emphasizes the themes in Basho's work and how haiku became associated with nature and the seasons. Choice (D) provides examples of possible subjects of Basho haiku and is therefore correct.

9. C   Difficulty: Hard
Category: Effective Language Use

Getting to the Answer: Consider what the sentence is communicating and if it can be made more concise. The sentence uses too many words to communicate its point. By combining ideas and eliminating wordiness, the sentence can flow more smoothly. Choice (C) is correct because it maintains the sentence's meaning while using fewer words.

10. B   Difficulty: Medium
Category: Effective Language Use

Getting to the Answer: Consider the precise relationship between Shiki and the other poets mentioned. The correct answer choice will describe his effect on them. It seems clear that Shiki's work influenced cummings and Pound. While "helped" and "aided" both generally suggest that his effect on them was positive, "inspired" is more accurate. Shiki had left his mark, and the other poets learned from him. Choice (B) is correct.

11. D   Difficulty: Medium
Category: Effective Language Use

Getting to the Answer: Read the sentence and determine whether its thoughts are joined logically. The two parts of the sentence are directly related; the writers are "taken with the brevity of the form" because of what it provides them. The sentence does not express this relationship as written, so eliminate A. Eliminate B and C because neither choice correctly relates the two parts of the sentence. Choice (D) correctly combines the sentence while maintaining the relationship between the two clauses.

12. A   Difficulty: Hard
Category: Effective Language Use

Getting to the Answer: Read the complete sentence. The correct answer will flow smoothly from the preceding sentence and place the different phrases of the sentence in a logical order based on their importance. Choice (A) is correct, as the existing sentence arranges the phrases in the most logical order. The sentence begins, "During his time there," smoothly transitioning from the previous sentence and providing nonessential context for the rest of the sentence. The main point is that Tesla invented the alternating current system. This is the first time the alternating current system has been named, so it should be written out fully, and the nonessential information, "what we know in our homes as AC power," should come last, set off by the comma.

13. D   Difficulty: Easy
Category: Development

Getting to the Answer: Identify the sentence that contributes the least relevant information to the focus, or purpose, of the paragraph and the passage as a whole. The paragraph introduces Tesla and his professional activities and accomplishments. The passage as a whole goes on to explore Tesla's scientific legacy. Sentence 5 provides accurate, but irrelevant, information regarding Tesla's personal interests and habits; therefore, the correct answer is choice (D).

14. A   Difficulty: Medium
Category: Effective Language Use

Getting to the Answer: Choose the most contextually appropriate word. Choice (A) is correct because

"implemented" most accurately conveys the idea that Westinghouse first carried out the use of alternating current, which had already been developed, during the exposition.

15. D   Difficulty: Easy
Category: Quantitative

Getting to the Answer: The correct answer will reflect the correct data contained in the timeline. The timeline states that Tesla and Westinghouse displayed the AC system at the Columbian Exposition in 1893, so choice (D) is correct.

16. B   Difficulty: Medium
Category: Development

Getting to the Answer: Identify the subject of the paragraph and consider what the author wants to convey about it. That is the central idea. Then, select the answer choice that correctly conveys the central idea of the paragraph as supported by the details in the preceding sentences. The paragraph discusses the importance of Tesla's development of alternating current and its impact on daily life. In particular, it distinguishes the legacy of Tesla relative to the contributions of Edison. For this reason, choice (B) is correct because it is the only answer choice that emphasizes that Tesla's AC system was crucial (not just incidental) to the success of Edison's bulbs as fixtures in everyday life. "However, bulbs alone do not light our homes" makes clear that Edison's invention would not have done so well without Tesla's.

17. B   Difficulty: Medium
Category: Organization

Getting to the Answer: The correct answer will provide a clear, smooth transition of ideas that connects the content of the previous and current paragraphs. It will also place sentences in logical sequence. The previous paragraph discusses the development of Tesla's AC technology, while the current paragraph discusses Tesla's other inventions. Choice (B) is correct because it links Tesla's development of alternating current with his other innovations. Moving sentence 4 to the beginning of the paragraph also provides a logical sequence of ideas.

18. C   Difficulty: Medium
Category: Quantitative

Getting to the Answer: Read the information next to 1883 in the timeline and find the answer choice that matches that content. The correct answer will correspond to the same event in the passage and timeline. According to the timeline, in 1883, Tesla used alternating current to power a motor. This date corresponds to the information in sentence 3 of paragraph 3, making choice (C) correct.

19. D   Difficulty: Easy
Category: Effective Language Use

Getting to the Answer: The correct answer will demonstrate economy of word choice and retain active voice while preserving the meaning of the sentence. The sentence communicates that Tesla's inventions contributed to the development of future technologies. Choice (D) is correct because it uses minimal verbiage to express that Tesla's inventions led to later inventions.

20. B   Difficulty: Medium
Category: Development

Getting to the Answer: Consider other information in the passage. The correct answer will identify and remove the least essential supporting information to streamline the rhetoric. The least essential information will not alter the meaning of the sentence and will most likely be irrelevant or redundant. The sentence communicates Tesla's impact on wireless communications. Choice (B) is correct because it provides examples that, while somewhat relevant, are nonessential.

21. B   Difficulty: Hard
Category: Sentence Formation

Getting to the Answer: The correct answer will align the modifier with its subject without disrupting the syntax of the remainder of the sentence. The sentence begins "Edison may have invented the lightbulb" and proceeds to contrast Edison's achievement with Tesla's. The second part of the sentence is a dependent clause connected with "but" and should lead off with its subject "Tesla," follow with the modifier "seeing no fame or fortune," and then proceed with the rest of the sentence. Choice (B) does so and is therefore correct.

22. D   Difficulty: Medium
Category: Effective Language Use

Getting to the Answer: Choose the most contextually appropriate word. Eliminate A, "pathfinder," because although Tesla was among the first to make advances toward the use of electricity—and the lightbulb—in daily life, he was neither the first nor the only one to do so. Choice (D) is correct because "pioneer" most correctly conveys the idea that Tesla was among the first.

CHAPTER 23

PRACTICE

4. A **Difficulty:** Medium
Category: Sentence Formation

Getting to the Answer: Words such as *while, when*, and *because* are subordinating conjunctions that work to join independent clauses with dependent clauses. Make sure that the subordinating conjunction fits the context of the sentence and makes the author's intent clear. Here, the author presents a contrast between the aspects of the Sun that are easily identifiable (light, heat) and other phenomena that are less obvious. At the same time, the author admits that all of these aspects of the Sun are always happening simultaneously. The current construction of "Yet, while" most clearly conveys the author's meaning of contrast. Choice (A) is correct.

5. D **Difficulty:** Hard
Category: Usage

Getting to the Answer: Pronouns need to agree with the noun or noun phrase to which they refer. The noun is often in the same sentence but can sometimes be found in preceding sentences. The noun phrase to which the pronoun refers is found at the end of the previous sentence: "the Sun's most volatile surface activity." Since "activity" is singular, the pronoun must agree with a singular noun. "They" is plural and is thus incorrect. Choice (D) is correct because it matches the singular noun.

6. B **Difficulty:** Medium
Category: Sentence Formation

Getting to the Answer: Pay close attention to modifier placement. If modifiers are misplaced or incorrectly used, they can change the author's meaning or harm the sentence's clarity. As the sentence is currently written, the modifier "powerful" is misplaced. The author's intent is to explain the power of the magnetic fields to prevent heat from reaching the Sun's surface. Choice (B) is correct because "powerful" is placed before "magnetic fields," thereby correctly modifying the noun.

PERFORM

7. C **Difficulty:** Medium
Category: Usage

Getting to the Answer: Active voice construction is almost always better than passive voice construction, as it has the subject of the sentence performing the action. This makes a sentence simpler and clearer. Choice (C) is correct because it is an active voice construction and is not interrupted by parentheticals set off by commas.

8. B **Difficulty:** Easy
Category: Sentence Formation

Getting to the Answer: When the passage presents a long, complex sentence, be sure that it is not a run-on that would be better presented as two or more separate sentences. The underlined section is a juncture within a very long sentence; this is made obvious by the comma and the transitional phrase "in fact." Before this juncture, the sentence discusses the accessibility of Eisenstein's work, and after, it addresses his lasting effect on film. These two ideas are more clearly presented in two separate sentences instead of the current run-on. Choice (B) is correct.

9. A **Difficulty:** Easy
Category: Sentence Formation

Getting to the Answer: If the underlined section is a coordinating conjunction—a word or phrase that joins two equally important phrases or clauses—pay attention to the appropriateness of the word choice. Keep clarity of the sentence and passage in mind. No change is necessary because "and" clearly demonstrates that Eisenstein was pushed out of one pursuit and into another. The other answer choices would confuse the reader and harm the author's clarity. Choice (A) is correct.

10. B **Difficulty:** Medium
Category: Sentence Formation

Getting to the Answer: Within complex sentences that contain parallel structure, make sure that verb conjugation, tense, and voice of the sentence are consistent. The underlined section is incorrect because it modifies a past-tense structure that was established earlier in the sentence with the phrase "He quickly found." The current construction blurs the author's clarity and intent. Choice (B) is correct because it is consistent with the past-tense structure already established.

11. D   Difficulty: Medium
Category: Usage

Getting to the Answer: Be aware of improper pronoun use, and keep in mind that not using a pronoun at all can also be incorrect. If the underlined section is a noun, consider whether a pronoun would be better suited for the quality of the narrative. Eisenstein's name is already mentioned in one other part of the sentence, so in this instance it is unnecessary to use it. A possessive pronoun is a better option as it improves the quality of the sentence by not unnecessarily repeating Eisenstein's name. Choice (D) is correct.

12. D   Difficulty: Medium
Category: Sentence Formation

Getting to the Answer: The correct use of modifiers includes vocabulary: making sure the word being used as a modifier has the appropriate definition for the context. Choice (D) is correct because "cumulative" is the correct word for the author's meaning. A montage is inherently cumulative: its meaning grows with the progression of each component shown.

13. C   Difficulty: Hard
Category: Sentence Formation

Getting to the Answer: Sentence fragments—stand-alone sentences that are missing either a subject or a predicate—should always be avoided because they are grammatically incorrect. Pay close attention to sentences that begin with "And," as they often can be combined with their preceding sentences. The sentence that begins with "And" is a sentence fragment because it has no subject. The best way to join this sentence with the previous sentence is to simply remove the period and make "And" lowercase. No other punctuation is needed. Choice (C) is correct.

14. A   Difficulty: Medium
Category: Sentence Formation

Getting to the Answer: Modifiers, while not always grammatically necessary, may be required for the author

to make a point or emphasize a detail. Scrutinize their use to determine which answer choice preserves the author's intent in the sentence and context. Choice (A) is correct because its use of the modifying phrases "enormously famous 1925 hit" and "1927 celebration of the October Revolution" is correct. Their use is also rhetorically effective, as it's clear to which film each refers, giving each movie context for the reader.

EXTRA PRACTICE

1. B   Difficulty: Medium
Category: Development

Getting to the Answer: Identify the common words in all the sentences of the opening paragraph. All the sentences in this paragraph refer to art as a form of communication throughout history, not to the devices required for digital communication; (B) is correct.

2. A   Difficulty: Easy
Category: Effective Language Use

Getting to the Answer: Determine how the word "prominent" is used in the sentence. The opening sentences of the passage describe art as a method of communication and the meeting place as an arena. Choice (A), "prominent," is an adjective meaning "noticeable," so it is the correct answer.

3. D   Difficulty: Easy
Category: Punctuation

Getting to the Answer: Determine whether the list of items is a series needing commas or semicolons. As the sentence is written, its many semicolons are unnecessary; none of the individual items in the list use commas. Since each item in the list is a simple word or phrase, commas are necessary, and choice (D) is correct.

4. C   Difficulty: Medium
Category: Effective Language Use

Getting to the Answer: Eliminate the redundant words from the sentence. Words with similar meanings, such as "create" and "craft," are unnecessary. Using the fewest words, choice (C) correctly conveys the meaning of the sentence.

5. B   Difficulty: Medium
Category: Effective Language Use

Getting to the Answer: Examine the sentence in relationship to the rest of the paragraph. The students are learning from the interactive settings, not teaching them. Choice (B), "hone," is the correct verb to describe how to sharpen or improve expertise.

6. D   Difficulty: Hard
Category: Organization

Getting to the Answer: Identify how the content of sentence 6 is related to the entire paragraph. The compilation of the portfolio happens as a result of the projects discussed in sentence 4 but before the graduates begin their job searches; (D) is correct.

7. A   Difficulty: Easy
Category: Punctuation

Getting to the Answer: Determine whether or not the two parts of the sentence can stand independently. The gerund phrase "taking on projects for external clients" cannot stand on its own because it lacks a subject. Choice (A) is correct.

8. C   Difficulty: Hard
Category: Development

Getting to the Answer: Identify the central idea of the paragraph in the topic sentence and the details presented in the support. The central idea is "graphic design features a variety of professional options." Only (C) supports the topic sentence because it identifies an option. All other choices discuss additional education or salary.

9. B   Difficulty: Easy
Category: Organization

Getting to the Answer: Determine the relationship between the two sentence parts. The two sentence parts present opposing ideas; (B), the subordinating conjunction "although," is correct.

10. C   Difficulty: Medium
Category: Sentence Formation

Getting to the Answer: Identify the two verbs describing how graphic designers feel about their careers. Parallel

ideas must be expressed in the same grammatical form. Correlative constructions require the transitive verb "satisfying" to be paired with the same form: "invigorating." Choice (C) is correct.

11. A   Difficulty: Hard
Category: Development

Getting to the Answer: Determine the main idea of the paragraph by closely examining the topic sentence. Choice (A) is the only option that adds relevant information to the rewards experienced by graphic designers in spite of the job competition.

12. A   Difficulty: Easy
Category: Punctuation

Getting to the Answer: Examine each answer choice and determine which presents the list in a grammatically correct manner with proper punctuation. The list is presented correctly as is, beginning with a colon and featuring the three items separated with commas with no additional information about the topic presented after the listed items. Choice (A) is correct.

13. C   Difficulty: Medium
Category: Effective Language Use

Getting to the Answer: Reread the sentence and select the answer choice that creates the most concise sentence. Minimize wordiness and awkward word combinations to ensure clarity. Choice (C) is correct as it creates the most concise sentence by removing unnecessary and awkward word choices while retaining the meaning of the sentence.

14. B   Difficulty: Hard
Category: Usage

Getting to the Answer: To avoid the passive voice, identify the subject and the object and make sure the subject comes before the verb. The sentence is passive as written, since the object ("educated guesses") should be preceded by the subject's actions. The verb "make" should come first and should be in the present tense. Choice (B) shows the correct construction of the sentence and eliminates the passive voice.

14. B   **Difficulty:** Medium
Category: Organization

Getting to the Answer: Study the surrounding sentences for context clues to determine which of the answer choices creates a logical flow of ideas. The preceding sentence discusses early humans using hands and feet to create music, and the following sentence discusses humans using tools to create music. The progression of ideas is a comparison of shared intentions and traits, so "Similarly," or choice (B), is correct.

15. C   **Difficulty:** Medium
Category: Sentence Formation

Getting to the Answer: Read the two underlined sentences and determine which answer choice best creates a logical and grammatically correct sentence. A grammatically correct sentence must contain a complete idea, utilizing both a subject and a predicate. Choice (C) is correct because it creates a logical, grammatically correct sentence with a subject and predicate.

16. D   **Difficulty:** Medium
Category: Organization

Getting to the Answer: Assess the central idea of both paragraphs and determine which answer choice creates an effective and logical transition from the previous idea while summarizing the next. The passage states music has affected all global cultures, and the noted paragraph explores two more examples showing how music is a social bonding tool. The correct answer, (D), is the only answer that creates a cohesive, logical transition while not limiting the number of cultures affected by music.

17. C   **Difficulty:** Hard
Category: Development

Getting to the Answer: Reread the sentence and select the answer choice that clearly conveys the author's full meaning. Sometimes adding a detail or two can improve a sentence and strengthen an author's claims. The author claims that directions for escape were embedded in well-known lyrics, implying that some people listening to the music may not have discovered the lyrics' true meaning. Choice (C) is correct, as it makes this statement clear and direct for the reader and strengthens the author's claim in a concise manner.

18. A   **Difficulty:** Medium
Category: Effective Language Use

Getting to the Answer: Review the rest of the sentence. Look for context clues that can help you determine which answer choice makes the most sense based on the information provided. The sentence states that as of 1910, headphones created a shift in how we listen to music, implying that headphones are a relatively new invention. Since "advent" is the only word meaning the headphones first appeared at a specific point in time, (A) is correct.

19. D   **Difficulty:** Easy
Category: Organization

Getting to the Answer: Read the entire paragraph for context. Then test the placement given in each answer choice to determine which one creates a paragraph with a logical progression of ideas. Choice (D) is correct because this sentence creates a transition into the subject discussed in the next paragraph.

20. D   **Difficulty:** Easy
Category: Punctuation

Getting to the Answer: The placement or lack of apostrophes can alter a noun's possessive meaning. Read the entire sentence to understand the author's intention. Which answer choice uses the correct punctuation to convey this idea? The nouns "Psychologists and sociologists" are not in possession of anything in this circumstance. Choice (D) correctly reflects this.

21. A   **Difficulty:** Medium
Category: Development

Getting to the Answer: Review the paragraph to assess areas in which the author may have left out facts or may have provided only partial information. Then determine which answer choice will have the greatest benefit to the reader. The author specifically mentions "recent studies" but does not cite any figures. Doing so will strengthen the importance of these studies, thus (A) is correct.

CHAPTER 24

PRACTICE

5. B   **Difficulty:** Medium
Category: Usage

Getting to the Answer: Make sure that comparisons use the correct construction that is aligned with the central idea and context of the passage. The author is making a comparison involving all North American animals—definitely a group larger than two. A superlative construction is appropriate, but it also needs to align with the thesis that the opossum is a very unusual animal. Choice (B) is correct because it is grammatically correct and fits the author's central idea.

6. D   **Difficulty:** Medium
Category: Usage

Getting to the Answer: When a pronoun is the subject of a sentence, make sure that its antecedent is clear. If it is not clear to which noun the pronoun is referring, replace the pronoun with the appropriate noun. The current construction of the sentence creates an ambiguity: does "It" refer to the opossum or the kangaroo? Since the passage describes the characteristics of the opossum, this sentence should be about that animal as well. Choice (D) is correct because it makes the sentence's subject clear to the reader.

7. C   **Difficulty:** Medium
Category: Usage

Getting to the Answer: Make sure that the proper prepositions are being used in the passage. The preposition "in" is incorrect, given the context. The author is describing "limitations *on* the amount of food . . . that can be stored . . . " Choice (C) is correct. If idioms are tricky, think of an analogous situation. A computer's limited warranty has limitations *on* the kinds of things you can do with it. It doesn't have limitations *in* those things.

8. C   **Difficulty:** Easy
Category: Usage

Getting to the Answer: Review a pronoun's antecedent to make sure there is agreement throughout the sentence or section. Early in this sentence, the author establishes the singular possessive form ("the opossum's") as the antecedent of the pronoun in the underlined section. Also, except for an earlier section that discusses "the female opossum," the author uses the non-gendered pronoun "it" when referring to the animal. Choice (C) is correct because it is singular, possessive, and non-gendered.

PERFORM

9. A   **Difficulty:** Medium
Category: Usage

Getting to the Answer: Read the sentence in its entirety to make sure there is no subject-verb disagreement. The verb in the underlined section, "were," appears after the parenthetical remark set aside by dashes. The current version of the subject, "airships," agrees with the verb. No change is necessary; choice (A) is correct.

10. B   **Difficulty:** Medium
Category: Usage

Getting to the Answer: Make sure that comparisons are in the appropriate format—comparative when comparing two things, superlative when comparing three or more things. In the previous sentence, the author states that the *Hindenburg* was "one of a kind." The ship was unique out of all airships, making superlative descriptions appropriate. Given the superlative construction and the author's focus on the ship's dimensions, you can infer that the Hindenberg was the "largest" airship of its time. Choice (B) is correct.

11. C   **Difficulty:** Medium
Category: Usage

Getting to the Answer: Complex sentences can often benefit from the use of pronouns, reducing wordiness and repetition. That said, make sure that the use of a pronoun will not introduce ambiguity into the sentence.

In a complicated sentence including multiple nouns, it is often better to avoid pronouns to preserve the clarity of the author's claims. Choice (C) is correct.

12. B   Difficulty: Hard
Category: Usage

Getting to the Answer: Check to see if the underlined section is part of an idiomatic expression, such as *either . . . or.* The sentence contains the first half of the idiomatic combination *not only . . . but also.* The use of "and" in this context is incorrect. Choice (B), "but also," is correct.

13. B   Difficulty: Easy
Category: Usage

Getting to the Answer: Pay attention to commonly confused words, such as *except* and *accept,* to make sure that careless mistakes do not go unaddressed in a passage. "It's" is a contraction of "it is" and is incorrect in this context. The sentence requires the singular possessive pronoun, "its." Choice (B) is correct.

14. C   Difficulty: Medium
Category: Usage

Getting to the Answer: Make sure the underlined section is using the appropriate preposition. If the verb "rest" refers to a direct object, the preposition "on" is required. Choice (C) is correct because it correctly constructs the idiom.

15. D   Difficulty: Easy
Category: Usage

Getting to the Answer: Examine any nouns that are used as synonyms within the same sentence. They should agree in number, and their shared meaning should either be easily understood or previously explained by the author. At this point in the passage, the author has already established that "balloon" is a synonym for "blimp" and "airship." The underlined section is therefore the correct term, but it disagrees in number with the rest of the sentence in which the associated noun ("airship") is singular. Choice (D) is correct because it is in numerical agreement with the previous noun.

16. B   Difficulty: Easy
Category: Usage

Getting to the Answer: Examine the sentence's use of pronouns for agreement with antecedents. The sentence's use of "their" as a possessive pronoun conflicts with the antecedent "the airship," which is singular. Choice (B) is correct because it is a singular possessive pronoun in agreement with its antecedent.

EXTRA PRACTICE

1. B   Difficulty: Medium
Category: Sentence Formation

Getting to the Answer: Compare the two parts of the sentence. Is the second part a subordinate or coordinate clause? "Since" is a conjunction used between subordinating ideas. These two clauses are coordinating and require a coordinating conjunction meaning "in addition to." Choice (B) is correct.

2. D   Difficulty: Medium
Category: Effective Language Use

Getting to the Answer: Analyze how the underlined word is used in the sentence. Test each answer choice to see if it improves the overall clarity of the text. The opening sentences of the passage are about how the cold weather makes starting cars difficult. When used as a verb, "credit" means to acknowledge (someone or something). Choice (D), "blame," means to hold responsible, and is correct.

3. D   Difficulty: Hard
Category: Organization

Getting to the Answer: Review how the content of sentence 3 is related to the entire paragraph. Recall that transitions help the reader understand logical relationships between ideas. What words in sentence 3 signal a transition? Sentence 4 explains what happens when the number of electrons increases. Because sentence 3 further develops the explanation of what happens when the number of electrons decreases, the transition "likewise" is a clue that it should follow sentence 4. Choice (D) is correct.

4. A   Difficulty: Hard
Category: Development

Getting to the Answer: Identify the key details in the paragraph. Then, summarize them to find the central idea. All of the sentences in this paragraph describe how a battery is constructed and works. Choice (A) is correct.

5. D   Difficulty: Easy
Category: Punctuation

Getting to the Answer: Determine if the items listed need to be treated as a series. Since there are only two items, no commas are needed. Choice (D) is correct.

6. C   Difficulty: Easy
Category: Usage

Getting to the Answer: Determine the tense and the number of the subject. Then, predict the verb form that matches. Since "lead oxide" is singular and the paragraph is written in present tense, choice (C) is correct.

7. C   Difficulty: Medium
Category: Effective Language Use

Getting to the Answer: Establish how the underlined word is used in the sentence; consider the connotations and denotations of the answer choices. Remember that the correct term should reflect the scientific subject matter. "Boundary" is a term meaning a limitation. "Circuit," a noun, is the scientific term that means circumference or course. Choice (C) is correct.

8. B   Difficulty: Hard
Category: Development

Getting to the Answer: Closely examine the topic sentence and the supporting details; identify the central idea of the paragraph. Choice (B) is the only option that adds supporting information about how a current flows through a battery charger.

9. D   Difficulty: Medium
Category: Effective Language Use

Getting to the Answer: Look at how the word is used in the sentence and analyze its grammatical function. Use context clues to determine which choice is correct. "Practicality" is an adverb meaning in a practical manner

and doesn't make sense here. "Probability" is a noun meaning likelihood, which is more appropriate. Choice (D) is correct.

10. A   Difficulty: Medium
Category: Usage

Getting to the Answer: Look for the antecedent of a pronoun to see if the pronoun agrees. The antecedent of "its" is "a battery," which is singular. The contraction "it's" is short for *it is* and is inappropriate here. Choice (A) is correct.

11. A   Difficulty: Hard
Category: Quantitative

Getting to the Answer: Study the graph carefully and consider how its data points connect to the content of the passage. The overall graph trend suggests that battery performance peaks at moderate temperatures, suffers slightly at higher temperatures, and declines greatly at lower ones. Since cold temperatures adversely affect the battery performance of an electric car, choice (A) is correct.

12. B   Difficulty: Hard
Category: Effective Language Use

Getting to the Answer: Consider the specific action being described by this word. Which answer choice is the most precise? The paragraph states that President Roosevelt asked Congress to declare war, an action that has a relationship to "The United States' entrance into World War II." This action led directly to war. Choice (B), "signaled," conveys the most direct relationship between these two ideas and it is therefore correct.

13. B   Difficulty: Medium
Category: Organization

Getting to the Answer: Define the relationship between these two clauses, as well as between this and the previous sentence. A semicolon links two complete but separate independent clauses within a sentence. The sentence states two things: "Japan had not capitulated," and "it had strengthened its expansionist aims." The relationship is one of opposites. Both (B) and C link the two parts of the sentence in the correct way. Only (B), however, maintains the correct relationship with the previous sentence.

14. C   Difficulty: Medium
Category: Usage

Getting to the Answer: Recall that the passive voice is used to describe a state of being. It requires an auxiliary verb and a past participle. The conflict in Japan is being described in the passive voice. To be grammatically correct, the verb form should be that of an auxiliary verb ("was") and a past participle ("understood"). Choice (C) is correct.

15. D   Difficulty: Hard
Category: Development

Getting to the Answer: Before reading the answer choices, think of a sentence that would make sentence 2 more credible if inserted here. Sentence 2 states that "American intelligence officials" had a theory about Japan's behavior. Therefore, the correct sentence will strengthen this idea. Choice (D) explains that as a consequence of America's wrong ideas about Japan, it had not bothered to defend Pearl Harbor well. This explanation supports the assertion made in sentence 2.

16. B   Difficulty: Medium
Category: Punctuation

Getting to the Answer: How can the relationship between Japan's plan and the phrase "destroy the Pacific Fleet" be clarified? The plan is to "destroy the Pacific Fleet." The two ideas are equivalent. The best way to convey this direct relationship is by introducing the phrase with a colon. Choice (B) is correct.

17. B   Difficulty: Medium
Category: Effective Language Use

Getting to the Answer: Identify the overall purpose and tone of the paragraph. The correct answer will convey the information needed to make the sentence effective without being excessively informal. In this sentence, Japan both plans and practices for months. These two ideas can be combined without changing the paragraph's informative tone. Choice (B) communicates the ideas of the sentence in the most elegant and neutral way, and it is therefore correct.

18. D   Difficulty: Medium
Category: Effective Language Use

Getting to the Answer: Consider whether the underlined text has any repetitive information. The correct answer will avoid excessive or redundant information. "8:00" means 8 o'clock, so "o'clock" is unnecessary. Choice (D) successfully communicates the time of day without being redundant.

19. A   Difficulty: Medium
Category: Sentence Formation

Getting to the Answer: Recall that a descriptive phrase that adds information without forming the main part of the sentence should use a participle, not a regular verb, in order to avoid creating a run-on sentence. Although the sentence should communicate that the bombs weighed "over a ton and a half," the main verb in this sentence is "destroyed." Therefore, the phrase should include the present participle "weighing." Choice (A) is correct.

20. C   Difficulty: Hard
Category: Effective Language Use

Getting to the Answer: Read around the underlined word to find clues to its meaning. Then, pick the answer that offers the clearest and most concise meaning. In this context, military equipment is typically described using the expression "sustained damage." While the other choices may make sense grammatically, choice (C) provides a clear and concise term that makes sense in context.

21. A   Difficulty: Hard
Category: Effective Language Use

Getting to the Answer: Describe the purpose of this paragraph in your own words before looking at the answer choices. The rest of the paragraph describes how Japan's attack had not meant to provoke war but resulted in the United States entering the war. Choice (A) sets up the next sentence, in which Roosevelt makes clear that the United States is willing to go to war with Japan.

22. A   **Difficulty:** Easy

Category: Quantitative

Getting to the Answer: Be careful not to bring in outside knowledge. The correct answer choice will be explicitly supported by information in the timeline. The timeline presents a group of historical events, only one of which is reflected in the answer choices. Other choices may or may not be true, but only the sentence as currently written draws its facts from the timeline. Choice (A) is correct.

CHAPTER 25

PRACTICE

7. D   **Difficulty:** Easy
Category: Punctuation

Getting to the Answer: Use commas to separate three or more items forming a series or list. This series contains four items. Separate each item with a comma and use a comma with the conjunction "and" to separate the final item from the rest of the series. Choice (D) is correct.

8. C   **Difficulty:** Hard
Category: Punctuation

Getting to the Answer: When a period is underlined, make sure it's being used correctly. The period correctly separates two sentences but breaks up the flow of the ideas. The second sentence contributes useful information regarding the results of using the "12-note scale." Make the second sentence a modifying phrase, and connect it to the sentence with a comma. Choice (C) is correct.

9. B   **Difficulty:** Medium
Category: Punctuation

Getting to the Answer: When you see a phrase set off by commas, always read the sentence without the phrase to determine if the phrase is nonessential. Although the sentence is still grammatically correct without the information that is set off by the commas, an essential part of the meaning is lost. The author is stating that it is the group setting that distinguishes the improvisation found in jazz from the improvisation found in other types of music. Choice (B) properly removes the commas that set off the phrase.

10. A   **Difficulty:** Easy
Category: Punctuation

Getting to the Answer: When an underlined section features an apostrophe after a noun, check the noun's number. This sentence is correct as written. Although there are many styles of music, the noun "music" is a collective noun and singular. Choice (A) correctly uses the singular possessive.

PERFORM

11. B   **Difficulty:** Medium
Category: Punctuation

Getting to the Answer: When a comma is underlined, check to see if the parts of the sentence before and after the comma need to be separated. In this sentence, the comma separates the subordinate conjunction "although" from the clause it introduces and breaks the link between the dependent clause and the main clause. Choice (B) correctly eliminates the unnecessary punctuation.

12. C   **Difficulty:** Hard
Category: Punctuation

Getting to the Answer: Make sure period use is warranted—determine whether or not the sentences should really be separate. Although the second sentence is an independent clause and could stand on its own, the information in the second sentence belongs in the previous sentence. Choice (C) correctly uses a colon to indicate a break in thought to provide additional explanatory information.

13. D   **Difficulty:** Hard
Category: Punctuation

Getting to the Answer: A period separates independent clauses into sentences and indicates a strong break in thought. Make sure the context of the sentences requires them to be separated. Since both clauses form complete sentences, look at the information they share. Each sentence has Mauritius as its subject and a verb phrase providing information about the island. Combine the two sentences by creating a compound predicate joined by the conjunction "and." Choice (D) is correct.

14. A   **Difficulty:** Medium
Category: Punctuation

Getting to the Answer: Although a parenthetical or non-restrictive phrase may appear in the beginning, middle, or end of a sentence, punctuation will always separate it from the rest of the sentence. Read the sentence without the parenthetical information to determine if the sentence still makes sense. This sentence is correct as written. Because the sentence makes logical sense without the phrase beginning with "making the dodo," the comma is necessary to correctly set off the phrase. Choice D may be tempting, but without the comma, the phrase incorrectly modifies "predators," suggesting that the predators themselves, not the dodo's failure to recognize the danger those predators posed, made the dodo easier to catch. Choice (A) is correct.

15. D   Difficulty: Easy
Category: Punctuation

Getting to the Answer: Separate three or more items in a series or list with commas. Separate the last two items with a comma and the conjunction "and." This series contains six distinct items. Separate each item with a comma and use the conjunction "and" with a comma to separate the final item from the rest of the series. Choice (D) is correct.

16. B   Difficulty: Easy
Category: Punctuation

Getting to the Answer: Watch out for easily confused words: keep straight your possessive determiners, contractions, and adverbs. "Who's" is a contraction for "who is" or "who has," which makes no sense in the context of the underlined portion. Choice (B) correctly uses "whose," the possessive form of the relative pronoun "who."

17. C   Difficulty: Medium
Category: Punctuation

Getting to the Answer: If a dash is used to introduce a break in thought, a second dash must be used to end the parenthetical phrase unless a period ends both the phrase and the sentence. Determine if the information after the dash is parenthetical or nonrestrictive by reading the sentence without that information. Although the phrase provides a description of how the "colonial powers" treated Mauritius, the sentence makes logical sense without it. The phrase is therefore parenthetical and must be properly set off. Only choice (C) correctly sets off the phrase with both an opening and closing dash.

18. A   Difficulty: Medium
Category: Punctuation

Getting to the Answer: Avoid using unnecessary punctuation. Reread the sentence to determine how its parts are related. This sentence is correct as written because

no punctuation is required. The phrase "through its advantageous geographic location and large labor force" completes the thought in the sentence by providing information on how Mauritius "balances" and "flourishes." Choice (A) is correct.

EXTRA PRACTICE

1. B   Difficulty: Medium
Category: Usage

Getting to the Answer: Consider the function of the underlined word in the sentence. The underlined word should be a plural possessive pronoun that refers to "coaches and trainers." Choice (B) is correct.

2. B   Difficulty: Medium
Category: Effective Language Use

Getting to the Answer: Think about the overall meaning of the sentence. Consider which answer choice most closely matches the author's intended meaning. The author explains that some people connect, or equate, the exercise-prompted burning feeling with burning calories. "Equate" is the most precise word to convey this meaning. Choice (B) is correct.

3. B   Difficulty: Medium
Category: Organization

Getting to the Answer: Two complete thoughts make up this sentence. Consider the relationship between the thoughts expressed on either side of the semicolon. The author presents contrasting ideas in this sentence. The relationship between these ideas is best expressed by inserting the transition word "instead" to indicate the contrast between the thoughts. Choice (B) is correct.

4. A   Difficulty: Hard
Category: Development

Getting to the Answer: The correct answer will include an idea that ties together all the information in the paragraph. Paraphrase the central idea into your own words. This paragraph is primarily about how muscles use glucose to get the energy they need to move. Choice (A) is correct because it most effectively states the central idea.

5. C **Difficulty:** Medium
Category: Usage

Getting to the Answer: Identify the noun in the clause. Determine whether the noun is singular or plural and what verb tense is used elsewhere in the sentence. The noun "cells" in this clause is plural, and the rest of the sentence is written in present tense. Choice (C) is correct because it features the plural present tense form of the verb "to continue."

6. B **Difficulty:** Medium
Category: Punctuation

Getting to the Answer: Determine the function of the phrase "found in vinegar" within the sentence. Remember that nonrestrictive elements must be set off from the rest of the sentence with commas before and after. The phrase "found in vinegar" modifies "acetic acid" and is not essential to the understanding of the sentence. Choice (B) is correct.

7. D **Difficulty:** Medium
Category: Effective Language Use

Getting to the Answer: Reread the sentence with each of the answer choices in place of the underlined word. All of the answer choices are similar in meaning, so think about the connotation of each one in relation to the overall meaning of the sentence. In this sentence, the connotation of "irritates" most precisely communicates the meaning of what the author is trying to convey to the reader: bothers. While "annoys" is similar to this meaning, it is mostly used when referring to people, not inanimate or biological objects like lactic acid. Choice (D) is correct.

8. C **Difficulty:** Medium
Category: Development

Getting to the Answer: Identify the central idea of paragraph 4. Think about which sentences are essential to understand the rest of the paragraph. The correct answer could be taken out without changing the meaning or the reader's understanding of the central idea. Although (C) is related to the central idea, the details in this sentence provide the least amount of support because they provide an example of a situation in which lactic acid builds up more quickly. The central idea of the paragraph, however, is the buildup and conversion of lactic acid during exercise. Choice (C) is correct.

9. C **Difficulty:** Medium
Category: Punctuation

Getting to the Answer: Determine whether two complete thoughts are expressed in this sentence. Two complete sentences, each with a subject and predicate, become a run-on without proper punctuation. As written, this is a run-on sentence. Placing a semicolon between the two complete thoughts makes the sentence grammatically correct. Choice (C) is correct.

10. B **Difficulty:** Easy
Category: Usage

Getting to the Answer: Read the entire sentence. Make sure that related pronouns agree in number and person. In this sentence, the author is referring to all human beings and uses "we" to do so. The underlined pronoun "you" does not match the use of the third person plural pronoun. Choice (B) is correct.

11. C **Difficulty:** Hard
Category: Quantitative

Getting to the Answer: The correct answer will both reflect the information presented in the graph and be an appropriate conclusion for the passage. Avoid answers like B that do not strengthen the central idea of the passage. Choice (C) is correct because it contains details presented in the graph that are relevant to the central idea of the passage and because it provides an appropriate conclusion to the passage.

12. B **Difficulty:** Medium
Category: Quantitative

Getting to the Answer: The table gives specific information about various bridges. Interpret the information to choose the correct answer choice. Choice (B) accurately reflects the information in the table since the Tower Bridge was not built until 1894.

13. B **Difficulty:** Medium
Category: Effective Language Use

Getting to the Answer: Watch out for answer choices that may have incorrect transition words or be incorrect in usage or in punctuation. Choice (B) joins the sentences concisely and correctly by using the conjunction "and" to connect the two complete ideas.

14. D   Difficulty: Medium
Category: Organization

Getting to the Answer: Study the relationship between the two parts of the sentence to determine which transition word would work logically. Substitute each transition word in the sentence to see which fits best. Only "however" (a contrast transition) in choice (D) creates a correct and logical relationship between the two parts of the sentence because it discusses the difficulties that were encountered in building the bridge.

15. B   Difficulty: Easy
Category: Effective Language Use

Getting to the Answer: The context of the sentence suggests which word would have the correct connotation. Substitute each word choice in the sentence to see how it fits with the context. Only choice (B) correctly fits the context of the sentence, which suggests that the bridge was something that people very much wanted; "longed" embodies this notion.

16. C   Difficulty: Easy
Category: Effective Language Use

Getting to the Answer: Watch out for answer choices like A, which are redundant. Be as direct and simple as possible. Additional adjectives do not add more meaning to this content. Choice (C) is the most concise and effective way of stating the information in the passage and is therefore correct.

17. D   Difficulty: Easy
Category: Usage

Getting to the Answer: Reread the sentence to identify the antecedent for the underlined pronoun and determine if the two agree. The antecedent in this sentence is "Roebling," which calls for a singular masculine possessive pronoun. Choice (D) is correct.

18. D   Difficulty: Medium
Category: Effective Language Use

Getting to the Answer: Consider the connotations of each word. Substitute each word choice back into the sentence to see how well it fits the context. Choice (D) fits with the context of the sentence, which suggests that such accidents do not happen often. While "special" in A and "exceptional" in B can indicate uniqueness, they are too positive. Choice (D) is correct.

19. C   Difficulty: Medium
Category: Sentence Formation

Getting to the Answer: Look at the other verb in the sentence to see if the verbs are parallel in structure. Choice (C) is the correct form of the verb that is parallel to "succumbed," which appears later in the sentence.

20. D   Difficulty: Hard
Category: Development

Getting to the Answer: To find the central idea of a paragraph, identify important details and summarize them. Then, find the choice that is the closest to your summary. Do not choose a detail rather than a central idea. The paragraph primarily discusses the hardships faced by workers building the bridge. Choice (D) most accurately summarizes the central idea of the paragraph.

21. B   Difficulty: Medium
Category: Sentence Formation

Getting to the Answer: Two complete thoughts should be two separate sentences. Be careful of inappropriate transition words. Choice (B) divides the two thoughts into two complete sentences by adding a period and capitalizing the first word of the second sentence and is therefore correct.

22. C   Difficulty: Hard
Category: Development

Getting to the Answer: To find the correct answer, look for the sentence that does not exclude any necessary details from the underlined portion. Choice (C) correctly maintains the author's inclusion of various details about when the bridge was completed and the significance of Emily's ride.

CHAPTER 26

PRACTICE

¶3: Second body paragraph

- **Introduce Feature 2 and provide a quote or paraphrase of the feature**

- Feature 2: Juxtaposition

  - ¶1 and ¶9: Stability vs. disorder: "strive for the values and ideals we believe in: freedom, justice" and" . . . the surest way to stability is through the very values of freedom, democracy and justice."

  - ¶2: Utilitarian vs. utopian: "more than ever before those two views are merging."

  - ¶4: Delayed vs. immediate information: slow communication of military battles in Queen Victoria's time vs. the immediate news reports of today

  - ¶5: Utilitarian vs. utopian views of international affairs: "So today, more than ever, 'their' problem becomes 'our' problem."

- **Specifically state how Feature 2 provides evidence to support the author's reasoning:** Provides evidence for author's reasoning by showing Blair's audience that the world has changed, and in the long run we must become one in common effort.

- **Discuss how Feature 2 reflects the author's thinking and the way the author ties his or her claim and evidence together:** Blair's repeated juxtapositions bring contrasts into sharp focus, making the alternatives crystal clear to the audience.

- **Analyze the effect Feature 2 is likely to have on the audience:** Emphasizes the need to present a united front, which reflects Blair's theme of world interdependence.

PERFORM

Prime Minister Blair also bolsters his argument by his use of juxtaposition, comparing situations and alternatives to show his audience that the world has changed, and in the long run we must become one in common effort. Blair notes the difference between stability and disorder in both the first and ninth paragraphs of this speech. He ties his discussion in the ninth paragraph with his opening statement by articulating that "the surest way to stability is through the very values of freedom, democracy and justice." In the second paragraph, he contrasts the utilitarian and utopian views of international affairs, not to give the audience a choice between the two but "to suggest that more than ever before those two views are merging." In the fourth paragraph he juxtaposes the slow communication of military battles in Queen Victoria's time with the immediate reports we see today, then follows this up in the fifth paragraph with "So today, more than ever, 'their' problem becomes 'our' problem." Blair puts quotation marks around the words "their" and "our" to emphasize that no one nation exists in isolation and no one problem is limited to one area. His repeated juxtapositions bring contrasts into sharp focus, making the alternatives crystal clear to the audience, while his emphasis on the need to present a united front again returns to his theme of world interdependence.

EXTRA PRACTICE

Adapted from "Freedom or Death," a speech delivered by Emmeline Pankhurst on November 13, 1913, in Hartford, Connecticut

1   Mrs. Hepburn, ladies and gentlemen:

2   Tonight I am not here to advocate woman suffrage. American suffragists can do that very well for themselves. <u>I am here as a soldier who has temporarily left the field of battle in order to explain what civil war is like when civil war is waged by women.</u> I am here as a person who, according to the law courts of my country, it has been decided, is of no value to the community at all: and I am adjudged because of my life to be a dangerous person.

purpose

war metaphor

3   (Now,) first of all I want to make you understand the <u>inevitableness of revolution and civil war, even on the part of women,</u> when you reach a certain stage in the development of a community's life. It is quite easy for you to understand the desirability of revolution <u>if I were a man.</u> If an Irish revolutionary had addressed this meeting, and many have addressed meetings all over the United States during the last twenty or thirty years, it would not be necessary for that revolutionary to explain the need of revolution beyond saying that the people of his country were denied—and by people, meaning men—were denied the right of self-government. That would explain the whole situation. <u>If I were a man</u> and I said to you, "I come from a country which professes to have representative institutions and (yet) denies me, a taxpayer, an inhabitant of the country, representative rights," you would at once understand that that human being, being a man, was justified in the adoption of revolutionary methods to get representative institutions. (But) since I am a woman it is <u>necessary in the twentieth century to explain why women have adopted revolutionary methods in order to win the rights of citizenship.</u>

hypothetical

must do this bc woman

4   You see, (in spite of) a good deal that we hear about revolutionary methods not being necessary for American women, we women, in trying to make our case clear, always have to make as part of our argument, and urge upon men in our audience the fact—a very simple fact—that women are human beings. <u>I want to put a few political arguments before you—not arguments for the suffrage, because I said when I opened, I didn't mean to do that—but arguments for the adoption of militant methods in order to win political rights.</u>

kinds of arguments for ev.

5   (Suppose) the men of Hartford had a grievance, and they laid that grievance before their legislature, and the legislature obstinately refused to listen to them, or to remove their grievance, what would be the

more hypothet.

proper and the constitutional and the practical way of getting their grievance removed? Well, <u>it is perfectly obvious</u> at the next general election, when the legislature is elected, <u>the men of Hartford would turn out that legislature and elect a new one: entirely change the personnel of an obstinate legislature</u>.

6 (But) let the men of Hartford <u>imagine</u> that they were not in the position of being voters at all, that they were governed without their consent being obtained, that the legislature turned an absolutely deaf ear to their demands, what would the men of Hartford do then? They couldn't vote the legislature out. They would have to make a <u>choice of two evils</u>: they would either have to <u>submit indefinitely to an unjust state of affairs</u>, or they would have <u>to rise up and adopt some of the antiquated means by which men in the past got their grievances remedied</u>. We know what happened when <u>your forefathers</u> decided that they must have representation for taxation, many, many years ago. When they felt they couldn't wait any longer, when they laid all the arguments before an obstinate British government that they could think of, and when their arguments were absolutely disregarded, when every other means had failed, they began by the tea party at Boston, and they went on until they had won the independence of the United States of America. <u>That is what happened in the old days</u>.

effects of men not having rights

ex. of Am. Rev.

7 <u>It is perfectly evident to any (logical mind)</u> that when you have got the vote, you can get out of any legislature whatever you want,(or,)if you cannot get it, you can send them about their business and choose other people who will be more attentive to your demands.(But) it is clear to the meanest intelligence that if you have not got the vote, you must either submit to laws just or unjust, administration just or unjust, or <u>the time inevitably comes when you will revolt against that injustice and use violent means to put an end to it</u>.

war = inevitable

Sample Student Response #1

Though Emmeline Pankhurst is a militant suffragist, she has not come to Hartford, Connecticut, to speak about suffrage. No, she makes that clear with the first line of her speech. Pankhurst does not want to explain why woman suffrage is just and necessary; she has come to explain why the way that she and her fellow suffragists fight for suffrage is just and necessary. She has come to justify not her cause but her methods, not her ideas but her strategies, not her goals but her tactics. Pankhurst claims that the government, by denying women the vote to begin with, has left them with only protest and revolt as a means to win political change. With her masterful use of historical examples, comparison, and irony, she positions her speech as a defense of her methods, but in doing so, also affirms her cause.

From the start, Pankhurst use historical examples to support her claim that the fight for woman suffrage is not merely a difference of opinion but a battle, as were the historical battles fought for Independence and Union. She immediately references "civil war," and proclaims herself a soldier who has come away from the battlefield "to explain what civil war is like when civil war is waged by women." Though she does not specify the War Between the States—a war which, being won only 50 years earlier could well be in the experience of her audience—her allusion is clear. She is not a reformer, an activist, or an ideologue. She is a soldier! She further compares the tactics used by women to those of American revolutionaries. Deprived of political representation, they, "began by the tea party at Boston, and . . . went on until they had won the independence of the United States of America." She claims that if she were a male revolutionary (as her audience might have been "in the old days"), no one would deny the right of her methods; it is only because she is a female revolutionary that there is any question. Her historical references are not limited to those of our forefathers but also encompass those of Ireland, claiming that the men of Hartford would immediately understand the need for Irish revolution simply by being told—by a man—that "the people of his country were denied—and by people, meaning men—were denied the right of self-government." Pankhurst emphasizes that revolution has always been a means to redress wrongs, and clearly states that the only reason it is questioned today is because "women have adopted revolutionary methods in order to win the rights of citizenship." By reminding her audience of the legitimacy of revolution, she compels them to ask the question: "if right for men, why not for women?" hoping to begin their reevaluation of women's right to citizenship.

Recognizing that the more she can make men understand the suffragettes' position in light of their own, the more they might understand its cause and correctness, Pankhurst makes several telling comparisons. Not only does she compare the male revolutionaries' rights to militancy to those of women, but she also compares their rights as citizens to women who have no such rights. She speaks of what citizens (men only) may do if they are dissatisfied with the government: "They would have to make a choice of two evils: they would either have to submit indefinitely to an unjust state of affairs, or they would have to rise up and adopt some of the antiquated means by which men in the past got their grievances remedied." Her contention is that women now face the same choice, but barring their ability to "turn out that legislature and elect a new one," they would need to use the same "antiquated" methods. Furthermore, Pankhurst makes the bold and clear comparison between women "of no value to the community at all," and "a very simple fact—that women are human beings." Even her use of the words "your forefathers," rather than "our forefathers," makes a comparison: this country was founded by men, with little regard for women. In making the comparisons between the political wrongs her audience faced and those now faced by women, Pankhurst again appeals to their emotions and sense of logic – other than gender, what is the difference between the rights of men and those of women?

Finally, Pankhurst is masterful in her use of irony throughout her speech. She begins with the irony that legally, she does not exist as a person, but has been judged "a dangerous person" because of her insistence on being heard. She speaks of adopting "antiquated means … many, many years ago," making militancy sound quaint and out of style, but supports it as a viable means of correcting wrongs. How ironic that the means that procured American independence is now deplored as "antiquated," merely because it is now in the wrong hands: those of women.

She addresses those of even the "meanest intelligence," pointing an imaginary finger at the self-satisfied men in her audience, giving them the benefit of logic which must bring them to the conclusion that, at this point, women have no other way to gain the vote but by revolutionary methods. Indeed, it is ironic that she consistently abjures the label of "suffragette" in favor of "soldier." Her rhetoric conflates the two, for the cause is one and the same. The irony of "us" vs. "them," when in reality all are human beings deserving of the same rights, brings the political divide home to the audience and undermines their ill-conceived and unjust assumptions.

Emmeline Pankhurst is a forceful, intelligent speaker, whose message to the men of Hartford is vigorous and assertive: female submission is not an option; the right to citizenship with its concomitant right to vote is just, and the same means by which men fought for freedom is a legitimate means open to women. She points out the historical acceptance of militancy, the comparisons between the choices American men faced when ill-used by England and those women face when ill-used by their government, and the incongruity between women's logical right to citizenship and the real state of affairs. Each element of her speech supports her primary idea, each one is intended to provoke the audience to rethink their stance either by logic or by inferred reproach, and each one goes beyond Pankhurst's stated reason for the speech to support the "inevitableness of revolution and civil war" to underscore that women will not stop until equality is achieved.

Reading—4: This writer demonstrates thorough comprehension of the source text. The writer clearly identifies Pankhurst's central purpose (*to explain why the way that she and her fellow suffragists fight for suffrage is just and necessary*), identifies important details, and skillfully includes textual evidence.

Analysis—4: This writer demonstrates a comprehensive understanding of the analytical task by developing a critical review of the source text. The writer identifies pieces of evidence Pankhurst uses and explains their importance in regard to the central argument.

Writing—4: This response is cohesive and demonstrates highly developed skill in the use and control of standard written English. The writer includes fully reasoned introduction and conclusion paragraphs that enhance the comprehensiveness of the essay. There is an intentional progression of ideas both within and among paragraphs. The writer includes a variety of sentence structures, demonstrates thoughtful word choice, and sustains a scholarly style and tone throughout the essay.

Sample Student Response #2

Emmeline Pankhurst does appear in Hartford, Connecticut, to speak about suffrage. From the start of her speech, she makes clear that she does not want to explain why woman suffrage is necessary. Rather, she means to explain why the way that she and her fellow suffragists fight for suffrage is necessary. Pankhurst looks at the battle for woman suffrage as a civil war. She calls herself a soldier sent to explain her tactics in the war, not the importance of her side in the war. In her speech, Pankhurst explains that she and the suffragists must use violent means to win change because it is the only means open to them. She asserts that they cannot win reform any other way precisely because suffrage is denied to them. In this way, she uses her defense of her methods to actually justify the underlying cause—suffrage for women.

Pankhurst grabs her audience's attention by calling woman suffrage not just a political debate but a civil war. In the same way, she makes herself more than a reformer or an activist; she declares herself a soldier. In this way, she gets men and woman to listen to what she has to say. Her references to revolution and civil war also call up America's own history, rooted in political revolt. In addition to this comparison, she compares the struggle of suffragists with that of Irish revolutionaries. Not only is the woman suffrage movement a political revolution, she seems to say, but also women (revolutionary and otherwise) are equal with men. If she were a man, she says no one would doubt her right to revolt, but because she's a woman, she and her fellow suffragists have to explain themselves.

Pankhurst also claims that the struggle for suffrage is really a fight for "the rights of citizenship." She implies that by denying women the right to vote, the government is denying them citizenships. In using this rhetoric, she makes the idea that suffrage is something to which women are entitled as citizens clear. This means that to deny woman suffrage is to deny them as citizens. She goes on to say "that women are human beings," making the debate over suffrage also a denial of women's humanity. By doing this, Pankhurst tries to appeal to her audience's emotions and sympathies. She begins by talking about the way she works for political change, but by calling attention to the battle and to women as citizens and humans, she really makes the case for suffrage itself.

Finally, Pankhurst ties it all together in her final paragraph. She even suggests that reason itself is on her side by stating that it's "perfectly evident to any logical mind" and "clear to the meanest intelligence" that if you can vote, you can change government peacefully, while if you can't vote, you have to resort to other means. For this reason, using even violent means of protest and revolt to win suffrage is just. Pankhurst concludes by claiming that her tactics are needed precisely because women can't vote. This argument rests on the assumption that woman suffrage itself is right and necessary, and in a circular kind of way, ends up defending suffrage as well as the tactics to win suffrage.

Reading—2: This writer demonstrates some comprehension of the source text. The writer shortly relates an overview of Pankhurst's central purpose (*she does not want to explain why woman suffrage is necessary*). However, the writer does not go beyond what can be interpreted from Pankhurst's speech and misunderstands some important details. There is very little textual evidence used in the response.

Analysis—2: This writer demonstrates a partial understanding of the analytical task, offering a limited analysis of the source text. The writer is able to identify pieces of evidence Pankhurst uses, but is ineffective in explaining their importance in regard to the central argument. Also, the lack of direct quotations or paraphrases from the text leaves much of the writer's analysis unsubstantiated. There is also a lack of focus on the features of the text most relevant to furthering Pankhurst's central argument.

Writing—2: This response has little cohesion and demonstrates limited skill in the use and control of standard written English. Rather than using the introduction and conclusion as touchstones of the response, the writer merely uses the four paragraphs (including the two body paragraphs) to describe Pankhurst's argument as it unfolds. There is limited progression of ideas within paragraphs but this progression is absent from the overall response. The sentence structures utilized are repetitive and the style and tone are nowhere near as formal and objective as they should be. While there are some careless grammatical and spelling errors, they do not detract from the author's intended meaning.

CHAPTER 27

PRACTICE

¶1: Introductory paragraph

- **Introductory statement:** *David Foster Wallace argues that while language is inherently political, how society expresses itself is a product of preexisting attitudes.*

- **Paraphrase the author's central idea or claim:** *Politically Correct English (PCE) is dangerous because using "politically correct" language doesn't get rid of elitism or unfairness.*

- **Specifically state the features the author uses to support the central idea or claim**

    - *Feature 1: Diction*

    - *Feature 2: Appeal to authority*

    - *Feature 3: Juxtaposition*

¶2: First body paragraph

- **Introduce Feature 1 and provide a quote or paraphrase of the feature**

    - Feature 1: Diction

        - *¶1: "insensitive and elitist and offensive and unfair"*

        - *¶2: "taken very seriously indeed"*

- **Specifically state how Feature 1 provides evidence to support the author's reasoning:** *Helps him subtly convey his central argument by using both politically correct and incorrect diction to make a point about language itself.*

- **Discuss how Feature 1 reflects the author's thinking and the way the author ties his or her claim and evidence together:** *Using informal and formal language side-by-side reinforces the fact that language itself, whether politically correct or not, is not indicative of societal attitudes.*

- **Analyze the effect Feature 1 is likely to have on the audience:** *By alternating between formal and informal diction, the author keeps the audience interested, which promotes further discussion.*

PERFORM

In his essay on the use of language, David Foster Wallace asserts that it is dangerous to promote strict use of Politically Correct English (PCE) because the use of PCE alone does not automatically make someone politically correct. Wallace effectively conveys the argument that PCE does not reverse instances of elitism or unfairness by using contrasting diction, appeals to authority, and juxtaposition.

Throughout the essay, Wallace uses both informal, colloquial diction and professional, academic diction. The seamless overlap of these two extremes not only forces Wallace's audience to pay attention but also reinforces the central argument that language itself, whether politically correct or not, is not indicative of societal attitudes or beliefs. In the first paragraph, Wallace writes that the "political realities of American life are themselves racially insensitive and elitist and offensive and unfair." The four adjectives Wallace uses to describe American political realities are progressively informal: "insensitive" could be considered PCE, while "unfair" evokes a child's temper tantrum. The use of four words that are similar in meaning but vary in sophistication to describe one concept strengthens Wallace's assertion that a point can be conveyed regardless of the type of language employed. The italicized word "indeed" in the second paragraph ("taken very seriously indeed") serves to emphasize that "prescriptive PCE is . . . silly." By highlighting the word "indeed" through italicization, Wallace underscores that the word itself does not enhance the statement in which it appears, but is merely a construction to enhance political correctness. By using both politically correct and incorrect diction, Wallace subtly enhances his central argument about how politically correct language is "sort of funny in a dark way, maybe."

EXTRA PRACTICE

Adapted from Vice President Spiro Agnew's 1969 speech "Television News Coverage."

1   Tonight I want to discuss the importance of the television news medium to the American people. No nation depends more on the intelligent judgment of its citizens. No medium has a more profound influence over public opinion. So, nowhere should there be more conscientious responsibility exercised than by the news media.

SA: TV should be responsible

2   Monday night a week ago, President Nixon delivered the <u>most important address</u> of his Administration, one of the <u>most important of our decade.</u> His subject was Vietnam. My hope, as his at that time, was to rally the American people to see the conflict through to a lasting and just peace in the Pacific. For 32 minutes, he reasoned with a nation that has suffered <u>almost a third of a million casualties in the longest war</u> in its history.

dramatic lang. emphasizes importance

3   When the President completed his address—an address, incidentally, that <u>he spent weeks</u> in the preparation of—his words and policies were subjected to <u>instant analysis and querulous criticism.</u> The audience of 70 million Americans was inherited by a small band of network commentators and self-appointed analysts, the majority of whom expressed in one way or another their hostility to what he had to say.

imagery = band of commentators

4   It was obvious that their minds were made up in advance. Those who recall the fumbling and groping that followed President Johnson's dramatic disclosure of his intention not to seek another term have seen these men in a genuine state of nonpreparedness. This was not it.

contrast w/ Johnson

5   One commentator twice contradicted the President's statement about the exchange of correspondence with Ho Chi Minh.[1] Another challenged the President's abilities as a politician. A third asserted that the President was following a Pentagon line. Others by the expressions on their faces, the tone of their questions, and the sarcasm of their responses, made clear their sharp disapproval.

supporting data = examples of bias

6   To guarantee in advance that the President's plea for national unity would be challenged, one network <u>trotted out</u> Averell Harriman for the occasion. All in all, Mr. Harriman offered a broad range of gratuitous advice challenging and contradicting the policies outlined by the President of the United States. Where the President had issued a call for unity, Mr. Harriman was encouraging the country not to listen to him.

AH = evidence of agenda

7   Now every American has a right to disagree with the President of the United States and to express publicly that disagreement. (But) the President of the United States has a right to communicate directly with the people who elected him, and the people of this country have the right to make up their own minds.

call to arms

8   When Winston Churchill rallied public opinion to stay the course against Hitler's Germany, he didn't have to contend with a gaggle of commentators raising doubts about whether he was reading public opinion right, or whether Britain had the stamina to see the war through. When President Kennedy rallied the nation in the Cuban missile crisis, his address to the people was not chewed over by a roundtable of critics who disparaged the course of action he'd asked America to follow.

parallel examples: WC rallying public vs Hitler; JFK rallying U.S. in crisis

media left them alone

9   At least 40 million Americans every night, it's estimated, watch the network news. Seven million of them view ABC, the remainder being divided between NBC and CBS. According to Harris polls and other studies, for millions of Americans the networks are the sole source of national and world news.

10 Now how is this network news determined? A small group of anchormen, commentators, and executive producers settle upon the 20 minutes or so of film and commentary that's to reach the public. This selection is made from the 90 to 180 minutes that may be available. Their powers of choice are broad.

contrast: small # elites vs millions

11 They decide what 40 to 50 million Americans will learn of the day's events in the nation and in the world. These men can create national issues overnight. They can make or break by their coverage and commentary a moratorium on the war. They can elevate men from obscurity to national prominence within a week. They can reward some politicians with national exposure and ignore others.

repetition of "they" & "they can" → emphasizes media power

12 The views of the majority of this fraternity do *not*—and I repeat, not— represent the views of America. Not only did the country receive the President's speech more warmly than the networks, but so also did the Congress of the United States.

13 Yesterday, the President was notified that 300 individual Congressmen and 50 Senators of both parties had endorsed his efforts for peace. As with other American institutions, perhaps it is time that the networks were made more responsive to the views of the nation and more responsible to the people they serve.

central idea = media should reflect how "the nation" feels but not distort or persuade them

[1]Ho Chi Minh—president of North Vietnam, the enemy of the U.S. in the Vietnam War

Sample Student Response #1

While many people today get their news from different online sources, in the 1960s, a majority of Americans got their news from newspapers and television networks. Television in particular was a popular source of news, and presidents like Richard Nixon sometimes used it to communicate policy decisions to the American people. After Nixon gave a televised address about Vietnam, some network news correspondents disagreed with the president's position. Vice President Agnew disagreed with the network's criticism of the president's address. His argument? Network news coverage unduly influenced and did not accurately reflect popular opinion of the president's position on Vietnam.

After giving his implicit support for the president's address, Agnew begins his critique of the networks by explaining their outsize influence relative to the number of Americans who watch the news. He notes that at least 40 million people watch the news, yet what they see on the programs is decided by a relatively small number of people like producers and commentators. Then he explains this outsize influence by writing that they can "create national issues overnight," they can "elevate men from obscurity," and even "reward some politicians with national exposure." This is true today as it was then, but how does Agnew feel about this influence? The reader can see Agnew's opinion in the language he uses. For example, he describes news analysts as "self-appointed," which diminishes the reliability of their opinion in the reader's eyes.

Agnew does not restrict his criticism of network coverage to undue influence. He also argues that the opinion expressed on the networks did not accurately reflect that of Americans as a whole. His evidence for this idea can be seen in the last paragraph where he explains that over 300 congressmen and 50 senators "endorsed his efforts for peace." This implies that the will of Congress is also that of the American people. He also explicitly attacks Averell Harriman by contrasting Harriman's position with the president's, noting that other leaders such as Churchill and Kennedy were not criticized by media pundits. Agnew does this to equate the popular choices these leaders made during World War II and the Cuban Missile Crisis with Nixon's choices about Vietnam. The implication is that Churchill and Kennedy were correct, so Nixon must be too.

Throughout his speech, Agnew portrays the news networks as a minority of people with undue influence who are presenting an outsize opinion of Nixon's speech that does not "represent the views of America." In the end, the reader is left questioning the veracity and reliability of media coverage, something that many Americans continue to do today in the age of the Internet.

Reading—4: The writer demonstrates thorough understanding of the source text as evidenced by use of direct quotations and paraphrases. The writer succinctly and accurately relays Agnew's central idea at the end of the introductory paragraph (*Network news coverage unduly influenced and did not accurately reflect popular opinion of the president's position on Vietnam*). The writer also references and cites many important details of Agnew's speech, making sure to interrelate them to the central idea. For example, at the end of the third paragraph, the writer states, *Agnew does this to equate the popular choices these leaders made during World War II and the Cuban Missile Crisis with Nixon's choices about Vietnam. The implication is that Churchill and Kennedy were correct, so Nixon must be too.* This response demonstrates thorough comprehension of the source text.

Analysis—3: This response offers effective analysis of the source text and demonstrates an understanding of the analytical task. The third paragraph is stronger than the second paragraph in that the writer cites evidence Agnew uses to support a claim and proceeds to explain why this evidence serves to advance Agnew's central argument. However, the second body paragraph is merely a summary of Agnew's speech.

Writing—3: The writer demonstrates effective use and control of standard written English in this mostly cohesive response. The introduction is not as focused as it should be; the writer focuses more on providing background information to Agnew's speech than presenting his or her own central claim. The manner in which the writer introduces his or her interpretation of Agnew's central idea (*His argument?*) is a bit too casual for an SAT Essay. Overall, the writing in this response is proficient. While the response is well written and conforms to standard written English, the fact that the writer does not provide his or her own central claim lowers the Writing score.

Sample Student Response #2

Today people get their news from different places like the Internet and television. But back in the 1960s, it was mainly from newspapers and television. Lots of people watched television news and presidents like Richard Nixon would explain their decisions on television to the American people. Nixon gave a speech about Vietnam and people on network news disagreed with what he said. In response, Vice President Agnew gave his own speech to support President Nixon. Agnew thought that the opinion of many in the network news was wrong because it was different than the opinion of a majority of Americans.

In his speech, we can see Agnew thinks they have too much power to influence opinion. He supports that idea with statements like the networks can "create national issues overnight" and "elevate men from obscurity." He doesn't think a small number of people should be able to do that.

We can also see that Agnew thinks a majority of Americans disagree with the opinion shown on networks. He says that a majority of Congress thinks that Nixon is right about Vietnam, so he probably thinks a lot of Americans must support Nixon's ideas about Vietnam too. He says that people supported Churchill and Kennedy, so they should support Nixon now. This is a good comparison, because he makes the readers think Nixon is a good leader like Kennedy and Churchill.

In conclusion, Agnew supports Nixon and doesn't approve of how the news networks are talking about him. He thinks the president knows what he's talking about when it comes to Vietnam. But now that we have the Internet, people have a choice about where to get their news.

Reading—2: This writer demonstrates some comprehension of the source text. The writer understands the surface function and central idea of Agnew's speech, but does not delve into important details; rather, he or she sticks to sweeping generalizations. Furthermore, the last sentence of the essay (*But now that we have the Internet, people have a choice about where to get their news*) veers from not only the central idea of Agnew's speech but also goes beyond the scope of the SAT Essay task.

Analysis—2: This writer demonstrates a partial understanding of the analytical task, offering a limited analysis of the source text. The writer summarizes Agnew's position and uses the third paragraph to partly discuss a comparison Agnew makes, but instead of accurately explaining how this comparison helps his argument, the writer qualifies it as "good." (*This is a good comparison, because he makes the readers think Nixon is a good leader like Kennedy and Churchill*)

Writing—2: This response has little cohesion and demonstrates limited skill in the use and control of standard written English. The writer never asserts his or her own central claim but merely describes the circumstances surrounding Agnew's speech. The lack of varied sentence structure and overuse of the third person plural (*we*) also contribute to this low Writing score. Overall, the language used is far too casual for an SAT Essay response.